Writers' & Artists' Y

Writers' & Artists' Yearbook 2003

Ninety-sixth Year of Issue

A directory for writers, artists, playwrights, writers for film, radio and television, designers, illustrators and photographers

A & C Black · London

37 Soho Square, London W1F 0BJ

A & C Black uses paper produced with elemental chlorine-free pulp, harvested from managed sustainable forests.

A CIP catalogue record for this book is available from the British Library.

ISBN 0-7136-6281-6

Printed and bound in France by Aubin
email sales@aubin-imprimeur.fr

Foreword

***Doris Lessing's** first novel was published in 1950. Many successful award-winning books have followed and her latest novel, The Sweetest Dream, has recently been published on both sides of the Atlantic.*

Since I began writing 70 or so years ago everything has changed for writers. Then "I want to be a writer" meant you were in apprenticeship to a hard craft taught by extensive reading of the best that has been written. It might take years to get your first book published. You were probably going to be poor, at least at first. There was room in this design for respect for those writers who could never command big sales, might never be known to more than a discriminating minority. Stendhal said he expected to be read and understood in a 100 years time by the happy few. He was wrong about his prospects but his stoic stance on solitary excellence was a banner that some of us, at least in our better moments, were happy to march under. Writing was a vocation, a dedication. To write for money was to sell out – never mind about Dr Johnson. Too much socialising and celebrity must be death to integrity. This was then understood by publishers: when my first book did well, they apologised for asking me to do an interview.

Dear dead days. Now, "I want to be a writer" usually means, I want the bright lights, a big advance, prizes, and the bigger the promotional tour the better.

This is true for a good many aspiring writers. There remains, and always will, a minority who know that what makes a real writer is the solitary hard slog. There are exceptions. Balzac thrived on society, and Victor Hugo was not averse to notice. Salman Rushdie can party all night and write the next day. But on the whole it is better for writers to shun the razzmatazz. Not much chance of that these days: the publishers see to that. Yet it is bad for a young writer to be exposed suddenly to a glare of attention. Not a few have written a good or promising first novel but then the second, written in time snatched from journalists and interviewers, might not be so good, or there might be a long wait for it. But it is no good saying what ought to be, what one might prefer: one has to work inside the limits of what is. You have to learn how to switch yourself into a public personality, for the duration of the tour or festival or promotion, and switch yourself off again, back into your working – your real – self.

Until recently, asked if I always intended to be a writer, I would say No, not until my twenties. So much for lying, twisty memory: I met a woman who remembered me from school, when we were 11, sitting on our beds in the dorm, and I said I was going to be a writer. I had been writing bits of this and that always, the first when I was seven. I wrote two novels when I was 17, but I was too raw to match up to my ambitions. One of them was social satire, about the bright young things of Salisbury, Southern Rhodesia (I was shortly to become one of them) and the other was … but I have no idea. Written in a kind of trance of delight at the easy way it all poured out, I could not read a word of it back. That taught me a lesson. If you have even mildly dodgy handwriting, do not use a pen.

I am glad to say I destroyed those two early novels and much else. I went on writing when I could, even when I had two small children and no sustained work was possible. I have always had to write in short concentrated bursts, because of pressures. All this time I was saying I was going to be a writer, and other people said it of me, on the strength of some cocky early stories in South African magazines. Young writers brought me their work to judge and I had not had much published myself. I look back on this with surprise. I had reached my mid-twenties, always saying I was a writer – and where was the evidence? I gave up my job in a lawyer's office and began on *The Grass is Singing*. I earned my living part time, and better than in a full-time office job, doing typing for Parliament and Select Committees. I was pregnant then and had a small child, luckily an easygoing one.

I finished *The Grass is Singing*. Now what to do? This was wartime. It took six weeks to get letters and packages to London. No airmail then, it had to be by sea, by convoy through the submarine-haunted oceans. When you launched your precious offspring into the mails you knew it might find a watery grave. I sent *The Grass is Singing* and some short stories to publishers and magazines, getting addresses from an old copy of the *Writers' and Artists' Yearbook*, sent to me by an old friend of my parents, who had been watching me floundering about in my provincial ignorance of the big literary world. Six weeks there, the usual delays, six weeks back. I am reading a book now about Matteo Ricci, a traveller to China in the 16th century, and when he wrote a letter home to Italy he knew it would take seven years for a reply.

Always keep a copy of what you send out. And do not believe the promises of friends, agents, impressarios when you trust them with a precious only copy. They will lose it and not know how it happened.

I got encouraging letters and began that collection of rejection slips which is essential discipline for every writer. It is not a bad thing to learn patience. The novel was rejected and by the time it had got back to me, I knew why. It was too long, three times the final length. Two thirds was social satire, but I had been too ambitious again, I did not have the lightness of touch. I threw away two thirds, and the rest became *The Grass is Singing*. It found a Johannesburg publisher who turned out to be a crook. He would take 50% of the proceeds, but he didn't publish it anyway: too politically risky.

Having at last reached London I sent short stories to Juliet O'Hea of Curtis Brown, recommended by the *Writers' and Artists' Yearbook*. She asked: Did I have a novel? I said Yes, but it was bespoke. She asked to see the contract, then said she had never seen such a shocking contract. She sent a telegram to the Johannesburg publisher threatening him with exposure, and sold the novel over the weekend to Michael Joseph. It was reprinted twice before publication, but I was green, and thought this happened to every writer. The book did well. But this success was preceded by years of writing, tearing up, rewriting. When I am asked for advice by young writers I say that what makes the difference between amateur writers and professionals is that the latter work hard, tear up, rewrite, and are always ready to let something go that doesn't match up. A ruthlessness towards one's dear progeny, that's the thing.

They ask, What is your routine? How do you write? Do your use a processor, a fountain pen, a quill? Do you write in the mornings or perhaps at night? Do you …? Hidden in this kind of questioning is the belief that there is some trick or secret recipe; this is because all one needs to write is a biro and an exercise book, a provisioning that gives an illusion of ease. Alas, no, the trick, the recipe, is hard work.

Doris Lessing, March 2002

Contents

**Classified index to listings for quick reference*

Literary agents

Art and illustration

Photography and picture research

Societies, prizes and festivals

Writers and artists online

Resources for writers

Publishing practice

Copyright and libel

Finance for writers and artists

Newspapers and magazines

Submitting material

Of the titles included in the newspapers and magazines section of the Yearbook, almost all offer opportunities to the writer. Many publications do not appear in our lists because the market they offer for the freelance writer is either too small or too specialised, or both. We give here some guidelines to bear in mind when submitting material to a newspaper or magazine.

Before submitting material to any newspaper or magazine it is advisable first to contact the relevant editor. The listings beginning on page 3 give the names of editors for each section of the national newspapers and a quick telephone call to a magazine will establish the name of the relevant commissioning editor together with an email address.

Magazine editors frequently complain to us about the unsuitability of many submissions. When submitting by post writers are advised, in their own interests, to enclose postage for the return of unsuitable material.

Study the market

Before submitting articles or features, always study carefully the editorial requirements of a magazine, not only for the subjects dealt with but for the approach, treatment, style and length. These comments will be obvious to the practised writer but the beginner can be spared much disappointment by buying copies of magazines and studying the market in depth.

The importance of studying the market cannot be overemphasised. It is an editor's job to know what readers want, and to see that they get it. Thus, freelance contributions must be tailored to fit a specific market; subject, theme, treatment, length, etc, must meet the editor's requirements. This is looked at further in *Writing for newspapers* on page 124 and *Writing magazine articles* on page 128. For additional information on markets, see the UK volume of *Willings Press Guide*, which is usually available at local reference libraries.

Most newspapers and many magazines these days expect copy to be sent by email. Editors who accept postal submissions expect them to be well presented: neatly typed, double spaced, with good margins, on A4 paper is the standard to aim at. If submitting articles on disk always verify with the editor that your system and theirs are compatible before sending. Most editors also require a hard copy (printout) in addition to the disk.

Illustrations

It is not advisable to send illustrations 'on spec'; check with the editor first. See page 131 for further information and *Digital imaging for writers* on page 571; listings of *Picture agencies and libraries* start on page 412.

For a list of magazines and newspapers willing to pay for cartoons, see *Newspapers and magazines which accept cartoons* on page 405, and *A serious look at marketing cartoons* (page 402) offers guidance for success.

Payment

It has always been our aim to obtain and publish the rates of payment offered for contributions by newspapers and magazines. Many publications, however, are reluctant to state a standard rate, since the value of a contribution may be dependent not upon length but upon the standing of the writer or of the information given. Many other periodicals, in spite of efforts to extract more precise information from them, prefer to state 'by negotiation' or 'by arrangement'.

A number of magazines will accept and pay for letters to the editor, brief fillers and gossip paragraphs, as well as puzzles and quizzes. *Magazines by subject area* on page 113 provides a rough guide to these markets.

Overseas contributions

The lists of overseas newspapers and magazines in the *Yearbook* contain only a selection of those journals which offer a market for the freelance writer. For fuller listings, refer to *Willings Press Guide Volume 2 Overseas*. The overseas market for stories and articles is small and editors often prefer their fiction to have a local setting. Some editors require their contributors to be residents of that country.

Some overseas magazine titles have little space for freelance contributions but many of them will consider outstanding work. Potential contributors should check whether it is acceptable to send material by email. Query proposals or finished articles mailed overseas should always be accompanied by return postage in the form of International Reply Coupons (IRCs). IRCs can be exchanged in any foreign country for stamps representing the minimum postage payable on a letter sent from one country to another.

Using an agent to syndicate material written from overseas is worth considering. Most agents operate on an international basis and are more aware of current market requirements. Again, return postage should always be included.

Newspapers and syndicates

The larger newspapers and magazines buy many of their stories, and the smaller papers buy general articles, through one or other of the well-known syndicates. Another avenue for writers is to send printed copies of their stories published at home to an agent for syndication overseas. Listings for *Syndicates, news and press agencies* start on page 133. Listings of *National newspapers UK and Ireland* start on page 3, and the names of editors are included in each.

Most of the larger UK and overseas newspapers depend for news on their own staffs and press agencies. The most important overseas newspapers have permanent representatives in Britain who keep them supplied, not only with news of especial interest to the country concerned, but also with regular summaries of British news and with articles on events of particular importance. While many overseas newspapers and magazines have a London office, it is usual for manuscripts from freelance contributors to be submitted to the headquarters' editorial office overseas.

See also ...

- *Regional newspapers UK and Ireland*, page 12
- Newspapers are listed together with magazines for *Australia* (page 99), *Canada* (page 105), *New Zealand* (page 108), *South Africa* (page 110) and *USA* (page 112)
- *Recent changes to newspapers and magazines*, page 123
- *Dos and don'ts on approaching a publisher*, page 237.

National newspapers UK and Ireland

The Business

292 Vauxhall Bridge Road,
London SW1V 1DE
tel 020-7961 0000 *fax* 020-7961 0101
Sun 50p
Editor-in-Chief Andrew Neil

Standalone Sunday newspaper for the business and financial community. All aspects of business news with in-depth features ranging from captains of industry to the entrepreneurial and small business sector. Wide economic coverage, IT news, and personal finance features. Length: from 200-word news stories to 2500-word features. Payment: by arrangement.

City Editor Rob Bailhache
Deputy Editor Ian Watson
Political Editor Andrew Porter
World Business Editor Sylvia Pfeifer

Daily Express

Ludgate House, 245 Blackfriars Road,
London SE1 9UX
tel 020-7928 8000 *fax* 020-7620 1654
Albert House, 17 Bloom Street,
Manchester M1 3HZ
tel 0161-236 2112
Editor Chris Williams
Daily Mon-Fri 35p Sat 50p
Supplements **Saturday, The Sport**

Exclusive news; striking photos. Leader page articles (600 words); facts preferred to opinions. Payment: according to value.

City Editor Stephen Kahn
Diary Editor Kathryn Spencer
Environment Editor John Ingham
Features Editor Yvonne Illsley
Foreign Editor Gabriel Milland
Health Editor Michael Day
Literary Editor Graham Ball
News Editor David Leigh
Political Editor Patrick O'Flynn
Sports Editor Bill Bradshaw
Women's Editor Lorna Frame

Saturday

fax 020-7922 2753
Editor Martin Smith
Free with paper

Daily Mail

Northcliffe House, 2 Derry Street, London W8 5TT
tel 020-7938 6000 *fax* 020-7937 3251
Editor Paul Dacre
Daily Mon-Fri 35p Sat 50p
Supplements **Weekend**

Highest payment for good, exclusive news. Ideas welcomed for leader page articles (500–800 words). Exclusive news photos always wanted. Founded 1896.

City Editor Alex Brummer
Diary Editor Nigel Dempster
Education Editor Tony Halpin
Features Editor Eric Bailey
Deputy Foreign Editor Gerry Hunt
Health Editor Lisa Collins
Industrial Editor Darren Behar
Literary Editor Jane Mays
Money Editor Tony Hazell
News Editor Tony Gallagher
Picture Editor Paul Silva
Political Editor David Hughes
Showbiz Editor Alison Boshoff
Sports Editor Colin Gibson
Travel Editor Mark Edmonds
Weekend Editor Heather McGlone

Daily Mirror

1 Canada Square, Canary Wharf,
London E14 5AP
tel 020-7293 3000 *fax* 020-7293 3409
Editor Piers Morgan
Daily Mon-Sat 32p
Supplements **The Look, Mirror Football Mania, The Ticket**

Top payment for exclusive news and news pictures. Freelance articles used, and ideas bought: send synopsis only. 'Unusual' pictures and those giving a new angle on the news are welcomed; also cartoons. Founded 1903.

Business Editor Clinton Manning
Features Editor Matt Kelly
Health Editor Jill Palmer
Letters Editor Geraldine Esau
News Editor Connor Hanna
Picture Editor Ian Down
Political Editor James Hardy
Sports Editor Dean Morse

Daily Record

1 Central Quay, Glasgow G3 8DA
tel 0141-309 3000 *fax* 0141-309 3340
website www.record-mail.co.uk/rm
London office 1 Canada Square, Canary Wharf, London E14 5AP
tel 020-7293 3000
Editor Peter Cox
Daily Mon-Fri 32p, Sat 35p
Supplements **Saturday**

Topical articles, from 300–700 words; exclusive stories of Scottish interest and exclusive colour photos.

Features Editor Jill Main
Health & Science Correspondent Judith Duffy
News Editor Tom Hamilton
Picture Editor Stuart Nicol
Political Editor Paul Sinclair
Sports Editor Alan Thomson
Women's Page Editor Jill Main

Saturday

Editor Angela Dewar
Free with paper

Lifestyle magazine and entertainment guide. Reviews, travel features, shopping, personalities. Payment: by arrangement. Illustrations: colour.

Daily Sport

19 Great Ancoats Street, Manchester M60 4BT
tel 0161-236 4466 *fax* 0161-236 4535
Editor David Beevers, *Editor-in-Chief* Tony Livesey
Daily Mon-Fri 35p

Factual stories and series. Length: up to 1000 words. Illustrations: b&w and colour photos, cartoons. Payment: £30–£5000. Founded 1988.

Features and News Editor Justin Dunn
Sports Editor Mark Smith

Daily Star

Ludgate House, 245 Blackfriars Road, London SE1 9UX
tel 020-7928 8000 *fax* 020-7922 7960
Editor Peter Hill
Daily Mon-Sat 30p

Hard news exclusives, commanding substantial payment. Major interviews with big-star personalities; short features; series based on people rather than things; picture features. Payment: short features £75–£100; full page £250–£300; double page £400–£600,otherwise by negotiation. Illustrations: line, half-tone. Founded 1978.

Deputy Editor Hugh Whittow
Entertainment Editor Gareth Morgan
Features Editor Dawn Neesom
News Editor Kieron Saunders
Political Editor tba
Sports Editor Jim Mansell

The Daily Telegraph

1 Canada Square, Canary Wharf, London E14 5DT
tel 020-7538 5000 *fax* 020-7538 6242
websites www.telegraph.co.uk
www.sport.telegraph.co.uk
www.travel.telegraph.co.uk
www.money.telegraph.co.uk
Editor Charles Moore
Daily Mon-Fri 45p Sat 75p
Supplements **Appointments, Arts & Books, dotcom.telegraph, Money-Go-Round, Motoring, Property, Telegraph Magazine, Television & Radio, T2, Weekend**

Articles on a wide range of subjects of topical interest considered. Preliminary letter and synopsis required. Length: 700–1000 words. Payment: by arrangement. Founded 1855.

Arts Editor Sarah Crompton
City Editor Neil Collins
Education Editor John Clare
Environment Editor Charles Clover
Fashion Editor Hilary Alexander
Features Editor Richard Preston
Foreign Editor Alec Russell
Health Features Editor Christine Doyle
Health News Editor Celia Hall
Literary Editor Kate Summerscale
Media Correspondent Tom Leonard
News Editor Richard Spencer
Picture Editor Bob Bodman
Political Editor George Jones
Sports Editor David Welch

Electronic Telegraph

email et@telegraph.co.uk
website www.telegraph.co.uk/
Editor Derek Bishton
Daily Free to Internet subscribers

Based on *The Daily Telegraph*.

Juiced

website www.juiced.com
Weekly Free to internet subscribers

Student magazine.

Planet

website www.the-planet.co.uk
Free to internet subscribers

Travel writing from the *Daily Telegraph* and the *Sunday Telegraph*.

Telegraph Magazine

Editor Michelle Lavery
Free with Sat paper

Short profiles (about 1600 words); articles of topical interest. Preliminary study of the magazine essential. Illustrations: all types. Payment: by arrangement. Founded 1964.

Financial Times

1 Southwark Bridge, London SE1 9HL
tel 020-7873 3000 *fax* 020-7873 3076
website www.ft.com
Editor Andrew Gowers
Daily Mon-Sat £1
Supplements **Business Books, Companies & Markets, Creative Business, FT Fund Management, FT-IT, How To Spend It, Surveys, Weekend FT, Weekend Money**

Articles of financial, commercial, industrial and economic interest. Length: 800–1000 words. Payment: by arrangement. Founded 1888.

Arts Editor Peter Aspden
Banking Editor Charles Pretzlik
City Editor Martin Dickson
Deputy Editor John Ridding
Features Editor John Gapper
Food & Travel Editor Jill James
Growing Business Correspondent Katherine Campbell
International Affairs Editor Quentin Peel
Investment Editor Philip Coggan
Lex Editor George Graham
Observer Editor Sunny Tucker
Political Editor Brian Groom
Surveys Editor Rhys David
US edition Editor Lionel Barber
Weekend FT Editor Julia Cuthbertson
World News Editor Edward Carr

The Guardian

119 Farringdon Road, London EC1R 3ER
tel 020-7278 2332 *fax* 020-7837 2114
164 Deansgate, Manchester M60 2RR
tel 0161-832 7200 *fax* 0161-832 5351
Editor Alan Rusbridger
Daily Mon-Fri 45p Sat 75p
Supplements **The Editor, Education, Friday Review, G2, Media Guardian, Office Hours, Online, Review, Society, Space, The Week, Weekend**

Few articles are taken from outside contributors except on its specialist pages. Length: not exceeding 1200 words. Illustrations: news and features photos. Payment: from £170.83 per 1000 words; from £50.94 for illustrations. Founded 1821.

Arts Editor Dan Glaister
Books Editor Claire Armitstead
Deputy Editor Georgina Henry
Deputy Editor (News) Paul Johnson
Economics Editor Victor Keegan
Education Editor Will Woodward
Fashion Editor Jess Cartner-Morley
Features Editor Ian Katz
Financial Editor Paul Murphy
Foreign Editor Ed Pilkington
Home Editor Harriet Sherwood
Media Editor Janine Gibson
News Editor Andrew Culf
Political Editor Michael White
Religious Editor Stephen Bates
Science Editor Tim Radford
Sports Editor Ben Clissitt
Travel Editor Charlie Burgess
Women's Editor Clare Margetson

Guardian Unlimited

website www.guardian.co.uk
Editor-in-Chief Emily Bell

Weekend

Editor Katherine Viner
Free with Sat paper

Features on world affairs, major profiles, food and drink, home life, the arts, travel, leisure, etc. Also good reportage on social and political subjects. Illustrations: b&w photos and line, cartoons. Payment: apply for rates.

The Herald

Scottish Media Newspapers Ltd,
200 Renfield Street, Glasgow G2 3PR
tel 0141-302 7000 *fax* 0141-333 1147
website www.theherald.co.uk
London office 3 Waterhouse Square, 138-142 Holborn, London EC1N 2NY
tel 020-7882 1060
Editor Mark Douglas-Home
Daily Mon-Fri 50p Sat 55p

Articles up to 1000 words. Founded 1783.

Arts Editor Keith Bruce
Assistant Editor Melanie Reid
Business Editor Robert Powell
Joint Deputy Editors Joan McAlpine and Kevin McKenna
Diary Editor Ken Smith
Executive Editor Colin McDiarmid
Features Editor Cate Devine
News Editor Magnus Llewellin
Sports Editor Donald Cowey

The Independent

Independent House, 191 Marsh Wall, London E14 9RS
tel 020-7005 2000 *fax* 020-7005 2628
Editor-in-Chief Simon Kelner
Daily Mon-Fri 50p Sat 90p
Supplements **Business Review, Education, The Information, Review, Traveller, Weekend Review, Your Money**

Occasional freelance contributions; preliminary letter advisable. Payment: by arrangement. Founded 1986.

Arts Editor Ian Irvine
Business & City Editor Jeremy Warner
Education Editor Richard Garner
Environment Editor Mike McCarthy
Features Editor Laurence Earle
Foreign Editor Leonard Doyle
Health Editor Jeremy Laurance

Literary Editor Boyd Tonkin
Media Editor Jojo Moyes
News Editor Adam Leigh
Picture Editor Lynn Cullen
Political Editor Andrew Grice
Sports Editor Paul Newman

The Independent Magazine

Editor Lisa Markwell
Free with Sat paper

Profiles and illustrated articles of topical interest; all material commissioned. Preliminary study of the magazine essential. Length: 500–3000 words. Illustrations: cartoons; commissioned colour and b&w photos. Payment: by arrangement. Founded 1988.

Independent on Sunday

Independent House, 191 Marsh Wall, London E14 9RS
tel 020-7005 2000 *fax* 020-7005 2999
Editor Tristan Davies, *Editor-at-Large* Janet Street-Porter
Sun £1.10
Supplements **Business, Life Etc, The Sunday Review, Smart Moves, Sportsweek, Travel**

News, features and articles. Illustrated, including cartoons. Payment: by negotiation. Founded 1990.

Arts Editor, Life Etc Marcus Field
Assistant Editor David Randall
Business Editor Jason Nissé
Comment Executive Editor Anne McElvoy
Deputy Editor Michael Williams
Environment Editor Geoffrey Lean
Features Editor, Life Etc Nick Coleman
Foreign Editor Ray Whitaker
News Editor Peter Victor
Picture Editor Sophie Batterbury
Political Editor Colin Brown
Sports Editor Neil Morton

The Sunday Review

tel 020-7293 2000 *fax* 020-7293 2027
Editor Andrew Tuck
Free with paper

Original features of general interest with potential for photographic illustration. Material mostly commissioned. Length: 1000–5000 words. Illustrations: transparencies. Payment: £150 per 1000 words.

Ireland on Sunday

Ireland on Sunday Ltd, Embassy House, Ballsbridge, Dublin 4, Republic of Ireland
tel (01) 6375800 *fax* (01) 6375880
email news@irelandonsunday.com
website www.irelandonsunday.com
Editor Paul Drury
Sun E1.20

Mid-market tabloid. Considers unsolicited material. Length: 2500 words (articles/features), 800 words (news). Payment: by negotiation. Founded 1997.

Features Editor Philip Nolan
Sports Editor Jack White

Irish Examiner

1-6 Academy Street, Cork, Republic of Ireland
tel (021) 4272722, 4802153 (newsroom)
fax (021) 4275477
email (department)@examiner.ie
website www.examiner.ie
Editor Tim Vaughan
Daily Mon-Sat IR90p

Features. Material mostly commissioned. Length: 1000 words. Payment: by arrangement. Founded 1841.

Features Editor Dan Buckley
News Editor Brian Carroll
Picture Editor John Donovan
Sports Editor Tony Leen

Irish Independent

Independent House, 90 Middle Abbey Street, Dublin 1, Republic of Ireland
tel (01) 7055333 *fax* (01) 8720304/8731787
Editor Vincent Doyle
Daily Mon-Sat E1.30

Special articles on topical or general subjects. Length: 700–1000 words. Payment: editor's estimate of value.

Business Editor Richard Curran
Deputy Editor Michael Wolsey
Diary Editor Angela Phelan
Features Editor Peter Carvosso
News Editor Philip Molloy
Picture Editor Danny Thornton
Political Editor Chris Glennon
Sports Editor Patrick J. Cunningham

Irish Times

11-15 D'Olier Street, Dublin 2, Republic of Ireland
tel (01) 6792022 *fax* (01) 6719407
Editor Conor Brady
Daily Mon-Sat E1.27

Mainly staff-written. Specialist contributions (800–2000 words) by commission on basis of ideas submitted. Payment: at editor's valuation. Illustrations: photos and line drawings.

Arts Editor Victoria White
Features Editor Sheila Wayman
Finance Editor Paul O'Neill
Foreign Editor Paul Gillespie
Literary Editor Caroline Walsh
News Editor Willy Clingan
Picture Editor Dermot O'Shea

Political Editor Geraldine Kennedy
Special Reports Editor Ray Comiskey
Sports Editor Malachy Logan

The Irish Times on the Web
website www.ireland.com

Mail on Sunday
Northcliffe House, 2 Derry Street, London W8 5TS
tel 020-7938 6000 *fax* 020-7937 3829
Editor Peter Wright
Sun £1
Supplements **Financial Mail on Sunday, Night & Day, Review, You**

Articles. Payment: by arrangement. Illustrations: line, half-tone; cartoons. Founded 1982.

City Editor Ben Laurance
Diary Editor Nigel Dempster
Features Editor Sian James
Literary Editor Susanna Gross
News Editor Paul Field
Picture Editor Liz Cocks
Political Editor Simon Walters
Sports Editor Malcolm Vallerius

Financial Mail on Sunday
tel 020-7938 6984
email fmos@mailonsunday.co.uk
website www.financialmail.co.uk
Editor Ben Laurance
Free with paper
Personal Finance Editor Jeff Prestridge

City, industry, business, and personal finance. News stories up to 1500 words. Payment by arrangement. Full colour illustrations and photography commissioned.

Night & Day
tel 020-7938 7051 *fax* 020-7937 7488
Editor Christena Appleyard
Free with paper

Interviews, entertainment-related features and TV listings. Length: 1000–3000 words. Illustrations: colour photos. Founded 1993.

Review
Editor Jim Gillespie

Investigative journalism, reportage, features, and film, TV, book and theatre reviews.

You
Editor Sue Peart
Deputy Editor Catherine Fenton
Free with paper

Women's interest features. Length: 500–2500 words. Payment: by arrangement. Illustrations: full colour and b&w drawings commissioned; also colour photos.

Morning Star
(formerly Daily Worker)
People's Press Printing Society Ltd, Cape House, 787 Commercial Road, London E14 7HG
tel 020-7538 5181 *fax* 020-7538 5125
email morsta@geo2.poptel.org.uk
Editor John Haylett
Daily Mon-Sat 50p

Newspaper for the labour movement. Articles of general interest. Illustrations: photos, cartoons, drawings. Founded 1930.

Arts, Media & Features Editor Kevin Russell
Diary Editor Mike Ambrose
Financial Editor Daniel Coysh
Foreign Editor Brian Denny
Health Editor Dan O'Neill
Industrial & News Editor Ian Morrison
Political Editor Mike Ambrose
Sports Editor Alex Reid

News of the World
1 Virginia Street, London E1 9XR
tel 020-7782 1000 *fax* 020-7583 9504
Editor Rebekah Wade, *Deputy Editor* Andy Coulson
Sun 60p

Uses freelance material. Payment: by negotiation. Founded 1843.

Assistant Editor (Features) Gary Thompson
Money Editor Peter Prendergast
News Editor Greg Miskia
Political Editor Ian Kirby
Royal Editor Clive Goodman
Sports Editor Mike Dunn
Travel Editor Jon Barnsley

Sunday Magazine
Phase 2, 5th Floor, 1 Virginia Street, London E1 9BD
tel 020-7782 7900 *fax* 020-7782 7474
Editor Judy McGuire
Free with paper

The Observer
119 Farringdon Road, London EC1R 3ER
tel 020-7278 2332 *fax* 020-7713 4250
Editor Roger Alton
Sun £1.20
Supplements **Business, Cash, Escape, Life, Observer Sport Monthly, Observer Food Monthly, Observer Review, The Observer TV, Sport**

Some articles and illustrations commissioned. Payment: by arrangement. Founded 1791.

Arts Editor Jane Ferguson
Business Editor Frank Kane
City Editor Richard Wachman
Economics Editor William Keegan
Fashion Editor Jo Adams
Foreign Editor Arnold Kemp
Literary Editor Robert McCrum

News Editor Andy Malone
OFM Editor Lucy Cavendish
OSM Editor Matt Tench
Picture Editor Greg Whitmore
Political Editor Kamal Ahmed
Review Editor Lisa O'Kelly
Screen Editor Akin Ojomu
Sports Editor Brian Oliver
Travel Editor Jeanette Hyde

Life
tel 020-7713 4175 *fax* 020-7239 9837
Editor Allan Jenkins
Free with paper

Commissioned features. Length: 2000–3000 words. Illustrations: first-class colour and b&w photos. Payment: NUJ rates; £150 per illustration.

The Observer Online
website www.observer.co.uk

Scotland on Sunday

108 Holyrood Road, Edinburgh EH8 8AS
tel 0131-620 8620 *fax* 0131-620 8491
tel 0141-332 6163
Editor John McLellan (acting)
Sun 70p

Features on all subjects, not necessarily Scottish. Payment: by arrangement. Founded 1988.

News Editor Peter Laing
Political Editor Jason Allardyce

Scotland on Sunday Magazine
Editor Deborah Collcutt
Free with paper

The Scotsman

Barclay House, 108 Holyrood Road,
Edinburgh EH8 8AS
tel 0131-620 8620 *fax* 0131-620 8615
Editor Iain Martin
Daily Mon-Fri 40p Sat 50p
Supplements **S2, Saturday Magazine**

Considers articles on political, economic and general themes which add substantially to current information. Prepared to commission topical and controversial series from proved authorities. Length: 800–1000 words. Illustrations: outstanding news pictures, cartoons. Payment: by arrangement. Founded 1817.

Arts Editor Andrew Eaton
Business Editor Ian Watson
Education Editor Seonag MacKinnon
Features Editor Charlotte Ross
Foreign Editor Andrew McLeod
Literary Editor David Robinson
News Editor Gordon Hay
Political Editor (Westminster) Fraser Nelson
Assistant Editor (Politics) Hamish Macdonell
Saturday Magazine Editor Sandra Colamartino
Sports Editor Donald Walker
S2 Editor Charlotte Ross

The Star

Independent Star Ltd, Star House,
62A Terenure Road North, Dublin 6w,
Republic of Ireland
tel (01) 4901228 *fax* (01) 4902193/4902188
Editor Gerard Colleran
Daily Mon-Sat E1.00

General articles relating to news and sport, and features. Length: 1000 words. Illustrations: colour photos. Payment: by negotiation. Founded 1989.

Deputy Editor Danny Smyth
News Editor Dave O'Connell
Picture Editor Bernard Phelan
Political Editor Stephen O'Brien
Sports Editor Eoin Brannigan

The Sun

News Group Newspapers Ltd, Virginia Street,
London E1 9XP
tel 020-7782 4000 *fax* 020-7488 3253
Editor David Yelland
Daily Mon-Fri 28p, Sat 30p
Supplements **Super Goals, The TV Mag**

Takes freelance material, including cartoons. Payment: by negotiation. Founded 1969.

Business Editor Ian King
Features Editor Sam Carlisle
Health Editor Jacqui Thornton
Letters Editor Sue Cook
News Editor Sue Thompson
Picture Editor John Edwards
Political Editor Trevor Kavanagh
Showbiz Editor Dominic Mohan
Sports Editor Ted Chadwick
Travel Editor Lisa Bielfeld
Women's Editor Sharon Hendry

The Sunday Business Post

80 Harcourt Street, Dublin 2,
Republic of Ireland
tel (01) 6026000 *fax* (01) 6796496/6796498
Editor Ted Harding
Sun E1.65

Features on financial, economic and political topics; also lifestyle, media and science articles. Illustrations: colour and b&w photos, graphics, cartoons. Payment: by negotiation. Founded 1989.

Arts Editor Jennifer O'Connell
The Market Editor Kathleen Barrington
IT Editor Gavin Daly
Media Editor Catherine O'Mahony
Newsdesk Fiona Ness
Political Editor Maol Muire Tynan

Sunday Express

Ludgate House, 245 Blackfriars Road, London SE1 9UX
tel 020-7928 8000 *fax* 020-7620 1653
Editor Martin Townsend
Sun £1
Supplements **Sunday Express 'S' Magazine**

Exclusive news stories, photos, personality profiles and features of controversial or lively interest. Length: 800–1000 words. Payment: top rates. Founded 1918.

City Editor Patrick Tooher
Features Editor Giulia Rhodes
Literary Editor Graham Ball
News Editor David Dillon
Political Editor Julia Llewelyn-Smith
Sports Editor Dave Harrison

Sunday Express 'S' Magazine

tel 020-7922 7297
Free with paper
Editor Louise Robinson (acting)

Sunday Herald

Scottish Media Publishing Ltd, 200 Renfield Street, Glasgow G2 3PR
tel 0141-302 7800 *fax* 0141-302 7809
website www.sundayherald.com
Editor Andrew Jaspan
Sun
Supplements **Directory, Seven Days, Sport, Sunday Herald Magazine**

News and stories about Scotland, its characteristics and people. Opportunities for freelances with quality contacts. Founded 1999.

Business Editor Kenny Kemp
Deputy Editor Richard Walker
Features Editor Charlene Sweeney
Magazine Editor Jane Wright
News Editor David Milne
Political Editor Douglas Fraser
Sports Editor David Dick

Sunday Independent

Independent House, 90 Middle Abbey Street, Dublin 1, Republic of Ireland
tel (01) 7055333 *fax* (01) 7055779
Editor Aengus Fanning
Sun £1.20

Special articles. Length: according to subject. Illustrations: topical or general interest, cartoons. Payment: at editor's valuation.

Business Editor Shane Ross
Deputy Editors Anne Harris, Willie Kealy
Political Editor Jody Corcoran
Sports Editor Adhamhnan O'Sullivan

Sunday Life

124 Royal Avenue, Belfast BT1 1EB
tel 028-9026 4300 *fax* 028-9055 4507
email betty.arnold@belfasttelegraph.co.uk
Editor Martin Lindsay
Sun 70p

Items of interest to Northern Ireland Sunday tabloid readers. Payment: by arrangement. Illustrations: colour and b&w pictures and graphics. Founded 1988.

Features Editor Sue Corbett
News Editor Martin Hill
Photographic Editor Fred Hoare
Sports Editor Jim Gracey
Women's Page Editor Sue Corbett

Sunday Mail

1 Central Quay, Glasgow G3 8DA
tel 0141-309 3000 *fax* 0141-309 3582
website www.record-mail.co.uk/rm
London office 1 Canada Square, Canary Wharf, London E14 5AP
Editor Allan Rennie
Sun 60p
Supplements **MailSport Monthly, 7-Days**

Exclusive stories and pictures (in colour if possible) of national and Scottish interest; also cartoons. Payment: above average.

Assistant Editor Andrew Sannholm
Deputy Editor Bob Caldwell
Features Editor Susie Cormack
Health Editor Dr Gareth Smith
News Editor Jim Wilson
Picture Editor Andrew Hosie
7-Days Editor Liz Steele
Showbiz Editor Billy Sloan
Sports Editor George Cheyne
Women's Page Editor Donna White

Sunday Mirror

1 Canada Square, Canary Wharf, London E14 5AP
tel 020-7293 3000 *fax* 020-7293 3939
website www.mirror.co.uk
Editor Tina Weaver
Sun 65p
Supplements **M Celebs**

Concentrates on human interest news features, social documentaries, dramatic news and feature photos. Ideas, as well as articles, bought. Payment: high, especially for exclusives. Founded 1963.

Associate Editor Mike Small
Deputy Editor Mark Thomas
Executive Editor (Pictures) Ivor Game
Editor (Sport) Steve McKenlay
Executive Editor (Features) Jane Johnson
News Editor Euan Stretch

The Sunday People

1 Canada Square, Canary Wharf, London E14 5AP
tel 020-7293 3000 *fax* 020-7293 3517
website www.thepeople.co.uk
Editor Neil Wallis
Sun 65p
Supplements **Sunday People Magazine**

Investigative features, single articles and series considered; pictures should be supplied with contributions if possible. Features should be of deep human interest, whether the subject is serious or light-hearted. Very strong sports following. Exclusivenews and news-feature stories also considered. Payment: rates high, even for tips that lead to published news stories.

Features Editor Dawn Alford
News Editor Ian Edmondson
Picture Editor Paula Derry
Political Editor Nigel Nelson
Sports Editor Lee Clayton

Sunday People Magazine

Editor Amanda Cable
Free with paper

Sunday Post

D.C. Thomson & Co. Ltd, 144 Port Dundas Road, Glasgow G4 0HZ
tel 0141-332 9933 *fax* 0141-331 1595
Albert Square, Dundee DD1 9QJ
tel (01382) 223131 *fax* (01382) 201064
Editor David Pollington
Sun 65p

Human interest, topical, domestic and humorous articles, and exclusive news. Payment: on acceptance.

The Sunday Post Magazine

tel (01382) 223131 *fax* (01382) 201064
Editor Maggie Dun
Monthly Free with paper

General interest articles. Length: 1000–2000 words. Illustrations: colour transparencies. Payment: varies. Founded 1988.

Sunday Sport

19 Great Ancoats Street, Manchester M60 4BT
tel 0161-236 4466 *fax* 0161-236 4535
Editor Mark Harris
Sun 60p

Founded 1986.

Assistant Editor Simon Dean
Deputy Editor Jon Wise
Executive Editor John Livesey
Features Editor Sarah Stephens
News Editor Paul Carter
Picture Editor Paul Currie
Sports Editor Marc Smith

Sunday Telegraph

1 Canada Square, Canary Wharf, London E14 5DT
tel 020-7538 5000 *fax* 020-7513 2504
Editor Dominic Lawson
Sun £1
Supplements **Appointments, City, Review, Sport, Sunday Telegraph Magazine, Travel**

Occasional freelance material accepted.

Arts Editor Suzannah Herbert
City Editor Robert Peston
Comment Editor Mark Law
Deputy Editor Matthew d'Ancona
Diary Editor Adam Helliker
Executive Editor Con Coughlin
Features Editor Anna Murphy
Foreign Editor Robin Gedye
Literary Editor Miriam Gross
News Editor Richard Ellis
Picture Editor Nigel Skelsey
Sports Editor John Ryan
Travel Editor Graham Boynton

Sunday Telegraph Magazine

tel 020-7538 7590 *fax* 020-7538 7074
email sunmag@telegraph.co.uk
Editor Lucy Tuck, *Executive Editor* Rebecca Tyrrel
Free with paper

All material is commissioned. Founded 1995.

The Sunday Times

1 Pennington Street, London E98 1ST
tel 020-7782 5000 *fax* 020-7782 5658
website www.sunday-times.co.uk
Editor John Witherow
Sun £1.10
Supplements **Appointments, Doors, Business, Culture, Funday Times, Money, News Review, Rich List, Sport, Style, The Sunday Times Magazine, Travel**

Special articles by authoritative writers on politics, literature, art, drama, music, finance and science, and topical matters. Payment: top rate for exclusive features. Founded 1822.

Culture Editor Helen Hawkins
Economics Editor David Smith
Education Correspondent Judith O'Reilly
Literary Editor Caroline Gascoigne
News Editor Charles Hymas
News Review Sarah Baxter
Chief Political Correspondent Eben Black
Sports Editor Alex Butler
Travel Editor Christine Walker

The Sunday Times Magazine

tel 020-7782 7000
Editor Robin Morgan
Free with paper

Articles and pictures. Illustrations: colour and b&w photos. Payment: by negotiation.

The Sunday Times Scotland

Times Newspapers Ltd, 124 Portman Street, Kinning Park, Glasgow G41 1EJ
tel 0141-420 5100 *fax* 0141-420 5262
Editor Dean Nelson
Free with *The Sunday Times*

News, features and sport. Illustrations: colour photos, cartoons and graphics. Payment: £100 per feature; £50 for illustrations. Founded 1988.

The Sunday Tribune

Tribune Publications plc, 15 Lower Baggot Street, Dublin 2, Republic of Ireland
tel (01) 661 5555 *fax* (01) 661 5302
email editorial@tribune.ie
Editor Matt Cooper
Sun £1
Supplements **People, Review**

Newspaper containing news (inc. foreign), articles, features and photo features. Length: 600–2800 words. Illustrations: colour and b&w photos and cartoons. Payment: £100 per 1000 words; £100 for illustrations. Founded 1980.

Arts Editor Lise Hand
Business Editor Brian Carey
Deputy Editor Paddy Murray
News Editor Martin Wall
Photo Desk Bea McMunn
Sports Editor Mark Jones
Supplements Editor Ros Dee

The Times

1 Pennington Street, London E98 1TT
tel 020-7782 5000 *fax* 020-7488 3242
website www.thetimes.co.uk
Editor Robert Thomson
Daily Mon-Fri 40p Sat 70p
Supplements **Crème, Football Handbook, London List, Money Play, Times 2, Times Law, The Times Magazine, Times Sport, Travel, Weekend**

Outside contributions considered from: experts in subjects of current interest and writers who can make first-hand experience or reflection come readably alive. Phone appropriate section editor. Length: up to 1200 words. Founded 1785.

Arts Editor Sarah Vine
Business/City Editor Patience Wheatcroft
Deputy Editor Ben Preston
Education Editor John O'Leary
Features Editor Anne Barrowclough
Foreign Editor Bronwen Maddox
Health Editor Nigel Hawkes
Industrial Correspondent Christine Buckley
Literary Editor Erica Wagner
Media Editor Ray Snoddy
News Editor John Wellman
Political Editor Philip Webster
Science Correspondent Mark Henderson
Sports Editor David Chappell
Weekend Times Editor Jane Wheatley

The Times Magazine

Editor Gill Morgan
Free with Sat paper

Features. Illustrated.

Wales on Sunday

Thomson House, Havelock Street, Cardiff CF10 1XR
tel 029-2058 3583 *fax* 029-2058 3725
Editor Alan Edmunds
Sun 60p

National Sunday newspaper of Wales offering comprehensive news, features and entertainments coverage at the weekend, with a particular focus on events in Wales. Accepts general interest articles, preferably with a Welsh connection. Founded 1989.

News Editor Ceri Gould
Senior Assistant Editor Mike Smith
Sports Editor Paul Abbandonato

Regional newspapers UK and Ireland

Regional newspapers are listed in alphabetical order under region. Some will accept and pay for letters to the editor, brief fillers, and gossip paragraphs, as well as puzzles and quizzes. See also Writing for newspapers on page 124.

Belfast

Belfast Telegraph

124-144 Royal Avenue, Belfast BT1 1EB
tel 028-9026 4000 *fax* 028-9033 1332 (also photographic), 9055 4540 (news only), 9055 4517 (features), 9055 4508 (sport)
email editor@belfasttelegraph.co.uk
website www.belfasttelegraph.co.uk
Editor Edmund Curran
Daily Mon-Sat 45p
Features Editor John Caruth
News Editor Paul Connolly
Picture Editor Gerry Fitzgerald
Sports Editor John Laverty

Any material relating to Northern Ireland. Payment: by negotiation. Founded 1870.

Irish News

113-117 Donegall Street, Belfast BT1 2GE
tel 028-9032 2226 *fax* 028-9033 7505
website www.irishnews.com
Editor Noel Doran
Daily Mon-Sat 45p
Business Editor Gary McDonald
Features Editor Joanna Braniff
News Editor Stephen McCaffery
Picture Editor Brendan Murphy
Sports Editor Thomas Hawkins

Articles of historical and topical interest. Payment: by arrangement. Founded 1855.

News Letter

46-56 Boucher Crescent, Boucher Road, Belfast BT12 6QY
tel 028-9068 0000 *fax* 028-9066 4412
email newsletter@mgn.co.uk
website www.newsletter.co.uk
Editor Geoff Martin
Daily Mon-Sat 35p
Features Editor Geoff Hill
Picture Editor tba
Sports Editor Brian Millar

Pro-Union. Founded 1737.

Channel Islands

Guernsey Press and Star

Braye Road, Vale, Guernsey GY1 3BW
tel (01481) 240240 *fax* (01481) 240235
Editor Richard Digard
Daily Mon-Sat 37p
Features Editor Suzanne Heneghan
News Editor James Falla
Sports Editor Rob Batiste

News and feature articles. Length: 500–700 words. Illustrations: colour and b&w photos. Payment: by negotiation. Founded 1897.

Jersey Evening Post

PO Box 582, Five Oaks, St Saviour, Jersey JE4 8XQ
tel (01534) 611611 *fax* (01534) 611622
email editorial@jerseyeveningpost.com
Editor Chris Bright
Daily Mon-Sat 40p
Features Editor Elaine Hanning
News Editor Sue le Ruez
Picture Editor Peter Mourant
Sports Editor Ron Felton

News and features with a Channel Islands angle. Length: 1000 words (articles/features), 300 words (news). Illustrations: colour and b&w. Payment: £90 (articles/features), £27 (news); £30. Founded 1890.

Cork

Evening Echo (Cork)

Cork Examiner Publications Ltd, 1-6 Academy Street, Cork, Republic of Ireland
tel (021) 4272722 *fax* (021) 4802135
Editor Maurice Gubbins
Daily Mon-Sat E1.27
Deputy Editor Vincent Kelly
News Editor Emma Connolly

Picture Editor Brian Lougheed
Sports Editor Liam Horan

Articles, features and news for the area. Illustrations: colour prints.

Dublin

Evening Herald

90 Middle Abbey Street, Dublin 1, Republic of Ireland
tel (01) 7055333
email eveningherald@unison.independent.ie
Editor Gerard O'Regan
Daily Mon-Sat E1.00
Deputy Editor Noirin Hegarty
Assistant Editors Dave Kenny, Ronan Price, Mark Evans
Associate Editor Frank Coghlan
Features Editor Dave Lawlor
Deputy Features Editor Sile McArdle
News Editor Martin Brennan
Deputy News Editor Stephen Rea
Assistant News Editor Bairbre Power
Picture Editor Declan Cahill
Sports Editor David Courtney

Articles. Payment: by arrangement. Illustrations: line, half-tone, cartoons.

East Anglia

Cambridge Evening News

Winship Road, Milton, Cambs. CB4 6PP
tel (01223) 434434 *fax* (01223) 434415
email colingrant@cambridge-news.co.uk
Editor Colin Grant
Daily Mon-Sat 35p
News Editor Helen King
Sports Editor Chris Gill

The voice of Mid-Anglia – news, views and sport. Illustrations: colour prints, b&w and colour graphics. Payment: by negotiation. Founded 1888.

East Anglian Daily Times

30 Lower Brook Street, Ipswich, Suffolk IP4 1AN
tel (01473) 230023 *fax* (01473) 233228
Editor Terry Hunt
Daily Mon-Fri 44p Sat 50p
Features Editor Julian Ford
News Editor Aynsley Davidson
Picture Editor Paul Nixon
Sports Editor Nick Garnham

Features of East Anglian interest, preferably with pictures. Length: 500 words. Illustrations: colour, b&w. Payment: negotiable; illustrations NUJ rates. Founded 1874.

Eastern Daily Press

Prospect House, Rouen Road, Norwich NR1 1RE
tel (01603) 628311 *fax* (01603) 612930
website www.ecn.co.uk
London office House of Commons Press Gallery, House of Commons, London SW1A 0AA
tel 020-7219 3384 *fax* 020-7222 3830
Editor Peter Franzen
Daily Mon-Wed 40p, Thur, Fri 45p, Sat 50p

Limited market for articles of East Anglian interest not exceeding 900 words. Founded 1870.

Evening News

Prospect House, Rouen Road, Norwich NR1 1RE
tel (01603) 628311 *fax* (01603) 219060
Editor David Bourn
Daily Mon-Sat 32p
Features Editor Derek James
News Editor Amanda Patterson
Picture Editor Nolan Lincoln
Sports Editor David Cuffley

Interested in local news-based features. Length: up to 500 words. Payment: NUJ or agreed rates. Founded 1882.

East Midlands

Burton Mail

Burton Daily Mail Ltd, 65-68 High Street, Burton on Trent DE14 1LE
tel (01283) 512345 *fax* (01283) 515351
Editor Paul Hazeldine
Daily Mon-Sat 32p
Deputy Editor Killoran Wills
Features Editor Bill Pritchard
News and Picture Editor Andy Parker
Sports Editor Rex Page

Features, news and articles of interest to Burton and south Derbyshire readers. Length: 400–500 words. Illustrations: colour and b&w. Payment: by negotiation. Founded 1898.

Chronicle & Echo, Northampton

Northamptonshire Newspapers Ltd, Upper Mounts, Northampton NN1 3HR
tel (01604) 467000 *fax* (01604) 467190
Editor Mark Edwards
Daily Mon-Sat 32p

Articles, features and news – mostly commissioned – of interest to the Northampton area. Length/illustrations: varies. Payment: by negotiation. Founded 1931.

Derby Evening Telegraph

Northcliffe House, Meadow Road, Derby DE1 2DW
tel (01332) 291111 *fax* (01322) 253027
website www.thisisderbyshire.co.uk

Editor Mike Norton
Daily Mon-Sat 29p
News Editor Michael Hill
News Features Editor Sarah Newton
Picture Editor Steve Mitchell
Sports Editor David Parkinson

Articles and news of local interest. Payment: by negotiation.

The Leicester Mercury

St George Street, Leicester LE1 9FQ
tel 0116-251 2512 *fax* 0116-253 0645
Editor Nick Carter
Daily Mon-Sat 27p

Occasional articles, features and news; submit ideas to editor first. Length/payment: by negotiation. Founded 1874.

Nottingham Evening Post

Castle Wharf House, Nottingham NG1 7EU
tel 0115-948 2000 *fax* 0115-964 4049
email nep.editorial@dial.pipex.com
website www.thisisnottingham.co.uk
Editor Graham Glen
Daily Mon-Sat 29p

Material on local issues considered. Founded 1878.

London

Evening Standard

Northcliffe House, 2 Derry Street, London W8 5EE
tel 020-7938 6000
website www.thisislondon.com
Editor Veronica Wadley
Daily Mon-Fri 35p
Features Editor Bernice Davison
News Editor Ian Walker
Picture Editor David Ofield
Sports Editor Martin Chilton

Articles of general interest considered, 1500 words or shorter; also news, pictures and ideas. Founded 1827.

ES Magazine

Editor Mimi Spencer
Weekly Free with paper

Feature ideas, exclusively about London. Payment: by negotiation. Illustrations: all types.

North

Evening Chronicle

Newcastle Chronicle and Journal Ltd, Groat Market, Newcastle upon Tyne NE1 1ED
tel 0191-232 7500 *fax* 0191-232 2256
Editor Paul Robertson
Daily Mon-Sat 30p
Features Editor Richard Ord
News Editor Mick Smith
Picture Editor Rod Wilson
Sports Editor Paul New

News, photos and features covering almost every subject of interest to readers in Tyne and Wear, Northumberland and Durham. Payment: by arrangement.

Evening Gazette

North Eastern Evening Gazette Ltd, Borough Road, Middlesbrough TS1 3AZ
tel (01642) 245401 *fax* (01642) 232014
email editor@eveninggazette.co.uk
Editor Steve Dyson
Daily Mon-Sat 27p

News, and topical and lifestyle features. Length: 600–800 words. Illustrations: line, half-tone, colour, graphics, cartoons. Payment: £75 per 1000 words; scale rate or by agreement for illustrations. Founded 1869.

Hartlepool Mail

Northeast Press Ltd, New Clarence House, Wesley Square, Hartlepool TS24 8BX
tel (01429) 274441 *fax* (01429) 869024
email mail.news@northeast-press.co.uk
Editor Harry Blackwood
Daily Mon-Sat 32p
Deputy Editor Neil Hunter
Picture Editor Dirk van der Werff
Sports Editor Roy Kelly

Features of local interest. Length: 500 words. Illustrations: colour, b&w photos, line. Payment: by negotiation. Founded 1877.

The Journal

Groat Market, Newcastle upon Tyne NE1 1ED
tel 0191-232 7500 *fax* 0191-261 8869
email jnl.newsdesk@ncjmedia.co.uk
Editor Gerard Henderson
Daily Mon-Sat 35p
Features Editor Jane Hall
News Editor Stephen Rouse
Picture Editor Simon Greener
Sports Editor Kevin Dinsdale

News, sport items and features of topical interest considered. Payment: by arrangement.

North-West Evening Mail

Newspaper House, Abbey Road, Barrow-in-Furness, Cumbria LA14 5QS
tel (01229) 840150 *fax* (01229) 840164/832141
Editor Bill Myers (acting)
Daily Mon-Sat 33p
News Editor Steve Hartley

Sports Editor Leo Clarke

'The Voice of Furness and West Cumbria.' Articles, features and news. Length: 500 words. Illustrations: b&w photos and occasional artwork. Payment: £30 (minimum); £10 for illustrations. Founded 1898.

The Northern Echo

Priestgate, Darlington, Co. Durham DL1 1NF
tel (01325) 381313 *fax* (01325) 380539
Editor Peter Barron
Daily Mon-Sat 32p
Features Editor Jenny Needham
News Editor Nigel Burton
Picture Editor Mike Gibb
Sports Editor Nick Loughlin

Articles of interest to North-East and North Yorkshire; all material commissioned. Preliminary study of newspaper advisable. Length: 800–1000 words. Illustrations: line, half-tone, colour – mostly commissioned. Payment: by negotiation. Founded 1870.

The Sunday Sun

Groat Market, Newcastle upon Tyne NE1 1ED
tel 0191-201 6251 *fax* 0191-230 0238
email scoop.sundaysun@ncjmedia.co.uk
Editor Peter Montellier
Sun 60p

Key requirements: immediate topicality and human sidelights on current problems. Particularly welcomed are special features of family appeal and news stories of special interest to the North of England. Length: 200–700 words. Payment: normal lineage rates, or by arrangement. Illustrations: photos. Founded 1919.

Sunderland Echo

Echo House, Pennywell, Sunderland, Tyne & Wear SR4 9ER
tel 0191-501 5800 *fax* 0191-534 5975
website www.sunderlandtoday.co.uk
Editor Andrew Smith
Daily Mon-Sat 32p

Local news, features and articles. Length: 500 words. Illustrations: colour and b&w photos, line, cartoons. Payment: negotiable. Founded 1875.

North West

Bolton Evening News

Newspaper House, Churchgate, Bolton, Lancs. BL1 1DE
tel (01204) 522345 *fax* (01204) 365068
email ben_editorial@boltoneveningnews.co.uk
tel (01204) 522345 *fax* (01204) 365068
email ben_editorial@newsquest.co.uk
Daily Mon-Sat 30p

Founded 1867.

Daily Post

PO Box 48, Old Hall Street, Liverpool L69 3EB
tel 0151-227 2000 *fax* 0151-236 4682
Editor Alastair Machray
Daily Mon-Sat 32p
Supplement **Daysix**
Features Editor Jane Haase
News Editor Andrew Edwards
Picture Editor Steve Shakeshaft
Sports Editor Richard Williamson

Articles of general interest and topical features of special interest to North West England and North Wales. No verse or fiction. Payment: according to value. News and feature illustrations. Founded 1855.

The Gazette, Blackpool

Blackpool Gazette & Herald Ltd, Avroe House, Avroe Crescent, Blackpool Business Park, Squires Gate, Blackpool FY4 2DP
tel (01253) 400888 *fax* (01253) 361870
email bpl_editorial@rim.co.uk
website www.blackpoolonline.co.uk
Editor tba, *Managing Director* Philip Welsh
Daily Mon-Sat 30p

Local news and articles of general interest, with photos if appropriate. Length: varies. Payment: on merit. Founded 1929.

Lancashire Evening Post

Oliver's Place, Fulwood, Preston PR2 9ZA
tel (01772) 254841 *fax* (01772) 880173
Editor Simon Reynolds
Daily Mon-Sat 30p

Topical articles on all subjects. Area of interest Wigan to Lake District, Lancs, and coast. Length: 600–900 words. Illustrations: colour and b&w photos, cartoons. Payment: by arrangement.

Lancashire Evening Telegraph

Newspaper House, High Street, Blackburn, Lancs. BB1 1HT
tel (01254) 678678
website www.thisislancashire.co.uk
Editor Kevin Young
Daily Mon-Sat 26p
News Editor Nick Nunn
Picture Editor John Napier
Sports Editor Neil Bramwell

Will consider general interest articles, such as property, motoring, finance, etc. Payment: by arrangement. Founded 1886.

Liverpool Echo

PO Box 48, Old Hall Street, Liverpool L69 3EB
tel 0151-227 2000 *fax* 0151-236 4682
website www.liverpool.com
Editor Mark Dickinson
Daily Mon-Sat 32p
Head of News Andrew Edwards
Picture Editor Stephen Shakeshaft
Sports Editor Ken Rogers

Articles of up to 600–800 words of local or topical interest; also cartoons. Payment: according to merit; special rates for exceptional material. Connected with, but independent of, the *Liverpool Daily Post*. Articles not interchangeable.

Manchester Evening News

164 Deansgate, Manchester M60 2RD
tel 0161-832 7200 editorial *fax* 0161-834 3814
features fax 0161-839 0968
Editor Paul Horrocks
Daily Mon-Sat 30p
Features Editor Maggie Henfield
News Editor Ian Wood
Picture Editor Simon Pendrigh
Sports Editor Peter Spencer

Feature articles of up to 1000 words, topical or general interest and illustrated where appropriate, should be addressed to the Features Editor. Payment: on acceptance.

Oldham Chronicle

PO Box 47, Union Street, Oldham, Lancs. OL1 1EQ
tel 0161-633 2121 *fax* 0161-627 0905
Editor Jim Williams
Daily Mon-Fri 30p

News and features on current topics and local history. Length: 1000 words. Illustrations: colour and b&w photos and line. Payment: £20–£25 per 1000 words; £16.32–£21.90 for illustrations. Founded 1854.

Northern Ireland – see Belfast

Scotland

Aberdeen Evening Express

Aberdeen Journals Ltd, PO Box 43, Lang Stracht, Mastrick, Aberdeen AB15 6DF
tel (01224) 690222 *fax* (01224) 699575
Editor Donald Martin
Daily Mon-Sat 32p
Features Editor Scott Begbie
News Editor Richard Prest
Sports Editor Jim Strachan

Lively evening paper. Illustrations: colour and b&w, cartoons. Payment: by arrangement.

The Courier and Advertiser

D.C. Thomson & Co. Ltd, 80 Kingsway East, Dundee DD4 8SL
tel (01382) 223131 *fax* (01382) 454590
email courier@dcthomson.co.uk
website www.thecourier.co.uk
London office 185 Fleet Street, London EC4A 2HS
tel 020-7400 1030 *fax* 020-7400 1089
Daily Mon-Sat 32p

Founded 1816 and 1801.

Dundee Evening Telegraph and Post

D.C. Thomson & Co. Ltd, 80 Kingsway East, Dundee DD4 8SL
tel (01382) 223131 *fax* (01382) 454590
London office 185 Fleet Street, London EC4A 2HS
tel 020-7400 1030 *fax* 020-7400 1089
Daily Mon-Fri 28p

Edinburgh Evening News

108 Holyrood Road, Edinburgh EH8 8AS
tel 0131-620 8620 *fax* 0131-620 8696
Editor Ian Stewart (acting)
Daily Mon-Sat 30p
Features Editor Sandra Dick
News Editor Jim G. Morrison
Picture Editor Tony Marsh
Sports Editor Martin Dempster

Features on current affairs, preferably in relation to our circulation area. Women's talking points, local historical articles; subjects of general interest; health and beauty, fashion.

Glasgow Evening Times

200 Renfield Street, Glasgow G2 3PR
tel 0141-302 7000 *fax* 0141-302 6600
website www.eveningtimes.co.uk
Editor Charles McGhee
Daily Mon-Sat 30p

Founded 1876.

Inverness Courier

PO Box 13, 9-11 Bank Lane, Inverness IV1 1QW
tel (01463) 233059 *fax* (01463) 243439
email editorial@inverness-courier.co.uk
Editor Jim Love
2 p.w. Tue 42p Fri 50p
News Editor Jack Gemmell
Sports Editor David Beck

Articles of Highland interest only. Unsolicited material accepted. Illustrations: colour and b&w photos. Payment: by arrangement. Founded 1817.

The Press and Journal
Lang Stracht, Aberdeen AB15 6DF
tel (01224) 690222
email pj.editor@ajl.co.uk
website www.thisisnorthscotland.co.uk
Editor Derek Tucker
Daily Mon-Sat 37p
Deputy Editor Kay Drummond
News Editor Fiona McWhirr
Picture Desk Kami Thomson
Sports Editor Jim Dolan

Contributions of Scottish interest. Payment: by arrangement. Illustrations: half-tone. Founded 1748.

The Sun
News International Newspapers, Scotland, 124 Portman Street, Kinning Park, Glasgow G41 1EJ
tel 0141-420 5200 *fax* 0141-420 5248
email thescottish-sun@the-sun.co.uk
Editor Bruce Waddell
Daily Mon-Sat 28p
Features Editor David Reynolds
News Editor Alan Muir
Picture Editor Mark Sweeney
Sports Editor Steve Wolstencroft

Scottish edition of *The Sun*. Illustrations: transparencies, colour and b&w prints, colour cartoons. Payment: by arrangement. Founded 1985.

South East

Evening Echo
Newspaper House, Chester Hall Lane, Basildon, Essex SS14 3BL
tel (01268) 522792 *fax* (01268) 469281
Editor Martin McNeill
Daily Mon-Fri 32p
Features Editor Sally King
News Editor Geraldine Underwood
Picture Editor Nick Ansell
Sports Editor Paul Alton

Mostly staff-written. Only interested in local material. Payment: by arrangement. Founded 1969.

Kent Today
395 High Street, Chatham, Kent ME4 4PQ
tel (01634) 830600 *fax* (01634) 829484
Daily Mon-Fri 25p
News Editor Sarah Clarke
Picture Editor Barry Hollis
Sports Editor Mike Rees

Paper with emphasis on local news and sport, plus regular feature pages. National news; with editions covering the Medway Towns, Gravesend and Dartford, Swale. Illustrations: line, half-tone.

The News, Portsmouth
The News Centre, Hilsea, Portsmouth PO2 9SX
tel 023-9266 4488 *fax* 023-92673363
email newsdesk@thenews.co.uk
website www.thenews.co.uk
Editor Mike Gilson
Daily Mon-Sat 32p
Features Editor John Millard
News Editor Colin McNeill
Picture Editor Steve Cutner
Sports Editor Colin Channon

Articles of relevance to southeast Hampshire and West Sussex. Payment by arrangement. Founded 1877.

Reading Evening Post
8 Tessa Road, Reading, Berks. RG1 8NS
tel 0118-918 3000 *fax* 0118-959 9363
Editor Andy Murrill
Daily Mon-Fri 25p
Features Editor Kate Magee
News Editor Ian Francis
Picture Editor Steve Templeman
Sports Editor Dave Wright

Topical articles based on current local news. Length: 800–1200 words. Payment: based on lineage rates. Illustrations: half-tone. Founded 1965.

The Southern Daily Echo
Newspaper House, Test Lane, Redbridge, Southampton SO16 9JX
tel 023-8042 4777 *fax* 023-8042 4770
Editor Ian Murray
Daily Mon-Sat 30p
Features Editor Andy Bissell
News Editor Gordon Sutter
Picture Editor Paul Collins
Sports Editor Dave King
Supplements Editor Emma Green

News, articles, features, sport. Length: varies. Illustrations: line, half-tone, colour. Payment: NUJ rates. Founded 1888.

Swindon Evening Advertiser
100 Victoria Road, Old Town, Swindon SN1 3BE
tel (01793) 528144 *fax* (01793) 542434
email editor@newswilts.co.uk
website www.thisiswiltshire.co.uk
Editor Simon O'Neill
Mon-Sat 32p

News and information relating to Swindon and Wiltshire only. Considers unsolicited material. Founded 1854.

South West

The Bath Chronicle

Bath Newspapers, Windsor House,
Windsor Bridge, Bath BA2 3AU
tel (01225) 322322 *fax* (01225) 322291
Editor David Gledhill
Daily Mon-Sat 32p
Features Editor Matt Mills
News Editor Paul Wiltshire
Picture Editor Kevin Bates
Sports Editor Neville Smith

Welcomes local news and features. Length: 200–500 words. Illustrations: colour photos. Payment: 8p–15.7p per printed line; £5 per photo where commissioned. Founded 1760.

Bristol Evening Post

Temple Way, Bristol BS99 7HD
tel 0117-934 3000
Editor Mike Lowe
Daily Mon-Sat 28p
Features Editor Matthew Shelley
News Editor Kevan Blackadder
Picture Editor Peter Watson
Sports Editor Chris Bartlett

Takes freelance news and articles. Payment: by arrangement. Founded 1932.

The Citizen

Gloucestershire Newspapers Ltd, St John's Lane,
Gloucester GL1 2AY
tel (01452) 424442 *fax* (01452) 420664
Editor Spencer Feeney
Daily Mon-Sat 30p

Local news and features for Gloucester and its districts. Length: 1000 words (articles/features), 300 words (news). Illustrations: colour. Payment: negotiable.

Dorset Echo

Newscom, Fleet House, Hampshire Road,
Weymouth, Dorset DT4 9XD
tel (01305) 830930 *fax* (01305) 830956
email newsdesk@dorsetecho.co.uk
Editor David Murdock
Daily Mon-Sat 28p
Features Editor Mike Clarke
News Editor Paul Thomas
Picture Editor Jim Tampin
Sports Editor Paul Baker

News and occasional features (1000–2000 words). Illustrations: b&w photos. Payment: by negotiation. Founded 1921.

Express & Echo

Express & Echo Publications Ltd, Heron Road,
Sowton, Exeter, Devon EX2 7NF
tel (01392) 442211 *fax* (01392) 442294/442287
Editor Steve Hall
Daily Mon-Sat 27p
Head of Content Sue Kemp
Picture Editor John Ffoulkes
Sports Editor Simon Mills

Features and news of local interest. Length: 500–800 words (features), up to 400 words (news). Illustrations: colour. Payment: lineage rates; illustrations negotiable. Founded 1904.

Gloucestershire Echo

Cheltenham Newspaper Co. Ltd,
1 Clarence Parade, Cheltenham, Glos. GL50 3NY
tel (01242) 271900 *fax* (01242) 271803
Editor Anita Syvret
Daily Mon-Sat 30p

Specialist articles with Gloucestershire connections; no fiction. Material mostly commissioned. Length: 350 words. Payment: £30 per article, negotiable. Founded 1873.

Sunday Independent (West of England)

Southern Newspapers plc, Burrington Way,
Plymouth PL5 3LN
tel (01752) 206600 *fax* (01752) 206164
Editor Nikki Rowlands
Sun 60p

News features on West Country topics; features/articles with a nostalgic theme; short quirky news briefs (must be original). Length: 600 words (features/articles), 300 words (news). Illustrations: colour, b&w. Payment: by arrangement. Founded 1808.

Western Daily Press

Bristol Evening Post and Press Ltd, Temple Way,
Bristol BS99 7HD
tel 0117-934 3000 *fax* 0117-934 3574
website www.westpress.co.uk
Editor Terry Manners
Daily Mon-Sat 34p

National, international or West Country topics for features or news items, from established journalists, with or without illustrations. Payment: by negotiation. Founded 1858.

The Western Morning News

Brest Road, Derriford, Plymouth PL6 5AA
tel (01752) 765500 *fax* (01752) 765535
Editor Barrie Williams
Daily Mon-Sat 34p
News Editor Laura Snook
Picture Editor Michael Cranmer
Sports Editor Rick Cowdery

Articles plus illustrations considered on West Country subjects. Founded 1860.

Wales

South Wales Argus

South Wales Argus Ltd, Cardiff Road, Maesglas, Newport, Gwent NP20 3QN
tel (01633) 777219 *fax* (01633) 777202
Editor Gerry Keighley
Daily Mon-Sat 32p

News and features of relevance to Gwent. Length: 500–600 words (features); 350 words (news). Illustrations: colour prints and transparencies. Payment: £30 (features), £20 (news) per item; £20–£25 (photos). Founded 1892.

South Wales Echo

Thomson House, Havelock Street, Cardiff CF10 1XR
tel 029-2058 3622/20223333 *fax* 029-2058 3624
Editor Alastair Milburn
Daily Mon-Sat 32p

Evening paper: news, sport, features, showbiz, news features, personality interviews. Length: up to 700 words. Illustrations: photos, cartoons. Payment: by negotiation. Founded 1884.

The Western Mail

Thomson House, Havelock Street, Cardiff CF10 1XR
tel 029-2058 3583 *fax* 029-2058 3652
Editor Neil Fowler
Daily Mon-Fri 35p Sat 40p

Articles of political, industrial, literary or general and Welsh interest are considered. Illustrations: topical general news and feature pictures, cartoons. Payment: according to value; special fees for exclusive news. Founded 1869.

West Midlands

Birmingham Evening Mail

28 Colmore Circus, Queensway, Birmingham B4 6AX
tel 0121-236 3366 *fax* 0121-625 1105
London office 1 Canada Square, Canary Wharf, London E14 5AP
tel 020-7293 3000 *fax* 020-7293 3793
Editor Roger Borrell
Daily Mon-Sat 32p

Features of topical Midland interest considered. Length: 400–800 words. Payment: by arrangement. Founded 1870.

The Birmingham Post

PO Box 18, 28 Colmore Circus, Birmingham B4 6AX
tel 0121-236 3366 *fax* 0121-625 1105
London office 22nd Floor, 1 Canada Square, Canary Wharf, London E14 5AP
tel 020-7293 3455 *fax* 020-7293 3400
Editor N. Hastilow
Daily Mon-Sat 37p
Features Editor Peter Bacon
News Editor Chris Russon
Picture Editor Paul Vokes
Sports Editor Mark Woodward

Authoritative and well-written articles of industrial, political or general interest are considered, especially if they have relevance to the Midlands. Length: up to 1000 words. Payment: by arrangement.

Coventry Evening Telegraph

Corporation Street, Coventry CV1 1FP
tel 024-7663 3633 *fax* 024-7655 0869
Editor Alan Kirby
Daily Mon-Sat 32p

Topical, illustrated articles with a Coventry or Warwickshire interest. Length: up to 600 words. Payment: by arrangement.

Express & Star

Queen Street, Wolverhampton WV1 1ES
tel (01902) 313131 *fax* (01902) 319721
email general@expressandstar.co.uk
website www.westmidlands.com
London office Room 110, Temple Chambers, Temple Avenue, London EC4Y 0DT
Editor Warren Wilson
Daily Mon-Sat 30p
Head of Features Jim Walsh
Head of News John Bray
Head of Pictures Tony Adams
Sports Editor Steve Gordos

Founded 1874.

The Sentinel

Staffordshire Sentinel Newspapers Ltd, Sentinel House, Etruria, Stoke-on-Trent ST1 5SS
tel (01782) 602525 *fax* (01782) 602616
email editor@thesentinel.co.uk
website www.thisisstaffordshire.co.uk
Editor Sean Dooley
Daily Mon-Sat 28p Sun 35p
Features Editor Julie Stickels
Business Correspondent Stephen Houghton
Managing Editor Roy Coates
News Editor Martin Tideswell
Picture Editor Trevor Slater
Sports Editor Alex Martin

Articles and features of topical interest to the north Staffordshire/south Cheshire area. Illustrations: colour and b&w. Payment: by arrangement. Founded 1873.

Shropshire Star

Ketley, Telford TF1 5HU
tel (01952) 242424 *fax* (01952) 254605
Editor Sarah Jane Smith
Daily Mon-Sat 32p
News Editor John Simcock
Picture Editor Paul Morstatt-Higgs
Sports Editor Keith Harrison
Supplements Dept Sharon Walters

Evening paper: news and features. No unsolicited material; write to features editor with outline of ideas. Payment: by arrangement. Founded 1964.

Sunday Mercury

Colmore Circus, Birmingham B4 6AZ
tel 0121-234 5567 *fax* 0121-233 0271
Editor David Brookes
Sun 60p
Deptuy Editor Paul Cole
Assistant Editor Tony Larner
Picture Editor Adam Fradgley
Sports Editor Lee Gibson

News specials or features of Midland interest. Illustrations: colour, b&w, cartoons. Special rates for special matter.

Yorkshire/Humberside

Evening Courier

PO Box 19, King Cross Street, Halifax HX1 2SF
tel (01422) 260200 *fax* (01422) 260341
email editor@halifaxcourier.co.uk
website www.halifaxcourier.co.uk
Editor Edward Riley
2 per day Mon-Sat 30p
Features Editor William Marshall
News Editor John Kenealy
Sports Editor Ian Rushworth

Articles of local interest and background to news events. Length: up to 500 words. Illustrations: colour photos. Payment: £25–£40 per article; photos per quality/size used. Founded 1832.

Evening Press

York and County Press, PO Box 29,
76-86 Walmgate, York YO1 9YN
tel (01904) 653051 *fax* (01904) 612853
email newsdesk@ycp.co.uk
website www.thisisyork.co.uk
Editor Elizabeth Page
Daily Mon-Sat 32p
Assistant Editors Chris Buxton, Bill Hearld
News Editor Francine Clee
Picture Editor Martin Oates
Sports Editor Martin Jarred

Articles of North and East Yorkshire interest, humour, personal experience of current affairs. Length: 500–1000 words. Payment: by arrangement. Illustrations: line, half-tone, cartoons. Founded 1882.

Grimsby Telegraph

80 Cleethorpe Road, Grimsby,
North East Lincolnshire DN31 3EH
tel (01472) 360360 *fax* (01472) 372257
email newsdesk@grimsbytelegraph.co.uk
website www.thisisgrimsby.co.uk
Editor Peter Moore
Daily Mon-Sat 28p
Features Editor Barrie Farnsworth
News Editor David Atkin
Picture Editor David Moss
Sports Editor Geoff Ford

Considers general interest articles. Illustrations: line, half-tone, colour, cartoons. Payment: by arrangement. Founded 1897.

The Huddersfield Daily Examiner

Examiner News & Information Services Ltd,
PO Box A26, Queen Street South,
Huddersfield HD1 2TD
tel (01484) 430000 *fax* (01484) 437789
email editor@examiner.co.uk
website www.examiner.co.uk
Editor John Williams
Daily Mon-Fri 32p
Features editor Andrew Flynn
Picture editor Neil Atkinson

No contributions required at present. Payment: £10–£15 (short features). Founded 1871.

The Star

York Street, Sheffield S1 1PU
tel 0114-276 7676 *fax* 0114-272 5978
website www.sheffweb.co.uk
Editor Peter Charlton
Daily Mon-Sat 27p
Features Editor Paul License
News Editor Bob Westerdale
Picture Editor Dennis Lound
Sports Editor Martin Smith

Well-written articles of local character. Length: about 500 words. Payment: by negotiation. Illustrations: topical photos, line drawings, graphics, cartoons. Founded 1887.

Telegraph & Argus

Hall Ings, Bradford, West Yorkshire BD1 1JR
tel (01274) 729511 *fax* (01274) 723634
email bradford.editorial@bradford.newsquest.co.uk
website www.thisisbradford.co.uk
Editor Perry Austin-Clarke
Daily Mon-Sat 28p

Assistant Editor (sport & pictures) Simon Waites
Assistant Editor (news & features) Damian Bates
Sports Editor Alan Birkinshaw

Evening paper: news, articles and features relevant to or about the people of West Yorkshire. Length: up to 1000 words. Illustrations: line, half-tone, colour. Payment: features from £15; line from £5, b&w and colour photos by negotiation. Founded 1868.

Yorkshire Evening Post

PO Box 168, Wellington Street, Leeds LS1 1RF
tel 0113-2432701 *fax* 0113-2388535
Editor N.R. Hodgkinson
Daily Mon-Sat 32p
Features Editor Anne Pickles
News Editor David Helliwell
Picture Editor Andy Manning
Sports Editor Phil Rostron

News stories and feature articles. Illustrations: colour and b&w, cartoons. Payment: by negotiation. Founded 1890.

Yorkshire Post

Wellington Street, Leeds LS1 1RF
tel 0113-243 2701 *fax* 0113-238 8537
website www.yorkshirepost.co.uk
London office 27 Albemarle Street, London W15 4DW
tel 020-7408 9636
Editor Tony Watson
Daily Mon-Sat 38p
Supplement **Yorkshire Post Magazine**
Features Editor Michael Hickling
Head of Content John Furbisher
Picture Editor Ian Day
Sports Editor Bill Bridge

Authoritative and well-written articles on topical subjects of general, literary or industrial interests. Length: max. 1200 words. Illustrations: photos and frequent pocket cartoons (single column width), topical wherever possible. Payment: by arrangement. Founded 1754.

Magazines UK and Ireland

Listings for regional newspapers start on page 12 and listings for national newspapers start on page 3. For quick reference, magazines are listed by subject area on page 113. See page 123 for recent changes to newspapers and magazines.

Accountancy

40 Bernard Street, London WC1N 1LD
tel 020-7833 3291 *fax* 020-7833 2085
email postmaster@theabg.demon.co.uk
website www.accountancymagazine.com
Editor Brian Singleton-Green
Monthly £57.50 p.a.

Articles on accounting, taxation, financial, legal and other subjects likely to be of professional interest to accountants in practice or industry, and to top management generally; cartoons. Payment: £140 per page. Founded 1889.

Accountancy Age

VNU Business Publications, VNU House, 32-34 Broadwick Street, London W1A 2HG
tel 020-7316 9236 *fax* 020-7316 9250
email accountancy_age@vnu.co.uk
website www.accountancyage.com
Editor Damian Wild
Weekly £2 (£100 p.a.)

Articles of accounting, financial and business interest. Illustrations: colour photos; freelance assignments commissioned. Payment: by arrangement. Founded 1969.

Accounting & Business

Association of Chartered Certified Accountants, 10-11 Lincolns Inn Fields, London WC2A 3BP
tel 020-7396 5966 *fax* 020-7396 5950
email john.prosser@accaglobal.com
website www.accaglobal.com
Editor John Rogers Prosser
10 p.a. £85 p.a.

Journal of the Association of Chartered Certified Accountants. Accountancy, finance and business topics of relevance to accountants and finance directors. Length: 1300 words. Payment: £150 per 1000 words. Illustrated. Founded 1998.

Ace Tennis Magazine

Tennis GB, 9-11 North End Road, London W14 8ST
tel 020-7605 8000 *fax* 020-7602 2323
email dominic.bliss@acemag.co.uk
Editor Dominic Bliss
11 p.a. £2.85

International high profile tennis, including interviews with top players, coaching articles, big tournament reports, health and fitness. Submit synopsis in first instance. Payment: 20p per word. Founded 1996.

Active Life

Lexicon Editorial Group Services, 16 Ennismore Avenue, London W4 1SF
tel 020-8994 3144 *fax* (01932) 343011
email activelife@lexicon-uk.com
Editor Helene Hodge
Monthly £1

Lifestyle advice for the over 50s, including holidays and health, fashion and food, finance and fiction, hobbies and home, personality profiles. Submit ideas in writing. Length: 600–1200 words. Illustrations: colour. Payment: £100 per 1000 words; photos by negotiation. Founded 1989.

Acumen

6 The Mount, Higher Furzeham, Brixham, South Devon TQ5 8QY
tel (01803) 851098
Editor Patricia Oxley
3 p.a. (Jan/May/Sept) £4.50, £12.50 p.a.

Poetry, literary and critical articles, reviews, literary memoirs, etc. Send sae with submissions. Payment: small. Founded 1985.

Aeroplane Monthly

IPC Magazines Ltd, King's Reach Tower, Stamford Street, London SE1 9LS
tel 020-7201 5040 *fax* 020-7261 5269
email aeroplane_monthly@ipcmedia.com
website www.aeroplanemonthly.com
Editor Michael Oakey
Monthly £3.30

Articles and photos relating to historical aviation. Length: up to 3000 words. Illustrations: line, half-tone, colour, cartoons. Payment: £60 per 1000 words, payable on publication; photos £10–£40; colour £80 per page. Founded 1973.

Africa Confidential

Blackwell Publishers Ltd, 73 Farringdon Road, London EC1M 3JQ
tel 020-7831 3511 *fax* 020-7831 6778
website www.africa-confidential.com
Editor Patrick Smith
Fortnightly £87 p.a. students, £347 p.a. institutions

News and analysis of political and economic developments in Africa. Unsolicited contributions welcomed, but must be exclusive and not published elsewhere. Length: 1200–word features, 200-word pointers. Payment: from £200 per 1000 words. No illustrations. Founded 1960.

Africa: St Patrick's Missions

St Patrick's, Kiltegan, Co. Wicklow, Republic of Ireland
tel (0508) 73600 *fax* (0508) 73622
email africa@spms.org
website www.spms.org
Editor Rev. Gary Howley
9 p.a. £5 p.a. (E9)

Articles of missionary and topical religious interest. Length: up to 1000 words. Illustrations: line, half-tone, colour.

African Business

IC Publications Ltd, 7 Coldbath Square, London EC1R 4LQ
tel 020-7713 7711 *fax* 020-7713 7970
email icpubs@dial.pipex.com
Editor Anver Versi
Monthly £2.50

Articles on business, economic and financial topics of interest to businessmen, ministers, officials concerned with African affairs. Length: 400–750 words; shorter coverage 100–400 words. Illustrations: line, half-tone. Payment: £80 per 1000 words; £1 per column cm for illustrations. Founded 1978.

Agenda

5 Cranbourne Court, Albert Bridge Road, London SW11 4PE
tel/fax 020-7228 0700
email agendapoetry@btinternet.com
Editor William Cookson, *Assistant Editor* Anita Money
Quarterly £26 p.a. (libraries, institutions and overseas: rates on application); £20 OAPs/students

Poetry and criticism. Study the journal before submitting MSS with an sae. Illustrations: half-tone. Payment: variable.

Air International

Key Publishing Ltd, PO Box 100, Stamford, Lincs. PE9 1XQ
tel (01780) 755131 *fax* (01780) 757261
email malcolm.english@keypublishing.com

Editor Malcolm English
Monthly £3.20

Technical articles on aircraft; features on topical aviation subjects – civil and military. Length: up to 5000 words. Illustrations: colour transparencies/prints, b&w prints/line drawings. Payment: £50 per 1000 words or by negotiation; £20 colour, £10 b&w. Founded 1971.

Air Pictorial International

HPC Publishing, Drury Lane, St Leonards-on-Sea, East Sussex TN38 9BJ
tel (01424) 720477 *fax* (01424) 443693/434086
Editor Barry C. Wheeler
Monthly £2.95

Covers all aspects of aviation. Many articles commissioned; will consider competent articles exploring fresh ground or presenting an individual point of view on technical matters. Illustrated, mainly with photos. Payment: by arrangement.

Amateur Gardening

IPC Media Ltd, Westover House, West Quay Road, Poole, Dorset BH15 1JG
tel (01202) 440840 *fax* (01202) 440860
email amateurgardening@ipcmedia.com
Editor Tim Rumball
Weekly £1.30

Topical, practical or newsy articles up to 1200 words of interest to keen gardeners. Payment: by arrangement. Illustrations: colour. Founded 1884.

Amateur Photographer

(incorporating Photo Technique)
IPC Magazines Ltd, King's Reach Tower, Stamford Street, London SE1 9LS
tel 020-7261 5100 *fax* 020-7261 5404
email amateurphotographer@ipcmedia.com
Editor Garry Coward-Williams
Weekly £1.95

Original articles of pictorial or technical interest, preferably illustrated with either photos or diagrams. Good instructional features especially sought. Length preferred: (unillustrated) 400–800 words; articles up to 1500 words; (illustrated) 2–4 pages. Payment: weekly, rates according to usage. Illustrations unaccompanied by text considered – indicate if material can be held on file. Founded 1884.

Amateur Stage

Platform Publications Ltd, Hampden House, 2 Weymouth Street, London W1W 5BT
tel 020-7636 4343 *fax* 020-7636 2323
email cvtheatre@aol.com
website www.amdram.org.uk/amstagel.htm
Editor Charles Vance
Monthly £2.40

Articles on all aspects of the amateur theatre, preferably practical and factual. Length: 600–2000 words. Illustrations: photos, line drawings. Payment: none. Founded 1946.

Ambit

17 Priory Gardens, London N6 5QY
tel 020-8340 3566
website www.ambitmag.co.uk
Poetry Editors Martin Bax, Henry Graham, Carol-Ann Duffy, *Prose Editors* J.G. Ballard, Geoff Nicholson, *Art Editor* Mike Foreman
Quarterly £6 inc. p&p (£24 p.a. UK, £26/$52 p.a. overseas; £35 p.a., £37/$74 p.a. institutions)

Poetry, short fiction, art, poetry reviews. New and established writers and artists. Payment: by arrangement. Illustrations: line, half-tone, colour. Founded 1959.

American Markets Newsletter

175 Westland Drive, Glasgow G14 9JQ
email sheila.oconnor@juno.com
Editor Sheila O'Connor
6 p.a. £34 p.a. (£63 for 2 years)

Editorial guidelines for US, Canadian and other overseas markets, plus information on press trips, non-fiction/fiction markets and writers' tips. Free syndication for all subscribers. Sample issue £5.95 (payable to S. O'Connor).

AN Magazine

AN: The Artists Information Company, 1st Floor, 7-15 Pink Lane, Newcastle upon Tyne NE1 5DW
tel 0191-241 8000 *fax* 0191-241 8001
email edit@anpubs.demon.co.uk
website www.anweb.co.uk
Contact Gillian Nicol, Magazine Coordinator
Monthly £3.50 (£28 p.a.)

Articles, news and features for visual and applied artists. Illustrations: transparencies, colour and b&w photos. Payment: £110 per 1000 words. Founded as *Artists Newsletter* in 1980.

Angler's Mail

IPC Media Ltd, King's Reach Tower, Stamford Street, London SE1 9LS
tel 020-7261 5778 *fax* 020-7261 6016
Editor Roy Westwood
Weekly £1

News items about coarse and sea fishing. Payment: by agreement.

Angling Times

EMAP Active, Bushfield House, Orton Centre, Peterborough PE2 5UW
tel (01733) 232600 *fax* (01733) 465844
email richard.lee@emap.com
Editor Richard Lee
Weekly £1

Articles, pictures, news stories, on all forms of angling. Illustrations: line, half-tone, colour. Payment: by arrangement. Founded 1953.

Animals and You

D.C. Thomson & Co Ltd, Albert Square, Dundee DD1 9QJ
tel (01382) 223131 *fax* (01382) 225511
185 Fleet Street, London EC4A 2HS
tel 020-7400 1030 *fax* 020-7400 1089
Monthly (Fri) £1.75

Features, stories and pin-ups for girls who love animals. Founded 1998.

Antiques & Art Independent

PO Box 1945, Comely Bank, Edinburgh EH4 1AB
tel (07000) 765 263 *fax* (07000) 268 478
email antiquesnews@hotmail.com
website www.antiquesnews.co.uk
Publisher/Editor Tony Keniston
Quarterly £2

Newspaper for the British antiques and art trade. News, gossip and controversial personal views on all aspects of the antiques world welcome. People stories only. Approach in writing with ideas. Length: 600 words (articles), 200 words (news). Illustrations: b&w prints. Payment: by negotiation. Founded 1997.

Antiques and Collectables

Merricks Media Ltd, Charlotte House, 12 Charlotte Street, Bath BA1 2NE
tel (01225) 786800 *fax* (01225) 786801
email info@antiques.collectables.co.uk
website www.antiques-collectables.co.uk
Editor Diana Cambridge
Monthly £2.60

Features on ceramics, furniture, glass, memorabilia, ephemera, etc aimed at the antiques trade and general collectors. Includes price guide and news. Write with idea in first instance. Length: 1500–2000 (features). Illustrations: transparencies and colour prints. Payment £100–£150. Founded 1998.

Apollo

1-2 Castle Lane, London SW1E 6DR
tel 020-7233 6640 *fax* 020-7630 7791
Editor David Ekserdjian
Monthly £7.80

Scholarly articles of about 3000 words on art, architecture, ceramics, furniture, armour, glass, sculpture, and any subject connected with art and collecting. Payment: by arrangement. Illustrations: half-tone, colour. Founded 1925.

Aquila

New Leaf Publishing Ltd, PO Box 2518, Eastbourne, East Sussex BN21 2BB
tel (01323) 431313 *fax* (01323) 731136
email info@aquila.co.uk
website www.aquila.co.uk
Editor Jackie Berry
Monthly £31.50 p.a. (£19.95 6 months)

Dedicated to encouraging children aged 8–13 to reason and create, and to develop a caring nature. Short stories and serials of up to 4 parts. Occasional features commissioned from writers with specialist knowledge. Approach in writing with ideas and sample of writing style, with sae. Length: 700–800 words (features), 1000–1100 words (stories or per episode of a serial). Illustrations: colour and b&w, cartoons. Payment: £75 (features); £90 (stories), £80 (per episode). Founded 1993.

The Architects' Journal

EMAP Business Communications, 151 Rosebery Avenue, London EC1R 4GB
tel 020-7505 6700 *fax* 020-7505 6701
Editor Isabel Allen
Weekly £1.80 (£78 p.a.)

Articles (mainly technical) on architecture, planning and building accepted only with prior agreement of synopsis. Illustrations: photos and drawings. Payment: by arrangement. Founded 1895.

Architectural Design

John Wiley & Sons Ltd, 4th Floor, International House, Ealing Broadway Centre, London W5 5DB
tel 020-8326 3800 *fax* 020-8326 3801
Editor Helen Castle
6 double issues p.a. £99 p.a. (£70 p.a. students)

International magazine comprising an extensively illustrated thematic profile, presenting architecture and critical interpretations of architectural history, theory and practice. Uncommissioned articles not accepted. Illustrations: drawings and photos, line (colour preferred). Payment: by arrangement. Founded 1930.

The Architectural Review

EMAP Construct, 151 Rosebery Avenue, London EC1R 4GB
tel 020-7505 6725 *fax* 020-7505 6701
email peter.davey@ebc.emap.com
website www.arplus.com/
Editor Peter Davey
Monthly £6.50

Articles on architecture and the allied arts. Writers must be thoroughly qualified. Length: up to 3000 words. Payment: by arrangement. Illustrations: photos, drawings, etc. Founded 1896.

Architecture Today

161 Rosebery Avenue, London EC1R 4QX
tel 020-7837 0143 *fax* 020-7837 0155
Editors Ian Latham, Mark Swenarton
10 p.a. £4 Free to architects

Mostly commissioned articles and features on today's European architecture. Length: 200–800 words. Illustrations: colour. Payment: by negotiation. Founded 1989.

Arena

EMAP Élan Ltd, Exmouth House, Pine Street, London EC1R 0JL
tel 020-7689 2251 *fax* 020-7689 0901
email editorial@arenamag.co.uk
Editor Anthony Noguera
Monthly £3.20

Profiles, articles on a wide range of subjects intelligently treated; art, architecture, politics, sport, business, music, film, design, media, fashion. Length: up to 3000 words. Illustrations: b&w and colour photos. Payment: £300 per 1000 words; varies for illustrations. Founded 1986.

Art Business Today

The Fine Art Trade Guild, 16-18 Empress Place, London SW6 1TT
tel 020-7381 6616 *fax* 020-7381 2596
email abt@fineart.co.uk
website www.fineart.co.uk/Abtonline/abt.htm
Editor Annabelle Ruston
5 p.a. £19 p.a.

Distributed to the fine art and framing industry. Covers essential information on new products and technology, market trends and business analysis. Length: 800–1600 words. Illustrations: colour photos, cartoons. Payment: by arrangement. Founded 1991.

Art Monthly

4th Floor, 28 Charing Cross Road, London WC2H 0DB
tel 020-7240 0389 *fax* 020-7497 0726
email info@artmonthly.co.uk
website www.artmonthly.co.uk
Editor Patricia Bickers
10 p.a. £3.50

Features on modern and contemporary visual artists and art history, art theory and art-related issues; exhibition and book reviews. All material commissioned. Length: 750–1500 words. Illustrations: b&w photos. Payment: features £100–£200; none for photos. Founded 1976.

The Art Newspaper

70 South Lambeth Road, London SW8 1RL
tel 020-7735 3331 *fax* 020-7735 3332
Editor Anna Somers Cocks
11 p.a. £4.50 (£47 p.a.)

International coverage of visual art, news, politics, law, exhibitions with some feature pages. Length: 200–1000 words. Illustrations: b&w photos. Payment: £120 per 1000 words. Founded 1990.

Art Review

Art Review Ltd, Hereford House, 23-24 Smithfield Street, London EC1A 9LB
tel 020-7236 4880 *fax* 020-7236 4881
email info@art-review.co.uk
Editor Meredith Etherington-Smith
Monthly £3.95

Art news, features and reviews. Commissioned work only. Payment: from £200 per 1000 words. Illustrations: line, colour. Founded 1949.

The Artist

The Artists' Publishing Co. Ltd, Caxton House, 63-65 High Street, Tenterden, Kent TN30 6BD
tel (01580) 763673
Editor Sally Bulgin
Monthly £2.45

Practical, instructional articles on painting for all amateur and professional artists. Payment: by arrangement. Illustrations: line, half-tone, colour. Founded 1931.

Artists and Illustrators

The Fitzpatrick Building, 188-194 York Way, London N7 9QR
tel 020-7700 8500 *fax* 020-7700 4985
email aim@quarto.com
Editor James Hobbs
Monthly £2.60

Practical and business articles for amateur and professional artists. Length: 1000–1500 words. Illustrations: colour transparencies. Payment: variable. Founded 1986.

Asian Times

Ethnic Media Group, Unit 2.01, Technology Centre, 65 Whitechapel Road, London E1 1DU
tel 020-7650 2000 *fax* 020-7560 2001
Editor Emenike Pio
Weekly 50p

News stories, articles and features of interest to Britain's Asian community. Founded 1983.

Astronomy Now

Pole Star Publications, PO Box 175, Tonbridge, Kent TN10 4ZY
tel (01903) 266165 *fax* (01732) 356230
email editorial@astronow.cix.co.uk
Managing Editor Steven Young
Monthly £2.70

Aimed at amateur and professional astronomers. Interested in news items and longer features on astronomy and some space-related activities. Writers' guidelines available (send sae). Length: 600–3000 words. Illustrations: line, half-tone, colour. Payment:5p per word; from £10 per photo. Founded 1987.

Athletics Weekly

Descartes Publishing Ltd, 83 Park Road, Peterborough PE1 2TN
tel (01733) 898440 *fax* (01733) 898441
email nigel.walsh@athletics-weekly.co.uk
Editor Nigel Walsh
Weekly £1.95

News and features on track and field athletics, road running, cross country, fell and race walking. Material mostly commissioned. Length: 800–2000 words. Illustrations: colour and b&w action and head/shoulder photos, line. Payment: varies. Founded 1946.

Attitude

Ludgate House, 245 Blackfriars Road, London SE1 9UX
tel 020-7928 0000 *fax* 020 7922 7600
email attitude@express.co.uk
Editor Adam Mattera
Monthly £2.75

Men's style magazine aimed primarily but not exclusively at gay men. Covers style/fashion, interviews, reviews, celebrities, humour. Illustrations: colour transparencies, b&w prints. Payment: £150 per 1000 words; £100 per full page illustration. Founded 1994.

The Author

84 Drayton Gardens, London SW10 9SB
tel 020-7373 6642
Editor Derek Parker
Quarterly £7

Organ of The Society of Authors. Commissioned articles from 1000–2000 words on any subject connected with the legal, commercial or technical side of authorship. Little scope for the freelance writer: preliminary letter advisable. Illustrations: line, occasional cartoons. Payment: by arrangement. Founded 1890.

Auto Express

Dennis Publishing Ltd, 30 Cleveland Street, London W1T 4JD
tel 020-7907 6200 *fax* 020-7907 6234
email editorial@autoexpress.co.uk
website www.autoexpress.co.uk
Editor David Johns
Weekly £1.50

News stories, and general interest features about drivers as well as cars. Illustrations: colour photos. Payment: features £350 per 1000 words; photos, varies. Founded 1988.

Autocar

Haymarket Publishing Ltd, 60 Waldegrave Road, Teddington, Middlesex TW11 8LG
tel 020-8267 5630 *fax* 020-8267 5759
email autocar@haynet.com
Editor Rob Aherne
Weekly £2.10

Articles on all aspects of cars, motoring and the motor industry: general, practical, competition and technical. Illustrations: line (litho), colour and electronic (Illustrator). Press day news: Thursday. Payment: varies; mid-month following publication. Founded 1895.

Back Street Heroes

Isis Building, 193 Marsh Wall, Thames Quay, London E14 9SG
tel 020-7772 8300 *fax* 020-7772 8585
Editor Stu Garland
Monthly £2.99

Custom motorcycle features plus informed lifestyle pieces. Illustrations: colour, cartoons. Payment: by arrangement. Founded 1983.

Balance

British Diabetic Association, 10 Queen Anne Street, London W1M 0BD
tel 020-7323 1531 *fax* 020-7637 3644
email balance@diabetes.org.uk
website www.diabetes.org.uk
Editor Martin Cullen
Bi-monthly £2

Articles on diabetes and related health and lifestyle issues. Length: 1000–2000 words. Payment: by arrangement. Illustrations: colour. Founded 1935.

The Banker

Maple House, Tottenham Court Road, London W1T 7LB
tel/fax 020-7896 2507
email stephen.timewell@ft.com
Editor Stephen Timewell
Monthly £189 p.a.

Articles on investment banking and finance, retail banking, banking technology, banking services and systems; bank analysis and top 1000 listings. Illustrations: half-tones and full colour of people, charts, tables, maps etc. Founded 1926.

Baptist Times

PO Box 54, 129 Broadway, Didcot, Oxon OX11 8XB
tel (01235) 517670 *fax* (01235) 517678
Editor John Capon
Weekly 50p

Religious or social affairs material, up to 1000 words. Payment: by arrangement. Illustrations: half-tone. Founded 1855.

BBC magazines – see page 294

The Beano

D.C. Thomson & Co. Ltd, Albert Square, Dundee DD1 9QJ
tel (01382) 223131 *fax* (01382) 322214
185 Fleet Street, London EC4A 2HS
tel 020-7400 1030 *fax* 020-7400 1089
Weekly 60p

Comic strips for children. Series, 11–22 pictures. Payment: on acceptance.

Fun Size Beano
2 p.m. 80p

Founded 1997.

Bella

H. Bauer Publishing, Academic House, 24-28 Oval Road, London NW1 7DT
tel 020-7241 8000 *fax* 020-7241 8056
Editor Jackie Highe, *Assistant Editor/Features Editor* Sue Ricketts
Weekly 62p

General interest magazine for women: practical articles on fashion and beauty, health, cooking, home, travel; real life stories, plus fiction up to 2000 words. Payment: by arrangement. Illustrations: line including cartoons, half-tone, colour. Founded 1987.

Best

The National Magazine Company, 33 Broadwick Street, London W1F 0DQ
tel 020-7439 5000 *fax* 020-7312 4176
Editor Louise Court, *Fiction Editor* Pat Richardson, *Features Editor* Charlotte Seligman
Weekly 64p

Short stories. No other uncommissioned work accepted, but always willing to look at ideas/outlines. Length: 1000 words for short stories, variable for other work. Illustrations: line, half-tone, colour, cartoons. Payment: by agreement. Founded 1987.

Best of British

Ian Beacham Publishing, Bank Chambers, 27A Market Place, Market Deeping, Lincs. PE6 8EA
tel/fax (01778) 342814
email mail@british.fsbusiness.co.uk
Editor-in-Chief Ian Beacham
Monthly £2.75

Nostalgic features about life in the 1930s, 1940s and 1950s together with stories celebrating interesting aspects of Britain today. Length: max. 1500 words. Illustrations: colour and b&w. Payment: from £30 (words); £20 (pictures). Founded 1994.

The Big Issue

1-5 Wandsworth Road, London SW8 2LN
tel 020-7526 3200
Editor tba
Weekly £1.20

Features, news, reviews, interviews – of general interest and on social issues. Length: features 500–2000 words. No short stories or poetry. Illustrations: colour and b&w photos and line. Payment: £160 per 1000 words. Founded 1991.

The Big Issue in the North

The Big Issue in the North Ltd, 135-141 Oldham Street, Manchester M4 1LL
tel 0161-834 6300 *fax* 0161-819 5000
Editor Kate Markey
Weekly £1

Articles of general interest and on social issues; arts features and news covering the north of England. No fiction or poetry, except by the homeless. Contact the news, arts or deputy editor to discuss ideas. Length: 1500 words (features/articles), 300–500 (news), 700 (arts features), 350 words (comment). Payment: £90 per 1000 words. Colour transparencies, puzzles and quizzes. Founded 1992.

The Big Issue in Scotland

The Big Issue in Scotland Ltd, 71 Oxford Street, Glasgow G5 9EP
tel 0141-418 7000 *fax* 0141-418 7061
email editorial@bigissuescotland.com
Editor Mel Young, *Send material to* Claire Black, Assistant Editor
Weekly £1

Features on human rights, animal issues, green issues, injustices, Scotland, medical, scientific, the paranormal, health and crime, plus news and reviews. Also international features/news. Length: 1000–2000 words (articles); 500–800 words (news). Illustrations: colour and b&w. Payment: £100 per 1000 words; £60 per photo/illustration. Founded 1993.

The Big Issue South West

5 Brunswick Court, Brunswick Square, Bristol BS2 8PE
tel 0117-908 0091 *fax* 0117-908 0093
email editorial@bigissuesouthwest.co.uk
website www.bigissuesouthwest.co.uk
Editor Rich Cookson
Weekly £1.20

Social news, general interest features and arts information for the South West. Considers unsolicited material. Length: 1200 words (articles/features), 100–1200 words (news). Payment: negotiable. Illustrations: colour, payment negotiable. Founded 1991.

Bike

EMAP Automotive Ltd, Media House, Lynchwood, Peterborough PE2 6EA
tel (01733) 468000 *fax* (01733) 468196
email bike@emap.com
Editor Tim Thompson
Monthly £3.50

Motorcycle magazine: interested in articles, features, news. Length: articles/features 1000–3000 words. Illustrations: colour and b&w photos. Payment: £150 per 1000 words; photos per size/position. Founded 1971.

Bird Keeper

IPC Magazines Ltd, King's Reach Tower, Stamford Street, London SE1 9LS
tel 020-7261 6116 *fax* 020-7261 6095
Editor Donald Taylor
Monthly £2.75

Articles on the care, health and breeding of pet birds, beginner bird keepers and how-to. Send synopsis of ideas. Payment: by negotiation. Founded 1988.

Bird Watching

EMAP Active Ltd, Bretton Court, Bretton, Peterborough PE3 8DZ
tel (01733) 264666 *fax* (01773) 282654
email david.cromack@emap.com
Editor David Cromack
Monthly £2.95

Broad range of bird-related features and photography, particularly looking at bird behaviour, bird news, reviews and birdwatching sites. Emphasis on providing accurate information in entertaining ways. Send synopsis first. Length: 1200 words. Illustrations: colour photos, cartoons, bird identification artwork. Payment: by negotiation. Founded 1986.

Birding World

Sea Lawn, Coast Road, Cley next the Sea, Holt, Norfolk NR25 7RZ
tel (01263) 740913 *fax* (01263) 741014
email steve@birdingworld.co.uk
website www.birdingworld.co.uk
Editor Steve Gantlett
Monthly £40 p.a. (£47 p.a. Europe; £51 p.a. rest of the world, airmail)

Magazine for keen birdwatchers. Articles and news stories about mainly European ornithology, with the emphasis on ground-breaking new material and identification. Length: up to 3000 words (articles); up to 1500 words (news). Illustrations: good quality colour photos of birds. Payment: up to £25 per 500 words; £10–£40 (illustrations). Founded 1987.

Birdwatch

Solo Publishing Ltd, 3rd Floor, Leroy House, 436 Essex Road, London N1 3QP
tel 020-7704 9495 *fax* 020-7704 2767
website www.birdwatch.co.uk
Editor Dominic Mitchell
Monthly £2.95

Topical articles on all aspects of birds and birding, including conservation, identification, sites and habitats, equipment, overseas expeditions. Length: 700–1500 words. Illustrations: colour slides, b&w photos, colour and b&w line. Payment: from £40 per 1000 words; colour: photos £15–£40, cover £75, line by negotiation; b&w: photos £10, line £10–£40. Founded 1991.

Bizarre

IFG, 9 Dallington Street, London EC1V 0BQ
tel 020-7687 7000 *fax* 020-77687 7096
email bizarre@ifgmags.com

Editor Joe Gardiner
Monthly £2.95
Features on strange events, adventure, cults, weird people, celebrities, etc. Study the magazine for style before submitting ideas by post or fax. No fiction. Length: 800–2000 words. Payment: £80 per 1000 words. Colour transparencies and prints: £200 perdps, £125 per page. Founded 1997.

Black Beauty & Hair

Hawker Publications, 2nd Floor, Culvert House, Culvert Road, London SW11 5DH
tel 020-7720 2108 *fax* 020-7498 3023
email info@blackbeauty.co.uk
website www.blackbeautyandhair.com
Editor Irene Shelley
Bi-monthly £2.20
Beauty and style articles relating specifically to the black woman; celebrity features. True-life stories and salon features. Length: approx. 1000 words. Illustrations: colour and b&w photos. Payment: £100 per 1000 words; photos £25–£75. Founded 1982.

Bliss!

EMAP Élan Ltd, Endeavour House, 189 Shaftesbury Avenue, London WC2H 8JG
tel 020-7437 9011 *fax* 020-7208 3591
website www.blissmag.co.uk
Editor Helen Johnston
Monthly £1.90
Glamorous young women's glossy magazine. Bright intimate American-style format, with real life stories and reports, beauty, fashion, talent, advice, quizzes. Payment: by arrangement. Founded 1995.

Blueprint

ETP Ltd, Rosebery House, 41 Springfield Road, Chelmsford CM2 6JJ
tel (01245) 491717 *fax* (01245) 499110
email ggibson@wilmington.co.uk
Editor Grant Gibson
12 p.a. £3.75
The magazine of modern architecture and design and contemporary culture. Interested in articles, features and reviews. Length: up to 2500 words. Illustrations: colour and b&w photos and line. Payment: negotiable. Founded 1983.

BMA News

British Medical Association, BMA House, Tavistock Square, London WC1H 9JP
tel 020-7383 6122 *fax* 020-7383 6566
Joint Editors Julia Bell, Caroline Jones
51 p.a. £60 p.a.
News and features. Length: 700–2000 words (features), 100–300 words (news). Illustrations: transparencies, colour and b&w artwork and cartoons. Payment: by negotiation. Founded 1966.

Boards

Yachting Press Ltd, 196 Eastern Esplanade, Southend-on-Sea, Essex SS1 3AB
tel (01702) 582245 *fax* (01702) 588434
email 106003.3405@compuserve.com
website www.boards.co.uk
Editor Bill Dawes
Monthly during summer, Bi-monthly during winter £2.80 (9 p.a.)
Articles, photos and reports on all aspects of windsurfing and boardsailing. Payment: by arrangement. Illustrations: line, halftone, colour, cartoons. Founded 1982.

The Book Collector

(incorporating Bibliographical Notes and Queries)
The Collector Ltd, PO Box 12426, London W11 3GW
tel/fax 020-7792 3492
email info@thebookcollector.co.uk
Editorial Board Nicolas Barker (Editor), A. Bell, J. Fergusson, T. Hofmann, D. McKitterick, Joan Winterkorn
Quarterly £40 p.a. (£42/$68 overseas)
Articles, biographical and bibliographical, on the collection and study of printed books and MSS. Payment: for reviews only. Founded 1952.

Book and Magazine Collector

Diamond Publishing Group Ltd, 43-45 St Mary's Road, London W5 5RQ
tel 020-8579 1082 *fax* 020-8566 2024
Editor Crispin Jackson
Monthly £3.20
Articles about collectable authors/publications/subjects. Articles must be bibliographical and include a full bibliography and price guide (no purely biographical features). Approach in writing with ideas. Length: 2000–4000 words. Illustrations: colour and b&w artwork. Payment: £35 per 1000 words. Founded 1984.

Books Ireland

11 Newgrove Avenue, Dublin 4, Republic of Ireland
tel (01) 2692185 *fax* (01) 260 4927
email booksi@eircom.net
Editor Jeremy Addis, *Features Editor* Shirley Kelly
Monthly (exc. Jan, Jul, Aug) E3 (E32 p.a.)

Reviews of Irish-interest and Irish-author books, articles of interest to librarians, booksellers and readers. Length: 800–1400 words. Payment: £80 per 1000 words. Founded 1976.

Books Magazine

39 Store Street, London WC1E 7DB
tel 020-7629 2900 *fax* 020-7419 2111
Editor Liz Thomson
Quarterly £1.50

Reviews, features, interviews with authors. No unsolicited MSS. Payment: negotiable but little bought in. Founded 1987.

The Bookseller

VNU Entertainment Media Ltd, 5th Floor, Endeavour House, 189 Shaftesbury Avenue, London WC2H 8TJ
tel 020-7420 6006 *fax* 020-7420 6103
email letters.to.editor@bookseller.co.uk
website www.thebookseller.com
Editor Nicholas Clee
Weekly £170 p.a.

Journal of the publishing and bookselling trades. While outside contributions are welcomed, most of the journal's contents are commissioned. Length: about 1000–1500 words. Payment: by arrangement. Founded 1858.

Bowls International

Key Publishing Ltd, PO Box 100, Stamford, Lincs. PE9 1XQ
tel (01780) 755131 *fax* (01780) 757261
Editor Melvyn Beck
Monthly £2.50

Sport and news items and features; occasional, bowls-oriented short stories. Illustrations: colour transparencies, b&w photos, occasional line, cartoons. Payment: sport/news approx. 25p per line, features approx. £50 per page; colour £25, b&w £10. Founded 1981.

British Birds

The Banks, Mountfield, Robertsbridge, East Sussex TN32 5JY
tel/fax (01580) 882039
Managing Editor Dr Roger Riddington
Monthly £56.50 p.a. (concessionary rates available)

Articles, papers and short notes on wild birds of Britain, Europe, North Africa and the Middle East, ranging from conservation and breeding biology to rarities and identification. Illustrations: line, half-tone, colour. Payment: token. Founded 1907.

British Deaf News

7 Empire Court, Albert Street, Redditch, Worcs. B97 4DA
tel (01527) 592034, 592044 (text)
fax (01527) 592083 *videophone* (01527) 595318
email editorial@britishdeafness.com
website www.britishdeafnews.com
Editor Catya Neilson
Monthly £1.75, £18 p.a. non-members (£14 p.a. BDA members)

Interviews, features, reviews, articles, news items, letters dealing with deafness. Payment: by arrangement. Illustrations: line, half-tone. Founded 1872.

The British Journal of Photography

Timothy Benn Publishing, 39 Earlham Street, London WC2H 9LT
tel 020-7306 7000 *fax* 020-7306 7017
email bjp.editor@bjphoto.co.uk
website www.bjphoto.co.uk
Editor Jon Tarrant
Weekly £1.95

Articles on professional, commercial and press photography, and on the more advanced aspects of amateur, technical, industrial, medical, scientific and colour photography. Illustrations: line, half-tone, colour. Payment: by arrangement. Founded 1854.

British Journalism Review

BJR Publishing Ltd, c/o University of Luton Press, Dept of Media Arts, University of Luton, 75 Castle Street, Luton, Beds. LU1 3AJ
tel (01582) 743297 *fax* (01582) 743298
email ulp@luton.ac.uk
Editor Geoffrey Goodman
Quarterly £25 p.a. (overseas rates on application)

Comment/criticism/review of matters published by, or of interest to, the media. Length: 1000–3000 words. Illustrations: b&w photos. Payment: by arrangement. Founded 1989.

British Medical Journal

BMA House, Tavistock Square, London WC1H 9JR
tel 020-7387 4499 *fax* 020-7383 6418
email editor@bmj.com
website www.bmj.com
Editor Richard Smith BSc, NB, ChBEDd, MFPHM, FRCPE
Weekly £7.90

Medical and related articles. Payment: by arrangement. Founded 1840.

British Philatelic Bulletin

Royal Mail, 2-14 Bunhill Row, London EC1Y 8HQ
fax 020-7847 3359
Editor J.R. Holman
Monthly 85p

Articles on any aspect of British philately – stamps, postmarks, postal history; also stamp collecting in general. Length: up to 1500 words (articles); 250 words (news). Payment: £45 per 1000 words. Illustrations: colour. Founded 1963.

British Postmark Bulletin
Fortnightly £10 p.a. (£21.75 p.a. overseas)

Articles on British postmarks – past and present. Founded 1971.

Broadcast

EMAP Media, 33-39 Bowling Green Lane, London EC1R 0DA
tel 020-7505 8014 *fax* 020-7505 8050
Editor Lucy Rouse
Weekly £2.60

News and authoritative articles designed for all concerned with the UK and international TV and radio industry, and with programmes and advertising on TV, radio, video, cable, satellite, digital. Illustrations: colour, b&w, line, cartoons. Payment: by arrangement.

Brownie

The Guide Association, 17-19 Buckingham Palace Road, London SW1W 0PT
tel 020-7834 6242
email MarionT@guides.org.uk, chq@guides.org.uk
website www.guides.org.uk
Editor Marion Thompson
Monthly £1.35

Official Magazine of The Guide Association. Short articles for Brownies (girls 7–10 years); fiction with Brownie background (700–800 words); puzzles; 'things to make', etc. Illustrations: colour. Payment: £50 per 1000 words; varies for illustrations.

Buckinghamshire Countryside

Beaumonde Publications Ltd, PO Box 5, Hitchin, Herts. SG5 1GJ
tel (01462) 431237 *fax* (01462) 422015
email info@hertscountryside.co.uk
Editor Sandra Small
Bi-monthly £1.25

Articles relating to Buckinghamshire. No poetry, puzzles or crosswords. Length: approx. 1000 words. Illustrations: colour transparencies and b&w prints, artwork. Payment: £30 per article. Founded 1995.

Building

The Builder Group plc, 7th Floor, Anchorage House, 2 Clove Crescent, London E14 2BE
tel 020-7560 4000 *fax* 020-7560 4014
email adrian_barrick@buildersgroup.co.uk
Editor Adrian Barrick
Weekly £2.40

Covers the entire professional, industrial and manufacturing aspects of the building industry. Articles on architecture and techniques at home and abroad considered, also news and photos. Payment: by arrangement. Founded 1842.

Building Design

CMP Information Ltd, City Reach, 5 Greenwich View Place, Millharbour, London E14 9NN
tel 020-7861 6467 *fax* 020-7861 6261
email bd@cmpinformation.com
Editor Robert Bevan
Weekly Controlled circulation

News and features on all aspects of building design. All material commissioned. Length: up to 1500 words. Illustrations: colour and b&w photos, line, cartoons. Payment: £150 per 1000 words; illustrations by negotiation. Founded 1970.

Built Environment

Alexandrine Press, PO Box 15, 51 Cornmarket Street, Oxford OX1 3EB
tel (01865) 724627 *fax* (01865) 792309
email representative@ara.i-way.co.uk
Editors Prof Sir Peter Hall, Prof David Banister
Quarterly £75 p.a.

Articles about architecture, planning and the environment. Preliminary letter advisable. Length: 1000–5000 words. Payment: by arrangement. Illustrations: photos and line.

Burlington Magazine

14-16 Duke's Road, London WC1H 9SZ
tel 020-7388 1228 *fax* 020-7388 1230
email editorial@burlington.org.uk
Editor Andrew Hopkins
Monthly £12.40

Deals with the history and criticism of art; book and exhibition reviews; illustrated monthly Calendar section. Potential contributors must have special knowledge of the subjects treated; MSS compiled from works of reference are unacceptable. Length: 500–5000 words. Payment: up to £100. Illustrations: b&w and colour photos. Founded 1903.

Buses

Ian Allan Publishing Ltd, Riverdene Business Park, Molesey Road, Hersham, Surrey KT12 4RG
tel (01932) 266600 *fax* (01932) 266601
email alan@millar1.demon.co.uk
website www.busesmag.com
Editor Alan Millar, PO Box 3759, Glasgow G41 5YN

tel 0141-427 6294 *fax* 0141-427 9594
Monthly £3.25

Articles of interest to both road passenger transport operators and bus enthusiasts. Preliminary enquiry essential. Illustrations: colour transparencies, half-tone, line maps. Payment: on application. Founded 1949.

Business Life

Cedar Communications, Haymarket House, 1 Oxenden Street, London SW1Y 4EE
tel 020-7925 2544 *fax* 020-7839 4508
website www.cedarcom.co.uk
Editor Alex Finer
Monthly Free

Inflight magazine for British Airways. Articles and features of interest to the European business traveller. All material commissioned; approach in writing with ideas. Length: 850–2500 words. Illustrations: colour photos and line. Payment: £250 per 1000 words; £100–£400 for illustrations. Founded 1985.

Business Scotland

Peebles Media Group, Bergius House, Clifton Street, Glasgow G3 7LA
tel 0141-567 6000 *fax* 0141-331 1395
Editor Graham Lironi
Monthly Controlled circulation

Features, profiles and news items of interest to business and finance in Scotland. Payment: by arrangement. Founded 1947.

Business Traveller

Perry Publications Ltd, Russell Square House, 10-12 Russell Square, London WC1B 5ED
tel 020-7580 9898 *fax* 020-7580 6676
email editorial@businesstraveller.com
website www.btonline.co.uk
Editor Julia Brookes
Monthly £2.90

Articles, features and news on consumer travel aimed at individual frequent international business travellers. Submit ideas with recent clippings and a CV. Length: varies. Illustrations: colour for destinations features; send lists to Deborah Miller, Picture Editor. Payment: on application. Founded 1976.

Cable Guide

Scorpio Multimedia, 1st Floor, 40 Bernard Street, London WC1N 1LE
tel 020-7419 8419 *fax* 020-7419 8400
website www.cableguide.co.uk
Editor Biddy Crews
Monthly £3.50

Features and interviews about programmes featured on cable TV, together with programme listings for cable channels. All material commissioned. Length: up to 1000 words. Illustrations: colour transparencies. Payment: £400 per 1000 words, photo fees negotiable. Founded 1986.

Cage & Aviary Birds

IPC Media Ltd, King's Reach Tower, Stamford Street, London SE1 9LS
tel 020-7261 6116 *fax* 020-7261 6095
Editor Donald Taylor
Weekly £1.10

News on all aspects of birds and birdkeeping. Practical articles on bird-keeping. First-hand knowledge only. Quality pictures always welcome. Illustrations: line, half-tone, colour. Payment: by arrangement. Founded 1902.

Caledonia

Scott House Publishing Ltd, 28 Melville Street, Edinburgh EH3 7HA
tel 0131-476 4670 *fax* 0131-476 4671
email dcurrie@scotthouse.co.uk
website www.caledonia-magazine.com
Editor Don Currie
Monthly £2.95

Contemporary features of Scottish interest on personalities, arts, interiors, lifestyle. Send proposal to the Editor. Length: variable. Payment: £250 per 1000 words. Founded 1999.

Camcorder User

(incorporating Video Editing and Desktop Video)
WVIP, 53-79 Highgate Road, London NW5 1TW
tel 020-7331 1000 *fax* 020-7331 1242
email rob.hull@wvip.co.uk
Editor Robert Hull
Monthly £3.25

Features on film/video-making techniques, specifically tailored to the amateur enthusiast. Material mostly commissioned. Length: 1000–2500 words. Illustrations: colour and b&w; contact editor for details. Payment: by arrangement. Founded 1988.

Campaign

Haymarket Business Publications Ltd, 22 Bute Gardens, London W6 7HN
tel 020-8267 4656 *fax* 020-8267 4915
email campaign@haynet.com
Editor Caroline Marshall
Weekly £2.50

News and articles covering the whole of

the mass communications field, particularly advertising in all its forms, marketing and the media. Features should not exceed 2000 words. News items also welcome. Press day, Wednesday. Payment: by arrangement.

Camping Magazine

Warner Group Publications, The Maltings, West Street, Bourne, Lincs. PE10 9PH
tel/fax (01778) 391116
Editor John Lloyd
Monthly £2.70

Covers the spectrum of camping and related activities in all shapes and forms – camping is more than a tent on a site! Lively, anecdotal articles written to guidelines and photos are welcome. Talk to editor first. Length: 500–1500 words on average. Illustrations: colour. Payment: by arrangement. Founded 1961.

Canal & Riverboat

PO Box 618, Norwich NR7 0QT
tel (01603) 708930 *fax* (01603) 708934
email bluefoxfilms@netscapeonline.co.uk
website www.canalandriverboat.com
Editor Chris Cattrall
Monthly £2.60

News, views and articles on UK inland waterways and cruising features, DIY articles and historical features. Length: 1500 words (articles/features), 300 words (news). Payment: £100; £25 (news). Illustrations: colour, plus b&w cartoons. Founded 1978.

Car

EMAP Automotive Ltd, 3rd Floor, Priory Court, 30-32 Farringdon Lane, London EC1R 3AU
tel 020-7017 3500 *fax* 020-7017 3530
email car@emap.com
Editor Greg Fountain
Monthly £3.50

Top-grade journalistic features on car driving, car people and cars. Length: 1000–2500 words. Payment: minimum £250 per 1000 words. Illustrations: b&w and colour photos to professional standards. Founded 1962.

Car Mechanics

Cudham Tithe Barn, Berrys Hill, Cudham, Kent TW16 3AG
tel (01959) 541444 or (01733) 203749
fax (01959) 541400
email info@kelsey.co.uk
Editor Phil Weeden
Monthly £2.80

Practical articles on maintaining, repairing and uprating modern cars for DIY plus the motor trade. Always interested in finding new talent for our rather specialised market but please study a recent copy before submitting ideas or features. Preliminary letter or phone call outlining feature recommended. Payment: by arrangement. Illustrations: line drawings, colour prints or transparencies. Rarely use words only; please supply text and pictures.

Caravan Magazine

IPC Country & Leisure Media Ltd, Focus House, Dingwall Avenue, Croydon CR9 2TA
tel 020-8774 0600 *fax* 020-8774 0939
website www.caravanmagazine.co.uk
Editor Rob McCabe
Monthly £2.90

Lively articles based on real experience of touring caravanning, especially if well illustrated by photos. General countryside or motoring material not wanted. Payment: by arrangement. Founded 1933.

Caribbean Times

(incorporating African Times)
Ethnic Media Group, Unit 2.01, Technology Centre, 65 Whitehchapel Road, London E1 1DU
tel 020-7650 2000 *fax* 020-7650 2004
email caribbeantimes@hotmail.com
Editor Ron Shillingford
Weekly 50p

News stories, articles and features of interest to Britain's African-Caribbean community. Founded 1981.

Carousel – The Guide to Children's Books

The Saturn Centre, 54-76 Bissell Street, Birmingham B5 7HX
tel 0121-622 7458 *fax* 0121-666 7526
email carousel.guide@virgin.net
website www.carouselguide.co.uk
Editor Jenny Blanch
3 p.a. £9.75 p.a. (£13 p.a. Europe; £16 p.a. rest of world)

Reviews of fiction, non-fiction and poetry books for children, plus in-depth articles; profiles of authors and illustrators. Length: 1200 words (articles); 150 words (reviews). Illustrations: colour and b&w. Payment: by arrangement. Founded 1995.

Cat World

Ashdown Publishing, Avalon Court, Star Road, Partridge Green, West Sussex RH13 8RY
tel (01403) 711511 *fax* (01403) 711521
email editor@catworld.co.uk

website www.catworld.co.uk
Editor Jo Rothery
Monthly £2.75

Bright, lively articles on any aspect of cat ownership. Articles on breeds of cats and veterinary articles by acknowledged experts only. No unsolicited fiction. All submissions by email or on disk. Illustrations: colour prints, transparencies, TIFFS. Payment: by arrangement. Founded 1981.

Caterer & Hotelkeeper

Reed Business Information Ltd, Quadrant House, The Quadrant, Sutton, Surrey SM2 5AS
tel 020-8652 8680 *fax* 020-8652 8973/8947
Editor Forbes Mutch
Weekly £1.90

Articles on all aspects of the hotel and catering industries. Length: up to 1500 words. Illustrations: line, half-tone, colour. Payment: by arrangement. Founded 1893.

Catholic Gazette

The Chase Centre, 114 West Heath Road, London NW3 7TX
tel 020-8458 3316 *fax* 020-8905 5780
email gazette@cms.org.uk
website www.cms.org.uk/gazette
Editor Fr. Peter Wilson
Monthly £1.20

Articles on evangelisation and the Christian life. Length: up to 2000 words. Payment: by arrangement. Founded 1910.

The Catholic Herald

Herald House, Lambs Passage, Bunhill Row, London EC1Y 8TQ
tel 020-7588 3101 *fax* 020-7256 9728
email editorial@catholicherald.co.uk
website www.catholicherald.co.uk
Editor Dr William Oddie
Weekly 70p

Independent newspaper covering national and international affairs from a Catholic/Christian viewpoint as well as church news. Length: articles 600–1200 words. Illustrations: photos of Catholic and Christian interest. Payment: by arrangement.

Catholic Pictorial

Media House, Mann Island, Pier Head, Liverpool L3 1DQ
tel 0151-236 2191 *fax* 0151-236 2216
Editor David Mahon
Weekly 60p

News and photo features (maximum 800 words plus illustration) of Merseyside, regional and national Catholic interest only; also cartoons. Has a strongly social editorial and is a trenchant tabloid. Payment: by arrangement. Founded 1961.

Catholic Times

1st Floor, St James's Buildings, Oxford Street, Manchester M1 6FP
tel 0161-236 8856 *fax* 0161-237 5590
Editor Stefano Hatfield
Weekly 70p

News (400 words) and news features (800 words) of Catholic interest. Illustrations: colour and b&w photos. Payment: £30–£80; photos £50. Relaunched 1993.

Cencrastus: Scottish & International Literature, Arts and Affairs

Unit One, Abbeymount Techbase, 2 Easter Road, Edinburgh EH8 8EJ
tel/fax 0131-661 5687
email cencrastus1@hotmail.com
Editor Raymond Ross, *Managing Editor* Zsvzsanna Varga
Quarterly £2.95 (back copies £2.50); £12 p.a.

Articles, short stories, poetry, reviews. Payment: by arrangement. Illustrations: line, half-tone. Founded 1979.

Chapman

4 Broughton Place, Edinburgh EH1 3RX
tel 0131-557 2207 *fax* 0131-556 9565
email editor@chapman-pub.co.uk
website www.chapman-pub.co.uk
Editor Joy Hendry
3 p.a. £18 p.a.

'Scotland's Quality Literary Magazine.' Poetry, short stories, reviews, criticism, articles on Scottish culture. Illustrations: line, half-tone, cartoons. Payment: £8.00 per page; illustrations by negotiation. Founded 1969.

Chartered Secretary

(formerly Administrator)
16 Park Crescent, London W1B 1AH
tel 020-7580 4741 *fax* 020-7612 7034
email chartsec@icsa.co.uk
website www.icsa.org.uk
Monthly £5 (£50 p.a. post free UK)

Official magazine of The Institute of Chartered Secretaries and Administrators. Practical and topical articles (1500+ words) on law, finance and management affecting company secretaries and other senior administrators in business, not-for-profit sector, local and central government and other institutions in Britain and overseas. Payment: by arrangement.

Chat
IPC Connect Ltd, King's Reach Tower, Stamford Street, London SE1 9LS
tel 020-7261 6565 *fax* 020-7261 6534
website www.ipcmedia.com
Editor Paul Merrill
Weekly 68p

Tabloid weekly for women; fiction. Length: up to 800 words. Payment: by arrangement. Founded 1986.

Child Education
Scholastic Ltd, Villiers House, Clarendon Avenue, Leamington Spa, Warks. CV32 5PR
tel (01926) 887799 *fax* (01926) 883331
website www.scholastic.co.uk
Editor Jeremy Sugden
Monthly £2.95

For teachers concerned with the education of children aged 4–8. Articles by specialists on practical teaching ideas and methods. Length: 600–1200 words. Payment: by arrangement. Profusely illustrated with photos and artwork; also large full colour picture posters. Founded 1924.

The China Quarterly
School of Oriental and African Studies, Thornhaugh Street, Russell Square, London WC1H 0XG
tel 020-7898 4063 *fax* 020-7898 4849
email chinaq@soas.ac.uk
Editor Dr Julia Strauss
Quarterly £39/$68 p.a. (£80/$135 institutions, £20/$35 students)

Articles on contemporary China. Length: 8000 words approx.

Choice
1st Floor, Kings Chambers, 39-41 Priestgate, Peterborough PE1 1FR
tel (01733) 555123 *fax* (01733) 427500
Editor-in-Chief Sue Dobson
Monthly £2.30

Pre- and retirement magazine for 50+ readership. Positive attitude to life – experiences, hobbies, holidays, finance, relationships. Most of the magazine commissioned. If suggesting feature material, include selection of cuttings of previously published work. Payment: by agreement, on publication. Founded 1974.

Christian Herald
Christian Media, 96 Dominion Road, Worthing, West Sussex BN14 8JP
tel (01903) 821082 *fax* (01903) 821081
email news@christianherald.org.uk
features@christianherald.org.uk
website www.christianherald.org.uk
Weekly 65p

Evangelical Christian paper with strong emphasis on news and current affairs. Features up to 800 words – profiles, the changing church, Christians, and contemporary culture (e.g. media, TV, music); cartoons. No short stories. Payment: £20–£60, depending on length/pictures used.

Church of England Newspaper
20-26 Brunswick Place, London N1 6DZ
tel 020-7417 5800 *fax* 020-7216 6410
Weekly 70p

Anglican news and articles relating the Christian faith to everyday life. Evangelical basis; almost exclusively commissioned articles. Study of paper desirable. Length: up to 1000 words. Illustrations: photos, line drawings, cartoons. Payment: c. £40 per1000 words; photos £22, line by arrangement. Founded 1828.

Church Times
33 Upper Street, London N1 0PN
tel 020-7359 4570 *fax* 020-7226 3073
email editor@churchtimes.co.uk
website www.churchtimes.co.uk
Editor Paul Handley
Weekly 70p

Articles on religious topics are considered. No verse or fiction. Length: up to 1000 words. Illustrations: news photos, sent promptly. Payment: £100 per 1000 words; Periodical Publishers' Association negotiated rates for illustrations. Founded 1863.

Classic & Sports Car
Haymarket Specialist Motoring Publications Ltd, Somerset House, Somerset Road, Teddington, Middlesex TW11 8RT
tel 020-8267 5399 *fax* 020-8267 5318
Editor James Elliott
Monthly £3.60

Features on classic cars and sportscars; shows, news and reviews, features and stories. Illustrations: half-tone, colour. Payment: £250 per 1000 words; varies for illustrations. Founded 1982.

Classic Boat & The Boatman
Focus House, Dingwall Avenue, Croydon CR9 2TA
tel 020-8774 0603 *fax* 020-8774 0943
email cb@ipcmedia.com
website www.classicboat.co.uk
Editor Dan Houston

Monthly £3.60

Cruising and technical features, restorations, events, new boat reviews, practical, maritime history; news. Study of magazine essential: read 3–4 back issues and send for contributors' guidelines. Length: 500–2000 words. Illustrations: colour and b&w photos; line drawings of hulls. Payment: £75–£100 per published page. Founded 1987.

Classic Cars

EMAP Automotive Ltd, Media House, Lynchwood, Peterborough Business Park, Peterborough PE2 6EA
tel (01733) 468219 *fax* (01733) 468888
email classic.cars@emap.com
Editor Martyn Moore
Monthly £3.50

Specialist articles on older cars. Length: from 500–4000 words (subject to prior contract). Illustrations: half-tone, colour, cartoons. Payment: by negotiation.

Classic Stitches

D.C. Thomson & Co. Ltd, 80 Kingsway East, Dundee DD4 8SL
tel (01382) 462276 *fax* (01382) 452491
email editorial@classicstitches.com
website www.classicstitches.com
Editor Mrs Bea Neilson
Bi-monthly £3.95

Creative needlework ideas and projects; needlework-based features on designers, collections, work-in-progress and exhibitions. Submissions also welcome for e-mag on website. Length: 1000–2000 words. Illustrations: colour photos, preferably not 35 mm. Payment: negotiable. Founded 1994.

Classical Music

Rhinegold Publishing Ltd, 241 Shaftesbury Avenue, London WC2H 8TF
tel 020-7333 1742 *fax* 020-7333 1769
email classical.music@rhinegold.co.uk
website www.rhinegold.co.uk
Editor Keith Clarke
Fortnightly £3.25

News, opinion, features on the classical music business. All material commissioned. Illustrations: b&w photos and line; colour covers. Payment: minimum £100 per 1000 words; from £50 for illustrations. Founded 1976.

Classics

SPL, Berwick House, 8-10 Knoll Rise, Orpington, Kent BR6 0PS
tel (01689) 887200 *fax* (01689) 876438
email classics@splpublishing.co.uk
Editor Andrew Charman
Monthly £3.50

News photos and stories of classic car interest and illustrated features on classic car history, repairs, maintenance and restoration. Study magazine before submitting material. Features must have high level of subject knowledge and technical accuracy. Length: up to 2000 words (features); 200 words (news). Illustrations: colour and b&w. Payment: £120 per 1000 words plus £100 per set of supporting photos (features); £120 per 1000 words plus photos based on £100 per page (news). Founded 1997.

Climber

Warners Group Publications plc, West Street, Bourne, Lincs. PE10 9PH
tel (01778) 391117
Editor Bernard Newman
Monthly £2.99

Articles on all aspects of rock climbing/mountaineering in Great Britain and abroad, and on related subjects. Study of magazine essential. Length: 1500–2000 words. Illustrations: colour transparencies. Payment: according to merit. Founded 1962.

Coin News

Token Publishing Ltd, Orchard House, Duchy Road, Heathpark, Honiton, Devon EX14 1YD
tel (01404) 46972 *fax* (01404) 44788
Editor John W. Mussell
Monthly £2.75

Articles of high standard on coins, tokens, paper money. Length: up to 2000 words. Payment: by arrangement. Founded 1964.

Commando

D.C. Thomson & Co. Ltd, Albert Square, Dundee DD1 9QJ
tel (01382) 223131 *fax* (01382) 322214
8 p.m. 80p

Fictional war stories told in pictures. Scripts: about 135 pictures. Synopsis required as an opener. New writers encouraged; send for details. Payment: on acceptance.

Commercial Motor

Reed Business Information Ltd, Quadrant House, The Quadrant, Sutton, Surrey SM2 5AS
tel 020-8652 3302/3303 *fax* 020-8652 8969
Editor-in-Chief Brian Weatherley

Weekly £1.70

Technical and road transport articles only. Length: up to 1500 words. Payment: varies. Illustrations: drawings and photos. Founded 1905.

Communicate

DMG World Media (UK) Ltd, Queensway House, 2 Queensway, Redhill, Surrey RH1 1QS
tel (01737) 768611 *fax* (01737) 855470
Editor Neil Tyler
Monthly Controlled circulation

Covers all aspects of telecommunications management: analysis pieces (200–700 words), features (1000–2000 words), case studies (300 words). Some material commissioned. Illustrations: colour photos, line, diagrams. Payment: by arrangement. Founded 1980.

Company

National Magazine House, 72 Broadwick Street, London W1V 2BP
tel 020-7439 5000
email company.mail@natmags.co.uk
Editor Sam Baker
Monthly £2.60

Articles on a wide variety of subjects, relevant to young, independent women. Most articles are commissioned. Payment: usual magazine rate. Illustrated. Founded 1978.

Computer Weekly

Reed Business Information Ltd, Quadrant House, The Quadrant, Sutton, Surrey SM2 5AS
tel 020-8652 3122 *fax* 020-8652 8979
website www.cw360.com
Editor Karl Schneider, *News Editor* Lindsay Clark
Weekly £2.20

Feature articles on IT-related topics for business/industry users. Length: 1200 words. Illustrations: b&w photos, line, cartoons. Payment: £250 per 1000 words; negotiable for illustrations. Founded 1966.

Computing

VNU Business Publications, VNU House, 32-34 Broadwick Street, London W1A 2HG
tel 020-7316 9158 *fax* 020-7316 9160
website www.computingnet.co.uk
Editor Colin Barker
Weekly £100 p.a.

Features and news items on corporate procurement and deployment of IT infrastructure, and on applications and implications of computers and telecommunications. Particular sections address the IT professional career development, and the desktop computing environment. Length: 1600–2200 words. Payment: by negotiation. Illustrations: colour photos, line drawings, cartoons. Founded 1973.

Condé Nast Traveller

Vogue House, Hanover Square, London W1S 1JU
tel 020-7499 9080 *fax* 020-7493 3758
email cntraveller@condenast.co.uk
website www.cntraveller.co.uk
Editor Sarah Miller
Monthly £3.20

Highly illustrated features on travel, style, food and wine, beauty and health. Illustrations: colour. Payment: by arrangement. Founded 1997.

Contemporary

Suite K101, Tower Bridge Business Complex, 100 Clements Road, London SE16 4DG
tel 020-7740 1704 *fax* 020-7252 3510
email info@contemporary-magazine.com
website www.contemporary-magazine.com
Editor Keith Patrick
Monthly £4.95

International magazine with extensive coverage of visual arts, architecture, fashion, film, photography, books, music, dance and sport. Also includes interviews, profiles and art news from around the world. Length: varies. Illustrations: colour transparencies. Payment: £100 per 1000 words; none for photos. Founded 1992; relaunched 2002.

Contemporary Review

(incorporating the Fortnightly)
Contemporary Review Co. Ltd, PO Box 1242, Oxford OX1 4FJ
tel/fax (01865) 201529
Editor Dr Richard Mullen, *Send material to* Dr Alex Kerr, Managing Editor
Monthly £3.25

Independent review dealing with questions of the day, chiefly politics, international affairs, religion, literature, the arts. Mostly commissioned, but with limited scope for freelance authors with authoritative knowledge. TS returned only if sae enclosed. Intending contributors should study journal first. Length: 2000–3000 words. No illustrations. Payment: £5 per page (500 words), 2 complimentary copies. Founded 1866.

Cosmetic World News

9 Onslow Square, London SW7 3NJ
tel 020-7589 0589 *fax* 020-7838 0908
email mamp@cosmeticworldnews.com
website www.cosmeticworldnews.com

Editor M.A. Murray-Pearce
Bi-monthly £96 p.a.

International news magazine of perfumery, cosmetics and toiletries industry. World-wide reports, photo-news stories, articles (500–1000 words) on essential oils and new cosmetic raw materials, and exclusive information on industry's companies and personalities welcomed. Payment: by arrangement. Illustrations: b&w and colour photos or colour separations. Founded 1949.

Cosmopolitan

National Magazine House, 72 Broadwick Street, London W1V 2BP
tel 020-7439 5000 *fax* 020-7439 5016
Editor-in-Chief Lorraine Candy
Monthly £2.70

Articles. Commissioned material only. Payment: by arrangement. Illustrated. Founded 1972.

Country

Summerhouse Publishing Ltd, St James Yarn Mill, Whitefriars, Norwich NR3 1XU
tel (01603) 664242 *fax* (01603) 664410
Editor Gill Crawley
Monthly £2.95

Magazine of the CGA. News and features covering rural events, countryside, leisure, heritage, homes and gardens. Some outside contributors used; approach in writing in first instance. Payment: by arrangement. Founded 1893.

Country Homes and Interiors

IPC Magazines Ltd, King's Reach Tower, Stamford Street, London SE1 9LS
tel 020-7261 6451 *fax* 020-7261 6895
Editor Deborah Barker
Monthly £2.80

Articles on property, country homes, interior designs. Illustrations: colour. Payment: from £250 per 1000 words. Founded 1986.

Country Life

IPC Media Ltd, King's Reach Tower, Stamford Street, London SE1 9LS
tel 020-7261 7058 *fax* 020-7261 5139
Editor Clive Aslet
Weekly £2.80

Illustrated journal chiefly concerned with British country life, social history, architecture and the fine arts, natural history, agriculture, gardening and sport. Length: about 1000 or 1300 words (articles). Illustrations: mainly colour photos. Payment:according to merit. Founded 1897.

Country Living

National Magazine House, 72 Broadwick Street, London W1F 9EP
tel 020-7439 5000 *fax* 020-7439 5093
website www.countryliving.co.uk
Editor Susy Smith
Monthly £3

Up-market home-interest magazine with a country lifestyle theme, covering interiors, gardens, crafts, food, wildlife, rural and green issues. Do not send unsolicited material or valuable transparencies. Illustrations: line, half-tone, colour. Payment: byarrangement. Founded 1985.

Country Quest

7 Aberystwyth Science Park, Aberystwyth, Ceredigion SY23 3AH
tel (01970) 615000 *fax* (01970) 624699
Editor Beverly Davies, *Send material to* Erica Jones
Monthly £2

Illustrated articles on matters relating to countryside, history and personalities of Wales and border counties. No fiction. Illustrated work preferred. Length: 700–1500 words. Payment: by arrangement.

Country Smallholding

Archant Regional Ltd, Fair Oak Close, Exeter Airport Business Park, Clyst Honiton, Exeter EX5 2UL
tel (01392) 117711 *fax* (01392) 445350
email editorial@countrysmallholding.com
website www.countrysmallholding.com
Editor Sara Priddle
Monthly £2.75

The magazine for smallholders. Practical, how-to articles, and seasonal features, on organic gardening, small-scale poultry and livestock keeping, country crafts, cookery and smallholdings. Approach editor in writing with ideas. Length: up to 2000 words.Payment. £40 per 1000 words; photos £10, £50 cover. Founded 1975 as *Home Farm*.

Country Walking

EMAP Active Ltd, Bretton Court, Bretton, Peterborough PE3 8DZ
tel (01733) 264666 *fax* (01733) 282653
Editor Nicola Dela-Croix
Monthly £2.95

Features. Length: 1200 words on average. Illustrations: colour transparencies. Payment: by arrangement. Founded 1987.

The Countryman

Countryman Publishing Ltd, Sheep Street, Burford, Oxon OX18 4LS
tel (01993) 824424
email burford@countrymanmagazine.co.uk
Editor David Horan
Monthly £1.95

Every department of rural life except field sports. Copy must be trustworthy, well-written, brisk, cogent and light in hand. Articles up to 1200 words. Skilful sketches of life and character from personal knowledge and experience. Dependable natural history based on writer's own observation. Really good matter from old unpublished letters and MSS. Study magazine before submitting material. Illustrations: b&w and colour photos and drawings, but all must be exclusive and out of the ordinary. Payment: min. £70 per 1000 words, usually more, according to merit. Founded 1927.

The Cricketer International

Ridge Farm, Lamberhurst Down, Kent TN3 8ER
tel (01892) 893000 *fax* (01892) 893010
email editorial@cricketer.co.uk
Editor Peter Perchard
Monthly £2.95

Articles on cricket at any level. Illustrations: line, half-tone, colour, cartoons. Payment: £85 per 1000 words; illustrations minimum £17.50. Founded 1921.

Critical Quarterly

Contributions Andrew Shail, School of English, Queen's Building, The Queen's Drive, Exeter EX4 4QH
website www.criticalquarterly.co.uk
Quarterly £21 p.a. (£88 p.a. institutions)

Fiction, poems, literary criticism. Length: 2000–5000 words. Study magazine before submitting MSS. Payment: by arrangement. Founded 1959.

Cumbria and Lake District Magazine

(formerly Cumbria)
Dalesman Publishing Company Ltd, Stable Courtyard, Broughton Hall, Skipton, North Yorkshire BD23 3AE
tel (01756) 701381 *fax* (01756) 701326
email editorial@dalesman.co.uk
Editor Terry Fletcher
Monthly £1.40

Articles of genuine rural interest concerning Lakeland and Cumbria. Short length preferred. Illustrations: line drawings and first-class photos. Payment: according to merit. Founded 1951.

Custom Car

Kelsey Publishing Ltd, Cudham Tithe Barn, Berry's Hill, Cudham, Kent TN16 3AG
tel (01959) 541444 *fax* (01959) 541400
email cc.mag@kelsey.co.uk
website www.kelsey.co.uk/custom
Editor Kev Elliott
Monthly £2.95

Customising, drag racing and hot rods. Length: by arrangement. Payment: by arrangement. Founded 1970.

Cycling Weekly

IPC Music and Sport Ltd, 5th Floor, Focus House, 9 Dingwall Avenue, Croydon CR9 2TA
tel 020-8774 0811 *fax* 020-8774 0952
email cycling@ipcmedia.com
Editor Robert Garbutt
Weekly £1.90

Racing and technical articles; topical photos with a cycling interest considered; cartoons. Length: not exceeding 1500 words. Payment: by arrangement. Founded 1891.

Cyphers

3 Selskar Terrace, Dublin 6, Republic of Ireland
tel/fax (01) 4978866
IR£9/$25 for 3 issues

Poems, fiction, articles on literary subjects, translations. Payment: £10 per page. Founded 1975.

Dairy Farmer

United Business Media International, 4 Friars Courtyard, Princes Street, Ipswich IP1 1RJ
tel (01473) 401379 *fax* (01473) 232822
email df@ubminternational.com
Editor Rachael Porter
Monthly Controlled circulation

In-depth, technical articles on all aspects of dairy farm management and milk marketing. Length: normally 800–1400 words with colour photos. Payment: by arrangement.

Dalesman

Dalesman Publishing Company Ltd, Stable Courtyard, Broughton Hall, Skipton, North Yorkshire BD23 3AE
tel (01756) 701381 *fax* (01756) 701326
email editorial@dalesman.co.uk
Editor Terry Fletcher
Monthly £1.60

Articles and stories of genuine rural interest concerning Yorkshire (1000–1500 words). Payment: according to merit. Illustrations: line drawings and first-class photos preferably featuring people. Founded 1939.

Dance Today!

The Dancing Times Ltd, 45-47 Clerkenwell Green, London EC1R 0EB
tel 020-7250 3006 *fax* 020-7253 6679
email dancetoday!@dancing-times.co.uk
website www.dancing-times.co.uk
Editor Bronya Seifert, *Editorial Adviser* Mary Clarke
Monthly £1.20

Ballroom and social dancing from every aspect, but chiefly from the serious competitive, teaching and medal test angles. Well-informed freelance articles are occasionally used, but only after preliminary arrangements. Payment: by arrangement. Illustrations: action photos preferred, b&w or colour. Founded 1956.

Dancing Times

The Dancing Times Ltd, 45-47 Clerkenwell Green, London EC1R 0EB
tel 020-7250 3006 *fax* 020-7253 6679
email dt@dancing-times.co.uk
website www.dancing-times.co.uk
Editor Mary Clarke, *Editorial Adviser* Ivor Guest
Monthly £2.30

Ballet, contemporary dance and all forms of stage dancing from general, historical, critical and technical angles. Well-informed freelance articles used occasionally, but only after preliminary arrangements. Payment: by arrangement. Illustrations: occasional line, action photos preferred; colour welcome. Founded 1910.

The Dandy

D.C. Thomson & Co. Ltd, Albert Square, Dundee DD1 9QJ
tel (01382) 223131 *fax* (01382) 322214
185 Fleet Street, London EC4A 2HS
tel 020-7400 1030 *fax* 020-7400 1089
Weekly 60p

Comic strips for children. 10–12 pictures per single page story, 18–20 pictures per 2-page story. Promising artists are encouraged. Payment: on acceptance.

Funsize Dandy

2 p.m. 80p

Founded 1997.

Darts World

World Magazines Ltd, 28 Arrol Road, Beckenham, Kent BR3 4PA
tel 020-8650 6580 *fax* 020-8654 4343
Editor Tony Wood
Monthly £2.20

Articles and stories with darts theme. Illustrations: half-tone, cartoons. Payment: £40–£50 per 1000 words; illustrations by arrangement. Founded 1972.

Day by Day

Woolacombe House, 141 Woolacombe Road, London SE3 8QP
tel 020-8856 6249
Editor Patrick Richards
Monthly 95p

Articles and news on non-violence and social justice. Reviews of art, books, films, plays, musicals and opera. Cricket reports. Short poems and very occasional short stories in keeping with editorial viewpoint. Payment: £2 per 1000 words. No illustrations required. Founded 1963.

Decanter

IPC Country & Leisure Media Ltd, 1st Floor, Broadway House, 2-6 Fulham Broadway, London SW6 1AA
tel 020-7610 3929 *fax* 020-7381 5282
email editorial@decantermagazine.com
website www.decanter.com
Editor Amy Wislocki
Monthly £3.40

Articles and features on wines, wine travel and food-related topics. Welcomes ideas for articles and features. Length: 1000–1800 words. Illustrations: colour. Payment: £230 per 1000 words. Founded 1975.

Derbyshire Life and Countryside

Heritage House, Lodge Lane, Derby DE1 3HE
tel (01332) 347087/8/9 *fax* (01332) 290688
Monthly £1.50

Articles, preferably illustrated, about Derbyshire life, people and history. Length: up to 800 words. Some short stories set in Derbyshire accepted; no verse. Payment: according to nature and quality of contribution. Illustrations: photos of Derbyshire subjects. Founded 1931.

Descent

Wild Places Publishing, 51 Timbers Square, Cardiff CF24 3SH
tel/fax 029-2048 6557
email descent@wildplaces.co.uk
website www.caving.uk.com
Editor Chris Howes
Bi-monthly £2.95

Articles, features and news on all aspects of cave and mine sport exploration. Submissions must match magazine style. Length: up to 2000 words (articles and features), up to 1000 words (news). Illustrations: colour and b&w. Payment: on consideration of material. Founded 1969.

The Dickensian

The Dickens Fellowship, Dickens House, 48 Doughty Street, London WC1N 2LX
Editor Dr Malcolm Andrews, School of English, Rutherford College, University of Kent, Canterbury, Kent CT2 7NX *fax* (01227) 827001
email M.Y.Andrews@ukc.ac.uk
3 p.a. £9.50 p.a. (£12 p.a. institutions; overseas rates on application)

Welcomes articles on all aspects of Dickens' life, works and character. Payment: none. Send contributions (enclose sae if return required) and editorial correspondence to the editor.

Director

116 Pall Mall, London SW1Y 5ED
tel 020-7766 8950 *fax* 020-7766 8840
Editor Joanna Higgins
Monthly £3.25

Authoritative business-related articles. Send synopsis of proposed article and examples of printed work. Length: 500–3000 words. Payment: by arrangement. Illustrations: colour. Founded 1947.

Dirt Bike Rider

Lancaster & Morecambe Newspapers Ltd, Victoria Street, Morecambe, Lancs. LA4 4AG
tel (01524) 32525 *fax* (01524) 842157
email sean.lawless@rim.co.uk
Editor Sean Lawless
Monthly £2.80

Features, track tests, coverage on all aspects of off-road motor-cycling. Length: up to 2000 words. Illustrations: half-tone, colour, cartoons. Founded 1981.

Disability Now

(published by Scope)
6 Market Road, London N7 9PW
tel 020-7619 7323 *fax* 020-7619 7331
Minicom 020-7619 733
email editor@disabilitynow.org.uk
website www.disabilitynow.org.uk
Editor Mary Wilkinson
Monthly £18 p.a., free to people on income support; tape version free to people with visual impairment or severe disability

Newspaper for people with different types of disability, carers and professionals, and anyone interested in disability. News and comment on anything of interest in the disability field: benefits, services, equipment, jobs, politics, motoring, holidays, sport, relationships, the arts. All regular contributors have a disability (unless they are a parent of someone with a disability). Preliminary letter desirable. Founded 1957.

Diva

Millivres Prowler Group Ltd, Worldwide House, 116-134 Bayham Street, London NW1 0BA
tel 020-7482 2576 *fax* 020-7284 0329
email edit@divamag.co.uk
website www.divamag.co.uk
Editor Gillian Rodgerson
Monthly £2.25

Lesbian life and culture: articles, features, news, short fiction. Length: 1000–2000 words (articles/features); 300–500 words (news); 1000–2000 words (short stories). Illustrations: colour and b&w. Payment: £10 per 100 words; £30–£50 per photo; £25–£80 per drawing. Founded 1994.

Diver

55 High Street, Teddington, Middlesex TW11 8HA
tel 020-8943 4288 *fax* 020-8943 4312
email enquiries@divermag.co.uk
website divernet@www.divernet.com
Editor Nigel Eaton
Monthly £3.20

Articles on sub aqua diving and related developments. Length: 1500–4000 words. Illustrations: line, half-tone and colour. Payment: by arrangement. Founded 1953.

Dogs Today

Pet Subjects Ltd, Town Mill, Bagshot Road, Chobham, Surrey GU24 8BZ
tel (01276) 858880 *fax* (01276) 858860
email dogstoday@dial.pipex.com
Editor Beverley Cuddy
Monthly £2.95

Study of magazine essential before submitting ideas. Interested in human interest dog stories, celebrity interviews, holiday features and anything unusual – all must be entertaining and informative and accompanied by illustrations. Length: 800–1200 words. Illustrations: colour, preferably transparencies, colour cartoons. Payment: negotiable. Founded 1990.

Dorset Life – The Dorset Magazine

7 The Leanne, Sandford Lane, Wareham, Dorset BH20 4DY
tel (01929) 551264 *fax* (01929) 552099
email office@dorsetlife.co.uk
Editor John Newth
Monthly £1.95

Articles (500–1200 words), photos (colour) and line drawings with a specifically Dorset theme. Payment: by arrangement. Founded 1967.

Drapers Record

EMAP Communications, Greater London House, Hampstead Road, London NW1 7EJ
tel 020-7391 3300 *fax* 020-7391 3403
email drapers.record@emap.com
website www.drapersrecord.com
Editor-in-Chief Eric Musgrave
Weekly £2.60

Business editorial aimed at fashion retailers, large and small. Payment: by negotiation. Illustrations: colour and b&w: photos, drawings and cartoons. Founded 1887.

Early Music

Oxford University Press, 70 Baker Street, London W1M 7DN
tel 020-7616 5902 *fax* 020-7616 5901
email jnl.early-music@oup.co.uk
website www.em.oupjournals.org
Editor Tess Knighton
Quarterly £10.50 (£46 p.a., institutions £92 p.a.)

Lively, informative and scholarly articles on aspects of medieval, renaissance, baroque and classical music. Payment: £20 per 1000 words. Illustrations: line, half-tone, colour. Founded 1973.

East Lothian Life

1 Beveridge Row, Belhaven, Dunbar, East Lothian EH42 1TP
tel/fax (01368) 863593
email info@east-lothian-life.co.uk
website www.east-lothian-life.co.uk
Editor Pauline Jaffray
Quarterly £2

Articles and features with an East Lothian slant. Length: up to 1000 words. Illustrations: b&w photos, line, cartoons. Payment: negotiable. Founded 1989.

Eastern Art Report

Eastern Art Publishing Group, PO Box 13666, 27 Wallorton Gardens, London SW14 8WF
tel 020-8392 1122 *fax* 020 8392 1422
email ear@eapgroup.com
Managing Sajid Rizvi, *Send material to* Shirley Rizvi, Executive Editor
Bi-monthly £6 (individual £30 p.a., institutions £60 p.a.)

Original, well-researched articles on all aspects of the visual arts – Islamic, Indian, Chinese and Japanese; reviews. Length of articles: min. 1500 words. Illustrations: colour transparencies, b&w photos; no responsibility accepted for unsolicited material. Payment: by arrangement. Founded 1989.

Eastern Eye

Ethnic Media Group, Unit 2, 65 Whitechapel Road, London E1 1DU
tel 020-7650 2000 *fax* 020-7650 2001
Editor Mujibul Islam
Weekly 70p

Articles, features and news of interest to British Asians. Magazine covers music, fashion, film gossip. Freelance material considered. Illustrations: colour. Founded 1989.

The Ecologist

Unit 18, Chelsea Wharf, 15 Lots Road, London SW10 0QJ
tel 020-7351 3578 *fax* 020-7351 3617
email sally@theecologist.org
Editors Zac Goldsmith
10 p.a. £3.50

Fully referenced articles on economic, social and environmental affairs from an ecological standpoint. Study magazine first for level and approach. Length: 1000–5000 words. Illustrations: line, half-tone. Payment: by arrangement.

Economica

STICERD, London School of Economics, Houghton Street, London WC2A 2AE
tel 020-7955 7855 *fax* 020-7955 6951
Editors Prof F.A. Cowell, Prof Alan Manning, Prof Tore Ellingsen
Quarterly £28 (apply for subscription rates)

Learned journal covering the fields of economics, economic history and statistics. Payment: none. Founded 1921; New Series 1934.

The Economist

25 St James's Street, London SW1A 1HG
tel 020-7830 7000
website www.economist.com
Editor Bill Emmott
Weekly £2.80

Articles staff-written. Founded 1843.

The Edge

65 Guinness Buildings, London W6 8BD
tel 020-7460 9444
email davec@theedge.abelgratis.co.uk
website www.theedge.abelgratis.co.uk
Editor David Clark
Quarterly £3.50

Interviews, features, reviews: books, films, music, modern popular culture; imaginative fiction – science fiction, modern urban fiction, horror, etc. Return postage essential. Payment: £30–£300 negotiable.

Edinburgh Review

22A Buccleugh Place, Edinburgh EH8 9LN
tel/fax 0131-651 1415
email Edinburgh.Review@ed.ac.uk
Editor Alex Thomson
Tri-annual £17 p.a. (individual)

Fiction, poetry, clearly written articles on Scottish and international cultural and philosophical ideas. Payment: by arrangement. Founded 1969.

Education Journal

17 Park Road, Hampton Hill, Middlesex TW12 1HE
tel/fax 020-8979 9473
Editor George Low
Monthly £38 p.a.

Features on policy, management and professional development issues. Major documents and reports gutted down to a brief digest; documents and research listings. Research section combining original reports and updates on research projects. Coverage of parliamentary debates and answers to parliamentary questions, giving statistical data by LEA. Reference section that includes coverage of all circulars, conference reports and opinion column. Length: 1000 words. Illustrations: photos, cartoons. Payment: by arrangement. Founded 1903; relaunched 1996.

EE Times

CMP Europe Ltd, City Reach, 5 Greenwich View Place, Millharbour, London E14 9NN
tel 020-7861 6417 *fax* 020-7861 6253
email cedwards@cmp-europe.com
Editor Chris Edwards
Weekly £3.25 (£85 p.a.)

News, reviews and features on the electronics industry. Length: 2000 words (features), 200 words (news). Illustrations: colour transparencies, colour and b&w artwork and cartoons. Payment: variable. Founded 1978.

Electrical Review

Cumulus Business Media, Anne Boleyn House, 9-13 Ewell Road, Cheam, Surrey SM3 8BZ
tel 020-8652 8736 *fax* 020-8652 8951
email b.evett@cumulusmedia.co.uk
Managing Editor Bill Evett
Fortnightly £3.50

Technical and business articles on electrical and control engineering; outside contributions considered. Electrical news welcomed. Illustrations: photos and drawings, cartoons. Payment: according to merit. Founded 1872.

Electrical Times

Cumulus Business Media, Anne Boleyn House, 9-13 Ewell Road, Cheam, Surrey SM3 8BZ
tel 020-8652 8736 *fax* 020-8652 8972
email b.evett@cumulusmedia.co.uk
Managing Editor Bill Evett
Monthly £3.50

Business and technical articles of interest to contractors and installers in the electrical industries and business services engineers, with illustrations as necessary. Length: 750–1000 words. Payment: negotiable. Illustrations: line, half-tone, colour, cartoons. Founded 1892.

Elle (UK)

EMAP Élan, Endeavour House, 189 Shaftesbury Avenue, London WC2H 8JG
tel 020-7437 9011 *fax* 020-7208 3599
Editor Sarah Bailey
Monthly £2.80

Commissioned material only. Payment: by arrangement. Illustrations: colour. Founded 1985.

Embroidery

The Embroiderers' Guild, PO Box 42B, East Molesey, Surrey KT8 9BB
email pppinpod@aol.com
website www.embroiderersguild.com
6 p.a. £4.55 (£27.30 p.a.)

Illustrated features on contemporary textile art. Reports on internationally renowned makers. In-depth articles on ethnographic embroidery. Looks inside important collections, and at the history and social history of embroidery. Plus book and exhibition reviews, news and opportunities. Payment: by arrangement.

Empire

Endeavour House, 189 Shaftesbury Avenue, London WC2H 8JG
tel 020-7439 9011 *fax* 020-7859 8613
website www.empireonline.com
Editor Emma Cochrane
Monthly £3

Guide to film and video: articles, features, news. Length: various. Illustrations: colour and b&w photos. Payment: approx. £300 per 1000 words; varies for illustrations. Founded 1989.

The Engineer

Centaur Communications Ltd, St Giles House, 50 Poland Street, London W1F 7AX
tel 020-7970 4106 *fax* 020-7970 4189
email george.coupe@centaur.co.uk
website www.e4engineering.com

Editor Sean Brierley
50 p.a. Controlled circulation (£118 p.a.)

Features and news on innovation and technology, including profiles, analysis. Length: news up to 800 words, features average 1000 words. Illustrations: colour transparencies or prints, artwork, line diagrams, graphs. Payment: by negotiation. Founded 1856.

Engineering

Gillard Welch Ltd, Chester Court, High Street, Knowle, Solihull
tel (01564) 771772 *fax* (01564) 774776
Editor Jonathan Ward
12 p.a. £5.95

'For innovators in technology, manufacturing and management': features and news. Contributions considered on all aspects of engineering. Illustrations: colour. Founded 1866.

The English Garden

Romsey Publishing Ltd, Glen House, Stag Place, London SW1E 5AQ
tel 020-7233 9191 *fax* 020-7931 0160
email editorial@theenglishgarden.co.uk
Editor Julia Watson
Monthly £2.95

Features and photography on English gardens, plant genera and garden design. Send written synopsis. Length: 1000 words. Illustrations: colour photos and artwork. Payment: variable. Founded 1997.

Envoi

44 Rudyard Road, Biddulph Moor, Stoke-on-Trent, Staffs. ST8 7JN
tel (01782) 517892
Editor Roger Elkin
3 p.a. £15 p.a.

New poetry, including sequences, collaborative works and translations, reviews, articles on modern poets and poetic style; poetry competitions; adjudicator's reports. Sample copy: £3.00. Payment: 1 complimentary copy. Founded 1957.

The Erotic Review

4th Floor, Maddox House, 1 Maddox Street, London W1S 2PZ
tel 020-7439 8999 *fax* 020-7437 3528
email editrice@eroticreview.org
website www.eroticreview.org
Editor Rowan Pelling, *Send material to* Pauline Morrison
Monthly £3.50

Up-market literary magazine for sensualists and libertines. Length: 1000 words (articles and features), 1000–2000 (short stories). Illustrations: colour and b&w prints, artwork and cartoons. Payment: £50–£75 (articles and features), £50–£75 (short stories); £50 (prints and artwork), £40 (cartoons). Founded 1997.

ES Magazine – see Evening Standard in Regional newspapers UK and Ireland, page 12

Esquire

National Magazine House, 72 Broadwick Street, London W1F 9EP
tel 020-7439 5000 *fax* 020-7439 5675
Editor Peter Howarth
Monthly £3.40

Quality men's general interest magazine – articles, features. No unsolicited material or short stories. Length: various. Illustrations: colour and b&w photos, line. Payment: by arrangement. Founded 1991.

Essential Water Garden

Aceville Publications Ltd, Castle House, 97 High Street, Colchester, Essex CO1 1TH
tel (01206) 505977 *fax* (01206) 505985
email demelzashea@genie.co.uk
Editor Demelza Shea
10 p.a. £2.80

Magazine for owners of all styles and sizes of water gardens, including fish-stocked pools. Practical projects and seasonal solutions. Illustrated step-by-step projects considered; also regular readers' garden feature. Illustrations: colour. Length: approx. 1000 words. Payment: by arrangement. Founded 1998.

Essentials

IPC Magazines Ltd, King's Reach Tower, Stamford Street, London SE1 9LS
tel 020-7261 6970
Editor Karen Livermore
Monthly £2

Features, plus fashion, health and beauty, cookery. Illustrations: colour. Payment: by negotiation. Founded 1988.

Essex Life & Countryside

Dugard House, Peartree Road, Stanway, Colchester CO3 5JX
tel (01206) 571348 *fax* (01206) 366982
Editor Carmen Konopka
Monthly £2.20

Features and profiles with Essex emphasis. Length: up to 1200 words. Illustrations: colour photos. Payment: negotiable. Founded 1952.

Essex Magazine
Acorn Magazines Ltd, The Old County School, Northgate Street, Bury St Edmunds, Suffolk IP33 1HP
tel (01284) 701190 *fax* (01284) 701680
Editor Pippa Bastin
Monthly £2.10

Magazine for residents of Essex and East Anglia covering history, people, places, environment, events, homes and gardens. Considers unsolicited material; no acknowledgement. Welcomes ideas for articles and features. Length: 1500 words features/articles. Illustrations: colour. Payment: £100 per 1500-word feature/article; £50 for front cover image. Founded 1999.

European Chemical News
Reed Business Information, Quadrant House, The Quadrant, Sutton, Surrey SM2 5AS
tel 020-8652 8147 *fax* 020-8652 3375
email ecne@rbi.co.uk
Editor John Baker
Weekly £335 p.a. Europe (£376 p.a. overseas)

Articles and features concerning business, markets and investments in the chemical industry. Length: 1000–2000 words; news items up to 400 words. Payment: £150–£180 per 1000 words.

Eventing
IPC Magazines Ltd, Room 2005, King's Reach Tower, Stamford Street, London SE1 9LS
tel 020-7261 5388 *fax* 020-7261 5429
Editor Kate Green
Monthly £3.10

News, articles, features, event reports and opinion pieces – all with bias towards the sport of horse trials. Mostly commissioned, but all ideas welcome. Length: up to 1500 words. Illustrations: colour and b&w, mostly commissioned. Payment: by arrangement; illustrations £30–£45. Founded 1984.

Evergreen
PO Box 52, Cheltenham, Glos. GL50 1YQ
tel (01242) 537900 *fax* (01242) 537901
Editor Roy Faiers
Quarterly £3.25

Articles about Britain's famous people and infamous characters, its natural beauty, towns and villages, history, traditions, odd customs, legends, folklore, etc; regular articles on old films, songs, radio programmes and variety acts. Length 250–2000 words. Also 'meaningful rather than clever' poetry. Illustrations: colour transparencies. Payment: £15 per 1000 words, £4 poems. Founded 1985.

Everyday Practical Electronics
Wimborne Publishing Ltd, 408 Wimborne Road East, Ferndown, Dorset BH22 9ND
tel (01202) 873872 *fax* (01202) 874562
email editorial@epemag.wimborne.co.uk
website www.epemag.wimborne.co.uk
Editor Mike Kenward
Monthly £2.85

Constructional and theoretical articles aimed at the student and hobbyist. Length: 1000–5500 words. Payment: £55–£90 per 1000 words. Illustrations: line, half-tone. Founded 1971.

Executive PA
Hobsons, Bateman Street, Cambridge CB2 1LZ
tel (01223) 273300 *fax* (01223) 273435
email penny.cottee@hobsons.co.uk
Editor Penny Cottee
Quarterly Complimentary

Business to business for working senior secretaries. Length: 700–1400 words. Illustrations: colour. Payment: £140 per 1000 words. Founded 1991.

Executive Woman
Saleworld Ltd, 2 Chantry Place, Harrow, Middlesex HA3 6NY
tel 020-8420 1210 *fax* 020-8420 1691/3
email info@execwoman.com
website www.execwoman.com
Editor Angela Giveon
Bi-monthly £2.50

News and features with a holistic approach to the world of successful working women. Strong business features; articles on management, personnel, networking and mentoring. Length: 500–1000 words. Illustrations: colour and b&w. Payment: £150 per 1000 words; £50–£100. Founded 1987.

The Face
EMAP Élan Ltd, Exmouth House, Pine Street, London EC1R 0JL
tel 020-7689 9999 *fax* 020-7689 0300
Editor Neil Stevenson
Monthly £2.70

Articles on music, fashion, films, popular youth culture. Contributors must be familiar with the magazine, its audience and culture. Illustrations: half-tone, colour. Payment: £250 per 1000 words; illustrations approx. £150 per page. Founded 1980.

Family Law

21 St Thomas Street, Bristol BS1 6JS
tel 0117-923 0600 *fax* 0117-925 0486
email familylaw@jordanpublishing.co.uk
website www.familylaw.co.uk
Editors Elizabeth Walsh, Miles McColl
Monthly £135 p.a.

Articles dealing with all aspects of the law as it affects the family, written from a legal or socio-legal point of view. Length: from 1000 words. Payment: by arrangement. No illustrations. Founded 1971.

Family Tree Magazine

61 Great Whyte, Ramsey, Huntingdon, Cambs. PE26 1HJ
tel (01487) 814050
Editor Sue Fearn
Monthly £2.50 (£27.50 p.a.)

Articles on any genealogically related topics. Payment: £40 per 1000 words. Founded 1984.

Farmers Weekly

Reed Business Information, Quadrant House, The Quadrant, Sutton, Surrey SM2 5AS
tel 020-8652 4911 *fax* 020-8652 4005
email farmers.weekly@rbi.co.uk
website www.fwi.co.uk
Editor Stephen Howe
Weekly £1.55

Articles on agriculture from freelance contributors will be accepted subject to negotiation. Founded 1934.

Fasttrack

1-3 Frederick's Place, London EC2R 8AB
tel 0161-817 3400 *fax* 0161-817 3401
email editor@fasttrack-digital.com
website www.goldensquare.com
Editor Marion Ainge
6 p.a. £15 p.a.

Upbeat magazine targeted mainly at female professional and executive personnel in the 20–40 age group. News and features – success stories, career changes, mentoring, current workplace issues, training opportunities, etc. Contact editor with ideas for contributions. Founded 1995.

FHM (For Him Magazine)

EMAP Élan Network, Mappin House, 4 Winsley Street, London W1W 8HF
tel 020-7436 1515 *fax* 020-7343 3000
email dan.elk@fhm.com
website www.fhm.com
Editor David Davies
Monthly £3.10

Features, fashion, grooming, travel (adventure) and men's interests. Length: 1200–2000 words. Illustrations: colour and b&w photos, line and colour artwork. Payment: by negotiation. Founded 1987.

The Field

IPC Media Ltd, King's Reach Tower, Stamford Street, London SE1 9LS
tel 020-7261 5198 *fax* 020-7261 5358
website www.thefield.co.uk
Monthly £3.20

Specific, topical and informed features on the British countryside and country pursuits, including natural history, field sports, gardening and rural conservation. Overseas subjects considered but opportunities for such articles are limited. No fiction or children's material. Articles, length 800–2000 words, by outside contributors considered; also topical 'shorts' of 200–300 words on all countryside matters. Illustrations: colour photos of a high standard. Payment: on merit. Founded 1853.

Film Review

Visual Imagination Ltd, 9 Blades Court, Deodar Road, London SW15 2NU
tel 020-8875 1520 *fax* 020-8875 1588
email filmreview@visimag.com
Editor Neil Corry
Monthly £2.80

Features and interviews on mainstream cinema; film and video reviews. No fiction. Length: 1000–3000 words (features), 350 words (reviews). Illustrations: colour and b&w. Payment: £80 per 1000 words; £20 for first image, £10 per additional image. Founded 1950.

Financial Adviser

FT Finance Ltd, Maple House, 149 Tottenham Court Road, London W1T 7LB
tel 020-7896 2525 *fax* 020-7896 2699/2588
Editor Hal Austin
Weekly (£90 p.a.) Free to financial intermediaries working in financial services

Topical personal finance news and features. Length: variable. Payment: by arrangement. Founded 1987.

Financial Mail on Sunday – see Mail on Sunday in National newspapers UK and Ireland, page 3

Fire

Queensway House, 2 Queensway, Redhill, Surrey RH1 1QS
tel (01737) 855431 *fax* (01737) 855418
Editor Andrew Lynch
Monthly £8 (£61 p.a.)

Articles on firefighting and fire prevention from acknowledged experts only. Length: 600 words. No unsolicited contributions. Illustrations: dramatic firefighting or fire brigade rescue colour photos. Also *Fire International*. Payment: by arrangement. Founded 1908.

Fishing News

Telephone House, 69-77 Paul Street, London EC2A 4LQ
tel 020-7017 4531 *fax* 020-7017 4536
email tim.oliver@informa.com
Editor Tim Oliver
Weekly £1

News and features on all aspects of the commercial fishing industry. Length: up to 1000 words (features), up to 500 words (news). Illustrations: colour and b&w photos. Payment: negotiable. Founded 1913

The Fix

(formerly Zene)
TTA Press, 5 Martins Lane, Witcham, Ely, Cambs. CB6 2LB
tel (01353) 777931
email ttapress@aol.com
website www.ttapress.com
Editor Andy Cox
Bi-monthly 12 p.a. (subscription only)

Reviews of short fiction, in-depth coverage of the world's magazines (both large and small) plus interviews, columns, news and views. Hundreds of markets for writers in every issue. Submissions welcome. Payment: negotiable. Founded 1995.

Flight International

Reed Business Information Ltd, Quadrant House, The Quadrant, Sutton, Surrey SM2 5AS
tel 020-8652 3842 *fax* 020-8652 3840
email flight.international@rbi.co.uk
website www.flightinternational.com
Editor Murdo Morrison
Weekly £2.40

Deals with all branches of aerospace: operational and technical articles, illustrated by photos, engineering cutaway drawings; also news, paragraphs, reports of lectures, etc. News press days: Thu, Fri. Illustrations: tone, line, colour. Payment: by agreement. Founded 1909.

Fly-Fishing & Fly-Tying

Rolling River Publications, Aberfeldy Road, Kenmore, Perthshire PH15 2HF
tel/fax (01887) 830526
email MarkB.ffft@btinternet.com
website www.flyfishing-and-flytying.co.uk
Editor Mark Bowler
8 p.a. £2.60

Fly-fishing and fly-tying articles, fishery features, limited short stories, fishing travel. Length: 800–2000 words. Illustrations: colour photos. Payment: by arrangement. Founded 1990.

Focus

Origin Publishing, 14th Floor, Tower House, Fairfax Street, Bristol BS1 3BN
tel 0117-927 9009 *fax* 0117-934 9008
Editor Emma Bayley
Monthly £2.95

'Tomorrow's science today.' Articles, features and news with a science-based or technical slant. All material is commissioned. Length: 500–3000 words (features), 50–200 words (news). Illustrations: colour prints, transparencies and artwork. Payment: £150–£200 per 1000 words; £200 per full-page photo (negotiable). Founded 1993.

Folio

64-65 North Road, St Andrews, Bristol BS6 5AQ
tel 0117-942 8491 *fax* 0117-942 0369
email editor@venue.co.uk
website www.venue.co.uk
Editor Dave Higgitt
Monthly Free

Articles, features, interviews and news on people, places and events with a local connection (Bristol, Bath and Cheltenham area). No short stories or poems. Unsolicited material considered. Length: 600–2000 words (features), variable (news). Illustrations: colour and b&w. Payment: by negotiation. Founded 1994.

Football Picture Story Library

D.C. Thomson & Co. Ltd, Albert Square, Dundee DD1 9QJ
tel (01382) 223131 *fax* (01382) 322214
185 Fleet Street, London EC4A 2HS
tel 020-7400 1030 *fax* 020-7400 1089
2 p.m. 80p

Football stories for boys told in pictures.

For Women

Fantasy Publications, 4 Selsdon Way, London E14 9GL
tel 020-7308 5363
Fiction Editor Elizabeth Coldwell
6-weekly £3.50

Women's magazine with erotic emphasis. Features on sex and health; erotic fiction and photos. Submit written synopsis for features; erotic fiction welcomed on spec. Fiction guidelines on receipt of sae. Length: 2000–3000 words. Illustrations: colour and b&w photos. Payment: £150 per story (fiction), features by arrangement. Founded 1992.

Fortean Times

Box 2409, London NW5 4NP
tel/fax 020-7485 5002
email rickard@forteantimes.com
website www.forteantimes.com/
Editors Bob Rickard, Paul Sieveking
Monthly £2.80

Journal of strange phenomena, experiences, related subjects and philosophies. Articles, features, news, reviews. Length: 500–3000 words; longer by arrangement. Illustrations: colour photos, line and tone art, cartoons. Payment: by negotiation. Founded 1973.

Fortnight – An Independent Review of Politics and the Arts

81 Botanic Avenue, Belfast BT7 1JL
tel 028-9023 2353/9031 1337/9032 4141
fax 028-9023 2650
email jofarrell@fortnight.org
website www.fortnight.org
Editors John O'Farrell, Mairtin Crawford
Monthly £2.20

Current affairs analysis, reportage, opinion pieces, cultural criticism, book reviews, poems. Illustrations: line, halftone, cartoons. Payment: by arrangement. Founded 1970.

FourFourTwo

Haymarket Leisure Publications Ltd, 38-42 Hampton Road, Teddington TW11 0JE
tel 020-8267 5337 *fax* 020-8267 5019
Editor Mat Snow
Monthly £3.20

Football magazine with 'adult' approach: interviews, in-depth features, issues pieces, odd and witty material. Length: 2000–3000 (features), 100–500 words (news/latest score). Illustrations: colour transparencies and artwork, b&w prints. Payment: £200 per 1000 words. Founded 1994.

FRANCE Magazine

Community Media Ltd, Cumberland House, Oriel Road, Cheltenham, Glos. GL50 1BB
tel (01242) 216050 *fax* (01242) 216074
email editorial@francemag.com
Editor Philip Faiers
Bi-monthly £3.99

Features and articles on the real France ranging from cuisine to customs to architecture to exploring the hidden France. Informed speculative submissions welcome. Length: 800–2500 words. Illustrations: colour transparencies (mounted and captioned). Payment: £100 per 1000 words; £50 per page/pro rata for illustrations. Founded 1989.

Freelance Market News

Sevendale House, 7 Dale Street, Manchester M1 1JB
tel 0161-228 2362 ext. 210 *fax* 0161-228 3533
email fmn@writersbureau.com
Editor Angela Cox
11 p.a.

Information on UK and overseas publications with editorial content, submission requirements and contact details. News of editorial requirements for writers. Features on the craft of writing, competitions, letters page. Founded 1968.

Freelance Photographer

(formerly Photon)
Icon Publications Ltd, Maxwell Place, Maxwell Lane, Kelso, Roxburghshire TD5 7BB
tel (01573) 226032 *fax* (01573) 226000
email david@maxwellplace.demon.co.uk
website www.freelancephotographer.co.uk/photon/
Editor David Kilpatrick
6 p.a. £2.95

Illustrated features on professional and craft photography. All material commissioned. Length: 750–2500 words. Illustrations: b&w and colour photos. Payment: £50–£300 per feature, including photos. Founded 1989.

The Friend

New Premier House, 150 Southampton Row, London WC1B 5BQ
tel 020-7387 7549
email editorial@thefriend.org
website www.thefriend.org
Editor Harry Albright
Weekly £1.20

Material of interest to the Religious

Society of Friends and like-minded people; political, social, economic or devotional, considered from outside contributors. Length: up to 1200 words. Illustrations: b&w or colour prints, b&w line drawings. Payment: not usually but will negotiate a small fee with professional writers. Founded 1843.

Fun Size Beano – see The Beano

Funsize Dandy – see The Dandy

The Furrow

St Patrick's College, Maynooth, Co. Kildare, Republic of Ireland
tel (01) 7083741 *fax* (01) 7083908
email furrow.office@may.ie
website www.thefurrow.ie
Editor Rev. Ronan Drury
Monthly E2.16

Religious, pastoral, theological, social articles. Length: 3000 words. Payment: average E20 per page (450 words). Illustrations: line, half-tone. Founded 1950.

The Garden

Bretton Court, Bretton Centre, Bretton, Peterborough PE3 8DZ
tel (01733) 264666 *fax* (01733) 282655
email thegarden@rhs.org.uk
Editor Ian Hodgson
Monthly £3.75

Journal of The Royal Horticultural Society. Features of horticultural or botanical interest on a wide range of subjects. Commissioned material only. Length: 1200–2500 words. Illustrations: 35mm or medium format colour transparencies, occasional b&w prints, botanical line drawings. Payment: varies. Founded 1866.

Garden Answers

EMAP Active Ltd, Bretton Court, Bretton, Peterborough PE3 8DZ
tel (01733) 264666 *fax* (01733) 282695
Editor Gail Major
Monthly £2.50

Commissioned features and articles on all aspects of gardening. Study of magazine essential. Approach by letter with examples of published work. Length: 750 words. Illustrations: colour transparencies and artwork. Payment: by negotiation. Founded 1982.

Garden News

EMAP Active Ltd, Apex House, Oundle Road, Peterborough PE2 9NP
tel (01733) 898100 *fax* (01733) 466857
email sarah.page@ecm.emap.com
Editor Sarah Page
Weekly £1

Up-to-date information on everything to do with plants, growing and gardening. Illustrations: line, colour, cartoons. Payment: by negotiation. Founded 1958.

Gay Times

Ground Floor, Worldwide House, 116-134 Bayham Street, London NW1 0BA
tel 020-7482 2576 *fax* 020-7284 0329
email edit@gaytimes.co.uk
Editor Vicky Powell
Monthly £2.95

Feature articles, full news and review coverage of all aspects of gay and lesbian life. Length: up to 2000 words. Illustrations: colour, line and half-tone, cartoons. Payment: by arrangement. Founded 1982.

Geographical Journal

Royal Geographical Society (with the Institute of British Geographers), Kensington Gore, London SW7 2AR
tel 020-7591 3026 *fax* 020-7591 3001
email journals@rgs.org
Editor Prof A. Millinglon
4 p.a. £30 (post free), (£81 p.a.)

Papers on all aspects of geography and development of current interest and concern. Large reviews section. Illustrations: photos, maps, diagrams. Founded 1893.

Geographical Magazine

(under licence from the Royal Geographical Society)
Campion Interactive Publishing Ltd, 124-8 Barlby Road, London W10 6BL
tel 020-8960 6400 *fax* 020-8960 6004
email magazine@geographical.co.uk
Editor Carolyn Fry
Monthly £3.25

Covers travel, culture, wildlife, exploration, science and history. Illustrations: top quality transparencies, vintage material. Payment: by negotiation. Founded 1935.

Geological Magazine

Cambridge University Press, The Edinburgh Building, Shaftesbury Road, Cambridge CB2 2RU
tel (01223) 312393
Editors Prof I.N. McCave, Dr N.H. Woodcock, Dr M.J. Bickle, Dr T.J. Palmer
Bi-monthly (£198 p.a. institutions, £42 p.a. students, US$324 USA/Canada/Mexico)

Original articles on all earth science topics containing the results of independent research by experts. Also reviews and notices of current geological literature, correspondence on geological subjects – illustrated. Length: variable. Payment: none. Founded 1864.

Gibbons Stamp Monthly

Stanley Gibbons Ltd, 5 Parkside, Ringwood, Hants BH24 3SH
tel (01425) 472363 *fax* (01425) 470247
email hjefferies@stanleygibbons.co.uk
Editor Hugh Jefferies
Monthly £2.40 (£28.80 p.a.)

Articles on philatelic topics. Contact the editor first. Length: 500–2500 words. Payment: by arrangement, £35 or more per 1000 words. Illustrations: photos, line, stamps or covers.

Girl About Town Magazine

Independent Magazines, Independent House, 191 Marsh Wall, London E14 9RS
tel 020-7005 5000 *fax* 020-7005 5333
Editor-in-Chief Bill Williamson
Weekly Free

Articles of general interest to women. Length: about 1100–1500 words. Payment: negotiable. Founded 1972.

Girl Talk – see page 294

Glamour

The Condé Nast Publications Ltd, 6-8 Old Bond Street, London W15 4PH
tel 020-7499 9080 *fax* 020-7491 2551
email features@glamourmagazine.co.uk
website www.glamour.com
Editor Jo Elvin, *Features Editor* Miranda Levy
Monthly £1.50

Lifestyle magazine containing fashion, beauty, real life features and celebrity news aimed at women aged 18–34. Feature ideas welcome; approach with brief outline. Length: 500–800 words. Payment: by arrangement. Founded 2001.

Golf Monthly

IPC Magazines Ltd, King's Reach Tower, Stamford Street, London SE1 9LS
tel 020-7261 7237 *fax* 020-7261 7240
email golfmonthly@ipcmedia.com
Editor Jane Carter
Monthly £3.10

Original articles on golf considered (not reports), golf clinics, handy hints. Illustrations: half-tone, colour, cartoons. Payment: by arrangement. Founded 1911.

Golf Weekly

EMAP Active Ltd, Bushfield House, Orton Centre, Peterborough PE2 5UW
tel (01733) 237111 *fax* (01733) 288025
email peter.masters@emap.com
Editor Peter Masters
Weekly £2.25

News, tournament reports and articles on golf of interest to golfers. Payment: 15p per word published. Illustrations: photos of golf news and new courses.

Golf World

EMAP Active Ltd, Bushfield House, Orton Centre, Peterborough PE2 5UW
tel (01733) 237111 *fax* (01733) 288025
Editor Neil Pope
Monthly £3.30

Expert golf instructional articles, 500–3000 words; general interest articles, personality features 500–3000 words. No fiction. No unsolicited material. Payment: by negotiation. Illustrations: line, half-tone, colour, cartoons. Founded 1962.

Good Housekeeping

National Magazine House, 72 Broadwick Street, London W1V 2BP
tel 020-7439 5000 *fax* 020-7439 5591
website www.natmags.co.uk
Editor-in-Chief Lindsay Nicholson
Monthly £2.70

Articles on topics of interest to intelligent women. No unsolicited features or stories accepted; approach by letter only. Homes, fashion, beauty and food covered by staff writers. Payment: magazine standards. Illustrations: commissioned. Founded 1922.

GQ

Vogue House, Hanover Square, London W1S 1JU
tel 020-7499 9080 *fax* 020-7495 1679
website www.gq/magazine.co.uk
Editor Dylan Jones
Monthly £3.10

Style, fashion and general interest magazine for men. Illustrations: b&w and colour photos, line drawings, cartoons. Payment: by arrangement. Founded 1988.

Granta

2-3 Hanover Yard, Noel Road, London N1 8BE
tel 020-7704 9776 *fax* 020-7704 0474
website www.granta.com
Editor Ian Jack
Quarterly £8.99 (£24.95 p.a.)

Original literary fiction, non-fiction and journalism. Study magazine before submitting work. No poems, essays or reviews. Length: determined by content. Illustrations: photos. Payment: by arrangement. Founded 1889; new series 1979.

Greetings Today

(formerly Greetings Magazine)
Lema Publishing, Unit No. 1, Queen Mary's Avenue, Watford, Herts. WD1 7JR
tel (01923) 250909 *fax* (01923) 250995
Publisher Malcolm Naish, *Editor* Vicky Hancocks
Monthly £45 p.a. (other rates on application)

Articles, features and news related to the greetings card industry; includes Artists Directory for aspiring artists wishing to attract the eye of publishers. Mainly written in-house; some material taken from outside. Length: varies. Illustrations: line, colour and b&w photos. Payment: by arrangement. Founded 1999; first published 1972.

The Grocer

(incorporating CTN – Confectioner, Tobacconist, Newsagent)
William Reed Publishing Ltd, Broadfield Park, Crawley, West Sussex RH11 9RT
tel (01293) 613400 *fax* (01293) 610333
email grocer.editorial@william-reed.co.uk
Editor Julian Hunt
Weekly £1.30

Trade journal: articles or news or illustrations of general interest to the grocery and provision trades. Payment: by arrangement. Founded 1861.

The Grower

Nexus Media Ltd, Nexus House, Azalea Drive, Swanley, Kent BR8 8HU
tel (01322) 660070 *fax* (01322) 616324
email editor.horticulture@nexusmedia.com
Editor Peter Rogers
Weekly £1.35

News and practical articles on commercial horticulture, covering all sectors including fruit, vegetable, salad crop and ornamentals. Founded 1923.

Guiding Magazine

17-19 Buckingham Palace Road, London SW1W 0PT
tel 020-7834 6242 *fax* 020-7828 8317
Acting Editor Victoria Wheater
Monthly

Official magazine of The Guide Association. Articles of interest to women of all ages, with special emphasis on youth work and the Guide Movement. Articles on simple crafts, games and the outdoors especially welcome. Length: 300–400 words. Illustrations:line, halftone, colour. Payment: £70 per 1000 words; £100 full colour spread.

H&E Naturist

New Freedom Publications Ltd, Burlington Court, Carlisle Street, Goole, East Yorkshire DN14 5EG
tel (01405) 769712 *fax* (01405) 763815
email newfreedom@btinternet.com
website www.healthandefficiency.co.uk
Editor Mark Nisbet
Monthly £3.25

Articles on naturist travel, clubs, beaches and naturist lifestyle experiences from the UK, Europe and the world. Length: 700–1500 words. Illustrations: line, colour transparencies and prints featuring naturists in natural settings; also cartoons, humorous fillers and features with naturist themes. Payment: by negotiation but guidelines for contributors and basic payment rates available on request.

Hairflair

Hairflair Magazines Ltd, Freebournes House, Freebournes Road, Witham, Essex CM8 3US
tel (01376) 534547 *fax* (01376) 534565
Editor Ruth Page
Bi-monthly £2.20

Hair, beauty, fashion – and related features – for the 16–35 age group. Preliminary letter essential. Length: 800–1000 words. Illustrations: colour and b&w photos. Payment: negotiable. Founded 1985.

Hampshire – The County Magazine

74 Bedford Place, Southampton SO15 2DF
tel 023-8022 3591/8033 3457
Monthly £2

Factual articles concerning all aspects of Hampshire and Hampshire life, past and present. Length: 400–1000 words. Payment: by arrangement. Illustrations: mainly colour photos. Founded 1960.

Harpers & Queen

National Magazine House, 72 Broadwick Street, London W1V 2BP
tel 020-7439 5000 *fax* 020-7439 5506
Editor Lucy Yeomans
Monthly £3.20

Features, fashion, beauty, art, theatre, films, travel, interior decoration – all commissioned. Illustrations: line, wash, full colour and 2- and 3-colour, and photos. Founded 1929.

Health Club Management

Leisure Media Company Ltd, Portmill House, Portmill Lane, Hitchin, Herts. SG5 1DJ
tel (01462) 471920 *fax* (01462) 433909
email catherinelarner@leisuremedia.com
website www.leisuremedia.co.uk
Editor Catherine Larner
Monthly £48 p.a. with *Leisure Management* magazine

Official publication of the Fitness Industry Association. Articles on the operation of health clubs, day spas, fitness and sports centres. Items on consumer issues and lifestyle trends as they affect club management are welcomed. Length: up to 1500 words. Illustrations: colour and b&w photos. Payment: by arrangement. Founded 1995.

Health & Fitness

Highbury WViP, 53-79 Highgate Road, London NW5 1TW
tel 020-7331 1000 *fax* 020-7331 1108
email editorial@hfonline.co.uk
website www.hfonline.co.uk
Editor Mary Comber
Monthly £2.60

Articles on all aspects of health and fitness. Illustrations: line, half-tone, colour. Payment: by arrangement. Founded 1984.

Hello!

Wellington House, 69-71 Upper Ground, London SE1 9PQ
tel 020-7667 8700 *fax* 020-7667 8716
Editor tba
Weekly £1.85

News-based features – showbusiness, celebrity, royalty; exclusive interviews. Payment: by arrangement. Illustrated. Founded 1988.

Here's Health

EMAP Esprit, Greater London House, Hampstead Road, London NW1 7EJ
tel 020-7347 1893 *fax* 020-7347 1897
Editor Collette Harris
Monthly £2.60

Articles on alternative medicine, complementary health, holistic living, environment, nutrition and natural treatment success stories. Preliminary letter and clippings essential. Length: 750–1800 words. Payment: on publication.

Hertfordshire Countryside

Beaumonde Publications Ltd, PO Box 5, Hitchin, Herts. SG5 1GJ
tel (01462) 431237 *fax* (01462) 422015
email info@hertscountryside.co.uk
Editor Sandra Small
Monthly £1.25

Articles of county interest. No poetry, puzzles or crosswords. Length: approx. 1000 words. Payment: £30 per 1000 words. Illustrations: line, half-tone. Founded 1946.

Hi-Fi News

IPC Country & Leisure Media Ltd, Focus House, Dingwall Avenue, Croydon CR9 2TA
tel 020-8774 0846 *fax* 020-8774 0940
email hi-finews@ipcmedia.com
Editor Steve Harris
Monthly £3.50

Articles on all aspects of high quality sound recording and reproduction; also extensive record review section and supporting musical feature articles. Audio matter is essentially technical, but should be presented in a manner suitable for music lovers interested in the nature of sound. Length: 2000–3000 words. Illustrations: line, half-tone. Payment: by arrangement. Founded 1956.

History Today

20 Old Compton Street, London W1D 4TW
tel 020-7534 8000
email admin@historytoday.com
website http://admin@historytoday.com
Editor Peter Furtado
Monthly £3.60

History in the widest sense – political, economic, social, biography, relating past to present; world history as well as British. Length: articles 3500 words; shorter news/views pieces 600–1200 words. Illustrations: from prints and original photos. Please do not send original material until publication is agreed. Payment: by arrangement. Founded 1951.

Home and Country

104 New King's Road, London SW6 4LY
tel 020-7731 5777 *fax* 020-7736 4061
Editor Susan Seager
Monthly £1.50

Journal of the National Federation of Women's Institutes for England and Wales. Publishes material related to the Federation's and members' activities; also considers articles of general interest to women, particularly country women, e.g. craft, environment, humour, health, rural life stories, of 800–1200 words. Illustrations: colour and b&w photos and drawings, cartoons. Payment: by arrangement. Founded 1919.

Home and Family

The Mothers' Union, Mary Sumner House, 24 Tufton Street, London SW1P 3RB
tel 020-7222 5533 *fax* 020-7222 1591
Editor Jill Worth
Quarterly £1.50

Short articles related to Christian family life. Payment: approx. £70 per 1000 words. Illustrations: colour photos. Founded 1954.

Home Words

G.J. Palmer & Sons Ltd, St Mary's Works, St Mary's Plain, Norwich, Norfolk NR3 3BH
tel (01603) 612914 *fax* (01603) 624483
email admin@scm-canterburypress.co.uk
Publisher G.A. Knights *Send material to* John King
Monthly

Illustrated C of E magazine insert. Articles of popular Christian interest with an Anglican slant (400–800 words) with relevant photos; also cartoons. Payment: by arrangement. Founded 1870.

Homes and Gardens

IPC Magazines Ltd, King's Reach Tower, Stamford Street, London SE1 9LS
tel 020-7261 5000 *fax* 020-7261 6247
Editor Isobel McKenzie-Price
Monthly £2.90

Articles on home interest or design, particularly well-designed British interiors (snapshots should be submitted). Length: articles, 900–1000 words. Illustrations: all types. Payment: generous, but exceptional work required; varies. Founded 1919.

Homestyle

Essential Publishing, 1-4 Eaglegate, East Hill, Colchester, Essex CO1 2PR
tel (01206) 796911 *fax* (01206) 796922
website www.essentialhomes.com
Editor Sally Narraway
Monthly £1.90

Ideas and practical features on home and garden improvements. Merchandise reviews. Length: 2–6 page spreads. Illustrations: colour transparencies. Payment: by negotiation. Founded 1992.

Horse & Hound

IPC Media Ltd, King's Reach Tower, Stamford Street, London SE1 9LS
tel 020-7261 6315 *fax* 020-7261 5429
email jenny_sims@ipcmedia.com
website www.horseandhound.co.uk
Editor Lucy Higginson
Weekly £1.80

Special articles, news items, photos, on all matters appertaining to equestrian sports. Payment: by negotiation.

Horse and Rider

Haslemere House, Lower Street, Haslemere, Surrey GU27 2PE
tel (01428) 651551 *fax* (01428) 653888
email djm@djmurphy.co.uk
website www.horseandridermagazine.co.uk
Editor Alison Bridge, *Assistant Editor* Danielle Pascoe
Monthly £2.70

Sophisticated magazine covering all forms of equestrian activity at home and abroad. Good writing and technical accuracy essential. Length: 1500–2000 words. Illustrations: photos and drawings, the latter usually commissioned. Payment: by arrangement. Founded 1959.

Horticulture Week

Haymarket Magazines Ltd, 174 Hammersmith Road, London W6 7JP
tel 020-8267 4977
Editor Pete Weston
Weekly £1.75 (£75 p.a.)

News, technical and business journal for the nursery and garden centre trade, landscape industry and public parks and sports ground staff. Outside contributions considered. No fiction. Length: 500–1500 words. Illustrations: line, half-tone, colour. Payment: by arrangement.

Hortus

Bryan's Ground, Stapleton, Nr Presteigne, Herefordshire LD8 2LP
tel (01544) 260001 *fax* (01544) 260015
email all@hortus.co.uk
website www.hortus.co.uk
Editor David Wheeler
Quarterly £32 p.a. (UK)

Articles on decorative horticulture: plants, gardens, history, design, literature, people; book reviews. Length: 1500–5000 words, longer by arrangement. Illustrations: line, half-tone and wood-engravings. Payment: by arrangement. Founded 1987.

Hospital Doctor

Reed Healthcare Publishing, Quadrant House, The Quadrant, Sutton, Surrey SM2 5AS
tel 020-8652 8745 *fax* 020-8652 8701
Editor Tim Burrowes
Weekly Free to 40,000 doctors. (£89 p.a.)

Commissioned features of interest to all

grades and specialities of hospital doctors; demand for news tip-offs. Length: features 800–1500 words. Illustrations: colour photos, transparencies, cartoons and commissioned artwork. Payment: £165 per 1000 wordsfeatures, £16 per 100 words news. Founded c.1977.

Hot Press

13 Trinity Street, Dublin 2, Republic of Ireland
tel (01) 2411500 *fax* (01) 2411539
email info@hotpress.ie
website www.hotpress.com
Editor Niall Stokes
Fortnightly E3.17

High-quality, investigative stories, or punchily written offbeat pieces, of interest to 16–39 year-olds, including politics, music, sport, sex, religion – whatever's happening on the street. Length: varies. Illustrations: colour with some b&w. Payment: by negotiation. Founded 1977.

Hotel and Catering Review

Jemma Publications Ltd, Marino House,
52 Glasthule Road, Sandycove, Co. Dublin
tel (01) 2800000 *fax* (01) 2801818
email fcorr@homenet.ie
Editor Frank Corr
Monthly IR£22 p.a.

Short news and trade news pieces. Length: approx. 200 words. Features. Payment: £100 per 1000 words. Illustrations: halftone, cartoons.

House & Garden

Vogue House, Hanover Square, London W1S 1JU
tel 020-7499 9080 *fax* 020-7629 2907
Editor Susan Crewe
Monthly £2.90

Articles (always commissioned), on subjects relating to domestic architecture, interior decorating, furnishing, gardening, household equipment, food and wine.

House Beautiful

National Magazine Co. Ltd, National Magazine House, 72 Broadwick Street, London W1F 9EP
tel 020-7439 5000 *fax* 020-7439 5595
Editor Sarah Whelan
Monthly £2.40

Specialist 'home' features for the homes of today. Preliminary study of magazine advisable. Payment: according to merit. Illustrated. Founded 1989.

Housebuilder

56-64 Leonard Street, London EC2A 4JX
tel 020-7608 5130
email ben.roskrow@house-builder.co.uk
website www.house-builder.co.uk
Editor Ben Roskrow, *Send material to* Allison Heller
11 p.a. £66 p.a.

Official Journal of the HouseBuilders Federation published in association with the National House-Building Council. Technical articles on design, construction and equipment of dwellings, estate planning and development, and technical aspects of house-building, aimed at those engaged in house and flat construction and the development of housing estates. Preliminary letter advisable. Length: articles from 500 words, preferably with illustrations. Payment: by arrangement. Illustrations: photos, plans, construction details, cartoons.

HQ Poetry Magazine

(The Haiku Quarterly)
39 Exmouth Street, Swindon SN1 3PU
tel (01793) 523927
Editor Kevin Bailey
3-4 p.a. £2.80 (4 issues £10 p.a. UK, £13 p.a. non-UK)

International in scope, publishes both experimental and traditional work. About one third of the content is devoted to haikuesque and imagistic poetry. Plus review section and articles. Payment: small. Founded 1990.

i-D Magazine

124 Tabernacle Street, London EC2A 4SA
tel 020-7490 9710 *fax* 020-7251 2225
email editor@i-Dmagazine.co.uk
Editor Avril Mair
Monthly £2.80

International fashion orientated magazine. Includes music, art, design and film. Illustrations: colour and b&w photos. Payment: £100 per 1000 words; photos £50 per page. Founded 1980.

Ideal Home

IPC Media Ltd, King's Reach Tower,
Stamford Street, London SE1 9LS
tel 020-7261 5000 *fax* 020-7261 6697
Acting Editor Jane Harbury
Monthly £2.60

Lifestyle magazine, articles usually commissioned. Contributors advised to study editorial content before submitting material. Payment: according to material. Illustrations: usually commissioned. Founded 1920.

The Illustrated London News

20 Upper Ground, London SE1 9PF
tel 020-7805 5555 *fax* 020-7805 5911
Editor Alison Booth
2-3 p.a. £2.50

Two special issues published annually: Summer and Christmas, plus occasional additional issues to tie in with major events. Focuses on London and the UK: culture, the arts, people, dining, fashion, entertainment. All material commissioned but ideas welcome. Founded 1842.

In Balance Health & Lifestyle Magazine

(formerly Herts. Holistic Health Magazine)
The Pintail Media Ltd, 50 Parkway,
Welwyn Garden City, Herts. AL8 6HH
tel (01707) 339007 *fax* (01707) 395550
email vrb@inbalancemagazine.com
website www.inbalancemagazine.com
Editor Val Reynolds Brown
Bi-monthly £1.50

Health and lifestyle magazine with therapy listings. Features on alternative therapies and related environmental issues. Ideas welcome. Length: 1000–3000 words. Payment: negotiable. Founded 1990.

In Britain

Premier Media Partners, Haymarket House,
1 Oxendon Street, London SW1Y 4EE
tel 020-7925 2544 *fax* 020-7976 1088
email in_britain@premiermp.com
Editor Andrea Spain
Monthly £2.75 (£23.95 p.a. UK/Europe; $39.95 US)

Upmarket features magazine about places and people in Britain. Very limited freelance material is accepted. Illustrated. Payment: by arrangement. Founded 1930.

In Dublin

6-7 Camden Place, Dublin 2, Republic of Ireland
tel (01) 4784322 *fax* (01) 4781055
Editor Declan Lawn
Fortnightly IR£1.95

Dublin-related news features, oddball items, humour and interviews. Length: 500–1000 words. Payment: £80 per 1000 words. Illustrated. Founded 1976.

The Independent Magazine – see The Independent in National newspapers UK and Ireland, page 3

Index on Censorship

Lancaster House, 33 Islington High Street,
London N1 9LH
tel 020-7278 2313 *fax* 020-7278 1878
email judith@indexoncensorship.org
website www.indexoncensorship.org
Editor-in-Chief Ursula Owen
Quarterly £9.50 (£32 p.a.)

Articles up to 3000 words dealing with all aspects of free speech and political censorship. Illustrations: b&w, cartoons. Payment: £75 per 1000 words. Founded 1972.

Infant Projects

Scholastic Ltd, Villiers House, Clarendon Avenue,
Leamington Spa, Warks. CV32 5PR
tel (01926) 887799 *fax* (01926) 337322
Editor Jeremy Sugden
Bi-monthly £3.15

Practical articles suggesting project activities for teachers of children aged 4–7; material mostly commissioned. Length: 500–1000 words. Illustrations: colour photos and line illustrations, colour posters. Payment: by arrangement. Founded 1978.

Inspirations For Your Home

SPL Publishing Ltd, Berwick House,
8-10 Knoll Rise, Orpington, Kent BR6 0PS
tel (01689) 887200
Editor Andrée Frieze
Monthly £2.90

Inspirational features on all aspects of home interest – home design, cookery, decorating, makeovers. Length: 800–1000 words. Payment: by arrangement. Founded 1993.

Insurance Age

Informa Group plc, 69-77 Paul Street,
London EC2A 4LQ
tel 020-7553 1665 *fax* 020-7553 1151
email jon.guy@informa.com
website www.insuranceage.com
Acting Editor Jon Guy
Monthly £5

News and features on general insurance and the broker market, personal, commercial, health and Lloyd's of London. Illustrations: transparencies. Payment: by negotiation. Founded 1979.

Insurance Brokers' Monthly

7 Stourbridge Road, Lye, Stourbridge,
West Midlands DY9 7DG
tel (01384) 895228 *fax* (01384) 893666
email info@brokersmonthly.co.uk
website www.brokersmonthly.co.uk
Editor Brian Susman
Monthly £4

Articles of technical and non-technical interest to insurance brokers and others engaged in the insurance industry.

Occasional articles of general interest to the City, on finance, etc. Length: 1000–1500 words. Payment: from £40 per 1000 words on last day of month following publication. Authoritative material written under true name and qualification receives highest payment. Illustrations: line and half-tone. Founded 1950.

InterMedia

International Institute of Communications, 35 Portland Place, London W1B 1AE
tel 020-7323 9622 *fax* 020-7323 9623
email martin@iicom.org
Editor Martin Sims
Bi-monthly £70 p.a. individuals, £150 p.a. library subscription

International journal concerned with policies, events, trends and research in the field of communications, broadcasting, telecommunications and associated issues, particularly cultural and social. Preliminary letter essential. Illustrations: b&w line. Payment: by arrangement. Founded 1970.

International Affairs

Royal Institute of International Affairs, Chatham House, 10 St James's Square, London SW1Y 4LE
tel 020-7957 5700 *fax* 020-7957 5710
email IA-CH@riia.org
website www.riia.org
Editor Caroline Soper
Quarterly £16 (£44 p.a.individuals, £123 p.a. institutions)

Serious long-term articles on international affairs; more than 100 books reviewed each quarter. Preliminary letter advisable. Article length: average 7000 words. Illustrations: none. Payment: by arrangement. Founded 1922.

Internet

EMAP Automotive Ltd, Priory Court, 30-32 Farringdon Lane, London EC1R 3AU
tel 020-7017 3691
website www.internet-magazine.com
Editor Dave Wilby
Monthly £3.75

Internet magazine for the serious home user and professional small business sector. No unsolicited contributions. Payment: by arrangement. Founded 1994.

Internet Made Easy

Paragon Publishing, Paragon House, St Peters Road, Bournemouth BH1 2JS
tel (01202) 299900 *fax* (01202) 299955
email internet@made-easy.net
website www.paragon.co.uk
Editor Rob Clymo
Monthly £2.99

Magazine for internet beginners. Includes practical tutorials on internet software; reviews of websites; net hardware and software; internet news and features. Send paragraph summaries for features to Editor in first instance. Length: 3–6 pages. Payment: £65 per page. Illustrations: colour and b&w including 3D rendering; payment negotiable. Founded 1999.

Interzone

217 Preston Drove, Brighton, East Sussex BN1 6FL
tel (01273) 504710
website www.sfsite.com/interzone
Editor David Pringle
Monthly £3 (£34 p.a.)

Science fiction and fantasy short stories, articles, interviews and reviews. Read magazine before submitting. Length: 2000–6000 words. Illustrations: line, half-tone, colour. Payment: by arrangement. Founded 1982.

Investors Chronicle

Maple House, 149 Tottenham Court Road, London W1T 7LB
tel 020-7896 2525 *fax* 020-7896 2078
Editor Matthew Vincent
Weekly £3.25

Journal covering investment and personal finance. Occasional outside contributions for surveys are accepted. Payment: by negotiation.

Ireland of the Welcomes

Irish Tourist Board, Baggot Street Bridge, Dublin 2, Republic of Ireland
tel (01) 6024000 *fax* (01) 6024335
email iow@irishtouristboard.ie
website www.irelandofthewelcomes.com
Editor Letitia Pollard
Bi-monthly £3.17

Articles on cultural, sporting or topographical aspects of Ireland; designed to arouse interest in Irish holidays. Mostly commissioned – preliminary letter advised. No unsolicited MSS. Length: 1200–1800 words. Payment: by arrangement. Illustrations: scenic and topical transparencies, line drawings, some cartoons. Founded 1952.

Ireland's Own

Channing House, Upper Rowe Street, Wexford, Republic of Ireland

tel (053) 40140 *fax* (053) 340191
Editors Sean Nolan, Phil Murphy
Weekly E85 cents

Short stories: non-experimental, traditional with an Irish orientation (2000–2500 words); articles of interest to Irish readers at home and abroad (750–1000 words); general and literary articles (750–1000 words). Monthly special bumper editions, each devoted to a particular seasonal topic. Suggestions for new features considered. Payment: varies according to quality and length. Illustrations: photos, cartoons. Founded 1902.

Irish Farmers Journal

Irish Farm Centre, Bluebell, Dublin 12, Republic of Ireland
tel (01) 4199500 *fax* (01) 4520876
email editdept@ifj.ie
website www.farmersjournal.ie
Editor Matthew Dempsey
Weekly E1.78

Readable, technical articles on any aspect of farming. Length: 700–1000 words. Payment: £100–£150 per article. Illustrated. Founded 1948.

Irish Journal of Medical Science

Royal Academy of Medicine, 6 Kildare Street, Dublin 2, Republic of Ireland
tel (01) 6623706 *fax* (01) 6611684
email journal@rami.ie
website www.rami.ie
Send material to Mr Thomas N. Walsh
Quarterly E35 (E130 p.a. EU, E160 p.a. outside EU)

Official Organ of the Royal Academy of Medicine in Ireland. Original contributions in medicine, surgery, midwifery, public health, etc; reviews of professional books, reports of medical societies, etc. Illustrations: line, half-tone, colour.

Irish Medical Times

24-26 Upper Ormond Quay, Dublin 7, Republic of Ireland
tel (01) 8176300 *fax* (01) 8176345
email editor@imt.ie
website www.imt.ie
Editor Aindreas McEntee
Weekly E4.25 (E198 p.a.)

Medical articles, also humorous articles with medical slant. Length: 850–1000 words. Payment: £60 per 1000 words. Illustrations: line, half-tone, colour, cartoons.

Irish Printer

Jemma Publications Ltd, 52 Glasthule Road, Sandycove, Co. Dublin, Republic of Ireland
tel (01) 2800000 *fax* (01) 2801818
email n.tynan@jemma.ie
Editor Nigel Tynan
Monthly E60.95 p.a. (E76.18 UK/overseas)

Technical articles and news of interest to the printing industry. Length: 800–1000 words. Illustrations: colour and b&w photos. Payment: E140 per 1000 words; photos £30. Founded 1974.

Irish Tatler

Smurfit Publications Ltd, 2 Clanwilliam Court, Lower Mount Street, Dublin 2, Republic of Ireland
tel (01) 2405367 *fax* (01) 6619757
Editor Vanessa Harriss
Monthly E3.56

General interest women's magazine: beauty, interiors, fashion, cookery, current affairs, reportage and celebrity interviews. Length: 2000–4000 words. Payment: by arrangement. In assoc. with ivenus.com

J17

EMAP Élan, Endeavour House, 189 Shaftesbury Avenue, London WC2H 8JG
tel 020-7208 3408 *fax* 020-7208 3590
Editor tba
Monthly £1.70

Articles of interest to girls aged 14–16: fashion, beauty, pop, and various features; investigative pieces; quizzes. Payment: by arrangement. Illustrations: colour. Founded 1983.

Jane's Defence Weekly

Sentinel House, 163 Brighton Road, Coulsdon, Surrey CR5 2YH
tel 020-8700 3700 *fax* 020-8763 1007
website http://jdw.janes.com
Editor Clifford Beal
Weekly £220 p.a. (5-year archive on CD-Rom)

International defence news; military equipment; budget analysis, industry, military technology, business, political, defence market intelligence. Payment: minimum £200 per 1000 words used. Illustrations: line, half-tone, colour. Founded 1984.

Jazz Journal International

Jazz Journal Ltd, 3 and 3A Forest Road, Loughton, Essex IG10 1DR
tel 020-8532 0456/0678 *fax* 020-8532 0440
Publisher/Editor-in-Chief Eddie Cook
Monthly £3.20

Articles on jazz, record reviews. Telephone or write before submitting material. Payment: by arrangement. Illustrations: photos. Founded 1948.

Jewish Chronicle

25 Furnival Street, London EC4A 1JT
tel 020-7415 1500
Editor Edward J. Temko
Weekly 60p

Authentic and exclusive news stories and articles of Jewish interest from 500–1500 words are considered. There is a lively arts and leisure section, as well as regular travel pages. Payment: by arrangement. Illustrations: of Jewish interest, either topical or feature. Founded 1841.

The Jewish Quarterly

PO Box 2078, London W1A 1JR
tel/fax 020-8830 5367 (editorial)
Editor Matthew Reisz
Quarterly £4.95 (£25 p.a., £35 p.a. Europe, £45 p.a. overseas)

Articles of Jewish interest, literature, history, music, politics, poetry, book reviews, fiction. Illustrations: half-tone. Founded 1953.

Jewish Telegraph

Telegraph House, 11 Park Hill, Bury Old Road, Prestwich, Manchester M25 0HH
tel 0161-740 9321 *fax* 0161-740 9325
email mail@jewishtelegraph.com
website www.jewishtelegraph.com
1 Shaftesbury Avenue, Leeds LS8 1DR
tel 0113-295 6000 *fax* 0113-295 6006
Harold House, Dunbabin Road, Liverpool L15 6XL
tel 0151-475 6666 *fax* 0151-475 2222
May Terrace, Giffnock, Glasgow G46 6LD
tel 0141-621 4422 *fax* 0141-621 4333
Editor Paul Harris
Weekly Man. 35p, Leeds 25p, Liverpool 25p, Glasgow 40p

Non-fiction articles of Jewish interest, especially humour. Exclusive Jewish news stories and pictures, international, national and local. Length: 1000–1500 words. Payment: by arrangement. Illustrations: line, half-tone, cartoons. Founded 1950.

Journal of Alternative and Complementary Medicine

9 Rickett Street, London SW6 1RU
tel 020-7385 0012 *fax* 020-7385 4566
Editor Graeme Miller
Monthly £2.95 (£33.50 p.a.)

Feature articles (up to 2000 words) and news stories (up to 250 words). Unsolicited material welcome but not eligible for payment unless commissioned. Illustrations: line, half-tone, colour. Payment: by negotiation. Founded 1983.

Junior Education

Scholastic Ltd, Villiers House, Clarendon Avenue, Leamington Spa, Warks. CV32 5PR
tel (01926) 887799 *fax* (01926) 883331
email juniored@scholastic.co.uk
Editor Tracy Lomas
Monthly £3.15

For teachers of 7–11 year-olds. Articles by specialists on practical teaching ideas, coverage of primary education news; posters; photocopiable material for the classroom. Length: 800–1000 words. Payment: by arrangement. Illustrated with photos and drawings; includes colour poster. Founded 1977.

Junior Focus

Scholastic Ltd, Villiers House, Clarendon Avenue, Leamington Spa, Warks. CV32 5PR
tel (01926) 887799 *fax* (01926) 883331
email jfocus@scholastic.co.uk
Editor Tracy Lomas
Monthly £3.15

Aimed at teachers of 7–11 year-olds, each issue is based on a theme, closely linked to the National Curriculum. Includes A1 and A3 full-colour posters, 12 pages of photocopiable material and 16 pages of articles. All material commissioned. Length: 800 words. Illustrations: photos and drawings. Payment: £100 per double-page spread; varies for illustrations. Founded 1982.

Justice of the Peace

Butterworths Tolley, 35 Chancery Lane, London WC2A 1EL
tel 020-7400 2828 *fax* 020-7400 2805
email jpn@butterworths.com
Editor Adrian Turner, *Send material to* Diana Rose
Weekly £232 p.a.

Professional journal. Articles on magisterial and local government law and associated subjects including family law, criminology, medico-legal matters, penology, police, probation. Information on articles and contributions sent on request. Length: 3000 words. Payment: £200 per feature article or £20 per column (articles). Founded 1837.

Kerrang!

EMAP Performance 2001, PO Box 2930, London W1A 6DZ
tel 020-7436 1515 *fax* 020-7312 8910
Editor Paul Rees

Weekly £1.70

News, reviews and interviews; music with attitude. All material commissioned. Illustrations: colour. Payment: by arrangement. Founded 1981.

Kids Alive! (The Young Soldier)

The Salvation Army, 101 Newington Causeway, London SE1 6BN
tel 020-7367 4910 *fax* 020-7367 4710
email kidsalive@salvationarmy.org.uk
Editor Ken Nesbitt
Weekly 20p (£26 p.a.)

Children's magazine: stories, pictures, cartoon strips, puzzles etc, Christian-based with emphasis on education re addictive substances. Payment: by arrangement. Illustrations: half-tone, line and 4-colour line, cartoons. Founded 1881.

Kids Out

Time Out Guides Ltd, Universal House, 251 Tottenham Court Road, London W1T 7AB
tel 020-7813 6018 *fax* 020-7813 6153
email meldakin@timeout.com
Editor Melanie Dakin
Monthly £2.50

Contains a comprehensive calendar of events in London for families, plus travel, education and parenting articles of interest to parents of under 16 year-olds in the London area. Also restaurant, game, book, software, film, shops and product reviews. For picture requirements call Kerri Miles 020-7813 6089. Length: 200–8000 words. Payment: £100 per 1000 words. Founded 1995.

The Lady

39-40 Bedford Street, Strand, London WC2E 9ER
tel 020-7379 4717 *fax* 020-7836 4620
website www.lady.co.uk
Editor Arline Usden
Weekly 80p

British and foreign travel, countryside, human-interest, celebrity interviews, animals, cookery, art and antiques, historic-interest and commemorative articles (preliminary letter advisable for articles dealing with anniversaries). Send proposals for articles by post or fax; do not phone. Length: 900–1200 words; Viewpoint: 500 words. Annual Short Story Competition in October with prize of £1000 plus. Winning entries printed in magazine. Payment: by arrangement. Founded 1885.

Lancashire Magazine

33 Beverley Road, Driffield, Yorkshire YO25 6SD
tel/fax (01377) 253232
Editor Winston Halstead
Bi-monthly £1.60

Articles about people, life and character of all parts of Lancashire. Length: 1000 words. Payment: £35–£40 approx. per published page. Illustrations: line, half-tone, colour. Founded 1977.

Lancet

84 Theobalds Road, London WC1X 8RR
tel 020-7611 4100 *fax* 020-7611 4466
website www.thelancet.com
Editor Dr Richard Horton
Weekly £5

Research papers, review articles, editorials, correspondence and commentaries on the international medicosocial scene. Consult the editor before submitting material. Founded 1823.

Land & Liberty

Suite 427, The London Fruit Exchange, Brushfield Street, London E1 6EL
tel 020-7377 8885 *fax* 020-7377 8886
email henrygeorge@charity.vfree.com
website www.henrygeorge.org.uk
Editor Fred Harrison
Quarterly £3.75 (£15 p.a.)

Articles on land economics, land taxation, land prices, land speculation as they relate to housing, the economy, production, politics. Study of journal essential. Length: up to 3000 words. Payment: by arrangement. Illustrations: half-tone. Founded 1894.

The Lawyer

Centaur Communications Group, 50 Poland Street, London W1V 4AX
tel 020-7970 4614 *fax* 020-7970 4640
email lawyer.edit@chiron.co.uk
website www.thelawyer.com
Editor Catrin Griffiths
Weekly £1.75 (£60 p.a.)

News, articles, features and views relevant to the legal profession. Length: 600–900 words. Illustrations: as agreed. Payment: £125–£150 per 1000 words. Founded 1987.

Legal Week

Global Professional Media Ltd, 99 Charterhouse Street, London EC1M 6HR
tel 020-7566 5600 *fax* 020-7253 8505
email jmalpas@gpmuk.com
website www.legalweek.net

Editor John Malpas
Weekly £2.45
News and features aimed at business lawyers. Length: 750–1000 words (features), 300 words (news). Payment: £150 upwards (features), £75–£100 (news). Considers unsolicited material and welcomes ideas for articles and features. Founded 1999.

Legal Director
Monthly
News and features for in-house lawyers.

Legal IT
Monthly
News and features for IT decision-makers in the legal industry.

The Leisure Manager

The Institute of Leisure and Amenity Management, ILAM House, Lower Basildon, Reading, Berks. RG8 9NE
tel (01491) 874800 *fax* (01491) 874801
email leisuremanager@ilam.co.uk
website www.ilam.co.uk
Editor Jonathan Ives
Monthly £40 p.a. (£50 p.a. overseas)
Official Journal of The Institute of Leisure and Amenity Management. Articles on amenity, children's play, tourism, leisure, parks, entertainment, recreation and sports management, cultural services. Payment: by arrangement. Illustrations: line, half-tone. Founded 1985.

Leisure Painter

63-65 High Street, Tenterden, Kent TN30 6BD
tel (01580) 763315 *fax* (01580) 765411
Editor Jane Stroud
Monthly £2.55
Instructional articles on painting and fine art. Payment: £75 per 1000 words. Illustrations: line, half-tone, colour, original artwork. Founded 1967.

Leviathan Quarterly

Bears Hay Farm, Brookhay Lane, Fradley, Lichfield WS13 8RG
tel (01543) 411161 *fax* (01543) 410679
email leviathanmh@hotmail.com
Editor Michael Hulse
Quarterly £5.95
Fiction, essays, poetry, criticism, interviews, photographs, drawings and symposia aimed at readers interested in literature and art. Considers unsolicited material. Length: 500–8000 words. Illustrations: b&w photos and artwork. Payment: negotiable. Founded 2001.

Life – see The Observer in National newspapers UK and Ireland, page 3

Life & Work: Magazine of the Church of Scotland

121 George Street, Edinburgh EH2 4YN
tel 0131-225 5722 *fax* 0131-240 2207
email lifework@dial.pipex.com
Editor Lynne Robertson
Monthly £1
Articles not exceeding 1200 words and news; occasional stories. Study the magazine and contact editor first. Payment: up to £100 per 1000 words, or by arrangement. Illustrations: photos and line drawings, colour illustrations, cartoons.

Lincolnshire Life

PO Box 81, Lincoln LN1 1HD
tel (01522) 527127 *fax* (01522) 560035
email editorial@lincolnshirelife.co.uk
website www.lincolnshirelife.co.uk
Editor Judy Theobald
Monthly £1.70
Articles and news of county interest. Approach in writing. Length: up to 1200 words. Illustrations: colour photos and line drawings. Payment: varies. Founded 1961.

The Linguist

The Institute of Linguists, Saxon House, 48 Southwark Street, London SE1 1UN
tel 020-7690 9665 *fax* 020-7607 6824
email linguist@patricia.treasure.co.uk
website www.linguistonline.co.uk
Editor Pat Treasure
Bi-monthly £6 (£30 p.a.)
Articles of interest to professional linguists in translating, interpreting and teaching fields. Articles usually contributed, but payment by arrangement. All contributors have special knowledge of the subjects with which they deal. Length: 1500–2000 words. Illustrations: line, half-tone.

The List

The List Ltd, 14 High Street, Edinburgh EH1 1TE
tel 0131-558 1191 *fax* 0131-557 8500
email editor@list.co.uk
Editor Mark Fisher
Fortnightly £2.20
Events guide for Glasgow and Edinburgh covering film, theatre, music, clubs, books, city life, art, and TV and video. Considers unsolicited material and welcomes ideas. Length: 200 words (articles), 800 words and above (features).

Illustrations: transparencies and colour prints. Payment: £20 (articles), from £60 (features); £25–£50. Founded 1985.

The Literary Review

44 Lexington Street, London W1F 0LW
tel 020-7437 9392 *fax* 020-7734 1844
Editor Nancy Sladek
Monthly £3 (£30 p.a.)

Reviews, articles of cultural interest, interviews, profiles, monthly poetry competition. Material mostly commissioned. Length: articles and reviews 800–1500 words. Illustrations: line and b&w photos. Payment: £25 per article; none for illustrations. Founded 1979.

Loaded

IPC Media Ltd, King's Reach Tower, Stamford Street, London SE1 9LS
tel 020-7261 5000 *fax* 020-7261 5557
email (features) tammy_butt@ipc.co.uk
(handbook) johnny-cigarettes@ipcmedia.com
website www.uploaded.com
Editor Keith Kendrick
Monthly £2.90

Magazine for men aged 18–30. Music, sport, sex, humour, travel, fashion, hard news and popular culture. Address longer features (2000 words) to Features Editor, and shorter items to Handbook Editor. Payment: by arrangement. Founded 1994.

LOGOS

5 Beechwood Drive, Marlow, Bucks. SL7 2DH
tel/fax (01628) 477577
email logos-marlow@dial.pipex.com
Editor Gordon Graham
Quarterly £45 p.a. (£90 p.a. institutions)

In-depth articles on publishing, librarianship and bookselling with international or interdisciplinary appeal. Length: 3500–7000 words. Payment: 25 offprints/copy of issue. Founded 1990.

The London Magazine: A Review of Literature and the Arts

32 Addison Grove, London W4 1ER
tel 020-8400 5882 *fax* 020-8994 1713
email editorial@londonmagazine.ukf.net
website www.londonmagazine.ukf.net
Editor Sebastian Barker
Bi-monthly £6.95 (£30 p.a.)

Poems, stories (2000–5000 words), literary memoirs, critical articles, features on art, photography, sport, theatre, cinema, music, architecture, events, reports from abroad, drawings and photographs. Sae essential (3 IRCs from abroad). Payment: by arrangement. Founded 1732.

London Review of Books

28 Little Russell Street, London WC1A 2HN
tel 020-7209 1101 *fax* 020-7209 1102
email edit@lrb.co.uk
Editor Mary-Kay Wilmers
Fortnightly £2.95

Features, essays, poems. Payment: by arrangement. Founded 1979.

MacUser

Dennis Publishing Ltd, 30 Cleveland Street, London W1T 4JD
tel 020-7907 6000 *fax* 020-7907 6369
email edit@macuser.co.uk
website www.macuser.co.uk
Editor Ian Betteridge
Fortnightly £3.10

News, reviews, tutorials and features on Apple Macintosh computer products and topics of interest to their users. Commissioned reviews of products compatible with Mac computers required. Occasional requirement for features relating to Mac-based design and publishing and general computing and internet issues. Ideas welcome. Length: 2500–5000 words (features), approx. 500 words (news), 300–2500 words (reviews). Illustrations: commissioned from Mac-based designers. Payment: £170 per 1000 words; competitive (artwork). Founded 1985.

Making Music

Nexus Media Ltd, Nexus House, Azalea Drive, Swanley, Kent BR8 8HU
tel (01322) 660070 *fax* (01322) 616319
email makingmusic@cerbernet.co.uk
website http://cerbernet.co.uk/makingmusic/
Editor Paul Quinn
Monthly £18 p.a.

Technical, musicianly and instrumental features on rock, pop, blues, dance, world, jazz, soul; little classical. Length: 500–2500 words. Payment: £95 per 1000 words. Illustrations: colour, including cartoons and photos. Founded 1986.

Management Today

174 Hammersmith Road, London W6 7JP
tel 020-8267 4610 *fax* 020-7267 4966
Editor Matthew Gwyther
Monthly £40 p.a.

Company profiles and analysis – columns from 1000 words, features up to 3000 words. Payment: £330 per 1000 words. Illustrations: colour transparencies, always commissioned. Founded 1966.

Marie Claire

European Magazines Ltd, 2 Hatfields, London SE1 9PG
tel 020-7261 5240 *fax* 020-7261 5277
email marieclaire@ipcmedia.com
Editor Marie O'Riordan
Monthly £2.60

Feature articles of interest to today's woman; plus fashion, beauty, health, food, drink and travel. Commissioned material only. Payment: by negotiation. Illustrated in colour. Founded 1988.

Market Newsletter

Bureau of Freelance Photographers, Focus House, 497 Green Lanes, London N13 4BP
tel 020-8882 3315/6 *fax* 020-8886 5174
email info@thebfp.com
website www.thebfp.com
Editor John Tracy
Monthly Private circulation

Current information on markets and editorial requirements of interest to writers and photographers. Founded 1965.

Marketing Week

St Giles House, 50 Poland Street, London W1F 7AX
tel 020-7970 4000 *fax* 020-7970 6721
website www.marketing-week.co.uk
Editor Stuart Smith
Weekly £2.30

Aimed at marketing management. Accepts occasional features and analysis. Length: 1000–2000 words. Payment: £200 per 1000 words. Founded 1978.

Maxim

Dennis Publishing Ltd, 30 Cleveland Street, London W1T 4JD
tel 020-7907 6410 *fax* 020-7907 6439
email editorial.maxim@dennis.co.uk
website www.maxim-magazine.co.uk
Editor Tom Loxley
Monthly £3.10

Glossy men's lifestyle magazine with news, features and articles. All material is commissioned. Length: 1500–2500 words (features), 150–500 words (news). Illustrations: transparencies. Payment: by negotiation. Founded 1995.

Medal News

Token Publishing Ltd, Orchard House, Duchy Road, Heathpark, Honiton, Devon EX14 1YD
tel (01404) 46972 *fax* (01404) 44788
email info@medal-news.com
website www.tokenpublishing.com
Editor John Mussell
10 p.a. £2.95

Well-researched articles on military history with a bias towards medals. Length: up to 2000 words. Illustrations: b&w preferred. Payment: £25 per 1000 words; none for illustrations. Founded 1989.

Media Week

Quantum Business Media Ltd, Quantum House, 19 Scarbrook Road, Croydon CR9 1LX
tel 020-8565 4323 *fax* 020-8565 4394
email patrickb@qpp.co.uk
Editor Patrick Barrett
Weekly £2

News and analysis of UK advertising media industry. Illustrations: full colour. Founded 1985.

Men Only

2 Archer Street, London W1V 8JJ
tel 020-7292 8000 *fax* 020-7734 5030
Publisher Paul Raymond, *Editor* Joanna Bounds
Monthly £2.60

High quality glamour photography; explicit sex stories (no erotic fiction); male interest features – sport, humour, entertainment, hedonism! Proposals welcome. Payment: by arrangement. Founded 1971.

Men's Health

Rodale Press Ltd, 7-10 Chandos Street, London W1M 0AD
tel 020-7291 6000 *fax* 020-7291 6060
website www.menshealth.co.uk
Editor Simon Geller
10 p.a. £3.20

Active pursuits, grooming, fitness, fashion, sex, career and general men's interest issues. Length 1000–4000 words. Ideas on any subject welcome. No unsolicited MSS. Payment: by arrangement. Founded 1994.

Methodist Recorder

122 Golden Lane, London EC1Y 0TL
tel 020-7251 8414
email editorial@methodistrecorder.co.uk
website www.methodistrecorder.co.uk
Editor Moira Sleight
Weekly 60p

Methodist newspaper; ecumenically involved. Limited opportunities for freelance contributors. Preliminary letter advised. Founded 1861.

Military Modelling

Nexus Special Interests Ltd, Nexus House, Azalea Drive, Swanley, Kent BR8 8HU
tel (01322) 660070 *fax* (01322) 667633
Editor Ken Jones
Monthly £2.75

Articles on military modelling. Length: up to 2000 words. Payment: by arrangement. Illustrations: line, half-tone, colour.

Mixmag

EMAP plc, Mappin House, 4 Winsley Street, London W1N 7AR
tel 020-7436 1515 *fax* 020-7312 8977
email mixmag@emap.com
website www.mixmag.net
Editor tba
Monthly £3.50

Clubbing magazine covering dance music, club culture, fashion and drugs. Considers unsolicited material. Length: 300–1000 words (articles), 2500–3000 (features). Payment: £200 per 1000 words. Illustrations: colour and b&w. Founded 1984.

Mizz

IPC Magazines Ltd, King's Reach Tower, Stamford Street, London SE1 9LS
tel 020-7261 7358 *fax* 020-7261 6032
email mizz@ipcmedia.com
website www.ipcmedia.com
Editor Sharon Christal
Fortnightly £1.40

Articles on any subject of interest to girls aged 10–14. Approach in writing. Payment: by arrangement. Illustrated. Founded 1985.

Model Boats

Nexus Special Interests Ltd, Nexus House, Azalea Drive, Swanley, Kent BR8 8HU
tel (01322) 660070 *fax* (01322) 667633
Editor John L. Cundell *tel* (01525) 382847
13 p.a. £2.30

Articles, drawings, plans, sketches of model boats. Payment: £25 per page; plans £100. Illustrations: line, half-tone. Founded 1964.

Model Engineer

Nexus Special Interests Ltd, Nexus House, Azalea Drive, Swanley, Kent BR8 8HU
tel (01322) 660070 *fax* (01322) 667633
Editor Mike Chrisp
Fortnightly £2.10

Detailed description of the construction of models, small workshop equipment, machine tools and small electrical and mechanical devices; articles on small power engineering, mechanics, electricity, workshop methods, clocks and experiments. Payment: up to£35 per page. Illustrations: line, half-tone, colour. Founded 1898.

Modern Language Review

Modern Humanities Research Association, c/o Maney Publishing, Hudson Road, Leeds LS9 7DL
Quarterly £91 p.a. UK/EC (£109 overseas, $218 USA)

Articles and reviews of a scholarly or specialist character on English, Romance, Germanic and Slavonic languages and literatures. Payment: none, but offprints are given. Founded 1905.

Modern Painters

3rd Floor, 52 Bermondsey Street, London SE1 3UD
tel 020-7407 9246 *fax* 020-7407 9242
email info@modernpainters.co.uk
Editor Karen Wright
Quarterly £5.99

Journal of modern fine arts and architecture – commissioned articles and features; also interviews. Length: 1000–2500 words. Payment: £120 per 1000 words. Illustrated. Founded 1986.

Modern Woman Nationwide

Meath Chronicle Ltd, Market Square, Navan, Co. Meath, Republic of Ireland
tel (046) 79600 *fax* (046) 23565
Editor Margot Davis
Monthly E63 cents

Articles and features on a wide range of subjects of interest to women over the age of 18 (e.g. politics, religion, health and sex). Length: 200–1000 words. Illustrations: colour and b&w photos, line drawings and cartoons. Payment: NUJ rates. Founded 1984.

Mojo

EMAP Metro, Mappin House, 4 Winsley Street, London W1W 8HF
tel 020-7436 1515 *fax* 020-7312 8296
email mojo@emap.com
website www.mojo4music.com
Editor Pat Gilbert
Monthly £3.50

Serious rock music magazine: interviews, news and reviews of books, live shows and albums. Length: up to 10,000 words. Illustrations: colour and b&w photos, colour caricatures. Payment: £225 per 1000 words; £150–£350 illustrations. Founded 1993.

MoneyMarketing

Centaur Communications, St Giles House, 50 Poland Street, London W1T 3QN
tel 020-7970 4000 *fax* 020-7943 8097
Editor John Lappin
Weekly £1.75

News, features, surveys and viewpoints. Length: features from 900 words. Illustrations: b&w photos, colour and b&w line. Payment: by arrangement. Founded 1985.

Moneywise

RD Publications Ltd, 11 Westferry Circus, Canary Wharf, London E14 4HE
tel 020-7715 8465 *fax* 020-7715 8725
website www.moneywise.co.uk
Editor David Ellis, *Send material to* Dominic Hiatt, Features Editor
Monthly £3.50

Financial and consumer interest features, articles and news stories. No unsolicited MSS. Length: 1500–2000 words. Illustrations: willing to see designers, illustrators and photographers for fresh new ideas. Payment: by arrangement. Founded 1990.

More!

EMAP Élan, Endeavour House, 189 Shaftesbury Avenue, London WC2H 8JG
tel 020-7208 3165 *fax* 020-7208 3595
Editor Marianne Jones
Fortnightly £1.45

Celebrities, fun, gossip and sexy features, 'how to' articles aimed at young women, including 'Men Unzipped' section. Serialised erotic fiction. Study of magazine essential. Length: 900–1100 words. Payment: £150 per 1000 words. Illustrated. Founded 1988.

Mother & Baby

EMAP Esprit, Greater London House, Hampstead Road, London NW1 7EJ
tel 020-7874 0200
website www.motherandbaby.co.uk
Editor Dani Zur
Monthly £1.99

Features and practical information including pregnancy and birth and babycare advice. Expert attribution plus real-life stories. Length: 1000–1500 words. Payment: by negotiation. Illustrated. Founded 1956.

Motor Boat and Yachting

IPC Media Ltd, King's Reach Tower, Stamford Street, London SE1 9LS
tel 020-7261 5333 *fax* 020-7261 5419
email mby@ipcmedia.com
website www.mby.com
Editor Alan Harper
Monthly £3.45

General interest as well as specialist motor boating material welcomed. Features up to 2000 words considered on all sea-going aspects. Payment: varies. Illustrations: photos (mostly colour and transparencies preferred). Founded 1904.

Motor Boats Monthly

IPC Magazines Ltd, King's Reach Tower, Stamford Street, London SE1 9LS
tel 020-7261 7256 *fax* 020-7261 7900
email mbm@ipcmedia.com
website www.motorboatsmonthly.co.uk
Editor Jane Kavanagh
Monthly £3.25

News on motorboating in the UK and Europe, cruising features and anecdotal stories. Mostly commissioned – send synopsis to editor. Length: news up to 200 words, features up to 4000 words. Illustrations: colour transparencies. Payment: by arrangement. Founded 1987.

Motor Caravan Magazine

IPC Country & Leisure, Focus House, Dingwall Avenue, Croydon CR9 2TA
tel 020-8774 0737 *fax* 020-8774 0939
email steve_rowe@ipcmedia.com
Editor Steve Rowe
Monthly £2.80

Practical features, touring features (home and abroad), motorhome tests. Length: up to 1500 words. Payment: £50 per page. Illustrations: line, half-tone, colour, cartoons. Founded 1985.

Motor Cycle News

EMAP Active Ltd, Media House, Peterborough Business Park, Lynchwood, Peterborough PE2 6EA
tel (01733) 468000 *fax* (01733) 468028
email mcn@emap.com
website www.motorcyclenews.com
Editor Adam Duckworth
Weekly £1.60

Features (up to 1000 words), photos and news stories of interest to motorcyclists. Founded 1955.

Motorcaravan Motorhome Monthly (MMM)

PO Box 44, Totnes TQ9 5XB
Editor Mike Jago
Monthly £2.80

Articles including motorcaravan travel, owner reports and DIY. Length: up to

2500 words. Payment: by arrangement. Illustrations: line, half-tone, colour prints and transparencies. Founded 1966 as Motor Caravan and Camping.

Ms London

Independent Magazines, Independent House, 191 Marsh Wall, London E14 9RS
tel 020-7005 5000 *fax* 020-7005 5333
Editor-in-Chief Bill Williamson
Weekly Free

Features and lifestyle pieces of interest to young professional working women with a contemporary London bias. All material commissioned. Length: 800–1400 words. Illustrations: no unsolicited illustrations; enquire first. Payment: by negotiation. Founded1968.

Mslexia

PO Box 656, Newcastle upon Tyne NE99 1PZ
tel 0191-261 6656 *fax* 0191-261 6636
email postbag@mslexia.demon.co.uk
website www.mslexia.co.uk
Editor Debbie Taylor, *Send material to* Melanie Ashby
4 p.a. £18.75 p.a.

Magazine for women writers which combines features and advice about writing, with new fiction and poetry by women. Considers unsolicited material. Length: up to 3000 words (short stories), articles/features by negotiation, up to 6 poems. Illustrations: mono art, photos, colour transparencies. Payment: by negotiation. Founded 1998.

Music Teacher

Rhinegold Publishing Ltd, 241 Shaftesbury Avenue, London WC2H 8TF
tel 020-7333 1747 *fax* 020-7333 1769
email music.teacher@rhinegold.co.uk
Editor Lucien Jenkins
Monthly £3.75

Information and articles for both school and private music teachers, including reviews of books, music, CD-Roms, videos and other music-education resources. Articles and illustrations must both have a teacher, as well as a musical, interest. Length: articles 1000–2000 words. Payment: £100 per 1000 words. Founded 1908.

Music Week

United Business Media International, 7th Floor, Ludgate House, 245 Blackfriars Road, London SE1 9UR
tel 020-7579 4143 *fax* 020-7579 4011
email mwnews@ubminternational.com
Editor Ajax Scott
Weekly £3.60 (£160 p.a.)

News and features on all aspects of producing, manufacturing, marketing and retailing music. Payment: by negotiation. Founded 1959.

Musical Opinion

2 Princes Road, St Leonards-on-Sea, East Sussex TN37 6EL
tel (01424) 715167 *fax* (01424) 712214
email musicalopinion2@aol.com
Editor Denby Richards
Quarterly (plus supplements) £5 (£28 p.a.)

Suggestions for contributions of musical interest, scholastic, educational, anniversaries, ethnic, and also relating to the organ world. Dance, video, CD, opera, festival, book, music reviews. All editorial matter must be commissioned. Payment: on publication. Illustrations: b&w and colour photos, cartoons. Founded 1877.

Musical Times

22 Gibson Square, London N1 0RD
Editor Antony Bye
4 p.a. For subscription rates *tel* (01442) 879097

Musical articles, reviews, 500–6000 words. All material commissioned; no unsolicited material. Illustrations: music. Founded 1844.

My Weekly

D.C. Thomson & Co. Ltd, 80 Kingsway East, Dundee DD4 8SL
tel (01382) 223131 *fax* (01382) 452491
email myweekly@dcthomson.co.uk
185 Fleet Street, London EC4A 2HS
tel 020-7400 1030 *fax* 020-7400 1089
Editor H.G. Watson
Weekly 58p

Serials, from 30,000–80,000 words, suitable for family reading. Short complete stories of 1000–3500 words with humorous, romantic or strong emotional themes. Articles on TV stars and on all subjects of women's interest. Contributions should appeal to women everywhere. Payment: on acceptance. Illustrations: colour and b&w. Founded 1910.

My Weekly Story Collection

D.C. Thomson & Co. Ltd, Albert Square, Dundee DD1 9QJ
tel (01382) 223131 *fax* (01382) 322214
185 Fleet Street, London EC4A 2HS
tel 020-7400 1030 *fax* 020-7400 1089
Editor Dorothy Hunter

4 p.m. 75p
35,000–37,500-word romantic stories aimed at the post-teenage market. Payment: by arrangement; competitive for the market. No illustrations.

The National Trust Magazine

The National Trust, 36 Queen Anne's Gate, London SW1H 9AS
tel 020-7222 9251 *fax* 020-7222 5097
website www.nationaltrust.org.uk
Editor Gaynor Aaltonen
3 p.a. Free to members

News and features on the conservation of historic houses, coasts and countryside in the UK. No unsolicited articles. Length: 1000 words (features), 200 words (news). Illustrations: colour transparencies and artwork. Payment: by arrangement; picture library rates. Founded 1969.

Natural World

River Publishing, Victory House, 14 Leicester Place, London WC2H 7QH
tel 020-7306 0304 *fax* 020-7306 0303
Editor Trevor Lawson
3 p.a. Free to members

National magazine of The Wildlife Trusts. Short articles on the work of the UK's 47 wildlife trusts. Unsolicited MSS not accepted. Length: up to 1200 words. Payment: by arrangement. Illustrations: line, colour. Founded 1981.

Naturalist

The University, Bradford BD7 1DP
tel (01274) 234212 *fax* (01274) 234231
email m.r.d.seaward@bradford.ac.uk
Editor Prof M.R.D. Seaward MSc, PhD, DSc
Quarterly £20 p.a.

Original papers on all kinds of British natural history subjects, including various aspects of geology, archaeology and environmental science. Length: immaterial. Illustrations: photos and line drawings. Payment: none. Founded 1875.

Nature

Macmillan Magazines Ltd, The Macmillan Building, 4 Crinan Street, London N1 9XW
tel 020-7833 4000 *fax* 020-7843 4596
email nature@nature.com
website www.nature.com
Editor Philip Campbell
Weekly £5.45

Devoted to scientific matters and to their bearing upon public affairs. All contributors of articles have specialised knowledge of the subjects with which they deal. Illustrations: line, half-tone. Founded 1869.

Nautical Magazine

Brown, Son & Ferguson, Ltd, 4-10 Darnley Street, Glasgow G41 2SD
tel 0141-429 1234 *fax* 0141-420 1694
email info@skipper.co.uk
website www.skipper.co.uk
Editor L. Ingram-Brown MIM, MBIM, MRIN
Monthly £29.40 p.a. (£33 p.a. overseas)

Articles relating to nautical and shipping profession, from 1500–2000 words; also translations. Payment: by arrangement. No illustrations. Founded 1832.

Needlecraft

Future Publishing Ltd, 30 Monmouth Street, Bath BA1 2BW
tel (01225) 442244 *fax* (01225) 732398
email debora.bradley@futurenet.co.uk
Editor Debora Bradley
Monthly £3.20

Mainly project-based stitching designs with step-by-step instructions. Features with tight stitching focus (e.g. technique, personality). Length: 1000 words. Illustrated. Payment: £150–£200. Founded 1991.

.net The Internet Magazine

Future Publishing Ltd, Beaufort Court, 30 Monmouth Street, Bath BA1 2BW
tel (01225) 442244 *fax* (01225) 732291
email netmag@futurenet.co.uk
website www.netmag.co.uk
Editor Paul Douglas
Monthly CD edition £4.49

Articles, features and news on the internet. Length: 1000–3000 words. Payment: negotiable. Illustrations: colour. Founded 1994.

New Beacon

RNIB, 224 Great Portland Street, London W1N 6AA
tel 020-7388 1266
Editor Ann Lee
Monthly £2

Articles on all aspects of living with a visual impairment (blindness or partial sight). Published in clear print, braille, disk and tape editions. Length: from 500 words. Payment: by arrangement. Illustrations: half-tone. Founded 1930; as *Beacon* 1917.

New Humanist

Rationalist Press Association, Bradlaugh House, 47 Theobald's Road, London WC1X 8SP
tel 020-7430 1371 *fax* 020-7430 1271

email jim.herrick@rationalist.org.uk
Editor Jim Herrick
Quarterly £2.50

Articles on current affairs, philosophy, science, literature and humanism. Length: 1000–3000 words. Illustrations: b&w photos. Payment: nominal; none for photos. Founded 1885.

New Impact

Anser House of Marlow, Courtyard Offices, 3 High Street, Marlow, Bucks. SL7 1AX
tel (01628) 481581 *fax* (01628) 475570
Managing Editor Elaine Sihera
Bi-monthly £45 p.a. (business), £35 p.a. (individual), £25 p.a. (faculties)

'Promoting enterprise, training and diversity.' Articles, features and news on any aspect of training, business and women's issues to suit a multicultural audience; also profiles of personalities, short stories. Length: 900–1000 words. Illustrations: b&wphotos if related to profiles. Payment: £50 (depending on merit); none for photos. Founded 1993.

New Internationalist

55 Rectory Road, Oxford OX4 1BW
tel (01865) 728181 *fax* (01865) 793152
email ni@newint.org
website www.newint.org
Editors Vanessa Baird, Katharine Ainger, David Ransom
Monthly £2.95 (£28.85 p.a.)

World issues, ranging from food to feminism to peace – examines one subject each month. Length: up to 2000 words. Illustrations: line, half-tone, colour, cartoons. Payment: £80 per 1000 words. Founded 1973.

New Law Journal

LexisNexis Butterworths Tolley, Halsbury House, 35 Chancery Lane, London WC2A 1EL
tel 020-7400 2500 *fax* 020-7400 2583
email newlaw.journal@butterworths.com
Acting Editor Jane Maynard
48 p.a. £4.75

Articles and news on all aspects of the legal profession. Length: up to 2000 words. Payment: by arrangement.

New Media Age

Centaur Newsletters, St Giles House, 50 Poland Street, London W1F 7AX
tel 020-7970 4000 *fax* 020-7943 8169
email michael.nutley@centaur.co.uk
Editor Michael Nutley
Weekly £164 p.a.

News and articles on online advertising, marketing, publishing and e-commerce. Phone first with ideas; no uncommissioned material. Length: 1000–3000 words (articles), 250 words (news). Payment: £180 per 1000 words. Founded 1995.

New Musical Express

(incorporating Melody Maker)
IPC Magazines Ltd, 25th Floor, King's Reach Tower, Stamford Street, London SE1 9LS
tel 020-7261 5000 *fax* 020-7261 5185
Editor tba
Weekly £1.50

Authoritative articles and news stories on the world's rock and movie personalities. Length: by arrangement. Preliminary letter or phone call desirable. Payment: by arrangement. Illustrations: action photos with strong news angle of recording personalities, cartoons.

New Scientist

RBI Ltd, 151 Wardour Street, London W1F 8WE
tel 020-8652 3500 *fax* 020-7331 2777
email enquiries@newscientist.com
website www.NewScientist.com
Editor Jeremy Webb
Weekly £2.20

Authoritative articles of topical importance on all aspects of science and technology. Intending contributors should study recent copies of the magazine and initially send only a 200–word synopsis of their idea. NB: Does not publish non-peer reviewed theories, poems or crosswords. Payment: varies but average £300 per 1000 words. Illustrations: all styles, cartoons; contact art dept.

New Statesman

(formerly New Statesman & Society)
Victoria Station House, 191 Victoria Street, London SW1E 5NE
tel 020-7828 1232 *fax* 020-7828 1881
email info@newstatesman.co.uk
Editor Peter Wilby
Weekly £2

Interested in news, reportage and analysis of current political and social issues at home and overseas, plus book reviews, general articles and coverage of the arts, environment and science seen from the perspective of the British Left but written in a stylish, witty and unpredictable way. Length: strictly according to the value of the piece. Illustrations: commissioned for specific articles, though artists' samples considered for future reference; occasional cartoons. Payment: by agreement. Founded 1913.

New Theatre Quarterly

Oldstairs, Kingsdown, Deal, Kent CT14 8ES
email simontrussler@lineone.net
Editors Clive Barker, Simon Trussler
Quarterly £18 (£32 p.a.)

Articles, interviews, documentation, reference material covering all aspects of live theatre. An informed, factual and serious approach essential. Preliminary discussion and synopsis desirable. Payment: by arrangement. Illustrations: line, half-tone. Founded 1985; as *Theatre Quarterly* 1971.

New Welsh Review

Chapter Arts Centre, Market Road, Cardiff CF5 1QE
tel/fax 029-2066 5529/2051 5014
email robin@nwrc.demon.co.uk
Editor Robin Reeves
Quarterly £5.40 (£20 p.a., £38 2 yrs)

Literary – critical articles, short stories, poems, book reviews, interviews and profiles. Especially, but not exclusively, concerned with Welsh writing in English. Theatre in Wales section. Length: (articles) up to 4000 words. Illustrations: line, half-tone, cartoons; colour cover. Payment: £15–£35 per 1000 words (articles); £10–£25 per poem, £40–£70 per short story, £15–£35 per review, £10–£20 per illustration. Founded 1988.

New Woman

EMAP Élan, Endeavour House, 189 Shaftesbury Avenue, London WC2H 8JG
tel 020-7437 9011 *fax* 020-7208 3585
email lizzi.hosking@hotmail.com
website www.newwoman.co.uk
Editor Sara Cremer
Monthly £2.60

Features up to 2000 words. Occasionally accepts unsolicited articles; enclose sae for return. No fiction. Payment: at or above NUJ rates. Illustrated. Founded 1988.

The New Writer

PO Box 60, Cranbrook, Kent TN17 2ZR
tel (01580) 212626 *fax* (01580) 212041
email editor@thenewwriter.com
website www.thenewwriter.com
Editor Suzanne Ruthven *Publisher* Merric Davidson
6 p.a. £3.95

Features, short stories from guest writers and from subscribers, poems, news and reviews. Seeks forward-looking articles on all aspects of the written word that demonstrate the writer's grasp of contemporary writing and current editorial/publishing policies. Length: approx. 1000 words (articles), longer pieces considered; 1000–2000 words (features). Payment: £20 per 1000 words (articles), £10 (stories), £3 (poems). Founded 1996.

Night and Day – see Mail on Sunday in National newspapers UK and Ireland, page 3

19

IPC Magazines Ltd, King's Reach Tower, Stamford Street, London SE1 9LS
tel 020-7261 6410
Editor Helen Bazuaye
Monthly £2.30

Glossy fashion and general interest magazine for young women aged 16–22, including beauty, celebrities and social features of strong contemporary interest. All illustrations commissioned. Payment: by arrangement. Founded 1968.

Nursery Education

Scholastic Ltd, Villiers House, Clarendon Avenue, Leamington Spa, Warks. CV32 5PR
tel (01926) 887799 *fax* (01926) 883331
email earlyyears@scholastic.co.uk
website www.scholastic.co.uk
Editor Susan Howard
Monthly £3.15

Practical theme-based activities for educators working with 3–5 year-olds. All ideas based on the Early Learning Goals. Material mostly commissioned.Length: 500–1000 words. Illustrations: colour and b&w; colour posters. Payment: by arrangement. Founded 1997.

Nursery World

Admiral House, 66-68 East Smithfield, London E1W 1BX
tel 020-7782 3120
Editor Liz Roberts
Weekly £1.20

For all grades of primary school, nursery and child care staff, nannies, foster parents and all concerned with the care of expectant mothers, babies and young children. Authoritative and informative articles, 800 or 1600 words, and photos, on all aspects of child welfare and early education, from 0–8 years, in the UK. Practical ideas and leisure crafts. No short stories. Payment: by arrangement. Illustrations: line, half-tone, colour.

Nursing Times

EMAP Healthcare, Greater London House,
Hampstead Road, London NW1 7EJ
tel 020-7874 0500 *fax* 020-7874 0505
Editor Tricia Reid
Weekly £1.10

Articles of clinical interest, nursing education and nursing policy. Illustrated articles not longer than 2000 words. Contributions from other than health professionals sometimes accepted. Press day: Monday. Illustrations: photos, line, cartoons. Payment: NUJ rates; by arrangement for illustrations. Founded 1905.

Office Secretary (OS Magazine)

Peebles Media Group, Brookmead House,
8 Thorney Leys Business Park, Witney,
Oxon OX8 7GE
tel (01993) 894500 *fax* (01993) 778884
email emmasmith@peeblesmedia.com
website http://os.deskdemon.com
Editor Emma Smith
Bi-monthly £20 p.a.

Serious features on anything of interest to senior secretaries and executive PAs. No unsolicited MSS; ideas only. Illustrations: colour transparencies and prints. Payment: by negotiation. Founded 1986.

OK! Magazine

Northern & Shell plc, Ludgate House,
245 Blackfriars Road, London SE1 9UX
tel 020-7928 8000 *fax* 020-7579 4607
Editor Nic McCarthy
Weekly £1.85

Exclusive celebrity interviews and photographs. Submit ideas in writing. Length: 1000 words. Illustrations: colour. Payment: £150–£250,000 per feature. Founded 1993.

The Oldie

65 Newman Street, London W1T 3EG
tel 020-7436 8801 *fax* 020-7436 8804
email theoldie@theoldie.co.uk
website www.theoldie.co.uk
Editor Richard Ingrams
Monthly £2.50

General interest magazine reflecting attitudes of older people but aimed at a wider audience. Welcomes features (800–2000 words) on all subjects. Enclose sae for reply/return of MSS. Illustrations: welcomes b&w and colour cartoons. Payment: approx. £80–£100 per 1000 words; minimum £45 for cartoons. Founded 1992.

Opera

36 Black Lion Lane, London W6 9BE
tel 020-8563 8893 *fax* 020-8563 8635
Editor John Allison
13 p.a. £3.45

Articles on general subjects appertaining to opera; reviews; criticisms. Length: up to 2000 words. Payment: by arrangement. Illustrations: photos.

Opera Now

241 Shaftesbury Avenue, London WC2H 8EH
tel 020-7333 1740 *fax* 020-7333 1769
email opera.now@rhinegold.co.uk
website www.rhinegold.co.uk
Editor Ashutosh Khandekar
Bi-monthly £4.95

Articles, news, reviews on opera. All material commissioned only. Length: 150–1500 words. Illustrations: colour and b&w photos, line, cartoons. Payment: £120 per 1000 words. Founded 1989.

Orbis

17 Greenhow Avenue, West Kirby, Wirral CH48 5EL
tel 0151-625 1446
email carolebaldock@hotmail.com
website www.poettext.com
Editor Carole Baldock
Quarterly £15/E32/$28 p.a.

Poetry, prose (1000 words), news, reviews, views, letters. Up to 4 poems by post; via email, up to 2 in body. Enclose sae/2 IRCs with all correspondence. Payment: £20–£40 plus year's subscription for Editor's Choice, poetry/pose; £50 Readers' Vote. Founded 1968.

Organic Gardening

Sandvoe, North Roe, Shetland ZE2 9RY
tel (01806) 533319
email organic.gardening@virgin.net
Editor Gaby Bartai Bevan
Monthly £2.55

Articles on all aspects of gardening by experienced organic gardeners. Unsolicited material welcome. Length: 600–2000 words. Illustrations: transparencies, colour and b&w photos, line drawings, cartoons. Payment: by arrangement. Founded 1988.

Other Poetry

29 Western Hill, Durham DH1 4RL
tel 0191-386 4058
website www.otherpoetry.com
Editors Michael Standen (managing), Richard Kell, Peter Bennet, James Roderick Burns
3 p.a. £3.50 (£10/$18 p.a.)

Poetry. Submit up to 6 poems with sae. Payment: £5 per poem. Founded 1979.

Our Dogs

Oxford Road Station Approach,
Manchester M60 1SX
tel 0161-236 2660 *fax* 0161-236 5534/0892
Editor William Moores
Weekly £1.60

Articles and news on the breeding and showing of pedigree dogs. Illustrations: b&w photos. Payment: by negotiation; £10 per photo. Founded 1895.

Outposts Poetry Quarterly

22 Whitewell Road, Frome,
Somerset BA11 4EL
tel/fax (01373) 466653
Editor Roland John *Founder* Howard Sergeant MBE, *Send material to* M. Pargitter
Quarterly £4 (£14 p.a.)

Poems, essays and critical articles on poets and their work; poetry competitions. Payment: by arrangement. Founded 1943.

Oxford Poetry

Magdalen College, Oxford OX1 4AU
email editors@oxfordpoetry.co.uk
website www.oxfordpoetry.co.uk
Editors Graham Nelson, Jenni Nutall
3 p.a. £3 (£9 p.a.)

Previously unpublished poems and translations, both unsolicited and commissioned; interviews, articles and reviews. Payment: none. Founded 1910; refounded 1983.

Park Home & Holiday Caravan

(formerly Mobile & Holiday Homes)
Focus House, Dingwall Avenue,
Croydon CR9 2TA
tel 020-8774 0600 *fax* 020-8774 0939
email phhc@ipcmedia.com
Editor Anne Webb
Monthly £2.50

Informative articles on residential mobile homes (park homes) and holiday static caravans – personal experience articles, site features, news items. No preliminary letter. Payment: by arrangement. Illustrations: line, half-tone, colour transparencies, cartoons. Founded 1960.

PC Answers

Future Publishing Ltd, 30 Monmouth Street,
Bath BA1 2BW
tel (01225) 442244 *fax* (01225) 732295
email pcanswers@futurenet.co.uk
website www.pcanswers.co.uk
Editor Nick Peers
13 p.a. £4.99

Reviews, news and practical/how-to features for home PC users, excluding games. Length: 2500 words (features). Illustrations: colour. Payment: by negotiation. Founded 1991.

PC Direct

VNU Business Publications, VNU House,
32-34 Broadwick Street, London W1A 2HG
tel 020-7316 9000 *fax* 020-7316 9151
website www.pcdirect.co.uk
Editor Paul Hales
Monthly £2.99

News, features, reviews and technical information for the direct computer buyer. All material commissioned. Length: 500–3000 words. Illustrations: colour photos and illustrations, including computer generated. Payment: £200 per 1000 words; varies for illustrations according to subject/media. Founded 1991.

PCS View

Public and Commercial Services Union,
160 Falcon Road, London SW11 2LN
tel 020-7924 2727 *fax* 020-7924 1847
email editor@pcs.org.uk
website www.pcs.org.uk
Editor Sharon Breen
10 p.a. Free to members

Well-written articles on civil service, trade union and general subjects considered. Send ideas for consideration before submitting full article. Length: 600 words. Also photos and humorous drawings of interest to civil servants. Illustrations: line, half-tone. Payment: NUJ rates.

Peace News

5 Caledonian Road, London N1 9DX
tel 020-7278 3344 *fax* 020-7278 0444
email editorial@peacenews.info
website www.peacenews.info
Submit material to The Editor
Quarterly £2.50

Political articles based on nonviolence in every aspect of human life. Illustrations: line, half-tone. No payment. Founded 1936.

Peninsular Magazine

Cherrybite Publications, Linden Cottage,
45 Burton Road, Little Neston, Cheshire CH64 4AE
tel 0151-353 0967
email helicon@globalnet.co.uk
website www.cherrybite.co.uk
Editor Shelagh Nugent

Quarterly £3.50

Literary magazine: essential to read a current issue before sending MSS. Regular competitions with prizes. Length: up to 4000 words. Payment: £5 per 1000 words. Founded 1996.

Pensions World

LexisNexis Butterworths Tolley, Tolley House, 2 Addiscombe Road, Croydon CR9 5AF
tel 020-8686 9141 *fax* 020-8212 1970
email stephanie_hawthorne@tolley.co.uk
website www.pensionsworld.co.uk
Editor Stephanie Hawthorne
Monthly £84 p.a.

Specialist articles on pensions, investment and law. No unsolicited articles; all material is commissioned. Length: 1500 words. Payment: by negotiation. Founded 1972.

People Management

Personnel Publications Ltd, 17 Britton Street, London EC1M 5TP
tel 020-7880 6200 *fax* 020-7336 7635
email editorial@peoplemanagement.co.uk
website www.peoplemanagement.co.uk
Editor Steve Crabb
Fortnightly £5 (£88 p.a.)

Journal of the Chartered Institute of Personnel and Development. News items and feature articles on recruitment and selection, training and development; pay and performance management; industrial psychology; employee relations; employment law; working practices and new practical ideas in personnel management in industry and commerce. Length: up to 2500 words. Payment: by arrangement. Illustrations: contact art editor.

People's Friend

D.C. Thomson & Co. Ltd, 80 Kingsway East, Dundee DD4 8SL
tel (01382) 223131 *fax* (01382) 452491
185 Fleet Street, London EC4A 2HS
tel 020-7400 1030 *fax* 020-7400 1089
Send material to The Editor
Weekly 50p

Fiction magazine for women of all ages. Includes personal and home interests, especially knitting and cookery. Serials (60,000–70,000 words) and complete stories (1500–3000 words) of strong romantic and emotional appeal. Considers stories for children. No preliminary letter required. Illustrations: colour and b&w. Payment: on acceptance. Founded 1869.

People's Friend Story Collection

D.C. Thomson & Co. Ltd, 2 Albert Square, Dundee DD1 9QJ
tel (01382) 223131 *fax* (01382) 322214
185 Fleet Street, London EC4A 2HS
tel 020-7400 1030 *fax* 020-7400 1089
Editor Shirley Blair
2 p.m. £1

50,000–55,000-word family and romantic stories aimed at 30+ age group. Payment: by arrangement. No illustrations.

Perfect Home

Fox Publishing Ltd, Lion House, Red Lion Street, Richmond, Surrey TW9 1RE
tel 020-8332 9090 *fax* 020-8332 9991
email zena.alli@fox-publishing.com
Editor Zena Alli
Monthly £2.80

Home-related features: readers' homes, makeovers, DIY, product testing/reviews, gardening. Length: 800–1000 words. Payment: by merit. Illustrated. Founded 1992.

Period Living & Traditional Homes

EMAP Élan, Endeavour House, 189 Shaftesbury Avenue, London WC2H 8JG
tel 020-7437 9011 *fax* 020-7434 0656
Editor Garry Mason
Monthly £2.85

Articles and features on decoration, furnishings, renovation of period homes; gardens, crafts, decorating in a period style. Illustrated. Payment: varies, according to work required. Founded 1990.

Personal Computer World

VNU House, 32-34 Broadwick Street, London W1A 2HG
tel 020-7316 9000 *fax* 020-7316 9313
email pcw@vnu.co.uk
website www.pcw.co.uk
Editor Dylan Armbrust
Monthly £3.25

Articles about computers, reviews and 'how to' advice. Length: 800–5000 words. Payment: from £150 per 1000 words. Illustrations: line, half-tone, colour. Founded 1978.

Personal Finance

Charterhouse Communications, Arnold House, 36-41 Holywell Lane, London EC2A 3SF
tel 020-7827 5454 *fax* 020-7827 0567
email martin.fagan@charterhouse-communications.co.uk
Editor Martin Fagan
Monthly £2.60

Articles and features on savings and

investment, general family finance, of interest both to new investors and financially aware readers. All material commissioned: submit ideas in writing to the editor in first instance. Illustrations: colour and b&w photos, colour line drawings. Payment: £200 per 1000 words; £90–£250 illustrations. Founded 1994.

Picture Postcard Monthly

15 Debdale Lane, Keyworth, Nottingham NG12 5HT
tel 0115-937 4079 *fax* 0115-937 6197
email reflections@argonet.co.uk
website www.postcardcollecting.co.uk
Editor Brian Lund
Monthly £2.40 (£28 p.a.)

Articles, news and features for collectors of old or modern picture postcards. Length: 500–2000 words. Illustrations: colour and b&w. Payment: £27 per 1000 words; 50p per print. Founded 1978.

Pig Farming

United Business Media International, Sovereign House, Sovereign Way, Tonbridge, Kent TN9 1RW
tel 020-8309 7000 *fax* (01732) 377128
Editor Roger Abbott
Monthly £28 p.a.

Practical, well-illustrated articles on all aspects of pigmeat production required, particularly those dealing with new ideas in pig management, feeding, housing, health and hygiene, product innovation and marketing. Length: 800–1200 words. Payment: by arrangement. Illustrations: line, half-tone, colour.

Pilot

PO Box 313, Teddington, Middlesex TW11 9WD
tel 020-8977 6595 *fax* 020-8977 5881
email pilotmagazine@pilotweb.co.uk
website www.pilotweb.co.uk
Editor Philip Whiteman
Monthly £3.25

Feature articles on general aviation, private and business flying. Illustrations: line, half-tone, colour, cartoons. Payment: £125–£1000 per article on acceptance; £30 per photo. Founded 1968.

The Pink Paper

72 Holloway Road, London N7 8NZ
tel 020-7296 6000 *fax* 020-7957 0046
email editorial @pinkpaper.co.uk
Editor Trist Reid-Smith
Weekly Free

National news magazine for lesbians and gay men. Features (500–1000 words) and news (100–500 words) plus lifestyle section (features 350–1000 words) on any gay-related subject. Illustrations: b&w photos and line plus colour 'scene' photos. Payment: £40–£90 for words; £30–£60 for illustrations. Founded 1987.

Planet

PO Box 44, Aberystwyth, Ceredigion SY23 3ZZ
tel (01970) 611255 *fax* (01970) 611197
email planet.enquiries@planetmagazine.org.uk
website www.planetmagazine.org.uk
Editor John Barnie
6 p.a. £3.25 (£15 p.a.)

Short stories, poems, topical articles on Welsh current affairs, politics, the environment and society. New literature in English. Length of articles: 1000–3500 words. Payment: £40 per 1000 words for prose; £25 minimum per poem. Illustrations: line, half-tone, cartoons. Founded 1970–9; relaunched 1985.

PN Review

(formerly Poetry Nation)
Carcanet Press Ltd, 4th Floor, Conavon Court, 12 Blackfriars Street, Manchester M3 5BQ
tel 0161-834 8730 *fax* 0161-832 0084
email pnr@carcanet.u-net.com
website www.carcanet.co.uk
Editor Michael Schmidt
6 p.a. £4.99 (£29.50 p.a.)

Poems, essays, reviews, translations. Submissions by post only. Payment: by arrangement. Founded 1973.

Poetry Ireland Review/Éigse Éireann

Bermingham Tower, Upper Yard, Dublin Castle, Dublin 2, Republic of Ireland
tel (01) 671 4632 *fax* (01) 671 4634
email poetry@iol.ie
Managing Editor Joseph Woods, *Editor* Michael Smith
Quarterly E7.99 (E30.50/$52 p.a.)

Poetry. Features and articles by arrangement. Payment: E32 per contribution or one year's subscription; E51 reviews. Founded 1981.

Poetry London

1A Jewel Road, London E17 4QU
tel/fax 020-8521 0776
email editors@plondon.demon.co.uk
website www.poetrylondon.co.uk
Editors Pascale Petit, Scott Verner, Martha Kapos, *Send material to* Katrine Herian, Business Manager
3 p.a. £11 p.a.

Poems of the highest standard, articles/reviews on any aspect of modern poetry. Comprehensive listings of poetry events and resources. Contributors must be knowledgeable about contemporary poetry. Payment: £20 minimum. Founded 1988.

Poetry Nottingham International

PO Box 6740, Nottingham NG5 1QG
Editor Julie Lumsden
Quarterly £2.75 (£10 p.a. UK, 17 p.a. overseas)

Poems; letters; articles up to 500 words on current issues in the poetry world. Payment: complimentary copy. Founded 1946.

Poetry Review

22 Betterton Street, London WC2H 9BX
tel 020-7420 9880 *fax* 020-7240 4818
email poetryreview@poetrysociety.org.uk
website www.poetrysociety.org.uk
Editors Robert Potts, David Herd
Quarterly £30 p.a. (£40 p.a. institutions, schools and libraries)

Poems, features and reviews; also cartoons. Send no more than 6 poems with sae. Preliminary study of magazine essential. Payment: £40 per poem.

Poetry Wales

38-40 Nolton Street, Bridgend CF31 3BN
tel (01656) 663018 *fax* (01656) 649226
email poetrywales@seren.force9.co.uk
website www.seren-books.com
Editor Robert Minhinnick, *Reviews Editor* Amy Wack
Quarterly £4 (£16 p.a.)

Poetry, criticism and commentary from Wales and around the world. Payment: by arrangement. Founded 1965.

Police Journal

Vathek Publishing, 5 Millennium Court, Derby Road, Douglas, Isle of Man IM2 3EW
tel (01624) 863256 *fax* (01624) 863254
email mlw@vathek.com
Publisher Mairwen Lloyd-Williams
Quarterly £74 p.a.

Articles of technical or professional interest to the Police Service throughout the world. Payment: none. Illustrations: line drawings. Founded 1928.

Police Review

The Quadrangle, 1st Floor, 180 Wardour Street, London W1F 8FY
tel 020-7851 9701 *fax* 020-7287 4765
Editor Catriona Marchant
Weekly £1.75

News and features of interest to the police and legal professions. Length: 200–2000 words. Illustrations: colour and b&w photos, line, cartoons. Payment: NUJ rates. Founded 1893.

The Political Quarterly

Blackwell Publishers Ltd, 108 Cowley Road, Oxford OX4 1JF
tel (01865) 791100
website www.blackwellpublishers.co.uk
Editors Tony Wright MP *and* Prof Andrew Gamble, *Literary Editor* Prof Donald Sassoon
Assistant Editor Gillian Bromley, 3 Fernhill Close, Kidlington, Oxford OX5 1BB
4 p.a. (£111 p.a. institutions, £21 p.a. individuals)

Topical aspects of national and international politics and public administration; takes a progressive, but not a party, point of view. Send articles to Assistant Editor. Length: average 5000 words. Payment: about £100 per article. Founded 1930.

Pony Magazine

Haslemere House, Lower Street, Haslemere, Surrey GU27 2PE
tel (01428) 651551 *fax* (01428) 653888
Editor Janet Rising
Monthly £1.90

Lively articles and short stories with a horsy theme aimed at readers aged 8–16 . Technical accuracy and young, fresh writing essential. Length: up to 800 words. Payment: by arrangement. Illustrations: drawings (commissioned), photos, cartoons. Founded 1949.

Popular Crafts

Nexus Special Interests Ltd, Nexus House, Azalea Drive, Swanley, Kent BR8 8HU
tel (01322) 660070 *fax* (01322) 616319
email debbie.moss@nexusmedia.com
website www.popularcrafts.com
Editor Debbie Moss
Monthly £2.75

Covers all kinds of crafts. Projects with full instructions, profiles and successes of craftspeople, news on craft group activities, readers' homes, celebrity interviews, general craft-related articles. Welcomes written outlines of ideas. Payment: by arrangement. Illustrated.

Post Magazine & Insurance Week

Timothy Benn Publishing Ltd, 39 Earlham Street, London WC2H 9LD
tel 020-7306 7000 *fax* 020-7306 7101
email postmag@benn.co.uk

website www.postmag.co.uk
www.insurancewindow.net
Editor Anthony Gould
Weekly £3 (£142 p.a.)

Commissioned specialist articles on topics of interest to insurance professionals; news, especially from overseas stringers. Illustrations: colour photos and illustrations, colour and b&w cartoons and line drawings. Payment: £200 per 1000 words; photos £30–£120, cartoons/line by negotiation. Founded 1840.

Poultry World

Quadrant House, The Quadrant, Sutton, Surrey SM2 5AS
tel 020-8652 4020 *fax* 020-8652 4042
email poultry.world@rbi.co.uk
Editor John Farrant
Monthly £2.30

Articles on poultry breeding, production, marketing and packaging. News of international poultry interest. Payment: by arrangement. Illustrations: photos, line.

PR Week

Haymarket Marketing Publications, 174 Hammersmith Road, London W6 7JP
tel 020-8267 4520 *fax* 020-8267 4509
Editor Kate Nicholas
Weekly Controlled circulation; £1.85 (£72 p.a.)

News and features on public relations. Length: approx. 800–3000 words. Payment: £185 per 1000 words. Illustrations: colour and b&w. Founded 1984.

Practical Boat Owner

Westover House, West Quay Road, Poole, Dorset BH15 1JG
tel (01202) 440820
email pbo@ipcmedia.com
website www.pbo.co.uk
Editor Rodger Witt
Monthly £3.20

Hints, tips and practical articles for cruising skippers – power and sail. Send synopsis first. Payment: by negotiation. Illustrations: photos or drawings. Founded 1967.

Practical Caravan

Haymarket Magazines Ltd, 60 Waldegrave Road, Teddington, Middlesex TW11 8LG
tel 020-8267 5629 *fax* 020-8267 5725
email practical.caravan@haynet.com
website www.practicalcaravan.com
Editor Carl Rodgerson
Monthly £2.80

Caravan-related travelogues, human interest features, technical and DIY matters. Length: 1500–2500. Illustrations: colour. Payment: £120 per 1000 words; negotiable. Founded 1967.

Practical Fishkeeping

EMAP Active Ltd, Bretton Court, Bretton, Peterborough PE3 8DZ
tel (01733) 264666
Editor Karen Youngs
Monthly £2.95

Practical fishkeeping in tropical and coldwater aquaria and ponds. Heavy emphasis on inspiration and involvement. Good colour photography always needed, and used. No verse or humour, no personal biographical accounts of fishkeeping unless practical. Payment: by worth. Founded 1966.

Practical Householder

Nexus Media Ltd, Nexus House, Azalea Drive, Swanley, Kent BR8 8HU
tel (01322) 660070 *fax* (01322) 667633
Editor John McGowan
Monthly £2.15

Articles about 1500 words in length, about practical matters concerning home improvement. Payment: according to subject. Illustrations: line, half-tone. Founded 1955.

Practical Parenting

IPC Media Ltd, King's Reach Tower, Stamford Street, London SE1 9LS
tel 020-7261 5058 *fax* 020-7261 6542
Editor-in-Chief Jayne Marsden
Monthly £2.20

Articles on parenting, baby and childcare, health, psychology, education, children's activities, personal birth/parenting experiences. Send synopsis, with sae. Illustrations: commissioned only; colour: photos, line. Payment: by agreement. Founded 1987.

Practical Photography

EMAP Active Ltd, Bretton Court, Bretton, Peterborough PE3 8DZ
tel (01733) 264666 *fax* (01733) 465246
email practical.photography@emap.com
Editor Will Cheung
Monthly £3.10

Aimed at anyone who seeks to take excellent quality pictures. Excellent potential for freelance pictures: must be first rate – technically and pictorially – and have some relevance to photographic technique. Freelance ideas for words welcome (the more unusual ideas stand the greatest chance of success). Send synopsis of feature ideas in first instance. Payment: negotiable but typically £80 per page and £120 per 1000 words. Founded 1959.

Practical Wireless

PW Publishing Ltd, Arrowsmith Court, Station Approach, Broadstone, Dorset BH18 8PW
tel (01202) 659910 *fax* (01202) 659950
email rob@pwpublishing.ltd.uk
Editor Rob Mannion G3XFD
Monthly £2.75

Articles on the practical and theoretical aspects of amateur radio and communications. Constructional projects. Write or email for advice and author's guide. Illustrations: in b&w and colour; photos, line drawings and wash half-tone for offset litho. Payment: by arrangement. Founded 1932.

Practical Woodworking

Nexus Special Interests Ltd, Nexus House, Azalea Drive, Swanley, Kent BR8 8HU
tel (01322) 660070 *fax* (01322) 616319
Editor Mark Chisholm
Monthly £2.75

Articles of a practical nature covering any aspect of woodworking, including woodworking projects, tools, joints or timber technology. Payment: £70 per published page. Illustrated.

The Practising Midwife

(formerly Modern Midwife)
Temple DPS Ltd, 23 New Mount Street, Manchester M4 4DE
tel/fax 0161-953 4003
email pracmid@aol.com
Editor Jennifer Hall, *Managing Editor* Jane Bowler
Monthly £35 p.a.

Disseminates research-based material to a wide professional audience. Research and review papers, viewpoints and news items pertaining to midwifery, maternity care, women's health and neonatal health with both a national and an international perspective. All articles submitted are anonymously reviewed by at least 2 external acknowledged experts. Length: 1000–2000 words (articles); 150–400 words (news); up to 1000 words (viewpoints). Illustrations: colour transparencies and artwork. Payment: by arrangement. Founded 1991.

The Practitioner

CMP Information Ltd, City Reach, 5 Greenwich View Place, Millharbour, London E14 9NN
tel 020-7861 6478 *fax* 020-7861 6544
email gmatkin@cmpinformation.com
Editor Gavin Atkin
Monthly £12.60 (£82.50 p.a. UK, $194.25 p.a. overseas)

Articles of interest to GPs and vocational registrars, and others in the medical profession. Payment: approx. £200 per 1500 words. Founded 1868.

Prediction

IPC Country & Leisure, Focus House, Dingwall Avenue, Croydon CR9 2TA
tel 020-8774 0600 *fax* 020-8774 0939
Acting Editor Marion Williamson
Monthly £2.50

Articles on astrology and all occult subjects. Length: up to 2000 words. Payment: by arrangement. Illustrations: for cover use only: large colour transparencies (i.e. not 35mm). Founded 1936.

Press Gazette

Quantum Business Media Ltd, Quantum House, 19 Scarbrook Road, Croydon CR9 1LX
tel 020-8565 4200 *fax* 020-8565 4395
Editor Philippa Kennedy
Weekly £1.90

News and features of interest to journalists and others working in the media. Length: 1200 words (features), 300 words (news). Payment: approx. £200 (features), news stories negotiable. Founded 1965.

Pride

Hamilton House, 55 Battersea Bridge Road, London SW11 3AX
tel 020-7228 3110 *fax* 020-7228 3130
Managing Editor Dionne St Hill
Monthly £2.30

Lifestyle magazine incorporating fashion and beauty, travel, food and entertaining articles for the young woman of colour. Length: 1000–3000 words. Illustrations: colour photos and drawings. Payment: £100 per 1000 words. Founded 1993; relaunched 1997, 1998.

Priests & People

Blackfriars, 64 St Giles, Oxford OX1 3LY
tel (01865) 514845
Editor Rev. D.C. Sanders OP
Monthly £2.50

Journal of pastoral theology especially for parish ministers and for Christians of

English-speaking countries. Illustrations: occasional b&w photos. Length and payment by arrangement.

Prima

National Magazine Company, 72 Broadwick Street, London W1F 9EP
tel 020-7439 5000 *fax* 020-7312 4100
Editor Maire Fahey
Monthly £2

Articles on fashion, crafts, health and beauty, cookery; features. Illustrations: half-tone, colour. Founded 1986.

Prima Baby

National Magazine Co Ltd, 72 Broadwick Street, London W1F 9EP
tel 020-7312 3852 *fax* 020-7312 3744
email prima.baby@natmags.co.uk
Editor Julie Goodwin
Monthly £1.95

Magazine for women covering all aspects of pregnancy and childbirth and life with children aged up to 3 years; plus health, beauty, fashion. Length: up to 1500 words. Illustrations: colour transparencies. Payment: by arrangement. Founded 1994.

Printing World

United Business Media International, Sovereign House, Sovereign Way, Tonbridge, Kent TN9 1RW
tel (01732) 377391 *fax* (01732) 377552
Editor Gareth Ward
Weekly £2.75 (£90 p.a., overseas US$206 p.a.)

Commercial, technical, financial and labour news covering all aspects of the printing industry in the UK and abroad. Outside contributions. Payment: by arrangement. Illustrations: line, half-tone, colour, cartoons. Founded 1878.

Private Eye

6 Carlisle Street, London W1V 5RG
tel 020-7437 4017 *fax* 020-7437 0705
email strobes@private-eye.co.uk
website www.private-eye.co.uk
Editor Ian Hislop
Fortnightly £1.20

Satire. Payment: by arrangement. Illustrations: b&w, line, cartoons. Founded 1961.

Professional Nurse

EMAP Healthcare Ltd, Greater London House, Hampstead Road, London NW1 7EJ
tel 020-7874 0384 *fax* 020-7874 0386
email pn@healthcare.emap.co.uk
Editor Carolyn Scott
Monthly £36 p.a.

Clinical articles of interest to the professional nurse. Length: articles: 2000–3000 words; letters: 250–500 words. Payment: by arrangement. Illustrations: commissioned. Founded 1985.

Professional Photographer

Archant Specialist Ltd, The Mill, Bearwalden Business Park, Wendens Ambo, Saffron Walden, Essex CB11 4GB
tel (01799) 544246 *fax* (01799) 544201
Editor Steve Hynes
Monthly £3.10

Articles on professional photography, including technical articles, photographer profiles and coverage of issues affecting the industry. Length: 1000–2000 words. Illustrations: colour and b&w prints and transparencies, or digital files; diagrams if appropriate. Payment: from £200. Founded 1961.

Prospect

Prospect Publishing Ltd, 4 Bedford Square, London WC1B 3RD
tel 020-7255 1281 *fax* 020-7255 1279
email editorial@prospect-magazine.co.uk
website www.prospect-magazine.co.uk
Editor David Goodhart
Monthly £3.80

Politics and current affairs. Essays, features, special reports, reviews, short stories, opinions/analysis. Length: 3000–6000 words (essays, special reports, short stories), 1000 words (opinions). Illustrations: colour and b&w. Payment: by negotiation. Founded 1995.

Publishing News

39 Store Street, London WC1E 7DB
tel 020-7692 2900
website www.publishingnews.co.uk
Editor Jane Ellis
Weekly £2

Articles and news items on the book publishing and bookselling industry. Payment: £120 per 1000 words. Founded 1979.

Pulse

CMP Information Ltd, City Reach, 5 Greenwich View Place, Millharbour, London E14 9NN
tel 020-7861 6483 *fax* 020-7861 6257
email pulse@cmpinformation.com
Editor Howard Griffiths
Weekly £141.25 p.a.

Articles and photos of direct interest to GPs. Purely clinical material can only be accepted from medically qualified authors. Length: up to 750 words. Payment: £150 average. Illustrations: b&w and colour photos. Founded 1959.

Q Magazine

EMAP Performance, Mappin House, 4 Winsley Street, London W1W 8HF
tel 020-7436 1515 *fax* 020-7312 8247
email q@ecm.emap.com
website www.q4music.com
Editor John McKie
Monthly £3

Glossy modern guide to more than just rock music. All material commissioned. Length: 1200–2500 words. Illustrations: colour and b&w photos. Payment: £180 per 1000 words; illustrations by arrangement. Founded 1986.

QWF

PO Box 1768, Rugby CV21 4ZA
tel (01788) 334302
email jo@qwfmagazine.co.uk
website www.qwfmagazine.co.uk
Editor Jo Good, *Send material to* Sally Zigmond, Assistant Editor, 18 Warwick Crescent, Harrogate, North Yorkshire HG2 8JA
Bi-monthly £3.95 (£23 p.a.)

Thought-provoking short stories by female writers (no traditional romances, domestic crises or mainstream fiction) and articles of general interest. Study magazine first. Length: up to 4000 words. Payment: £5 (articles), £10 (short stories). Annual short story competition (up to 5000 words) in any style or genre, on any theme; first prize: £200. Founded 1994.

RA Magazine

Royal Academy of Arts, Burlington House, Piccadilly, London W1J 0BD
tel 020-7300 5820 *fax* 020-7300 5881
Editor Mira Hudson
Quarterly £4.50

Topical articles relating to the Royal Academy, its history and its exhibitions. Length: 500–1800 words. Illustrations: consult editor. Payment: £200 per 1000 words; illustrations by negotiation. Founded 1983.

Racing Post

Trinity Mirror, Floor 23, One Canada Square, Canary Wharf, London E14 5AP
tel 020-7293 3291 *fax* 020-7293 3758
email editor@racingpost.co.uk
website www.racingpost.co.uk
Editor Chris Smith
Mon-Fri £1.10 Sat £1.20

News on horseracing, greyhound racing and sports betting. Founded 1986.

Radio Control Models and Electronics

Nexus Special Interests Ltd, Nexus House, Azalea Drive, Swanley, Kent BR8 8HU
tel (01322) 660070 *fax* (01322) 667633
Editor Graham Ashby
Monthly £2.85

Well-illustrated articles on topics related to radio control. Payment: £45 per published page. Illustrations: line, half-tone. Founded 1960.

Radio Times

BBC Worldwide Ltd, 80 Wood Lane, London W12 0TT
tel 020-8433 3400 *fax* 020-8433 3160
email radio.times@bbc.co.uk
website www.radiotimes.com
Editor Gill Hudson
Weekly 85p

Articles that preview the week's programmes on British TV and radio. All articles are specially commissioned – ideas and synopses are welcomed but not unsolicited MSS. Length: 600–2500 words. Payment: by arrangement. Illustrations: mostly in colour; photos, graphic designs or drawings.

Rail

EMAP Active Publications, Bretton Court, Bretton, Peterborough PE3 8DZ
tel (01733) 264666 *fax* (01733) 282720
email rail@emap.com
Managing Editor Nigel Harris
Fortnightly £2.30

News and in-depth features on current UK railway operations. Length: 2000–3000 words (features), 250–400 words (news). Illustrations: colour and b&w photos and artwork. Payment: £75 per 1000 words; £20 per photo except cover (£70). Founded 1981.

Railway Gazette International

Reed Business Information, Quadrant House, The Quadrant, Sutton, Surrey SM2 5AS
tel 020-8652 8608 *fax* 020-8652 3738
website www.railwaygazette.com
Editor Murray Hughes
Monthly £68 p.a.

Deals with management, engineering, operation and finance of railways worldwide. Articles of practical interest on these subjects are considered and paid for if accepted. Illustrated articles, of 1000–3000 words, are preferred. A preliminary letter is required.

Railway Magazine

IPC Media Ltd, King's Reach Tower, Stamford Street, London SE1 9LS
tel 020-7261 5821 *fax* 020-7261 5269
Editor Nick Pigott
Monthly £3.05

Illustrated magazine dealing with all railway subjects; no fiction or verse. Articles from 1500–2000 words accompanied by photos. Preliminary letter desirable. Payment: by arrangement. Illustrations: colour transparencies, half-tone and line. Founded 1897.

The Rambler

The Ramblers' Association, 2nd Floor, Camelford House, 87-90 Albert Embankment, London SE1 7TW
tel 020-7339 8500 *fax* 020-7339 8501
email ramblers@london.ramblers.org.uk
website www.ramblers.org.uk
Editor Christopher Sparrow
Quarterly Free to members

Magazine of The Ramblers' Association. Articles on walking, access to countryside and related issues. Material mostly commissioned. Length: about 1000 words. Illustrations: colour slides. Payment: by agreement. Founded 1935.

Reader's Digest

The Reader's Digest Association Ltd, 11 Westferry Circus, Canary Wharf, London E14 4HE
tel 020-7715 8000
email excerpts@readersdigest.co.uk
website www.readersdigest.co.uk
Editor Katherine Walker
Monthly £2.50

Original anecdotes – £200 for up to 150 words – are required for humorous features. Booklet 'Writing for Reader's Digest' available £4.50 post free.

Reality

Redemptorist Publications, Orwell Road, Rathgar, Dublin 6, Republic of Ireland
tel (01) 4922488 *fax* (01) 4922654
Editor Rev. Gerry Moloney CSSR
Monthly 85p

Illustrated magazine for Christian living. Articles on all aspects of modern life, including family, youth, religion, leisure. Illustrated articles, b&w photos only. Short stories. Length: 1000–1500 words. Payment: by arrangement; average £50 per 1000 words. Founded 1936.

Red

EMAP Élan, Endeavour House, 189 Shaftesbury Avenue, London WC2H 8JG
tel 020-7437 9011 *fax* 020-7208 3218
Editor Trish Halpin, *Send material to* Andrea Childs, Assistant Editor
Monthly £2.80

High-quality articles on topics of interest to women aged 35–45: humour, memoirs, interviews and well-researched investigative features. Approach with ideas in writing in first instance. Length: 1500 words upwards. Illustrations: transparencies. Payment: NUJ rates. Founded 1998.

Red Pepper

Socialist Newspaper (Publications) Ltd, 1B Waterlow Road, London N19 5NJ
email redpepper@redpepper.org.uk
website www.redpepper.org.uk
Editor Hilary Wainwright, *Send material to* David Castle, Deputy Editor
Monthly £1.95

Independent radical magazine: news and features on politics, culture and everyday life of interest to the left and greens. Material mostly commissioned. Length: news/news features 200–800 words, other features 800–2000 words. Illustrations: b&w photos, cartoons, graphics. Payment: for investigations, otherwise only exceptionally. Founded 1994.

Reform

(published by United Reformed Church)
86 Tavistock Place, London WC1H 9RT
tel 020-7916 8630 *fax* 020-7916 2021 (fao 'Reform')
email reform@urc.org.uk
Editor David Lawrence
Monthly £1.30 (£11 p.a.)

Articles of religious or social comment. Length: 600–1000 words. Illustrations: line, half-tone, colour, cartoons. Payment: by arrangement. Founded 1972.

Report

ATL, 7 Northumberland Street, London WC2N 5DA
tel 020-7782 1517 *fax* 020-7925 0529
email info@atl.org.uk
website www.askatl.org.uk
Editor Heather Pinnell
8 p.a. £2.50 (£15 p.a. UK; £27 p.a. overseas)

The magazine from the Association of Teachers and Lecturers (ATL). Features, articles, comment, news about nursery, primary, secondary and further education. Payment: minimum £120 per 1000 words.

Retail Week

Emap Retail, Angel House, 338-346 Goswell Road, London EC1V 7QP
tel 020-7520 1500 *fax* 020-7520 1752
Editor Neill Denny
Weekly Controlled circulation (£105 p.a.)

Features and news stories on all aspects of retail management. Length: up to 1000 words. Illustrations: colour photos. Payment: by arrangement. Founded 1988.

The Rialto

PO Box 309, Aylsham, Norwich NR11 6LN
website www.therialto.co.uk
Editor Michael Mackmin
3 p.a. £4.25 (£12 p.a., £9 p.a. low income)

Poetry and criticism. Sae essential. Payment: by arrangement. Founded 1984.

Right Start

McMillan-Scott plc, Adam House, 7-10 Adam Street, The Strand, London WC2N 6AA
tel 020-7403 0840 *fax* 020-7378 6883
Editor Lynette Lowthian
Bi-monthly £1.95

Features on all aspects of preschool and infant education, child health and behaviour. No unsolicited MSS. Length: 800–1500 words. Illustrations: colour photos, line. Payment: varies. Founded 1989.

Rugby World

IPC Media Ltd, Kings Reach Tower, Stamford Street, London SE1 9LS
tel 020-7261 6830 *fax* 020-7261 5419
email Paul_Morgan@ipcmedia.com
Editor Paul Morgan
Monthly £3.10

Features and exclusive news stories on rugby. Length: approx. 1200 words. Illustrations: colour photos, cartoons. Payment: £120. Founded 1960.

Runner's World

Rodale Ltd, 7-10 Chandos Street, London W1M 0AD
tel 020-7291 6000 *fax* 020-7291 6080
email rwedit@rodale.co.uk
website www.runnersworld.co.uk
Editor Steven Seaton
Monthly £3

Articles on jogging, running, health and fitness. Payment: by arrangement. Illustrations: line, half-tone, colour. Founded 1979.

Running Fitness

Kelsey Publishing Ltd, Arcade Chambers, Westgate Arcade, Peterborough PE1 1PY
tel (01733) 347559 *fax* (01733) 352749
email paul.larkins@kelsey.co.uk
Editor Paul Larkins
Monthly £3

Practical articles on all aspects of running lifestyle, especially road running training and events, and advice on health, fitness and injury. Illustrations: colour photos, cartoons. Payment: by negotiation. Founded 1985.

RUSI Journal

Whitehall, London SW1A 2ET
tel 020-7930 5854 *fax* 020-7321 0943
email journal@rusi.org
website www.rusi.org
Contact Editorial Manager
Bi-monthly £7.50

Journal of the Royal United Services Institute for Defence Studies. Articles on international security, the military sciences, defence technology and procurement, and military history; also book reviews and correspondence. Length: 3000–3500 words. Illustrations: b&w photos, colour transparencies, maps and diagrams. Payment: £12.50 per printed page upon publication.

Safety Education

Royal Society for the Prevention of Accidents, Edgbaston Park, 353 Bristol Road, Birmingham B5 7ST
tel 0121-248 2000 *fax* 0121-248 2001
website www.rospa.org.uk
Editor Janice Cave
3 p.a. £9.50 p.a. for members of Safety Education Department (£11.32 p.a. non-members)

Articles on every aspect of good practice in safety education including safety of teachers and pupils in school, and the teaching of road, home, water, leisure and personal safety by means of established subjects on the school curriculum. All ages. Commissioned material only. Illustrations: line, half-tone, colour. Payment: by negotiation. Founded as *Child Safety* 1937; became *Safety Training* 1940; 1966.

Saga Magazine

The Saga Building, Middelburg Square, Folkestone, Kent CT20 1AZ
tel (01303) 771523 *fax* (01303) 776699
Editor Emma Soames
Monthly £15.95 p.a.

Articles relevant to interests of 50-plus age group, and profiles of celebrities in same age group. Mostly commissioned or written in-house, but genuine exclusives always welcome. Length: 1200–1600 words. Illustrations: colour transparencies, commissioned colour artwork. Payment: competitive rate. Founded 1984.

Sainsbury's Magazine

New Crane Publishing, 20 Upper Ground, London SE1 9PD
tel 020-7633 0266 *fax* 020-7401 9423
Editor Sue Robinson
Monthly £1

Features: general, food and drink, health, beauty, homes; all material commissioned. Length: from 1500 words. Illustrations: colour and b&w photos and line illustrations. Payment: varies; £300 per full page for illustrations. Founded 1993.

Satellite Times

Everpage Ltd, The Stables, West Hill Grange, North Road, Horsforth
tel 0113-258 5008 *fax* 0113-258 9745
email info@satellitetimes.co.uk
Editor-in-Chief Juliet Cross
Monthly £2.30

TV and film personality articles and interviews, sports articles, music, competitions. Payment: from £120 per 1000 words. Founded 1988.

The School Librarian

The School Library Association, Unit 2, Lotmead Business Village, Lotmead Farm, Wanborough, Swindon SN4 0UY
tel (01793) 791787 *fax* (01793) 791786
email info@sla.org.uk
website www.sla.org.uk
Editor Ray Lonsdale, DILS, University of Wales, Aberystwyth, Ceredigion SY23 3AS
Quarterly Free to members (£55 p.a.)

Official journal of the School Library Association. Articles on school library management, use and skills, and on authors and illustrators, literacy, publishing. Reviews of books, CD-Roms, websites and other library resources from preschool to adult. Length: 1800–3000 words (articles). Payment: by arrangement. Founded 1937.

Science Progress

Science Reviews, PO Box 314, St Albans, Herts. AL1 4ZG
tel (01724) 847322 *fax* (01727) 847323
email scilet@scilet.com
Editors Prof David Phillips, Prof Robin Rowbury
Quarterly £181 p.a. ($276 p.a. overseas)

Articles of 6000 words on new scientific developments, written so as to be intelligible to workers in other disciplines. Imperative to submit synopsis before full-length article. Payment: by arrangement. Illustrations: line, half-tone.

Scientific Computing World

Cambridge Publishers Ltd, 53-54 Sydney Street, Cambridge CB2 3HX
tel (01223) 477411 *fax* (01223) 327356
website www.scientific-computing.com
Editor Dr Tom Wilkie
6 p.a. Free to qualifying subscribers

Features on hardware and software developments for the scientific community, plus news articles and reviews. Length: 800–2000 words. Illustrations: colour transparencies, photos, electronic graphics. Payment: by negotiation. Founded 1994.

Scotland on Sunday Magazine – see Scotland on Sunday in National newspapers UK and Ireland, page 3

The Scots Magazine

D.C. Thomson & Co. Ltd, 2 Albert Square, Dundee DD1 9QJ
tel (01382) 223131 *fax* (01382) 322214
email mail@scotsmagazine.com
website www.scotsmagazine.com
Monthly £1.35

Articles on all subjects of Scottish interest. Short stories, poetry, but must be Scottish. Illustrations: colour and b&w photos. Payment: £22 per 1000 words; from £12–£40. Founded 1739.

Scottish Book Collector

c/o 8 Lauriston Street, Edinburgh EH3 9DJ
tel 0131-228 4837 *fax* 0131-228 3904
email jennie@scotbooksmag.demon.co.uk
website www.scotbooksmag.demon.co.uk
Editor Jennie Renton
Quarterly £3

Articles on collecting Scottish books; literary/bibliographical articles on books published in Scotland or by Scottish writers. Length: 1500–2500 words. Payment: £25 per article. Founded 1987.

The Scottish Farmer

SMG Magazines Ltd, 200 Renfield Street, Glasgow G2 3PR
tel 0141-302 7700 *fax* 0141-302 7799
Editor Alasdair Fletcher
Weekly £1.50

Articles on agricultural subjects. Length: 1000–1500 words. Payment: £80 per

1000 words. Illustrations: line, half-tone, colour. Founded 1893.

Scottish Field

Special Publications, Royston House, Caroline Park, Edinburgh EH5 1QJ
tel 0131-551 2942 *fax* 0131-551 2938
email editor@scottishfield.co.uk
Editor Archie Mackenzie
Monthly £2.90

Will consider all material with a Scottish link and good photos. Payment: by negotiation. Founded 1903.

Scottish Home and Country

42A Heriot Row, Edinburgh EH3 6ES
tel 0131-225 1724 *fax* 0131-225 8129
email magazine@swri.demon.co.uk
website www.swri.org.uk
Editor Liz Ferguson
Monthly 80p

Articles on crafts, cookery, travel, personal experience, DIY; humorous rural stories; fashion, health, books. Length: up to 1000 words, preferably illustrated. Illustrations: colour prints/transparencies, b&w, cartoons. Payment: by arrangement. Founded 1924.

Scottish Memories

Lang Syne Publishers Ltd, Strathclyde Business Centre, 120 Carstairs Street, Glasgow G40 4DJ
tel 0141-554 9944 *fax* 0141-554 9955
email www.argyll
website internet.co.uk/scotmem
Editor George Forbes
Monthly £2.25

Features on any aspect of Scottish nostalgia or history, from primeval times to the 1990s. Contact editor with an outline in first instance. Length: 1000 words. Illustrations: colour and b&w. Payment: £70 per 1000 words; £20 per photo. Founded 1993.

Scouting Magazine

Gilwell House, Gilwell Park, London E4 7QW
tel 020-8433 7100 *fax* 020-8433 7103
Editor Anna Sorensen Thomson
Monthly £1.85

Magazine of the Scout Association. Ideas, news, views, features and programme resources for Leaders and Supporters. Training material, accounts of Scouting events and articles of general interest with Scouting connections. Illustrations: photos – action shots preferred rather than static posed shots for use with articles or as fillers or cover potential, cartoons. Payment: on publication by arrangement.

Screen International

EMAP Business Publishing, 33-39 Bowling Green Lane, London EC1R 0DA
tel 020-7505 8080 *fax* 020-7505 8117
email ScreenInternational@compuserve.com
website www.screendaily.com
Managing Editor Leo Barraclough
Weekly £2.50

International news and features on the international film business. No unsolicited material. Length: variable. Payment: by arrangement.

Scuba World

Freestyle Publications Ltd, Alexander House, Ling Road, Tower Park, Poole, Dorset BH12 4NZ
tel (01202) 735090 *fax* (01202) 733969
email fraines@freepubs.co.uk
website www.freepubs.co.uk
Editor Frank Raines
Monthly £3

The official magazine of the Sub-Aqua Association. Articles, features, news and short stories related to diving. Unsolicited material welcome. Length: 1300–1400 words (articles/features); 200–300 words (news); 800 words (short stories); 2000 words (interviews). Payment: negotiable. Founded 1990.

Sea Angler

EMAP Active Ltd, Bushfield House, Orton Centre, Peterborough PE2 5UW
tel (01733) 237111 *fax* (01733) 465658
Editor Mel Russ
Monthly £2.60

Topical articles on all aspects of sea-fishing around the British Isles. Payment: by arrangement. Illustrations: colour. Founded 1973.

Sea Breezes

Media House, Tromode, Douglas, Isle of Man IM4 4SB
tel (01624) 696573 *fax* (01624) 661655
Editor A.C. Douglas
Monthly £2.50

Factual articles on ships and the sea past and present, preferably illustrated. Length: up to 4000 words. Illustrations: line, half-tone, colour. Payment: by arrangement. Founded 1919.

Sewing World

Traplet Publications Ltd, Traplet House, Severn Drive, Upton Upon Seven, Worcs. WR8 0JL
tel (01684) 595300 *fax* (01684) 594586

email sw@traplet.co.uk
Editor Wendy Gardiner
Monthly £2.75

'Sewing magazine for sewing machine enthusiasts.' Articles and step-by-step projects. Length: 1000–1500 words (articles). Illustrations: colour. Payment: £100 per article including illustrations. Founded 1995.

She

National Magazine House, 72 Broadwick Street, London W1F 9EP
tel 020-7439 5000 *fax* 020-7312 3981
Editor Eve Cameron, *Send material to* Cayte Williams, Features Editor
Monthly £2.70

No unsolicited MSS. Ideas with synopses welcome on subjects ranging from health and relationships to child care. Payment: NUJ freelance rates. Illustrations: photos. Founded 1955.

She Kicks

(formerly ONtheBALL)
Design Works, William Street, Gateshead, Tyne & Wear NE10 0JP
tel 0191-420 8383 *fax* 0191-420 4950
Editor Jennifer O'Neill
Bi-monthly £1.80

News, features and reviews of women's football in the UK and abroad. Aimed at the player rather than the spectator, it includes training tips and articles on tactics in the game, etc and addresses a wide range of both serious and humorous issues relating to the women's game. Length: 1000 words (features/articles), 100 words (news), 500 words (stories). Illustrations: colour. Founded 1996.

Sherlock Holmes – The Detective Magazine

(formerly The Sherlock Holmes Gazette)
69 Greenhead Road, Huddersfield HD1 4ER
tel/fax (01484) 426957
email overdale@btinternet.com
website www.pmh.uk.com/sherlock.htm
Editor David Stuart Davies
6 p.a. £3.50

Articles relating to Sherlock Holmes and Conan Doyle, and crime fiction and writers. Also short stories. Length: 1600 words (articles), 7000–12,000 words (short stories). Illustrations: colour and b&w prints. Payment: £20–£25 (articles), short stories by negotiation. Founded 1991.

Ships Monthly

IPC Country & Leisure (Marine), 222 Branston Road, Burton-on-Trent, Staffs. DE14 3BT
tel (01283) 542721 *fax* (01283) 546436
Editor Iain Wakefield
Monthly £2.50

Illustrated articles of shipping interest – both mercantile and naval, preferably of 20th and 21st century ships. Well-researched, factual material only. No short stories or poetry. 'Notes for Contributors' available. Mainly commissioned material; preliminary letter essential, with sae. Payment: by arrangement. Illustrations: half-tone and line, colour transparencies and prints. Founded 1966.

Shoot

IPC Magazines Ltd, King's Reach Tower, Stamford Street, London SE1 9LS
tel 020-7261 6287 *fax* 020-7261 6019
Editor Colin Mitchell
Monthly £2.60

Football magazine. Features, profiles of big names in football. Length: 500–2000 words (features). Illustrations: colour transparencies. Payment: negotiable. Founded 1969.

Shooting Times and Country Magazine

IPC Magazines Ltd, King's Reach Tower,, Stamford Street, London SE1 9LS
tel 020-7261 6180 *fax* 020-7261 7179
Editor Julian Murray-Evans
Weekly £1.70

Articles on fieldsports, especially shooting, and on related natural history and countryside topics. Unsolicited MSS not encouraged. Length: up to 2000 words. Payment: by arrangement. Illustrations: photos, drawings, colour transparencies. Founded 1882.

The Shop: A Magazine of Poetry

Skeagh, Schull, Co. Cork, Republic of Ireland
email wakeman@iolfree.ie
Editors John and Hilary Wakeman
3 p.a. E19 p.a.

Poems on any subject in any form and occasional essays on poetry, especially Irish poetry. No submissions by email. No illustrations required. Length: 2000–3000 words (essays); any (poems). Payment: by arrangement. Founded 1999.

The Short Wave Magazine

Arrowsmith Court, Station Approach, Broadstone, Dorset BH18 8PW
tel (01202) 659910 *fax* (01202) 659950
email kevin.nice@pwpublishing.ltd.uk
website www.pwpublishing.ltd.uk
Editor Kevin Nice
Monthly £3.25 (£36 p.a.)

Technical and semi-technical articles, 500–5000 words, on design, construction and operation of radio receiving equipment. Radio-related photo features welcome. Payment: £55 per page. Illustrations: line, half-tone, colour. Founded 1937.

Shout

D.C. Thomson & Co. Ltd, Albert Square, Dundee DD1 9QJ
tel (01382) 223131 *fax* (01382) 200880
email shout@dcthomson.co.uk
185 Fleet Street, London EC4A 2HS
tel 020-7400 1030 *fax* 020-7400 1089
Editor-in-Chief Jackie Brown
Fortnightly £1.50

Colour gravure magazine for 12–16 year-old girls. Pop, film and 'soap' features and pin-ups; general features of teen interest; emotional features, fashion and beauty advice. Illustrations: colour transparencies. Payment: on acceptance. Founded 1993.

The Shropshire Magazine

77 Wyle Cop, Shrewsbury, Shropshire SY1 1UT
tel (01743) 361979 *fax* (01743) 362128
Editor Keith Parker
Monthly £1.50

Articles on topics related to Shropshire, including countryside, history, characters, legends, education, food; also home and garden features. Length: up to 1500 words. Illustrations: colour. Founded 1950.

Sight and Sound

British Film Institute, 21 Stephen Street, London W1T 1LN
tel 020-7255 1444 *fax* 020-7436 2327
Editor Nick James
Monthly £3.25

Topical and critical articles on the cinema of any country; reviews of every film theatrically released in the UK; book reviews; reviews of every video released; regular columns from around the world. Length: 1000–5000 words. Payment: by arrangement. Illustrations: relevant photos, cartoons. Founded 1932.

The Sign

G.J. Palmer & Sons Ltd, St Mary's Works, St Mary's Plain, Norwich, Norfolk NR3 3BH
tel (01603) 615995 *fax* (01603) 624483
email terencestalbans@aol.com
Publisher G.A. Knights
Monthly 5p

Leading national insert for C of E parish magazines. Articles of interest to parishes. No poems. Items should bear the author's name and address; return postage essential or send by email. Length: up to 450 words, accompanied by photos/illustrations. Payment: by arrangement. Founded 1905.

Signal, Approaches to Children's Books

Lockwood, Station Road, South Woodchester, Stroud, Glos. GL5 5EQ
tel (01453 75) 5566/2208 *fax* (01453 87) 8599
Editor Nancy Chambers
3 p.a. £4.75 (£13.25 p.a.)

Articles on any aspect of children's books or the children's book world. Length: no limit but average 2500–3000 words. Payment: £3 per printed page. Illustrations: line occasionally. Founded 1970.

Ski and Board

The Ski Club of Great Britain, The White House, 57-63 Church Road, London SW19 5SB
tel (0845) 4580780 *fax* (0845) 4580781
email s&b@skiclub.co.uk
website www.skiclub.co.uk
Editor Arnie Wilson
Monthly (Oct-Jan) £2.95

Articles, features, news, true life stories, ski tips, equipment reviews, resort reports – all in connection with skiing and snowboarding. Welcomes ideas for articles and features. Length: 600–2000 words. Illustrations: colour transparencies, colour and b&w artwork and cartoons. Payment: £200 per 1000 words; £100–£200 per photo/illustration. Founded 1903.

The Skier and The Snowboarder Magazine

Mountain Marketing Ltd, PO Box 386, Sevenoaks, Kent TN13 1AQ
tel (0845) 3108303 *fax* (01732) 779266
email skierandsnowboarder@hotmail.com
Editor Frank Baldwin
5 p.a. (July–May) £2.95

Ski features, based around a good story.

Length: 800–1000 words. Illustrations: colour action ski photos. Payment: by negotiation. Founded 1984.

Slimmer, Healthier, Fitter

Aceville Publications Ltd, Castle House, 97 High Street, Colchester CO1 1TH
tel (01206) 505933 *fax* (01206) 505935
email slimmer@aceville.com
Editor Helen Tudor
10 p.a. £1.95

Features on health, nutrition, slimming. Personal weight loss stories. Sae essential. Length: 600 or 1200 words. Payment: by arrangement. Founded 1972.

Slimming Magazine

EMAP Esprit, Greater London House, Hampstead Road, London NW1 7EJ
tel 020-7347 1854 *fax* 020-7347 1863
Editor Alison Hall
11 p.a. £2.10

Articles on psychology, lifestyle and health related to diet and nutrition. Approach editor in writing with ideas. Length: 1000–1500 words. Payment: by negotiation. Founded 1969.

Smallholder

Hook House, Hook Road, Wimblington, March, Cambs. PE15 0QL
tel/fax (01354) 741182
email edit@smallholder.co.uk
website www.smallholder.co.uk
Editor Liz Wright
Monthly £2.30

Articles of relevance to small farmers about livestock and crops, organics, conservation, poultry, equipment. Items relating to the countryside considered. Send for copy. Payment: £30 per 1000 words or by arrangement. Illustrations: line, half-tone, cartoons. Founded 1985.

Smash Hits

EMAP Performance, Mappin House, 4 Winsley Street, London W1W 8HF
tel 020-7436 1515 *fax* 020-7636 5792
email smash-hits@emap.com
Editor tba
Fortnightly £1.90

News interviews and posters of pop, TV and film stars. Illustrations: colour photos. Payment: varies.

Snooker Scene

Cavalier House, 202 Hagley Road, Edgbaston, Birmingham B16 9PQ
tel 0121-454 2931 *fax* 0121-452 1822
email editor@snookerscene.com
website www.snookerscene.com
Editor Clive Everton
Monthly £2.50 (£25 p.a.)

News and articles about the snooker and billiards scene for readers with more than a casual interest in the games. Payment: by arrangement. Illustrations: photos. Founded 1971.

Snoop

Snoop Publications Ltd, 5A High Street, Southall, Middlesex UB1 3HA
tel 020-8571 7700 *fax* 020-8571 6006
email editor@snooplife.com
website www.snooplife.com
Editor Raj Kaushal
Monthly £3

Entertainment and lifestyle magazine for second and third generation UK Asians (16–35 year-olds): interviews, music, films, fashion, gossip and gigs. Features and articles by arrangement. Founded 1997.

Solicitors Journal

Sweet & Maxwell, 100 Avenue Road, London NW3 3PF
tel 020-7393 7000 *fax* 020-7393 7880
email solicitorsjournal@sweetandmaxwell.co.uk
Weekly £149 for 48 issues

Articles, by practising lawyers or specialist journalists, on subjects of practical interest to solicitors. Articles on spec should be sent on disk or by email. Length: up to 1800 words. Payment: by negotiation. Founded 1856.

Somerset Magazine

Eastern Counties Newspapers, 23 Market Street, Crewkerne, Somerset TA18 7JU
tel (01460) 270011 *fax* (01460) 270022
Managing Publisher Jenny Nicholls
Monthly £2.25

Articles, features with particular reference to Somerset locations, facilities and other interests. Length: 1000–1500 words. Illustrations: half-tone, colour. Payment: by arrangement. Founded 1977 as Somerset & West.

The Songwriter

International Songwriters Association, PO Box 46, Limerick City, Republic of Ireland
tel (061) 228837
Editor James D. Liddane
Monthly Available to members only

Articles on songwriting and interviews with music publishers and recording company executives. Length: 400–5000 words. Payment: by arrangement. Illustrations: photos. Founded 1967.

Songwriting and Composing

Sovereign House, 12 Trewartha Road, Praa Sands, Penzance, Cornwall TR20 9ST
tel (01736) 762826 *fax* (01736) 763328
email songmag@aol.com
website www.songwriters-guild.co.uk
General Secretary Carole Jones
Quarterly Free to members

Magazine of the Guild of International Songwriters and Composers. Short stories, articles, letters relating to songwriting, publishing, recording and the music industry. Payment: negotiable upon content £25–£60. Illustrations: line, halftone. Founded 1986.

The Spark Magazine

Blue Sax Publishing Ltd, 86-88 Colston Street, Bristol BS1 5BB
tel 0117-914 3434 *fax* 0117-914 3444
email john@spark.u-net.com
website www.thespark.co.uk
Editor John Dawson, *Send material to* Katj Noakes, Deputy Editor
Quarterly Free (5 p.a.)

'A free... thinking magazine about positive change for the West Country.' Features on health, fitness, the environment, social and community issues. Welcomes ideas for features and articles. Send A4 envelope for writers' guidelines. Length: varies. Illustrations: colour cover. Payment: £6.50 per 100 words. Founded 1993.

The Spectator

56 Doughty Street, London WC1N 2LL
tel 020-7405 1706 *fax* 020-7242-0603
Editor Boris Johnson, *Publisher* Kimberly Fortier
Weekly £2.40

Articles on current affairs, politics, the arts; book reviews. Illustrations: colour and b&w, cartoons. Payment: on merit. Founded 1828.

Sport First

20-26 Brunswick Place, London N1 0DZ
tel 020-7490 7575 *fax* 020-7490 7666
email editorial@sportfirst.com
website www.sportfirst.com
Editor James Eastham
Weekly £1

Tabloid Sunday newspaper covering all sports. Length: 800 words (articles), 300–800 words (news). No unsolicited contributions. Payment: £100 per 1000 words. Founded 1998.

Springboard

144 Alexandra Road, Great Watering, Essex SS3 0GW
tel (01702) 216247
email slieberman@tinyonline.co.uk
Editor Sandra Lieberman
Quarterly £8 p.a.

Articles on writing, competition news, markets. Winning articles, stories and poems from internal competitions – £45 prize money each quarter. Includes copy of *The Curate's Egg*, poetry submissions for which contributors receive free copy. Founded 1990.

The Squash Player

460 Bath Road, Longford, Middlesex UB7 0EB
tel (01753) 775511 *fax* (01753) 775512
email editor@squashplayer.co.uk
Editor Ian McKenzie
10 p.a. £40 p.a.

Covers all aspects of playing squash. All features are commissioned – discuss ideas with editor. Length: 1000–1500 words. Illustrations: unusual photos (e.g. celebrities), cartoons. Payment: £75 per 1000 words; £25–£40 for illustrations. Founded 1971.

Staffordshire Life Magazine

Staffordshire Newsletter Ltd, The Publishing Centre, Derby Street, Stafford ST16 2DT
tel (01785) 257700 *fax* (01785) 253287
email editor@staffordshirelife.co.uk
Editor Philip Thurlow-Craig
11 p.a. £1.50

County magazine for Staffordshire. Historical articles; features on county personalities. No short stories. Contact the editor in first instance. Length: 500–800 words. Illustrations: colour transparencies and prints. Founded 1948; relaunched 1980.

The Stage

(incorporating Television Today)
Stage House, 47 Bermondsey Street, London SE1 3XT
tel 020-7403 1818 *fax* 020-7357 9287
email editor@thestage.co.uk
website www.thestage.co.uk
Editor Brian Attwood
Weekly £1

Original and interesting articles on professional stage and broadcasting topics may be sent for the editor's consideration. Length: 500–800 words. Payment: £100 per 1000 words. Founded 1880.

Stamp Lover

National Philatelic Society, British Philatelic Centre, 107 Charterhouse Street, London EC1M 6PT
tel 020-7336 0882
email nps@philately.org.uk
Editor Michael Furnell
6 p.a. £2

Original articles on stamps and postal history. Illustrations: line, half-tone. Payment: by arrangement. Founded 1908.

Stamp Magazine

IPC Media Ltd, Focus Network, 9 Dingwall Avenue, Croydon CR9 2TA
tel 020-8774 0772 *fax* 020-8774 0939
Editor Steve Fairclough
Monthly £2.40

Informative articles and exclusive news items on stamp collecting and postal history. No preliminary letter. Payment: by arrangement. Illustrations: line, half-tone, colour. Founded 1934.

Stand Magazine

School of English, University of Leeds, Leeds LS2 9JT
tel 0113-233 4794 *fax* 0113-233 4791
email stand@leeds.ac.uk
website http://saturn.vcu.edu/~dlatane/stand.html
Managing Editor Jon Glover
Quarterly £6.50 plus p&p (£25 p.a.)

Poetry, short stories, translations, literary criticism. Send sae/IRCs for return. Payment: £50 per 1000 words (prose); £40 per poem. Founded 1952.

Staple

35 Carr Road, Walkley, Sheffield S6 2WY
Editors Ann Atkinson, Elizabeth Barrett
3 p.a. £10 p.a. (£15 p.a. overseas)

Poetry, short fiction, articles. Payment: £5 per poem, £10 fiction/articles. Founded 1982.

Starburst

Visual Imagination Ltd, 9 Blades Court, Deodar Road, London SW15 2NU
tel 020-8875 1520 *fax* 020-8875 1588
email starburst@vismag.com
website www.wisimag.com
Editor Andrew Cartmel
Monthly plus 4 specials p.a. £3.25

Features and interviews on all aspects of science fiction. Length: 2000 words. Illustrations: colour and b&w photos. Payment: £80 per 1000 words; £10–20 per image. Founded 1977.

Studies, An Irish quarterly review

35 Lower Leeson Street, Dublin 2, Republic of Ireland
tel (01) 6766785 *fax* (01) 6762984
email studies@s-j.ie
website www.studiesirishreview.com
Editor Rev. Fergus O'Donoghue SJ
Quarterly E6.35

General review of social comment, literature, history, the arts. Articles written by specialists for the general reader. Critical book reviews. Preliminary letter. Length: 3500 words. Founded 1912.

Studio Sound

Miller Freeman Entertainment Ltd, 8 Montague Close, London SE1 9UR
tel 020-7940 8500 *fax* 020-7407 7102
Editor Tim Goodyer
Monthly £5

Articles on all aspects of professional sound recording. Technical and operational features on the functional aspects of sound recording, AV postproduction and broadcast; general features on studio affairs. Length: widely variable. Payment: by arrangement. Illustrations: line, half-tone, colour. Founded 1959.

Suffolk Norfolk Life

Today Magazines Ltd, Barn Acre House, Saxtead Green, Woodbridge, Suffolk IP13 9QJ
tel (01728) 685 832 *fax* (01728) 685 842
email todaymagazines@btopenworld.com
website www.today-magazines.com
Editor William Locks
Monthly £1.25

Articles relevant to Suffolk and Norfolk – current topics plus historical items, art, leisure, etc. Considers unsolicited material and welcomes ideas for articles and features. Length: 900–1000 words. Illustrations: transparencies, colour and b&w prints, b&w artwork and cartoons. Payment: £25–£40 per article. Founded 1980.

Sugar

Attic Futura (UK) Ltd, 17-18 Berners Street, London W1T 3LN
tel 020-7664 6400 *fax* 020-7070 3409
Editor Jennifer Stringer
Monthly £2

Magazine for young women aged 13–17. Fashion, beauty, entertainment, features. Interested in real-life stories (1200 words), quizzes. Payment: by arrangement. Opportunities for freelance writers, illustrators and designers. Founded 1994.

Sunday Express 'S' Magazine – see Sunday Express in National newspapers UK, page 3

Sunday Magazine – see News of the World in National newspapers UK and Ireland, page 3

Sunday People Magazine – see Sunday People in National newspapers UK and Ireland, page 3

The Sunday Post Magazine – see Sunday Post in National newspapers UK and Ireland, page 3

The Sunday Review – see Independent on Sunday in National newspapers UK and Ireland, page 3

Sunday Telegraph Magazine Sunday Telegraph in National newspapers UK and Ireland, page 3

The Sunday Times Magazine – see The Sunday Times in National newspapers UK and Ireland, page 3

Swimming Magazine

(formerly Swimming Times)
Swimming Times Ltd, Harold Fern House, Derby Square, Loughborough LE11 5AL
tel (01509) 618766 *fax* (01509) 618768
Editor Peter Hassall
Monthly £1.80, £20 p.a.

Official journal of the Amateur Swimming Association and the Institute of Swimming Teachers and Coaches. Reports of major events and championships; news and features on all aspects of swimming including synchronised swimming, diving and water polo, etc; accompanying photos where appropriate; short fiction with a swimming theme. Unsolicited material welcome. Length: 800–1500 words. Payment: by arrangement. Founded 1923.

The Tablet

1 King Street Cloisters, Clifton Walk, London W6 0QZ
tel 020-8748 8484 *fax* 020-8748 1550
email thetablet@thetablet.co.uk
website www.thetablet.co.uk/
Editor John Wilkins
Weekly £1.55

The senior Catholic weekly. Religion, philosophy, politics, society, books and arts. International coverage. Freelance work welcomed. Length: 1500 words. Illustrations: cartoons. Payment: by arrangement. Founded 1840.

Take a Break

H. Bauer Publishing Ltd, Academic House, 24-28 Oval Road, London NW1 7DT
tel 020-7241 8000 *fax* 020-7241 8052
Editor John Dale
Weekly 68p

Lively, tabloid women's weekly. True life features, celebrities, health and beauty, family, travel; short stories (up to 1500 words); lots of puzzles. Payment: by arrangement. Illustrated. Founded 1990.

Take a Break's Take a Puzzle

H. Bauer Publishing, Academic House, 24-28 Oval Road, London NW1 7DT
tel 020-7241 8229 *fax* 020-7241 8009
email take.puzzle@bauer.co.uk
Editor Rachel Plumridge
Monthly £1.55

Puzzles. Fresh ideas always welcome. Illustrations: colour transparencies and b&w prints and artwork. Work supplied on Mac-compatible disk preferred. Payment: from £25 per puzzle, £30–£90 for picture puzzles and for illustrations not an integral part of a puzzle. Founded 1991.

tate: the art magazine

Vogue House, Hanover Square, London W1S 1JU
tel 020-7499 9080 *fax* 020-7460 6406
Editor Robert Violette
Bi-monthly £4

Independent visual arts magazine: features, news, interviews, reviews, previews and opinion pieces. Length: up to 3000 words but always commissioned. Illustrations: colour and b&w photos. Payment: negotiable. Founded 1993; relaunched 2002.

Tatler

Vogue House, Hanover Square, London W1S 1JU
tel 020-7499 9080 *fax* 020-7409 0451
website www.tatler.co.uk
Editor Geordie Greig
Monthly £3.30

Smart society magazine favouring sharp articles, profiles, fashion and the arts. Illustrations: colour, b&w, but all commissioned. Founded 1709.

The Teacher

National Union of Teachers, Hamilton House, Mabledon Place, London WC1H 9BD
tel 020-7380 4708 *fax* 020-7387 8458
Editor Mitch Howard
8 p.a. Free to NUT members

Articles, features and news of interest to all those involved in the teaching profession. Length: 750 words. Payment: NUJ rates to NUJ members. Founded 1872.

Technology Ireland

Enterprise Ireland, Strand Road, Dublin 4, Republic of Ireland
tel (01) 206 6337 *fax* (01) 206 6342
Editor Tom Kennedy
Monthly IR£33 p.a. (IR£38 p.a. overseas)

Articles, features, reviews, news on current business, innovation and technology. Length: 1500–2000 words. Illustrations: line, half-tone, colour. Payment: varies. Founded 1969.

Telegraph Magazine – see The Daily Telegraph in National newspapers UK and Ireland, page 3

Television

Reed Business Information Ltd, Quadrant House, The Quadrant, Sutton, Surrey SM2 5AS
tel 020-8652 8120 *fax* 020-8652 8956
Monthly £2.80

Articles on the technical aspects of domestic TV and video equipment, especially servicing, long-distance TV, constructional projects, satellite TV, video recording, teletext and viewdata, test equipment, monitors. Payment: by arrangement. Illustrations: photos and line drawings for litho. Founded 1950.

Tempo

Boosey & Hawkes, Music Publishers Ltd, 295 Regent Street, London W1B 2JH
tel 020 7580 2060 *fax* 020-7436 5675
email tempo2@boosey.com
website www.temporeview.com
Editor Calum MacDonald
Quarterly £4 (£19.50 p.a.)

Authoritative articles on contemporary music. Length: 2000–4000 words. Payment: by arrangement. Illustrations: music type, occasional photographic or musical supplements.

Tennis World

Market Link Publishing plc, The Mill, Bearwalden Business Park, Wendens Ambo, Saffron Walden
tel (01799) 544200 *fax* (01799) 544201
Editor Alastair McIver
Monthly £2.50

Tournament reports, topical features, personality profiles, instructional articles. Length: 600–1500 words. Payment: by arrangement. Illustrations: line, half-tone, colour.

TES Primary

TSL Education Ltd, Admiral House, 66-68 East Smithfield, London E1W 1BX
tel 020-7782 3000 *fax* 020-7782 3200
email primary@tes.co.uk
website www.tesprimary.com
Editor Diane Hofkins
Monthly £2.50

Inspirational, practical and informative magazine for primary teachers, with pull-out posters in each issue. Seeks original ideas for teaching, and subject-based features on science, history, art, etc. Considers unsolicited material. Length: 500–1500 words (articles/features). Payment: £75–£350. Founded 2000.

TGO (The Great Outdoors) Magazine

SMG Magazines Ltd, 200 Renfield Street, Glasgow G2 3PR
tel 0141-302 7700 *fax* 0141-302 7799
email tgo@calmags.co.uk (editorial)
Editor Cameron McNeish
Monthly £2.60

Articles on walking or lightweight camping in specific areas, preferably illustrated. Length: 1200–1800 words. Payment: by arrangement. Illustrations: colour. Founded 1978.

that's life!

H. Bauer Publishing Ltd, Academic House, 24-28 Oval Road, London NW1 7DT
tel 020-7241 8000 *fax* 020-7241 8008
Editor Christabel Smith
Weekly 57p

Dramatic true life stories about women. Length: average 1000 words. Illustrations: colour photos and cartoons. Payment: £650. Founded 1995.

Therapy Weekly

EMAP Healthcare Ltd, Greater London House, Hampstead Road, London NW1 7EJ
tel 020-7874 0360 *fax* 020-7874 0368
Editor Melissa Oliveck
Weekly Free to NHS and local authority therapists (£47.50 p.a.)

Articles of interest to chartered physiotherapists, occupational therapists and speech and language therapists. Guidelines to contributors available. Send proposals only initially. Length: up to 1000 words. Illustrations: colour and b&w photos, line, cartoons. Payment: by arrangement. Founded 1974 as *Therapy*.

The Third Alternative

TTA Press, 5 Martins Lane, Witcham, Ely, Cambs. CB6 2LB
tel (01353) 777931
email ttapress@aol.com
website www.ttapress.com
Editor Andy Cox
Bi-monthly £3.75 (£21 for 6 issues)

Extraordinary new fiction: science fiction, fantasy, horror, slipstream. Also interviews with, and profiles of, authors and film-makers. Send sae with all submissions. Considers unsolicited material and welcomes ideas for articles and features. Length: 3000–4000 words (articles and features), short stories unrestricted. Illustrations: send samples and portfolios. Payment: £30 per 1000 words. Founded 1994.

Third Way

St Peter's, Sumner Road, Harrow, Middlesex HA1 4BX
tel 020-8423 8494 *fax* 020-8423 5367
email editor@thirdway.org.uk
10 p.a. £2.90

Aims to present biblical perspectives on the political, social and cultural issues of the day. Payment: by arrangement on publication. Founded 1977.

This Caring Business

1 St Thomas' Road, Hastings, East Sussex TN34 3LG
tel (01424) 718406 *fax* (01424) 718460
email vivshep@aol.com
Editor Michael J. Monk
Monthly £50 p.a.

Specialist contributions relating to the commercial aspects of nursing and residential care, including hospitals. Payment: £100 per 1000 words. Illustrations: line, half-tone. Founded 1985.

This England

PO Box 52, Cheltenham, Glos. GL50 1YQ
tel (01242) 537900
Editor Roy Faiers
Quarterly £3.75

Articles on towns, villages, traditions, customs, legends, crafts of England; stories of people. Length: 250–2000 words. Payment: £25 per page and pro rata. Illustrations: line, half-tone, colour. Founded 1968.

Time Out

Time Out Group Ltd, Universal House, 251 Tottenham Court Road, London W1T 7AB
tel 020-7813 3000 *fax* 020-7813 6001
website www.timeout.com
Editor Laura Lee Davies
Weekly £2.20

Listings magazine for London covering all areas of the arts, plus articles of consumer and news interest. Illustrations: colour and b&w. Payment by negotiation. Founded 1968.

The Times Educational Supplement

Admiral House, 66-68 East Smithfield, London E1W 1BX
tel 020-7782 3000 *fax* 020-7782 3202 (news), 020-7782 3919 (features)
email friday@tes.co.uk (feature outlines), teacher@tes.co.uk (curriculum-related outlines)
website www.tes.co.uk
Editor Bob Doe
Weekly £1.20

Articles on education written with special knowledge or experience; news items; books, arts and equipment reviews. Advisable to check with news or picture editor before submitting. Outlines of feature ideas should be faxed or emailed. Illustrations: suitable photos and drawings of educational interest, cartoons. Payment: standard rates, or by arrangement.

Times Educational Supplement Scotland

Scott House, 10 South St Andrew Street, Edinburgh EH2 2AZ
tel 0131-557 1133 *fax* 0131-558 1155
Editor Neil Munro
Weekly £1.20

Articles on education, preferably 800–1000 words, written with special knowledge or experience. News items about Scottish educational affairs. Illustrations: line, half-tone. Payment: by arrangement. Founded 1965.

Times Higher Education Supplement

Admiral House, 66-68 East Smithfield, London E1W 1BX
tel 020-7782 3000 *fax* 020-7782 3300
Editor John O'Leary
Weekly £1.20

Articles on higher education written with special knowledge or experience, or articles dealing with academic topics. Also news items. Illustrations: suitable photos and drawings of educational interest. Payment: by arrangement. Founded 1971.

The Times Literary Supplement

Admiral House, 66-68 East Smithfield, London E1W 1BX
tel 020-7782 3000 *fax* 020-7782 3100
Editor Peter Stothard
Weekly £2.40

Will consider poems for publication, literary discoveries and articles, particularly of an opinionated kind, on literary and cultural affairs. Payment: by arrangement.

The Times Magazine – see The Times in National newspapers UK and Ireland, page 3

Today's Fishkeeper

(formerly The Aquarist and Pondkeeper)
TRMG Ltd, 1 Forum Place, Winchester Court, Hatfield, Herts. AL10 0RN
tel (01707) 273999 *fax* (01707) 276555
Editor Derek Lambert
Monthly £2.75

Illustrated authoritative articles by professional and amateur biologists, naturalists and aquarium hobbyists on all matters concerning life in and near water, conservation and herpetology. Length: about 1000 words. Illustrations: line, half-tone, colour, cartoons. Payment: by arrangement. Founded 1924.

Today's Pilot

Key Publishing Ltd, PO Box 100, Stamford, Lincs. PE9 1XQ
tel (01780) 755131 *fax* (01780) 757261
email dave.unwin@keypublishing.com
website www.todayspilot.co.uk
Editor Dave Unwin
Monthly £2.95

General aviation magazine providing information and inspiration for the recreational aviator. Considers unsolicited material. Length: 3000 words (articles/features), 1000 words (news). Illustrations: colour. Payment: negotiable (words); £20 per image. Founded 2000.

Today's Golfer

EMAP Active Ltd, Bushfield House, Orton Centre, Peterborough PE2 5UW
tel (01733) 237111 *fax* (01733) 288014
Editor Paul Hamblin
Monthly £3.10

Specialist features and articles on golf instruction, equipment and courses. Founded 1988.

Top of the Pops – see page 294

Top Santé Health & Beauty

Emap Elán, Endeavour House, 189 Shaftesbury Avenue, London WC2H 8JG
tel 020-7437 9011 *fax* 020-7208 3514
Editor Juliette Kellow
Monthly £2

Articles, features and news on all aspects of health and beauty. Ideas welcome. Length: 1–2 pages. Illustrations: colour photos and drawings. Payment: £200 per 1000 words; illustrations by arrangement. Founded 1993.

Total Film

99 Baker Street, London W1U 6FP
tel 020-7317 2600 *fax* 020-7317 0275
email totalfilm@futurenet.co.uk
Editor Matt Mueller
Monthly £3

Movie magazine covering all aspects of film. Email ideas before submitting material. Not seeking interviews or reviews. Length: 400 words (news items); 1000 words (funny features). Payment: £150 per 1000 words; free–£1500 per picture. Founded 1996.

Trail

(formerly Trail Walker)
Emap Active Ltd, Bretton Court, Bretton, Peterborough PE3 8DZ
tel (01733) 264666 *fax* (01733) 282653
email trail@emap.com
Editor Edward Kenyon
Monthly £2.95

Outdoor activity magazine focusing mainly on high level walking with some scrambling, moutain biking and climbing. Send sae for guidelines for overseas features and This Weekend routes. Send features to Features Editor. Illustrations: colour and b&w. Payment: negotiable.

Traveller

Wexas Ltd, 45 Brompton Road, London SW3 1DE
tel 020-7589 0500 *fax* 020-7581 1357
email traveller@wexas.com
website www.traveller.org.uk
Editor Jonathan Lorie
Quarterly Free to UK travel club members; back numbers £2.50 (£3 overseas), payable to Wexas

Serious travel writing. Narrative features describe personal journeys to remarkable places (mainly non-Western). Unsolicited material considered if prose and pictures are excellent. See website for guidelines. Length: 1600–2000 words. Illustrations: transparencies only. Payment: £150 per 1000 words; colour £35 (£100 cover). Founded 1970.

Tribune

9 Arkwright Road, London NW3 6AN
tel 020-7433 6410
Editor Mark Seddon, *Reviews Editor* Caroline Rees
Weekly £1.25

Political, literary, with Socialist outlook. Informative articles (about 700 words), news stories (250–300 words). No unsolicited reviews or fiction. Payment: by arrangement. Illustrations: cartoons, photos.

Trout and Salmon

EMAP Active Ltd, Bushfield House, Orton Centre, Peterborough PE2 5UW
tel (01733) 237111 *fax* (01733) 465820
email sandy.leventon@emap.com
Editor Sandy Leventon
Monthly £2.80

Articles of good quality with strong trout or salmon angling interest. Length: 400–2000 words, accompanied if possible by colour transparencies or good-quality colour prints. Payment: by arrangement. Illustrations: line, colour transparencies and prints, cartoons. Founded 1955.

Truck & Driver

Reed Business Information, Quadrant House, The Quadrant, Sutton, Surrey SM2 5AS
tel 020-7652 3682 *fax* 020-7652 8988
Editor Dave Young
Monthly £2.10

News, articles on trucks, personalities and features of interest to truck drivers. Words (on disk or electronically) and picture packages preferred. Length: approx. 2000 words. Illustrations: colour transparencies and artwork, cartoons. Payment: negotiable. Founded 1984.

Trucking

A & S Publishing, Messenger House, 35 St Michael's Square, Gloucester GL1 1HX
tel (01452) 317750 *fax* (01452) 415817
Editor Richard Simpson
Monthly £2.20

For truck drivers, owner-drivers and operators: news, articles, features and technical advice. Length: 750–2500 words. Illustrations: mostly 35 mm colour transparencies. Payment: by negotiation. Founded 1983.

TV Quick

H. Bauer Publishing Ltd, Academic House, 24-28 Oval Road, London NW1 7DT
tel 020-7241 8000 *fax* 020-7241 8066
Editor Lori Miles
Weekly 65p

TV listings magazine featuring TV-related material. Payment: by arrangement. Founded 1991.

TVTimes Magazine

IPC Media Ltd, 10th Floor, King's Reach Tower, Stamford Street, London SE1 9LS
tel 020-7261 7000 *fax* 020-7261 7777
Editor Mike Hollingsworth
Weekly 72p

Features with an affinity to ITV, BBC1, BBC2, Channels 4 and 5, satellite and radio personalities and TV generally. Length: by arrangement. Photographs: commissioned only. Payment: by arrangement.

U magazine

Smurfit Communications, 2 Clanwilliam Court, Lower Mount Street, Dublin 2, Republic of Ireland
tel (01) 240 5300 *fax* (01) 661 9757
email letters@umagazine.ie
Editor Fionnuala McCarthy
Monthly E3.43

Fashion and beauty magazine for 18–25 year-old Irish women, with celebrity interviews, talent profiles, real-life stories, sex and relationship features, plus regular pages on the club scene, movies, music and film. Also travel, interiors, health, food, horoscopes. Material mostly commissioned. Payment: varies. Founded 1978.

Ulster Grocer

Greer Publications, 5B Edgewater Business Park, Belfast Harbour Estate, Belfast BT3 9JQ
tel 028-9078 3200 *fax* 028-9078 3210
email kathyj@writenow.prestel.co.uk
Editor Kathy Jensen
Monthly Controlled circulation

Topical features (1000–1500 words) on food/grocery retailing and exhibitions; news (200 words) with a Northern Ireland basis. All features commissioned; no speculative articles accepted. Illustrations: colour photos. Payment: features £275, product news £160. Founded 1972.

Under Five Contact

Pre-school Learning Alliance, 69 Kings Cross Road, London WC1X 9LL
tel 020-7833 0991 *fax* 020-7837 4942
email pla@pre-school.org.uk
Editor Ann Henderson
10 p.a. £30 p.a.

Articles on the role of adults – especially parents/preschool workers – in young children's learning and development, including children from all cultures and those with special needs. Length: 1000 words. Payment: £75 per article. Founded 1962.

The Universe

1st Floor, St James's Buildings, Oxford Street, Manchester M1 6FP
tel 0161-236 8856 *fax* 0161-236 8530
Editor Joe Kelly
Weekly 50p

Catholic Sunday newspaper. News stories, features and photos on all aspects of Catholic life required; also cartoons. MSS should not be submitted without sae. Payment: by arrangement. Founded 1860.

Vanity Fair

The Condé Nast Publications Ltd, Vogue House, Hanover Square, London W1S 1JU
tel 020-7499 9080 *fax* 020-7493 1962
website www.vanityfair.co.uk
London Editor Henry Porter
tel 020-7221 6228 *fax* 020-7221 6269
Monthly £2.80

Media, glamour and politics for grown-up readers. No unsolicited material. Payment: by arrangement. Illustrated.

The Vegan

The Vegan Society, Donald Watson House, 7 Battle Road, St Leonards-on-Sea, East Sussex TN37 7AA
tel (01424) 427393 *fax* (01424) 717064
email editor@vegansociety.com
website www.vegansociety.com
Editor Rick Savage
Quarterly £2.50

Articles on health, nutrition, cookery, vegan lifestyle, land use, animal rights. Length: approx. 1000 words. Payment: by arrangement. Illustrations: photos, cartoons, line drawings – foods, animals, livestock systems, crops, people, events; colour for cover. Founded 1944.

Venue

Ventrogreen Ltd, 64-65 North Road, Bristol BS6 5AQ
tel 0117-942 8491 *fax* 0117-942 0369
email editor@venue.co.uk
website www.venue.co.uk
Editor Nigel Tassell
Fortnightly £1.90

Listings magazine for Bristol and Bath combining comprehensive entertainment information with local features, profiles and interviews. Length: by agreement. Illustrations: colour. Payment: £8.50 per 100 words. Founded 1982.

Veterinary Review

John C. Alborough Ltd, Lion Lane, Needham Market, Suffolk IP6 8NT
tel (01449) 723800 *fax* (01449) 723801
email enquiries@jca.uk.com
Editor Anna Cooper
Monthly £60 p.a.

News, articles – both topical and general – and product listings for veterinarians. Payment: negotiable.

Animal Health News

Editor Rachael Porter
Bi-monthly £30 p.a.

News, articles and product listings for the agricultural supply trade.

Viz Comic

PO Box 1PT, Newcastle upon Tyne NE99 1PT
fax 0191-241 4244
email viz.comic@virgin.net
website www.viz.co.uk
Contact Editorial Cabinet
10 p.a. £1.85

Cartoons, spoof tabloid articles, spoof advertisements. Illustrations: half-tone, line, cartoons. Payment: £300 per page (cartoons). Founded 1979.

Vogue

Vogue House, Hanover Square, London W1S 1JU
tel 020-7499 9080 *fax* 020-7408 0559
website www.vogue.co.uk
Editor Alexandra Shulman
Monthly £3.20

Fashion, beauty, health, decorating, art, theatre, films, literature, music, travel, food and wine. Length: articles from 1000 words. Illustrated.

The Voice

Blue Star House, 234-244 Stockwell Road, London SW9 9SP
tel 020-7737 7377 *fax* 020-7274 8994
email newsdesk@the-voice.co.uk
Editor-in-Chief Mike Best
Weekly 75p

News, general and arts features of interest to black readers. Illustrations:

colour and b&w photos. Founded 1982.

woman2woman

Last Mon of each month

Supplement addressing the needs and aspirations of young Black Britons with a focus on a female readership.

Wanderlust

PO Box 1832, Windsor SL4 1YT
tel (01753) 620426
website www.wanderlust.co.uk
Editor Lyn Hughes
Bi-monthly £3.50

Features on independent, adventure and special-interest travel. Send sae or visit website for 'Guidelines for contributors'. Length: up to 2500 words. Illustrations: high-quality colour slides (send stocklist first). Payment: by arrangement. Founded 1993.

The War Cry

The Salvation Army, 101 Newington Causeway, London SE1 6BN
tel 020-7367 4900 *fax* 020-7367 4710
email warcry@salvationarmy.org.uk
website www.salvationarmy.org/warcry
Editor Major Nigel Bovey
Weekly 20p (£26 p.a.)

Voluntary contributions: Christian comment on contemporary issues, human interest stories of personal Christian faith; puzzles. Illustrations: line and photos, cartoons. Founded 1879.

Waterways World

Waterways World Ltd, The Well House, High Street, Burton-on-Trent, Staffs. DE14 1JQ
tel (01283) 742951 *fax* (01283) 742957
email wwedit@the-wellhouse.com
Editor Hugh Potter
Monthly £2.60

Feature articles on all aspects of inland waterways in Britain and abroad, including historical material; factual and technical articles preferred. No short stories or poetry. Send sae for 'Notes for WW Contributors'. Payment: £40 per 1000 words. Illustrations: colour transparencies or prints, line. Founded 1972.

Wedding and Home

IPC Magazines Ltd, King's Reach Tower, Stamford Street, London SE1 9LS
tel 020-7261 7471 *fax* 020-7261 7459
email weddingandhome@ipcmedia.com
Editor tba, *Deputy Editor* Helen Salmon
Bi-monthly £3.95

Ideas and inspiration for modern brides. Fashion and beauty, information for grooms, real life weddings, planning advice, gift list ideas and honeymoon features. Unsolicited features not accepted. Founded 1985.

Weekend – see The Guardian in National newspapers UK and Ireland, page 3

The Weekly News

D.C. Thomson & Co. Ltd, Albert Square, Dundee DD1 9QJ
tel (01382) 223131
137 Chapel Street, Manchester M3 6AA
tel 0161-834 5122
144 Port Dundas Road, Glasgow G4 0HZ
tel 0141-332 9933
185 Fleet Street, London EC4A 2HS
tel 020-7400 1030
Send material to Rod Cameron, Deputy Editor
Weekly 50p

Real-life dramas of around 1200 words told in the first person. Non-fiction series with lively themes or about interesting people. Keynote throughout is strong human interest. Joke sketches. Illustrations: cartoons. Payment: on acceptance.

Weight Watchers Magazine

Bloomsbury House Ltd, 1 Cecil Court, 49-55 London Road, Enfield, Middlesex EN2 6DN
tel 020-8342 2222 *fax* 020-8342 2223
8 p.a. £1.95

Features: health, beauty, news, astrology; food-orientated articles; success stories. All material commissioned. Length: ½–3 pages. Illustrations: colour photos and cartoons. Payment: by arrangement.

West Lothian Life

Ballencrieff Cottage, Ballencrieff Toll, Bathgate, West Lothian EH48 4LD
tel (01506) 632728 *fax* (01506) 635444
email wll@pages.clara.net
website http://home.clara.net/pages
Editor Susan Coon
Quarterly £2

Articles, profiles etc with a West Lothian angle. Length: 800–3000 words. Illustrations: colour and b&w photos, b&w artwork and cartoons. Payment: £20 per 1000 words. Founded 1995.

What Camcorder

(formerly Video Camera)
Highbury WViP, 53-79 Highgate Road, London NW5 1TW

tel 020-7331 1000 *fax* 020-7331 1242
email jake.williams@wvip.co.uk
Editor Jake Williams
Monthly £3.25

Technique articles aimed at the beginner on how to use camcorders and equipment tests of camcorders and accessories. Material mostly commissioned. Length: 1000–1800 words. Illustrations: colour photos, diagrams. Payment: £95 per 1000 words; £70 per page for illustrations. Founded 2000.

What Car?

Haymarket Motoring Magazines Ltd, 60 Waldegrave Road, Teddington, Middlesex TW11 8LG
tel 020-8267 5688 *fax* 020-8267 5750
Editor Rob Aherne
Monthly £3.60

Road tests, buying guide, consumer stories and used car features. No unsolicited material. Illustrations: colour and b&w photos, line drawings. Payment: by negotiation. Founded 1973.

What Laptop & Handheld PC

Crimson Publishing, 14 Northfields, London SW18 1UU
tel 020-8875 5600 *fax* 020-8875 5601
email letters@whatlaptop.co.uk
website www.whatlaptop.co.uk
Editor Ian Delaney
Monthly £2.99

Non-technical news, reviews and help for anyone who wants to buy or has bought a portable computer. Discuss ideas for features with Editor in first instance; welcomes ideas for features. Length: up to 1600 words. Payment: by arrangement. Founded 1999.

What's on TV

IPC Media Ltd, 10th Floor, King's Reach Tower, Stamford Street, London SE1 0LS
tel 020-7261 7769 *fax* 020-7261 7739
Editor Colin Tough
Weekly 40p

Features on TV programmes and personalities. All material commissioned. Length: up to 500 words. Illustrations: colour and b&w photos, cartoons. Payment: by agreement. Founded 1991.

Wine

Quest Magazines Ltd, Wilmington Publishing, 6-8 Underwood Street, London N1 7JQ
tel 020-7549 2572 *fax* 020-7549 8622
email wine@wilmington.co.uk
Editor Chris Losh
12 p.a. £3.30

Articles, features and news on new developments in wine and spirits; travelogues, tastings and profiles. Illustrations: colour. Payment: £180 per 1000 words. Founded 1983.

Wisden Cricket Monthly

The New Boathouse, 136-142 Bramley Road, London W10 6SR
tel 020-7565 3000 *fax* 020-7565 3090
email wcm@wisden.com
website www.wisden.com
Editor Stephen Fay
Monthly £3.25

Cricket articles of exceptional interest (unsolicited pieces seldom used). Length: up to 3000 words. Payment: by arrangement. Illustrations: half-tone, colour. Founded 1979.

Woman

IPC Magazines Ltd, King's Reach Tower, Stamford Street, London SE1 9LS
tel 020-7261 5000 *fax* 020-7261 5997
Editor Carole Russell
Weekly 68p

Human interest stories and practical articles of varying length on all subjects of interest to women. Payment: by arrangement. Illustrations: colour transparencies and photos. Founded 1937.

Woman Alive

(formerly Christian Woman)
Christian Media Centre Ltd, Garcia Estate, Canterbury Road, Worthing, West Sussex BN13 1EH
tel (01903) 821082 *fax* (01903) 821081
email womanalive@christianmedia.org.uk
Editor Elizabeth Trundle
Monthly £2

Aimed at women aged 25 upwards. Celebrity interviews, topical features, Christian issues, 'Day in the life of' profiles of women in interesting occupations, Christian testimonies, fashion, beauty, health, crafts. Unsolicited material should include colour slides or photos. Length: 'Day in the life of'/testimonies 750 words, interviews/features 1300 words. Payment: £72 per 1000 words published. Founded 1982.

Woman and Home

(incorporating Living)
IPC Magazines Ltd, King's Reach Tower, Stamford Street, London SE1 9LS
tel 020-7261 5000 *fax* 020-7261 7346

Acting Editor Sarah Kilby
Monthly £1.90

Centres on the personal and home interests of the lively minded mature, modern woman. Articles dealing with fashion, beauty, leisure pursuits, gardening, home style; features on topical issues, people and places. Fiction: complete stories from 3000–4500 words in length. Illustrations: commissioned colour photos and sketches. Please note: non-commissioned work is rarely accepted and regrettably cannot be returned. Founded 1926.

The Woman Writer

Enquiries to Zoe King, The Secretary, SWWJ, Calvers Farm, Thelverton, Diss, Norfolk IP21 4NG
email zoe@zoeking.com
website www.swwj.co.uk
Editor tba
3 p.a. Free to members

Periodical of the Society of Women Writers and Journalists. See under Societies section for further information. Founded 1894.

Woman's Weekly Fiction Special

IPC Media Ltd, King's Reach, Stamford Street, London SE1 9LS
tel (0870) 4445000 *fax* 020-7261 6322
Editor Olwen Rice
Bi-monthly £1.30

25 stories each issue of 1000–8000 words of varied emotional interest, including romance, humour and mystery. Payment: by arrangement. Illustrations: full colour. Founded 1998.

Woman's Own

IPC Connect Ltd, King's Reach Tower, Stamford Street, London SE1 9LS
tel 020-7261 5000
Editor Elsa McAlonan
Weekly 66p

Modern women's magazine aimed at the 20–35 age group. No unsolicited features or fiction. Illustrations: colour and b&w: interior decorating and furnishing, fashion. Address work to relevant department editor. Payment: by arrangement.

Woman's Way

Smurfit Communications, 2 Clanwilliam Court, Lower Mount Street, Dublin 2, Republic of Ireland
tel (01) 240 5300 *fax* (01) 661 9757
email ltaylor@smurfit-comms.ie
Editor Lucy Taylor
Weekly E1.27

Human interest, personality interviews, features on fashion, beauty, celebrities and investigations, short stories. Length: 1800 words. Payment: approx. E65–E130. Founded 1963.

Woman's Weekly

IPC Media Ltd, King's Reach Tower, Stamford Street, London SE1 9LS
tel (0870) 4445000 *fax* 020-7261 6322
Editor Gilly Sinclair
Weekly 66p

Lively, family-interest magazine. One serial, averaging 4000 words each instalment, of strong emotional interest, and several short stories of 1000–2500 words of general interest. Celebrity and strong human interest features; also inspirational and entertaining personal stories. Payment: by arrangement. Illustrations: full colour fiction illustrations, small sketches and photos. Founded 1911.

Women's Health

WVIP, 53-79 Highgate Road, London NW5 1TW
tel 020-7331 1000 *fax* 020-7331 1108
email tracey.smith@wvip.co.uk
Editor Tracey Smith
Monthly £2.50

Lifestyle magazine for women covering a wide range of issues from fashion and fitness to health and beauty, including alternative therapies and food. Length: 1800–2000 words. Payment: by negotiation. Founded 1998.

The Woodworker

Nexus Special Interests Ltd, Nexus House, Azalea Drive, Swanley, Kent BR8 8HU
tel (01322) 660070
Editor Mark Ramuz
Monthly £2.65

For the craft and professional woodworker. Practical illustrated articles on cabinet work, carpentry, wood polishing, wood turning, wood carving, rural crafts, craft history, antique and period furniture; also wooden toys and models, musical instruments; timber procurement, conditioning, seasoning; tool, machinery and equipment reviews. Payment: by arrangement. Illustrations: line drawings and photos.

The Word

Divine Word Missionaries, 3 Pembroke Road, Dublin 4, Republic of Ireland
tel/fax (01) 6606646
email wordeditor@eircom.net

Editor Michael Cleere
Monthly E95 cents
General interest magazine with religious emphasis. Illustrated articles up to 2000 words and good picture features. Payment: by arrangement. Illustrations: photos and large colour transparencies. Founded 1936.

Workbox Magazine

Ebony Media Ltd, Heathlands Business Park, Heathlands Road, Liskeard, Cornwall PL14 4DH
tel (01579) 340100 *fax* (01579) 340200
email workbox@ebony.co.uk
website www.ebony.co.uk/workbox
Editor Victor Briggs
Bi-monthly £1.95
Features, of any length, on all aspects of needlecrafts. No 'how-to' articles. Send sae with enquiries and submissions. Illustrations: good colour transparencies. Payment: by agreement. Founded 1984.

World Fishing

Nexus Media Ltd, Nexus House, Azalea Drive, Swanley, Kent BR8 8HU
tel (01322) 660070 *fax* (01322) 616324
Editor Mark Say
Monthly £49 p.a.
International journal of commercial fishing. Technical and management emphasis on catching, processing and marketing of fish and related products; fishery operations and vessels covered worldwide. Length: 500–1500 words. Payment: by arrangement. Illustrations: photos and diagrams for litho reproduction. Founded 1952.

The World of Interiors

The Condé Nast Publications Ltd, Vogue House, Hanover Square, London W1S 1JU
tel 020-7499 9080 *fax* 020-7493 4013
email interiors@condenast.co.uk
website www.worldofinteriors.co.uk
Editor Rupert Thomas
Monthly £3.60
All material commissioned: send synopsis/visual reference for article ideas. Length: 1000–1500 words. Illustrations: colour photos. Payment: £500 per 1000 words; photos £125 per page. Founded 1981.

World Soccer

IPC Media Ltd, King's Reach Tower, Stamford Street, London SE1 9LS
tel 020-7261 5737 *fax* 020-7261 7474
Editor Gavin Hamilton
Monthly £2.70
Articles, features, news concerning football, its personalities and worldwide development. Length: 600–2000 words. Payment: by arrangement. Founded 1960.

The World Today

The Royal Institute of International Affairs, Chatham House, 10 St James's Square, London SW1Y 4LE
tel 020-7957 5712 *fax* 020-7957 5710
email wt@riia.org
website www.theworldtoday.org/wt.html
Editor Graham Walker, *Send material to* Michelle Mannion, Assistant Editor
Monthly £2.50
Analysis of international issues and current events by journalists, diplomats, politicians and academics. Length: 1400–2300 words. Payment: nominal. Founded 1945.

World's Children

Save the Children, 17 Grove Lane, London SE5 8RD
tel 020-7703 5400 *fax* 020-7708 2508
email publications@scfuk.org.uk
website www.savethechildren.org.uk
Contact Frances Ellery (Head of Publications)
Quarterly Sent free to regular donors
Magazine of Save the Children. Articles on child welfare and rights, related to Save the Children's work overseas and in the UK. No unsolicited features. Illustrations: colour and b&w photos. Founded 1920.

Writers' Forum

(incorporating World Wide Writers)
Writers' International Ltd, PO Box 3229, Bournemouth BH1 1ZS
website www.worldwidewriters.com
Publisher John Jenkins
10 p.a. £3 (£28 p.a., £40 Europe)
Welcomes articles on any aspect of the craft and business of writing. Length: 800–2000 words. Payment: by arrangement. Poetry and short story competitions in each issue. Founded 1993.

Writers' News

PO Box 168, Wellington Street, Leeds LS1 1RF
tel 0113-238 8333 *fax* 0113-238 8330
Editor Derek Hudson
Monthly £44.90 p.a. (£39.90 p.a. CC/DD)
News, competitions and articles on all aspects of writing. Length: 400–1500 words. Illustrations: line, half-tone. Payment: by arrangement. Founded 1989.

Writing Magazine

PO Box 168, Wellington Street, Leeds LS1 1RF
tel 0113-238 8333 *fax* 0113-238 8330
Editor Derek Hudson
Bi-monthly £3 (free to *Writers' News* subscribers)

Articles on all aspects of writing. Length: 400–1500 words. Illustrations: full colour, line, half-tone. Payment: by arrangement. Founded 1992.

Yachting Monthly

IPC Meida Ltd, King's Reach Tower, Stamford Street, London SE1 9LS
tel 020-7261 6040 *fax* 020-7261 7555
Editor Sarah Norbury
Monthly £3.40

Articles on all aspects of seamanship, navigation, the handling of sailing craft, and their design, construction and equipment. Well-written narrative accounts of cruises in yachts. Length: up to 2250 words (articles), up to 2500 words (narratives). Illustrations: colour transparencies and prints, cartoons. Payment: quoted on acceptance. Founded 1906.

Yachting World

IPC Media Ltd, King's Reach Tower, Stamford Street, London SE1 9LS
tel 020-7261 6800 *fax* 020-7261 6818
email yachting_world@ipc.media.com
website www.yachting-world.com
Editor Andrew Bray
Monthly £3.50

Practical articles of an original nature, dealing with sailing and boats. Length: 1500–2000 words. Payment: varies. Illustrations: colour transparencies, drawings, cartoons. Founded 1894.

Yachts and Yachting

196 Eastern Esplanade, Southend-on-Sea, Essex SS1 3AB
tel (01702) 582245 *fax* (01702) 588434
email editorial@yachtsandyachting.com
website www.yachtsandyachting.com
Editor Gael Pawson
Fortnightly £3.10

Short articles which should be technically correct. Payment: by arrangement. Illustrations: line, half-tone, colour. Founded 1947.

Yorkshire Ridings Magazine

33 Beverley Road, Driffield, Yorkshire YO25 6SD
tel/fax (01377) 253232
Editor Winston Halstead
Bi-monthly £1.40

Articles exclusively about people, life and character of the 3 Ridings of Yorkshire. Length: up to 1000 words. Payment: approx. £35–£40 per published page. Illustrations: colour, b&w photos; prints preferred. Founded 1964.

You – see Mail on Sunday in National newspapers UK and Ireland, page 3

You & Your Wedding

Nat Mag Specialist Media (AIM), Silver House, 31-35 Beak Street, London W1F 9DL
tel 020-7440 3838 *fax* 020-7734 5383
website www.youandyourwedding.co.uk
Editor Carole Hamilton
Bi-monthly £3.95

Articles, features and news covering all aspects of planning a wedding. Submit ideas in writing only. Illustrations: colour. Payment: £300 per 1000 words.

Young People Now

National Youth Agency, 17-23 Albion Street, Leicester LE1 6GD
tel 0116-285 3760 *fax* 0116-285 3775
email ypn@nya.org.uk
website www.nya.org.uk
Editor Tim Burke
Monthly £2 (£22.80 p.a.)

Informative articles, highlighting issues of concern to all those who work with young people, including youth workers, probation and social services, Connexions Service, teachers and volunteers. Guidelines for contributors available on request. Founded 1989.

Young Writer

Glebe House, Weobley, Herefordshire HR4 8SD
tel/fax (01544) 318901
email editor@youngwriter.org
website www.youngwriter.org
Editor Kate Jones
3 p.a. £2.75 (£7.50 for 3 issues)

Specialist magazine for young writers under 18 years: ideas for them and writing by them. Includes interviews with famous writers by children, fiction and non-fiction pieces, poetry; also explores words and grammar, issues related to writing (e.g. dyslexia), plus competitions with prizes. Length: 750 or 1500 words (features), up to 400 words (news), 750 words (short stories – unless specified otherwise in a competition), poetry of any length. Illustrations: colour – drawings by children, snapshots to accompany features. Payment: most children's material is published without payment; £25–£100 (features); £15 (cover cartoon). Founded 1995.

Your Cat Magazine

BPG (Stamford) Ltd, Roebuck House,
33 Broad Street, Stamford, Lincs. PE9 1RB
tel (01780) 766199 *fax* (01780) 766416
email suebpgroup@talk21.com
Editor Sue Parslow
Monthly £2.65

Practical advice on the care of cats and kittens, general interest items and news on cats, and true life tales and fiction. Length: 800–1500 (articles), 200–300 (news), up to 1000 (short stories). Illustrations: colour transparencies and prints. Payment: £80 per 1000 words. Founded 1994.

Your Dog Magazine

BPG (Stamford) Ltd, Roebuck House,
33 Broad Street, Stamford, Lincs. PE9 1RB
tel (01780) 766199 *fax* (01780) 766416
email sarahbpgroup@talk21.com
Editor Sarah Wright
Monthly £2.95

Articles and information of interest to dog lovers; features on all aspects of pet dogs. Length: approx. 1500 words. Illustrations: colour transparencies, prints and line drawings. Payment: £80 per 1000 words. Founded 1994.

Yours

Emap Esprit Ltd, Bushfield House, Orton Centre, Peterborough PE2 5UW
tel (01733) 237111 *fax* (01733) 288129
Editor-in-Chief Neil Patrick
Monthly £1.15

Features and news about and/or of interest to the over-60s age group, including nostalgia and short stories. Study of magazine essential; approach in writing in first instance. Length: articles up to 1000 words, short stories up to 1800 words. Illustrations: preferably colour transparencies/prints but will consider good b&w prints/line drawings, cartoons. Payment: at editor's discretion or by agreement. Founded 1973.

Zest

National Magazine House, 72 Broadwick Street, London W1F 9EP
tel 020-7439 5000 *fax* 020-7312 3750
email zest.mail@natmags.co.uk
Editor Alison Pylkkanen
Monthly £2.80

Health and beauty magazine. Commissioned material only: health, fitness and beauty, features, news and shorts. Length: 50–2000 words. Illustrations: colour and b&w photos and line. Payment: by arrangement. Founded 1994.

Newspapers and magazines overseas

Listings are given for newspapers and magazines in Australia (below), Canada (page 105), New Zealand (page 108) and South Africa (page 110). For information on submitting material to the USA, see page 112. Newspapers are listed under the towns in which they are published.

Australia

(Adelaide) Advertiser

121 King William Street, Adelaide, SA 5000
tel (08) 8206 2000 *fax* (08) 8206 3669
London office PO Box 481, 1 Virginia Street, London E1 9BD
tel 020-7702 1355 *fax* 020-7702 1384
Editor Mel Mansell
Daily Mon-Fri 90c Sat $1.30

Descriptive and news background material, 400–800 words, preferably with pictures; also cartoons. Founded 1858.

(Adelaide) Sunday Mail

121 King William Street, Adelaide, SA 5000
postal address GPO Box 339, Adelaide, SA 5001
tel (08) 8206 2000 *fax* (08) 8206 3646
website www.news.com.au
Editor K. Porter
Weekly $1.50

Founded 1912.

AQ – Journal of Contemporary Analysis

Australian Institute of Political Science, PO Box 145, Balmain, NSW 2041
tel (02) 9810 5642 *fax* (02) 9810 2406
website www.aips.net.au
6 p.a. $60.50 p.a. individuals/schools, $104.50 p.a. organisations ($105 overseas)

Peer-reviewed articles for the informed non-specialist on politics, law, economics, social issues, etc. Length: 3500 words preferred. Payment: none. Founded 1929.

Art and Australia

Fine Art Publishing Pty Ltd, 42 Chandos Street, St Leonards, NSW 2065
tel (02) 9966 8400 *fax* (02) 9966 0355
email info@gbpub.com.au
website www.artaustralia.com
Editor Laura Murray Cree
Quarterly $14.50 (plus £6 postage), $108 p.a.

Articles with a contemporary perspective on Australia's traditional and current art, and on international art of Australian relevance, plus exhibition and book reviews. Length: 2000–3000 words (articles), 600–1200 words (reviews). Payment: $250 per 1000 words. Colour transparencies. Founded 1916 as *Art in Australia*.

Aussie Post

(formerly Australasian Post)
Pacific Publications Pty Ltd, 35-51 Mitchell Street, McMahons Point, NSW 2060
postal address Private Bag 9100, North Sydney, NSW 2059
tel (02) 9464 3129 *fax* (02) 9464 3169
email aussiepost@pacpubs.com.au
Editor Gill Chalmers
Weekly $3.50

Feature stories about Australia and Australians, both urban and rural; characters and achievers, known and unknown; short stories and poems. Material mostly commissioned. Length: 750–1000 words. Illustrations: colour transparencies. Payment: $300–500 per feature/illustration. Founded 1864.

Australian Bookseller & Publisher

D.W. Thorpe, 18 Salmon Street, Port Melbourne, Victoria 3207
tel (03) 9245 7370 *fax* (03) 9245 7395
email bookseller.publisher@thorpe.com.au
website www.thorpe.com.au
Editor Andrew Wilkins
Monthly $80 p.a. ($110 p.a. NZ/Asia; $150 p.a. USA/Canada; $140 p.a. UK/Europe)

Founded 1921.

Australian Camera

Horwitz Publications Pty Ltd, 55 Chandos Street, St Leonards, NSW 2065
tel (02) 9901 6100 *fax* (02) 9901 6198
email paulb@horwitz.com.au
Editor Paul Burrows
Monthly $5.95

Magazine for amateur photographers and digital imaging enthusiasts covering techniques, test reports, new products. Considers unsolicited material. Welcomes ideas for articles and features. Length: 750–1500 words (features/articles). Illustrations: colour prints and transparencies. Payment: $300–$500. Founded 1979.

The Australian Financial Review

GPO Box 506, Sydney, NSW 2001
tel (02) 9282 2512 *fax* (02) 9282 3137
Editor Glenn Burge
London office 1 Bath Street, London EC1V 9LB
tel 020-7688 2777 *fax* 020-7688 3499
New York office Suite 1720, 317 Madison Avenue, New York, NY 10017
tel 212-398-9494
Daily Mon-Fri $2.20

Investment business and economic news and reviews; government and politics, production, banking, commercial, and Stock Exchange statistics; company analysis. General features in Friday *Weekend Review* supplement.

Australian Flying

Yaffa Publishing Group, 17-21 Bellevue Street, Surry Hills, NSW 2010
tel (02) 9281 2333 *fax* (02) 9281 2750
email shelleyross@yaffa.com.au
Editor Shelley Ross
London office 2 Milford Road, London W13 9HZ
tel 020-8579 4836
Contact Robert Logan
6 p.a. $5.95

Covers the Australian aviation industry, from light aircraft to airliners. Payment: by arrangement.

Australian Geographic

PO Box 321, Terrey Hills, NSW 2084
tel (02) 9473 6777 *fax* (02) 9473 6701
website www.australiangeographic.com.au
Editor Terri Cowley (managing)
Quarterly $49.50 p.a.

Articles and features about Australia, particularly life, technology and wildlife in remote parts of the country. Material mostly commissioned. Length: articles, 300–800 words, features, 2000–3000 words. Illustrations: all commissioned. Payment: from $500 per 1000 words; illustrations by negotiation. Founded 1986.

Australian Home Beautiful

Private Bag 9700, North Sydney, NSW 2059
tel (02) 9464 3218 *fax* (02) 9464 3263
email homebeaut@pacpubs.com.au
Editor Andrea Jones
Monthly $5.90

Interior decoration, furnishing, gardening, cookery, etc. Unsolicited MSS not accepted. Founded 1925.

Australian House and Garden

54 Park Street, Sydney, NSW 1028
postal address GPO Box 4088, Sydney, NSW 1028
tel (02) 9282 8456 *fax* (02) 9267 4912
email h&g@acp.com.au
Editor Anny Friis
Monthly $5.95

Factual articles dealing with interior decorating, home design, gardening, wine, food. Preliminary letter essential. Payment: by arrangement. Illustrations: line, half-tone, colour. Founded 1948.

Australian Journal of International Affairs

Department of International Relations, RSPAS, Australian National University, Canberra, ACT 0200
tel (06) 249 2169 *fax* (06) 279 8010
Editor Dr Ramesh Thakur, Vice-Rector (Peace & Governance), United Nations University, 53-70 Jingumae 5-chome, Shibuya-ku, Tokyo 150-8925, Japan
3 p.a. Personal rate A$64 p.a., institutions A$132 p.a. (Australia); other rates on application

Scholarly articles on international affairs. Length: 3000–7000 words. Payment: none.

Australian Journal of Politics and History

School of Political Science and International Studies and the Department of History, University of Queensland, St Lucia, Queensland 4067
tel (07) 3365 3163 *fax* (07) 3365 1388
email i.ward@mailbox.uq.edu.au
Editor Ian Ward and Andrew Bonnell
4 p.a. $66/£38 p.a. individuals; $144/£110 institutions

Australian, European, Asian, Pacific and international articles. Special feature: regular surveys of Australian Foreign Policy and State and Commonwealth politics. Length: 8000 words max. Illustrations: line, only when necessary. Payment: none.

Australian Photography

Yaffa Publishing Group, 17-21 Bellevue Street, Surry Hills, NSW 2010
tel (02) 9281 2333 *fax* (02) 9281 2750
email robertkeeley@yaffa.com.au
Editor Robert Keeley
London office 2 Milford Road, London W13 9HZ
tel 020-8579 4836
Contact Robert Logan
Monthly $4.95

Illustrated articles: picture-taking techniques, technical. Length: 1200–2500 words with colour and/or b&w prints or slides. Payment: $80 per page. Founded 1950.

Australian Powerboat

Yaffa Publishing Group, GPO Box 606, Sydney, NSW 2001
tel (02) 9281 2333 *fax* (02) 9281 2750
Editor Graham Lloyd
London office 2 Milford Road, London W13 9HZ
tel 020-8579 4836
Contact Robert Logan
Bi-monthly $5.20

Articles and news on boats and boating, racing, water skiing and products. Length: 1500 words (articles), 200 words (news). Illustrations: colour (transparencies preferred). Payment: $100 per 1000 words; from $30. Founded 1976.

Australian Short Stories

73 Mooltan Street, Flemington, Victoria 3031
tel (03) 9370 4858
Editor Howard Firkin
Quarterly $9.95

Contemporary short stories from around the world. Length: 500–5000 words. Illustrations: b&w artwork. Payment $90 per 1000 words; $70 illustrations. Founded 1983.

The Australian Women's Weekly

Australian Consolidated Press Ltd, 54 Park Street, Sydney, NSW 1028
postal address GPO Box 4178, Sydney, NSW 1028
tel (02) 9282 8000 *fax* (02) 9267 4459
email dthomas@acp.com.au
Editor Deborah Thomas
Monthly $4.95

Fiction and features. Length: fiction 1000–5000 words; features 750–1500 words plus colour or b&w photos. Payment: according to length and merit. Fiction illustrations: sketches by own artists and freelances.

The Big Issue Australia

GPO Box 4911VV, Melbourne, Victoria 3001
tel (03) 9663 4522 *fax* (03) 9663 4252
email bigissue@infoxchange.net.au
Editor Simon Castles
Fortnightly $3

Profiles and features of general interest and on social issues, plus international and local news, arts reviews. No fiction. Length: 1000–2500 words (features), up to 900 words (news), 250 words (reviews). Payment: 15c per word (features and news), $30 (reviews). Colour and b&w cartoons (approx. $100). Founded 1996.

(Brisbane) The Courier-Mail

Queensland Newspapers Pty Ltd, Campbell Street, Bowen Hills, Brisbane, Queensland 4006
tel (07) 3666 8000 *fax* (07) 3666 6696
email cmletters@qnp.newsltd.com.au
website www.news.com.au
Editor-in-Chief C. Mitchell
Daily $1

(Brisbane) The Sunday Mail

Queensland Newspapers Pty Ltd, PO Box 130, Campbell Street, Bowen Hills, Brisbane, Queensland 4006
tel (07) 3666 6276 *fax* (07) 3666 6787
email smletters@qnp.newsltd.com.au
Editor Michael Prain
Weekly $1.50

Anything of general interest. Length: up to 1500 words. Illustrations: line, photos, b&w and colour, cartoons. Rejected MSS returned if postage enclosed.

Dance Australia

Yaffa Publishing Group, Box 606, GPO Sydney, NSW 2001
tel (02) 9281 2333 *fax* (02) 9281 2750
email dance@yaffa.com.au
Editor Karen van Ulzen
London office 2 Milford Road, London W13 9HZ
tel 020-8579 4836
Contact Robert Logan
Bi-monthly $5.50

Articles and features on all aspects of dance in Australia. Material mostly commissioned, but will consider unsolicited contributions. Illustrations: b&w photos, line drawings, cartoons. Payment: $200 per 1000 words; illustrations by negotiation. Founded1980.

Dolly

GPO Box 5201, Sydney, NSW 1028
tel (02) 9282 8437 *fax* (02) 9267 4911
website www.ninemsn.com.au/dolly
Editor Virginia Knight

Monthly $4.40

Features on teen fashion, health and beauty, personalities, music, social issues and how to cope with growing up, etc. Length: not less than 1000 words. Illustrations: colour, b&w, line, cartoons. Payment: by arrangement. Founded 1970.

EA Today Magazine

PO Box 199, Alexandria, NSW 1435
tel (02) 9353 0620 *fax* (02) 9353 0613
email electaus@fpc.com.au
website www.electronicsaustralia.com.au
Editor Graham Cattley
Monthly $6.95

Articles on technical TV and radio, hi-fi, popular electronics. Length: up to 2000 words. Payment: by arrangement. Illustrations: line, half-tone, cartoons.

Fishing World Magazine

Yaffa Publishing Group, 17-21 Bellevue Street, Surry Hills, NSW 2010
tel (02) 9281 2333 *fax* (02) 9281 2750
website www.yaffa.com.au/fw
Editor Jim Harnwell
London office 2 Milford Road, London W13 9HZ
tel 020-8579 4836
Contact Robert Logan
Monthly $4.95

Rock, surf, stream, deep sea and game fishing, with comprehensive sections on gear, equipment and boats. Payment: by arrangement.

Geo Australasia

Hallmark Editions, PO Box 84, Hampton, Victoria 3188
tel (03) 9555 7377 *fax* (03) 9555 7599
email hallmark@halledit.com.au
Editor Peter Stirling
Bi-monthly $7.95 ($55 p.a. surface mail, $85 p.a. airmail)

Non-fiction articles on wildlife, adventure, culture and lifestyles, natural history and the environment in Australia, New Zealand, the Pacific and SE Asia. Length: 1500–3000 words. Payment: $600–$1500 by arrangement. Illustrations: photos, colour transparencies. Founded 1978.

Harper's Bazaar

ACP Publishing Pty Ltd, 54 Park Street, Sydney, NSW 2000
tel (02) 9282 8703 *fax* (02) 9267 4456
email bazaar@acp.com.au
Editor Karin Upton Baker
10 p.a. $6.50

Fashion, health and beauty, celebrity news, plus features. Length: 3000 words. Illustrations: colour and b&w photos. Payment: $500 per 1000 words; $150. Founded 1998.

HQ Magazine

Level 2, 115-117 Coopers Street, Surry Hills, NSW 2010
tel (02) 9281 3111 *fax* (02) 9281 3122
email hq@terraplanet.com
website www.terraplanet.com
Editor Alex Craig
Monthly $7.95

General interest features and profiles for a literate readership. Length: 1500–5000 words. Illustrations: colour and b&w photos. Payment: by negotiation. Founded 1989.

(Launceston) Examiner

Box 99A, PO Launceston, Tasmania 7250
tel (03) 633 67111 *fax* (03) 633 47328
Editor Rod Scott
Daily 90c

Accepts freelance material. Payment: by arrangement.

Meanjin

Meanjin Company Ltd, 131 Barry Street, Carlton, Victoria 3054
tel (03) 8344 6950 *fax* (03) 9347 2550
email meanjin@unimelb.edu.au
website www.meanjin.unimelb.edu.au
Editor Dr Ian Britain
Quarterly $19.95

Cultural commentary, fiction, poetry, essays and discussion of contemporary issues, e.g. biography, drugs, travel. See website for submission guidelines. Payment: $50 per poetry item, min. $100 prose. Founded 1941.

(Melbourne) Age

The Age Company Ltd, 250 Spencer Street, Melbourne, Victoria 3000
tel (03) 9600 4211 *fax* (03) 9601 2412
London office 1 Bath Street, London EC1V 9LB
tel 020-7688 2777 *fax* 020-7688 3499
Associate Publisher and Editor Michael Gawenda, *Managing Editor* Malcolm Schmidtke
Daily Mon-Fri $1.10, Sat $1.90, Sun $1.50

Independent liberal morning daily; room occasionally for outside matter. *Good Weekend* and *Sunday Life* (illustrated weekend magazines); *News Extra*; *Saturday Extra* (includes literary reviews). Accepts occasional freelance material.

(Melbourne) Herald Sun

HWT Tower, 40 City Road, Southbank, Victoria 3006
tel (03) 9292 1686 *fax* (03) 9292 2112
Editor Peter Blunden
Send material to Darrell Richardson, Syndications Manager
Daily Mon-Fri $1 Sat $1.20 Sun $1.50

Accepts freelance articles, preferably with illustrations. Length: up to 750 words. Illustrations: half-tone, line, cartoons. Payment: on merit.

(Melbourne) Sunday Herald Sun

HWT Tower, 40 City Road, Southbank, Victoria 3006
tel (03) 9292 2000 *fax* (03) 9292 2080
Editor Alan Howe
Weekly $1.40

Accepts freelance articles, preferably with illustrations. Length: up to 2000 words. Illustrations: colour. Payment: on merit.

New Woman

Level 6, 187 Thomas Street, Haymarket, NSW 2000
tel (02) 9581 9400 *fax* (02) 9211 9540
Editor Sue Wheeler
Monthly $5.95

Irreverent and humorous style of magazine for the single, professional woman aged 25–35. Includes celebrity gossip, fashion, beauty, sex and relationships, and entertainment reviews. Founded 1989.

NW Magazine

54 Park Street, Sydney, NSW 2000
tel (02) 9282 8285 *fax* (02) 9264 6005
Editor Louisa Hatfield
Weekly $3.50

News and features on celebrities, food, new products, fashion and astrology. Illustrated. Payment: by negotiation. Founded 1993.

Overland

PO Box 14146 MCMC, Melbourne, Victoria 8001
tel (03) 9688 4163 *fax* (03) 9688 4883
email overland@vu.edu.au
Editor Ian Syson
Quarterly $36 p.a.

Literary and cultural. Australian material preferred. Payment: by arrangement. Illustrations: line, half-tone, cartoons.

People Magazine

54 Park Street, Sydney, NSW 2000
tel (02) 9288 9648 *fax* (02) 9267 4365
Editor Tom Foster
Weekly $3.30

National weekly news-pictorial. Mainly people stories. Photos depicting exciting happenings, glamour, show business, unusual occupations, rites, customs. Payment: $300 per page, text and photos.

(Perth) The Sunday Times

34-40 Stirling Street, Perth, Western Australia 6000
tel (08) 9326 8476 *fax* (08) 9226 8316
Editor Brett McCarthy
Weekly $1.30

Topical articles to 800 words. Payment: on acceptance. Founded 1897.

(Perth) The West Australian

50 Hasler Road, Osborne Park, Western Australia 6017
tel (08) 9482 3111 *fax* (08) 9482 3452
Editor Brian Rogers
Daily Mon-Fri 88c Sat $1.60

Articles and sketches about people and events in Australia and abroad. Length: 300–700 words. Payment: Award rates or better. Illustrations: line, half-tone. Founded 1833.

Quadrant

437 Darling Street, Balmain, NSW 2041
postal address PO Box 82, Balmain, NSW 2041
tel (02) 9818 1155 *fax* (02) 9818 1422
email quadrantmonthly@ozemail.com.au
Literary Editor Les Murray
Editor P.P. McGuinness
Monthly $7 (10 p.a.)

Articles, short stories, verse, etc. Prose length: 2000–5000 words. Payment: min. $90 articles/stories, $60 reviews, $40 poems; illustrations by arrangement.

Reader's Digest (Australia)

PO Box 4353, Sydney, NSW 2001
tel (02) 9690 6111 *fax* (02) 9690 6211
Editor-in-Chief Tony Spencer-Smith
Monthly $5.44

Articles on Australian subjects by commission only. No unsolicited MSS accepted. Length: 2500–5000 words. Payment: up to $6000 per article; brief filler paragraphs, $50–$250. Illustrations: half-tone, colour.

Rock

Wild Publications Pty Ltd, PO Box 415, Prahran, Victoria 3181
tel (03) 9826 8482 *fax* (03) 9826 3787
email rock@wild.com.au
website www.rock.com.au
Editor Lucy Monie
Quarterly $8.99

Australian rockclimbing and mountaineering articles, features and news. Length: 2000 words (articles/features), 200 words (news). Illustrations: colour transparencies. Payment: $85 per page (words and pictures). Founded 1978.

Scuba Diver

Yaffa Publishing Group, 17-21 Bellevue Street, Surry Hills, NSW 2010
tel (02) 9281 2333 *fax* (02) 9281 2750
email yaffa@flex.com.au
Editor Sue Crowe
London office 2 Milford Road, London W13 9HZ
tel 020-8579 4836
Contact Robert Logan
Bi-monthly $6.50

News, features, articles and short stories on scuba diving. Length: 1500 words (articles/features), 300–800 words (news), 800–1000 (short stories). Illustrations: colour. Payment: $70 per page, negotiable (words and pictures).

The Sun-Herald

GPO Box 506, Sydney, NSW 2001
tel (02) 9282 2822 *fax* (02) 9282 2151
London office John Fairfax (UK) Ltd, 1 Bath Street, London EC1V 9LB
tel 020-7688 2777 *fax* 020-7688 3499
Editor Philip McLean
Weekly $1.50

Topical articles to 1000 words; news plus sections on current affairs, entertainment, finance, sport and travel. Payment: by arrangement.

(Sydney) The Daily Telegraph

News Ltd, 2 Holt Street, Surry Hills, NSW 2010
tel (02) 9288 3000 *fax* (02) 9288 3311
Editor-in-Chief Col Allan
Daily Mon-Fri 90c Sat $1.20

Modern feature articles and series of Australian or world interest. Length: 1000–2000 words. Payment: according to merit/length.

The Sydney Morning Herald

PO Box 506, Sydney, NSW 2001
tel (02) 9282 2858
London office 1 Bath Street, London EC1V 9LB
tel 020-7688 2777 *fax* 020-7688 3499
Editor Phil Scott
Daily $1.10

Saturday edition has pages of literary criticism and also magazine articles, plus glossy colour magazine. Topical articles 600–4000 words. Payment: varies, but minimum $100 per 1000 words. Illustrations: all types. Founded 1831.

(Sydney) The Sunday Telegraph

News Ltd, 2 Holt Street, Surry Hills, Sydney, NSW 2010
tel (02) 9288 3000 *fax* (02) 9288 3311
Editor Jeni Cooper
Weekly $1.40

News and features. Illustrations: transparencies. Payment: varies. Founded 1935.

Vogue Australia

170 Pacific Highway, Greenwich, NSW 2065
postal address Locked Bag 2550, Crows Nest, NSW 1585
tel (02) 9964 3817 *fax* (02) 9964 3763
Editor Kirstie Clements
Monthly $5.90

Articles and features on fashion, beauty, health, business, people and the arts of interest to the modern woman of style and high spending power. Ideas welcome. Length: from 1000 words. Illustrations: colour and b&w. Founded 1959.

Wild

Wild Publications Pty Ltd, PO Box 415, Prahran, Victoria 3181
tel (03) 9826 8482 *fax* (03) 9826 3787
email wild@wild.com.au
website www.wild.com.au
Editor Lucy Monie
4 p.a. $7.99

'Australia's wilderness adventure magazine.' Illustrated articles of first-hand experiences of the Australian wilderness, plus book and track reviews, product tests. Send sae for guidelines for contributors. Length: 2500 words (articles), 200 words (news). Colour transparencies. Payment: $125 per published page. Founded 1981.

Woman's Day

54-58 Park Street, Sydney, NSW 2000
tel (02) 9282 8000 *fax* (02) 9267 4360
Editor-in-Chief Philip Barker
Weekly $3.30

National women's magazine; news, show business, fiction, fashion, general articles, cookery, home economy.

Canada

The Beaver: Canada's History Magazine

Canada's National History Society, Suite 478, 167 Lombard Avenue, Winnipeg, Manitoba R3B 0T6
tel 204-988-9300 *fax* 204-988-9309
website www.historysociety.ca
Editor Annalee Greenberg
Bi-monthly $27.50 p.a. ($31.50 USA, $33.50 p.a. elsewhere)

Articles, historical and modern, on Canadian history. Length: 1500–4000 words, with illustrations. Payment: on acceptance. Illustrations: b&w and colour archival photos/drawings. Founded 1920.

Books in Canada

6021 Yonge Street, Ste 1014, Toronto, Ontario M2M 3W2
tel 416-222-7139 *fax* 416-222-9384
email olgo.stein@sympatico.ca
Editor Adrian Stein
6 p.a. $27.98 p.a.

Commissioned reviews, informed criticism and articles on Canadian literary, intellectual and political books. Query first – do not send unsolicited material. Payment: 10c per word. Founded 1971.

C international contemporary art

PO Box 5, Station B, Toronto, Ontario M5T 2T2
tel 416-539-9495 *fax* 416-539-9903
email general@cmagazine.com
Editor Si Si Penaloza
Quarterly US$8.25

Arts and artists' projects, features, reviews. Accepts submissions. Length: features (varies), reviews (500 words). Illustrations: transparencies, photos. Payment: $250–$500 features, $100 reviews. Founded 1972.

The Canadian Forum

35 Britain Street, 3rd Floor, Toronto, Ontario M5A 1R7
tel 416-362-0726 *fax* 416-362-3939
email canadian.forum@sympatico.ca
Editor Robert Chodos
10 p.a. $4 ($28 p.a.)

Articles on public affairs and the arts; book reviews. Length: up to 2500 words. Payment: varies. Illustrations: line and photos.

Canadian Literature

University of British Columbia, Buchanan E158, 1866 Main Mall, Vancouver, BC V6T 1Z1
tel 604-882-2780 *fax* 604-822-5504
Editor E.M. Kröller
4 p.a. $45 p.a. individual; $60 p.a. institutions (outside Canada add $20 postage)

Articles on Canadian writers and writing in English and French. No fiction. Length: up to 5000 words. Payment: none. Founded 1959.

Canadian Theatre Review (CTR)

Dept of Drama, University of Guelph, Guelph, Ontario N1G 2W1
Contact Editorial Committee
Quarterly $10.50 ($35 p.a.)

Feature and review articles on Canadian theatre aimed at theatre professionals, academics and general audience; book and play reviews. Send MSS accompanied by PC compatible disk. Length: 2000–3000 words. Illustrations: b&w. Payment: $200–275 (features/articles), $75 (book/play reviews). Founded 1974.

Canadian Writer's Journal

PO Box 5180, New Liskeard, Ontario P0J 1P0
tel 705-647-5424 *fax* 705-647-8366
email cwj@cwj.ca
website www.cwj.ca
Editor Deborah Ranchuk
Bi-monthly $30 p.a.

News on markets and articles on writers' aspirations for dedicated apprentice and professional Canadian writers. Considers unsolicited material. Founded 1984.

Chatelaine

777 Bay Street, Toronto, Ontario M5W 1A7
tel 416-596-5425
Editor Rona Maynard
Monthly $2.99

Women's interest articles; Canadian angle preferred. Payment: on acceptance; from $1000.

Chickadee

The Owl Group, Bayard Press Canada, 49 Front Street East, 2nd Floor, Toronto, Ontario M5E 3B1
tel (416) 340 2700 *fax* (416) 340 9769
email hilary@owl.on.ca
website www.owlkids.com
Editor Hilary Bain
9 p.a. $2.95 ($24 p.a. Canada, US$14.95 USA, $34 rest of world)

Highly illustrated mix of stories and activities on the theme of the world around kids; aimed at children aged 6–9. Length: 10–100 words (articles), 800–900 words (fiction). Illustrations: colour. Payment: $250 (fiction). Founded 1979.

The Dalhousie Review

Dalhousie University, Halifax, Nova Scotia B3H 3J5
tel 902-494-2541 *fax* 902-494-3561
email Dalhousie.Review@dal.ca
website www.dal.ca/~dalrev/
Associate Editors Ronald Huebert, Trevor Ross
3 p.a. ($32.10 p.a., $85.60 for 3 years; ($40/$100 outside Canada)

Articles on history, literature, political science, philosophy, sociology, popular culture, fine arts; short fiction; verse; book reviews. Usually not more than 3 stories and 10–12 poems in any one issue. Length: prose, up to 5000 words; verse, less than 40 words. Contributors receive 2 copies of issue and 10 offprints of their work.

Equinox

11450 Albert-Hudon Blvd, Montreal, Montreal, QC H1G 3J9
tel 514-327-4464 *fax* 514-327-0514
email eqxmag@globetrotter.net
Editor Martin Silverstone
Bi-monthly ($22.95 p.a. Canada; Can.$29 p.a. USA; Can.$35 elsewhere)

Magazine of discovery in science, human cultures, technology and geography. Accepts articles on hard science topics (length: 250–350 words); welcomes queries (2–3-page outline) for specific assignments. No phone queries please. Illustrations: colour transparencies. Payment: by arrangement. Founded 1982.

The Fiddlehead

Campus House, 11 Garland Court,
UNB PO Box 4400, Fredericton, NB E3B 5A3
tel 506-453-3501
email fid@nbnet.nb.ca
website www.lib.unb.ca/texts/fiddlehead
Editor Ross Leckie
Quarterly US$10 (US$25 p.a.)

Reviews, poetry, short stories. Payment: approx. $20 per printed page. Founded 1945.

(Hamilton) The Spectator

44 Frid Street, Hamilton, Ontario L8N 3G3
tel 905-526-3333
website www.hamiltonspectator.com
Publisher Ms Jagoda S. Pike
Daily Mon-Fri 75c Sat $1.75

Articles of general interest, political analysis and background; interviews, stories of Canadians abroad. Length: 800 words maximum. Payment: rate varies. Founded 1846.

Inuit Art Quarterly

2081 Merivale Road, Ottawa, Ontario K2G 1G9
tel 613-224-8189 *fax* 613-224-2907
email iaq@inuitart.org
website www.inuitart.org
Editor Marybelle Mitchell
Quarterly $6.25

Features, original research, artists' perspectives, news. Freelance contributors are expected to have a thorough knowledge of the arts. Length: varies. Illustrations: colour and b&w photos and line. Payment: by arrangement. Founded 1985.

Journal of Canadian Studies

Trent University, Peterborough, Ontario K9J 7B8
tel 705-748-1279 *fax* 705-748-1564
email jcs_rec@trentu.ca
Editors Robert M. Campbell, Kerry Cannon
Quarterly US$50 p.a. (US$60 p.a. institutions)

Major academic review of Canadian studies. Articles of general as well as scholarly interest on history, politics, literature, society, arts. Length: 7000–10,000 words.

The Malahat Review

University of Victoria, PO Box 1700 STN CSC, Victoria, BC V8W 2Y2
tel 250-721-8524
email malahat@uvic.ca (queries only)
website http://web.uvic.ca/malahat
Editor Marlene Cookshaw
Quarterly $30 p.a. ($40 p.a. overseas)

Short stories, poetry, short plays, reviews. Payment: $30 per magazine page. Illustrations: half-tone. Founded 1967.

Performing Arts & Entertainment in Canada (PA&E)

104 Glenrose Avenue, Toronto, Ontario M4T 1K8
tel 416-484-4534 *fax* 416-484-6214
Editor Sarah Hood
Quarterly $8 p.a. ($14 p.a. elsewhere)

Feature articles on Canadian theatre, music, dance and film artists and organisations; technical articles on scenery, lighting, make-up, costumes, etc. Length: 600–1200 words. Payment: $150-$175, one month after publication. Illustrations: b&w photos, colour slides. Founded 1961.

Photo Life

1 Dundas Street West, Suite 2500, PO Box 84, Toronto, Ontario M5G 1Z3
tel 800-905-7468 *fax* 800-664-2739
email editor@photolife.com
website www.photolife.com
Editor Suzie Ketene

6 p.a. $3.95
Covers all aspects of photography of interest to amateur and professional photographers. Length: 800–1500 words. Illustrations: colour and b&w photos. Payment: by arrangement. Founded 1976.

Queen's Quarterly

Queen's University, Kingston, Ontario K7L 3N6
tel 613-533-2667 *fax* 613-533-6822
email qquarter@post.queensu.ca
website http://info.queensu.ca/quarterly
Editor Dr Boris Castel
Quarterly $6.50 ($20 p.a.; $40 p.a. institutions)
A multidisciplinary scholarly journal aimed at the general educated reader – articles, short stories and poems. Length: 2500–3500 words (articles), 2000 (stories). Payment: by negotiation. Founded 1893.

Quill & Quire

70 The Esplanade, Suite 210, Toronto, Ontario M5E 1R2
tel 416-360-0044 *fax* 416-955-0794
email info@quillandquire.com
Editor Scott Anderson
12 p.a. $59.95 p.a. (outside Canada $95p.a.)
Articles of interest about the Canadian book trade. Payment: from $100. Illustrations: line, half-tone. Subscription includes Canadian Publishers Directory (2 p.a.). Founded 1935.

Reader's Digest (Canada)

1100 René Levesque Blvd. W, Montreal, Quebec H3B 5H5
tel 514-940-0751
Editor Murray Lewis
Monthly $3.25
Original articles on all subjects of broad general appeal, thoroughly researched and professionally written. Outline or query only. Length: 3000 words approx. Payment: from $2700. Also previously published material. Illustrations: line, half-tone, colour.

(Toronto) The Globe and Mail

444 Front Street West, Toronto, Ontario M5V 2S9
Editor Edward Greenspon
Daily 60c
Unsolicited material considered. Payment: by arrangement. Founded 1844.

Toronto Life

59 Front Street East, Toronto, Ontario M5E 1B3
tel 416-364-3333 *fax* 416-861-1169
Editor John Macfarlane
Monthly $3.95
Articles, profiles on Toronto and Torontonians. Illustrations: line, half-tone, colour. Founded 1966.

Toronto Star

One Yonge Street, Toronto, Ontario M5E 1E6
tel 416-367-2000
London office Level 4A, PO Box 495, Virginia Street, London E1 9XY
tel 020-7833 0791
Daily Mon-Fri 30c Sat$1 Sun 75c
Features, life, world/national politics. Payment: by arrangement. Founded 1892.

(Vancouver) Province

200 Granville Street, Suite 1, Vancouver, BC V6C 3N3
tel 604-605-2063 *fax* 604-606-2720
Editor-in-Chief Vivienne Sosnowski
Daily Mon-Fri 60c Sun $1
Founded 1898.

Vancouver Sun

200 Granville Street, Vancouver, BC V6C 3N3
tel 604-605-2180 *fax* 604-605-2323
email nreynolds@pacpress.southam.ca
website www.vancouversun.com
London office Southam News of Canada, 8 Heath Mansions, Hampstead Grove, London NW3 6SL
tel 020-7435 5103
Editor-in-Chief Neil Reynolds
Daily Mon-Thu 75c Fri, Sat $1.40
Mix arts magazine. Travel, Op-Ed pieces considered. Payment: by arrangement.

Wascana Review of Contemporary Poetry & Short Fiction

c/o English Department, University of Regina, Regina, Sask. S4S 0A2
tel 306-585-4302 *fax* 306-585-4827
website www.uregina.ca./wrhome.htm
Editor Michael Trussler
Bi-annual $10 p.a. ($12 p.a. outside Canada)
Criticism, short stories, poetry, reviews. Manuscripts from freelance writers welcome. Length: prose, not more than 6000 words; verse, up to 100 lines. Payment: $3 per page for prose; $10 per printed page for verse; $3 per page for reviews. Contributors also receive 2 free copies and a year's subscription. Founded 1966.

Winnipeg Free Press

1355 Mountain Avenue, Winnipeg, MB R2X 3B6
tel 204-697-7000 *fax* 204-697-7412
Editor Nicholas Hirst
Daily Mon-Fri 25c Sat $1.25 Sun 35c
Some freelance articles. Payment: $100. Founded 1872.

New Zealand

(Auckland) New Zealand Herald

PO Box 32, Auckland
tel (09) 379 5050 *fax* (09) 373 6421
email editor@herald.co.nz
website www.nzherald.co.nz
Editor Tim Murphy *Editor-in-Chief* Gavin Ellis
Daily Mon-Fri $1 Weekend $2

Topical and informative articles 800–1100 words. Payment: minimum $150–$300. Illustrations: colour negatives or prints. Founded 1863.

(Auckland) Sunday News

PO Box 1327, Auckland
tel (09) 302 1300 *fax* (09) 358 3003
email editor@sunday-news.co.nz
Editor Clive Nelson
Weekly Sun $1.10

News, sport and showbiz, especially with New Zealand interest. Illustrations: colour and b&w photos. Founded 1963.

(Auckland) Sunday Star-Times

News Media Auckland Ltd, PO Box 1327, Auckland 1
tel (09) 302 1300 *fax* (09) 309 0258
email feedback@star-times.co.nz
Editor Suzanne Chetwin
Sun $1.50

(Christchurch) The Press

Private Bag 4722, Christchurch
tel (03) 379 0940 *fax* (03) 364 8238
email editorial@press.co.nz
Editor Paul Thompson
Daily 80c

Articles of general interest not more than 800 words. Illustrations: photos and line drawings, cartoons. Payment: by arrangement.

(Dunedin) Otago Daily Times

PO Box 181, Dunedin
tel (03) 477 4760 *fax* (03) 474 7422
email odt.editor@alliedpress.co.nz
website www.odt.co.nz
Editor R.L. Charteris
Daily 80c

Any articles of general interest up to 1000 words, but preference is given to NZ writers. Topical illustrations and personalities. Payment: current NZ rates. Founded 1861.

Hawke's Bay Today

PO Box 180, Karamu Road North, Hastings
tel (06) 878 5155 *fax* (06) 876 0655
Editor L. Pierard
Daily 70c

Limited requirements. Payment: $50 upwards for articles, $15 upwards for photos. Illustrations: web offset.

(Invercargill) The Southland Times

PO Box 805, Invercargill
tel (03) 218 1909 *fax* (03) 214 9905
email editor@stl.co.nz
website www.press.co.nz
Editor F.L. Tulett
Mon-Fri 70c Sat 80c

Articles of up to 800 words on topics of Southland interest. Payment: by arrangement. Illustrations: line, half-tone, colour, cartoons. Founded 1862.

Management Magazine

Profile Publishing, PO Box 5544, Auckland
tel (09) 630 8940 *fax* (09) 630 1046
email sprofile@iconz.co.nz
Editor Sherrill Tapsell
Monthly $5.95

Articles on the practice of management skills and techniques, individual and company profiles, coverage of business trends and topics. A NZ/Australian angle or application preferred. Length: 2000 words. Payment: by arrangement; minimum 23c per word. Illustrations: photos, line drawings.

The Nelson Mail

PO Box 244, 15 Bridge Street, Nelson
tel (03) 548 7079 *fax* (03) 546 2802
email nml@nelsonmail.co.nz
Editor Bill Moore
Daily 70c

Features, articles on NZ subjects. Length: 500–1000 words. Payment: up to $100 per 1000 words. Illustrations: half-tone, colour.

(New Plymouth) The Daily News

PO Box 444, Currie Street, New Plymouth
tel (06) 758 0559 *fax* (06) 758 6849
email editor@tnl.co.nz
Editor Lance G. Butcher
Daily 90c

Articles preferably with a Taranaki connection. Payment: by negotiation. Illustrations: half-tone, cartoons. Founded 1857.

New Zealand Woman's Day

Private Bag 92512, Auckland
tel (09) 308 2718 *fax* (09) 357 0978
Editor Louise Wright
Weekly $3.25

Celebrity interviews, exclusive news stories, short stories, gossip. Length: 1000 words. Illustrations: colour transparencies; payment according to use. Payment: by arrangement. Founded 1989.

New Zealand Woman's Weekly

PO Box 90-119 AMC, Auckland 1
tel (09) 360 3820 *fax* (09) 360 3829
email editor@nzww.co.nz
Editor Rowan Dixon
Weekly $3.10

Articles and features of general interest to women aged 30+ and their families: celebrities, news, health, food, fashion, DIY and home improvement, short stories. Considers unsolicited material and welcomes ideas for features and articles. Length: 800–2000 words (features/articles), 500–1500 (fiction). Illustrations: colour. Payment: on acceptance. Founded 1932.

NZ House & Garden

PO Box 6341, Wellesley Street, Auckland
tel (09) 353 1010 *fax* (09) 353 1020
Editor Kate Coughlan
Monthly $8.95

Upmarket magazine that celebrates New Zealand's most interesting houses and beautiful gardens. Inspiration for food and entertaining, and a resource for decor. Considers unsolicited material. Welcomes ideas for articles and features. Length: 500–800 words. Payment: $400. Illustrations: colour transparencies. Founded 1994.

She

Private Bag 92512, Wellesley Street, Auckland 1036
tel (09) 308 2735 *fax* (09) 302 0667
email she@acpnz.co.nz
Editor Leonie Dale
Monthly $6.20

Lifestyle magazine for women aged 25–40. Length: 1000–2000 words (features and profiles). Illustrations: colour. Payment: negotiable. Founded 1996.

Straight Furrow

Rural Press, PO Box 4233, Auckland
tel (09) 376 9786 *fax* (09) 376 9780
Editor Susan Topless

Fortnightly News and features of interest to the farming/rural sector with emphasis on agri-political issues. Length: 500 words news, 1000 words features. Illustrations: colour and b&w photos. Payment: 30c per published word; $15 per published photo. Founded 1933.

Takahe

Takahe Collective Trust, PO Box 13335, Christchurch 8001
tel (03) 359 8133
3 p.a. $25 for 4 issues ($35 international)

Quality short fiction and poetry by both new and established writers. Payment: approx. $30 per issue. Founded 1989.

The Timaru Herald

PO Box 46, Bank Street, Timaru
tel (03) 684 4129 *fax* (03) 688 1042
email editor@timaruherald.co.nz
Editor D.H. Wood
Daily 65c

Topical articles. Payment: by arrangement. Illustrations: colour or b&w prints.

(Wellington) The Evening Post

PO Box 3740, 40 Boulcott Street, Wellington
tel (04) 474 0444 *fax* (04) 474 0237, (04) 474 0536 (editor)
email editor@evpost.co.nz
Editor Tim Pankhurst
Daily Mon-Fri 80c Sat $1

General topical articles, 600 words. Payment: NZ current rates or by arrangement. News illustrations, cartoons. Founded 1865.

Your Home and Garden

Australian Consolidated Press (New Zealand) Ltd, Private Bag 92512, Wellesley Street, Auckland
tel (09) 308 2700 *fax* (09) 377 6725
Editor Claire McCall
Monthly $5.95

Advice, ideas and projects for homeowners – interiors and gardens. Length: 1000 words. Illustrations: good quality colour transparencies. Payment: 30c per word/ $75 per transparency. Founded 1991.

South Africa

Bona

Caxton Magazines, PO Box 32083, Mobeni 4060, KwaZulu-Natal
tel (031) 422-041
Monthly R5.50

Articles on fashion, cookery, sport, music of interest to black people. Length: up to 3000 words. Payment: by arrangement. Illustrations: line, half-tone, colour, cartoons.

(Cape Town) Cape Times

Newspaper House, 5th Floor, 122 St George's Mall, Cape Town 8001
postal address PO Box 56, Cape Town 8000
tel (021) 488-4911 *fax* (021) 488 4744
Editor Chris Whitfield
London office Mediaforce Ltd, 1 Gunpowder Square, Fleet Street, London EC4A 3EP
tel 020-7583 2100 *fax* 020-7353 2111
Daily R3.10

Contributions must be suitable for a daily newspaper and must not exceed 800 words. Illustrations: photos of outstanding South African interest. Founded 1876.

Car

PO Box 180, Howard Place 7450
tel (021) 530-3153 *fax* (021) 532-2698
email car@rsp.co.za
website www.cartoday.com
Editor John Wright
Monthly R13.95

New car announcements with pictures and full colour features of motoring interest. Payment: by arrangement. Illustrations: colour, cartoons. Founded 1957.

Daily Dispatch

Dispatch Media (Pty) Ltd, 35 Caxton Street, East London 5201
tel (043) 702-2000 *fax* (043) 743 5155
email eledit@iafrica.com
website www.dispatch.co.za
postal address PO Box 131, East London 5200
Editor Gavin Stewart
Daily Mon-Sat R2

Newspaper for the Eastern Cape region. Features of general interest, especially successful development projects in developing countries. Colour and b&w photographs, artwork, cartoons. Contributions welcome. Length: approx. 1000 words (features). Payment: R250; R62 photographs. Founded 1872.

(Durban) The Mercury

Independent Newspapers KwaZulu-Natal Ltd, PO Box 950, Durban 4000
tel (031) 308-2332 *fax* (031) 308-2357
Editor D. Pather
Daily Mon-Fri R2.80

Serious background news and inside details of world events. Length: 700–900 words. Illustrations: photos of general interest. Founded 1852.

Farmer's Weekly

Caxton Magazines, PO Box 1797, Pinegowie, Johannesburg 2123
tel (011) 889-0836
email farmersweekly@caxton.co.za
Editor Chris Burgess
Weekly R7.95

Articles, generally illustrated, up to 1000 words, on all aspects of practical farming and research with particular reference to conditions in Southern Africa. Includes women's section which accepts suitable, illustrated articles. Illustrations: line, half-tone, colour, cartoons. Payment: according to merit. Founded 1911.

Femina Magazine

Associated Magazines, Box 3647, Cape Town 8000
tel (021) 464-6200 *fax* (021) 461 4290
email femina@assocmags.co.za
Editor Clare O'Donoghue
Monthly R15.95

For busy young professionals, often with families. Humour, personalities, real-life drama, medical breakthroughs, popular science, news-breaking stories and human interest. Payment: by arrangement.

Garden and Home

Caxton Magazines, PO Box 32083, Mobeni 4060
tel (031) 910-5713
Editor Les Abercrombie
Monthly R17.95

Well-illustrated articles on gardening suitable for southern hemisphere. Articles for home section on furnishings, decor ideas, food. Payment: by arrangement. Illustrations: half-tone, colour, cartoons.

Independent Newspapers (South Africa) Ltd

PO Box 56, Cape Town 8000
tel (021) 488-4911 *fax* (021) 488-4762
website www.iol.co.za
Cape Town **Argus** Daily R2.70
Saturday Argus R5.60
Sunday Argus R5.60
Cape Times Daily R3.10

Accepts articles of general and South African interest; also cartoons. Payment: in accordance with an editor's assessment.

Independent Newspapers Gauteng

PO Box 1044, Johannesburg 2000
tel (011) 633-9111 *fax* (011) 836-8398
website www.iol.co.za
Johannesburg **The Star** Daily R2.40
Saturday Star R3.20
Sunday Independent R6
Pretoria **Pretoria News** Daily R2.50

Accepts articles of general and South African interest; also cartoons. Payment: in accordance with an editor's assessment.

Independent Newspapers Kwa-Zulu Natal Ltd

18 Osborne Street, Greyville, Durban 4023
tel (031) 308-2400 *fax* (031) 308-2427
website www.iol.co.za
Durban **Daily News** R2.40
Ilanga Bi-weekly R1.40
The Mercury Daily R3.20
The Post Bi-weekly R3.40
Independent on Saturday R3.20

Accepts articles of general and South African interest; also cartoons. Payment: in accordance with an editor's assessment.

(Johannesburg) Sunday Times

PO Box 1742, Saxonwold 2132
tel (011) 280-5102 *fax* (011) 280-5111
email suntimes@sundaytimes.co.za
Editor M.W. Robertson
Sun R6

Illustrated articles of political or human interest, from a South African angle if possible. Maximum 1000 words long and 2 or 3 photos. Shorter essays, stories and articles of a light nature from 500–750 words. Payment: average rate £100 a column. Illustrations: colour and b&w photos, line drawings.

Living and Loving

Caxton Magazines, PO Box 32083, Mobeni 4060, KwaZulu-Natal
tel (031) 910 5785/6
Editor Fiona Wayman
Monthly R11.95

Parenting magazine: from pregnancy to preschool. Articles about behaviour and development in the first 7 years of life. First-person parenting experiences – pregnancy and the growing child. Medical news/breakthroughs of interest to parents worldwide. Payment: by merit, on acceptance and publication. Founded 1970.

Natal Witness

Box 362, Pietermaritzburg, KwaZulu-Natal 3201
tel (033) 355-1111 *fax* (033) 355-1122
email features@witness.co.za
Editor J.H. Conyngham
Daily R2.60

Accepts topical articles. All material should be submitted direct to the editor in Pietermaritzburg. Length: 500–1000 words. Payment: average of R350 per 1000 words. Founded 1846.

Southern Cross

PO Box 2372, Cape Town 8000
tel (021) 465-5007 *fax* (021) 465-3850
email scross@global.co.za
Editor Gunther Simmermacher
Weekly R3

National English-language Catholic weekly. Catholic news reports, world and South African. Length: 550-word articles. Illustrations: photos of Catholic interest from freelance contributors. Payment: 12c per word; illustrations R23.10.

Woman's Value

Media 24, PO Box 1802, Cape Town 8000
tel (021) 406-2205 *fax* (021) 406-2929
email tleroux@womansvalue.com
website www.womansvalue.com
Editor Terena le Raix
Monthly R11.95

Features on beauty, food, finance, knitting, needlecraft, crafts, home and garden, health and parenting; short stories. 1000-word accounts of experiences published on the 'My own story' page. Length: up to 1200 words (features/ stories). Payment: by negotiation. Colour transparencies. Founded 1980.

World Airnews

PO Box 35082, Northway, Durban 4065
tel (031) 564-1319 *fax* (031) 563-7115
Editor Tom Chalmers
Monthly £36 p.a.

Aviation news and features with an African angle. Payment: by negotiation.

Your Family

PO Box 473016, Parklands 2121, Gauteng
tel (011) 889-0749
Editor Patti Garlick
Monthly R10.95

Cookery, knitting, crochet and home-crafts. Family drama, happy ending. Payment: by arrangement. Illustrations: continuous tone, colour and line, cartoons.

USA

The Yearbook does not contain a detailed list of US magazines and journals. The Overseas volume of Willings Press Guide is the most useful general reference guide to US publications, available in most reference libraries. For readers with a particular interest in the US market, the publications listed here will be helpful (please make payments to the US in US funds).

American Markets Newsletter

175 Westland Drive, Glasgow G14 9JQ
e-mail sheila.oconnor@juno.com
Editor Sheila O'Connor
6 p.a. £34 p.a. (£63 for 2 years)

Editorial guidelines for US, Canadian and other overseas markets, plus information on press trips, non-fiction/fiction markets and writers' tips. Free syndication. Sample issue £5.95 (payable to S. O'Connor).

Willings Press Guide

Waymaker Ltd, Chess House,
34 Germain Street, Chesham, Bucks. HP5 1SJ
tel 0870-7360010 (UK), (1494) 797225 (int.)
fax 0870-7360011 (UK), (1494) 797224
e-mail willings@waymaker.co.uk
website www.willingspress.com
£265 2-volume set; or £180 UK volume, £190 international volume

Two volumes contain details of over 50,000 newspapers, broadcasters, periodicals and special interest titles in the UK and internationally. Usually available at local reference libraries or direct from the publisher. Also available as an online product.

The Writer

Kalmbach Publishing Co., 21027 Crossroads Circle, PO Box 1612, Waukesha, WI 53187
Monthly $29 p.a. ($39 p.a. Canada and foreign)

Contains articles of instruction on all writing fields, lists of markets for MSS and special features of interest to freelance writers everywhere. The Writer Books also publishes books on writing fiction, non-fiction, poetry, articles, plays, etc.

Writer's Digest

Writer's Digest Books, 4700 East Galbraith Road, Cincinnati, OH 45236
($36 plus $10 surface post, $75 airmail)

Monthly magazine for writers who want to write better and sell more; aims to inform, instruct and inspire the freelance.

Writer's Digest Books

Writer's Digest Books, 4700 East Galbraith Road, Cincinnati, OH 45236

Also publishes annually *Novel and Short Story Writer's Market, Children's Writer's and Illustrator's Market, Poet's Market, Photographer's Market, Artist's & Graphic Designer's Market, Guide to Literary Agents* and many other books on creating and selling writing and illustrations.

The Writer's Handbook

The Writer Books, Kalmbach Publishing Co., Dept W1966, 21027 Crossroads Circle, PO Box 986, Waukesha, WI 53187
$29.95 plus $5.50 shipping & handling; $7.50 s&h plus 7% GST Canada; $10.50 s&h foreign

Contains more than 3000 quality magazine and book markets, and hundreds of additional literary resources, plus 60 articles with advice from America's most successful writers.

Writer's Market

Writer's Digest Books (address above)
($27.99 plus $4 p&p)

An annual guidebook giving editorial requirements and other details of over 4000 US markets for freelance writing. Also available on CD-Rom.

Submitting manuscripts

When submitting material to US journals, include a covering letter, together with return postage in the form of International Reply Coupons (IRC). IRCs can be exchanged in any foreign country for stamps representing the minimum postage payable on a letter sent from one country to another. Make it clear what rights are being offered for sale as some editors like to purchase MSS outright, thus securing world copyright, i.e. the traditional British market as well as the US market. Send the MSS direct to the US office of the journal and not to any London office.

In many cases it is best to send a preliminary letter giving a rough outline of your article or story (enclose IRCs for a reply). Most magazines will send a leaflet giving guidance to authors.

Magazines by subject area

These lists can be only a broad classification. They should be regarded as a pointer to possible markets and should be used with discrimination. Addresses for magazines start on page 21.

Fiction (see also Literary)

Active Life
Acumen
Ambit
Aquila
Australian Short Stories (Aus.)
The Australian Women's Weekly (Aus.)
Back Street Heroes
Bella
Best
Brownie
Cencrastus: Scottish & International Literature, Arts and Affairs
Chapman
Chat
Chickadee (Can.)
Critical Quarterly
The Dalhousie Review (Can.)
Day by Day
Diva
The Edge
The Erotic Review
The Fiddlehead (Can.)
Fly-Fishing & Fly-Tying
For Women
Interzone
Ireland's Own
The Jewish Quarterly
The Lady
The London Magazine: A Review of Literature and the Arts
The Malahat Review (Can.)
More!
Mslexia
My Weekly
My Weekly Story Collection
New Impact
The New Writer
New Zealand Woman's Day (NZ)
New Zealand Woman's Weekly (NZ)
Overland (Aus.)
Peninsular Magazine
People's Friend
People's Friend Story Collection
Planet
Practical Caravan
Pride
Prospect
Quadrant (Aus.)
QWF
Railway Magazine
Reality
The Scots Magazine
Scuba Diver (Aus.)
Springboard
Stand Magazine
Staple
Starburst
Takahe (NZ)
Take a Break
The Third Alternative
The Times Literary Supplement
Wascana Review of Contemporary Poetry & Short Fiction (Can.)
Woman and Home
Woman's Weekly Fiction Special
Woman's Day (Aus.)
Woman's Own
Woman's Way
Woman's Weekly
Writers' Forum
Young Writer
Your Cat Magazine
Yours

Letters to the Editor

Amateur Gardening
The Australian Women's Weekly (Aus.)
Bella
Best
The Big Issue
Birding World
Bizarre
Caravan Magazine
Chartered Secretary
Child Education
Country Smallholding
Day by Day
Dolly (Aus.)
The Economist
Electrical Times
The Engineer
FHM (For Him Magazine)
Freelance Market News
H&E Naturist
Here's Health
Ideal Home
Jewish Telegraph
Modern Painters
Moneywise
Mother & Baby
Motor Boat and Yachting
Motor Caravan Magazine
My Weekly
New Law Journal
New Zealand Woman's Day (NZ)
Nursery Education
NW Magazine (Aus.)
Park Home & Holiday Caravan
People's Friend
Personal Finance
Police Journal
Practical Caravan
Practical Householder
Practical Parenting
Practical Photography
Prima
Retail Week
Saga Magazine
Shout

Ski and Board
Slimmer, Healthier, Fitter
Slimming Magazine
Take a Break
Television
that's life!
Third Way
TV Quick
The Weekly News
West Lothian Life
What's on TV
Woman's Day (Aus.)
Woman's Way
Woman's Weekly
Writers' Forum
Writers' News
Writing Magazine
Yours

Gossip paragraphs

Australian Bookseller & Publisher (Aus.)
The Big Issue
Broadcast
Campaign
Church of England Newspaper
Classical Music
Country Life
Dirt Bike Rider
Drapers Record
Electrical Times
Eventing
Femina Magazine (SA)
FHM (For Him Magazine)
Film Review
Garden News
Geographical Magazine
Golf Weekly
Golf World
Hampshire – The County Magazine
Horse & Hound
Irish Medical Times
Irish Printer
The Lawyer
Making Music
Marketing Week
Mojo
Music Week
My Weekly
New Statesman
New Welsh Review
Nursing Times
Opera Now
The Pink Paper
Pride
Radio Times
Retail Week
Rugby World
Runner's World
Running Fitness
Satellite Times
Shoot
Shout
The Stage
The Tablet
tate: the art magazine
The Voice
World Soccer
Writers' News
Writing Magazine

Brief filler paragraphs

Active Life
Africa Confidential
Amateur Gardening
American Markets Newsletter
The Architects' Journal
Athletics Weekly
Australian Bookseller & Publisher (Aus.)
Bella
The Big Issue
Boards
Broadcast
Cage & Aviary Birds
Cencrastus: Scottish & International Literature, Arts and Affairs
Classic Cars
Communicate
Country Life
Country Smallholding
The Countryman
Decanter
Drapers Record
Electrical Times
Eventing
Executive PA
Femina Magazine (SA)
Film Review
Flight International
Freelance Market News
Garden News
Geographical Magazine
Gibbons Stamp Monthly
Golf Weekly
Golf World
Greetings Today
H&E Naturist
Hampshire – The County Magazine
Health & Fitness
Horse & Hound
Horticulture Week
Hortus
Hotel and Catering Review
Insurance Age
Inuit Art Quarterly (Can.)
Ireland of the Welcomes
Ireland's Own
Irish Medical Times
Irish Printer
Jane's Defence Weekly
Jewish Telegraph
Justice of the Peace
Kids Out
The Lawyer
Making Music
Marketing Week
Model Engineer
My Weekly
New Welsh Review
Nursing Times
Opera Now
Overland (Aus.)
Picture Postcard Monthly
Pig Farming
The Pink Paper
Police Review
Pony Magazine
Post Magazine & Insurance Week
Practical Fishkeeping
Pride
Radio Times
Reader's Digest
Reader's Digest (Australia) (Aus.)
Retail Week
Runner's World
Running Fitness
Satellite Times
The School Librarian
Sea Breezes
Shoot
Slimmer, Healthier, Fitter
Snooker Scene
Somerset Magazine
The Songwriter
Southern Cross (SA)
The Stage
Stamp Lover
Studio Sound
The Tablet
tate: the art magazine
Technology Ireland
Trucking
Waterways World
Weight Watchers Magazine
The Woodworker
World Airnews (SA)
World Fishing
World Soccer
Writers' News
Writing Magazine
Your Dog Magazine

Puzzles and quizzes

The following take puzzles and/or quizzes on an occasional or, in some cases, regular basis. Ideas must be tailored to suit each publication: approach in writing in the first instance.

Active Life
Baptist Times
The Big Issue in the North
Bird Watching
Birding World
Brownie
Cage & Aviary Birds
Catholic Gazette
Chickadee (Can.)
Choice
Country Life
The Dandy
Darts World
Dirt Bike Rider
Disability Now
Dolly (Aus.)
Electrical Times
The Engineer
Essex Magazine
Farmer's Weekly (SA)
Film Review
Fire
Fishing World Magazine (Aus.)
Football Picture Story Library
Garden and Home (SA)
Golf Monthly
Guiding Magazine
Hertfordshire Countryside
Horse & Hound
Hospital Doctor
Hotel and Catering Review
Housebuilder
Irish Medical Times
J17
Kids Alive! (The Young Soldier)
Kids Out
Living and Loving (SA)
Making Music
(Melbourne) Herald Sun (Aus.)
More!
Nursing Times
Opera
Opera Now
Park Home & Holiday Caravan
Performing Arts & Entertainment in Canada (PA&E) (Can.)
Picture Postcard Monthly
Practical Caravan
Practical Photography
Publishing News
Reality
Runner's World
Running Fitness
Satellite Times
Shoot
Shout
Snooker Scene
Southern Cross (SA)
The Spectator
Sugar
The Tablet
Take a Break's Take a Puzzle
The Times Literary Supplement
The Universe
Waterways World
West Lothian Life
Woman's Way
The Woodworker
The Word
World Soccer
Your Family (SA)

UK ethnic weekly newspapers

Asian Times
Caribbean Times
Eastern Eye
The Voice

Women's interest magazines (see also Health and home)

The Australian Women's Weekly (Aus.)
Bella
Best
Black Beauty & Hair
Bliss!
Bona (SA)
Chat
Chatelaine (Can.)
Company
Cosmopolitan
Diva
Elle (UK)
Essentials
Executive PA
Executive Woman
Femina Magazine (SA)
For Women
Girl About Town Magazine
Glamour
Good Housekeeping
Hairflair
Harpers & Queen
Harper's Bazaar (Aus.)
Hello!
Home and Country
Home Words
HQ Magazine (Aus.)
Irish Tatler
The Lady
Living and Loving (SA)
Marie Claire
Modern Woman Nationwide
More!
Mother & Baby
Ms London
Mslexia
My Weekly
My Weekly Story Collection
New Woman (Aus.)
New Woman
New Zealand Woman's Day (NZ)
New Zealand Woman's Weekly (NZ)
19
Nursery World
Office Secretary (OS Magazine)
OK! Magazine
People's Friend
The Pink Paper
Pride
Prima
Prima Baby
Red
She (NZ)
She
She Kicks
Sugar
Take a Break
Tatler
that's life!
U magazine
Vanity Fair
Vogue
Vogue Australia (Aus.)
Wedding and Home
Woman
Woman Alive
Woman and Home
Woman's Weekly Fiction Special
Woman's Day (Aus.)
Woman's Own
Woman's Value (SA)
Woman's Way
Woman's Weekly
Women's Health
World's Children
You & Your Wedding
Your Family (SA)

Men's interest magazines

Arena
Attitude
Country
Esquire
FHM (For Him Magazine)
Gay Times
GQ
Loaded
Maxim
Men Only
Men's Health
The Pink Paper

Children's and young adult magazines

Animals and You
Aquila
The Beano
Brownie
Chickadee (Can.)
Commando
The Dandy
Dolly (Aus.)
Football Picture Story Library
Hot Press
i-D Magazine
J17
Mizz
Pony Magazine
Scouting Magazine
Shoot
Shout
Smash Hits
Young Writer

Subject articles

Advertising, design, printing and publishing (see also Literary)

Arena
Australian Bookseller & Publisher (Aus.)
The Author
British Journalism Review
Campaign
The Face
Freelance Market News
Greetings Today
Irish Printer
Media Week
New Media Age
PR Week
Press Gazette
Printing World
Publishing News

Agriculture, farming and horticulture

Country Life
Country Smallholding
The Countryman
Dairy Farmer
Farmers Weekly
Farmer's Weekly (SA)
The Field
The Grower
Horticulture Week
Irish Farmers Journal
Pig Farming
Poultry World
The Scottish Farmer
Smallholder
Straight Furrow (NZ)

Architecture and building

The Architects' Journal
Architectural Design
The Architectural Review
Architecture Today
Blueprint
Building
Building Design
Built Environment
Country Homes and Interiors
Country Life
Education Journal
Homes and Gardens
House & Garden
Housebuilder
Ideal Home

Art and collecting

AN Magazine
Antiques & Art Independent
Antiques and Collectables
Apollo
Art Business Today
Art Monthly
The Art Newspaper
Art Review
The Artist
Artists and Illustrators
The Book Collector
Book and Magazine Collector
Burlington Magazine
C international contemporary art (Can.)
Coin News
Contemporary
Country Life
Eastern Art Report
Embroidery
Gibbons Stamp Monthly
The Illustrated London News
Inuit Art Quarterly (Can.)
Leisure Painter
Medal News
Modern Painters
RA Magazine
Stamp Lover
Stamp Magazine
tate: the art magazine

Aviation

Aeroplane Monthly
Air International
Air Pictorial International
Australian Flying (Aus.)
Flight International
Pilot
Today's Pilot
World Airnews (SA)

Blind and partially sighted

Published by the Royal National Institute for the Blind in braille unless otherwise stated (see under Book publishers UK and Ireland)

3-FM
Absolutely Boys (also disk)
Absolutely Girls (also disk)
Access IT (also disk)
After Hours
Aphra (women's magazine; also disk)
BBC on Air (also disk)

Blast Off! (also disk)
Braille Chess Magazine
Braille Journal of Physiotherapy
Braille at Bedtime
Braille Music Magazine (also disk)
Braille Radio Times
Braille TV Times (5 regions)
Broadcast Times (disk only)
Busy Solicitor's Digest (also disk)
Channels of Blessing (also disk)
Come Gardening
Compute IT (also disk)
Contention (also disk)
Conundrum (also disk)
Daily Bread (also disk)
Diane (Moon)
Eye Contact (also print)
Good Vibrations (also disk)
High Browse (also print, tape and disk)
Light of the Moon (Moon)
The Moon Magazine (Moon)
Money Matters (also disk)
New Beacon (also print, tape and disk)
News to You? (also print, tape and disk)
Physiotherapists' Quarterly
Piano Tuners' Quarterly (also print, tape and disk)
Progress (also disk)
Rhetoric (also disk)
Scientific Enquiry (also disk)
Shaping Up (also disk)
Shop Window (also disk)
Slugs and Snails (also disk)
SP (Starting Price: men's magazine; also disk)
Spotlight (also print, tape and disk)
Sugar and Spice (also disk)
Theological Times (also tape and disk)
Upbeat (also disk)
You & Your Child (also disk)
VisAbility (also print and tape)
Welcome to a World of ... (also disk)

Business, industry and management

Business Life
Business Scotland
Chartered Secretary
Communicate
Cosmetic World News
Director
European Chemical News
Executive PA
Executive Woman
Fasttrack
Fire
Fishing News
Land & Liberty
Management Magazine (NZ)
Management Today
New Impact
Office Secretary (OS Magazine)
People Management
The Political Quarterly
The Woodworker

Cinema and films

Campaign
The Edge
Empire
Film Review
New Statesman
Screen International
Sight and Sound
Studio Sound
Total Film

Computers

Computer Weekly
Computing
Internet
MacUser
.net The Internet Magazine
PC Answers
PC Direct
Personal Computer World
Scientific Computing World
What Laptop & Handheld PC

Economics, accountancy and finance

Accountancy
Accountancy Age
Accounting & Business
Active Life
Africa Confidential
African Business
The Australian Financial Review (Aus.)
The Banker
Business Scotland
Choice
Contemporary Review
Economica
The Economist
Financial Adviser
The Grower
Insurance Age
Insurance Brokers' Monthly
Investors Chronicle
Land & Liberty
MoneyMarketing
Moneywise
New Statesman
Pensions World
Personal Finance
Post Magazine & Insurance Week
Tribune

Education

Amateur Stage
Aquila
Carousel – The Guide to Children's Books
Child Education
Education Journal
Guiding Magazine
Infant Projects
Junior Education
Junior Focus
The Linguist
Modern Language Review
Music Teacher
New Impact
New Statesman
Nursery Education
Nursery World
Practical Parenting
Reality
Report
Right Start
Safety Education
The School Librarian
The Teacher
TES Primary
The Times Educational Supplement
Times Educational Supplement Scotland
Times Higher Education Supplement
Tribune
Under Five Contact
World's Children
Young People Now

Engineering and mechanics (see also Architecture, Aviation, Business, Motor transport, Nautical, Radio, Sciences)

Car Mechanics
EA Today Magazine (Aus.)
EE Times
Electrical Review
Electrical Times
The Engineer
Engineering

European Chemical News
Everyday Practical Electronics
Fire
Model Engineer
Practical Woodworking
Rail
Railway Gazette International
Railway Magazine

Gardening

Amateur Gardening
Country
Country Life
Country Smallholding
The English Garden
Essential Water Garden
The Field
The Garden
Garden and Home (SA)
Garden Answers
Garden News
Homestyle
Hortus
House & Garden
NZ House & Garden (NZ)
Organic Gardening

Health and home (see also Women's interest magazines)

Active Life
Australian Home Beautiful (Aus.)
Australian House and Garden (Aus.)
Black Beauty & Hair
British Deaf News
Choice
Classic Stitches
Country Homes and Interiors
Country Living
Garden and Home (SA)
H&E Naturist
Health & Fitness
Here's Health
Home and Family
Homes and Gardens
Homestyle
House & Garden
House Beautiful
Ideal Home
In Balance Health & Lifestyle Magazine
Inspirations For Your Home
Kids Out
NZ House & Garden (NZ)
Perfect Home
Period Living & Traditional Homes
Practical Householder
Practical Parenting
Prediction
Prima Baby
Running Fitness
Safety Education
Saga Magazine
Sainsbury's Magazine
Scottish Home and Country
Slimmer, Healthier, Fitter
Slimming Magazine
The Vegan
Weight Watchers Magazine
Wine
Woman's Value (SA)
Women's Health
The World of Interiors
Your Family (SA)
Your Home and Garden (NZ)
Yours
Zest

History and archaeology

Best of British
Coin News
Evergreen
Geographical Magazine
History Today
The Illustrated London News
In Britain
The National Trust Magazine
Picture Postcard Monthly
Scottish Memories
Studies, An Irish quarterly review

Hotel, catering and leisure

Caterer & Hotelkeeper
Health Club Management
Hotel and Catering Review
The Leisure Manager

Humour and satire

Private Eye
Viz Comic

Inflight magazines

Business Life

Legal and police

Family Law
Justice of the Peace
The Lawyer
Legal Week
New Law Journal
Police Journal
Police Review
Solicitors Journal

Leisure interests, pets (see also Nautical, Sports)

Ace Tennis Magazine
Astronomy Now
Bird Keeper
Bird Watching
Birding World
Birdwatch
Boards
British Birds
British Philatelic Bulletin
Camping Magazine
Canal & Riverboat
Caravan Magazine
Classic Stitches
Classics
Climber
Country Walking
Decanter
Dogs Today
Family Tree Magazine
The Field
Folio
Gibbons Stamp Monthly
Guiding Magazine
The List
Military Modelling
Mixmag
Model Boats
Model Engineer
Motor Caravan Magazine
Motorcaravan Motorhome Monthly (MMM)
Needlecraft
Our Dogs
Park Home & Holiday Caravan
Popular Crafts
Practical Caravan
Practical Fishkeeping
Radio Control Models and Electronics
The Rambler
Scottish Field
Scouting Magazine
Scuba World
Sewing World
Stamp Lover
Stamp Magazine
Swimming Magazine
Time Out

Venue
Wine
The Woodworker
Workbox Magazine
Your Cat Magazine
Your Dog Magazine

Literary (see also Poetry)

American Markets Newsletter
Australian Bookseller & Publisher (Aus.)
Australian Short Stories (Aus.)
The Author
The Book Collector
Books in Canada (Can.)
Books Ireland
Books Magazine
The Bookseller
British Journalism Review
The Canadian Forum (Can.)
Canadian Literature (Can.)
Canadian Writer's Journal (Can.)
Carousel – The Guide to Children's Books
Cencrastus: Scottish & International Literature, Arts and Affairs
Chapman
Contemporary Review
Critical Quarterly
The Dalhousie Review (Can.)
The Dickensian
The Edge
Edinburgh Review
The Fiddlehead (Can.)
The Fix
Granta
Index on Censorship
Journal of Canadian Studies (Can.)
Leviathan Quarterly
The Literary Review
LOGOS
The London Magazine: A Review of Literature and the Arts
London Review of Books
The Malahat Review (Can.)
Market Newsletter
Meanjin (Aus.)
Modern Language Review
Mslexia
New Statesman
New Welsh Review
The New Writer
The Oldie
Orbis
Outposts Poetry Quarterly
Overland (Aus.)
Peninsular Magazine
Planet
Prospect
Publishing News
Quadrant (Aus.)
Queen's Quarterly (Can.)
Quill & Quire (Can.)
QWF
Reality
Scottish Book Collector
Signal, Approaches to Children's Books
The Spectator
Springboard
Stand Magazine
Starburst
Studies, An Irish quarterly review
Takahe (NZ)
The Third Alternative
The Times Literary Supplement
Tribune
Wascana Review of Contemporary Poetry & Short Fiction (Can.)
The Woman Writer
Writers' Forum
Writers' News
Writing Magazine
Young Writer

Local government and civil service

Justice of the Peace
PCS View

Marketing and retailing

Drapers Record
Greetings Today
The Grocer
Marketing Week
Retail Week
Ulster Grocer

Medicine and nursing

Balance
BMA News
British Deaf News
British Medical Journal
Disability Now
Hospital Doctor
Irish Journal of Medical Science
Irish Medical Times
Journal of Alternative and Complementary Medicine
Lancet
Nursery World
Nursing Times
The Practising Midwife
The Practitioner
Professional Nurse
Pulse
Therapy Weekly
This Caring Business
Veterinary Review
Young People Now

Military

Jane's Defence Weekly
RUSI Journal

Motor transport and cycling

Auto Express
Autocar
Back Street Heroes
Bike
Buses
Car (SA)
Car
Car Mechanics
Classic & Sports Car
Classic Cars
Classics
Commercial Motor
Custom Car
Cycling Weekly
Dirt Bike Rider
Motor Cycle News
Truck & Driver
Trucking
What Car?

Music and recording

Arena
Classical Music
Early Music
The Face
Hi-Fi News
i-D Magazine
Jazz Journal International
Kerrang!
Making Music
Mojo
Music Teacher
Music Week
Musical Opinion
Musical Times
New Musical Express
Opera
Opera Now
Q Magazine
Smash Hits
The Songwriter
Songwriting and Composing
Studio Sound
Tempo

Natural history (see also Agriculture, Rural life)

Bird Keeper
Bird Watching
Birding World
Birdwatch
British Birds
Cage & Aviary Birds
Cat World
Chickadee (Can.)
Dogs Today
The Ecologist
Equinox (Can.)
Geo Australasia (Aus.)
Geographical Magazine
Guiding Magazine
The National Trust Magazine
Natural World
Naturalist
Nature
Our Dogs
Today's Fishkeeper

Nautical and marine

Australian Powerboat (Aus.)
Canal & Riverboat
Classic Boat & The Boatman
Diver
Motor Boat and Yachting
Motor Boats Monthly
Nautical Magazine
Practical Boat Owner
Sea Breezes
Ships Monthly
Yachting Monthly
Yachting World
Yachts and Yachting

Photography

Amateur Photographer
Australian Camera (Aus.)
Australian Photography (Aus.)
The British Journal of Photography
Camcorder User
Freelance Photographer
Market Newsletter
Photo Life (Can.)
Practical Photography
What Camcorder

Poetry

**Magazines that only take the occasional poem: check with the editor before submitting*

Acumen
Agenda
Ambit
Best of British*
Brownie*
Cencrastus: Scottish & International Literature, Arts and Affairs
Chapman
Chickadee (Can.)
Contemporary Review*
The Countryman*
The Cricketer International*
Critical Quarterly
Cumbria and Lake District Magazine
Cyphers
Dalesman*
The Dalhousie Review (Can.)
Day by Day*
East Lothian Life*
Edinburgh Review
Envoi
The Erotic Review*
Evergreen*
The Fiddlehead (Can.)
Fortnight – An Independent Review of Politics and the Arts
Home and Country*
HQ Poetry Magazine
Infant Projects
Jewish Chronicle*
The Jewish Quarterly*
The Lady*
Lancet*
Leviathan Quarterly
The Literary Review
The London Magazine: A Review of Literature and the Arts
London Review of Books
The Malahat Review (Can.)
Meanjin (Aus.)
Mslexia*
New Humanist*
New Welsh Review
The New Writer*
Orbis
Other Poetry
Outposts Poetry Quarterly
Overland (Aus.)
Oxford Poetry
Peninsular Magazine
People's Friend*
Planet
PN Review
Poetry Ireland Review/Éigse Éireann
Poetry London
Poetry Nottingham International
Poetry Review
Poetry Wales
Pride
Quadrant (Aus.)
Reform*
The Rialto
The Scots Magazine*
Scuba Diver* (Aus.)
The Shop: A Magazine of Poetry
Songwriting and Composing*
The Spectator*
Springboard
Stand Magazine
Staple
Takahe (NZ)
Third Way*
This England*
The Times Literary Supplement*
Traveller*
Tribune*
Wascana Review of Contemporary Poetry & Short Fiction (Can.)
West Lothian Life*
Writers' Forum*
Young Writer*
Yours

Politics

Africa Confidential
Australian Journal of International Affairs (Aus.)
Australian Journal of Politics and History (Aus.)
The China Quarterly
Christian Herald
Contemporary Review
Fortnight – An Independent Review of Politics and the Arts
The Illustrated London News
International Affairs
Justice of the Peace
New Internationalist
New Statesman
Peace News
The Political Quarterly
Prospect
Red Pepper
Studies, An Irish quarterly review
Tribune
The World Today

Radio, TV and video

Broadcast
Cable Guide
Campaign
EA Today Magazine (Aus.)
Empire
Film Review
Hi-Fi News
InterMedia
New Statesman
Opera Now
Practical Wireless
Radio Times
Satellite Times
The Short Wave Magazine
The Stage
Studio Sound
Television
Tribune
TV Quick
TVTimes Magazine
What's on TV

Religion, philosophy and New Age

Baptist Times
Catholic Gazette
The Catholic Herald
Catholic Pictorial
Catholic Times
Christian Herald
Church of England Newspaper
Church Times
Contemporary Review
Day by Day
Fortean Times
The Friend
The Furrow
Home and Family
Home Words
Jewish Chronicle
The Jewish Quarterly
Jewish Telegraph
Kids Alive! (The Young Soldier)
Life & Work: Magazine of the Church of Scotland
Methodist Recorder
New Humanist
Priests & People
Reality
Reform
The Sign
Southern Cross (SA)
Studies, An Irish quarterly review
The Tablet
Third Way
The Universe
The War Cry
Woman Alive
The Word

Rural life and country (see also Natural history)

Aussie Post (Aus.)
Buckinghamshire Countryside
Country
Country Life
Country Quest
The Countryman
Cumbria and Lake District Magazine
Dalesman
Derbyshire Life and Countryside
Dorset Life – The Dorset Magazine
East Lothian Life
Essex Life & Countryside
Essex Magazine
Evergreen
The Field
Hampshire – The County Magazine
Hertfordshire Countryside
In Britain
Lancashire Magazine
Lincolnshire Life
The National Trust Magazine
The Rambler
The Scots Magazine
Scottish Field
Scottish Home and Country
Shooting Times and Country Magazine
The Shropshire Magazine
Somerset Magazine
The Spark Magazine
Staffordshire Life Magazine
This England
Waterways World
West Lothian Life
Yorkshire Ridings Magazine

Sciences

Equinox (Can.)
Focus
Geological Magazine
Nature
New Scientist
Science Progress
Scientific Computing World
Technology Ireland

Sports and games (see also Leisure interests, Motor transport, Nautical)

Ace Tennis Magazine
Angler's Mail
Angling Times
Athletics Weekly
Australian Powerboat (Aus.)
Bowls International
The Cricketer International
Darts World
Descent
Eventing
The Field
Fishing World Magazine (Aus.)
Fly-Fishing & Fly-Tying
FourFourTwo
Golf Monthly
Golf Weekly
Golf World
Horse & Hound
Horse and Rider
Our Dogs
Racing Post
Rock (Aus.)
Rugby World
Runner's World
Running Fitness
Scottish Field
Scuba Diver (Aus.)
Scuba World
Sea Angler
She Kicks
Shoot
Shooting Times and Country Magazine
Ski and Board
The Skier and The Snowboarder Magazine
Snooker Scene
Sport First
The Squash Player
Swimming Magazine
Tennis World
Today's Golfer
Trout and Salmon
Wisden Cricket Monthly
The Word
World Fishing
World Soccer

Theatre, drama and dancing (see also Cinema, Music)

Amateur Stage
The Canadian Forum (Can.)
Canadian Theatre Review (CTR) (Can.)
Dance Australia (Aus.)
Dance Today!
Dancing Times
The Illustrated London News
In Britain
New Statesman
New Theatre Quarterly
Performing Arts & Entertainment in Canada (PA&E) (Can.)
Radio Times
Reality
The Stage
Tribune
TVTimes Magazine

Travel and geography

Australian Geographic (Aus.)
Caledonia
Caravan Magazine
The China Quarterly
Condé Nast Traveller
Country Quest
Equinox (Can.)
FRANCE Magazine
Geo Australasia (Aus.)
Geographical Journal
Geographical Magazine
The Illustrated London News
In Britain
In Dublin
Ireland of the Welcomes
Natal Witness (SA)
Traveller
Wanderlust
Wild (Aus.)

Recent changes to newspapers and magazines

The following changes have taken place since the last edition of the Yearbook.

Changes of name and mergers

Ace *now* Ace Tennis Magazine
The Aquarist and Pondkeeper *now* Today's Fishkeeper
Ballroom Dancing Times *now* Dance Today!
cva (Contemporary Visual Arts) *now* Contemporary
Electronics Times *now* EE Times
Essex Countryside *now* Essex Life & Countryside
Grimsby Evening Telegraph *now* Grimsby Telegraph
Health and Efficiency – H&E Magazine *now* H&E Naturist
HouseBuilder *now* Housebuilder
IT (Irish Tatler) *now* Irish Tatler
ONtheBALL *now* She Kicks
Practical Parenting's Complete Guide to Pregnancy *merged with* Practical Parenting
Staple New Writing *now* Staple
Sunday Business *now* The Business
Swiming Times *now* Swimming Magazine
Trucking International *now* Trucking
The World of Embroidery *now* Embroidery
World Wide Writers *merged with* Writers' Forum

Titles ceased publication

Art & Design
Bunty Monthly
Celebrity Looks
Cool Magazine
DPICT
Farming News
Good Health
Homes & Ideas
Hot Air
Magpie
My Weekly Puzzle Time
The New Zealand Farmer
Peakland Walker
Print it! magazine
Real Money
Shine
Signal, Approaches to Children's Books (last issue Summer 2003)
Sky Magazine
Total Football
Woman's Journal
Your Garden

Writing for newspapers

A newspaper may be only ink on paper but it's alive, feeding on topicality, originality and the quality of writing on its pages. The contributors an editor longs to hear from identify with the readers and understand what they want. Such contributors are never short of work and enjoy great personal satisfaction. ***Jill Dick*** *looks at newspapers from the freelance's point of view.*

Freelance writers are essential in newspaper production. The sense of excitement, of being reborn every week, every day or even several times a day, and of living on a fast-moving platform of people and events makes papers grow and thrive – and the work of freelances, each with a fresh view of the outside world, is invaluable.

Newspapers offer writers an enormous variety of markets. In the UK and Ireland there are more than two dozen national daily and Sunday papers, plus dozens of supplements, representing thousands of separate opportunities a year for freelance contributions. The nationals fall into three groups – quality, middle-range and popular – each with its own characteristics, ranging from *The Times* and the *Daily Telegraph*, to the *Daily Mail* and the *Daily Star*; from the *Observer* to the *Sunday People* and from the *Sunday Express* to the *Sunday Mirror*. Add to these hundreds of evening and weekly regional newspapers and an increasing number of free papers – and the total is staggering.

The size and quality of the readership are vital elements in market study. Advertisers want to know this too, and freelance writers can benefit greatly from the information advertisers use for their own purposes. It is not unusual for a serious Sunday newspaper to reserve 50% of the whole paper for advertisements and to carry as many as 150 display and several thousand classified ads in a single edition.

Advertisers (with big money at stake) take pains to target the readers most likely to buy their wares or use their services: editors have the same idea in mind when considering whether to accept or reject work from freelances. Will this particular copy encourage readers to buy the paper or make them pleased they did so to the extent that they will buy the next edition too? That's how close you need to get to the readers for consistent success.

There is no better way of finding out who the readers are and how they think and live than making a close, regular and up-to-date study of the papers you'd like to write for. Analyse their content, their page layout and format and discover why they print what they do. Even such attention to detail isn't infallible, for at best it can only reveal what they printed and were interested in yesterday or last week. As for what they'll want tomorrow and next week …

Ideas

If ideas jostle for priority in your head almost without thinking you may have a natural bent for newspaper writing. Even if they don't, remember journalism is a craft which almost anyone can learn, and gathering ideas is just part of it. No matter where you live or work, whom you meet, how you spend your time or what your hobbies and interests may be, you'll find a story. Feature, filler, news item, article, review, regular series, specialist column, interview, diary item, letter, anecdote, profile, preview; in buying a paper readers instinctively ask themselves, 'What's in it for me?' You are providing the answer. To help you there are several well-established market guides, the best being the *Writers' & Artists' Yearbook*, *Willings Press Guide* and *Benns Media*.

To provide a list of topics to write about would be counter-productive. Dry lists of ideas can encourage stultified thinking; countless writers have stared at such lists and tried to wrench inspiration from them; countless editors have seen (and rejected) the results. In any case, more is needed than an idea. A unique slant on one may be the pointer to a worthwhile venture but a newspaper 'story' is most likely to be successful when it arrives in your head eager, if not desperate, to be told.

Whatever your chosen topic, remember that fishermen bait their hooks not with what they like, but with what fish like. There are many hard lessons to learn about freelancing and one of the toughest is that you have to write not just the stories that appeal to you, but the stories that will sell.

It pays to look ahead, particularly in ways other writers may not. This is not always easy to do and you will have to work hard on your copy before ever writing a word. Research can never be skimped. A thinly researched piece quickly lands on the reject pile if another author has taken more time and trouble to delve into the subject than you have. The real value of research lies not only in the facts and figures you have unearthed but also in the greater understanding you can give your readers from what you have yourself understood. The internet offers easy and rapid results to any researcher but must be used with caution (see *The writer's toolkit*, page 567). It has no overall controlling body and I (or anyone else) could put up a website of wholly invented 'facts'; a wise writer will always confirm research material elsewhere. Reference libraries offer extensive facilities for researching anything and everything, but the most comprehensive single volume to help you is *Research for Writers* by Ann Hoffmann (see further reading, page 132). As your pile of researched material grows so will your interest and enthusiasm. To write well you have to be interested in what you're writing, or at least make yourself interested. If you're not, why should anyone else be?

Style

Style is of equal importance. Beginners sometimes think the lifespan of a newspaper, particularly a daily, is so short that it's not worth bothering about style. This is a big mistake.

Written work submitted to editors or features editors needs to stop them in their tracks or at least intrigue them sufficiently to contact you about development of a point here or getting a picture there. So important is this 'must have' attribute that such features are called 'page-stoppers' in newspaper offices.

Remember the importance of character in newspaper articles: papers are alive because people are alive. Show rather than tell and use the active rather than the passive voice. Write using all five senses, in short sentences when you want to quicken the pace. Never be afraid to evoke emotion to give your copy a human face, mindful that writing for newspapers is always practical work. Too often journalists fail to give characters life – even though the people featured in their copy are alive, not fictional creations. Features may be based entirely on facts but it is their relevance to people that makes them viable. Make yourself the bringer of comfort, an inspiration, an instructor or a wallower in nostalgia. Give readers information about education, medical services, local transport, job opportunities; all are important to people. Above all, let your originality show through – in what you say and how you say it.

But a couple of warnings: be careful not to fill your piece with little more than your own opinion and personal experiences; unless you are famous or well known in the locality, such views are unlikely to be required. And remember that if your story is tagged to a news event (as some of the best often are), whatever its theme, be sure it is not out of date, having been overtaken by more recent events.

Original freelance copy on an editor's desk is more welcome than a tea-break. A good feature writer can write about virtually anything. When you do so make it strong; plunge right into your story, make the readers laugh, cry, want to know more, swear, feel encouraged, understand something or someone better, agree, disagree – or whatever you choose – but make sure they do or feel *something*.

Specialist spots

Writing a regular page/halfpage/column/corner is not a commission won without effort, often over a number of years. Editors will want to know you will be able to sustain an unlimited time at the job, that your copy will constantly be fresh and innovative and, most importantly, that it will always arrive on time. But when satisfied about these criteria, most are only too glad to hand over responsibility for a portion of the paper and know it is being handled efficiently. Making editors aware of your worth by previously selling them other copy is a good basis for seeking a regular column for yourself.

The golden rule that applies for all copy is that (short of real and rare emergencies) it must never be late. To be calm about accepting deadlines you need to plan ahead carefully, to accept your own limits in terms of the research needed for a particular job and the time it is likely to take you to write it and (the best and only true safety net) to have plenty of copy ready in your private store.

What types of regular columns are popular with readers? Their themes are boundless: nature, profiles of famous people, chess, horoscopes, self-help, crosswords, competitions, children's and women's pages, young mothers, pop music, pets, food – anything that interests people will make a good column. As writing a column will get you known and your work constantly read you should be prepared for the feedback from readers. This can be one of the most rewarding aspects of column-running if you don't let it take up too much of your writing time. And at the end of every month you are guaranteed a pre-negotiated fee without having to invoice anyone.

A few topics generally fall into a separate category: travel, sport, motoring, business and finance among them. These are nearly always covered by staff writers and freelance contributions to these sections have to be exceptional, if not unique.

Reviews

The distinctive task of reviewing books, drama, films, videos, radio and television programmes is seldom work for beginners. Sometimes a person who is not even thought of as a writer but who is famous in another sphere might be invited to contribute – a politician or a top sportsman, perhaps – to attract readers with the name of the reviewer rather than the quality of the review but the established papers have their own trained and experienced staff reviewers.

How, then, do you gain experience? For all categories of reviewing it is at the discretion of editors (or features editors) that you may be given a chance. And the only way to build up a solid reputation is to keep writing the copy they want when (or preferably just before) they want it.

Reporting

National dailies and Sunday papers rely on staff reporters and news agencies to maintain a flow of news and reports from prearranged locations, as do leading regional papers. With competition fierce between them, none can afford to miss the capturing and reporting of events as they happen; there can be little or no room for the *ad hoc* freelance in these circumstances.

The local and regional scene is very different. With a sound reputation for filing local news stories a freelance reporter may find work as a regular contributor or on the staff of a local paper, and will soon discover that local reporters are hard working folk at the very root of a paper's activities. They are likely to be out and about collecting information from tip-offs supplied by the office, waiting to file the latest news on a 'running' story or they might be engaged on any one of a dozen duties in the circulation area. It's the place where many a leading journalist began learning the craft.

Reporters carry considerable responsibility in a challenging job that should not be undertaken without careful consideration. Being committed to maintaining a flow of news from a small town or village or district can be a chore when you want to go on holiday, or if you are ill, or if you just don't feel like doing it. But the first rule of the job is not to let your community down. Doing the 'calls' will be a regular task. This means you will call on the people or organisations likely to tell you what's going on: the police and fire stations, local hospitals, the town hall, the Citizens Advice Bureau, the morgue, the courts, schools, health clinics, community centres – anywhere and everywhere in the locality where a spokesperson is able and willing to give you news or the basis of a news story to pass on to readers of the paper.

Being a reporter will almost certainly bring you more rewards than cash. Your writing skills will benefit by making quick decisions about your copy, learning how to present it clearly in print and over the phone; you will develop an increasing awareness of what is and what is not newsworthy and your confidence will increase.

Letters, fillers, anecdotes and humour

Writers may complain that computerised page layout leaves fewer spaces for small items but (as in all marketing) it is a matter of finding your own openings. It is sometimes worthwhile amassing a good collection of fillers and filing them to an editor as a single package. Fillers, be they Letters to the Editor, snippets to make readers laugh or small pieces of general interest, are covered by the same copyright protection as their weightier brothers: the original copy belongs to the writer and only an exact copy of it by an unauthorised person infringes that copyright. Other people taking up the ideas in themes or fillers are quite free to develop them as they wish – in fact Letters to the Editor are generally chosen with just this in mind: that the original may generate sufficient interest for other readers to write more letters with their views.

To a freelance writer nothing observed or overheard is ever wasted. Humour is nearly always welcome and the newspaper world is full of surprises: a writer friend persuaded the editor of her evening paper that a 'funny' corner would give readers at least one thing to laugh at every day. That's her column now and readers love it. It's easy to laugh at humour, not easy to write it and virtually impossible to teach someone how to do it. If you can, you're lucky.

Business

Never be deterred by the fact that a freelance writer must also be a seller – or be afraid to discuss what you will be paid for work accepted. Bona fide freelances have to deal with tax self-assessment but with this status you can claim many benefits, setting some of your expenses against tax and even working at a tax loss. To satisfy the Inland Revenue you must demonstrate that you are a professional writer, that you are trying to make a profit and that you are eligible to be taxed in such a capacity. This means your taxable income from writing will be the amount you receive in fees less expenses wholly and exclusively incurred in the pursuit of your writing. If you hold another full-time job it may not be easy to substantiate your writing credentials, but being able to produce genuine records and receipts and to demonstrate a proper businesslike approach to your writing work will be to your advantage.

Perhaps the most important rule to observe is this: never give your copy away or sell it for less than its fair value. Above all, write what editors want – that's the simple recipe. A newspaper may be only ink on paper but it's alive, feeding on topicality, originality and the quality of the writing on its pages. The contributor an editor longs to hear from identifies with readers and understands what they want. Such a contributor has plenty to write about, works hard to achieve success and enjoys great personal satisfaction.

Jill Dick has spent many years working for national, regional and local newspapers as a feature writer, columnist, reviewer and departmental editor. Her published books include *Freelance Writing for Newspapers* and *Writing for Magazines* (A & C Black), and *The Writers' Circles Handbook* (see page 510).

Writing magazine articles

For the would-be writer there can be little doubt that magazine articles offer the easiest way to get into print. ***John Hines*** *offers guidance to potential contributors.*

The article market is vast and is growing steadily. New magazines appear almost daily and, although some founder, many of them survive. The subject material covered by these magazines is so varied that few writers would find their special interests not included.

The magazines range from the modest budget publications to the expensive glossies. Beginners can cut their teeth on the lower end of the market, knowing that, although the fees are modest, the competition is small. These publications provide an excellent start for building skills, self-confidence and credibility. The opportunity for steadily moving up-market is there for the taking, until the writer reaches the level which fulfils his or her ambitions.

The idea

Established article writers usually have files bulging with ideas. They will include newspaper and magazine clippings, jottings from television and radio programmes and personal observations. Almost anything which intrigues the writer or fires the imagination is worth a place in the ideas file. There is an adage in the writing world that it pays to write about what you know. Certainly this is a good idea, for you write more comfortably and competently on a familiar subject, but the wise diversify as well.

In selecting subjects, it is most rewarding to pick those which interest you or, better still, fascinate you. They provide absorbing research and can result in articles rich in original thought with your enthusiasm showing through. As a freelance, you have the luxury of being able to pick and choose, so why not select those articles which are a pleasure to write?

Market study

Successful writers know that effective market study is vital. Any editor will tell you that the vast majority of unsolicited material which lands on their desk is quite unsuitable. The material may be wrong in length, style or choice of subject. Yet studying a copy of the magazine could have helped to avoid these mistakes.

A number of magazines produce guidelines for prospective contributors. Some of these are basic, but others may be very specific. The latter can be invaluable. It is worthwhile enquiring if such guidelines are available.

Try to read at least two recent copies of the magazine for which you are aiming to write. Analyse it carefully. Check the number of articles which are staff written (the staff are usually listed in the front of the magazine). By studying several issues you may also discover that there are contributors with regular slots and so deduce the opportunities which exist for the freelance.

If the magazine looks promising, study the type of subject which the editor favours. Check the approximate length of the average article. Ask yourself if the magazine's style is one with which you would be comfortable or to which you could adapt.

Few writers seem to study the advertisements and this is a big mistake. Advertising agencies spend a great deal of money on painstaking expert research, aimed at identifying the typical reader. By studying the advertisements you can benefit from this valuable information which can be most helpful when slanting your article to the readers' interests.

Willings Press Guide, Vol. 1 is an excellent comprehensive source of information on the UK print media. In particular, its classified index can be invaluable for finding a market for those difficult-to-place articles. If you are interested in selling to foreign markets, *Vol. 2* gives international coverage, apart from the UK. There is now a CD-Rom that covers even more titles than the printed volumes.

Studying the *Writers' & Artists' Yearbook* can give you a good insight into the requirements of many magazines, even including the fees they pay.

Writers' News includes much useful market information (see further reading, page 132). However, the finest market information is that which freelances compile for themselves from personal experience. A card filing system is useful here but, like all market information, its value depends on its being kept up to date.

Research and accuracy

Although some articles can be written from personal experience or knowledge, most articles require some sound current research. Public libraries can be very helpful, particularly if you enlist the help of a qualified librarian rather than a library assistant. The copyright libraries, of which the British Library is the best known, are superb. Would-be researchers must establish their bona fides before being issued with a ticket.

All facts should be checked for accuracy, going back to the source wherever possible. The books of others are not infallible, even reference books. Errors can be embarrassing and inevitably attract unwelcome letters from readers. File your researched material away for future use; an effective filing system is essential. The best book on the subject is *Research for Writers* by Ann Hoffmann (see further reading, page 132).

The internet can offer a vast amount of research material, particularly in the form of published articles. As some internet sources may include information of dubious quality, your routine check for accuracy should be made conscientiously.

Research may entail interviewing people and this is a skill which the freelance should consider developing. For effective interviews, sound preparation is important. Research in advance as much as possible about the interviewee and their field of interest. Make a list of important questions in logical sequence. But be prepared to divert from your questions and follow any unexpected revelations. If you use a tape recorder, test it beforehand and always carry spare batteries and tapes. It is essential to have a notebook as a back-up and to carry spare pens.

Sensitivity and courtesy should be the criteria for all interviewing for normal articles. Start with easy general questions. Guide the interview gently, but firmly. Wind up the interview as you began, on an easy note. The interviewee should be left with the feeling that it has been an enjoyable experience. Some interviewees ask if they can vet the finished article. You should always politely refuse, but do offer to allow them to withdraw anything they may regret saying. For more information on interviewing technique, see *Freelance Writing for Newspapers* and *The Way to Write Magazine Articles* in the further reading list on page 132.

Non-linear thinking

A stumbling block for many inexperienced writers is beginning their article, particularly when faced with a daunting mass of notes, clippings and research references. Related research material must be associated and the various aspects considered in order of importance. However, when marshalling material, we often tend to arrange it in a linear fashion, rather like a shopping list. This tends to restrict our thinking on each point.

It has been found that non-linear thinking stimulates ideas and their logical development. I use this method as a framework for my articles, particularly those which are complex. Non-linear flow-of-thought patterns are easy to compile and to use. The subject is written in the centre of a large sheet of paper with the major aspects to be covered radiating from it. From these, further spurs are drawn, filling in other important material. Less significant points are added on minor spurs until all aspects are covered. Never discard these patterns; file them away for future use as a valuable concise reference to your research material.

A detailed explanation of this method, together with illustrations of typical non-linear patterns, is given in *The Way to Write Magazine Articles*; and more general coverage can be found in *Use Your Head* (see further reading, page 132).

The article structure

We all develop our own style, but it is important to learn to modify it to suit the requirements of our market. The majority of articles are relatively short and must put over their story crisply without wasting words. Often this can best be done with fairly short sentences and relatively short paragraphs. Never write long convoluted sentences which require reading more than once to understand.

The opening

The first paragraph of an article has special importance. It must grip the editor's attention immediately, its purpose being to force the editor to read on. You can often make your opening irresistible by selecting a point from your article which is intriguing, startling or even audacious.

The body

The body of the article must fulfil the promise of that good first paragraph. It is here that the main text or message of your article will be unfolded. Your thought patterns will help you to move logically from one aspect to the next in a smooth progression and ensure that nothing important is left out.

The end

The poor article appears to finish when the writer runs out of ideas. A good ending must aim to tie up any loose ends positively. The way it does this depends a great deal on the subject. It can be speculative – a look into the future, perhaps. It might go back to answer a question posed in the beginning. Avoid a mere recap of the main text for this gives a weak ending. Try to set aside some 'meat' to include in the ending; this could leave the reader with a strong point to ponder over.

Dialogue

Dialogue can breathe life into an article and give it sparkle. It must be used judiciously, for over-use may unbalance the article. It is often effective when used appropriately as the first sentence of an article.

The typescript

The conventional layout of a typescript is described in *Dos and don'ts on approaching a publisher* on page 237. However, an article for the British magazine market needs the addition of a typed cover sheet with the writer's name and address in the top right-hand corner, the article's title centred halfway down the page followed by the writer's name. If you are using a pseudonym it goes here, not at the top.

About two-thirds down the page on the left should be the number of words in the article and two or three lines' space below, the rights which you are offering the editor. For normal practical purposes this would be First British Serial Rights, usually abbreviated to 'FBSR offered' – see below. The cover sheet is not used for USA markets.

An increasing number of editors are asking writers to submit their articles on disk or by email. It pays you to provide this facility if you can. You should always verify with the editor that your system and theirs are compatible before submission. You will find that most editors also require a hard copy (printout) in addition to the disk or electronic copy.

Illustrations

Good illustrations enhance an article, making it more saleable. The writer/illustrator also receives an extra fee. It is self-evident that all article writers should try to produce that editors' delight – the words and pictures package. If you are a reasonable photographer, you are halfway there. If you are not, there is little excuse for not trying with one of the fully automatic cameras which are available today.

Study magazines to see, not only whether they use black and white or colour, but also the way they use illustrations. Do they tend to be small and plentiful to assist in the understanding of the text? Does the editor favour large dramatic pictures, sometimes covering as much as a whole page or even two? Finally, can your pictures match those in the magazine?

Your pictures must be pin-sharp and properly exposed. They must avoid all the basic mistakes of composition which are outlined in any photographic primer. For black and white you should submit glossy, borderless prints, 254 x 203mm (10 x 8in). Transparencies are demanded by many quality magazines for their colour illustrations, but a growing number of periodicals will consider colour prints. You must always confirm that a magazine uses colour prints before submitting them. For covers, some magazines use 35mm transparencies, but many prefer a larger format. The quality of digital reproduction is improving rapidly, making it acceptable to a much wider range of magazines. For those markets that still require transparencies, digital reproductions are invaluable as proofs (see *Digital imaging for writers*, page 571). Illustrations are covered in depth in *The Way to Write Magazine Articles* (see further reading, page 132).

Rights

By offering First British Serial Rights you are inviting the magazine to publish your article once and for the first time in Britain. You are retaining the right to sell it elsewhere in the world. Some editors will try to wring all rights from you. Do not give way as it leaves the magazine free to sell your article worldwide and pocket the proceeds.

Second British Serial Rights are rarely sold, but a magazine may ask to buy them if they see your article in print and wish to reproduce it themselves. You would normally accept, but as Second Rights earn lower fees than First Rights, it is not worth making a particular effort to sell them. It pays to rewrite the original article, reslanting it to suit the new market and possibly introducing some new material. This effectively makes it a new article for which the First Rights may be legitimately offered.

The sales strategy

Probably the most common reason for good articles failing to get published is lack of a sound sales strategy. A surprisingly large number of writers complete a good article and then peddle it hopefully around the markets. This is quite the wrong way. Your article must always be written specifically for the market you have in mind. Your sales strategy should begin the moment you look at your material and can say: 'Yes, there is enough here for a good article.' You then use your market study to find a number of likely magazines which might publish such an article.

Query letters

The sound query letter is essential for sustained success in the article-writing field. Examine your list of possible magazines and arrange them in order of your preference. Select the top one and write your query letter to its editor. Keep it brief and state your idea for the article, mentioning any special slant you have in mind. If you are qualified in any way to write such an article or if you have a 'track-record' of writing in that field, you should say so. Also mention if you have suitable illustrations.

Ask the editor how many words he or she would like to see. It is particularly important to ask for the magazine's rates for contributors. Always enclose an sae. The query letter is your initial shop-window and its quality should be the best of which you are capable. If the editor turns down the idea, write immediately to the next magazine on your list and so on.

If the editor likes your idea, you may get a commission, but if you are unknown it is more likely that you will be asked to submit the article on spec.

An acceptance is the usual outcome from an editor's expression of interest. As you become better at matching subject to magazine, writing shrewd query letters and producing sound articles, your rejections should drop to virtually nil.

On acceptance, the professional freelance looks around for another outlet. Writing is easy, it is the research which takes the time. Make sure you get the maximum from your research (see above).

Payment

Some magazines pay on acceptance, but the majority pay on publication. Avoid those magazines which hold your material on spec with no guarantee of ultimate publication. Never be afraid to question offers of low rates, for many editors will negotiate. If low rates are not improved upon, be professional and withdraw the offer of your article.

If a magazine defaults on payment, you should always consider pursuing the matter, even as far as the Small Claims Court. The Society of Authors has an excellent pamphlet on Small Claims procedure (free to members; £5, post free, to non-members).

The pathway to successful article writing

- have a good idea for a subject;
- find a suitable market;
- produce an interesting and well-written article for that market;
- submit a professional-looking typescript;
- have a sound sales strategy throughout.

Fresh fields

When you have written articles extensively on a subject, it may be worth considering whether the subject is suitable for a non-fiction book (see *The Way to Write Non-fiction*, further reading, page 132). If so, your articles could be valuable as evidence of your writing skills, your knowledge of the subject and the wide interest the subject can generate. Many writers have used their published articles as a means of gaining an advance contract for a non-fiction book.

John Hines is a freelance writer and lecturer covering a wide range of interests, but specialises in health and the environment. He lectures extensively on writing, both in the UK and abroad.

Further reading

Buzan, Tony, *Use Your Head*, BBC, revised edn, 1995

Dick, Jill, *Freelance Writing for Newspapers*, A & C Black, 2nd edn, 1998

Dick, Jill, *Writing for Magazines*, A & C Black, 2nd edn, 1996

Hines, John, *The Way to Write Magazine Articles*, Hamish Hamilton, 1995

Hines, John, *The Way to Write Non-fiction*, Hamish Hamilton, 1990

Hoffmann, Ann, *Research for Writers*, A & C Black, 6th edn, 1999

Howard, Godfrey, *The English Guide*, Pan Macmillan, 1994, o.p.

Keeble, Richard, *The Newspaper Handbook*, Routledge, 2001

The Oxford Writers' Dictionary, Oxford 1990

Peak, Steve and Fisher, Paul (eds), *The Media Guide*, Fourth Estate, annual

Waterhouse, Keith, *On Newspaper Style*, Penguin 1993, o.p.

Willings Press Guide, Media Information Ltd, annual

Writers' News, Yorkshire Post Newspapers, see page 96

Syndicates, news and press agencies

Before submitting material, you are strongly advised to make preliminary enquiries and to ascertain terms of work. Strictly speaking, syndication is the selling and reselling of previously published work although some news and press agencies handle original material.

Academic File Information Services

Eastern Art Publishing Group, PO Box 13666, 27 Wallorton Gardens, London SW14 8WF
tel 020-8392 1122 *fax* 020-8392 1422
email afis@eapgroup.com
website www.eapgroup.com
Managing Editor Sajid Rizvi, *Executive Editor* Shirley Rizvi

Feature and photo syndication with special reference to the developing world and immigrant communities in the West. Founded 1985.

Advance Features

Stubbs Wood Cottage, Hammerwood, East Grinstead, West Sussex RH19 3QE
tel/fax (01342) 850480
website www.advancefeatures.uk.com
Managing Editor Peter Norman

Crosswords: daily, weekly and theme; general puzzles. Daily and weekly cartoons for the regional, national and overseas press (not single cartoons).

Alpha incorporating London News Service

63 Gee Street, London EC1V 3RS
tel 020-7336 0632 *fax* 020-7253 8419
Managing Director Ray Blumire

Worldwide syndication of features and photos.

The Associated Press Ltd

(News Department), The Associated Press House, 12 Norwich Street, London EC4A 1BP
tel 020-7353 1515 *fax* 020-7353 8118

Atlantic Syndication Partners

17-18 Haywards Place, London EC1R 0EQ
tel 020-7566 0360 *fax* 020-7566 0388
Contact Nick York

Worldwide syndication of newspaper features, photos, cartoons, strips and book serialisations. Agency represents the international syndication of Associated Newspapers (*Daily Mail*, *Mail on Sunday*, *Evening Standard*).

Australian Associated Press

12 Norwich Street, London EC4A 1QJ
tel 020-7353 0153 *fax* 020-7583 3563

News service to the Australian, New Zealand and Pacific Island press, radio and TV. Founded 1935.

Neil Bradley Puzzles

Linden House, 73 Upper Marehay, Ripley, Derbyshire DE5 JF
tel (01773) 741500 *fax* (01773) 741555
email bradcart@aol.com
Director Neil Bradley

Supplies visual puzzles to national and regional press; emphasis placed on variety and topicality with work based on current media listings. Work supplied on disk or prints to Mac or PC. Daily single frame and strip cartoons. Contact for free booklet and disk demo. Founded 1981.

Bulls Presstjänst AB

Tulegatan 39, Box 6519, S-11383 Stockholm, Sweden
tel (08) 55520600 *fax* (08) 55520665
email kontakt@bulls.se
website www.bulls.se

Bulls Pressedienst GmbH
Eysseneckstrasse 50, D-60322 Frankfurt am Main, Germany
tel (069) 959 270 *fax* (069) 959 27111
email sales@bullspress.de

Bulls Pressetjeneste A/S
Ebbells Gate 3, N-0183 Oslo, Norway
tel 22 98 26 60 *fax* 22 20 49 78
email bullsosl@online.no

Bulls Pressetjeneste
Ostbanegade 9, 1th, DK-2100 Copenhagen, Denmark

tel 35 38 90 99 *fax* 35 38 25 16
email kjartan@bulls.dk
Oy Fennopress AB – a Bulls company
Arabianranta 6, FIN-00560, Helsinki, Finland
tel (09) 612 96 50 *fax* (09) 656 092
email illeka@bullspress.fi
Bulls Press
ul. Chocimska 28, Pokoj 509, 00-791 Warsawa, Poland
tel (22) 845 90 10 *fax* (22) 845 90 11
email krzysztof@bulls.com.pl
Bulls Press
Mere Pst 8, EE 0001 Tallinn, Estonia
tel (2) 61 30 663 *fax* (2) 64 64 133
email bulls@online.ee

Market newspapers, magazines, weeklies and advertising agencies in Sweden, Denmark, Norway, Finland, Iceland, Poland, The Baltic States, Germany, Austria and German-speaking Switzerland.

Syndicates human interest picture stories; topical and well-illustrated background articles and series; photographic features dealing with science, people, personalities, glamour; genre pictures for advertising; condensations and serialisations of best-selling fiction and non-fiction; cartoons, comic strips, film and TV rights, merchandising and newspaper graphics online.

The Canadian Press

Associated Press House, 12 Norwich Street, London EC4A 1QE
tel 020-7353 6355 *fax* 020-7583 4238
Chief Correspondent Helen Branswell

London Bureau of the national news agency of Canada. Founded 1919.

Celebritext

F6 Broadway Studios, 28 Tooting High Street, London SW17 0RG
tel/fax 020-8672 5100
email info@celebritext.com
website www.celebritext.com
Contact Lee Howard

Specialises in music and film celebrity interviews. Commission: 50%. Founded 2000.

Central Press Features

Temple Way, Bristol BS99 7HD
tel 0117-934 3600 *fax* 0117-934 3639
email mail@central-press.co.uk
website www.central-press.co.uk
Editor Ken Elkes

Supplies features, cartoons, crosswords, horoscopes and graphics strips to newspapers, magazines and other publications (including Internet sites) in 50 countries. Included in over 100 daily and weekly services are columns of international interest on health and beauty, medicine, employment, sports, house and home, motoring, computers, film and video, children's features, gardening, celebrity profiles, food and drink, finance and law. Also runs a parliamentary service and TV listings service, as well as supplying editorial material for advertising features.

Children's Express UK

Exmouth House, 3-11 Pine Street, London EC1R 0JH
tel 020-7833 2577 *fax* 020-7278 7722
email enquiries@childrensexpress.btinternet.com
website www.childrens-express.org
Chief Executive Christopher Wyle, *Chairman* Stephanie Williams

Offers young people aged 8–18 the opportunity to write on issues of importance to them, for newspapers, radio and TV. It operates after school and at weekends. Founded 1995.

J.W. Crabtree and Son

Cheapside Chambers, 43 Cheapside, Bradford BD1 4HP
tel (01274) 732937 (office), (01535) 655288 (home)
fax (01274) 732937

News, general and sport. Founded 1919.

Daily & Sunday Telegraph Syndication

The Telegraph Group Ltd, 1 Canada Square, Canary Wharf, London E14 5DT
tel 020-7538 7505 *fax* 020-7538 7319
email syndicat@telegraph.co.uk

News, features, photography; worldwide distribution and representation.

Environmental & Occupational Health Research Foundation

Penrose House, Birtles Road, Whirley, Cheshire SK10 3JQ
tel/fax (01625) 615323
email eorhfl@aol.com
Managing Editor Peggy Bentham

Undertakes individual commissions and syndicates articles to diverse science and technology journals and general consumer media. Peer reviewed and accredited contributors from academia and professional institutions.

Euro-Digest Features

34A Compton Avenue, Brighton BN1 3PS
tel (01273) 233615 *fax* (01273) 203622
Directors Edward Whitehead, Andrew C.F. Whitehead, Kirsty Tranter

Represents European press. Human interest and travel features. Occasional news items. Particularly interested in material from Scotland, Northern Ireland and Wales. Commission: by arrangement, according to subject, etc.

Europa-Press

Saltmätargatan 8, 1st Floor, Box 6410, S-113 82, Stockholm
tel 8-34 94 35 *fax* 8-34 80 79
email tord@europapress.se
Managing Director Tord Steinsvik

Market: newspapers, magazines, weeklies and websites in Sweden, Denmark, Norway, Finland, and the Baltic states. Syndicates high quality features of international appeal such as topical articles, photo-features – b&w and colour, women's features, short stories, serial novels, non-fiction stories and serials with strong human interest, crime articles, popular science, cartoons, comic strips.

Europress Features (UK)

18 St Chads Road, Didsbury, Nr Manchester M20 9WH
tel 0161-445 2945
email freddy_12_gb@hotmail.com

Representation of newspapers and magazines in Europe, Australia, United States. Syndication of top-flight features with exclusive illustrations – human interest stories – showbusiness personalities. 30–35% commission on sales of material successfully accepted; 40% on exclusive illustrations.

Express Enterprises

(division of Express Newspapers plc)
Ludgate House, 245 Blackfriars Road, London SE1 9UX
tel 020-7922 7903 *fax* 020-7922 7871

Text and pictures from all Express titles. Archive from 1900. Numerous strips and political cartoons. Material handled worldwide for freelance journalists.

Frontline Photo Press Agency

18 Wall Street, Norwood, South Australia 5067
postal address PO Box 162, Kent Town, SA 5071
tel (08) 8333 2691 *fax* (08) 8364 0604
email info@frontline.net.au
website www.frontline.net.au
Director Carlo Irlitti

Photographic press agency. Services provided: news, interviews, features, articles and photos for newspapers, magazines and other media. Digital photo wire services.

Syndicates sports, celebrity, travel, men's, women's, human and general interest features and articles with photos. Welcomes approaches from individuals and organisations abroad. Assignments undertaken. Rates negotiable. Founded 1988.

Gemini News Service

9 White Lion Street, London N1 9PD
tel 020-7278 1111 *fax* 020-7278 0345
email gemini@panoslondon.org.uk
website www.gemininewsservice.com
Editor Dipankar De Sarkar

Network of freelance contributors and specialist writers all over the world. Specialists in news-features of international, topical and development interest. Preferred length 800–1200 words.

Graphic Syndication

4 Reyntiens View, Odiham, Hants RG29 1AF
tel (01256) 703004
email sensible@sensible.screaming.net
website www.members.tripod.co.uk/mike_flanagan
Manager M. Flanagan

Cartoon strips and single frames supplied to newspapers and magazines in Britain and overseas. Terms: 50%. Founded 1981.

India-International News Service

Head office Jute House, 12 India Exchange Place, Calcutta 700001, India
tel 2209563, 4791009
Proprietor Eur Ing H. Kothari BSc, DWP(Lond), FIMechE, FIE, FVI, FInstD(Lond), FRAS, FRSA

'Calcutta Letters' and Air Mail news service from Calcutta. Specialists in industrial and technical news.

INS (International News Service) and Irish News Service

7 King's Avenue, Minnis Bay, Birchington-on-Sea, East Kent CT7 9QL
tel (01843) 845022
Editor and Managing Director Barry J. Hardy PC, *Photo Editor* Jan Vanek, *Secretary* K.T. Byrne

News, sport, book and magazine reviews (please forward copies), TV, radio, photographic department; also equipment for TV films, etc.

International Fashion Press Agency

Penrose House, Birtles Road, Whirley, Cheshire SK10 3JQ
tel/fax (01625) 615323
email ifpressagy@aol.com
Directors P. Bentham (managing), P. Dyson, S. Fagette, L.C. Mottershead, L.B. Fell, T.R. Fox

Monitors and photographs international fashion collections and developments in textile and fashion industry. Specialist writers on health, fitness, beauty and personalities. Undertakes individual commissioned features. Supplies syndicated columns/pages to press, radio and TV (NUJ staff writers and photographers).

International Press Agency (Pty) Ltd

PO Box 67, Howard Place 7450, South Africa
tel (021) 531 1926 *fax* (021) 531 8789
email inpra@iafrica.com
Manager Mrs T. Temple
UK office 17 Fairmount Road, London SW2 2BJ
tel 020-8674 9283
Managing Editor Mrs U.A. Barnett PhD

South African agents for many leading British, American and continental press firms for the syndication of comic strips, cartoons, jokes, feature articles, short stories, serials, press photos for the South African market. Founded 1934.

Joker Feature Service (JFS)

PO Box 253, 6040 AG, Roermond, The Netherlands
tel (0475) 337338 *fax* (0475) 315663
email j.f.s@tip.nl
Managing Director Ruud Kerstens

Feature articles, serial rights, tests, cartoons, comic strips and illustrations, puzzles. Handles TV features, books, Internet sites; also production for merchandising.

Knight Features

20 Crescent Grove, London SW4 7AH
tel 020-7622 1467 *fax* 020-7622 1522
email peter@knightfeatures.co.uk
Director Peter Knight, *Associates* Ann King-Hall, Gaby Martin, Andrew Knight, Samantha Ferris

Worldwide selling of strip cartoons and major features and serialisations. Exclusive agent in UK and Republic of Ireland for United Feature Syndicate and Newspaper Enterprise Association of New York. Founded 1985.

London News Service – see Alpha incorporating London News Service

Maharaja Features Pvt. Ltd

5-226 Sion Road East, Bombay 400022, India
tel 22-4097951 *fax* 22-4097801
email mahafeat@bom2.vsnl.net.in
website www.welcomeindia.com/maharaja
Editor Mrs R. Ravi, *Managing Editor* K.R.N. Swamy

Syndicates feature and pictorial material, of interest to Asian readers, to newspapers and magazines in India, UK and abroad. Specialists in well-researched articles on India by eminent authorities for publication in prestige journals throughout the world. Also topical features 1000–1500 words. Illustrations: b&w prints and colour transparencies.

Mirrorpix

22nd Floor, 1 Canada Square, Canary Wharf, London E14 5AP
tel 020-7293 3700 *fax* 020-7293 2712
email desk@mirrorpix.com
website www.mirrorpix.com
Contact sales desk

Supplies publishing material and international rights for news text and pictures from Trinity Mirror Newspapers and other large publishing houses. Extensive picture library of all subjects.

National Association of Press Agencies (NAPA)

41 Lansdowne Crescent, Leamington Spa, Warks. CV32 4PR
tel (01926) 424181 *fax* (01926) 424760
website www.napa.org.uk
Directors Denis Cassidy, Chris Johnson, Barrie Tracey, Peter Steele, John Quinn

NAPA is a network of independent, established and experienced press agencies serving newspapers, magazines, TV and radio networks. Founded 1983.

National Sports Reporting

Ground Floor, 13-16 Faro Close, Coates Hill Road, Bromley, Kent BR1 2RR
tel 020-8467 1951
email 100654.463@compuserve.com
Editor Christopher Harte, *Managers* Michael Latham (Northern Region), David Fox (South West Region), Diana Harding (South East Region), Dave Hammond (Scotland)

News and reporting service for sporting events. Research facilities for radio and TV, particularly sports documentaries. Commission: NUJ rates. Founded 1994.

New Blitz Literary & TV Agency

Via di Panico 67, 00186 Rome, Italy
postal address CP 30047-00193, Rome 47, Italy

tel/fax (06) 686 4859
email blitzgacs@inwind.it
Manager Giovanni A.S. Congiu

Syndicates worldwide: cartoons, comic strips, humorous books with drawings, feature and pictorial material, topical, environment, travel. Average rates of commission 60/40%, monthly report of sales, payment 60 days after the date of monthly report.

Chandra S. Perera

Cinetra, 437 Pethiyagoda, Kelaniya-11600, Sri Lanka
tel 94-1-911885 *fax* 94-1-323910/674-737/674-738 ATTN CHANDRA PERERA
email cinetraww@dialogsl.net comsvc01@slt.lk ATTN CHANDRA PERERA
Cinetra Worldwide Createch (Pvt) Ltd, 126/3rd floor, 10B YMBA Building, Fort, Colombo 1, Sri Lanka
tel 94-1-323910

Press and TV news, news films on Sri Lanka and Maldives, colour and b&w photo news and features, photographic and film coverages, screenplays and scripts for TV and films, press clippings. Broadcasting, TV and newspapers; journalistic features, news, broadcasting and TV interviews.

Pixfeatures

5 Latimer Road, Barnet, Herts. EN5 5NU
tel 020-8449 9946 *fax* 020-8441 2725
Contact Peter Wickman
Spanish office tel 00349 6647 6379 *Contact* Roy Wickman

News agency and picture library. Specialises in selling Spanish pictures and features to British and European press.

The Press Association

292 Vauxhall Bridge Road, London SW1V 1AE
tel 020-7963 7000 *fax* 020-7963 7192
website www.pa.press.net
Chief Executive/Editor-in-Chief Paul Potts, *Managing Director* Steven Brown

PA News Fast and accurate news, photography and information to print, broad cast and electronic media in the UK and Ireland.

PA Sport In-depth coverage of national and regional sports, transmitting a huge range of stories, results, pictures and updates every day.

PA Listings Page- and screen-ready information from daily guides to 7-day supplements on sports results, TV and radio listings, arts and entertainment, financial and weather listings tailored to suit requirements.

PA Digital Top quality content including news and sport for a wide range of multimedia customers.

PA WeatherCentre Continuously updated information on present and future weather conditions; consultancy services for media and industry. Founded 1868.

Press Features Syndicate

9 Paradise Close, Eastbourne, East Sussex BN20 8BT
tel (01323) 728760
Editor Harry Gresty

Specialises in photo-features, both b&w and colour. Seeks human interest, oddity, glamour, pin-ups, scientific, medical, etc, material suitable for marketing through own branches in London, San Francisco, Paris, Hamburg, Milan, Stockholm, Amsterdam (for Benelux), Helsinki.

Press Gang News

137 Endlesham Road, London SW12 8JN
tel 020-8673 4229 020-8673 7778
fax 020-8673 3205
email mail@pressgangnews.co.uk
website www.pressgangnews.co.uk
Partners Mark Christy, Sarah Christy

National news, features and photographic news agency. Seeks good journalists and photographers; considers material from freelance journalists. Keen to receive stories, press releases, etc from individual members of the public and from organisations, etc. Founded 1996.

Rann Communication

6th Floor, 117 King William Street, Adelaide, SA 5000, Australia
postal address GPO Box 958, Adelaide, SA 5000, Australia
tel (08) 8211 7771 *fax* (08) 8212 2272
email chrisrann@rann.com.au
Proprietor C.F. Rann

Full range of professional PR, press releases, special newsletters, commercial and political intelligence, media monitoring. Welcomes approaches from organisations requiring PR representation or press release distribution. Founded 1982.

Reuters Group plc

85 Fleet Street, London EC4P 4AJ
tel 020-7250 1122

UK Features

38 The Woodlands, Esher, Surrey KT10 8DB
tel 020-8398 5676 *fax* 020-8398 9051
email robincorry@ukfeatures.com
Proprietor Robin Corry

Human interest and general features. Payment: £150–£250 for an early tip-off. Founded 1979.

United Press International

80 Silverthorne Road, London SW8 3XA
tel 020-7675 9960 (news), 020-7675 9967 (admin), 020-7675 9992 (business development)
fax 020 7579 0871
email www.upi.com

Universal Pictorial Press & Agency Ltd

29-31 Saffron Hill, London EC1N 8SW
tel 020-7421 6000 *fax* 020-7421 6006
email postmaster@uppa.demon.co.uk
Managing Director T.R. Smith

Photographic news agency and picture library: the UK's leading archive for British and international personalities from 1944 to present. Digital archive from 1994 with full ISDN facilities. Founded 1929.

Visual Humour

5 Greymouth Close, Stockton-on-Tees TS18 5LF
tel/fax (01642) 581847
email peterdodsworth@btclick.com
website enquiries@businesscartoons.co.uk
Contact Peter Dodsworth

Daily and weekly humorous cartoon strips; also single panel cartoon features (not single cartoons) for possible syndication in the UK and abroad. Picture puzzles also considered. Submit photocopy samples only initially, with sae. Founded 1984.

Books

Submitting material

Each year, thousands of typescripts are submitted to publishers by hopeful authors but only a small proportion are accepted for publication. Some are needlessly rejected either because they were sent to an inappropriate publisher, or because the publisher's submission procedure was not followed. We give here some guidelines to consider before submitting material.

First, and most importantly, choose the right publisher. It is a waste of time and money to send the typescript (or manuscript, abbreviated to MS) of a novel to a publisher who publishes no fiction, or poetry to one who publishes no verse. By studying the entries in the *Yearbook*, examining publishers' lists of publications, or by looking for the names of suitable publishers in the relevant sections in libraries and bookshops, you will find the names of several publishers which might be interested in seeing your material.

Secondly, approach the publisher in the way they prefer. Many publishers will not accept unsolicited material – you must enquire first if they would be willing to read the whole work. A few publishers are prepared to speak on the telephone, allowing you to describe, briefly, the work on offer. Most prefer a preliminary letter; and many publishers, particularly of fiction, will only see material submitted through a literary agent. It has to be said that some publishing houses, the larger ones in particular, may well employ all three methods!

Enclose a synopsis of the work, and two or three sample chapters, with your preliminary letter, plus return postage (International Reply Coupons if you are writing from outside the country or if you are submitting material from the UK to the Irish Republic). Writers have been known to send out such letters in duplicated form, an approach unlikely to stimulate a publisher's interest. Remember, also, that whilst every reasonable care will be taken of material in the publishers' possession, responsibility cannot be accepted if material is lost or damaged. Never send your only copy of the typescript. For more information, see *Dos and don'ts on approaching a publisher* on page 237. An alphabetical listing of publishers' names and addresses follows on page 141. For classified lists, see below.

Fiction

See page 209 for a list of *Publishers of fiction*, by fiction genre. A full list of *Literary agents* starts on page 345.

Poetry

Publishers which consider poetry for adults are listed in *Publishers of poetry* on page 280. See also the article *Poetry into print* on page 269 and *Poetry organisations* on page 275.

Children's books

The market for children's books is considered in *Writing and the children's book market* on page 241 and the list of *Children's book publishers and packagers* on page 248, which includes publishers of poetry for children. A list of *Literary agents for children's books* is on page 367.

Small presses

It is beyond the scope of the *Yearbook* to list all the many smaller publishers which have either a limited output, or that specialise in poetry, avant-garde or other fringe publishing. We include details of some of the better-known small poetry houses.

Self-publishing

Authors are strongly advised not to pay for the publication of their work. A reputable firm of publishers will undertake publication at its own expense, except possibly for works of an academic nature. See *Doing it on your own* on page 251 for an introduction to self-publishing, *Vanity publishing* on page 260, and *Publishing agreements* on page 617.

See also ...

- *Book publishers* in *Australia*, page 212; in *Canada*, page 215; in *New Zealand*, page 218; in *South Africa*, page 220; and in the *USA*, page 222
- *Who owns whom in publishing*, page 258
- *Top hundred chart of 2001 paperback fastsellers*, page 261
- *Book packagers*, page 203
- *Publishers of plays*, page 342
- *How to get an agent*, page 343
- *Literary agents*, page 345
- *E-publishing*, page 551
- *The writer's toolkit*, page 567

Book publishers UK and Ireland

**Member of the Publishers Association or Scottish Publishers Association*
†Member of the Irish Book Publishers' Association

AA Publishing
Automobile Association, Fanum House, Basingstoke, Hants RG21 4EA
tel (0990) 448866 *fax* (01256) 322575
website www.theAA.com
Managing Director Stephen Mesquita, *Editorial Director* Michael Buttler

Travel, atlases, maps, leisure interests, including Essential Guides, Spiral Guides, City Packs and Explorer Travel Guides. Founded 1979.

Abacus – see Time Warner Books UK

ABC-Clio Europe
(formerly Clio Press Ltd)
Old Clarendon Ironworks, 35A Great Clarendon Street, Oxford OX2 6AT
tel (01865) 311350 *fax* (01865) 311358
email oxford@abc-clio.ltd.uk
website www.abc-clio.com
Senior Acquisitions Editor Dr Robert G. Neville

General and academic reference: encyclopedias in history, mythology, literature, ethnic studies; bibliography. Publishes *The Clio Montessori Series*, and CD-Rom and web versions of abstracting services in American studies and history. Branch of ABC-CLIO Inc. Founded 1971.

Absolute Press
Scarborough House, 29 James Street West, Bath BA1 2BT
tel (01225) 316013 *fax* (01225) 445836
email sales@absolutepress.demon.co.uk
website www.absolutepress.demon.co.uk
Publisher Jon Croft, *Directors* Amanda Bennett (sales), Bronwen Douglas (marketing)

General list: cookery, food-related topics, wine, lifestyle, popular culture, travel, gay travel. Streetwise maps, accordian fold, and laminated city maps. No fiction. *Outlines* series of monographs on gay and lesbian artists. No unsolicited MSS. Founded 1979.

Academic Press – see Harcourt Publishers Ltd

Academy Editions – acquired by Wiley Europe Ltd

Access Press – former imprint of HarperCollins Publishers

Ace Books – see Age Concern Books

Acorn Editions – see James Clarke & Co. Ltd

Actinic Press – see Cressrelles Publishing Co. Ltd

Addison-Wesley – imprint of Pearson Education

Adlard Coles Nautical – see A & C Black Publishers Ltd

Age Concern Books
(formerly Ace Books)
Age Concern England, 1268 London Road, London SW16 4ER
tel 020-8765 7200 *fax* 020-8765 7211
email books@ace.org.uk
Publisher Richard Holloway

Health and care, advice, finance, gerontology. Founded 1973.

Airlife Publishing Ltd
101 Longden Road, Shrewsbury, Shrops. SY3 9EB
tel (01743) 235651 *fax* (01743) 350409
email airlife@airlifebooks.com
website www.airlifebooks.com
Directors Jonathan Parker (managing), Colin Strachan (finance), Anne Walker (rights)

Aviation, technical and general, military, military history. Founded 1976.

Aladdin/Watts – see The Watts Publishing Group Ltd

Ian Allan Publishing Ltd

Riverdene Business Park, Molesey Road, Hersham, Surrey KT12 4RG
tel (01932) 266600 *fax* (01932) 266601
email info@ianallanpub.co.uk
website www.ianallanpub.co.uk
Publishing Manager Peter Waller

Transport: railways, aircraft, shipping, road; naval and military history; reference books and magazines; sport and cycling guides; no fiction.

Dial House (imprint)
General: sport, cycling.

Midland Publishing (imprint)
Transport: railways, aviation; naval and military history.

Oxford Publishing Company (imprint)
Transport: railways, road.

George Allen & Unwin Publishers – acquired by HarperCollins Publishers

J.A. Allen

Clerkenwell House, 45-7 Clerkenwell Green, London EC1R 0HT
tel 020-7251 2661 *fax* 020-7490 4958
Publisher Caroline Burt

Horse and equestrianism including bloodstock breeding, racing, polo, dressage, horse care, carriage driving, breeds, veterinary and farriery. Books usually commissioned but willing to consider any serious, specialist MSS on the horse and related subjects. Imprint of **Robert Hale Ltd**. Founded 1926.

W.H. Allen – acquired by Virgin Books Ltd

Allen Lane – see The Penguin Group (UK)

Allison & Busby Ltd

Suite 111, Bon Marché Centre, 241-251 Ferndale Road, London SW9 8BJ
tel 020-7738 7888 *fax* 020-7733 4244
email all@allisonbusby.co.uk
website www.allisonandbusby.ltd.uk
Publishing Director David Shelley, *Editor* Debbie Hatfield, *Press Officer* Fiona Hague

Literary fiction, crime fiction. Biography and history with a literary theme. Writers' Guides. New proposals accepted (send synopsis and sample pages initially) but sae essential.

The Alpha Press – see Sussex Academic Press

AN The Artists Information Company

1st Floor, 7-15 Pink Lane, Newcastle upon Tyne NE1 5DW
tel 0191-241 8000 *fax* 0191-241 8001
email edit@anpubs.demon.co.uk
website www.anweb.co.uk
AN Magazine Co-ordinator Gillian Nicol

Provides information, advice and critical debate on contemporary visual arts practice through *AN magazine* (monthly), its website, and a programme of artists' training and professional development for Northern England. Founded 1980.

Andersen Press Ltd

20 Vauxhall Bridge Road, London SW1V 2SA
tel 020-7840 8700 (editorial) *fax* 020-7233 6263
email andersenpress@randomhouse.co.uk
website www.andersenpress.co.uk
Managing Director/Publisher Klaus Flugge, *Directors* Philip Durrance, Joëlle Flugge (company secretary), Janice Thomson (editorial)

Children's books: picture books, novelties, junior and teenage fiction (send synopsis and full MS with sae); no short stories or poetry. International co-productions. Founded 1976.

The Angels' Share – see Neil Wilson Publishing Ltd

Anness Publishing

88-89 Blackfriars Road, London SE1 8HA
tel 020-7401 2077 *fax* 020-7633 9499
Managing Director Paul Anness, *Publisher* Joanna Lorenz

Practical illustrated books on lifestyle, cookery, crafts, gardening, Mind, Body & Spirit, health and children's non-fiction. Founded 1989.

Aquamarine (hardback imprint)
Lifestyle, cookery, crafts and gardening.

Hermes House (imprint)
Illustrated promotional books on practical subjects.

Lorenz Books (hardback imprint)
Lifestyle, cookery, crafts, gardening, Mind, Body & Spirit, health and children's non-fiction.

Southwater (paperback imprint)
Lifestyle, cookery, crafts, gardening, Mind, Body & Spirit, health and children's non-fiction.

Antique Collectors' Club Ltd

Sandy Lane, Old Martlesham, Woodbridge, Suffolk IP12 4SD

tel (01394) 389950 *fax* (01394) 389999
email sales@antique-acc.com
website www.antique-acc.com
Managing Director Diana Steel

Fine art, antiques, gardening and garden history, architecture. Founded 1966.

Anvil Books/The Children's Press*

45 Palmerston Road, Dublin 6, Republic of Ireland
tel (01) 4973628 *fax* (01) 4968263
Directors Rena Dardis (managing), Margaret Dardis (editorial)

Anvil: Irish history and biography. Only considers MSS by Irish-based authors and of Irish interest. Send synopsis with IRCs (no UK stamps); unsolicited MSS not returned. Children's Press: adventure, fiction, ages 9–14. Founded 1964.

Anvil Press Poetry

Neptune House, 70 Royal Hill, London SE10 8RF
tel 020-8469 3033 *fax* 020-8469 3363
email anvil@anvilpresspoetry.com
website www.anvilpresspoetry.com
Director Peter Jay

Poetry. Submissions only with sae. Founded 1968.

Apple Press – see Quarto Publishing plc in Book packagers, page 207

Appletree Press Ltd*†

14 Howard Street South, Belfast BT7 1AP
tel 028-9024 3074 *fax* 028-9024 6756
email reception@appletree.ie
website www.appletree.ie
Director John Murphy

Gift books, biography, cookery, guidebooks, history, Irish interest, literary criticism, music, photographic, social studies, sport, travel. Founded 1974.

Aquamarine – see Anness Publishing Ltd

Arc Publications

Nanholme Mill, Shaw Wood Road, Todmorden, Lancs. OL14 6DA
tel (01706) 812338 *fax* (01706) 818948
Partners Rosemary Jones, Tony Ward (general editor), Angela Jarman, *Associate Editors* John Kinsella (international), Jean Boase-Beier (translation)

Poetry. MSS with sae only.

Arcadia Books Ltd

15-16 Nassau Street, London W1W 7AB
tel 020-7436 9898 *fax* 020-7637 7357
email info@arcadiabooks.co.uk
website www.arcadiabooks.co.uk
Managing Director Gary Pulsifer, *Publishing Director* Daniela de Groote

Original paperback fiction, fiction in translation, autobiography, biography, travel, gender studies, gay books. Submissions via literary agents only. Founded 1996.

Architectural Press – see Reed Educational and Professional Publishing Ltd

Arkana – former imprint of The Penguin Press

E.J. Arnold – former imprint of Nelson Thornes Ltd

Edward Arnold – now part of Hodder Arnold – see Hodder Headline Ltd

Arrow Books Ltd – see Random House Group Ltd

Art Trade Press Ltd

9 Brockhampton Road, Havant, Hants PO9 1NU
tel 023-9248 4943
Editorial Director J.M. Curley

Publishers of *Who's Who in Art*.

Ashgate Publishing Ltd

Gower House, Croft Road, Aldershot, Hants GU11 3HR
tel (01252) 331551 *fax* (01252) 344405
email info@ashgatepub.co.uk
Editors Sarah Markham (social sciences), Katherine Hodkinson (social work and public service), John Hindley (aviation management), Thomas Gray (history), Pamela Edwardes (art history), Rachel Lynch (music and literary studies), Sarah Lloyd (philosophy and theology), Val Rose (regional science), Kirsten Howgate (politics and international relations), John Irwin (legal studies)

Publishes a wide range of academic research in the social sciences and humanities, professional practice publications in the management of business and public services, and illustrated books on art, architecture and design. Founded 1967.

Gower (imprint)
Editor Jonathan Norman

Business, management and training.

Lund Humphries (imprint)
Editor Lucy Myers

Art and design.

Variorum (imprint)
Editor John Smedley

History.

Ashmolean Museum Publications

Beaumont Street, Oxford OX1 2PH
tel (01865) 278009/27801 *fax* (01865) 278018
website www.ashmol.ox.ac.uk
Contact Susan Moss

Fine and applied art of Europe and Asia, archaeology, history, numismatics. No unsolicited MSS. Photographic archive. Founded 1683.

Aslib

(The Association for Information Management)
Staple Hall, Stone House Court, London EC3A 7PB
tel 020-7903 0000 *fax* 020-7903 0011
email pubs@aslib.com
website www.aslib.com
Head of Publications Sarah Blair

Information management, librarianship, information science, general reference, translation, copyright, the internet, knowledge management, records management, computing. Founded 1924.

Aspect Guides – see Peter Collin Publishing Ltd

Associated University Presses – see Golden Cockerel Press

Athlone – see The Continuum International Publishing Group Ltd

Atlantic Books

Ormond House, 26-27 Boswell Street, London WC1N 3JZ
tel 020-7269 1610 *fax* 020-7430 0916
email enquiries@groveatlantic.co.uk
Managing Director/Publisher Toby Mundy

Literary fiction, history, current affairs, biography, politics, reference, autobiography. No unsolicited submissions. Wholly owned subsidiary of **Grove/Atlantic Inc.**, New York. Founded 2000.

Atlantic Europe Publishing Co. Ltd

Greys Court Farm, Greys Court, Henley-on-Thames, Oxon RG9 4PG
tel (01491) 628188 *fax* (01491) 628189
email info@atlanticeurope.com
website www.AtlanticEurope.com
Directors Dr B.J. Knapp, D.L.R. McCrae

Children's colour illustrated information books, co-editions and primary class books: science, geography, technology, mathematics, history. No MSS accepted by post. In the first instance email. Associate company: **Earthscape Editions** (see Book packagers). Founded 1990.

Atrium Press – see Attic Press

Attic Press[†]

Crawford Business Park, Crosses Green, Cork, Republic of Ireland
tel (021) 4321725 *fax* (021) 4315329
email S.Wilbourne@ucc.ie
website www.iol.ie/~atticirl/
Publisher Sara Wilbourne

Books by and about women in the areas of social and political comment, women's studies, reference guides and handbooks. Imprint of **Cork University Press**. Founded 1984.

Aureus Publishing Ltd

24 Mafeking Road, Cardiff CF23 5DQ
tel/fax 029-2045 5200
email meuryn.hughes@aureus.co.uk
website www.aureus.co.uk
Director Meuryn Hughes

Rock and pop, autobiography, sport, aviation, religion; music. Founded 1993.

Aurum Press Ltd

25 Bedford Avenue, London WC1B 3AT
tel 020-7637 3225 *fax* 020-7580 2469
email firstname.surname@aurumpress.co.uk
website www.aurumpress.co.uk
Directors Bill McCreadie (managing), Piers Burnett (editorial), Graham Eames (sales), Sheila Murphy (non-executive), Khalil Abu-Shawareb (non-executive)

General, illustrated and non-illustrated adult non-fiction: biography and memoirs, military, visual arts, film, sport, travel, fashion, home interest. Imprints: Argentum (photography), Jacqui Small (lifestyle). Founded 1977.

Award Publications Ltd

1st Floor, 27 Longford Street, London NW1 3DZ
tel 020-7388 7800 *fax* 020-7388 7887
Managing Director Ron Wilkinson

Children's books: full colour picture story books; early learning, information and activity books. No unsolicited material. Founded 1954.

Azure Books – see Society for Promoting Christian Knowledge

Bernard Babani (Publishing) Ltd

The Grampians, Shepherds Bush Road, London W6 7NF
tel 020-7603 2581/7296 *fax* 020-7603 8203
Directors S. Babani, M.H. Babani BSc (Eng)

Practical handbooks on radio, electronics and computing.

Baillière Tindall Ltd – see Harcourt Publishers Ltd

Duncan Baird Publishers

6th Floor, Castle House, 75-76 Wells Street, London W1T 3QH
tel 020-7323 2229 *fax* 020-7580 5692
Directors Duncan Baird (managing), Bob Saxton (editorial), Roger Walton (art), Alex Mitchell (international sales), Nick Foster (financial)

Non-fiction, illustrated reference. Founded 1992.

Bantam – see Transworld Publishers

Bantam Children's Books – see Random House Group Ltd

Bantam Press – see Transworld Publishers

Barefoot Books Ltd

124 Walcot Street, Bath BA1 5BG
tel (01225) 322400 *fax* (01225) 322499
email info@barefootbooks.co.uk
website www.barefootbooks.co.uk
Publisher Tessa Strickland

Children's picture books and audiobooks: myth, legend, fairytale. No unsolicited MSS. Founded 1993.

Barrie & Jenkins – former imprint of Random House Group Ltd

Bartholomew – see HarperCollins Publishers

B.T. Batsford Ltd

64 Brewery Road, London N7 9NT
tel 020-7697 3000 *fax* 020-7697 3001
email batsford@chrysalisbooks.co.uk
website www.batsford.com
Director Roger Huggins

Chess and bridge, art techniques, film, fashion and costume, practical craft, gardening, embroidery, lace, woodwork. Part of Chrysalis Books Ltd. Founded 1843.

BBC Worldwide Ltd* – see page 294

Belitha Press

64 Brewery Road, London N7 9NT
tel 020-7697 3000 *fax* 020-7697 3003
email info@belithapress.co.uk
website www.belithapress.co.uk
Head of Children's Books Steve Evans, *Publisher* Chester Fisher

Illustrated children's non-fiction: literacy, art, atlases, geography, history, natural history, reference, science. Part of Chrysalis Books Ltd. Founded 1980.

Bell & Hyman Ltd – acquired by HarperCollins Publishers

David Bennett Books Ltd

64 Brewery Road, London N7 9NT
tel 020-7697 3000 *fax* 020-7697 3001
email info@db-books.co.uk
website www.db-books.co.uk
Head of Children's Books Steve Evans, *Publisher* Chester Fisher

Highly illustrated children's fiction and non-fiction; baby books, interactive play books and gift books for the young. Part of Chrysalis Books Ltd. Founded 1989.

Berg Publishers

150 Cowley Road, Oxford OX4 1JJ
tel (01865) 245104 *fax* (01865) 791165
email enquiry@bergpublishers.com
Managing Director Kathryn Earle

Social anthropology, cultural studies, dress and fashion studies, European studies, politics, history. Founded 1983.

Berkswell Publishing Co. Ltd

PO Box 420, Warminster, Wilts. BA12 9XB
tel (01985) 840189 *fax* (01985) 840243
email churchwardens@btinternet.com
Directors J.N.G. Stidolph, S.A. Abbott

Books of local interest, field sports; *The Churchwarden's Yearbook*, church and parish administration. Ideas and MSS welcome.

Berlitz Publishing Co. Ltd

Lincoln House, 296-302 High Holborn, London W1V 7JH
tel 020-7611 9640 *fax* 020-7611 9656
email publishing@berlitz.co.uk
Managing Director Roger Kirkpatrick

Travel, language and related multimedia. Founded 1970.

BFI Publishing

British Film Institute, 21 Stephen Street, London W1P 2LN
tel 020-7255 1444 *fax* 020-7636 2516
website www.bfi.org.uk
Head of Publishing Andrew Lockett

Film and media studies; general books on films and directors. Founded 1982.

Big Fish

64 Brewery Road, London N7 9NT
tel 020-7697 3000 *fax* 020-7697 3003
email info@bigfishonline.co.uk
website www.bigfishonline.co.uk

Head of Children's Books Steve Evans, *Publisher* Chester Fisher

Highly interactive non-fiction children's books for UK trade and co-editions. Part of Chrysalis Books Ltd. Founded 2001.

Clive Bingley Ltd – see Facet Publishing

Birlinn Ltd

West Newington House, 10 Newington Road, Edinburgh EH9 1QS
tel 0131-668 4371 *fax* 0131-668 4466
email info@birlinn.co.uk
website www.birlinn.co.uk
Directors Hugh Andrew, Hubert Andrew

Scottish history, local interest/history, Scottish humour, guides, military, adventure, history, archaeology, vernacular architecture, sport, general non-fiction. Imprint: John Donald. Founded 1992.

Birnbaum – see HarperCollins Publishers

Black Ace Books

PO Box 6557, Forfar DD8 2YS
tel (01307) 465096 *fax* (01307) 465494
website www.blackacebooks.com
Publisher Hunter Steele, *Art, Publicity and Sales* Boo Wood

Fiction, Scottish and general; new editions of outstanding recent fiction. Some biography, history, psychology and philosophy. No submissions without first visiting website for latest list details and requirements. Imprints: Black Ace Books, Black Ace Paperbacks. Founded 1991.

Black Lace – see Virgin Books Ltd

A & C Black Publishers Ltd*

37 Soho Square, London W1D 3QZ
tel 020-7758 0200 *fax* 020-7758 0222
email enquiries@acblack.com
website www.acblack.com
Chairman Nigel Newton, *Managing Director* Jill Coleman, *Directors* Colin Adams, Jenny Aspinall, Charles Black, Sarah Fecher (children's books), Oscar Heini (production), Paul Langridge (rights), Janet Murphy (Adlard Coles Nautical), Kathy Rooney, Terry Rouelett (distribution), David Wightman (sales)

Children's and educational books (including music) for 3–15 years (preliminary enquiry appreciated – fiction guidelines available on request); ceramics, art and craft, drama, ornithology, reference (*Who's Who, Whitaker's Almanack*), sport, theatre, travel, books for writers. Subsidiary of Bloomsbury Publishing plc. Founded 1807.

Adlard Coles Nautical (imprint)
Nautical.

Christopher Helm (imprint)
Ornithology.

The Herbert Press (imprint)
Visual arts.

Pica Press (imprint)
Ornithology.

Black Swan – see Transworld Publishers

BlackAmber Books Ltd

PO Box 10812, London SW7 4ZG
tel/fax 020-7373 3178
email info@blackamber.com
website www.blackamber.com
Publisher Rosemarie Hudson

Literary fiction and non-fiction and work in translation by British and European Black and Asian writers. For novel submissions send one-page synopsis together with first 3 chapters and sae; for non-fiction, send a detailed outline with some accompanying material plus a one-page CV and sae. Founded 1998.

Blackstaff Press Ltd†

Blackstaff House, Wildflower Way, Apollo Road, Belfast BT12 6TA
tel 028-9066 8074 *fax* 028-9066 8207
email info@blackstaffpress.com
website www.blackstaffpress.com
Managing Director Anne Tannahill

Fiction, poetry, biography, history, politics, natural history, humour, education. Founded 1971.

Blackstone Press Ltd – acquired by Oxford University Press

The Blackwater Press – see Folens Publishing Company

Blackwell Publishers*

(Basil Blackwell Ltd)
108 Cowley Road, Oxford OX4 1JF
tel (01865) 791100 *fax* (01865) 791347
Directors Nigel Blackwell (chairman), René Olivieri (managing), Mark Houlton

Economics, education (academic), geography, history, industrial relations, linguistics, literature and criticism, politics, psychology, social anthropology, social policy and administration, sociology, theology, business studies, professional, law, reference, feminism, information technology, philosophy, cultural studies. Founded 1922.

Shakespeare Head Press (imprint)
Finely printed books; scholarly works.

Blackwell Science Ltd*

Osney Mead, Oxford OX2 0EL
tel (01865) 206206 *fax* (01865) 721205
website www.blackwell-science.com
Chairman Nigel Blackwell, *Managing Director* Robert Campbell, *Directors* Jonathan Conibear, Martin Wilkinson (finance), John Strange (production)

Medicine, nursing, dentistry, veterinary medicine, life sciences, earth sciences, chemistry, professional including construction, allied health. Founded 1939.

Fishing News Books (imprint)
tel (01865) 206081
Publisher Nigel Balmforth
Commercial fisheries, aquaculture, fish biology.

Blake Publishing

(incorporating Smith Gryphon Ltd)
3 Bramber Court, 2 Bramber Road, London W14 9PB
tel 020-7381 0666 *fax* 020-7381 6868
email words@blake.co.uk

Popular non-fiction, including biographies and true crime. No unsolicited fiction. Founded 1991.

John Blake Publishing Ltd

(incorporating Metro Books)
3 Bramber Court, 2 Bramber Road, London W14 9PB
tel 020-7381 0666 *fax* 020-7381 6868
email words@blake.co.uk

Popular non-fiction, including biographies, true crime, food and drink, health. No unsolicited fiction. Acquired Metro Publishing Ltd 2001.

Bloodaxe Books Ltd

Highgreen, Tarset, Northumberland NE48 1RP
tel (01434) 240500 *fax* (01434) 240505
email editor@bloodaxebooks.demon.co.uk
Directors Neil Astley, Simon Thirsk

Poetry, literary criticism. No submissions from new authors this year. Founded 1978.

Bloomsbury Publishing Plc*

38 Soho Square, London W1D 3HB
tel 020-7494 2111 *fax* 020-7434 0151
website www.bloomsburymagazine.com
Chairman and Chief Executive Nigel Newton, *Directors* Liz Calder (publishing), Alexandra Pringle (publishing), Alan Wherry (USA), Kathleen Farrar (international), Kathy Rooney (reference), David Ward (sales), Minna Fry (marketing), Katie Collins (publicity), Ruth Logan (rights), Penny Edwards (production), Arzu Tahsin (paperbacks), Sarah Odedina (children's), Colin Adams (finance), Will Webb (design), Jill Coleman

Fiction, biography, illustrated, reference, travel, children's, trade paperback and mass market paperback. Founded 1986.

Boatswain Press Ltd – now Nautical Data Ltd

Bodley Head Children's – see Random House Group Ltd

Booth-Clibborn Editions

12 Percy Street, London W1T 1DW
tel 020-7637 4255 *fax* 020-7637 4251
email info@book-clibborn.com
website www.booth-clibborn-editions.co.uk

Illustrated books on art, popular culture, graphic design, photography. Founded 1974.

Bounty – see Octopus Publishing Group

Bowker

Windsor Court, East Grinstead House, East Grinstead, West Sussex RH19 1XA
tel (01342) 336149 *fax* (01342) 336192
email customer.services@bowker.co.uk
website www.bowker.co.uk
Managing Director Jacki Heppard

Print and electronic publishers of bibliographies and serials databases, trade and reference directories and library and information titles. Part of the Cambridge Information Group.

Boxtree – see Macmillan Publishers Ltd

Marion Boyars Publishers Ltd

24 Lacy Road, London SW15 1NL
tel 020-8788 9522 *fax* 020-8789 8122
Directors Arthur Boyars, Catheryn Kilgarriff

Literary fiction, psychology, feminism, music, drama, cinema, dance, biography. Will only consider material submitted through an agent.

Boydell & Brewer Ltd

PO Box 9, Woodbridge, Suffolk IP12 3DF

Medieval studies, history, literature, archaeology, art history. No unsolicited MSS. Founded 1969.

Bradt Travel Guides Ltd

19 High Street, Chalfont St Peter, Bucks SL9 9QE
tel (01753) 893444 *fax* (01753) 892333
email info@bradt-travelguides.com
website www.bradt-travelguides.com

Managing Director Hilary Bradt

Guides for the adventurous traveller who seeks off-beat places and 'the dreamer who would like to travel there but never will'. Bradt series: *Country Guides, Trekking Guides, Rail Guides, Road Guides, Wildlife Guides.* Founded 1973.

Brandon/Mount Eagle Publications†

(incorporating Brandon Book Publishers Ltd, 1982)
Cooleen, Dingle, Co. Kerry, Republic of Ireland
tel (353) 66 9151463 *fax* (353) 66 9151234
Publisher Steve MacDonogh

Fiction, biography and current affairs. No unsolicited MSS.

Brassey's (UK) Ltd

64 Brewery Road, London N7 9NT
tel 020-7697 3000 *fax* 020-7697 3001
website www.brasseys.com
Editorial John Lee

Military technology, military history and illustrated military reference works. Part of Chrysalis Books Ltd. Founded 1886.

Conway Maritime Press (imprint)
Editorial John Lee

Highly illustrated reference books on naval history and maritime culture, ship design and ship modelling.

Putnam Aeronautical Books (imprint)
Editorial John Lee

Highly illustrated reference books on specialist aviation histories and studies of aerospace manufacturers.

Nicholas Brealey Publishing

3-5 Spafield Street, London EC1R 4QB
tel 020-7239 0360 *fax* 020-7239 0370
website www.nbrealey-books.com
Managing Director Nicholas Brealey

Critical issues facing business in the new century – from leadership to personal development, from science applied to business success to an understanding of global change. Acquired Intercultural Press, US publisher of books and training materials on crossing cultures. Founded 1992.

Breedon Books Publishing Co. Ltd

Breedon House, 3 The Parker Centre,
Derby DE21 4SZ
tel (01332) 384235 *fax* (01332) 292755
email anton@breedonbooks.co.uk
Directors Anton Rippon (chairman and editorial), Patricia Rippon, Graham Hales (production)

Heritage, local history, archive photography, local guidebooks, sports history – especially soccer. No fiction. Preliminary letter essential. Founded 1981.

Breese Books Ltd

164 Kensington Park Road, London W11 2ER
tel 020-7727 9426 *fax* 020-7229 3395
email martin@sherlockholmes.co.uk
website www.sherlockholmes.co.uk
Publisher Martin Breese

Conjuring books, Sherlock Holmes pastiches and *Breese's Guide to Modern First Editions.* All work is commissioned and unsolicited submissions are not required. Founded 1980.

Brilliant Publications*

1 Church View, Sparrow Hall Farm,
Edlesborough, Dunstable LU6 2ES
tel (01525) 229720 *fax* (01525) 229725
email editorial@brilliantpublications.co.uk
website www.brilliantpublications.co.uk
Managing Director Priscilla Hannaford

Books for teachers and others concerned with the education of 0–13 year-olds. All areas of the curriculum published. Study catalogue or visit website before sending proposal. Founded 1993.

Brimax Books – see Octopus Publishing Group

Bristol Classical Press – see Gerald Duckworth & Co. Ltd

Britannica.co.uk.ltd – see Encyclopaedia Britannica International Ltd

The British Library (Publications)*

Publishing Office, The British Library,
96 Euston Road, London NW1 2DB
tel 020-7412 7704 *fax* 020-7412 7768
email blpublications@bl.uk
website www.bl.uk
Managers David Way (publishing), Lara Speicher (managing editor), Catherine Britton (sales and marketing)

Book arts, bibliography, music, maps, oriental, manuscript studies, history, literature, facsimiles, audio-visual, and multimedia CD-Rom. Founded 1973.

British Museum Press*

46 Bloomsbury Street, London WC1B 3QQ
tel 020-7323 1234 *fax* 020-7436 7315
website www.britishmuseum.co.uk
Managing Director Andrew Thatcher, *Head of Sales & Marketing* Alasdair MacLeod

General and specialised adult and children's books on art history, archaeology, numismatics, history, oriental art and archaeology, horology, ethnography. Division of The British Museum Company Ltd. Founded 1973.

Brockhampton Press – **see Caxton Publishing Group**

Andrew Brodie Publications
PO Box 23, Wellington, Somerset TA21 8YX
tel (01823) 665493 *fax* (01823) 665345
email andrew@andrewbrodie.co.uk
website www.andrewbrodie.co.uk
Maths and English for pupils and teachers. Founded 1992.

Brown, Son & Ferguson, Ltd*
4-10 Darnley Street, Glasgow G41 2SD
tel 0141-429 1234 (24 hours) *fax* 0141-420 1694
email info@skipper.co.uk
website www.skipper.co.uk
Editorial Director L. Ingram-Brown
Nautical books; plays; Scout, Cub Scout, Brownie Guide and Guide story books. Founded 1860.

Brunner-Routledge – **see Psychology Press Ltd**

Bryntirion Press
(formerly Evangelical Press of Wales)
Bryntirion, Bridgend CF31 4DX
tel (01656) 655886 *fax* (01656) 665919
email office@evangelicalmvt-wales.org
website www.evangelicalmvt-wales.org
Press Manager Huw Kinsey
Theology and religion (in English and Welsh). Founded 1955.

Burns & Oates – **see The Continuum International Publishing Group Ltd**

Buster Books – **see Michael O'Mara Books Ltd**

Butterworth–Heinemann UK – **see Reed Educational and Professional Publishing Ltd**

Cadogan Guides
Network House, 1 Ariel Way, London W12 7SL
tel 020-8600 3550 *fax* 020-8600 3599
email cadoganguides@morrispub.co.uk
website www.cadoganguides.com
Editorial Director Vicki Ingle
Travel guides. Founded 1982.

Calder Publications Ltd
51 The Cut, London SE1 8LF
tel 020-7633 0599 *fax* 020-7928 5930
email info@calderpublications.com
website www.calderpublications.com
Director John Calder
European, international and British fiction and plays, art, literary, music and social criticism, biography and autobiography, essays, humanities and social sciences, European classics. No unsolicited MSS. Inquiry letters must include an sae. Series include: *English National Opera Guides, Scottish Library, New Writing and Writers, Opera Library, Historical Perspectives, Thought Bites.*

Calmann and King Ltd – **see Laurence King Publishing Ltd**

Cambridge University Press*
The Edinburgh Building, Shaftesbury Road, Cambridge CB2 2RU
tel (01223) 312393 *fax* (01223) 315052
email information@cambridge.org
website www.cambridge.org
Chief Executive of the Press and University Printer Stephen R.R. Bourne
Anthropology and archaeology, art and architecture, astronomy, biological sciences, classical studies, computer science, dictionaries, earth sciences, economics, educational (primary, secondary, tertiary), educational software, engineering, film, English language teaching, history, language and literature, law, mathematics, medical sciences, music, philosophy, physical sciences, politics, psychology, reference, technology, social sciences, theology, religion. Journals (humanities, social sciences, science and professional). The Bible and Prayer Book. Founded 1534.

Cameron & Hollis
PO Box 1, Moffat, Dumfriesshire DG10 9SU
tel (01683) 220808 *fax* (01683) 220012
email editorial@cameronbooks.co.uk
website www.cameronbooks.co.uk
Directors Ian A. Cameron, Jill Hollis
Modern art, decorative art, collecting and film (serious critical works only). Founded 1979.

Campbell Books – **see Macmillan Publishers Ltd**

Canongate Books Ltd*
14 High Street, Edinburgh EH1 1TE
tel 0131-557 5111 *fax* 0131-557 5211
email info@canongate.co.uk
website www.canongate.net

Publisher Jamie Byng, *Directors* David Graham (managing), Ronnie Shanks (finance), Judy Moir (editorial), Caroline Graham (production)

Adult general non-fiction and fiction: literary fiction, art, travel, mountaineering, Scottish interest, philosophy, religion, history and biography. No unsolicited MSS. Founded 1973.

Canongate Classics (imprint)
Senior Editor Rory Watson

Reprint series of key works of Scottish literature ranging from fiction to poetry, to biography, philosophy and travel.

Canongate Crime (imprint)
Senior Editor Karen McCrossan

Crime fiction and non-fiction – hard-boiled, literary and noir, including Canongate Crime Classics.

Canopus Publishing Ltd

Suite 2, Piccadilly House, London Road, Bath BA1 6PL
tel/fax (01225) 789850
email robin@canopusbooks.com
website www.canopusbooks.com
Director Robin Rees

Popular science and astronomy. Founded 1999.

Canterbury Press Norwich

St Mary's Works, St Mary's Plain, Norwich, Norfolk NR3 3BH
tel (01603) 612914 *fax* (01603) 624483
email admin@scm-canterburypress.co.uk
website www.scm-canterburypress.co.uk
Publisher Christine Smith

C of E doctrine, theology, liturgy, general interest, reference, diary, guide and resource, histories and associated religious topics, hymn books. Division of SCM-Canterbury Press Ltd, a subsidiary of Hymns Ancient & Modern Ltd.

Jonathan Cape – see Random House Group Ltd

Jonathan Cape Children's Books – see Random House Group Ltd

Carcanet Press Ltd

4th Floor, Conavon Court, 12-16 Blackfriars Street, Manchester M3 5BQ
tel 0161-834 8730 *fax* 0161-832 0084
email pnr@carcanet.u-net.com
website www.carcanet.co.uk
Director Michael Schmidt

Poetry, *Fyfield* series, Oxford Poets, translations. Founded 1969.

Carlton Publishing Group

20 Mortimer Street, London W1T 3JW
tel 020-7612 0400 *fax* 020-7612 0401
email enquiries@carltonbooks.co.uk
website www.carlton.com
Managing Director Jonathan Goodman, *Publishing Director* Piers Murray Hill

TV tie-ins, lifestyle, computer games, sport, health, New Age, quizzes and puzzles, popular science and history, rock 'n' roll; illustrated leisure and entertainment. No unsolicited MSS; synopses and ideas welcome. Imprints: Carlton Books, André Deutsch, Granada Media, Manchester United Books. Owned by Carlton Communications. Founded 1992.

Frank Cass & Co. Ltd

Crown House, 47 Chase Side, Southgate, London N14 5BP
tel 020-8920 2100 *fax* 020-8447 8548
email info@frankcass.com
website www.frankcass.com
Directors Frank Cass (chairman), Stewart Cass (managing), A.E. Cass, H.J. Osen, M.P. Zaidner, Hon. C. Callman

History, economic and social history, military and strategic studies, politics, international affairs, development studies, African studies, Middle East studies, sports studies, law, business management and academic journals in all of these fields.

Woburn Press (imprint)
Educational.

Cassell (academic, professional and contemporary studies list) – see The Continuum International Publishing Group Ltd

Cassell – see Weidenfeld & Nicolson

Cassell Illustrated – see Octopus Publishing Group

Cassell Military – see Weidenfeld & Nicolson

Cat's Whiskers – see The Watts Publishing Group Ltd

Kyle Cathie Ltd

122 Arlington Road, London NW1 7HP
tel 020-7692 7215 *fax* 020-7692 7260
email general.enquiries@kyle-cathie.com
website www.kylecathie.com
Publisher and Managing Director Kyle Cathie

Health, beauty, food and drink, gardening, reference, style, design, Mind, Body & Spirit. Founded 1990.

Catholic Truth Society
40-46 Harleyford Road, London SE11 5AY
tel 020-7640 0042 *fax* 020-7640 0046
email editorial@cts.online.org.uk
website www.cts-online.org.uk
Chairman Most Rev. Peter Smith DCL, LLB, *General Secretary* Fergal Martin LLB, LLM

General books of Roman Catholic and Christian interest, bibles, prayer books, RE, and booklets of doctrinal, historical, devotional or social interest. MSS of 11,000–15,000 words with up to 6 illustrations considered for publication as pamphlets. Founded 1868.

Cavendish Publishing Ltd*
The Glass House, Wharton Street, London WC1X 9PX
tel 020-7278 8000 *fax* 020-7278 8080
email info@cavendishpublishing.com
website www.cavendishpublishing.com
Executive Chairman Sonny Leong, *Managing Director* Jeremy Stein, *Managing Editor* Cara Annett

A wide range of legal and medico-legal books and journals. Founded 1990.

Caxton Publishing Group
20 Bloomsbury Street, London WC1B 3QA
tel 020-7636 7171 *fax* 020-7636 1922
Directors John Maxwell (managing), Jack Cooper (deputy managing)

Reprints, promotional books, remainders. Imprints: Caxton Editions, Brockhampton Press, Knight Paperbacks.

CBD Research Ltd
15 Wickham Road, Beckenham, Kent BR3 5JS
tel 020-8650 7745 *fax* 020-8650 0768
email cbd@cbdresearch.com
website www.cbdresearch.com
Directors G.P. Henderson, S.P.A. Henderson, A.J.W. Henderson

Directories, reference books, bibliographies, guides to business and statistical information. Founded 1961.

Chancery House Press (imprint)
Unusual non-fiction/reference works. Preliminary letter and synopsis with return postage essential.

Centaur Press – acquired by Open Gate Press

Century – see Random House Group Ltd

Chambers Harrap Publishers Ltd*
7 Hopetoun Crescent, Edinburgh EH7 4AY
tel 0131-556 5929 *fax* 0131-556 5313
email admin@chambersharrap.co.uk
Managing Director Maurice Shepherd, *Publishing Manager* Patrick White

English language and bilingual dictionaries, reference. No unsolicited MSS. Write enclosing CV and synopsis.

Chancery House Press – see CBD Research Ltd

Geoffrey Chapman – see The Continuum International Publishing Group Ltd

Chapman Publishing*
4 Broughton Place, Edinburgh EH1 3RX
tel 0131-557 2207 *fax* 0131-556 9565
email editor@chapman-pub.co.uk
website www.chapman-pub.co.uk
Editor Joy Hendry

Poetry and drama: *Chapman New Writing Series.* Founded 1970.

Paul Chapman Publishing Ltd
6 Bonhill Street, London EC2A 4PU
tel 020-7374 0645 *fax* 020-7374 8741
website www.paulchapmanpublishing.co.uk
Consultant P.R. Chapman, *Commissioning Editor* Marianne Lagrange

Education. Subsidiary of **SAGE Publications Ltd**.

Chartered Institute of Personnel and Development
CIPD House, Camp Road, London SW19 4UX
tel 020-8263 3382 *fax* 020-8263 3850
email publish@cipd.co.uk
website www.cipd.co.uk/publications
Publishing Manager Sarah Brown

Personnel management, training and development.

Chatham Publishing – see Gerald Duckworth & Co. Ltd

Chatto & Windus – see Random House Group Ltd

Cherrytree Books – see Zero to Ten Ltd

The Chicken House – see Egmont Books

Child's Play (International) Ltd
Ashworth Road, Bridgemead, Swindon, Wilts. SN5 7YD
tel (01793) 616286 *fax* (01793) 512795
email allday@childs-play.com

website www.childs-play.com
Chairman Adriana Twinn, *Publisher* Neil Burden
Children's educational books: board picture, activity and play books; fiction and non-fiction. Founded 1972.

Chivers Press Ltd
Windsor Bridge Road, Bath BA2 3AX
tel (01225) 335336 *fax* (01225) 310771
website www.chivers.co.uk
Directors Julian Batson (managing), Nicole Kirkman (publishing), Michael Bowen (finance)
Large print books and complete and unabridged audiobooks: general fiction, crime, romance, mystery/thrillers, westerns, non-fiction. Does not publish original books. Imprints: Chivers Large Print, Chivers Audio Books, Black Dagger Crime, Windsor Large Print, Galaxy Children's Large Print, Cavalcade. Founded 1979.

Christian Education*
(incorporating International Bible Reading Association)
1020 Bristol Road, Selly Oak, Birmingham B26 6LB
tel 0121-472 4242 *fax* 0121-472 7575
email enquiries@christianeducation.org.uk
website www.christianeducation.org.uk
Training material for children and youth workers in the Church. Worship resources for use in primary schools. Christian drama and musicals, Activity Club material and Bible reading resources. Resources and journals for teachers of RE.

Churchill Livingstone – see Harcourt Publishers Ltd

Cicerone Press
2 Police Square, Milnthorpe, Cumbria LA7 7PY
tel (015395) 62069 *fax* (015395) 63417
email info@cicerone.demon.co.uk
website www.cicerone.co.uk
Managing Director Jonathan Williams
Guidebooks to the great outdoors – walking, mountaineering, climbing, cycling, etc in Britain, Europe, and worldwide. Founded 1969.

Cico Books
32 Great Sutton Street, London EC1V 0NB
tel 020-7253 7960 *fax* 020-7253 7967
email mail@cicobooks.co.uk
Directors Mark Collins (managing), Lucinda Richards (publishing)
Lifestyle and interiors and Mind, Body & Spirit. Founded 1999.

Cima Books – now Cico Books

Clarendon Press – former imprint of Oxford University Press

T & T Clark – see The Continuum International Publishing Group Ltd

James Clarke & Co. Ltd*
PO Box 60, Cambridge CB1 2NT
tel (01223) 350865 *fax* (01223) 366951
email publishing@lutterworth.com
website www.lutterworth.com
Managing Director Adrian Brink
Theology, academic, reference books. Founded 1859.
Acorn Editions (imprint)
Sponsored books.
Lutterworth Press (subsidiary)
The arts, biography, children's books (fiction, non-fiction, picture, rewards), educational, environmental, general, history, leisure, philosophy, science, sociology, theology and religion.
Patrick Hardy Books (imprint)
Children's fiction.

Cló Iar-Chonnachta Teo.†
Indreabhán, Conamara, Co. Galway, Republic of Ireland
tel (091) 593307 *fax* (091) 593362
email cic@iol.ie
website www.cic.ie
Director Micheál Ó Conghaile, *General Manager* Deirdre O'Toole
Irish-language – novels, short stories, plays, poetry, songs, history; cassettes (writers reading from their works in Irish and English). Promotes the translation of contemporary Irish fiction and poetry into other languages. Founded 1985.

CMP Information Ltd
Riverbank House, Angel Lane, Tonbridge, Kent TN9 1SE
tel (01732) 377591 *fax* (01732) 368324
Directories for business and industry, including *Benn's Media* and *The Knowledge*, guides for the media and film and TV markets respectively. Subsidiary of United Business Media.

Co & Bear Productions*
565 Fulham Road, London SW6 1ES
tel 020-7385 0888 *fax* 020-7385 0101
email info@cobear.co.uk
Publisher Beatrice Vincenzini
High quality illustrated books on lifestyle, photography, art. Imprints:

Scriptum Editions, Cartago. Founded 1996.

Peter Collin Publishing Ltd
32-34 Great Peter Street, London SW1P 2DB
tel 020-7222 1155 *fax* 020-7222 1551
email info@petercollin.com
website www.petercollin.com
Directors S.M.H. Collin (managing), P.H. Collin, F. Collin

Specialised dictionaries covering many subjects – from business to computing, medicine to tourism, law to banking. Bilingual language dictionaries in various subjects and languages. Founded 1985.

Aspect Guides (imprint)
email info@aspectguides.com
website www.aspectguides.com

Travel guides including the *French Entrée* series, *Everybody's Guides*, *Access Guides*, *Before You Go*.

Collins – see HarperCollins Publishers

Collins & Brown
64 Brewery Road, London N7 9NT
tel 020-7697 3000 *fax* 020-7697 30001
Directors Colin Ziegler (publishing), Frank Chambers (international rights, sales), Richard Samson (UK sales and marketing)

Lifestyle and interiors, gardening, photography, practical arts, health and beauty, hobbies and crafts, natural history, history, ancient civilisation and general interest. Part of Chrysalis Books Ltd. Founded 1989.

Paper Tiger (imprint)
Contact Colin Ziegler

Science fiction and fantasy art.

Colourpoint Books*
Unit D5, Ards Business Centre, Jubilee Road, Newtownards, Co. Down BT23 4YH
tel (028) 9182 0505 *fax* (028) 9182 1900
email info@colourpoint.co.uk
website www.colourpoint.co.uk
Directors Sheila Johnston (commissioning editor), Norman Johnston (transport editor), *Administrator* Michelle Chambers, *Sales Manager* Lawrence Greet

Educational textbooks; transport – shipping, aviation, buses, road and railways; religion; Irish interest. Initial approach in writing please, with full details of proposal and sample chapters. Include return postage. Founded 1993.

The Columba Press†
55A Spruce Avenue, Stillorgan Industrial Park, Blackrock, Co. Dublin, Republic of Ireland
tel (1) 2942556 *fax* (1) 2942564
email info@columba.ie
website www.columba.ie
Publisher and Managing Director Seán O'Boyle

Religion (Roman Catholic and Anglican) including pastoral handbooks, spirituality, theology, liturgy and prayer; counselling and self-help. Founded 1985.

Conran Octopus – see Octopus Publishing Group

Conservative Policy Forum
(formerly the Conservative Political Centre)
32 Smith Square, London SW1P 3HH
tel 020-7984 8086 *fax* 020-7984 8272
email cpf@conservative-party.org.uk
Director Dr Greg Clark

Politics, current affairs. Founded 1945 as the Conservative Political Centre.

Constable & Robinson Ltd*
3 The Lanchesters, 162 Fulham Palace Road, London W6 9ER
tel 020-8741 3663 *fax* 020-8748 7562
email enquiries@constablerobinson.com
website www.constablerobinson.com
Non-Executive Chairman Benjamin Glazebrook, *Managing Director* Nick Robinson, *Directors* Jan Chamier, Nova Jayne Heath, Adrian Andrews

Unsolicited sample chapters, synopses and ideas welcome with return postage. Do not send MSS; no email submissions. Founded 1890 (Constable); 1983 (Robinson).

Constable (imprint: hardbacks)
Editorial Director Carol O'Brien

Biography, crime fiction, general and military history, travel and endurance, climbing, landscape photography, outdoor-pursuits guidebooks.

Robinson (imprint: paperbacks)
Senior Commissioning Editor Krystyna Green

Crime fiction, science fiction, *Daily Telegraph* health books, the Mammoth series, psychology, true crime, military history, *Smarties* children's books.

Constable Publishers – see Constable & Robinson Ltd

Consumers' Association – see Which? Ltd

The Continuum International Publishing Group Ltd

The Tower Building, 11 York Road, London SE1 7NX
tel 020-7922 0880 *fax* 020-7922 0881
email info@continuumbooks.com
website www.continuumbooks.com
Chairman and Chief Executive Philip Sturrock, *Directors* Robin Baird-Smith (publishing: religious and general), Philip Davies (editorial: religious and biblical studies – Sheffield Academic Press), Geoffrey Green (publishing: academic religious and theological – T & T Clark), Anthony Haynes (editorial: professional, philosophy and social sciences), Janet Joyce (publishing: journals, humanities and history), Frank Roney (finance), Ed Suthon (sales and marketing)

Serious non-fiction, academic and professional, including scholarly monographs and educational texts and reference works in history, politics and social thought; literature, criticism, performing arts; religion and spirituality; education, psychology, women's studies, business. Imprints: Athlone, Burns & Oates, Cassell (academic, professional and contemporary studies lists), Geoffrey Chapman, T & T Clark, Handsel Press, Leicester University Press, Mansell Publishing, Mowbray, Pinter, Sheed & Ward, Sheffield Academic Press.

Conway Maritime Press – see Brassey's (UK) Ltd

Thomas Cook Publishing

PO Box 227, Units 19-21, The Thomas Cook Business Park, Peterborough PE3 8XX
tel (01733) 416477 *fax* (01733) 416688
email publishing-sales@thomascook.com
website www.thomascookpublishing.com
Managing Director Kevin Fitzgerald

Travel guides, rail maps and timetables. Founded 1875.

Leo Cooper – see Pen & Sword Books Ltd

Corgi – see Transworld Publishers

Corgi Children's Books – see Random House Group Ltd

Cork University Press†

Crawford Business Park, Crosses Green, Cork, Republic of Ireland
tel (021) 4902980 *fax* (021) 4315329
email corkunip@ucc.ie
website www.corkuniversitypress.com
Publisher Sara Wilbourne

Irish literature, history, cultural studies, medieval studies, English literature, musicology, poetry, translations. Founded 1925.

Cornwall Books – see Golden Cockerel Press

Coronet – see Hodder Headline Ltd

Council for British Archaeology

Bowes Morrell House, 111 Walmgate, York YO1 9WA
tel (01904) 671417 *fax* (01904) 671384
email info@britarch.ac.uk
website www.britarch.ac.uk
Director George Lambrick, *Publications Officer* Jane Thorniley-Walker

British archaeology – academic; practical handbooks; general interest archaeology. Founded 1944.

Countryside Books

2 Highfield Avenue, Newbury, Berks. RG14 5DS
tel (01635) 43816 *fax* (01635) 551004
website www.countrysidebooks.co.uk
Partners Nicholas Battle, Suzanne Battle

Books of local or regional interest, usually on a county basis: walking, outdoor activities, local history; also genealogy, aviation. Founded 1976.

Countrywise Press – see Barry Rose Law Publishers Ltd

Crescent Moon Publishing

PO Box 393, Maidstone, Kent ME14 5XU
tel (01622) 729593
email jrobinson@crescentmoon.org.uk
website www.crescentmoon.org.uk
Director Jeremy Robinson, *Editors* C. Hughes, B.D. Barnacle

Literature, poetry, fine art, cultural studies, media, cinema, feminism. Submit sample chapters or 6 poems plus sae, not complete MSS. Founded 1988.

Cressrelles Publishing Co. Ltd

10 Station Road Industrial Estate, Colwall, Malvern, Herefordshire WR13 6RN
tel/fax (01684) 540154
email simonsmith@cressrelles4drama.fsbusiness.co.uk
Directors Leslie Smith, Simon Smith

General publishing. Founded 1973.

Actinic Press (imprint)

Chiropody.

J. Garnet Miller (imprint)

Plays and theatre textbooks.

Kenyon-Deane (imprint)
Plays and drama textbooks for amateur dramatic societies. Plays for women.

Croner.CCH Group Ltd

145 London Road, Kingston-upon-Thames, Surrey KT2 6SR
tel 020-8247 1262 *fax* 020-8547 2637
email info@.croner.cch.co.uk
website www.croner.cch.co.uk
Managing Director Hans Thijs

Law, taxation, finance, insurance, looseleaf and online information services. Founded 1948.

Crown House Publishing Ltd*

Crown Buildings, Bancyfelin, Carmarthen SA33 5ND
tel (01267) 211345 *fax* (01267) 211882
email books@crownhouse.co.uk
website www.crownhouse.co.uk
Directors Martin Roberts (chairman), Glenys Roberts, David Bowman (editorial), Karen Bowman

Psychology, personal growth, stress management, business, education, health. Founded 1998.

The Crowood Press

The Stable Block, Ramsbury, Marlborough, Wilts. SN8 2HR
tel (01672) 520320 *fax* (01672) 520280
email enquiries@crowood.com
website www.crowood.com
Directors John Dennis (chairman), Ken Hathaway (managing)

Sport, motoring, aviation, military, climbing, walking, fishing, country sports, farming, natural history, gardening, DIY, crafts, dogs, equestrian, games. Founded 1982.

Current Science Group

34-42 Cleveland Street, London W1T 4LB
tel 020-7323 0323 *fax* 020-7580 1938
email csg@cursci.co.uk
website www.current-science-group.com
Chairman Vitek Tracz

Biological sciences, medicine, pharmaceutical science, internet communities, electronic publishing.

James Currey Ltd

73 Botley Road, Oxford OX2 0BS
tel (01865) 244111 *fax* (01865) 246454
Directors James Currey, Prof Wendy James FBA, Dr Douglas H. Johnson, Keith Sambrook

Academic studies of Africa, Caribbean, Third World: history, anthropology, archaeology, economics, agriculture, politics, literary criticism, sociology. Founded 1985.

Curzon Press Ltd – now RoutledgeCurzon – see Taylor & Francis Group plc

Cygnus Arts – see Golden Cockerel Press

Dalesman Publishing Co. Ltd

Stable Courtyard, Broughton Hall, Skipton, North Yorkshire BD23 3AE
tel (01756) 701381 *fax* (01756) 701326
email editorial@dalesman.co.uk
Chairman T.J. Benn, *Chief Executive* C.G. Benn, *Managing Director* R. Flanagan

Countryside books and magazines covering the North of England. Founded 1939.

Terence Dalton Ltd

Water Street, Lavenham, Sudbury, Suffolk CO10 9RN
tel (01787) 249289 *fax* (01787) 248267
Directors T.A.J. Dalton, E.H. Whitehair

Contract publisher for the Chartered Institution of Water and Environmental Management. Founded 1966.

The C.W. Daniel Company Ltd

1 Church Path, Saffron Walden, Essex CB10 1JP
tel (01799) 521909 *fax* (01799) 513462
email cwdaniel@dial.pipex.com
website www.cwdaniel.com
Directors Ian Miller, Jane Miller

Natural healing, Bach Flower Remedies, homoeopathy, aromatherapy, mysticism. Founded 1902.

L.N. Fowler & Co Ltd (imprint)
Directors Ian Miller, Jane Miller
Mysticism, astrology.

Health Science Press (imprint)
Directors Ian Miller, Jane Miller
Homoeopathy.

Neville Spearman Publishers (imprint)
Editorial Director Sebastian Hobnut
Mysticism, metaphysical.

Darton, Longman & Todd Ltd*

1 Spencer Court, 140-142 Wandsworth High Street, London SW18 4JJ
tel 020-8875 0155 *fax* 020-8875 0133
email editorial@darton-longman-todd.co.uk
Editorial Director Brendan Walsh

Religious books and bibles, including the following themes: bible study, spirituality, prayer and meditation, anthologies, daily readings, healing, counselling and pastoral care, bereavement, personal growth, mission, political, environmental and social issues, biography/autobiography, theological and historical studies. Founded 1959.

Darwen Finlayson Ltd – see Phillimore & Co. Ltd

David & Charles Ltd

Brunel House, Newton Abbot, Devon TQ12 4PU
tel (01626) 323200 *fax* (01626) 323317
Acting Managing Director Budge Wallis

High quality illustrated non-fiction specialising in crafts, hobbies, art techniques, gardening, natural history, equestrian, DIY. Founded 1960.

David Fickling Books – see Random House Group Ltd

Christopher Davies Publishers Ltd

PO Box 403, Swansea SA1 4YF
tel/fax (01792) 648825
Directors Christopher Talfan Davies (editorial), K.E.T. Colayera, D.M. Davies

History, leisure, sport, general books of Welsh interest, *Triskele Books*. Founded 1949.

Giles de la Mare Publishers Ltd

PO Box 25351, London NW5 1ZT
tel 020-7485 2533 *fax* 020-7485 2534
email gilesdelamare@dial.pipex.com
Chairman Giles de la Mare

Non-fiction: art, architecture, biography, history, music, travel. Telephone before submitting MSS. Founded 1995.

Dean – see Egmont Books

Dedalus Ltd

24 St Judith's Lane, Sawtry, Cambs. PE28 5XE
tel/fax (01487) 832382
email DedalusLimited@compuserve.com
website www.dedalusbooks.com
Chairman Juri Gabriel, *Directors* Eric Lane (managing), Robert Irwin (editorial), Lindsay Thomas (marketing), Mike Mitchell (translations)

Original fiction in English and in translation; Dedalus European Classics, Dedalus concept books. Founded 1983.

J.M. Dent – now incorporated into The Orion Publishing Group Ltd

André Deutsch Ltd

20 Mortimer Street, London W1T 3JW
tel 020-7612 0400 *fax* 020-7612 0401
Managing Director Jonathan Goodman, *Publishing Director* Piers Murray Hill

Subsidiary of Carlton Publishing Group. Founded 1950.

André Deutsch (imprint)
Film/TV, popular entertainment, music, comedy, sport, biography, history and current affairs, popular culture, cookery/craft.

Granada Media Group (imprint)
Official TV tie-in books, publishing interests of Liverpool Football Club.

Manchester United Books (imprint)
Publishing interests of Manchester United Football Club.

Dial House – see Ian Allan Publishing Ltd

diehard

91-93 Main Street, Callander FK17 8BQ
tel (01877) 339449
Edinburgh office 3 Spittal Street, Edinburgh EH3 9DY
tel 0131-229 7252
Directors Ian William King (managing), Sally Evans King (marketing)

Scottish poetry. Founded 1993.

Discovery Walking Guides Ltd

10 Tennyson Close, Dallington, Northampton NN5 7HJ
tel/fax (01604) 752576
website www.walking.demon.co.uk/
Chairman Rosamund C. Brawn

'Warm island' walking guides and plant and flower guides to European holiday destinations; 'Tour & Trail' digital cartographic large-scale maps, 'Drive' touring maps, '34 Walks' guide books. Founded 1994.

John Donald – see Birlinn Ltd

Dorling Kindersley – see The Penguin Group (UK)

Doubleday (UK) – see Transworld Publishers

Doubleday Children's Books – see Random House Group Ltd

Dref Wen

28 Church Road, Whitchurch, Cardiff CF14 2EA
tel 029-2061 7860 *fax* 029-2061 0507
Directors Roger Boore, Anne Boore, Gwilym Boore, Alun Boore

Original Welsh language novels for children and adult learners. Original, adaptations and translations of foreign and English language full-colour picture story books for children. Educational material for primary/secondary schoolchildren in Wales and England. Founded 1970.

Dryden Press – see Harcourt Publishers Ltd

Dublar Scripts
204 Mercer Way, Romsey, Hants SO51 7QJ
tel (01794) 501377 *fax* (01794) 502538
email scripts@dublar.freeserve.co.uk
website www.dublar.co.uk
Managing Director Robert Heather
Pantomimes, one-act and full-length plays. Drama and comedy. Imprint: Sleepy Hollow Pantomimes (pantomime scripts). Founded 1994.

Gerald Duckworth & Co. Ltd
61 Frith Street, London W1D 3JL
tel 020-7434 4242 *fax* 020-7434 4420
email info@duckworth-publishers.co.uk
website www.ducknet.co.uk
Directors Stephen Hill (chairman), Gillian Hawkins (Coo and sales and marketing), Deborah Blake (editorial)
General trade publishers with a strong academic division. Imprints: Bristol Classical Press and Chatham Publishing; naval and maritime history. Founded 1898.

Dunedin Academic Press*
Hudson House, 8 Albany Street, Edinburgh EH1 3QB
tel 0131-473 2397 *fax* (01250) 870937
Director Anthony Kinahan
All types of academic books and books of Scottish interest. Founded 2000.

Martin Dunitz Ltd
The Livery House, 7-9 Pratt Street, London NW1 0AE
tel 020-7482 2202 *fax* 020-7267 0159
email info@dunitz.co.uk
website www.dunitz.co.uk
Managing Director Martin Dunitz
Specialist medical and dentistry books, journals and slide atlases. A member of the **Taylor & Francis Group plc**. Founded 1978.

Earthlight – see Simon & Schuster

Earthscan Publications Ltd – see Kogan Page Ltd

East-West Publications (UK) Ltd
8 Caledonia Street, London N1 9DZ
tel 020-7837 5061 *fax* 020-7278 4429
Chairman L.W. Carp
General non-fiction, Eastern studies, sufism. No unsolicited MSS; please write first. Founded 1977.

Ebury Press – see Random House Group Ltd

Edinburgh University Press*
22 George Square, Edinburgh EH8 9LF
tel 0131-650 4218 *fax* 0131-662 0053
Chairman Tim Rix, *Managing Director* Timothy Wright, *Editorial Director* Ms Jackie Jones
Academic and general publishers. Archaeology, cultural studies, Islamic studies, geography, history, linguistics, literature (criticism), philosophy, politics, Scottish studies, American studies, religious studies.

Polygon (imprint)
tel 0131-650 4223
New international and Scottish fiction, poetry, short stories, popular Scottish and international general interest. No unsolicited poetry accepted.

Polygon at Edinburgh (imprint)
tel 0131-650 4223
Scottish language, literature and culture, Scottish history and politics, celtic and folklore.

Éditions Aubrey Walter
27 Old Gloucester Street, London WC1 3XX
email aubrey@gmppubs.co.uk
Publisher Aubrey Walter
Visual work by gay artists and photographers, usually in the form of a monograph showcasing one artist's work. Work may be submitted on disk, email, transparency, photocopy or photograph.

The Educational Company of Ireland
Ballymount Road, Walkinstown, Dublin 12, Republic of Ireland
tel (01) 4500611 *fax* (01) 4500993
email info@edco.ie
website www.edco.ie
Executive Directors F.J. Maguire (chief executive), R. McLoughlin, *Financial Controller* A. Harrold, *Sales and Marketing Manager* M. Harford-Hughes, *Publisher* F. Fahy
Trading unit of Smurfit Ireland Ltd. Educational MSS on all subjects in English or Irish language.

Educational Explorers
11 Crown Street, Reading, Berks. RG1 2TQ
tel (01734) 873101 *fax* (01734) 873103
email explorers@cuisenaire.co.uk
website www.cuisenaire.co.uk
Directors M.J. Hollyfield, D.M. Gattegno
Educational, mathematics: *Numbers in*

colour with Cuisenaire Rods*, languages: *The Silent Way*, literacy, reading: *Words in Colour*; educational films. No unsolicited material. Founded 1962.

Egmont Books*

239 Kensington High Street, London W8 6SA
tel 020-7761 3500 *fax* 020-7761 3510
email firstname.surname@ecb.egmont.com
Chief Executive Julie Goldsmith, *Managing Director* Susannah McFarlane

Children's books: picture books, fiction (ages 4–16), illustrated non-fiction, licensed character list. Publishes under Egmont and Dean.

The Chicken House

2 Palmer Street, Frome, Somerset BA11 1DS
tel (01373) 454488 *fax* (01373) 454499
email chickenhouse@doublecluck.com
Managing Director Barry Cunningham

Fiction and non-fiction for 7+, picture books. An Egmont joint venture company.

Element – see HarperCollins Publishers

11:9 – see Neil Wilson Publishing Ltd

Edward Elgar Publishing Ltd

Glensanda House, Montpellier Parade, Cheltenham, Glos. GL50 1UA
tel (01242) 226934 *fax* (01242) 262111
email info@e-elgar.co.uk
website www.e-elgar.co.uk
Managing Director Edward Elgar

Economics and other social sciences. Founded 1986.

Elliot Right Way Books

Kingswood Buildings, Brighton Road, Lower Kingswood, Tadworth, Surrey KT20 6TD
tel (01737) 832202 *fax* (01737) 830311
email info@right-way.co.uk
Managing Directors Clive Elliot, Malcolm Elliot

Independent publishers of practical non-fiction 'how to' paperbacks. The low-price *Right Way* and *Right Way Plus* series include games, pastimes, horses, pets, motoring, sport, health, business, public speaking and jokes, financial and legal, cookery and etiquette. Similar subjects are covered in the *Clarion* series of large-format paperbacks, sold in supermarkets and bargain bookshops. No freelance proof-readers or editors required. Founded 1946.

Aidan Ellis Publishing

Whinfield, Herbert Road, Salcombe, Devon TQ8 8HN
tel (01548) 842755 *fax* (01548) 844356
email aidan@aepub.demon.co.uk
website www.aepub.co.uk
Publisher Aidan Ellis

Non-fiction: gardening, maritime, biography, general. Founded 1971.

ELM Publications

Seaton House, Kings Ripton, Huntingdon, Cambs. PE28 2NJ
tel (01487) 773238 *fax* (01487) 773359
website www.elm-training.co.uk
Managing Director Sheila Ritchie

Educational books and resources; books and training aids (tutor's packs and software) for business and management; software simulations; library and information studies. Actively seeking good, tested management skills training materials. Telephone in the first instance, rather than send MSS. Founded 1977.

Elm Tree Books – former imprint of Hamish Hamilton/Penguin

Elsevier Science Ltd*

The Boulevard, Langford Lane, Kidlington, Oxford OX5 1GB
tel (01865) 843000 *fax* (01865) 843010
Managing Director/Coo Gavin Howe, *Editorial Director (Social Sciences)* B. Barret, *Editorial Director (Materials Science and Engineering)* Peter Desmond

Journal, magazine and book publishers in science, technology and medicine. Imprints: Pergamon, Elsevier Applied Science, Elsevier Trends Journals, Butterworth Heinemann Journals. Division of Reed Elsevier (UK) Ltd

Encyclopaedia Britannica (UK) Ltd

2nd Floor, Unity Wharf, Mill Street, London SE1 2BH
tel 020-7500 7800 *fax* 020-7500 7878
website www.britannica.co.uk
Managing Director Leah Mansoor

Enitharmon Press

26B Caversham Road, London NW5 2DU
tel 020-7482 5967 *fax* 020-7284 1787
email books@enitharmon.co.uk
website www.enitharmon.co.uk
Director Stephen Stuart-Smith

Poetry, literary criticism, fiction, translations, artists' books. No unsolicited MSS. No freelance editors or proofreaders required. Founded 1967.

Epworth Press

c/o Methodist Publishing House, 4 John Wesley Road, Peterborough PE4 6ZP
tel (01733) 325002 *fax* (01733) 384180

Editorial Committee Rev. Gerald Burt (editorial secretary), Dr Valerie Edden, Dr E. Dorothy Graham, Rev. Dr Emmanuel M. Jacob, Rev. Dr Ivor H. Jones, Rev. Dr John A. Newton (chairman), Rev. Michael J. Townsend, Rev. Dr Neil G. Richardson

Religion, theology, church history, worship, Bible commentaries.

Eurobook Ltd – see Peter Lowe (Eurobook Ltd)

Euromonitor plc

60-61 Britton Street, London EC1M 5UX
tel 020-7251 8024 *fax* 020-7608 3149
email info@euromonitor.com
website www.euromonitor.com
Directors T.J. Fenwick (managing), R.N. Senior (chairman)

Business and commercial reference, marketing information, European and International Surveys, directories. Founded 1972.

Europa Publications Ltd

11 New Fetter Lane, London EC4P 4EE
tel 020-7583 9855 *fax* 020-7842 2249
email sales@europapublications.co.uk
Directors R. Horton (managing), P. Kelly (editorial), *General Manager* J.G. North

Directories, international relations, reference, yearbooks. A member of **Taylor & Francis Group plc**.

Evangelical Press of Wales – see Bryntirion Press

Evans Brothers Ltd*

2A Portman Mansions, Chiltern Street, London W1M 1LE
tel 020-7487 0920 *fax* 020-7487 0921
email sales@evansbooks.co.uk
website www.evansbooks.co.uk
Directors S.T. Pawley (managing), Brian D. Jones (international publishing), A.O. Ojora (Nigeria), *UK Publisher* Su Swallow

Educational books, particularly preschool, school library and teachers' books for the UK, including the Rainbows series of graded information books for 5–8 year-olds; primary and secondary for Africa, the Caribbean and Brazil. Part of the Evans Publishing Group. Founded 1908.

Everyman – see The Orion Publishing Group Ltd

Everyman Publishers plc

Gloucester Mansions, 140A Shaftesbury Avenue, London WC2H 8HD
tel 020-7539 7600 *fax* 020-7379 4060
Publisher David Campbell, *Finance Director* Mark Bicknell

Everyman's Library (cloth reprints of the classics); *Everyman's Library Children's Classics*; *Everyman's Library Pocket Poets*; *Everyman Guides*; *Everyman City Guides*; *Everyman City Map Guides*; *Everyman Chess*. No unsolicited submissions.

Exley Publications Ltd

16 Chalk Hill, Watford, Herts. WD19 4BG
tel (01923) 250505 *fax* (01923) 818733/249795
Directors Dalton Exley, Helen Exley (editorial), Lincoln Exley, Richard Exley

Popular colour giftbooks for an international market. No unsolicited MSS. Founded 1976.

Faber & Faber Ltd*

3 Queen Square, London WC1N 3AU
tel 020-7465 0045 *fax* 020-7465 0034
website www.faber.co.uk
Chief Executive Stephen Page, *Directors* John Bodley, Walter Donohue, Valerie Eliot, Matthew Evans, Laurence Longe, Julian Loose, Nigel Marsh, Jon Riley, David Tebbutt

High quality general fiction and non-fiction; all forms of creative writing, including plays. Write to Sales Dept for current catalogues. Unsolicited submissions for the children's list not accepted. For information on submission procedure ring 020-7465 0189. For practical and security reasons submissions by fax or on disk cannot be accepted, except by special arrangement. Allow 6–8 weeks for a response. Freelance editors and proofreaders without in-house experience need not apply.

Fabian Society

11 Dartmouth Street, London SW1H 9BN
tel 020-7227 4900 *fax* 020-7976 7153
email info@fabian-society.org.uk
website www.fabian-society.org.uk
General Secretary Michael Jacobs

Current affairs, political thought, economics, education, environment, foreign affairs, social policy. Also controls NCLC Publishing Society Ltd. Founded 1884.

Facet Publishing*

7 Ridgmount Street, London WC1E 7AE
tel 020-7255 0590 *fax* 020-7255 0591
email info@facetpublishing.co.uk
website www.facetpublishing.co.uk
Managing Director Janet Liebster

Library and information science, information technology, reference works, directories, bibliographies.

Clive Bingley Ltd (imprint)
Library and information science, reference.
Library Association Publishing (imprint)
Library and information science, information technology, reference works, directories, bibliographies.

CJ Fallon

Lucan Road, Palmerstown, Dublin 20, Republic of Ireland
tel (01) 6166400 *fax* (01) 6166499
email editorial@cjfallon.ie
Executive Directors H.J. McNicholas (managing), P. Tolan (financial), N. White (editorial)
Educational text books. Founded 1927.

Falmer Press – now RoutledgeFalmer

Farming Press

United Business Media International, Sovereign House, Sovereign Way, Tonbridge, Kent TN9 1RW
tel (01732) 377539 *fax* (01732) 377465
email cwicks@ubminternational.com
website www.farmingpress.com
Publishing Manager Alison Stevens
Technical agriculture, farm machinery, veterinary; books, videos, audio, CD-Roms. Founded 1951.

Fernhurst Books

Duke's Path, High Street, Arundel, West Sussex BN18 9AJ
tel (01903) 882277 *fax* (01903) 882715
email sales@fernhurstbooks.co.uk
website www.fernhurstbooks.co.uk
Publisher Tim Davison
Sailing, watersports. Founded 1979.

Financial Times Prentice Hall – imprint of Pearson Education

First and Best in Education Ltd*

(incorporating Hamilton House Publishing)
Earlstrees Court, Earlstrees Road, Corby, Northants. NN17 4HH
tel (01536) 399004 *fax* (01536) 399012
email info@firstandbest.co.uk
website www.firstandbest.co.uk
Contact Anne Cockburn (editor)
Education-related books. Currently actively recruiting new writers for schools; ideas welcome. Sae must accompany submissions. Founded 1992.

Fishing News Books – see Blackwell Science Ltd

Fitzroy Dearborn Publishers

310 Regent Street, London W1B 3AX
tel 020-7636 6627 *fax* 020-7636 6982
email post@fitzroydearborn.co.uk
website www.fitzroydearborn.com
Managing Director Daniel Kirkpatrick, *Senior Commissioning Editor* Lesley Henderson, *Publisher* Roda Morrison
Reference books: history, media studies, design, art, literature, philosophy and religion, music, business, science, international affairs, social sciences. Founded 1994.

Five Star – see Serpent's Tail

Flambard Press

Stable Cottage, East Fourstones, Hexham, Northumberland NE47 5DX
tel (01434) 674360 *fax* (01434) 674178
Managing Editor Peter Lewis, *Deputy Editor* Margaret Lewis
Poetry and fiction (literary and crime). Only hard-copy submissions with sae considered. Preliminary letter required. Founded 1990.

Flame – see Hodder Headline Ltd

Flamingo – see HarperCollins Publishers

Flicks Books

29 Bradford Road, Trowbridge, Wilts. BA14 9AN
tel (01225) 767728 *fax* (01225) 760418
email flicks.books@dial.pipex.com
Partners Matthew Stevens (publisher), Aletta Stevens
Cinema, TV, related media. Founded 1986.

Floris Books*

15 Harrison Gardens, Edinburgh EH11 1SH
tel 0131-337 2372 *fax* 0131-347 9919
email floris@floris.demon.co.uk
Editors Christopher Moore, Gale Winskill
Religion, science, Celtic studies, craft; children's books: picture and board books, activity books. Founded 1978.
Flyways (imprint)
Children's fiction paperbacks for the more able reader.
Kelpies (imprint)
Children's fiction from Scotland.

Focal Press – see Reed Educational and Professional Publishing Ltd

Fodor Guides – see Random House Group Ltd

Folens Ltd*

Apex Business Centre, Boscombe Road, Dunstable LU5 4RL
tel (0870) 609 1237 *fax* (0870) 609 1236
email folens@folens.com

website www.folens.com
Managing Director Malcolm Watson

Primary and secondary educational books, learn at home books. Founded 1987.

Folens Publishing Company

Hibernian Industrial Estate, Greenhills Road, Tallaght, Dublin 24, Republic of Ireland
tel (01) 4137200 *fax* (01) 4137282
Chairman Dirk Folens, *Directors* John O'Connor (managing), Margaret Burns (secondary), Deirdre Whelan (primary)

Educational (primary, secondary, comprehensive, technical, in English and Irish).

The Blackwater Press† (imprint)
General non-fiction, Irish interest.

Fontana Press – former imprint of HarperCollins Publishers

G.T. Foulis & Co. – see Haynes Publishing, Special Interest Publishing Division

W. Foulsham & Co. Ltd

The Publishing House, Bennetts Close, Slough, Berks. SL1 5AP
tel (01753) 526769 *fax* (01753) 535003
Managing Director B.A.R. Belasco, *Editorial Director* W. Hobson

Life issues. General know-how, cookery, health and alternative therapies, hobbies and games, gardening, sport, travel guides, DIY, collectibles, popular new age. Imprints: Foulsham, Quantum (Mind, Body & Spirit, popular philosophy and practical psychology). Founded 1819.

Foundery Press – see Methodist Publishing House

Fount – see HarperCollins Publishers

Four Courts Press†

Fumbally Court, Dublin 8, Republic of Ireland
tel (01) 4534668 *fax* (01) 4534672
email info@four-courts-press.ie
website www.four-courts-press.ie
Managing Director Michael Adams

Academic books in the humanities, especially history, Celtic and medieval studies, art, theology. Founded 1970.

Fourth Estate – see HarperCollins Publishers

L.N. Fowler & Co. Ltd – see The C.W. Daniel Company Ltd

Framework Press Educational Publishers Ltd*

Heinemann, Halley Court, Jordan Hill, Oxford OX2 8EJ
tel (01865) 314194 *fax* (01865) 314116
email nigel.kelly@repp.co.uk
Publisher Nigel Kelly

School management, professional development, raising attainment, PSHE and Citizenship. Founded 1983.

Free Association Books

57 Warren Street, London W1T 5NR
tel 020-7388 3182 *fax* 020-7388 3187
email fab@fa-b.com
website www.fa-b.com
Publisher and Managing Director T.E. Brown

Social sciences, psychoanalysis, psychotherapy, counselling, cultural studies, social welfare, addiction studies, child and adolescent studies. Also contemporary fiction, including works in translation. No poetry, science fiction or fantasy. Founded 1984.

Free Press – see Simon & Schuster

W.H. Freeman

Palgrave Publishers Ltd, Houndmills, Basingstoke, Hants RG21 6XS
tel (01256) 332807 *fax* (01256) 330688

Science, medicine, economics, psychology, archaeology.

Samuel French Ltd*

52 Fitzroy Street, London W1T 5JR
tel 020-7387 9373 *fax* 020-7387 2161
email theatre@samuelfrench-london.co.uk
website www.samuelfrench-london.co.uk
Directors Charles R. Van Nostrand (chairman, USA), Vivien Goodwin (managing), Amanda Smith, Paul Taylor, *Consultant* John Bedding

Publishers of plays and agents for the collection of royalties. Founded 1830.

FT Law & Tax – incorporated into Sweet & Maxwell

David Fulton Publishers Ltd*

Ormond House, 26-27 Boswell Street, London WC1N 3JZ
tel 020-7405 5606 *fax* 020-7831 4840
email mail@fultonpublishers.co.uk
website www.fultonpublishers.co.uk
Chairman David Fulton, *Managing Director/Publisher* David Hill, *Marketing Director* Rachael Robertson

Initial and continuing teacher education (special needs, primary and secondary), educational management and psychology. Unsolicited MSS not returned. Part of Granada Learning Ltd. Founded 1987.

Funfax – see The Penguin Group (UK)

Gaia Books Ltd
66 Charlotte Street, London W1P 1LR
tel (01453) 752985 *fax* (01453) 752987
Managing Director Joss Pearson
Illustrated reference books on ecology, natural living, health, mind. Submissions (outline and sample chapter) with sae to managing director.

Gairm Publications
(incorporating Alex MacLaren & Sons)
29 Waterloo Street, Glasgow G2 6BZ
tel/fax 0141-221 1971
Editorial Director Derick Thomson
(Gaelic and Gaelic-related only) dictionaries, language books, novels, poetry, music, children's books, quarterly magazine, *Gairm*. Founded 1952.

The Gallery Press
Loughcrew, Oldcastle, Co. Meath, Republic of Ireland
tel/fax (049) 8541779
email gallery@indigo.ie
Editor/Publisher Peter Fallon
Poetry, drama, occasionally fiction, by Irish authors. Allied company: Deerfield Publications Inc., USA. Founded 1970.

Garland Science – see Taylor & Francis Group plc

Garnet Miller – see Cressrelles Publishing Co. Ltd

Garnet Publishing Ltd
8 Southern Court, South Street, Reading RG1 4QS
tel (01189) 597847 *fax* (01189) 597356
email enquiries@garnet-ithaca.demon.co.uk
Editorial Manager Emma G. Hawker
Art, architecture, photography, fiction, religious studies, travel and general, mainly on Middle and Far East, and Islam. Founded 1991.

Ithaca Press (imprint)
Post-graduate academic works, especially on the Middle East.

South Street Press (imprint)
Non-fiction, including *Behind the Headlines* series.

Gateway Books – see Gill & Macmillan Ltd

The Gay Men's Press
(Millivres Prowler Ltd)
PO Box 3220, Brighton BN2 5AU
tel (01273) 672823 *fax* 01273) 672159
email peterburton@easicom.com
Commissioning Editor Peter Burton
Gay-related issues: primarily fiction from literary to popular; limited non-fiction.

Geddes & Grosset*
David Dale House, New Lanark ML11 9DJ
tel (01555) 665000 *fax* (01555) 665694
email info@gandg.sol.co.uk
Publishers Ron Grosset, Mike Miller
Popular reference, children's picture books, non-fiction and activity books. Founded 1988.

Geographia – now Bartholomew – see HarperCollins Publishers

Stanley Gibbons Publications
Parkside, Christchurch Road, Ringwood, Hants BH24 3SH
tel (01425) 472363 *fax* (01425) 470247
email sales@stangib.demon.co.uk
Chief Executive T. McQuillan
Philatelic handbooks, stamp catalogues and albums. Founded 1856.

Robert Gibson & Sons Glasgow Ltd
17 Fitzroy Place, Glasgow G3 7SF
tel 0141-248 5674 *fax* 0141-221 8219
website robert.gibsonsons@btinternet.com
Directors R.G.C. Gibson, M. Pinkerton, H.C. Crawford, N.J. Crawford (editorial)
Educational and textbooks. Founded 1885.

Gill & Macmillan Ltd†
Hume Avenue, Park West, Dublin 12, Republic of Ireland
tel (01) 500 9500 *fax* (01) 500 9599
website www.gillmacmillan.ie
Biography or memoirs, educational (secondary, university), history, literature, cookery, current affairs, guidebooks. Founded 1968.

Gateway Books (imprint)
Spirituality, ecology, metaphysics and alternative science.

Newleaf (imprint)
Mind, Body & Spirit, popular psychology, self-help, health and healing, lifestyle.

Tivoli (imprint)
Popular fiction.

Ginn & Co. – see Reed Educational and Professional Publishing Ltd

Mary Glasgow – former imprint of Nelson Thornes Ltd

Godsfield Press Ltd

Laurel House, Station Approach, Arlesford, Hants SO24 9JH
tel (01962) 736677 *fax* (01962) 738610
email enquiries@godsfieldpress.com
Publisher Debbie Thorpe

Highly illustrated books for adults in the area of Mind, Body & Spirit with an emphasis on practical application and personal spiritual awareness. Founded 1994.

Golden Cockerel Press

16 Barter Street, London WC1A 2AH
tel 020-7405 7979 *fax* 020-7404 3598
email lindesay@btinternet.com
Contact Tamar Lindesay

Academic.

Associated University Presses (imprint)
Literary criticism, art, music, history, film, theology, philosophy, Jewish studies, politics, sociology.

Cornwall Books (imprint)
Antiques, history, film.

Cygnus Arts (imprint)
The arts.

The Goldsmith Press

Newbridge, Co. Kildare, Republic of Ireland
tel (045) 433613 *fax* (045) 434648
email de@iol.ie
website www.irishpoems.com
Directors V. Abbott, D. Egan, *Secretary* B. Ennis

Literature, art, Irish interest, poetry. Unsolicited MSS not returned. Founded 1972.

Gollancz – see The Orion Publishing Group Ltd

Victor Gollancz Ltd – now incorporated into The Orion Publishing Group Ltd

Gomer Press

Llandysul, Ceredigion SA44 4QL
tel (01559) 362371 *fax* (01559) 363758
email gwasg@gomer.co.uk
website www.gomer.co.uk
Directors Jonathan Lewis, John H. Lewis, Mairwen Prys Jones, *Editors* Bethan Mair, Gordon Jones, Francesca Rhydderch

Literature and non-fiction with a Welsh background or relevance: biography, history, aspects of Welsh culture, children's books. No unsolicited MSS; preliminary enquiry essential. Founded 1892.

Government Supplies Agency

Publications Division, Office of Public Works, 51 St Stephen's Green, Dublin 2, Republic of Ireland
tel (01) 6476000 *fax* (01) 6476843

Irish government publications.

Gower Publishing Ltd – see Ashgate Publishing Ltd

Grafton – now HarperCollins Paperbacks

Graham & Whiteside Ltd

High Holborn House, 50-51 Bedford Row, London WC1R 4LR
tel 020-7067 2500 *fax* 020-7067 2600
email sales@major-co-data.com
Directors A.M.W. Graham, R.M. Whiteside, P.L. Murphy

Directories for international business and professional markets. Founded 1995.

Granada Media Group – see André Deutsch Ltd

Granta Publications

2-3 Hanover Yard, Noel Road, London N1 8BE
tel 020-7704 9776 *fax* 020-7354 3469
website www.granta.com
Publishing Director Neil Belton, *Magazine Editor* Ian Jack

Literary fiction, memoir, political non-fiction, travel, history, etc. Founded 1982.

Green Books

Foxhole, Dartington, Totnes, Devon TQ9 6EB
tel/fax (01803) 863843
email edit@greenbooks.co.uk
website www.greenbooks.co.uk
Publisher John Elford

Environment (practical and philosophical). No fiction or children's books. No MSS; submit synopsis with covering letter, preferably by email. Founded 1987.

Green Print – see Merlin Press Ltd

Greenhill Books/Lionel Leventhal Ltd

Park House, 1 Russell Gardens, London NW11 9NN
tel 020-8458 6314 *fax* 020-8905 5245
email LionelLeventhal@compuserve.com
website www.greenhillbooks.com
Directors Lionel Leventhal (managing), Mark Wray (sales)

Military history. Founded 1984.

Gresham Books Ltd
The Gresham Press, 46 Victoria Road, Oxford OX2 7QD
tel (01865) 513582 *fax* (01865) 512718
email greshambks@btinternet.com
website www.gresham-books.co.uk
Chief Executive Paul Lewis

Hymn books, Prayer books, Service books, school histories.

Grub Street Publishing
The Basement, 10 Chivalry Road, London SW11 1HT
tel 020-7924 3966/738 1008 *fax* 020-7738 1009
email post@grubstreet.co.uk
website www.grubstreet.co.uk
Principals John B. Davies, Anne Dolamore

Adult non-fiction: military, aviation history, cookery, wine. Founded 1992.

Guild of Master Craftsman Publications Ltd
Castle Place, 166 High Street, Lewes, East Sussex BN7 1XU
tel (01273) 477374/47844 *fax* (01273) 487692
Managing Director Alan Phillips

Practical, illustrated crafts, including photography, needlecrafts, dolls' houses, woodworking and other leisure and hobby subjects. Founded 1979.

Guinness World Records
338 Euston Road, London NW1 3BD
tel 020-7891 4567 *fax* 020-7891 4501

Guinness World Records, *Guinness British Hit Singles*, *Guinness World Records* Prime Time TV shows. A Gullane Entertainment company. Founded 1954.

Gullane Children's Books
Winchester House, 259-269 Old Marylebone Road, London NW1 5XJ
tel 020-7616 7200 *fax* 020-7616 7201
Directors Alison Ritchie (editorial), Paula Burgess (art)

Picture books, novelty books, board books, and giftsets for under-7 age group. A Gullane Entertainment company.

Gwasg Bryntirion Press – see Bryntirion Press

Gwasg y Dref Wen – see Dref Wen

Peter Halban Publishers Ltd
22 Golden Square, London W1F 9JW
tel 020-7437 9300 *fax* 020-7437 9512
email books@halbanpublishers.com
website www.halbanpublishers.com
Directors Martine Halban, Peter Halban

General non-fiction; history and biography; Jewish subjects and Middle East. No unsolicited MSS considered; preliminary letter essential. Founded 1986.

Haldane Mason Ltd
59 Chepstow Road, London W2 5BP
tel 020-7792 2123 *fax* 020-7221 3965
email haldane.mason@dial.pipex.com
Directors Ron Samuel, Sydney Francis

Illustrated general non-fiction: children's, cookery, health, New Age, lifestyle, popular reference, sport. Opportunities for freelances. Founded 1992.

Robert Hale Ltd
Clerkenwell House, 45-47 Clerkenwell Green, London EC1R 0HT
tel 020-7251 2661 *fax* 020-7490 4958
Directors John Hale (managing and editorial), Robert Kynaston (financial), Martin Kendall (marketing)

Adult general non-fiction and fiction. Founded 1936.

Hambledon and London
102 Gloucester Avenue, London NW1 8HX
tel 020-7586 0817 *fax* 020-7586 4970
email office@hambledon.co.uk
website www.hambledon.co.uk
Managing Director Martin Sheppard, *Commissioning Director* Tony Morris

History. Winner, *The Sunday Times* Small Publisher of the Year Award 2001–2. Founded in 1980 as Hambledon Press.

Hamilton House Publishing – see First and Best in Education Ltd

Hamish Hamilton – see The Penguin Group (UK)

Hamlyn – see Octopus Publishing Group

Handsel Press – see The Continuum International Publishing Group Ltd

Harcourt Publishers Ltd
Harcourt Place, 32 Jamestown Road, London NW1 7BY
tel 020-7424 4200 *fax* 020-7482 2293/485 4752
website www.harcourt-international.com
Managing Director Peter H. Lengemann

Scientific and medical.

Academic Press (division)
Managing Director Jan Velterop

Academic and reference.

Baillière Tindall Ltd (division)
Managing Director Andrew Stevenson

Medical, veterinary, nursing, pharmaceutical books and journals.

Churchill Livingstone (division)
Managing Director Andrew Stevenson
Medical, nursing, pharmaceutical books and journals.

Dryden Press (division)
Managing Director Peter H. Lengemann
Educational books (college, university), economics, business.

Holt Rinehart & Winston (division)
Managing Director Peter H. Lengemann
Educational books.

Mosby International (division)
6th Floor, Lynton House, 7-12 Tavistock Square, London WC1H 9LB
tel 020-7388 7676 *fax* 020-7391 6555
Managing Director Derrick Holman

W.B. Saunders Co. Ltd (division)
Managing Director Andrew Stevenson
Medical and scientific.

Patrick Hardy Books – see James Clarke & Co. Ltd

Harlequin Mills & Boon Ltd*

Eton House, 18-24 Paradise Road, Richmond, Surrey TW9 1SR
tel 020-8288 2800 *fax* 020-8288 2899
Directors Andy Low (managing), Stuart Barber (financial), Angela Meredith (production), Alan Dawson (retail sales and marketing), Karin Stoecker (editorial), Liz Bulow (direct marketing), Mike Creffield (information technology), Jackie McGee (human resources)
Founded 1908.

Medical™ (imprint)
Senior Editor S. Hodgson
Romance fiction.

Mills & Boon® (imprint)
Senior Editors T. Shapcott, S. Bell
Contemporary romance fiction in paperback and hardback.

Mira Books® (imprint)
Senior Editor L. Fildew
Women's fiction.

Silhouette® (imprint)
Senior Editor L. Stonehouse
Popular romantic women's fiction.

Historical™ (imprint)
Senior Editor L. Fildew
Romance fiction.

Red Dress Ink™ (imprint)
Senior Editor Samantha Bell
Contemporary women's fiction with energy and attitude.

HarperCollins Publishers*

77-85 Fulham Palace Road, London W6 8JB
tel 020-8741 7070 *fax* 020-8307 4440
website www.fireandwater.com
Ceo/Publisher Victoria Barnsley
All fiction and trade non-fiction must be submitted through an agent. Unsolicited submissions should be made in the form of a typewritten synopsis. Founded 1819.

HarperCollins General Books (division)
Managing Director Amanda Ridout

HarperCollins (imprint)
Publishing Directors Nick Sayers (fiction), Lynne Drew (fiction), Michael Fishwick (non-fiction), Arabella Pike (non-fiction), Susan Watt (fiction/non-fiction)
General trade fiction and non-fiction.

Collins Crime (imprint)
Publishing Director Julia Wisdom

Willow (imprint)
Publishing Director Michael Doggart
Sport.

Flamingo (imprint)
Publishing Director Philip Gwyn Jones
Original and engaging literary fiction and topical non-fiction.

Fourth Estate (imprint)
Managing Director/Publisher Christopher Potter
Current affairs, literature, popular culture, fiction, humour, politics, science, popular reference.

HarperCollins Audio (imprint)
Publishing Director Rosalie George
Selection of fiction and non-fiction recordings of adult and children's titles by famous name readers.

HarperCollins Entertainment (imprint)
Publishing Director Val Hudson
Media-related books from film companions to autobiographies and TV tie-ins.

Estates
Publishing Director David Brawn
Authors include Agatha Christie, J.R.R. Tolkoin, C.S. Lewis. Imprint: Tolkein.

Thorsons/Element (imprint)
Managing Director Belinda Budge
Mind, Body & Spirit.

Voyager (imprint)
Publishing Director Jane Johnson
Science fiction/fantasy.

Collins Children's (division)
Acting Managing Director Katie Fulford, *Publishing Directors* Gail Penston (picture books and properties), Gillie Russell (fiction)

Quality picture books and book and tape sets for under 7s; fiction for age 6 up to young adult. Imprints: Lions, Collins Picture Books, Collins Jet, Collins Teacher.

Collins (division)
Managing Director Thomas Webster, *Publishing Director, Collins Reference* Sarah Bailey
Reference, including encyclopedias, guides and handbooks, phrase books and manuals on popular reference, art instruction, illustrated, cookery and wine, crafts, DIY, gardening, military, natural history, pet care, Scottish, pastimes. Imprints: Collins, Collins Gem, Colins New Naturalist Library, Times Books, Jane's.

Collins/Times Maps and Atlases (division)
Publishing Directors Juliet Lawler (international titles), Mike Cottingham (UK titles)
Maps, atlases, street plans and leisure guides. Imprints: Access Press, Bartholomew, Birnbaum, Nicholson.

Collins Dictionaries/COBUILD (imprint)
Publishing Director Lorna Sinclair Knight
Bilingual and English dictionaries, English dictionaries for foreign learners.

Collins Education (division)
Managing Director tba
Books, CD-Roms and online material for UK schools and colleges.

Letterland (imprint)
Home learning titles from preschool to further education.

Harrap – see Chambers Harrap Publishers Ltd

The Harvill Press – see Random House Group Ltd

Haynes Publishing
Sparkford, Yeovil, Somerset BA22 7JJ
tel (01963) 440635 *fax* (01963) 440023
Directors J.H. Haynes (chairman), A.C. Haynes, I.P. Mauger, K.C. Fullman (managing), D.J. Hermelin, M. Minter, M.J. Hughes, G.R. Cook
Car and motorcycle service and repair manuals, car handbooks/servicing guides; DIY books for the home; car, motorcycle, motorsport and leisure activities.

Haynes Motor Trade Division (imprint)
Editorial Director Matthew Minter
Car and motorcycle service and repair manuals and technical data books.

Haynes Special Interest Publishing Division (imprint)
Editorial Director Mark Hughes
Cars, motorcycles, motorsport, related biographies, maintenance and renovation.

Headland Publications
Editorial office Ty Coch, Galltegfa, Llanfwrog, Ruthin, Denbighshire LL15 2AR
and 38 York Avenue, West Kirby, Wirral CH48 3JF
Director and Editor Gladys Mary Coles
Poetry, anthologies of poetry and prose. No unsolicited MSS. Founded 1970.

Headline – see Hodder Headline Ltd

Headline Book Publishing Ltd – see Hodder Headline Ltd

Headway – see Hodder Headline Ltd

Health Science Press – see The C.W. Daniel Company Ltd

Heinemann Educational – see Reed Educational and Professional Publishing Ltd

Heinemann English Language Teaching – now Macmillan Heinemann English Language Teaching

Heinemann Young Books – former imprint of Egmont Books

William Heinemann – see Random House Group Ltd

Christopher Helm – see A & C Black Publishers Ltd

The Herbert Press – see A & C Black Publishers Ltd

Hermes House – see Anness Publishing

Hermes Penton Science Ltd – see Kogan Page Ltd

Nick Hern Books Ltd
The Glasshouse, 49A Goldhawk Road, London W12 8QP
tel 020-8749 4953 *fax* 020-8735 0250
email info@nickhernbooks.demon.co.uk
website www.nickhernbooks.co.uk
Publisher Nick Hern
Theatre, professionally produced plays, screenplays. Initial letter required. Founded 1988.

Hilmarton Manor Press
Calne, Wilts. SN11 8SB
tel (01249) 760208 *fax* (01249) 760379

email mailorder@hilmartonpress.co.uk
website www.hilmartonpress.co.uk
Editorial Director Charles Baile de Laperriere

Fine art, antiques, visual arts, wine. Founded 1964.

Hippo – see Scholastic Children's Books

Hippopotamus Press

22 Whitewell Road, Frome, Somerset BA11 4EL
tel/fax (01373) 466653
Editors Roland John, Anna Martin

Poetry, essays, criticism. Publishes *Outposts Poetry Quarterly*. Poetry submissions from new writers welcome. Founded 1974.

Historical™ – see Harlequin Mills & Boon Ltd

Hobsons Publishing plc

Challenger House, 42 Adler Street, London E1 1EE
tel 020-7958 5000 *fax* 020-7958 5001
Chairman Martin Morgan, *Directors* Chris Letcher (managing), Frances Halliwell, David Harrington, Tanja Kuveljic

Database publisher of educational and careers information under licence to CRAC (Careers Research and Advisory Centre). Also publishes accommodation guides under Johansens brand. Founded 1974.

Hodder & Stoughton – see Hodder Headline Ltd

Hodder Children's Books – see Hodder Headline Ltd

Hodder Christian – see Hodder Headline Ltd

Hodder Headline Ltd*

338 Euston Road, London NW1 3BH
tel 020-7873 6000 *fax* 020-7873 6024
Chairman Richard Handover, *Group Chief Executive* Tim Hely Hutchinson, *Directors* Martin Neild (managing, Headline), Jamie Hodder-Williams (managing, Hodder & Stoughton General), Mary Tapissier (managing, Hodder Children's Books), Charles Nettleton (managing, Hodder & Stoughton Religious), Malcolm Edwards (managing, Australia and New Zealand), Philip Walters (managing, Hodder Arnold), Colin Fairbain (finance), Tony Bryars (managing, Bookpoint)

Founded 1986.

Headline Book Publishing Ltd (division)
Managing Director Martin Neild, *Publishing Directors* Jane Morpeth (fiction), Heather Holden-Brown (non-fiction)

Publishes under Headline and Review. Commercial and literary fiction (hardback and paperback), and popular non-fiction including autobiography, biography, food and wine, gardening, history, popular science, sport, TV tie-ins.

Hodder Children's Books (division)
Managing Director Mary Tapissier, *Deputy Managing Director* Charles Nettleton, *Publishing Director* Margaret Conroy, *Editorial Directors* Anne McNeil, Anne Clark, Venetia Gosling

Publishes under Hodder Children's Books (picture books, fiction and non-fiction) and Hodder Wayland (illustrated non-fiction and reference).

Hodder Arnold (division)
Directors Philip Walters (managing), Tim Gregson-Williams (deputy managing), Elisabeth Tribe (schools publishing), Katie Roden (consumer education), Georgina Bentliff (health sciences), Mary Attree (journals and reference books), Alyssum Ross (production & design), Catherine Newman (sales & marketing)

Publishes under Hodder & Stoughton Educational, Teach Yourself, Headway. Textbooks for the primary, secondary, tertiary and further education sectors and for self-improvement. Academic and professional books and journals.

Hodder & Stoughton General (division)
Managing Director Jamie Hodder-Williams, *Non-fiction* Roland Philipps, *Sceptre* Carole Welch, *Fiction* Carolyn Mays, *Audio* Rupert Lancaster

Publishes under Hodder & Stoughton, Coronet, Flame, New English Library, Sceptre, Lir, Mobius. Commercial and literary fiction; biography, autobiography, history, self-help, humour, Mind, Body & Spirit, travel and other general interest non-fiction; audio. All unsolicited MSS to the Submissions Editor, Betty Schwartz.

Hodder & Stoughton Religious (division)
Managing Director Charles Nettleton, *Publishing Director* Judith Longman

Publishes under New International Version of the Bible, Hodder Christian Books, Help Yourself, Bibles. Christian books, biography, self-help, gift, health.

Hogarth Press – former imprint of Random House Group Ltd

Hollis Publishing Ltd

Harlequin House, 7 High Street, Teddington, Middlesex TW11 8EL
tel 020-8977 7711 *fax* 020-8977 1133
email gary@hollis-pr.co.uk
website www.hollis-pr.co.uk

Managing Director Gary Zabel

Publications include *Hollis Press & PR Annual*, *Hollis Sponsorship Yearbook*, *Advertisers Annual*, *Marketing Handbook*, Hollis Europe, *A.S.K. Hollis* (Directory of Associations) and *SHOWCASE* (International Music Business Guide).

Holt, Rinehart & Winston – see Harcourt Publishers Ltd

Honno Ltd (Welsh Women's Press)

Honno Editorial Office, c/o UTC, King Street, Aberystwyth, Ceredigion SY23 2LT
tel/fax (01970) 623150
email editor@honno.co.uk
website www.honno.co.uk
Editor Janet Thomas

Literature written by women in Wales or with a Welsh connection. All subjects considered – fiction, non-fiction, poetry, autobiographies. Honno is a community collective. Founded 1986.

Hopscotch Educational Publishing Ltd*

29 Waterloo Place, Leamington Spa, Warks. CV32 5LA
tel (01926) 744227 *fax* (01926) 744228
email sales@hopscotchbooks.com
website www.hopscotchbooks.com
Editorial Director Margot O'Keeffe, *Creative Director* Frances Mackay

National Curriculum subjects for primary teachers. Founded 1997.

House of Lochar

Isle of Colonsay, Argyll PA61 7YR
tel/fax (01951) 200232
email lochar@colonsay.org.uk
website www.colonsay.org.uk/lochar.html
Managing Director Georgina Hobhouse, *Editorial Director* Kevin Byrne

Scottish history, transport, Scottish literature. Founded 1995.

How To Books Ltd

3 Newtec Place, Magdalen Road, Oxford OX4 1RE
tel (01865) 793806 *fax* (01865) 248780
email info@howtobooks.co.uk
website www.howtobooks.co.uk
Publisher and Managing Director Giles Lewis, *Commissioning Editor* Nikki Read

Reference. Practical books that inspire. Subjects covered include small business and self-employment, business and management, career development, living and working abroad, home and family reference, personal development, study skills and student guides, creative writing. Book proposals welcome. Authors are given assistance and guidance in the development of their books. Founded 1991.

Hugo's Language Books Ltd

80 Strand, London WC2R 0RL
tel 020-7010 3000 *fax* 020-7010 6060

Hugo's language books and courses. Owned by Pearson plc. Founded 1864.

Hunt & Thorpe – see John Hunt Publishing Ltd

John Hunt Publishing Ltd

(incorporating Hunt & Thorpe, Arthur James Ltd)
46A West Street, New Alresford, Hants SO24 9AU
tel (01962) 736880 *fax* (01962) 736881
email john@johnhunt-publishing.com
Director John Hunt

Children's and adult religious, full colour books for the international market. MSS welcome; send sae. Founded 1989.

O-Books (imprint)
Global spirituality.

C. Hurst & Co. (Publishers) Ltd*

38 King Street, London WC2E 8JZ
tel 020-7240 2666, (night) 020-7624 8713
fax 020-7240 2667
email hurst@atlas.co.uk
website www.hurstpub.co.uk
Directors Christopher Hurst, Michael Dwyer

Scholarly 'area studies' covering contemporary history, politics, sociology and religion of Europe, former USSR, Middle East, Asia and Africa. Founded 1967.

Hutchinson – see Random House Group Ltd

Hutchinson Children's – see Random House Group Ltd

ICSA Publishing Ltd*

16 Park Crescent, London W1B 1AH
tel 020-7612 7020 *fax* 020-7323 1132
email icsa.pub@icsa.co.uk
website www.icsapublishing.co.uk
Joint Managing Directors Clare Grist Taylor, Susan Richards

Publishing company of the Institute of Chartered Secretaries and Administrators. Professional business information for the corporate, public and not-for-profit sectors in a range of formats. Founded 1981.

In Pinn – see Neil Wilson Publishing Ltd

Institute of Physics Publishing
Dirac House, Temple Back, Bristol BS1 6BE
tel 0117-929 7481 *fax* 0117-930 1186
email nicki.dennis@iop.org
website www.bookmarkphysics.iop.org
Head of Books Publishing Nicki Dennis
Monographs, graduate texts, conference proceedings and reference works in physics and physics-related science and technology; also popular science titles.

Institute of Public Administration†
Vergemount Hall, Clonskeagh, Dublin 6, Republic of Ireland
tel (01) 2697011 *fax* (01) 2698644
email tmcnamara@ipa.ie
website www.ipa.ie
Head of Publishing Tony McNamara
Government, economics, politics, law, public management, social policy and administrative history. Founded 1957.

Inter-Varsity Press*
38 De Montfort Street, Leicester LE1 7GP
tel 0116-255 1754 *fax* 0116-254 2044
email ivp@uccf.org.uk
website www.ivpbooks.com
Managing Editor S. Carter
Theology and religion.

Internet Handbooks Ltd
Unit 5, Dolphin Building, Queen Anne's Battery, Plymouth PL4 0LP
tel (01752) 202301
email post@internet-handbooks.co.uk
website www.internet-handbooks.co.uk
Director Roger Ferneyhough
Practical internet guides. Founded 1997.

Irish Academic Press Ltd
44 Northumberland Road, Ballsbridge, Dublin 4, Republic of Ireland
tel (01) 6688244 *fax* (01) 6601610
email info@iap.ie
website www.iap.ie
Directors Stewart Cass, Frank Cass, Michael Philip Zaidner, *Administrator* Rachel Milotte
Publishes under the imprints **Irish University Press** and **Irish Academic Press**. Scholarly books especially in 19th and 20th century history, literature, heritage and culture. Founded 1974.

IRS/Eclipse – see LexisNexis Butterworths Tolley

Ithaca Press – see Garnet Publishing Ltd

Arthur James Ltd – incorporated into John Hunt Publishing Ltd

Jane's Information Group
163 Brighton Road, Coulsdon, Surrey CR5 2YH
tel 020-8700 3700 *fax* 020-8700 3704
website www.janes.com
Managing Director Alfred Rolington
Professional publishers in hardcopy and electronic multimedia of military, aviation, naval, defence, non-fiction, reference, police, geo-political. Consumer books in association with **HarperCollins Publishers**.

Jarrold Publishing
(incorporating Pitkin and Unichrome brands)
Whitefriars, Norwich NR3 1TR
tel (01603) 763300 *fax* (01603) 662748
Directors Caroline Jarrold (managing), Margot Russell-King (commercial – stationery), Heather Hook (commercial – heritage & leisure), David Loombe (finance)
UK travel guidebooks, pictorial books and calendars. Unsolicited MSS, synopses and ideas welcome but approach in writing before submitting to Sarah Letts, Managing Editor. Division of Jarrold & Sons Ltd. Founded 1770.

Jordan Publishing Ltd
21 St Thomas Street, Bristol BS1 6JS
tel 0117-923 0600 *fax* 0117-925 0486
website www.jordanpublishing.co.uk
Managing Director Richard Hudson
Law and business administration. Also specialist Family Law imprint (including the *Family Law Journal*). Books, looseleaf services, serials, CD-Roms and online.

Michael Joseph – see The Penguin Group (UK)

The Journeyman Press – see Pluto Press

Karnak House
300 Westbourne Park Road, London W11 1EH
tel/fax 020-7243 3620
Directors Amon Saba Saakana (managing), Seheri Sujai (art)
Specialists in African/Caribbean studies worldwide: anthropology, education, Egyptology, fiction, history, language, linguistics, literary criticism, music, parapsychology, philosophy, prehistory. Founded 1979.

Kelpies – imprint of Floris Books

The Kenilworth Press Ltd
Addington, Buckingham MK18 2JR
tel (0129 671) 5101 *fax* (0129 671) 5148
email mail@kenilworthpress.co.uk

website www.kenilworthpress.co.uk
Directors David Blunt, Deirdre Blunt

Equestrian, including official publications for the British Horse Society. Founded 1989. Incorporates Threshold Books; founded 1970.

Kenyon-Deane – see Cressrelles Publishing Co. Ltd

Laurence King Publishing Ltd

(formerly Calmann & King Ltd)
71 Great Russell Street, London WC1B 3BP
tel 020-7430 8850 *fax* 020-7430 8880
email enquiries@calmann-king.co.uk
website www.laurence-king.com
Directors Robin Hyman (chairman), Laurence King (managing), Lesley Ripley Greenfield (editorial: college and fine arts), Philip Cooper (editorial: architecture and design), Judith Rasmussen (production), John Stoddart (financial)

Illustrated books on art, architecture, design, graphic design, film and photography. Founded 1976.

Kingfisher Publications plc

(formerly Larousse plc)
New Penderel House, 283-288 High Holborn, London WC1V 7HZ
tel 020-7903 9999 *fax* 020-7242 4979
email sales@kingfisherpub.co.uk
Directors Géraud de Durand (finance), John Richards (production)

Kingfisher (imprint)
Publishing Director, Non-fiction Gillian Denton, *Acting Publishing Director, Fiction* Suzanne Carnell

Children's books. No unsolicited MSS or synopses considered.

Jessica Kingsley Publishers*

116 Pentonville Road, London N1 9JB
tel 020-7833 2307 *fax* 020-7837 2917
email post@jkp.com
website www.jkp.com
Director Jessica Kingsley

Psychology, psychotherapy, psychiatry, arts therapies, social work, special needs (especially autism and Asperger's Syndrome), education, law, anthropology. Founded 1987.

Kluwer Academic/Plenum Publishers

241 Borough High Street, London SE1 1GB
tel 020-7940 7490 *fax* 020-7940 7495
email mail@plenum.co.uk
Managing Director Dr Ken Derham, *Editor* Joanna Lawrence

Postgraduate, professional scientific, technical and medical, and reference books. Founded 1966.

Knight Paperbacks – see Caxton Publishing Group

Charles Knight – see LexisNexis Butterworths Tolley

Knockabout Comics

10 Acklam Road, London W10 5QZ
tel 020-8969 2945 *fax* 020-8968 7614
email knockcomic@aol.com
website www.knockabout.com
Editors Tony Bennett, Carol Bennett

Humorous and satirical graphic novels for an adult readership. Founded 1975.

Kogan Page Ltd*

120 Pentonville Road, London N1 9JN
tel 020-7278 0433 *fax* 020-7837 6348
website www.kogan.page.co.uk
website www.earthscan.co.uk *Managing Director* Philip Kogan, *Directors* Pauline Goodwin (editorial), Peter Chadwick (production and editorial), Gordon Watts (financial), Philip Mudd (editorial), Julie McNair (sales)

Education, training, educational and training technology, journals, business and management, human resource management, transport and distribution, marketing, sales, advertising and PR, finance and accounting, directories, small business, careers and vocational, personal finance, environment. Founded 1967.

Earthscan Publications Ltd (subsidiary)
website www.earthscan.com
Directors Philip Kogan, Jonathan Sinclair-Wilson (editorial)

Third World and environmental issues: politics, sociology, environment, economics, current events, geography, health.

Hermes Penton Science Ltd (subsidiary)
Directors Philip Kogan, Sami Menasce

Engineering science, physics, chemistry, structural engineering, communication science, materials science.

Penton Press (imprint)
Director Philip Kogan

Engineering science, materials science, surface technology, information systems and networks.

Ladybird – see The Penguin Group (UK)

Lawrence & Wishart Ltd

99A Wallis Road, London E9 5LN
tel 020-8533 2506 *fax* 020-8533 7369

email lw@l-w-bks.demon.co.uk
website www.l-w-bks.co.uk
Directors S. Davison (editorial), J. Rodrigues, B. Kirsch, M. Seaton, J. Rutherford, A. Greenaway, G. Andrews

Cultural studies, current affairs, history, socialism and Marxism, political philosophy, politics, popular culture.

Leicester University Press – see The Continuum International Publishing Group Ltd

Lennard Publishing

Windmill Cottage, Mackerye End, Harpenden, Herts. AL5 5DR
tel (01582) 715866
email stephenson@lennardqap.co.uk
Directors K.A.A. Stephenson, R.H. Stephenson

Sponsored books, special commissions. No unsolicited MSS. Division of Lennard Associates Ltd.

Letts Educational*

Chiswick Centre, 414 Chiswick High Road, London W4 5TF
tel 020-8996 3333 *fax* 020-8742 8390
email mail@lettsed.co.uk
website www.lettsed.co.uk/
Directors Stephen Baker (managing), Wayne Davies (publishing), Andrew Thraves (publishing), Lee Warren (finance)

Accountancy and taxation; children's; computer science; economics; educational and textbooks; industry, business and management; mathematics and statistics; vocational training and careers; homework and revision books. Associate and subsidiary companies: Granada Learning, nferNelson, Black Cat, Granada Media, Semerc. Founded 1979.

Lewis Masonic

Riverdene Business Park, Molesey Road, Hersham, Surrey KT12 4RG
tel (01932) 266600 *fax* (01932) 266601

Masonic books; *Masonic Square Magazine*. Founded 1870.

LexisNexis Butterworths Tolley

Halsbury House, 35 Chancery Lane, London WC2A 1EL
tel 020-7400 2500 *fax* 020-7400 2842
email customer_services@butterworths.com
website www.butterworths.com
Managing Director Paul Virik

Division of Reed Elsevier (UK) Ltd.

Butterworths (imprint)
Legal and tax and accountancy books, journals, looseleaf and electronic services.

IRS/Eclipse (imprint)
Company and employment law.

Charles Knight (imprint)
Looseleaf legal works and periodicals on local government law, construction law and technical subjects.

Tolley (imprint)
Law, taxation, accountancy, business.

John Libbey & Co. Ltd

PO Box 276, Eastleigh SO50 5YS
tel (023) 8065 0208 *fax* (023) 8065 0259
email johnlibbey@aol.com
Director John Libbey

Medical: nutrition, obesity, epilepsy, neurology, nuclear medicine. Film/cinema, animation. Founded 1979.

Library Association Publishing – see Facet Publishing

Libris Ltd

26 Lady Margaret Road, London NW5 2XL
tel 020-7482 2390 *fax* 020-7485 2730
Directors Nicholas Jacobs, S.A. Kitzinger

Literature, literary biography, German studies, bilingual poetry. Founded 1986.

The Lilliput Press Ltd†

62-63 Sitric Road, Dublin 7, Republic of Ireland
tel (01) 6711647 *fax* (01) 6711233
email info@lilliput.ie
website www.lilliputpress.ie
Managing Director Antony T. Farrell

General and Irish literature: essays, biography/autobiography, fiction, criticism; Irish history; philosophy; contemporary culture; nature and environment. Founded 1984.

Frances Lincoln Ltd

4 Torriano Mews, Torriano Avenue, London NW5 2RZ
tel 020-7284 4009 *fax* 020-7485 0490
email reception@frances-lincoln.com
Directors John Nicoll (managing), Anne Fraser (editorial, adult books), Janetta Otter-Barry (editorial, children's books)

Illustrated, international co-editions: gardening, interiors, health, spirituality, art, gift, children's books. Founded 1977.

Lion Publishing plc*

Mayfield House, 256 Banbury Road, Oxford OX2 7DH
tel (01865) 302750 *fax* (01865) 302757
email enquiries@lion-publishing.co.uk
website www.lion-publishing.co.uk
Directors Denis Cole, Tony Wales, Rebecca Winter

(editorial), Paul Clifford (managing), John O'Nions, Roy McCloughry

Reference, paperbacks, illustrated children's books, educational, gift books, religion and theology; all reflecting a Christian position. No adult fiction. Send preliminary letter before submitting MSS. Founded 1971.

Lions – see HarperCollins Publishers

Lir – see Hodder Headline Ltd

Little Tiger Press – see Magi Publications

Little, Brown and Company (UK) – see Time Warner Books UK

Liverpool University Press

4 Cambridge Street, Liverpool L69 7ZU
tel 0151-794 2233 *fax* 0151-794 2235
email robblo@liv.ac.uk
website www.liverpool-unipress.co.uk
Publisher Robin Bloxsidge

Academic and scholarly books in a range of disciplines. Special interests: art history, European and American literature, science fiction criticism, all fields of history, archaeology, population studies, sociology, urban and regional planning. New series established include *Liverpool Latin American Studies* and *Studies in Social and Political Thought*. Founded 1899.

Livewire – see The Women's Press

Logaston Press

Little Logaston, Logaston, Woonton, Almeley, Herefordshire HR3 6QH
tel (01544) 327344
email logastonp@aol.com
Proprietor Andy Johnson

History, social history, archaeology and guides to rural west Midlands and central and south Wales. Founded 1985.

Lonely Planet Publications

10A Spring Place, London NW5 3BH
tel 020-7428 4800 *fax* 020-7428 4828
email go@lonelyplanet.co.uk
website www.lonelyplanet.com/
Directors Tony Wheeler, Maureen Wheeler, *UK Publisher* Katharine Leck

Country and regional guidebooks, city guides, phrasebooks, walking guides, travel atlases, city maps, diving and snorkelling guides, pictorial books, condensed guides, restaurant guides, health guides, food guides, cycling guides, wildlife guides, first-time travel guides, classic overland routes, and travel photography. Also digital travel guides (*CitySync*), a commercial slide library (Lonely Planet Images) and a TV company. London office established 1991.

Longman – imprint of Pearson Education

Lorenz Books – see Anness Publishing

Peter Lowe (Eurobook Ltd)

PO Box 52, Wallingford, Oxon OX10 0XU
tel (01865) 340110 *fax* (01865) 340087
email eurobook@compuserve.com
Director P.S. Lowe

Publishers of popular science and related subjects. Age 12+ but no general or teen fiction. Founded 1968.

Lund Humphries – see Ashgate Publishing Ltd

Lutterworth Press – see James Clarke & Co. Ltd

Macdonald Young Books – now Hodder Children's Books – see Hodder Headline Ltd

McGraw-Hill Education*

McGraw-Hill House, Shoppenhangers Road, Maidenhead, Berks. SL6 2QL
tel (01628) 502500 *fax* (01628) 770224
email (contact)@mcgraw-hill.com
website www.mcgraw-hill.co.uk
Directors Simon Allen (managing – EMEA), Alan Martin (operations), Rupert Mitchell (professional, Northern Europe), Murray St Leger (higher education sales & marketing, Northern Europe), Melissa Rosati (higher education, editorial)

Technical, scientific, professional reference.

Macmillan Children's Books Ltd – see Macmillan Publishers Ltd

Macmillan Education Ltd – see Macmillan Publishers Ltd

Macmillan Heinemann ELT – see Macmillan Publishers Ltd

Macmillan Online Publishing – see Macmillan Publishers Ltd

Macmillan Publishers Ltd*

The Macmillan Building, 4 Crinan Street, London N1 9XW
tel 020-7833 4000 *fax* 020-7843 4640
Chief Executive Richard Charkin, *Directors* M. Barnard, C.J. Paterson, G.R.U. Todd, D. North, Dr A. Thomas, D.J.G. Knight

Macmillan Children's Books Ltd (division)
20 New Wharf Road, London N1 9RR
tel 020-7014 6000 *fax* 020-7014 6001
Managing Director Kate Wilson, *Publishing Director (Picture Books and Gift Books)* Alison Green, *Editorial Director (Campbell Books)* Dereen Taylor, *Publishing Director (Fiction, Non-fiction and Poetry)* Sarah Davies, *Associate Publisher (Fiction)* Marion Lloyd, *Editorial Director (Poetry and Non-fiction)* Gaby Morgan

Publishes under Macmillan, **Pan**, Baby Campbell, Campbell Books, Young **Picador**. Picture books, fiction, poetry, non-fiction, early learning, pop-up, novelty, board books. No unsolicited material.

Pan Macmillan (division)
20 New Wharf Road, London N1 9RR
tel 020-7014 6000 *fax* 020-7014 6001
Publisher (Macmillan) Jeremy Trevathan, *Managing Director* David North, *Editorial Directors* Imogen Taylor (fiction), Peter Lavery (thrillers), Georgina Morley (non-fiction), *Publishing Manager (Macmillan Audio* Alison Muirden, *Publishing Director (Macmillan, Pan and Picador)* Maria Rejt

Novels, crime, science fiction, fantasy and horror. Autobiography, biography, business, gift books, health and beauty, history, humour, natural history, travel, philosophy, politics and world affairs, psychology, theatre and film, gardening and cookery, encyclopedias. Publishes under **Boxtree**, Macmillan, **Pan**, **Picador**, **Sidgwick & Jackson**.Founded 1843.

Boxtree (imprint)
fax 020-7881 8280
Publisher Gordon Wise, *Channel 4 Projects* Charlie Carman

TV and film tie-ins (adult and children's non-fiction); illustrated and general non-fiction; mass market paperbacks linked to TV, film, rock and sporting events; humour.

Pan (imprint)
Publisher Clare Harington

Fiction: novels, crime, science fiction, fantasy and horror. Non-fiction: sports, theatre and film, travel, gardening and cookery, encyclopedias, general. Founded 1947.

Picador (imprint)
Publishing Director Maria Rest

Literary international fiction and non-fiction, poetry. Founded 1972.

Sidgwick & Jackson (imprint)
Publisher Gordon Wise

Military and war, music, pop and rock. MSS, synopses and ideas welcome. Send to submissions editor, with return postage. Founded 1908.

Macmillan Education Ltd (division)
Macmillan Oxford, Between Towns Road, Oxford OX4 3PP
tel (01865) 405700 *fax* (01865) 405701
Chairman Christopher Paterson, *Joint Managing Directors* Mike Esplen, Christopher Harrison, *Publishing Directors* Sue Bale, Alison Hubert, *Finance Director* Paul Emmett

English language teaching materials. School and college textbooks and materials in all subjects for international markets.

Macmillan Heinemann English Language Teaching
Macmillan Oxford, Between Towns Road, Oxford OX4 3PP
tel (01865) 405700 *fax* (01865) 405701
Chairman Christopher Paterson, *Managing Directors* Mike Esplen, Chris Harrison, *Director, ELT Publishing* Sue Bale

English language teaching materials.

Palgrave Publishers Ltd (division)
Managing Director D. Knight, *Publishing Directors* J. Dixon (academic), S. Kennedy (politics), S. Rutt (professional business and management), F. Arnold (humanities and social sciences), Christopher Glennie (business, computer science and engineering)

Textbooks and monographs in academic, professional and vocational subjects.

Macmillan Online Publishing (division)
Managing Director Ian Jacobs, *Production Director* John Peacock, *Executive Web Producer* Sara Lloyd, *Editorial and Publishing Director* Jane Turner

Reference works in academic, professional and vocational subjects, online resources. Founded 2000.

Magi Publications

1 The Coda Centre, 189 Munster Road, London SW6 6AW
tel 020-7385 6333 *fax* 020-7385 7333
website www.littletigerpress.com
Publisher Monty Bhatia, *Editors* Ramona Reihill, Julie Evans

Little Tiger Press (imprint)
email info@littletiger.co.uk

Quality children's picture books and novelty books. New material will be considered from authors and illustrators, but enquire first. Founded 1987.

Mainstream Publishing Co. (Edinburgh) Ltd*

7 Albany Street, Edinburgh EH1 3UG
tel 0131-557 2959 *fax* 0131-556 8720
email enquiries@mainstreampublishing.com
website www.mainstreampublishing.com
Directors Bill Campbell, Peter MacKenzie, Fiona Brownlee (marketing), Sharon Atherton (publicity), Ray Cowie (sales), Neil Graham (production), Ailsa Bathgate (editorial)

Biography, autobiography, art, photography, sport, health, guidebooks, humour, literature, current affairs, history, politics. Founded 1978.

Mainstream Sport (imprint)
Sport.

Mammoth – former imprint of Egmont Books

Management Books 2000 Ltd

(incorporating Mercury Books)
Forge House, Limes Road, Kemble, Cirencester, Glos. GL7 6AD
tel (01285) 771441 *fax* (01285) 771055
email M.B.2000@virgin.net
website www.mb2000.com
Directors N. Dale-Harris, R. Hartman, *Publisher* James Alexander

Practical books for working managers and business professionals: management, business and lifeskills, and sponsored titles. Unsolicited MSS, synopses and ideas for books welcome.

Manchester United Books – see André Deutsch Ltd

Manchester University Press*

Oxford Road, Manchester M13 9NR
tel 0161-275 2310 *fax* 0161-274 3346
email mup@man.ac.uk
website www.manchesteruniversitypress.co.uk
Chief Executive David Rodgers

Works of academic scholarship: literary criticism, cultural studies, media studies, art history, design, architecture, history, politics, economics, international law, modern language texts. Textbooks and monographs. Founded 1904.

Mandrake of Oxford

PO Box 250, Oxford OX1 1AP
tel (01865) 243671 *fax* (01865) 432929
email krm@mandrake.uk.net
website www.mandrake.uk.net
Directors Mogg Morgan, Kym Morgan

Occult and bizarre. Founded 1986.

Mansell Publishing – see The Continuum International Publishing Group Ltd

Manson Publishing Ltd*

73 Corringham Road, London NW11 7DL
tel 020-8905 5150 *fax* 020-8201 9233
email manson@man-pub.demon.co.uk
website www.manson-publishing.co.uk
Managing Director Michael Manson

Medical, scientific, veterinary. Founded 1992.

Mantra

5 Alexandra Grove, London N12 8NU
tel 020-8445 5123 *fax* 020-8446 7745
email sales@mantrapublishing.com
website www.mantralingua.com
Managing Director M. Chatterji

Children's multicultural picture books; multilingual friezes/posters; dual language books/cassettes; South Asian literature/teenage fiction; CD-Roms and videos. Founded 1984.

Marino Books – see The Mercier Press

Marshall Pickering – former imprint of HarperCollins Publishers

Martin Books

88 Regent Street, Cambridge CB2 1DP
tel (01223) 448770 *fax* (01223) 448777
Editorial Director Janet Copleston

Cookery, gardening, illustrated non-fiction and sponsored publishing. Imprint of Simon & Schuster UK Ltd.

Kenneth Mason Publications Ltd

The Book Barn, Westbourne, Hants PO10 8RS
tel (01243) 377977 *fax* (01243) 379136
Directors Kenneth Mason (chairman), Piers Mason (managing), Michael Mason, Anthea Mason

Nautical, slimming, health, fitness; technical journals. Founded 1958.

Kevin Mayhew Ltd

Buxhall, Suffolk IP14 3BW
tel (01449) 737978 *fax* (01449) 737834
email info@kevinmayhewltd.com
Directors Kevin Mayhew (chairman), Gordon Carter (managing) Ray Gilbert (purchasing), Jonathan Bugden (sales)

Christianity: prayer and spirituality, pastoral care, preaching, liturgy worship, children's, youth work, drama, instant art. Music: hymns, organ and choral, contemporary worship, piano and instrumental. Contact Editorial Dept before sending MSS/synopses. Founded 1976.

Medical™ – see Harlequin Mills & Boon Ltd

Mentor Books[†]

43 Furze Road, Sandyford Industrial Estate, Dublin 18, Republic of Ireland
tel (353) 1-2952112 *fax* (353) 1-2952114
email all@mentorbooks.ie
website www.mentorbooks.ie
Managing Director Daniel McCarthy, *Managing Editor* Claire Haugh

General: adult fiction and non-fiction, children's, guide books, biographies, history. Educational: languages, history, geography, business, maths. Founded 1979.

The Mercat Press*

10 Coates Crescent, Edinburgh EH3 7AL
tel 0131-225 5324 *fax* 0131-226 6632
email enquiries@mercatpress.com
Managing Editors Seán Costello, Tom Johnstone

Scottish books of general and academic interest. No new fiction or poetry. Founded 1970.

The Mercier Press[†]

5 French Church Street, Cork, Republic of Ireland
tel (021) 4275014 *fax* (021) 4274969
email books@mercier.ie
website www.mercier.ie
Directors G. Eaton (chairman), J.F. Spillane (managing), M.P. Feehan, J. O'Donoghue

Irish literature, folklore, history, politics, humour, education, theology, law. Founded 1944.

Marino Books (imprint)
16 Hume Street, Dublin 2, Republic of Ireland
tel (01) 6615299 *fax* (01) 6618583
email books@marino.ie
Publisher Jo O'Donoghue

Fiction, children's fiction, current affairs, health, mind & spirit, general non-fiction.

Merehurst Ltd – see Murdoch Books UK Ltd

Merlin Press Ltd

PO Box 30705, London WC2E 8QD
tel 020-7836 3020 *fax* 020-7497 0309
email info@merlinpress.co.uk
Managing Director Anthony Zurbrugg

Radical history and social studies. Letters/synopses only please.

Green Print (imprint)
Green politics and the environment.

Merrell Publishers Ltd

42 Southwark Street, London SE1 1UN
tel 020-7403 2047 *fax* 020-7407 1333
email mail@merrellpublishers.com
website www.merrellpublishers.com
Publisher Hugh Merrell, *Editorial Director* Julian Honer, *Sales Manager* Emilie Nangle, *Art Director* Matt Hervey

Art, architecture, photography and design.

Methodist Publishing House

4 John Wesley Road, Werrington, Peterborough PE4 6ZP
tel (01733) 325002 *fax* (01733) 384180
email sales@mph.org.uk
Chief Executive Brian Thornton

Hymn and service books, general religious titles, church supplies. Founded 1773.

Foundery Press (imprint)
Ecumenical titles.

Methuen Academic – now incorporated into Routledge

Methuen Children's Books – former imprint of Egmont Books

Methuen Publishing Ltd

215 Vauxhall Bridge Road, London SW1V 1EJ
tel 020-7798 1600 *fax* 020-7828 2098
Managing Director Peter Tummons, *Publishing Director* Max Eilenberg, *Sales Manager* Haydn Jones, *Publicity Manager* Margot Weale

Literary fiction and non-fiction: biography, autobiography, travel, history, sport, drama, humour, film, performing arts, plays. No unsolicited MSS. Synopses considered.

Metro Publishing Ltd – see John Blake Publishing Ltd

Michelin Travel Publications

Hannay House, 39 Clarendon Road, Watford, Herts. WD17 1JA
tel (01923) 205240 *fax* (01923) 205241
website www.viamichelin.com
Head of Travel Publications J. Lewis

Tourist, hotel and restaurant guides, maps and atlases; children's activity books.

Midland Publishing – see Ian Allan Publishing Ltd

Milestone Publications

62 Murray Road, Horndean, Waterlooville PO8 9JL
tel (023) 9259 7440 *fax* (023) 9259 1975

email info@gosschinaclub.co.uk
website www.gosscrestedchina.co.uk
Managing Director Lynda J. Pine

Goss & Crested heraldic china, antique porcelain. Publishing and bookselling division of Goss & Crested China Club. Founded 1967.

Harvey Miller Publishers

2 Byron Mews, Fleet Road, London NW3 2NQ
tel 020-7284 4359 *fax* 020-7267 8764
email johan.van.der.beke@brepols.com
website www.brepols.com
Publisher Johan Van der Beke

Art history. Imprint of Brepols Publishers.

Miller's – see Octopus Publishing Group

J. Garnet Miller – see Cressrelles Publishing Co. Ltd

Miller Freeman Information Services – now CMP Information Ltd

Mills & Boon® – see Harlequin Mills & Boon Ltd

Mira Books® – see Harlequin Mills & Boon Ltd

The MIT Press – see under USA in Overseas book publishers, page 228

Mitchell Beazley – see Octopus Publishing Group

Mobius – see Hodder Headline Ltd

Mojo Books – former imprint of Canongate Books Ltd

Monarch Books

Concorde House, Grenville Place, London NW7 3SA
tel 020-8959 3668 *fax* 020-8959 3678
email tonyc@angushudson.com
website www.angushudson.com
Editorial Director Tony Collins

Christian books: issues of faith and society; leadership, mission, evangelism. Submit synopsis/2 sample chapters only with return postage.

Morrigan Book Company

Killala, Co. Mayo, Republic of Ireland
tel/fax (096) 32555
email morrigan@online.ie
Publisher Gerry Kennedy, *Administrator* Hilary Kennedy, *Editor* Gillian Brennan

Non-fiction: general Irish interest, biography, history, local history, folklore and mythology. Founded 1979.

Mosby International – see Harcourt Publishers Ltd

Mount Eagle Publications Ltd – see Brandon/Mount Eagle Publications

Mowbray – see The Continuum International Publishing Group Ltd

MQ Publications Ltd

12 The Ivories, 6-8 Northampton Street, London N1 2HY
tel 020-7359 2244 *fax* 020-7359 1616
email mail@mqpublications.com
Ceo Zaro Weil

Lifestyle, Mind, Body & Spirit, inspirational, photography, cookery, popular culture, biography, gift books. Founded 1993.

Murdoch Books UK Ltd

Ferry House, 51-57 Lacy Road, London SW15 1PR
tel 020-8355 1480 *fax* 020-8355 1499
Ceo Robert Oerton, *Publisher* Catie Ziller

Cookery, gardening, DIY, homes and interiors, crafts and hobbies, cake decorating. Imprint: Merehurst Ltd.

John Murray (Publishers) Ltd*

50 Albemarle Street, London W1S 4BD
tel 020-7493 4361 *fax* 020-7499 1792
Directors Grant McIntyre (general editorial), Judith Reinhold (educational marketing)

General: art and architecture, biography and autobiography, letters and diaries, travel, exploration and guidebooks, Middle East, Asia, India and subcontinent, general history, health education, aviation, craft and practical. No unsolicited MSS please. Also self teaching in all subjects in *Success Studybook* series. Acquired by Hodder Headline Ltd. Founded 1768.

National Christian Education Council – see Christian Education

The National Trust

36 Queen Anne's Gate, London SW1H 9AS
tel 020-7222 9251 *fax* 020-7447 6641
Publisher Margaret Willes

History, cookery, architecture, gardening, guidebooks, children's non-fiction. No unsolicited MSS. Founded 1895.

The Natural History Museum Publishing Division

Cromwell Road, London SW7 5BD
tel 020-7942 5336 *fax* 020-7942 5010
email publishing@nhm.ac.uk
website www.nhm.ac.uk/publishing
Head of Publishing Jane Hogg

Natural sciences; entomology, botany, geology, mineralogy, palaeontology, zoology, history of natural history. Founded 1881.

Nautical Books – now Adlard Coles Nautical – see A & C Black Publishers Ltd

Nautical Data Ltd

The Book Barn, Westbourne, Hants PO10 8RS
tel (01243) 377977 *fax* (01243) 379136
Directors Piers Mason, Michael Benson-Colpi

Yachting titles, nautical almanacs.

Naxos AudioBooks

18 High Street, Welwyn, Herts. AL6 9EQ
tel (01438) 717808 *fax* (01438) 717809
email naxos_audiobooks@compuserve.com
website www.naxosaudiobooks.com
Managing Director Nicolas Soames

Classic literature, modern fiction, non-fiction, drama and poetry available on CD and cassette. Also junior classics and classical music. Founded 1994.

NCVO Publications

(incorporating Bedford Square Press)
Regent's Wharf, 8 All Saints Street, London N1 9RL
tel 020-7713 6161 *fax* 020-7713 6300
email ncvo@ncvo-vol.org.uk
website www.ncvo-vol.org.uk
Head of Publications Maria Kane

Imprint of the National Council for Voluntary Organisations. Practical guides, reference books, directories and policy studies on voluntary sector concerns including management, employment, trustee development, legal and finance. No unsolicited MSS accepted.

Neate Publishing*

33 Downside Road, Winchester SO22 5LT
tel (01962) 841479 *fax* (01962) 841743
email bobbie@neatepublishing.co.uk
website www.neatepublishing.co.uk
Directors Bobbie Neate (managing), Ann Langran, Maggie Threadingham

Non-fiction books and posters for primary children. Founded 1999.

Thomas Nelson Ltd – see Nelson Thornes Ltd

Nelson Thornes Ltd*

Delta Place, 27 Bath Road, Cheltenham, Glos. GL53 7TH
tel (01242) 267100 *fax* (01242) 221914
email name@nelsonthornes.com
website www.nelsonthornes.com
Directors Oliver Gadsby (managing), Adrian Ford, Brian Carvell, Paul Vinson, Adrian Wheaton, Peter Oates, Sonia Raphael

Print and electronic publishers for the educational market: primary, secondary, further education, higher education, professional. Part of the Wolters Kluwer Group of Companies.

New Beacon Books

76 Stroud Green Road, London N4 3EN
tel 020-7272 4889 *fax* 020-7281 4662
Directors John La Rose, Sarah White, Michael La Rose, Janice Durham

Small specialist publishers: general non-fiction, fiction, poetry, critical writings, concerning the Caribbean, Africa, African-America and Black Britain. No unsolicited MSS. Founded 1966.

New Cavendish Books

3 Denbigh Road, London W11 2SJ
tel 020-7229 6765/792 9984 *fax* 020-7792 0027
email narisa@new-cav.demon.co.uk
website www.newcavendishbooks.co.uk

Specialist books for the collector; art reference, Thai guidebooks. Founded 1973.

River Books (associate imprint)
The art and architecture of Southeast Asia.

New English Library – see Hodder Headline Ltd

New Holland Publishers (UK) Ltd*

Garfield House, 86 Edgware Road, London W2 2EA
tel 020-7724 7773 *fax* 020-7258 1293
email postmaster@nhpub.co.uk
website www.newhollandpublishers.com
Managing Director John Beaufoy, *Publishing Director* Yvonne McFarlane

Illustrated non-fiction books on natural history, travel, cookery, needlecrafts and handicrafts, interior design, DIY, gardening, fishing, Mind, Body & Spirit, travel guides, sport, general books. New proposals accepted (send CV and synopsis and sample chapters in first instance; sae essential).

New Island Books†

2 Brookside, Dundrum Road, Dundrum, Dublin 14, Republic of Ireland
tel (01) 2986867/2989937 *fax* (01) 2982783

email staff@newisland.ie
Directors Edwin Higel (managing), Fergal Stanley
Fiction, poetry, drama, humour, biography, current affairs. Founded 1992.

New Playwrights' Network
10 Station Road Industrial Estate, Colwall, Nr Malvern, Herefordshire WR13 6RN
tel/fax (01684) 540154
email simonsmith@cressrelles4drama.fsbusiness.co.uk
Publishing Director Leslie Smith
General plays for the amateur, one-act and full length.

New Theatre Publications
13 Mossgrove Road, Timperley, Altringham, Cheshire WA15 6LF
tel 0161-283 1924
email plays4theatre@btinternet.com
website www.plays4theatre.com
Directors Paul Beard, Ian Hornby
Plays for the professional and amateur stage. Founded 1987.

Newleaf – see Gill & Macmillan Ltd

Newnes – see Reed Educational and Professional Publishing Ltd

Nexus – see Virgin Books Ltd

Nexus Special Interests Ltd
Nexus House, Azalea Drive, Swanley, Kent BR8 8HU
tel (01322) 660070 *fax* (01322) 616319
Publisher Dawn Frosdick-Hopley
Modelling, model engineering, woodworking, aviation, military, boats, crafts.

nferNELSON Publishing Co. Ltd*
Darville House, 2 Oxford Road East, Windsor, Berks. SL4 1DF
tel (01753) 858961 *fax* (01753) 856830
email information@nfer-nelson.co.uk
website www.nfer-nelson.co.uk
Director, Education Anne Eastgate
Testing, assessment and management publications and services for education, business and health care. Founded 1981.

Nia – see the X Press

Nicholson – see HarperCollins Publishers

James Nisbet & Co. Ltd
Pirton Court, Hitchin, Herts. SG5 3QA
tel/fax (01462) 713444
Directors Miss E.M. Mackenzie-Wood, Mrs A.A.C. Bierrum
Business management. Founded 1810.

NMSI
Science Museum, Exhibition Road, London SW7 2DD
tel 020-7942 4361 *fax* 020-7942 4362
email publicat@nmsi.ac.uk
website www.nmsi.ac.uk/publications
Publications Manager Ela Ginalska
History of science and technology, public understanding of science, history of photography, railway history, museum guides.

Northcote House Publishers Ltd
Horndon House, Horndon, Tavistock, Devon PL19 9NQ
tel (01822) 810066 *fax* (01822) 810034
Directors B.R.W. Hulme, A.V. Hulme (secretary)
Education and education management, educational dance and drama, literary criticism (*Writers and their Work*). Founded 1985.

W.W. Norton & Company
Castle House, 75-76 Wells Street, London W1T 3QT
tel 020-7323 1579 *fax* 020-7436 4553
Managing Director Alan Cameron
English and American literature, economics, music, psychology, science. Founded 1980.

NWP – see Neil Wilson Publishing Ltd

O-Books – see John Hunt Publishing Ltd

Oak Tree Press
19 Rutland Street, Cork, Republic of Ireland
tel (021) 431 3855 *fax* (021) 431 3496
email info@oaktreepress.com
website www.oaktreepress.com
Directors Brian O'Kane, Rita O'Kane, Ron Immink
Business management, enterprise, accountancy and finance, law. Founded 1991.

Oberon Books
(incorporating Absolute Classics)
521 Caledonian Road, London N7 9RH
tel 020-7607 3637 *fax* 020-7607 3629
email oberon.books@btinternet.com
website www.oberonbooks.com
Managing Director Charles Glanville, *Publisher* James Hogan
New and classic play texts, programme texts and general theatre books. Founded 1986.

The O'Brien Press Ltd
20 Victoria Road, Rathgar, Dublin 6, Republic of Ireland
tel (01) 492 3333 *fax* (01) 492 2777
email books@obrien.ie
website www.obrien.ie

Directors Michael O'Brien, Ide ní Laoghaire, Ivan O'Brien

Adult: business, true crime, biography, music, travel, sport, Celtic subjects, food and drink, history, humour, politics, reference. Children's: fiction for every age from tiny tots to teenage; illustrated fiction series – *Pandas* (age 5+), *Flyers* (age 6+) and *Red Flag* (8+); substantial novels (10+) – contemporary, historical, fantasy. Some non-fiction, mainly historical and art and craft, resource books for teachers. No poetry, adult fiction or academic. Unsolicited MSS (sample chapters only), synopses and ideas for books welcome – submissions will not be returned. Founded 1974.

The Octagon Press Ltd

PO Box 227, London N6 4EW
tel 020-8348 9392 *fax* 020-8341 5971
email octagon@schredds.demon.co.uk
website www.octagonpress.com
Managing Director George R. Schrager

Psychology, philosophy, Eastern religion. Unsolicited MSS not accepted. Founded 1972.

Octopus Publishing Group

2-4 Heron Quays, London E14 4JP
tel 020-7531 8400 *fax* 020-7531 8650
email firstname.lastname@octopus-publishing.co.uk
website www.octopus-publishing.co.uk
Chief Executive Derek Freeman, *Executive Directors* Laura Bamford, Helen Barlow

Bounty (imprint)
tel 020-7531 8601 *fax* 020-7531 8607
email bountybooksinfo-bp@bountybooks.co.uk
Publisher/Managing Director Alison Goff

Promotional publishing, adult books.

Brimax Books (imprint)
tel 020-7531 8598 *fax* 020-7531 8607
email brimax@brimax.octopus.co.uk
Managing Director Des Higgins

Mass market picture books for children.

Conran Octopus (imprint)
tel 020-7531 8628 *fax* 020-7531 8627
email info-co@conran-octopus.co.uk
website www.conran-octopus.co.uk
Publishing Director Lorraine Dickie

Quality illustrated books, particularly lifestyle, cookery, gardening.

Hamlyn (imprint)
tel 020-7531 8573 *fax* 020-7537 0514
email info-ho@hamlyn.co.uk
website www.hamlyn.co.uk
Publisher/Managing Director Alison Goff

Popular illustrated non-fiction, particularly cookery, health and parenting, home and garden, sport and reference.

Miller's (imprint)
The Cellars, High Street, Tenterden, Kent TN30 6BN
tel (01580) 766411 *fax* (01580) 766100
email firstname.lastname@millers.uk.com
Publisher/Managing Director Jane Aspden

Quality illustrated books on antiques and collectables.

Mitchell Beazley (imprint)
tel 020-7531 8400 *fax* 020-7531 8650
email info-mb@mitchell-beazley.co.uk
Publisher/Managing Director Jane Aspden

Quality illustrated books, particularly antiques, gardening, craft and interiors, wine.

Philip's (imprint)
tel 020-7531 8459 *fax* 020-7531 8460
email george.philip@philips-maps.co.uk
website www.philips-maps.co.uk
Publisher/Managing Director John Gaisford

Atlases, maps, astronomy, encyclopedias, globes.

Cassell Illustrated (imprint)
tel 020-7531 8400 *fax* 020-7531 8650
email info-ci@cassell-illustrated.co.uk
website www.cassell-illustrated.co.uk
Publishing Director Polly Powell

Illustrated books for the international market specialising in gardening, history and heritage, health and humour.

Oldcastle Books Ltd

18 Coleswood Road, Harpenden, Herts AL5 1EP
tel/fax (01582) 761264
email ion@noexit.co.uk
website www.noexit.co.uk
www.pocketessentials.com www.highstakes.com
Director Ion Mills

Imprints: No Exit Press (crime fiction), High Stakes (gambling), Pocket Essentials (reference guides). Founded 1985.

The Oleander Press

16 Orchard Street, Cambridge CB1 1JT
tel (01223) 357768
website www.oleanderpress.com
Managing Director Dr Jeremy Toner

Travel, language, literature, Libya, Arabia and Middle East, Cambridgeshire, history, humour, reference. Preliminary letter required before submitting MSS; please send sae for reply. Founded 1960.

Michael O'Mara Books Ltd

9 Lion Yard, Tremadoc Road, London SW4 7NQ
tel 020-7720 8643 *fax* 020-7627 8953
website www.mombooks.com

Chairman Michael O'Mara, *Managing Director* Lesley O'Mara

General non-fiction: biography, humour, history, ancient history, anthologies and royal books. Founded 1985.

Buster Books (imprint)

Children's.

Omnibus Press/Music Sales Ltd

8-9 Frith Street, London W1D 3JB
tel 020-7434 0066 *fax* 020-7434 3310
email music@musicsales.co.uk
Chief Editor Chris Charlesworth

Rock music biographies, books about music. Founded 1976.

On Stream Publications Ltd

Currabaha, Cloghroe, Blarney, Co. Cork, Republic of Ireland
tel/fax (353) 21-4385798
email info@onstream.ie
website www.onstream.ie
Owner Rosalind Crowley

Cookery, wine, travel, human interest non-fiction, local history, academic and practical books. Founded 1986.

Oneworld Publications

185 Banbury Road, Oxford OX2 7AR
tel (01865) 310597 *fax* (01865) 310598
email info@oneworld-publications.com
website www.oneworld-publications.com
Directors Juliet Mabey (publisher), Novin Doostdar (publisher), Helen Coward (managing)

Religion, world religions, inter-religious dialogue, Islamic studies, philosophy, history, psychology, self-help, teenage non-fiction. Founded 1984.

Onlywomen Press Ltd

40 St Lawrence Terrace, London W10 5ST
tel 020-8354 0796 *fax* 020-8960 2817
email onlywomenpress@cs.com
Managing Director Lilian Mohin

Lesbian feminist: theory, fiction, poetry, crime fiction and cultural criticism. Founded 1974.

Open Books Publishing Ltd

Willow Cottage, Cudworth, Nr Ilminster, Somerset TA19 0PS
tel/fax (01460) 52565
email patrickta@aol.com
Directors P. Taylor (managing), C. Taylor

Gardening. Founded 1974.

Open Gate Press*

(incorporating Centaur Press, founded 1954)
51 Achilles Road, London NW6 1DZ
tel 020-7431 4391 *fax* 020-7431 5129
email books@opengatepress.co.uk
website www.opengatepress.co.uk
Directors Jeannie Cohen, Elisabeth Petersdorff, George Frankl, Sandra Lovell

Psychoanalysis, philosophy, social sciences, religion, animal welfare, the environment. Founded 1988.

Open University Press*

Celtic Court, 22 Ballmoor, Buckingham MK18 1XW
tel (01280) 823388 *fax* (01280) 823233
email enquiries@openup.co.uk
website www.openup.co.uk
Directors John Skelton (managing), Jacinta Evans (editorial), Sue Hadden (production), Barry Clarke (financial), Barbara Martin (sales)

Education, management, psychology, sociology, criminology, counselling, cultural and media studies, health and social welfare, gender studies, public policy. Founded 1977.

Orbit – see Time Warner Books UK

Orchard Books – see The Watts Publishing Group Ltd

The Orion Publishing Group Ltd*

Orion House, 5 Upper St Martin's Lane, London WC2H 9EA
tel 020-7240 3444 *fax* 020-7379 6158
Directors Jean-Louis Lisimachio (chairman), Anthony Cheetham (chief executive), Peter Roche (managing)

No unsolicited MSS; approach in writing in first instance. Founded 1992.

Orion Paperbacks (division)
Managing Director Susan Lamb

Mass market fiction and non-fiction under **Everyman**, **Orion** and **Phoenix** imprints.

Orion Trade (division)
Directors Malcolm Edwards (managing), Jane Wood (publishing), Trevor Dolby (publishing, non-fiction and audio books)

Hardcover fiction (crime, science fiction, fantasy) and non-fiction.

Gollancz (imprint)
Contact Simon Spanton, Jo Fletcher

Science fiction and fantasy.

Orion Children's Books (division)
Managing Director and Publisher Judith Elliott

Children's fiction and non-fiction.

Osprey Publishing Ltd

Elms Court, Chapel Way, Botley, Oxford OX2 9LP
tel (01865) 727022 *fax* (01865) 727017/727019
email info@ospreypublishing.com
website www.ospreypublishing.com
Managing Director William Shepherd, *Finance*

Director Sarah Lough, *Director, American Operations* Bill Corsa
Illustrated history, military history and aviation from around the world. Founded 1969.

Peter Owen Ltd

73 Kenway Road, London SW5 0RE
tel 020-7373 5628/370 6093 *fax* 020-7373 6760
email admin@peterowen.com
website www.peterowen.com
Directors Peter L. Owen (managing), Antonia Owen (editorial)
Art, belles lettres, biography, literary fiction, general non-fiction, sociology, theatre. No highly illustrated books. Do not send fiction without first speaking to the Editorial Dept unless by an established novelist. First novels rarely published.

Oxford Illustrated Press – see Haynes Publishing, Special Interest Publishing Division

Oxford Publishing Company – see Ian Allan Publishing Ltd

Oxford University Press*

Great Clarendon Street, Oxford OX2 6DP
tel (01865) 556767 *fax* (01865) 556646
email enquiry@oup.co.uk
website www.oup.co.uk
Chief Executive and Secretary to the Delegates Henry Reece, *Group Finance Director* Roger Boning, *Academic Division Managing Director* Ivon Asquith, *UK Educational Division Managing Director* Fiona Clarke, *ELT Division Managing Director* Peter Mothersole, *UK Personnel Director* John Williams
Anthropology, archaeology, architecture, art, belles-lettres, bibles, bibliography, children's books (fiction, non-fiction, picture), commerce, current affairs, dictionaries, drama, economics, educational (infants, primary, secondary, technical, university), English language teaching, electronic publishing, essays, foreign language learning, general history, hymn and service books, journals, law, maps and atlases, medical, music, oriental, philosophy, poetry, political economy, prayer books, reference, science, sociology, theology and religion, educational software. Trade paperbacks published under the imprint of Oxford Paperbacks. Founded 1478.

Paladin – now Flamingo – see HarperCollins Publishers

Palgrave Publishers Ltd – see Macmillan Publishers Ltd

Pan – see Macmillan Publishers Ltd

Pan Macmillan Ltd – see Macmillan Publishers Ltd

Pandora Press – see Rivers Oram Press

Paper Tiger – see Collins & Brown

Parkgate Books – see Collins & Brown

Paternoster

PO Box 300, Carlisle, Cumbria CA3 0QS
tel (01228) 512512 *fax* (01228) 593388
email info@paternoster-publishing.com
Publisher Mark Finnie
Biblical studies, Christian theology, ethics, history, mission. Imprints: Paternoster Press, Authentic Lifestyle, Partnership, Regnum, Rutherford House, Challenge, Paternoster Periodicals, SP Media.

Stanley Paul – former imprint of Random House Group Ltd

Pavilion Books Ltd

64 Brewery Road, London N7 9NT
tel 020-7697 3000 *fax* 020-7697 3001
Publisher Vivien James, *UK Sales and Marketing Director* Richard Samson
Cookery, gardening, travel, humour, sport, photography, art. Part of Chrysalis Books Ltd. Founded 1980.

Pavilion Children's Books

64 Brewery Road, London N7 9NT
tel 020-7697 3000 *fax* 020-7697 3001
email info@pavilionbooks.co.uk
website www.pavilionbooks.co.uk
Head of Children's Books Steve Evans, *Publisher* Chester Fisher
Children's high quality illustrated fiction and non-fiction. Part of Chrysalis Books Ltd. Founded 1980.

Pavilion Publishing (Brighton) Ltd

The Ironworks, Cheapside, Brighton BN1 4GD
tel (01273) 623222 *fax* (01273) 625526
email info@pavpub.com
website www.pavpub.com
Directors Jan Alcoe, Chris Parker, Julie Gibson
Health and social care training: learning disability, mental health, community care management, older people, looked-after young people, community justice, drugs, supported housing. Founded 1987.

Payback Press – former imprint of Canongate Books Ltd

Pearson Education*

Edinburgh Gate, Harlow, Essex CM20 2JE
tel (01279) 623623 *fax* (01279) 431059
email firstname.lastname@pearsoned-ema.com
website www.pearsoned.com
President/Ceo, Pearson Education Europe, Middle East & Africa Nigel Portwood, *President, Pearson Education Ltd* Rod Bristow

Materials for school pupils, students and practitioners globally. Imprints include Longman, Financial Times Prentice Hall, Addison-Wesley, Prentice Hall.

Pelham Books – former imprint of Michael Joseph/Penguin

Pen & Sword Books Ltd

47 Church Street, Barnsley, South Yorkshire S70 2AS
tel (01226) 734222 *fax* (01226) 734438
email charles@pen-and-sword.co.uk
website www.pen-and-sword.co.uk
Managing Director Charles Hewitt, *Publishing Manager* Henry Wilson

Military history. Imprints: Leo Cooper, Pen & Sword Military Classics.

Wharncliffe* (imprint)
Local history.

Penguin Group (UK)*

80 Strand, London WC2R 0RL
tel 020-7010 3000 *fax* 020-7010 6060
website www.penguin.co.uk
Ceo Anthony Forbes Watson, *Managing Director* Helen Fraser

Penguin General Books (division)
Managing Director Tom Weldon, *Publishing Directors* Tony Lacey (Viking/Hamish Hamilton/Penguin), Juliet Annan (Viking/Hamish Hamilton/Penguin), Simon Prosser (Hamish Hamilton/Penguin), Louise Moore (Michael Joseph/Penguin fiction)

No unsolicited MSS or synopses.

Hamish Hamilton (imprint)
Fiction, belles-lettres, biography and memoirs, current affairs, history, literature, politics, travel. No unsolicited MSS or synopses.

Michael Joseph (imprint)
Biography and memoirs, current affairs, fiction, history, humour, travel, health, spirituality and relationships, sports, general leisure, illustrated books. No unsolicited MSS or synopses.

Penguin (imprint)
Adult paperback books – wide range of fiction, non-fiction, TV and film tie-ins. No unsolicited MSS or synopses.

Viking (imprint)
Fiction, general non-fiction; literature, biography, autobiography, current affairs, history, travel, popular culture, reference. No unsolicited MSS or synopses.

Penguin Press (division)
Publishing Directors Stuart Proffitt, Nigel Wilcockson, Simon Winder, Stefan McGrath

Serious adult non-fiction, reference, specialist and classics. Imprint: Allen Lane. Series: Penguin Classics, Penguin Modern Classics. Approach in writing only.

Warne (division)
website www.peterrabbit.com
Managing Director Sally Floyer

Classic children's publishing and merchandising including *Beatrix Potter*™, *Flower Fairies*, *Orlando*. No unsolicited MSS or synopses.

Ventura (division)
website www.funwithspot.com
Managing Director Sally Floyer

Producer and packager of *Spot* titles by Eric Hill. No unsolicited MSS or synopses.

Puffin (division)
website www.puffin.co.uk
Managing Director Francesca Dow

Children's hardback and paperback list, publishing in virtually all fields including fiction, non-fiction, poetry, picture books, media-related titles. No unsolicited MSS or synopses.

Penguin Audiobooks (division)
Contact Victoria Williams

Penguin eBooks
Contact Jeremy Ettinghausen

Dorling Kindersley (a Penguin company)
Publisher Christopher Davis, *Managing Director* Andrew Welham

High quality illustrated non-fiction for adults and children: health, atlases, travel, cookery, gardening, crafts and reference. Imprints: Ladybird, Funfax. Bought by Pearson plc in 2000. Founded 1974.

Penguin
Adult and children's lists include fiction, non-fiction, poetry, drama, classics, reference and special interest areas. Reprints and new work. Owned by Pearson plc.

Rough Guides (a Penguin company)
website www.roughguides.com

Publisher Mark Ellingham, *Directors* Martin Dunford, John Fisher, Jonathan Buckley, Susanne Hillen, Richard Trillo

Travel guides, phrasebooks, maps, music guides, reference books, music CDs.

Pergamon – see Elsevier Science Ltd

Peterloo Poets

The Old Chapel, Sand Lane, Calstock, Cornwall PL18 9QX
tel (01822) 833473 *fax* (01822) 833989
email poets@peterloo.fsnet.co.uk
website www.peterloopoets.co.uk
Publishing Director Harry Chambers, *Trustees* Brian Perman, David Selzer, Rose Taw, *Honorary President* Charles Causley CBE

Poetry. Founded 1976.

Phaidon Press Ltd

Regent's Wharf, All Saints Street, London N1 9PA
tel 020-7843 1000 *fax* 020-7843 1010
Publisher Richard Schlagman, *Managing Director* Andrew Price, *Directors* Amanda Renshaw, Frances Johnson, Nigel Watts-Morgan

Fine art and art history, architecture, design, decorative arts, photography, music, fashion, film.

Philip's – see Octopus Publishing Group

Phillimore & Co. Ltd

(incorporating Darwen Finlayson Ltd)
Shopwyke Manor Barn, Chichester, West Sussex PO20 6BG
tel (01243) 787636 *fax* (01243) 787639
email bookshop@phillimore.co.uk
website www.phillimore.co.uk
Directors Philip Harris JP (chairman), Noel Osborne MA, FSA (managing), Hilary Clifford Brown (marketing), Nicola Willmot (production)

Local and family history; architectural history, archaeology, genealogy and heraldry; also Darwen County History series and History from the Sources series. Founded 1897.

Phoenix House – see The Orion Publishing Group Ltd

Piatkus Books

5 Windmill Street, London W1T 2JA
tel 020-7631 0710 *fax* 020-7436 7137
email info@piatkus.co.uk
website www.piatkus.co.uk
Managing Director Judy Piatkus, *Directors* Philip Cotterell (marketing), Gill Bailey (editorial)

Fiction, biography, history, self-help, health, Mind, Body & Spirit, business, careers, women's interest, how-to and practical, popular psychology, cookery, parenting and childcare, paranormal. Founded 1979.

Pica Press – see A & C Black Publishers Ltd

Picador – see Macmillan Publishers Ltd

Piccadilly Press

5 Castle Road, London NW1 8PR
tel 020-7267 4492 *fax* 020-7267 4493
email books@piccadillypress.co.uk
website www.piccadillypress.co.uk
Directors Brenda Gardner (publisher and managing), Philip Durrance (secretary)

Early picture books, parental advice trade paperbacks, trade paperback teenage non-fiction and humorous teenage fiction. Founded 1983.

Pimlico – see Random House Group Ltd

Pinter – see The Continuum International Publishing Group Ltd

Pipers' Ash Ltd

Pipers' Ash, Church Road, Christian Malford, Chippenham, Wilts. SN15 4BW
tel (01249) 720563 *fax* (0870) 0568916
email pipersash@supamasu.com
website www.supamasu.com
Editorial Director Alfred Tyson

Poetry, contemporary short stories, science fiction stories; short novels, biographies, plays, philosophy, translations, children's, general non-fiction. New authors with talent and potential encouraged. Founded 1976.

Pitkin Unichrome Ltd – see Jarrold Publishing

Pitman Publishing – now Financial Times Prentice Hall; see Pearson Education

The Playwrights Publishing Company

70 Nottingham Road, Burton Joyce, Notts. NG14 5AL
tel 0115-931 3356
email playwrightspublishingco@yahoo.co.uk
Proprietor Liz Breeze, *Consultant* Tony Breeze

One-act and full-length drama: serious work and comedies, for mixed cast, all women or schools. Reading fee and sae required. Founded 1990.

Plexus Publishing Ltd

55A Clapham Common Southside, London SW4 9BX

tel 020-7622 2440 *fax* 020-7622 2441
email plexus@plexusuk.demon.co.uk
website www.plexusbooks.com
Directors Terence Porter (managing), Sandra Wake (editorial)

Film, music, biography, popular culture, fashion. Imprint: Eel Pie. Founded 1973.

Pluto Press*
345 Archway Road, London N6 5AA
tel 020-8348 2724 *fax* 020-8348 9133
email pluto@plutobooks.com
website www.plutobooks.com
Directors Roger van Zwanenberg (managing), Anne Beech (editorial), *Head of Sales* Simon Liebesny, *Head of Marketing* Melanie Patrick

Sociology, economics, history, politics, cultural, international, women's studies, legal studies, Irish studies, Black studies, Third World and development, anthropology, media studies. Imprint: Journeyman Press. Founded 1968.

Pocket Books – **see Simon & Schuster**

Point – **see Scholastic Children's Books**

The Policy Press
University of Bristol, 34 Tyndall's Park Road, Bristol BS8 1PY
tel 0117-9546800 *fax* 0117-9737308
email tpp-info@bristol.ac.uk
website www.policypress.org.uk
Publishing Director Alison Shaw, *Editorial and Production Manager* Dawn Louise Rushen, *Marketing and Sales Manager* Julia Mortimer

Social science publisher, specialising in social and public policy, social work and social welfare. Founded 1996.

Policy Studies Institute (PSI)
100 Park Village East, London NW1 3SR
tel 020-7468 0468 *fax* 020-7388 0914
email pubs@psi.org.uk

Economic, cultural, social and environmental policy, political institutions, social sciences.

Polity Press
65 Bridge Street, Cambridge CB2 1UR
tel (01223) 324315 *fax* (01223) 461385
Directors Anthony Giddens, David Held, John Thompson

Social and political theory, politics, sociology, history, psychology, media and cultural studies, philosophy, literary theory, feminism, human geography, anthropology. Founded 1983.

Polygon – **see Edinburgh University Press**

Poolbeg Group Services Ltd
123 Grange Hill, Baldoyle, Dublin 13, Republic of Ireland
tel (01) 8321477 *fax* (01) 8321430
email poolbeg@poolbeg.com
Directors Kieran Devlin (managing), Philip MacDermott (chairman), Paula Campbell (publisher)

Fiction, public interest, women's interest, history, politics, current affairs. Imprints: Poolbeg, Poolbeg for Children. Founded 1976.

Portland Press Ltd
59 Portland Place, London W1B 1QW
tel 020-7580 5530 *fax* 020-7323 1136
email editorial@portlandpress.com
website www.portlandpress.com
Directors Rhonda C. Oliver (managing), Chris J. Finch (finance), John Day (IT), Adam Marshall (marketing)

Biochemistry and molecular life science books for graduate, post-graduate and research students. Illustrated science books for children: Making Sense of Science series. Founded 1990.

Prentice Hall – **imprint of Pearson Education**

Princeton University Press – Europe
3 Market Place, Woodstock, Oxon OX20 1SY
tel (01993) 814500 *fax* (01993) 814504
email admin@pupress.co.uk
website http://pup.princeton.edu
Publishing Director – Europe Richard Baggaley

Economics, finance and mathematics. Part of **Princeton University Press**, USA. European office founded 1999.

Prion Books
Imperial Works, Perren Street, London NW5 3ED
tel 020-7482 4248 *fax* 020-7482 4203
Managing Director Barry Winkleman

Popular culture, humour, drink, literary and historical reprints, health and beauty. Founded 1982.

Profile Books Ltd
58A Hatton Garden, London EC1N 8LX
tel 020-7404 3001 *fax* 020-7404 3003
email info@profilebooks.co.uk
website www.profilebooks.co.uk
Publisher and Managing Director Andrew Franklin, *Editorial Director* Stephen Brough

General non-fiction: current affairs, politics, social sciences, history, psychology, business, management. Also publishes in association with the *Economist* and the

London Review of Books. No unsolicited MSS; phone or send preliminary letter. Founded 1996.

Psychology Press Ltd

27 Church Road, Hove, East Sussex BN3 2FA
tel (01273) 207411 *fax* (01273) 205612
email info@psypress.co.uk
website www.psypress.co.uk

Psychology textbooks and monographs. Member of the **Taylor and Francis Group plc**.

Brunner-Routledge (imprint)
Clinical psychology and psychiatry.

Puffin – see The Penguin Group (UK)

Putnam Aeronautical Books – see Brassey's (UK) Ltd

Quadrille Publishing

5th Floor, Alhambra House,
27-31 Charing Cross Road, London WC2H 0LS
tel 020-7839 7117 *fax* 020-7839 7118
Directors Alison Cathie (managing), Jane O'Shea and Anne Furniss (editorial), Mary Evans (art), Marlis Ironmonger (commercial), Vincent Smith (production)

Illustrated non-fiction: cookery, craft, health and medical, gardening, interiors, magic. Founded 1994.

Quantum – see W. Foulsham & Co. Ltd

Quartet Books Ltd

27 Goodge Street, London W1T 2LD
tel 020-7636 3992 *fax* 020-7637 1866
email quartetbooks@easynet.co.uk
Chairman N.I. Attallah, *Managing Director* Jeremy Beale, *Publishing Director* Stella Kane

General fiction and non-fiction, foreign literature in translation, classical music, jazz, contemporary music, biography. Member of the Namara Group. Founded 1972.

Queen Anne Press

Windmill Cottage, Mackerye End, Harpenden, Herts. AL5 5DR
tel (01582) 715866
email stephenson@lennardqap.co.uk
Directors K.A.A. Stephenson, R.H. Stephenson

Sporting yearbooks, sponsored titles and special commissions. No unsolicited MSS. Division of Lennard Associates Ltd.

Quiller Publishing Ltd

Wykey House, Wykey, Shrewsbury, Shrops. SY4 1JA
tel (01939) 261616 *fax* (01939) 261606
email info@quillerbooks.com
Managing Director Andrew Johnston

Quiller Press (imprint)
Specialises in sponsored books and publications sold through non-book trade channels as well as bookshops: architecture, biography, business and industry, collecting, cookery, DIY, gardening, guidebooks, humour, reference, sports, travel, wines and spirits.

Swan Hill Press (imprint)
Country and field sports activities.

Radcliffe Medical Press Ltd

18 Marcham Road, Abingdon, Oxon OX14 1AA
tel (01235) 528820 *fax* (01235) 528830
email contact.us@radcliffemed.com
website www.radcliffe-oxford.com
Directors Andrew Bax (managing), Gill Nineham (editorial), Margaret McKeown (financial), *Head of Marketing* Gregory Moxon

Primary care, child health, palliative care, nursing, pharmacy, dentistry, healthcare organisation and management. Founded 1987.

Ragged Bears Publishing Ltd

Milborne Wick, Sherborne, Dorset DT9 4PW
tel (01963) 251600 *fax* (01963) 250889
email info@raggedbears.co.uk
website www.raggedbears.co.uk
Managing Director Henrietta Stickland, *Submissions Editor* Barbara Lamb

Preschool and primary age picture and novelty books. Takes very few unsolicited ideas as the list is small. Send sae for return of MSS; do not send original artwork. Imprints: Ragged Bears, Spindlewood. Founded 1984.

Random House Group Ltd*

20 Vauxhall Bridge Road, London SW1V 2SA
tel 020-7840 8400 *fax* 020-7233 8791
email randomhouse.co.uk
Chairman/Ceo Gail Rebuck, *Directors* Simon Master (deputy chairman), Ian Hudson (managing), Larry Finlay (joint managing, Transworld), Mark Gardiner (finance), Brian Davies (managing director, overseas operations)

Subsidiary of Bertelsmann AG.

Arrow Books Ltd (imprint)
tel 020-7840 8516 *fax* 020-7233 6127
Director Andy McKillop (publishing)
Fiction, non-fiction, fantasy, crime, humour, film tie-ins.

Jonathan Cape (imprint)
tel 020-7840 8576 *fax* 020-7233 6117
Directors Dan Franklin (managing), Robin Robertson, Tom Maschler
Biography and memoirs, current affairs,

drama, fiction, history, poetry, travel. Imprint: Yellow Jersey Press (sport).

Century (imprint)
tel 020-7840 8555 *fax* 020-7233 6127
Directors Kate Parkin (managing), Mark Booth, Oliver Johnson
Fiction, classics, romance, biography, autobiography, general non-fiction, film tie-ins; *Century Business Books*.

Chatto & Windus (imprint)
tel 020-7840 8522 *fax* 020-7233 6123
Directors Alison Samuel (publishing), Penny Hoare, Tasja Dorkofikis (publicity)
Art, belles-lettres, biography and memoirs, current affairs, drama, essays, fiction, history, poetry, politics, philosophy, translations, travel, hardbacks and paperbacks. No unsolicited MSS.

Ebury Press Special Books (division)
tel 020-7840 8400 *fax* 020-7840 8406
Directors Fiona MacIntyre (publisher), Sarah Bennie (publicity)
Art and antiques, biography, buddhism, cookery, gardening, health and beauty, homes and interiors, personal development, spirituality, sport, entertainment, travel guides, TV tie-ins. Unsolicited MSS welcome.

Fodor Guides (imprint of **Ebury Press**)
Worldwide annual travel guides.

The Harvill Press (imprint)
Publisher Christopher MacLehose, *Editorial Director* Margaret Stead
English-language and world literature in translation (literary fiction, non-fiction and some narrative thrillers); monographs in the fields of ethnography, art, horticulture and natural history. Unsolicited MSS only accepted with sae. Founded 1946.

William Heinemann (imprint)
tel 020-7840 8400 *fax* 020-7233 8791
Publishing Directors Kirsty Fowkes (fiction), Ravi Mirchandani (non-fiction), Karen Gibbings (publicity)
Fiction and general non-fiction: crime, thrillers, women's fiction, history, biography, science. No unsolicited MSS and synopses considered.

Hutchinson (imprint)
tel 020-7840 8564 *fax* 020-7233 7870
Directors Sue Freestone (publishing), Anthony Whittome, Paul Sidey (editorial), Sarah Whale (publicity)
Belles-lettres, biography, memoirs, thrillers, crime, current affairs, general history, politics, translations, travel, film tie-ins.

Pimlico (imprint)
tel 020-7840 8630 *fax* 020-7233 6117
Publishing Director Will Sulkin
History, biography, literature.

Vintage (imprint)
tel 020-7840 8400
Publisher Caroline Michel, *Associate Publishing Director* Will Sulkin
Quality fiction and non-fiction.

Random House Audio Books
tel 020-7840 8400
Manager Victoria Williams

Bantam Children's (imprint)
Publisher Philippa Dickinson
Paperback young adult books and series.

Random House Children's Books (division)
61-63 Uxbridge Road, London W5 5SA
tel 020-8579 2652 *fax* 020-8579 5479
Chairman Philippa Dickinson, *Publishing Director* Caroline Roberts, *Publisher (Cape)* Tom Maschler
Publishes under Bodley Head Children's, Jonathan Cape Children's Books, Hutchinson Children's, Red Fox. Picture books, fiction, poetry, music, non-fiction, audio cassettes.

Corgi Children's Books (imprint)
Publisher Philippa Dickinson
Children's paperback picture books, fiction and poetry.

Doubleday Children's Books (imprint)
Publisher Philippa Dickinson
Hardback picture books, fiction and poetry for children.
Also: Expert Gardening Books, *Frommer's* Travel Guides, *Cliffs Notes*.

David Fickling (imprint)
31 Beaumont Street, Oxford OX1 2NP
tel (01865) 339000 *fax* (01865) 339009
email dfickling@randomhouse.co.uk
Publisher David Fickling, *Editor* Bella Pearson
Quality children's fiction and picture books.

Rider (imprint of **Ebury Press**)
Publishing Director Fiona MacIntyre, *Editorial Consultant* Judith Kendra
Buddhism, religion and philosophy, psychology, ecology, health and healing, mysticism, meditation and yoga.

Secker and Warburg (imprint)
tel 020-7840 8649 *fax* 020-7233 6117
Directors Geoff Mulligan (editorial), Tasja Dorkofikis (publicity)

Literary fiction, general non-fiction. No unsolicited MSS/synopses.

Transworld Publishers Ltd (division)
See page 196.

Vermilion (imprint of **Ebury Press**)

Ransom Publishing Ltd*

Ransom House, Unit 1, Brook Street, Watlington, Oxon OX9 5PP
tel (01491) 613711 *fax* (01491) 613733
email ransom@ransompublishing.co.uk
website www.ransom.co.uk
Directors Jenny Ertle (managing), Steve Rickard (creative)

Preschool, primary and secondary education: literacy, numeracy and science multimedia. Founded 1995.

The Reader's Digest Association Ltd*

11 Westferry Circus, Canary Wharf, London E14 4HE
tel 020-7715 8000 *fax* 020-7715 8600
Managing Director A.T. Lynam-Smith, *Editorial Directors* Katherine Walker (magazine), Cortina Butler (books)

Monthly magazine, condensed and series books; DIY, computers, puzzles, gardening, medical, handicrafts, law, touring guides, encyclopedias, dictionaries, nature, folklore, atlases, cookery, music; videos.

Reaktion Books

77-79 Farringdon Road, London EC1M 3JU
tel 020-7404 9930 *fax* 020-7404 9931
email info@reaktionbooks.co.uk
website www.reaktionbooks.co.uk
Editorial Director Michael R. Leaman

Art history, design, architecture, history, cultural studies, film studies, Asian studies, travel writing, photography. Founded 1985.

Rebel Inc. – former imprint of Canongate Books Ltd

Red Dress Ink™ – see Harlequin Mills & Boon Ltd

Red Fox – see Random House Group Ltd

Reed Books – now Octopus Publishing Group

Reed Business Information

Windsor Court, East Grinstead House, Wood Street, East Grinstead, West Sussex RH19 1XA
tel (01342) 326972 *fax* (01342) 335612
email information@reedinfo.co.uk
website www.reedbusiness.com
Managing Director John Minch

Directories and reference books covering professional and industrial sectors, including *Kompass*, *Kelly's*, *Dial* and *The Bankers' Almanac*. Part of Reed Elsevier plc. Founded 1983.

William Reed Directories

Broadfield Park, Crawley, West Sussex RH11 9RT
tel (01293) 613400 *fax* (01293) 610322
email directories@william-reed.co.uk
website www.william-reed.co.uk
Director Mark de Lange, *Editorial Manager* Sulann Staniford, *Group Sales Manager* Simon Hughes

Publishers of leading business-to-business directories and reports, including *The Grocer Directory of Buyers and Retailers* and *The Grocer Directory of Manufacturers and Suppliers*.

Reed Educational and Professional Publishing Ltd*

Halley Court, Jordan Hill, Oxford OX2 8EJ
tel (01865) 310533 *fax* (01865) 314641
email reed.educational@repp.co.uk
website www.repp.co.uk
Chief Executive John Philbin

Division of Reed Elsevier (UK) Ltd.

Architectural Press (imprint)
website www.architecturalpress.com
Publisher Neil Warnock-Smith

Architecture, the environment, planning, townscape, building technology; general.

Butterworth–Heinemann UK (imprint)
Linacre House, Jordan Hill, Oxford OX2 8EJ
tel (01865) 310366 *fax* (01865) 310898
website www.bh.com
Managing Director Philip Shaw

Books and electronic products across business, technical, medical fields for students and professionals.

Focal Press (imprint)
website www.focalpress.com
Publisher Jenny Welham

Professional, technical and academic books on photography, broadcasting, film, television, radio, audiovisual and communication media.

Ginn & Co. (imprint)
fax (01865) 314189
Managing Director Paul Shuter

Textbook/other educational resources for primary schools.

Heinemann Educational (imprint)
Managing Director Bob Osborne

Textbooks, literature and other educational resources for all levels.

Newnes (imprint)
fax (01865) 314641
website www.newnespress.com
Publisher Matthew Deans
Technical books in electronics and engineering.

Rigby Heinemann (imprint)
fax (01865) 314189
Managing Director Paul Shuter
Textbook/other educational resources for primary schools.

Religious and Moral Education Press

St Mary's Works, St Mary's Plain, Norwich, Norfolk NR3 3BH
tel (01603) 612914 *fax* (01603) 624483
email admin@scm-canterburypress.co.uk
website www.scm-canterburypress.co.uk
Publisher Mary Mears
Books for primary and secondary school pupils, college students, and teachers on religious, moral, personal and social education. Division of SCM-Canterbury Press Ltd, a subsidiary of Hymns Ancient & Modern Ltd.

Review – **see Hodder Headline Ltd**

Reynolds & Hearn Ltd

61A Priory Road, Kew, Richmond, Surrey TW9 3DH
tel 020-8940 5198 *fax* 020-8940 7679
email richard.reynolds@rhbooks.com
website www.rhbooks.com
Directors Richard Reynolds (managing), Marcus Hearn (editorial), David O'Leary, Geoffrey Wolfson
Film, TV, entertainment, media. Founded 1999.

Rider – **see Random House Group Ltd**

Rigby Heinemann – **see Reed Educational and Professional Publishing Ltd**

Rivelin Grapheme Press

Merlin House, Church Street, Hungerford, Berks. RG17 0JG
tel (01488) 684645 *fax* (01488) 683018
Director Snowdon Barnett
Poetry. Send introductory letter enclosing one short poem. Founded 1984.

River Books – **see New Cavendish Books**

Rivers Oram Press

144 Hemingford Road, London N1 1DE
tel 020-7607 0823 *fax* 020-7609 2776
email ro@riversoram.demon.co.uk
Directors Elizabeth Rivers Fidlon (managing), Anthony Harris
Non-ficton: social and political science, current affairs, social history, gender studies, sexual politics, cultural studies and photography. Founded 1991.

Pandora Press (imprint)
Managing Editor Caroline Lazar
Feminist press publishing. General non-fiction: biography, arts, media, health, current affairs, reference and sexual politics.

Robinson Publishing Ltd – **see Constable & Robinson Ltd**

Robson Books

64 Brewery Road, London N7 9NT
tel 020-7697 3000 *fax* 020-7697 3001
Publisher Jeremy Robson
General non-fiction, biography, music, humour, sport. Unsolicited MSS discouraged; ideas with synopses welcome with sae. Part of Chrysalis Books Ltd. Founded 1973.

George Ronald

46 High Street, Kidlington, Oxon OX5 2DN
tel/fax (01235) 529137
email sales@grpubl.demon.co.uk
Managers W. Momen, E. Leith
Religion, specialising in the Baha'i Faith. Founded 1939.

Barry Rose Law Publishers Ltd

Little London, Chichester, West Sussex PO19 1PG
tel (01243) 775552/783637 *fax* (01243) 779278
email books@barry-rose-law.co.uk
Law, local government, police, legal history. Founded 1972.

Countrywise Press
Reprints in paperback of hardcover books from Barry Rose; some non-law titles.

Rough Guides – **see The Penguin Group (UK)**

Round Hall Ltd

43 Fitzwilliam Place, Dublin 2, Republic of Ireland
tel (01) 6625301 *fax* (01) 6625302
email info@roundhall.ie
Director and General Manager Elanor McGarry
Law. Part of Thomson Legal & Regulatory (Europe) Ltd.

Roundhouse Publishing Ltd

Millstone, Limers Lane, Northam, North Devon EX39 2RG
tel (01237) 474474 *fax* (01237) 474774
email roundhouse.group@ukgateway.net
website www.roundhouse.net
Publisher Alan T. Goodworth

Film, cinema, and performing arts; reference books. No unsolicited MSS. Founded 1991.

Route

School Lane, Glasshoughton, Castleford, West Yorkshire WF10 4QH
tel (01977) 603028 *fax* (01977) 512819
email books@route-online.com
website www.route-online.com
www.openingline.co.uk www.artcircus.com
Contact Ian Daley

Fiction imprint of Yorkshire Art Circus. Specialises in contemporary fiction and has a commitment to new writing. Looking for novels/novellas and publishes an annual collection of short fiction (check for current theme). Unsolicited MSS discouraged; send for fact sheet or visit website for submission guidelines. Also manages the writers programme, The Opening Line. Route Events facilitate the development of performance poetry.

Routledge – see Taylor & Francis Group plc

RoutledgeFalmer – see Taylor & Francis Group plc

RoutledgeCurzon – see Taylor & Francis Group plc

Royal National Institute for the Blind

PO Box 173, Peterborough, Cambs. PE2 6WS
tel (0845) 7023153 *fax* (01733) 371555
email cservices@rnib.org.uk
website www.rnib.org.uk
textphone (0845) 7585691

Magazines, catalogues and books for blind and partially sighted people, to support daily living, leisure, learning and employment reading needs. Produced in braille, audio, large/legible print, disk and Moon. For complete list of magazines see page 116. Founded 1868.

Ryland Peters & Small

Kirkman House, 12-14 Whitfield Street, London W1T 2RP
tel 020-7436 9090 *fax* 020-7436 9790
email info@rps.co.uk
Directors David Peters (managing), Gabriella Le Grazie (art), Alison Starling (publishing), Joanna Everard (rights), Meryl Silbert (production)

High-quality illustrated books on cookery, lifestyle, interior design and gardening. Founded 1995.

SAGE Publications Ltd*

6 Bonhill Street, London EC2A 4PU
tel 020-7374 0645 *fax* 020-7374 8741
email info@sagepub.co.uk
website www.sagepub.co.uk
Directors Stephen Barr (managing), Peter Heilbrunn, Ian Eastment, Mike Birch, Ziyad Marar, Richard Fidczuk, Michael Melody (USA), Sara Miller McCune (USA), Paul R. Chapman

Social sciences, behavioural sciences, humanities, STM, software. Founded 1971.

Saint Andrew Press*

121 George Street, Edinburgh EH2 4YN
tel 0131-225 5722 *fax* 0131-220 3113
email cofs.standrew@dial.pipex.com
website www.standrewpress.com
Head of Publishing Ann Crawford

Publishing house of the Church of Scotland: publishes books that explore Christianity, spirituality, faith and ethical and moral issues, as well as more general Scottish works of fiction and non-fiction; children's.

St Pauls

St Pauls Publishing, 187 Battersea Bridge Road, London SW11 3AS
tel 020-7978 4300 *fax* 020-7978 4370
email editions@stpauls.org.uk
website www.stpauls.ie

Theology, ethics, spirituality, biography, education, general books of Roman Catholic and Christian interest. Founded 1948.

Salamander

64 Brewery Road, London N7 9NT
tel 020-7697 3000 *fax* 020-7700 4552
Directors Colin Gower (publishing), Richard Samson (UK sales)

Cookery, crafts, military, natural history, music, gardening, hobbies, transport, sports. Part of Chrysalis Books Ltd. Founded 1973.

Salariya Book Company Ltd

Book House, 25 Marlborough Place, Brighton BN1 1UB
tel (01273) 603306 *fax* (01273) 693857
email salariya@salariya.com
website www.salariya.com
Director David Salariya

Children's non-fiction. Imprint: Book House. Founded 1989.

W.B. Saunders Co. Ltd – see Harcourt Publishers Ltd

S.B. Publications

c/o 19 Grove Road, Seaford, East Sussex BN25 1TP
tel (01323) 893498 *fax* (01323) 893860
email sales@sbpublications.swinternet.co.uk
website www.sbpublications.swinternet.co.uk
Proprietor Lindsay Woods

Local history, local themes (e.g. walking books, guides), maritime history, transport, specific themes. Founded 1987.

Sceptre – see Hodder Headline Ltd

Schofield & Sims Ltd

Dogley Mill, Fenay Bridge, Huddersfield HD8 0NQ
tel (01484) 607080 *fax* (01484) 606815
email schofield_and_sims@compuserve.com
Managing Director J. Stephen Platts

Educational: nursery, infants, primary; posters. Founded 1901.

Scholastic Children's Books*

Commonwealth House, 1-19 New Oxford Street, London WC1A 1NU
tel 020-7421 9000 *fax* 020-7421 9001
email publicity@scholastic.co.uk
Publisher Richard Scrivener

Imprint of **Scholastic Ltd**.

Hippo (imprint)

Children's paperbacks – fiction and non-fiction. No unsolicited MSS.

Point (imprint)

Fiction for 12+.

Scholastic Press (imprint)

Literary fiction and picture books.

Scholastic Ltd*

Villiers House, Clarendon Avenue, Leamington Spa, Warks. CV32 5PR
tel (01926) 887799 *fax* (01926) 883331
website www.scholastic.co.uk
Directors D.M.R. Kewley (managing), M.R. Robinson (USA), R.M. Spaulding (USA), D.J. Walsh (USA)

Children's Division

Publisher Richard Scrivener

See **Scholastic Children's Books**.

Direct Marketing

Managing Director, Book Fair Division Mike Robinson, *Managing Director, Book Club Division* Mike Crossley, *Managing Director, Trade Sales and Marketing* Gavin Lang

Children's book clubs and school book fairs.

Educational Division

Publishing Director Anne Peel

Publishers of books for teachers (*Bright Ideas* and other series), primary classroom resources and magazines for teachers (*Child Education*, *Junior Education* and others). Founded 1964.

Scholastic Press – see Scholastic Children's Books

Science Museum Publications – see NMSI

SCM Press*

9-17 St Albans Place, London N1 0NX
tel 020-7359 8033 *fax* 020-7359 0049
email admin@scm-canterburypress.co.uk
website www.scm-canterburypress.co.uk
Publishing Director Alex Wright

Theological books with special emphasis on interdisciplinary, culturally engaged contemporary theology and its relationship to postmodernity and secular life and thought. Division of SCM-Canterbury Press Ltd. Founded 1929.

Scottish Children's Press

Unit 13D, Newbattle Abbey Business Annexe, Newbattle Road, Dalkeith EH22 3LJ
tel 0131-660 4757 *fax* 0131-660 6414
email info@scottishbooks.com
website www.scottishbooks.com
Directors Avril Gray, Brian Pugh

Scottish fiction, Scottish non-fiction and Scots language, children's writing. Unsolicited MSS not accepted; send letter only in first instance.

SCP Publishers Ltd*

(trading as Scottish Cultural Press)
Unit 13D, Newbattle Abbey Business Annexe, Newbattle Road, Dalkeith EH22 3LJ
tel 0131-660 6366 *fax* 0131-660 6414
email info@scottishbooks.com
website www.scottishbooks.com
Directors Brian Pugh, Avril Gray

Literature, poetry, history, archaeology, biography and environmental history. Unsolicited MSS not accepted; send letter only in first instance. Founded 1992.

Scribner – see Simon & Schuster

Scripture Union

207-209 Queensway, Bletchley, Milton Keynes, Bucks. MK2 2EB
tel (01908) 856000 *fax* (01908) 856111
email postmaster@scriptureunion.org.uk

Christian books and Bible reading materials for people of all ages; educational and worship resources for churches; children's fiction and non-fiction; adult non-fiction. Founded 1867.

Seafarer Books
102 Redwald Road, Rendlesham, Woodbridge, Suffolk IP12 2TE
tel (01394) 420789
email info@seafarerbooks.com
website www.seafarerbooks.com
Commissioning Editor Patricia Eve

Books on traditional sailing, mainly narrative.

Search Press Ltd
Wellwood, North Farm Road, Tunbridge Wells, Kent TN2 3DR
tel (01892) 510850 *fax* (01892) 515903
email searchpress@searchpress.com
Directors Martin de la Bédoyère (managing), Rosalind Dace (editorial)

Arts, crafts, leisure, gardening. Founded 1970.

Secker and Warburg – see Random House Group Ltd

Seren
First Floor, 38-40 Nolton Street, Bridgend CF31 3BN
tel (01656) 663018 *fax* (01656) 649226
email mickfelton@seren.force9.co.uk
Director Mick Felton

Poetry, fiction, drama, history, film, literary criticism, biography, art – mostly with relevance to Wales. Founded 1981.

Serpent's Tail
4 Blackstock Mews, London N4 2BT
tel 020-7354 1949 *fax* 020-7704 6467
email info@serpentstail.com
website www.serpentstail.com
Director Peter Ayrton

Fiction and non-fiction in paperback; literary and non-mainstream work, and work in translation. Approach with query letter please; do not send complete MSS. Sae essential as is familiarity with list. Imprint: Five Star. Founded 1986.

Seven Dials – see Weidenfeld & Nicolson

Severn House Publishers
9-15 High Street, Sutton, Surrey SM1 1DF
tel 020-8770 3930 *fax* 020-8770 3850
email editorial@severnhouse.com
website www.severnhouse.com
Chairman Edwin Buckhalter, *Publishing Director* Amanda Stewart

Hardcover adult fiction for the library market: romances, crime, thrillers, detective, adventure, war, science fiction. No unsolicited MSS.

Shakespeare Head Press – see Blackwell Publishers

Sheed & Ward Ltd – see The Continuum International Publishing Group Ltd

Sheffield Academic Press – see The Continuum International Publishing Group Ltd

Sheldon Press – see Society for Promoting Christian Knowledge

Sheldrake Press
188 Cavendish Road, London SW12 0DA
tel 020-8675 1767 *fax* 020-8675 7736
email mail@sheldrakepress.demon.co.uk
website www.sheldrakepress.demon.co.uk
Publisher J.S. Rigge

History, travel, architecture, cookery, music; stationery. Founded 1979.

Shepheard-Walwyn (Publishers) Ltd
Suite 604, 50 Westminster Bridge Road, London SE1 7QY
tel 020-7721 7666 *fax* 020-7721 7667
email books@shepheard-walwyn.co.uk
Directors A.R.A. Werner, M.M. Werner

History, biography, political economy, philosophy; illustrated gift books; Scottish interest. Founded 1971.

Shire Publications Ltd
Cromwell House, Church Street, Princes Risborough, Bucks. HP27 9AA
tel (01844) 344301 *fax* (01844) 347080
email shire@shirebooks.co.uk
website www.shirebooks.co.uk
Director J.W. Rotheroe

Discovering paperbacks, Shire Albums, Shire Archaeology, Shire Natural History, Shire Ethnography, Shire Egyptology, Shire Garden History. Founded 1962.

Short Books Ltd
15 Highbury Terrace, London N5 1UP
tel 020-7226 1607 *fax* 020-7226 4169
email rebecca@sbco.demon.co.uk
website www.theshortbookco.com
Editorial Directors Rebecca Nicolson, Aurea Carpenter

Short (less than 40,000 words) books of narrative non-fiction bridging the gap between journalism and publishing: history, biography, journalism. Founded 1999.

Sidgwick & Jackson – see Macmillan Publishers Ltd

Sigma Press

1 South Oak Lane, Wilmslow, Cheshire SK9 6AR
tel (01625) 531035 *fax* (01625) 536800
email info@sigmapress.co.uk
website www.sigmapress.co.uk
Partners Graham Beech, Diana Beech

Leisure: country walking, cycling, regional heritage, sport, cookery, health, folklore; biographies. Founded 1979.

Signet Books – former imprint of Michael Joseph/Penguin

Silhouette® – see Harlequin Mills & Boon Ltd

Simon & Schuster*

Africa House, 64-78 Kingsway, London WC2B 6AH
tel 020-7316 1900 *fax* 020-7316 0331/2
website www.simonsays.co.uk
Directors Ian Chapman (managing), Suzanne Baboneau (publishing), James Kellow (sales and marketing), Diane Spivey (rights), Helen Gummer (non-fiction publisher)

Commercial and literary fiction; general and serious non-fiction; children's. No unsolicited MSS. Founded 1986.

Earthlight (imprint)
Science fiction and fantasy.

Pocket Books (imprint)
Mass-market fiction and non-fiction paperbacks.

Scribner (imprint)
Literary fiction and non-fiction.

Simon & Schuster Audioworks
Fiction, non-fiction and business.

Free Press (imprint)
Serious adult non-fiction: history, biography, current affairs, science.

Simon & Schuster Children's Publishing
Fiction and non-fiction.

Skoob Russell Square

10 Brunswick Centre, off Bernard Street, London WC1N 1AE
tel 020-7278 8760 *fax* 020-7278 3137
email books@skoob.com
website www.skoob.com
Editorial M. Lovell

Literary guides, cultural studies, oriental literature. No unsolicited material. Founded 1979.

Smith Gryphon Ltd – see Blake Publishing

Colin Smythe Ltd*

PO Box 6, Gerrards Cross, Bucks. SL9 8XA
tel (01753) 886000 *fax* (01753) 886469
website www.colinsmythe.co.uk
Directors Colin Smythe (managing and editorial), Peter Bander van Duren, A. Norman Jeffares, Ann Saddlemyer, Leslie Hayward

Biography, phaleristics, heraldry, Irish literature and literary criticism, folklore, crafts and history. Founded 1966.

Society for Promoting Christian Knowledge*

Holy Trinity Church, Marylebone Road, London NW1 4DU
tel 020-7387 5282 *fax* 020-7388 2352
email publishing@spck.org.uk
Director of Publishing Simon Kingston

Founded 1698.

Azure Books (imprint)
Editor Alison Barr
Biography and letters, personal growth and relationships, history, humour, spirituality, travel.

Sheldon Press (imprint)
Editorial Director Joanna Moriarty
Popular medicine, health, self-help, psychology, business.

SPCK (imprint)
Editorial Director Joanna Moriarty
Theology and academic, liturgy, prayer, spirituality, biblical studies, educational resources, mission, gospel and culture.

Society of Genealogists Enterprises Ltd

14 Charterhouse Buildings, Goswell Road, London EC1M 7BA
tel 020-7251 8799 *fax* 020-7250 1800
email sales@sog.org.uk
website www.sog.org.uk/
Managing Director Robert I.N. Gordon, *General Manager* Andrew Rylah

Local and family history books, fiche, disks, CDs, software and magazines plus extensive library facilities.

South Street Press – see Garnet Publishing Ltd

Southwater – see Anness Publishing Ltd

Souvenir Press Ltd

43 Great Russell Street, London WC1B 3PD
tel 020-7580 9307/8
Managing Director Ernest Hecht BSc (Econ), BCom

Archaeology, biography and memoirs, educational (secondary, technical), fiction, general, humour, practical handbooks, psychiatry, psychology, sociology, sports, games and hobbies, travel, supernatural, parapsychology, illustrated books.

SPCK – see Society for Promoting Christian Knowledge

Neville Spearman Publishers – see The C.W. Daniel Company Ltd

Specialist Crafts Ltd

(formerly Dryad)
PO Box 247, Leicester LE1 9QS
tel 01162-697711 *fax* 01162-697722
email post@speccrafts.co.uk
website www.speccrafts.co.uk
Director N. Beavon

'How to' booklets on various art and craft skills. *Specialist Crafts 500* series full colour craft booklets and patterns. Suppliers of over 12,000 art and craft items.

Spellmount Ltd

The Old Rectory, Staplehurst, Kent TN12 0AZ
tel (01580) 893730 *fax* (01580) 893731
email enquiries@spellmount.com
website www.spellmount.com
Proprietor Jamie A.G. Wilson

Ancients, 15th through to 20th century history/military history. Send sae with submissions please. Founded 1984.

Spindlewood – see Ragged Bears Publishing Ltd

Spon Press – see Taylor & Francis Group plc

Springer-Verlag London Ltd

Sweetapple House, Catteshall Road, Godalming, Surrey GU7 3DJ
tel (01483) 418800 *fax* (01483) 415151
email postmaster@svl.co.uk
website www.springer.co.uk
Managing Director John Watson, *Executive Directors* D. Goetz, R. Gebauer

Medicine, computing, engineering, astronomy, mathematics. Founded 1972.

Stacey International

128 Kensington Church Street, London W8 4BH
tel 020-7221 7166 *fax* 020-7792 9288
email enquiries@stacey-international.co.uk
Directors Max Scott (managing), Kitty Carruthers (publishing executive), Tom Stacey (consultant)

Illustrated non-fiction, encyclopedic books on regions and countries, Islamic and Arab subjects, world affairs, art, travel, belles-lettres. Founded 1974.

Stainer & Bell Ltd

PO Box 110, Victoria House, 23 Gruneisen Road, London N3 1DZ
tel 020-8343 3303 *fax* 020-843 3024
email post@stainer.co.uk
website www.stainer.co.uk
Directors Keith Wakefield (joint managing), Carol Wakefield (joint managing and secretary), Antony Kearns, Andrew Pratt, Nicholas Williams

Books on music, religious communication. Founded 1907.

Harold Starke Publishers Ltd*

Pixey Green, Stadbroke, Eye, Suffolk IP21 5NG
tel (01379) 388334 *fax* (01379) 388335
203 Bunyan Court, Barbican, London EC2Y 8DH
tel 020-7588 5195
Directors Harold K. Starke, Naomi Galinski (editorial)

Specialist, scientific, medical, reference.

Stationery Office (Ireland) – see Government Supplies Agency

Stenlake Publishing*

54-58 Mill Square, Catrine Ayrshire KA5 6RD
tel (01290) 552233 *fax* (01290) 551122
email sales@stenlake.co.uk
website www.stenlake.co.uk
Proprietor Richard Stenlake, *Editorial Director* Oliver van Helden

Scottish interest: history, railways, transport, canals, mining. Founded 1997.

Patrick Stephens Ltd – acquired by Sutton Publishing Ltd

Stride Publications

11 Sylvan Road, Exeter, Devon EX4 6EW
email editor@stridebooks.co.uk
website www.stridebooks.co.uk
Managing Editor Rupert M. Loydell

Poetry, literary experimental novels and short fiction collections, contemporary music and visual arts, interviews. No submissions are currently being sought. Founded 1980.

Summersdale Publishers Ltd

46 West Street, Chichester, West Sussex PO19 1RP
tel (01243) 771107 *fax* (01243) 786300
email info@summersdale.com
liz@summersdale.com
website www.summersdale.com
Commissioning Editor Elizabeth Kershaw

Fiction and non-fiction. Specialist areas: travel literature, international fiction, biography and history, humour and gift books. No poetry or children's literature. Founded 1990.

Sunflower Books
12 Kendrick Mews, London SW7 3HG
tel/fax 020-7589 1862
email mail@sunflowerbooks.co.uk
website www.sunflowerbooks.co.uk/
Directors P.A. Underwood (editorial), J.G. Underwood, S.J. Seccombe
Travel guidebooks.

Sussex Academic Press
PO Box 2950, Brighton BN2 5SP
tel (01273) 699533 *fax* (01273) 621262
email edit@sussex-academic.co.uk
website www.sussex-academic.co.uk
Editorial Director Anthony Grahame
Theology and religion, British history and Middle East studies. Founded 1994.
The Alpha Press (imprint)
Religion, history, sport.

Sutton Publishing Ltd
Phoenix Mill, Thrupp, Stroud, Glos. GL5 2BU
tel (01453) 731114 *fax* (01453) 731117
email publishing@sutton-publishing.co.uk
website www.suttonpublishing.co.uk
Directors Keith Fullman (managing), Peter Clifford (publishing), Jeremy Yates-Round (sales and marketing)
General academic and specialist publishers of high-quality illustrated books: history, military, biography, archaeology, heritage. Founded 1978.
Patrick Stephens Ltd (imprint)
Aviation, maritime and military. New titles and new editions now published under Sutton imprint.

Swan Hill Press – see Quiller Publishing Ltd

Swedenborg Society
20-21 Bloomsbury Way, London WC1A 2TH
tel 020-7405 7986 *fax* 020-7831 5848
email swed.soc@netmatters.co.uk
website www.swedenborg.co.uk
The Writings of Swedenborg.

Sweet & Maxwell*
100 Avenue Road, London NW3 3PF
tel 020-7393 7000 *fax* 020-7393 7010
Directors Wendy Beecham (managing), Jim Glover, Aris Kassimatis, Hilary Lambert, Wendy Newman, Martin Redfern, Jackie Rhodes
Law. Part of Thomson Legal & Regulatory (Europe) Ltd. Founded 1799; incorporated 1889.

Take That Ltd
PO Box 200, Harrogate, North Yorkshire HG1 2YR
tel (01423) 507545 *fax* (01423) 526035
email sales@takethat.co.uk
website www.takethat.co.uk
Managing Director Chris Brown
Internet/computing, business, finance, gambling. Send sae with synopsis/samples. Founded 1986.

Tamarind Ltd
PO Box 52, Northwood, Middlesex HA6 1UN
tel 020-8866 8808 *fax* 020-8866 5627
email info@tamarindbooks.co.uk
website www.tamarindbooks.co.uk
Managing Director Verna Wilkins
Multicultural children's picture books and posters. All books give a high positive profile to black children. Unsolicited material welcome with return postage. Founded 1987.

Tango Books – imprint of Sadie Fields Productions Ltd, book packagers

Tarquin Publications
Stradbroke, Diss, Norfolk IP21 5JP
tel (01379) 384218 *fax* (01379) 384289
email tarquin-books.demon.co.uk
website www.tarquin-books.demon.co.uk
Partners Gerald Jenkins, Margaret Jenkins
Mathematics and mathematical models; paper cutting, paper engineering and pop-up books for intelligent children. No unsolicited MSS; send suggestion or synopsis in first instance. Founded 1970.

Tate Publishing
The Lodge, Millbank, London SW1P 4RG
tel 020-7887 8869/70 *fax* 020-7887 8878
email tgpl@tate.org.uk
website www.tate.org.uk
Chief Executive Celia Clear, *Publishing Director* Roger Thorp, *Senior Manager* Brian McGahon, *Production Manager* Tim Holton, *Head of Licensing* Jo Matthews, *Head of Products* Rosey Blackmore
Publishers for Tate in London, Liverpool and St Ives. Exhibition catalogues, art books (contemporary, modern and from 1500 if British) and diaries, posters, etc. Also product development, picture library and licensing. Division of Tate Enterprises Ltd. Founded 1995.

I.B.Tauris & Co. Ltd
6 Salem Road, London W2 4BU
tel 020-7243 1225 *fax* 020-7243 1226
email mail@ibtauris.com
website www.ibtauris.com
Directors I. Bagherzade (chairman and publisher), Jonathan McDonnell (managing)

History, biography, politics, international relations, current affairs, Middle East, cultural and media studies, film, art, archaeology, travel guides. Founded 1983.
Tauris Academic Studies (imprint)
Academic monographs on history, political science and social sciences.
Tauris Parke Books (imprint)
Illustrated books on architecture, design, photography, cultural history and travel.
Tauris Parke Paperbacks (imprint)
Non-fiction trade paperbacks: biography, history, travel, cinema, art, cultural history.

Taylor & Francis Group plc*

11 New Fetter Lane, London EC4P 4EE
tel 020-7583 9855 *fax* 020-7842 2298
email info@tandf.co.uk
website www.tandf.co.uk
Chief Executive David J. Smith, *Managing Director, Taylor & Francis Books Ltd* Roger Horton

The company is making its books available through the Taylor & Francis Electronic Library imprint.
Europa Publications (imprint)
See page 159.
Garland Science (imprint)
Science textbooks and scholarly works.
Psychology Press Ltd
See page 185.
Routledge (imprint)
website www.routledge.com
Addiction, anthropology, archaeology, Asian studies, business, classical studies, counselling, criminology, development and environment, dictionaries, economics, education, geography, health, history, Japanese studies, library science, language, linguistics, literary criticism, media and culture, nursing, performance studies, philosophy, politics, psychiatry, psychology, reference, social administration, social studies/sociology, women's studies.
RoutledgeFalmer (imprint)
Education books.
Spon Press (imprint)
Architecture, civil engineering, construction, leisure and recreation management, sports science.
Taylor & Francis (imprint)
Educational (university), science: physics, mathematics, chemistry, electronics, natural history, pharmacology and drug metabolism, toxicology, technology, history of science, ergonomics, production engineering, remote sensing, geographic information systems.
RoutlegeCurzon (imprint)
Academic/scholarly books in the social sciences, particularly Asian studies.

Teach Yourself – see Hodder Headline Ltd

Telegraph Books

Telegraph Group Ltd, 1 Canada Square, Canary Wharf, London E14 5DT
tel 020-7538 6826 *fax* 020-7538 6064
Publisher Susannah Charlton

Business, personal finance, crosswords, sport, travel and guides, cookery and wine, general, gardening, history – all by *Telegraph* journalists and contributors, and co-published with major publishing houses. Founded 1920.

Tempus Publishing Group Ltd

The Mill, Brimscombe Port, Stroud, Glos. GL5 2QG
tel (01453) 883300 *fax* (01453) 883233
Directors Alan Sutton (chief executive), Paul Raffle (finance), Michael Walton (operations), Kirsty Sutton (operations, USA), Peter Kemmis Betty (publishing)

Local history: England, Scotland, Ireland, Wales; sport; industrial and transport history, archaeology. Founded 1993.

Thames & Hudson Ltd*

181A High Holborn, London WC1V 7QX
tel 020-7845 5000 *fax* 020-7845 5050
email mail@thameshudson.co.uk
website www.thamesandhudson.com
Directors T. Neurath (managing), E. Bates, C. Kaine, C. Ferguson, J. Camplin, P. Hughes, S. Baron, B. Meek, P. Meades, J. Neurath, T. Evans, T. Naylor, N. Stangos, N. Palfreyman

Illustrated non-fiction for an international audience, especially art, architecture, graphic design, garden and landscape design, archaeology, cultural history, historical reference, fashion, photography, ethnic arts, mythology and religion.

Thames Publishing

c/o William Elkin Music Services, Station Road Industrial Estate, Salhouse, Norwich NR13 6NS
tel (01603) 721302 *fax* (01603) 721801
email sales@elkinmusic.co.uk
website www.elkinmusic.co.uk
Publishing Manager E.B. Bishop

Books about music (not pop), particularly British composers and musicians. Preliminary letter essential. Founded 1970.

D.C. Thomson & Co. Ltd – Publications

2 Albert Square, Dundee DD1 9QJ
London office 185 Fleet Street, London EC4A 2HS

Publishers of newspapers and periodicals. Children's books (annuals), based on weekly magazine characters; fiction. For fiction guidelines, send a large sae to Central Fiction Dept.

Stanley Thornes (Publishers) Ltd – see Nelson Thornes Ltd

Thorsons – see HarperCollins Publishers

Time Warner Books UK

(formerly Little, Brown and Company (UK))
Brettenham House, Lancaster Place, London WC2E 7EN
tel 020-7911 8000 *fax* 020-7911 8100
Chief Executive David Young, *Directors* Ursula Mackenzie (publisher), Barbara Boote (editorial), Alan Samson (editorial), David Kent (home sales), Nigel Batt (financial), Terry Jackson (marketing)

Hardback and paperback fiction, general non-fiction and illustrated books. No unsolicited MSS. Founded 1988.

Abacus (division)
Editorial Director Richard Beswick

Trade paperbacks.

Orbit (imprint)
Editorial Director Tim Holman

Science fiction and fantasy paperbacks.

Virago (division)
Publisher Lennie Goodings

Fiction, including Modern Classics Series, biography, autobiography and general non-fiction which highlight all aspects of women's lives.

Warner (division)
Editorial Directors Barbara Boote, Alan Samson, Hilary Hale

Paperbacks: original fiction and non-fiction; reprints.

X Libris (imprint)
Editor Sarah Shrubb

Erotic fiction for women.

Times Books – see HarperCollins Publishers

Titan Books

144 Southwark Street, London SE1 0UP
tel 020-7620 0200 *fax* 020-7620 0032
email readerfeedback@titanemail.com
Publisher and Managing Director Nick Landau, *Editorial Director* Katy Wild

Graphic novels, including *Simpsons* and *Batman*, featuring comic strip material; film and TV tie-ins and cinema reference books, including *Star Wars* and *Star Trek*. No fiction or children's proposals and no unsolicited material without preliminary letter please; send large sae for current author guidelines. Division of Titan Publishing Group Ltd. Founded 1981.

Tivoli – see Gill & Macmillan Ltd

Tolkien – see HarperCollins Publishers

Tolley – see LexisNexis Butterworths Tolley

Town House and Country House†

Trinity House, Charleston Road, Ranelagh, Dublin 6, Republic of Ireland
tel (01) 4972399 *fax* (01) 4970927
email books@townhouse.ie
Directors Treasa Coady, Jim Coady

General illustrated non-fiction, popular and literary fiction, art, archaeology and biography. Imprints: TownHouse, Simon and Schuster/TownHouse, Pocket/TownHouse, Scribner/TownHouse, Earthlight/TownHouse. Founded 1981.

Transworld Publishers*

61-63 Uxbridge Road, London W5 5SA
tel 020-8579 2652 *fax* 020-8579 5479
email info@transworld-publishers.co.uk
Chairman Mark Barty-King, *Joint Managing Directors* Larry Finlay, Patrick Janson-Smith (publishing), *Deputy Managing Director* Barry Hempstead (operations)

Division of **Random House Group Ltd**; subsidiary of Bertelsmann AG.

Bantam (imprint)
Publishing Director Francesca Liversidge

Paperback general fiction and non-fiction.

Bantam Press (imprint)
Publishing Director Sally Gaminara

Fiction, general, cookery, business, crime, health and diet, history, humour, military, music, paranormal, self-help, science, travel and adventure, biography and autobiography.

Black Swan (imprint)
Editorial Director Bill Scott-Kerr

Paperback quality fiction.

Corgi (imprint)
Editorial Director Bill Scott-Kerr

Paperback general fiction and non-fiction.

Doubleday (UK) (imprint)
Publisher Marianne Velmans
General fiction and non-fiction.

Treehouse Children's Books
2nd Floor Offices, Old Brewhouse,
Lower Charlton Trading Estate, Shepton Mallet,
Somerset BA4 5QE
tel (01749) 330529 *fax* (01749) 330544
email richard.powell4@virgin.net
Editorial Director Richard Powell
Preschool children's books and novelty books. Imprint of Emma Treehouse Ltd. Founded 1989.

Trentham Books Ltd*
Westview House, 734 London Road, Oakhill,
Stoke-on-Trent, Staffs. ST4 5NP
tel (01782) 745567 *fax* (01782) 745553
email tb@trentham.books.co.uk
website www.trentham-books.co.uk
Editorial office 28 Hillside Gardens,
London N6 5ST
tel 020-8348 2174
Directors Dr Gillian Klein (editorial), Barbara Wiggins (executive)
Education (including specialist fields – multi-ethnic issues, equal opportunities, bullying, design and technology, early years), social policy, sociology of education, European education, women's studies. Does not publish books for use by parents or children, or fiction, biography, reminiscences and poetry. Founded 1978.

Trotman & Company Ltd
2 The Green, Richmond,
Surrey TW9 1PL
tel 020-8486 1150 *fax* 020-8486 1161
website www.trotmanpublishing.co.uk
Chairman A.F. Trotman, *Managing Director* Toby Trotman, *Commissioning Editor* Rachel Lockhart
Higher education guidance, careers, classroom resources. Founded 1970.

TSO (The Stationery Office)*
Head office St Crispins, Duke Street,
Norwich NR3 1PD
tel (0870) 6005522 *fax* (0870) 6005533
website www.tso.co.uk
Chief Executive Ian Burns, *Coo* Fred Perkins, *Commercial Director* Peter Miller, *Sales & Marketing Director* J. Hook
Publishing and information management services: business, current affairs, directories, general, pharmaceutical, professional, reference, National Curriculum, Learning to Drive.

Ulric Publishing
PO Box 55, Church Stretton, Shrops. SY6 6WR
tel (01694) 781354 *fax* (01694) 781372
email books@ulric-publishing.com
website www.ulric-publishing.com
Directors Ulric Woodhams, Elizabeth Follows
Military and political history – World War Two; automobilia – classic cars; travel – unique adventures. No unsolicited MSS. Founded 1992.

University of Exeter Press*
Reed Hall, Streatham Drive, Exeter,
Devon EX4 4QR
tel (01392) 263066 *fax* (01392) 263064
email uep @exeter.ac.uk
website www.ex.ac.uk/uep/
Publisher Simon Baker
Academic and scholarly books on history, local history (Exeter and the South West), archaeology, classical studies, English literature, film history, performance studies, medieval studies, linguistics, modern languages, European studies, maritime studies, mining history. Founded 1958.

University of Wales Press
10 Columbus Walk, Brigantine Place,
Cardiff CF10 4UP
tel 029-2049 6899 *fax* 029-2049 6108
email press@press.wales.ac.uk
website www.wales.ac.uk/press
Director Susan Jenkins
Academic and educational (Welsh and English). Publishers of *Welsh History Review, Studia Celtica, Llên Cymru, Efrydiau Athronyddol, Contemporary Wales, Welsh Journal of Education, Journal of Celtic Linguistics, ALT-J (Association for Learning Technology Journal), Kantian Review. Founded 1922.*

Merlin Unwin Books
Palmers House, 7 Corve Street, Ludlow,
Shropshire SY8 1DB
tel (01584) 877456 *fax* (01584) 877457
email books@merlinunwin.co.uk
website www.countrybooksdirect.com
Proprietor Merlin Unwin
Fishing and country books. Founded 1990.

Unwin Hyman Academic – incorporated into Routledge; see Taylor and Francis Group plc

Unwin Hyman Ltd – acquired by HarperCollins Publishers

Usborne Publishing*

Usborne House, 83-85 Saffron Hill,
London EC1N 8RT
tel 020-7430 2800 *fax* 020-7430 1562
email mail@usborne.co.uk
Directors Peter Usborne, Jenny Tyler (editorial), Robert Jones, David Lowe, Keith Ball, David Harte, Lorna Hunt

Children's books: reference, practical, computers, craft, natural history, science, languages, history, geography, preschool, fiction. Founded 1973.

V&A Publications

160 Brompton Road, London SW3 1HW
tel 020-7942 2966 *fax* 020-7942 2977
website www.vandashop.co.uk/books
Head of Publications Mary Butler

Popular and scholarly books on fine and decorative arts, architecture, contemporary design, fashion and photography. Founded 1980.

Vallentine Mitchell

Crown House, 47 Chase Side,
London N14 5BP
tel 020-8920 2100 *fax* 020-8447 8548
email info@vmbooks.com
website www.vmbooks.com
Directors Frank Cass (chairman), Stewart Cass, A.E. Cass, H.J. Osen, Hon. C.V. Callman, M.P. Zaidner

Jewish history, Jewish thought, Judaism, Holocaust studies.

Van Nostrand Reinhold – acquired by John Wiley & Sons Inc.; see overseas book publishers, page 236

Variorum – see Ashgate Publishing Ltd

Vega Books Ltd

1st Floor, 64 Brewery Road, London N7 9NT
tel 020-7697 3000 *fax* 020-7697 3001
email vega@chrysalisbooks.co.uk
Publisher Will Steeds

Mind, Body & Spirit. Part of Chrysalis Books Ltd. Founded 2001.

Ventura – see The Penguin Group (UK)

Veritas Publications[†]

Veritas House, 7-8 Lower Abbey Street, Dublin 1, Republic of Ireland
tel (01) 8788177 *fax* (01) 8786507
email publications@veritas.ie
website www.veritas.ie

Liturgical and Church resources, religious school books for primary and post-primary levels, biographies, academic studies, and general books on religious, moral and social issues.

Vermilion – see Random House Group Ltd

Verso Ltd

6 Meard Street, London W1V 3HR
tel 020-7437 3546 *fax* 020-7734 0059
email verso@verso.co.uk
Directors George Galfalvi (executive chairman), Gavin Everall (sales and marketing), Robin Blackburn, Tariq Ali, Perry Anderson

Politics, sociology, economics, history, philosophy, cultural studies. Founded 1970.

Viking – see The Penguin Group (UK)

Vintage – see Random House Group Ltd

Virago – see Time Warner Books UK

Virgin Books Ltd

Thames Wharf Studios, Rainville Road,
London W6 9HA
tel 020-7386 3300 *fax* 020-7386 3360
Directors K.T. Forster (managing), Sir Richard Branson, *Management* Carolyn Thorne (editorial director, illustrated), Julia Bullock (rights), Jamie Moore (marketing), Beckie Parker (publicity), Ray Mudie (sales), Fiona Langdon (sales)

Virgin (imprint)
Editorial Carolyn Thorne (travel), Jonathan Taylor (sport), Stuart Slater (music), Kirstie Addis (general), Mark Wallace (general)

Popular culture: entertainment, showbiz, arts, film and TV, music, humour, biography and autobiography, popular reference, true crime, sport, travel.

Black Lace (imprint)
Senior Editor Kerri Sharp

Erotic fiction by women for women.

Nexus (imprint)
Editor Paul Copperwaite

Erotic fiction.

Virtue Books Ltd

Edward House, Tenter Street, Rotherham S60 1LB
tel (01709) 365005 *fax* (01709) 829982
email info@virtue.co.uk
website www.virtue.co.uk
Directors Peter E. Russum, Margaret H. Russum

Books for the professional chef: catering and drink.

The Vital Spark – see Neil Wilson Publishing Ltd

VNR – see Wiley Europe Ltd

VNU Entertainment Media UK Ltd*

Endeavour House, 189 Shaftesbury Avenue, London WC2H 8TJ
tel 020-7420 6000 *fax* 020-7836 2909
Directors Jonathan Nowell, Chris Ostrom, Paul Pounsford, Richard Knight

Reference including *The Bookseller* (1858), *Whitaker's Books in Print* (1874), and other book trade directories.

Voyager – see HarperCollins Publishers

Walker Books Ltd

87 Vauxhall Walk, London SE11 5HJ
tel 020-7793 0909 *fax* 020-7587 1123
email mail@walkerbooks.co.uk
Directors David Heatherwick, David Lloyd, Karen Lotz, Tammy Johnstone, Roger Alexander (non-executive), Michel Blake, Sarah Foster, Harold G. Gould OBE (non-executive), Mike McGrath, Henryk Wesolowski, Jane Winterbotham, *Company Secretary* Richard Wilkinson

Children's: picture books, non-fiction and novelty titles; junior and teenage fiction. Founded 1979.

Warburg Institute

University of London, Woburn Square, London WC1H 0AB
tel 020-7862 8949 *fax* 020-7862 8955
email warburg@sas.ac.uk
website www.sas.ac.uk/warburg/

Cultural and intellectual history, with special reference to the history of the classical tradition.

Ward Lock – former imprint of Weidenfeld & Nicolson

Ward Lock Educational Co. Ltd

BIC Ling Kee House, 1 Christopher Road, East Grinstead, West Sussex RH19 3BT
tel (01342) 318980 *fax* (01342) 410980
email wle@lingkee.com
website www.wardlockeducational.com
Directors Au Bak Ling (chairman, Hong Kong), Au King Kwok (Hong Kong), Au Wai Kwok (Hong Kong), Albert Kw Au (Hong Kong), *General Manager* Penny Kitchenham

Primary and secondary pupil materials, Kent Mathematics Project: KMP BASIC and KMP Main series covering Reception to GCSE, Reading Workshops, Take Part Series and Take Part Starters, teachers' books, music books, Target Series for the National Curriculum: Target Science and Target Geography, religious education. Founded 1952.

Warne – see The Penguin Group (UK)

Warner – see Time Warner Books UK

Warner/Chappell Plays Ltd – see Josef Weinberger Plays Ltd

The Watts Publishing Group Ltd*

96 Leonard Street, London EC2A 4XD
tel 020-7739 2929 *fax* 020-7739 2318
Directors Marlene Johnson (managing/publishing, Orchard), Philippa Stewart (publishing, Franklin Watts), Clare Somerville (sales), Elaine Ward (production), Zosia Knopp (rights)

Cat's Whiskers (imprint)
Publishing Director Philippa Stewart

Children's picture books.

Orchard Books (division)
Publishing Director M. Johnson

Children's picture books, fiction, poetry, novelty books, board books.

Franklin Watts (division)
Publishing Director Philippa Stewart

Children's illustrated non-fiction, reference, education. Imprint: Aladdin/Watts.

Franklin Watts – see The Watts Publishing Group Ltd

Wayland – now Hodder Wayland – see Hodder Headline Ltd

Websters International Publishers Ltd

2nd Floor, Axe & Bottle Court, 70 Newcomen Street, London SE1 1YT
tel 020-7940 4700 *fax* 020-7940 4701
Chairman and Publisher Adrian Webster, *Managing Director* Jean-Luc Barbanneau, *Publishing Director* Susannah Webster

Wine, food, travel, health. Founded 1983.

Weidenfeld & Nicolson

Orion House, 5 Upper St Martin's Lane, London WC2H 9EA
tel 020-7240 3444 *fax* 020-7379 6158
Managing Director Adrian Bourne, *Publishing Director* Richard Milner

Biography and autobiography, current affairs, history, travel, fiction, literary fiction. Part of the Orion Publishing Group Ltd.

Weidenfeld & Nicolson Illustrated
Editor-in-Chief Michael Dover

Quality illustrated non-fiction: gardening, cookery, wine, art and design, health and lifestyle, history, popular culture, archaeology, British heritage, literature, fashion, architecture, natural history, sport and adventure.

Cassell Military (imprint)
Publishing Director Ian Drury
Military history and militaria.

Seven Dials (imprint)
Managing Editor Nic Cheetham
Quality illustrated paperbacks: food and drink, gardening, heritage, history, lifestyle, art.

Cassell Reference (imprint)
Publishing Director Richard Milbank
Language and general interest reference. In association with Peter Crawley: *Master Bridge Series*.

Josef Weinberger Plays Ltd

12-14 Mortimer Street, London W1T 3JJ
tel 020-7580 2827 *fax* 020-7436 9016
email general.info@jwmail.co.uk
website www.josef-weinberger.com
Stage plays only, in both acting and trade editions. Preliminary letter essential.

Wharncliffe – see Pen & Sword Books Ltd

Which? Ltd

2 Marylebone Road, London NW1 4DF
tel 020-7770 7000 *fax* 020-7770 7660
email books@which.net
Chief Executive Sheila McKechnie, *Head of Which? Books* Robert Gray
Part of Consumers' Association. Founded 1957.

Which? Books (imprint)
Travel, restaurant, hotel and wine guides, medicine, law and personal finance for the layman, gardening, careers, DIY – all branded *Which? Books*.

J. Whitaker & Sons Ltd – see VNU Entertainment Media UK Ltd

Whittet Books Ltd

Hill Farm, Stonham Road, Cotton, Stowmarket, Suffolk IP14 4RQ
tel (01449) 781877 *fax* (01449) 781898
email annabel@whittet.dircon.co.uk
Directors Annabel Whittet, John Whittet
Natural history, countryside, poultry, pets, horses. Founded 1976.

Whurr Publishers Ltd*

19B Compton Terrace, London N1 2UN
tel 020-7359 5979 *fax* 020-7226 5290
email info@whurr.co.uk
Managing Director Colin Whurr
Disorders of human communication, medicine, psychology, psychiatry, psychotherapy, occupational therapy, physiotherapy, nursing, for professional markets only. Founded 1987.

Wiley Europe Ltd*

(incorporating Interscience Publishers)
The Atrium, Southern Gate, Chichester, West Sussex PO19 8SQ
tel (01243) 779777 *fax* (01243) 775878
email europe@wiley.co.uk
website www.wileyeurope.com
Managing Director/Senior Vice President J.H. Jarvis, *Director, STM Publishing* M. Davis, *Senior Vice President, P&T Publishing* S. Smith
Physics, chemistry, mathematics, statistics, engineering, architecture, computer science, biology, medicine, earth science, psychology, business, economics, finance. Imprints: Betty Crocker, Bible, Capstone, Cliffsnotes, Current Protocols, Ernst & Sohn, Expressexec, For Dummies, Frommer's, Howell Book House, Interscience, Jossey-Bass, Jossey-Bass/Pfeiffer, J.K. Lasser, Red Hat Press, Scripta Technica, The Unofficial Guide, Visual, Webster's New World, Wiley Academy, Wiley-Heyden, Wiley-Interscience, Wiley-Liss, ValuSource, WILEY-VCH, VNR.

Willow – see HarperCollins Publishers

Neil Wilson Publishing Ltd*

303A The Pentagon Centre, 36 Washington Street, Glasgow G3 8AZ
tel 0141-221 1117 *fax* 0141-221 5363
email info@nwp.sol.co.uk
website www.nwp.co.uk
Managing Director Neil Wilson

The Angels' Share (imprint)
website www.angelshare.co.uk
Whisky-related matters (leisure, reference, history, memoir); other food and drink categories.

11:9 (imprint)
tel 0141-204 1109
website www.11-9.co.uk
Scottish Arts Council/National Lottery-funded project to bring new Scottish fiction writing to the marketplace.

In Pinn (imprint)
website www.theinpinn.co.uk
The outdoors: travel, hillwalking, climbing, fishing.

NWP (imprint)
Scottish interest subjects including history, biography, culture and reference.

The Vital Spark (imprint)
website www.vitalspark.co.uk
Scottish humour.

Philip Wilson Publishers Ltd

7 Deane House, 27 Greenwood Place, London NW5 1LB
tel 020-7284 3088 *fax* 020-7284 3099
email pwilson@philip-wilson.co.uk
website www.philip-wilson.co.uk
Chairman P. Wilson, *Director* S. Prohaska, *Managing Editor* C. Venables, *Production Manager* N. Turpin

Fine and applied art, collecting, museums. Founded 1975.

The Windrush Press

Windrush House, Adlestrop, Moreton-in-Marsh, Glos. GL56 0YN
tel (01608) 658758/652012 *fax* (01608) 659345
email gcs@windrushpublishingservices.com
Managing Director Geoffrey Smith, *Publishing Director* Victoria Huxley

History, military history, *The Traveller's History* series, ancient mysteries. Publishes in association with the Orion Group. Founded 1987.

Woburn Press – see Frank Cass & Co. Ltd

The Women's Press

34 Great Sutton Street, London EC1V 0LQ
tel 020-7251 3007 *fax* 020-7608 1938
website www.the-womens-press.com
Managing Director Emma Drew

Books by women in the areas of literary and crime fiction, biography and autobiography, health, culture, politics, handbooks, literary criticism, psychology and self-help, the arts. Founded 1978.

Livewire (imprint)
Books for teenagers and young women.

Wooden Books

The Walkmill, Cascob, Presteigne, Powys LD8 2NT
tel (01547) 560251 *fax* (01547) 560113
website www.wooden-books.com
Directors John Martineau (managing), Anthony Brandt (secretary), Michael Glickman (overseas), Katie L'Estrange (design)

Magic, mathematics, ancient sciences, esoteric. Illustrators needed. Founded 1996.

Woodhead Publishing Ltd

Abington Hall, Abington, Cambridge CB1 6AH
tel (01223) 891358 *fax* (01223) 893694
email wp@woodhead-publishing.com
website www.woodhead-publishing.com
Managing Director Martin Woodhead

Materials engineering, welding, textiles, finance, investment, banking, business, food science and technology. Founded 1989.

Wordsworth Editions Ltd*

Cumberland House, Crib Street, Ware, Herts SG12 9ET
tel (01920) 465167 *fax* (01920) 462267
email editorial@wordsworth-editions.com
website www.wordsworth.editions.com
Directors Michael Trayler (managing), Helen Trayler (operations), Laelia Hartnoll (editorial), Dennis Hart (sales)

Reprints of classic books: literary, children's, exploration, military; myth, legend and folklore; poetry; reference. Founded 1987.

X Libris – see Time Warner Books UK

The X Press

PO Box 25694, London N17 6FP
tel 020-8801 2100 *fax* 020-8885 1322
email vibes@xpress.co.uk
Editorial Director Dotun Adebayo, *Marketing Director* Steve Pope

Black interest popular novels, particularly reflecting contemporary ethnic experiences. *Black Classics* series: reprints of classic novels by black writers. Founded 1992.

Nia (imprint)
Literary black fiction.

Y Lolfa Cyf.

Talybont, Ceredigion SY24 5AP
tel (01970) 832304 *fax* (01970) 832782
email ylolfa@ylolfa.com
website www.ylolfa.com
Director Garmon Gruffudd, *Editor* Lefi Gruffudd

Welsh-language popular fiction and non-fiction, music, children's books; Welsh-language tutors; Welsh politics in English and a range of Welsh-interest books for the tourist market. Founded 1967.

Yale University Press London*

23 Pond Street, London NW3 2PN
tel 020-7431 4422 *fax* 020-7431 3755
email firstname.lastname@yaleup.co.uk
Managing Director John Nicoll

Art, architecture, history, economics, political science, literary criticism, Asian and African studies, religion, philosophy, psychology, history of science. Founded 1961.

Yellow Jersey Press – see Random House Group Ltd

Young Picador – see Macmillan Publishers Ltd

Zed Books Ltd*

7 Cynthia Street, London N1 9JF
tel 020-7837 4014 (general) *fax* 020-7833 3960
email zed @ zedbooks.demon.co.uk
website www.zedbooks.demon.co.uk
Editors Robert Molteno, Barbara Clarke

Social sciences on international issues; women's studies, politics, development and environmental studies; area studies (Africa, Asia, Caribbean, Latin America, Middle East and the Pacific). Founded 1976.

Zero to Ten Ltd*

327 High Street, Slough, Berks SL1 1TX
tel (01753) 578499 *fax* (01753) 578488
email annamcquinn@zerototen.co.uk
Publishing Director Anna McQuinn

Non-fiction for children aged 0–10: board books, toddler books, first story books, etc. Part of the Evans Publishing Group. Founded 1997.

Cherrytree Books (imprint)
UK Publisher Su Swallow

Non-fiction children's books for schools and the trade.

Zigzag

64 Brewery Road, London N7 9NT
tel 020-7697 3000 *fax* 020-7697 3003
email zigzag@chrysalisbooks.co.uk
Head of Children's Books Steve Evans, *Publisher* Chester Fisher

Illustrated non-fiction, most including CD-Roms or other additional features. Part of Chrysalis Books Ltd. Relaunched 2001.

Zoë Books Ltd

15 Worthy Lane, Winchester, Hants SO23 7AB
tel (01962) 851318
email enquiries@zoebooks.co.uk
website www.zoebooks.co.uk
Directors I.Z. Dawson (managing publishing), C.W. Dawson, J.T. Dawson

Publishers of children's information books for the school and library markets in the UK; specialists in co-editions for world markets. No unsolicited MSS. No opportunities for freelances. Founded 1990.

Audiobook publishers

BBC Worldwide Ltd
Chivers Press Ltd
HarperCollins Publishers
Hodder Headline Ltd
Naxos Audiobooks
Random House Audio Books
Simon & Schuster Audioworks

Book packagers

Many modern illustrated books are created by book packagers, whose special skills are in the areas of book design and graphic content. In-house desk editors and art editors match up the expertise of specialist writers, artists and photographers who usually work on a freelance basis.

act-two ltd

(formerly Two-Can Design)
346 Old Street, London EC1V 9RB
tel 020-7684 4000 *fax* 020-7613 3371
email info@act-two.co.uk
Directors Andrew Jarvis (chairman), Sara Lynn (creative)

Creative development and packaging of children's products including books, magazines, partworks, CD-Roms and websites.

Aetos Ltd

69 Warminster Road, Bathampton,
Bath & NE Somerset BA2 6RU
tel (01225) 425745 *fax* (01225) 444966
email ron@aetos.co.uk
General Manager Athina Adams-Florou, *Publishing Manager* Ron Adams

Full packaging/production service, from original concept to delivery of film or finished copies. Specialises in illustrated educational and general interest books. Publishers' commissions undertaken. Opportunities for freelances.

Aladdin Books Ltd

28 Percy Street, London W1P 0LD
tel 020-7323 3319 *fax* 020-7323 4829
email aladdin@dircon.co.uk
Directors Charles Nicholas, Bibby Whittaker

Full design and book packaging facility specialising in children's non-fiction and reference. Founded 1980.

Albion Press Ltd

Spring Hill, Idbury, Oxon OX7 6RU
tel (01993) 831094 *fax* (01993) 831982
Directors Emma Bradford, Neil Philip

Quality integrated illustrated titles. Specialises in children's books. Supply finished books. Publishers' commissions undertaken. No unsolicited MSS. Founded 1984.

Alphabet & Image Ltd

Marston House, Marston Magna, Yeovil, Somerset BA22 8DH
tel (01935) 851331 *fax* (01935) 851372
Directors Anthony Birks-Hay, Leslie Birks-Hay

Complete editorial, picture research, photographic, design and production service for illustrated books on ceramics, fine art, horticulture, architecture, history, etc. Imprint: Marston House. Founded 1972.

Amber Books Ltd

Bradley's Close, 74-77 White Lion Street, London N1 9PF
tel 020-7520 7600 *fax* 020-7520 7606/7607
email enquiries@amberbooks.co.uk
website www.amberbooks.co.uk
Managing Director Stasz Gnych, *Deputy Managing Director* Sara Ballard, *Publishing Manager* Judith Samuelson, *Head of Production* Peter Thompson, *Military Editor* Charles Catton, *Design Manager* Mark Batley, *Picture Manager* Lisa Wren

Illustrated non-fiction. Subject areas include military, aviation, transport, crime, general reference and maritime. Opportunities for freelances. Imprints: Brown Books Ltd. Founded 1989.

Andromeda Oxford Ltd

11-13 The Vineyard, Abingdon, Oxon OX14 3PX
tel (01235) 550296 *fax* (01235) 550330
email mail@andromeda.co.uk
website www.andromeda.co.uk
Directors David Holyoak (managing), Graham Bateman (publishing), Clive Sparling (production), Simon Matthews (finance), Christopher Collier (sales), Linda Cole (creative)

Produces for the international market adult and junior reference books: history, natural history, geography, science, art; children's information and activity books. Founded 1986.

BCS Publishing Ltd

2nd Floor, Temple Court, 109 Oxford Road, Cowley, Oxford OX4 2ER
tel (01865) 770099 *fax* (01865) 770050
email bcs-publishing@dial.pipex.com
Managing and Art Director Steve McCurdy

Specialises in the preparation of illustrated non-fiction; provides a full creative, design, editorial and production service. Opportunities for freelances. Commissioned work undertaken.

Bender Richardson White

PO Box 266, Uxbridge, Middlesex UB9 5NX
tel (01895) 832444 *fax* (01895) 835213
email brw@brw.co.uk
Partners Lionel Bender, Kim Richardson, Ben White

Book and multimedia packaging, specialising in children's natural history, science and family information. Opportunities for freelances. Founded 1990.

BLA Publishing Ltd

BIC Ling Kee House, 1 Christopher Road, East Grinstead, West Sussex RH19 3BT
tel (01342) 318980 *fax* (01342) 410980
Directors Au Bak Ling (chairman, Hong Kong), Albert Kw Au (Hong Kong)

High quality illustrated reference books, particularly science dictionaries and encyclopedias, for the international market. Founded 1981.

Book Packaging and Marketing

3 Murswell Lane, Silverstone, Towcester, Northants. NN12 8UT
tel/fax (01327) 858380
Proprietor Martin F. Marix Evans

Illustrated general and informational non-fiction and reference for adults, especially military history, travel, countryside. Product development and project management; editorial and marketing consultancy. Very limited opportunities for freelances. Founded 1990.

Breslich & Foss Ltd

20 Wells Mews, London W1T 3HQ
tel 020-7580 8774 *fax* 020-7580 8784
Directors Paula G. Breslich, K.B. Dunning

Books produced from MS to bound copy stage from in-house ideas. Specialising in the arts, crafts, gardening, health, gift and novelty, children's. Founded 1978.

Brown Packaging Books Ltd

Bradley's Close, 74-77 White Lion Street, London N1 9PF
tel 020-7520 7600 *fax* 020-7520 7606/7607
email enquiries@amberbooks.co.uk
website www.amberbooks.co.uk
Managing Director Stasz Gnych, *Deputy Managing Director* Sara Ballard, *Publishing Manager* Judith Samuelson, *Head of Production* Peter Thompson, *Military Editor* Charles Catton, *Design Manager* Mark Batley, *Picture Manager* Lisa Wren

Highly illustrated non-fiction. Subject areas include military, aviation, transport, crime, general reference and maritime. Opportunities for freelances. Imprint: Brown Books Ltd. Founded 1989.

The Brown Reference Group Ltd

8 Chapel Place, Rivington Street, London EC2A 3DQ
tel 020-7920 7500 *fax* 020-7920 7501
email info@brownpartworks.co.uk
website www.brownpartworks.co.uk
Marketing Director Sharon Hutton

Book, partwork and continuity set packaging services for trade, promotional and international publishers. Opportunities for freelances. Founded 1989.

Brown Wells & Jacobs Ltd

Foresters Hall, 25-27 Westow Street, London SE19 3RY
tel 020-8771 5115 *fax* 020-8771 9994
email graham@popking.demon.co.uk
website www.bwj.org
Director Graham Brown

Design, editorial, illustration and production of high quality non-fiction illustrated children's books. Specialities include pop-ups and novelties. Opportunities for freelances. Founded 1979.

C&B Packaging

64 Brewery Road, London N7 9NT
tel 020-7697 3000 *fax* 020-7697 3001
email roger.bristow@cb-packaging.co.uk
Managing Director Roger Bristow

Quality illustrated non-fiction book production from conception: editorial/design, reproduction, print. Opportunities for freelances. Division of **Collins & Brown**. Part of Chrysalis Books Ltd. Founded 1998.

Calmann & King Ltd – see Laurence King Publishing Ltd

Cambridge Language Services Ltd

Greystones, Allendale, Northumberland NE47 9PX
tel/fax (01434) 683200
email paul@oakleaf.demon.co.uk
Managing Director Paul Procter

Suppliers to publishers, societies and other organisations of customised database management systems, with advanced retrieval mechanisms, and electronic publishing systems for the preparation of dictionaries, reference books, encyclopedias, catalogues, journals, archives. PC (windows) based. Founded 1982.

Cambridge Publishing Management Ltd

149B Histon Road, Cambridge CB4 3JD
tel (01223) 367288 *fax* (01223) 368237
email initial.surname@cambridgepm.co.uk
website www.cambridgepm.co.uk
Managing Director Jackie Dobbyne, *Publishing Director* Julia Morris

Full editorial and book production service, from market research to delivery of film or electronic files. Specialises in education, ELT, travel and illustrated non-fiction – particularly architecture and art history. Opportunities for freelances. Founded 1999.

Cameron Books

PO Box 1, Moffat, Dumfriesshire DG10 9SU
tel (01683) 220808 *fax* (01683) 220012
email editorial@cameronbooks.co.uk
website www.cameronbooks.co.uk
Directors Ian A. Cameron, Jill Hollis

Illustrated non-fiction: fine arts (including environmental and land art), film, the decorative arts, crafts, architecture, design, antiques, collecting, natural history, environmental studies, social history, food. Founded 1976.
Edition: Design, editing, typesetting, production work from concept to finished book for galleries, museums, institutions and other publishers. Founded 1975.

Canopus Publishing Ltd

Suite 2, Piccadilly House, London Road, Bath BA1 6PL
tel/fax (01225) 789850
email robin@canopusbooks.com
website www.canopusbooks.com
Director Robin Rees

Highly illustrated popular science and astronomy titles for international markets. Founded 1999.

Carroll & Brown Ltd

20 Lonsdale Road, London NW6 6RD
tel 020-7372 0900 *fax* 020-7372 0460
email mail@carrollandbrown.co.uk
Directors Amy Carroll (managing), Denise Brown (creative)

Editorial and design through to final film and printing of cookery, health, craft, Mind, Body & Spirit, and lifestyle titles. Opportunities for freelances. Founded 1989.

Roger Coote Publishing

Gissing's Farm, Fressingfield, Eye, Suffolk IP21 5SH
tel (01379) 588044 *fax* (01379) 588055
email rgc@ndirect.co.uk
Director Roger Goddard-Coote

High quality illustrated children's non-fiction titles for trade, institutional and international markets. Commissions undertaken. Freelance opportunities for editors and designers. Founded 1989.

Cowley Hunter Robinson Ltd

8 Belmont, Bath BA1 5DZ
tel (01225) 339999 *fax* (01225) 339995
Directors Lee Robinson (chairman), Clyde Hunter (managing), Stewart Cowley (publishing), Rob Kendrew (production)

Children's international co-editions. Novelty format creation. Licence and character publishing developments. Information and early learning. Founded 1998.

Design Eye Ltd

4th Floor, The Fitzpatrick Building, 188-194 York Way, London N7 9QP
tel 020-7700 7654 *fax* 020-7700 3890
Managing Director Jeffrey Nobbs

Packager and publisher of interactive kit books for adults and children: arts and crafts, science, history and fiction. Opportunities for freelances. Member of the Quarto Group. Founded 1988.

Diagram Visual Information Ltd

195 Kentish Town Road, London NW5 2JU
tel 020-7482 3633 *fax* 020-7482 4932
email diagramvis@aol.com
Director Bruce Robertson

Research, writing, design and illustration of reference books, supplied as film or disk. Opportunities for freelances. Founded 1967.

Earthscape Editions

Greys Court Farm, Greys Court, Henley on Thames, Oxon RG9 4PG
tel (01491) 628188 *fax* (01491) 628189
Partners B.J. Knapp, D.L.R. McCrae

High quality, full colour, illustrated children's text and information books, including co-editions, for education and library market. No unsolicited MSS accepted. Founded 1987.

Eddison Sadd Editions Ltd

St Chad's House, 148 King's Cross Road, London WC1X 9DH
tel 020-7837 1968 *fax* 020-7837 2025
email reception@eddisonsadd.co.uk
Directors Nick Eddison, Ian Jackson, David Owen, Elaine Partington, Charles James, Susan Cole

Illustrated non-fiction books and kits for the international co-edition market. Broad, popular list with emphasis on Mind, Body & Spirit and complementary health. Founded 1982.

First Rank Publishing

5 Rochester Gardens, Hove, East Sussex BN3 3AW
tel (01273) 326376
email byron@firstrank.co.uk
website www.firstrank.co.uk
Proprietor Byron Jacobs

Packager and publisher of sports, games and leisure books. No unsolicited MSS but ideas and synopses welcome. Payment usually fees. Also provides editorial, production and typesetting services. Founded 1996.

Focus Publishing

11A St Botolph's Road, Sevenoaks, Kent TN13 3AJ
tel (01732) 742456 *fax* (01732) 743381
email focus-publishing@netway.co.uk
website www.focus-publishing.co.uk
Partners Guy Croton, Caroline Watson

Illustrated non-fiction: gardening, wine and food, sex and health, sport, aviation, DIY and crafts, transport. Opportunities for freelances. Founded 1997.

Graham-Cameron Publishing & Illustration

The Studio, 23 Holt Road, Sheringham, Norfolk NR26 8NB
tel (01263) 821333 *fax* (01263) 821334
Directors Mike Graham-Cameron, Helen Graham-Cameron

Educational and children's books; information publications; sponsored publications. Illustration agency with 37 artists. Editorial and production services. NB: No unsolicited MSS. Founded 1984.

Hardlines Ltd

Park Street, Charlbury, Oxon OX7 3PS
tel (01608) 811255 *fax* (01608) 811442
email info@hardlines.co.uk
website www.hardlines.co.uk
Managing Director R. Hickey, *Directors* P. Wilkinson, G. Walker

Primary, secondary academic education (geography, science, modern languages) and co-editions (travel guides, gardening, cookery). Multimedia (CD-Rom programming and animations). Opportunities for freelances. Founded 1985.

Hart McLeod Ltd

14 Greenside, Waterbeach, Cambridge CB5 9HP
tel (01223) 861495 *fax* (01223) 862902
email hmcl@dial.pipex.com
Directors Graham Hart, Chris McLeod

Primarily educational and general non-fiction with particular experience of revision books, school texts, ELT. Opportunities for freelances. Founded 1985.

Angus Hudson Ltd

Concorde House, Grenville Place, London NW7 3SA
tel 020-8959 3668 *fax* 020-8959 3678
email coed@angushudson.com
website www.angushudson.com
Directors Nicholas Jones (managing), Stephen Price (production), Rodney Shepherd (operations), Geoffrey Benge

Adult and children's Christian books including international co-editions. Publishing imprints: Candle Books and Monarch Books. Founded 1971.

The Ivy Press Ltd

The Old Candlemakers, West Street, Lewes, East Sussex BN7 2NZ
tel (01273) 487440 *fax* (01273) 487441
email surname@ivypress.co.uk
Directors Peter Bridgewater, Jenny Manstead, Terry Jeavons, Sophie Collins

Illustrated books on art, lifestyle, popular culture and design. Opportunities for freelances. Founded 1995.

Lennard Books

Windmill Cottage, Mackerye End, Harpenden, Herts. AL5 5DR
tel (01582) 715866
email stephenson@lennardqap.co.uk
Directors K.A.A. Stephenson, R.H. Stephenson

Commissioned projects only. Division of Lennard Associates Ltd.

Lexus Ltd

60 Brook Street, Glasgow G40 2AB
tel 0141-556 0440 *fax* 0141-556 2202
email pt@lexus.win-uk.net
Director P.M. Terrell

Reference book publishing (especially bilingual dictionaries) as contractor, packager, consultant; translation. Founded 1980.

Lionheart Books
10 Chelmsford Square, London NW10 3AR
tel 020-8459 0453 *fax* 020-8451 3681
email lionheart.brw@btinternet.com
Partners Lionel Bender (editorial), Madeleine Bender (editorial), Ben White (design)

Handles all aspects of editorial and design packaging of, mostly, children's illustrated science, natural history and history projects. Founded 1985.

Market House Books Ltd
2 Market House, Market Square, Aylesbury, Bucks. HP20 1TN
tel (01296) 484911 *fax* (01296) 437073
email books@mhbref.com
website www.mhbref.com
Directors Dr Alan Isaacs, Dr John Daintith, P.C. Sapsed

Compilation of dictionaries, encyclopedias, and reference books. Founded 1970.

Marshall Cavendish Partworks Ltd
119 Wardour Street, London W1F 0UW
tel 020-7734 6710 *fax* 020-7734 6221
website www.marshallcavendish.co.uk
New Product Development Manager Ann Davies

Cookery, crafts, gardening, do-it-yourself, general illustrated non-fiction. Founded 1969.

Marshall Editions Ltd
The Old Brewery, 6 Blundell Street, London N7 9BH
tel 020-7700 6700 *fax* 020-7700 4191
email info@marshalleditions.com

Highly illustrated non-fiction for adults and children, including health, gardening, lifestyle, self-improvement, leisure, popular science and visual information for children. Founded 1977.

Monkey Puzzle Media Ltd
Gissing's Farm, Fressingfield, Eye, Suffolk IP21 5SH
tel (01379) 588044 *fax* (01379) 588055
email rgc@ndirect.co.uk
Director Roger Goddard-Coote

High-quality illustrated children's and adult non-fiction for trade, institutional and mass markets worldwide. Publishers' commissions undertaken.

Orpheus Books Ltd
2 Church Green, Witney, Oxon OX28 4AW
tel (01993) 774949 *fax* (01993) 700330
email info@orpheusbooks.com
Executive Director Nicholas Harris (editorial, design and marketing)

Children's illustrated non-fiction/reference. Opportunities for freelance artists. Founded 1992.

Pinwheel Ltd
Station House, 8-13 Swiss Terrace, London NW6 4RR
tel 020-7586 5100 *fax* 020-7483 1999
email angela.brooksbank@pinwheel.co.uk
shaheen.bilgrami@pinwheel.co.uk
website www.pinwheel.co.uk
Art Director Angela Brooksbank, *Commissioning Editor* Shaheen Bilgrami

Novelty books for children under 5. opportunities for freelances. Founded 1995.

Playne Books Ltd
Chapel House, Trefin, Haverfordwest, Pembrokeshire SA62 5AU
tel (01348) 837073 *fax* (01348) 837063
email playne.books@virgin.net
Design and Production David Playne, *Editor* Gill Davies

Specialises in highly illustrated adult non-fiction and books for very young children. All stages of production undertaken from initial concept (editorial, design and manufacture) to delivery of completed books. Include sae for return of work. Founded 1987.

Mathew Price Ltd
The Old Glove Factory, Bristol Road, Sherborne, Dorset DT9 4HP
tel (01935) 816010 *fax* (01935) 816310
email mathewp@mathewprice.com
Chairman Mathew Price

Illustrated fiction and non-fiction children's books for all ages for the international market. Specialist in flap, pop-up, paper-engineered titles. Founded 1983.

Quarto Children's Books Ltd
3rd Floor, The Fitzpatrick Building, 188-194 York Way, London N7 9QP
tel 020-7607 3322 *fax* 020-7700 2951
Editorial Director Beck Ward, *Managing Director* Jeffrey Nobbs

Highly illustrated children's non-fiction.

Apple Press (imprint)
Leisure, domestic and craft pursuits; cookery, gardening, sport, transport, children's.

Quarto Publishing plc/Quintet Publishing Ltd
The Old Brewery, 6 Blundell Street, London N7 9BH
tel 020-7700 6700 *fax* 020-7700 4191
Publisher (Quarto) Piers Spence, *Publisher (Quintet)* Oliver Salzmann, *Directors* L.F. Orbach, R.J. Morley, M.J. Mousley

International co-editions. Founded 1976/1984.

Sadie Fields Productions Ltd

Penthouse Studio, 4C/D West Point, 36-37 Warple Way, London W3 0RG
tel 020-8996 9970 *fax* 020-8996 9977
email sales@tangobooks.co.uk
Directors Sheri Safran, David Fielder

Creates and produces international co-editions of books, plus pop-up, touch-and-feel, and other novelty books for children. Imprint: Tango Books. Founded 1983.

Savitri Books Ltd

115J Cleveland Street, London W1P 5PN
tel 020-7436 9932 *fax* 020-7580 6330
email munni@savitribooks.demon.co.uk
Director Mrinalini S. Srivastava

Packaging, publishing, design, production. Founded 1983.

Studio Cactus Ltd

13 Southgate Street, Winchester, Hants SO23 9DZ
tel (01962) 878600 *fax* (01962) 850209
email mail@studiocactus.co.uk
website www.studiocactus.co.uk
Editorial Director Damien Moore, *Art Director* Amanda Lunn

High-quality illustrated non-fiction books for the international market. Undertakes book packaging/production service, from initial concept to delivery of final electronic files. Opportunities for freelances. Founded 1998.

Tangerine Designs Ltd

2 High Street, Freshford, Bath BA2 7WE
tel (01225) 722382 *fax* (01225) 722856
email tangerinedesigns@aol.com
website www.tangerinedesigns.co.uk
Managing Director Christine Swift

Packagers and co-edition publishers of children's novelty books including licensed titles. Innovative new concepts sought. Foreign rights and co-edition agent to publishers. Freelance enquiries invited (in writing only). Founded 2000.

The Templar Company plc

Pippbrook Mill, London Road, Dorking, Surrey RH4 1JE
tel (01306) 876361 *fax* (01306) 889097
email info@templar.co.uk
website www.templarco.co.uk
Directors Amanda Wood, Ruth Huddleston, Elaine Hunt

Children's gift, novelty, picture and illustrated information books; most titles aimed at international co-edition market. Established links with major co-publishers in USA, Australia and throughout Europe.

Toucan Books Ltd

3rd Floor, 89 Charterhouse Street, London EC1M 6PE
tel 020-7250 3388 *fax* 020-7250 3123
Directors Robert Sackville West, Adam Nicolson, Jane MacAndrew

International co-editions; editorial, design and production services. Founded 1985.

Tucker Slingsby Ltd

Roebuck House, 288 Upper Richmond Road West, London SW14 7JG
tel 020-8876 6310 *fax* 020-8876 4104
email firstname@tuckerslingsby.co.uk
Directors Janet Slingsby, Del Tucker

Creation, editorial and design to disk, film or finished copy of children's books, magazines and general interest adult books. Commissioned work undertaken. Opportunities for freelances and picture book artists. Founded 1993.

Ventura Publishing Ltd

80 Strand, London WC2R 0RL
tel 020-7010 3000 *fax* 020-7010 6707
email funwithspot@penguin.co.uk
website www.funwithspot.com
Managing Director Sally Floyer

Specialises in production of the *Spot* books by Eric Hill.

Wordwright Books

8 St Johns Road, Saxmundham, Suffolk IP17 1BE
tel (01728) 604204 *fax* (01728) 604029
email wordwright@clara.co.uk
Director Charles Perkins

Full packaging/production service – from concept to delivery of film or finished copies. Produces illustrated non-fiction. Also assesses and prepares MSS for the US market. Publishes a small general fiction list. Founded 1987.

Working Partners Ltd

1 Albion Place, London W6 0QT
tel 020-8748 7477 *fax* 020-8748 7450
email enquiries@workingpartnersltd.co.uk
website www.workingpartnersltd.co.uk
Chairman Ben Baglio, *Managing Director* Chris Snowdon, *Creative Director* Rod Ritchie, *Editorial Director* Deborah Smith

Children's and young adult fiction – series, trilogies, single titles. Founded 1995.

Publishers of fiction

Addresses for Book publishers UK and Ireland start on page 141.

Adventure/thrillers

Allison & Busby Ltd
Arcadia Books Ltd
Bantam
Bantam Press
Black Ace Books
Black Swan
Blackstaff Press Ltd
Bloomsbury Publishing Plc
Breese Books Ltd
Chatto & Windus
Faber & Faber Ltd
Gairm Publications
The Gay Men's Press
Robert Hale Ltd
Headline Book Publishing Ltd
Honno Ltd (Welsh Women's Press)
Macmillan Publishers Ltd
Mentor Books
The Orion Publishing Group Ltd
Penguin Group (UK)
Piatkus Books
Pipers' Ash Ltd
Random House Group Ltd
Souvenir Press Ltd
Summersdale Publishers Ltd
Time Warner Books UK
Town House and Country House
Vintage
Virago
Warner

Crime/mystery/suspense

Allison & Busby Ltd
Arcadia Books Ltd
Arrow Books Ltd
Bantam
Bantam Press
Black Ace Books
Black Swan
Bloomsbury Publishing Plc
Breese Books Ltd
Canongate Books Ltd
Corgi
Coronet
Everyman Publishers plc
Faber & Faber Ltd
Flambard Press
Gairm Publications
The Gay Men's Press
Robert Hale Ltd
Hamish Hamilton
HarperCollins Publishers
Headline Book Publishing Ltd
William Heinemann
Hodder & Stoughton
Honno Ltd (Welsh Women's Press)
Hutchinson
Michael Joseph
Macmillan Publishers Ltd
Mentor Books
Methuen Publishing Ltd
New English Library
Oldcastle Books Ltd
Michael O'Mara Books Ltd
Onlywomen Press Ltd
The Orion Publishing Group Ltd
Pan
Penguin Group (UK)
Piatkus Books
Polygon
Random House Group Ltd
Sceptre
Serpent's Tail
Severn House Publishers
Souvenir Press Ltd
Summersdale Publishers Ltd
Time Warner Books UK
Town House and Country House
Transworld Publishers
Viking
Vintage
Virago
The Women's Press
The X Press

Gay/lesbian

Arcadia Books Ltd
Bantam
Black Swan
Corgi
The Gay Men's Press
Hamish Hamilton
HarperCollins Publishers
Honno Ltd (Welsh Women's Press)
Macmillan Publishers Ltd
MQ Publications Ltd
Michael O'Mara Books Ltd
Onlywomen Press Ltd
Penguin Group (UK)
Polygon
Sceptre
Serpent's Tail
Summersdale Publishers Ltd
Time Warner Books UK
Transworld Publishers
Vintage
Virago
The Women's Press

General

Abacus
Allison & Busby Ltd
Bantam
Bantam Press
Black Ace Books
Black Swan
Blackstaff Press Ltd
Bloomsbury Publishing Plc
Calder Publications Ltd
Jonathan Cape
Century
Chatto & Windus
Cló Iar-Chonnachta Teo.
Corgi
Crescent Moon Publishing
Doubleday (UK)
Gairm Publications
The Gallery Press
Garnet Publishing Ltd
Victor Gollancz Ltd
Robert Hale Ltd
Hamish Hamilton
HarperCollins Publishers
Headline Book Publishing Ltd
William Heinemann
Hodder & Stoughton
Honno Ltd (Welsh Women's Press)

John Hunt Publishing Ltd
Hutchinson
Michael Joseph
Karnak House
Macmillan Publishers Ltd
Marino Books
Mentor Books
Methuen Publishing Ltd
MQ Publications Ltd
New English Library
New Island Books
The Oleander Press
Michael O'Mara Books Ltd
The Orion Publishing Group Ltd
Pan
Paternoster
Penguin Group (UK)
Piatkus Books
Pocket Books
Poolbeg Group Services Ltd
Random House Group Ltd
Route
Sceptre
SCP Publishers Ltd
Secker and Warburg
Seren
Serpent's Tail
Severn House Publishers
Simon & Schuster
Souvenir Press Ltd
Summersdale Publishers Ltd
Time Warner Books UK
Town House and Country House
Viking
Vintage
Virago
Warner
The Women's Press
Y Lolfa Cyf.

Historical

Allison & Busby Ltd
Bantam
Bantam Press
Birlinn Ltd
Black Ace Books
Blackstaff Press Ltd
Jonathan Cape
Doubleday (UK)
Everyman Publishers plc
Flambard Press
The Gay Men's Press
Victor Gollancz Ltd
Robert Hale Ltd
HarperCollins Publishers
Headline Book Publishing Ltd
William Heinemann
Hodder & Stoughton
Honno Ltd (Welsh Women's Press)
John Hunt Publishing Ltd
Hutchinson
Michael Joseph
Karnak House
Macmillan Publishers Ltd
Mentor Books
Methuen Publishing Ltd
MQ Publications Ltd
The Oleander Press
Onlywomen Press Ltd
The Orion Publishing Group Ltd
Pan
Penguin Group (UK)
Random House Group Ltd
Sceptre
SCP Publishers Ltd
Severn House Publishers
Souvenir Press Ltd
Summersdale Publishers Ltd
Time Warner Books UK
Vintage
Virago
Warner
The Women's Press

Literary

Abacus
Allison & Busby Ltd
Arcadia Books Ltd
Atlantic Books
Bantam
Bantam Press
Black Ace Books
Black Swan
BlackAmber Books Ltd
Blackstaff Press Ltd
Bloomsbury Publishing Plc
Marion Boyars Publishers Ltd
Calder Publications Ltd
Canongate Books Ltd
Jonathan Cape
Cassell
Chapman Publishing
Chatto & Windus
Corgi
Crescent Moon Publishing
Dedalus Ltd
Doubleday (UK)
Enitharmon Press
Everyman Publishers plc
Faber & Faber Ltd
Flambard Press
Flamingo
The Gay Men's Press
Victor Gollancz Ltd
Gomer Press
Granta Publications
Robert Hale Ltd
Hamish Hamilton
HarperCollins Publishers
The Harvill Press
Headline Book Publishing Ltd
William Heinemann
Hodder & Stoughton
Honno Ltd
Hutchinson
Karnak House
Libris Ltd
The Lilliput Press Ltd
Macmillan Publishers Ltd
Mentor Books
The Mercier Press
Methuen Publishing Ltd
New Beacon Books
The Oleander Press
The Orion Publishing Group Ltd
Peter Owen Ltd
Pan
Paternoster
Penguin Group (UK)
Piatkus Books
Picador
Polygon
Quartet Books Ltd
Random House Group Ltd
Sceptre
SCP Publishers Ltd
Secker and Warburg
Seren
Serpent's Tail
Simon & Schuster
Skoob Russell Square
Souvenir Press Ltd
Summersdale Publishers Ltd
Time Warner Books UK
Town House and Country House
Viking
Vintage
Virago
The Women's Press
The X Press

Romantic

Bantam
Bantam Press
Black Swan
Corgi
Coronet
Doubleday (UK)
Robert Hale Ltd
Harlequin Mills & Boon Ltd
Headline Book Publishing Ltd
William Heinemann
Hodder & Stoughton
Honno Ltd (Welsh Women's Press)
Macmillan Publishers Ltd
Mentor Books
Monarch Books
The Orion Publishing Group Ltd
Pan
Piatkus Books
Random House Group Ltd

Severn House Publishers
Silhouette®
Time Warner Books UK
Transworld Publishers
Warner

Science fiction/fantasy

Arrow Books Ltd
Bantam
Bantam Press
Black Swan
Corgi
Coronet
Gollancz
Victor Gollancz Ltd
HarperCollins Publishers
Headline Book Publishing Ltd
Hodder & Stoughton
Honno Ltd (Welsh Women's Press)
Macmillan Publishers Ltd
New English Library
Orbit
The Orion Publishing Group Ltd
Pan
Penguin Group (UK)
Pipers' Ash Ltd
Random House Group Ltd
Simon & Schuster
Souvenir Press Ltd
Time Warner Books UK
Voyager
The Women's Press

Short stories

Blackstaff Press Ltd
Breese Books Ltd
Jonathan Cape
Chapman Publishing
Chatto & Windus
Everyman Publishers plc
Faber & Faber Ltd
Flambard Press
Gairm Publications
Hamish Hamilton
William Heinemann
Hodder & Stoughton
Honno Ltd (Welsh Women's Press)
Karnak House
Macmillan Publishers Ltd
Methuen Publishing Ltd
Pan
Penguin Group (UK)
Pipers' Ash Ltd
Polygon
Random House Group Ltd
SCP Publishers Ltd
Secker and Warburg
Seren
Town House and Country House
The Women's Press
Y Lolfa Cyf.

Other

Ethnic

Arcadia Books Ltd
Honno Ltd (Welsh Women's Press)
MQ Publications Ltd
Skoob Russell Square
Souvenir Press Ltd
Summersdale Publishers Ltd
The Women's Press
The X Press

Erotic

Black Lace
Honno Ltd (Welsh Women's Press)
Nexus
Souvenir Press Ltd
Summersdale Publishers Ltd
The Women's Press
X Libris
The X Press

Graphic

Knockabout Comics
Titan Books

Horror

Mentor Books
Titan Books
Warner

Humour

Black Swan
Breese Books Ltd
Corgi
Everyman Publishers plc
Victor Gollancz Ltd
Methuen Publishing Ltd
The Oleander Press
Michael O'Mara Books Ltd
The Orion Publishing Group Ltd
Paternoster
Piccadilly Press
Souvenir Press Ltd
Summersdale Publishers Ltd
Warner
The Women's Press

New/experimental

Calder Publications Ltd
Canongate Books Ltd
Crescent Moon Publishing
Faber & Faber Ltd
Flambard Press
Honno Ltd (Welsh Women's Press)
Polygon
Quartet Books Ltd
Seren
Serpent's Tail
Stride Publications
Summersdale Publishers Ltd
The X Press

Translations

Arcadia Books Ltd
Calder Publications Ltd
Enitharmon Press
Everyman Publishers plc
Faber & Faber Ltd
Flambard Press
Gomer Press
The Harvill Press
Honno Ltd (Welsh Women's Press)
The Oleander Press
The Orion Publishing Group Ltd
Peter Owen Ltd
Pipers' Ash Ltd
Quartet Books Ltd
Seren
Serpent's Tail
Skoob Russell Square
Souvenir Press Ltd
Summersdale Publishers Ltd
The Women's Press

War

Calder Publications Ltd
The Orion Publishing Group Ltd
Pipers' Ash Ltd
Severn House Publishers
Souvenir Press Ltd
Summersdale Publishers Ltd

Westerns

Robert Hale Ltd
Pipers' Ash Ltd

Book publishers overseas

Listings are given for book publishers in Australia (below), Canada (page 215), New Zealand (page 218), South Africa (page 220) and the USA (page 222).

Australia

**Member of the Australian Publishers Association*

Access Press

54 Railway Parade, Bassendean, Western Australia 6054
postal address PO Box 446, Bassendean, Western Australia 6054
tel (08) 9379 3188 *fax* (08) 9379 3199
Managing Editor Helen Weller

Australiana, poetry, children's, history, general. Privately financed books published and distributed. Founded 1979.

Allen & Unwin Pty Ltd*

83 Alexander Street, Crows Nest, NSW 2065
postal address PO Box 8500, St Leonards, NSW 1590
tel (02) 8425 0100 *fax* (02) 9906 2218
email info@allenandunwin.com
website www.allenandunwin.com

General trade, including fiction and children's books, academic, especially social science and history.

Michelle Anderson Publishing Pty Ltd*

86 Bourke Street, Melbourne, Victoria 3000
tel (03) 9662 2282 *fax* (03) 9662 2527
email hocpub@collinsbooks.com.au
website http://hillofcontent@bizland.com
Directors M. Slamen, Michelle Anderson

Health and Mind, Body & Spirit. Licensed imprint of Hill of Content.

The Australian Council for Educational Research Ltd*

19 Prospect Hill Road, Private Bag 55, Camberwell, Victoria 3124
tel (03) 9277 5555 *fax* (03) 9277 5500
email info@acer.edu.au
website www.acerpress.com.au

Range of books and kits: for teachers, trainee teachers, parents, psychologists, counsellors, students of education, researchers.

Blackwell Publishing Asia Pty Ltd

550 Swanston Street, Carlton South, Victoria 3053
tel (03) 9347 0300 *fax* (03) 9347 5001
email info@blackwellpublishing.com
website www.blackwellpublishingasia.com
Group President Mark Robertson

Medical, healthcare, life, earth sciences, professional.

Cambridge University Press Australian Branch*

477 Williamstown Road, Port Melbourne, Victoria 3207
tel (03) 8671 1411 *fax* (03) 9676 9955
email info@cambridge.edu.au
website www.cambridge.edu.au
Director Sandra McComb

Academic, educational, reference, English as a second language.

Dominie Pty Ltd

Drama Department, 8 Cross Street, Brookvale, NSW 2100
tel (02) 9905 0201 *fax* (02) 9905 5209
email dominie@dominie.com.au
website www.dominie.com.au

Australian representatives of publishers of plays and agents for the collection of royalties for Samuel French Ltd, incorporating Hanbury Plays and Samuel French Inc., The Society of Authors, Bakers Plays of Boston, Nick Hern Books, Pioneer Drama and Dramatic Publishing.

Harcourt Australia Pty Ltd

30-52 Smidmore Street, Marrickville, NSW 2204
tel (02) 9517 8999 *fax* (02) 9550 6007
Managing Director Fergus Hall

Novels, children's, academic, medical and scientific books. Imprints: Harcourt Brace; Holt, Rinehart and Winston; W.B. Saunders/Ballière Tindall; Saunders College; The Psychological Corporation; Academic Press, Churchill Livingstone; Morgan Kaufmann; Industrial Press; Technomic Publishing, Mosby. Established 1972.

HarperCollins Publishers (Australia) Pty Limited Group*
25-31 Ryde Road, Pymble, NSW 2073
postal address PO Box 321, Pymble, NSW 2073
tel (02) 9952 5000 *fax* (02) 9952 5555
Managing Director Brian Murray
Literary fiction and non-fiction, popular fiction, reference, biography, autobiography, current affairs, sport, lifestyle, health/self-help, humour, true crime, travel, Australiana, history, business, gift/stationery, religion.

Hill of Content Publishing Co. Pty Ltd – see Michelle Anderson Publishing Pty Ltd

Hodder Headline Australia Pty Ltd*
Level 22, 201 Kent Street, Sydney, NSW 2000
tel (02) 8248 0800 *fax* (02) 2848 0810
email auspub@hha.com.au
website www.hha.com.au
Directors Malcolm Edwards (managing), Lisa Highton, Mary Drum, David Cocking
General, children's. No unsolicited MSS.

Kangaroo Press – see Simon & Schuster (Australia) Pty Ltd

Lawbook Co.*
PO Box 3502, Rozelle, NSW 2039
tel (02) 8587 7000 *fax* (02) 8587 7100
email service@thomson.com.au
website www.lawbookco.com.au
Law.

LexisNexis Butterworths Australia*
Tower 2, 475-495 Victoria Avenue, Chatswood, NSW 2067
postal address Level 9, Locked Bag 2222, Chatswood Delivery Centre, Chatswood, NSW 2067
tel (02) 9422 2222 *fax* (02) 9422 2444
website www.butterworths.com.au
Managing Director Murray Hamilton, *Editorial/Deputy Managing Director* J. Broadfoot
Legal, tax and commercial. Division of Reed International Books Australia Pty Ltd.

Lonely Planet Publications*
Corner Maribyrnong and Parker Streets, Footscray 3011, Victoria
tel (03) 8379 8000 *fax* (03) 8379 8079
email talk2us@lonelyplanet.com.au
website www.lonelyplanet.com
Travel guidebooks, phrasebooks, travel literature, pictorial books, city maps; diving and snorkelling, walking, health, restaurant, pre-departure guidebooks, world food, condensed pocket guides. Offices in London, Paris and Oakland, USA. Founded 1973.

Lothian Books*
Level 5, 132-136 Albert Road, South Melbourne, Victoria 3205
tel 613-9694-4900 *fax* 613-9645-0705
email books@lothian.com.au
website www.lothian.com.au
Chairman/Managing Director P. Lothian, *Directors* B. Hilliard
Juveniles, health, gardening, reference, Australian history, business, sport, biography, New Age, humour.

Macmillan Education Australia Pty Ltd*
Melbourne office Locked Bag 1, Prahran, Victoria 3181
tel (03) 9825 1025 *fax* (03) 9825 1010
email mea@macmillan.com.au
Sydney office Level 2, St Martin's Tower, 31 Market Street, Sydney, NSW 2000
tel (02) 9264 0522 *fax* (02) 9264 0770
email measyd@macmillan.com.au
Directors Richard Charkin (chief executive – UK), Ross Gibb (executive chairman), Shane Armstrong (managing), Peter Huntley (sales), Sandra Iversen (primary publishing), Rex Parry (secondary publishing), George Smith (production), *Company Secretary/Financial Controller* Terry White
Educational books.

Melbourne University Press*
268 Drummond Street, Carlton, Victoria 3053
postal address PO Box 278, Carlton South, Victoria 3053
tel (03) 9342 0300 *fax* (03) 9342 0399
email mup-info@unimelb.edu.au
website www.mup.com.au
Director John Meckan
Academic, scholastic and cultural; educational textbooks and books of reference. Imprint: Miegunyah Press. Founded 1922.

Mimosa Publications Pty Ltd – see Weldon Russell Pty Ltd

Pan Macmillan Australia Pty Ltd*
Level 18, 31 Market Street, Sydney, NSW 2000
tel (02) 9285 9100 *fax* (02) 9285 9190
email pansyd@macmillan.com.au
website www.macmillan.com.au
Directors Ross Gibb (chairman), James Fraser (publishing), Roxarne Burns (publishing), Siv Toigo (finance), Peter Phillips (sales), Jeannine Fowler (publicity and marketing)
Commercial and literary fiction; children's fiction, non-fiction and character products; non-fiction; sport.

Penguin Books Australia Ltd*
250 Camberwell Road, Camberwell, Victoria 3124
postal address PO Box 257, Ringwood, Victoria 3134
tel (03) 9871 2400 *fax* (03) 9870 9618
website www.penguin.com.au
Ceo P.J. Field, *Publishing Director* R.P. Sessions
Fiction, general non-fiction, current affairs, sociology, economics, environmental, travel guides, anthropology, politics, children's, health, cookery, gardening, pictorial and general books relating to Australia under Penguin Books and Viking imprints. Founded 1946.

Random House Australia Pty Ltd*
20 Alfred Street, Milsons Point, NSW 2061
tel (02) 9954 9966 *fax* (02) 9954 4562
email random@randomhouse.com.au
website www.randomhouse.com.au
Managing Director Margaret Seale, *Coo* Andrew Davis, *Head of Publishing, Random House* Jane Palfreyman, *Head of Publishing, Bantam Doubleday* Fiona Henderson, *Children's Publisher* Linsay Knight, *Illustrated Publisher* James Mills-Hicks, *Head of Sales* Amanda Roberts, *Head of Media & Marketing* Maggie Hamilton, *Business Manager* Andrew Leake, *Rights Manager* Nerrilee Weir
General fiction and non-fiction; children's, illustrated. MSS submissions – for Random House and Transworld Publishing, unsolicited non-fiction accepted, unbound in hard copy addressed to Submissions Editor. Fiction submissions are only accepted from previously published authors, or authors represented by an agent or accompanied by a report from an accredited assessment service.
Imprints: Arrow, Avon, Ballantine, Bantam, Black Swan, Broadway, Century, Chatto & Windus, Corgi, Crown, Dell, Doubleday, Ebury, Fodor, Heinemann, Hutchinson, Jonathan Cape, Knopf, Mammoth UK, Minerva, Pantheon, Pavilion, Pimlico, Random House, Red Fox, Rider, Vermillion, Vintage, Virgin. Agencies: BBC Worldwide. Subsidiary of Bertelsmann AG.

Reed Educational & Professional Publishing Australia*
22 Salmon Street, Port Melbourne, Victoria 3207
tel (03) 9245 7111 *fax* (03) 9245 7333
Managing Director David O'Brien
Art, chemistry, chemical engineering, environmental studies, geography, geology, health, nutrition, history, mathematics, physics, languages. Primary, Secondary; electronic publishing. Division of Reed Elsevier Australia. Founded 1982.

Reeve Books
54 Railway Parade, Bassendean, Western Australia 6054
postal address PO Box 446, Bassendean, Western Australia 6054
tel (08) 9379 3188 *fax* (08) 9379 3199
Managing Director/Editor Helen Weller
Biography, local history, general non-fiction. Commissioned works only. Founded 1987.

Rigby Heinemann – now Reed Educational & Professional Publishing Australia

Samuel French Ltd – see Dominie Pty Ltd

Scholastic Australia Pty Ltd*
PO Box 579, Gosford, NSW 2250
tel (02) 4328 3555 *fax* (02) 4323 3827
website www.scholastic.com.au
Managing Director Ken Jolly
Children's fiction/non-fiction; educational materials for elementary schools, teacher reference. Founded 1968.

Simon & Schuster (Australia) Pty Ltd
20 Barcoo Street, East Roseville, NSW 2069
postal address PO Box 507, East Roseville, NSW 2069
tel (02) 9415 9900 *fax* (02) 9417 4292
Managing Director Jon Attenborough, *Publisher* Angelo Loukakis
Fiction and general non-fiction including anthropology, child care, hobbies, house and home, how-to, craft, biography, motivation, management, outdoor recreation, sport, travel. Imprints: Simon & Schuster Australia, Kangaroo Press.

Thomson Learning Australia*
102 Dodds Street, Southbank, Victoria 3006
tel (03) 9685 4111 *fax* (03) 9685 4199
email customerservice@thomsonlearning.com.au
website www.thomsonlearning.com.au
Educational books.

Transworld Publishers (Aust) Pty Ltd – merged with Random House Australia Pty Ltd

University of Queensland Press
PO Box 6042, St Lucia, Queensland 4067
tel (07) 3365 2127 *fax* (07) 3365 7579
email uqp@uqp.uq.edu.au
website www.uqp.uq.edu.au
General Manager L.C. Muller
Scholarly works, tertiary texts, Australian fiction, young adult fiction, poetry, history, general interest. Founded 1948.

University of Western Australia Press*
UWA, 35 Stirling Hwy, Nedlands 6009, Western Australia
tel (08) 9380 3670 *fax* (08) 9380 1027
email uwap@cyllene.uwa.edu.au
website www.uwapress.uwa.edu.au
Natural history, history, maritime history, critical studies, women's studies, general non-fiction, contemporary issues, children's picture books, young fiction. Imprints: Cygnet Books, Staples, Tuart House, UWA Press. Founded 1954.

UNSW Press
University of New South Wales, UNSW Sydney NSW 2052
tel (02) 9664 0900 *fax* (02) 9664 5420
email info.press@unsw.edu.au
website www.unswpress.com.au
Managing Director Dr Robin Derricourt, *Publishing Manager* John Elliot
Science, ecology, natural history, botany and horticulture; cultural studies, politics, history; general reference; tertiary textbooks. Founded 1962.

Viking – see Penguin Books Australia Ltd

Wild & Woolley Pty Ltd*
PO Box 41, Glebe, NSW 2037
tel (02) 9692 0166 *fax* (02) 9552 4320
website www.fastbooks.com.au
Director Pat Woolley
Offers short-run paperback printing, promotion, marketing and distribution for self-publishing writers. Founded 1974.

John Wiley & Sons Australia, Ltd*
33 Park Road, Milton, Queensland 4064
tel (07) 3859 9755 *fax* (07) 3859 9715
email brisbane@johnwiley.com.au
Managing Director P. Donoughue
Educational, technical, atlases, professional, reference, trade. Imprints: John Wiley & Sons, Jacaranda Press. Founded 1954.

Wrightbooks Pty Ltd – acquired by John Wiley & Sons Australia, Ltd*

Canada

**Member of the Canadian Publishers' Council*
†Member of the Association of Canadian Publishers

Addison-Wesley Canada – merged with Prentice Hall Canada to form Pearson Education Canada

Annick Press Ltd†
15 Patricia Avenue, Toronto, Ontario M2M 1H9
tel 416-221-4802 *fax* 416-221-8400
email annick@annickpress.com
website www.annickpress.com
Co-editors Rick Wilks, Colleen MacMillan
Preschool to juvenile fiction and non-fiction. Founded 1975.

CDG Books Canada Inc.
99 Yorkville Avenue, Suite 400, Toronto, Ontario M5R 3K5
tel 416-963-8830 *fax* 416-923-4821
Trade book publishers. Founded 1905.

The Charlton Press
PO Box 94, Station Main, Thornhill, Ontario L3T 3N1
tel 416-488-1418 *fax* 416-488-4656
email chpress@charltonpress.com
website www.charltonpress.com
President W.K. Cross
Collectibles, Numismatics, Sportscard price catalogues. Founded 1952.

Doubleday Canada*
1 Toronto Street, Suite 300, Toronto, Ontario M5C 2V6
tel 416-364-4449 *fax* 416-957-1587
Chairman John Neale, *Publisher* Maya Mavjee
General trade non-fiction: current affairs, politics; fiction; children's illustrated. Division of **Random House of Canada Ltd**. Founded 1942.

Douglas & McIntyre Ltd†

2323 Quebec Street, Suite 201, Vancouver, BC V5T 4S7
tel 604-254-7191 *fax* 604-254-9099
email dm@douglas-mcintyre.com

General list, including Greystone Books imprint: Canadian biography, art and architecture, natural history, history, native studies, Canadian fiction. Children's division (Groundwood Books) specialises in fiction and illustrated flats. No unsolicited MSS. Founded 1964.

ECW Press Ltd†

2120 Queen Street E, Suite 200, Toronto, Ontario M4E 1E2
tel 416-694-3348 *fax* 416-698-9906
email info@ecwpress.com
website www.ecwpress.com
President Jack David, *Secretary-Treasurer* Robert Lecker

Popular culture, sports, humour, general trade books, biographies, guidebooks. Founded 1979.

Fitzhenry & Whiteside Ltd†

195 Allstate Parkway, Markham, Ontario L3R 4T8
tel 905-477-9700 *fax* 905-477-9179
email godwit@fitzhenry.ca
tel 1-800-387-9776 (toll free) *fax* 1-800-260-9777
Director Sharon Fitzhenry

Trade, educational, children's books. Founded 1966.

Gage Learning Corporation†

164 Commander Boulevard, Toronto, Ontario M1S 3C7
tel 416-293-8141 *fax* 416-293-9009

Publishers of elementary and secondary school textbooks; professional and reference materials. Founded 1844.

Gold Eagle Books – see Harlequin Enterprises Ltd

Harcourt Canada Ltd*

55 Horner Avenue, Toronto, Ontario M8Z 4X6
tel 416-255-4491 *fax* 416-255-4046
email firstname_lastname@harcourt.com
website www.harcourtcanada.com
President Wendy Cochran

Educational materials from K–Grade 12, testing and assessment. Imprints: Harcourt Religion (formerly Brown-ROA), Harcourt Brace & Company, Holt, Rinehart and Winston, MeadowBrook Press, The Psychological Corporation, Therapy Skill Builders/Communications Skill Builders. Founded 1922.

Harlequin Enterprises Ltd*

225 Duncan Mill Road, Don Mills, Ontario M3B 3K9
tel 416-445-5860 *fax* 416-445-8655
website www.eharlequin.com
President & Publisher Donna Hayes, *Vice President, Editorial* Isabel Swift

Women's fiction, romance, action adventure, mystery. Founded 1949.

Gold Eagle Books (imprint)
Editorial Director Randall Toye
Series action adventure fiction.

Harlequin Books (imprint)
Editorial Director Randall Toye
Contemporary and historical romance fiction in series.

Mira Books (imprint)
Editorial Director Dianne Moggy
Women's fiction: contemporary and historical dramas, family sagas, romantic suspense and relationship novels.

Red Dress Ink (imprint)
Editorial Director Tara Gavin
Women's fiction for the 20-somethings.

Silhouette Books (imprint)
Editorial Director Tara Gavin
Contemporary romance fiction in series.

Steeple Hill (imprint)
Editorial Director Tara Gavin
Contemporary inspirational romantic fiction in series.

Worldwide Mystery (imprint)
Editorial Director Randall Toye
Contemporary mystery fiction. Reprints only.

HarperCollins Publishers Ltd*

Suite 2900, Hazelton Lanes, 55 Avenue Road, Toronto, Ontario M5R 3L2
tel 416-975-9334 *fax* 416-975-9884
website www.harpercanada.com
President David Kent

Publishers of literary fiction and non-fiction, business books, history, politics, biography, spiritual and children's books. Founded 1989.

Irwin Publishing Ltd†

325 Humber College Blvd, Toronto, Ontario M9W 7C3
tel 416-798-0424 *fax* 416-798-1384
email irwin@irwin-pub.com
President Brian O'Donnell, *Chairman* Jack Stoddart

Educational books at the elementary, high school and college levels.

Key Porter Books Ltd†
70 The Esplanade, 3rd Floor, Toronto, Ontario M5E 1R2
tel 416-862-7777 *fax* 416-862-2304
email aporter@keyporter.com
website www.keyporter.com
Publisher/Ceo Anna Porter, *President* Diane Davy, *Editor-in-Chief* Clare McKeon

Fiction, nature, history, Canadian politics, conservation, humour, biography, autobiography, health, children's books. Founded 1981.

Kids Can Press Ltd†
29 Birch Avenue, Toronto, Ontario M4V 1E2
tel 416-925-5437 *fax* 416-960-5437
email info@kidscan.com
Publisher Valerie Hussey

Juvenile/young adult books.

Knopf Canada*
33 Yonge Street, Suite 210, Toronto, Ontario M5E 1G4
tel 416-777-9477 *fax* 416-777-9470
website www.randomhouse.com
Publisher, Vice-President Louise Dennys

Literary fiction and non-fiction. Division of **Random House of Canada Ltd**. Founded 1991.

LexisNexis Butterworths
75 Clegg Road, Markham, Ontario L6G 1A1
tel 905-479-2665 *fax* 905-479-2826
email info@lexisnexis.ca

Law and accountancy. Division of Reed Elsevier plc.

Lone Pine Publishing
10145-81 Avenue, Edmonton, Alberta T6E 1W9
tel 780-433-9333 *fax* 780-433-9646
Chairman Grant Kennedy, *President* Shane Kennedy

Natural history, recreation and wildlife guidebooks, gardening, popular history. Founded 1980.

McClelland & Stewart Ltd†
481 University Avenue, Suite 900, Toronto, Ontario M5G 2E9
tel 416-598-1114 *fax* 416-598-7764
website www.mcclelland.com
Chairman Avie Bennett, *President/Publisher* Douglas M. Gibson

General. Founded 1906.

McGill-Queen's University Press†
3430 McTavish Street, Montreal, Quebec H3A 1X9
tel 514-398-3750 *fax* 514-398-4333
email mqup@mqup.ca
website www.mqup.ca
Queen's University, Kingston, Ontario K7L 3N6
tel 613-533-2155 *fax* 613-533-6822
email mqup@qucdn.queensu.ca

Academic, non-fiction, poetry. Founded 1969.

McGraw-Hill Ryerson Ltd*
300 Water Street, Whitby, Ontario L1N 9B6
tel 905-430-5000 *fax* 905-430-5020
website www.mcgrawhill.ca

Educational and trade books.

Mira Books – see Harlequin Enterprises Ltd

Nelson*
(formerly Nelson Thomson Learning)
1120 Birchmount Road, Toronto, Ontario M1K 5G4
tel 416-752-9100 *fax* 416-752-9646
President/Ceo George W. Bergquist, *Senior Vice President, Finance/Cfo* Lesley Gouldie, *Senior Vice President, School* Greg Pilon, *Vice President, Higher Education* Ron Kelly, *Vice President, Media Services* Susan Cline, *Vice President, Operations* Ed Berman, *Vice President, Human Resources* Marlene Nyilassy, *Editorial Director, Higher Education* Evelyn Veitch, *Director of Publishing, School* David Steele, *Director of Marketing, Higher Education* James Rozsa, *Director of Sales, School* James Reeve, *Director of Information Systems & Technology* Bruce Sharron

Educational publishing: school (K–12), college and university, career education, measurement and guidance, professional and reference, ESL titles. Founded 1914.

Oberon Press
400-350 Sparks Street, Ottawa, Ontario K1R 7S8
tel/fax 613-238-3275

General.

Oxford University Press, Canada*
70 Wynford Drive, Don Mills, Ontario M3C 1J9
tel 416-441-2941 *fax* 416-444-0427
website www.oup.com/ca
President Joanna Gertler

General, educational and academic.

Pearson Education Canada*
(formerly Prentice Hall Canada and Addison-Wesley Canada)
26 Prince Andrew Place, Toronto, Ontario M3C 2T8
tel 416-447-5101 *fax* 416-443-0948
website www.pearsoned.ca
President Tony Vander Woude

Academic, technical, educational, children's and adult, trade.

Penguin Books Canada Ltd*
10 Alcorn Avenue, Suite 300, Toronto, Ontario M4V 3B2
tel 416-925-2249 *fax* 416-925-0068
website www.penguin.ca
Joint President, Publisher and Editor-in-Chief Cynthia Good, *Joint President and Ceo* Don Howard, *Cfo* Tim Man

Literary fiction, memoir, non-fiction (history, business, current events). Founded 1974.

Pippin Publishing Corporation
Suite 232, 85 Ellesmere Road, Toronto, Ontario M1R 4B9
tel 416-510-2918 *fax* 416-510-3359
email jld@pippinpub.com
website www.pippinpub.com
President/Editorial Director Jonathan Lovat Dickson

ESL/EFL, teacher reference, adult basic education, school texts (all subjects).

Random House of Canada Limited*
One Toronto Street, Suite 300, Toronto, Ontario M5C 2V6
tel 416-364 4449 *fax* 416-364-6863
website www.randomhouse.com
Chairman John Neale

Imprints: Ballantine Canada, Doubleday Canada, Knopf Canada, Random House Canada, Seal Books, Vintage Canada. Subsidiary of Bertelsmann AG. Founded 1944.

Red Dress Ink – see Harlequin Enterprises Ltd

Silhouette Books – see Harlequin Enterprises Ltd

Steeple Hill – see Harlequin Enterprises Ltd

Stoddart Publishing Co. Ltd†
895 Don Mills Road, 400-2 Park Centre, Toronto, Ontario M3C 1W3
tel 416-445-3333 *fax* 416-445-5967
website www.stoddartpub.com

Fiction and non-fiction.

Tundra Books Inc.†
481 University Avenue, Suite 900, Toronto, Ontario M5G 2E9
tel 416-598-4786 *fax* 416-598-0247

High quality children's picture books.

University of Toronto Press Inc.†
10 St Mary Street, Suite 700, Toronto, Ontario M4Y 2W8
tel 416-978-2239 *fax* 416-978-4738
email publishing@utpress.utoronto.ca
website www.utpress.utoronto.ca
President/Publisher George L. Meadows

Worldwide Mystery – see Harlequin Enterprises Ltd

New Zealand

**Member of the New Zealand Book Publishers' Association*

Auckland University Press*
University of Auckland, Private Bag 92019, Auckland
tel (09) 373-7528 *fax* (09) 373-7465
email aup@auckland.ac.nz
website www.auckland.ac.nz/aup
Director Elizabeth Caffin

NZ history, NZ poetry, Maori and Pacific studies, politics, sociology, literary criticism, art history, biography, media studies, women's studies. Founded 1966.

David Bateman Ltd*
30 Tarndale Grove, Bush Road, Albany, Auckland
postal address PO Box 100242, North Shore Mail Centre, Auckland 1330
tel (09) 415-7664 *fax* (09) 415-8892
email bateman@bateman.co.nz
website www.bateman.co.nz
Chairman/Publisher David L. Bateman, *Directors* Janet Bateman, Paul Bateman (joint managing), Paul Parkinson (joint managing)

Natural history, gardening, encyclopedias, sport, art, cookery, historical, juvenile, travel, motoring, maritime history, business, art, lifestyle. Founded 1979.

Bush Press Communications Ltd
4 Bayview Road, Hauraki Corner, Takapuna
postal address PO Box 33-029, Takapuna, Auckland 1309
tel/fax (09) 486-2667
email bush.press@clear.net.nz
Governing Director/Publisher Gordon Ell

NZ non-fiction, particularly outdoor, nature, travel, architecture, crafts, Maori, popular history; children's non-fiction. Founded 1979.

The Caxton Press
113 Victoria Street, Christchurch, PO Box 25-088
tel (03) 366-8516 *fax* (03) 365-7840
Director E.B. Bascand

Biography, history, natural history, travel, gardening. Founded 1935.

Dunmore Press Ltd*
PO Box 5115, Palmerston North
tel (06) 358-7169 *fax* (06) 357-9242
email dunmore@xtra.co.nz
website www.dunmore.co.nz
Directors Murray Gatenby, Sharmian Firth
Education, history, sociology, business studies, general non-fiction. Founded 1970.

Godwit Publishing Ltd – acquired by Random House New Zealand Ltd

HarperCollins Publishers (New Zealand) Ltd*
PO Box 1, Auckland
tel (09) 443-9400 *fax* (09) 443-9403
website www.harpercollins.co.nz
Publishers of general literature, teen fiction, non-fiction, reference, children's.

Hodder Moa Beckett Publishers Ltd*
PO Box 100-749, North Shore Mail Centre, Auckland 1330
tel (09) 478-1000 *fax* (09) 478-1010
email admin@hoddermoa.co.nz
Managing Director Kevin Chapman, *Managing Editor* Linda Cassells, *Executive Editor* Warren Adler
Sport, gardening, cooking, travel, atlases, general.

LexisNexis Butterworths New Zealand*
205-207 Victoria Street, Wellington 1
postal address PO Box 472, Wellington 1
tel (04) 385-1479 *fax* (04) 385-1598
email Russell.Gray@butterworths.co.nz
website www.butterworths.co.nz
Managing Director Russell Gray
Law, business, academic.

Mallinson Rendel Publishers Ltd*
Level 5, 15 Courteney Place, PO Box 9409, Wellington
tel (04) 802-5012 *fax* (04) 802-5013
email publisher@mallinsonrendel.co.nz
Director Ann Mallinson
Children's books. Founded 1980.

Nelson Price Milburn Ltd*
1 Te Puni Street, Petone
postal addres PO Box 38-945, Wellington Mail Centre, Wellington
tel (04) 568-7179 *fax* (04) 568-2115
email npm@xtra.co.nz
Children's fiction, primary school texts, especially school readers and maths, secondary educational.

New Zealand Council for Educational Research*
Box 3237, Education House, 178-182 Willis Street, Wellington 1
tel (04) 384-7939 *fax* (04) 384-7933
email info@nzcer.org.nz
website www.nzcer.org.nz
Director Robyn Baker, *Publisher* Bev Webber
Education, including educational policy and institutions, early childhood education, educational achievement tests, Maori education, curriculum and assessment, etc. Founded 1934.

Pearson Education New Zealand Ltd*
Private Bag 102908, North Shore Mail Centre, Glenfield, Auckland 10
tel (09) 444-4968 *fax* (09) 444-4957
email rosemary.stagg@pearsoned.co.nz
NZ educational books.

Random House New Zealand Ltd*
Private Bag 102950, North Shore Mail Centre, Auckland 10
tel (09) 444-7197 *fax* (09) 444-7524
Managing Director M. Moynahan
Fiction, general non-fiction, gardening, cooking, art, business, health.
Subsidiary of Bertelsmann AG. Founded 1977.

Reed Publishing (New Zealand) Ltd*
(incorporating Reed Consumer Books and Heinemann Education)
39 Rawene Road, Private Bag 34901, Birkenhead, Auckland 10
tel (09) 480-4950 *fax* (09) 480-4999
Chairman John Philbin, *Managing Director* Alan Smith
NZ literature, specialist and general titles, primary, secondary and tertiary textbooks. Imprints: BBC, Egmont, Brimax, Butterworth-Heinemann, CIS Heinemann, Conran, George Philip, Ginn UK, Heinemann Australia, Heinemann NZ, Heinemann UK, Heinemann USA, Huia Jasons, John Murray, Kyle Cathie, Longacre, Mammoth, Mitchell Beazley, Quadrille, Reed NZ, Ryland Peters, Rigby Australia, Rigby USA, Virgin Publishing.

Scholastic New Zealand Ltd*
21 Lady Ruby Drive, East Tamaki, Auckland
postal address Private Bag 94407, Greenmount, Auckland
tel (09) 274-8112 *fax* (09) 274-8114
General Manager David Peagram, *Publishing Manager* Christine Dale
Children's books. Founded 1962.

Shortland Publications*

10 Cawley Street, Ellerslie, Auckland 5
tel (09) 526-6200 *fax* (09) 526-4448
Submissions Louise Williams, Shortland Publications, Private Bag 11904, Ellerslie, Auckland 5
email Louise_Williams@mcgraw-hill.com

International primary reading market: potential authors should familiarise themselves with Shortland products. Currently seeking submissions for: *Emergent/early and fluency reading material* – 8–24pp, stories need to be simple and to feature supports for the child learning to read, e.g. repetition of vocabulary and sentence structure. *Short fiction* (ages 9–12) – MSS up to 1500 words long. Looking for fresh ideas. *Cocky Circle* – 24pp read-to books for 2–6 year-olds. Stories must lend themselves to a different illustration on each page. Fantasy and humour are always good sellers. All submissions should cater for an international market; include sae. Founded 1984.

University of Otago Press*

University of Otago, PO Box 56, Dunedin
tel/fax (03) 479-8807 (03) 479-8385
email university.press@otago.ac.nz
Managing Editor Wendy Harrex

Student texts and scholarly works in many disciplines and general books, including Maori and women's studies, natural history and environmental studies, health and fiction. Also publishes journals including *Landfall* and the *Women's Studies Journal*. Founded 1958.

Victoria University Press*

Victoria University of Wellington, PO Box 600, Wellington
tel (04) 463-6580 *fax* (04) 463-6581
email victoria-press@vuw.ac.nz
website www.vup.vuw.ac.nz
Publisher Fergus Barrowman

Academic, scholarly books on NZ history, sociology, law; Maori language; fiction, plays, poetry. Founded 1974.

Viking Sevenseas Ltd

23B Ihakara Street, Paraparaumu
tel/fax (04) 902-9990
email vikings@paradise.net.nz
Managing Director M.B. Riley

Natural history books on New Zealand only.

South Africa

**Member of the Publishers' Association of South Africa*

Ad Donker (Pty) Ltd – see Jonathan Ball Publishers (Pty) Ltd

Jonathan Ball Publishers (Pty) Ltd

10-14 Watkins Street, Denver Ext. 4, Johannesburg
postal address Box 33977, Jeppestown 2043
tel (011) 622-2900 *fax* (011) 622-3553

Ad Donker (imprint)
Africana, literature, history, academic.

Jonathan Ball (imprint)
General publications, reference books, South African business, history, politics.

Delta Books (imprint)
General South African trade non-fiction.

Cambridge University Press*

(African Branch)
Dock House, Portswood Ridge,
Victoria & Alfred Waterfront, Cape Town 8001
tel (021) 419-8414
email information@cup.co.za
website www.cambridge.org
Director Hanri Pieterse

African Branch of CUP, responsible for sub-Saharan Africa and English-speaking Caribbean. Publishes distance learning material and textbooks for various African countries, as well as primary reading materials in 28 local African languages.

Delta Books – see Jonathan Ball Publishers (Pty) Ltd

Jacklin Enterprises (Pty) Ltd

PO Box 521, Parklands 2121
tel (011) 265-4200 *fax* (011) 314-2984
email mjacklin@jacklin.co.za
Managing Director M.A.C. Jacklin

Children's fiction and non-fiction; Afrikaans large print books. Subjects include aviation, natural history, romance, general science, technology and transportation. Imprints: Mike Jacklin, Kennis Onbeperk, Daan Retief.

Juta & Company Ltd*

PO Box 14373, Kenwyn 7790, Cape Town
tel (021) 797-5101 *fax* (021) 762-0248
email books@juta.co.za
website www.juta.co.za
Ceo Rory Wilson

School, academic, professional, law and electronic. Founded 1853.

Maskew Miller Longman (Pty) Ltd*
c/o Forest Drive & Logan Way, Pinelands 7405, Cape Town
postal address PO Box 396, Cape Town 8000
tel (021) 531-7750 *fax* (021) 531-4877
email administrator@mml.co.za
website www.mml.co.za
Educational and general publishers.

Oxford University Press Southern Africa*
Vasco Boulevard, N1 City, Cape Town 7460
postal address PO Box 12119, N1 City, Cape Town 7463
tel (021) 595-4400 *fax* (021) 595-4430
email oxford@oup.co.za
Managing Director Kate McCallum

David Philip Publishers (Pty) Ltd*
PO Box 23408, Claremont 7735, Western Cape
tel (21) 6744-136 *fax* (21) 6743-358
email information@dpp.co.za
website www.dpp.co.za
Managing & Marketing Director Bridget Impey, *Publishing Director* Russell Martin, *Non-executive Directors* David Philip, Marie Philip, Wilmot James, G.J. Gerwel, Njabulo Ndebele, Steve Kromberg, Alec Davis, Mike Tissong, Mike Siluma, Zwelakhe Sisulu
Academic, history, social sciences, politics, biography, belles-lettres, reference books, fiction, cartoons, educational. Founded 1971.

Ravan Press
c/o Macmillan SA, Old Trafford 4, Isle of Houghton, Houghton 2198
postal address PO Box 32484, Braamfontein 2017
tel (011) 484-0916 *fax* (011) 484-3129
South African studies: history, politics, social studies; fiction, literature, children's, educational. Founded 1972.

Shuter and Shooter (Pty) Ltd*
230 Church Street, Pietermaritzburg 3201, KwaZulu-Natal
postal address PO Box 109, Pietermaritzburg 3200, KwaZulu-Natal
tel (033) 3946-830/3948-881 *fax* (033) 3427-419
email dryder@shuter.co.za
website www.shuter.co.za
Publishing Director D.F. Ryder
Primary and secondary educational, science, biology, history, maths, geography, English, Afrikaans, biblical studies, music, teacher training, agriculture, accounting, early childhood, dictionaries, African languages. Founded 1925.

Struik Publishers (Pty) Ltd
Cornelius Struik House, 80 McKenzie Street, Cape Town 8001
tel (021) 462-4360 *fax* (021) 462-4379
Managing Director Steve Connolly
General illustrated non-fiction. Division of New Holland Publishing (Pty) Ltd.

Unisa Press*
PO Box 392, Pretoria 0003
tel (012) 429-3051 *fax* (012) 429-3221
email unisa-press@unisa.ac.za
website www.unisa.ac.za/dept/press/ index.html
Head Phoebe Van Der Walt
Theology and all academic disciplines. Publishers of University of South Africa. Imprint: UNISA. Founded 1957.

University of Natal Press*
Private Bag X01, Scottsville, KwaZulu-Natal
tel (033) 260 5226 *fax* (33) 260 5801
email books@nu.ac.za
website www.unpress.co.za
Publisher Glenn Cowley
South African social, political, economic and military history, gender, natural sciences, African poetry and literature, genealogy, education, biography. Founded 1948.

Van Schaik Publishers*
PO Box 12681, Hatfield, Pretoria 0028
tel (012) 342-2765 *fax* (012) 430-3563
email vanschaik@vanschaiknet.com
website www.vanschaiknet.com
Publishers of school books in English, Afrikaans and African languages. Specialists in textbooks and books for the corporate market. Founded 1914.

Witwatersrand University Press*
PO Wits, Johannesburg 2050
tel (011) 484-5910 *fax* (011) 484-5971
email witspress@wup.wits.ac.za
website http://witspress.wits.ac.za

Zebra Press
80 McKenzie Street Gardens, Cape Town 8001
postal address PO Box 1144, Cape Town 8000
tel (021) 462-4360 *fax* (021) 462-4379
email info@struik.co.za
Business, contemporary, humour. Imprint of Struik Publishers. Division of New Holland Publishing (South Africa) (Pty) Ltd.

USA

**Member of the Association of American Publishers Inc.*

Abbeville Press
22 Cortlandt Street, 32nd Floor, New York, NY 10007
tel 212-577-5555 *fax* 212-577-5579
Publisher/President Robert Abrams
Art and illustrated books. Founded 1977.

Abingdon Press
PO Box 801, Nashville, TN 37202-0801
tel 615-749-6404 *fax* 615-749-6512
website www.abingdon.org
Senior Vice President, Publishing Harriett Jane Olson
General interest, professional, academic and reference – primarily directed to the religious market.

Harry N. Abrams Inc.*
100 Fifth Avenue, New York, NY 10011
tel 212-206-7715 *fax* 212-645-8437
Ceo/President/Editor-in-Chief Paul Gottlieb
Art and architecture, photography, natural sciences, performing arts, children's books. No fiction. Founded 1949.

Applause Theatre and Cinema Book Publishers
151 West 46th Street, 8th Floor, New York, NY 10036
tel 212-575-9265 *fax* 646-562-5852
Ceo John Cerullo
Performing arts. Founded 1980.

Arcade Publishing
141 Fifth Avenue, New York, NY 10010
tel 212-475-2633 *fax* 212-353-8148
email arcadeinfo@arcadepub.com
website www.arcadepub.com
President/Editor-in-Chief Richard Seaver, *Publisher/Marketing Director* Jeannette Seaver, *General Manager/Executive Editor* Cal Barksdale, *Editors* Greg Comer, Darcy Falkenhagen
General trade, including adult hard cover and paperbacks. No unsolicited MSS.

Atlantic Monthly Press – see Grove/Atlantic Inc.

Avery – see The Putnam Publishing Group

Avon Books – see HarperCollins Publishers

Walter H. Baker Company
PO Box 699222, Quincy, MA 02269
tel 617-745-0805 *fax* 617-745-9891
website www.bakersplays.com
President Charles Van Nostrand, *General Manager* Kurt Gombar, *UK Agent* Samuel French Ltd
Plays and books on the theatre. Also agents for plays. Founded 1845.

The Ballantine Publishing Group*
1540 Broadway, New York, NY 10036
tel 212-782-9000 *fax* 212-302-7985
website www.randomhouse.com
President/Publisher Gina Centrello
Trade and mass-market general fiction, science fiction and non-fiction. Imprints: Ballantine Books, Ballantine Wellspring, Del Rey, Fawcett, Ivy, Library of Contemporary Thought, One World. Division of **Random House Inc.**

Bantam Dell Publishing Group*
1540 Broadway, New York, NY 10036
tel 212-782-9000 *fax* 212-302-7985
website www.randomhouse.com
President/Publisher Irwyn Applebaum
General fiction and non-fiction. Imprints: Bantam Hardcover, Bantam Mass Market, Bantam Trade Paperback, Crimeline, Delacorte Press, Dell, Delta, Dial Press, Domain, DTP, Fanfare, Island, Spectra. Division of **Random House Inc.**

Barron's Educational Series Inc.
250 Wireless Boulevard, Hauppage, NY 11788
tel 516-434-3311 *fax* 516-434-3723
website www.barronseduc.com
Chairman/Ceo Manuel H. Barron, *President/Publisher* Ellen Sibley
Test preparation, juvenile, cookbooks, Mind, Body & Spirit, crafts, business, pets, gardening, family and health, art, study guides, school guides. Founded 1941.

Beacon Press
25 Beacon Street, Boston, MA 02108
tel 617-742-2110 *fax* 617-723-3097
Director Helene Atwan
General non-fiction in fields of religion, ethics, philosophy, current affairs, gender studies, environmental concerns, African-American studies, anthropology and women's studies, nature.

Berkley Books – see Berkley Publishing Group

Berkley Publishing Group

375 Hudson Street, New York, NY 10014
tel 212-366-2000 *fax* 212-366-2666
email online@penguinputnam.com
website www.penguinputnam.com
President, Mass Market Paperbacks Leslie Gelbman

Fiction and general non-fiction. Imprints: Ace Books, Berkley Books, Boulevard, Diamond Books, HP Books, Jam, Jove, Perigee, Prime Crime, Riverhead Books (trade paperback). Division of **Penguin Putnam Inc.** Founded 1954.

Berkley Books (imprint)
President and Publisher Leslie Gelbman

Fiction and general non-fiction for adults. Imprints: Ace Books, Berkley Books, Boulevard Books, Diamond Books, Jam, Jove, Prime Crime. Founded 1954.

HP Books (imprint)
Editorial Director, Automotive Michael Lutfy

Non-fiction trade paperbacks. Founded 1964.

Perigee Books (imprint)
Vice President/Publisher John Duff

Non-fiction paperbacks: psychology, spirituality, reference, etc. Founded 1980.

Riverhead Books (Trade Paperback)
Editor Christopher Knutsen

Fiction and general non-fiction for adults. Founded 1995.

Betterway Books – see Writer's Digest Books

Bloomsbury USA

Suite 300, 175 Fifth Avenue, New York, NY 10010
tel 212-674-5151 *fax* 212-780-0115
Publisher Alan Wherry, *Editorial Director, Adult Books* Karen Rinaldi, *Executive Editor, Adult Books* Colin Dickerman, *Editorial Director, Children's Books* Victoria Arms, *Director of Marketing and Publicity (Children's)* Kate Kubert

Literary fiction, general non-fiction, children's books. Branch of **Bloomsbury UK**. Founded 1998.

BlueHen – see The Putnam Publishing Group

R.R. Bowker*

121 Chanlon Road, New Providence, NJ 07974
tel 908-464-6800 *fax* 908-464-3553
President Ira T. Siegel

Bibliographies and reference tools for the book trade and literary and library worlds, available in hardcopy, on microfiche, online and CD-Rom. Reference books for music, art, business, computer industry, cable industry and information industry. Division of Reed Elsevier Inc.

Boyds Mills Press

815 Church Street, Honesdale, PA 18431
tel 570-253-1164 *fax* 570-253-0179
website www.boydsmillpress.com
Publisher Kent Brown Jr, *President* Clay Winters, *Editorial Director* Larry Rosler, *Art Director* Tim Gillner, *Manuscript Coordinator* Kathryn Yerkes

Fiction, non-fiction, and poetry trade books for children. Founded 1990.

Burford Books

PO Box 388, Short Hills, NJ 07078
tel 973-258-0960 *fax* 973-258-0113
email info@burfordbooks.com
website www.burfordbooks.com
President Peter Burford

Outdoor activities: golf, sports, fitness, nature, travel. Founded 1997.

Cambridge University Press*

(North American Branch)
40 West 20th Street, New York, NY 10011
tel 212-924-3900 *fax* 212-691-3239
website www.cambridge.org
Director Richard L. Ziemacki

Candlewick Press

2067 Massachusetts Avenue, Cambridge, MA 02140
tel 617-661-3330 *fax* 617-661-0565
website www.candlewick.com
Editorial Director/Associate Publisher Liz Bicknell, *Executive Editor* Mary Lee Donovan, *Editorial Director (novelty)* Joan Powers, *Editor-at-Large* Amy Ehrlich

Children's books – 6 months to 14 years: board books, picture books, novels, non-fiction, novelty books. Submit material through a literary agent. Subsidiary of **Walker Books Ltd**, UK. Founded 1991.

Carroll & Graf Publishers Inc.

161 William Street, 16th Floor, New York, NY 10038
tel 646-375-2570 *fax* 646-375-2571
website www.carrollandgraf.com
President/Publisher Herman Graf, *Subrights* Martine Ballen, *Foreign Rights* Lena Dixon

Mystery and crime, popular fiction, history, biography, literature, literary fiction. Founded 1983.

Chronicle Books

85 Second Street, 6th Floor, San Francisco, CA 94105
tel 415-537-3730 *fax* 415-537-4460

website www.chroniclebooks.com
Publisher Jack Jensen, *Associate Publishers* Christine Carswell, Craig Hetzer, Nion McEvoy, Victoria Rock

Cooking, art, fiction, general, children's, gift, new media, gardening, regional, nature. Founded 1967.

Coffee House Press

27 N 4th Street, Suite 400, Minneapolis, MN 55401
tel 612-338-0125 *fax* 612-338-4004
UK Representation Nancy Green Madia
tel 212-864-0425 *fax* 212-316-2121

Literary fiction and poetry; collectors' editions. Founded 1984.

Columbia University Press*

61 West 62nd Street, New York, NY 10023
tel 212-459-0600 *fax* 212-459-3677
website www.columbia.edu/cu/cup
UK Office 1 Oldlands Way, Bognor Regis, West Sussex PO22 9SA
tel (0243) 842165 *fax* (0243) 842167
Editorial Director Jennifer Crewe

General reference works in print and electronic formats, translations and serious non-fiction of more general interest.

Concordia Publishing House

3558 S Jefferson Avenue, St Louis, MO 63118
tel 314-268-1000 *fax* 314-268-1329

Religious books, Lutheran perspective. Few freelance MSS accepted; query first. Founded 1869.

Contemporary Books

130 East Randolph Street, Suite 900, Chicago, IL 60601
tel 312-233-7500 *fax* 312-233-7570
Vice President Philip Ruppel

Non-fiction. Imprints: Peter Bedrick, Contemporary Books, Country Roads Press, Jamestown Publishers, Lowell House, Masters Press, National Textbook Co., NTC Business Books, Passport Books, Quilt Digest Press, VGM Career Horizons. Division of the McGraw-Hill Companies.

The Continuum International Publishing Group Inc.

370 Lexington Avenue, New York, NY 10017-6503
tel 212-953-5858 *fax* 212-953-5944
email contin@tiac.net
website www.continuum-books.com
Chairman/Publisher Philip Sturrock

General non-fiction, education, literature, psychology, politics, sociology, literary criticism, religious studies. Founded 1999.

Cornell University Press*

(including ILR Press and Comstock Publishing Associates)
Sage House, 512 East State Street, Ithaca, NY 14850
tel 607-277-2338 *fax* 607-277-2374
email cupressinfo@cornell.edu
website www.cornellpress.cornell.edu
Director John G. Ackerman

Scholarly books. Founded 1869.

Council Oak Books

1290 Chestnut Street, Suite 2, San Francisco, CA 94109
tel 415-931-6868 *fax* 415-931-5353
email calla@sky4.com
Publishing Director Melissa Lilly, *Editor-in-Chief* Kevin Bentley

Non-fiction: native American, multicultural, life skills, life accounts, Earth awareness, meditation. Founded 1984.

The Countryman Press

PO Box 748, Rte 12N, Mount Tom Building, Woodstock, VT 05091
tel 802-457-4826 *fax* 802-457-1678
email countrymanpress@wwnorton.com
website www.countrymanpress.com
Editorial Director Kermit Hummel

Outdoor recreation guides for anglers, hikers, cyclists, canoeists and kayakers, US travel guides, New England non-fiction, how-to books, country living books, books on nature and the environment, classic reprints and general non-fiction. No unsolicited MSS. Division of **W.W. Norton & Co. Inc.** Founded 1973.

Crown Publishing Group*

299 Park Avenue, New York, NY 10170
tel 212-572-2408 *fax* 212-940-7408
President/Publisher Jenny Frost

General fiction, non-fiction, illustrated books. Imprints: Bell Tower, Clarkson Potter, Crown Publishers Inc., Harmony Books, Three Rivers Press. Division of **Random House Inc.**

DAW Books Inc.

375 Hudson Street, 3rd Floor, New York, NY 10014
tel 212-366-2096 *fax* 212-366-2090
email daw@penguinputnam.com
website www.dawbooks.com
Publishers Elizabeth R. Wollheim, Sheila E. Gilbert

Science fiction, fantasy, horror, mainstream thrillers: originals and reprints. Imprints: DAW/Fantasy, DAW/Fiction, DAW/Science Fiction. Affiliate of **Penguin Putnam Inc.** Founded 1971.

Dial Books for Young Readers – see Penguin Putnam Books for Young Readers

Doubleday Broadway Publishing Group*
1540 Broadway, New York, NY 10036
tel 212-782-9000 *fax* 212-302-7985
website www.randomhouse.com
President/Publisher Stephen Rubin
General fiction and non-fiction. Imprints: Anchor Bible Dictionary, Anchor Bible Reference Library, Currency, Doubleday, Doubleday Bible Commentary, Doubleday/Galilee, Doubleday/Image, Nan A. Talese, The New Jerusalem Bible. Division of **Random House Inc.**

Dover Publications Inc.
31 E 2nd Street, Mineola, NY 11501
tel 516-294-7000 *fax* 516-742-5049
Vice-President, Editorial Paul Negri
Art, architecture, antiques, crafts, juvenile, food, history, folklore, literary classics, mystery, language, music, math and science, nature, design and ready-to-use art. Founded 1941.

Dutton
(formerly Dutton/Signet)
375 Hudson Street, New York, NY 10014
tel 212-366-2000 *fax* 212-366-2666
email online@penguinputnam.com
website www.penguinputnam.com
Vice President/Editor-in-Chief Brian Tart
Fiction and general non-fiction for adults. Imprint: Dutton. Division of **Penguin Putman Inc.**

Dutton Children's Books – see Penguin Putnam Books for Young Readers

Facts On File Inc.
132 West 31st Street, 17th Floor, New York, NY 10001-2006
tel 212-967 8800 *fax* 212-967 9196
President Mark McDonnell, *Editorial Director* Laurie E. Likoff
General reference books and services for colleges, libraries, schools and general public. Founded 1940.

Farrar, Straus and Giroux
19 Union Square West, New York, NY 10003
tel 212-741-6900 *fax* 212-633-9385
website www.fsgbooks.com
President/Publisher Jonathan Galassi, *Editor-in-Chief* John Glusman
General publishers.

Fodor's Travel Publications Inc. – see Random House Inc.

Four Walls Eight Windows*
39 West 14th Street, Room 503, New York, NY 10011
tel 212-206-8965 *fax* 212-206-8799
email edit@4w8w.com
website www.4w8w.com
Publisher John Oakes
Fiction, history, current affairs, biography, environment, health. No unsolicited submissions accepted. Founded 1987.

Samuel French Inc.
45 West 25th Street, New York, NY 10010
tel 212-206-8990 *fax* 212-206-1429
Play publishers and authors' representatives (dramatic).

David R. Godine, Publisher Inc.
9 Hamilton Place, Boston, MA 02108
tel 617-451-9600 *fax* 617-350-0250
email info@godine.com
website www.godine.com
President David R. Godine
Fiction, photography, poetry, art, biography, children's, essays, history, typography, architecture, nature and gardening, music, cooking, words and writing, and mysteries. No unsolicited MSS. Founded 1970.

Golden Books Family Entertainment
888 Seventh Avenue, New York, NY 10106
tel 212-547-6700 *fax* 212-547-6788
Chairman/Ceo Richard E. Snyder, *Coo* Richard Collins
Children's books, educational workbooks and products, electronic books and software, children's videos. Founded 1907.

Greenwillow Books – see HarperCollins Publishers

Grosset & Dunlap – see Penguin Putnam Books for Young Readers

Grove/Atlantic Inc.*
841 Broadway, New York, NY 10003-4793
tel 212-614-7850 *fax* 212-614-7886
Publisher Morgan Entrekin
MSS of permanent interest, fiction, biography, autobiography, history, current affairs, social science, belles-lettres, natural history. Imprints: Atlantic Monthly Press, Grove Press.

Harcourt Trade Division*

525 B Street, Suite 1900, San Diego, CA 92101
tel 619-231-6616 *fax* 619-699-6320
website www.harcourtbrace.com
President/Publisher, Adult Books Dan Farley, *Vice President/Publisher, Children's Books* Louise Pelan

General publishers. Fiction, history, biography, etc. Division of Harcourt Inc.

HarperCollins Publishers*

10 East 53rd Street, New York, NY 10022
tel 212-207-7000 *fax* 212-207-7145
website www.harpercollins.com
HarperCollins SanFrancisco 1160 Battery Street, San Francisco, CA 94111
tel 415-477-4400 *fax* 415-477-4444
President/Ceo Jane Friedman

Fiction, history, biography, poetry, science, travel, cookbooks, juvenile, educational, business, technical and religious. No unsolicited material; all submissions must come through a literary agent. Founded 1817.

HarperCollins General Books Group (division)
President/Publisher Cathy Hemming

HarperInformation (division)
Imprints: HarperBusiness, HarperResource, Access Travel, William Morrow Cookbooks.

HarperSanFrancisco (division)
Imprint: HarperSanFrancisco.

HarperTrade (division)
Imprints: HarperCollins, Perennial, Cliff Street Books, The Ecco Press, Quill, Amistad, HarperAudio, Large Print Editions, Rayo, Fourth Estate, ReganBooks and PerfectBound (e-books)

Morrow/Avon (division)
Imprints: William Morrow, Avon, HarperTorch, Eos, HarperEntertainment.

HarperCollins Children's Books Group
1350 6th Avenue, New York, NY 10019
tel 212-261-6500
President/Publisher Susan Katz

Imprints: Greenwillow Books, Joanna Cotler Books, Laura Geringer Books, HarperCollins Children's Books, HarperFestival, HarperTrophy, Avon, HarperTempest.

Harvard University Press*

79 Garden Street, Cambridge, MA 02138-1499
tel 617-495 2600 *fax* 617-495-5898
website www.hup.harvard.edu
Director William P. Sisler, *Editor-in-Chief/ Assistant Director* Aida D. Donald

History, philosophy, literary criticism, politics, economics, sociology, music, science, classics, social sciences, behavioural sciences, law.

Hastings House/Daytrips Publishers

2601 Wells Avenue, Suite 161, Fern Park, FL 32730
tel 407-339-3600 *fax* 407-339-5900
email PLeers@aol.com hhousebks@aol.com
website www.HastingsHouseBooks.com
Publisher Peter Leers

Travel, general non-fiction.

D.C. Heath and Co. – acquired by Houghton Mifflin Company

Hill and Wang

19 Union Square West, New York, NY 10003
tel 212-741-6900 *fax* 212-633-9385
website www.fsgbooks.com
Publisher Elisabeth Sifton, *Editor* Thomas Le Bien, *Consulting Editor* Arthur W. Wang

General non-fiction, history, drama. Division of **Farrar, Straus and Giroux**. Founded 1956.

Hippocrene Books Inc.

171 Madison Avenue, New York, NY 10016
tel 212-685-4371 *fax* 212-779-9338
email orders@hippocrenebooks.com
website www.hippocrenebooks.com
President/Editorial Director George Blagowidow

Foreign language books, international cookbooks, foreign language dictionaries, love poetry, travel, military history, Polonia, general trade. Founded 1971.

Holiday House

425 Madison Avenue, New York, NY 10017
tel 212-688-0085
President John Briggs, *Vice-President/Editor-in-Chief* Regina Griffin

General children's books. Send query letter before submitting MSS. Always include sae. No multiple submissions, please. Founded 1935.

Henry Holt and Company LLC*

115 West 18th Street, New York, NY 10011
tel 212-886-9200 *fax* 212-633-0748
President/Publisher John Sterling

History, biography, nature, science, self-help, novels, mysteries; books for young readers; trade paperback line, computer books. Founded 1866.

Houghton Mifflin Company*

222 Berkeley Street, Boston, MA 02116
tel 617-351-5000

Fiction and non-fiction – history, political science, biography, nature (Peterson Guides), and gardening guides; reference, both adult and juvenile. Imprints: Mariner (original and reprint paperbacks). No unsolicited MSS. Founded 1832.

HP Books – see Berkley Publishing Group

Hyperion*

77 West 66 Street, New York, NY 10023-6298
tel 212-456-0110 *fax* 212-456-0157
website www.hyperionbooks.com
President Robert Miller, *Vice-President/Publisher* Ellen Archer, *Vice-President/Publisher (Hyperion Books for Children)* Lisa Holton

General fiction and non-fiction, children's books. Division of Buena Vista Publishing, formerly Disney Book Publishing Inc. Founded 1990.

Indiana University Press

601 North Morton Street, Bloomington, IN 47404-3797
tel 812-855-8817 *fax* 812-855-8507
email iupress@indiana.edu
website www.indiana.edu/~iupress
Director Peter-John Leone

African studies, Russian and East European studies, music, history, women's studies, Jewish studies, African-American studies, film, folklore, philosophy, medical ethics, archaeology, anthropology, paleontology. Reference and high level trade books. Founded 1950.

International Marine Publishing

PO Box 220, Camden, Maine 04843
tel 207-236-4837 *fax* 207-236-6314
email nancy_dowling@mcgraw-hill.com
website www.internationalmarine.com
www.raggedmountainpress.com
Editorial Director Jonathan F. Eaton

Imprints: International Marine (boats, boating and sailing); Ragged Mountain Press (sport, adventure/travel, natural history). Division of the McGraw-Hill Companies. Founded 1992.

The Johns Hopkins University Press*

2715 North Charles Street, Baltimore, MD 21218-4319
tel 410-516-6971 *fax* 410-516-6968
Director James D. Jordan

History, literary criticism, classics, politics, economic development, environmental studies, biology, medical genetics, consumer health, history, religion. Founded 1878.

Knopf Publishing Group*

299 Park Avenue, New York, NY 10170
tel 212-572-2600 *fax* 212-572-8700
website www.randomhouse.com
President Sonny Mehta

General literature, fiction, belles-lettres, sociology, politics, history, nature, science, etc. Imprints: Alfred A. Knopf Inc., Anchor, Everyman's Library, Pantheon Books, Schocken Books, Vintage Books. Division of **Random House Inc.**

Krause Publications

700 East State Street, Iola, WI 54990-0001
tel 715-445-2214 *fax* 715-445-4087
email info@Krause.com
website www.Krause.com
Acquisitions Editor Paul Kennedy

Antiques and collectibles: coins, stamps, automobiles, toys, trains, firearms, comics, records; sewing and crafts, ceramics, outdoors, hunting.

Little, Brown & Company*

1271 Avenue of the Americas, New York, NY 10020
tel 212-522-8700
Chief Executive Larry Kirshbaum

General literature, fiction, non-fiction, biography, history, trade paperbacks, books for boys and girls. Art and photography books under the Bulfinch Press imprint.

Llewellyn Publications

PO Box 64383, St Paul, MN 55164-0383
email info@llewellyn.com
website www.llewellyn.com
President Carl Llewellyn Weschcke, *Vice President* Gabriel Weschcke

New Age, occult, astrology, magic. Founded 1901.

The Lyons Press

123 West 18th Street, 6th Floor, New York, NY 10011
tel 212-620-9580 *fax* 212-929-1836
President/Publisher Tony Lyons

Outdoor sport, natural history, sports, art, general fiction and non-fiction. Founded 1978.

McGraw-Hill*

11 West 19th Street, New York, NY 10011
tel 212-337 4098
website www.mcgraw-hill.com
Group Vice-President Theodore Nardin

Professional and reference: engineering, scientific, business, architecture, encyclopedias; college textbooks; high school and vocational textbooks: business, secretarial, career; trade books; training materials for industry. Division of The McGraw-Hill Companies.

McPherson & Company

PO Box 1126, Kingston, NY 12402
tel/fax 845-331-5807
email bmcpher@ulster.net
website www.mcphersonco.com
Publisher Bruce R. McPherson

Literary fiction; non-fiction: art criticism, writings by artists, film-making, etc; occasional general titles (e.g. anthropology). No poetry. No unsolicited MSS; query first. Founded 1974.

Microsoft Press*

One Microsoft Way, Redmond, WA 98052-6399
tel 425-882-8080 *fax* 425-936-7329
Publisher James Brown, *Editorial Director* Kim Fields

Computer books. Division of Microsoft Corp. Founded 1983.

Milkweed Editions

1011 Washington Avenue South, Suite 300, Minneapolis, MN 55415
tel 612-332-3192 *fax* 612-215-2550
website www.milkweed.org
www.worldashome.org
Publisher/Editor Emilie Buchwald

Fiction, poetry, essays, the natural world, children's novels (ages 8–14). Founded 1979.

The MIT Press*

5 Cambridge Center, Cambridge, MA 02142-1493
tel 617-253-5646 *fax* 617-258-6779
website mitpress.mit.edu
Director Frank Urbanowski, *Editor-in-Chief* Laurence Cohen

Architecture, art and design, cognitive sciences, neuroscience, linguistics, computer science and artificial intelligence, economics and finance, philosophy, environment and ecology, natural history. Founded 1961.

Morehouse Publishing Co.

PO Box 1321, Harrisburg, PA 17105
tel 717-541-8130 *fax* 717-541-8128
President Kenneth Quigley, *Publisher* Debra Farrington

Religious books, spirituality, children's.

William Morrow – see HarperCollins Publishers

The Naiad Press Inc.

PO Box 10543, Tallahassee, FL 32302
tel 850-539-5965 *fax* 850-539-9731
website www.naiadpress.com
Ceo Barbara Grier

Lesbian fiction; non-fiction: bibliographies, biographies, essays. Founded 1973.

NAL

375 Hudson Street, New York, NY 10014
tel 212-366-2000 *fax* 212-366-2666
email online@penguinputnam.com
website www.penguinputnam.com
President, Mass Market Paperbacks Leslie Gelbman, *Vice President/Publisher* Kara Welch

Fiction and general non-fiction. Imprints: Mentor, Meridian, New American Library, Onyx, Roc, Signet, Signet Classics, Topaz. Division of **Penguin Putnam Inc.** Founded 1948

Thomas Nelson Publisher

501 Nelson Place, Nashville, TN 37214-1000
tel 615-889-9000 *fax* 615-391-5225
Executive Vice President, Thomas Nelson Publishing Group Lee Gessner

Bibles, religious, non-fiction and fiction general trade books. Founded 1798.

North Light Books – see Writer's Digest Books

W.W. Norton & Company Inc.

500 Fifth Avenue, New York, NY 10110
tel 212-354-5500 *fax* 212-869-0856
website www.wwnorton.com

General fiction and non-fiction, music, boating, psychiatry, economics, family therapy, social work, reprints, college texts, science.

Orchard Books

555 Broadway, New York, NY 10012
tel 212-343-6782 *fax* 212-343-4890
website www.scholastic.com
Editorial Director Ken Geist

Books for children and young adults; picture books, fiction. Imprint of **Scholastic Inc.** Founded 1987.

Ottenheimer Publishers Inc.

5 Park Center Court, Suite 300, Onwings Mill, MD 21117
tel 410-902-9100 *fax* 410-902-7210
Directors Allan T. Hirsh, Jr, Allan T. Hirsh, III

Juvenile and adult non-fiction, reference. Founded 1890.

The Overlook Press*

141 Wooster Street, New York, NY 10012
tel 212-673-2210 *fax* 212-673-2296
website www.overlookpress.com
President and Publisher Peter Mayer, *Publishing Director* Tracy Carns

Non-fiction, fiction, children's books.

Oxford University Press Inc.*

198 Madison Avenue, New York, NY 10016
tel 212-726-6000 *fax* 212-726-6455
website www.oup-usa.org

Scholarly, professional, reference, bibles, college textbooks, religion, medical, music.

Pantheon Books – imprint of Knopf Publishing Group

Peachtree Publishers Ltd

1700 Chattahoochee Avenue, Atlanta, GA 30318-2112
tel 404-876-8761 *fax* 404-875-2578
email hello@peachtree-online.com
website www.peachtree-online.com
President and Publisher Margaret Quinlin, *Editorial Director* Kathy Landwehr

Children's picture books, novels and non-fiction books. Adult non-fiction subjects include self-help, parenting, education, health, regional guides. For children's books, send complete MS; for all others, send query letter with 3 sample chapters and table of contents. Founded 1977.

Pelican Publishing Company*

PO Box 3110, Gretna, LA 70054
tel 504-368-1175 *fax* 504-368-1195
email editorial@pelicanpub.com
website www.pelicanpub.com www.epelican.com
Publisher/President Milburn Calhoun

Art and architecture, cookbooks, travel, music, business, children's. Founded 1926.

Penguin AudioBooks – see Viking Penguin

Penguin Books – see Viking Penguin

Penguin Putnam Books for Young Readers

345 Hudson Street, New York, NY 10014
tel 212-366-2000 *fax* 212-366-2666
email online@penguinputnam.com
website www.penguinputnam.com
President Douglas Whiteman

Children's: picture books, board and novelty books, young adult novels, mass merchandise products. Imprints: Dial Books for Young Readers, Dutton Children's Books, Dutton Interactive, Phyllis Fogelman Books, Grosset & Dunlap, PaperStar, Philomel, Planet Dexter, Platt & Munk, Playskool, Price Stern Sloan, PSS, Puffin Books, G.P. Putnam's Sons, Viking Children's Books, Frederick Warne. Division of **Penguin Putnam Inc.** Founded 1997.

Dial Books for Young Readers (imprint)
fax 212-414-3394
President/Publisher Nancy Paulsen, *Editorial Director* Laura Hornik, *Vice President/Publisher, Phyllis Fogelman Books* Phyllis Fogelman

Children's fiction and non-fiction, picture books, board books, interactive books, novels.

Dutton Children's Books (imprint)
President/Publisher Stephanie Lurie, *Editorial Director, Dutton Children's Trade* Donna Brooks

Picture books, young adult novels, non-fiction photographic books. Founded 1852.

Grosset & Dunlap (imprint)
President/Publisher, Grosset & Dunlap Debra Dorfman

Children's: picture books, activity books, fiction and non-fiction. Imprints: Grosset & Dunlap, Platt & Munk, Somerville House USA, Planet Dexter. Founded 1898.

Price Stern Sloan (imprint)
Vice President/Publisher Jon Anderson

Children's books: novelty/lift-flaps, activity books, middle-grade fiction, middle-grade and YA non-fiction, cutting-edge graphic readers, picture books, books plus. Imprints: Crazy Games, Doodle Art, Planet Dexter, Serendipity, Troubador Press, Wee Sing. Founded 1963.

Puffin Books (imprint)
President/Publisher Tracy Tang, *Associate Publisher/Managing Editor* Gerard Mancini

Children's paperbacks. Founded 1935.

G.P. Putnam's Sons (imprint)
President/Publisher Nancy Paulsen

Children's hardcover and paperback

books. Imprints: G.P. Putnam's Sons, Philomel Books, PaperStar. Founded 1838.

Viking Children's Books (imprint)
President Regina Hayes
Fiction, non-fiction, picture books. Founded 1925.

Frederick Warne (imprint)
Original publisher of Beatrix Potter's *Tales of Peter Rabbit*. Founded 1865.

Penguin Putnam Inc.

(formerly Penguin USA and Putnam Berkley)
375 Hudson Street, New York, NY10014
tel 212-366-2000 *fax* 212-366-2666
email online@penguinputnam.com
website www.penguinputnam.com
President, The Penguin Group David Wan, *President* Susan Pearson Kennedy, *Ceo* David Shanks

Publisher of consumer books in both hardcover and paperback for adults and children; also produces maps, calendars, audiobooks and mass merchandise products. Adult imprints: Ace, Ace/Putnam, Allen Lane The Penguin Press, Avery, Berkley Books, BlueHen, Boulevard, DAW, Dutton, Grosset/Putnam, HP Books, Jove, Mentor, Meridian, Onyx, Penguin, Penguin Classics, Penguin Compass, Perigee, Plume, Prime Crime, Price Stern Sloan Inc., Putnam, G.P. Putnam's Sons, Riverhead Books, Roc, Signet, Signet Classics, Jeremy P. Tarcher, Topaz, Viking, Viking Compass, Viking Studio, Marian Wood Books. Children's imprints: Dial Books for Young Readers, Dutton Children's Books, Grosset & Dunlap, PaperStar, Philomel Books, Planet Dexter, Price Stern Sloan Inc., Puffin, G.P. Putnam's Sons, Viking Children's Books, Wee Sing, Frederick Warne. Divisions: **Berkley Publishing Group**, **Dutton**, **Plumo**, **NAL**, **Penguin Putnam Books for Young Readers**, **The Putnam Publishing Group**, **Viking Penguin**.

Penn State University Press*

820 North University Drive, USB1, Suite C, University Park, PA 16802
tel 814-865-1327 *fax* 814-863-1408
website www.psupress.org
Editor-in-Chief Peter Potter

Art history, literary criticism, religious studies, philosophy, political science, sociology, history, Russian and East European studies, Latin American studies and medieval studies. Founded 1956.

Perigee Books – see Berkley Publishing Group

The Permanent Press and Second Chance Press

4170 Noyac Road, Sag Harbor, NY 11963
tel 631-725-1101 *fax* 631-725-8215
website www.thepermanentpress.com
Directors Martin Shepard, Judith Shepard

Quality fiction. Founded 1978.

Plume

375 Hudson Street, New York, NY 10014
tel 212-366-2000 *fax* 212-366-2666
email online@penguinputnam.com
website www.penguinputnam.com
Publisher Kathryn Court, *President* Clare Ferraro, *Editor-in-Chief* Trena Keating

Fiction and general non-fiction for adults. Division of **Penguin Putnam Inc.**

Pocket Books*

1230 Avenue of the Americas, New York, NY 10020
tel 212-698-7000 *fax* 212-698-7007
website www.SimonSays.com
President/Publisher Judith M. Curr, *Vice President/Editorial Director* Emily Bestler

General fiction and non-fiction, trade hardcovers and paperbacks, mass market paperbacks. Imprints: Archway Paperbacks, Minstrel Books. Division of Simon & Schuster Adult Publishing Group. Founded 1939.

Price Stern Sloan – see Penguin Putnam Books for Young Readers

Princeton University Press*

Princeton, NJ 08540
postal address 41 William Street, Princeton, NJ 08540
tel 609-258-4900 *fax* 609-258-6305
website www.pup.princeton.edu
Director Walter Lippincott, *Editor-in-Chief* Terry Vaughn

Scholarly and scientific books on all subjects. Founded 1905.

Puffin Books – see Penguin Putnam Books for Young Readers

The Putnam Publishing Group

375 Hudson Street, New York, NY 10014
tel 212-366-2000 *fax* 212-366-2666
email online@penguinputnam.com
website www.penguinputnam.com

General trade books for adults; books on cassette. Imprints: Avery, BlueHen, G.P. Putnam's Sons, Riverhead Books, Jeremy P. Tarcher, Tarcher/Penguin, Putnam Berkley Audio, Marian Wood Books. Division of **Penguin Putnam Inc.**

G.P. Putnam's Sons (adult) – see The Putnam Publishing Group

G.P. Putnam's Sons (children's) – see Penguin Putnam Books for Young Readers

Rand McNally

PO Box 7600, Chicago, IL 60680
tel 847-329-2178
Chairman John Macomber, *President/Ceo* Norman E. Wells, Jr

Maps, guides, atlases, educational publications, globes and children's geographical titles and atlases in print and electronic formats.

Random House Inc.*

1540 Broadway, New York, NY 10036
tel 212-782-9000 *fax* 212-302-7985
299 Park Avenue, New York, NY 10170, *and* 280 Park Avenue, New York, NY 10017
tel 212-572-2600 *fax* 212-572-8700
website www.randomhouse.com
Chairman/Ceo Peter Olson, *President/Coo* Erik Engstrom

General fiction and non-fiction, children's books. Subsidiary of Bertelsmann AG.

Random House Audio Publishing Group (division)
President Jenny Frost

BDD Audio Publishing, Random House Audio Publishing.

Random House Children's Media Group (division)
President Kristina Peterson

Imprints: Children's Publishing (Crown Books for Young Readers, CTW Publishing, Delacorte Press, Disney Books, Doubleday Books for Young Readers, Dragonfly Books, First Choice Chapter Books, Knopf Books for Young Readers, Knopf Paperbacks, Laurel-Leaf, Picture Yearling, Random House Children's Publishing, Skylark, Starfire, Yearling Books); Children's Media.

Random House Diversified Publishing Group (division)
President Jenny Frost

Random House Large Print Publishing; Random House Value Publishing (Children's Classics, Crescent Books, Derrydale, Gramercy Books, Testament Books, Wings Books).

The Random House Information Group (division)
President Bonnie Ammer

Imprints: Fodor's Travel Publications, Living Language, Princeton Review, Random House Reference, Random House Puzzles and Games.

Random House Trade Publishing Group (division)
President/Editor-in-Chief Ann Godoff

Imprints: Random House Adult Trade Books, The Modern Library, Villard Books.

Riverhead Books (Hardcover) – see The Putnam Publishing Group

Riverhead Books (Trade Paperback) – see Berkley Publishing Group

Rizzoli International Publications Inc.

300 Park Avenue South, New York, NY 10010
tel 212-387-3400 *fax* 212-387-3535
Publisher Marta Hallett

Art, architecture, photography, fashion, gardening, design, gift books, cookbooks. Founded 1976.

Rodale Book Group

400 South 10th Street, Emmaus, PA 18098
tel 610-967-5171 *fax* 610-967-8961
Executive Editor, Rodale General Books Stephanie Tade, *Senior Editor, Spirituality* Troy Juliar, *Editor-in-Chief, Women's Health Books* Tami Booth, *Executive Editor, Cooking* Anne Egan, *Executive Editor, Home Arts* Ellen Phillips, *Executive Editor, Organic Living Books* Margot Schupf, *Executive Editor, Sports & Fitness Books* Steve Madden, *Executive Editor, Men's Health Books* Jeremy Katz

General health, women's health, men's health, senior health, alternative health, fitness, healthy cooking, gardening, pets, spirituality/inspiration, trade health. Founded 1930.

Rough Guides – see Viking Penguin

Routledge

29 West 35th Street, New York, NY 10001
tel 212-216-7800 *fax* 212-563-2269
Vice President and Publisher Linda Hollick, *Vice President and Publishing Director, Humanities* William P. Germano, *Publishing Director, Social Sciences* Karen Wolny, *Publishing Director,*

Reference Sylvia K. Miller

Literary criticism, history, philosophy, psychology and psychiatry, politics, women's studies, education, anthropology, sociology, urban studies, religion, lesbian and gay studies, classical studies, reference. Subsidiary of Taylor & Francis Books Inc.

Running Press Book Publishers

125 S 22 St, Philadelphia, PA 19103-4399
tel 215-567-5080 *fax* 215-568 2919
President Stuart Teacher, *Publisher* Carlo DeVito, *Design Director* Bill Jones, *Production Director* Peter Horodowich, *Editorial Director* Jennifer Worick

Art, craft/how-to, general non-fiction, children's books. Imprints: Courage Books, Running Press Miniature Editions. Founded 1972.

Rutgers University Press*

100 Joyce Kilmer Avenue, Piscataway, NJ 08854-8099
tel 732-445-7762 *fax* 732-445-7039
website http://rutgerspress.rutgers.edu
Directors Marlie Wasserman, *Editor-in-Chief* Leslie Mitchner

Women's studies, anthropology, film and media studies, sociology, public health, popular science, cultural studies, literature, religion, history of medicine, Asian-American studies, African-American studies, American history, American studies, art history, regional titles. Founded 1936.

St Martin's Press Inc.*

175 Fifth Avenue, New York, NY 10010
tel 212-674-5151 *fax* 212-420-9314

Trade, reference, college.

Schocken Books – imprint of Knopf Publishing Group

Scholastic Inc.*

555 Broadway, New York, NY 10012
tel 212-343-6100 *fax* 212-343-6930
website www.scholastic.com
Chairman/President/Ceo Richard Robinson, *Executive Vice President, Book Group* Barbara Marcus, *Executive Vice President, Scholastic Entertainment* Deborah Forte, *Executive Vice President, Educational Publishing* Julie McGee

Innovative textbooks, magazines, technology and teacher materials for use in both school and the home. Founded 1920.

Scribner – imprint of Simon & Schuster Adult Publishing Group

Sheridan House Inc.*

145 Palisade Street, Dobbs Ferry, NY 10522
tel 914-693-2410 *fax* 914-693-0776
email sheribks@aol.com
website www.sheridanhouse.com
President Lothar Simon

Sailing, nautical, travel. Founded 1940.

Simon & Schuster Adult Publishing Group*

1230 Avenue of the Americas, New York, NY 10020
tel 212-698-7000 *fax* 212-698-7007
President/Publisher Carolyn K. Reidy

General fiction and non-fiction. Imprints: Fireside, The Free Press, Kaplan, MTV®, PB Press, Pocket Books, Scribner, Scribner Paperback Fiction, S&S Libros en Espanol, Simon & Schuster, S&S Source, Sonnet, Star Trek®, Touchstone, Wall Street Journal Books, Washington Square Press VHI®. Division of Simon & Schuster. Founded 1924.

Simon & Schuster Children's Publishing Division*

1230 Avenue of the Americas, New York, NY 10020
tel 212-698-2112 *fax* 212-698-2793
President Kristina Peterson

Preschool to young adult, fiction and non-fiction, trade, library and mass market. Imprints: Aladdin Paperbacks, Atheneum Books for Young Readers, Little Simon, Margaret K. McElderry Books, Simon & Schuster Books for Young Readers, Simon Spotlight. Division of Simon & Schuster. Founded 1924.

Soho Press Inc.

853 Broadway, New York, NY 10003
tel 212-260-1900 *fax* 212-260-1902
email soho@sohopress.com
website www.sohopress.com
Publisher Juris Jurjevics, *Associate Publisher* Laura Hruska

Literary fiction, commercial fiction, mystery, thrillers, travel, memoir, general non-fiction. Founded 1986.

Stackpole Books

5067 Ritter Road, Mechanicsburg, PA 17055-6921
tel 717-796-0411 *fax* 717-796-0412
email sales@stackpolebooks.com
website www.stackpolebooks.com
Directors David Detweiler (chairman), David Ritter (president), Judith Schnell (editorial)

Nature, outdoor sports, Pennsylvania, crafts and hobbies, history, military history. Founded 1930.

Stanford University Press*

Palo Alto, CA 94304-1124
tel 650-723-9434 *fax* 650-725-3457
website www.sup.org
Director Geoffrey Burn

Scholarly non-fiction, college text, professional.

Strawberry Hill Press

21 Isis Street, Apt 102, San Francisco, CA 94103-4365
President Jean-Louis Brindamour PhD, *Executive Vice-President/Art Director* Ku Fu-Sheng, *Treasurer* Edward E. Serres

Health, self-help, cookbooks, philosophy, religion, history, drama, science and technology, biography, mystery, Third World. No unsolicited MSS; preliminary letter and return postage essential. Founded 1973.

Jeremy P. Tarcher – see The Putnam Publishing Group

Ten Speed Press

PO Box 7123, Berkeley, CA 94707
tel 510-559-1600 *fax* 510-524-1052
email order@tenspeed.com
website www.tenspeed.com
President Philip Wood, *Publisher and Vice President* Kirsty Melville

Career/business, cooking, general non-fiction, health, women's interest, self-help, practical guides, children's. Founded 1971.

Theatre Arts Books

29 West 35th Street, New York, NY 10001
tel 212-216-7877
Publishing Director William Germano

Theatre, performance, dance and allied books – acting techniques, voice, movement, costume, etc; a few plays. Imprint of **Routledge**.

Time Life Inc.*

2000 Duke Street, Alexandria, VA 22314
tel 703-838-7000 *fax* 703-838-7225
President/Ceo Steven L. Janas

Non-fiction: art, cooking, crafts, food, gardening, health, history, home maintenance, nature, photography, science. Subsidiary of Time Warner Inc. Founded 1961.

Tor Books

175 Fifth Avenue, 14th Floor, New York, NY 10010
tel 212-388-0100 *fax* 212-388-0191

Fiction: general, historical, western, suspense, mystery, horror, science fiction, fantasy, humour, juvenile, classics (English language); non-fiction: adult and juvenile. Affiliate of **St Martin's Press Inc**. Founded 1980.

Tuttle Publishing/Periplus Editions

153 Milk Street, Boston, MA 02109
tel 617-951-4080 *fax* 617-951-4045
website www.tuttlepublishing.com
Periplus Editions, 5 Little Road 08-01, Singapore 536983
tel 65-280-3320 *fax* 65-280-6290
Ceo Eric Oey, *Editorial Director* Ed Walters

Asian art, culture, cooking, gardening, Eastern philosophy, martial arts, health. Founded 1948.

United Publishers Group – see Hastings House Book Publishers

The University of Alabama Press*

Box 870380, Tuscaloosa, AL 35487
tel 205-348-5180 *fax* 205-348-9201
Director Daniel J.J. Ross, *Managing Editor* Kristin Harpster Lawrence

American and Southern history, African-American studies, religion, rhetoric and communication, Judaic studies, literary criticism, anthropology and archaeology. Founded 1945.

The University of Arkansas Press

The University of Arkansas, 201 Ozark Avenue, Fayetteville, AR 72701
tel 501-575-3246 *fax* 501-575-6044
email uaprinfo@cavern.uark.edu
Director Lawrence J. Malley

Biography, history, humanities, literary criticism, Middle East studies, African-American studies, poetry. Founded 1980.

University of California Press*

2120 Berkeley Way, Berkeley, CA 94720
tel 510-642-4247 *fax* 510-643-7127
Director James H. Clark

Publishes scholarly books, books of general interest, series of scholarly monographs and scholarly journals.

University of Chicago Press*

1427 East 60th Street, Chicago, IL 60637
tel 773-702-7700 *fax* 773-702-9756
Director Paula Barker Duffy

Scholarly books and monographs, religious and scientific books, general trade books, and 44 scholarly journals.

University of Illinois Press*

1325 South Oak Street, Champaign, IL 61820
tel 217-333-0950 *fax* 217-244-8082
Director Willis G. Regier

American studies (history, music, literature, religion), working-class and ethnic studies, communications, regional studies, architecture, philosophy and women's studies. Founded 1918.

The University of Massachussetts Press

PO Box 429, Amherst, MA 01004-0429
tel 413-545-2217 *fax* 413-545-1226
website www.umass.edu/umpress
Director Bruce G. Wilcox

Scholarly books and works of general interest: American studies and history, black and ethnic studies, women's studies, cultural criticism, architecture and environmental design, literary criticism, poetry, fiction, philosophy, political science, sociology, books of regional interest. Founded 1964.

The University of Michigan Press

839 Greene Street, PO Box 1104, Ann Arbor, MI 48106
tel 734-764-4388 *fax* 734-615-1540
email um.press@umich.edu
website www.press.umich.edu/
Director Philip Pochoda, *Assistant Director* Mary Erwin, *Executive Editor* LeAnn Fields, *Managing Editor* Christina Milton

Scholarly and general interest works in literature, classics, history, theatre, women's studies, political science, law, anthropology, economics, jazz; textbooks in English as a second language; regional trade titles. Founded 1930.

University of Missouri Press

2910 LeMone Boulevard, Columbia, MO 65201
tel 573-882-7641 *fax* 573-884-4498
website www.system.missouri.edu/upress
Director/Editor-in-Chief Beverly Jarrett, *Acquisitions Editor* Clair Willcox

American and European history, African American studies, American, British and Latin American literary criticism, journalism, political philosophy, art history, regional studies; short fiction. Founded 1958.

University of New Mexico Press

1720 Lomas Boulevard NE, Albuquerque, NM 87131-1591
tel 505-277-2346 *fax* 505-277-9270
email unmpress@unm.edu
website www.unmpress.com
Director Luther Wilson

Western history, anthropology and archaeology, Latin American studies, photography, multicultural literature, poetry. Founded 1929.

The University of North Carolina Press*

PO Box 2288, 116 South Boundary Street, Chapel Hill, NC 27514
tel 919-966-3561 *fax* 919-966-3829
Director Kate Douglas Torrey

American history, American studies, Southern studies, European history, women's studies, Latin American studies, political science, anthropology and folklore, classics, regional trade. Founded 1922.

University of Oklahoma Press

1005 Asp Avenue, Norman, OK 73019-0445
tel 405-325-2000 *fax* 405-325-4000
Director John N. Drayton

History of American West, American Indian studies, Mesoamerican studies, classical studies, women's studies, natural history, political science. Founded 1928.

University of Pennsylvania Press

4200 Pine Street, Philadelphia, PA 19104-4011
tel 215-898-6261 *fax* 215-898-0404
website www.upenn.edu/pennpress
Director Eric Halpern

American and European history, anthropology, art, architecture, business, cultural studies, economics, ancient studies, human rights, literature, health, sociology, Pennsylvania regional studies. Founded 1890.

University of Tennessee Press*

110 Conference Center Building, Knoxville, TN 37996-4108
tel 865-974-3321 *fax* 865-974-3724
email gadair@utk.edu
website www.sunsite.utk.edu/utpress
Director Jennifer Siler

American studies: women's studies, African-American studies, ethnomusicology, folklore, history, religion, anthropology, political science, vernacular architecture, material culture, literature.

Native American studies; cultural and ethnic studies; studies in most disciplines on Appalachia and the Southeast; literary fiction. Founded 1940.

University of Texas Press*
PO Box 7819, Austin, TX 78713-7819
tel 512-471-7233 *fax* 512-232-7178
email utpress@uts.cc.utexas.edu
website www.utexas.edu/utpress/
Director Joanna Hitchcock, *Assistant Director and Editor-in-Chief* Theresa May, *Assistant Director and Financial Officer* Joyce Lewandowski
Scholarly non-fiction: anthropology, classics and the Ancient World, conservation and the environment, film and media studies, geography, Latin American and Latino studies, Middle Eastern studies, natural history, ornithology, Texas and Western studies. Founded 1950.

University of Washington Press
PO Box 50096, Seattle, WA 98145-5096
tel 206-543-4050 *fax* 206-543-3932
Director Patrick Soden
Anthropology, Asian-American studies, Asian studies, art and art history, aviation history, environmental studies, forest history, Jewish studies, literary criticism, marine sciences, Middle East studies, music, regional studies, including history and culture of the Pacific Northwest and Alaska, Native American studies, resource management and public policy, Russian and East European studies, Scandinavian studies. Founded 1909.

University Press of Kansas
2501 West 15th Street, Lawrence, KS 66049-3905
tel 785-864-4154 *fax* 785-864-4586
email upress@ku.edu
website www.kansaspress.ku.edu
Director Fred Woodward, *Editor-in-Chief* Michael Briggs, *Senior Production Editor* Melinda Wirkus, *Assistant Director/Marketing Manager* Susan K. Schott
American history (political, social, cultural, environmental), military history, American political thought, American presidency studies, law and constitutional history, political science. Founded 1946.

Van Nostrand Reinhold – acquired by John Wiley & Sons

Viking – see Viking Penguin

Viking Children's Books – see Penguin Putnam Books for Young Readers

Viking Penguin
375 Hudson Street, New York, NY 10014
tel 212-366-2000 *fax* 212-366-2666
email online@penguinputnam.com
website www.penguinputnam.com
Chairman Susan Petersen Kennedy, *President* Clare Ferraro
Fiction and general non-fiction for adults. Imprints: Stephen Greene Press, Pelham, Penguin Books, Penguin Classics, Penguin Compass, Rough Guides, Viking, Viking Compass, Penguin AudioBooks, Allen Lane The Penguin Press. Division of **Penguin Putnam Inc.** Founded 1975.

Penguin AudioBooks (imprint)
Senior Editor David Highfill
Imprints: Penguin AudioBooks, Penguin HighBridge Audio. Founded 1990.

Penguin Books (imprint)
President/Publisher Kathryn Court
Fiction and general non-fiction for adults. Imprints: Penguin, Penguin Classics, Penguin Compass, Penguin 20th Century Classics. Founded 1935.

Rough Guides (imprint)
345 Hudson Street, New York, NY 10014
tel 212-414-3635 *fax* 212-414-3352
email rough@panix.com
website www.roughguides.com
Publisher Martin Dunford
Trade paperbacks, travel guides, phrasebooks, music reference, music CDs and internet reference. Founded 1982.

Viking (imprint)
Associate Publisher Paul Slovak
Fiction and general non-fiction for adults. Founded 1925.

Walker & Co.
435 Hudson Street, New York, NY 10014
tel 212-727-8300 *fax* 212-727-0984
Publisher George Gibson, *Mystery* Michael Seidman, *Juvenile* Emily Easton
General publishers, biography, popular science, health, business, mystery, history, juveniles. Founded 1960.

Frederick Warne – see Penguin Putnam Books for Young Readers

Warner Books Inc.*
1271 Avenue of the Americas, New York, NY 10020
tel 212-522-7200 *fax* 212-522-7991
Ceo Laurence K. Kirshbaum, *President/Coo/Publisher* Maureen Mahon Egen
Paperback originals and reprints, fiction

and non-fiction, trade paperbacks and hardcover books, audio books, gift books. Subsidiary of Time Warner Inc. Founded 1961.

WaterBrook Press*

5446 North Academy, Suite 200, Colorado Springs, CO 80918
tel 719-590-4999 *fax* 719-590-8977
website www.randomhouse.com
President/Publisher Dan Rich

Broad range of Christian fiction and non-fiction. Imprint: Harold Shaw Publishing. Division of **Random House Inc.**

Watson-Guptill Publications

770 Broadway, New York, NY 10003
tel 646-654-5500 *fax* 646-654-5486
email info@watsonguptill.com
website www.watsonguptill.com
Associate Publisher & Vice-President, Marketing and Sales Harriet Pierce, *Senior Acquisitions Editors* Candy Raney, Bob Nirkind, Victoria Craven, Joy Aquilino

Art, crafts, how-to, comic/cartooning, photography, performing arts, architecture and interior design, graphic design, music, entertainment, writing, reference, children's. Imprints: Amphoto Books, Back Stage Books, Billboard Books, Watson-Guptill, Whitney Library of Design. Founded 1937.

Franklin Watts

90 Sherman Turnpike, Danbury, CT 06816
tel 203-797-3500 *fax* 203-797-6986

School and library books for grades K–12.

Westminster John Knox Press

100 Witherspoon Street, Louisville, KY 40202-1396
tel 502-569-5042 *fax* 502-569-5113
email wjk@ctr.presbypub.com
website www.wjkbooks.com
Director Jack Keller

Religious, academic, reference, general

John Wiley & Sons Inc.*

605 Third Avenue, New York, NY 10158-0180
tel 212-850-6000 *fax* 212-850-6088
email info@wiley.com
website www.wiley.com
President/Ceo William J. Pesce

Specialises in scientific and technical books and journals, textbooks and educational materials for colleges and universities, as well as professional and consumer books and subscription services. Subjects include business, computer science, electronics, engineering, environmental studies, reference books, science, social sciences, multimedia, and trade paperbacks. Founded 1807.

Marian Wood Books – see The Putnam Publishing Group

Writer's Digest Books

4700 East Galbraith Road, Cincinnati, OH 45236
tel 513-531-2690 *fax* 513-891-7185

Market Directories, books for writers, photographers and songwriters.

Betterway Books (imprint)
How-to in home building, remodelling, woodworking, home organisation, theatre, genealogy.

North Light Books (imprint)
Fine art, decorative art, crafts, graphic arts instruction books.

Yale University Press*

302 Temple Street, New Haven, CT 06511
postal address PO Box 209040, New Haven, CT 06520
tel 203-432-0960 *fax* 203-432-0948/2394
email firstname.lastname@yale.edu
website www.yale.edu/yup/
Director John G. Ryden

Scholarly books and art books.

Dos and don'ts on approaching a publisher

You want the book you've written to be published. So how do you set about it? Where will you send the typescript? Probably to a publisher, but to which one? ***Michael Legat*** *offers guidelines on how to proceed.*

Finding a publisher

Do your market research in public libraries and bookshops, and especially in *Writers' and Artists' Yearbook*, to find out which publishers bring out the kind of book you have written. While looking at the *Yearbook* entries, note which publishers are willing to consider books submitted to them directly, rather than through an agent, and which require a letter of enquiry first. Incidentally, if you are hoping to interest an agent, they almost all want an enquiry letter first.

Enquiry letters

An enquiry letter should be business-like. Don't grovel ('it would be an honour to be published by so distinguished a firm'), don't make jokes ('my Mum says it's smashing, but maybe you'll think she's prejudiced'), don't be aggressive ('I have chosen you to publish my book, kindly send me your terms by return'). It is a good idea to write to whichever editor in the publishing house is responsible for books of the kind you have written (a phone call will provide this information – but take care to get the right title and spelling of the editor's name). Enclose a stamped addressed envelope. Look at the examples of the two poor enquiry letters followed by a good one on page 239.

You may have noticed that none of the letters refers to sending a disk or email. Such submissions may well become standard in a few years' time, but that stage has not yet been reached. However, once a book has been accepted, the publisher will certainly want a copy of the book on disk if it is available.

```
                          10 Any Street, Any Town,
                                        Any County

Messrs Dickens and Thackray,
83 Demy Street,
London WC45 9BM                         12th March

Dear Sirs,

May I please send for your
consideration the novel I have
written.

Yours sincerely,


L. Hopeful
```

This letter is far too brief. It gives no information about the kind of novel the author wishes to submit, nor of its length, it doesn't include a sae, and it doesn't even reveal the writer's sex. And since the writer doesn't use a question mark and has misspelt 'Thackeray', it's a good bet that the book will need meticulous and time-consuming copy-editing.

Presentation

Assuming that a publishing firm agrees to look at your book, the editor will expect to see a well-presented typescript (sometimes called a manuscript, abbreviated to MS). Here are some dos and don'ts about its appearance.

Use a typewriter or a word processor, or get a secretarial service to translate your handwriting on to a disk. Don't expect a publisher to read a handwritten script,

12 Any Street, Any Town,
Any County

Messrs Dickens and Thackeray,
83 Demy Street,
London WC45 9BM 14th March

Dear Sirs,

May I please send you the novel I have written, which I want to get published? It's called Wendy Chiltern. That's the name of the heroine. I am a 76-year-old grandmother, but all my friends say that I am very young for my age and I can certainly claim to be 'with it'. I belong to the Townswomen's Guild, and I do a lot of work at the local Church, and I play Bridge regularly, so you can tell my mind's still as sharp as ever.

I have been writing ever since I was a little girl, without trying to get anything published, but my friends have persuaded me to try my luck with this book. One of them said it was better than anything by Jackie Collins. Any publisher would jump at it, she said. They are all so enthusiastic, that I just had to 'have a go'…

The book is 57 pages long. It is properly typed, and all the spelling mistakes have been corrected. I should tell you that I am aware that the novel has some faults. It is just a little slow to get started, but once you're into it I am sure you won't be able to put it down.

If your reply is favourable, I shall bring the typescript to your office and perhaps you could spare me a few minutes to talk about it.

Yours sincerely,

Louise Hopeless (Mrs)

This letter is far too long, and includes masses of irrelevant information about the author. The fact that the lady's friends said they liked the book is no recommendation – what else are they going to say to their friend? And no editor is going to be tempted by a slow beginning, however honest it may be for the author to point it out. The book is almost certainly typed in single spacing with minuscule margins, and even so will be a long way short of book-length. And publishers do not spend time interviewing would-be authors – the lady should leave the typescript at reception, and let it speak for itself.

even if you have a fine Italian hand.

Choose a good quality white A4 paper (preferably not continuous listing paper, or if you must use it, at least separate the pages and remove the perforated edges). Whatever paper you use don't type on both sides, and don't use single spacing (which publishers abhor, and usually refuse to read) – one side of the paper only and double spacing is the rule. And do leave a good margin, at least 3 cm, all around the text, using the same margins throughout, so as to have the same number of lines on each page (except at the beginning and end of chapters). Double spacing and good margins allow space for your last-minute corrections to the typescript, for any copy-editor's amendments, and for instructions to the printer. And, not least in importance, a typescript in that style is much easier to read.

Always begin chapters on a new page. Justify on the left hand side only. Don't use blank lines between paragraphs (in the style of most typed letters nowadays), but indent the first line of each paragraph a few spaces. Blank lines should be used only to indicate a change of subject, or time, or scene, or viewpoint.

Be consistent in your choice of variant spellings, capitalisation, use of subheadings, etc. Make up your mind whether you are going to use -ise or -ize suffixes, for example, and whether, if 'village hall' appears in your text, you will type 'village hall' or Village Hall'.

For plays, use capitals for character names and underline stage directions or print them in italics. Use single spacing for dialogue, but leave a blank line between one character's speech and that of the next character to speak.

Poetry should be typed in exactly the way that the poem would appear in a printed version, using single or double spacing and various indentations as the poet wishes.

A good enquiry letter. The writer has (we can presume) found out to whom to address the letter, and how the lady spells her name. The letter is brief, but gives a clear picture of what the novel is about, and suggests its possible market, telling the publisher all that is necessary at this stage. It makes the two points that the writer has had some success with her work (do always include such details, provided that they are for professional publications), and that she intends to write other books. It also asks about the possibility of sending a synopsis and specimen chapters rather than the complete book, and that is in fact the way in which most publishers nowadays like to see new material (especially for non-fiction books, but also for novels). Of course, no enquiry letter, however satisfactory, can guarantee a favourable response, but at least with this one no editorial hackles should rise.

14 Any Street, Any Town,
Any County

Ms Ann Clarke,
Messrs Dickens and Thackeray,
83 Demy Street,
London WC45 9BM 16th March

Dear Ms Clarke,

May I please send you my novel, My Son, my Son, for your kind consideration? It is approximately 87,000 words in length and is a contemporary story, telling of the devastating effect on the marriage of the central characters when their 17-year-old son announces that he is gay. It is aimed at the same market as that of Joanna Trollope, although my characters might be described as a little further down the class scale.

I have written a number of articles which have been published not only in my local newspaper, but in a couple of cases in 'The Lady', and once in 'The Observer'. This is my first work of fiction, but I have two other novels with similar backgrounds in mind.

I enclose a sae and look forward to hearing from you. Perhaps you will let me know whether you would prefer to see a synopsis and specimen chapters, or the entire book.

Yours sincerely,

Lucilla Possible

Organising the pages

Number the pages (or 'folios', as publishers like to call them) straight through from beginning to end. Don't start each chapter at folio 1. If you need to include an extra folio after, say, folio 27, call it folio 27a and write at the foot of folio 27: 'Folio 27a follows'. Then write at the foot of 27a: 'Folio 28 follows'. Obviously, if you want to insert more than one page, you would use '27a', '27b', '27c', and so on. Some writers like to use part of the book's title as well as the folio number: 'Harry 27', for example, but this is not essential.

Create a title page for the book, showing the title and your name or pseudonym. Add your name and address in the bottom right hand corner, and also type it on the last folio of the typescript, in case the first folio becomes detached. You can also add a word count, if you wish (if using the word-counting facility on your word processor, round the figure up or down to the nearest thousand or five thousand). If you want to include a list of your previously published books, a dedication, a quotation, a list of contents or of illustrations, an assertion of your moral rights, or any similar material, use a separate page for each item. Leave these pages unnumbered or use small roman figures – i, ii, iii, etc – so that the first folio to have an Arabic number will be the first page of your text.

When fastening the typescript together, don't use pins (which scratch), paperclips (which pick up other papers from a busy editor's desk), or staples (which make it difficult to read). Don't ever fasten the pages together in one solid lump, and it's best to avoid ring binders too. Don't use plastic folders – they are slippery and can very easily cascade off a pile on the editor's desk (which won't please the editor). Almost all publishers prefer to handle each folio separately, so put the typescript into a wallet-type folder, or more than one if necessary. Put the title of the book and your name and address on the outside of the folder.

If illustrations form a large part of your book and you expect to provide them yourself they should be included with the typescript, and equally a selection should accompany a synopsis and specimen chapters. Send copies rather than originals. If your book is for children don't complete all the illustrations until the publisher has decided on the size of the book and the number of illustrations. If you have a friend who wants to supply illustrations for your book, do make sure that they will be up to publishing standard before you accept the offer. You may put off a children's publisher by suggesting an illustrator – they like to choose.

Waiting for a decision

Many publishers take what seems to be an unconscionable time to give a verdict on typescripts submitted to them. However, a decision whether or not to publish may not be easy, and several readings and consultations with other departments in the publishing house often have to take place before the editor can be sure of the answer. If you have heard nothing after two months, send a polite letter of enquiry; if you get no response, ask for your typescript back, and try another publisher.

Don't expect to be given reasons for rejection. Publishers do not have time to spend on books and authors which they are not going to publish. However, if the rejection letter contains any compliments on your work, you can take them at face value – publishers tend not to encourage authors unless they mean it.

Copyright material

Copyright exists as soon as you (or anyone else) records anything original to you on paper or film or disk. If you want to quote or otherwise use any material which is someone else's copyright, even if it is a short extract, you will have to get permission to do so, and possibly pay a fee. This applies not only to the text of a book, but also to letters and photographs, the copyright of which belongs to the letter-writer and photographer respectively. You must always give full acknowledgement to the source of the material. Use copyright material without such clearance and acknowledgement, and you are guilty of plagiarism – and another name for plagiarism is stealing. There are some circumstances in which you may use small amounts of text under a rule called 'Fair Dealing'. If your book has been accepted for publication, the publisher will be able to give you advice on the matter. (See also articles on copyright starting on page 627.)

Proofs

When your book is accepted by a publisher you may be asked to do further work on it, and a copy-editor will probably check the typescript line by line and word by word. As the author you should see the final copy before it goes to the printer, and this is almost your last chance to make any changes, whether they are simply the correction of literals or are more extensive than that.

At a later stage you will be sent proofs from the printer, which you will have to read with great care. Any errors which the printer has made are corrected without charge, but if you alter anything else, the publisher will have to pay for the changes and will be entitled to pass on to you any costs which exceed 10–15% of the cost of composition (i.e. the setting of the book in type). That sounds as though it gives you a lot of leeway, but alterations at proof stage are hugely expensive, so avoid them if you possibly can.

Michael Legat became a full-time writer after a long and successful publishing career. He is the author of a number of highly regarded books on publishing and writing.

See also...

- *Submitting material*, page 139
- *Writing and the children's book market*, page 241
- *How to get an agent*, page 343
- *Copyright questions*, page 627
- *British copyright law*, page 629

Writing and the children's book market

Over 10,700 new children's titles were published in the UK last year. ***Chris Kloet*** *suggests how a potential author can best ensure that their work is published.*

Children's book publishing can be difficult for the first-time writer to break into. It is a diverse, overcrowded market, with many thousands of titles currently in print, available both in the UK and from elsewhere via the internet. Children's publishers tend to fill their lists with commissioned books by writers they publish regularly, so they may lack space or be reluctant to take a risk with an untried author. This is a selective, highly competitive, market-led business. Since every new book is expected to meet its projected sales target, your writing must demonstrate solid sales potential, as well as strength and originality, if it is to stand a chance of being published.

Is your work right for today's market? Literary tastes and fashions change. Publishers cater to children whose reading is now almost certainly different from that of your own childhood. In the present electronic media-driven age, few want cosy tales about fairies and bunnies, jolly talking cars or magic teapots. Nor anything remotely imitative. Editors choose original, lively material – something witty, innovative and pacey. They look for polished writing with a fresh, contemporary voice that speaks directly and engages today's critical, media-savvy young readers, who are often easily bored.

Develop a sense of the market so that you can judge the potential for your work. Read widely and critically across the children's book spectrum for an overview, especially noting recent titles. As you read, pay attention to the different categories, series, genres and publishers' imprints. This will help you to pinpoint likely publishers. Before submitting your typescript, ensure that your targeted publisher currently publishes in your particular form or genre. Request catalogues from their marketing department; check out their website. Consult the publisher's entry under *Book publishers UK and Ireland* (see page 141). Many publishing houses now stipulate 'No unsolicited MSS or synopses'. Don't spend your time and postage sending work to them; choose instead a publisher who accepts unsolicited work.

You might consider approaching a literary agent who knows market trends, publishers' lists and the faces behind them (see *Literary agents for children's books*, page 367). Most editors regard agents as filters and may prefer submissions from them, knowing that a preliminary critical eye has been cast over them.

Picture books

Books for babies and toddlers are often board books and novelties. Unless you are also a professional illustrator (see *Illustrating for children's books*, page 245) they present few opportunities for a writer. Picture books are aimed at children aged between two and five or six, and are usually 32 pages long giving 12–14 double-page spreads, and illustrated in colour.

Although a story written for this format should be simple, it must be structured, with a compelling beginning, middle and end. The theme should interest and be appropriate for the age and experience of its audience. As the text is likely to be reread, it should possess a satisfying rhythm (but beware of rhymes). Ideally, it should be fewer than 1000 words (and could be much shorter), must offer scope

Publisher	Series name	Length	Age group	Comments
Andersen Press	Tigers	3000–5000 words 64 pages	6–9	B&w illustrations throughout
A & C Black	Black Cats	12,000 words 96 pages	10–12	Short comic novels; b&w illustrations
	Chameleons	1200 words 48 pages	5–7	Colour illustrations throughout
Bloomsbury	Young Fiction	2500 words 64 pages	5–7	B&w illustrations throughout
	Middle Fiction	6000 words 64 pages	7–9	B&w illustrations throughout
Collins Children's Books	Roaring Good Reads	2000–8000 words	7–9	B&w illustrations throughout
	Middle Fiction	8000–15,000 words	9–11	
	Collins Voyager	20,000 words+	9–14	Fantasy
	Collins Flamingo	30,000–60,000 words	13–16	Contemporary fiction
Egmont Books	Blue Bananas	1000 words 48 pages	5+	Colour illustrations
	Red Bananas	2000 words 48 pages	6+	Colour illustrations
	Yellow Bananas	3000 words 48 pages	7+	Colour illustrations
	Go Bananas	1000–3000 words 48 pages	5–9	Curriculum-based strand
Franklin Watts	Leapfrog	500–700 words 32 pages	4–6	Colour illustrations throughout
	Hopscotch	1000 words 32 pages	6–8	Colour illustrations throughout
Hodder Children's Books	Bite	35,000+ words	11+	Contemporary fiction
	Silver	35,000+ words	10+	Fantasy and science fiction
	Signature	35,000+ words	11+	Literary fiction
Kingfisher	I Am Reading	1200 words 48 pages	5+	Colour illustrations throughout
Orchard Books	Crunchies	1000–1500 words	5–7	B&w line illustrations
	Super Crunchies	5000 words	7–9	B&w line illustrations
	Red Apples	20,000–25,000 words	9–11	
	Black Apples	30,000–40,000 words	12+	
Penguin Group	Colour Young Puffin	1000–2500 words 32–64 pages	6–8	Colour illustrations
	Young Puffin	8000–10,000 words 96–128 pages	7–9	B&w line illustrations
Scholastic Children's Books	Young Hippo	3500–10,000 words 64–128 pages	5–8	B&w illustrations throughout
	Hippo	15,000–25,000 words	8–12	
	Point	30,000 words	12+	
Walker Books	Story Books	6000–10,000 words	4–7	Stories around central character
	Sprinters	2000 words	6–8	B&w illustrations throughout
	Junior fiction	15,000–25,000 words	8–12	
	Teenage fiction	25,000–40,000 words	12+	

for illustration and, finally, it needs strong international appeal. Reproducing full-colour artwork is costly and the originating publisher must be confident of achieving co-productions with publishers overseas, to keep unit costs down. It has to be said: it is a tough field.

Submit a picture book text typed either on single-sided A4 sheets, showing page breaks, or as a series of numbered pages, each with its own text. Do not go into details about illustrations, but simply note anything that is not obvious from the text that needs to be included in the pictures.

Younger fiction

This area of publishing presents opportunities for the new writer. It covers stories written for the post-picture book stage, when children are reading their first whole novels. Texts vary in length and complexity, depending on the age and fluency of the reader, but tend to be between 1000 and 8000 words long.

Publishers bring out titles under the umbrella of various series, each targeted at a particular level of reading experience and competency. Categories are: beginning or first readers, developing or newly confident, confident, and fluent readers. Note that these are not the same as reading schemes published for the schools market and do not require a restricted vocabulary. Stories for the bottom end of the age range are usually short, straight-through narratives illustrated throughout in colour, whereas those for older children are broken down into chapters and may be illustrated in black and white. The table opposite lists publishers' requirements for some currently published series. Check that your material is correct in terms of length and interest level when approaching a publisher with a submission for a series.

Genre fiction

Another area in children's publishing is that of genre fiction. Usually published in paperback series, titles are sometimes the work of a single author, but might also be novels from several authors writing in a similar vein. Some fiction aimed at teenagers is published in genre series although it is much less popular than in recent years.

General fiction

Many novels for children aged 9–12 are published, not in series, but as 'standalone' titles, each judged on its own merits. The scope for different types of stories is wide – adventure stories, fantasies, historical novels, science fiction, ghost and horror stories, humour, and stories of everyday life. Generally, their length is 20,000–40,000 words. Anything longer may present the publisher with an unpalatably high price point for the book. This is a rough guide and is by no means fixed. For example, J.K. Rowling's phenomenally successful *Harry Potter* novels generally weigh in at between 300–600 closely printed pages.

Perhaps more than in other areas of juvenile fiction, the individual editor's tastes will play a significant part in the publishing decision, i.e they want authors' work which *they* like. They also need to feel confident of a new writer's ability to go on to write further books for their lists – nobody is keen to invest in an author who is just a one-book wonder.

When submitting your work it is probably best to send the entire typescript (see *Dos and don'ts on approaching a publisher*, page 237). Although some people advise sending in a synopsis with the first three chapters, a prospective publisher will need to see whether you can sustain a reader's interest to the end of the book.

Teenage fiction

As noted earlier, some of the published output for teenaged readers is published in series, sometimes under different series genres. Increasingly, though, publishers are targeting this area of the market with edgy, hard-hitting novels about contemporary teenagers, which they publish as standalone titles. There is also a current vogue for 'young adult' novels that have a crossover appeal to an adult readership.

This is particularly true of certain types of historical fiction by writers such as Jamila Gavin, Adele Geras and Kevin Crossley-Holland, and of several fantasy writers. For example, Philip Pullman's *The Amber Spyglass* was the first children's book to be the overall winner of the Whitbread Book of the Year award.

Non-fiction

The last few years have seen fundamental and striking changes in the type of information books published for the young. Hitherto the province, by and large, of specialist publishers catering for the educational market, the field has now broadened to encompass an astonishing range of presentations and formats which are attractive to the young reader. Although the illustrated text book approach still has its place in schools, increasingly, children are wooed into learning about many topics via entertaining and accessible paperback series such as the *Horrible Histories* published by Scholastic, and a host of similar series from other publishers. In writing for this market, it goes without saying that you must research your subject thoroughly and be able to put it across clearly, with an engaging style. Familiarise yourself with the relevant parts of the National Curriculum. Check out the various series and ask the publishers for any guidelines. You will be well advised to check that there is a market for your book before you actually write it, as researching a subject can be both time consuming and costly. Submit a proposal to your targeted publisher, outlining the subject matter and the level of treatment, and your ideas about the audience for your book.

Chris Kloet worked as Children's Publisher (1984–97) at Victor Gollancz Ltd, and is now Fiction Publisher at Hodder Children's Books. She has written and reviewed children's books and has lectured widely on the subject.

Illustrating for children's books

The world of children's publishing is big business. The huge range of books published each year all carry artwork – lots of it. ***Maggie Mundy*** *offers guidance for people who are at the start of their career in illustrating for children's books.*

The portfolio

Your portfolio should reflect the best of you and your work, and should speak for itself. Keep its content simple – if too many styles are included, for instance, your work will not leave a lasting impression.

Include some artwork other than those carried out for college projects, e.g. an illustration from a timeless classic to show your abilities, and something modern which reflects your own taste and the area in which you wish to work.

If your strength is for black and white illustration, include pieces with and without tone and with or without a wash. Some publishers want line and tone and some want only line. As cross hatching and stippling can add a lot of extra time to an illustration deadline, it might be advisable to leave out these samples. If you can, include a selection of humour as it can be used effectively in educational books and elsewhere. It is best not to sign and date your work: some artworks can stand the test of time and still look good after a year or two, but if it looks dated … so is the illustrator!

An A3 portfolio is probably the ideal size. Place your best piece of artwork on the opening page and your next best piece on the last page. See *Freelancing for beginners* on page 383 for further information on portfolio presentation.

Looking at the market

Start by looking thoroughly at what is being published today for children. Take your studies to branches of big retail chains, some independent bookshops, as well as your local library (a helpful librarian should be able to tell you which are the most borrowed books). Absorb the picture books, explore the novelty books, look at the variety of colour covers, and note the range of black line illustrations inside books for children and teenagers. Make a list of the publishers you think may be able to use your particular style.

By making these investigations you will gain an insight into not only the current trends and styles but also the much favoured, oft-published classic children's literature. Most importantly, it will help you identify your market.

In books for a young age range every picture must tell the story – some books have no text and the illustrations say it all. Artwork should be uncluttered, shapes clear, and colour bright. If this does not appeal to you, go up a year or two and note the extra details that are added to the artwork (which still tells the story). Children now need to see more than just clear shapes: they need extra details added to the scene – e.g. a quirky spider hanging around, or a mouse under the bed.

Children are your most critical audience: never think that you can got away with 'any old thing'. Indeed, at the Bologna Book Fair it is a panel of children which judges what they consider to be the best picture book.

Current trends

Innovative publishers are always on the lookout for something new in illustration styles: something completely different from the tried and tested. More and more they are turning to European and overseas illustrators, often sourced from the Bologna Book Fair exhibitions and illustrators catalogue.

Today, virtually any medium can be used on any colour paper. Belgian Marjolein Pottie is another young illustrator to watch out for. Her picture books are done on black paper, using the paper itself to make the outlines. A new discovery in the UK, her latest book, *Musical Beds*, is published by Simon & Schuster in both the UK and the USA.

Always strive to improve on your work. Don't be afraid to try out something different and to work it up into acceptable examples. Above all, don't get left behind.

Making approaches for work

With your portfolio arranged and your target audience in mind, compile a list of publishing houses, packagers and magazines which you think may be suitable for your work.

An agent should know exactly where to place your work, and this may be the easier option (see below). However, you may wish to market yourself by making and going to appointments until you crack your first job.

Alternatively, you could make up a simple broadsheet comprising a black and white and two or three colour illustrations, together with your contact details, and have it colour photocopied or printed. Another inexpensive option is to have your own CDs made up and to send them instead. Send a copy to either the Art Director, the Creative Director or the Senior Commissioning Editor (for picture books) of each potential client on your list. Try to find out the name of the person you would like to see your work. Wait at least a week and then follow up your mailing with a phone call to ask if someone would like to see your portfolio.

Also consider investing in your own website which you can easily update yourself (see *Setting up a website*, page 556).

Know your capabilities

Know your strengths, but be even more aware of your weaknesses. You will gain far more respect if you admit to not being able to draw something particularly well than by going ahead and producing an embarrassing piece of artwork and having it rejected. You will be remembered for your professional honesty and that client may well try to give you a job where you can use your expertise.

Publishers need to know that you can turn out imaginative, creative artwork while closely following a text or brief, and be able to meet their deadline. It may take an illustrator three weeks to prepare roughs for 32 pages, three weeks to finish the artwork, plus a week to make any corrections. In addition, time has to be allowed for the roughs to be returned. On this basis, how many books can an illustrator realistically take on? Scheduling is of paramount importance (see below).

You will need to become familiar with 'publishing speak' – terms such as gutters, full bleed, holding line, overlays, vignettes, tps, etc. If you don't know the meaning of a term, ask – after all, if you have only recently left college you will not be expected to know all the jargon.

In the course of your work you will have to deal with such issues as contracts, copyright, royalties, public lending rights, rejection fees, etc. The Association of Illustrators, which exists to give help to illustrators in all areas, is well worth joining.

Organising your workload

When you have reached the stage when you have jobs coming through on a fairly regular basis, organise a comprehensive schedule for yourself so you do not overburden yourself with work. Include on it when roughs have to be submitted, how much work you can fit in while waiting for their approval, the deadline for the artwork, and so on. A wall chart can be helpful for this but another system may work better for you. It is totally unacceptable to deliver artwork late. If you think that you might run over time with your work, let your client know in advance as it may be possible to reach a new agreement for delivery.

Payment

There are two ways in which an illustrator may be paid for a commission for a book: a flat fee on receipt and acceptance of the artwork, or by an advance against a royalty of future sales. The advance offered could be less than a flat fee but it may result in higher earnings overall. If the book sells well, the illustrator will receive royalty payments twice a year for as long the book is in print.

You need to know from the outset how you are going to be paid. If it is by a flat fee, you may be given an artwork order with a number to be quoted when you invoice. Always read through orders to make sure you understand the terms and conditions. If you haven't been paid within 30 days, send a statement to remind the client, or make a quick phone call to ask when you can expect to receive payment.

With a royalty offer, a contract will be drawn up and this must be checked carefully. One of the clauses will state the breakdown of how and when you will be paid.

Once you have illustrated your first book you should register with the Public Lending Right office (see page 623) so that you can receive a yearly payment on all UK library borrowings. You will need to cooperate with the author regarding percentages before submitting your own form. The PLR office will give you a reference number, and you then submit details to them of each book you illustrate. It mounts up and is a nice little earner!

Agents

The role of the agent is to represent the illustrator to the best of their ability and to the illustrator's best advantage. A good agent knows the marketplace and will promote illustrators' work where it will count. An agent may ask you to do one or two sample pieces to strengthen your portfolio, giving them a better chance of securing work for you.

Generally speaking, agents will look after you, your work schedules, payments, contracts, royalties, copyright issues, and try to ensure you have a regular flow of work which you not only enjoy but will stretch your talents to taking on bigger and better jobs. Without exposing your weaknesses, check that you have adequate time in which to do a job and that you are paid a fair rate for the work.

Some illustrators manage well without an agent, and having one is not necessarily a pathway to fame and fortune. Choose carefully: you need to both like and trust the agent and vice versa.

Agents' charges range from 25% to 30%. Find out from the outset how much a prospective agent will charge.

Finally

Do not be downhearted if progress is at first slow. Everyone starts by serving an apprenticeship, and it is a great opportunity to learn, absorb and soak up as much of the business as possible. Ask questions, get all the advice you can, and use what you learn to improve your craft and thereby your chances of landing a job. Publishers are always on the lookout for fresh talent and new ideas, and one day your talent will be the one they want.

Maggie Mundy has been representing illustrators for children's books since 1983. Her agency represents 25 European and British illustrators for children's books.

Children's book publishers and packagers

A quick reference guide to children's book publishers and packagers by subject area. Listings for Book publishers UK and Ireland start on page 141 and listings for Book packagers start on page 203.

Picture books

Book publishers
Andersen Press Ltd
Award Publications Ltd
Bantam Children's Books
Barefoot Books Ltd
David Bennett Books Ltd
Bloomsbury Publishing Plc
Bodley Head Children's
Jonathan Cape Children's Books
Child's Play (International) Ltd
Christian Education
James Clarke & Co. Ltd
Dref Wen
Egmont Books
Evans Brothers Ltd
Everyman Publishers plc
Floris Books
Gairm Publications
Geddes & Grosset
Gomer Press
Gullane Children's Books
HarperCollins Publishers
Heinemann Young Books
Hippo
Hodder & Stoughton
Hodder Headline Ltd
Hunt & Thorpe
John Hunt Publishing Ltd
Hutchinson Children's
Kingfisher Publications plc
Ladybird
Frances Lincoln Ltd
Lion Publishing plc
Peter Lowe (Eurobook Ltd)
Lutterworth Press
Macmillan Children's Books Ltd
Magi Publications
Mammoth
Mantra
Methuen Children's Books
The O'Brien Press Ltd
Michael O'Mara Books Ltd
Orchard Books
The Orion Publishing Group Ltd
Oxford University Press
Paternoster
Pavilion Children's Books
Piccadilly Press
Puffin
Ragged Bears Publishing Ltd
Red Fox
Saint Andrew Press
Scholastic Children's Books
Scottish Children's Press
Scripture Union
Tamarind Ltd
Time Warner Books UK
Transworld Publishers
Usborne Publishing
Ventura
Walker Books Ltd
Warne
The Watts Publishing Group Ltd
Zero to Ten Ltd

Book packagers
act-two ltd
Aladdin Books Ltd
Albion Press Ltd
Breslich & Foss Ltd
Brown Wells & Jacobs Ltd
Graham-Cameron Publishing & Illustration
Angus Hudson Ltd
Marshall Editions Ltd
Mathew Price Ltd
Tangerine Designs Ltd
The Templar Company plc
Tucker Slingsby Ltd
Ventura Publishing Ltd

Fiction

Book publishers
Andersen Press Ltd
Anvil Books/The Children's Press
Bantam Children's Books
Barefoot Books Ltd
David Bennett Books Ltd
A & C Black Publishers Ltd
Bloomsbury Publishing Plc
Bodley Head Children's
Breese Books Ltd
Brimax Books
Jonathan Cape Children's Books
Child's Play (International) Ltd
Christian Education
James Clarke & Co. Ltd
Cló Iar-Chonnachta Teo.
Dref Wen
Egmont Books
Evans Brothers Ltd
Everyman Publishers plc
Faber & Faber Ltd
Floris Books
Gairm Publications
Gomer Press
Patrick Hardy Books
HarperCollins Publishers
Heinemann Young Books
Hippo
Hodder & Stoughton
Hodder Headline Ltd
Honno Ltd (Welsh Women's Press)
John Hunt Publishing Ltd
Hutchinson Children's
Kingfisher Publications plc
Ladybird
Frances Lincoln Ltd
Lion Publishing plc
Peter Lowe (Eurobook Ltd)
Lutterworth Press
Macmillan Children's Books Ltd
Mammoth

Mantra
Marino Books
Kevin Mayhew Ltd
Mentor Books
The Mercier Press
Methuen Children's Books
The O'Brien Press Ltd
Michael O'Mara Books Ltd
Orchard Books
The Orion Publishing Group Ltd
Oxford University Press
Pavilion Children's Books
Pipers' Ash Ltd
Point
Poolbeg Group Services Ltd
Puffin
Ragged Bears Publishing Ltd
Red Fox
Robinson Publishing Ltd
Saint Andrew Press
Scholastic Press
Scottish Children's Press
Scripture Union
Simon & Schuster
D.C. Thomson & Co. Ltd – Publications
Transworld Publishers
Usborne Publishing
Walker Books Ltd
The Watts Publishing Group Ltd
The Women's Press
Y Lolfa Cyf.

Book packagers

Graham-Cameron Publishing & Illustration
Quarto Children's Books Ltd
Working Partners Ltd

Non-fiction

Book publishers

Aladdin/Watts
Anness Publishing
Apple Press
Atlantic Europe Publishing Co. Ltd
Award Publications Ltd
Bantam Children's Books
Belitha Press
David Bennett Books Ltd
Big Fish
A & C Black Publishers Ltd
Boxtree
Brimax Books
Child's Play (International) Ltd
James Clarke & Co. Ltd
Dref Wen
Egmont Books
Evans Brothers Ltd
Faber & Faber Ltd
First and Best in Education Ltd
Folens Ltd
Geddes & Grosset
Gomer Press
HarperCollins Publishers
Heinemann Young Books
Hippo
Hodder & Stoughton
Hodder Headline Ltd
Hopscotch Educational Publishing Ltd
John Hunt Publishing Ltd
Kingfisher Publications plc
Ladybird
Frances Lincoln Ltd
Lion Publishing plc
Peter Lowe (Eurobook Ltd)
Lutterworth Press
Macmillan Children's Books Ltd
Mantra
Mentor Books
The National Trust
Neate Publishing
NMSI
The O'Brien Press Ltd
Michael O'Mara Books Ltd
The Orion Publishing Group Ltd
Oxford University Press
Paternoster
Pavilion Children's Books
Piccadilly Press
Pipers' Ash Ltd
Portland Press Ltd
Puffin
Saint Andrew Press
Salariya Book Company Ltd
Schofield & Sims Ltd
Scholastic Children's Books
Scottish Children's Press
Scripture Union
Simon & Schuster
Tamarind Ltd
Tango Books
Time Warner Books UK
Transworld Publishers
Usborne Publishing
Walker Books Ltd
Warne
The Watts Publishing Group Ltd
The Women's Press
Y Lolfa Cyf.
Zero to Ten Ltd
Zigzag
Zoë Books Ltd

Book packagers

act-two ltd
Aladdin Books Ltd
Andromeda Oxford Ltd
Bender Richardson White
BLA Publishing Ltd
Breslich & Foss Ltd
The Brown Reference Group Ltd
Brown Wells & Jacobs Ltd
Cambridge Publishing Management Ltd
Roger Coote Publishing
Design Eye Ltd
Earthscape Editions
Graham-Cameron Publishing & Illustration
Hart McLeod Ltd
Lionheart Books
Marshall Editions Ltd
Monkey Puzzle Media Ltd
Orpheus Books Ltd
Quarto Children's Books Ltd
Wordwright Books

Other

Activity and novelty

Book publishers

Andersen Press Ltd
Apple Press
Award Publications Ltd
David Bennett Books Ltd
Big Fish
A & C Black Publishers Ltd
Bloomsbury Publishing Plc
Brimax Books
Child's Play (International) Ltd
Christian Education
James Clarke & Co. Ltd
Dref Wen
Egmont Books
First and Best in Education Ltd
Floris Books
Geddes & Grosset
Gullane Children's Books
Heinemann Young Books
Hippo
Hodder Headline Ltd
John Hunt Publishing Ltd
Kingfisher Publications plc
Ladybird
Frances Lincoln Ltd
Lion Publishing plc
Lutterworth Press
Macmillan Children's Books Ltd
Magi Publications
Mammoth
Kevin Mayhew Ltd
Mentor Books
Methuen Children's Books
Michelin Travel Publications
The O'Brien Press Ltd
Michael O'Mara Books Ltd
Orchard Books
Oxford University Press

Pavilion Children's Books
Pipers' Ash Ltd
Puffin
Robinson Publishing Ltd
Scholastic Children's Books
Scottish Children's Press
Scripture Union
Tango Books
Tarquin Publications
Transworld Publishers
Treehouse Children's Books
Usborne Publishing
Walker Books Ltd
Warne
Zigzag

Book packagers

act-two ltd
Aladdin Books Ltd
Andromeda Oxford Ltd
Breslich & Foss Ltd
Brown Wells & Jacobs Ltd
Cowley Hunter Robinson Ltd
Design Eye Ltd
Graham-Cameron Publishing & Illustration
Angus Hudson Ltd
Marshall Cavendish Partworks Ltd
Pinwheel Ltd
Playne Books Ltd
Mathew Price Ltd
Quarto Children's Books Ltd
Sadie Fields Productions Ltd
Tangerine Designs Ltd
The Templar Company plc
Tucker Slingsby Ltd

Audiobooks

Book publishers

Barefoot Books Ltd
Child's Play (International) Ltd
Dref Wen
Egmont Books
HarperCollins Publishers
Hodder Children's Books
Ladybird
Mantra
The O'Brien Press Ltd
Random House Group Ltd
St Pauls
Scholastic Children's Books
Scripture Union

Multimedia

Book publishers

Big Fish
Christian Education
Cló Iar-Chonnachta Teo.
Ginn & Co.
HarperCollins Publishers
Heinemann Educational
Macmillan Children's Books Ltd
Mantra
Nelson Thornes Ltd
Oxford University Press
Paternoster
Puffin
Random House Group Ltd
Ransom Publishing Ltd
St Pauls
Warne
Zigzag

Book packagers

act-two ltd
Andromeda Oxford Ltd

Poetry

Book publishers

Anvil Press Poetry
Bantam Children's Books
Belitha Press
A & C Black Publishers Ltd
Bloomsbury Publishing Plc
Bodley Head Children's
Jonathan Cape Children's Books
James Clarke & Co. Ltd
Dref Wen
Evans Brothers Ltd
Everyman Publishers plc
Faber & Faber Ltd
Gairm Publications
Gomer Press
HarperCollins Publishers
Heinemann Young Books
Hutchinson Children's
Kingfisher Publications plc
Frances Lincoln Ltd
Lutterworth Press
Macmillan Children's Books Ltd
Mammoth
Methuen Children's Books
Orchard Books
Oxford University Press
Paternoster
Pipers' Ash Ltd
Puffin
Red Fox
Saint Andrew Press
Scholastic Children's Books
Scottish Children's Press
Transworld Publishers
Walker Books Ltd
The Watts Publishing Group Ltd

Book packagers

Albion Press Ltd
Graham-Cameron Publishing & Illustration

Religion

Book publishers

A & C Black Publishers Ltd
Canterbury Press Norwich
Catholic Truth Society
Christian Education
James Clarke & Co. Ltd
Dref Wen
Gresham Books Ltd
HarperCollins Publishers
Hunt & Thorpe
John Hunt Publishing Ltd
Kingfisher Publications plc
Frances Lincoln Ltd
Lion Publishing plc
Lutterworth Press
Mantra
Marshall Pickering
Kevin Mayhew Ltd
Oxford University Press
Paternoster
George Ronald
Saint Andrew Press
St Pauls
Scripture Union
Society for Promoting Christian Knowledge
Usborne Publishing
Veritas Publications

Book packagers

Albion Press Ltd
Graham-Cameron Publishing & Illustration
Angus Hudson Ltd

Doing it on your own

Reasons for self-publishing are varied. Many highly respected comtemporary and past authors have published their own works. **Peter Finch** *introduces the concept and outlines the implications of such an undertaking.*

Why bother?

You've tried all the usual channels and been turned down; your work is uncommercial, specialised, technical, out of fashion; you are concerned with art while everyone else is obsessed with cash; you need a book out quickly; you want to take up small publishing as a hobby; you've heard that publishers make a lot of money out of their authors and you'd like a slice – all reason enough. But be sure you understand what you are doing before you begin.

But isn't this cheating? It can't be real publishing – where is the critical judgement? Publishing is a respectable activity carried out by firms of specialists. Writers of any ability never get involved.

But they do. Start self-publishing and you'll be in good historical company: Horace Walpole, Balzac, Walt Whitman, Virginia Woolf, Gertrude Stein, John Galsworthy, Rudyard Kipling, Beatrix Potter, Lord Byron, Thomas Paine, Mark Twain, Upton Sinclair, W.H. Davies, Zane Grey, Ezra Pound, D.H. Lawrence, William Carlos Williams, Alexander Pope, Robbie Burns, James Joyce, Anaïs Nin and Lawrence Stern. All these at some time in their careers dabbled in doing it themselves. William Blake did nothing else. He even made his own ink, handprinted his pages and got Mrs Blake to sew on the covers.

But today it's different?

Not necessarily. This is not vanity publishing we're talking about although if all you want to do is produce a pamphlet of poems to give away to friends then self-publishing will be the cheapest way. Doing it yourself today can be a valid form of business enterprise. Being twice shortlisted for major literary prizes sharpened Timothy Mo's acumen. Turning his back on mass-market paperbacks, he published *Brownout on Breadfruit Boulevard* on his own. Billy Hopkin's Headline bestseller of Lancashire life, *High Hopes*, began as a self-published title. Susan Hill self-produced her short stories, *Listening to the Orchestra*, and as an example to us all Jill Paton Walsh's self-published *Knowledge of Angels* was shortlisted for the Booker Prize.

Can anyone do it?

Certainly. If you are a writer then a fair number of the required qualities will already be in hand. The more able and practical you are then the cheaper the process will be. The utterly inept will need to pay others to help them, but it will still be self-publishing in the end.

Where do I start?

With research. Read up on the subject. Make sure you know what the parts of a book are. Terms like *verso*, *recto*, prelims, typeface and point size all have to lose their mystery. You will not need to become an expert but you will need a certain familiarity. Don't rush. Learn.

What about ISBN numbers?

International Standard Book Numbers – a standard bibliographic code, individual to each book published, are used by booksellers and librarians alike. They are issued by the Standard Book Numbering Agency at a cost of £50 plus VAT for ten. Self-publishers may balk at this apparently inordinate expense but the ISBN is the device used by the trade to track titles and if you are serious about your book should be regarded as essential. The Agency issues a free information pack; see *FAQs about ISBNs* on page 621.

Next?

Put your book together – be it the typed pages of your novel, your selected poems or your story of how it was sailing round the world – and see how large a volume it will make.

If you have no real idea of what your book should look like, go to your local bookshop and hunt out a few contemporary examples of volumes produced in a style you would like to emulate. Take your typescript and your examples round to a number of local printers and ask for a quote.

Low print run printers

Start by asking a few local printers for quotes. It is also worth trying:

Able Publishing
13 Station Road, Knebworth, Herts SG3 6AP
tel (01438) 814316 *fax* (01438) 815232
email fp@ablepublishing.co.uk
website www.ablepublishing.co.uk

Biddles Ltd – Short Run Printing
Woodbridge Park Estate, Woodbridge Road, Guildford, Surrey GU1 1DA
tel (01483) 502224/(01553) 769072
fax (01483) 576150
email shortrun@biddles.co.uk
website www.biddles.co.uk/html/services_srb1.htm

The Fast Print Network
Unit 1 Southfolds Road, Corby, Northants NN18 9EU
tel (01536) 742430 *fax* (01536) 741766
email info@fast-print.net
website www.fast-print.net

Antony Rowe Ltd
Bumper's Farm, Chippenham, Wilts. SN14 6LH
tel (01249) 659705 *fax* (01249) 445535
email sales@antonyrowe.co.uk
website www.antonyrowe.co.uk

How much?

It depends. How long is a piece of string? Unit cost is important: the larger the number of copies you have printed the less each will cost. Print too many and the total bill will be enormous. Printing has gone through somewhat of a revolution in recent years. The arrival of digital processes and on-demand machines such as the Docutech have reduced costs and, for the first time, made short runs economic. But books are still not cheap.

Can I make it cost less?

Yes. Do some of the work yourself. If you want to publish poems and you are prepared to use a text set by a word processor, you will make a considerable saving. Many word processing programs have desktop publishing (DTP) facilities which will enhance the look of your text. Could you accept home production, run the pages off on an office photocopier, then staple the sheets? Editions made this way can be very presentable.

For longer texts keyed in on a word processor, savings can be made by supplying the work on disk directly to a printer. They can import your text into their program without the need for any rekeying. But be prepared to shop around.

Home binding, if your abilities lie in that direction, can save a fair bit. What it all comes down to is the standard of production you want and indeed at whom your book is aimed. Books for the commercial marketplace need to look like their fellows; specialist publications can afford to be more eccentric.

Who decides how it looks?

You do. No one should ever ask a printer simply to produce a book. You should plan the design of your publication with as much care as you would a house extension. Spend as much time and money as you can on the cover. It is the part of the book your buyer will see first. If you're stuck, employ a book designer.

How many copies should I produce?

Poetry books sell about 300 copies, new novels sometimes manage 1000, literary paperbacks 10,000, mass-market blockbusters over a million. But that is generally where there is a sales team and whole distribution organisation behind the book. Do not, on the one hand, end up with a prohibitively high unit cost by ordering too few copies. One hundred of anything is usually a waste of time. On the other hand can you really sell 3000? Will shops buy in dozens? They will probably only want twos and threes. Take care. Research your market first.

How do I sell it?
With all your might. This is perhaps the hardest part of publishing. It is certainly as time consuming as both the writing of the work and the printing of it put together. To succeed here you need a certain flair and you should definitely not be of a retiring nature. If you intend selling through the trade (and even if you don't you are bound to come into contact with bookshop orders at some stage), your costing must be correct and worked out in advance. Shops will want at least 35% (with national chains asking for even more) of the selling price as discount. You'll need about the same again to cover your distribution, promotion and other overheads, leaving the final third to cover production costs and any profit you may wish to make. Multiply your unit production cost by at least four. Commerical publishers often multiply by as much as nine.

Do not expect the trade to pay your carriage costs. Your terms should be 35% post free on everything bar single copy orders. Penalise these by reducing your discount to 25%. Some shops will suggest that you sell copies to them on sale or return. This means that they only pay you for what they sell and then only after they've sold it. This is a common practice with certain categories of publications and often the only way to get independent books into certain shops; but from the self-publisher's point of view it should be avoided if at all possible. Cash in hand is best but expect to have your invoices paid by cheque at a later date. Buy a duplicate pad in order to keep track of what's going on. Phone the shops you have decided should take your book or turn up in person and ask to see the buyer. Letters and sample copies sent by post will get ignored. Get a freelance distributor to handle all of this for you if you can. But expect to be disappointed. Independent book representatives willing to take on a one-off title are as rare as hen's teeth. If you can contract one they will want another 12% or so commission on top of the shops' discount – but expect to have to go it alone.

What about promotion?
A vital aspect often overlooked by beginners. Send out as many review copies as you can, all accompanied by slips quoting selling price and name and address of the publisher. Never admit to being that person yourself. Invent a name: it will give your operation a professional feel. Ring up newspapers and local radio stations ostensibly to check that your copy has arrived but really to see if they are prepared to give your book space. Buying advertising space rarely pays for itself but good local promotion with 100% effort will generate dividends.

What about depositing copies at the British Library?
Under the Copyright Acts the British Library, the Bodleian Library, Oxford, the University Library, Cambridge, the National Library of Scotland, the Library of Trinity College Dublin and the National Library of Wales are all entitled to a free copy of your book which must be sent to them within one month of publication. One copy should go direct to the Legal Deposit Office at the British Library, Boston Spa, Wetherby, West Yorkshire LS23 7BY. The other libraries use an agent, Carryl M. Allardice, Agent for the Copyright Libraries, 100 Euston Street, London NW1 2HQ. Contact her directly to find out how many copies she requires.

What if I can't manage all this myself?
You can employ others to do it for you. If you are a novelist and you opt for a package covering everything, it could set you back more than £10,000. A number of

publishers and associations advertise such services in writers' journals and in the Sunday classifieds. 'Authors. Publish with us.' is a typical ploy. They will do a competent job for you, certainly, but you will still end up having to do the bulk of the selling yourself. It is a costly route, fraught with difficulty. Do the job on your own if you possibly can.

And what if it goes wrong?

Put all the unsolds under the bed or give them away. It has happened to lots of us. Even the big companies who are experienced at these things have their regular flops. It was an adventure and you did get your book published. On the other hand you may be so successful that you'll be at the London Book Fair selling the film rights and wondering if you've reprinted enough.

Can the internet help?

The web has yet to take the place of traditional print. However, a good number of authors are setting up their own home pages. From these they advertise themselves and their works, and offer downloadable samples and, in some cases, their complete books. No one has yet made a fortune here and the number of 'hits' some sites claim to get are questionable. Nonetheless, this method of self-promotion comes highly recommended. Self-publishers, if they are not already familiar with the internet, should get on board now. *The Internet: A Writer's Guide* (see further reading) is a good place to start; see also *Setting up a website* on page 556.

Currently, the internet is thick with operators offering to promote or publish work electronically. These range from companies which post sample chapters and then charge readers a fee for the complete work to professional e-book developers who offer books fully formatted for use on devices such as the Rocket E-book or the Palm (see *E-publishing*, page 551). The jury is still out on where this flux of technological change is going, but if you'd like to test the waters, visit Jane Dorner's site at www.internetwriter.co.uk or romance writer Mary Wolf's list of e-publishers at http://coredcs.com/~mermaid/epub.html.

Peter Finch runs Academi, the Welsh National Literature Promotion Agency and Society of Writers. He is a poet, former bookseller and small publisher and author of the *How to Publish Yourself*. His website contains further advice for self-publishers (www.peterfinch.co.uk).

Further reading

Baverstock, Alison, *Marketing Your Book: An Author's Guide*, A & C Black, 2001

Coleman, Vernon, *How to Publish Your Own Book*, Blue Books, 1998

Dawes, John (ed.), *The Best of Write to Publish!*, John Dawes Publications, 2002

Domanski, Peter and Irvine, Philip, *A Practical Guide to Publishing Books Using Your PC*, Domanski Irvine Books, 1997

Dorner, Jane, *The Internet: A Writer's Guide*, A & C Black, 2nd edn, 2001

Finch, Peter, *How to Publish Yourself*, Allison & Busby, 4th edn, 2000

Ross, Tom and Marilyn, *The Complete Guide to Self-Publishing*, Writer's Digest Books, 4th edn, 2002

Spicer, Robert, *Publishing a Book*, How To Books, 3rd edn, 1998, o.p.

Woll, Thomas, *Publishing for Profit*, Kogan Page, 2000

Helping to market your book

*Authors can enhance their publisher's efforts to sell their book and in this article **Alison Baverstock** offers guidance on how they can help. The information is also relevant to self publishers.*

Having a book accepted for publication is immensely satisfying – all the more so if in the process you have amassed a thick pile of rejection letters spanning several years. At this stage, some authors decide that, having committed themselves to work with a professional publishing house, this is the end of their involvement in the process. They will move on thankfully to the writing of their next book.

Once you have delivered your manuscript, and it has been accepted for publication, a publisher should handle all aspects of your book's subsequent development, from copy editing and production to promotion and distribution. But there is a sound pragmatism in remaining vigilant. When it comes to the marketing of your book, there is a huge amount that you can do to help it sell.

The challenging marketplace

Each year in Britain alone, over 100,000 books get published or come out in new editions. All compete for the attention of the same review editors, the same stock buyers in bookshops, and the largely static number of regular book-buying members of the general public. It follows that anything an author can do to help 'position' the book, to make it sound different, or just more interesting than those it competes with, will be a huge advantage.

The marketing of books is not usually an area of high spending and there are many reasons why. Books are cheap (a novel costs about the same as a cinema ticket, and much less than a round of drinks), the publishers' profit margins are low, booksellers claim a percentage of the purchase price as discount (35–50%), and books sell in relatively small quantities (a mass market novel selling 15,000 copies may be considered a 'bestseller' – compare that with the sales figures for CDs or computer games). Your publisher will probably try to make maximum use of (free) publicity to stimulate demand using low-cost marketing techniques. They are far more likely to arrange for the insertion of a simple leaflet as a loose insert in a relevant publication, or organise a specific mailing to members of a relevant society, than book television or billboard advertising. Your assistance in helping them reach the market could be most important.

Examine your resources

Think in detail about what resources you have at your disposal that would help make your book sell, and tell your publisher. Most houses send out an Authors' Publicity Form about six months before publication, asking you for details of your book and how you feel it can best be marketed. Whilst the house will probably not be able to fulfil all your ambitions (mass market advertising is not possible for every book), they will be particularly interested in your contacts. For example, were you at school with the person who is now a features writer on *The Times*? Even if you have not spoken since, they may still remember your name. Do your children attend the same school as a contact on your local paper? Do you belong to a society or professional organisation that produces a newsletter for members, organises a conference or regular dining club? All these communication channels provide opportunities for publishers to send information on your book to potential purchasers.

Even greater things may be achieved if you set up the arrangements yourself. Can you arrange for an editorial mention of your book in a society journal (which will carry more weight than an advertisement) or organise for your publisher to take advertising space at a reduced rate? Remember that the less it costs your publishing house to reach each potential customer, the more of the market they will be able to cover out of their planned budgetary spend.

Offer a peg to your publisher

In trying to stimulate demand for a book, publishers try to achieve publicity (or coverage in the media) at the time of publication. The most usual way of getting this is for the in-house publicist to write a press release about you and your book and send this out to journalists in the hope that they will be interested enough to write about you, or even better decide to interview you.

Your publishing house will need 'pegs' on which to hang stories about you and your book, and it is helpful if you volunteer these rather than waiting to be asked. So, think back over your career and life in general. What is interesting about you? Are there any stories that arise out of the research for the book; incidents that give a flavour of the book and you as a writer?

Try to look at your life as others might see it; events or capabilities you take for granted might greatly interest other people. For example, novelist Catherine Jones is married to a former soldier, and has moved house 15 times in 20 years. In that time she has produced three children and has had appointments with over 40 different classroom teachers. She speaks about her life in a very matter of fact way, but when she wrote her first novel, *Army Wives* (Piatkus), the media were quite fascinated by a world they clearly knew nothing about. They found military jargon particularly compelling, and this proved a wonderful (and headline-producing) peg on which to promote her book.

Make yourself available

For a mass market title, any publicity that can be achieved will need to be orchestrated at the time of publication. By this time the publisher will hopefully have persuaded booksellers to take stock and the books will be in the shops. If the publicity is successful, but peaks before the books are available to buy, you have entirely missed the boat. If there is no publicity on publication, and no consequent demand, the bookseller has the right to return the books to the publisher and receive a credit note. And in these circumstances it will be *extremely* difficult to persuade them to restock the title having been let down once.

Timing is therefore absolutely crucial, so make yourself available at the time of publication (this is not the time to take your well-earned break). Remember too that, unless you are a very big star, each different newspaper or programme approached will consider its own requirements exclusively, and will not be interested in your own personal scheduling. Not all journalists work every day, and even if they do they like to decide on their own priorities. If you ask for an interview to be rescheduled, it may be dropped completely.

Don't assume that only coverage in the national media is worth having and turn your nose up at local radio and newspapers; they can reach a very wide audience and be particularly effective in prompting sales. You may be able to extend the amount of time and space you get by suggesting a competition or reader/listener offer. Local journalists usually have a much friendlier approach than those who work on the nationals, so if you are a novice to the publicity process this can be a much easier start, and an opportunity to build your confidence.

Contributing text for marketing

At several stages in the production process your publisher may request your input. You may be asked to provide text for the book jacket or for an author profile, to check information that will be included in the publisher's annual catalogue, or to provide biographical information for their website.

Think in detail about the words you have been asked for, who will read them and in what circumstances, and then craft what you write accordingly. For example, the text on a fiction book jacket (or 'blurb') should not retell the story or give away the plot; rather it should send signals that convey atmosphere, whet the appetite of the reader and show what kind of book they can expect. The potential customer is likely to be reading the blurb in a hurry, perhaps whilst standing in a bookshop being jostled by other shoppers, so it is best to keep it brief.

A non-fiction blurb should establish what the book will do for the reader and what your qualifications are for writing it. Again, keep the details short. The key factor is relevance – what have you done, and what are you qualified to do, that is relevant to the publication in hand?

For both categories of book a third party recommendation will help enormously as this provides objective proof of what a book is like and how useful it is. When books have come out as hardbacks, then extracts from the review coverage can be used on the paperback edition. For previously unpublished authors, a relevant quotation is very helpful instead. Do you know anyone established in the appropriate field who could provide an endorsement for what you have written? Can you contact them and ask them to help? The endorsement does not have to be from someone famous, just someone relevant. For example, a children's book endorsed as a gripping read by a 10-year-old with an interesting name, or an educational text endorsed by a student who had just passed her exams could both be effective.

You may be asked to check your details in a publisher's catalogue. Bear in mind that your entry will sit alongside everything else they publish, so it must be factual and clear.

If you are asked to write website copy, be sure to look at the relevant site before you draft something. Think about the context in which your material will be seen and read (by whom, how often and for how long) and use this information as the basis for writing.

Marketing after publication

Although most of the effort in marketing your book will inevitably occur at the time of publication (because next month's schedule will bring forward further titles that need the marketing department's attention), there is a great deal of opportunity to carry on selling your book afterwards.

So, if you are asked to speak at a conference or run a training course, ask if your book can be included in the package available to delegates, either as part of the overall price or at a reduced rate. Ask the publishing house for simple flyers (leaflets) on your book which you can hand out on suitable occasions. Then ask the organisers to put a copy inside the delegate pack, on every seat, or in a pile at the back of the hall (or preferably all three!).

Give your publishing house the details of speaking engagements or conferences at which they could usefully mount a display of all their titles (your own included). Even though they published your book, you cannot reasonably expect them to be specialists in every specific field you know intimately, so give them *all* the details they need. For a conference this would include the full title (not just the initials you refer to it by), the organiser's address and contact numbers (not the chairperson's address to which you should send associated papers), the precise dates and times, and any associated deadlines (e.g. stand bookings placed before a certain date may be cheaper). Finally, try to plan ahead rather than passing on key details at the last minute (this is one of publishers' most common complaints about authors!).

After 10 years in publishing **Alison Baverstock** set up her own marketing consultancy, specialising in running campaigns for the book trade and training publishers to market more effectively. She is a well-established speaker on the book business and has written widely on how to market books. Her most recent title is *Marketing Your Book: An Author's Guide* (A & C Black, 2001).

Who owns whom in publishing

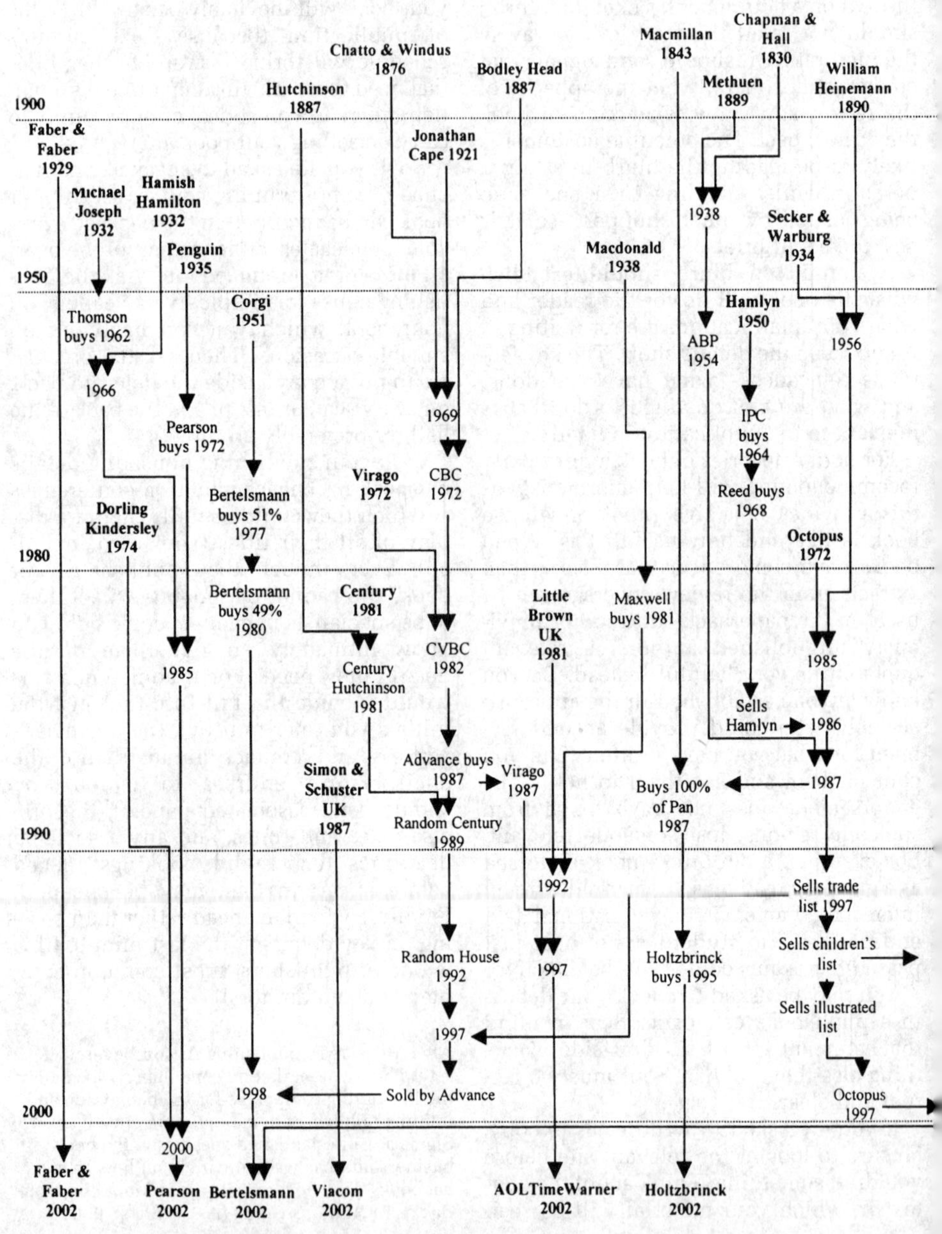

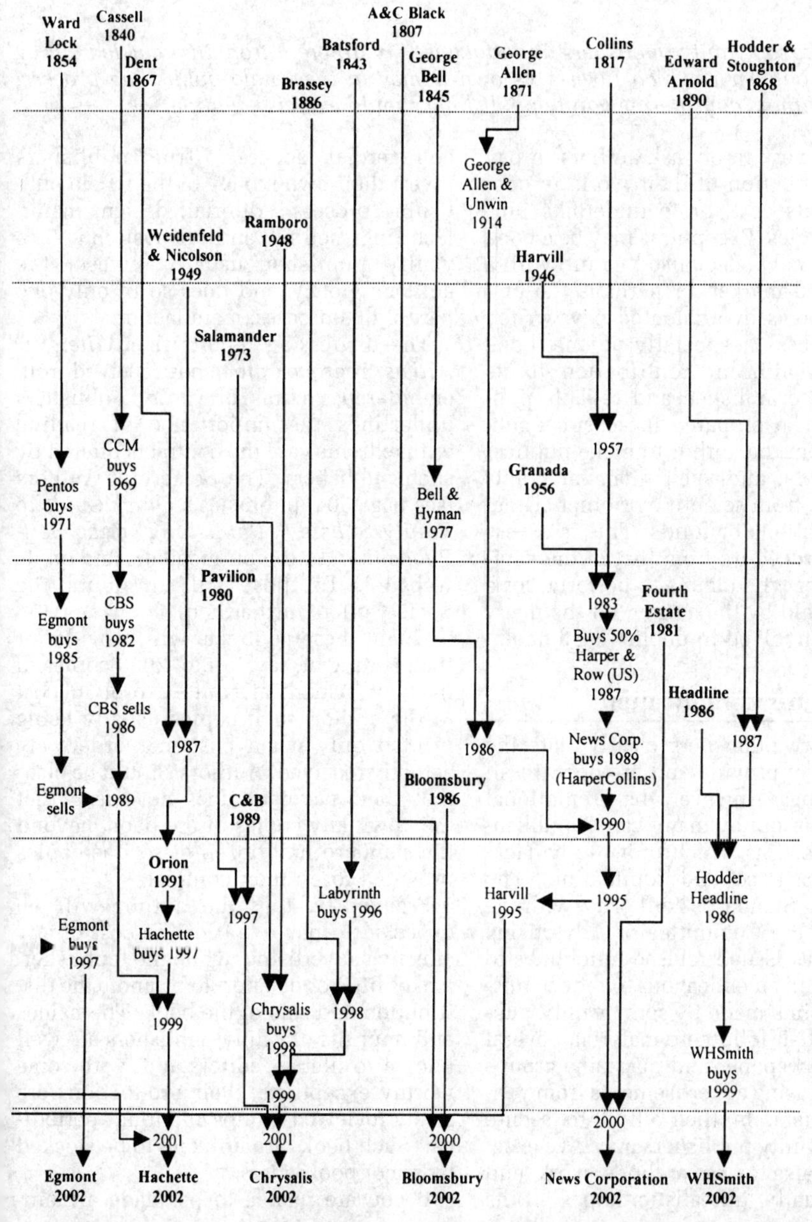
Ward Lock 1854
Cassell 1840
Dent 1867
A&C Black 1807
Batsford 1843
Brassey 1886
George Bell 1845
George Allen 1871
Collins 1817
Edward Arnold 1890
Hodder & Stoughton 1868
George Allen & Unwin 1914
Ramboro 1948
Weidenfeld & Nicolson 1949
Harvill 1946
Salamander 1973
CCM buys 1969
Pentos buys 1971
1957
Granada 1956
Bell & Hyman 1977
Pavilion 1980
CBS buys 1982
Egmont buys 1985
1983
Buys 50% Harper & Row (US) 1987
Fourth Estate 1981
Headline 1986
CBS sells 1986
1987
1986
News Corp. buys 1989 (HarperCollins)
1987
Egmont sells
1989
C&B 1989
Bloomsbury 1986
1990
Orion 1991
1997
Labyrinth buys 1996
Harvill 1995
1995
Hodder Headline 1986
Egmont buys 1997
Hachette buys 1997
1999
Chrysalis buys 1998
1998
WHSmith buys 1999
1999
2000
2001
2001
2000
Egmont 2002
Hachette 2002
Chrysalis 2002
Bloomsbury 2002
News Corporation 2002
WHSmith 2002

Vanity publishing

The job vanity publishers undertake is very different from that carried out by a publisher, which invests its own money in the whole publishing process. Authors considering vanity publishing should exercise caution.

Publishers very rarely ask authors to pay for the production of their work, to contribute to its cost, or to undertake purchase of copies. Exceptions may be a book of an extremely specialised nature with a very limited market, or perhaps the first book of poems by a talented new writer. In such cases, especially if the book makes a significant contribution to its subject, an established and reliable publisher may be prepared to accept a subvention from the author to make publication possible, and such financial grants often come from scientific or other academic foundations or funds. This is a very different procedure from that of the vanity publisher who claims to perform, for a fee to be paid by the author, all the many functions involved in publishing a book.

Manufacture *v.* publication

Some vanity publishers clearly state the services they provide and are open in all their dealings. However, the promotional material sent out by many vanity publishers makes claims which prove to be lacking in substance and foundation. The Advertising Standards Authority, with the support of the Committee of Advertising Practice, has issued revised guidelines to advertisers in an endeavour to reduce misleading claims made by some vanity publishers in their follow-up material. Several national newspaper and magazine groups are now refusing advertisements from vanity publishers. In their effort to secure business, vanity publishers may give exaggerated praise to an author's work and arouse equally unrealistic hopes of its commercial success. True publishers invest their own money in the whole publishing process: editorial, design, manufacturing, selling and distribution. The vanity publisher usually invests the author's money, and does so in only one part of this process: manufacture.

The distressing reports the *Writers' & Artists' Yearbook* office has received from embittered victims of vanity publishers underlines the importance of reading with extreme care the contracts offered by such publishers. The Society of Authors (see page 504) publishes a *Quick Guide to Vanity/Subsidy Publishing and Self-Publishing* (£1 to non-members and on its website). To those still in doubt the Society offers further help.

Often, these contracts will provide for the printing of, say, 'up to' 2000 copies of the book, usually at a quite exorbitant cost to the author, such copies usually being printed only when customer orders are actually received. Authors should be clear that their payment does not mean that they own any copies of the book, beyond the standard half dozen or so free copies provided for in their contract.

Frequently, too, the author will be expected to pay extra for the cost of any effective advertising, while the 'publisher' makes little or no effort to promote the distribution and sale of the book. The names and imprints of vanity publishers are well known to literary editors and, with some worthy exceptions, their productions are rarely reviewed in any important periodical. Such books are unlikely to be stocked by major booksellers.

If you are unable to persuade a mainstream publisher to take your typescript and decide to publish at your own expense, you could consider the possibility of self-publishing (see page 251). If you decide to approach a vanity publisher do so with caution and do not expect any commercial gain from your investment. Having checked that the sum asked for is a reasonable one, and the publisher will provide the services you require, take the attitude that you are paying simply for the pleasure of seeing your work in print. You are less likely to be disappointed.

E-publishing

Electronic publishing is a very new market, and it is risky – not least because it costs almost nothing to set up a website, compared with the high costs of publishing a book in traditional form. Some e-publishers ask the author to pay for electronic publication – either in the form of money, or by granting the e-publisher the right to act as agent if the work is ever exploited in more traditional ways in the future. Others may ask you to join a 'book club' which all the other members are, like you, only joining as a way of getting their own books published.

The main problem with e-publishing is getting readers to visit the relevant website and, if that hurdle can be overcome, getting them to purchase your book. But an e-publisher which is just one of a rapidly growing number of broadly similar sites, each offering a random selection of titles (not necessarily all good quality) covering a range of subject areas, may not be the best home for your work. If you do go ahead, at least make sure that you can terminate the contract after no more than three years.

See also *E-publishing* on page 551.

Top hundred chart of 2001 paperback fastsellers

Every year since 1979 ***Alex Hamilton*** *has compiled for the Guardian a chart of the 100 topselling paperbacks published for the first time during that year by British publishers. Here he describes its terms of reference, and sets the context.*

A distinction must be made between 'bestsellers' and the term used here – 'fastsellers'. Bestsellers have the real commercial pedigree. Sometimes they make a strong showing in the fastseller lane, but among bestselling authors are hundreds whose books began slowly and only over many years vindicate the faith of the original publisher. D.H. Lawrence and George Orwell are two whose sales in their lifetimes were modest, but posthumous interest spectacular.

Poetry

While serious poets never repeat Lord Byron's triumph in becoming a bestseller and 'famous overnight', and the only two works with short lines in two decades of fastsellers were collections of comic verse, a poet such as Eliot, not to mention Shakespeare and Chaucer, will eventually rack up sales in millions. And an outside event, such as the Nobel Prize for Seamus Heaney in 1995, produces an immediate harvest. In 1998, the late Poet Laureate, Ted Hughes, with the last book of his life, *Birthday Letters*, headed the hardcover selling lists with 145,000 copies, and won every award for which the book could qualify.

Fiction and non-fiction

The staple of publishing has long been Bibles, classic authors, cookbooks, dictionaries and other reference books.

Although fiction dominates counter sales and library borrowings, the top individual titles for the 20th century, with figures over 20 million copies, include most of these categories. For example, *The Guinness Book of Records*, over many editions, has passed 85 million copies. However, gross figures of 50–300 million copies are claimed for worldwide hardcover, paperback and translation editions of prolific authors such as Agatha Christie, Alistair MacLean, Mickey Spillane, Stephen King and Catherine Cookson.

The fastseller list on pages 264–7 is limited to paperbacks that appeared for the first time in that year from British publishers. These are defined in the trade as 'frontlist', and those that remain in print become 'backlist'. It is tempting to enter backlist titles revived as screen tie-ins, but except when the figure is very large, I exclude them.

Looking at the figures

From 1979 until the 1990s recession there were always between 102 and 125 titles that passed the 100,000 mark, but the figure has risen this year to 164. The expansion results partly from widespread competitive discounting by chain booksellers, supermarket interest, and the focus of many high street bookshops. Ubiquitous 'top 10' charts reinforce the successes (of the frontlist, that is; the backlist tends to suffer).

A distortion for titles published at the end of the year looks likely, but actually it rarely makes much difference. Electronic stock control enables booksellers to match ordering to demand. The significant sale of new paperbacks, particularly by established authors, takes place within a few weeks of their appearance, although a few do enter the magic circle of bestsellers: *Captain Corelli's Mandolin* by Louis de Bernières has gone on to sell 2 million copies after achieving only 60,000 in its first year.

The authors

Over 20 years, the lists indicate conservative attitudes among buyers. Fewer than 10% of authors come from outside the Anglo-American axis (which divides this year 64–26). Few appear in the top 25 who have not appeared somewhere on the list in previous years. (2000 provided two exceptions; this year there are three, including the impressive entry of a first novel by Zadie Smith). Once established on it, authors have only to turn in a regular supply of similar works to stay there. However, like typecast actors, they may find too late that they are captives of the market.

Leading figures of the 1980s were Wilbur Smith, Stephen King, Dick Francis, Barbara Taylor Bradford, Len Deighton, Catherine Cookson, Jeffrey Archer, Danielle Steel and Victoria Holt. To these (minus Holt, who died) the 1990s added regular front-runners in John Grisham and Maeve Binchy, with Patricia Cornwell and Jilly Cooper as top 10 reliables. J.K. Rowling is the new dead cert. Cookson, King, Francis and Steel are the only four in every list since 1979. (And Francis has announced that this year's title will be his last book). Such authors' names are like a brand. While only seven of 2000 titles were volumes of short stories, two had sales over 750,000, because they were by Frederick Forsyth and Jeffrey Archer, and two reached 500,000 (Archer and Rosamund Pilcher).

More than half the buyers of books have always been women but for most of the 1980s hardly more than a quarter of the authors were. In the 1990s their presence gradually increased, and in 2000 they at last achieved parity, to reach 53% in 2001.

Genres

More than 80 of the top 100 paperback fastsellers are usually fiction. Regular elements of the non-fiction remainder have dealt in diets, horoscopes, jokes, showbiz lives and, latterly, history. Cookery books, being basically tools in daily use, are essentially hardcover bestsellers (with more than 4 million in two years for Jamie Oliver's cookbooks). Of fiction, genres fill most slots, particularly adventure and naval yarns, crime, horror, family sagas and a mixed bag of romances. The 'chicklit' fashion for humorous accounts of young women's urban experience, sharing flats, holding a job, finding a man, is evolving into 'mumlit' – and in due course perhaps 'nanlit'.

Though there is a lesser vogue for 'ladlit', there is no longer an obvious category of 'men's fiction', once supplied by such as Mickey Spillane and Harold Robbins (world sales reached 130 million in his 1970s heyday). Currently the heroics of SAS men, typified by Andy McNab, are the substitute. In the 1970s and early 1980s, with authors such as Russell Braddon and Sven Hassel, hot war outsold sex. But the balloon of the cold war spy story, inflated by Ian Fleming and crewed by Len Deighton, John le Carré, *et al*, fell with the Berlin Wall. Much depends on the policies of the White House and the Kremlin, and the aftermath of recent terrorist action.

Science fantasy does better than experimental science fiction. Westerns never figured, despite the fame of Zane Grey, Louis L'Amour and J.T. Edson. Contrary to widespread opinion, erotica have never made publishers an opulent living. Imprints dedicated to soft porn must be content with sales around 25,000, and their living is made more precarious by material on the internet. Comic books, on the edge of being non-books, and collections of cartoonists of genius, appear *passim*, and quickly fade. Travellers' tales had no significant presence until the American Bill Bryson's flattering farewell journey around Britain sold more copies in one year (1996) than any other travelogue has in 20. But newcomer Pete McCarthy has the best mileage since.

Heavyweight to juvenile

Hardly more than a dozen titles in any list could count on reviews from serious book pages. However, in recent years the Booker Prize has taken winners into the fastseller list (witness Arundati Roy in 1998, the highest to date). When it works, this award seems to establish books rather than authors, and not all winners reappear. Still, the potential of non-category fiction is evinced by Humberto Eco's *The Name of the Rose*, Tom Wolfe's *The Bonfire of the Vanities* and Salman Rushdie's *Midnight's Children*, all well over half a million copies.

The phenomenon at the century's end was a series by J.K. Rowling about a schoolboy wizard called Harry Potter. (Her position at 0 above the current list may seem eccentric: but precise figures were not available at the time of going to press – this is an educated guess. With four of seven Potter titles published, they sell 50,000 a week in Britain (incidentally boosting the status of children's book publishing) and the total claimed for 40 countries is 72 million. Rowling quickly became as popular with children as the late Roald Dahl and Terry Pratchett, who is equally at home on the wilder shores of technology, and whose 42 titles with Transworld sell 1,850,000 copies a year. Mention must also be made of American horror writer R.L. Stine, claiming worldwide sales of 220 million for 60 children's books.

The year 2001

The new element for the trade in recent years has been freedom from retail price maintenance and widespread discounting on top hardcover titles. For a few, surprisingly high figures are reported. (Thus, Harris's grotesque thriller *Hannibal* sold 800,000 copies, and Sir Alex Ferguson's *Managing My Life* 600,000). Paperbacks are less affected, but perhaps 20% should be deducted from the aggregate money gross shown. The most common price point has moved on from £5.99 to £6.99.

In a market with a surplus of books, the fastsellers' performance seems still the most stable element. The aggregate went up from 30.5 million to 33 million, with the notional turnover improved from £194.7 million to 225.8 million (the first 25 titles account for 15.5 million books and £106.4 million). Export suffers badly from the strength of the pound, particularly against the Australian dollar and the South African rand; its share seems stuck on 22%, the lowest ever.

Alex Hamilton is a journalist and award-winning travel writer, and the author of several novels and volumes of short stories.

No	Title	Genre	Author	Imprint
0	Harry Potter: The Goblet of Fire	Juvenile	J.K. Rowling (Br.)	Bloomsbury
1	The Brethren	Thriller	John Grisham (US)	Arrow
2	Scarlet Feather	Novel	Maeve Binchy (Ire.)	Orion
3	A Child Called "It"	Autobiog.	Dave Pelzer (US)	Orion
4	White Teeth	Novel	Zadie Smith (Br.)	Penguin
5	The Last Precinct	Crime	Patricia Cornwell (US)	Warner
6	Sushi for Beginners	'Chicklit'	Marian Keyes (Ire.)	Penguin
7	Marrying the Mistress	Novel	Joanna Trollope (Br.)	Black Swan
8	The Lost Boy	Autobiog.	Dave Pelzer (US)	Orion
9	The Falls	Crime	Ian Rankin (Br.)	Orion
10	Down Under	Travel	Bill Bryson (US)	Black Swan
11	The Bear and the Dragon	Thriller	Tom Clancy (US)	Penguin
12	The Blind Assassin	Novel	Margaret Atwood (Can.)	Virago
13	Winter Solstice	Novel	Rosamunde Pilcher (Br.)	Coronet
14	The Sky is Falling	Thriller	Sidney Sheldon (US)	HarperCollins
15	No Angel	Saga	Penny Vincenzi (Br.)	Orion
16	McCarthy's Bar	Travel	Pete McCarthy (Br.)	Sceptre
17	Blackberry Wine	Novel	Joanna Harris (Br.)	Black Swan
18	The Wedding	Novel	Danielle Steel (US)	Corgi
19	Eden: The Guide	Guide	Various (Br.)	Eden
20	Kate Hannigan's Girl	Novel	Catherine Cookson (Br.)	Corgi
21	Shattered	Thriller	Dick Francis (Br.)	Pan
22	Roses are Red	Thriller	James Patterson (US)	Headline
23	When We Were Orphans	Novel	Kazuo Ishiguro (Br.)	Faber
24	Cradle and All	Thriller	James Patterson (US)	Headline
25	A Darkness More than Night	Thriller	Michael Connelly (US)	Orion
26	The House on Hope Street	Novel	Danielle Steel (US)	Corgi
27	The Shape of Snakes	Crime	Minette Walters (Br.)	Pan
28	Journey	Novel	Danielle Steel (US)	Corgi
29	The Truth	Fantasy	Terry Pratchett (Br.)	Corgi
30	Looking Back	Saga	Josephine Cox (Br.)	Headline
31	Firewall	Thriller	Andy McNab (Br.)	Corgi
32	The Constant Gardener	Novel	John Le Carré (Br.)	Coronet
33	To Cut a Long Story Short	Stories	Jeffrey Archer (Br.)	HarperCollins
34	Let It Shine	Saga	Josephine Cox (Br.)	Headline
35	Bad Blood	Autobiog.	Lorna Sage (Br.)	Fourth Estate
36	Fortune's Rocks	Novel	Anita Shreve (US)	Abacus
37	Deadly Decisions	Crime	Kathy Reichs (US)	Arrow
38	Broken	Novel	Martina Cole (Br.)	Headline
39	The Dare Game	Juvenile	Jacqueline Wilson (Br.)	Corgi Yearling
40	Where You Belong	Romance	Barbara Taylor Bradford (Br.)	HarperCollins
41	Rosie of the River	Novel	Catherine Cookson (Br.)	Corgi
42	The Prometheus Deception	Thriller	Robert Ludlum (US)	Orion
43	No Logo	Sociology	Naomi Klein (Can.)	Flamingo
44	Band of Brothers	War	Stephen Ambrose (US)	Pocket
45	Atlantis Found	Thriller	Clive Cussler (US)	Penguin
46	The Holiday	Romance	Erica James (Br.)	Orion
47	Code to Zero	Thriller	Ken Follett (Br.)	Pan
48	Turning Thirty	'Ladlit'	Mike Gayle (Br.)	Flame
49	English Passengers	Novel	Matthew Kneale (Br.)	Penguin
50	The Naked Chef	Cookery	Jamie Oliver (Br.)	Penguin

Price	Month	Home	Export	Total	Gross (RRP)	No
£6.99	July	1,403,520	443,216	1,846,736	£12,908,685	**0**
£6.99	Jan	730,237	429,658	1,159,895	£8,107,666	**1**
£6.99	Apr	702,813	450,502	1,153,315	£8,061,672	**2**
£5.99	Jan	876,603	105,133	981,736	£5,880,599	**3**
£6.99	Jan	608,282	183,167	791,449	£5,532,229	**4**
£6.99	June	470,133	164,011	634,144	£4,432,667	**5**
£6.99	June	402,257	206,457	608,714	£4,254,911	**6**
£6.99	Feb	512,870	62,811	575,681	£4,024,010	**7**
£6.99	Oct	465,408	100,208	565,616	£3,953,656	**8**
£6.99	Nov	399,770	158,873	558,643	£3,904,915	**9**
£7.99	Sept	426,959	99,967	526,926	£4,210,139	**10**
£6.99	Aug	306,299	220,458	526,757	£3,682,031	**11**
£7.99	Sept	371,521	146,918	518,439	£4,142,328	**12**
£6.99	May	406,028	101,323	507,351	£3,546,383	**13**
£5.99	July	363,731	114,700	478,431	£2,865,802	**14**
£6.99	May	302,526	146,779	449,305	£3,140,642	**15**
£6.99	Mar	415,152	27,642	442,794	£3,095,130	**16**
£6.99	Apr	368,092	71,293	439,385	£3,071,301	**17**
£6.99	Apr	338,632	88,813	427,445	£2,987,841	**18**
£3.50	Mar	409,025	0	409,025	£1,431,588	**19**
£5.99	Mar	318,487	78,811	397,298	£2,379,815	**20**
£6.99	Sept	243,478	151,832	395,310	£2,763,217	**21**
£6.99	June	298,743	90,707	389,450	£2,722,256	**22**
£6.99	Mar	317,282	69,549	386,831	£2,703,949	**23**
£6.99	Jan	278,496	95,881	374,377	£2,616,895	**24**
£6.99	Oct	255,808	106,166	361,974	£2,530,198	**25**
£5.99	Aug	297,075	63,306	360,381	£2,158,682	**26**
£6.99	Aug	273,394	77,294	350,688	£2,451,309	**27**
£6.99	Nov	265,660	83,994	349,654	£2,444,081	**28**
£5.99	Nov	260,802	88,681	349,483	£2,093,403	**29**
£5.99	Feb	312,229	31,823	344,052	£2,060,871	**30**
£6.99	Oct	284,919	42,224	327,143	£2,286,730	**31**
£6.99	Oct	220,308	104,810	325,118	£2,272,575	**32**
£5.99	Mar	236,394	87,021	323,415	£1,937,256	**33**
£5.99	Oct	293,262	21,217	314,479	£1,883,729	**34**
£6.99	July	297,717	13,685	311,402	£2,176,700	**35**
£6.99	Jan	230,177	75,959	306,136	£2,139,891	**36**
£5.99	Mar	225,074	76,663	301,737	£1,807,405	**37**
£6.99	June	248,393	31,513	279,906	£1,956,543	**38**
£4.99	Mar	261,891	11,847	273,738	£1,365,953	**39**
£5.99	Feb	221,461	48,703	270,164	£1,618,282	**40**
£5.99	Sept	202,205	65,230	267,435	£1,601,936	**41**
£6.99	Oct	154,550	112,454	267,004	£1,866,358	**42**
£8.99	Jan	179,650	79,150	258,800	£2,326,612	**43**
£5.99	June	246,668	10,101	256,769	£1,538,046	**44**
£6.99	Jan	160,849	92,667	253,516	£1,772,077	**45**
£5.99	June	192,502	58,001	250,503	£1,500,513	**46**
£6.99	June	117,619	132,606	250,225	£1,749,073	**47**
£6.99	Feb	216,385	32,296	248,681	£1,738,280	**48**
£6.99	Apr	212,777	29,756	242,533	£1,695,306	**49**
£12.99	Apr	217,187	19,464	236,651	£3,074,096	**50**

No	Title	Genre	Author	Imprint
51	Death in Holy Orders	Crime	P.D. James (Br.)	Faber
52	Beneath the Skin	Crime	Nicci French (Br.)	Penguin
53	Lord of Rings Off. Movie Guide	Cinema	Brian Sibley (Br.)	HC Tolkien
54	Lethal Seduction	Romance	Jackie Collins (Br.)	Pocket
55	One-Hit Wonder	'Chicklit'	Lisa Jewell (Br.)	Penguin
56	Whispers in the Sand	Romance	Barbara Erskine (Br.)	HarperCollins
57	Trust Me	Saga	Lesley Pearse (Br.)	Penguin
58	Glass Palace	Novel	Amitav Ghosh (India)	HarperCollins
59	Faceless	Novel	Martina Cole (Br.)	Headline
60	The Empty Chair	Thriller	Jeffery Deaver (US)	Coronet
61	From the Corner of his Eye	Thriller	Dean Koontz (US)	Headline
62	Edge of Danger	Thriller	Jack Higgins (Br.)	HarperCollins
63	Bleeding Hearts	Thriller	Ian Rankin (Br.)	Orion
64	Pastures Nouveaux	Novel	Wendy Holden (Br.)	Headline
65	The Amber Spyglass	Juvenile	Philip Pullman (Br.)	Scholastic
66	A Mad World My Masters	Autobiog.	John Simpson (Br.)	Pan
67	The Lion's Game	Thriller	Nelson DeMille (US)	Warner
68	Grail Quest: Harlequin	Novel	Bernard Cornwell (US)	HarperCollins
69	Omerta	Thriller	Mario Puzo (US)	Arrow
70	Someone Like You	Romance	Cathy Kelly (Ire.)	HarperCollins
71	Warlock	Adventure	Wilbur Smith (SA)	Macmillan
72	The Visitor	Thriller	Lee Child (Br.)	Bantam
73	Summertime	Novel	Charlotte Bingham (Br.)	Bantam
74	The Darwin Awards	Humour	Wendy Northcutt (US)	Orion
75	Emotionally Weird	Novel	Kate Atkinson (Br.)	Black Swan
76	Honeymoon	'Chicklit'	Amy Jenkins (Br.)	Flame
77	Hades Factor	Thriller	Ludlum & Lynds (US)	HarperCollins
78	Stalker	Thriller	Faye Kellerman (US)	Headline
79	Witch Hunt	Thriller	Ian Rankin (Br.)	Orion
80	Girls' Night Out, Boys' Night In	Stories	Ed: Jessica Adams (Br.)	HarperCollins
81	Talking to Addison	'Chicklit'	Jenny Colgan (Br.)	HarperCollins
82	Miss Garnet's Angel	Novel	Salley Vickers (Br.)	HarperCollins
83	The Season	Novel	Charlotte Bingham (Br.)	Bantam
84	Dust to Dust	Crime	Tami Hoag (US)	Orion
85	Killing the Shadows	Crime	Val McDermid (Br.)	HarperCollins
86	My Favourite Goodbye	'Chicklit'	Sheila O'Flanagan (Ire.)	Headline
87	True	Autobiog.	Martin Kemp (Br.)	Orion
88	The Best a Man Can Get	Novel	John O'Farrell (Br.)	Black Swan
89	Bonesetter's Daughter	Novel	Amy Tan (US)	Flamingo
90	Vicky Angel	Juvenile	Jacqueline Wilson (Br.)	Corgi Yearling
91	Millie's Fling	'Chicklit'	Jill Mansell (Br.)	Headline
92	Hit List	Thriller	Chris Ryan (Br.)	Arrow
93	Sea Change	Novel	Robert Goddard (Br.)	Corgi
94	Grasshopper	Crime	Barbara Vine (Br.)	Penguin
95	Between Males	Novel	Fiona Walker (Br.)	Coronet
96	Kitchen Confidential	Biog./cook	Anthony Bourdain (US)	Bloomsbury
97	Prodigal Summer	Novel	Barbara Kingsolver (US)	Faber
98	Olivia's Luck	'Chicklit'	Catherine Alliott (Br.)	Headline
99	My Sister's Child	Saga	Lyn Andrews (Br.)	Headline
100	Anil's Ghost	Novel	Michael Ondaatje (Can.)	Picador

Price	Month	Home	Export	Total	Gross (RRP)	No
£12.99	Mar	107,372	125,754	233,126	£3,028,307	**51**
£6.99	Mar	152,804	76,598	229,402	£1,603,520	**52**
£10.99	Nov	104,320	122,181	226,501	£2,489,246	**53**
£5.99	May	182,775	39,461	222,236	£1,331,194	**54**
£6.99	Sept	203,270	15,386	218,656	£1,528,405	**55**
£5.99	Aug	185,917	30,974	216,891	£1,299,177	**56**
£6.99	Mar	182,563	33,357	215,920	£1,509,281	**57**
£6.99	June	188,827	26,286	215,113	£1,503,640	**58**
£9.99	Oct	194,974	19,700	214,674	£2,144,593	**59**
£5.99	May	159,642	53,978	213,620	£1,279,584	**60**
£6.99	Aug	138,532	73,511	212,043	£1,482,181	**61**
£5.99	Oct	166,752	45,010	211,762	£1,268,454	**62**
£5.99	July	161,412	50,102	211,514	£1,266,969	**63**
£5.99	July	192,369	18,644	211,013	£1,263,968	**64**
£6.99	Sept	200,991	9,083	210,074	£1,468,417	**65**
£7.99	Sept	207,129	2,466	209,595	£1,674,664	**66**
£6.99	Aug	124,166	84,205	208,371	£1,456,513	**67**
£5.99	June	173,636	34,009	207,645	£1,243,794	**68**
£6.99	May	127,860	79,315	207,175	£1,448,153	**69**
£5.99	Apr	170,245	34,407	204,652	£1,225,865	**70**
£12.99	Oct	152,446	50,533	202,979	£2,636,697	**71**
£5.99	Apr	150,715	48,997	199,712	£1,196,275	**72**
£5.99	July	129,906	69,453	199,359	£1,194,160	**73**
£5.99	Jan	162,641	35,697	198,338	£1,188,045	**74**
£6.99	Mar	167,257	30,887	198,144	£1,385,027	**75**
£6.99	May	165,870	30,112	195,982	£1,369,914	**76**
£6.99	Mar	134,353	60,447	194,800	£1,361,652	**77**
£5.99	Apr	143,258	51,057	194,315	£1,163,947	**78**
£5.99	Mar	150,009	43,800	193,809	£1,160,916	**79**
£6.99	July	180,745	12,274	193,019	£1,349,203	**80**
£5.99	Jan	174,518	18,042	192,560	£1,153,434	**81**
£6.99	Apr	153,507	34,816	188,323	£1,316,378	**82**
£5.99	Mar	112,472	75,332	187,804	£1,124,946	**83**
£5.99	Aug	117,439	69,602	187,041	£1,120,376	**84**
£6.99	May	158,727	26,419	185,146	£1,294,171	**85**
£5.99	Nov	157,096	23,301	180,397	£1,080,578	**86**
£6.99	Jan	175,802	4,210	180,012	£1,258,284	**87**
£6.99	June	174,503	4,700	179,203	£1,252,629	**88**
£6.99	Oct	165,527	13,612	179,139	£1,252,182	**89**
£4.99	Oct	166,372	10,952	177,324	£884,847	**90**
£5.99	Aug	155,420	20,795	176,215	£1,055,528	**91**
£5.99	June	138,432	35,040	174,072	£1,042,091	**92**
£5.99	Dec	129,993	41,685	171,678	£1,028,351	**93**
£5.99	May	93,301	78,212	171,513	£1,027,363	**94**
£5.99	Mar	139,249	30,147	169,396	£1,014,682	**95**
£7.99	Mar	116,677	52,040	168,717	£1,348,049	**96**
£7.99	June	133,727	33,549	167,276	£1,336,535	**97**
£6.99	May	142,829	24,351	167,180	£1,168,588	**98**
£5.99	Mar	163,697	2,048	165,745	£992,813	**99**
£6.99	May	116,597	46,420	163,017	£1,139,489	**100**

Book clubs

Artists' Choice
Artists' Choice Ltd, PO Box 3, Huntingdon, Cambs. PE28 0QX
tel (01832) 710201 *fax* (01832) 710488
website www.artists-choice.co.uk
www.acaward.com

Quarterly.

Baker Books
Manfield Park, Cranleigh, Surrey GU6 8NU
tel (01483) 267888 *fax* (01483) 267409
email bakerbooks@dial.pipex.com
website www.bakerbooks.co.uk

School book clubs – Rainbow for ages 2–5 and Funfare for ages 5–11. Two per term.

BCA
Greater London House, Hampstead Road, London NW1 7TZ
tel 020-7760 6500 *fax* 020-7760 6901
website www.booksdirect.co.uk

Ancient & Medieval History Book Club, Arts Guild, Computer Books Direct, Books for Children, Escape (The Fiction Club), Escape (The Travel Book Club), Fantasy & SF Book Club, The History Guild, Home Software World, Just Good Books, Mango, Military and Aviation Book Society, Mind Body & Spirit, Moments (The Romantic Fiction Club), The Mystery & Thriller Club, QPD (Quality Paperbacks Direct), The Professional Book Club, Railway Book Club, The Softback Preview, Taste (A Fresh Approach to Food), World Books.

Cygnus Book Club
PO Box 15, Llandeilo, Carmarthenshire SA19 6YX
tel (01550) 777977/777701 *fax* (01550) 777569
email enquiries@cygnus-books.co.uk
website www.cygnus-books.co.uk

Includes psychology and self-help, diet, health and exercise, world religions, new economics and education, green issues, mythology, spirituality. Monthly.

The Folio Society
44 Eagle Street, London WC1R 4FS
tel 020-7400 4222 *fax* 020-7400 4242

Fine editions of classic literature.

Letterbox Library
71-73 Allen Road, London N16 8RY
tel 020-7503 4801 *fax* 020-7503 4800
email info@letterboxlibrary.com
website www.letterboxlibrary.com

Multicultural and non-sexist children's books. Quarterly.

Poetry Book Society
Book House, 45 East Hill, London SW18 2QZ
tel 020-8870 8403 *fax* 020-8877 1615
email info@poetrybooks.co.uk
website www.poetrybooks.co.uk

Quarterly. See pages 275 and 488.

Readers Union Ltd
Brunel House, Ford Close, Newton Abbot, Devon TQ12 4PU
tel (01626) 323200 *fax* (01626) 323318

Includes Country Sports Book Society, The Craft Club, Craftsman Book Society, Equestrian Book Society, Gardeners Book Society, Needlecrafts with Cross Stitch Book Society, Photographic Book Society.

The Red House Book Club
Windrush Park, Witney, Oxon OX29 0XD
tel (01993) 893456 *fax* (01993) 893424
website www.redhouse.co.uk

Mail order book supplier specialising in children's and parenting books. Also available online.

Writers' Bookshelf
PO Box 168, Wellington Street, Leeds LS1 1RF
tel 0113-238 8333 *fax* 0113-238 8330
email janet.evans@writersnews.co.uk

Books for writers.

Poetry

Poetry into print

***John Whitworth** has submitted hundreds of poems and has had dealings with a number of publishers of poetry. He gives advice here 'from the handle end of the long spoon that poets use to sup with those they would persuade or bamboozle into printing, even paying for, their work.'*

Constant readers of these columns may suppose that I do not update my material. Be assured that I do – magazines and publishers wax and wane and I try to keep abreast. But, even in these days of publishing on the internet (rather like making your poems into paper boats and sending them down the Yangtse it seems to me), the basics seem to stay the same and my general advice likewise. If your poems are good they will find a publisher if you persevere. Do I believe this? Yes I do and so should you.

There are two things to say at the outset. Do not expect to make more than pin money *directly* from publication of your work. You may, in the fullness of time, make quite a tidy sum *indirectly* – I mean you get work because you are a published poet: readings, workshops, reviewing and so forth, if you like any of that sort of thing. But if you get £50 for a poem from a national magazine you may feel very satisfied, and as for your published slim volumes – they will not sell in four figures, nor do the publishers, except in a very few instances, expect them to. In a sense, nearly all poetry publishing is vanity publishing. Nobody is in it for the money.

And, secondly, as one poet put it to me, do not have too much respect for the taste of individual literary editors. She is right. An editor is not God (whatever he or she thinks). Remember that, though it can be hard if you are diffident (and most poets are). But this person is just like you; the fact that he or she (nearly always he) is warming an editorial chair may mean many things. It certainly does not mean papal infallibility. If Snooks of the *Review* sends back your work, despatch it immediately to Snurd of the *Supplement*. And if Snurd concurs with Snooks, they may both be wrong, indeed neither may actually have read through (or at all) what you sent. Grit your teeth and send to Snarl and then to Snivel. Do not be discouraged by rejection. If your poems are as good as you can make them and have been submitted in as professional a way as you can manage, then just keep on sending them out. I started writing poems in 1968, wrote my first good one in 1972, and was paid my first proper money (£40 from the Arts Council) in 1976. The first book was published in 1980. So patience and a thick skin are big advantages.

It does help, of course, to have read the magazine you are making submissions to. This will prevent you sending your bawdy ballad to *The Times Literary Supplement (TLS)* or concrete poetry to the *Literary Review*. And I am assuming that you actually are interested in the craft of poetry and the names of, say, Milton, Tennyson and Eliot mean something to you. You will also be interested to know what Heaney, Harrison and Hannah actually do. You don't have to like it, but you ought to want to know about it. If no one is writing anything remotely like your work, perhaps you should ask yourself why that might be. On the other hand, remember the words of Charlie Coburn, the old music-hall singer: 'I sang my song to them, and they didn't like it. So I sang it again, and they still didn't like it. So I sang it a third time and one of them thought he might just get to like it if I changed the tune and altered the words. So I sang it again, just exactly the same way, and after a bit they all liked it.'

Submitting your work to magazines

I asked a number of poets about this. Some of them said they never submitted to magazines at all, because they disliked being rejected. I must say I think that a rather craven attitude, but you *can* carve out a poetic reputation through workshops and readings. You must be good at putting yourself about in public and have the time and energy to expend on it. All who did submit work regularly agreed on a number of basics:

• Submit your poem on an A4 sheet, typed or printed out from a word processor. One poet, David Phillips, reckoned his percentage of successful submissions had gone up appreciably since he bought his word processor, and he assumed it was because his work now looked much more professional. It might be, of course, that it has just got better. Do not type it in italic, capitals or mock cursive. Keep it simple.

• Put your name and address at the bottom of each poem. Editors, reasonably, do not keep your letters, only the poems that interest them. You might consider one of those rubber stamps. I know a number of poets who have them, though I don't myself.

• Fold the poem once and put it into the sort of envelope designed to take A4 folded once. I don't know why poets like to scrunch their verses into tiny envelopes, but don't do it. Don't go to the other extreme either and send it decorated with admonitions not to bend, etcetera. Include a stamped, self-addressed envelope of the same size. This really is important. Shakespeare himself would be consigned to the wpb without an appropriate sae.

• Do not send just one poem. Do not send 20 poems. Send enough to give a reasonable flavour of your work – say about four or five. Long poems are less likely to be accepted than short poems. If you write different kinds of things, then make sure your selection covers a fair few of these kinds. Send what you think of as your best work, but do not be surprised if what is finally accepted is the one you put in at the last minute, 'to make the others look better' as Larkin lugubriously puts it. And if an editor says he or she likes your work and would like to see more, then send more as soon as possible. The editor wasn't just being polite. Editors aren't. It was said because it was meant.

• At this point there is generally some po-faced stuff about never sending the same poem to more than one editor simultaneously. As it happens, I don't do this, but some well-known poets do. And indeed, if Snurd of the *Supplement* sits on your poems for six months, what are you supposed to do, since the polite follow-up letter recommended will, almost certainly, have no effect at all, except to waste your time and your stamps? The real reason for not making multiple submissions is the embarrassment when the same poem is accepted by two editors at once. I once, inadvertently, won two microscopic prizes in poetry competitions for the same poem. What did I do? I kept my mouth shut and cashed the cheques, that's what I did.

• You wouldn't have been daft enough to send off your *only* copies of poems to Snurd, would you? *Of course* he lost them and it's all your own silly fault. No you can't sue him but you'll know better next time. Send photocopies and keep your originals. Editors don't mind photo-

Submitting poems

- Submit poems on an A4 sheet, simply typed.
- Put your name and addess at the bottom of each sheet.
- Fold the sheet only once and use an A5 envelope.
- Send about four or five poems.
- Consider whether to submit the same poem simultaneously to more than one editor.
- Always keep copies of your poems.
- Include a short covering letter.

copies. Why should they? They look a lot better than the original all covered in Tippex.

• Keep your covering letter short, but if you have been published in reputable places then it will do no harm to say so. This advice comes from Duncan Forbes. Selling poems is very like selling anything else, so blow your own trumpet, but don't blow for too long. Don't ask the editor for help in the advancement of your poetic career. Being rude won't help either. Artists are supposed to be rude and a lot of them are, too, but it hasn't actually helped them to anything except an ulcer or a punch on the nose.

Which magazines?

You could start with the *TLS* but I wouldn't advise it. One editor (not from the *TLS*) said honestly that he tended to reject, more or less unread, poems from anyone he had never heard of. Before you play with the big boys perhaps you ought to have some sort of a record in the little magazines. Some pay and some do not. What matters is not the cash but whether you feel proud or ashamed to be seen in the thing. The Poetry Library at the South Bank Centre (Royal Festival Hall, London SE1 8XX) publishes a list of poetry magazines, and if you can get along there (open 11am–8pm except Mondays), you can nose around among the back numbers and see what is appealing to you. If you can't do that, then a letter with an sae will get you the list (see also page 276).

Judge where you think you will fit in, and buy yourself a big sheet of second-class stamps. Send off your work and be prepared to be reasonably patient. Most editors reply in the end. Little magazines have a high mortality rate, so be prepared for a particularly crushing form of disappointment – having your work accepted by a magazine which promptly ceases publication. It happens to us all; it goes on happening to me. The Poetry Library also sends out for an sae of 40p a satisfying wodge of bumph about poetry publishing in general. Worth the money.

Some inexperienced poets seem very worried that editors will filch their 'ideas' and pay them nothing, but poems are not made up of ideas; they are made up of words, and if anyone prints your poem without permission they are infringing your copyright and you can threaten them with all sorts of horrible things. But, honestly, this is a buyer's market, and even the editor of that badly photocopied rag has more material than can be used.

There seems to be a new kind of organisation that solicits poems. Often with names like Global or International, they don't ask for money up front, so are not exactly vanity presses. But they encourage you in marketers' prose to buy superduper anthologies for £40 or so. Harmless, I suppose, but I'd rather appear in something less pretentious along with some poets I had actually heard of.

Subscribe to *Poetry Review*, the magazine of the Poetry Society. It's quarterly, expensive and the best in the UK. Peter Forbes, who edited it for some considerable time (after a succession of short-lived editorships, including a spell by the Poet Laureate) made it so. Now he has hung up his red pen and it is being edited jointly by Robert Potts, the literary journalist, and David Herd of the University of Kent. They are into people like Geoffrey Hill and John Ashbery, so complexity and difficulty may be 'in' now, or more 'in' than they were under Forbes, who is certainly a hard act to follow.

Most magazines pay badly. More important is the quality of the poems and the articles (down to the editor) and the quality of the production (down to the size of the grant because poetry magazines never make money). The best looking one I know is *Ambit* (super artwork but still takes forever to look at submissions). Other good magazines include two Welsh productions, *Poetry Wales* and the *New Welsh Review;* and the *Rialto* from Norwich (great covers and some interesting articles). *PN Review*, an offshoot of Michael Schmidt's Carcanet, is good. The earlier savagery of its reviews seems to have been toned down lately. I'm not sure if that is good or bad. Last year it seemed the end for *London Magazine* after the death of Alan Ross, but it has risen again under the new editorship of the poet and son of a poet, Sebastian Barker. Two newcomers (new to me) are *Metre* and *Thumbscrew*. *Metre*, edited in the UK by another poet, David Wheatley, at the University of Hull, is a very superior production, looking like those other superior magazines generated on the best US campuses – aggressively traditional as you would expect from the name. *Thumscrew* comes out of Oxford and is learned and rude – what did you think? Both good places to be seen in. *Stand* has been relaunched and reformatted under the editorship of Jon Glover. It now lives at the School of English in the University of Leeds. *Poetry London* is still good and Pascale Petit keeps the turn-around pretty brisk. The best I have seen from Scotland is *Chapman*. *Connections* is in Kent again after a brief sojourn in Wales.

Plenty of little magazines do not pay at all, except in copies. That does not mean you should ignore them – a reputation is built up by getting into such places. Some you might try are *Acumen*, *Outposts*, and *Envoi*, all long-running magazines of a good standard. The *Frogmore Papers,* edited by Jeremy Page, is also good, and I like *Equinox* from Barbara Diordi. *Tabla* is annual; you can get into it through their competition (see page 537). This is no more that a personal choice; I am sure there are other excellent magazines which I haven't seen.

The two literary heavyweights are, of course, the *The Times Literary Supplement (TLS)* and the *London Review of Books (LRB)*. Both publish good poetry. The *Spectator* is publishing poetry again, but not very often. Send in submissions but don't hold your breath.

Have you tried abroad? The Post Office will tell you about International Reply Coupons, and there is a good article by Bonny Yuill on this in *Connections* (Winter 98/99).

Small press information

Photon Press
The Light House, 37 The Meadows, Berwick-upon-Tweed, Northumberland TD15 1NY
Light's List, now in its 17th year, is a list of over 1500 magazines worldwide. It costs £2.50 including p&p.

The Poetry Library
Royal Festival Hall, South Bank Centre, London SE1 8XX
tel 020-7921 0943/0664 *fax* 020-7921 0939
Lists of poetry magazines, poetry bookshops, current competitions, etc. See also page 276.

Book publication

Every poet wants to get a book out. How do you do it? One pretty sure way is to win a big prize in a competition, the National or the biennial Arvon or Harry Chambers' Peterloo. Otherwise, you wait until you have reached the stage of having had two or three dozen poems published in reputable places; then you type out enough poems for a collection, traditionally 64pp but collections seem to be getting longer, and send them out, keeping your own copy and including return postage. I suppose you do. I first got published by talking to Anthony Thwaite in a pub; everybody needs a slice of luck. I know some excellent poets who are still trying to place their first book and, contrariwise, there are books … Poetry, like most things, goes in fashions. But don't be in a hurry. Wait until you have a reputation in the magazines and small presses. Neil Astley at Bloodaxe reckons more than 90% of what comes through his letterbox he sends back, and he has usually had an eye on the successful ones before they got around to submitting.

Who do you send out to? Faber are still out in front (though they did turn down Larkin's *The Less Deceived*, the most influential book of English poems in the last 50 years). It is not that their poets are better, but Faber promote them heavily and care about them. And being a Faber poet puts you in the company of Eliot and Larkin. Penguin have revived their excellent *Modern Poets* series and have 12 titles so far. Most other big publishers do poetry – fortunes wax and wane with the person, often a poet, nearly always a man, in the editorial chair.

But being published by a household name does not mean selling thousands – hundreds are more common. Publishers like to have poetry on their list as a badge of virtue, but often they don't want to know much about it, they don't promote it and they don't persist with it. The book sinks or swims, and usually it sinks. (Publishers that consider poetry for adults are listed in *Publishers of poetry* on page 280; *Children's book publishers and packagers* on page 248 includes publishers of poetry for children.)

Specialist poetry presses (some, though not all of which, publish nothing but poetry) produce books that look every bit as good and, in most cases, sell every bit as well (or badly). Bloodaxe, Peterloo and Carcanet, none of them London-based, are leaders in the field.

Bloodaxe sounds fearsomely dismissive, but the name is from a Viking who conquered Northumbria. They have more titles and possibly better poets than Faber but they still fail the railway bookstall test. 'From traditional formalists to post-modernists', says Neil Astley. Half the poets on his list are women – good if you are a woman.

Carcanet publish Elizabeth Jennings, Sophie Hannah and the Wizard of Oz, Les Murray, which indicates Michael Schmidt's catholicity and willingness to go outside this country. He snapped up the homeless OUP authors. He now publishes Robert Graves too. He welcomes submissions but wishes people would first read some books on his list to get an idea of house style. Good advice.

Harry Chambers at Peterloo has a reputation for publishing late starters. Kirkpatrick Dobie's first book came out in the poet's 84th year – excellent! Dana Gioia, the American 'new formalist', Ann Drysdale and quizzical Ursula Fanthorpe are his biggest guns.

Back in the metropolis, Anvil has Carol Ann Duffy and Michael Hamburger along with lots of poetry in translation. Harry Chambers' Peterloo Press continues to flourish in the mainstream. The big publishing event of 2003 will be *The Collected Poems of Ursula Fanthorpe*. Substantial Selected Poems are also scheduled from David Sutton, John Mole and the Canadian prizewinner, Brian Bartlet.

Enitharmon Press has gained a new lease of life, thanks to long-awaited Arts Council support. Senior poets (Alan Brownjohn, U.A. Fanthorpe, Anthony Thwaite), jostle with a younger generation (Jane Duran, Duncan Forbes) and interesting newcomers like Judy Gahagan. One to watch! Seren, the imprint of Poetry Wales, publishes the lively Sheena Pugh and Paul Groves, who isn't obviously Welsh. Headland has Simon Rae of the *Guardian* fame. A welcome new face is Leviathan (Oxford, Portland, Amsterdam) – really Michael Hulse, one of the editors of *Stand*. It seems quite hard to get the books though, unless, as I did, you contact the distributors (Drake International Services in Oxford) direct. But honestly, there are lots (really *lots*) more small presses and information on them can be obtained through the organisations listed in the box.

Competitions

Some poets are snooty about these (perhaps they don't win?) and of course competitions are supposed to make money for the organisers. But in my experience, they (judge, organiser, entrant, prizewinner) are honest and unknowns sometimes win big prizes, and often pick up smaller ones. Many a poet's published career has started with a competition win. I like it when the judge is a published poet – a badge of respectability, I think. Try the small ones. Prize money of £200 or less deters big names (not me though!).

You might consider subscribing to *Writers News*, now owned by the *Yorkshire Post*. Their literary competitions specifically exclude published poets like me and their stuff on poetry is good, if elementary. It's also a good place to find out about other competitions. If you can do light verse, why not enter the competitions run by the *Spectator* and the *New Statesman*? I've won sometimes, Wendy Cope used to, and so have a couple of members of my local writing groups. Lots of kudos, some money and the occasional bottle of scotch. Go for it! For more information on current competitions, see page 278 and *Prizes and awards* on page 512.

Getting on radio

Michael Conaghan, who has had many poems broadcast, says BBC local radio – more talk than its commercial equivalent – is the place to start. Find out who is responsible for Arts programming and contact them. "Short punchy, topical work is probably what they want, and events/festivals concentrate their minds wonderfully. Nationally, Radio 1's Mark Radcliffe is a notable friend to poets."

Poetry on the internet

There is a lot of this. Just type in poetry and up it comes. There are competitions too, mostly American, and I've entered some. No dollars yet I have to report. The poet Peter Howard writes an internet column for *Poetry Review* and has his own excellent site. Try it. Try other people's too. Why not set up your own? See also page 278.

Poetry for children

Not a dustbin for grown-up rejects. There seems to be a market in the USA. Over here, you can self-publish books of poems and flog them locally. Schools pay poets (some with more brass neck than talent) to give readings and workshops. Poet Lindsay Macrae thinks it helps to be young and female (she is), but Roger McGough and Kit Wright are old(ish) and male. There is an inner circle of editors attached to publishers who trawl likely names for inclusion in anthologies; I said in the last edition that I'd never had a poem accepted by this route – I have now had four, so it does work after all. How do you break into this charmed circle? You get a book published. How do you do that? With great difficulty at present. Chris Reid did it privately and won a prize.

Vanity/subsidy publishing

Never give a publisher money. That is what they give to you. If you want your work in print and nobody will do it for you without a cheque, then do it yourself. See *Doing it on your own* on page 251. You could buy yourself a secondhand word processor with the money you save by not answering that advertisement!

Making your poems better

Read more poetry, and I mean modern poetry. You can't write it if you don't read it. There are some good how-to books. In the UK, *Writing Poetry* (A & C Black) is by John Whitworth (i.e. me). *Writing Poetry and Getting Published* by Matthew Sweeney and John Hartley Williams (Hodder) is good too. *The Practice of Poetry* (Harper Perennial), edited by Robin Behn and Chase Twichell, is the best book of this kind I know of in the USA. John Hollander's *Rhyme's Reason* (Yale) is excellent on poetic forms; he writes all the examples himself. Similar ground is covered by E.O. Parrott and the competition-winning crew in *How to be Well-Versed in Poetry* (Penguin). *The Princeton Handbook of Poetic Terms* by Alex Preminger (Princeton) is what is says.

John Whitworth has published 7 books of poetry, including *From the Sonnet History of Modern Poetry* and, for children, *The Complete Poetical Works of Phoebe Flood* (Hodder). He has been a Faber anthologist, both judge and prizewinner in national poetry competitions, and has been published in national newspapers and on radio and television.

Poetry organisations

*Poetry is one of the easiest writing art forms to begin with, though the hardest to excel at or earn any money from. Many organisations offer advice, information and resources to writers and readers at all levels, and as many as possible are included here. **Christina Patterson**, director of the **Poetry Society** lists below the organisations which can help poets take their poetry further.*

Where to get involved

The Poetry Society

22 Betterton Street, London WC2H 9BX
tel 020-7420 9880 *fax* 020-7240 4818
email info@poetrysociety.org.uk
website www.poetrysociety.org.uk

The Poetry Society was set up to help poetry and poets thrive in Britain and is a registered charity funded by the Arts Council of England. The Society offers advice and information to all, with a more comprehensive level of information available to members. Membership is open to anyone interested in poetry and includes 4 issues each of the magazine *Poetry Review* and the newsletter *Poetry News*.

The Society also publishes education resources (see later); promotes National Poetry Day; runs a critical service called Poetry Prescription (£50 for 100 lines – 20% discount to members); provides an education advisory and training service, school membership, youth membership and a thriving website. A range of events and readings take place at the Poetry Café and the BT Poetry Studio at the Society's headquarters in Covent Garden.

Competitions run by the Society include the National Poetry Competition, the largest open poetry competition in Britain each year with a first prize of £5000, the biannual European Poetry Translation Prize and the Simon Elvin Young Poet Awards. Membership: £35 full, £25 concessions. Founded 1909.

Poetry Ireland

Upper Yard, Dublin Castle, Dublin 1, Republic of Ireland
tel (01) 671 4632
email poetry@iol.ie
website www.poetryireland.ie

Poetry Ireland is the national poetry organisation for Ireland. It is grant-aided by both the Northern and Southern Arts Councils of Ireland and is a resource centre with the Austin Clarke Library of over 10,000 titles. It publishes the quarterly magazine *Poetry Ireland Review* and the bi-monthly newsletter *Poetry Ireland News*. Poetry Ireland organises readings in Dublin and nationally, and runs a Writers-in-Schools Scheme.

The Poetry Book Society

Book House, 45 East Hill, London SW18 2QZ
tel 020-8870 8403 *fax* 020-8877 1615
email info@poetrybooks.co.uk
website www.poetrybooks.co.uk
Director Clare Brown

This unique book club for readers of poetry was founded in 1953 by T.S. Eliot, and is funded by the Arts Council of England. Every quarter, selectors choose one outstanding publication (the PBS Choice), and recommend 4 other titles. Members can receive some or all of these books free and are also offered substantial discounts on other poetry books. The Poetry Book Society also administers the T.S. Eliot Prize (see page 520), produces the quarterly membership magazine, the *Bulletin*, and has an education service providing teaching materials for primary and secondary schools. Write for details.

The British Haiku Society

Lenacre Ford, Woolhope, Hereford HR1 4RF
Secretary David Walker
tel (01432) 860328
email davidawalker@btinternet.com
website www.britishhaikusociety.org

The Society runs 'The Hackett' annual haiku competition; organises tutorials, workshops and critical comment; and provides information to promote the appreciation of haiku, senryu, tanka and renga. It publishes the journal *Blithe Spirit* (4 p.a.), a newsletter for its members called the *Brief* (4 p.a.), as well as books and the *Haiku Kit* – a teachers' guide for schools suitable for all age groups. Write for membership details. Founded 1990.

Survivors Poetry

Diorama Arts Centre, 34 Osnaburgh Street, London NW1 3ND
tel 020-7916 5317 *fax* 020-7916 0830
email survivor@survivorspoetry.org.uk

Survivors Poetry provides poetry workshops, performances, readings, publishing, networking and training for survivors of mental distress in London and the UK. Survivors Poetry is funded by the Arts Council of England and was founded in 1991 by 4 poets who have had first-hand experience of the mental health system. It works in partnership with local and national arts, mental health, community, statutory and disability organisations. Its outreach project has established a network of 30 writers' groups in the UK.

Where to get information

Your local library should have information about the local poetry scene. Many libraries are actively involved in promoting poetry as well as having modern poetry available for loan. Local librarians promote writing activities with, for example, projects like Poetry on Loan and Poetry Places information points in West Midlands Libraries.

The Poetry Library

Level 5, Royal Festival Hall, London SE1 8XX
tel 020-7921 0943/0664 *fax* 020-7921 0939
email poetrylibrary@rfh.org.uk
website www.poetrylibrary.org.uk

The principal roles of the Poetry Library are to collect and preserve all poetry published in the UK since about 1912 and to act as a public lending library. The Library also keeps a wide range of international poetry. It has 2 copies of each title available and a collection of about 40,000 titles in English and English translation. The Library also provides an education service (see later).

Founded in 1953 by the Arts Council, the Library runs an active information service, which includes a unique noticeboard for lost quotations, and tracing authors and publishers from extracts of poems. Current awareness lists are available for magazines, publishers, competitions, bookshops, groups and workshops, evening classes and festivals on receipt of a large sae. The Library also stocks a full range of British poetry magazines as well as a selection from abroad. When visiting the Library, look out for the Voice Box, a performance space for literature; a programme is available from 020-7921 0906.

Open 11am–8pm Tuesday to Sunday. Membership: free with proof of identity and current address.

The Northern Poetry Library

County Library, The Willows, Morpeth, Northumberland NE61 1TA
tel (01670) 534514 (poetry enquiries)
tel (01670) 534524 (poetry dept)

The Northern Poetry Library has over 14,000 titles and magazines covering poetry published since 1945. For information about epic through to classic poetry, a full text database is available of all poetry from 600–1900. A postal lending service is available to members, who pay for return postage. Membership is free to anyone living in the areas of Tyne and Wear, Durham, Northumberland, Cumbria and Cleveland. Founded 1968.

The Scottish Poetry Library

5 Crichton's Close, Canongate, Edinburgh EH8 8DT
tel 0131-557 2876 *fax* 0131-557 8393
email inquiries@spl.org.uk
website www.spl.org.uk

The Scottish Poetry Library is run along similar lines to the Poetry Library in London. It specialises in 20th century poetry written in Scotland, in Scots, Gaelic and English. It also collects some pre-20th-century poetry and contemporary poetry from all over the world. Information and advice is given, and visits by individuals, groups and schools are welcome. Borrowing is free of charge and there is a membership scheme (£20 p.a.), which includes use of the members' reading room and a regular newsletter. It has branches in libraries and arts centres throughout Scotland and also runs a library touring service. Readings and exhibitions are regularly organised, particularly during the Edinburgh Festival. Founded 1984.

Poeziecentrum

Hoornstraat 11, B-9000 Ghent, Belgium
tel 0032 9 225 2225
fax 0032 9 225 9054

Poeziecentrum (poetry centre) offers general information about translated and non-translated poetry. It has a library of 20,000 titles (including English, Scottish, American, Canadian and South African poetry), 600 magazines and 5000 archives including press cuttings, periodicals and biographical information. It also promotes the study of poetry (particularly in schools), offers advice on writing, publishing and competitions, and publishes many collections, including its own magazine *Poezierant* (bi-monthly). Founded 1980.

Regional Arts Offices

website www.arts.org.uk

Local literature officers can provide information on local poetry groups, workshops and societies (see page 490). Many Regional Arts Offices give grant aid to local publishers and magazines and help fund festivals, literature projects and readings, and some run critical services.

The internet

You can get many links with good internet poetry magazines through the following:
The Poetry Kit www.poetrykit.org
The Poetry Society of America
www.poetrysociety.org

Where to get poetry books

See the Poetry Book Society on page 275. The Poetry Library provides a list of bookshops stocking poetry. For second-hand mail order poetry books try:

Peter Riley
27 Sturton Street, Cambridge CB1 2QG
tel (01223) 576422
email priley@dircon.co.uk

The Poetry Bookshop
The Ice House, Brook Street, Hay-on-Wye HR3 5BQ
tel (01497) 821812

Where to celebrate poetry

Festival information should be available from Regional Arts Offices (see page 490). See also *Literature festivals* on page 544.

The British Council

Information Officer, Literature Dept,
The British Council, 11 Portland Place,
London W1N 4EJ
tel 020-7930 8466 *fax* 020-7389 3199
website www.britishcouncil.org/arts/literature

Send a large sae or visit the website for a list of forthcoming festivals.

Where to perform

In London, Express Excess and Vice Verso are 2 of the liveliest venues and they regularly feature the best performers, while Poetry Unplugged at the Poetry Café is famous for its weekly open mike nights (Tuesdays 7.30pm). Other performance venues listed below have readings. For up-to-date information, read *Time Out* and *What's On in London*).

Apples and Snakes Performance Poetry
Battersea Arts Centre, Lavender Hill,
London SW11
tel 020-7223 2223

Coffee House Poetry
Troubadour Coffee House, 265 Old Brompton Road, London SW5 *tel* 020-7370 1434

Express Excess
The Enterprise, 2 Haverstock Hill, London NW3
tel 020-7485 2659

Poetry Café
22 Betterton Street, London WC2
tel 020-7420 9888

Vice Verso
Bread and Roses, 68 Clapham Manor Street, London SW4 *tel* 020-8341 6085

Voice Box
Level 5, Royal Festival Hall, London SE1
tel 020-7960 4242

For venues outside London, check local listings, and ask at libraries and Regional Arts Offices (see page 490).

Competitions

There are now hundreds of competitions to enter and as the prizes increase, the highest being £5000 (first prize in the National Poetry Competition and the Arvon Foundation International Poetry Competition), so does the prestige associated with winning such competitions.

To decide which competitions are worth entering, make sure you know who the judges are and think twice before paying large sums for an anthology of 'winning' poems which will only be read by entrants wanting to see their own work in print. The Poetry Library publishes a list of competitions each month (available free on receipt of a large sae). See also *Poetry into print* on page 269 and *Prizes and awards* on page 512.

Literary prizes are given annually to published poets and as such are non-competitive. An A–Z guide to literary prizes can be found on the Booktrust website (www.booktrust.org.uk).

Where to write poetry

The Arvon Foundation

The Arvon Foundation at Lumb Bank
Hebden Bridge, West Yorkshire HX7 6DF
tel (01422) 843714 *fax* (01422) 843714
website www.arvonfoundation.org
The Arvon Foundation at Totleigh Barton
Sheepwash, Beaworthy, Devon EX21 5NS
tel (01409) 231338 *fax* (01409) 231144
The Arvon Foundation at Moniack Mhor
Teavarren, Kiltarlity, Beauly,
Inverness-shire IV4 7HT
tel (01463) 741675 *fax* (01463) 741733

The Arvon Foundation's 3 centres run 5-day residential courses throughout the year to anyone over the age of 16, providing the opportunity to live and work with professional writers. Writing genres explored include poetry, narrative, drama, writing for children, song writing and the performing arts. Bursaries are available to those receiving benefits. Founded in 1968.

The Poetry School

1A Jewel Road, London E17 4QU
tel/fax 020-8223 0401 *tel* 020-8985 0090
email poetryschl@aol.com

Using London venues, the Poetry School offers a core programme of tuition in reading and writing poetry. It provides a forum to share experience, develop skills and extend appreciation of both traditional and innovative aspects of poetry.

The Poet's House/Teach na hÉigse

Clonbarra, Falcarragh, County Donegal,
Republic of Ireland
tel 00 353 74 65470 *fax* 00 353 74 65471
email phouse@iol.ie

The Poet's House runs 3 10-day poetry courses in July and August. An MA degree in creative writing is validated by Lancaster University, and the Irish Language Faculty includes Cathal O'Searcaigh. The poetry faculty comprises 30 writers, including Paul Durcan and John Montagu.

Ty Newydd

Taliesin Trust, Ty Newydd, Llanystumdwy,
Criccieth, Gwynedd LL52 0LW
tel (01766) 522811 *fax* (01766) 523095
email tynewydd@dial.pipex.com

Ty Newydd runs week-long writing courses encompassing a wide variety of genres, including poetry, and caters for all levels, from beginners to published poets. All the courses are tutored by published writers. Writing retreats are also available.

Write Away

East Midlands Arts, Mountfields House,
Epinal Way, Loughborough, Leics. LE11 0QE
tel (01509) 218292 *fax* (01509) 262214
website www.arts.org.uk
Contact Lisa Pacynko

A varied programme of residential writing courses. Details on application.

Internet and local groups

On the internet. It is worth searching for discussion groups and chat rooms on the internet. There are plenty of them; John Kinsella's is highly recommended, which is junk mail-resistant and highly informative:
John Kinsella's poetryetc@jiscmail.ac.uk
The Poetry Kit www.poetrykit.org/wkshops2.htm

Locally. Local groups vary enormously so it is worth shopping around to find one that suits your poetry. Up-to-date information can be obtained from Regional Arts Offices.

The Poetry Library publishes a list of groups for the Greater London area which will be sent out on receipt of a large sae.

Help for young poets and teachers

The Poetry Library

Children's Section, Royal Festival Hall,
London SE1 8XX
tel 020-7921 0664
website www.poetrylibrary.org.uk

For young poets, the Poetry Library has about 4000 books incorporating the SIGNAL Collection of Children's Poetry. It also has a multimedia children's section, from which cassettes and videos are available to engage children's interest in poetry.

The Poetry Library has an education service for teachers and writing groups. Its information file covers all aspects of poetry in education. There is a separate collection of books and materials for teachers and poets who work with children in schools, and teachers may join a special membership scheme to borrow books for the classroom.

National Association of Writers in Education (NAWE)

PO Box 1, Sheriff Hutton, York YO60 7YU
tel/fax (01653) 618429
email paul@nawe.co.uk
website www.nawe.co.uk

NAWE is a national organisation, which aims to widen the scope of writing in education, and coordinate activities between writers, teachers and funding bodies. It publishes the magazine *Writing in Education* and is author of a writers' database which can identify writers who fit the given criteria (e.g. speaks several languages, works well with special needs, etc) for schools, colleges and the community. Publishes *Reading the Applause: Reflections on Performance Poetry by Various Artists*. Write for membership details.

Poetry Society Education

The Poetry Society, 22 Betterton Street,
London WC2H 9BX
tel 020-7420 9894 *fax* 020-7240 4818
email education@poetrysociety.org.uk
website www.poetrysociety.org.uk

For 30 years the Poetry Society has been introducing poets into classrooms, providing teachers' resources and producing colourful, accessible publications for pupils. A publication celebrating National Poetry Day is sent free to every school, giving an insight into the best of contemporary poetry.

Schools membership (£50 secondary, £30 primary) offers publications, training opportunities for teachers and poets, a free subscription to *Poems on the Underground* and a consultancy service giving advice on working with poets in the classroom. Poetryclass, an INSET training project funded by the DfES, employs poets to train teachers at primary and secondary level. People aged 11–18 can join the Society and receive poetry books and posters, quarterly copies of *Poetry News*, and a Young Writer's Pack giving advice on developing writing skills.

Poetry Society publications for schools include *The Poetry Book for Primary Schools* and *Jumpstart Poetry in the Secondary School*, a young poets pack and posters for school Key Stage 1 to GCSE requirements. A full catalogue of poetry resources, details of youth membership, the Foyle Young Poets of the Year Award, school membership and education residencies are available from the Education Department.

Young poetry competitions

Children's competitions are included in the competition list provided by the Poetry Library (free on receipt of a large sae).

Foyle Young Poets of the Year Award

The Poetry Society, 22 Betterton Street,
London WC2H 9BX
tel 020-7420 9894 *fax* 020-7240 4818
email education@poetrysociety.org.uk
website www.poetrysociety.org.uk

Free entry for 11–18 year-olds with unique prizes.

Further reading

Baldwin, Michael, *The Way to Write Poetry*, Hamish Hamilton, 1982, o.p.
Chisholm, Alison, *The Craft of Writing Poetry*, Allison & Busby, 1992, repr. 2001
Chisholm, Alison, *A Practical Poetry Course*, Allison & Busby, 1994
Corti, Doris, *Writing Poetry*, Writers News, 1994
Fairfax, John, and John Moat, *The Way to Write*, Elm Tree Books, 2nd edn revised, 1998
Finch, Peter, *How to Publish Your Poetry*, Allison & Busby, 2nd edn, 1998
Forbes, Peter, *Scanning the Century*, Penguin Books, 1999
Hamilton, Ian, *The Oxford Companion to Twentieth Century Poetry in English*, OUP, 1994, POD
Hyland, Paul, *Getting into Poetry*, Bloodaxe, 2nd edn, 1997
Livingstone, Dinah, *Poetry Handbook for Readers and Writers*, Macmillan, 1992
O'Brien, Sean, *The Firebox*, Picador, 1998
Reading the Applause: Reflections on Performance Poetry by Various Artists, NAWE, 1999
Riggs, Thomas, (ed.) *Contemporary Poets*, St James Press, 7th edn, 2000
Roberts, Philip Davies, *How Poetry Works*, Penguin Books, 2nd edn, 2000
Sansom, Peter, *Writing Poems*, Bloodaxe, 1994, reprinted 1997
Sweeney Matthew, and John Williams, *Teach Yourself Writing Poetry*, Hodder and Stoughton, 1997
Whitworth, John, *Writing Poetry*, A & C Black, 2001

USA

Breen, Nancy, *Poet's Market*, Writer's Digest Books, USA, 2003
Fulton, Len, *Directory of Poetry Publishers*, Dustbooks, USA, 18th edn, 2002–3
Fulton, Len, *The International Directory of Little Magazines and Small Presses*, Dustbooks, USA, 38th edn, 2002–3
Preminger, Alex, *New Princeton Encyclopedia of Poetry and Poetics*, Princeton University Press, 3rd edn, 1993

Publishers of poetry

Anvil Press Poetry
Arc Publications
Blackstaff Press Ltd
Bloodaxe Books Ltd
Calder Publications Ltd
Jonathan Cape
Carcanet Press Ltd
Chapman Publishing
Chatto & Windus
Cló Iar-Chonnachta Teo.
Crescent Moon Publishing
diehard
Enitharmon Press
Everyman Publishers plc
Faber & Faber Ltd
Flambard Press
Gairm Publications
The Gallery Press
The Goldsmith Press
Gomer Press
Headland Publications
Hippopotamus Press
Honno Ltd (Welsh Women's Press)
Libris Ltd
The Lilliput Press Ltd
Liverpool University Press
Methuen Publishing Ltd
MQ Publications Ltd
New Beacon Books
New Island Books
The Oleander Press
Onlywomen Press Ltd
Oxford University Press
Payback Press
Penguin Group (UK)
Peterloo Poets
Pipers' Ash Ltd
Polygon
Random House Group Ltd
Rivelin Grapheme Press
Saint Andrew Press
SCP Publishers Ltd
Seren
Skoob Russell Square
Stride Publications
Town House and Country House

Television, film and radio

Writing for television

Writing for television can be an extremely rewarding career. ***Anji Loman Field*** *says anyone with the right aptitude and attitude can succeed, and here she gives sound advice for the potential screenwriter.*

The markets

There are various openings for new writers in television, but apart from competitions and special projects these are hardly ever advertised. The BBC's latest information on opportunities for new writers can be found at www.bbc.co.uk/writersroom. The openings fall into four categories:

Single drama

There are fewer slots nowadays for the single play – a 30- or even 60-minute one-off drama is highly unlikely to find a market. Occasionally broadcasters will gather single 90-minute plays together under a collective banner (e.g. Screens One and Two; Love Bites; Obsession) but it's best to think of individual projects as either standalone 90-minute television films, two-parters or even four-parters. Ask television companies for their current guidelines on single drama and film.

Series and serials

Although it has been known for a new writer to sell an original series or serial, it is a relatively rare occurrence. Writers with a track record of writing for existing strands are far more likely to be taken seriously. Long-running soaps like *EastEnders*, *Emmerdale* and *Family Affairs* are often in the market for new writers, but check first. If the door is open, a good 'calling card script' is usually the way in. Submit an original piece of work in a similar genre that is at least an hour long and shows your ability to create believable characters, write sparkling dialogue and tell a compelling story. You may be invited to try out for one of these long-running shows.

Dramatisations/adaptations

A new writer is extremely unlikely to be commissioned to adapt or dramatise someone else's work for television. However, if there's something you really want to adapt and you can afford to take out an 'option' on the rights (or already own them, if it is your own novel or play) then write the script on spec. If you have a good script and can show that you own the rights, you could succeed.

Situation comedy

This is the one area where production companies and broadcasters are desperate for new talent, and there are several competitions open to new writers. If you are a good comedy writer and market your work well, you will undoubtedly succeed (see 'Writing situation comedy' below).

Aptitude and attitude

The first prerequisite in writing for television is that you enjoy the medium, and actually watch the kinds of shows that you would be interested in writing for. A cynical approach will always show through. And before sitting down to write that first television script, arm yourself with the appropriate skills by examining the medium as a whole.

- **Tape the kind of show you'd like to write for and analyse it.** How many scenes are there? What length are they? How much of the story happens 'off camera'? Knowing the answers to these questions will help you to understand the grammar of screen, and enable you to write a more professional script.

• **Study the structure of story telling.** There are plenty of books on the subject, and although it is never a good idea to follow structural paradigms to the letter, absorb as much information as possible so that the essential 'rules' on character, motivation and plot filter through into your writing.

• **Read scripts.** Some are published in book form, but a huge variety of scripts are also available from specialist book shops such as Offstage (*tel* 020-7485 4996) and the Screenwriter's Store (*tel* 020-8469 2244).

• **If you want to write sitcom, see as many live recordings of shows as possible.** This enables you to understand the techniques involved in television production, and particularly the physical constraints imposed by the studio. Free tickets for sitcom recordings are always available – phone the broadcasters for information.

• **Be realistic.** Don't make your first project too ambitious in terms of screen time, locations or special effects. If you can 'contain the action' and make your first script affordable to shoot, it is far more likely to be taken seriously.

Learning the craft

Even the most successful and experienced screenwriters say they never stop learning. Some have been lucky enough to learn the skill of writing for the screen in a subliminal way. For example, Lynda La Plante (*Prime Suspect*) was an actress with plenty of opportunity for studying scripts and production techniques before she turned her hand to writing; John Sullivan (*Only Fools and Horses*) worked in the props department at the BBC on countless sitcoms, and used to take the scripts home to study. But there are other ways to learn. Script workshops are particularly useful.

There are many courses and workshops available. These range from small self-help groups, where writers give each other feedback on their work, to full- and part-time Screenwriting MA courses at universities (e.g. in London, Sheffield, Leicester, Bournemouth, Manchester and Leeds). Evening classes are springing up in local colleges, and there are even script workshops on the internet. The BBC's Learning Zone site is worth checking out, at bbc.co.uk/education/lzone/master/index.shtml. Workshops can help in the following ways:

• **Discipline**. The hardest thing most writers ever have to do is sit down and face that blank screen or page. Joining a script workshop – where you *have* to deliver an outline or a treatment, or the next 20 pages of your script by a certain date – provides the push that so many writers need.

• **Feedback**. Reading and giving feedback on other people's work helps you to focus on getting your own script right. It is also good to get used to the idea of showing your own work to others and getting their feedback. Television writing is generally a collaborative process and writers need to be pleasant to work with, and receptive to ideas. Knowing when to argue a point and when to concede are crucial skills which can be developed in good writing workshops.

• **Rewriting**. Learn to Love the Rewrite. It is such a major achievement to get to the end of a first draft that it is all too easy to rush to the post box and send it off to several production companies at once. *Four Weddings and a Funeral*, a Channel 4-funded project, went through 17 rewrites before finally reaching the screen. So before you post your masterpiece:

• Leave it to 'settle' for a few days and do something completely different – allow your head to clear completely. Then re-read the script from beginning to end – from as objective a viewpoint as possible – and make necessary changes.

• Get feedback so that you're sure your script is ready to send. Be warned: knowing how to read and analyse a script properly is a particular skill. Unless they are equipped in this area, *never* ask your friends or relations to read your script. Their comments could either lull you into a false sense of security or destroy your confidence for ever. Feedback from other writers in your workshop group is best.

Useful information

Euroscript
Suffolk House, 1-8 Whitfield Place, London W1T 5JU
tel/fax 020-7387 5880
email euroscript@netmatters.co.uk
website www.euroscript.co.uk
A script development organisation aiming to place great screenplays at the heart of the industry. Originally funded by the European Union's Media II programme, the service is now worldwide. Professional development support is provided for screenwriters, producers and production companies through consultancy, Film Story Competition (deadlines: 30 April and 31 October each year) and international workshops.

London Film & Video Development Agency
114 Whitfield Street, London W1T 5EF
tel 020-7383 7755
(incorporating the London Production Fund *tel* 020-7383 7766)
website www.lfvda.demon.co.uk
Offers grants that enable writers, producers and directors to make their projects. Consult website or send sae for further information.

National Association of Television Program Executives (NATPE)
452 Oakleigh Road North, London N20 0RZ
tel 020-8361 3793 *fax* 020-8368 3824
website www.natpe.org
Contact Pam Smithard
Non-profit TV programming and content association dedicated to the continued growth and success of the global TV marketplace. Year-round activities include the annual conference and exhibition, which reaches tens of thousands of key decisionmakers in virtually every sector of the TV industry.

PACT (Producers Alliance for Cinema and Television)
45 Mortimer Street, London W1W 8HJ
tel 020-7331 6000 *fax* 020-7331 6700
Serves the feature film and independent TV production sector. The *PACT Directory* lists contacts in all areas (£30 to non-members). (See also page 485.)

Regional Arts Offices
Many Offices offer grants that enable writers, producers and directors to make their projects. Contact your local Arts Office for details (see page 490).

The Screenwriters' Workshop
(formerly London Screenwriters' Workshop)
Suffolk House, 1-8 Whitfield Place, London W1T 5JU
tel/fax 020-7387 5511
email screenoffice@cwcom.net
screenoffice@tiscali.co.uk
website www.lsw.org.uk
Runs regular courses, workshops and events; publishes a quarterly newsletter. Educational charity. (See also page 495.)

The Spotlight
7 Leicester Place, London WC2H 7RJ
tel 020-7437 7631
Publishes a book called *Contacts*, which contains useful information and contact addresses. The 2003 edition is available from October.

The Writers' Guild of Great Britain
430 Edgware Road, London W2 1EH
tel 020-7723 8074
website www.writers.org.uk/guild
Trade union-affiliated organisation for professional writers. Negotiates rates for TV drama with the BBC and the ITV Network Centre. (See also page 506.)

There are some organisations (including the Screenwriters' Workshop) which offer a professional script feedback service for a moderate fee.

Writing situation comedy

Situation comedy writing is the most lucrative area of television, and deservedly so. Have you ever tried making an audience laugh several times a minute for 25 minutes for at least six weeks running, and maybe (in the case of *Last of the Summer Wine*) for 20 long years?

Despite its name, sitcom is less about situation and much more about character. It is better to start with funny and engaging characters in mind and then (if it isn't part and parcel of the character) find the perfect situation in which to place them than it is to begin with the premise 'nobody's ever set a sitcom in a nuclear power station before'. It is not the setting that makes the audience laugh, it is the characters.

A good exercise in seeing if you can write funny material is to write an episode of an existing sitcom. If *Fawlty Towers* is your all-time favourite, study a few episodes and then try your own. It will never get made, but you'll learn a lot in the process – and sample scripts like this are often useful as calling card scripts.

Some of the broadcast companies issue guidelines on writing situation comedy. Phone the comedy departments at the BBC, LWT and Carlton for information, or the Programme Support Unit at Channel 4 (*tel* 020-7396 4444) for their excellent 'beginner's guide to sitcom writing' pack – available for a small fee.

Competitions

Broadcasters occasionally run writing competitions or 'new writing initiatives'. Check their websites – and general screen-writers' websites – for up-to-date information. Also, watch out for annual awards run by organisations such as PAWS (People's Awareness of Science), the BBC (e.g. the Dennis Potter Play of the Year Award, see page 533), and the Orange Prize for Screenwriting (*website* www.orangeprize.com *tel* (07970) 111999). Details can be found in the trade press and via relevant websites and screen-writing organisations. See also *Prizes and awards* section on page 512.

Breaking in

Do you need an agent?

Many new writers are keen to get an agent before they attempt to sell anything, but this can be an arduous process and there are few agents prepared to take on a completely untried writer.

The best way to get an agent is to first get an offer of a deal on a project. Most *bona fide* production companies and broad-casters will happily recommend a selection of agents to writers they want to do business with. If you can phone an agent and say 'so-and-so wants to option/ commission my project and has recom-mended you as an agent' s/he is far more likely to be interested. And at that point you can pick and choose the agent who is right for you, rather than going with the first one to say "yes".

Selling yourself

Once you are sure you have a good script, where do you send it? If you've done your homework, you will already know which channel is the most likely to be interested. But often it is better to send to an independent production company rather than directly to a broadcaster, so do a bit more research. Check out the companies that are making the kind of show you've written and approach them first.

A preliminary letter or phone call can save you time and money because some smaller companies simply don't have the resources to read unsolicited material. If you feel that a certain production company is absolutely right for your project, write a letter giving a brief synopsis of the project and asking if they will read the script. If they agree, your script will join the 'solicited' pile. And if it fits the bill, they may even pick it up and develop it. But don't expect overnight results. It can some-times take many months before scripts are even read by small and/or busy companies.

Sending your script directly to a broadcaster can lead to a commission, but unless you target a particular producer whose work you admire you will probably have less control over who you work with.

Being 'discovered'

If you can get your work 'rehearse-read' by actors in front of an audience it will help your writing, and may even lead to discovery. Many script readings are attended by development executives from television and production companies and there are many stories of individuals being picked up from such projects. TAPS (Television Arts Performance Showcase) (*tel* 01932 592151), Player–Playwrights (*tel* 020-

8883 0371) and the Screenwriters' Workshop, all organise rehearsed readings.

Development hell

This is the place between finding someone who wants to produce your script and waiting for the 'suits' at the television companies to give the final go-ahead for the project. In the meantime you will have been paid, perhaps just an option fee, or maybe a commission fee for a script or two. Either way, *never put all your eggs in one development basket.* Aim eventually to have several projects bubbling under for every one that comes to the boil.

A realistic optimism is required for this game. Don't believe anything wonderful will happen until you actually have that signed contract in front of you. In the meantime keep writing, keep marketing and, if you possibly can, keep making contacts in the industry. If you're good at schmoozing, go to as many industry events as possible and make new contacts. If you can send a script to a producer with a covering letter saying 'I heard your talk the other day ...' you will immediately arouse interest.

Coping with rejection

The standard rejection letter is the worst part of this business. When it is accompanied by your returned script – looking decidedly un-read – it is very easy to become disillusioned. The trick is this: change your mental attitude to the point where if you don't receive at least one rejection letter in the post every day, you feel rejected! So long as you are absolutely sure that your work is good, keep sending it out. Sooner or later you'll get a nicer, more personalised rejection letter, and then eventually perhaps even a cup of tea with the producer ...

Selling ideas

Completely new writers do occasionally sell ideas but are much more likely to sell the idea alone, i.e. the 'format rights', and will probably end up not writing the script. If you have a great calling card script or two, or have had a few episodes of something produced, your ideas will be taken much more seriously. At this stage you might well sell a project on the basis of a short outline or synopsis, and be paid to write the script(s).

All scripts must be typed and properly formatted if they are to be taken seriously. If you dread the practical aspects of getting your script onto the page it might be worth investing in a screenwriting software program for your computer. They take the pain out of screenwriting by auto-formatting and numbering the pages and scenes, thus enabling you to move scenes around and restructure your script with ease. Such facilities allow writers to concentrate wholly on the creative process and can therefore be quite liberating, even for those who type well. Contact the Screenwriters' Store for details and advice.

Summary

Writing for television is not generally something that can be taken up as a hobby. It may look easy but huge amounts of work and commitment are required in order to succeed. If that doesn't put you off, and it is what you really want to do, then go for it. And good luck!

Anji Loman Field worked as a television producer for several years before turning to writing. She has since written drama, comedy drama and animation for film and television, and has taught writing at the Screenwriters' Workshop, the Royal College of Art and the London Institute.

Further reading

Friedmann, Julian, *How to Make Money Scriptwriting*, Boxtree, 1995, o.p.
Kelsey, Gerald, *Writing for Television*, A & C Black, 3rd edn, 1999
Seger, Linda, *Making a Good Script Great*, Samuel French Inc. (pbk), 1994
Vogler, Christopher, *The Writer's Journey*, Pan, 2nd revised edn, (pbk), 1999
Wolfe, Ronald, *Writing Comedy*, Robert Hale, (pbk), 1997

Writing drama for radio

*Writing drama for radio allows a freedom which none of the other performing arts can give. **Lee Hall** guides the radio drama writer to submit a script which will be both well received and merit production.*

With upwards of 300 hours of radio drama commissioned each year, radio is an insatiable medium and, therefore, one which is constantly seeking new blood. It is no surprise to find that many of our most eminent dramatists, such as Pinter and Stoppard, did important radio work early in their careers.

Although the centrality of radio has been eclipsed somewhat by television and fringe theatre, it continues to launch new writers, and its products often find popular recognition in other media (for example, the film version of Anthony Mingella's *Truly Madly Deeply*). Because radio is often cited as the discoverer and springboard of so many talents, this should not obscure the fact that many writers make a living primarily out of their radio writing and the work itself is massively popular, with plays regularly getting audiences of over 500,000 people.

For the dramatist, the medium offers a variety of work which is difficult to find anywhere else: serials, dramatisations, new commissions of various lengths (from a couple of minutes to several hours), musicals, soap operas, adaptations of the classics, as well as a real enthusiasm to examine new forms.

Because it is no more expensive to be in the Hindu Kush than to be in a laundrette in Deptford, the scope of the world is only limited by the imagination of the writer. However, though radio drama in the 'Fifties and 'Sixties was an important conduit for absurdism, there is a perceived notion that radio drama on the BBC is domestic, Home Counties and endlessly trotting out psychological trauma in a rather naturalistic fashion. This is not a fair assessment of the true range of work presented. The BBC itself is anxious to challenge this idea and as the face of broadcasting changes, there is a conscious move to attract new audiences with new kinds of work.

Get to know the form

Listen to as many plays as possible, read plays that are in print, and try to analyse what works, what doesn't and why. This may seem obvious, but it is easy to fall back on your preconceived notions of what radio plays are. The more you hear other people's successes and failures, the more tools you will have to discriminate when it comes to your own work.

Plays on radio tend to fit into specific time slots: 30, 60, 75, 90 minutes, and each slot will have a different feel – an afternoon play will be targeted at a different audience from one at 10.30pm.

A radio play will be chosen on artistic grounds but nevertheless a writer should be familiar with the market. This should not be seen as an invitation merely to copy forms or to try to make your play 'fit', but an opportunity to gain some sense of what the producers are dealing with. Producers are looking for new and fresh voices, ones which are unique, open new areas or challenge certain preconceptions. This is not to suggest you should be wilfully idiosyncratic but to be aware that it is the individuality of your 'voice' that people will notice.

Write what you feel strongly about, in the way that most attracts you. It should be bold, personal, entertaining, challenging and stimulating. Radio has the scope to explore drama that wouldn't get produced in theatres or on television, so treat it as the most radical forum for new writing. How many times have you listened to the radio with the sense that you've heard it all before? Never feel limited by what exists but be aware how your voice can enrich the possibilities of the future.

Who to approach

Opportunities for writing for radio in the UK are dominated by the BBC. Whilst there are increasing opportunities with independent stations, BBC Radio Drama overwhelms the field. Its output is huge. The variety of the work – from soaps to the classics – makes it the true national repertory for drama in its broadest sense. However, the BBC is increasingly commissioning productions from independent producers, so you can:

- send your unsolicited script to the BBC's New Writing Initiative (see page 291) where it will be assessed by a reader. If they find it of interest they will put you in contact with a suitable producer.
- approach a producer directly. This may be a producer at the BBC or at an independent company (see page 323). Both will give a personal response based on their own taste, rather than an institutional one.

Producers have a broad role: they find new writers, develop projects, edit the script, cast the actors, record and edit the play, and even write up the blurb for the *Radio Times*. Because of this intense involvement, the producer needs to have a strong personal interest in the writer or writing when they take on a project.

The system of commissioning programmes at the BBC is such that staff producers or independent production companies offer projects to commissioning editors to decide upon. Thus, a writer must be linked to a producer in the first instance to either get their play produced or get a commission for a new piece of work. Therefore, going direct to a producer can be a convenient short cut, but it requires more preparation.

Approaching a producer

Discovering and developing the work of new writers is only a small part of a producer's responsibilities, so be selective. Do your homework – there is little point in sending your sci-fi series to a producer who exclusively produces one-off period comedies.

To help decide which producer will be the most receptive to your work, become familiar with the work of each producer you are intersted in and the type of writers they work with. Use the *Radio Times* to help with your research and listen to as many of their plays as possible. It is well worth the effort in order to be sure to send your play to the right person. If you can quote the reasons why you've chosen them in particular, it can only help to get a congenial reception. It will also give you confidence in their response, as the comments – good or bad – will be from someone you respect.

Submitting your work

Don't stuff your manuscript into an envelope as soon as you've written 'The End'. You owe it to yourself to get the script into the best possible state before anyone sees it. First impressions matter and time spent refining will pay dividends in attracting attention.

Ask a person you trust to give you some feedback. Try to edit the work yourself, cutting things that don't work and spending time revising and reinventing anything which you think could be better. Make sure that what you send is the best you can possibly do.

Producers have mountains of scripts to read. The more bulky your tome the less enthusiastically it will be received. (It's better to send a sparkling 10-page sample than your whole 300-page masterpiece.) Try to make the first scene excellent. The more you can surprise, engage or delight in the first few pages, the more chance the rest will be carefully read. The adage that a reader can tell whether a play is any good after the first three pages might be wholly inaccurate but it reflects a cynicism versed by the practice of script reading. The reader will probably approach your script with the expectation that it is unsuitable, and part of getting noticed is jolting them out of their complacency.

Have your script presentably typed. Make sure your letter of introduction is well informed and shows that you haven't just picked a name at random. Do not send it to more than one producer at a time, as this is considered bad etiquette. And don't expect an instantaneous response – it may take a couple of months before you receive a reply. Don't be afraid of calling up if they keep you waiting for an unreasonable length of time, but don't badger people as this will inevitably be counterproductive.

Finally

Don't be discouraged by rejection and *don't* assume that because one person has rejected your script that it is no good. It is all a question of taste. Use the criticism positively to help your work, not as a personal attack.

Lee Hall has written several plays for BBC Radio, including the award-winning *Spoonface Steinberg*, which he has since adapted for TV and theatre. His translations of theatre plays include Brecht's *Mr Puntilla and His Man Matti* and *Mother Courage*, and Goldoni's *The Servant with Two Masters*. His play *Cooking with Elvis* was nominated for an Olivier Award for Best New Comedy, and his screenplay for *Billy Elliot* was Oscar nominated.

Digital broadcasting

Digital broadcasting is expanding rapidly. ***David Teather*** *introduces this new media and looks at the implications for writers.*

Digital broadcasting offers choice from hundreds of channels and the chance to offer interactive services to viewers. As many as 10 digital services are able to occupy the frequency previously occupied by one analogue service. Picture quality is far sharper using digital transmission.

Interactive services are so far only being used for e-commerce – for instance, Sky's television shopping and banking service Open. But a number of broadcasters are beginning to explore different ways of using the services for entertainment. In its coverage of Wimbledon, for instance, the BBC used the Sky Digital service to allow viewers to choose which court they wanted to watch. Ultimately, viewers will be able to link straight from a programme to associated websites, merchandising or online discussion points covering issues raised in a show. Digital transmission costs are also much lower which makes it more commercially viable for niche channels to exist.

The technical explanation

The BBC offers this definition: "Digital Broadcasting is transmission by converting sound and picture into binary digits – a series of ones and noughts. Digital signals are more robust than analogue signals and can occupy parts of the spectrum unavailable to analogue. A process of compression also allows many digital services within the space taken by one analogue service."

The story so far

The first company to launch digital services was Sky which now has 6 million digital subscribers. Its customer numbers for pay-TV stations had plateaued, but are now rising again as a result of digital broadcasting.

Of the cable companies, Telewest began its digital services at the end of 1999 and NTL (which now owns Cable & Wireless) started in mid 2000. The plug was pulled on ITV Digital, a joint venture between Carlton Communications and Granada which enabled digital services to be sent via traditional roof-top aerials, in April 2002. ITV Digital had attracted 1.3 million subscribers but was heavily loss making.

The uptake of digital services was given a huge boost when the fierce competition for subscribers led Sky to scrap the £200 charge for the set-top boxes needed to unscramble the digital signal.

The government is aiming to switch off analogue and would like to do so before 2010. By that time, digital set-top boxes should have been replaced by television sets able to receive digital signals – but sales so far have been slow. The switch-off date for analogue is highly political because it will cause an inevitable outcry when old sets become useless.

Free to air

There are a number of free-to-air digital channels. The BBC has, controversially, set up three new channels: BBC Choice shows reruns from the previous week as well as some entertainment-based original programming; BBC4, an arts-based channel (previously BBC Knowledge); and BBC News 24 – as the name suggests – screens news 24 hours a day. Rival companies such as Sky have argued that the licence fee should not be used to prop up stations like News 24 in a commercial marketplace. The BBC is planning to relaunch Choice as a youth channel called BBC3. During the day, BBC3 and BBC4 will run two new children's channels, Cbeebies, for a preschool audience and CBBC for older children.

ITV Network's ITV2 also shows 'catch-up' episodes of programmes like *Coronation Street*, as well as trumpeting a large number of US imports, including a late night double bill of Jerry Springer and David Letterman. ITV is also planning a family of channels including movies and sport.

All of the five existing free-to-air channels are also available in digital format.

Video on demand

The next step in the digital revolution is video on demand. A number of companies are trialling systems, including the cable firms and a new breed of young companies, such as Video Networks and Kingston Communications. Users will be able to download films or television programmes at will, and fast forward, pause and rewind them. Programme-makers like the BBC have already sold packages to some of the video-on-demand firms and writers need to consider the implications for the potential sell-on of copyright.

Video on demand could become widespread with the advent of a technology called ADSL (Asymmetrical Digital Subscriber Line), which upgrades existing copper telephone wires for high bandwidth use such as pay-TV without the need to dig up roads. ADSL is becoming more widely available on BT's networks. A ban on broadcasting being carried over BT's lines has now been lifted but costs are still prohibitively high.

Digital technology in the next few years will enable video-quality film to be sent over mobile phone networks. The mobile phone industry is expecting to have the networks and handsets with larger screens available by 2003.

New channels, new opportunities?

The explosion of new channels may suggest that there will be an equally huge demand for new writing talent to help fill the extra airtime. Through a joint venture with Flextech Television, the BBC has six pay-TV channels, including UK Gold, UK Play and UK Drama. The evidence so far, however, is that money is being spent largely on three things: sports rights, movies and US imports. Most original programming on pay-TV channels is very low budget and is far more likely to be a cookery or pop music show than original drama.

Unfortunately, rather than playing to their own strengths, the BBC and ITV appear to be drawn into competing with the entertainment channels at their level. "Once upon a time the BBC set the standards of quality and everyone else had to try and compete," says one writer. "That doesn't happen any more. Now the BBC competes with the others for crap."

The level of competition among broadcasters now also means that where original drama is being commissioned it is often low budget. In fact, many writers believe that in the short term digital technology has not opened opportunities at all and see the future as pretty bleak. Management gurus, though, maintain that 'content is king' and that those broadcasters who triumph will be the ones who produce the most compelling programming.

Copyrights

The Writers' Guild notes a recent case where a writer saw a 30-year-old show he had penned being repeated again and again on a pay-TV channel and demanded to know why he wasn't being paid. It turned out that he had signed his rights away in 1972.

If the explosion of channels made possible by digital technology isn't leading to a wave of new commissioning then writers could at least hope for healthier repeat fees. The culture of broadcasters forcing writers to sign away their rights for a lump sum so that they can show a programme whenever they like is becoming increasingly prevalent. The usual royalty is 5.6% of the sale price, which gives the owner the right to show the programme a set number of times over a given period.

Broadcasters blame the need to sell to the US market programmes which are unencumbered by copyright issues. When selling work, writers should remember how many more times, potentially, a programme will appear on air because of the growth in distribution platforms, and therefore at least try to protect their rights. The rapid changes in technology has also led writers' unions to recommend that contracts over the shortest space of time possible are agreed.

Original programming

There are at last some encouraging signs, however, led by Channel 4 and followed by Sky. Channel 4 has long supported new writing talent through its backing of British film and has found its own pay-TV distribution outlet with FilmFour.

Sky One commits an annual £90 million to original programming with mixed results – probably the most successful has been the football drama *Dream Team*. However, Sky's original programming has largely been forced upon it as the cost of acquiring top US content has soared due to increased competition – the reason why it lost the rights to show *Friends* and *ER*, two of Sky One's biggest ratings pullers, to Channel 4. Sky's commitment to original programming is also uncertain after the departure of Elisabeth Murdoch who championed British-produced content at Sky. Channel 4 has begun to commission original programming for its new digital channel, E4.

Sky Pictures is trying to emulate the success of FilmFour, albeit from a mass audience pitch. Its first two films were a biopic of footballer George Best and *Saving Grace* staring Brenda Blethyn. In early 2000, NTL, now Britain's largest cable company, committed its first spend to original programming.

Digital radio

The attributes of digital radio are similar to those of television. It was supposed to be the next revolution, but it has yet to catch on. The growth of stations is still in its infancy. In London, for instance, there will be three so-called 'multiplexes' of eight stations awarded to various consortia of existing radio groups. Interactive services will be on offer with the most obvious for radio including up-to-date traffic or weather reports displayed on a digital monitor on request. Digital radio could also lead to music or programming on demand similar to that of digital television programming.

A number of stations are now being broadcast in both digital and analogue as well as a growing number in digital alone. The BBC is committed to five new radio stations including one devoted to the spoken word where new commissioning should be available. So far, though, the industry has been held back by the prohibitive cost of hardware – the radios currently cost around £300.

David Teather is at the *Guardian*.

BBC network television and radio

The following outlines the new structure of the BBC.

The new structure

Major restructuring, introduced by BBC Director-General Greg Dyke on 3 April 2000, resulted in the creation of four programming divisions:

- Drama, Entertainment and Children;
- Factual and Learning;
- Sport; and
- News.

BBC Broadcast and BBC Production have been abolished. In the areas of sport, children's and education, commissioning and programme-making are now integrated. A New Media division is now developing the BBC's interactive television online activities.

Television genre commissioners in drama, entertainment and features now work with the television channel controllers to strengthen the BBC's output in these areas.

The disbanding of the Independent Commissioning Group has not diminished the value the BBC now places on the contribution of independents. However, in future they will take the same commissioning routes as in-house producers.

The restructuring also gives output guarantees for in-house departments, including Nations and English Regions, and longer term commissions to enable better planning and a greater focus on creativity.

website www.bbc.co.uk/
Director, Television Jana Bennett
Director, Sport Peter Salmon
Controller, BBC 1 Lorraine Heggessy
Controller, BBC 2 Jane Root
Controller, BBC Choice Stuart Murphy
Controller, BBC4 Roly Keating
Controller, Children's (CBBC) Nigel Pilkard
Director, Radio Jenny Abramsky
Controller, Radio 1 Andy Parfitt
Controller, Radio 2 Jim Moir
Controller, Radio 3 Roger Wright
Controller, Radio 4 Helen Boaden
Controller, Radio 5 Live Bob Shennan

Drama, Entertainment and Children

Director Alan Yentob

Drama

BBC Television Centre, Centre House,
Wood Lane, London W12 7SB
tel 020-8743 8000
The New Writing Initiative
Room 6058, BBC Broadcasting House,
London W1A 1AA
tel 020-7580 4468
Drama Development in the North
BBC New Broadcasting House, Oxford Road,
Manchester M60 1SJ
tel 0161-200 2020
BBC Broadcasting Centre
Pebble Mill Road, Birmingham B5 7QQ
tel 0121-432 8888

Drama has departments in London, Birmingham and Manchester and produces a broad range of plays, serials, series and readings for TV, film, BBC Radio 3, BBC Radio 4 and BBC World Service.

Unsolicited scripts for TV and film, single plays and radio drama, are co-ordinated by the New Writing Initiative. Scripts should be submitted one at a time. The Initiative also produces detailed guidelines on script construction, markets and contacts (for address see above). Since competition is fierce, reading the guidelines is advisable before submitting a script. All writers submitting scripts are considered for the Initiative's highly targeted writing schemes and workshops.

The Manchester team also operates radio drama workshops, primarily for writers in the North of England. For further information contact Drama Development in the North.

The Birmingham radio team reads the unsolicited scripts of writers in the Midlands, East Anglia and South West but does not have a formal new writing department. The TV operation also reads unsolicited scripts on an informal basis. Both offices are based at BBC Broadcasting Centre.

Controller, Continuing Drama Series Mal Young
Head of Films and Single Drama David Thompson
Head of Development Television Series Serena Cullen
Head of Development Television Serials Pippa Harris
Controller, Drama Commissioning Jane Tranter
Head of Independents Drama Gareth Neame
Controller, Innovation and Factual Drama Susan Spindler
Senior Executive Producer Hilary Salmon
Head of Development Films Tracey Scoffield
Casting Executive, Drama Series Jane Deitch
Head of Radio Drama and New Services Kate Rowland
Executive Producer TV Drama Series, Birmingham Richard Langridge
Development Co-ordinator TV Drama, Birmingham Terry Barker
Executive Producer Radio Drama and Editor, The Archers, Birmingham Vanessa Whitburn
Executive Producer Radio Drama, Manchester Sue Roberts
Head of Drama, BBC World Service Gordon House
New Writing Initiative Co-ordinator Lucy Hannah

Entertainment

BBC Television Centre, Wood Lane, London W12 7RJ
tel 020-8743 8000
website www.bbc.co.uk/entertainment

Entertainment welcomes new half-hour TV situation comedy scripts and material is reviewed by its Comedy Script Unit. Radio is also a good entry point for new comedy writers, performers and ground-breaking innovative series such as sketch shows and panel games.

The department produces *Writers Guidelines*, a detailed information pack which includes advice on how to write radio and TV scripts, current trends, available markets, contacts, free audience opportunities and further reading (available by sending an A4 first class sae to Comedy Script Unit, Room 4088). Writers are strongly advised to read the *Writers Guidelines* before submitting scripts one at a time, as competition is high.

Controller, Entertainment Commissioning Jane Lush
Editor, Radio Entertainment John Pidgeon
Head of Comedy Geoffrey Perkins
Head of Comedy Entertainment Jon Plowman
Editor, Comedy Sophie Clarke-Jervoise
Script Executive Bill Dare
Head of Music Entertainment Trevor Dann

Children's

BBC Television Centre, Wood Lane, London W12 7RJ
tel 020-8743 8000

There are opportunities for new writers in this highly competitive area. Unsolicited material is read by the department, preferably in the form of synopses of ideas. The preferred genres are contemporary comedy and drama.

Controller, Children's Programmes Nigel Pickard
Head of Drama Elaine Sperber
Head of Entertainment Chris Bellinger
Development Executive Greg Childs

Factual and Learning

Joint Directors Glenwyn Benson, Michael Stevenson

General Factual

BBC Television Centre, Wood Lane, London W12 7RJ
tel 020-8743 8000
Controller, Commissioning Nicola Moody
Controller, General Factual Anne Morrison
Head of Production, General Factual Steve Wallis
Managing Editor, General Factual Donna Taberer

Entertainment and Features, Manchester

BBC New Broadcasting House, PO Box 27, Oxford Road, Manchester M60 1SJ
tel 0161-200 2020

A bi-media department which makes programmes for both radio and TV. It is responsible for a wide range of factual, entertainment and music programming, and specialises in spotting new comedy talent and aims to see all new stand-up performers/writers in the North West. Write with details of events to Comedy Entertainment, Room 4033.

Head of Entertainment and Features, Manchester Wayne Garvie

General Factual, Bristol

BBC Broadcasting House, Whiteladies Road, Bristol BS8 2LR
tel 01179-732211

Produces a range of factual leisure, documentary and animation programmes for radio and TV along with supporting websites.

Head of Programmes, General Factual, Bristol Tom Archer
Creative Directors Andy Batten-Foster, Mark Hill, Tessa Finch
Joint Editors, Radio Fiona Couper, Elizabeth Burke
Executive Producer, Animation Helen Nabarro

Network Production, Birmingham

BBC Birmingham, Pebble Mill Road, Birmingham B5 7QQ
tel 0121-432 8888

A vast range of radio and TV programming which encompasses Asian, consumer affairs, leisure, lifestyle, motoring, music and rural affairs.

Head of Programmes vacant
Managing Editor, General Factual Paresh Solanki
Editor, Factual Radio and Countryfile Andrew Thorman
Editor, Radio Drama and The Archers Vanessa Whitburn
Editor, Specialist Programmes, Radio Dave Barber

Specialist Factual

BBC Television Centre, Wood Lane, London W12 7RJ
tel 020-8743 8000
Acting Controller Keith Scholey
Acting Deputy Commissioner Emma Swain
Head of Production Kelvin Jones
Managing Editor Clare Brigstocke

Natural History Unit

BBC Broadcasting House, Whiteladies Road, Bristol BS8 2LR
tel 01179-732211

Makes specialist programmes with established experts.

Head of Natural History Unit Keith Scholey
Head of Development Alistair Fothergill
Commercial Director Ailish Heneberry
Editor Radio Julian Hector

Religion and Ethics

BBC New Broadcasting House, PO Box 27, Oxford Road, Manchester M60 1SJ
tel 0161-200 2020

Produces a wide range of religious, moral and ethical programmes for radio and TV which, while recognising Christianity as the UK's dominant faith, explores a wide range of faiths and issues.

Head of Religion and Ethics Alan Bookbinder

News

BBC Television Centre, Wood Lane, London W12 7RJ
tel 020-8743 8000

BBC News is the biggest news organisation in the world with over 2000 journalists, 50 bureaux worldwide and 13 networks and services across TV, radio and new media.

Director, News Richard Sambrook
Assistant Director and Head of Political Programmes Mark Damazer
Head of Current Affairs Peter Horrocks
Head of Radio News Steve Mitchell
Head of New Media Richard Deverell
Head of TV News Roger Mosey
Head of Newsgathering Adrian Van Klaveren
Executive Editor Radio Daily Current Affairs Anne Koch
Managing News Editor, News 24 Peter Knowles

Sport

BBC Television Centre, Wood Lane, London W12 7RJ
tel 020-8743 8000

Multimedia coverage of a wide range of sports in the UK and worldwide.

Director, Sport Peter Salmon
Executive Editor, Magazines and Documentaries Philip Bernie
Executive Editor, Radio Gordon Turnbull
Executive Editor, Television Dave Gordon

World Service

Bush House, Strand, London WC2B 4PH
tel 020-7240 3456
website www.bbc.co.uk/worldservice

BBC World Service provides radio

services in English and 42 other languages, via short wave and in an increasing number of cities around the world, on MW and FM. The English service is also available 24 hours a day in real audio on the internet. Classic contemporary drama, novels, short stories, soap operas and poetry are all a feature of its English service, plus a wide range of arts, documentaries, education, features, music, religious affairs, science, sports and youth programmes. In addition, BBC World Service provides on-the-spot coverage of world news, giving a global perspective of international events.
Director, BBC World Service Mark Byford
Director, English Network and News and Programme Commissioning Phil Harding

Worldwide

BBC Woodlands, 80 Wood Lane,
London W12 0TT
tel 020-8433 2000
website www.bbcworldwide.com

BBC Worldwide Ltd is the commercial arm of the BBC. It makes money from broadcast-related businesses and returns cash to the BBC to invest in new programming. Publishing forms a significant part of its activities.
Chief Executive Rupert Gavin
Managing Director, UK Regions and Deputy CE Peter Teague

Audio cassettes and CDs. Around 130 audio cassettes and CDs of BBC radio and TV programmes are released every year, mainly comedy, readings and dramatised serials. Pitch ideas to:
Publishing Director Jan Paterson

Books. Ideas for books that would extend audience enjoyment of a BBC radio or TV programme should be pitched, according to subject matter, via a short synopsis to:
Commissioning Editor, Factual Sally Potter
Commissioning Editor, Factual/Drama Emma Shackleton
Commissioning Editors, Lifestyle Vivien Bowler, Nicky Copeland
Commissioning Editor, Sport and Entertainment Benn Dunn

Magazines. Freelance contributions are regularly used by BBC Worldwide magazines, but the use of unsolicited material is rare as the editorial links closely to BBC programme content. Ideas for articles that clearly fit the remit of a magazine should be pitched via a short written summary to the Editor.
Eve Jane Bruton
Gardens Illustrated Clare Foster
Radio Times Gill Hudson
BBC Good Food Orlando Murrin
BBC Gardeners' World Adam Pasco
BBC Good Homes Julie Savill
BBC History Magazine Greg Neale
BBC Homes & Antiques Mary Carroll
BBC Top Gear Magazine Kevin Blick
BBC Music Magazine Helen Wallace
BBC Wildlife Magazine Rosamund Kidman Cox (BBC Bristol address)

All ideas for BBC children's and teen magazines (*Top of the Pops*, *It's Hot*, *Girl Talk*, *BBC Learning is Fun*, *Noddy*, *BBC Toybox*, *Teletubbies*, *Bob the Builder*, *Roar*, *The Magic Key* and *Tweenies*) should be sent to the magazine concerned.

Nations and Regions

BBC Henry Wood House, Langham Place,
London W1A 1AA
tel 020-7580 4468

BBC Nations and Regions is responsible for over 80% of all the BBC's domestic output – about 7000 hours of TV and over 250,000 of radio. BBC Northern Ireland, BBC Scotland and BBC Wales produce a growing number of programmes for the BBC's TV and radio networks, as well as providing comprehensive services for viewers and listeners in their own nations. The BBC's English Regions are responsible for 11 TV regional news and current affairs services across England; for 39 BBC local radio stations and 50 local 'Where I Live' websites with their emphasis on news and information for their local communities.
Director, National & Regional Broadcasting Pat Loughrey

BBC Northern Ireland

BBC Broadcasting House, Ormeau Avenue,
Belfast BT2 8HQ
tel 028-9033 8000
website www.bbc.co.uk/ni

BBC Northern Ireland produces a broad spectrum of radio and TV programmes, both for the BBC's networks and for its home audience. Output includes news and current affairs, documentaries, education, entertainment, sport, music, Irish language and religious programmes. It also has a thriving drama department which reads unsolicited scripts across all genre, i.e. single, serials, series, feature films and the short film scheme *Northern Lights*, which is aimed at new talent from within Northern Ireland.

In addition to making network radio programmes, broadcasting on BBC Radio 1, 2, 3, 4, and 5 Live and BBC World Service, BBC Northern Ireland also makes programmes for its local radio listeners.

Controller, BBC Northern Ireland Anna Garragher
Head of Broadcasting Tim Cooke
Head of News and Current Affairs Andrew Colman
Head of Factual and Learning Bruce Batten
Entertainment and Events Mike Edgar
Head of Drama Robert Cooper
Editor, Radio Foyle Ana Leddy
Head of Marketing and Development Peter Johnston
Head of Resources Stephen Beckett

BBC Radio Ulster

BBC Broadcasting House, Ormeau Avenue, Belfast BT2 8HQ
tel 028-9033 8000

BBC Radio Foyle

8 Northland Road, Londonderry BT48 7JO
tel 028-7126 2244

BBC Scotland

BBC Broadcasting House, Queen Margaret Drive, Glasgow G12 8DG
tel 0141-339 8844
website www.bbc.co.uk/scotland

BBC Scotland is the BBC's most varied production centre outside London, providing BBC TV and radio networks and BBC World Service with pivotal drama, comedy, entertainment, children's, leisure, documentaries, religion, education, arts, music, special events news, current affairs and political coverage. Internet development is also a key element of production activity.

Its drama department, along with Scottish Screen, is responsible for the highly successful initiative, *Tartan Shorts*, which promotes film-making in the nation and provides a platform for emerging Scottish creative talent, including actors, writers, directors and producers.

In addition to making network output, more than 850 hours of TV programming per year is transmitted on BBC1 Scotland and BBC2 Scotland. BBC Radio Scotland is the country's only national radio station, and is on air 18 hours a day, 7 days a week. Local programmes are also broadcast on Radio Scotland's FM frequency in the Northern Isles, and there are daily local bulletins for listeners in the Highlands, Grampian, Borders, and the southwest. BBC Radio Nan Gaidheal provides a Gaelic service on a separate FM frequency for around 40 hours a week.

Controller, BBC Scotland John McCormick
Head of Programmes Ken MacQuarrie
Head of Network Programmes Colin Cameron
Head of News and Current Affairs Blair Jenkins
Head of Drama Barbara McKissack

BBC Radio Scotland

BBC Broadcasting House, Queen Margaret Drive, Glasgow G12 8DG
tel 0141-338 8844

BBC Radio Nan Gaidheal

Rosebank, Church Street, Stornoway, Isle of Lewis PA87 2LS
tel (0851) 705000

BBC Wales

BBC Broadcasting House, Llandaff, Cardiff CF5 2YQ
tel 029-2032 2000
website www.bbc.co.uk/wales

BBC Wales provides a wide range of services in Welsh and in English, on radio, TV and online. This includes more than 20 hours a week of programmes on BBC1 Wales and BBC2 Wales including the new BBC Wales digital services. Regular output includes the flagship news programme *Wales Today*, the current affairs strand *Week In Week Out*, and the rugby magazine *Scrum V*. A further 10 hours are shown on the Welsh-language channel S4C including the news programme *Newyddion*, the nightly drama serial *Pobol y Cwm* plus a range of programmes for schools. Its 2 radio stations, BBC Radio Wales,

broadcasting in English, and BBC Radio Cymru, broadcasting in Welsh, each provide 18 hours a day of news, entertainment, music and sports output. Political coverage on all services has expanded as a result of the creation of the National Assembly for Wales. BBC Wales also makes popular drama, documentaries, education and music programmes for audiences throughout the UK, including the biennial *Cardiff Singer of the World* competition, accompanied by the BBC National Orchestra of Wales.
Controller, BBC Wales Menna Richards
Head of Programmes (English) Clare Hudson
Head of Programmes (Welsh) Keith Jones
Head of News and Current Affairs Aled Eirug
Editor, Radio Wales Julie Barton
Editor, Radio Cymru Aled Glynne Davis
Head of Drama Matthew Robinson
Head of Sport Nigel Walker
Head of Factual Adrian Davis
Head of Arts Paul Islwyn Thomas
Head of Music David Jackson
Music Director, BBC National Orchestra of Wales David Murray

BBC Radio Cymru (Welsh language)
BBC Broadcasting House, Llandaff, Cardiff CF5 2YQ
tel 029-2032 2000

BBC Radio Wales (English language)
BBC Broadcasting House, Llandaff, Cardiff CF5 2YQ
tel 029-2032 2000

BBC regional television and local radio

The BBC's English Regions are responsible for 11 TV regional news and current affairs services across England, and for 40 BBC local radio stations with their emphasis on news and information for their local communities.

BBC English regions (TV and radio)

BBC Birmingham, Pebble Mill Road, Birmingham B5 7QQ
tel 0121-432 8888
Controller, English Regions Andy Griffee
Head of Programming Craig Henderson
Head of New Services Julie Allen

BBC East

St Catherine's Close, All Saints Green, Norwich NR1 3ND
tel (01603) 619331
Head of Regional and Local Programmes David Holdsworth

BBC Radio Cambridgeshire
PO Box 96, Hills Road, Cambridge CB2 1LD
tel (01223) 259696

BBC Essex
198 New London Road, Chelmsford CM2 9AB
tel (01245) 616000

BBC Radio Norfolk
Norfolk Tower, Surrey Street, Norwich NR1 3PA
tel (01603) 617411

BBC Radio Northampton
Broadcasting House, Abington Street, Northampton NN1 2BE
tel (01604) 239100

BBC Radio Suffolk
Broadcasting House, St Matthew's Street, Ipswich IP1 3EP
tel (01473) 250000

BBC Three Counties Radio
PO Box 3CR, Luton, Beds. LU1 5XL
tel (01582) 637400

BBC East Midlands

London Road, Nottingham NG2 4UU
tel 0115-955 0500
Head of Regional and Local Programmes Alison Ford

BBC Radio Derby
PO Box 269, Derby DE1 3HL
tel (01332) 361111

BBC Radio Leicester
Epic House, Charles Street, Leicester LE1 3SH
tel 0116-251 6688

BBC Radio Lincolnshire
Radio Buildings, PO Box 219, Newport, Lincoln LN1 3XY
tel (01522) 511411

BBC Radio Nottingham
York House, Mansfield Road, Nottingham NG1 3JB
tel 0115-955 0500

BBC South East

The Great Hall, Mount Pleasant Road, Tunbridge Wells, Kent TN1 1QQ
tel (01892) 675550
Head of Regional and Local Programmes Laura Ellis

BBC London 94.9 FM
35C Marylebone High Street, London W1A 4LG
tel 020-7224 2424

BBC Radio Kent
The Great Hall, Mount Pleasant Road, Tunbridge Wells, Kent TN1 1QQ
tel (01892) 675550

BBC South East London
35C Marylebone High Street, London W1A 4LG
tel 020-7224 2424

BBC Southern Counties Radio
Broadcasting Centre, Guildford GU2 5AP
tel (01483) 306306

BBC North

Broadcasting Centre, Woodhouse Lane, Leeds LS2 9PX
tel 0113-244 1188
Head of Regional and Local Programmes Colin Philpott

BBC Radio Humberside
9 Chapel Street, Hull HU1 3NU
tel (01482) 323232

BBC Radio Leeds
Broadcasting Centre, Woodhouse Lane, Leeds LS2 9PN
tel 0113-244 2131

BBC Radio Sheffield
54 Shoreham Street, Sheffield S1 4RS
tel 0114-273 1171

BBC Radio York
20 Bootham Row, York YO3 7BR
tel (01904) 641351

BBC North East and Cumbria

Broadcasting Centre, Barrack Road, Newcastle upon Tyne NE99 2NE
tel 0191-232 1313
Head of Regional and Local Programmes Olwyn Hocking

BBC Radio Cleveland
PO Box 95FM, Newport Road, Middlesbrough TS1 5DG
tel (01642) 225211

BBC Radio Cumbria
Annetwell Street, Carlisle CA3 8BB
tel (01228) 592444

BBC Radio Newcastle
Broadcasting Centre, Barrack Road, Newcastle upon Tyne NE99 1RN
tel 0191-232 4141

BBC North West

New Broadcasting House, Oxford Road, Manchester M60 1SJ
tel 0161-200 2020
Head of Regional and Local Programmes Martin Brooks

BBC GMR
PO Box 951, Oxford Road, Manchester M60 1SD
tel 0161-200 2000

BBC Radio Lancashire
26 Darwen Street, Blackburn, Lancs. BB2 EA
tel (01254) 262411

BBC Radio Merseyside
55 Paradise Street, Liverpool L1 3BP
tel 0151-708 5500

BBC South

Broadcasting House, Havelock Road, Southampton SO14 7PW
tel 023-80226201
Head of Regional and Local Programmes Eve Turner

BBC Radio Berkshire
PO Box 1044, Reading, Berks. RG4 8FH
tel 0118-946 4200

BBC Radio Oxford
PO Box 95.2, Oxford OX2 7YL
tel (08459) 311444

BBC Radio Solent
Broadcasting House, Havelock Road,
Southampton SO14 7PW
tel 023-8063 1311

BBC South West

Broadcasting House, Seymour Road,
Mannamead, Plymouth PL3 5BD
tel (01752) 229201
Head of Regional and Local Programmes Leo Devine

BBC Radio Cornwall
Phoenix Wharf, Truro, Cornwall TR1 1UA
tel (01872) 275421

BBC Radio Devon
PO Box 1034, Plymouth PL3 5BD
tel (01752) 260323
PO Box 1034, Exeter EX4 4DB
tel (01392) 215651

BBC Radio Guernsey
Commerce House, Les Banques, St Peter Port,
Guernsey GY1 2HS
tel (01481) 728977

BBC Radio Jersey
18 Parade Road, St Helier, Jersey JE2 3PL
tel (01534) 870000

BBC West

Broadcasting House, Whiteladies Road,
Bristol BS8 2LR
tel 0117-973 2211
Head of Regional and Local Programmes Andrew Wilson

BBC Radio Bristol
PO Box 194, Bristol BS99 7QT
tel 0117-974 1111

BBC Radio Gloucestershire
London Road, Gloucester GL1 1SW
tel (01452) 308585

BBC Radio Somerset Sound
(part of Radio Bristol)
14-15 Paul Street, Taunton,
Somerset TA1 3PF
(01823) 252437

BBC Wiltshire Sound
Broadcasting House, Prospect Place,
Swindon SN1 3RW
tel (01793) 513626

BBC West Midlands

Pebble Mill Road, Birmingham B5 7QQ
tel 0121-432 8888
Head of Regional and Local Programmes Roy Roberts

BBC Coventry & Warwickshire
Holt Court, 1 Greyfriars Road,
Coventry CV1 2WR
tel (02476) 231231

BBC Hereford & Worcester
Hylton Road, Worcester WR2 5WW
tel (01905) 748485

BBC Radio Shropshire
2-4 Boscobel Drive, Shrewsbury SY1 3TT
tel (01743) 248484

BBC Radio Stoke
Cheapside, Hanley,
Stoke on Trent ST1 1JJ
tel (01782) 208080

BBC Radio WM
PO Box 206, Broadcasting Centre,
Pebble Mill Road, Birmingham B5 7SD
tel 0121-432 8484

BBC broadcasting rights and terms

Contributors are advised to check latest details of fees with the BBC.

Rights and terms – television

Specially written material

Fees for submitted material are paid on acceptance. For commissioned material, half the fee is paid on commissioning and half on acceptance as being suitable for television. All fees are subject to negotiation above the minima.

- Rates for one performance of a 60-minute original television play are a minimum of £4728 for a play written by a beginner and a 'going rate' of £7450 for an established writer, or *pro rata* for shorter or longer timings.
- Fees for a 50-minute episode in a series during the same period are a minimum of £3900 for a beginner and a 'going rate' of £5634 for an established writer.
- Fees for a 50-minute dramatisation are a minimum of £2721 for a beginner and a 'going rate' of £4010 for an established writer.
- Fees for a 50-minute adaptation of an existing stage play or other dramatic work are a minimum of £1640 for a beginner and a 'going rate' of £2403 for an established writer.

Specially written light entertainment sketch material

- The rates for sketch material range from £40 per minute for beginners with a 'going rate' of £70 for established writers.
- The fee for a quickie or news item is half the amount of the writer's per minute rate.
- Fees for submitted material are payable on acceptance and for commissioned material half on signature and half on acceptance.

Published material

- Prose works: £20.64 per minute.
- Poems: £23.97 per half minute.

Stage plays and source material for television

- Fees for stage plays and source novels are negotiable.

Rights and terms – radio

Specially written material

Fees are assessed on the basis of the type of material, its length, the author's status and experience in writing for radio. Fees for submitted material are paid on acceptance. For commissioned material, half the fee is paid on commissioning and half on acceptance as being suitable for broadcasting.

- Rates for specially written radio dramas in English (other than educational programmes) are £45.16 a minute for beginners and a 'going rate' of £68.74 a minute for established writers. This rate covers two broadcasts.

Specially written short stories

- Fees range from £139 for 15 minutes.

Published material

Domestic radio

- Dramatic works: £13.64 per minute.
- Prose works: £13.64 per minute.
- Prose works required for dramatisation: £10.63 per minute.
- Poems: £13.64 per half minute.

World Service Radio (English)

- Dramatic works: £6.83 per minute for

broadcasts within a seven-day period.
- Prose works: £6.83 per minute for broadcasts within a seven-day period.
- Prose works required for dramatisation: £5.32 per minute for broadcasts within a seven-day period.
- Poems: £6.83 per half minute for broadcasts within a seven-day period.
- Foreign Language Services are approximately one-fifth of the rate for English Language Services.

Television and radio

Repeats in BBC programmes

- Further proportionate fees are payable for repeats.

Use abroad of recordings of BBC programmes

If the BBC sends abroad recordings of its programmes for use by overseas broadcasting organisations on their own networks or stations, further payments accrue to the author, usually in the form of additional percentages of the basic fee paid for the initial performance or a royalty based on the percentage of the distributors' receipts. This can apply to both sound and television programmes.

Value Added Tax

There is a self-billing system for VAT which covers radio, World Service and television for programmes made in London.

Talks for television

Contributors to talks will be offered the standard television talks contract which provides the BBC certain rights to broadcast the material in a complete, abridged and/or translated manner, and which provides for the payment of further fees for additional usage of the material whether by television, domestic radio or external broadcasting. The contract also covers the assignment of material and limited publication rights. Alternatively, a contract taking in all standard rights may be negotiated. Fees are arranged by the contract authorities in London and the Regions.

Talks for radio

Contributors to talks for domestic radio and World Service broadcasting may be offered either:
- the standard talks contract which takes rights and provides for residual payments, as does the television standard contract; or
- an STC (Short Talks Contract) which takes all rights except print publication rights where the airtime of the contribution does not exceed five minutes and which has set fees or disturbance money payable; or
- an NFC (No Fee Contract) where no payment is made which provides an acknowledgement that a contribution may be used by the BBC.

Independent national television

BSkyB
Grant Way, Isleworth, Middlesex TW7 5QD
tel 020-7705 3000 *fax* 020-7705 3030/3113
website www.sky.com

Channel 5 Broadcasting Ltd
22 Long Acre, London WC2E 9LY
tel 020-7550 5555 *fax* 020-7550 5554
website www.channel5.co.uk

The fifth and last national 'free-to-air' terrestrial 24-hour TV channel. Commissions a wide range of programmes to suit all tastes.

Channel 4 Television Corporation
124 Horseferry Road, London SW1P 2TX
tel 020-7396 4444 *fax* 020-7306 8347
website www.channel4.com

Commissions and purchases programmes (it does not make them) for broadcast during the whole week throughout the United Kingdom (except Wales). Also broadcasts subscription film channel FilmFour and digital entertainment channel E4.

GMTV
London Television Centre, Upper Ground, London SE1 9TT
tel 020-7827 7000 *fax* 020-7827 7001

GMTV1 is ITV's national breakfast TV service, 6.00–9.25am, 7 days a week. GMTV2 is GMTV's cable and digital channel shown on ITV2 daily 6.00–9.25am.

Independent Television Commission (ITC)
33 Foley Street, London W1W 7TL
tel 020-7255 3000 *fax* 020-7306 7800
email publicaffairs@itc.org.uk
website www.itc.co.uk

Licenses and regulates all commercially funded TV services in the UK, including cable and satellite services as well as terrestrial services.

ITN
200 Gray's Inn Road, London WC1X 8XZ
tel 020-7833 3000
website www.itn.co.uk

Provides the national news programmes for ITV, Channel 4 and Channel 5.

ITV Network Ltd
200 Gray's Inn Road, London WC1X 8HF
tel 020-7843 8000 *fax* 020-7843 8158
website www.itv.co.uk

NTL
NTL House, Bartley Wood Business Park, Bartley Way, Hook, Hants RG27 9UP
tel (01256) 752000 *fax* (01256) 752100
website www.ntl.co.uk

S4C
Parc Ty Glas, Llanishen, Cardiff CF14 5DU
tel 029-20747444 *fax* 029-20754444
email s4c@s4c.co.uk
website www.s4c.co.uk

The Welsh Fourth Channel. S4C's analogue service broadcasts 32 hours per week in Welsh: 22 hours are commissioned from independent producers and 10 hours are produced by the BBC. Most of Channel 4's output is rescheduled to complete this service. S4C's digital service broadcasts 12 hours per day in Welsh.

Teletext Ltd
101 Farm Lane, London SW6 1QJ
tel 020-7386 5000 *fax* 020-7386 5002
email editor@teletext.co.uk
website www.teletext.co.uk

Independent regional television

It is advisable to check before submitting any ideas/material – in all cases, scripts are preferred to synopses. Programmes should be planned with natural breaks for the insertion of advertisements. These companies also provide some programmes for Channel 4.

Anglia Television Ltd

Anglia House, Norwich NR1 3JG
tel (01603) 615151 *fax* (01603) 631032
email angliatv@angliatv.com
website www.angliatv.com

Provides programmes for the East of England, daytime discussion programmes, documentaries and factual programmes for UK and international broadcasters.

Border Television plc

The Television Centre, Carlisle CA1 3NT
tel (01228) 25101

Provides programmes for, Cumbria, the Borders and the Isle of Man, during the whole week. Ideas for programmes, but not drama programmes, are considered from outside sources. Suggestions should be sent to Neil Robinson, Director of Programmes.

Carlton Broadcasting

101 St Martin's Lane, London WC2N 4AZ
tel 020-7240 4000 *fax* 020-7240 4171

Provides ITV programmes for London and the South East from Monday to Friday.

Carlton Broadcasting, Central Region

Gas Street, Birmingham B1 2JT
tel 0121-643 9898 *fax* 0121-643 4897
Carlton Studios, Lenton Lane, Nottingham NG7 2NA
tel 0115-986 3322 *fax* 0115-964 5552
Unit 9, Windrush Court, Abingdon Business Park, Abingdon, Oxon OX1 1SA
tel (01235) 554123 *fax* (01235) 524024

Provides ITV programmes for the East, West and South Midlands 7 days a week.

Carlton Broadcasting, West Country Region

Langage Science Park, Plymouth PL7 5BQ
tel (01752) 333333 *fax* (01752) 333444
email westcountryregion@carltontv.co.uk

Provides programmes for South West England throughout the week. In-house production mainly news, regional current affairs and topical features; other regional features commissioned from independent producers. Conduit to the Network for independent production packages.

Channel Television

The Television Centre, St Helier, Jersey JE1 3ZD
tel (01534) 816816 *fax* (01534) 816817
email broadcast@channeltv.co.uk

Provides programmes for the Channel Islands during the whole week relating mainly to Channel Islands news, events and current affairs.

Grampian Television plc

Queens Cross, Aberdeen AB15 4XJ
tel (01224) 846846 *fax* (01224) 846800
email gtv@grampiantv.co.uk
Harbour Chambers, Dock Street, Dundee DD1 3HW
tel (01382) 591000 *Ifax* (01382) 591010
23-25 Huntly Street, Inverness IV3 5PR
tel (01463) 242624

Provides programmes for North Scotland during the whole week.

Granada Television Ltd

Granada Television Centre, Manchester M60 9EA
tel 0161-832 7211 and
Upper Ground, London SE1 9LT
tel 020-7620 1620

The ITV franchise holder for the North West of England. Produces programmes across a broad range for both its region and the ITV Network. Writers are advised to make their approach through agents who would have some knowledge of Granada's current requirements.

HTV Ltd

HTV Wales, The Television Centre, Culverhouse Cross, Cardiff CF5 6XJ
tel 029-2059 0590 and
email public.relations@htv-wales.co.uk
website www.htvwales.com
HTV West, The Television Centre, Bristol BS4 3HG
tel 01179-722 722
email presspr@htv-west.co.uk
website www.htvwest.com

Provides programmes for Wales and West of England during the whole week. Produces programmes for home and international sales.

LWT

The London Television Centre, London SE1 9LT
tel 020-7620 1620
website www.granadamedia.com

Broadcasts to Greater London and much of the Home Counties area from Friday 5.15pm to Monday 6.00am (excluding 6.00–9.25am on Sat/Sun).

Meridian Broadcasting

Television Centre, Southampton, Hants SO14 0PZ
tel 023-8022 2555 *fax* 023-8033 5050
website www.meridiantv.com

The ITV franchise holder for the South and South East. Meridian produces quality drama, factual, sport and children's programming for the ITV network.

Scottish Television – Network Production

3 Waterhouse Square, 138-142 Holborn, London EC1N 2YN
tel 020-7882 1000 *fax* 020-7882 1005
website www.smg.plc.uk

Wholly owned subsidiary of SMG plc, making drama and other programmes for the ITV network. The SMG plc Television Division also includes Ginger Television.

• Material (STV): ideas and formats for long-form series with or without a Scottish flavour. Approach Controller of Drama, Eric Coulter.

• Material (Ginger): produces compelling programmes for groups of all ages. Programming includes *TFI Friday* and *The Priory*. Contact: Clare Barton.

Tyne Tees Television Ltd

The Television Centre, City Road, Newcastle upon Tyne NE1 2AL
tel 0191-261 0181 *fax* 0191-261 2302
email tyne.tees@granadamedia.com

Serving the North of England 7 days a week, 24 hours a day.

UTV

Havelock House, Ormeau Road, Belfast, Northern Ireland BT7 1EB
tel 028-9032 8122 *fax* 028-9024 6695
email info@utvplc.com
website www.utv.co.uk

Provides programmes for Northern Ireland.

Yorkshire Television Ltd

The Television Centre, Leeds LS3 1JS
tel 0113-243 8283 *fax* 0113-244 5107

Yorkshire Television is a Network Company which produces many programmes for the ITV Network and the Yorkshire area 7 days a week. Material preferred submitted through agents. Wholly owned subsidiary of Granada Media Group.

Presenting scripts for television and film

Whether your aim is to write a feature film or a screenplay for television, the discipline of the visual medium calls for a special appreciation and understanding. ***Jean McConnell*** *advises on how to prepare and lay out your manuscript and how to submit it to a production company for consideration.*

What is a screenplay?

A screenplay should tell a story in terms of visual action and dialogue spoken by the characters. A script for a full-length feature film running about one and a half hours will be about 100–130 pages long. Whether it is a feature film, a short film for children, say, or a documentary, it is better to present a version which is too short rather than too long.

Elaborate camera directions are not necessary as a shooting script will be made at a later stage. Your job is to write the master scenes, clearly broken down into each incident and location.

Layout

Individual companies may vary slightly in their house style but the general layout of a screenplay, either for a feature film or television film, is illustrated on page 305. The following points should be noted.

- Each scene should be numbered on the left and given a title which indicates whether the scene is an interior or an exterior, where it takes place, and the lighting conditions, i.e. day or night. The situation of each scene should be standardised; don't call your 'sitting room' a 'lounge' the next time you come to it, or people will think you mean a different place.
- Note that the dialogue is spaced out, with the qualifying directions such as '(frowning)' on a separate line, slightly inset from the dialogue. Double space each speech from the previous one.
- Always put the names of the characters in CAPITALS, except when they occur in the actual dialogue. Double space the stage directions from the dialogue, but single space the lines of the stage directions themselves.
- Use A4 size paper. Leave at least a 4cm margin on the left and a reasonably wide right-hand margin. It is false economy to cram the page. Use one side of the sheet only.
- Only give the camera directions when you feel it to be essential. For instance, if you want to show something from a particular character's point of view, or if you think you need it to make a point, i.e. 'HARRY approaches the cliff edge and looks down. LONG SHOT – HARRY'S POINT OF VIEW. ALICE fully clad is walking into the sea. CUT TO: CLOSE UP OF HARRY'S HORRIFIED FACE.' Note the camera directions are put in capital letters on a separate line, as in the specimen page.
- Character sketches should appear in the body of the screenplay, e.g. PETE enters. He is a man you wouldn't want to meet in a dark alley.

Preparation of manuscript

The title page should give the name and nature of your piece. Also include your (or your agent's) address. The second page should give a list of the main characters.

13. INT. LIVING ROOM DAY

SUNNIE is on the telephone, listening, bewildered.

SUNNIE
… But Mr Phelps led me to believe my husband was to be released. You're now saying there's no definite news and never has been? Then why …! Oh never mind.

She puts the receiver down, numb and despairing.

14. INT. JACKIE'S CELL NIGHT

JACKIE is scratching a mark on the wall, keeping check on the days. A woman's terrible screaming starts up somewhere in the building. JACKIE leans against the wall, listening. The screaming stops abruptly.

JACKIE
(beating the wall in a frenzy)
What's happening! Is that my wife? Sunnie!

The cell door bursts open. Several Arabs in noisy altercation are glimpsed in the passage outside. Two GUARDS rush in. They unchain JACKIE, roughly, unnervingly.

JACKIE
Where are you taking me?

They manhandle JACKIE out of the door.

15. INT. BRITISH CONSULATE DAY

PHELPS ushers SUNNIE into his office. She is blazing. His manner is placating, irritation under the surface.

PHELPS
(as they come in)
I don't know where you …

SUNNIE
(speaking at the same time)
From a British newspaper, that's where! They'd been told officially, officially mind, that Jackie Mann was dead!

PHELPS indicates a seat. SUNNIE ignores it.

Add a front and back cover and bind your screenplay, securing the pages firmly. Make sure you have saved it on disk or retain a master copy. Never part with the only copy you possess. If you do, it will surely get lost.

Submission

Try to get an agent. A good agent will give you a fair opinion of your work and, if your work is worthwhile, he or she will know the particular film company which will want to buy it. Remember that if film companies state that they will only consider material sent through an agent, they definitely mean it.

If you are sending your manuscript to a company direct, it is advisable to first check as far as possible in case it is already working on a similar idea.

Attach a stamped, addressed envelope to your manuscript whether sending it through an agent or direct. Most companies have a story department, to which you should address your material. As story editors are very busy people, you can make their life easier by complying with the submission notes listed in the box.

Accept that this is really a tough market, namely because:

- films cost so much to make today that the decision to go ahead is only taken after a great many important factors have been satisfied and an even greater number of important people are happy about it;
- writing a screenplay calls for knowledge and appreciation of the technicalities of film-making, as well as the ability to combine dialogue, action and pictures in the language of the medium.

Submission notes

If you have based your screenplay on someone else's published work you should make the fact clear in a covering letter, stating that:

- the material is no longer in copyright, or
- you yourself own the copyright, or at least an option on it, or
- you have not obtained the copyright but have reason to believe that there would be no difficulty in doing so.

Apart from a note of any relevant credits you may already possess, do not regale the editor with your personal details, unless they bear a direct relation to the material submitted. For instance, if your story concerns a brain surgeon, then it would be relevant for the editor to know that you actually are one. Otherwise, trust your work to stand on its own merit.

There is no need to mention if your work has been turned down by other companies, however regretfully. The comments of others will not influence a story editor one way or the other.

Do not suggest actors or actresses you would like to play your characters. This decision is entirely out of your hands.

Don't pester the company if you don't get a reply, or even an acknowledgement, for some weeks. Most companies will formally acknowledge receipt and then leave you in limbo for at least six weeks. However, after about three months or so, a brief letter politely asking what has happened is in order. A telephone call is unlikely to be helpful. It is possible the company may have liked your work enough to have sent it to America, or to be getting further readers' opinions on it. This all takes time. If they don't like it, you will certainly get your manuscript back in due course.

The treatment

If a producer likes the idea of your screenplay, he or she may ask to see a treatment. A treatment can range from a basic outline through to a synopsis of the story with a breakdown of the main characters and some of the key scenes written in detail. Its aim is to demonstrate the style and general flavour of the piece. The producer may want it before reading your whole script or to interest colleagues. It may be no more than half a dozen pages but it is likely to be your major selling document. So do your best to thrill the producer to the core in a couple of minutes flat.

Television and film producers

Jean McConnell advises on submitting a screenplay for consideration.

The recommended approach for placing material is through a recognised literary agent. Most film companies have a story department to which material can be sent for consideration by its editors. If you choose to submit material direct, first check with the company to make sure it is worth your while.

It is a fact that many of the feature films these days are based on already best-selling books. However, there are some companies, particularly those with a television outlet, which will sometimes accept unsolicited material if it seems to be exceptionally original.

When a writer submits material direct to a company, some of the larger ones – usually those based in the United States – may request that a Release Form be signed before they are prepared to read it. This document is ostensibly designed to absolve the company from any charge of plagiarism if they should be working on a similar idea; and also to limit their liability in the event of any legal action. Writers must make up their own minds whether they wish to sign this but, in principle, it is not recommended.

It should be noted that there are a number of independent companies making films specifically for television presentation. These are included in the list below of companies currently in active production.

Jean McConnell is a founder member of the Writers' Guild of Great Britain. She has written screenplays, radio and stage plays, and books. She is a member of the Crime Writers' Association and the Society of Women Writers and Journalists.

Aardman Animations

Gas Ferry Road, Bristol BS1 6UN
tel 0117-984 8485 *fax* 0117-984 8486
website www.aardman.com
Head of Script Development Mike Cooper, *Development Executive (Shorts & Series)* Helen Brunsdon

Specialists in model animation. No unsolicited treatments. Founded 1972.

Absolutely Productions

Alhambra House, 27-31 Charing Cross Road, London WC2H 0AU
tel 020-7930 3113 *fax* 020-7930 4114
email info@absolutely-uk.com
website www.absolutely-uk.com
Contact Miles Bullough

Drama and comedy screenplays for cinema and TV, and TV entertainment programmes. Founded 1989.

British Lion

Pinewood Studios, Iver, Bucks. SL0 0NH
tel (01753) 651700 *fax* (01753) 656844
Contact Peter Snell

Screenplays and treatments for cinema; TV drama and sitcoms. No unsolicited material. Founded 1927.

Brook Lapping Productions Ltd

6 Anglers Lane, London NW5 3DG
tel 020-7428 3100 *fax* 020-7284 0626
Directors Anne Lapping, Brian Lapping, Phillip Whitehead, Norma Percy

TV documentaries and current affairs.

Carlton Television Productions

35-38 Portman Square, London W1H 0NU
tel 020-7486 6688 *fax* 020-7486 1132
Director of Programmes Steve Hewlett

Comprises Carlton Television Productions, Planet 24 and Action Time and makes programmes for all UK major broadcasters (ITV, BBC, Channel 4, Channel 5 and Sky) and regional programmes for Carlton Central, Carlton London and Carlton Westcountry. Carlton Television Productions' Drama department encourages the submission of scripts and outlines from professional writers through an agent.

Catalyst Film and Television International Ltd

Brook Green Studios, 186 Shepherds Bush Road, London W6 7NL
tel 020-7603 7030 *fax* 020-7603 9519
Contact Head of Drama Development

Screenplays/novels for adaptation for TV. Only considers material submitted through an agent or publisher. Founded 1991.

Celador Productions Ltd

39 Long Acre, London WC2E 9LG
tel 020-7240 8101 *fax* 020-7845 9541

All material should be submitted through an agent.

Chatsworth Television Ltd

97-99 Dean Street, London W1D 3TE
tel 020-7734 4302 *fax* 020-7437 3301
email television@chatsworth-tv.co.uk
website www.chatsworth-tv.co.uk
Managing Director Malcolm Heyworth

Entertainment, factual and drama. Sister companies in TV distribution and licensing. Founded 1980.

Children's Film and Television Foundation Ltd

Elstree Film and Television Studios, Borehamwood, Herts. WD6 1JG
tel 020-8953 0844 *fax* 020-8207 0860
email annahome@cftf.onyxnet.co.uk

Involved in the development and co-production of films for children and the family, both for the theatric market and for TV.

Collingwood O'Hare Entertainment and Convergence Productions

10-14 Crown Street, London W3 8SB
tel 020-8993 3666 *fax* 020-8993 9595
email info@crownstreet.co.uk
Contact Helen Stroud, Head of Development

Animation series for children (COE), documentary series, and drama films and series (Convergence). Limited development capacity – generates own ideas/projects. Prefers material to be submitted through an agent. Founded 1988.

Company Pictures

Suffolk House, 1-8 Whitfield Place, London W1T 5JU
tel 020-7380 3900 *fax* 020-7380 1166
email enquiries@companypictures.co.uk
Contact George Faber, Charles Pattinson

Screenplays for TV drama and feature films. All material should be submitted through an agent. Founded 1997.

Cosgrove Hall Films Ltd

8 Albany Road, Chorlton-Cum-Hardy, Manchester M21 0AW
tel 0161-882 2500 *fax* 0161-882 2555
email animation@chf.co.uk
Contact Nicola Davies, Assistant Script Editor

Screenplays for cinema and TV for animation (drawn, model or CGI) or a 'live action'/animation mix. Series material especially welcome, preschool to adult. Founded 1976.

The Walt Disney Company Ltd

3 Queen Caroline Street, London W6 9PE
tel 020-8222 1000 *fax* 020-8222 2795

Screenplays not accepted by London office. Must be submitted by an agent to The Walt Disney Studios in Burbank, California.

Fabulist Productions Ltd

49 Cambert Way, London SE3 9YA
email submissions@fabulistproductions.com
website www.fabulistproductions.com
Contact Louis Mesiha, Thomas Templeton

Screenplays for feature films and TV dramas; documentaries. Submissions from beginners welcome. Send full scripts, synopsis and covering letter with sae for return of material. Founded 2000.

Fairwater Films Ltd

68 Vista Rise, Llandaff, Cardiff CF5 2SD
tel/fax 029-2057 8488
email tbarnes@netcomuk.co.uk
Managing Director Tony Barnes

Animation for cinema and TV; live action entertainment. All material should be submitted through an agent. Founded 1982.

Feelgood Fiction Ltd

49 Goldhawk Road, London W12 8QP
tel 020-8746 2535 *fax* 020-8740 6177
email feelgood@feelgoodfiction.co.uk
Managing Director Philip Clarke, *Drama Producer* Laurence Bowen

Film and TV drama.

The First Film Company Ltd

38 Great Windmill Street, London W1D 7LU
tel 020-7439 1640 *fax* 020-7437 2062
Producers Roger Randall-Cutler, Robert Cheek

Screenplays for cinema. All material should be submitted through an agent. Founded 1984.

Focus Films Ltd

The Rotunda Studios, rear of 116-118 Finchley Road, London NW3 5HT
tel 020-7435 9004 *fax* 020-7431 3562
email focus@pupix.demon.co.uk
Contact Lucinda Van Rie

Screenplays for cinema. Will only consider material submitted through an agent. Founded 1982.

Mark Forstater Productions Ltd

27 Lonsdale Road, London NW6 6RA
tel 020-7624 1123 *fax* 020-7624 1124
Contact Rosie Homan

Film and TV production. No unsolicited scripts, please.

Front Page Films

507 Riverbank House, 1 Putney Bridge Approach, London SW6 3JD
Contact Script Editor

Screenplays for cinema. Founded 1985.

Gaia Communictions

Sanctuary House, 35 Harding Avenue, Eastbourne, East Sussex BN22 8PL
tel (01323) 727183 *fax* (01323) 734809
email production@gaiacommunications.co.uk
website www.gaiacommunications.co.uk
Director Robert Armstrong, *Script Editor* Loni von Gruner

Specialises in Southeast regional documentary programmes, particularly historical and tourist. Founded 1987.

Noel Gay Television

Shepperton Studios, Studios Road, Shepperton, Middlesex TW17 0QD
tel (01932) 592569 *fax* (01932) 592172
email ngtv@noelgay.co.uk
website www.noelgay.co.uk
Contact Lesley McKirdy

Treatments for TV; entertainment, comedy and drama. Founded 1987.

Granada Film

4th Floor, 48 Leicester Square, London WC2H 7FB
tel 020-7389 8555 *fax* 020-7930 8499
email granada.film@granadamedia.com
Head of Film Pippa Cross

Screenplays for cinema: major commercial feature films and smaller UK-based films. No unsolicited material. Founded 1989.

Hartswood Films

Twickenham Studios, The Barons, St Margaret's, Twickenham, Middlesex TW1 2AW
tel 020-8607 8736 *fax* 020-8607 8744
Producers Beryl Vertue, Sue Vertue, Elaine Cameron

Screenplays for cinema and TV; comedy and drama. No unsolicited material. Founded 1981.

Hat Trick Productions Ltd

10 Livonia Street, London W1F 8AF
tel 020-7434 2451 *fax* 020-7287 9791
website www.hattrick.com
Contact Denise O'Donoghue

Situation and drama comedy series and light entertainment shows. Founded 1986.

The Jim Henson Company

30 Oval Road, London NW1 7DE
tel 020-7428 4000 *fax* 020-7428 4001
website www.henson.com
Executive VP & Co-Head, Jim Henson Television Group Worldwide Angus Fletcher, *Director of Development, Jim Henson Television* Sophie Finston

Screenplays for cinema and TV; fantasy, family and children's programmes – usually involving puppetry or animatronics. All material should be submitted through an agent. Founded 1979.

Mike Hopwood Productions Ltd

Winton House, Stoke Road, Stoke-on-Trent ST4 2RW
tel (01782) 848800 *fax* (01782) 749447
Contact Development Executive

Screenplays for cinema; drama and factual TV programmes. No unsolicited material. Founded 1991.

Ignition Films Ltd

1 Wickham Court, Bristol BS16 1DQ
tel 0117-958 3087 *fax* 0117-965 7674
email ignition@wickham-court.demon.co.uk
website www.wickham-court.demon.co.uk
Contact Alison Sterling

Screenplays for cinema and TV. Material only accepted through agents. Founded 1999.

Illuminations

19-20 Rheidol Mews, Rheidol Terrace, London N1 8NU
tel 020-7288 8400 *fax* 020-7359 1151
email linda@illumin.co.uk
website www.illumin.co.uk
Contact Linda Zuck

Screenplays for TV; cultural documentaries, arts and entertainment for broadcast TV. Founded 1982.

Little Bird Company Ltd

9 Grafton Mews, London W1P 5LG
tel 020-7380 3980 *fax* 020-7380 3981

email firstname@littlebird.co.uk
Contact N. Mirza
Screenplays for cinema and TV. Founded 1982.

Little Dancer Ltd

Avonway, 3 Naseby Road, London SE19 3JJ
tel 020-8653 9343
email Littdan99@cs.com
Producer Robert Smith
Screenplays for cinema and TV; drama. Founded 1992.

LWT and United Productions

London TV Centre, Upper Ground, London SE1 9LT
tel 020-7620 1620
Controller of Drama Michele Buck
Producers of TV and film. Founded 1996.

Malone Gill Productions Ltd

27 Campden Hill Road, London W8 7DX
tel 020-7937 0557 *fax* 020-7376 1727
email malonegill@cs.com
Contact Georgina Denison
TV programmes. Founded 1978.

Maya Vision International Ltd

43 New Oxford Street, London WC1A 1BH
tel 020-7836 1113 *fax* 020-7836 5169
email info@mayavisionint.com
website www.mayavisionint.com
Producer/Director Rebecca Dobbs
Features, TV dramas and documentaries. No unsolicited scripts. Founded 1982/3.

Monogram Productions Ltd

45-49 Mortimer Street, London W1W 8HX
tel 020-7470 0035
Managing Director Eileen Quinn
Screenplays for cinema and TV; drama series and serials only. All material should be submitted through an agent. Founded 1997; merged with Scottish Independent Wark Clements 2001.

MW Entertainments

48 Dean Street, London W1D 5BF
tel 020-7734 7707 *fax* 020-7734 7727
email mw@michaelwhite.co.uk
Screenplays for cinema. Treatments and synopses only. Founded 1963.

Penumbra Productions Ltd

80 Brondesbury Road, London NW6 6RX
tel 020-7328 4550 *fax* 020-7328 3844
email nazpenumbra@aol.com
Contact H.O. Nazareth
Contemporary social-issue drama and docs for feature films and TV; non-broadcast videos to commissions. Send synopsis only, not scripts, preferably by email. Founded 1981.

Picture Palace Films Ltd

13 Egbert Street, London NW1 8LJ
tel 020-7586 8763 *fax* 020-7586 9048
email info@picturepalace.com
website www.picturepalace.com
Contact Malcolm Craddock
Screenplays for cinema and TV; low budget films; TV drama series. Material only considered if submitted through an agent. Founded 1971.

Planet 24 Productions Ltd

195 Marsh Wall, London E14 9SG
tel 020-7345 2424 *fax* 020-7345 9400
email info@planet24.com
website www.planet24.com
Managing Director Mary Durkan
Light entertainment, factual entertainment, music, features and computer animation. Wholly owned subsidiary of Carlton Communications Plc.

Portobello Pictures Ltd

64A Princedale Road, London W11 4NL
tel 020-7379 5566 *fax* 020-7379 5599
Contact Eric Abraham
Screenplays for cinema. Founded 1987.

Praxis Films Ltd

PO Box 290, Market Rasen, Lincs. LN3 6BB
tel/fax (01472) 399976
email info@praxisfilms.com
website www.praxisfilms.com
Contact Lori Wheeler, Head of Development
Documentaries, news, current affairs, all factual genres for TV. No drama/movies. Proposals via website preferred. Founded 1985.

September Films Ltd

Glen House, 22 Glenthorne Road, London W6 0NG
tel 020-8563 9393 *fax* 020-8741 7214
email september@septemberfilms.com
website www.septemberfilms.com
Head of Production Elaine Day, *Head of Drama and Film Development* Nadine Mellor
Factual entertainment and documentary specialists expanding further into TV drama and film. Founded 1993.

SH Production

Green Dene Cottage, Honeysuckle Bottom, East Horsley, Surrey KT24 5TD
tel/fax (01483) 281792
Contact Robert Symes

Broadcast and non-broadcast commercial material, English and German voiceovers for films, video production. Founded 1988.

Specific Films

25 Rathbone Street, London W1T 1NQ
tel 020-7580 7476 *fax* 020-7494 2676
Contact Michael Hamlyn

Feature-length films.

Spice Factory UK Ltd

81 The Promenade, Peacehaven, East Sussex BN10 8LS
tel (01273) 585275, 587495 *fax* (01273) 585304
email script@spicefactory.co.uk
Contact Lucy Shuttleworth, Head of Development

Treatment and/or synopsis for feature length films. Enclose sae. Founded 1995.

Talisman Films Ltd

5 Addison Place, London W11 4RJ
tel 020-7603 7474 *fax* 020-7602 7422
email email@talismanfilms.com
Contact Eva Arnold

Screenplays for cinema and TV. Material only considered if submitted through an agent. Single page treatments accepted. Founded 1991.

TalkBack Productions

20-21 Newman Street, London W1T 1PG
tel 020-7861 8000 *fax* 020-7861 8001

TV situation comedies and comedy dramas, features, straight drama. Send unsolicited material to PA to Managing Director; material through an agent to Peter Fincham. Founded 1981.

Tiger Aspect Productions

Drama 5 Soho Square, London W1V 5DE
tel 020-7434 0672 *fax* 020-7544 1665
Comedy 7 Soho Street, London W1D 3DQ
tel 020-7434 0700 *fax* 020-7434 1798
email general@tigeraspect.co.uk
website www.tigeraspect.co.uk

TV drama, comedy and sitcoms. All material should be submitted through an agent. Founded 1993.

Twentieth Century Fox Productions Ltd

Twentieth Century House, 31-32 Soho Square, London W1D 3AP
tel 020-7437 7766 *fax* 020-7434 2170

Will not consider unsolicited material.

Twenty Twenty Television

20 Kentish Town Road, London NW1 9NX
tel 020-7284 2020 *fax* 020-7284 1810
email mail@twentytwentytv.co.uk
Executive Producers Claudia Milne, Paul Woolwich

Current affairs, documentaries, science and educational programmes, drama. Founded 1982.

Warner Bros. Productions Ltd

Warner House, 98 Theobald's Road, London WC1X 8WB
tel 020-7984 5000

Screenplays for cinema. Will only consider material submitted through an agent.

Warner Sisters Film & TV Ltd

The Cottage, Pall Mall Deposit, 124 Barlby Road, London W10 6BL
tel 020-8960 3550 *fax* 020-8960 3880

Screenplays for cinema and TV; TV programmes. All material should be submitted through an agent. Founded 1984.

Working Title Films

Films 76 Oxford Street, London W1N 9FD
tel 020-7307 3000 *fax* 020-7307 3003
email dan.shepherd@unistudios.com
website www.workingtitlefilms.com
Chairmen Tim Bevan and Eric Fellner,
Head of Development Debra Hayward (films)
TV 77 Shaftesbury Avenue, London W1V 8HQ
tel 020-7494 4001 *fax* 020-7255 8600
Head of Television Simon Wright
WT2 76 Oxford Street, London W1N 9FD
Head of Development Natascha Wharton

Screenplays for films; TV drama and comedy; low budget films (WT2).

World Productions Ltd

Norman House, 105-109 Strand, London WC2R 0AA
tel 020-7240 1444 *fax* 020-7240 3740
email firstname@world-productions.com
website www.world-productions.com
Contact Office Manager

Screenplays for TV; TV drama series and serials.

Zenith Entertainment Ltd

43-45 Dorset Street, London W1U 7NA
tel 020-7224 2440 *fax* 020-7224 3194
email general@zenith-entertainment.co.uk

Screenplays for cinema; TV drama. No unsolicited scripts.

Independent national radio

Commercial Radio Companies Association (CRCA)

77 Shaftesbury Avenue, London W1D 5DU
tel 020-7306 2603 *fax* 020-7470 0062
email info@crca.co.uk
website www.crca.co.uk

CRCA is the trade body for UK commercial radio. It represents commercial radio to Government, the Radio Authority, copyright societies and other organisations concerned with radio. CRCA is a source of advice to members and acts as a clearing house for radio information.

CRCA runs the Radio Advertising Clearance Centre. It jointly owns Radio Joint Audience Research Ltd (RAJAR) with the BBC, JICRIT Ltd (an electronic means of buying, selling and accounting for radio advertisements) with the IPA, and also owns the Network Chart Show, sponsored by Pepsi.

CRCA is a founder member of the Association of European Radios (AER), which lobbies European institutions on behalf of commercial radio.

Classic FM

7 Swallow Place, London W1B 2AG
tel 020-7343 9000 *fax* 020-7344 2700
email enquiries@classicfm.co.uk
website www.classicfm.com

Digital One Ltd

7 Swallow Place, London W1R 7AA
tel 020-7518 2620 *fax* 020-7518 2605
email info@digitalone.co.uk
website www.ukdigitalradio.com

Commercial digital radio multiplex operator. Founded 1999.

IRN (Independent Radio News)

6th Floor, 200 Gray's Inn Road, London WC1X 8XZ
tel 020-7430 4090 *fax* 020-7430 4092
email news@irn.co.uk
website www.irn.co.uk

National news provider to all UK commercial radio stations, including live news bulletins, sport and financial news, and coverage of the House of Commons.

Oneword

Landseer House, 19 Charing Cross Road, London WC2H 0ES
tel 020-7976 3030 *fax* 020-7930 9460
email info@oneword.co.uk
website www.oneword.co.uk
Managing Director Ben Budworth

Book readings, plays, comedy, reviews and commentaries for national transmission on Digital Radio, SkyDigital and the internet. Founded 2000.

The Radio Authority

Holbrook House, 14 Great Queen Street, London WC2B 5DG
tel 020-7430 2724 *fax* 020-7405 7062
email info@radioauthority.org.uk
website www.radioauthority.org.uk

Licenses and regulates Independent Radio. Plans frequencies, awards licences, regulates programming and advertising, and plays an active role in the discussion and formulation of policies which affect the Independent Radio industry and its listeners.

TalkSPORT

18 Hatfields, London SE1 8DJ
tel 020-7636 1089 *fax* 020-7636 1053

Virgin 1215

1 Golden Square, London W1F 9DJ
tel 020-7434 1215 *fax* 020-7434 1197
email reception@virginradio.co.uk
website www.virginradio.co.uk

Independent local radio

**Stations offering some/occasional opportunities for creative input from local writers. Check with the station before submitting material.*

England

Alton/Haslemere
Delta FM 102, 65 Weyhill, Haslemere,
Surrey GU27 1HN
tel (01428) 651931 *fax* (01428) 658971
email studio@deltafm.freeserve.co.uk

Aylesbury
Mix 96, Friars Square Studios, 11 Bourbon Street,
Aylesbury, Bucks. HP20 2PZ
tel (01296) 399396 *fax* (01296) 398988
email mix@mix96.co.uk
website www.mix96.co.uk

Barnstaple
Lantern FM, Unit 2B, Lauder Lane, Barnstaple,
Devon EX31 3TA
tel (01271) 340340 *fax* (01271) 340345

Basingstoke
107.6 Kestrel FM, 2nd Floor,
Paddington House, The Walks Shopping Centre,
Basingstoke RG21 7LJ
tel (01256) 694000 *fax* (01256) 694111

Bassetlaw
Trax 107.9 FM, PO Box 444, Worksop,
Notts. S80 1GP
tel (01909) 500611 *fax* (01909) 500445

Bath
Bath FM, Station House, Ashley Avenue,
Lower Weston, Bath BA1 3DS
tel (01225) 471571 *fax* (01225) 471681
email studio@bath.fm
website http://bath.fm

Bedford
96.9 Chiltern FM, 55 Goldington Road,
Bedford MK40 3LT
tel (01234) 272400 *fax* (01234) 325137

Birmingham
96.4 FM BRMB *and* Capital Gold (1152 AM),
9 Brindleyplace, 4 Oozells Square,
Birmingham B1 2DJ
tel 0121-245 5000 *fax* 0121-245 5245
email info@brmb.co.uk

Birmingham
Galaxy 102.2, 1 The Square, 111 Broad Street,
Birmingham B15 1AS
tel 0121-695 0000 *fax* 0121-695 0055
email firstname.surname@galaxy1022.co.uk

Birmingham
Radio XL 1296 AM, KMS House, Bradford Street,
Birmingham B12 0JD
tel 0121-753 5353 *fax* 0121-753 3111

Blackpool
The Wave 96.5, 965 Mowbray Drive,
Blackpool, Lancs. FY3 7JR
tel (01253) 304965 *fax* (01253) 301965
email any@thewavefm.co.uk

Bolton & Bury
Tower FM, The Mill, Brownlow Way,
Bolton BL1 2RA
tel (01204) 387000 *fax* (01204) 534065

Bournemouth
2CR FM *and* Classic Gold 828, 5 Southcote Road,
Bournemouth BH1 3LR
tel (01202) 259259 *fax* (01202) 255244

Bradford
Sunrise FM, Sunrise House, 30 Chapel Street,
Little Germany, Bradford BD1 5DN
tel (01274) 735043 *fax* (01274) 728534

Bradford, Huddersfield & Halifax
Classic Gold 1278/1530 AM *and* The Pulse,
Pennine House, Forster Square, Bradford BD1 5NE
tel (01274) 203040 *fax* (01274) 203130
email general@pulse.co.uk

Bridgwater
BCR FM, PO Box 1074, Bridgwater TA6 4WE
tel (01278) 727701 *fax* (01278) 727705
email studio@bcrfm.co.uk
website www.bcrfm.co.uk

Bridlington
Yorkshire Coast Radio – Bridlington,
Old Harbourmaster's Office, Harbour Road,
Bridlington, East Yorkshire YO15 2NR
tel (01262) 404400 *fax* (01262) 404404

Brighton*
Surf 107, PO Box 107, Brighton BN1 1QG
tel (01273) 386107 *fax* (01273) 273107
email info@Surf107.co.uk

Bristol & Bath
Classic Gold 1260 AM, PO Box 2000,
1 Passage Street, Bristol BS99 7SN
tel 0117-984 3200 *fax* 0117-984 3202
email reception@classicgold.musicradio.com
website www.classicgold.co.uk

Bristol & Bath
GWR FM, PO Box 2000, 1 Passage Street,
Bristol BS99 7SN
tel 0117-984 3200 *fax* 0117-984 3202
email reception@gwrfm.musicradio.com
website www.gwrfm.co.uk

Cambridge
Star 107.9, Sturton Street,
Cambridge CB1 2QF
tel (01223) 722300 *fax* (01223) 577686
email firstname.surname@star1079.co.uk
website www.star1079.co.uk

Cambridge & Newmarket
Q103 FM, Enterprise House, The Vision Park,
Chivers Way, Histon, Cambridge CB4 9WW
tel (01223) 235255 *fax* (01223) 235161
email reception@q103.musicradio.com

Canterbury
106 CTFM Radio, 16 Lower Bridge Street,
Canterbury, Kent CT1 2HQ
tel (01227) 789106 *fax* (01227) 785106
email e-mail@ctfm.co.uk

Carlisle
CFM, PO Box 964, Carlisle CA1 3NG
tel (01228) 818964 *fax* (01228) 819444
email news@cfmradio.com
website www.cfmradio.com

Chelmsford
Dream 107.7, 6th Floor, Cater House, High Street,
Chelmsford, Essex CM1 1AL
tel (01245) 259400 *fax* (01245) 259558
email reception@dream107.com
website www.dream107.com

Cheltenham
Star 107.5 FM, Cheltenham Film Studios,
1st Floor, West Suite, Arle Court, Matherley Lane,
Cheltenham, Glos. GL51 6PN
tel (01242) 699555 *fax* (01242) 699666
website www.ukrd.com

Chesterfield & North Derbyshire
Peak 107 FM, Radio House, Foxwood Road,
Chesterfield S41 9RF
tel (01246) 269107 (01246) 269933
email info@peak107.co.uk
website www.peak107.co.uk

Chichester, Bognor Regis & Littlehampton
Spirit FM, Dukes Court, Bognor Road, Chichester,
West Sussex PO19 8FX
tel (01243) 773600 *fax* (01243) 786464
email info@spiritfm.net
website www.spiritfm.net

Colchester
SGR Colchester, Abbeygate Two,
9 Whitewell Road, Colchester CO2 7DE
tel (01206) 575859 *fax* (01206) 561199

Cornwall, Plymouth & West Devon
Pirate FM102·2/8, Carn Brea Studios, Wilson Way,
Redruth, Cornwall TR15 3XX
tel (01209) 314400 *fax* (01209) 314345
email enquiries@piratefm102.co.uk

Coventry
Classic Gold 1359 *and* Mercia FM, Hertford Place,
Coventry CV1 3TT
tel (01203) 868200 *fax* (01203) 868202
email mercia@musicradio.com

Coventry
Kix 96, Watch Close, Spon Street,
Coventry CV1 3LN
tel 024-7652 5656 *fax* 024-7655 1744
email kix962@aol.com

Darlington
Alpha 103.2, Radio House, 11 Woodland Road,
Darlington, Co. Durham DL3 7BJ
tel (01325) 255552 *fax* (01325) 255551
email admin@alpharadio.demon.co.uk

Derby
Ram FM, 35-36 Irongate, Derby DE1 3GA
tel (01332) 851100 *fax* (01332) 851199

Doncaster
Trax FM, PO Box 444, Doncaster DN4 5GW
tel (01302) 341166 *fax* (01302) 326104

Dover & Folkestone
Neptune Radio, PO Box 1068, Dover CT16 1GB
tel (01304) 202505 *fax* (01304) 212717

East of England
Vibe FM, Reflection House, The Anderson Centre,
Olding Road, Bury St Edmunds IP33 3TA
tel (01284) 718800 *fax* (01284) 718839
email studios@vibefm.co.uk

East Lancashire
Asian Sound Radio, Globe House, Southall Street,
Manchester M3 1LG
tel 0161-288 1000 *fax* 0161-288 9000
email asr@aol.com

East Midlands
106 Century FM, City Link, Nottingham NG2 4NG
tel 0115-910 6100 *fax* 0115-910 6107
email info106@centuryfm.com
website www.centuryfm.com

Eastbourne*
Sovereign Radio, 14 St Mary's Walk, Hailsham, East Sussex BN27 1AF
tel (01323) 442700 *fax* (01323) 442866
email info@1075sovereignradio.com
website www.1075country.com

Exeter & Torbay
Classic Gold Digital 666/954 *and* Gemini FM, Hawthorn House, Exeter Business Park, Exeter, Devon EX1 3QS
tel (01392) 444444 *fax* (01392) 354202
email colin.slade@musicradio.com
gemini@geminifm.musicradio.com

Fenland*
Star 107.1, 46 Camel Road, Littleport, Ely, Cambs. CB6 1EW
tel (01353) 865100 *fax* (01353) 865105
email mail@star1071.co.uk

Gloucestershire
Severn Sound, Bridge Studios, Eastgate Centre, Gloucester GL1 1SS
tel (01452) 313200 *fax* (01452) 313213
email reception@severnsound-musicradio.com

Great Yarmouth & Lowestoft
The Beach, PO Box 103.4, Lowestoft, Suffolk NR32 2TL
tel (07000) 001035 *fax* (07000) 001036
email 103.4@thebeach.co.uk

Grimsby, Cleethorpes, Immingham
Compass FM, PO Box 297, Grimsby DN32 0XR
tel (01472) 346666
email enquiries@compassfm.co.uk

Guernsey
Island FM, 12 Westerbrook, St Sampson, Guernsey GY2 4QQ, Channel Islands
tel (01481) 242000 *fax* (01481) 249676
email kevin@islandfm.guernsey.net
website www.islandfm.guernsey.net

Guildford
County Sound Radio 1566 AM *and* 96.4 The Eagle, Dolphin House, North Street, Guildford, Surrey GU1 4AA
tel (01483) 300964 *fax* (01483) 531612
email onair@964eagle.co.uk

Harlow
Mercury FM, Latton Bush Centre, Southern Way, Harlow, Essex CM18 7BU
tel (01279) 432415 *fax* (01279) 445289
email studios@ten17.co.uk

Harrogate
97.2 Stray FM, PO Box 972, Station Parade, Harrogate HG1 5YF
tel (01423) 522972 *fax* (01423) 522922
email @972strayfm.co.uk

Hastings
107.8 Arrow FM, Priory Meadow Centre, Hastings, East Sussex TN34 1PJ
tel (01424) 461177 *fax* (01424) 422662
email info@arrowfm.co.uk
website www.arrowfm.co.uk

Havering
Soul City 107.5 FM, Lambourne House, 7 Western Road, Romford, Essex RM1 3LD
tel (01708) 731643 *fax* (01708) 730383

Hereford, Worcester & Kidderminster
Wyvern FM, 5 Barbourne Terrace, Worcester WR1 3JZ
tel (01905) 612212 *fax* (01905) 746637
email wyvernfm@musicradio.com
website www.koko.com

Hertford, Ware, Hatfield, Welwyn Garden City & Stevenage
hertbeat fm, The Pump House, Knebworth Park, Herts SG3 6HQ
tel (01438) 810900 *fax* (01438) 815100
email info@hertbeat.com
website www.hertbeat.com

High Wycombe
Swan FM, PO Box 1170, High Wycombe, Bucks HP13 6YT
tel (01494) 446611 *fax* (01494) 445400

Hinckley, Nuneaton & surrounding area
Fosseway Radio, PO Box 107, Hinckley, Leics. LE10 1WR
tel (01455) 614151 *fax* (01455) 616888
email enquiries@fossewayradio.co.uk

Huddersfield
Home 107.9, The Old Stableblock, Lockwood Park, Huddersfield HD1 3UR
tel (01484) 321107 *fax* (01484) 311107
email info@home1079.com

Humberside
Magic 1161 AM *and* 96.9 Viking FM, Commercial Road, Hull HU1 2SG
tel (01482) 325141 *fax* (01482) 587067
website www.magic1161.co.uk
www.vikingfm.co.uk

Ipswich & Bury St Edmunds
SGR-FM *and* Classic Gold Amber (Suffolk), Alpha Business Park, 6-12 White House Road, Ipswich IP1 5LT
tel (01473) 461000 *fax* (01473) 741200
email sgrfm.co.uk

Isle of Man*
Manx Radio, PO Box 1368, Broadcasting House, Douglas, Isle of Man IM99 1SW
tel (01624) 682600 *fax* (01624) 682604
email postbox@manxradio.com
website www.manxradio.com www.radiott.com

Isle of Wight
Isle of Wight Radio, Dodnor Park,
Newport PO30 5XE
tel (01983) 822557 *fax* (01983) 822109
email admin@iwradio.co.uk

Jersey
Channel 103 FM, 6 Tunnell Street, St Helier,
Jersey JE2 4LU, Channel Islands
tel (01534) 888103 *fax* (01534) 887799
email chan103@itl.net

Kendal & Windermere
Lakeland Radio, Lakeland Food Park,
Plumgarths, Crook Road, Kendal LA8 8QJ
tel (01539) 737380 *fax* (01539) 737390

Kent
Capital Gold (1242 and 603) *and* Invicta FM,
Radio House, John Wilson Business Park,
Whitstable, Kent CT5 3QX
tel (01227) 772004 *fax* (01227) 771558
email info@invictaradio.co.uk

Kettering, Corby, Wellingborough*
Connect FM, Unit 1, PO Box 1074, Centre 2000,
Kettering, Northants. NN16 8PU
tel (01536) 412413 *fax* (01536) 517390
email info@connectfm.co.uk

Kings Lynn
KL.FM 96·7, 18 Blackfriars Street, Kings Lynn,
Norfolk PE30 1NN
tel (01553) 772777 *fax* (01553) 766453
email klfmradio.co.uk

Kingston upon Thames
107.8 FM Thames Radio, Brentham House,
45C High Street, Hampton Wick,
Kingston upon Thames KT1 4DG
tel 020-8288 1300 *fax* 020-8288 1312
email events@thamesradio.co.uk
website www.thamesradio.co.uk

Knowsley*
KCR 106.7 FM, The Studios, Cables Retail Park,
Prescot, Knowsley L34 5SW
tel 0151-290 1501 *fax* 0151-290 1505

Leeds
96.3 Aire FM *and* Magic 828, 51 Burley Road,
Leeds LS3 1LR
tel 0113-283 5500 *fax* 0113-283 5501

Leicester
Leicester Sound, Granville House, Granville Road,
Leicester LE1 7RW
tel 0116-256 1300 *fax* 0116-256 1303
email leicestersound@musicradio.com

Leicester
Sabras, Radio House, 63 Melton Road,
Leicester LE4 6PN
tel 0116-261 0666 *fax* 0116-266 7776

Lincolnshire & Newark*
Lincs FM, Witham Park, Waterside South,
Lincoln LN5 7JN
tel (01522) 549900 *fax* (01522) 549911
email enquiries@lincsfm.co.uk

Liverpool
Radio City 96·7 *and* Magic 1548, St Johns Beacon,
1 Houghton Street, Liverpool L1 1RL
tel 0151-472 6800 *fax* 0151-472 6821
website www.radiocity.co.uk

London
Choice FM, 291-299 Borough High Street,
London SE1 1JG
tel 020-7378 3969 (South London),
020-8348 1033 (North London) *fax* 020-7378 3911
(South London), 020-7378 3911 (North London)
email info@choicefm.com
website www.choicefm.com

London
Millennium 106.8 FM, 2-6 Basildon Road,
Abbey Wood, London SE2 0EW
tel 020-8311 3112 *fax* 020-8312 1930
website www.millennium1068.com

London, Greater
95.8 Capital FM *and* Capital Gold (1548),
30 Leicester Square, London WC2H 7LA
tel 020-7766 6000 *fax* 020-7766 6100

London, Greater
Heart 106·2, The Chrysalis Building,
Bramley Road, London W10 6SP
tel 020-7468 1062 *fax* 020-7470 1062
email initial.surname@heart1062.co.uk

London, Greater
Jazz FM 102.2, 26-27 Castlereagh Street,
London W1H 5DL
tel 020-7706 4100 *fax* 020-7723 9742
email info@jazzfm.com

London, Greater
Kiss 100 FM *and* Magic 105.4 FM, Mappin House,
4 Winsley Street, London W1W 8HF
Magic tel 020-7955 1054 *fax* 020-7975 8227
Kiss tel 020-7975 8100 *fax* 020-7975 8150

London, Greater
LBC 1152 AM *and* ITN News Direct 97·3 FM,
200 Gray's Inn Road, London WC1X 8XZ
tel 020-7973 1152 *fax* 020-7973 8833
email news@lbc.co.uk editor@newsdirect.co.uk

London, Greater
963/972 Liberty Radio, Liberty House,
The Grove, London E15 1EL
tel 020-8221 4040 *fax* 020-8221 4044
email liberty963@aol.com

London, Greater*
Premier Christian Radio, Glen House, Stag Place,
London SW1E 5AG

tel 020-7316 1300 *fax* 020-7233 6706
email premier@premier.org.uk
website www.premier.org.uk

London, Greater
Ritz 1035 AM, 33-35 Wembley Hill Road, Wembley, Middlesex HA9 8RT
tel 020-8733 1300 *fax* 020-8733 1393
website www.officialritz1035.com

London, Greater
Spectrum Radio, 4 Ingate Place, London SW8 3NS
tel 020-7627 4433 *fax* 020-7627 3409
email name@spectrumradio.net
website www.spectrumradio.net

London, Greater
Sunrise Radio, Sunrise House, Merrick Road, Southall, Middlesex UB2 4AU
tel 020-8574 6666 *fax* 020-8813 9800

London, Greater
Virgin 105.8, 1 Golden Square, London W1F 9DJ
tel 020-7434 1215 *fax* 020-7434 1197
email reception@virginradio.co.uk
website www.virginradio.com

London, Greater
Xfm, 30 Leicester Square, London WC2H 7LA
tel 020-7766 6600 *fax* 020-7766 6601

London (Lewisham)
Fusion 107.3, Astra House, Arklow Road, London SE14 6EB
tel 020-8691 9202 *fax* 020-8691 9193
website www.fusion1073.com

London (North)
London Greek Radio, Florentia Village, Vale Road, London N4 1TD
tel 020-8800 8001 *fax* 020-8800 8005
email sales@lgr.co.uk
website www.lgr.co.uk

London (North)
London Turkish Radio, 185B High Road, London N22 6BA
tel 020-8881 0606/2020 *fax* 020-8881 5151
email LTR1584am@aol.com

Loughborough, Charnwood and North West Leicestershire
107 Oak FM, Waldron Court, Prince William Road, Loughborough LE11 5GD
tel (01509) 211711 *fax* (01509) 246107
website www.oak.fm

Ludlow
Sunshine 855, Unit 11, Burway Trading Estate, Ludlow, Shropshire SY8 1EN
tel (01584) 873795 *fax* (01584) 875900

Luton/Bedford
Chiltern FM *and* Classic Gold 792/828, Chiltern Road, Dunstable, Beds. LU6 1HQ
tel (01582) 676200 *fax* (01582) 676231/201
email chilternfm@musicradio.com

Macclesfield
Silk FM, Radio House, Bridge Street, Macclesfield, Cheshire SK11 6DJ
tel (01625) 268000 *fax* (01625) 269010
email mail@silkfm.com
website www.silkfm.com

Manchester
Key 103 *and* Magic 1152, Castle Quay, Castlefield, Manchester M5 4PR
tel 0161-288 5000 *fax* 0161-288 5001

Manchester
Big 1458 AM, 4th Floor, Quay West, Trafford Wharf Road, Trafford Park, Manchester M17 1FL
tel 0161-607 0420 *fax* 0161-607 0401

Eastern Greater Manchester*
96.2 The Revolution, PO Box 962, Oldham OL1 3JF
tel 0161-621 6500 *fax* 0161-621 6521

Greater Manchester, Merseyside & South & Central Lancashire
Galaxy 102, 5th Floor, The Triangle, Hanging Ditch, Manchester M4 3TR
tel 0161-279 0300 *fax* 0161-279 0301
website www.galaxy102.co.uk

Mansfield & Ashfield
Mansfield 103.2 FM, The Media Suite, Brunts Business Centre, Samuel Brunts Way, Mansfield, Notts. NG18 2AH
tel (01623) 646666 *fax* (01623) 660606

Medway towns
Mercury 107.9 FM, Berkeley House, 186 High Street, Rochester ME1 1EY
tel (01634) 841111 *fax* (01634) 841122
email mercurystudio@kmradio.co.uk

Merseyside
Juice 107.6 FM, 27 Fleet Street, Liverpool L1 4AR
tel 0151-707 3107 *fax* 0151-707 3109
email mail@juiceliverpool.com
website www.juice.fm

Milton Keynes
FM 103 Horizon, Broadcast Centre, Vincent Avenue, Crownhill Industry, Milton Keynes MK8 0AB
tel (01908) 269111 *fax* (01908) 564063
email fm103horizon@musicradio

Morecambe Bay
The Bay 96.9 FM, PO Box 969, St George's Quay, Lancaster LA1 3LD
tel (01524) 848747 *fax* (01524) 848787
email (staffname)@thebay.fm

Newbury*
Kick FM, The Studios, 42 Bone Lane, Newbury, Berks. RG14 5SD
tel (01635) 841600 *fax* (01635) 841010
email mail@kickfm.com
website www.kickfm.com

North East England
Century Radio, Century House, PO Box 100, Gateshead NE8 2YX
tel 0191-477 6666 *fax* 0191-477 1771
email name@centurynortheast.com

North West England
105.4 Century FM, Laser House, Waterfront Quay, Salford Quays, Manchester M5 2XW
tel 0161-400 0105 *fax* 0161-400 0173
email info1054@centuryfm.co.uk
website www.centuryfm.co.uk

North West England
Jazz FM 100.4, The World Trade Centre, Exchange Quay, Manchester M5 3EJ
tel 0161-877 1004 *fax* 0161-877 1005
email jazzinfo@jazzfm.com

Northampton
Classic Gold 1557 *and* Northants 96, 19-21 St Edmunds Road, Northampton NN1 5DY
tel (01604) 795600 *fax* (01604) 795601
email reception@northants96.musicradio.com

Norwich
Broadland 102·4 FM *and* Classic Gold Amber, St George's Plain, 47-49 Colegate, Norwich NR3 1DB
tel (01603) 630621 *fax* (01603) 671176
website www.koko.com

Nottingham & Derby
96 Trent FM *and* Classic Gold Gem, 29-31 Castle Gate, Nottingham NG1 7AP
tel 0115-952 7000 *fax* 0115-912 9302
email admin@gemam.musicradio.com
admin@trentfm.musicradio.com

Oxford
Fusion 107.9, Suite 41, Westgate Centre, Oxford OX1 1PD
tel (01865) 724442 *fax* (01865) 726161
email mail@oxygen.demon.co.uk

Oxford & Banbury
FOX FM, Brush House, Pony Road, Oxford OX4 2XR
tel (01865) 871000 *fax* (01865) 871036
email fox@foxfm.co.uk
website www.foxfm.co.uk

Peterborough
Classic Gold 1332 AM *and* 102·7 Hereward FM, PO Box 225, Queensgate Centre, Peterborough PE1 1XJ
tel (01733) 460460 *fax* (01733) 281445

Peterborough
Lite FM, 2nd Floor, 5 Church Street, Peterborough PE1 1XB
tel (01733) 898106 *fax* (01733) 898107

Plymouth
Classic Gold 1152 *and* 97FM Plymouth Sound, Earl's Acre, Plymouth PL3 4HX
tel (01752) 275600 *fax* (01752) 275605
email mail@plymouthsound.musicradio.com

Poole, Bournemouth & surrounding area*
Fire 107.6 FM, Quadrant Studios, Old Christchurch Road, Bournemouth BH1 2AD
tel (01202) 318100 *fax* (01202) 318110
email info@fire1076.com
website www.fire1076.com

Portsmouth, Havant, Gosport & Fareham*
107.4 The Quay, Media House, Tipner Wharf, Twyford Avenue, Portsmouth PO2 8PE
tel (02392) 364141 *fax* (02392) 364151

Preston & Blackpool
Magic 999 *and* Rock FM, PO Box 999/PO Box 974, Preston, Lancs. PR1 1XR
tel (01772) 556301 *fax* (01772) 201917

Reading, Basingstoke & Andover
2-TEN FM *and* Classic Gold 1431/1485, PO Box 2020, Reading RG31 7FG
tel 0118-945 4400 *fax* 0118-928 8513
email mail2tenfm@musicradio.com

Reigate & Crawley
102.7 Mercury FM *and* Classic Gold 1521, The Stanley Centre, Kelvin Way, Crawley, West Sussex RH10 9SE
tel (01293) 519161 *fax* (01293) 560927
email firstname.surname@musicradio.com
website www.koko.com

Rugby
107.1 Rugby FM, Suites 4-6, Dunsmore Business Centre, Spring Street, Rugby CV21 3HH
tel (01788) 541100 *fax* (01788) 541070

Rutland*
Rutland Radio, 40 Melton Road, Oakham, Rutland LE15 6AY
tel (01572) 757868 *fax* (01572) 757744
email enquiries@rutlandradio.co.uk
website www.rutlandradio.co.uk

St Albans & Watford
Mercury 96.6, Unit 5, The Metro Centre, Dwight Road, Watford WD18 9UP
tel (01923) 205470 *fax* (01923) 205471
email rebecca.paddick@musicradio.com
website www.koko.com

Salisbury
Spire FM, City Hall Studios, Malthouse Lane, Salisbury, Wilts. SP2 7QQ

tel (01722) 416644 *fax* (01722) 416688
email admin@spirefm.co.uk

Scarborough
Yorkshire Coast Radio, PO Box 962, Scarborough, North Yorkshire YO12 5YX
tel (01723) 500962 *fax* (01723) 501050
email info@yorkshirecoastradio.com
website www.yorkshirecoastradio.com

Severn Estuary
Galaxy 101, Millennium House, 26 Baldwin Street, Bristol BS1 1SE
tel 0117-901 0101 *fax* 0117-901 4666
email addressee@galaxy101.co.uk

Shaftesbury
97.4 Vale FM, Longmead, Shaftesbury SP7 8QQ
tel (01747) 855711 *fax* (01747) 855722

Slough, Windsor & Maidenhead
Star 106·6, The Observatory Shopping Centre, Slough, Berks. SL1 1LH
tel (01753) 551066 *fax* (01753) 512277
email onair@starfm.co.uk

Solent area
Wave 105.2 FM, 5 Manor Court, Barnes Wallis Road, Segensworth East, Fareham PO15 5TH
tel (01489) 481050 *fax* (01489) 481060
email studio@wave105.com

South Hampshire
Capital Gold (1170 and 1557) *and* Ocean FM *and* Power FM, Radio House, Whittle Avenue, Segensworth West, Fareham PO15 5SH
tel (01489) 589911 *fax* (01489) 589453
email info@oceanradio.co.uk

South Yorkshire
Hallam FM *and* Magic AM, Radio House, 900 Herries Road, Sheffield S6 1RH
tel 0114-209 1000 *fax* 0114-285 3159
email programmes@hallamfm.co.uk
@magicam.co.uk

Southampton
South City FM, City Studios, Marsh Lane, Southampton SO14 3ST
tel 023-8022 0020 *fax* 023-8022 0060
email info@southcityfm.co.uk
website www.southcityfm.co.uk

South-East Staffordshire
Centre FM, 5-6 Aldergate, Tamworth, Staffs B79 7DJ
tel (01827) 318000 *fax* (01827) 318002
website www.centrefm.com

Southend & Chelmsford
Classic Gold Breeze, Radio House, Clifftown Road, Southend-on-Sea, Essex SS1 1SX
tel (01702) 333711 *fax* (01702) 345224
email david.hoffman@classicgolddigital.com
website www.classicgolddigital.com

Southern Gloucestershire
FM 107 The Falcon, Brunel Mall, London Road, Stroud, Glos. GL5 2BP
tel (01453) 767369 *fax* (01453) 757107
email info@thefalcon.org
website www.thefalcon.org

Southport
107.9 Dune FM, The Power Station, Victoria Way, Southport PR8 1RR
tel (01704) 502500 *fax* (01704) 502540
email dunefm@aol.com

Stockport
Imagine FM, Regent House, Heaton Lane, Stockport SK4 1BX
tel 0161-609 1400 *fax* 0161-609 1401
email recipient@imaginefm.net

Stoke-on-Trent
Signal One *and* Signal's BIG (1170 AM), Stoke Road, Stoke-on-Trent ST4 2SR
tel (01782) 441300 *fax* (01782) 441301
email initialsurname@signalradio.com

Stratford upon Avon*
FM 102 – The Bear, The Guard House Studios, Banbury Road, Stratford upon Avon CV37 7HX
tel (01789) 262636 *fax* (01789) 263102
email studio@thebear.co.uk
website www.thebear.co.uk

Sunderland*
Sun FM, PO Box 1034, Sunderland SR5 2YL
tel 0191-548 1034 *fax* 0191-548 7171
email studio@sun-fm.com
website www.sun-fm.com

East Sussex
Capital Gold (1323 and 945) *and* Southern FM, Radio House, PO Box 2000, Brighton BN41 2SS
tel (01273) 430111 *fax* (01273) 430098

Swindon & West Wiltshire
Classic Gold 936/1161 AM *and* GWR FM 97.2/102.2, PO Box 2000, Swindon SN4 7EX
tel (01793) 842600 *fax* (01793) 842602
email reception@gwrfm.musicradio.com

Teesside
TFM *and* Magic 1170, Radio House, Yale Crescent, Thornaby, Stockton-on-Tees TS17 6AA
tel (01642) 888222 *fax* (01642) 868288

Telford*
Telford FM, PO Box 1074, Telford TF3 3WG
tel (01952) 280011 *fax* (01952) 280010

Tendring*
Dream 100 FM, Northgate House, St Peters Street, Colchester CO1 1HT
tel (01206) 764466 *fax* (01206) 715102
email info@Dream100.com

Thanet
TLR, Imperial House, 2-14 High Street, Margate, Kent CT9 1DH
tel (01843) 220222 *fax* (01843) 299666
email reception@tlrfm.co.uk

Tunbridge Wells & Sevenoaks
Mercury 96.2 FM, 1 East Street, Tonbridge, Kent TN9 1AR
tel (01732) 369200 *fax* (01732) 369201

Tyne & Wear
Galaxy 105-106, Kingfisher Way, Silverlink Business Park, Tyne & Wear NE28 9NX
tel 0191-206 8000
website www.galaxy1056.co.uk

Tyne & Wear
Magic 1152 *and* Metro FM, Longrigg, Swalwell, Newcastle upon Tyne NE99 1BB
tel 0191-420 0971 *fax* 0191-488 9222

Wakefield
Ridings FM, 2 Thornes Office Park, Monckton Road, Wakefield WF2 7AN
tel (01924) 367177 *fax* (01924) 367133
email enquiries@ridingsfm.co.uk

Warrington, Widnes & Runcorn
107.2 Wire FM, Warrington Business Park, Long Lane, Warrington WA2 8TX
tel (01925) 445545 *fax* (01925) 657705
email wirefm.com

West Cumbria
CFM, PO Box 964, Carlisle CA1 3NG
tel (01228) 818964 *fax* (01228) 819444
email news@cfmradio.com
website www.cfmradio.com

West Midlands
100·7 Heart FM, 1 The Square, 111 Broad Street, Birmingham B15 1AS
tel 0121-695 0000 *fax* 0121-696 1007
email firstname.surname@heartfm.co.uk

West Midlands*
Saga 105.7 FM, 3rd Floor, Crown House, Beaufort Court, Birmingham B16 0LD
tel 0121-452 1057 *fax* 0121-452 3222

West Somerset
Quay West Radio, Harbour Studios, The Esplanade, Watchet, Somerset TA23 0AJ
tel (01984) 634900 *fax* (01984) 634811
email quaywestradio@csi.com

Weymouth & Dorchester
Wessex FM, Radio House, Trinity Street, Dorchester, Dorset DT1 1DJ
tel (01305) 250333 *fax* (01305) 250052

Wigan & St Helens
102.4 Wish FM, Orrell Lodge, Orrell Road, Wigan WN5 8HJ
tel (01942) 761024 *fax* (01942) 777694
email general@wishfm.com

Winchester*
Win FM, PO Box 1072, The Brooks, Winchester SO23 8FT
tel (01962) 841071 *fax* (01962) 841079
email admin@winfm.co.uk

Wirral
The Buzz 97.1, Media House, Claughton Road, Birkenhead CH41 6EY
tel 0151-650 1700 *fax* 0151-647 5427

Wolverhampton
107.7 The Wolf, 10th Floor, Mander House, Wolverhampton WV1 3NE
tel (01902) 571070 *fax* (01902) 571079
email studio@thewolf.co.uk

Wolverhampton, Shrewsbury & Telford
Beacon Radio FM *and* Classic Gold WABC, 267 Tettenhall Road, Wolverhampton WV6 0DE
tel (01902) 461300 *fax* (01902) 461299

Yeovil & Taunton
Orchard FM, Haygrove House, Taunton TA3 7BT
tel (01823) 338448 *fax* (01823) 320444

York
Minster FM, PO Box 123, Dunnington, York YO19 5ZX
tel (01904) 488888 *fax* (01904) 488811
email mail@minsterfm.demon.co.uk
website www.minsterfm.demon.co.uk

Yorkshire
Galaxy 105, Josephs Well, Hanover Walk, Leeds LS3 1AB
tel 0113-213 0105 *fax* 0113-213 1055
email name@galaxy105.co.uk

Yorkshire Dales, with Skipton
Fresh AM, Gargrave Road, Skipton, North Yorkshire BD23 1YD
tel (01756) 799991 *fax* (01756) 799771

Northern Ireland

Belfast
Citybeat 96.7, PO Box 967, Belfast BT9 5DF
tel (028) 9020 5967 *fax* (028) 9020 0023
website www.citybeat.co.uk

Coleraine*
Q97.2 Causeway Coast Radio, 24 Cloyfin Road, Coleraine BT52 2NU
tel (028) 703 59100 *fax* (028) 703 26666

Londonderry
Q102·9 FM, The Riverside Suite, Old Waterside Railway Station, Duke Street, Londonderry BT47 6DH

tel (028) 7134 4449/311000 *fax* (028) 7131 1177
email q102@iol.ie
website http://q102-fm.com

Northern Ireland
Cool FM, PO Box 974, Belfast BT1 1RT
tel (01247) 817181 *fax* (01247) 814974
email music@coolfm.co.uk

Northern Ireland
Downtown Radio, Newtownards,
Co. Down BT23 4ES
tel (028) 9181 5555 *fax* (028) 9181 8913
email programmes@downtown.co.uk

Omagh & Enniskillen
Q101.2 FM Radio West, 42A Market Street,
Omagh BT78 1EH
tel 028-8224 5777
1 Belmore Mews, Enniskillen BT74 6AA
fax 028-6632 0777

Scotland

Aberdeen
Northsound One *and* Northsound Two,
45 Kings Gate, Aberdeen AB15 4EL
tel (01224) 337000 *fax* (01224) 400003
email northsound1@srh.co.uk,
northsound2@srh.co.uk

Arbroath*
RNA FM, Radio North Angus, Arbroath Infirmary,
Rosemount Road, Arbroath, Angus DD11 2AT
tel (01241) 879660 *fax* (01241) 439664
website www.radionorthangus.co.uk

Mid Argyll, Kintyre and Surrounding Islands
Argyll FM, 27-29 Longrow, Campbelltown,
Argyll PA28 6ER
tel (01586) 551800 *fax* (01586) 551888
email argyllfm1065@aol.com

Ayr
West FM *and* West Sound AM,
Radio House, 54A Holmston Road,
Ayr KA7 3BE
tel (01292) 283662 *fax* (01292) 283665
email westfm@srh.co.uk, westsound@srh.co.uk

The Borders
Radio Borders, Tweedside Park,
Galashiels TD1 3TD
tel (01896) 759444 *fax* (01896) 759494

Central Scotland
Beat 106 Ltd, The Fourwinds Pavilion,
Pacific Quay, Glasgow G51 1EB
tel 0141-566 6106 *fax* 0141-566 6110
email info@beat106.com
website www.beat106.com

Central Scotland*
Real Radio, PO Box 101, Glasgow Business Park,
Glasgow G69 6GA
tel 0141-781 1011 *fax* 0141-781 1112
email firstname.surname@realradiofm.com

Dumbarton
Castle Rock FM 103, Pioneer Park Studios,
Unit 3, 80 Castlegreen Street, Dumbarton G82 1JB
tel (01389) 734422 *fax* (01389) 734380
email info@castlerockfm.com

Dumfries & Galloway
South West Sound, Unit 40, The Loreburne Centre,
High Street, Dumfries DG1 2BD
tel (01387) 250999 *fax* (01387) 265629
website www.westsoundfm.co.uk

Dundee*
Wave 102 FM, 8 South Tay Street, Dundee DD1 1PA
tel (01382) 901000 *fax* (01382) 900999
email studio@wave102.co.uk
website www.wave102.co.uk

Dundee/Perth*
Radio Tay AM* *and* Tay FM, 6 North Isla Street,
Dundee DD3 7JQ
tel (01382) 200800 *fax* (01382) 423252
email tayam@radiotay.co.uk,
tayfm@radiotay.co.uk

Edinburgh
Forthone *and* Forth 2, Forth House, Forth Street,
Edinburgh EH1 3LE
tel 0131-556 9255 *fax* 0131-558 3277
email info@forthone.com info@forth2.com
website www.forthone.com www.forth2.com

Fife
Kingdom FM, Haig House, Haig Business Park,
Balgonie Road, Markinch, Fife KY7 6AQ
tel (01592) 753753 *fax* (01592) 757788
email kingdomfm@aol.com

Fort William
Nevis Radio, Inverlochy, Fort William PH33 6LU
tel (01397) 700007 *fax* (01397) 701007
email studio@nevisradio.co.uk

Forth Valley including Stirling & Falkirk
Central FM, 201 High Street, Falkirk FK1 1DU
tel (01324) 611164 *fax* (01324) 611168

Glasgow
Clyde 1 *and* Clyde 2, Clydebank Business Park,
Clydebank, Glasgow G81 2RX
tel 0141-565 2200 *fax* 0141-565 2265
website www.clyde1.com www.clyde2.com

Inverness
Moray Firth Radio, PO Box 271, Scorguie Place,
Inverness IV3 8UJ
tel (01463) 224433 *fax* (01463) 243224
website www.morayfirth.co.uk

Inverurie
NECR, Town House, Kintore, Inverurie AB51 0US
tel (01467) 632909 *fax* (01467) 632969

Lanarkshire
Clan FM, Radio House, Rowantree Avenue, Newhouse Industrial Estate, Newhouse, Lanarkshire ML1 5RX
tel (01698) 733107
email studio@clanfm.com
website www.clanfm.com

Oban*
Oban FM, 132 George Street, Oban, Argyll PA34 5NT
tel (01631) 570057 *fax* (01631) 570530

Paisley
96.3 QFM, 65 Sussex Street, Kinning Park, Glasgow G41 1DX
tel 0141-429 9430 *fax* 0141-429 9431

Peterhead
Waves Radio Peterhead, Unit 2, Blackhouse Industrial Estate, Peterhead AB42 1BW
tel (01779) 491012 *fax* (01779) 490802
email waves@radiophd.freeserve.co.uk
website www.wavesfm.com

Pitlochry & Aberfeldy*
Heartland FM, Atholl Curling Rink, Lower Oakfield, Pitlochry, Perthshire PH16 5HQ
tel (01796) 474040 *fax* (01796) 474007
website www.heartlandfm.co.uk

Shetland
SIBC, Market Street, Lerwick, Shetland ZE1 0JN
tel (01595) 695299 *fax* (01595) 695696
email info@sibc.co.uk
website www.sibc.co.uk

Ullapool*
Lochbroom FM, Mill Street, Ullapool, Ross-shire IV26 2UN
tel (01854) 613131 *fax* (01854) 613132
email radio@lochbroomfm.co.uk
website www.lochbroomfm.co.uk

Western Isles
Isles FM, PO Box 333, Stornoway, Isle of Lewis HS1 2PU
tel (01851) 703333 *fax* (01851) 703322
email amoqbel@lineone.net

Wales

Bridgend
Bridge FM, PO Box 1063, Bridgend CF31 1WF
tel (01656) 647777 *fax* (01656) 673611
website www.bridge.fm

Caernarfon
Champion 103 FM, Llys y Dderwen, Parc Menai, Bangor, Gwynedd LL57 4BN
tel (01248) 671888 *fax* (01248) 671971
email zowie.williams@musicradio.com

Cardiff & Newport
Red Dragon FM *and* Capital Gold AM, Atlantic Wharf, Cardiff CF10 4DJ
tel 029-2066 2066 *fax* 029-2066 2060
email mail@rdfm.co.uk

Ceredigion*
Radio Ceredigion, Yr Hen Ysgol Gymraeg, Ffordd Alexandra, Aberystwyth, Ceredigion SY23 1LF
tel (01970) 627999 *fax* (01970) 627206
email news@radioceredigion.f9.co.uk

Heads of South Wales Valleys
Valleys Radio, Festival Park, Victoria, Ebbw Vale NP23 8XW
tel (01495) 301116 *fax* (01495) 300710
email admin@valleysradio.co.uk

Montgomeryshire
Radio Maldwyn, The Studios, The Park, Newtown, Powys SY16 2NZ
tel (01686) 623555 *fax* (01686) 623666
email radio.maldwyn@ukonline.co.uk

North Wales Coast
Coast FM, Media House, Conway Road, Colwyn Bay LL28 5AB
tel (01492) 534555 *fax* (01492) 535248

Pembrokeshire
Radio Pembrokeshire, 14 Old School, Narberth, Pembrokeshire SA67 7DU
email info@radiopembrokeshire.com

Swansea
Swansea Sound, PO Box 1170, Victoria Road, Gowerton, Swansea SA4 3AB
tel (01792) 511170 *fax* (01792) 511171
email admin@swanseasound.co.uk

Swansea
The Wave 96·4 FM, PO Box 964, Victoria Road, Gowerton, Swansea SA4 3AB
tel (01792) 511964 *fax* (01792) 511965
email admin@thewave.co.uk

Wrexham & Chester
MFM 103.4 *and* Classic Gold Marcher 1260, The Studios, Mold Road, Gwersyllt, Wrexham LL11 4AF
tel (01978) 752202 *fax* (01978) 759701

Independent radio producers

Many writers approach independent production companies direct and, increasingly, BBC Radio is commissioning independent producers to make programmes.

Cork Campus Radio

Level 3, Áras na Mac Léinn,
University College Cork, Cork City,
Republic of Ireland
tel (021) 4902170 *fax* (021) 4903108
email radio@ucc.ie
Contact Sinéad O'Donnell, Station Manager

Actively produces dramatic works by new writers; stories of 1800–2000 words from the annual Fallen Leaves Short Story Competition; and the weekly *On the Road* documentary series. Oxygen 2001 SMEDIA Award winner – best student radio station. Founded 1995.

Fast Forward Productions

22 Fleshmarket Close, Edinburgh EH1 1DY
tel 0131-220 0200 *fax* 0131-220 2297
Producer Adrian Quine

Aviation. Founded 1994.

Festival Productions

PO Box 70, Brighton BN1 1EJ
tel (01273) 669595 *fax* (01273) 669596
email post@festivalradio.com
website www.festivalradio.com
Managing Director Daniel Nathan

Plays, docs, features and programmes. Founded 1989.

The Fiction Factory

14 Greenwich Church Street, London SE10 9BJ
tel 020-8853 5100 *fax* 020-8293 3001
email radio@fictionfactory.co.uk
website www.fictionfactory.co.uk
Creative Director John Taylor

Plays, dramatisations, documentaries and features mainly for BBC network radio and the World Service. Original radio drama scripts considered if targeted at existing BBC slots. Script reading fee except for submissions from established writers – some student exemptions. No charge for considering programme ideas and outlines. Founded 1993.

Heavy Entertainment Ltd

208-209 Canalot Studios, 222 Kensal Road,
London W10 5BN
tel 020-8960 9001/2 *fax* 020-8960 9003
Company Directors David Roper, Nick St George

Audiobooks, radio documentaries and commercials. Showreels and promotional audio. Studio available for hire. Founded 1992.

Mike Hopwood Productions Ltd

Winton House, Stoke Road, Stoke-on-Trent,
Staffs. ST4 2RW
tel (01782) 848800 *fax* (01782) 749447
Editor Mike Hopwood

Plays, docs, comedy, soaps, light entertainment. No unsolicited material. Founded 1991.

Mediatracks

93 Columbia Way, Blackburn,
Lancs. BB2 7EA
tel (01254) 691197 *fax* (01254) 723505
email info@mediatracks.co.uk
Contact Steve Johnson

Music and general interest docs for BBC local radio network. Founded 1987.

Mr Punch Audio Books

139 Kensington High Street,
London W8 6SU
tel 020-7368 0088 *fax* 020-7368 0051
Director Stewart Richards

Plays and dramatisations for broadcast on BBC Radio 4 and for audiobooks. Founded 1993.

Penumbra Productions Ltd

80 Brondesbury Road, London NW6 6RX
tel 020-7328 4550 *fax* 020-7328 3844
email nazpenumbra@aol.com
Contact R. Elsgood

Drama and documentaries for Radio 3 only. Send synopses by email. Founded 1981.

Quantum Radio Productions Ltd

22 Fleshmarket Close, Edinburgh EH1 1DY
tel 0131-220 0200 *fax* 0131-220 2297
email quine@quantumradio.demon.co.uk
Producer Adrian Quine

Sponsored syndicated radio programmes.

SH Radio

Green Dene Cottage, Honeysuckle Bottom, East Horsley, Surrey KT24 5TD
tel/fax (01483) 281792
Contact Robert Symes

Broadcast and non-broadcast commercial material (English and German). Founded 1988.

Smooth Operations

PO Box 286, Cambridge CB1 4TW
tel (01223) 880835 *fax* (01223) 881647
email nick@smoothoperations.com
Contact Nick Barraclough
6 Millgate, Delph, Oldham OL3 5JG
tel (01457) 873752 *fax* (01457) 878500
email john@smoothoperations.com
website www.smoothoperations.com
Contact John Leonard

Music-based docs and series. Founded 1992.

Testbed Productions

5th Floor, 14-16 Great Portland Street, London W1N 5AB
tel 020-7436 0555 *fax* 020-7436 2800
Directors Viv Black, Nick Baker

Docs and other programmes; ideas for interviews, feature series, magazine, plays and panel/quiz games. Founded 1992.

Whistledown Productions Ltd

PO Box 36633, London SE1 4NQ
tel 020-7403 4940 *fax* 020-7403 9952
Contact David Prest, Managing Director

Social, historical and popular culture documentaries as well as authored narratives, biographical features and magazine programmes for BBC network radio. Also syndicated tapes and other work for commercial companies. Founded 1998.

Television and radio overseas

Opportunities are outlined here for submitting material to television and radio companies in Australia, Canada, Republic of Ireland, New Zealand and South Africa.

Australia

Australian Broadcasting Corporation (ABC)

Box 9994, Sydney, NSW 2001
tel 612-9333-1500 *fax* 612-9333-5305
email comments@your.abc.net.au
website www.abc.net.au
Manager for Europe Australian Broadcasting Corporation, 54 Portland Place, London W1N 4DY

Provides TV, radio and online programmes in a national broadcasting service; operates Radio Australia internationally.

ABC TV restricts its production resources to work closely related to the Australian environment. ABC radio also looks principally to Australian writers for the basis of its drama output. However, ABC radio is interested in reading or auditioning new creative material of a high quality from overseas sources and this may be submitted in script or taped form. No journalistic material is required. Talks on international affairs are commissioned.

Federation of Australian Commercial Television Stations (FACTS)

44 Avenue Road, Mosman, NSW 2088
tel (02) 9960 2622 *fax* (02) 9969 3520
Ceo Julie Flynn

Represents all 48 commercial TV stations.

Federation of Australian Radio Broadcasters Ltd

PO Box 299, St Leonards, NSW 1590
tel (02) 9906 5944 *fax* (02) 9906 5128
Ceo Joan Warner

Association of privately owned commercial radio stations.

Canada

Canadian Broadcasting Corporation

250 Lanark Avenue, PO Box 3220, Stn. 'C',
Ottawa, Ontario K1Y 1E4
tel 613-724-1200
email commho@ottawa.cbc.ca
website www.cbc.radio-canada.ca

CTV Inc.

9 Channel Nine Court, Toronto, Ontario M1S 4B5
tel 416-332-5000 *fax* 416-332-5054

Ireland

Broadcasting Commission of Ireland

(formerly IRTC)
2-5 Warrington Place, Dublin 2,
Republic of Ireland
tel (01) 676 0966 *fax* (01) 676 0948
email info@bci.ie
website www.bci.ie

Under the Irish Broadcasting Act 2001, the name and role of the Independent Radio & Television Commission (IRTC) was changed to the Broadcasting Commission of Ireland. Consequentially, it now has a much expanded remit. In addition to its functions contained in the Radio & Television Act 1988, its new functions include the licensing of new TV services on terrestrial, cable, MMDS and satellite platforms, as well as the development of codes of programming and advertising standards for TV and radio services.

To date, its activities have included the establishment of:

- an independent TV programme service (TV3);
- a national radio service (100–102 Today FM);
- 23 local commercial radio services;
- 2 special interest radio services;
- 14 community/community of interest radio services;
- 7 hospital/institutional radio services;
- approximately 20 short-term special event licences per annum.

It is envisaged that further licences will be granted in 2002/3 for both commercial and non-commercial radio stations.

Radio Telefís Éireann (RTÉ)

Donnybrook, Dublin 4,
Republic of Ireland
tel (01) 208 3111 *fax* (01) 208 3080
website www.rte.ie

The Irish national broadcasting service operating radio and TV.

Television Ongoing production of an urban drama serial. Currently of interest: drama series for mainstream audiences, serials (preferably contemporary) and situation comedies (preferably set in Ireland or of strong Irish interest), with preferred length of commercial half hour or one hour. Proposals for serials and series suitable for a young adult Network 2 audience, either cutting edge or humorous, which could exploit a low-cost DV production model are of particular interest. Full scripts will not be considered – treatments and series/serial outlines only, except in cases where projects are already part funded. Before submitting material to the Drama or Entertainment departments, authors are advised to write to the department in question to establish initial interest, timing of commissioning rounds, etc.

Radio Ongoing production of hour-long dramas each week. Occasional full 2-hour productions and seasons of drama. Short stories (length 13–14 minutes) in Irish or English suitable for broadcasting; plays (running 28 or 58 minutes) are welcome. Guidelines on writing for radio drama are available from the RTÉ Radio Drama Department, Radio Centre, Donnybrook, Dublin 4.

New Zealand

The Radio Network of New Zealand Ltd

Private Bag 92198, Auckland
tel (09) 373-0000 *fax* (09) 367-4650
Ceo John McElhinney

A radio company controlling a NZ-wide group of commercial radio stations in metropolitan and provincial markets. The station brand groups are Newstalk ZB, Classic Hits, ZM, Easy Listening i, Hauraki, Radio Sports Network, and Community.

Television New Zealand Ltd

PO Box 3819, Auckland
tel (09) 916-7000 *fax* (09) 379-4907
website www.tvnz.co.nz
Chairman Ross Armstrong, *Ceo* Ian Fraser

A Crown-owned company, TVNZ is charged with operating a commercially successful TV business, acting with social responsibility in the provision of quality services. Of particular importance is the provision of TV programmes which reflect and foster New Zealand's identity and culture, and which are in the overall national interest. TVNZ broadcasts on 2 nationwide channels with a web presence via the organisation's internet portal, nzoom.com.

Local and international activities include programme production, outside broadcasting services (through subsidiary company Moving Pictures), multimedia development, merchandising, Teletext, signal distribution and programming supply and transmission consultancy services in Australia, South-East Asia and the Pacific.

South Africa

South African Broadcasting Corporation (SABC)

Private Bag X1, Auckland Park 2006
tel (011) 714-9111 *fax* (011) 714-3106
website www.sabc.co.za

Television Operates 6 TV services (4 free-to-air and 2 pay-TV). Three of the free-to-air channels, SABC1, SABC2 and SABC3, accept scripts in English for drama and comedy, either for one-off programmes or series.

Radio Operates 19 internal radio networks and one external radio service. The service which makes the greatest use of written material in English is SAFM.

Drama One-hour plays of all kinds welcomed. Half-hour plays are occasionally broadcast.

Short stories Short stories of all kinds (1500–1800 words) are welcomed.

Children's programmes Short stories, plays and serials (maximum 15 minutes) may be submitted.

Talks Most are locally commissioned, but outstanding material of particular interest may be submitted (3–10 minutes).

Theatre

Marketing a stage play

Despite the financial problems facing many subsidised theatres and the mounting costs of commercial productions, there are still plenty of companies interested in producing new plays and supporting new writers. Indeed, the sheer number and variety of such companies can be daunting. ***Ben Jancovich*** *examines the options.*

Selecting the theatre

Given the financial costs of submitting a play and the emotional strain in waiting for a response, it is important to take the time to research where a submission is most likely to gain a positive response. Start by recognising the disparate nature of contemporary outlets for new plays. Study the box (right) and decide on which kind of theatre company you should concentrate your efforts.

Clearly, the sheer volume of plays submitted to certain companies and the specific requirements of others make a blanket marketing campaign likely to be neither practical nor successful. An in-depth examination is needed on how to give your submission a head start.

Submitting your play

If the subject matter, form or the references in the play are specific enough, start by submitting your play to a theatre company which is likely to be predisposed towards those aspects of your play. For instance, if your play is about disability, you will want to be aware that the *raison d'etre* of the Graeae Theatre Company is to explore this theme. Likewise, if you have written a play for children you should know about the Polka Theatre for Children in Wimbledon. There is a danger of compartmentalising both writers and companies but, if your play has a distinct selling point, do the research and work to that strength.

Similarly, if your play details the life or history of a specific locale or region, send a copy of your script to the repertory theatre for that area – they may well have an interest in plays with a local appeal.

If a character in your play has a specific and discernible quality for which you think a particular actor may be uniquely suitable, it may be worth contacting them through their agent. Of course, there is no point in

Types of theatre companies

- **Metropolitan new writing theatre companies:** Largely London-based theatres which specialise in new writing, such as Hampstead Theatre, Royal Court, Bush Theatre, Soho Theatre, etc.
- **Regional repertory theatre companies:** Theatres based in towns and cities across the country which may do new plays as part of their repertoire.
- **Commercial producing managements:** Unsubsidised profit-making theatre producers who may occasionally be interested in new plays to take on tour or to present in the West End.
- **Small and/or middle-scale touring companies:** Companies – mostly touring – which may exist to explore or promote specific themes or are geared towards specific kinds of audiences.
- **Independent theatre practitioners:** For example, actors who may be looking for interesting plays in which to appear.
- **Independent theatre producers:** For example, young directors or producers who are looking for plays to produce at the onset of their career.
- **Drama schools and amateur dramatics companies.**

contacting an actor merely because they are famous – they will already receive many more scripts than they could ever read. Therefore, only consider doing this if there is genuinely something specific about the play that demands their attention.

Further options

If your play does not obviously fit any such niche, there are still plenty of companies which are keen to read exciting new writing irrespective of subject matter.

Metropolitan new writing companies, the regional repertory theatres and commercial producers are all, to different degrees, in the market for new plays. Additionally, and often most successfully, there is the plethora of young directors and other practitioners who institute productions under the aegis of their own independent theatre companies. An all-inclusive list of these latter organisations would be daunting, so research their interests and be selective. Reading reviews in the national and local press and listings magazines, such as *Time Out*, will give you some idea of which are the most productive and successful companies and practitioners.

Choosing which company to approach can be difficult as past productions and achievements rarely give precise indications of the way a company wants to move forward. Likewise, the notion of a successful 'commercial' company or play is not straightforward. For example, recent new plays with youthful, urban and often violent content have proved big commercial hits despite appearing anathema to the cliché of a well-made West End play.

Amateur companies/drama schools

Two other avenues to consider are amateur theatres and drama schools. Certain amateur theatre companies, such as the Questors Theatre in Ealing, have premiered plays by both new and established writers. The Leisure Department of your local council should be able to give information on groups which exist in your area.

One good reason for approaching such a company is that they are often the only organisations (apart from the RSC and RNT) which can afford to mount large cast plays. It is a reality of modern theatre that, if you write a play requiring a cast of more than 10, it will prove financially problematic for many companies.

Similar considerations are at work regarding drama schools, with the added incentive that the people involved – directors and actors – may form an attachment to the play and want to work on it professionally elsewhere. *Contacts* lists and gives contact details of the drama schools which are recognised by and accredited to the Conference of Drama Schools.

How to approach a company

Although some details may be obvious, they are worth noting and of course much depends on who you are approaching. At the very least, only ever submit a script which is legible, typed and bound, and always include a stamped addressed envelope large enough for its return. Find out the name and position of the best person to receive and assess your script. Do this not only a matter of courtesy but also because it will help if you need to follow up anything at a later date.

Do your best to ensure that you are happy with the script as it stands. Mistakes are inevitable but it is unprofessional to send rewrites before the original draft has even been read. Obviously, always keep a copy of your play.

Some theatres employ a literary manager or dramaturg whose job is specifically to facilitate the passage of plays through the administrative and artistic channels. In such cases, submissions should be simple and, under their management, the theatre should always be willing and ready to read plays by writers previously unknown to them (although some may not be interested in musicals, revues or translations and adaptations).

However, in the majority of cases there will be no one person whose main function is to deal with writers and their plays. Therefore, you will need to be particularly rigorous in finding out the theatre's policy (remember that due to the pressure of work, dealing with writers may not be the highest of priorities).

Some companies may only accept submission of scripts through agents or with some sort of recommendation. Others may want a brief description of the play so they can decide whether it is worth their time looking at it. They may want this either sent by post, or they may prefer a brief telephone conversation.

What to expect

Since working practices vary from organisation to organisation, the response you can expect and how long before you get it will also vary. After submitting your script, do not expect any response for two to three months. If you have heard nothing from the company after six months, make a gentle inquiry. Obviously, badgering the company for a response is unlikely to work to your advantage.

The company is likely to give one or more of the following responses:

- a straightforward rejection of the play;
- an explanation for the rejection;
- the offer of a 'getting to know you' meeting;
- a more formal dramaturgical meeting to discuss possible textual changes or clarifications;
- a reading or workshop on the play;
- advice on where else to send the play;
- an offer of a more formal recommendation for the play to colleagues working elsewhere;
- an offer of a production.

On the offer of a production you should be clear what rights you retain, and what remuneration is offered. This will depend largely on what kind of company or venue you are talking to. It is always advisable to talk to either the Writers' Guild of Great Britain (see page 506), the Theatre Writers' Union or an agent before you agree to anything.

Agents

When you enter into any kind of contractual relationship with a theatre company you should find an agent. An agent can help you on all the legal aspects of selling a play and ensure that your rights are protected. He or she will also help to promote you and your work and in guiding your career. As the relationship between you and your agent is crucial to your long-term development as a writer, meet as many agents as possible to seek out someone with whom you feel at ease and have an affinity. See *Literary agents for television, film, radio and theatre* on page 382.

Useful addresses

Arts Council of England
14 Great Peter Street, London SW1P 3NQ
email info.drama@artscouncil.org.uk
website www.artscouncil.org.uk
Contact The Drama Director
Publishes a brochure, *Schemes for Writers & Theatre Companies*, which gives details of various forms of assistance available to playwrights and to theatres wishing to commission new plays. The Council awards Bursaries (e.g. the John Whiting Award) and helps writers who are being commissioned or encouraged by a theatre company. A number of Resident Dramatists' Attachment Awards are available. See also page 459.

Writernet
(formerly New Playwrights Trust)
Cabin V, Clarendon Buildings, 25 Horsell Road, London N5 1XL
tel 020-7609 7474
website www.writernet.org.uk
A useful organisation which provides members with the fruits of its extensive knowledge of the industry through publications, forums and databases.

The Spotlight
7 Leicester Place, London WC2H 7BP
tel 020-7437 7631
Publishes a book, *Contacts*, which contains all the addresses for professional organisations and theatre companies listed in the article.

New writing support agencies

Aside from theatre companies and practitioners, there is a burgeoning industry of organisations which exist to help writers develop their craft, their contacts and their appreciation of the industry. One cross-over organisation is the National Theatre Studio, which is part of the Royal National Theatre but exists more as a service to theatre artists and the industry at large rather than directly for the scheduling of the company's three theatres. The national organisation Writernet exists to provide information through publications, forums and databases.

Attached to and supported by most of the Regional Arts Offices are regional forums such as Stagecoach for the West Midlands. It is worth making contact with such organisations, especially if you are based outside one of the metropolitan areas as they can act on your behalf. Some are very good at the national promotion of the work of their local writers, while others are more active in putting writers and directors in contact with each other. Contact your local Regional Arts Office (for details see page 490) or repertory theatre for more information.

Bursaries and prizes

There are various schemes run by theatre companies, television companies and independent organisations to financially assist writers. These fall into two categories: bursaries and prizes. Bursaries relate to the writer rather than their work, and can sometimes include an attachment to a theatre or arts organisation. Some writers can apply for themselves (e.g. the Arts Council's Writers' Bursaries; see page 513), while for other awards a theatre company applies on the writer's behalf.

Prizes usually (though not always) relate to the judging of a play. Because the prize for such a scheme may be either a production or sufficient money to encourage one to happen, it is worth familiarising yourself with the various schemes and their deadlines. This is best done either through Writernet or by being in contact with the regional forums, mentioned above. Also, monitor the Press, especially the *Observer*, the *Author*, *Amateur Stage* and the *Stage*.

Ben Jancovich is Assistant Commissioning Editor (Drama) at Channel 4 Television. Previously he was Script Editor at Company Television, Literary Manager of Hampstead Theatre and Literary Assistant at the Royal Shakespeare Company. He has directed plays and worked as a freelance theatre critic.

Theatre producers

This list is divided into London theatres (below), provincial theatres (page 334) and touring companies (page 339). See also Marketing a stage play on page 327.

London

Bush Theatre

Shepherd's Bush Green, London W12 8QD
tel 020-7602 3703 *fax* 020-7602 7614
email info@bushtheatre.co.uk
website www.bushtheatre.co.uk
Literary Manager Nicola Wilson
Welcomes unsolicited full-length stage scripts (plus one small and one large sae). Commissions writers, including those at an early stage in their career. Produces 9 premieres a year.

Michael Codron Plays Ltd

Aldwych Theatre Offices, Aldwych, London WC2B 4DF
tel 020-7240 8291 *fax* 020-7240 8467

Robert Fox Ltd

6 Beauchamp Place, London SW3 1NG
tel 020-7584 6855 *fax* 020-7225 1638
email rf@robertfoxltd.com
Small independent theatre, film and TV producer. Stages one production per year. Welcomes scripts from new writers. Founded 1980.

Hampstead Theatre

Swiss Cottage Centre, Avenue Road, London NW3 3EX
tel 020-7722 9224 *fax* 020-7722 3860
Contact Jeanie O'Hare

A brand new Theatre is due to open in Autumn 2002: an intimate space with a flexible stage and an auditorium which can expand to seat 325. The artistic policy is the production of the best British and international new plays. All plays are read and discussed, with feedback given to all writers with potential (usually 2–3 months to respond). Include postage with submissions. Plays cannot be accepted by email.

Bill Kenwright Ltd

BKL House, 106 Harrow Road, London W2 1RR
tel 020-7446 6200 *fax* 020-7446 6222
email info@kenwright.com
Managing Director Bill Kenwright, *General Manager* John Dalston

Commercial producing management presenting revivals and new works for the West End and for touring theatres.

King's Head Theatre

115 Upper Street, London N1 1QN
tel 020-7226 8561 *fax* 020-7226 8507
Contact Dan Crawford, Artistic Director

Off-West End theatre producing revivals/new works. No unsolicited submissions.

Lyric Theatre Hammersmith

King Street, London W6 0QL
tel 020-8741 0824 *fax* 020-8741 5965
email enquiries@lyric.co.uk
website www.lyric.co.uk
Directors Simon Mellor, Neil Bartlett

A producing theatre as well as a receiving venue for work by new writers, translators, performers and composers. Unsolicited scripts for in-house productions not accepted.

Man in the Moon Theatre

392 King's Road, London SW3 5UZ
tel 020-7351 5701 *fax* 020-7351 1873
Programming Director Nick Elsen

65-seat theatre. Part of each season is reserved for new writing which links with the season theme. Phone theatre for details. Plays scheduled in seasons of 3–4 months for in-house productions.

Moral Support

28 Chalcot Square, London NW1 8YA
tel (07958) 418515
website www.moralsupportonline.org
Contact Zoe Klinger

The company brings together writers, musicians and other freelance practitioners to create new work with the emphasis on producing new writing and performance styles, to be performed in a variety of locations. Its performance technique has been described as 'an utterly original theatrical language'. Available for commissions of new plays, performance and dance. Established 1997.

The Old Red Lion Theatre

418 St John Street, London EC1V 4NJ
tel/fax 020-7833 3053
Artistic Director Ken McClymont

Interested in contemporary pieces, especially from unproduced writers. No funding: incoming production company pays to rent the theatre. Sae essential with enquiries. Founded 1977.

Orange Tree Theatre

1 Clarence Street, Richmond, Surrey TW9 2SA
tel 020-8940 0141 *fax* 020-8332 0369
email admin@orange-tree.demon.co.uk
website www.orangetreetheatre.co.uk

Producing venue. The theatre does not currently have a literary manager and no longer has a studio theatre. New works presented generally come from agents or through writers' groups.

Polka Theatre for Children

240 The Broadway, London SW19 1SB
tel 020-8545 8320 *fax* 020-8545 8365
email polkatheatre@dial.pipex.com
website www.polkatheatre.com
Artistic Director Vicky Ireland

Exclusively for children, the Main Theatre seats 300 and the Adventure Theatre seats 80. Programmed for 18 months to 2 years in advance. Theatre of new writing, with targeted commissions; contact Director of New Writing. Founded 1967.

The Questors Theatre

Mattock Lane, London W5 5BQ
tel 020-8567 0011 *fax* 020-8567 8736
email enquiries@questors.org.uk
website www.questors.org.uk
Theatre Manager Paul Maurel, *Contact for new work* Hilary Shearing

Largest community theatre in Europe producing around 20 shows a year, specialising in modern and classical world drama. No unsolicited scripts.

Really Useful Theatres

Manor House, 21 Soho Square, London W1D 3QP
tel 020-7494 5200 *fax* 020-7434 1217
email info@rutheatres.com
website www.rutheatres.com
Production Director Nica Burns

Owns 13 West End theatres: Adelphi, Apollo, Cambridge, Duchess, Garrick, Gielgud, Her Majesty's, London Palladium, Lyric Shaftesbury Avenue, New London, Palace, Queens and Theatre Royal Drury Lane. Now commissions new plays from both established writers and new talent. Founded 1978.

Royal Court Theatre

(English Stage Company Ltd)
Sloane Square, London SW1W 8AS
tel 020-7565 5050 *fax* 020-7565 5002
Literary Manager Graham Whybrow

New plays.

Royal National Theatre

South Bank, London SE1 9PX
tel 020-7452 3323 *fax* 020-7452 3350
Literary Manager Jack Bradley

Limited opportunity for the production of unsolicited material, but submissions welcome. No synopses or treatments. Send to Literary Manager, together with an sae with return postage for the script.

Royal Shakespeare Company

Barbican Theatre, Barbican, London EC2Y 8BQ
tel 020-7628 3351 *fax* 020-7382 2320
Artistic Director Adrian Noble, *Dramaturg* Paul Sirett

The RSC is a classical theatre company based in Stratford-upon-Avon. It has recently transformed itself to create the opportunity for different ensemble companies to work on distinct projects that will open both in Stratford and at various venues in London. The Company also has an annual residency in Newcastle and tours both nationally and internationally.

As well as Shakespeare, English classics and foreign classics in translation, ambitious new plays counterpoint the RSC's repertory, especially those which celebrate language. The Dramaturgy Department is proactive rather than reactive, and seeks out the plays and playwrights it wishes to commission. It will read translations of classic foreign works submitted, or of contemporary works where the original writer and/or translator is known. It is unable to read unsolicited works from less established writers, and can only return scripts if an sae is enclosed with the submission.

Soho Theatre and Writers' Centre

21 Dean Street, London W1D 3NE
tel 020-7287 5060 *fax* 020-7287 5061
email writers@sohotheatre.com
website www.sohotheatre.com
Artistic Director Abigail Morris, *Literary Manager* Ruth Little

Always on the look out for new plays and playwrights and welcome unsolicited scripts. These are read by a professional panel who write a detailed critical report. Also offer various levels of workshop facilities, including rehearsed reading and platform performances, for promising playwrights, and in-depth script development with the Artistic Director and Literary Manager. See also the Verity Bargate Award on page 515.

The Steam Industry

Finborough Theatre, 118 Finborough Road, London SW10 9ED
tel 020-7244 7439 *fax* 020-7835 1853
Contact Neil McPherson (Director, Finborough Theatre)

Produces 1–2 seasons each year featuring new plays alongside well-known classics. Writers whose work is produced have developed a relationship with the company over a period of time. Does not accept unsolicited scripts and only occasionally attends rehearsed readings. Founded 1994.

Tabard Theatre

2 Bath Road, London W4 1LW
tel 020-8995 6035 *fax* 020-8994 5985
email Hamish.Gray@btopenworld.com
Artistic Director Hamish Gray

Managed by Two Colour Theatre Company which produces their own work regularly. Also welcomes visiting companies. Aims to produce new writing, rarely staged classics and regular new play readings.

TEG Productions

11-15 Betterton Street, London WC2H 9BP
tel 020-7379 1066 *fax* 020-7836 9454
email teg@plays.demon.co.uk
Contact Jeremy Meadow

Produces 2–4 new plays with commercial potential and revivals per year, all with 'star' casting. Welcomes scripts from new writers. Founded 1997.

Theatre of Comedy Company

Shaftesbury Theatre, 210 Shaftesbury Avenue, London WC2H 8DP
tel 020-7379 3345 *fax* 020-7836 8181
Contact Keith Murray

Commercial producing management creating a broad range of plays. Welcomes new scripts from writers. Founded 1983.

Theatre Royal, Stratford East

Gerry Raffles Square, London E15 1BN
tel 020-8534 7374 *fax* 020-8534 8381
website www.stratfordeast.com
Artistic Director Philip Hedley *Associate Director* Mr Kerry Michael

Middle-scale producing theatre. Specialises in new writing: currently developing contemporary British musicals. Welcomes new plays that are unproduced, full in length, and which relate to its diverse multicultural, Black and Asian audience.

The Tricycle Theatre Company

Tricycle Theatre, 269 Kilburn High Road, London NW6 7JR
tel 020-7372 6611 *fax* 020-7328 0795
Contact Nicolas Kent

Metropolitan new writing theatre company with particular focus on Black and Irish writing. Script-reading service but fee charged for unsolicited scripts.

Triumph Proscenium Productions Ltd

Suite 4, Waldorf Chambers, 11 Aldwych, London WC2B 4DA
tel 020-7343 8800 *fax* 020-7343 8801
email dcwtpp@aol.com

Unicorn Theatre for Children

Admin offices St Mark's Studios, Chillingworth Road, London N7 8QJ
tel 020-7700 0702 *fax* 020-7700 3870
email admin@unicorntheatre.com
website www.unicorntheatre.com
Administrative Director Christopher Moxon, *Artistic Director* Tony Graham, *Associate Director* Emily Gray

Six productions a year for children aged 4–12 and their families – new writing and adaptations.

Warehouse Theatre

Dingwall Road, Croydon CR0 2NF
tel 020-8681 1257 *fax* 020-8688 6699
email warehous@dircon.co.uk
website www.warehousetheatre.co.uk
Artistic Director Ted Craig

South London's new writing theatre. Seats 100–120. Produces 3–5 in-house plays a year and co-produces with companies which share the commitment to new work. It continues to build upon a tradition of discovering and nurturing new writers: activities include a monthly writers' workshop and the annual International Playwriting Festival (see page 526). Unsolicited scripts are welcome but it is more advisable to submit plays via the Festival. Also hosts youth theatre workshops and Saturday morning children's theatre.

Michael White

48 Dean Street, London W1D 5BF
tel 020-7734 7707 *fax* 020-7734 7727
Contact Olivia Harris

Provincial

Abbey Theatre

26 Lower Abbey Street, Dublin 1, Republic of Ireland
tel (01) 8872200 *fax* (01) 8729177
Artistic Director Ben Barnes, *Managing Director* Brian Jackson

Mainly produces plays written by Irish authors or on Irish subjects. Foreign classics are however regularly produced.

Actual Theatre

25 Hamilton Drive, Glasgow G12 8DN
tel/fax 0141-339 0654
Artistic Director Susan C. Triesman

Produces 'difficult and taboo subjects' as well as experimental theatre. Welcomes scripts from new writers. Founded 1980.

Yvonne Arnaud Theatre Management Ltd

Millbrook, Guildford, Surrey GU1 3UX
tel (01483) 440077 *fax* (01483) 564071
email yat@yvonne-arnaud.co.uk
website www.yvonne-arnaud.co.uk
Contact James Barber

Producing theatre which also receives productions.

The Belgrade Theatre

Belgrade Square, Coventry CV1 1GS
tel 024-7625 6431 *fax* 024-7655 0680
email admin@belgrade.co.uk
website www.belgrade.co.uk
Contact Denise Atcheson

Produces new plays developed in conjunction with Theatre Absolute, through the Writing House.

Birmingham Repertory Theatre Ltd

Broad Street, Birmingham B1 2EP
tel 0121-245 2000 *fax* 0121-245 2100
email info@birmingham-rep.co.uk
website www.birmingham-rep.co.uk
Artistic Director Jonathon Church, *Executive Director* Stuart Rogers, *Literary Manager* Ben Payne

Aims to provide a platform for the best work from new writers from both within and beyond the West Midlands region. The development, commissioning and production of new writing takes place across the full range of the theatre's programme including: the Main House (capacity 830); the Door (capacity 190 max.), a space dedicated to new work; and its annual Community tours. Unsolicited submissions are welcome principally from the point of view of beginning a relationship with a writer. Priority in such development work is given to writers from the region.

The Bootleg Theatre Company

23 Burgess Green, Bishopdown, Salisbury, Wilts. SP1 3EL
tel (01722) 421476
email colin@bootlegtheatrecompany.fsnet.co.uk
Contact Colin Burden

Metropolitan new writing theatre company and independent theatre practitioner. Stages 2 productions per year. Welcomes scripts from new writers. Founded 1985.

Bristol Old Vic

Theatre Royal, King Street, Bristol BS1 4ED
tel 0117-949 3993 *fax* 0117-949 3996
website www.bristol-old-vic.co.uk
Associate Director Gareth Machin, *Executive Director* Sarah Smith

Programme includes class plays in the Theatre Royal (650 seats) and new writing in the New Vic Studio (150 seats). Plays must have enough popular appeal to attract an audience of significant size. Will read and report on unsolicited scripts for a fee of £25 per script.

Also seeks emerging talent to the Basement, a profit share venue (50 seats) committed to producing one-act plays by unproven writers. Will read plays free of charge but no report can be provided. New Vic Studio often receives productions of new plays from visiting companies.

The Byre Theatre of St Andrews

Abbey Street, St Andrews KY16 9LA
tel (01334) 476288 *fax* (01334) 475370
email enquiries@byretheatre.com
website www.byretheatre.com
Artistic Director Ken Alexander

Offers a year-round programme of contemporary and classic drama, dance, concerts, opera, comedy and innovative education and community events. Operates a blend of in-house and touring productions. Maintains a policy of producing new and established work. Education programme caters for all ages with Youth workshops and Haydays (for 50+). Offers support for new writing through the Byre Writers, a well-established playwrights group.

Chester Gateway Theatre Trust Ltd

Hamilton Place, Chester CH1 2BH
tel (01244) 318603 *fax* (01244) 317277

website www.gateway-theatre.org
Chief Executive Jasmine Hendry
Mid-scale theatre with 2 in-house productions per year. Also presents a diverse programme of theatre, dance, comedy and music. Education and access department undertakes schools drama tours and writers' workshops.

Chichester Festival Theatre Ltd

Chichester Festival Theatre, Oaklands Park, Chichester, West Sussex PO19 4AP
tel (01243) 784437 *fax* (01243) 787288
email admin@cft.org.uk
website www.cft.org.uk
Theatre Director Andrew Welch
Festival Season May–Oct in Festival and Minerva Theatres; rest of year seasons of touring plays, opera, ballet, dance, jazz, orchestral concerts. Also presents own productions in Minerva Theatre Oct–April.

Clwyd Theatr Cymru

Mold, Flintshire CH7 1YA
tel (01352) 756331 *fax* (01352) 701558
email drama@celtic.co.uk wjames@clwyd-theatr-cymru.co.uk
website www.clwyd-theatr-cymru.co.uk
Director Terry Hands, *Literary Manager* William James
Produces a season of plays each year performed by a core ensemble, along with tours throughout Wales (in English and Welsh). Plays are a mix of classics, revivals, contemporary drama and new writing. Considers plays by Welsh writers or with Welsh themes.

Colchester Mercury Theatre Ltd

Balkerne Gate, Colchester, Essex CO1 1PT
tel (01206) 577006 *fax* (01206) 769607
email mercury.theatre@virgin.net
Contact (Playwrights' Group) Adrian Stokes
Regional repertory theatre presenting works to a wide audience. Produces some new work, mainly commissioned. Runs local Playwrights' Group for adults with a serious commitment to writing plays.

The Coliseum Theatre

Fairbottom Street, Oldham OL1 3SW
tel 0161-624 1731 *fax* 0161-624 5318
Chief Executive Kevin Shaw
Interested in new work, particularly plays set in the North. Contact by letter with scenario initially.

Contact Theatre Company

Oxford Road, Manchester M15 6JA
tel 0161-274 3434 *fax* 0161-274 0640
Artistic Director John E. McGrath
Interested in working with and for young people aged 13–30. Send sae for writers' guidelines.

Derby Playhouse Ltd

Theatre Walk, Eagle Centre, Derby DE1 2NF
tel (01332) 363271 *fax* (01332) 547200
email admin@derbyplayhouse.demon.co.uk
website www.derbyplayhouse.demon.co.uk
Artistic Director Mark Clements
Regional repertory company. Unsolicited scripts: send a letter with synopsis, a resumé of your writing experience and any 10 pages of your script. A review of this material will determine whether a complete copy of the script is required.

Druid Theatre Company

Druid Theatre, Chapel Lane, Galway, Republic of Ireland
tel (091) 568617/568660 *fax* (091) 563109
email info@druidtheatre.com
Managing Director Fergal McGrath, *Artistic Director* Garry Hynes
Producing company presenting a wide range of national and international plays. Emphasis on new Irish writing.

The Dukes

Moor Lane, Lancaster LA1 1QE
tel (01524) 598505 *fax* (01524) 598519
Artistic Director Ian Hastings

Dundee Repertory Theatre

Tay Square, Dundee DD1 1PB
tel (01382) 227684
website www.dundeereptheatre.co.uk
Artistic Director Hamish Glen
Regional repertory theatre company. Concentrates resources on commissions for contemporary Scottish writers.

Everyman Theatre

Regent Street, Cheltenham, Glos. GL50 1HQ
tel (01242) 512515 *fax* (01242) 224305
email admin@everymantheatre.org.uk
website www.everymantheatre.org.uk
Chief Executive Philip Bernays, *Artistic Director* Sue Colverd
Regional presenting and producing theatre promoting a wide range of plays. Small-scale experimental, youth and educational work encouraged in The Other Place studio theatre. Contact the Artistic Director before submitting material.

Everyman and Playhouse Theatres
Liverpool and Merseyside Theatres Trust Ltd, 13 Hope Street, Liverpool L1 9BH
tel 0151-708 0338 *fax* 0151-709 0398
email info@everyman.org.uk
website http://everyman.merseyworld.com/
Executive Director Jo Beddoe, *General Manager* Tim Brunsden
Produces and presents theatre.

Focus Theatre Company (Scotland)
c/o The Ramshorn Theatre, 98 Ingram Street, Glasgow G1 1ES
tel 0141-552 3489 *fax* 0141-553 2036
email ramshorn.theatre@strath.ac.uk
Artistic Director Susan C. Triesman
Produces women's plays and feminist work. Also holds workshops. Welcomes scripts from new writers. Founded 1982.

Grand Theatre
Singleton Street, Swansea SA1 3QJ
tel (01792) 475242 *fax* (01792) 475379
email swansea.grand.theatre@business.ntl.com
website www.swanseagrand.co.uk
General Manager Gary Iles
Regional receiving theatre.

Haymarket Theatre Company
The Haymarket Theatre, Wote Street, Basingstoke, Hants RG21 7NW
tel (01256) 323073 *fax* (01256) 357130
email info@haymarket.org.uk
website www.haymarket.org.uk
Produces up to 8 main house shows a year plus a full and integrated education programme. Interested in co-producing and up to 4 visiting shows. Introducing a 3-year ensemble acting company-in-residence.

Leicester Haymarket Theatre
Belgrave Gate, Leicester LE1 3YQ
tel 0116-253 0021 *fax* 0116-251 3310
email enquiry@leicesterhaymarkettheatre.org
website www.leicesterhaymarkettheatre.org
Regional producing theatre company.

Library Theatre Company
St Peter's Square, Manchester M2 5PD
tel 0161-234 1913 *fax* 0161-228 6481
Contact Artistic Director
Contemporary drama, classics, plays for children. Aims to produce drama which illuminates the contemporary world; scripts from new writers considered.

Live Theatre
27 Broad Chare, Quayside, Newcastle upon Tyne NE1 3DF
tel 0191-232 1232
email info@live.org.uk
website www.live.org.uk
Enquiries Wendy Barnfather, *Script Submissions* Jeremy Herrin
New writing theatre company and venue. Stages 3–4 productions per year of new writing, comedy, musical-comedy, etc.

LLt
Unity Theatre, 1 Hope Place, Liverpool L1 9BG
tel 0151-709 4332 *fax* 0151-709 7182
email lltpro@dircon.co.uk
Contact Paul Goetzee
New writing development company. Promising scripts developed to production standard, and links created with other new writing theatres and organisations. Send sae for return of script. Founded 1983.

The New Theatre Co
The New Theatre, Temple Bar, 43 East Essex Street, Dublin 2, Republic of Ireland
tel (1) 6703361 *fax* (1) 6711943
email info@thenewtheatre.com
website www.thenewtheatre.com
Joint Artistic Directors Anthony Fox, Ronian Wilmot
Innovative theatre producing plays by classic as well as Irish writers whose work deals with issues pertaining to contemporary Irish society. Welcomes scripts from new writers. Founded 1997.

New Vic Theatre
Etruria Road, Newcastle under Lyme ST5 0JG
tel (01782) 717954 *fax* (01782) 712885
email VicTheatre@aol.com
Artistic Director Gwenda Hughes, *General Manager* Nick Jones
Europe's first purpose built theatre in the round, presenting classics, adaptations, contemporary plays, new plays.

The New Wolsey Theatre
Civic Drive, Ipswich, Suffolk IP1 2AS
tel (01473) 295911 *fax* (01473) 295910
Chief Executive Sarah Holmes, *Artistic Associate* Peter Rowe, *Artistic Associate, Community & Education* Mary Swan
Mixed economy theatre. New writing and co-productions always condsidered.

Northcott Theatre
Stocker Road, Exeter, Devon EX4 4QB
tel (01392) 223999
Artistic Director Ben Crocker
Regional producing theatre company.

Northern Stage (Theatrical Productions) Ltd

Newcastle Playhouse, Barras Bridge, Newcastle upon Tyne NE1 1RH
tel 0191-232 3366 *fax* 0191-261 8093
email info@northernstage.com
website www.northernstage.com
Artistic Director Alan Lyddiard

Major company producing and presenting international work.

Nottingham Playhouse

Nottingham Theatre Trust Ltd, Wellington Circus, Nottingham NG1 5AF
tel 0115-947 4361 *fax* 0115-947 5759
website www.nottinghamplayhouse.co.uk/playhouse
Chief Executive Stephanie Sirr, *Artistic Director* Giles Croft

Works closely with communities of Nottingham and Nottinghamshire. Takes 6 months to read unsolicited MSS.

Nuffield Theatre

University Road, Southampton SO17 1TR
tel 023-8031 5500 *fax* 023-8031 5511
Script Executive tba

Repertory theatre producing straight plays and musicals, and some small-scale fringe work. Interested in new plays.

Octagon Theatre

Howell Croft South, Bolton BL1 1SB
tel (01204) 529407 *fax* (01204) 556502
Executive Director John Blackmore, *Personal Assistant* Lesley Etherington, *Artistic Director* Mark Babych, *Associate/Activ8 Director* Sue Reddish

Fully flexible professional theatre. Year round programme of own productions and visiting companies.

The Palace Theatre Watford Ltd

Clarendon Road, Watford, Herts. WD1 1JZ
tel (01923) 235455 *fax* (01923) 819664
Contact Lawrence Till

Regional repertory theatre. Produces 8 plays each year, both classic and contemporary drama. Welcomes synopses of new plays before submitting scripts.

Peacock Theatre

The Abbey Theatre, 26 Lower Abbey Street, Dublin 1, Republic of Ireland
tel (01) 8872200 *fax* (01) 8729177
Artistic Director Ben Barnes, *Managing Director* Brian Jackson, *Peacock Theatre Director* Ali Curran

Experimental theatre associated with the Abbey Theatre; mostly new writing.

Perth Theatre Ltd

185 High Street, Perth PH1 5UW
tel (01738) 472700 *fax* (01738) 624576
email theatre@perth.org.uk
website www.perth.org.uk/perth/theatre.htm
Artistic Director Michael Winter, *General Manager* Paul Hackett

Combination of 3- and 4-weekly repertoire of plays and musicals, incoming tours and studio productions.

Plymouth Theatre Royal

Theatre Royal, Royal Parade, Plymouth PL1 2TR
tel (01752) 230340 *fax* (01752) 225892
Chief Executive Adrian Vinken, *Artistic Director* Simon Stokes

Major regional theatre company which encourages new writing. All scripts are read and considered for production.

Queen's Theatre, Hornchurch

(Havering Theatre Trust Ltd)
Billet Lane, Hornchurch, Essex RM11 1QT
tel (01708) 456118 *fax* (01708) 452348
email info@queens-theatre.co.uk
Artistic Director Bob Carlton

500-seat producing theatre serving outer East London with permanent company of actors/musicians presenting 8 mainhouse and 2 TIE productions each year. Treatments welcome; unsolicited scripts may be returned unread. Queen's Theatre Writer's Group showcases new work Sept–March; contact Education Manager for details.

The Ramshorn Theatre/Strathclyde Theatre Group

98 Ingram Street, Glasgow G1 1ES
tel 0141-552 3489 *fax* 0141-553 2036
email ramshorn.theatre@strath.ac.uk
Contact Susan C. Triesman (Director of Drama, University of Strathclyde)

Develops new writing (including experimental) through Ramshorn New Playwrights Initiative. Founded 1992.

Royal Exchange Theatre Company Ltd

St Ann's Square, Manchester M2 7DH
tel 0161-833 9333 *fax* 0161-832 0881
website www.royalexchange.co.uk
Executive Director Patricia Weller

Varied programme of major classics, new plays, musicals, contemporary British and European drama; also explores the creative work of diverse cultures.

Royal Lyceum Theatre Company

Royal Lyceum Theatre, Grindlay Street, Edinburgh EH3 9AX
tel 0131-248 4848 *fax* 0131-228 3955
email royallyceumtheatre@cableinet.co.uk
website www.lyceum.org.uk
Artistic Director Kenny Ireland

Edinburgh's busiest repertory company, producing an all-year-round programme of classic, contemporary and new drama. Interested in work of Scottish writers.

Salisbury Playhouse

Malthouse Lane, Salisbury, Wilts. SP2 7RA
tel (01722) 320117 *fax* (01722) 421991
email info@salisburyplayhouse.com
Artistic Director Joanna Read

Regional repertory theatre producing a broad programme of classical and modern plays and new writing.

Scarborough Theatre Trust Ltd

Stephen Joseph Theatre, Westborough, Scarborough, North Yorkshire YO11 1JW
tel (01723) 370540 *fax* (01723) 360506
email response@sjt.uk.com
website www.webart.co.uk/clients/sjt/
Literary Manager Laura Harvey

Regional repertory theatre company which produces about 10 plays a year, around half of which are premieres. The theatre has an excellent reputation for comedy. Plays should have a strong narrative and a desire to entertain, though nothing too lightweight will be considered. Enclose a sae with all submissions.

Sheffield Theatres

(Crucible, Crucible Studio & Lyceum)
55 Norfolk Street, Sheffield S1 1DA
tel 0114-249 5999 *fax* 0114-249 6003
Chief Executive Grahame Morris

Large-scale producing house with distinctive thrust stage; smallish studio; Victorian proscenium arch theatre used mainly for touring productions.

Sherman Theatre

Senghennydd Road, Cardiff CF24 4YE
tel 029-2064 6901 *fax* 029-2064 6902
General Manager Margaret Jones

Plays mainly for 15–25 age range, plus under 7's Christmas show. Founded 1974.

Show of Strength Theatre Company Ltd

74 Chessel Street, Bedminster, Bristol BS3 3DN
tel 0117-902 0235
Artistic Director Sheila Hannon

Small-scale company committed to producing new and unperformed work. Theatre season: Sept–Dec. Send sae for return of MSS. Founded 1986.

Swan Theatre

The Moors, Worcester WR1 3EF
tel (01905) 726969 *fax* (01905) 723738
Artistic Director Jenny Stephens

A building-based producing theatre company with a mixed programme, including some new plays. No unsolicited scripts.

Theatre Royal

Windsor, Berks. SL4 1PS
tel (01753) 863444 *fax* (01753) 831673
Executive Producer Bill Kenwright, *Executive Director* Mark Piper

Regional producing theatre presenting a wide range of productions from classics to new plays.

Traverse Theatre

10 Cambridge Street, Edinburgh EH1 2ED
tel 0131-228 3223 *fax* 0131-229 8443
email roxana@traverse.co.uk
hannah@traverse.co.uk katherine@traverse.co.uk
website www.traverse.co.uk
Literary Director Roxana Silbert, *Literary Development Officer* Hannah Rye, *International Literary Associate* Katherine Mendelsohn

Scotland's new writing theatre with a special interest in Scottish writers and writers based in Scotland. Will read unsolicited scripts but an sae must be included for return of script.

The West Yorkshire Playhouse

Playhouse Square, Quarry Hill, Leeds LS2 7UP
tel 0113-213 7800 *fax* 0113-213 7250
email mail@wyp.org.uk
Artistic Director Jude Kelly, *Literary Manager* Alex Chisholm

Twin auditoria complex; community theatre. Has a policy of encouraging new writing from Yorkshire and Humberside region. Send sample of script with an sae for its return to the Literary Manager.

York Citizens' Theatre Trust Ltd

Theatre Royal, St Leonard's Place, York YO1 7HD
tel (01904) 658162 *fax* (01904) 611534
Chief Executive Ludo Keston, *Artistic Director* Damian Cruden

Repertory productions, tours.

Touring companies

Actors Touring Company

Alford House, Aveline Street, London SE11 5DQ
tel 020-7735 8311 *fax* 020-7735 1031
email atc@atc-online.com
Executive Producer Emma Dunton

Small to medium-scale company producing innovative contemporary work for young audiences.

Compass Theatre Company

Carver Street Institute, 24 Rockingham Lane, Sheffield S1 4FW
tel 0114-275 5328 *fax* 0114-278 6931
email info@compasstheatrecompany.com
website www.compasstheatrecompany.com
Artistic Director Neil Sissons, *General Manager* Craig Dronfield

Touring classical theatre nationwide. Does not produce new plays.

Eastern Angles

Sir John Mills Theatre, Gatacre Road, Ipswich IP1 2LQ
tel (01473) 218202 *fax* (01473) 384999
email admin@easternangles.co.uk
website www.easternangles.co.uk
Contact Jill Streatfeild

Touring company producing new work with a regional theme. Stages 3 productions per year. Welcomes scripts from new writers. Founded 1982.

Graeae Theatre Company

Interchange Studios, Hampstead Town Hall Centre, 213 Haverstock Hill, London NW3 4QP
tel 020-7681 4755 *minicom* 020-7681 4757
fax 020-7681 4756
email info@graeae.org
website www.graeae.org
Executive Producer Roger Nelson, *Artistic Director* Jenny Sealey, *Administrator* Annette Cumper

Small-scale company. Welcomes scripts from disabled writers. Founded 1980.

The Hiss & Boo Company Ltd

1 Nyes Hill, Wineham Lane, Bolney, West Sussex RH17 5SD
tel (01444) 881707 *fax* (01444) 882057
email ian@hissboo.co.uk

Not much scope for new plays, but will consider comedy thrillers/chillers and plays/musicals for children. Send synopsis first. Plays/synopses will be returned only if accompanied by an sae.

Hull Truck Theatre Co. Ltd

Hull Truck Theatre, Spring Street, Hull HU2 8RW
tel (01482) 224800 *fax* (01482) 581182
email admin@hulltruck.co.uk
website www.hulltruck.co.uk
Executive Director Joanne Gower

World-renowned small-cast touring company presenting popular and accessible theatre. Produces some new work, mainly commissioned.

The London Bubble

(Bubble Theatre Company)
3-5 Elephant Lane, London SE16 4JD
tel 020-7237 4434 *fax* 020-7231 2366
email admin@londonbubble.org.uk
website www.londonbubble.org.uk

M6 Theatre Company

Hamer C.P. School, Albert Royds Street, Rochdale, Lancs. OL16 2SU
tel (01706) 355898 *fax* (01706) 711700
email info@m6theatre.freeserve.co.uk
Contact Jane Milne

Theatre-in-education company providing high quality theatre for children, young people and community audiences.

New Perspectives Theatre Company

The Old Library, Leeming Street, Mansfield, Notts. NG18 1NG
tel (01623) 635225 *fax* (01623) 635240
email info@newperspectives.co.uk
website www.newperspectives.co.uk
Artistic Director Gavin Stride, *Literary Manager* Esther Richardson

Has a policy of employing writers for new work. Also home of the Literary Manager for the East Midlands Theatres, a post focused on developing East Midlands writers which has the support of the Nottingham Playhouse, Leicester Haymarket Theatre, Northampton Theatres and Derby Playhouse.

New Victoria Theatre

The Peacocks, Woking, Surrey GU21 1GQ
tel (01483) 747422 *fax* (01483) 740477
Contact Michael Lynas *tel* (01908) 547599

Large-scale touring house. Interested to co-produce or produce.

NITRO

(formerly Black Theatre Co-operative Ltd)
6 Brewery Road, London N7 9NH
tel 020-7609 1331 *fax* 020-7609 1221
email btc@dircon.co.uk
website www.nitro.co.uk
Artistic Director Felix Cross, *General Manager* Philip Deverell, *Administrator* Natasha Graham

Commissions and produces new and innovative musical theatre writing by black writers, that expresses the contemporary aspirations, cultures and issues that concern black people.

NTC Touring Theatre Company

(formerly Northumberland Theatre Company)
The Playhouse, Bondgate Without, Alnwick, Northumberland NE66 1PQ
tel (01665) 602586 *fax* (01665) 605837
email admin@ntc-touringtheatre.co.uk
website www.ntc-touringtheatre.co.uk
Artistic Director Gillian Hambleton

Performs a wide cross-section of work: new plays, extant scripts, classic and modern. Particularly interested in non-naturalism, physical theatre and plays with direct relevance to rural audiences.

Out of Joint

7 Thane Works, Thane Villas, London N7 7PH
tel 020-7609 0207 *fax* 020-7609 0203
email ojo@outofjoint.co.uk
website www.outofjoint.co.uk
Contact Max Stafford-Clark

Touring company producing new plays and some revivals. Welcomes scripts from writers. Founded 1993.

Oxford Stage Company

131 High Street, Oxford OX1 4DH
tel (01865) 723238 *fax* (01865) 790625
email info@oxfordstage.co.uk
website www.oxfordstage.co.uk
Contact Executive Producer

A middle-scale touring company presenting 4 productions per year: revivals of established masterpieces, modern classics, and new work. Founded 1989.

Paines Plough

4th Floor, 43 Aldwych, London WC2B 4DN
tel 020-7240 4533 *fax* 020-7240 4534
email office@painesplough.com
website www.painesplough.com
Artistic Director Vicky Featherstone, *Associate Director* John Tiffany, *Literary Associate* Lucy Morrison

Tours new plays by British writers nationwide. The company believes that the playwright's voice should be at the centre of contemporary theatre and works with new and experienced writers. A programme of workshops and readings develops new work. Provides support for commissioned writers to push themselves, with the aim to produce the most ambitious and challenging of new theatre writing. Considers all unsolicited scripts from UK writers – send sae for return of script.

Proteus Theatre Company

Queen Mary's College, Cliddesden Road, Basingstoke, Hants RG21 3HF
tel (01256) 354541 *fax* (01256) 356186
email info@proteustheatre.com
website www.proteustheatre.com
Artistic Director Mark Helyar, *Associate Director* Deborah Wilding, *General Manager* Julie Bladon

Small-scale touring company particularly committed to new writing and new work, education and community collaborations. Produces 3 touring shows per year plus several urban and rural community projects. Founded 1979.

Quicksilver National Touring Theatre

4 Enfield Road, London N1 5AZ
tel 020-7241 2942 *fax* 020-7254 3119
email talktous@quicksilvertheatre.org
website www.quicksilvertheatre.org
Joint Artistic Director/Ceo Guy Holland, *Joint Artistic Director* Carey English

A professional touring theatre company which brings live theatre to theatres and schools all over the country. Delivers good stories, original music, kaleidoscopic design and poignant, often humorous, new writing to entertain and make children and adultsthink. Two to three new plays a year for 3–5 year-olds, 7–11 year-olds and 6+ years and families. Founded 1977.

Red Ladder Theatre Company

3 St Peters Buildings, York Street, Leeds LS9 8AU
tel 0113-245 5311 *fax* 0113-245 5351
email wendy@redladder.co.uk
website www.redladder.co.uk
Artistic Director Wendy Harris

Theatre performances for young people (14–25) in youth clubs and small-scale theatre venues. Commissions at least two new plays each year. Runs Asian Theatre School, an annual theatre training programme for young Asians in Yorkshire.

Red Shift Theatre Company

TRG2 Trowbray House, 108 Weston Street, London SE1 3QB
tel 020-7378 9787 *fax* 020-7378 9789
email mail@redshifttheatreco.co.uk
website www.redshifttheatreco.co.uk
Artistic Director Jonathan Holloway

Productions include adaptations, classics, new plays. No commissions planned before 2004.

7:84 Theatre Company (Scotland)

333 Woodlands Road, Glasgow G3 6NG
tel 0141-334 6686 *fax* 0141-334 3369

email admin@784theatre.com
website www.784theatre.com

Presents 2–3 productions per year of political new writing and relevant classical texts. Welcomes scripts from new writers. Founded 1973.

Shared Experience Theatre

The Soho Laundry, 9 Dufour's Place, London W1F 7SJ
tel 020-7434 9248 *fax* 020-7287 8763
email admin@setheatre.co.uk
website www.setheatre.co.uk
Joint Artistic Directors Nancy Meckler, Polly Teale

Middle-scale touring company presenting 2 productions per year: innovative adaptations or translations of classic texts, and some new writing. Tours nationally and internationally. Founded 1975.

Snap People's Theatre Trust

29 Raynham Road, Bishop's Stortford, Herts. CM23 5PE
tel (01279) 461607 *fax* (01279) 506694
email info@snaptheatre.co.uk
Contact A. Graham

Produces classic adaptations, children's theatre and new writing. Welcomes scripts from new writers. Founded 1979.

Solent Peoples Theatre (SPT)

135 St Mary Street, Southampton SO14 1NX
tel 023-8063 4381 *fax* 023-8063 5717
email solent@solentpeoples.demon.co.uk
Artistic Director Mollie Guilfoyle, *General Manager* Susan Carpenter

SPT has developed its artistic programme through participatory projects, to incorporate a multimedia, cross art form approach to theatre that will offer richer opportunities and experience to both community and company. Works with diverse groups/individuals for whom an integrated approach to the creation/presentation of new work in performance makes that work more exciting, relevant and accessible.

The Sphinx Theatre Co. Ltd

25 Short Street, London SE1 8LJ
tel 020-7401 9993/4 *fax* 020-7401 9995
Artistic Director Sue Parrish

Women writers only.

Talawa Theatre Company

3rd Floor, 23-25 Great Sutton Street, London EC1V 0DN
tel 020-7251 6644 *fax* 020-7251 5969
email hq@talawa.com
Artistic Director Yvonne Brewster

Scripts from new writers considered. Particularly interested in scripts from black writers and plays portraying a black experience.

Theatre Centre

Units 7 & 8, Toynbee Workshops, 3 Gunthorpe Street, London E1 7RQ
tel 020-7377 0379 *fax* 020-7377 1376
email admin@theatre-centre.co.uk
website www.theatre-centre.co.uk
General Manager Jackie Alexis

New writing company producing and touring nationally and internationally. Professional theatre for young people – schools, arts centres, venues.

Theatre Workshop

34 Hamilton Place, Edinburgh EH3 5AX
tel 0131-225 7942 *fax* 0131-220 0112
Contact Robert Rae

Cutting edge, professional, inclusive theatre company. Plays include new writing/community/ children's/disabled. Scripts from new writers considered.

Tiebreak Theatre Company

Heartsease High School, Marryat Road, Norwich NR7 9DF
tel (01603) 435 209 *fax* (01603) 435 184
email info@tiebreak-theatre.com
website www.tiebreak-theatre.com
Contact Nicola Khandpur, General Manager

Presents 3 productions per year of children's and young people's theatre for schools and venues. Founded 1981.

Publishers of plays

Playwrights are reminded that it is unusual for a publisher of trade editions of plays to publish plays which have not had at least reasonably successful, usually professional, productions on stage first. See listings beginning on page 141 for addresses.

Brown, Son & Ferguson, Ltd
Calder Publications Ltd
Chapman Publishing
Cló Iar-Chonnachta Teo.
Cressrelles Publishing Co. Ltd
Dublar Scripts
Everyman Publishers plc
Faber & Faber Ltd
Samuel French Ltd
The Gallery Press
Nick Hern Books Ltd
Kenyon-Deane
Kevin Mayhew Ltd
Methuen Publishing Ltd
J. Garnet Miller
New Playwrights' Network
New Theatre Publications
Oberon Books
The Oleander Press
Pipers' Ash Ltd
The Playwrights Publishing Company
SCP Publishers Ltd
Seren
Skoob Russell Square
Colin Smythe Ltd
Ward Lock Educational Co. Ltd
Josef Weinberger Plays Ltd

Literary agents

How to get an agent

New writers and illustrators wishing to have their work published frequently ask whether it is worth their while finding an agent. ***Philippa Milnes-Smith*** *demystifies the role of the literary agent.*

This article is for all those who are prepared to dedicate themselves to the pursuit of publication. If you are currently experiencing just a vague interest in being a writer or illustrator, stop reading now. You are unlikely to survive the rigorous commercial assessment to which your work will be subjected. If you are a children's writer or illustrator do not think that the process will be any easier. It's just as tough, if not tougher.

So, what is a literary agent and why would I want one?

You will probably already have noticed that contacts for many publishers are provided in the *Writers' and Artists' Yearbook*. This means that there is nothing to prevent you from pursuing publishers directly yourself. Indeed, if you can answer a confident 'yes' to all the questions below, and have the time and resources to devote to this objective, you probably don't need an agent:

1. Do you have a thorough understanding of the publishing market and its dynamics?
2. Do you know who are the best publishers for your book and why? Can you evaluate the pros and cons of each?
3. Are you financially numerate and confident of being able to negotiate the best commercial deal available in current market conditions?
4. Are you confident of being able to understand fully and negotiate a publishing or other media contract?
5. Do you enjoy the process of selling yourself and your work?
6. Do you want to spend your creative time on these activities?

An agent's job is to deal with all of the above on your behalf. A good agent will do all of these well.

So, is that is all an agent does?

Agents aren't all the same. Some will provide more editorial and creative support; some will help on longer term career planning; some will be subject specialists; some will involve themselves more on marketing and promotion. Such extras may well be taken into consideration in the commission rates charged.

I have decided I definitely do want an agent. Where do I begin?

When I left publishing and talked generally to the authors and illustrators I knew, a number of them said it was now more difficult to find an agent than a publisher. Why is this? The answer is a commercial one. An agent will only take someone on if they can see how and why they are going to make money for the client and themselves. To survive, an agent needs to make commission and to do this they need projects they can sell. An agent also knows that if he/she does not sell a client's work, the relationship isn't going to last long.

So the agent just thinks about money?

Well, some agents may just think about money. And it might be all you care about. But good agents do also care about the quality of work and the clients they represent. They are professional people who commit themselves to doing the best job they can. They also know that good personal relationships count – and that they help everyone enjoy business more. This means that, if and when you get as far as talking to a prospective agent, you should ask yourself the questions: 'Do I have a good rapport with this person? Do I think we will get along? Do I understand and trust what they are saying?' Follow your instinct – more often than not it will be right.

So how do I convince an agent that I'm worth taking on?

Start with the basics. Make your approach professional. Make sure you only approach an appropriate agent who deals with the category of book you are writing/illustrating. Phone to check to whom you should send your work and whether there are any particular ways your submission should be made (if it's not clear from the listings in this *Yearbook*). Only submit neat, typed work on single-sided A4 paper. Send a short covering letter with your manuscript explaining what it is, why you wrote it, what the intended audience is and providing any other *relevant* context. Always say if and why you are uniquely placed and qualified to write a particular book. Provide your professional credentials, if any. If you are writing an autobiography, justify why it is of public interest and why your experiences set you apart. Also, provide a CV (again, neat, typed, relevant) and a stamped addressed envelope for the return of your manuscript. Think of the whole thing in the same way as you would a job application, for which you would expect to prepare thoroughly in advance. You might only get one go at making your big sales pitch to an agent. Don't mess it up by being anything less than thorough.

And if I get to meet an agent?

Treat it like a job interview (although hopefully it will be more relaxed than this). Be prepared to talk about your work and yourself. An agent knows that a prepossessing personality in an author is a great asset for a publisher in terms of publicity and marketing – they will be looking to see how good your interpersonal skills are.

And if an agent turns my work down? Should I ask them to look again? People say you should not accept rejection.

No means no. Don't pester. It won't make an agent change his/her mind. Instead, move on to the next agency – the agent there might feel more positive. The agents who reject you may be wrong. But the loss is theirs.

Even if an agent turns my work down, isn't it worth asking for help with my creative direction?

No. Agents will often provide editorial advice for clients but will not do so for non-clients. Submissions are usually sorted into two piles of 'yes, worth seeing more' and 'rejections'. There is not another pile of 'promising writer but requires further tutoring'. Creative courses and writers' and artists' groups are better options to pursue for teaching and advice (see *Writers' circles*, page 509, *Websites for writers*, page 561, *Creative writing courses*, page 574 and *Editorial, literary and production services*, page 576). It is, however, important to practise and develop your creative skills. You wouldn't expect to be able to play football without working at your ball skills or practise as a lawyer without studying to acquire the relevant knowledge. If you are looking to get your work published, you are going to have to compete with professional writers and artists – and those who have spent years working at their craft.

If I haven't put you off yet, it just remains for me to say good luck – and don't forget to buy plenty of stamps, envelopes and A4 paper.

Philippa Milnes-Smith is a literary agent and children's specialist at the agency LAW (Lucas Alexander Whitley). She was previously Managing Director of Puffin Books.

Literary agents UK and Ireland

**Full member of the Association of Authors' Agents*

A & B Personal Management Ltd

Paurelle House, 91 Regent Street,
London W1B 4EL
tel 020-7734 6047/8 *fax* 020-7734 6318
Directors R.W. Ellis, R. Ellis

Full-length MSS. Scripts for TV, theatre, cinema; also novels, fiction and non-fiction (home 12.5%, overseas 15%), performance rights (12.5%). No unsolicited material: write first before submitting synopsis. No reading fee for synopsis, plays or screenplays, but fee charged for full-length MSS. Return postage required. Founded 1982.

Abbey Agency (Literary Services)

83 High Street, Graveley,
Cambridgeshire PE19 6PL
tel (01480) 839150
email admin@abbeyagency.com
Proprietor Faith Dakin

General fiction and non-fiction. Full-length MSS (home 10%, overseas 12.5%). Aims to encourage new writers. Send preliminary letter with sae. Reading fee charged for unpublished authors.

Authors include John Daniels, Derek M. Fox, Stephen Najda, Mike Vardy. Founded 1999.

Sheila Ableman Literary Agency

122 Arlington Road, London NW1 7HP
tel/fax 020-7485 3409
email sheila@ableman.freeserve.co.uk
Contact Sheila Ableman

Non-fiction including history, science, biography, autobiography (home 15%, US/translation 20%). Specialises in TV tie-ins and ghost writing. No poetry, children's, cookery, gardening or sport. Unsolicited MSS welcome. Approach in writing with publishinghistory, CV, synopsis, 3 chapters and sae for return. No reading fee. Founded 2000.

The Susie Adams Rights Agency

8 Sullivan Road, London SE11 4UH
tel 020-7582 6765 *fax* 020-7582 7279
email SusieARA@aol.com
Agent Susie Adams

Subsidiary rights agent on behalf of packagers and publishers: foreign language and co-editions worldwide, UK serial, book club, merchandise and other sub rights. No authors. Founded 1998.

The Agency (London) Ltd*

24 Pottery Lane, London W11 4LZ
tel 020-7727 1346 *fax* 020-7727 9037
email info@theagency.co.uk
Executives Stephen Durbridge, Leah Schmidt, Sebastian Born, Julia Kreitman, Bethan Evans, Wendy Gresser, Hilary Delamere, Katie Haines, Ligeia Marsh

Represents writers for theatre, film, TV, radio and children's book writers and illustrators. Also film and TV rights in novels and non-fiction. Adult novels represented only for existing clients. Commission: 10% unless sub-agents employed overseas; works in conjunction with agents in USA and overseas. No unsolicited MSS. Founded 1995.

Gillon Aitken Associates Ltd*

29 Fernshaw Road, London SW10 0TG
tel 020-7351 7561 *fax* 020-7376 3594
email reception@aitkenassoc.demon.co.uk
Contacts Gillon Aitken, Clare Alexander

Fiction and non-fiction (home 10%, USA 15%, translation 20%). No plays or scripts unless by existing clients. Send preliminary letter with short synopsis, 3 sample chapters and return postage. No reading fee.

Clients include Pat Barker, John Cornwell, Linda Davies, Sarah Dunant, Sebastian Faulks, Niall Fergusson, Helen Fielding, Germaine Greer, Susan Howatch, Candia McWilliam, V.S. Naipaul, Jonathan

Raban, Piers Paul Read, Gillian Slovo, Colin Thubron, A.N. Wilson. Founded 1977.

Michael Alcock Management

96 Farringdon Road, London EC1R 3EA
tel 020-7837 8137 *fax* 020-7837 8787
email alcockmgt@aol.com
Agents Michael Alcock, Anna Power

Fiction and non-fiction (home 15%, overseas 20%, performance rights 15%). General non-fiction, mainly biography, history, current affairs, health and lifestyle; literary and commercial fiction. No reading fee. Send letter, CV including previous writing and media experience, and synopsis and first 3 chapters with sae.

Authors include Tamsin Blanchard, James Burke, Barbara Currie, Tom Dixon, Yehudi Gordon, Mark Griffiths, Joanna Hall, Lisa Hilton, Lynne Robinson, Barnaby Rogerson, Barry Turner, Lowri Turner. Founded 1997.

Jacintha Alexander Associates – see Lucas Alexander Whitley

Darley Anderson Literary, TV and Film Agency*

Estelle House, 11 Eustace Road, London SW6 1JB
tel 020-7385 6652 *fax* 020-7386 9689
020-7385 5571
email darley.anderson@virgin.net
Proprietor Darley Anderson, *Associates* Elizabeth Wright (love stories and 'tear jerkers'/women's fiction), Kerith Biggs (crime/foreign rights), Hayley Wood (non-fiction), Carrie Goodman (children's books/TV)

Popular commercial fiction and non-fiction, and children's fiction; selected scripts for film and TV. Special fiction interests: all types of thrillers and crime (American/hard boiled/cosy/historical); young male fiction and women's fiction including contemporary, 20th century romantic sagas, love stories, 'tear jerkers', women in jeopardy and erotica; thrillers, horror; comedy (TV and books); and all types of American and Irish novels.

Special non-fiction interests: investigative books, revelatory history and science, TV tie-ins, sports books, celebrity autobiographies, true life women in jeopardy, diet, beauty, health, animals, cookery, gardening, popular psychology, self improvement, inspirational, popular religion and supernatural (home 15%, US 20%, translation 20–25%, film/TV/radio 20%). No poetry, plays or academic books. Can arrange author PR and author publicity and specialist financial advice; editorial guidance on selected MSS. Preliminary letter, synopsis and first 3 chapters. Return postage/sae must accompany submission to receive reply. No reading fee. Overseas associates: APA Talent & Literary Agency (LA/Hollywood), Liza Dawson Associates (New York) and leading foreign agents worldwide.

Authors include Richard Asplin, Anne Baker, Catherine Barry, Paul Carson, Caroline Carver, Lee Child, Martina Cole, John Connolly, Joseph Corvo, Margaret Dickinson, Rose Doyle, Joan Jonker, Rani Manicka, Carole Matthews, Lesley Pearse, Allan Pease, Adrian Plass, Carmen Reid, Mary Ryan, Fred Secombe, Rebecca Shaw, Peter Sheridan, Kwong Kuen Shan, Linda Taylor.

Anubis Literary Agency

79 Charles Gardner Road, Leamington Spa, Warks. CV31 3BG
tel (01926) 832644 *fax* (01926) 311607
Partners Steve Calcutt and Maggie Heavey

Full-length MSS. Mainstream adult and literary fiction (home 15%, overseas 20%). Especially interested in crime fiction and thrillers, science fiction, fantasy and horror. No reading fee. Will suggest revision. Send preliminary letter with synopsis. No phone calls. Works with the **Marsh Agency** on translation rights.

Clients include Georgie Hale, Tim Lebbon, Adam Roberts, Elon Salmon, Zoe Sharp, Lesley Asquith, Steve Savile. Founded 1994.

Associated Publicity Holdings Ltd

7 Kensington Church Court, London W8 4SP
tel 020-7937 5277 *fax* 020-7937 2833
email Jonathan.Harris@aph-agent.demon.co.uk
Managing Director Jonathan G. Harris

Full-length MSS. Fiction and non-fiction, particularly sport, history, archaeology, biographies, thrillers and crime novels (home 15%, overseas 20%), performance, film and TV rights (15%). Send outline, 2 sample chapters and sae. Works with foreign agencies. No reading fee. Founded 1987.

Author Literary Agents

53 Talbot Road, London N6 4QX
tel 020-8341 0442 *mobile* (07989) 318245
email agile@authors.co.uk
Contact John Havergal

As well as writing for book publishers and screen producers, also handles new content and design ideas for retail markets such as calendar, gift, greeting, game, toy and stationery. Send sae, half-1-page (max.) outline and writing/work sample for quick saleability rating (writing: 15% UK, 25% overseas/translations; non-writing, e.g. illustration, plastic and digital media: 25% publishing, 33.3% non-publishing – all rates plus VAT). Founded 1997.

Don Baker Associates

25 Eley Drive, Rottingdean, East Sussex BN2 7FH
tel/fax (01273) 386842
Directors Donald Baker, Katy Quayle

Full-length MSS. Fiction, film, TV and theatre scripts (home 12.5%, overseas 15%). Reading fee. Send sae. No unsolicited MSS. Founded 1996.

Blake Friedmann Literary, TV & Film Agency Ltd*

122 Arlington Road, London NW1 7HP
tel 020-7284 0408 *fax* 020-7284 0442
email firstname@blakefriedmann.co.uk
Directors Carole Blake, Julian Friedmann, Barbara Jones, Conrad Williams, Isobel Dixon

Full-length MSS. Fiction: thrillers, women's novels and literary fiction; non-fiction: investigative books, biography, travel; no poetry or plays (home 15%, overseas 20%). Specialises in film and TV rights; place journalism and short stories for existing clients only. Represented worldwide in 26 markets. Preliminary letter, synopsis and first 2 chapters preferred. No reading fee.

Authors include Gilbert Adair, Jane Asher, Edward Carey, Elizabeth Chadwick, Stephanie Dowrick, Barbara Erskine, Ann Granger, Maeve Haran, John Harvey, Ken Hom, Glenn Meade, Lawrence Norfolk, Gregory Norminton, Joseph O'Connor, Sheila O'Flanagan, Sian Rees, Michael Ridpath, Tim Sebastian. Founded 1977.

David Bolt Associates

12 Heath Drive, Send, Surrey GU23 7EP
tel/fax (01483) 721118

Specialises in biography, fiction, theology. Full-length MSS (home 10%, overseas 19%; all other rights including film, video and TV 10%). No unsolicited short stories or play scripts. Will sometimes suggest revision. Works in association with overseas agencies worldwide. Preliminary letter essential. Reading fee terms on application.

Authors include Chinua Achebe, David Bret, John Cannon, Keith Cory-Jones, Nicci Mackay, Joseph Rhymer, Colin Wilson.

The Book Bureau Literary Agency

7 Duncairn Avenue, Bray, Co. Wicklow, Republic of Ireland
tel (01) 276 4996 *fax* (01) 276 4834
Managing Director Geraldine Nichol

Full-length MSS (home 10%, USA 15%, translation 20%). Fiction preferred – thrillers, Irish novels, literary fiction, women's novels and general commercial. No horror, science fiction, children's or poetry. Strong editorial support. No reading fee. Preliminary letter, synopsis and 5 sample chapters. Return postage essential. Works with agents overseas. Founded 1998.

BookBlast Ltd

PO Box 20184, London W10 5AU
tel 020-8968 3089 *fax* 020-8932 4087
Director G. de Chamberet

Full-length MSS (home 12%, overseas 20%), TV and radio (15%), film (20%). Fiction and non-fiction; traditional and underground literature. Radio, TV and film rights sold mainly in works by existing clients. No unsolicited material; no submissions on disk, by fax or by email. Preliminary letter, synopsis, 3–4 sample chapters and biographical information. Return postage essential. No reading fee. Founded 1997.

Authors include Jamika Ajalon, Stephen Barber, Rupert Bogarde, Garth Cartwright, Luis Domingues, S.I. Martin, Stephen Morris, Christov Rühn, Onyekachi Wambu.

Alan Brodie Representation Ltd

(incorporating Michael Imison Playwrights)
211 Piccadilly, London W1J 9HF
tel 020-7917 2871 *fax* 020-7917 2872
email info@alanbrodie.com
website www.alanbrodie.com
Directors Alan Brodie, Sarah McNair, Alison Lee

Specialises in stage plays, radio, TV, film

(home 10%, overseas 15%); no prose fiction or general MSS. Represented in all major countries. No unsolicited scripts; recommendation from known professional required.

Rosemary Bromley Literary Agency

Avington, Winchester, Hants SO21 1DB
tel/fax (01962) 779656
email rosemarybromley.juvenilia@clara.co.uk

Specialises in biography, travel, leisure, cookery, health (home 10%, overseas from 15%.) No poetry. No unsolicited MSS. Send full details of work on offer with return postage. No fax, telephone or email enquiries. For children's books see **Juvenilia**.

Felicity Bryan*

2A North Parade, Banbury Road, Oxford OX2 6LX
tel (01865) 513816 *fax* (01865) 310055

Fiction and general non-fiction; no light romance, science fiction, short stories, plays or young children's (home 10%, overseas 20%). Translation rights handled by Andrew Nurnberg Associates; works in conjunction with US agents. Return postage essential.

Brie Burkeman*

14 Neville Court, Abbey Road, London NW8 9DD
tel (0709) 223 9113 *fax* (0709) 223 9111
email brie.burkeman@mail.com
Proprietor Brie Burkeman

Commercial and literary full-length fiction and non-fiction and film/TV/theatre scripts (home 15%, overseas 20%). No academic text, poetry, short stories, musicals or short films. No reading fee but return postage essential. Unsolicited email attachments will be deleted without opening. Also independent film and TV consultant to literary agents. Founded 2000.

Calitz Associates

Suite 127, 2 Old Brompton Road,
London SW7 3DQ
tel (07092) 185544 *fax* (07092) 185545
email info@calitz-associates.com
Proprietor Chris Calitz

Commercial and literary full-length fiction and non-fiction (mainly health, lifestyle and natural history) and film/TV scripts (home 15%, overseas 20%). No plays, short stories, poetry or academic books. Aims particularly to encourage new writers. No reading fee. Will suggest revision. No unsolicited MSS. Send letter, CV and synopsis (for fiction, first 3 chapters); return postage essential. Founded 2000.

Campbell Thomson & McLaughlin Ltd*

1 King's Mews, London WC1N 2JA
tel 020-7242 0958 *fax* 020-7242 2408
Directors John McLaughlin, Charlotte Bruton

Full-length book MSS (home 10%, overseas up to 20% including commission to foreign agent). No poetry, plays or TV/film scripts, short stories or children's books. Preliminary letter with sae essential. No unsolicited synopses or MSS. No reading fee. USA agents represented: Raines & Raines, The Fox Chase Agency, Inc. Representatives in most European countries.

Capel & Land Ltd

29 Wardour Street, London W1D 6PS
tel 020-7734 2414 *fax* 020-7734 8101
email georgina@capelland.co.uk
Agents Georgina Capel (literary), Robert Caskie (film), Anita Land (TV)

Literary and commercial fiction, history, biography; film and TV (home/overseas 15%). No reading fee; will suggest revision.

Clients include Julie Burchill, Andrew Greig, Eamonn Holmes, Jean Marsh, Rt Hon. Dr Mo Mowlam, Cristina Odone, Jeremy Paxman, Henry Porter, Andrew Roberts, Simon Sebag Montefiore, Louis Theroux, Lucy Wadham. Founded 1999.

Casarotto Ramsay & Associates Ltd

(formerly Margaret Ramsay Ltd and Casarotto Company Ltd)
National House, 60-66 Wardour Street,
London W1V 4ND
tel 020-7287 4450 *fax* 020-7287 9128
email agents@casarotto.uk.com
Directors Jenne Casarotto, Giorgio Casarotto, Tom Erhardt, Tracey Hyde, Sara Pritchard, Mel Kenyon, Charlotte Kelly, Jodi Shields

MSS – theatre, films, TV, sound broadcasting only (10%). Works in conjunction with agents in USA and other foreign countries. Preliminary letter essential. No reading fee.

Authors include Paul Abbott, Alan Ayckbourn, J.G. Ballard, Peter Barnes, Edward Bond, Caryl Churchill, Pam Gems, Christopher Hampton, David Hare, Nick Hornby, Amy Jenkins, Neil

Jordan, Frank McGuiness, Phyllis Nagy, Mark Ravenhill, Willy Russell, Martin Sherman, Shawn Slovo, Fay Weldon, Timberlake Wertenbaker, David Wood. Founded 1992.

Celia Catchpole

56 Gilpin Avenue, London SW14 8QY
tel 020-8255 7200 *fax* 020-8288 0653

Specialises as agent for children's writers and illustrators (home 10% writers, 15% illustrators; overseas 20%). No unsolicited MSS. Founded 1996.

Chapman & Vincent

The Mount, Sun Hill, Royston, Herts. SG8 9AT
tel (01763) 245005 *fax* (01763) 243033
email ChapmanVincent@camnews.net
Directors Jennifer Chapman, Gilly Vincent

Original non-fiction and (occasionally) quality fiction (home 15%; overseas 20%). No children's, genre fiction or poetry. No reading fee. Clients come mainly from personal recommendation. No phone calls; no submissions by fax or email. Send synopsis and 2 sample chapters with sae.

Authors include George Carter, Leslie Geddes-Brown, Sara George, Rowley Leigh, John Miller, Dorit Peleg. Founded 1995.

Mic Cheetham Literary Agency

11-12 Dover Street, London W1S 4LJ
tel 020-7495 2002 *fax* 020-7495 5777
website www.miccheetham.com
Director Mic Cheetham

General and literary fiction, science fiction, some non-fiction (home 10%, overseas 20%); film, TV and radio rights (10–15%); will suggest revision. Works with the **Marsh Agency** for foreign rights. No unsolicited MSS. Founded 1994.

Judith Chilcote Agency*

8 Wentworth Mansions, Keats Grove, London NW3 2RL
tel 020-7794 3717
email judybks@aol.com
Director Judith Chilcote

Commercial fiction, non-fiction – sports, self-help and health, cookery, autobiography and biography, current affairs, TV tie-ins (home 15%, overseas 20–25%). No short stories, science fiction, children's, poetry. Works in conjunction with overseas agents and New York affiliate. No reading fee but preliminary letter with 3 chapters only, CV and sae essential. Founded 1990.

Teresa Chris Literary Agency

43 Musard Road, London W6 8NR
tel 020-7386 0633
Director Teresa Chris

All fiction, especially crime, women's commercial, general and literary fiction; all non-fiction, especially biography, history, health, cooking, arts and crafts. No science fiction, horror, fantasy, short stories, poetry, academic books (home 10%, USA 15%, rest 20%). Own US office: Thompson & Chris Literary Agency. No reading fee. No unsolicited MSS. Send introductory letter describing work, first 3 chapters and sae. Founded 1988.

Christy & Moore Ltd – see Sheil Land Associates Ltd

Mary Clemmey Literary Agency*

6 Dunollie Road, London NW5 2XP
tel 020-7267 1290 *fax* 020-7482 7360

High quality fiction and non-fiction with an international market (home 10%, overseas 20%), performance rights (15%). No children's books, science fiction or fantasy. TV, film, radio and theatre scripts from existing clients only. Works in conjunction with US agent. No reading fee. No unsolicited MSS. Approach by letter (including sae). Founded 1992.

Jonathan Clowes Ltd*

10 Iron Bridge House, Bridge Approach, London NW1 8BD
tel 020-7722 7674 *fax* 020-7722 7677
Directors Jonathan Clowes, Ann Evans

Literary and commercial fiction and non-fiction, film, TV, theatre and radio (home 15%, overseas 20%). No reading fee. No unsolicited MSS. Works in association with agents overseas. Founded 1960.

Clients include Sir Kingsley Amis Estate, Dr David Bellamy, Len Deighton, David Harsent, Elizabeth Jane Howard, Damian Lanigan, Doris Lessing, David Nobbs, Gillian White.

Elspeth Cochrane Personal Management

South Bank Commercial Centre, 140 Battersea Park Road, London SW11 4NB
tel 020-7622 0314 *fax* 020-7622 5815
email elspethc@dircon.co.uk
Contact Elspeth Cochrane

Send synopsis with covering letter and

sae in first instance (home and overseas 12.5%), performance rights (12.5%). No reading fee.

Authors include Nick Hennegan, Royce Ryton, Robert Tanitch. Founded 1960.

Rosica Colin Ltd

1 Clareville Grove Mews, London SW7 5AH
tel 020-7370 1080 *fax* 020-7244 6441
Directors Sylvie Marston, Joanna Marston

All full-length MSS (excluding science fiction and poetry); also theatre, film and sound broadcasting (home 10%, overseas 10–20%). No reading fee, but may take 3–4 months to consider full MSS. Send synopsis only in first instance, with letter outlining writing credits and whether MS has been previously submitted, plus return postage.

Authors include Richard Aldington, Simone de Beauvoir (in UK), Samuel Beckett (publication rights), Steven Berkoff, Alan Brownjohn, Sandy Brownjohn, Donald Campbell, Nick Dear, Neil Donnelly, J.T. Edson, Bernard Farrell, Rainer Werner Fassbinder (in UK), Jean Genet, Mary Halpin, Franz Xaver Kroetz, Don McCamphill, Heiner Müller (in UK), Graham Reid, Botho Strauss (in UK), Anthony Vivis, Wim Wenders (in UK). Founded 1949.

Conville & Walsh Ltd

118-120 Wardour Street, London W1F 0TU
tel 020-7287 3030 *fax* 020-7287 4545
email submissions@convilleandwalsh.com
info@convilleandwalsh.com
Directors Clare Conville, Patrick Walsh, Sam North (film/TV)

Literary and commercial fiction plus serious and narrative non-fiction. No reading fee; will suggest revision.

Authors include Jez Alborough, The Estate of Francis Bacon, John Burningham, Kate Cann, Mike Cordy, Jane Cumberbatch, Mike Dash, Steve Erikson, Caron Freeborn, Katy Gardner, Martin Gorst, Christopher Hart, Dermot Healy, Tom Holland, James Holland, Sebastian Horsley, David Huggins, Vivien Kelly, Kris Kenway, P.J. Lynch, Hector Macdonald, Harland Miller, Jacqui Murhall, Philip Oppenheim, Rebbecca Ray, Patrick Redmond, Candace Robb, Niamh Sharkey, Nicky Singer, Simon Singh, Adam Wishart, Isabel Wolff. Founded 2000.

Jane Conway-Gordon*

(in association with Andrew Mann Ltd)
1 Old Compton Street, London W1D 5JA
tel 020-7494 0148 *fax* 020-7287 9264

Full length MSS, performance rights (home 15%, overseas 20%). Represented in all foreign countries. No reading fee but preliminary letter and return postage essential. Founded 1982.

Coombs Moylett Literary Agency

3 Askew Road, London W12 9AA
tel 020-8740 0454 *fax* 020-8354 3065
email lisamoylett@dial.pipex.com
Proprietor Lisa Moylett

Specialises in crime, thrillers, contemporary women's fiction and literary fiction (home 10%; overseas 15%). Send first 3 chapters and synopsis. Will help with revision as appropriate. Return postage essential.

Rupert Crew Ltd*

1A King's Mews, London WC1N 2JA
tel 020-7242 8586 *fax* 020-7831 7914
email rupertcrew@compuserve.com
Directors Doreen Montgomery, Caroline Montgomery

International representation, handling volume and subsidiary rights in fiction and non-fiction properties (home 15%, elsewhere 20%); no plays, poetry, journalism or short stories. No reading fee, but preliminary letter and return postage essential. Also acts independently as publishers' consultants. Founded 1927 by F. Rupert Crew.

Curtis Brown Group Ltd*

Haymarket House, 28-29 Haymarket, London SW1Y 4SP
tel 020-7396 6600 *fax* 020-7396 0110
email cb@curtisbrown.co.uk
Chairman Paul Scherer, *Group Managing Director* Jonathan Lloyd, *Financial Director* Mark Collingbourne, *Australia: Managing Director* Fiona Inglis, *Books London* Jonathan Lloyd, Anna Davis, Jonny Geller, Hannah Griffiths, Ali Gunn, Camilla Hornby, Anthea Morton-Saner, Peter Robinson, Vivienne Schuster, Michael Shaw, Janice Swanson
Books Edinburgh 37 Queensferry Street, Edinburgh EH2 4QS
tel 0131-225 1286/1288 *fax* 0131-225 1290
email cb@curtisbrown.co.uk
Contact Giles Gordon, *Foreign Rights* Diana Mackay, Carol Jackson, Kate Cooper,

Film/TV/Theatre Nick Marston (Managing Director, Media Division), Ben Hall, Philip Patterson, *Presenters* Sue Freathy, Julian Beynon

Agents for the negotiation in all markets of novels, general non-fiction, children's books (home 10%, overseas 20%) and associated rights (including multimedia), as well as film, theatre, TV and radio scripts. Outline for non-fiction and short synopsis for fiction with 2 or 3 sample chapters and autobiographical note. No reading fee. Return postage essential. Also represents directors, designers and presenters. Return postage essential. Founded 1899.

Judy Daish Associates Ltd

2 St Charles Place, London W10 6EG
tel 020-8964 8811 *fax* 020-8964 8966
Agents Judy Daish, Sara Stroud, Tracey Elliston

Theatre, film, TV, radio (rates by negotiation). No unsolicited MSS. Founded 1978.

Caroline Davidson Literary Agency

5 Queen Anne's Gardens, London W4 1TU
tel 020-8995 5768 *fax* 020-8994 2770

Handles novels and non-fiction of all kinds, including reference works (12.5%). Send preliminary letter with detailed, well thought-out book proposal/synopsis and/or first 50 pages of novel, CV, and large sae. Return postage essential. No reading fee. Quick response.

Authors include Susan Aldridge, Nigel Barlow, Anna Beer, Stuart Clark, Naomi Craft, Andrew Dalby, Emma Donoghue, Cindy Engel, Robert Feather, Chris Greenhalgh, Paul Hillyard, Tom Jaine, Huon Mallalieu. Founded 1988.

Merric Davidson Literary Agency

12 Priors Heath, Goudhurst,
Kent TN17 2RE
tel/fax (01580) 212041
email mdla@msn.com
Contact Merric Davidson, Wendy Suffield

Specialising in contemporary adult fiction (home 10%, overseas 20%). No unsolicited MSS. Preliminary letter with synopsis, author information and sae. No initial reading fee, may suggest revision, subsequent editorial advice by arrangement.

Authors include Alys Clare, Francesca Clementis, Murray Davies, Harold Elletson, Alison Habens, Frankie Park, Mark Pepper, Simon Scarrow, Luke Sutherland. Founded 1990.

Felix De Wolfe

Garden Offices, 51 Maida Vale, London W9 1SD
tel 020-7289 5770 *fax* 020-7289 5731

Theatre, films, TV, sound broadcasting, fiction (home 10–15%, overseas 20%). Works in conjunction with many foreign agencies.

DGA

55 Monmouth Street, London WC2H 9DG
tel 020-7240 9992 *fax* 020-7395 6110
email assistant@davidgodwinassociates.co.uk
Directors David Godwin, Heather Godwin

Literary fiction and general non-fiction (home 10%, overseas 20%). No reading fee; send sae for return of MSS. Founded 1995.

Dorian Literary Agency (DLA)

Upper Thornehill, 27 Church Road,
St Marychurch, Torquay, Devon TQ1 4QY
tel/fax (01803) 312095
Proprietor Dorothy Lumley

General fiction, and specialising in popular fiction: women's fiction from romance, historicals to contemporary; crime from historical to noir and thrillers; science fiction, fantasy (but cautious about humorous/soft fantasy, i.e. unicorns), dark fantasyand horror. Adult and young adult, but no children's for under 10, poetry or drama (home 10–12.5%, USA 15%, translation 20%). No reading fee. Contact initially by mail with letter, outline and 1–3 chapters – please avoid faxes/email. Return postage/sae essential.

Authors include Gillian Bradshaw, Brian Lumley, Amy Myers, Stephen Jones, Rosemary Rowe. Founded 1986.

Robert Dudley Agency

8 Abbotstone Road, London SW15 1QR
tel 020-8788 0938 *fax* 020-8780 3586
email rdudley@btinternet.com
Proprietor Robert Dudley

Specialises in history, biography, sport, humour, health, management, politics, IT and personal development (home 10%, overseas 15%; film/TV/radio 15%, 20%). No reading fee. Will suggest revision.

Authors include Steve Biko, Peter Collins, David Osler, Simon Phillips, Tim Phillips, Sol Shulman. Founded 2000.

Toby Eady Associates Ltd

3rd Floor, 9 Orme Court, London W2 4RL
tel 020-7792 0092 *fax* 020-7792 0879
email toby@tobyeady.demon.co.uk

jessica@tobyeady.demon.co.uk
website www.tobyeadyassociates.co.uk
Contact Toby Eady, Jessica Woollard
Fiction and non-fiction (home 10–15%, overseas 20%). Special interests: China, Middle East, Africa, India. No film, TV scripts or poetry. Approach by personal recommendation, letter. Overseas associates for USA, France, Germany, Holland, Scandinavia, Italy, Spain and China.

Authors include Jung Chang, Fadia Faqir, Liu Hong, Ma Jian, David Landau, Kanan Makiya, Nuha Al Radi, Amir Taheri, Annie Wang, Xinran Xue, Julia Blackburn, Mark Burnell, John Carey, Bernard Cornwell, Kuki Gallmann, Francesca Marciano, Shyama Perera, Fiammetta Rocco, Rachel Seiffert, Ann Wroe. Founded 1968.

Eddison Pearson Ltd

West Hill House, 6 Swains Lane, London N6 6QU
tel 020-7700 7763 *fax* 020-7700 7866
email box1@eddisonpearson.com
Contact Clare Pearson
Children's books and scripts, literary fiction and non-fiction, poetry (home 10%, overseas 15%). No unsolicited MSS. Enquire by letter enclosing brief writing sample and sae. Email enquiries welcome but no email submissions please. No reading fee. May suggest revision where appropriate.

Authors include Valerie Bloom, Sue Heap, Abdullah Hussein.

Edwards Fuglewicz*

49 Great Ormond Street, London WC1N 3HZ
tel 020-7405 6725 *fax* 020-7405 6726
Partners Ros Edwards and Helenka Fuglewicz
Literary and commercial fiction (but no science fiction, horror or fantasy); non-fiction: biography, history, popular culture (home 15%, USA/translation 20%). No scripts. Unsolicited MSS welcome. In first instance send covering letter, synopsis and up to 3 sample chapters plus sae for return of MSS. Submissions on disk or by email are not acceptable. No reading fee. Founded 1996.

Faith Evans Associates*

27 Park Avenue North, London N8 7RU
tel 020-8340 9920 *fax* 020-8340 9410
Small agency (home 15%, overseas 20%). New clients by personal recommendation only. Sub-agents in most countries. No phone calls, scripts or unsolicited MSS.

Authors include Melissa Benn, Shyam Bhatia, Madeleine Bourdouxheh, Eleanor Bron, Caroline Conran, Helen Falconer, Alicia Foster, Midge Gillies, Ed Glinert, Jim Kelly, Helena Kennedy, Seumas Milne, Tom Paulin, Sheila Rowbotham, Lorna Sage, Rebecca Stott, Hwee Hwee Tan, Marion Urch, Harriet Walter, Elizabeth Wilson. Founded 1987.

John Farquharson Ltd – see Curtis Brown Group Ltd

Janet Fillingham Associates

52 Lowther Road, London SW13 9NU
tel 020-8748 5594 *fax* 020-8748 7374
email jfillassoc@aol.com
Director Janet Fillingham
Film and TV only (home 10%, overseas 15–20%). Strictly no unsolicited MSS; professional recommendation required. Founded 1992.

Film Rights Ltd

Mezzanine, Quadrant House, 80-82 Regent Street, London W1B 5AU
tel 020-7734 9911 *fax* 020-7437 0561
email information@filmrights.ltd.uk
website www.filmrights.ltd.uk
Directors Brendan Davis, Joan Potts
Theatre, films, TV and sound broadcasting (home 10%, overseas 15%). Represented in USA and abroad. Founded 1932.

Laurence Fitch Ltd

(incorporating The London Play Company 1922)
Mezzanine, Quadrant House, 80-82 Regent Street, London W1B 5AU
tel 020-7734 9911 *fax* 020-7437 0561
email information@laurencefitch.com
website www.laurencefitch.com
Directors F.H.L. Fitch, Joan Potts, Brendan Davis
Theatre, films, TV and sound broadcasting (home 10%, overseas 15%). Also works with several agencies in USA and in Europe.

Authors include The Estate of the Late Dodie Smith, Ray Coony, John Chapman, Carlo Ardito, John Graham, Edward Taylor, Dawn Lowe-Watson, Peter Coke, Glyn Robbins.

Jill Foster Ltd

9 Barb Mews, Brook Green, London W6 7PA
tel 020-7602 1263 *fax* 020-7602 9336
Theatre, films, TV and sound broadcast-

ing (12.5%). Particularly interested in film and TV comedy and drama. No novels or short stories. No reading fee. Preliminary letter essential. Founded 1978.

Fox & Howard Literary Agency

4 Bramerton Street, London SW3 5JX
tel/fax 020-7352 8691
Partners Chelsey Fox, Charlotte Howard

General non-fiction: biography, history and popular culture, reference, business, gardening, Mind, Body and Spirit, self-help and health (home 10–15%, overseas 20%); will suggest revision where appropriate. No reading fee, but preliminary letter and synopsis with sae essential.

Authors include Sarah Bartlett, Tony Clayton Lea, Maryon Stewart, Jane Struthers. Founded 1992.

Fraser & Dunlop Ltd, Fraser & Dunlop Scripts Ltd – see PFD

French's

78 Loudoun Road, London NW8 0NA
tel 020-7483 4269 *fax* 020-7722 0754
Directors John French, Mark Taylor

All MSS; specialises in novels and screenplays (home/overseas 10%); theatre, films, TV, radio (10%). Reading service available, details on application. Sae must be enclosed with all MSS.

Futerman, Rose & Associates*

Heston Court Business Park, 19 Camp Road, London SW19 4UW
tel 020-8947 0188 *fax* 020-8286 4861
email guy@futermanrose.co.uk
website www.futermanrose.co.uk
Contacts Guy Rose, Alexandra Groom, Christopher Oxford

Scripts for film, TV and theatre; commercial fiction and non-fiction with film potential, biography, show business (literature: 12.5–17.5%; drama/screenplays: 15 20%). No unsolicited MSS. Send preliminary letter with a brief resumé, detailed synopsis andsae. Overseas associates.

Clients include Alexandra Connor, Frank Dickens, Martin Dillon, Iain Duncan Smith, Royston Ellis, Charles Fourie, Russell Warren Howe, Sue Lenier, John McVicar, Angela Meredith, Valerie Grosvenor Myer, Yvonne Ridley, Gordon Thomas, Simon Woodham. Founded 1984.

Jüri Gabriel

35 Camberwell Grove, London SE5 8JA
tel/fax 020-7703 6186

Quality fiction and non-fiction (current specialisation: popular academic – but anything that shows wit and intelligence); radio, TV and film, but mainly selling these rights in existing works by existing clients. Full-length MSS (home 10%, overseas 20%), performance rights (10%); will suggest revision where appropriate. No short stories, articles, verse or books for children. No reading fee; return postage essential. Jüri Gabriel is the chairman of Dedalus (publishers).

Authors include Diana Constance, Miriam Dunne, Pat Gray, Robert Irwin, 'David Madsen', Richard Mankiewicz, David Miller, Prof Cedric Mims, John Outram, Stefan Szymanski, Dr Terence White,. Dr Robert Youngson.

Eric Glass Ltd

25 Ladbroke Crescent, London W11 1PS
tel 020-7229 9500 *fax* 020-7229 6220
Directors Janet Glass, Daniela Szmigielska

Full-length MSS only; also theatre, films, TV, and sound broadcasting. No unsolicited MSS. Founded 1932.

David Godwin Associates – see DGA

Annette Green Authors' Agency

6 Montem Street, London N4 3BE
tel 020-7281 0009 *fax* 020-7686 5884
email annettekgreen@aol.com
Partners Annette Green, David Smith

Full-length MSS (home 15%, overseas 20%). Literary and general fiction and non-fiction, upmarket popular culture, celebrity biography/autobiography. No dramatic scripts, poetry, children's, SF or fantasy. No reading fee. Preliminary letter, synopsis, sample chapter and sae essential.

Authors include Nick Barlay, Bill Broady, Dr Jerry Brotton, Emma Gold, Justin Hill, Max Kinnings, Maria McCann, Ian Marchant, Prof Charles Pasternak, Owen Sheers, Rev. Victor Stock, Elizabeth Woodcraft. Founded 1998.

Christine Green Authors' Agent*

6 Whitehorse Mews, Westminster Bridge Road, London SE1 7QD
tel 020-7401 8844 *fax* 020-7401 8860

Fiction and general non-fiction. Full-length MSS (home 10%, overseas 20%). Works in conjunction with agencies in Europe and Scandinavia. No reading fee, but preliminary letter and return postage essential. Founded 1984.

Louise Greenberg
The End House, Church Crescent, London N3 1BG
tel 020-8349 1179 *fax* 020-8343 4559
email louisegreenberg@msn.com
Full-length MSS (home10%, overseas 20–25%). Literary fiction and non-fiction. No reading fee. Return postage and sae essential. Founded 1997.

Greene & Heaton Ltd*
37 Goldhawk Road, London W12 8QQ
tel 020-8749 0315 *fax* 020-8749 0318
Directors Carol Heaton, Judith Murray, Charles Elliott, Antony Topping
Full-length MSS, fiction and non-fiction (home 10%, overseas 20%). No plays, TV or film scripts, science fiction, fantasy. Works in conjunction with agencies in most countries. Reply and/or return of MSS only if sae and/or return postage supplied. Founded 1962.

Gregory & Company Authors' Agents*
3 Barb Mews, London W6 7PA
tel 020-7610 4676 *fax* 020-7610 4686
email info@gregoryandcompany.co.uk
website www.gregoryandcompany.co.uk
Contact Jane Gregory, *Editorial* Broo Doherty, *Rights* Jane Barlow, Claire Morris
Fiction and general non-fiction (home 20%, USA/translation/radio/film/TV 20%). Special interests (fiction): literary, commercial, crime, suspense and thrillers. Particularly interested in books which will also sell to publishers abroad. No original plays, film or TV scripts (only published books are sold to film and TV), science fiction, fantasy, poetry, academic or children's books. No reading fee. Editorial advice given to own authors. No unsolicited MSS: send preliminary letter with CV, synopsis, first 3 chapters and future writing plans plus return postage. Short submissions by fax or email. Represented throughout Europe, Asia and USA. Founded 1987.

David Grossman Literary Agency Ltd
118A Holland Park Avenue, London W11 4UA
tel 020-7221 2770 *fax* 020-7221 1445
Full-length MSS (home 10–15%, overseas 20% including foreign agent's commission), performance rights (15%). Works in conjunction with agents in New York, Los Angeles, Europe, Japan. No reading fee, but preliminary letter required. Founded 1976.

The Rod Hall Agency Ltd
3 Charlotte Mews, London W1T 4DZ
tel 020-7637 0706 *fax* 020-7637 0807
email office@rodhallagency.com
website www.rodhallagency.com
Directors Rod Hall, Clare Barker
Specialises in writers for stage, screen and radio but also deals in TV and film rights in novels and non-fiction (home 10%, overseas 15%). No reading fee.

Clients include Simon Beaufoy, Jeremy Brock, Dario Fo, Lee Hall, Susan Hill, Arthur Hopcraft, Liz Lochhead, Martin McDonagh, Andrea Newman, Simon Nye. Founded 1997.

Margaret Hanbury*
27 Walcot Square, London SE11 4UB
tel 020-7735 7680 *fax* 020-7793 0316
email maggie@mhanbury.demon.co.uk
Personally run agency specialising in quality fiction and non-fiction (home 15%, overseas 20%). No unsolicited approaches this year.

Authors include George Alagiah, J.G. Ballard, Simon Callow, Judith Lennox. Founded 1983.

Antony Harwood Ltd
109 Riverbank House, 1 Putney Bridge Approach, London SW6 3JD
tel 020-7384 9209 *fax* 020-7384 9206
email mail@antonyharwood.com
Contacts Antony Harwood, James Macdonald Lockhart
General and genre fiction; general non-fiction (home 10%, overseas 15–20%). Will suggest revision.

Authors include Ethan Coen, Louise Doughty, Robert Edric, Peter F. Hamilton, Alan Hollinghurst, A.L. Kennedy, Douglas Kennedy, Chris Manby, George Monbiot, Tim Parks. Founded 2000.

Richard Hatton Ltd
29 Roehampton Gate, London SW15 5JR
tel 020-8876 6699 *fax* 020-8876 8278
Director Richard Hatton
Stage plays; TV, cinema and radio scripts

only (15%). No reading fee. Preliminary letter with outline and sae only. No unsolicited MSS. Founded 1954.

A.M. Heath & Co. Ltd*

79 St Martin's Lane, London WC2N 4RE
tel 020-7836 4271 *fax* 020-7497 2561
Directors William Hamilton, Sara Fisher, Sarah Molloy, Victoria Hobbs

Full-length MSS. Literary and commercial fiction and non-fiction, children's (home 10–15%, USA 20%, translation 20%), performance rights (15%). No screenplays, poetry or short stories except for established clients. No reading fee. Agents in USA and all European countries and Japan.

Clients include Joan Aiken, Bella Bathurst, Anita Brookner, Helen Cresswell, Patricia Duncker, Geoff Dyer, Katie Fforde, Graham Hancock, Tobias Hill, Hilary Mantel, Tim Pears, Ricardo Pinto, Susan Price, Adam Thorpe, Barbara Trapido. Founded 1919.

David Higham Associates Ltd*

(incorporating Murray Pollinger)
5-8 Lower John Street, Golden Square, London W1F 9HA
tel 020-7434 5900 *fax* 020-7437 1072
email dha@davidhigham.co.uk
Managing Director Anthony Goff, *Books* Veronique Baxter, Anthony Goff, Bruce Hunter, Jacqueline Korn, *Foreign Rights* Ania Corless, *Film/TV/Theatre* Gemma Hirst, Nicky Lund, Georgina Ruffhead

Agents for the negotiation of all rights in fiction, general non-fiction, children's fiction and picture books, plays, film and TV scripts (home 10%, USA/translation 20%). USA associate agency: Harold Ober Associates Inc. Represented in all foreign markets. Preliminary letter and return postage essential. No reading fee. Founded 1935.

Vanessa Holt Ltd*

59 Crescent Road, Leigh-on-Sea, Essex SS9 2PF
tel (01702) 473787 *fax* (01702) 471890
email vanessa@holtlimited.freeserve.co.uk

General adult fiction and non-fiction (home 15%, overseas 20%, TV/film/radio 15%). Works in conjunction with foreign agencies in all markets. No reading fee, but preliminary letter and sae essential. Founded 1989.

Valerie Hoskins Associates

20 Charlotte Street, London W1T 2NA
tel 020-7637 4490 *fax* 020-7637 4493
email vha@vhassociates.co.uk
Proprietor Valerie Hoskins, *Agent* Rebecca Watson

Film, TV and radio; specialises in animation (home 12.5%, overseas max. 20%). No unsolicited MSS; preliminary letter essential. No reading fee, but sae essential. Works in conjunction with US agents.

Tanja Howarth Literary Agency*

19 New Row, London WC2N 4LA
tel 020-7240 5553 *fax* 020-7379 0969
email tanja.howarth@virgin.net

Full-length MSS. General fiction and non-fiction, thrillers, contemporary and historical women's novels and sagas (home 15%, USA/translation 20%). Represented in the USA by various agents. No unsolicited MSS, and no submissions by fax or email. Founded 1970.

ICM Ltd

Oxford House, 76 Oxford Street, London W1D 1BS
tel 020-7636 6565 *fax* 020-7323 0101
email writers@icmlondon.co.uk
Directors Duncan Heath, Susan Rodgers, Sally Long-Innes, Paul Lyon-Maris, *Literary Agents* Susan Rodgers, Jessica Sykes, Catherine King, Greg Hunt, Hugo Young, Michael McCoy, Duncan Heath, Paul Lyon-Maris

Specialises in scripts for film, theatre, TV, radio (home 10%, overseas 10%).

IMG Literary UK

The Pier House, Strand on the Green, London W4 3NN
tel 020-8233 5000 *fax* 020-8233 5001
Chairman Mark H. McCormack, *Agents* Sarah Wooldridge (London), Mark Reiter and Lisa Queen (New York), Fumiko Matsuki (Japan)

Celebrity books, sports-related books, commercial fiction, non-fiction and how-to business books (home 15%, US 20%, elsewhere 25%). No theatre, children's, academic or poetry.

Intercontinental Literary Agency*

33 Bedford Street, London WC2E 9ED
tel 020-7379 6611 *fax* 020-7379 6790
email ila@ila-agency.co.uk
Contacts Nicki Kennedy, Sam Edenborough, Mary Esdaile

Represents translation rights for PFD, London, Harold Matson Company Inc., New York, The Turnbull Agency (John Irving) Inc., and Lucas Alexander Whitley Ltd. Founded 1965.

International Literary Representation & Management LLC

186 Bickenhall Mansions, Bickenhall Street, London W1U 6BX
tel 020-7224 1748 *fax* 020-7224 1802
email info@yesitive.com
website www.yesitive.com
Vice President for Europe Peter Cox

European office of US agency. Represents authors with major international potential. Commission by agreement. Only considers submissions if guidelines found on website have been followed. No unsolicited MSS. No radio or theatre scripts. No reading fee.

Clients include Daniel Altieri, Brian Clegg, Brian Cruver, Prof Devra Lee Davis, Dr Patrick Dixon, Senator Orrin Hatch, Commodore Scott Jones USN, Michael J. Nelson, Michelle Paver, Saxon Roach, Tom Stevenson, Mary Tabor. Founded 1993.

International Scripts

1A Kidbrooke Park Road, London SE3 0LR
tel 020-8319 8666 *fax* 020-8319 0801
Directors H.P. Tanner, J. Lawson

Specialises in full-length contemporary and women's fiction, biographies, business and general non-fiction (home 15%, overseas 20%), performance rights (15–20%); no poetry or short stories. Works with overseas agents. Preliminary letter and sae required.A £30 editorial contribution plus return postage may be requested for reading MSS.

Authors include Jane Adams, Zita Adamson, Simon Clark, Cory Daniells, Charla Devereux, Paul Devereux, Dr James Fleming, James Gibbins, Ed Gorman, Peter Haining, Julie Harris, Robert A. Heinlein, Anna Jacobs, Michael Jefferson-Brown, Anne Jones, Richard Laymon, Nick Oldham, Mary Ryan, John and Anne Spencer, Janet Woods. Founded 1979.

Barrie James Literary Agency

(incorporating New Authors Showcase)
Rivendell, Kingsgate, Torquay TQ2 8QA
tel (01803) 326617
email mail@newauthors.org.uk
website www.newauthors.org.uk
Contact Barrie E. James

Internet site for new writers and poets to display their work to publishers and others. No unsolicited MSS. First contact: send sae. Founded 1997.

Janklow & Nesbit (UK) Ltd

29 Adam & Eve Mews, London W8 6UG
tel 020-7376 2733 *fax* 020-7376 2915
email queries@janklow.co.uk
Directors Tif Loehnis, Claire Paterson

Commercial and literary fiction and non-fiction. No unsolicited MSS. Send informative covering letter and return postage with full outline (non-fiction), synopsis and 3 sample chapters (fiction). US and foreign rights handled by **Janklow & Nesbit Associates** in New York.

John Johnson (Authors' Agent) Ltd*

Clerkenwell House, 45-47 Clerkenwell Green, London EC1R 0HT
tel 020-7251 0125 *fax* 020-7251 2172
email johnjohnson@btinternet.com
Contacts Andrew Hewson, Margaret Hewson, Elizabeth Fairbairn

Full-length MSS (home 10%, USA 15–20%, translation 20%). General fiction and non-fiction. No science fiction, technical or academic material. Scripts from existing clients only. No unsolicited MSS; send preliminary letter and sae. No reading fee. Founded1956.

Jane Judd Literary Agency*

18 Belitha Villas, London N1 1PD
tel 020-7607 0273 *fax* 020-7607 0623

General non-fiction and fiction (home 10%, overseas 20%). Special interests: women's fiction, crime, thrillers, narrative non-fiction. No short stories, film/TV scripts, poetry or plays. No reading fee, but preliminary letter with synopsis, first chapter and sae essential. Works with agents in USA and most foreign countries. Founded 1986.

Juvenilia

Avington, Winchester, Hants SO21 1DB
tel/fax (01962) 779656
email juvenilia@clara.co.uk
Contact Mrs Rosemary Bromley

Full-length MSS for the children's market, fiction and non-fiction (home 10%, overseas from 15%), illustration (10%), performance rights (10%). Short stories only if specifically for picture books, radio or TV. No unsolicited MSS; preliminary letter with sae and full details essential. Postage for acknowledgement and return of material imperative. No fax, telephone or email enquiries. Founded 1973.

Michelle Kass Associates*

36-38 Glasshouse Street, London W1B 5DL
tel 020-7439 1624 *fax* 020-7734 3394
Proprietor Michelle Kass

Full-length MSS. Literary fiction and drama scripts for film (home 10%, overseas 15–20%). Will suggest revision where appropriate. Works with agents overseas. No reading fee. Absolutely no unsolicited MSS without a preliminary phone call. Founded 1991.

Frances Kelly Agency*

111 Clifton Road, Kingston-upon-Thames, Surrey KT2 6PL
tel 020-8549 7830 *fax* 020-8547 0051

Full-length MSS. Non-fiction: general and academic, reference and professional books, all subjects (home 10%, overseas 20%), TV, radio (10%). No reading fee, but no unsolicited MSS; preliminary letter with synopsis, CV and return postage essential. Founded 1978.

Peter Knight Agency

20 Crescent Grove, London SW4 7AH
tel 020-7622 1467 *fax* 020-7622 1522
email peter@knightfeatures.co.uk
Director Peter Knight, *Associates* Ann King-Hall, Gaby Martin, Andrew Knight, Samantha Ferris

Motor sports, cartoon books, business, history, and factual and biographical material. No poetry, science fiction or cookery. Overseas associates: United Media (USA), Auspac Media (Australia). No unsolicited MSS. Send letter accompanied by CV and sae with synopsis of proposed work.

Clients include David Kerr Cameron, Frank Dickens, Christopher Hilton, Gray Jolliffe, Angus McGill, Chris Maslanka, Barbara Minto. Founded 1985.

Labour & Management Ltd

Milton House, Milton Street, Waltham Abbey, Essex EN9 1EZ
tel/fax (01992) 711511/614527
email triciasumner@email.msn.com
Director Tricia Sumner

Writers for film, theatre, TV, radio. Also full-length MSS, fiction and non-fiction (home 12.5%, overseas 20%). Special interests (not exclusively): multicultural, gay, feminist, anti-establishment. No new authors taken on except by recommendation.

Clients include Marion Baraitser, Kathleen Kiirik Bryson, John R. Gordon, Barry Grossman, Angela Lanyon, Chris Madoch, Roland Moore, Jeremy Rayner. Founded 1995.

LAW Ltd (Lucas Alexander Whitley)*

(incorporating Jacintha Alexander Associates)
14 Vernon Street, London W14 0RJ
tel 020-7471 7900 *fax* 020-7471 7910
email firstname@lawagency.co.uk
Contact Mark Lucas, Julian Alexander, Araminta Whitley, Philippa Milnes-Smith, Celia Hayley, Lucinda Cook, Peta Nightingale, Alice Saunders, Helen Mulligan

Full-length adult and children's commercial and literary fiction and non-fiction (home 15%, US and translation 20%). No poetry, plays, textbooks, or fantasy. Film and TV scripts handled for established clients only. Unsolicited MSS considered; send brief covering letter, short synopsis and 2 sample chapters. Sae essential. No submissions by email. Overseas associates. Founded 1996.

Cat Ledger Literary Agency*

20-21 Newman Street, London W1T 1PG
tel 020-7861 8226 *fax* 020-7861 8001

General non-fiction and fiction but no short stories, film/TV scripts, poetry or plays (home 10%, overseas 20%). No reading fee but preliminary letter, synopsis and sae essential. Represented in all foreign countries.

Barbara Levy Literary Agency*

64 Greenhill, Hampstead High Street, London NW3 5TZ
tel 020-7435 9046 *fax* 020-7431 2063
Director Barbara Levy, *Associate* John Selby

Full-length MSS. Fiction and general non-fiction (home 10%, overseas by arrangement). Film and TV rights for existing clients only. No reading fee, but preliminary letter with synopsis and sae essential. Translation rights handled by the **Marsh Agency**; works in conjunction with US agents. Founded 1986.

Limelight Management*

33 Newman Street, London W1T 1PY
tel 020-7637 2529 *fax* 020-7637 2538
email limelight.management@virgin.net
website www.limelightmanagement.com
Directors Fiona Lindsay, Linda Shanks

Full-length and short MSS. Food, wine, health, crafts, gardening, interior design (home 15%, overseas 20%), TV and radio rights (10–20%); will suggest revision where appropriate. No reading fee. Founded 1991.

The Christopher Little Literary Agency*

10 Eel Brook Studios, 125 Moore Park Road, London SW6 4PS
tel 020-7736 4455 *fax* 020-7736 4490
email christopher@christopherlittle.net
christianname@christopherlittle.net
Contacts Christopher Little, Kellee Nunley, Emma Schlesinger

Commercial and literary full-length fiction and non-fiction (home 15%; US, Canada, translation, audio, motion picture 20%). No poetry, plays, science fiction, fantasy, textbooks, illustrated children's or short stories. Film scripts for established clients only. No reading fee. No unsolicited submissions. Founded 1979.

London Independent Books

26 Chalcot Crescent, London NW1 8YD
tel 020-7706 0486 *fax* 020-7724 3122
Proprietor Carolyn Whitaker

Specialises in commercial, fantasy and teenage fiction, show business, travel. Full-length MSS (home 15%, overseas 20%), films, TV and sound broadcasting (15%). Will suggest revision of promising MSS. No reading fee.

Authors include Eric Braun, Keith Gray, Tim Mackintosh-Smith, Glenn Mitchell, Connie Monk, Richard Morgan, Kevin Rushby, Emma Sinclair, Chris Wooding. Founded 1971.

Andrew Lownie Literary Agency*

17 Sutherland Street, London SW1V 4JU
tel 020-7828 1274 *fax* 020-7828 7608
email lownie@globalnet.co.uk
website www.andrewlownie.co.uk
Director Andrew Lownie

Full-length MSS. Biography, history, reference, current affairs, and packaging journalists and celebrities for the book market (worldwide 15%). No reading fee; will suggest a revision.

Authors include Theo Aronson, Juliet Barker, Guy Bellamy, the Joyce Cary Estate, Tom Devine, Peter Evans, David Fisher, Jonathan Fryer, Laurence Gardner, Timothy Good, Lawrence James, Leo McKinstry, Julian Maclaren-Ross Estate, Norma Major, Sir John Mills, Tom Pocock, Nick Pope, Martin Pugh, John Rae, Richard Rudgley, Desmond Seward, David Stafford, Andrew Wheatcroft, Alan Whicker; *The Oxford Classical Dictionary*, *The Cambridge Guide to Literature in English*. Founded 1988.

Lucas Alexander Whitley – see LAW Ltd

Jennifer Luithlen Agency

88 Holmfield Road, Leicester LE2 1SB
tel 0116-273 8863 *fax* 0116-273 5697
Agents Jennifer Luithlen, Penny Luithlen

Not looking for new clients. Children's books; adult fiction: crime, historical, saga (home 10%, overseas 20%), performance rights (15%). Founded 1986.

Lutyens & Rubinstein*

231 Westbourne Park Road, London W11 1EB
tel 020-7792 4855 *fax* 020-7792 4833
Directors Sarah Lutyens, Felicity Rubinstein
Submissions Susannah Godman

Fiction and non-fiction, commercial and literary (home 15%, overseas 20%). Send outline/2 sample chapters and sae. No reading fee. Founded 1993.

Duncan McAra

28 Beresford Gardens, Edinburgh EH5 3ES
tel/fax 0131-552 1558
email duncanmcara@hotmail.com

Literary fiction; non-fiction: art, architecture, archaeology, biography, military, Scottish, travel (home 10%, overseas 20%). Preliminary letter with sae essential. No reading fee. Founded 1988.

Eunice McMullen Children's Literary Agent Ltd

Low Ibbotsholme Cottage, Off Bridge Lane, Troutbeck Bridge, Windermere, Cumbria LA23 1HU
tel (01539) 448551 *fax* (01539) 442289
email eunicemcmullen@totalise.co.uk
Director Eunice McMullen

All types of children's books, particularly picture books (home 10%, overseas 15%). No unsolicited scripts. Telephone enquiries only.

Authors include Wayne Anderson, Reg Cartwright, Ross Collins, Jason Cockcroft, Charles Fuge, Susie Jenkin-Pearce, Maggie Kneen, David Melling, Sue Porter, Angela McAllister, Susan Winter, David Wood. Founded 1992.

Andrew Mann Ltd*

(in association with Jane Conway-Gordon)
1 Old Compton Street, London W1D 5JA
tel 020-7734 4751 *fax* 020-7287 9264
Directors Anne Dewe, Tina Betts

Full-length MSS. Scripts for TV, cinema, radio and theatre (home 15%, USA and Europe 20%). Associated with agents worldwide. No reading fee, but no unsolicited MSS without preliminary enquiry and sae. Founded 1974.

Manuscript ReSearch

PO Box 33, Bicester, Oxon OX6 7PP
tel (01869) 323447 *fax* (01869) 324096
Proprietor T.G. Jenkins

Now concentrating on film/TV and radio scripts. No reading fee, but sae for script return essential. Founded 1988.

Marjacq Scripts

34 Devonshire Place, London W1G 6JW
tel 020-7935 9499 *fax* 020-7935 9115
email enquiries@marjacq.com
website www.marjacq.com
Contact Mark Hayward

Full-length MSS (home10%, overseas 20%). Crime, thrillers, science fiction, women's commercial fiction. Will suggest revision.

Authors include Benita Brown, Richard Craze, James Follett, Ros Jay, Jeannie Johnson, Elizabeth Lord, Michael Taylor, R.D. Wingfield. Founded 1974.

The Marsh Agency Ltd*

11-12 Dover Street, London W1S 4LJ
tel 020-7399 2800 *fax* 020-7399 2801
email enquiries@marsh-agency.co.uk
website www.marsh-agency.co.uk
Director Paul Marsh

Specialises in international rights, selling English and foreign language writing. No TV, film, radio or theatre. Unsolicited submissions (outline and sample chapters) accepted by email. See also **Paterson Marsh Ltd**.

Clients include British, American and Canadian agencies and publishers as well as individual authors. Founded 1994.

Judy Martin

The Basement, 94 Goldhurst Terrace, London NW6 3HS
tel 020-7372 8422 *fax* 020-7372 8423

Fiction, non-fiction, biography and popular culture (home 15%, overseas 20%). No plays, poetry, cookery, gardening or children's stories. Translation rights handled by the **Marsh Agency**. No reading fee, but sae required for all unsolicited MSS, together with details of publishing history. Founded 1990.

Martinez Literary Agency

60 Oakwood Avenue, London N14 6QL
tel 020-8886 5829
Contacts Françoise Budd, Mary Martinez

Fiction, children's books, arts and crafts, interior design, alternative health and complementary medicine, cookery, autobiographies, popular music, sport and memorabilia (home 15%; US, overseas and translation 20%; performance rights 20%). Not acceptingany new writers. Founded 1988.

Blanche Marvin

21A St John's Wood High Street, London NW8 7NG
tel/fax 020-7722 2313

Full-length MSS (15%), performance rights. No reading fee but return postage essential.

Authors include Christopher Bond.

MBA Literary Agents Ltd*

62 Grafton Way, London W1T 5DW
tel 020-7387 2076 *fax* 020-7387 2042
email firstname@mbalit.co.uk
Contact Diana Tyler, John Richard Parker, Meg Davis, Laura Longrigg

Handles fiction and non-fiction, and TV, film, radio and theatre scripts (home 15%, overseas 20%; theatre, TV, radio 10%; films 10–20%). No unsolicited material. Works in conjunction with agents in most countries. UK representative for **Writers House LLC**, the Donald Maass Agency and the **Jabberwocky Literary Agency**.

Clients include Campbell Armstrong, A.L. Barker, *The Chap Magazine*, Estate of Harry Bowling, Jeffrey Caine, Glenn Chandler, Andrew Cowan, Patricia Finney, Maggie Furey, Sue Gee, Joanna Hines, the estate of B.S. Johnson, Anne McCaffrey, Paul Magrs, Susan Oudot, Sir Roger Penrose, Anne Perry, Gervase Phinn, Iain Sinclair, Steve Strange, Mark Wallington, Douglas Watkinson, Paul Wilson, Valerie Windsor. Founded 1971.

Midland Exposure

4 Victoria Court, Oadby, Leicester LE2 4AF
tel 0116-271 8332 *fax* 0116-281 2188
email partners@midlandexposure.co.uk
website www.midlandexposure.co.uk
Partners Cari Crook and Lesley Gleeson

Women's magazine fiction only (home initially 25%, overseas 20%). Phone for current reading fee rates. Will suggest revision. Founded 1996.

Laura Morris Literary Agency

21 Highshore Road, London SE15 5AA
tel 020-7732 0153 *fax* 020-7732 9022
email laura.morris@ukgateway.net
Director Laura Morris

Literary fiction, film studies, biography, media, cookery, culture/art, humour (home 10%, overseas 20%). No unsolicited MSS.

Authors include Peter Cowie, Laurence Marks and Maurice Gran, David Thomson, Brian Turner. Founded 1998.

William Morris Agency (UK) Ltd*

52-53 Poland Street, London W1F 7LX
tel 020-7534 6800 *fax* 020-7534 6900
website www.wma.com
Managing Director Stephanie Cabot

Worldwide theatrical and literary agency with offices in New York, Beverly Hills and Nashville, and associates in Sydney. Handles film and TV scripts, TV formats; fiction and general non-fiction (film/TV 10%, UK books 15%, US books and translation 20%). No unsolicited material; MSS only when preceded by letter. No reading fee. London office founded 1965.

Judith Murdoch Literary Agency

19 Chalcot Square, London NW1 8YA
tel 020-7722 4197

Full-length fiction only (home 15%, overseas 20%). No thrillers, science fiction/ fantasy, poetry, short stories or children's. Approach by letter, *not* telephone, sending the first 2 chapters and synopsis. Return postage/sae essential. Editorial advice given; no reading fee. Translation rights handled by the **Marsh Agency**. Founded 1993.

Negotiate Ltd

99 Caiyside, Edinburgh EH10 7HR
tel 0131-445 7571
email florence@negweb.com
website www.negotiate.co.uk
Contact Florence Kennedy

Specialises in the negotiation of author's contracts and subsidiary rights. Established authors only or new authors with draft contract from a publisher. Preliminary letter or fax please. Founded 1986.

Maggie Noach Literary Agency*

22 Dorville Crescent, London W6 0HJ
tel 020-8748 2926 *fax* 020-8748 8057
email m-noach@dircon.co.uk

General fiction and non-fiction, especially biography, travel, history and current events; non-illustrated children's books. Full-length MSS (home 15%, US/translation 20%). No scientific, academic or specialist non-fiction; no poetry, plays, short stories or books for the very young. Very few new clients taken on as it is considered vital to give individual attention to each author's work. Unsolicited MSS not welcome. Approach by letter (not by telephone), giving a brief description of the book and enclosing 2 sample chapters. Return postage essential. No reading fee. Founded 1982.

Andrew Nurnberg Associates Ltd*

Clerkenwell House, 45-47 Clerkenwell Green, London EC1R 0HT
tel 020-7417 8800 *fax* 020-7417 8812
email all@nurnberg.co.uk

Specialises in the sale of translation rights of English and American authors into European languages.

Alexandra Nye, Writers & Agents

Craigower, 6 Kinnoull Avenue, Dunblane, Perthshire FK15 9JB
tel (01786) 825114
Director Alexandra Nye

Literary fiction, Scottish history, biographies; no poetry or plays (home 10%, overseas 20%, translation 15%). Preliminary letter with synopsis preferred; sae essential for return. Reading fee for supply of detailed report on MSS. Founded 1991.

Deborah Owen Ltd*

78 Narrow Street, Limehouse, London E14 8BP
tel 020-7987 5119/5441 *fax* 020-7538 4004
Contact Deborah Owen, Michal Shault

Small agency specialising in representing authors direct around the world. International fiction and non-fiction – books which can be translated into a number of languages (home 10%, USA/translation 15%). No new authors.

Clients include Penelope Farmer, Amos Oz, Delia Smith. Founded 1971.

David O'Leary Literary Agency

10 Lansdowne Court, Lansdowne Rise, London W11 2NR
tel 020-7229 1623 *fax* 020-7727 9624
email d.o'leary@virgin.net

Popular and literary fiction and non-fiction. Special interests: Ireland, history, science (home 10%, overseas 20%, performance rights 15%). Will suggest revision; no reading fee. Write or call before submitting MSS; please enclose sae.

Authors include Alexander Cordell, David Crackanthorpe, Jim Lusby, Derek Malcolm, Ken Russell. Founded 1988.

Mark Paterson & Associates – see Paterson Marsh Ltd

Paterson Marsh Ltd*

(merged with the Marsh Agency Ltd 2001)
11-12 Dover Street, London W15 4LJ
tel 020-7399 2800 *fax* 020-7399 2801
email paterson@patersonmarsh.co.uk
website www.patersonmarsh.co.uk
Contact Mark Paterson, Stephanie Ebdon

Book-length MSS; general but with special experience in psychoanalysis, psychotherapy, history and education (20% worldwide including sub-agents' commission). No fiction, articles or short stories except for existing clients. Preliminary letter with synopsis, sample material and return postage essential.

Authors include Sigmund Freud, Anna Freud, Hugh Brogan, Donald Winnicott, Peter Moss, Sir Arthur Evans, Dorothy Richardson, Hugh Schonfield, Georg Groddeck, Patrick Casement, John Seely. Founded 1955.

John Pawsey

60 High Street, Tarring, Worthing,
West Sussex BN14 7NR
tel/fax (01903) 205167

General non-fiction, particularly biography, popular culture and sport; crime, thriller, suspense and genuinely original fiction only (home 10–15%, overseas 19–25%). No unsolicited material, poetry, short stories, journalism, children's or original film and stage scripts. Preliminary letter and return postage with all correspondence essential. Works in association with agencies in the USA, Europe and the Far East. Will suggest revision if MS sufficiently promising. No reading fee.

Authors include Jonathan Agnew, Jennie Bond, Patricia Hall, Elwyn Hartley Edwards, Dr David Lewis, Peter Hobday, Jon Silverman. Founded 1981.

Maggie Pearlstine Associates Ltd*

31 Ashley Gardens, Ambrosden Avenue,
London SW1P 1QE
tel 020-7828 4212 *fax* 020-7834 5546
email post@pearlstine.co.uk

General non-fiction and fiction. Special interests: history, current affairs, biography, health (home 10–12.5%; overseas, journalism and media 20%). Translation rights handled by Gillon Aitken Associates Ltd. No children's, poetry, horror, science fiction, short stories or scripts. Seldom takes on new authors. Prospective clients should write an explanatory letter and enclose a sae and the first chapter only. No submissions accepted by fax, email or from abroad. No reading fee.

Authors include Debbie Beckerman, John Biffen, Matthew Baylis, Kate Bingham, Menzies Campbell, Kim Fletcher, Fiona Harrold, Roy Hattersley, Rachel Holmes, Charles Kennedy, Mark Leonard, Claire Macdonald, Eleanor Mills, Dr Raj Persaud, Prof Lesley Regan, Hugo Rifkind, Winifred Robinson, Jackie Rowley, Henrietta Spencer-Churchill, Alan Stewart, Prof Robert Winston. Founded 1989.

The Peters Fraser and Dunlop Group Ltd – see PFD

PFD*

(incorporating A.D. Peters & Co. Ltd, Fraser & Dunlop Scripts Ltd, Fraser & Dunlop Ltd, June Hall Literary Agency Ltd, Watergate Film Services Ltd)
Drury House, 34-43 Russell Street,
London WC2B 5HA
tel 020-7344 1000 *fax* 020-7836 9539
email postmaster@pfd.co.uk
website www.pfd.co.uk
Joint Chairmen Anthony Jones and Tim Corrie, *Managing Director* Anthony Baring, *Books* Caroline Dawnay, Michael Sissons, Pat Kavanagh, Charles Walker, Rosemary Canter, Rosemary Scoular, Robert Kirby, Simon Trewin, James Gill, *Serial* Pat Kavanagh, Carol Macarthur, *Film/TV* Tim Corrie, Anthony Jones, Norman North, Charles Walker, Vanessa Jones, St John Donald, Natasha Galloway, Louisa Thompson, Jago Irwin, *Actors* Maureen Vincent, Ginette Chalmers, Dallas Smith, Lindy King, Ruth Cooper, Ruth Young, Lucy Brazier, *Theatre* Kenneth Ewing, St John Donald, Nicki Stoddart, Rosie Cobbe, *Children's* Rosemary Canter, *New Media* Rosemary Scoular, *Translation Rights* Intercontinental Literary Agency, *US Illustrators' Representation* Harriet Kasak

Handles the full range of books including fiction, children's and non-fiction as well as scripts for film, theatre, radio and TV, actors and multimedia projects (home 10%; US and translation 20%). Has 75 years of international experience in all media. Send a full outline for non-fiction and short synopsis for fiction with 2 or 3 sample chapters and autobiographical note. Screenplays/TV scripts should be addressed to the 'Film & Script Dept'. The Children's Dept does not accept unsolicited written material but welcomes work from illustrators seeking representation. Material submitted on an exclusive basis preferred; in any event it should be disclosed if material is being submitted to other agencies or publishers. Return postage essential. No reading fee. No guaranteed response to submissions by email.

Pollinger Ltd

(formerly Laurence Pollinger Ltd, successor of Pearn, Pollinger and Higham)
3rd Floor, Goldsmith's House,
137-141 Regent Street, London W1B 4HZ
tel/fax 020-7025 7820
email info@pollingerltd.com
website www.pollingerltd.com
Chairman Paul Woolf, *Managing Director* Lesley Pollinger, *Adult List* Lorella Belli, *Children's List* Linda Jennings, *Permissions/Foreign Rights* Heather Chalcroft, *Consultant* Gerald Pollinger

All types of general trade adult and children's fiction and non-fiction books; intellectual property development; illustrators/photographers (home 15%, translation 20%). Unsolicited material considered only if preceded by letter or email. Overseas and media associates, including Oak Media.

Clients include Roy Apps, Dougie Brimson, Michael Coleman, Michael Cox, Philip Gross, Gene Kemp, Adrienne Kennaway, Gary Latham, Alan McDonald, Nicha Minhas, Gary Paulsen, Nicholas Rhea, Sue Welford; also the estates of H.E. Bates, Louis Bromfield, Erskine Caldwell, Vera Chapman, D.H. Lawrence, John Masters, Alan Moorehead, W. Heath Robinson, William Saroyan, Clifford D. Simak and other notables. Founded 2002.

Murray Pollinger – see David Higham Associates Ltd

Shelley Power Literary Agency Ltd*

13 rue du Pre Saint Gervais, 75019 Paris, France
tel 42 38 36 49 *fax* 40 40 70 08
email shelley.power@wanadoo.fr

General fiction and non-fiction. Full-length MSS (home 10%, USA and translation 19%). No children's books, poetry or plays. Works in conjunction with agents abroad. No reading fee, but preliminary letter with return postage as from UK or France essential. No submissions by email. Also based in the UK. Founded 1976.

Elizabeth Puttick Literary Agency

46 Brookfield Mansions, Highgate West Hill, London N6 6AT
tel 020-8340 6383 *fax* 020-8340 6384
email agency@puttick.com
website www.puttick.com
Director Elizabeth Puttick

Full-length MSS (home 15%, overseas 20%). General non-fiction with special interest in self-help, Mind, Body & Spirit, health, childcare, cookery, business, science, biography, history, current affairs, women's issues, illustrated books, TV and film tie-ins. No poetry, drama, children's books. No reading fee. Send preliminary letter with synopsis; return postage essential.

Authors include William Bloom, Robin Bloor, Ann-Marie Gallagher, Emma Restall Orr, Eddie and Debbie Shapiro. Founded 1995.

PVA Management Ltd

Hallow Park, Worcester WR2 6PG
tel (01905) 640663 *fax* (01905) 641842
email pva@pva.co.uk
Managing Director Paul Vaughan

Full-length MSS. Non-fiction only (home 15%, overseas 20%, performance rights 15%). Please send synopsis and sample chapters together with return postage.

Radala & Associates

17 Avenue Mansions, Finchley Road, London NW3 7AX
tel 020-7794 4495 *fax* 020-7431 7636
email bt.press@lineone.net
Contacts Richard Gollner, Neil Hornick, Anna Swan, Andy Marino
Creative/editorial consultancy Robert Lambolle
tel 020-8455 4564
email ziph@appleonline.net

Quality fiction, non-fiction, performing and popular arts, psychotherapy (home 10%, USA 15–20%, translation 20%). Send a short letter plus synopsis (2pp max.), and first 2 chapters if a novel plus sae for return. Only considers writers with solid publication/production track records. Also provides editorial services and initiates in-house projects. Overseas associates: **Writers House** (Albert Zuckermann), New York, plus agents throughout Europe. Founded 1970.

Margaret Ramsay Ltd – now Casarotto Ramsay & Associates Ltd

The Lisa Richards Agency

46 Upper Baggot Street, Dublin 4, Republic of Ireland
tel (01) 660 3534 *fax* (01) 660 3545
email fogrady@eircom.net
Contact Faith O'Grady

Fiction, non-fiction, children's (home 10%, UK 15%, overseas 20%). Translation rights handled by the **Marsh Agency**. No reading fee.

Authors include Martin Malone, Pauline McLynn, David O'Doherty, Damien Owens, Annie Sparrow. Founded 1998.

Rogers, Coleridge & White Ltd*

20 Powis Mews, London W11 1JN
tel 020-7221 3717 *fax* 020-7229 9084
Directors Deborah Rogers, Gill Coleridge, Patricia White (USA), David Miller, Laurence Laluyaux, *Consultant* Ann Warnford-Davis, *USA Associate* International Creative Management, Inc.

Full-length book MSS, including children's books (home 10%, USA 15%, translation 20%). No unsolicited MSS please, and no submissions by fax or email. Founded 1967.

Elizabeth Roy Literary Agency

White Cottage, Greatford, Nr Stamford, Lincs. PE9 4PR
tel/fax (01778) 560672

Children's fiction and non-fiction – writers and illustrators (home 10–15%, overseas 20%). Will suggest revision. Preliminary letter, synopsis and sample chapters essential with names of publishers and agents previously contacted. Return postage essential. No reading fee. Founded 1990.

Uli Rushby-Smith

72 Plimsoll Road, London N4 2EE
tel/fax 020-7354 2718
Director Uli Rushby-Smith

Fiction and non-fiction, literary and commercial (home 15%, USA/foreign 20%). UK representatives of **Curtis Brown Ltd**, New York (children's books) and Penguin Canada, Penguin South Africa, Columbia University Press (USA), Alice Toledo Agency (Netherlands). Send outline, sample chapters and return postage; no reading fee. Founded 1993.

Saddler Literary Agency

9 Curzon Road, London W5 1NE
tel 020-8998 4868 *fax* 020-8998 8851
email john@saddlerj.fsnet.co.uk
Proprietor John Saddler

Quality fiction and non-fiction (home 10%, overseas 20%). No reading fee. Will suggest revision. Founded 2001.

Rosemary Sandberg Ltd

6 Bayley Street, London WC1B 3HB
tel 020-7304 4110 *fax* 020-7304 4109
Directors Rosemary Sandberg, Ed Victor, Graham Greene CBE

Children's – writers and illustrators, general fiction and non-fiction. Absolutely no unsolicited MSS: client list is full. Founded 1991.

The Sayle Literary Agency*

Bickerton House, 25-27 Bickerton Road, London N19 5JT
tel 020-7263 8681 *fax* 020-7561 0529
email info@sayleliteraryagency.com
website www.sayleliteraryagency.com
Proprietor Rachel Calder

Fiction: general and crime. Non-fiction: current affairs, social issues, travel, biographies, historical (home 10%, US/translation 20%). No plays, poetry, textbooks, children's, technical, legal or medical books. No unsolicited MSS. No reading fee but preliminary letter and return postage essential. Overseas associates: Elaine Markson Literary Agency, Darhansoff, Verrill and Feldman, and Anne Edelstein Literary Agency USA. Translation rights handled by the **Marsh Agency**. Film and TV rights handled by **Sayle Screen Ltd**

Sayle Screen Ltd*

11 Jubilee Place, London SW3 3TD
tel 020-7823 3883 *fax* 020-7823 3363
email info@saylescreen.com
website www.saylescreen.com
Agents Jane Villiers, Matthew Bates, Toby Moorcroft, Cathy Kehoe

Specialises in scripts for film, TV, theatre and radio (home 10%, overseas 15–20%). Works in conjunction with agents in

New York and Los Angeles. No reading fee but preliminary letter and return postage essential. Represents film and TV rights in fiction and non-fiction for the **Sayle Literary Agency** and **BlackAmber Books**.

The Sharland Organisation Ltd

The Manor House, Manor Street, Raunds, Northants. NN9 6JW
tel (01933) 626600 *fax* (01933) 624860
email tsoshar@aol.com
Directors Mike Sharland, Alice Sharland

Specialises in film, TV, stage and radio rights throughout the world (home 15%, overseas 20%); also negotiates multimedia, interactive TV deals and computer game contracts. Works in conjunction with overseas agents. Preliminary letter and return postage is essential. Founded 1988.

Sheil Land Associates Ltd*

(incorporating Richard Scott Simon Ltd 1971 and Christy & Moore Ltd 1912)
43 Doughty Street, London WC1N 2LH
tel 020-7405 9351 *fax* 020-7831 2127
email info@sheilland.co.uk
Agents UK and US Sonia Land, Luigi Bonomi, Sam Boyce, Vivien Green, Amanda Preston, *Film/theatre/TV* John Rush, Roland Baggot, *Foreign* Amelia Cummins

Full-length general, commercial, quality and literary fiction and non-fiction, including: social politics, history, military history, gardening, thrillers, crime, romance, fantasy, drama, biography, travel, cookery, humour, UK and foreign estates (home 15%, USA/translation 20%). Also theatre, film, radio and TV scripts. Welcomes approaches from new clients either to start or to develop their careers. Preliminary letter with sae essential. No reading fee. Overseas associates: Georges Borchardt, Inc. (Richard Scott Simon). UK representatives for Farrar, Straus & Giroux, Inc. US film and TV representation: CAA, APA and others.

Clients include Peter Ackroyd, John Blashford-Snell, Seve Ballesteros, Melvyn Bragg, Stephanie Calman, Catherine Cookson Estate, Anna del Conte, Elizabeth Corley, Seamus Deane, Alan Drury, Erik Durschmied, Alan Garner, Bonnie Greer, Susan Hill, Richard Holmes, HRH The Prince of Wales, John Humphrys, James Long, Richard Mabey, Colin McDowell, Richard Madeley and Judy Finnigan, Patrick O'Brian Estate, Esther Rantzen, Pam Rhodes, Jean Rhys Estate, Martin Riley, Colin Schindler, Tom Sharpe, Martin Stephen, Brian Sykes, Jeffrey Tayler, Alan Titchmarsh, Rose Tremain, John Wilsher, Paul Wilson, Chris Woodhead. Founded 1962.

Anthony Sheil

29 Fernshaw Road, London SW10 0TG
tel 020-7351 7561 *fax* 020-7376 3594
email reception@aitkenassoc.demon.co.uk
Proprietor Anthony Sheil

Quality and literary fiction (home 10%, overseas 20%). No reading fee. Works in conjunction with **Gillon Aitken Associates Ltd**.

Authors include Caroline Alexander, John Banville, Josephine Cox, John Fowles, John Keegan, Robert Wilson.

Caroline Sheldon Literary Agency*

London office 71 Hillgate Place, London W8 7SS
tel 020-7727 9102
mailing address Thorley Manor Farm, Thorley, Yarmouth, Isle of Wight PO41 0SJ
tel (01983) 760205
Proprietor Caroline Sheldon

Full-length MSS. General fiction, women's fiction, and children's books (home 10%, overseas 20%). No reading fee. Synopsis and first 3 chapters with large sae in case of return required initially. Founded 1985.

Jeffrey Simmons

10 Lowndes Square, London SW1X 9HA
tel 020-7235 8852 *fax* 020-7235 9733

Specialises in fiction (no science fiction, horror or fantasy), biography, autobiography, show business, personality books, law, crime, politics, world affairs. Full-length MSS (home from 10%, overseas from 15%). Will suggest revision. No reading fee, but preliminary letter essential.

Richard Scott Simon Ltd – **see Sheil Land Associates Ltd***

Sinclair-Stevenson

3 South Terrace, London SW7 2TB
tel/fax 020-7581 2550
Directors Christopher Sinclair-Stevenson, Deborah Sinclair-Stevenson

Full-length MSS (home 10%, USA/translation 20%). General – no children's books. No reading fee; will suggest a revision. Founded 1995.

Robert Smith Literary Agency Ltd*

12 Bridge Wharf, 156 Caledonian Road,
London N1 9UU
tel 020-7278 2444 *fax* 020-7833 5680
email robertsmith.literaryagency@virgin.net
Partners Robert Smith and Anne Smith

Non-fiction: autobiography and biography, health and nutrition, Mind, Body and Spirit, cookery, lifestyle, popular culture, music, TV and film tie-ins, true crime, investigative journalism, illustrated books (home 15%, overseas 20%). No unsolicited MSS. Will suggest revision.

Authors include Stewart Evans, Neil and Christine Hamilton, James Haspiel, Christine Keeler, Roberta Kray, Norman Parker, Mike Reid, Keith Skinner, Douglas Thompson. Founded 1997.

Abner Stein*

10 Roland Gardens, London SW7 3PH
tel 020-7373 0456 *fax* 020-7370 6316
Contact Abner Stein, Arabella Stein

Full-length and short MSS (home 10%, overseas 20%). No reading fee, but no unsolicited MSS; preliminary letter and return postage required.

Micheline Steinberg Playwrights' Agent

409 Triumph House, 187-191 Regent Street,
London W1R 7WF
tel 020-7287 4383 *fax* 020-7287 4384
email SteinPlays@aol.com

Full-length MSS – theatre, films, TV, radio (home 10%, overseas 15%). Dramatic Associate for **Pollinger Ltd**; works in conjunction with agents in USA and other countries. No reading fee, but preliminary letter essential and return postage with MSS. Founded 1987.

Rochelle Stevens & Co.

2 Terretts Place, Upper Street, London N1 1QZ
tel 020-7359 3900 *fax* 020-7354 5729
email info@rochellestevens.com
Proprietor Rochelle Stevens, *Associates* Frances Arnold, Lucy Fawcett

Drama scripts for film, TV, theatre and radio (10%); will suggest revision where appropriate. No reading fee, but preliminary letter and return postage essential. Founded 1984.

Shirley Stewart Literary Agency

3rd Floor, 21 Denmark Street, London WC2H 8NA
tel 020-7836 4440 *fax* 020-7836 3482
Director Shirley Stewart

Specialises in literary fiction and general non-fiction (home 10–15%, overseas 20%). No poetry, plays, film scripts, science fiction, fantasy or children's books. No reading fee. Send preliminary letter, synopsis and first 3 chapters plus return postage.Founded 1993.

The Susijn Agency

3rd Floor, 64 Great Titchfield Street,
London W1W 7QH
tel 020-7580 6341 *fax* 020-7580 8626
email info@thesusijnagency.com
website www.thesusijnagency.com
Director Laura Susijn

Specialises in world rights in English and non-English language literature: literary fiction and general non-fiction (home 10–15%, overseas 15–20%, theatre/film/TV/ radio 15%). Send synopsis and 2 sample chapters. No reading fee.

Authors include Peter Ackroyd, Robin Baker, Radhika Jha, Anita Nair, Joydeep Roy-Bhattacharya, Karl Shaw, Paul Sussman, Stephen Thompson, Alex Wheatle, Adam Zameenzad. Founded 1998.

The Tennyson Agency

10 Cleveland Avenue, London SW20 9EW
tel/fax 020-8543 5939
email agency@tenagy.co.uk
website www.tenagy.co.uk
Theatre, TV & Film Scripts Christopher Oxford, *Arts/Humanities* Adam Sheldon

Scripts and related material for theatre, film and TV (home 15%, overseas 20%). Will suggest revision. No reading fee.

Clients include Vivienne Allen, Iain Grant, Philip Hurd-Wood, Joanna Leigh, John Ryan, Walter Saunders, Diana Ward. Founded 2002.

J.M. Thurley Management

30 Cambridge Road, Teddington,
Middlesex TW11 8DR
tel 020-8977 3176 *fax* 020-8943 2678
email JMThurley@aol.com
Contact Jon Thurley

Specialises in commercial and literary full-length fiction and commercial work for film and TV. No plays, poetry, short stories, articles or fantasy. No reading fee but preliminary letter and sae essential. Editorial/creative advice provided to clients (home 15%, overseas 20%). Links with leading US and European agents. Founded 1976.

Lavinia Trevor*
The Glasshouse, 49A Goldhawk Road, London W12 8QP
tel 020-8749 8481 *fax* 020-8749 7377

Fiction and non-fiction, including popular science, for the general reader. No children's books or science fiction. No reading fee. Brief autobiographical letter and approx. first 50 pages required plus sae. Founded 1993.

Jane Turnbull*
13 Wendell Road, London W12 9RS
tel 020-8743 9580 *fax* 020-8749 6079

Fiction and non-fiction (home 10%, USA/translation 20%), performance rights (15%). No science fiction, romantic fiction, children's or short stories. Works in conjunction with **Gillon Aitken Associates Ltd** for sale of translation rights. No reading fee. Preliminary letter and sae essential; no unsolicited MSS. Founded 1986.

United Authors Ltd
11-15 Betterton Street, London WC2H 9BP
tel 020-7470 8886 *fax* 020-7470 8887
email utdauthors@clara.net

Fiction, non-fiction, children's, biography, travel. Full-length MSS (home 10%, overseas 15%), short MSS (12%/20%), film and radio (15%/20%), TV (15%/15%). Will suggest revision.

Authors include Charlotte Bingham, John Bingham (estate), Terence Brady, Sydney Gilliatt, Peter Willet. Founded 1998.

Ed Victor Ltd*
6 Bayley Street, Bedford Square, London WC1B 3HE
tel 020-7304 4100 *fax* 020-7304 4111
Executive Chairman Ed Victor, *Joint Managing Directors* Sophie Hicks, Margaret Phillips, *Directors* Carol Ryan, Graham C. Greene *H*cbe, Leon Morgan, Hitesh Shah

Full-length MSS, fiction and non-fiction, but no short stories, film/TV scripts, poetry or plays (home 15%, USA 15%, translation 20%), performance rights (15%). Represented in all foreign markets. No unsolicited MSS.

Authors include Eoin Colfer, Sir Ranulph Fiennes, Frederick Forsyth, A.A. Gill, Josephine Hart, Jack Higgins, Erica Jong, Nigella Lawson, Kathy Lette, Allan Mallinson, Nigel Nicolson, Anne Robinson, and the estates of Douglas Adams, Raymond Chandler, Dame Iris Murdoch, Sir Stephen Spender, Irving Wallace. Founded 1976.

Robin Wade Literary Agency
31 Ivory House, East Smithfield, London E1W 1AT
tel 020-7488 4171 *fax* 020-7488 4172
email rw@rwla.com
website www.rwla.com
Director Robin Wade, *Associate* Jo Kitching

General fiction and non-fiction, but no poetry, plays or short stories (home 10%, overseas 20%). Send descriptive preliminary email. No reading fee. Founded 2001.

Watson, Little Ltd*
Capo Di Monte, Windmill Hill, London NW3 6RJ
tel 020-7431 0770 *fax* 020-7431 7225
email sz@watsonlittle.com
Directors Sheila Watson, Amanda Little, Sugra Zaman

Full-length MSS. Special interests: business books, popular science, psychology, all leisure activities, popular culture, history, fiction; no short stories, plays or younger fiction (home 15%, serial 15%, translation 19%, US 24%; electronic rights 20%; all other rights including film, video and TV 10%). Works in association with US agencies and many foreign agencies. Preliminary letter please.

A.P. Watt Ltd*
20 John Street, London WC1N 2DR
tel 020-7405 6774 *fax* 020-7831 2154 (books) 020-7430 1952 (drama)
email apw@apwatt.co.uk
website www.apwatt.co.uk
Directors Caradoc King, Linda Shaughnessy, Derek Johns, Jo Frank, Georgia Garrett, Nick Harris

Full-length MSS; dramatic works for all media (home 10%, US and foreign 20% including commission to foreign agent). No poetry. No reading fee. No unsolicited MSS. Founded 1875.

WCA Licensing
3 Calais Street, London SE5 9LP
tel 020-7564 5898 *fax* 020-7564 3501
email ecollins@wca.co.uk
Partners Elaine Collins and Arabella Woods

Specialises in non-fiction: cookery, lifestyle, gardening, etc, TV tie-ins (home 15%, overseas 20%). No reading fee; will suggest a revision. Founded 1993.

Josef Weinberger Plays Ltd

(formerly Warner/Chappell Plays Ltd)
12-14 Mortimer Street, London W1T 3JJ
tel 020-7580 2827 *fax* 020-7436 9616

Specialises in stage plays. Works in conjunction with overseas agents. No unsolicited MSS; preliminary letter essential. Founded 1938.

Dinah Wiener Ltd*

12 Cornwall Grove, London W4 2LB
tel 020-8994 6011 *fax* 020-8994 6044

Full-length MSS only, fiction and general non-fiction (home 15%, overseas 20%), film and TV in association (15%). No plays, scripts, poetry, short stories or children's books. No reading fee, but preliminary letter and return postage essential.

Jonathan Williams Literary Agency

Ferrybank House, 6 Park Road, Dun Laoghaire, Co. Dublin, Republic of Ireland
tel/fax (01) 2803482
Director Jonathan Williams

General fiction and non-fiction, preferably by Irish authors (home 10%). Will suggest revision; usually no reading fee. Return postage appreciated (no British stamps – please use International Reply Coupons). Founded 1981.

Elisabeth Wilson

24 Thornhill Square, London N1 1BQ
fax 020-7609 6045

Rights agent and consultant; illustrated books, non-fiction (no children's). Founded 1979.

The Wylie Agency (UK) Ltd

4-8 Rodney Street, London N1 9JH
tel 020-7843 2150 *fax* 020-7843 2151
Contacts Andrew Wylie (president), Rose Gaete, Helen Allen

Literary fiction and non-fiction (home 10%, overseas 20%, USA 15%). No unsolicited MSS; send preliminary letter with 2 sample chapters and sae in first instance. Founded 1996.

Literary agents for children's books

The following literary agents will consider work suitable for children's books, from both authors and illustrators. See also Writing and the children's book market on page 241 and Art agents and commercial art studios on page 390.

The Agency (London) Ltd
Darley Anderson Literary, TV and Film Agency
Celia Catchpole
Curtis Brown Group Ltd
Eddison Pearson Ltd
A.M. Heath & Co. Ltd
David Higham Associates Ltd
Juvenilia
The Christopher Little Literary Agency
Jennifer Luithlen Agency
Eunice McMullen Children's Literary Agent Ltd
Andrew Mann Ltd
Martinez Literary Agency
Maggie Noach Literary Agency
PFD
Pollinger Ltd
The Lisa Richards Agency
Rogers, Coleridge & White Ltd
Elizabeth Roy Literary Agency
Rosemary Sandberg Ltd
Caroline Sheldon Literary Agency
United Authors Ltd
Ed Victor Ltd
A.P. Watt Ltd

Literary agents overseas

Before submitting material, writers are advised to send a preliminary letter with an sae (or an International Reply Coupon) and to ascertain terms. Listings for overseas literary agents other than in the USA start on page 377.

**Member of the Association of Authors' Representatives*

USA

American Play Company Inc.

19 West 44th Street, Suite 1204, New York, NY 10036
tel 212-921-0545 *fax* 212-869-4032
President Sheldon Abend

AMG/Renaissance

9465 Wilshire Boulevard, Beverly Hills, CA 90212
tel 310-860-8000 *fax* 310-860-8100
Partners Alan Nevins, Joel Gotler, Irv Schwartz, *Managers* Judi Farkas, Michael Prevett, Noah Lukeman

Full-length MSS. Fiction and non-fiction, plays (home 15%, overseas 20%), film and TV rights (home 10%, overseas 20%), performance rights. No unsolicited MSS; query first, submit outline. No reading fee. Founded 1934.

The Axelrod Agency*

49 Main Street, PO Box 357, Chatham, NY 12037
tel 518-392-2100 *fax* 518-392-2944
President Steven Axelrod

Full-length MSS. Fiction and non-fiction, software (home 15%, overseas 20%), film and TV rights (15%); will suggest revision where appropriate. Works with overseas agents. No reading fee. Founded 1983.

The Balkin Agency Inc.*

PO Box 222, Amherst, MA 01004
tel 413-548-9835 *fax* 413-548-9836
email balkin@crocker.com
Director Richard Balkin, *European and British Representative* Chandler Crawford Agency USA

Full-length MSS – adult non-fiction only (home 15%, overseas 20%). Query first. May suggest revision. No reading fee.

Virginia Barber Literary Agency Inc., The Writers Shop – see William Morris Agency Inc.

Berman, Boals & Flynn Inc.*

208 West 30th Street, Suite 401, New York, NY 10001
tel 212-868-1068 *fax* 212-868-1052
Agents Judy Boals, Jim Flynn

Dramatic writing only (and only by recommendation).

Georges Borchardt Inc.*

136 East 57th Street, New York, NY 10022
tel 212-753-5785 *fax* 212-838-6518
Directors Georges Borchardt, Anne Borchardt

Full-length and short MSS (home/British/performance 15%, translations 20%). Agents in most foreign countries. No unsolicited MSS. No reading fee. Founded 1967.

Brandt & Hochman Literary Agents Inc.*

1501 Broadway, New York, NY 10036
tel 212-840-5760
British Representative A.M. Heath & Co. Ltd

Full-length and short MSS (home 15%, overseas 20%), performance rights (15%). No reading fee.

The Helen Brann Agency Inc.*

94 Curtis Road, Bridgewater, CT 06752
tel 860-354-9580 *fax* 860-355-2572

Carlisle & Company*

24 East 64 Street, New York, NY 10021
tel 212-813-1881 *fax* 212-813-9567
website www.carlisleco.com
Directors Michael V. Carlisle, Emma Parry, Christy D. Fletcher

Narrative non-fiction, science, history,

biography, literary fiction (home 15%, overseas 20%). Founded 1998.

Maria Carvainis Agency Inc.*
1350 Avenue of the Americas, Suite 2905, New York, NY 10019
tel 212-5245-6365 *fax* 212-245-7196
President Maria Carvainis, *Executive Vice President* Frances Kuffel

Fiction: all categories (except science fiction and fantasy), especially literary and mainstream; mystery, thrillers and suspense; young adult; historical, Regency and contemporary women's fiction. Non-fiction: politics and film history, biography and memoir, medicine and women's issues; business, finance, psychology, popular science (home 15%, overseas 20%). Maria Carvainis views the author's editorial needs and career development as integral components of the literary agent's role, in addition to the negotiation of intricate contracts. Works in conjunction with foreign, TV and movie agents. No reading fee. Query first; no unsolicited MSS. No queries by fax or email.

Frances Collin Literary Agent*
PO Box 33, Wayne, PA 19087-0033
tel 610-254-0555

Full-length MSS (specialisations of interest to UK writers: mysteries, women's fiction, history, biography, science fiction, fantasy) (home 15%, overseas 20%), performance rights (20%). No screenplays. Works in conjunction with agents worldwide. No reading fee. No unsolicited MSS please. Letter queries must include sufficient IRCs. Founded 1948; successor to Marie Rodell-Frances Collin Literary Agency.

Don Congdon Associates Inc.*
156 Fifth Avenue, Suite 625, New York, NY 10010
tel 212-645-1229 *fax* 212-727-2688
email dca@doncongdon.com
Agents Don Congdon, Michael Congdon, Susan Ramer, Cristina Concepcion

Full-length and short MSS. General fiction and non-fiction (home 15%, overseas 19%), performance rights (15%); will sometimes suggest revision. Works with co-agents overseas. No reading fee but no unsolicited MSS – query first with return postage or sase for reply. Does not accept phone calls from querying authors. Founded 1983.

Richard Curtis Associates Inc.
171 East 74th Street, Floor 2, New York, NY 10021
tel 212-772-7363 *fax* 212-772-7393
website http://curtisagency.com
President Richard Curtis

All types of commercial fiction and non-fiction (home 15% overseas 20%), film, TV rights (15%). Works in conjunction with overseas agents. Will suggest revision. No reading fee. Send sase with all queries. Founded 1970.

Curtis Brown Ltd*
10 Astor Place, New York, NY 10003
tel 212-473-5400
Ceo Timothy Knowlton
Contact Query Department
1750 Montgomery Street, San Francisco, CA 94111
tel 415-954-8566
President Peter Ginsberg

Fiction and non-fiction, juvenile, film and TV rights. No unsolicited MSS; query first with sase. No reading fee; no handling fees.

Joan Daves Agency
21 West 26th Street, New York, NY 10010
tel 212-685-2663 *fax* 212-685-1781
Director Jennifer Lyons, *Assistant* Christopher Ladner

Sample chapter or detailed outline of non-fiction projects (home 15%, overseas 20%, film 15%). No reading fee. Subsidiary of **Writers House LLC**. Founded in 1952 by Joan Daves.

Sandra Dijkstra Literary Agency*
PMB 515, 1155 Camino Del Mar, Del Mar, CA 92104-2605
tel 858-755-3115 *fax* 858-792-1494
President Sandra Dijkstra

Fiction and non-fiction: narrative, history, business, psychology, science, memoir/biography, contemporary, women's, suspense; selected children's projects (home 15%, overseas 20%). Works in conjunction with foreign and film agents. No longer accepts unsolicited MSS. Founded 1981.

Donadio & Olson Inc.*
121 West 27th Street, Suite 704, New York, NY 10001
tel 212-691-8077 *fax* 212-633-2837

Owner Candida Donadio, *Associates* Edward Hibbert, Neil Olson, Peter Steinberg, Ira Silverberg

Literary fiction and non-fiction.

Jane Dystel Literary Management*

One Union Square West, New York, NY 10003
tel 212-627-9100 *fax* 212-627-9313
website www.dystel.com
President Jane D. Dystel, *Vice-President* Miriam Goderich, Jo Fagan, Stacey Glick, Michael Bourret

General fiction and non-fiction: literary and commercial fiction; narrative non-fiction; self-help; cookbooks; parenting; children's books; science fiction/fantasy. Full-length and short MSS (home 15%, overseas 10%); film, TV and radio (15%). No reading fee. Founded 1991.

Peter Elek Associates/The Content Company, Inc.

5111 JFK Boulevard East, West New York, NJ 07093
tel 201-558-0323 *fax* 201-558-0307
email info@theliteraryagency.com
website www.theliteraryagency.com
Directors Peter Elek, Helene W. Elek *Submissions* Lauren Mactas

Full-length fiction/non-fiction. Illustrated adult non-fiction: style, culture, popular history, popular science, current affairs; juvenile picture books (home 15%, overseas 20%), performance rights (20%); will sometimes suggest revision. Works with overseas agents. No reading fee. Experienced in licensing for multimedia, online and off-line. Founded 1979.

Ann Elmo Agency Inc.*

60 East 42nd Street, New York, NY 10165
tel 212-661-2880 *fax* 212-661-2883
Director Lettie Lee

Full-length fiction and non-fiction MSS (home 15%, overseas 20%), theatre (15%). Works with foreign agencies. No reading fee. Send query letter only with sase or IRC.

ForthWrite Literary Agency

23852 W. Pacific Coast Hwy, Suite 701, Malibu, CA 90265
tel 310-456-5698 *fax* 310-456-6589
email agent@kellermedia.com
website www.kellermedia.com
Owner Wendy Keller

ly non-fiction: business, self-help pop- r psychology, how-to. Subjects ude: animals, art, horticulture/gardening, archaeology, European history (especially English), biography, health (especially homeopathy and alternative medicines), parenting, coffee table (illustrated) books, crafts (bobbin lace, handicrafts, etc), nature, psychology. Send IRC with query. Response in 8 weeks. Founded 1988.

The Fox Chase Agency Inc.

Walnut Hill Plaza, Suite 140,
150 South Warner Road, King of Prussia, PA 19406
tel 610-341-9840 *fax* 610-341-9842

Jeanne Fredericks Literary Agency Inc.*

221 Benedict Hill Road, New Canaan, CT 06840
tel/fax 203-972-3011
email jfredrks@optonline.net

Quality non-fiction, especially health, science, women's issues, gardening, antiques and decorative arts, biography, cookbooks, popular reference, business, natural history (home 15%, overseas 20%). No reading fee. Query first, enclosing sase. Member of Authors Guild. Founded 1997.

Robert A. Freedman Dramatic Agency Inc.*

(formerly Harold Freedman Brandt & Brandt Dramatic Dept. Inc.)
1501 Broadway, Suite 2310, New York, NY 10036
tel 212-840-5760

Plays, motion picture and TV scripts. Send letter of enquiry first, with sase.

Samuel French Inc.*

45 West 25th Street, New York, NY 10010
tel 212-206-8990 *fax* 212-206-1429
President Charles R. Van Nostrand

Play publishers; authors' representatives.

Sarah Jane Freyman Literary Agency

(formerly Stepping Stone Literary Agency)
59 West 71st Street, Suite 9B, New York, NY 10023
tel 212-362-9277 *fax* 212-501-8240
President Sarah Jane Freymann

Book-length fiction and general non-fiction. Special interest in serious non-fiction, mainstream commercial fiction, contemporary women's fiction, Latino-American, Asian-American, African American fiction and non-fiction. Non-fiction: women's issues, biography, health/fitness, psychology, self-help, spiritual, natural science, cookbooks, pop culture. Works in conjunction with **Abner Stein** in London. No reading fee. Founded 1974.

Jay Garon-Brooke Associates Inc. – see Pinder, Lane & Garon-Brooke Associates Ltd

Gelfman Schneider Literary Agents Inc.*

250 West 57th Street, Suite 2515, New York, NY 10107
tel 212-245-1993 *fax* 212-245-8678
Directors Jane Gelfman, Deborah Schneider

General adult fiction and non-fiction (home 15%, overseas 20%). Works in conjunction with **Curtis Brown**, London. Will suggest revision. No reading fee but please send sase for return of material.

Sebastian Gibson Agency

PO Box 13350, Palm Desert, CA 92255-3350
tel 760-322-2446 *fax* 760-322-3857
Proprietor Sebastian Gibson

Full length MSS (home 20%, overseas 20%). All categories of fiction, particularly novels with interesting characters and well-woven plots. Especially interested in legal and psychological thrillers, historical novels, mystery/suspense and action/adventure or espionage with romance sub-plots and interesting twists, crime/police with humorous/gritty elements, medical dramas, sagas, and any well-written novel with unusual characters. Send query letter with synopsis and first 3 chapters and IRCs.

Goodman Associates, Literary Agents*

500 West End Avenue, New York, NY 10024
tel 212-873-4806
Partners Arnold P. Goodman, Elise Simon Goodman

Adult book length fiction and non-fiction (home 15%, overseas 20%). No reading fee. Founded 1976.

Sanford J. Greenburger Associates Inc.*

55 Fifth Avenue, New York, NY 10003
tel 212-206-5600 *fax* 212-463-8718
website www.greenburger.com
Contacts Heide Lange, Faith Hamlin, Beth Vesel, Theresa Park, Elyse Cheney, Daniel Mandel, PeterMcGuigan

Fiction and non-fiction, film and TV rights. No unsolicited MSS; query first. No reading fee.

The Joy Harris Literary Agency Inc.*

156 Fifth Avenue, Suite 617, New York, NY 10010-7002
tel 212-924-6269 *fax* 212-924-6609
email gen.office@jhlitagent.com
President Joy Harris

John Hawkins & Associates Inc.*

(formerly Paul R. Reynolds Inc.)
71 West 23rd Street, Suite 1600, New York, NY 10010
tel 212-807-7040 *fax* 212-807-9555
website www.jhaliterary.com
President John Hawkins, *Vice-President* William Reiss, *Foreign Rights* Moses Cardona, *Permissions* Matthew Miele, *Other Agents* Elinor B. Sidel, Warren Frazier, Anne Hawkins

Fiction, non-fiction, juvenile. Founded 1893.

The Jeff Herman Agency LLC

332 Bleecker Street, Suite 631, New York, NY 10014
tel 212-941-0540 *fax* 212-941-0614
email jeff@jeffherman.com
website www.jeffherman.com

Business, reference, popular psychology, computers, health, spirituality, general non-fiction (home/overseas 15%); will suggest revision where appropriate. Works with overseas agents. No reading fee. Founded 1986.

Frederick Hill Bonnie Nadell Inc.

1842 Union Street, San Francisco, CA 94123
tel 415-921-2910 *fax* 415-921-2802
Branch office 505 North Robertson Blvd, Los Angeles, CA 90048
tel 310-860-9605 *fax* 310-860-9672

Full-length fiction and non-fiction (home 15%, overseas 20%). Send query letter initially. Works in conjunction with agents in Scandinavia, France, Germany, Holland, Japan, Spain. No reading fee. Founded 1979.

IMG Literary – see Mark Reiter IMG Literary

International Creative Management Inc.*

40 West 57th Street, New York, NY 10019
tel 212-556-5600 *fax* 212-556-5665

No unsolicited MSS; send query letter.

Janklow & Nesbit Associates

445 Park Avenue, New York, NY 10022
tel 212-421-1700 *fax* 212-980-3671, 212-355 1403
email postmaster@janklow.com
Partners Morton L. Janklow, Lynn Nesbit, *Senior Vice President* Anne Sibbald
Agents Tina Bennett, Amy Howell, Luke Janklow, Richard Morris, Eric Simonoff, *Foreign rights* Cullen Stanley, Dorothy Vincent, Cecile Barendsma, Kate Schafer

Commercial and literary fiction and non-fiction. No unsolicited MSS. Works in conjunction with **Janklow & Nesbit (UK) Ltd**. Founded 1989.

JCA Literary Agency Inc.*

27 West 20th Street, Suite 1103, New York, NY 10011
tel 212-807-0888
Contacts Jeff Gerecke, Tony Outhwaite, Peter Steinberg

Adult fiction and non-fiction. No unsolicited MSS; query first.

Barbara S. Kouts, Literary Agent*

PO Box 560, Bellport, NY 11713
tel 631-286-1278 *fax* 631-286-1538

Full-length MSS. Fiction and non-fiction, children's and adult (home 15%, overseas 20%); will suggest revision. Works with overseas agents. No reading fee. Send query letter first. Founded 1980.

The Lazear Agency Inc./Talkback

800 Washington Avenue North, Suite 660, Minneapolis, MN 55401
tel 612-332-8640 *fax* 612-332-4648
Contacts Jonathon Lazear, Wendy Lazear, Christi Cardenas, Julie Mayo

Fiction: full-length MSS; non-fiction: proposals. Adult fiction and non-fiction; film and TV rights; foreign language rights; audio, video and electronic rights (home 15%, overseas 20%). No reading fee. No unsolicited MSS; 2–3 page query first with sase for response. No faxed queries.

Talkback: A Speaker's Bureau: book packaging and select entertainment management. Founded 1984.

Lescher & Lescher Ltd*

47 East 19th Street, New York, NY 10003
tel 212-529-1790 *fax* 212-529-2716
Directors Robert Lescher, Susan Lescher

Full-length and short MSS (home 15%, overseas 25%). No unsolicited MSS; query first with sase. No reading fee. Founded 1966.

Ellen Levine Literary Agency Inc.*

Suite 1801, 15 East 26th Street, New York, NY 10010
tel 212-899-0620 *fax* 212-725-4501
Contacts Elizabeth Kaplan, Diana Finch, Louise Quayle, *UK Representative* A.M. Heath

Full-length MSS: biography, contemporary affairs, women's issues, history, science, literary and commercial fiction (home 15%, overseas 20%); in conjunction with co-agents, theatre, films, TV (15%). Will suggest revision. Works in conjunction with agents in Europe, Japan, Israel, Brazil, Argentina, Australia, Far East. No reading fee; preliminary letter and sase and US postage essential. Founded 1980.

Margret McBride Literary Agency*

7744 Fay Avenue, Suite 201, La Jolla, CA 92037
tel 858-454-1550 *fax* 858-454-2156
President Margret McBride

Business, mainstream fiction and non-fiction; no poetry or children's books (home 15%, overseas 25%). No reading fee. Submit query letter with sase to Margret McBride. Founded 1981.

Gerard McCauley Agency Inc.*

PO Box 844, Katonah, NY 10536
tel 914-232-5700

Specialises in history, biography, public affairs for the general reader.

Anita D. McClellan Associates*

50 Stearns Street, Cambridge, MA 02138
tel 617-576-6950
Director Anita D. McClellan

General fiction and non-fiction. Full-length MSS (home 15%, overseas 20%). Will suggest revision for agency clients. No unsolicited MSS. Send preliminary letter and sase bearing US postage or IRC.

McIntosh & Otis Inc.*

353 Lexington Avenue, New York, NY 10016
tel 212-687-7400 *fax* 212-687-6894
Adult Eugene H. Winick, Samuel L. Pinkus, Elizabeth Winick, *Juvenile* Christina Biamonte, Tracey Adams, *Film and TV* Evva Joan Pryor

Adult and juvenile literary fiction and non-fiction, film and TV rights. No unsolicited MSS; query first with outline, sample chapters and sase. No reading fee. Founded 1928.

Carol Mann Agency*
55 Fifth Avenue, New York, NY 10003
tel 212-206-5635 *fax* 212-675-4809
Associates Carol Mann, Gareth Esersky, James Fitzgerald

Psychology, popular history, biography, pop culture, general non-fiction; fiction (home 15%, overseas 20%). Works in conjunction with foreign agents. No reading fee. Founded 1977.

Mildred Marmur Associates Ltd*
2005 Palmer Avenue, PMB 127, Larchmont, NY 10538-2469
tel 914-834-1170 *fax* 914-834-2840
email marmur@westnet.com, lebowitz@westnet.com
President Mildred Marmur, *Associate* Jane Lebowitz

Serious non-fiction. Full-length and short MSS (home licences 15%, overseas licences 20%), performance rights (15%). Works with co-agents in all major countries. No reading fee. Queries must include sase or International Reply Coupons. Founded 1987.

The Evan Marshall Agency*
Six Tristam Place, Pine Brook, NJ 07058-9445
tel 973-882-1122 *fax* 973-882-3099
email evanmarshall@thenovelist.com
website www.thenovelist.com
President Evan Marshall

General fiction (home 15%, overseas 20%). Works in conjunction with overseas agents. Will suggest revision; no reading fee. Founded 1987.

The Marton Agency Inc.*
1 Union Square, Suite 612, New York, NY 10003-3303
tel 212-255-1908 *fax* 212-691-9061
email info@martonagency.com
Owner Tonda Marton

Stage plays only.

Harold Matson Company Inc.*
276 Fifth Avenue, New York, NY 10001
tel 212-679-4490 *fax* 212-545-1224

Full-length MSS (home 15%, UK 19%, translation 19%). No unsolicited MSS. No reading fee. Founded 1937.

Scott Meredith Literary Agency LP
1675 Broadway, New York, NY 10019
tel 212-698-0785 *fax* 212-977-5997
website www.writingtosell.com
President Arthur Klebanoff, *Vice-President* Lisa J. Edwards, *Director, Subsidiary Rights* Barry N. Malzberg

Full-length and short MSS. General fiction and non-fiction. Single fee charged for readings, criticism and assistance in revision. Founded 1946.

Helen Merrill Ltd
295 Lafayette Street, Suite 915, New York, NY 10012

No unsolicited MSS. No books. No phone calls or faxes.

William Morris Agency Inc.*
(incorporating the Writers Shop, formerly Virginia Barber Literary Agency)
1325 Avenue of the Americas, New York, NY 10019
tel 212-586-5100
Executive VP Owen Laster, *Senior VPs* Jennifer Rudolph Walsh, Suzanne Gluck, Virginia Barber, Joni Evans, Mel Berger, *Agents* Manie Barron, Jay Mandel, Tracy Fisher, *Foreign Rights Director* Tracy Fisher, *Foreign Rights Coordinator* Shana Kelly, *First Serial and Audio Manager* Karen Gerwin

General fiction and non-fiction (home 15%, overseas 20%), performance rights (15%. Will suggest revision. No reading fee.

Multimedia Product Development Inc.*
410 South Michigan Avenue, Suite 724, Chicago, IL 60605
tel 312-922-3063 *fax* 312-922-1905
Contact Jane Jordan Browne, Scott Mendel

General fiction and non-fiction (home 15%, overseas 20%), performance rights (15%). Works in conjunction with foreign agents. Will suggest revision; no reading fee. Founded 1971.

Jean V. Naggar Literary Agency*
216 East 75th Street, Suite 1E, New York, NY 10021
tel 212-794-1082
President Jean V. Naggar, *Agents* Alice Tasman, Jennifer Weltz (rights)

Mainstream commercial and literary fiction (no formula fiction); non-fiction: psychology, science, biography (home 15%, overseas 20%), performance rights (15%). Works in conjunction with foreign agents. No reading fee. Founded 1978.

New England Publishing Associates Inc.*
PO Box 5, Chester, CT 06412
tel 860-345-READ *fax* 860-345-3660
email nepa@nepa.com

website www.nepa.com
Contact Elizabeth Frost-Knappman, Edward W. Knappman, Ron Formica, Kris Schiavi, Vicki Harlow

Serious non-fiction for the adult market (home 15%, overseas varies), performance rights (varies). Works in conjunction with foreign publishers. No reading fee; will suggest revision – if undertaken. London representative: Scott Ferris; Asia: Amer-Asia. Dramatic rights: **AMG/ Renaissance**, Beverly Hills. Founded 1982.

Harold Ober Associates Inc.*

425 Madison Avenue, New York, NY 10017
tel 212-759-8600 *fax* 212-759-9428
Directors Phyllis Westberg, Emma Sweeney, Wendy Schmalz, Knox Burger, Alex Smithline

Full-length MSS (home 15%, British 20%, overseas 20%), performance rights (15%). Will suggest revision. No reading fee. Founded 1929.

Fifi Oscard Agency Inc.

110 W 40th Street, New York, NY 10018
tel 212-764-1100 *fax* 212-840-5019
email fifioscard@aol.com
Agents Fifi Oscard, Peter Sawyer, Carolyn French, Carmen La Via, Kevin McShane

Full-length MSS (home 15%, overseas 20%), theatrical performance rights (10%). Will suggest revision. Works in conjunction with many foreign agencies. No reading fee, but no unsolicited submissions.

James Peter Associates Inc.

PO Box 670, Tenafly, NJ 07670
tel 201-568-0760 *fax* 201-568-2959
email bertholtje@compuserve.com
Contact Bert Holtje, Gene Brissie

Non-fiction, especially history, politics, popular culture, health, psychology, reference, biography (home 15%, overseas 20%). Foreign rights handled by: Bobbe Siegel, 41 West 83rd Street, New York, NY 10024. Will suggest revision. No reading fee. Founded 1971.

The Pimlico Agency Inc.

Box 20447, Cherokee Station, New York, NY 10021
tel 212-628-9729 *fax* 212-535-7861
Contacts Christopher Shepard, Catherine Brooks, *Directors* Kay McCauley, Kirby McCauley

Adult non-fiction and fiction. No unsolicited MSS.

Pinder, Lane & Garon-Brooke Associates Ltd

159 West 53rd Street, Suite 14, New York, NY 10019
tel 212-489-0880 *fax* 212-586-9346
London Representative Abner Stein

Specialises in fiction and non-fiction: biographies and lifestyle. Writer must be referred by an editor or a client. Will not read unsolicited MSS.

PMA Literary and Film Management Inc.

Old Chelsea Station, PO Box 1817, New York, NY 10011
tel 212-929-1222 *fax* 212-206-0238
email pmalitfilm@aol.com
website www.pmalitfilm.com
President Peter Miller

Full-length MSS. Specialises in commercial fiction (especially thrillers), true crime, non-fiction (all types), and all books with global publishing and film/ TV potential (home 15%, overseas 25%), films, TV (10–20%). Works in conjunction with agents worldwide. Preliminary enquiry with career goals, synopsis and resumé essential. Founded 1976.

Helen Rees Literary Agency

123 N. Washington Street, Boston, MA 02114
tel 617-723 5232 *fax* 617-723 5211
email reesliterary@aol.com
Contact Joan Mazmanian, *Associates* Barbara Rifkind, Ann Collette

Business books, self-help, biography, autobiography, political, literary fiction (home 15%). Works with foreign agent. No reading fee. Submit query letter with sase. Founded 1982.

Mark Reiter IMG Literary

825 Seventh Avenue, 9th Floor, New York, NY 10019
tel 212-489-5400 *fax* 212-246 1118

Fiction (no science fiction) and non-fiction. Send query letter with sase.

Renaissance – A Literary Talent Agency – see AMG/Renaissance

Rosenstone/Wender*

38 East 29th Street, 10th Floor, New York, NY 10016
tel 212-725-9445 *fax* 212-725-9447
Contact Phyllis Wender, Susan Perlman Cohen, Sonia Pabley

Fiction, non-fiction, film and TV rights.

No unsolicited MSS; query first. No reading fee.

Russell & Volkening Inc.*

50 West 29th Street, Suite 7E, New York, NY 10001
tel 212-684-6050 *fax* 212-889-3026
Contact Timothy Seldes, Joseph Regal

General fiction and non-fiction, film and TV rights. No screenplays. No unsolicited MSS; query first with letter and sase. No reading fee.

Susan Schulman Literary & Dramatic Agents Inc.*

454 West 44th Street, New York, NY 10036
tel 212-713-1633 *fax* 212-581-8830
email schulman@aol.com

Agents for negotiation in all markets (with co-agents) of fiction, general non-fiction, children's books, academic and professional works, and associated subsidiary rights including plays and film (home 15%, UK 7.5%, overseas 20%). Return postage required.

The Shukat Company Ltd*

340 West 55th Street, Suite 1A, New York, NY 10019
tel 212-582-7614 *fax* 212-315-3752
email staff@shukat.com
President Scott Shukat, *Contact* Maribel Rivas, Lysna Scriven-Marzani

Theatre, films, TV, radio (15%). No reading fee. No unsolicited material accepted.

The Spieler Agency

154 West 57th Street, Room 135, New York, NY 10019
tel 212-757-4439 *fax* 212-333-2019
email spielerlit@aol.com
Directors F. Joseph Spieler, Lisa M. Ross, John F. Thornton, Deirdre Mullane

Full- and short-length MSS. History, politics, ecology, business, consumer reference, some fiction (home 15%, overseas 20%). No reading fee. Query first with sample and sase. Founded 1982.

Philip G. Spitzer Literary Agency*

50 Talmage Farm Lane, East Hampton, NY 11937
tel 631-329-3650 *fax* 631-329-3651

General fiction and non-fiction; specialises in mystery/suspense, sports, politics, biography, social issues.

Sterling Lord Literistic Inc.

65 Bleecker Street, New York, NY 10012
tel 212-780-6050 *fax* 212-780-6095
Directors Peter Matson, Sterling Lord, Philippa Brophy

Full-length and short MSS (home 15%, overseas 20%), performance rights (15%). Will suggest revision. No reading fee.

Gloria Stern Agency

12535 Chandler Boulevard, Suite 3, North Hollywood, CA 91607-1934
tel/fax 818-508-6296
Director Gloria Stern

Fiction and films, electronics and multimedia (home 10%, overseas 15%). Reading fee for evaluation; consultation fee for revisions; some author expenses for placing MSS. Founded 1984.

Roslyn Targ Literary Agency Inc.*

105 West 13th Street, New York, NY 10011
tel 212-206-9390 *fax* 212-989-6233
email roslyntarg@aol.com

Fiction and non-fiction: query with outline, publication history and CV. Fiction: query with synopsis or outline, and CV and publication history. All submissions require sase. No phone queries. Affiliates in most foreign countries. No reading fee.

Ralph M. Vicinanza Ltd*

303 West 18th Street, New York, NY 10011
tel 212-924-7090
Contact Ralph Vicinanza, Christopher Lotts, Christopher Schelling

Fiction: literary, women's, 'multicultural', popular (especially science fiction, fantasy, thrillers), children's. Non-fiction: history, business, science, biography, popular culture. Foreign rights specialists. New clients by professional recommendationonly. No unsolicited MSS.

Austin Wahl Agency Inc.

1820 North 76th Court, Elmwood Park, IL 60707-3631
tel 708-456-2301 *fax* 708-456-2031
President Thomas Wahl

Full-length and short MSS (home 15%, overseas 20%), theatre, films, TV (10%). No reading fee; professional writers only. Founded 1935.

Wallace Literary Agency Inc.

177 East 70th Street, New York, NY 10021
tel 212-570-9090 *fax* 212-772-8979
Director Lois Wallace

Full-length MSS. No cookery, humour, how-to; film, TV, theatre for agency clients. Will suggest revision. No unsolicited MSS; no faxed queries. Will only answer queries with return postage. Founded 1988.

T.C. Wallace Ltd*

Suite 1001, 425 Madison Avenue, New York, NY 10017
tel 212-759-8600 *fax* 212-759-9428
email twallace@mindspring.com
Managing Director Tom Wallace

Full-length MSS. Non-fiction: history, biography, travel, memoirs. Fiction: thrillers, mystery novels, literary fiction (home 15%, overseas 20%. No unsolicited MSS. No reading fee. Will suggest a revision. Founded 1998.

Watkins/Loomis Agency Inc.

133 East 35th Street, New York, NY 10016
tel 212-532-0080 *fax* 212-889-0506
President Gloria Loomis, *Contact* Katherine Fausset

Fiction and non-fiction. No unsolicited MSS; query first with sase. No reading fee. Representatives: **Abner Stein** (UK), Marsh Agency (foreign).

Sandra Watt and Associates

8033 Sunset Boulevard, Suite 4053, Hollywood, CA 90046
tel 213-653-2339
Owner Sandra Watt

Lead women's fiction, suspense, mysteries, New Age, cyber-punk; psychological self-help, gardening, single-volume reference works; screenplays (home 15%, overseas 25%), films (10%). Works in conjunction with foreign agents. Will suggest revision; no reading fee; $100 marketing fee for unpublished authors. Founded 1978.

Wecksler-Incomco

170 West End Avenue, New York, NY 10023
tel 212-787-2239 *fax* 212-496-7035
email jacinny@aol.com
President Sally Wecksler, *Associate* Joann Amparan-Close

Illustrated books, non-fiction, business books, some literary fiction, children's books (home 15%, overseas 20%); will suggest revision where appropriate. No reading fee. Founded 1971.

Rhoda Weyr Agency*

151 Bergen Street, Brooklyn, NY 11217
tel 718-522-0480 *fax* 718-522-0410

General non-fiction and fiction, particularly science, history, biography (home 15%, overseas 20%, performance rights 15%). No unsolicited submissions. Co-agents in all foreign markets. Founded 1983.

Writers House LLC*

21 West 26th Street, New York, NY 10010
tel 212-685-2400 *fax* 212-685-1781
President Albert Zuckerman, *Executive Vice-President* Amy Berkower

Fiction and non-fiction, including all rights; film and TV rights. No screenplays or software. Write a one-page letter in first instance, saying what's wonderful about your book, what it is about and why you are the best person to write it. No reading fee. Founded 1974.

The Writers Shop – see William Morris Agency Inc.

The Wylie Agency Inc.

250 West 57th Street, New York, NY 10107
tel 212-246-0069 *fax* 212-586-8953
email mail@wylieagency.com
Directors Andrew Wylie (president), Sarah Chalfant

Literary fiction/non-fiction. No unsolicited MSS accepted. London office: **The Wylie Agency UK Ltd**.

Mary Yost Associates Inc.

59 East 54th Street, Suite 72, New York, NY 10022
tel 212-980-4988

Full-length and short MSS (home and overseas 10%). Works with individual agents in all foreign countries. Will suggest revision. No reading fee. Founded 1958.

Overseas literary agents – other

Most of the agents listed here work in association with an agent in London. Before submitting a typescript, writers are advised to send a preliminary letter and to ascertain terms.

Argentina

International Editors Co.
Avenida Cabildo 1156, 1426 Buenos Aires
tel 54-11-4788-2992 *fax* 54-11-4786-0888

The Nancy H. Smith Literary Agency
(formerly The Lawrence Smith Agency)
Ayacucho 1867, 2B, Buenos Aires 1112
tel/fax (54 11) 4804 5508
email meg@interlink.com.ar
Contact Margaret Murray
London office 30 Acton Lane, London W4 5ED
tel 020-8995 4769 *fax* 020-8747 4012
email distobart@cs.com
Contact Diana Stobart
Founded 1938.

Australia

Curtis Brown (Australia) Pty Ltd
27 Union Street, Paddington, Sydney, NSW 2021
tel (02) 9331 5301/9361 6161 *fax* (02) 9360 3935
email info@curtisbrown.com.au

Literary Resources
26 Robert Street, Willoughby, NSW 2068
fax (02) 9967 2102
email dougnanc@ozemail.com.au
Principal Doug Nancarrow
Full-length and short MSS, adult fiction (home 10%, overseas 20%), performance rights (10%); will suggest revision. Works with overseas agents. Reading fee. Founded 1992.

Brazil

Agencia Literária Balcells Mello e Souza Riff/BMSR
Rua Visconde de Pirajá, 414 s1 1108 Ipanema, 22410-002 Rio de Janeiro, RJ
tel (55-21) 2287-6299 *fax* (55-21) 2267-6393
email lucia@bmsr.com.br
Contact Lucia de Mello e Souza Riff

Karin Schindler and Suely Pedro dos Santos Rights Representatives
Caixa Postal 19051, 04505-970 São Paulo, SP
tel 55-11-5041-9177 *fax* 55-11-5041-9077
email sysantos@internetcom.com.br

Canada

Acacia House Publishing Services Ltd
51 Acacia Road, Toronto, Ontario M4S 2K6
tel/fax 416-484-8356
email fhanna.acacia@rogers.com
Managing Director Mrs Frances A. Hanna, *Vice President* Bill Hanna
Literary fiction/non-fiction, quality commercial fiction, most non-fiction, except business books (15% English worldwide, 25% translation, performance 20%). No science fiction, horror or occult. Works with overseas agents. Query first with sample of 50pp max. Include return postage. Founded 1985.

Authors' Marketing Services Ltd
55 Kennedy Avenue, Toronto M65 2X6
tel 416-763 8797 *fax* 416-763-1504
email authorslhoffman@cs.com
Director Larry Hoffman
Adult fiction, biography and autobiography (home 15%, overseas 20%). Reading fee charged for unpublished writers; will suggest a revision. Founded 1978.

Anne McDermid & Associates
92 Willcocks Street, Toronto, Ontario M5S 1C8
tel 416-324 8845 *fax* 416-324 8870
email anne@mcdermidagency.com
website www.mcdermidagency.com
Director Anne McDermid
Literary fiction and non-fiction, and quality commercial fiction; no children's literature (home 15%, US 15%, overseas 20%). No reading fee. Founded 1996.

Eastern Europe

Aura-Pont, Theatrical and Literary Agency Ltd
Radlická 99, Prague 5, Czech Republic
tel/fax (420) 2 51 55 02 07
email aura-pont@aura-pont.cz
website www.aura-pont.cz
Director Zuzana Jezková
Handles authors' rights in books, theatre, film, TV, radio, software – both Czech

and foreign (home 10%, overseas 15%). Founded 1990.

DILIA, Theatrical and Literary Agency
Krátkého 1, 190 03 Prague 9, Czech Republic
tel (420) 2 83 89 15 87 *fax* (420) 2 83 89 35 99
email info@dilia.cz
website www.dilia.cz
Theatrical and literary agency.

Lex Copyright
Szemere utca 21, 1054 Budapest, Hungary
tel (36) 1 332 9340 *fax* (36) 1 331 6181
email lexcopy.bp@mail.datanet.hu
Director Dr Gyorgy Tibor Szanto
Specialises in representing American and British authors in Hungary. Founded 1991.

Lita
Mozartova 9, CS-81530, Bratislava, Slovakia
tel (421) 7 313623 *fax* (421) 7 580 2246
Slovak Literary Agency.

Andrew Nurnberg Associates Prague, s.r.o
Seifertova 81, 130 00 Prague 3, Czech Republic
tel (420) 2 22 78 20 41 *fax* (420) 2 22 78 23 08
email nurnprg@mbox.vol.cz
Contact Petra Tobisková

Prava I Prevodi Literary Agency Permissions & Rights Ltd
Koste Jovanovica 18, 11000 Belgrade, Yugoslavia
tel (381) 11 460 290 *fax* (381) 11 472 146
email ana@pip.co.yu office@pip.co.yu
Director Jovan Milenkovic, *Foreign Rights* Ana Milenkovic
Specialises in representing American and British authors in former Eastern Europe (15 languages). Founded 1983.

France

Bureau Littéraire International
1 rue Alfred Laurant,
F-92100 Boulogne Billancourt
tel (1) 46 05 39 11
Contact Geneviéve Ulmann

Agence Hoffman
77 Boulevard Saint-Michel, 75005 Paris
tel (1) 43 26 56 94 *fax* (1) 43 26 34 07
email hoffman@starnet.fr

Agence Michelle Lapautre
6 rue Jean Carriès, 75007 Paris
tel (1) 47 34 82 41 *fax* (1) 47 34 00 90
email lapautre@club-internet.fr

La Nouvelle Agence
7 rue Corneille, 75006 Paris
tel (1) 43 25 85 60 *fax* (1) 43 25 47 98
email lnaparis@aol.com
Contact Mary Kling

Germany (see also Switzerland)

Agence Hoffman
Bechsteinstrasse 2, 80804 Munich
tel 089-308 48 07 *fax* 089-308 21 08

Michael Meller Literary Agency
Sandstrasse 33, 80335 Munich
tel (089) 366371 *fax* (089) 366372
email info@melleragency.com
website www.melleragency.com
Full-length MSS. Fiction and non-fiction, screenplays for films and TV (home 15%, overseas 20%). Own US office. No reading fee. Founded 1988.

Thomas Schlück GmbH
Literary Agency, Hinter der Worth 12,
Garbsen 30827
tel 05131-497560 *fax* 05131-497589
email mail@schlueckagent.de
website www.schlueckagent.de

India

Ajanta Books International
1 U.B. Jawahar Nagar, Bungalow Road,
Delhi 110007
tel 7415016, 3926182 *fax* 91-11-7415016
email ajantabi@ndf.vsnl.net.in ajantabi@id.cth.net
Proprietor S. Balwant
Full-length MSS in social sciences and humanities (commission varies according to market – Indian books in Indian and foreign languages, foreign books into Indian languages). Will suggest revision; charges made if agency undertakes revision; reading fee. Founded 1975.

Israel

I. Pikarski Ltd Literary Agency
200 Hayarkon Street, PO Box 4006,
Tel Aviv 61040
tel 03-5270159/5231880 *fax* 03-5270160
email gabpikar@inter.net.il
Director Ilana Pikarski
General trade publishing and merchandising rights. Founded 1977.

Italy

Eulama SRL
Via Guido de Ruggiero 28, 00142 Rome
tel (06) 540 73 09 *fax* (06) 540 87 72
Directors Harald Kahnemann, Karin von Prellwitz, Norbert von Prellwitz, Pina Ocello von Prellwitz
Quality fiction and non-fiction; Latin American literature; represents publishers, authors and agencies in Europe and the world. Founded 1962.

Grandi Associati SRL
Via Caradosso 12, 20123 Milan
tel (02) 469 55 41/481 89 62 *fax* (02) 481 95108
email agenzia@grandieassociati.it
website www.grandieassociati.it
Directors Laura Grandi, Stefano Tettamanti
Provides publicity and foreign rights consultation for publishers and authors as well as sub-agent services; will suggest revision where appropriate. Reading fee. Founded 1988.

ILA – International Literary Agency – USA
I-18010 Terzorio-IM
tel (018) 448 4048 *fax* (018) 448 7292
email libri.gg@dmw.it
Publishers' and authors' agent, interested only in series of best-selling and mass market books by proven, published authors with a track record. Also interested in published books on antiques and collectibles. Founded 1969.

Agenzia Letteraria Internazionale SRL
Via Valpetrosa 1, 20123 Milano
tel (02) 865445, 861572 *fax* (02) 876222
email alidmb@tin.it

New Blitz Literary & TV Agency
Via di Panico 67, 00186 Rome
postal address CP 30047-00193, Rome 47
tel/fax (06) 686 4859
email blitzgacs@inwind.it
Literary Department Giovanni A.S. Congiu

Japan

The English Agency (Japan) Ltd
Sakuragi Building 4F, 6-7-3 Minami Aoyama, Minato-ku, Tokyo 107-0062
tel 03-3406 5385 *fax* 03-3406 5387
Managing Director William Miller
Handles work by English-language writers living in Japan; arranges Japanese translations for internationally established publishers, agents and authors; arranges Japanese contracts for Japanese versions of all media. Standard commission: 10%. Own representatives in New York and London. No reading fee. Founded 1979.

Orion Literary Agency
1-7-12-4F Kanda-Jimbocho, Chiyoda-ku, Tokyo 101
tel 03-3295-1405 *fax* 03-3295-4366

Netherlands

Auteursbureau Greta Baars-Jelgersma
Villa Beau Rivage, Maasstaete 40, 6585 CB, Mook (L)
tel (024) 6963336 *fax* (024) 6963293
Literature; illustrated co-productions, including children's, art, handicraft, hobby and nature (home/overseas 20%). Works with overseas agents. Occasionally charges a reading fee. Founded 1951.

Internationaal Literatuur Bureau B.V.
Postbus 10014, 1201 DA, Hilversum
tel (035) 621 35 00 *fax* (035) 621 57 71
email mkohn@planet.nl
Contact Menno Kohn

New Zealand

Glenys Bean Writer's Agent
PO Box 60509, Titirangi, Auckland
tel (09) 812 8486 *fax* (09) 812 8188
email g.bean@clear.net.nz
Adult and children's fiction, educational, non-fiction, film, TV, radio (10%–20%). Send preliminary letter, synopsis and sae. Represented by **Sanford Greenburger Associates Ltd** (USA). Translation/foreign rights: Paul Marsh Agency. Founded 1989.

Richards Literary Agency
49C Aberdeen Road, Castor Bay, Auckland 9
postal address PO Box 31240, Milford, Auckland 9
tel (09) 410-5681 *fax* 09) 479-6389
Partners Ray Richards, Nicki Richards Wallace
Full-length MSS, fiction, non-fiction, adult, juvenile, educational, academic books; films, TV, radio (home 10%, overseas 10–20%). Preliminary letter, synop-

sis with sae required. No reading fee. Co-agents in London and New York. Founded 1977.

Portugal

Ilidio da Fonseca Matos

Avenida Gomes Pereira, 105-3°-B, 1500-326 Lisbon
tel (21) 716 2988 *fax* (21) 715 4445
email ilidio.matos@oninet.pt

Russia

Prava I Perevody

(Permissions and Rights Ltd, Moscow)
Bolshaya Bronnaya Street 6A, Moscow 103670
tel 095) 203 5280 *fax* (095) 203 0229
email prava@aha.ru
Director Konstantin Palchikov

Specialises in representing US and British authors in Russia, Latvia, Lithuania, Estonia and Ukraine. Founded 1993.

Scandinavia, inc. Finland and Iceland

Bookman Literary Agency

Bastager 3, DK-2950 Vedbaek, Denmark
tel (45) 45 89 25 20 *fax* (45) 45 89 25 01
email ihl@bookman.dk

Handles rights in Denmark, Sweden, Norway, Finland and Iceland for foreign authors.

Gösta Dahl & Son, AB

Aladdinsvägan 14, S-167 61 Bromma, Sweden
tel 08 25 62 35 *fax* 08 25 11 18

Leonhardt & Høier Literary Agency aps

Studiestraede 35, DK-1455 Copenhagen K, Denmark
tel 33 13 25 23 *fax* 33 13 49 92
email anneli@leonhardt-hoier.dk

Lennart Sane Agency AB

Holländareplan 9, S-374 34 Karlshamm, Sweden
tel 0454 123 56 *fax* 0454 149 20
Directors Lennart Sane, Elisabeth Sane, Ulf Töregård

Fiction, non-fiction, children's books. Founded 1969.

Sane Töregård Agency

Holländareplan 9, S-374 34 Karlshamn, Sweden
tel (46) 454 12356 *fax* (46) 454 14920
email ulf.toregard@sanetoregard.se
Directors Lennart Sane, Elisabeth Sane, Ulf Töregård

Represents authors, agents and publishers in Scandinavia and Holland for rights in fiction, non-fiction and children's books. Founded 1995.

South Africa

Frances Bond Literary Services

32B Stanley Teale Road, Westville North 3630, KwaZulu-Natal
postal address PO Box 223, Westville 3630
tel (031) 2624532 *fax* (031) 2622620
email fbond@mweb.co.za
Managing Editor Frances Bond, *Chief Editor* Eileen Molver

Full length MSS. Fiction and non-fiction; juvenile and children's literature. Consultancy service on contracts and copyright. Preliminary phone call or letter and sase required. Founded 1985.

International Press Agency (Pty) Ltd

PO Box 67, Howard Place 7450
tel (021) 5311926 *fax* (021) 5318789
email inpra@iafrica.com
Manager Terry Temple
UK office Ursula A. Barnett, 17 Fairmount Road, London SW2 2BJ
tel/fax 020-8674 9283

Literary Dynamics

Postnet Suite 222, Private Bag X10, Musgrave 4062
tel/fax (031) 2080045
email literary@saol.com
website www.literarydynamics.trading.net
Managing Editor Isabel Cooke

Full-length MSS, fiction and non-fiction, screenplays. Reading fee for in-depth evaluation. Public speaking consultant, company profiles, project reports, editorial services. Founded 1985.

Sandton Literary Agency

PO Box 785799, Sandton 2146
tel (011) 4428624
Directors J. Victoria Canning, M. Sutherland

Full-length MSS and screenplays; lecture agents. Professional editing. Write enclosing sae or phone first. Works in conjunction with Renaissance-Swan Film Agency Inc., Los Angeles, USA. Founded 1982.

Spain

ACER Literary Agency

Amor de Dios 1, 28014 Madrid
tel 1-369-2061 *fax* 1-369-2052
Directors Elizabeth Atkins, Laure Merle d'Aubigné

Represents UK, US, French and German publishers for Spanish and Portuguese translation rights; represents Spanish- and Portuguese-language authors (home/overseas 10%); will suggest revision where appropriate. £20 reading fee. Founded 1959.

Agencia Literaria Carmen Balcells S.A.

Diagonal 580, 08021 Barcelona
tel 93-200-89-33 *fax* 93-200-70-41
email ag-balcells@ag-balcells.com
Contact Gloria Gutiérrez

Mercedes Casanovas Literary Agency

Iradier 24, 08017 Barcelona
tel 93-212-47-91 *fax* 93-417-90-37

Literature, non-fiction, children's books (home 10%, overseas 20%). Works with overseas agents. No reading fee. Founded 1980.

International Editors Co., S.A.

Rambla Catalunya 63, 3°-1a, 08007 Barcelona
tel 93-215-88-12 *fax* 93-487-35-83
email ieco@es.inter.net

RDC Agencia Literaria SL

C. Fernando VI, No 13-15, Madrid 28004
tel 91-308-55-85 *fax* 91-308-56-00
Director Raquel de la Concha

Representing foreign fiction, non-fiction, children's books and Spanish authors. No reading fee.

Lennart Sane Agency AB

Paseo de Mejico 65, Las Cumbres-Elviria, E-29600 Marbella (Malaga)
tel 95-283-41-80 *fax* 95-283-31-96
email lennart.sane@telia.com

Fiction, non-fiction, children's books, film and TV scripts. Founded 1965.

Julio F. Yañez

Agencia Literaria S.L., Via Augusta 139, 6°-2a, 08021 Barcelona
tel 93-200-71-07, 93-200-54-43 *fax* 93-209-48-65
email yanezag@retemzil.es

Switzerland

Paul & Peter Fritz AG Literary Agency

Jupiterstrasse 1, CH-8032 Zürich
tel (01) 388 41 40 *fax* (01) 388 41 30
email info@fritzagency.com
Postfach 1773, CH-8032 Zürich

Represents authors, agents and publishers in German-language areas.

Liepman AG

Maienburgweg 23, CH-8044 Zürich
tel (01) 261 76 60 *fax* (01) 261 01 24
Contacts Eva Koralnik, Ruth Weibel

Represents authors, agents and publishers from all over the world for German translation rights, and selected international authors for world rights.

Mohrbooks AG, Literary Agency

Klosbachstrasse 110, CH-8032 Zürich
tel (01) 251 16 10 *fax* (01) 262 52 13
email info@mohrbooks.com
Contact Sabine Ibach, Sebastian Ritscher

Niedieck Linder AG

Zollikerstrasse 87, Postbox, CH-8034 Zürich
tel (01) 381 65 92 *fax* (01) 381 65 13
website www.nlagency.ch

Represents German-language authors and Italian-language authors on the German market.

Literary agents for television, film, radio and theatre

Listings for these and other literary agents start on page 345.
**US literary agents*

A & B Personal Management Ltd
American Play Company Inc.*
AMG/Renaissance*
Author Literary Agents
Berman, Boals & Flynn Inc.*
Blake Friedmann Literary, TV & Film Agency Ltd
Alan Brodie Representation Ltd
Calitz Associates
Capel & Land Ltd
Casarotto Ramsay & Associates Ltd
Jonathan Clowes Ltd
Elspeth Cochrane Personal Management
Rosica Colin Ltd
Jane Conway-Gordon
Richard Curtis Associates Inc.*
Curtis Brown Group Ltd
Curtis Brown Ltd
Judy Daish Associates Ltd
Felix De Wolfe
Robert Dudley Agency
Ann Elmo Agency Inc.*
Janet Fillingham Associates
Film Rights Ltd
Laurence Fitch Ltd
Jill Foster Ltd
Robert A. Freedman Dramatic Agency Inc.*
Samuel French Inc.*
French's
Futerman, Rose & Associates
Jüri Gabriel
Eric Glass Ltd
Antony Harwood Ltd
Richard Hatton Ltd
David Higham Associates Ltd
Valerie Hoskins Associates
ICM Ltd
Juvenilia
Michelle Kass Associates
The Lazear Agency Inc./Talkback*
Ellen Levine Literary Agency Inc.*
Limelight Management
Andrew Mann Ltd
Manuscript ReSearch
Martinez Literary Agency
The Marton Agency Inc.*
Blanche Marvin
MBA Literary Agents Ltd
Helen Merrill Ltd
William Morris Agency Inc.*
William Morris Agency (UK) Ltd
Multimedia Product Development Inc.*
Fifi Oscard Agency Inc.*
PFD
PMA Literary and Film Management Inc.*
PVA Management Ltd
Radala & Associates
Rosenstone/Wender*
Sayle Screen Ltd
Susan Schulman Literary & Dramatic Agents Inc.*
The Sharland Organisation Ltd
Sheil Land Associates Ltd
The Shukat Company Ltd*
Micheline Steinberg Playwrights' Agent
Sterling Lord Literistic Inc.*
Gloria Stern Agency*
Rochelle Stevens & Co.
The Tennyson Agency
J.M. Thurley Management
Austin Wahl Agency Inc.*
Watkins/Loomis Agency Inc.*
A.P. Watt Ltd
Sandra Watt and Associates*
Josef Weinberger Plays Ltd

Art and illustration

Freelancing for beginners

Full-time posts for illustrators are not only highly specialised but, sadly, very rare. Because the needs of those who commission illustration tend to change on a regular basis, most artists have little choice but to offer their skills to a variety of clients in order to make a living. ***Fig Taylor*** *describes the opportunities open to the freelance illustrator.*

As a freelance illustrator you will be entering a hugely competitive arena and a professional attitude towards targeting, presenting, promoting and delivering your work will be vital to your success. Equally crucial is a realistic understanding of how the illustration industry works and of your place within the scheme of things. Without adequate research into your chosen field of interest it is all too easy to approach inappropriate clients – a frustrating and disheartening experience for both parties, to say nothing of its being both expensive and time-consuming.

Who commissions illustration?

Magazines and newspapers

Whatever your eventual career goals, your first stop for research should be your largest local newsagent. Most illustrators receive their first commissions from editorial clients who, whilst offering comparatively modest fees, are actively keen to try out fresh talent. Briefs are by and large fairly loose, though deadlines can be short, particularly in the case of daily and weekly publications. However, fast turnover also ensures a swift appearance in print – positive proof of your professional status to clients in other, more lucrative, spheres. Given then that it is possible to use the editorial field as a springboard, it is essential to appreciate its breadth when seeking to identify your own individual market. Between them, magazines and newspapers accommodate an infinite variety of illustrative styles and techniques. Don't limit your horizons by approaching only the most obvious titles and/or those you would read yourself. Consider also trade and professional journals, free publications and those available on subscription from membership organisations or charities. Remember, the more potential clients you uncover, the brighter your future will be.

Greetings cards

Many decorative, humorous and fine art-biased illustrators are interested in providing designs for greetings cards and giftwrap, where there is a definite market for their skills. As with editorial, fees are unlikely to be high but many small card companies are keen to use new or lesser known artists. You may be expected to produce samples of artwork on a speculative basis prior to receiving a definite commission – therefore it makes sense to target those companies who are likely to be most responsive (see *Winning the greeting card game*, page 395).

In addition to card shops and the gift departments of larger stores (many of whom employ commissioning buyers for their own ranges), you may find trade fairs such as London's bi-annual Top Drawer and Birmingham's International Spring and Autumn Shows yield the best results for your research. Geared primarily towards buyers, trade fairs offer you the opportunity to check out the forthcoming ranges of numerous card, stationery and giftware manufacturers as well as enabling you to make contacts.

Be warned, however, that most exhibitors will be far too busy selling to go through your work there and then. It is best to make a separate appointment to do this after the fair has ended. For further details, contact Top Drawer organisers, Clarion Events Ltd, or Trade Promotion Services Ltd, which organise the International Gift Fairs (see page 386).

Book publishing

With the exception of adult illustrated non-fiction, where the emphasis is on decorative, specialist and technical illustration, the majority of pro-illustration publishers are interested in full-colour figurative work for use on paperback and hardback book covers. Strong, realistic work which shows the figure in a narrative context is invaluable to those who commission massmarket fiction, which includes such genres as historical and contemporary romance, thrillers, family sagas, horror, science fiction and fantasy. On the whole, publishing deadlines are civilised and massmarket covers well paid. Illustrators whose work is more stylised or experimental would be better advised to approach those smaller imprints and independent publishing houses which deal with more literary, upmarket fiction. Although fees are significantly lower and commissions less frequent, briefs are less restrictive and a wider range of styles can be accommodated.

Children's publishers use a diversity of styles, covering the gamut from baby books, activity and early-learning through to full-colour picture books, older children's novels with black and white spot illustrations and teenage fiction and non-fiction. Author/illustrators are particularly welcomed by picture book publishers – though, whatever your style, you must be able to draw children well and to sustain a character throughout a narrative. See *Illustrating for children's books* on page 245.

Design

It is unnecessary for you to have design training in order to approach a design group for illustration work. However, it is advisable that you be in print. Both designers and their clients – who are largely uncreative and will ultimately be footing the bill – will be impressed and reassured by relevant, published work. Although fees are higher than those in editorial and publishing, this third-party involvement generally means a more restrictive brief. Deadlines may vary while styles favoured range from conceptual through to realistic, decorative, humorous and technical.

For research purposes, look at *Design Week* or the monthly *Creative Review* (both published by Centaur Communications), or the monthly *Graphics International* (published by Market Link Publishing). Design groups have different biases and specialities – for instance, some might concentrate on packaging or website design while others may deal exclusively with corporate and financial literature.

The Creative Handbook (published by Reed Business Information), available at some reference libraries, carries many listings. Individual contact names are also available at a price from File FX, which specialises in providing creative suppliers with up-to-date information on commissioning clients in all spheres.

Advertising

As with design, you should ideally be quite well established before seeking commissions in advertising. Fees can be high, deadlines short and clients extremely demanding. Illustration has been enjoying something of a renaissance with agencies of late, particularly in areas relating to lifestyle such as food, travel and alcohol. A fairly wide range of styles are used and commissions might be incorporated into direct mail or press advertising, hoardings or animated for television – fees will vary depending on whether a campaign is locally or nationally based.

Most agencies employ an art buyer to look at portfolios. A good one will know what each creative team is working on at any given time and may refer you to specific art directors. Agency listings and client details may be found in *AL*

(Account List File, published by the BRAD Group, a subsidiary of EMAP Media), available at reference libraries. File FX can supply individual contact names. Magazines such as *Creative Review* and Haymarket's weekly, *Campaign*, also carry agency news.

Portfolio presentation

Obviously, the more outlets you can find for your talents the better. However, do not be tempted to develop a myriad of styles in an attempt to please every client you see. Firstly it's unlikely that you will and secondly, in the UK market, you'll stand a better chance of being remembered for one strong, consistent style. You'll also get far more commissions that way. Thus, when assembling your professional portfolio, try to exclude samples which are, in your own eyes, weak, irrelevant, uncharacteristic or simply unenjoyable to do – it is worth noting that even published work counts for little if the content is substandard. For maximum impact, aim to focus solely on your strengths. Should you be one of those rare, multi-talented individuals who find it hard to limit themselves stylistically, try splitting conflicting media or subject matter into separate portfolios geared towards different types of clients.

Having no formal illustrative training need not be a handicap providing your portfolio accurately reflects the needs of potential clients. With this in mind, some find it useful to assemble 'mock-ups' using existing magazine layouts. By responding to the copy, working in proportion to original images and replacing them with your own illustrations, both you and the client will be able to see how your work will look in context. Eventually, as you become more established, you'll be able to augment these with published pieces.

Ideally, your folder should be of the zip-up, ringbound variety and never any bigger than A2 as clients usually have very little desk space. Complexity of style and diversity of subject matter will be key elements in deciding how many pieces to include but all should be neatly, consistently mounted on lightweight paper or card and placed inside protective plastic leaves. Professional photographs of originals are acceptable to clients, as are good quality lasercopies or bubblejet prints. However, tacky, out-of-focus snapshots are not. Also avoid including too many sketchbooks and academic studies – particularly life drawings, which are anathema to clients. It will be taken for granted that you know how to draw from observation.

Interviews and beyond

Making appointments can be hard work but clients take a dim view of spontaneous visits from passing illustrators. Having identified the most relevant person to see (either from a written source or by asking the company directly), clients are best approached by letter or telephone call. Most magazines and publishing houses are happy to see freelances, though portfolio 'drop-offs' are becoming increasingly common within the industry. Some clients will automatically take photocopies of your work for their files. However, it is always advisable to have some form of self-promotional material to leave behind, such as a disk, CD, full-colour postcard or advertising tearsheet. In the case of larger companies, it is also worth asking your contact if others might be interested in your work. An introduction by word of mouth has a distinct advantage over cold-calling.

Cleanliness, punctuality and enthusiasm are more important to clients than the kind of clothes you wear – as is a professional attitude towards taking and fulfilling a brief. A thorough understanding of what a job entails is paramount from the outset. You will need to know all your client's requirements regarding roughs; format, size and flexibility of artwork; preferred medium and whether the image is to be executed in colour or black and white. You will also need to know when the deadline is. Never, under any circumstances, agree to undertake a commission unless you are certain you can deliver on time and always work within your limitations. Talent is nothing without reliability.

Useful addresses

Archant Specialist
The Mill, Bearwalden Business Park, Wendens Ambo, Saffron Walden, Essex CB11 4GB
tel (01799) 544200
email editorial.graphicsintl@virgin.net
Publishes *Graphics International.*

Boomerang Media Ltd
PO Box 141, Aldershot, Hants GU12 4XX
tel (01252) 368368

BRAD Group
33-39 Bowling Green Lane, London EC1R 0DA
tel 020-7505 8000
website www.brad.co.uk
Publishes *ALF* (Account List File).

Centaur Communications
49-50 Poland Street, London W1V 4AX
tel 020-7439 4222
email patrickb@centaur.co.uk
website www.creativereview.co.uk
www.design-week.co.uk
Publishes *Design Week, Creative Review.*

Clarion Events Ltd
Earls Court Exhibition Centre, London SW5 9AT
tel 020-7370 8210
website www.topdraweronline.com
Organises Top Drawer.

Elfande Ltd
Surrey House, 31 Church Street, Leatherhead, Surrey KT22 8EF
tel (01372) 220300 *fax* (01372) 220340
email mail@contact-uk.com
website www.contact-uk.com
Publishes *Contact Illustrators, Visionists* and *New Talent 11.*

File FX
Unit 11, 83-93 Shepperton Road, London N1 3DF
tel 020-7226 6646
email info@filefx.demon.co.uk
Specialises in providing creative suppliers with up-to-date information on commissioning clients in all spheres.

Association of Illustrators
81 Leonard Street, London EC2A 4QS
tel 020-7613 4328 *fax* 020-7613 4417
website www.aoisupplement.co.uk
Publishes *Survive – the Illustrators Guide to a Professional Career, Rights – the Illustrators Guide to Professional Practice* and *Images.* See also page 478.

Reed Business Information
Windsor Court, East Grinstead House, Wood Street, East Grinstead, West Sussex RH19 1XA
tel (01342) 332028 *fax* (01342) 332037
email phewson@reedinfo.co.uk
website www.chb.com
Publishes *The Creative Handbook.*

Trade Promotion Services Ltd
19th Floor, Leon House, 233 High Street, Croydon CR0 9XT
tel 020-8277 5844
email info@emap.com
website www.springfair.com
www.autumnfair.com
Organises the International Gift Fairs.

Self-promotion

There are many ways an illustrator can ensure their work stays uppermost in the industry's consciousness, some involving more expense than others. For those with their own computer/scanner set-up, artwork can be digitised, stored on a suitable application such as KPT Quickshow, which offers a simple slideshow format, or a more sophisticated application such as iView or Extensis Portfolio. Images can also be emailed to clients or copied onto a zip disk or CD. (Floppy disks can be used for this purpose but capacity is limited and they are rapidly becoming obsolete.) Should you opt for CD but lack a compatible writer, a reputable image bureau will be happy to do the necessary.

Prestigeous hardback annuals such as Elfande's *Contact Illustrators* and the digitally oriented *Visionists* (see box), enjoy a high profile, thanks to the extensive free distribution to commissioners. This kind of advertising does not come cheap, however, and, in the case of the Association of Illustrators' *Images*, only those selected to exhibit are permitted to buy pages for their winning entries. A more affordable alternative for recent graduates is Elfande's recently launched softback annual, *New Talent*, which is substantially cheaper to advertise in than the hardback publications and covers illustration, mixed media and photography. *New Talent* also benefits from free distribution to commissioners but, on the downside, you can only ever appear in it once.

Free publicity can be had courtesy of Boomerang Media Ltd, who will print samples of appropriate work to go in postcard advertising racks. These appear in cafés, bars, cinemas, health clubs, universities and schools.

As more and more commissioners turn towards the internet for inspiration, websites are becoming a viable and affordable method of self-promotion for illustrators (see *Setting up a website* on page 556). Those who advertise in *Contact* and *Visionists* are automatically entitled to a web portfolio of 12 images with links back to individual websites. This facility is also offered to *New Talent* advertisers at a discount and as an optional extra. Currently, even those who choose not to advertise in Elfande's annuals can promote their work on the *Contact* website independently. The AOI website features work from recent *Images* annuals together with contact details and links.

Be organised!

Once your career is off the ground it is imperative to keep organised records of all your commissions. Contracts can be verbal as well as written, though details – financial and otherwise – should always be confirmed in writing and duplicated for your files. Likewise, file away corresponding client faxes, letters and order forms. *Survive – the Illustrators Guide to a Professional Career* and *Rights – the Illustrators Guide to Professional Practice* (both published by the Association of Illustrators) offer artists a wealth of practical, legal and ethical information. Subjects covered include contracts, licences, royalties, copyright and ownership of artwork.

Money

Try not to undertake a commission before agreeing on a fee, although this may not always prove practicable in the case of rush jobs. Most publishing and editorial fees are fixed and, unfortunately, there are no hard and fast rules for negotiation where design and advertising are concerned. As a pointer, however, take into consideration the type of client involved and the distribution of the final printed product – obviously a national 48-sheet poster advertising a well-known supermarket chain is likely to pay better than a local press advertisement for a poodle parlour! Some illustrators find it helpful to work out a daily rate incorporating various overheads such as the cost of computer equipment, rent, heating, materials, travel and telephone charges – while others prefer to negotiate on a flat fee basis. Some clients will actually tell you if they have a specific figure in mind, though you may have to put them on the spot. Certainly, as you become more established, you'll be able to use comparable jobs as benchmarks when negotiating a fee.

Basic book-keeping – making a simple, legible record of all your financial transactions, both incoming and outgoing – will be vital to your sanity once the tax inspector starts to loom. It will also make your accountant's job easier, thereby saving you money. If your annual turnover is less than £15,000, it is unnecessary to provide the Inland Revenue with detailed accounts of your earnings. Information regarding your turnover, allowable expenses and net profit may simply be entered on your tax return. Although an accountant is not integral to this process, many find it advantageous to employ one. The tax system is complicated and dealing with the Inland Revenue can be stressful, intimidating and time-consuming – not least since the recent introduction of 'self-assessment'. Accountants offer invaluable advice on tax allowances, National Insurance and tax assessments as well as dealing expertly with the Revenue on your behalf – thereby enabling you to attend to the business of illustrating. See *Show me the money!* on page 388, *Income tax* on page 663, *Social security contributions* on page 673 and *Social security benefits* on page 680.

Show me the money!

Fee negotiation can be a confusing and complicated business for illustrators – not least because jobs can vary so tremendously. **Fig Taylor** *offers a guide to money matters for the freelance illustrator.*

The type of client, the purpose for which you are being commissioned and the usage of your work can all affect the fee you may expect to receive, as can your own professional attitude. Even experienced artists are capable of undervaluing their skills and allowing themselves to be exploited, particularly during a lean period. Add to this the fact that many work in relative isolation – while even those who don't can be reluctant to compare fees with fellow illustrators for fear their peers might be doing better than they are! Here is a rough guide to staying out of trouble and earning your due.

Licence *v.* copyright

Put simply, copyright is the right to reproduce a piece of work – in this instance illustration – anywhere, *ad infinitum*, for any purpose, for a very long time (70 years after your death, to be exact, if you are an EU citizen). It is therefore an exceedingly valuable commodity. By law, copyright automatically belongs to you, the creator of the artwork, unless you agree to sell it to another party. In most cases, clients really have no need to purchase it. The recommended alternative is for you to grant them a licence instead, governing the precise usage of your artwork (see also page 634). This is far cheaper from the client's perspective and, should they subsequently decide to use your work for some purpose other than those outlined in your initial agreement, will benefit you too – as a separate fee will have to be negotiated. Incidentally, even if you were ill-advised enough to sell the copyright, the artwork would still belong to you unless you had also agreed to sell that. (For more detailed information on copyright and contractual matters refer to *Rights – the Illustrators Guide to Professional Practice* and *Survive – the Illustrators Guide to Professional Practice* – see box on page 386, *Copyright questions* on page 627 and *British copyright law* on page 629.)

What if a job goes horribly wrong?

Most commissioners will not expect you to work for nothing unless you are involved in a speculative pitch, in which case it will be up to you to decide if the possible pros outweigh the cons of getting involved. Assuming you have given a job your best shot – i.e. carried out the client's instructions to the letter – it is customary to receive a rejection fee even if the client doesn't care for the outcome. The customary rate is 25% at rough/developmental stage and 50% at finished artwork stage. Cancellation fees, on the other hand, are paid when a commission is cancelled through no fault of the illustrator or, on occasion, even the client. Customary rates in this instance are 25% before rough stage, 33% on delivery of roughs and 100% on delivery of artwork.

Swings and roundabouts

Editorial and publishing fees are almost always fixed. Generally they are considerably lower than advertising and design fees which tend to be negotiable. Not all illustrators work for such a wide variety of clients but it's worth noting that jobs involving lots of money and middlemen tend to be tightly art-directed and more creatively restrictive. An editorial commission paying peanuts, on the other hand, can offer compensation by allowing the artist more creative freedom.

Biting the bullet

So, you've paid your editorial dues and now hanker after design and/or advertising commissions. Just how does one go about the gentle art of negotiation? Well, firstly, you've got to learn some self respect. This means disabusing yourself of the notion that the client is doing you a whopping big favour by descending to your sad, unworthy level because – newsflash! – he *needs* your professional skills to bring his ideas to life. In short, you're worth the money and he knows it, so take a deep breath and read on:

• Before you can quote on a job, you'll need to know exactly what it entails. For what purpose is your work to be used? Will it be used several times and/or for more than one purpose? Will its use be local or national? For how long is the client intending to use it? Who is your client and how soon do they want the work? Are you up against anybody else (who could possibly undercut you)?

• Now ask them what the budget is. Believe it or not, there's a fair chance they might tell you.

• Whether they are forthcoming about funds or not, don't feel you have to pluck a figure out of thin air or agree to their offer immediately. Play for time. Tell them you need to review your current workload and that you'll get back to them within a brief, specified period of time. If nothing else, haggling over the phone is less daunting than haggling face to face.

• If you've had no comparable commissions to date and are a member of the AOI, check out the going rate by calling them for advice on pricing. Failing that, try a friendly client or a fellow illustrator who's worked on similar jobs.

• Have in mind a bottom-line price you're prepared to do the job for and always ask for slightly more than your ideal fee. The client will invariably try to beat you down. (You may find it useful to break down your asking price in order to explain to him exactly what it is he's paying for. How you do this is up to you. Some illustrators charge by the hour, some by the job. Others charge extra for something needed yesterday, time spent researching, model hire if applicable and so on.)

• Lastly, remember that it pays to be flexible. If your initial quote exceeds that client's budget and you really want the job, you can always tell him you're open to further negotiation. If, on the other hand, the job looks suspiciously thankless, stick to your guns. If the client agrees to your exorbitant demands, the job might start to look more appetising!

Getting paid

Of course, this is not the end of the story. Once you've traded terms and conditions, done the job and invoiced the client, you'll then have the unenviable task of getting your hands on your fee. It is customary to send your invoice to the accounts department, stating payment within 30 days. It is also customary for them to ignore this entreaty, regardless of the wolf at your door, and pay you when it suits them. Magazines are the most prompt payers, taking something in the region of four to six weeks. Everyone else takes 60 to 90 days, no matter what.

Be organised when you're chasing up your hard-earned fee. Send out a statement the moment your 30 days has elapsed and call the accounts department as soon as you like. Take names, write down dates and the gist of their feeble excuses ("It's in the post", "He's in a meeting", "He's on holiday and forgot to sign the cheque before he went"), and keep on chasing. You're bound to wear down their resistance eventually. And don't worry about your incessant nagging scuppering your chance of working for the client ever again – these decisions are solely down to the art department and they think you're a gem.

Should payment *still* not be forthcoming three months downs the line, it might be advisable to ask your commissioner to follow things up on your behalf. Chances are they'll be horrified you haven't been paid yet and things will be speedily resolved. In the meantime, you'll have had a good deal of practice of talking money – which can only make things easier in the long run.

Fig Taylor initially began her career as an illustrators' agent in 1983. For 17 years she has been resident 'portfolio surgeon' at the Association of Illustrators and also operates as a private consultant to non-AOI member artists. In addition, she lectures extensively in Business Awareness to BA and HND illustration students.

Art agents and commercial art studios

Before submitting work, artists are advised to make preliminary enquiries and to ascertain terms of work. Commission varies but averages 25–30%. The Association of Illustrators (see page 478) provides a valuable service for illustrators, agents and clients.

**Member of the Society of Artists Agents*
†Member of the Association of Illustrators

Advocate†

Advocate Gallery, 372 Old York Road, London SW18 1SP
tel (07000) 238622 *fax* 020-8788 0388
email authors/hoffman@cs.com
website www.advocate-art.com
Director Edward Burns

Represents 80 artists working in all mediums and styles. Supplies greeting card and book publishers, and editorial and design industries. 5 specialised agents. Strong in secondary right sales and image licensing. Operates as a co-operative. Founded 1996.

Allied Artists

5 Fauconberg Road, London W4 3JZ
tel 020-8995 5500 *fax* 020-8995 8844
email info@alliedartists.ltd.uk
website www.alliedartists.ltd.uk
Contacts Gary Mills (director), Mary Burtenshaw

Represents over 40 artists specialising in highly finished realistic figure illustrations, stylised juvenile illustrations for children's books, and cartoons for magazines, books, plates, prints, cards and advertising. Extensive library of stock illustrations.

Arena*†

Quantum Artists Ltd, 108 Leonard Street, London EC2A 4RH
tel 020-7613 4040 *fax* 020-7613 1441
email info@arenaworks.com
website www.info@arenaworks.com
Contact Tamlyn Francis

Represents 35 artists working mostly for book covers, children's books and design groups. Average commission 30%. Founded 1970.

The Art Market*†

51 Oxford Drive, London SE1 2FB
tel 020-7407 8111 *fax* 020-7407 8222
email info@artmarketillustration.com
website www.artmarketillustration.com
Director Philip Reed

Represents 20 artists creating illustrations for publishing, design and advertising. Founded 1989.

Associated Freelance Artists Ltd

124 Elm Park Mansions, Park Walk, London SW10 0AR
tel 020-7352 6890 *fax* 020-7352 8125
email pekes.afa@virgin.net
Directors Eva Morris, Doug FitzMaurice

Freelance illustrators mainly in

children's educational fields, and some greeting cards.

Aviation Artists, The Guild of

Unit 410, Bondway Business Centre, 71 Bondway, London SW8 1SQ
tel/fax 020-7735 0634
email admin@gava.org.uk
website www.gava.org.uk
President Michael Turner PGAVA, *Secretary* Ian Burnstock

Professional body of 350 artists specialising in aviation art in all mediums. The Guild sells, commissions and exhibits members' work. Commission: 25%. Founded 1971.

Beehive Illustration

105 Watermoor Road, Cirencester, Glos. GL7 1LD
tel (01285) 885149 *fax* (01285) 641291
email paul@beehiveillustration.co.uk
website www.beehiveillustration.co.uk
Owners Paul Beebee, Karen Beebee

Represents 40 artists specialising in education and general children's publishing illustration. Commission: 25%. Founded 1990.

Sarah Brown Agency†

10 The Avenue, London W13 8PH
tel 020-8998 0390 *fax* 020-8843 1175
email sbagency@globalnet.co.uk
website www.sbagency.com
Contact Brian Fennelly

Illustrations for publishing and advertising. Sae essential for unsolicited material. Commission: 25% UK, 33.3% USA. Founded 1977.

Central Illustration Agency*†

36 Wellington Street, London WC2E 7BD
tel 020-7240 8925/836 1106 *fax* 020-7836 1177
email c.illustration.a@dial.pipex.com
website www.centralillustration.com
Director Brian Grimwood, Louisa St Pierre

Illustrations for design, publishing, animation and advertising. Commission: 30%. Founded 1983.

David Lewis Illustration Agency†

Worlds End Studios, 134 Lots Road, London SW10 0RJ
tel 020-7435 7762, *mobile* (07931) 824674
fax 020-7435 1945
email davidlewis34@hotmail.com
Director David Lewis, *Associate Director* Robin Broadway

Considers all types of illustration for a variety of applications but mostly suitable for book and magazine publishers, design groups, recording companies and corporate institutions. Also offers a comprehensive selection of images suitable for subsidiary rights purposes. Please send return postage with samples. Commission: 30%. Founded 1974.

Début Art†

30 Tottenham Street, London W1T 4RJ
tel 020-7636 1064 *fax* 020-7580 7017
email debutart@coningsbygallery.demon.co.uk
website www.debutart.com
Directors Andrew Coningsby, Luke Wilson, Benjamin Cox

Represents 60 artists working in mixed media, digital, photographic 3D and 2D collage and montage. Commission: 25%. Founded 1985.

Barry Everitt Associates

23 Mill Road, Stock, Essex CM4 9LJ
tel (01277) 840639 *fax* (01277) 841223
Contact Barry M. Everitt

Design and art resource specialising in licensing reproduction rights for greetings cards, fine art prints, calendars, giftware, etc. Always pleased to see the work of new and established artists and illustrators. Colour copies or photographs required initially with sae for return or reply.

Folio Illustrators' & Designers' Agents*†

10 Gate Street, Lincoln's Inn Fields, London WC2A 3HP
tel 020-7242 9562 *fax* 020-7242 1816
email all@folioart.demon.co.uk
website www.folioart.co.uk

All areas of illustration. Please send sae with samples. Founded 1976.

Graham-Cameron Illustration†

The Studio, 23 Holt Road, Sheringham, Norfolk NR26 8NB
tel (01263) 821333 *fax* (01263) 821334
Partners Mike Graham-Cameron, Helen Graham-Cameron

Represents 37 artists. Undertakes all forms of illustration for publishing and communications. Specialist in educational and children's books. Send sae with samples. Founded 1988.

John Hodgson Agency*†

38 Westminster Palace Gardens, Artillery Row, London SW1P 1RR
tel 020-7580 3773 *fax* 020-7222 4468

Publishing (children's picture books) and advertising. Sae with samples please. Commission: 25%. Founded 1965.

Illustration Ltd*†
1 Vicarage Crescent, London SW11 3LP
tel 020-7228 8882 *fax* 020-7228 8886
email team@illustrationweb.com
website www.illustrationweb.com
Contact Harry Lyon-Smith, Marie-Claire Carver, Vanessa Dell
Illustrations and animation for international advertisers, designers and publishers. Commission: 33.3% or 25%.

Image by Design
Norton Cottage, High Street, Norton St Philip, Bath BA2 7LH
tel (01373) 834666 *fax* (01373) 834777
email info@imagebydesign-licensing.co.uk
website www.imagebydesign-licensing.co.uk
Contact Burniece M. Brown
Artwork for prints, greetings cards, calendars, posters, stationery, jigsaw puzzles, tableware, ceramics. Commission: negotiable. Founded 1987.

The Inkshed*†
98 Columbia Road, London E2 7QB
tel 020-7613 2323 *fax* 020-7613 2726
email makecontact@globalnet.co.uk
website www.inkshed.co.uk
Partners Tim Woolgar, Jacqueline Hollister, *Contact* Elaine Smith, Abby Glassfield (agents)
Represents 30 artists who work across the board – advertising, design, publishing, editorial. Commission: 25%. Founded 1985.

Kathy Jakeman Illustration†
Richmond Business Centre, 23-24 George Street, Richmond, Surrey TW9 1HY
tel 020-8332 7755 *fax* (07071) 225 115
email kathy@kji.co.uk
website www.kji.co.uk
Illustration for publishing – especially children's, also design, editorial and advertising. Please send sae with samples. Commission: 25%.

Libba Jones Associates
Hopton Manor, Hopton, Nr Wirksworth, Derbyshire DE4 4DF
tel (01629) 540353 *fax* (01629) 540577
email ljassociates@easynet.co.uk
website www.libbajonesassociates.com
Contacts Libba Jones, Ieuan Jones
High quality artwork and design for china, greetings cards and giftwrap, jigsaw puzzles, calendars, prints, posters, stationery, book illustration, fabric design. Submission of samples required for consideration. Founded 1983.

JWL
Parlington Hall, Aberford, West Yorkshire LS25 3EG
tel 0113-281 3913 *fax* 0113-281 3911
email info@jwl.uk.com
Managing Director Janet Woodward, *Manager* Pamela Dash
International art licensing agency. Licensing concepts, artwork and children's TV projects for merchandise. Properties include *Rambling Ted, Kit 'n' Kin*. Freelance contributions welcome but ideas must be well developed. Samples with sae.

Lavapepper Ltd†
40 Weir Road, London SW12 0NA
tel (07050) 192354 *fax* (07050) 286 044
email its@lavapepper.com
website www.lavapepper.com
Directors Izabella Knights, James Muchmore
Seeks strong, idiosyncratic styles, including computer-generated images and collage. Look at website for styles before sending samples with sae. Commission 25–35%. Founded 1998.

John Martin & Artists Ltd
30 Maple Street, London W1T 6HA
tel 020-7734 9000 *fax* (01245) 382055
website www.jm-a.co.uk
Contacts Bernard Bowen-Davies, Pythia Ashton-Jewell
Represents 40 illustrators, mainly producing artwork for children's fiction/ non-fiction and educational books. Please include return postage with submissions. Founded 1956.

Meiklejohn Illustration*†
5 Risborough Street, London SE1 0HF
tel 020-7593 0500 *fax* 020-7593 0501
email mjn@mjgrafix.demon.co.uk
website www.theartbook.com
www.meiklejohn.co.uk
Contacts Paul Meiklejohn, Malcolm Sanders
All types of illustration.

N.E. Middleton
Richmond Business Centre, 23-24 George Street, Richmond, Surrey TW9 1HY
tel 020-8332 7755 *fax* (07071) 225 115
Designs for greetings cards, stationery, prints, calendars and china. Sae with samples, please.

Maggie Mundy Illustrators' Agency
14 Ravenscourt Park Mansions, Dalling Road, London W6 0HG
tel 020-8748 2029 *fax* 020-8748 0353
email maggiemundy@compuserve.com
Represents 20 artists in varying styles of illustration for children's books. The Agency's books are closed.

NB Illustration†
40 Bowling Green Lane, London EC1R 0NE
tel 020-7278 9131 *fax* 020-7278 9121
email info@nbillustration.co.uk
website www.nbillustration.co.uk
Directors Joe Najman, Charlotte Berens, Paul Najman
Represents 20+ artists and will consider all material for the commercial illustration market. Sae essential. Commission: 30%. Founded 2000.

The Organisation*†
The Basement, 69 Caledonian Road, London N1 9BT
tel 020-7833 8268 *fax* 020-7833 8269
email organise@easynet.co.uk
website www.organisart.co.uk
Contact Lorraine Owen
Various styles of illustration supplied for book work in adult, children's and educational markets. Also for print, advertising, packaging and editorial. Average commission: 30%. Sae essential for unsolicited samples. Founded 1986.

Oxford Designers & Illustrators
Aristotle Lane, Oxford OX2 6TR
tel (01865) 512331 *fax* (01865) 512408
email richard@odi-illustration.co.uk
website www.o-d-i.com
Studio of 25 full-time illustrators working for publishers, business and industry. All types of artwork including science, technical, airbrush, graphic, medical, biological, botanical, natural history, figure, cartoon, maps, diagrams, and charts. Artwork supplied as PDF files or on a CD, Zip optical disk or ISDN, Mac or PC, with both b&w and colour proofs. Not an agency. Founded 1968.

Pennant Inc.*†
16 Littleton Street, London SW18 3SY
tel 020-8947 4002 *fax* 020-8946 7667
email matt@pennantinc.co.uk
website www.pennantinc.co.uk
Director Matthew Doyle
Illustrations for publishing, design and advertising. Samples must be accompanied by an sae. Commission: 30%. Founded 1992.

Pink Barge
13 Wyndham Place, London W1H 2PY
tel 020-7486 1053 *fax* 020-7262 1130
Director Maggee Barge
Represents 20 artists working in advertising, publishing and corporate art. Commission: 25%. Founded 1982.

Linda Rogers Associates†
PO Box 330, 163 Half Moon Lane, London SE24 9WB
tel 020-7501 9106 *fax* 020-7501 9175
email lr@lindarogers.net
website www.lindarogers.net
Partners Linda Rogers and Peter Sims
Represents 65 illustrators and author/illustrators in all fields of illustration. Specialises in children's books, educational, information books; adult leisure books and magazines. Reply only with sae. Artwork samples only viewed via post, *not* email. Commission: 25%. Founded 1973.

SGA Illustration Agency†
(formerly Simon Girling & Associates)
18 High Street, Hadleigh, Suffolk IP7 5AP
tel (01473) 824083 *fax* (01473) 827846
email info@sgadesignart.com
website www.sgadesignart.com
Represents over 50 illustrators. Mainly working within publishing (early learning through to teenage). Also manages projects from conception to final film. See website for portfolio of illustration samples. Commission: 30%. Founded 1985.

Specs Art†
93 London Road, Cheltenham, Glos. GL52 6HL
tel (01242) 515951 *fax* (01242) 518862
email roland@specsart.com
website www.specsart.com
Partners Roland Berry and Stephanie Prosser
High quality illustration work for advertisers, publishers and all other forms of visual communication. Specialises in licensed character illustration.

Temple Rogers Artists' Agency
120 Crofton Road, Orpington, Kent BR6 8HZ
tel (01689) 826249 *fax* (01689) 896312
Contact Patrick Kelleher
Illustrations for children's educational books and magazine illustrations. Commission: by arrangement.

Vicki Thomas Associates

195 Tollgate Road, London E6 5JY
tel 020-7511 5767 *fax* 020-7473 5177
Consultant Vicki Thomas

Considers the work of illustrators and designers working in greetings and gift industries, and promotes such work to gift, toy, publishing and related industries. Written application and b&w photo copies required. Commission: 30%. Founded 1985.

Thorogood Illustration Ltd*†

5 Dryden Street, London WC2E 9NW
tel 020-7829 8468/9 *fax* 020-7497 1300
email draw@thorogood.net
website www.thorogood.net
Directors Doreen Thorogood, Stephen Thorogood

Represents 30 artists for advertising, design, publishing and animation work. Please send return postage with samples. Commission: 30%. Founded 1977.

TWO:Design London Ltd

Studio 20, The Arches, Hartland Road, London NW1 8HR
tel 020-7267 1118 *fax* 020-7482 0221
email studio@twodesign.net
website www.twodesign.net
Directors Graham N. Peake, David M. Coventon

Studio providing comprehensive services: design, photography, image creation and manipulation, typesetting, artworking, marketing, point-of-sale material, etc. Specialists in general books, magazines and periodicals. Founded 1997.

Ulric Design

PO Box 55, Church Stretton, Shropshire SY6 6WR
tel (01694) 781354 *fax* (01694) 781372
Directors Ulric Woodhams, Elizabeth Follows

Studio offering high quality bespoke graphics, corporate ID and illustration.

Wildlife Art Ltd†

Studio 16 Muspole Workshops, 25-27 Muspole Street, Norwich, Norfolk NR3 1DJ
tel (01603) 617868 *fax* (01603) 219017
email info@wildlife-art.co.uk

Illustrations of all things natural, including gardening and food. Clients range from children's/adults' books to design and advertising agencies. Sae must be included with work submitted for consideration. Commission: 30%. Founded 1992.

Michael Woodward Fine Art

Parlington Hall, Aberford, West Yorkshire LS25 3EG
tel 0113-281 3913 *fax* 0113-281 3911
email art@mwc.com
website www.woodward-fineart.co.uk
Managing Director Michael Woodward

Artist management company representing: Anthony Christian, Terry Durham, Jude Roberts, David Greenwood. Own publishing division. Artists should send transparencies or laser copies of work with biography, plus sae. Division of MWC Group. Founded 1996.

Winning the greeting card game

The UK population spends £1 billion a year on greeting cards yet finding a route into this fiercely competitive industry is not always easy. ***Jacqueline Brown*** *steers artists through the greeting card maze.*

The UK greeting card industry leads the world on two counts – design and innovation and per capita send. On average people in the UK send 44 cards a year, 85% of which are bought by women.

But just how do you, as an artist, go about satisfying this voracious appetite of the card-sending public? There are two main options: either to become a greeting card publisher yourself or to supply existing greeting card publishers with your artwork and be paid a fee for doing so.

The idea of setting up your own greeting card publishing company may sound exciting, but this decision should not be taken lightly. Going down this route will involve taking on all the set up and running costs of a publishing company as well as the production, selling and administrative responsibilities. This often leaves little time for you to do what you do best – creating the artwork.

There are estimated to be around 800 greeting card publishers in the UK, ranging in size from one-person operations to multinational corporations, roughly 200 of which are regarded as 'serious' publishers (see page 398). Not all of them accept freelance artwork, but a great many do. Remember, whatever the size of the company, all publishers rely on good designs.

Finding the right publishers

While some publishers concentrate on producing a certain type of greeting card (e.g. humorous, fine art or juvenile), the majority publish a variety of greeting card ranges. Unfortunately, this makes it more difficult for you as an artist to target the most appropriate potential publishers for your work. There are various ways in which you can research the market, quickly improve your publisher knowledge and, therefore, reduce the amount of wasted correspondence:

- **Go shopping.** Browse the displays in card shops, newsagents and other high street shops, department stores and gift shops. This will not only give you an insight into what is already available but also which publishers may be interested in your work. Most publishers include their contact details on the backs of the cards.
- **Trade fairs.** There are a number of trade exhibitions held during the year at which

Some greeting card language

Own brand/bespoke publishers. These design specific to a retailer's needs.

Spring Seasons. The industry term to describe greeting cards for Valentine's Day, Mother's Day, Easter and Father's Day. Publishers generally launch these ranges all together in June/July.

Greeting card types. Traditional; cute or whimsical; contemporary/quirky art; juvenile; handmade or hand-finished; fine art; photographic, humorous.

Finishes and treatments. Artists will not be expected to know the production techniques and finishes, but a working knowledge is often an advantage. Some of the most commonly used finishes and treatments include: embossing (raised portion of a design), die-cutting (where the card is cut into a shape or includes an aperture), foiling (metallic film) and flitter (a glitter-like substance).

publishers exhibit their greeting card ranges to retailers and overseas distributors. By visiting these exhibitions, you will gain a broad overview of the design trends in the industry, as well as the current ranges of individual publishers. Some publishers are willing to meet artists and look through their portfolios on the stand but others are not. If you believe your work could be relevant for them, ask for a contact name and follow it up afterwards. Have a supply of business cards handy, perhaps illustrated with some of your work, to leave with publishers.

Types of publishers

There are two broad categories of publisher – wholesale and direct-to-retail – each employing a different method of distribution to reach the retailer.

Wholesale publishers distribute their products to the retailer via greeting card wholesalers or cash-and-carry outlets. They work on volume sales and have a rapid turnover of designs, many being used with a variety of different captions. For example, the same floral design may be used for cards for mothers, grandmothers, aunts and sisters. It is therefore usual for the artist to leave a blank space on the design to accommodate the caption. Until recently, wholesale publishers were generally only interested in traditional, cute and juvenile designs, but they now publish across the board, including contemporary, humorous ranges.

Direct-to-retail (DTR) publishers supply retailers via sales agents or reps. Most greeting cards sold through specialist card shops and gift shops are supplied by DTR publishers, which range from multinational corporations down to small, trendy niche publishing companies. These publishers market series of ranges based on distinctive design themes or characters. Categories of DTR cards include contemporary art/fun, fine art, humour, children's, photographic and traditional.

Approaching a publisher

Unfortunately, there is no standard way of approaching and submitting work to a card publisher. The first step is to establish that the publisher you wish to approach accepts work from freelance artists; then find out their requirements for submission and to whom it should be addressed.

It is always better to send several examples of your work to show the breadth of your artistic skills. Some publishers prefer to see finished designs while others are happy with well-presented sketches. *Never* send originals: instead send photocopies, laser copies or photographs, and include at least one design in colour. Never be tempted to sell similar designs to two publishers – a bad reputation will follow you around.

Some publishers will be looking to purchase individual designs for specific sending occasions while others will be more intent on looking for designs which could be developed to make up a range. Bear in mind that publishers work a long way in advance, e.g. Christmas ranges are launched to the retailers in January. Development of a range may take up to six months prior to launching.

Also remember that cards in retail outlets are rarely displayed in their entirety. Therefore, when designing a card make sure that some of the 'action' appears in the top half.

When interest is shown

Some publishers respond to submissions from artists immediately while others prefer to deal with them on a monthly basis. A publisher's response may be in the form of a request for more submissions of a specific design style or of a specific character. This speculative development work is usually carried out free of charge. Always meet your deadline (news travels fast in the industry).

A publisher interested in buying your artwork will probably then issue you with a contract. This may cover aspects such as the terms of payment; rights of usage of the design (e.g. is it just for greeting cards or will it include giftwrap and/or stationery?); territory of usage (most publishers want worldwide rights); and ownership of copyright or license period.

There is no set industry standard rate of pay for greeting card artists. Publishers pay artists either on a per design or per

Further information

The Greeting Card Association
United House, North Road, London N7 9DP
tel 020-7619 0396
email gca@max-publishing.co.uk
website www.greetingcardassociation.org.uk
The UK trade association for greeting card publishers. Produces information leaflets on design and on writing, each with a list of members accepting free-lance work. See website (due online Aug 2002), or write to Sharon Little enclosing an A4 sae (postage £1); pack includes free copy of *Progressive Greetings Worldwide* or one of its relevant supplements.

Trade fairs

Spring Fair Birmingham, NEC
Contact TPS *tel* 020-8277 5800
Takes place 2–6 Feb 2003

Autumn Fair Birmingham, NEC
Contact TPS *tel* 020-8277 5800
Takes place 7–11 Sept 2003

Top Drawer, Earls Court
Contact Clarion Events *tel* 020-7370 8359
Takes place 19–21 Jan 2003, May 2003

Home and Gift, Harrogate
Contact Clarion Events *tel* 020-7370 8359
Takes place 13–16 July 2003

Trade magazines

Progressive Greetings Worldwide
Max Publishing, United House, North Road, London N7 9DP
tel 020-7700 6740 *fax* 020-7609 4222
12 p.a. (£40 p.a.)
The official magazine of the Greeting Card Association. Provides an insight to the industry, including an up-to-date list of publishers. Also includes special supplements such as *Focus on Art Cards* (annual) and *Focus on Humorous Cards.*

Progressive Greetings hosts The Henries, the greeting card industry awards. The September edition includes details of the finalists in the different categories and the November issue features the winners.

Greetings Today
(formerly Greetings Magazine)
Lema Publishing, Unit No. 1, Queen Mary's Avenue, Watford, Herts. WD1 7JR
tel (01923) 250909 *fax* (01923) 250995
Publisher Malcolm Naish, *Editor* Vicky Hancocks
Monthly £45 p.a. (other rates on application)
Articles, features and news related to the greetings card industry. Includes Artists Directory for aspiring artists wishing to attract the eye of publishers. Runs seminars for small publishers and artists.

range basis in one of the following ways:

- **Flat fee.** A one-off payment is made to the artist for ownership of a design for an unlimited period. The industry standard is around £200–£250 for a single design, and payment on a sliding scale for more than one design.
- **Licensing fee.** The publisher is granted the right to use a piece of artwork for a specified number of years, after which the full rights revert to the artist. Payment to the artist is approximately £150 upwards per design.
- **Licensing fee plus royalty.** As above plus a royalty payment on each card sold. Artists would generally receive a minimum of £100 for the licensing fee plus 3% of the trade price of each card sold.
- **Advance royalty deal.** A goodwill advance on royalties is paid to the artist. In the case of a range, the artist would receive a goodwill advance of say £500–£1000 plus 5% additional royalty payment once the threshold is reached.
- **Royalty only.** The artist receives regular royalty payments, generally paid quarterly, based on the number of cards sold. Artists should expect a sales report and royalty statement.

The fees stated above should only be regarded as a rough guideline. Fees and advances are generally paid on completion of artwork. Publishers which have worldwide rights pay royalties for sales overseas to artists, although these will be on a *pro rata* basis to the export trade price.

Jacqueline Brown is editor of *Progressive Greetings Worldwide* and general secretary of the Greeting Card Association.

Card and stationery publishers which accept illustrations and verses

Before submitting work, artists are advised to write giving details of the work they have to offer, and asking for requirements.

**Member of the Greeting Card Association*

Andrew Brownsword Collection – see Hallmark Cards Plc

Card Connection Ltd*
Park House, South Street, Farnham, Surrey GU9 7QQ
tel (01252) 892300 *fax* (01252) 892363
email ho@card-connection.co.uk
Managing Director Adrian Atkinson, *Senior Product and Marketing Manager* Alison Mahoney
Cute, humour, traditional, floral, contemporary, photography. Submit artwork, colour copies or 5 x 4in transparencies of originals. Humour verses only. Founded 1992.

Carlton Cards Ltd*
Mill Street East, Dewsbury, West Yorkshire WF12 9AW
tel (01924) 465200
Marketing Director Keith Auty, *Creative Director* Linda Marshall
All types of artwork, any size; submit as colour roughs, colour copies or transparencies. Especially interested in humorous artwork and ideas.

Caspari Ltd*
9 Shire Hill, Saffron Walden, Essex CB11 3AP
tel (01799) 513010 *fax* (01799) 513101
Managing Director Keith Entwisle
Traditional fine art/classic images; 5 x 4in transparencies. No verses. Founded 1990.

The Classic Card Company Ltd – see Hallmark Cards Plc

Gallery Five Ltd*
121 King Street, London W6 9JG
tel 020-8741 8394 *fax* 020-8741 4444
Send samples of work FAO 'Gallery Five Art Studio'. Colour photocopies, Mac-formatted zip/CD/floppy acceptable, plus sae. Founded 1961.

Gemma International Ltd*
Linmar House, 6 East Portway, Andover, Hants. SP10 3LU
tel (01264) 388400 *fax* (01264) 366243
website www.gemma-international.co.uk
Directors L. Rudd-Clarke, M. Rudd-Clarke, A. Parkin, T. Rudd-Clarke, W. O'Loughlin, R. Howard
Cute, contemporary, leading-edge designs for children, teens and young adults, and mainstream adult humour. Considers humorous verses. Founded 1984.

Gibson Greetings International Ltd
Gibson House, Hortonwood 30, Telford, Shropshire TF1 7YF
tel (01952) 608333 *fax* (01952) 605259
email jan_taylor@gibson-greetings.co.uk
Product Director Jan Taylor
All everyday and seasonal illustrations: cute, humorous, juvenile, traditional and contemporary designs, as well as surface pattern. Greeting card traditional and humorous verse. Founded 1991.

The Gordon Fraser Gallery – see Hallmark Cards Plc

Graphic Humour Ltd
4 Britannia House, Point Pleasant, Wallsend, Tyne & Wear NE28 6HA
tel 0191-295 4200 *fax* 0191-295 3916
email enquiries@graphic-humour.demon.co.uk
website www.graphic-humour.demon.co.uk
Risqué and everyday artwork ideas for greetings cards; short, humorous copy. Founded 1984.

Greetings Cards By Noel Tatt Ltd

t/a Noel Tatt Group,
Appledown House, Barton Business Park,
Appledown Way, New Dover Road, Canterbury,
Kent CT1 3TE
tel (01227) 811600 *fax* (01227) 811601
email mail@noeltatt.co.uk
Directors Jarle Tatt, Diane Tatt, Richard Parsons,
Ian Hylands

Greetings cards, giftwrap. Founded 1988.

Hallmark Cards Plc*

Bingley Road,
West Yorkshire BD9 8SD
Submissions Mr Richmond Denton (illustrations),
Paul Treacy (words)

Illustrations: all subjects considered. Submit colour copies and/or transparencies but not original artwork. Ensure that all work is named and include an sae. Words: verses, captions, jokes, etc considered.

Hanson White – UKG Speciality Products

9th Floor, Wettern House, 56 Dingwall Road,
Croydon, Surrey CR0 0XH
tel 020-8260 1200 *fax* 020-8260 1213
email hannah.turpin@ukgsp.co.uk
david.blake@ukgsp.co.uk
Artwork Submissions Editor Hannah Turpin,
Copy Submissions Editor Hannah Turpin
(everyday), David Blake (seasonal)

Humorous artwork and cartoons for greeting cards, including Christmas, Valentine's Day, Mother's Day and Father's Day. Humorous copy lines, punchline jokes, poems and rhymes; guidelines available. Founded 1958.

Images & Editions*

Bourne Road, Essendine, Nr Stamford,
Lincs. PE9 4UW
tel (01780) 757118 *fax* (01780) 754629
Contact Joanne Forrow (director)

Greetings card artwork: cute, floral, animals. Founded 1984.

Jarrold Publishing

Whitefriars, Norwich NR3 1TR
tel (01603) 763300 *fax* (01603) 662748
email publishing@jarrold.com
website www.jarrold-publishing.co.uk
Managing Director Caroline Jarrold, *Submissions*
Rose Joy (01603) 677331

Decorative colour artwork – floral, kitchen, animals. Humour. Calendars only; no cards. Please send sae with all submissions to Rose Joy. Founded 1770.

Jodds*

PO Box 353, Bicester, Oxon OX27 0GS
tel (01869) 278550 *fax* (01869) 278551
email design@joddscards.com
website www.joddscards.com
Partners M. Payne and J.S. Payne

Contemporary art style greetings cards; must give out a warm feel. Submit colour photocopies with sae. No verses. Founded 1988.

Leeds Postcards

4 Granby Road, Leeds LS6 3AS
email xtine@leedspostcards.com
website www.leedspostcards.com
Contact Christine Hankinson

Publisher and distributor of postcards worldwide. Artwork that challenges and amuses. See website for suitability. Send copies of artwork with sae. Founded 1979.

Ling Design Ltd*

The Old Brewery, Newtown, Bradford on Avon,
Wilts. BA15 1NF
tel (01225) 863991 *fax* (01225) 863992
Creative Director Kirsten Boyd

Artwork for greetings cards and giftwrap.

Medici*

Grafton House, Hyde Estate Road,
London NW9 6JZ
tel 020-8205 2500 *fax* 020-8205 2552
Contact The Art Department

Requirements: full colour or black and white paintings/sketches/etchings/ designs suitable for reproduction as greeting cards. Send preliminary letter with brief details of work and colour copies.

The Paper House Group plc

Waterwells Drive, Gloucester, Glos. GL2 4PH
tel (01452) 888999 *fax* (01452) 888912
email chris.hobbs@paperhouse.co.uk
website www.paperhouse.co.uk
Product Director Chris Wilcox

Publishers of greeting cards specialising in cartoon humour illustration, contemporary art styles and traditional verse design in special occasions and family birthday.

Paper Studios

4 Britannia House, Point Pleasant, Wallsend,
Tyne and Wear NE28 6HA
tel 0191-295 4200 *fax* 0191-295 3916
email paperstudios@graphic-humour.demon.co.uk
Directors Alan Picton, Mike Rowell

Traditional, floral and cute designs for greetings cards for all occasions – artwork and 35mm transparencies. Verses considered. Founded 1999.

Paperlink Ltd*
356 Kennington Road, London SE11 4LD
tel 020-7582 8244 *fax* 020-7587 5212
Directors Louise Tighe, Jo Townsend, Tim Porte, Tim Purcell

Publishers of ranges of humorous and contemporary art greetings cards, giftwrap, calendars, notelets, mugs, prints. Produce products under licence for charities. Founded 1986.

Pepperpot
Royston Road, Duxford, Cambridge CB2 4QY
tel (01223) 836825 *fax* (01223) 833321
Publishing Controller Linda Worsfold

Gift stationery, photo albums, gift cards. Colour illustrations; cute/traditional/ floral. Submit original artwork or 5 x 4in transparencies. No verses. Division of Copywrite Designs Ltd.

Pineapple Park Ltd*
58 Wilbury Way, Hitchin, Herts. SG4 0TP
tel (01462) 442021 *fax* (01462) 440418
email info@pineapplepark.co.uk
Directors Peter M. Cockerline, Sarah M. Parker

Illustrations and photographs for publication as greetings cards. Contemporary, cute, humour: submit artwork or laser copies with sae. Transparencies of animals, babies, children and floral. Humour copy/jokes accepted without artwork. Also concepts for ranges.

Powell Publishing
57 Coombe Valley Road, Dover, Kent CT17 0EX
tel (01304) 213999 *fax* (01304) 240151
Directors B.W. Powell (chairman), T.J. Paulett (managing)

Greetings card publishers. Interested in Christmas designs for the charity card market. Division of Powell Print Ltd.

Nigel Quiney Publications Ltd
Cloudesley House, Shire Hill, Saffron Walden, Essex CB11 3FB
tel (01799) 520200 *fax* (01799) 520100
website www.nigelquiney.com
Contact Ms J. Arkinstall, Product & Marketing Director

Everyday and seasonal greetings cards and giftwrap including fine art, photographic, humour, fun art, contemporary and cute. Submit colour copies, photographs or transparencies: no original artwork please.

Rainbow Cards Ltd*
Kingswood Business Park, Holyhead Road, Albrighton, Wolverhampton, West Midlands WV7 3AU
tel (01902) 374347 *fax* (01902) 376001
email sales@rainbowcards.co.uk

Artwork for humorous and traditional greetings cards. Founded 1976.

Really Good*
Osney Mead, Oxford OX2 0ES
tel (01865) 246888 *fax* (01865) 246999
Director David Hicks

Fun and funny cards, stationery and gifts. Allow plenty of time for review. Do not send originals. No verses. Founded 1987.

Felix Rosenstiel's Widow & Son Ltd
Fine Art Publishers, 33-35 Markham Street, London SW3 3NR
tel 020-7352 3551 *fax* 020-7351 5300
email sales@felixr.com
website www.felixr.com

Invites offers of original oil paintings and strong watercolours of a professional standard for reproduction as picture prints for the picture framing trade. Any type of subject considered; send photographs of work.

Royle Publications Ltd – see **The Paper House Group plc**

Santoro Graphics Ltd
Rotunda Point, 11 Hartfield Crescent, London SW19 3RL
tel 020-8781 1100 *fax* 020-8781 1101
email enquiries@santorographics.com
Directors Lucio Santoro, Meera Santoro (art)

Publishers of innovative and award-winning designs for greetings cards, giftwrap and gift stationery. Bold contemporary images with an international appeal. Subjects covered: quirky and humorous, whimsical, 'Fifties, 'Seventies, futuristic! Submit photographs or colour photocopies. Founded 1985.

Scandecor Ltd
3 The Ermine Centre, Hurricane Close, Huntingdon, Cambs. PE29 6WY
tel (01480) 456395 *fax* (01480) 456269
Managing Director Derek Shirley

Drawings all sizes. Founded 1967.

Second Nature Ltd*

10 Malton Road, London W10 5UP
tel 020-8960 0212 *fax* 020-8960 8700
email rods@secondnature.co.uk
website www.secondnature.co.uk
Publishing Director Rod Schragger

Contemporary artwork for greetings cards; jokes for humorous range; short modern sentiment; verses. Founded 1981.

W.N. Sharpe Ltd – see Hallmark Cards Plc

Solomon & Whitehead Ltd

Lynn Lane, Shenstone, Staffs. WS14 0DX
tel (01543) 480696 *fax* (01543) 481619
email sales@fineartgroup.co.uk

Fine art prints, limited editions and originals, framed and unframed.

Soul*

Osney Mead, Oxford OX2 0ES
tel (01865) 434444 *fax* (01865) 454444
Director David Hicks

Publishers of contemporary, fine and quirky art. Allow plenty of time for review. Please do not send originals. Sister company of Really Good.

Trumpet Limôn

Osney Mead, Oxford OX2 0ES
tel (01865) 240140 *fax* (01865) 454444

Publishers of limited edition prints. Allow plenty of time for review. Please do not send originals.

Twin Oaks Publishing – see Nigel Quiney Publications Ltd

Valentines – see Hallmark Cards Plc

Webb Ivory (Burton) Ltd

Queen Street, Burton-on-Trent, Staffs. DE14 3LP
tel (01283) 566311
email enquiries@webb-ivory.co.uk

High-quality Christmas cards and paper products.

Wishing Well Studios Ltd*

Kellet Close, Martland Park, Wigan, Lancs. WN5 0LP
tel (01942) 218888 *fax* (01942) 218899
email info@wishingwell.co.uk
website www.wishingwell.co.uk
Directors David Evans, Brian Phillips

Traditional, cute, contemporary and humorous images. Send samples, colour photocopies or mock-ups, *not* originals. Considers verses and jokes.

A serious look at marketing cartoons

*There are many freelance opportunities for comic artists and illustrators. In this article, **John Byrne** explores potential markets and offers guidance for success.*

Despite fears that 21st century innovations like computer graphics and 3D animation might supersede the appeal of simple pen and ink drawings, opportunities for the aspiring cartoonist are in fact more plentiful than every before. Many of the most lucrative multimedia and merchandising properties in recent years, from *Dilbert* to *X-men*, started life as cartoons. Freelance cartooning has its share of ups and downs, but the most important skill is not so much artistic creativity as creative marketing of your individual talent. Many cartoonists are certainly accomplished artists, but today funny ideas and sharp captions are just as important as the visuals. Writers with comic flair may consider collaborating with an artist or even trying their own simple drawings.

Research and presentation

See page 405 for *Newspapers and magazines which accept cartoons*.

Study the publication you are planning to submit to. What cartoon subjects feature most frequently, especially for joke or 'gag' cartoons (see 'Markets', below): married couples? children? animals? Are all the cartoons domestic or office based, or is there a mixture? Are the characters drawn in semi-realistic or more distorted styles? Are the jokes mainly in the captions or is the humour visual?

Be aware of changing fashions in humour. Thanks to Gary Larson's *The Far Side* the pun, formerly derided as a low form of wit, is currently very much in vogue. Consider technical details: Are the cartoons colour or black and white? What shape are they? It is pointless sending portrait-shaped cartoons to publications that only use landscape ones.

While many magazines still typeset cartoon captions, some also accept hand-drawn captions or balloons. Avoid spelling mistakes for which cartoonists are notorious and which often result in rejection of otherwise saleable drawings. This can also happen if a clever cartoon becomes illegible when reduced to printed size. Editors often squeeze cartoons into very small spaces – be sure your drawings are simple and bold enough to survive reduction.

It is useful to have a knowledge of copyright and libel. See *British copyright law* on page 629 and *Libel* on page 653.

Submitting cartoons

A preliminary letter saves wasted effort and can yield useful information. Busy editors find unsolicited phone calls very unamusing – but one call you will need to make is to check exactly who to address your letter to: full-time cartoon editors are rare and the person who chooses cartoons can be anyone from the art director to the person in charge of the puzzle page. Sending a number of cartoons together increases the chance of at least one being accepted, but quality is better than quantity. A few good jokes will get a better response when the editor doesn't have to extract them from a mountain of 'fillers'.

Rejections

While current fashions in cartoons encompass a wide range of styles, both visual and in terms of being funny,

Useful organisations

For specialist advice, and to meet other members of what can be a solitary profession, make contact with:

Cartoon Art Trust
7 Brunswick Centre, London WC1N 1AF
tel 020-7278 7172

The Cartoonists Guild and The Cartoonists' Club of Great Britain
46 Strawberry Vale, Twickenham TW1 4SE
tel 020-8892 3621 *fax* 020-8891 5946
website www.ccbg.org.uk

Comics Creators Guild
22 St James' Mansions, West End Lane, London NW6 2AA
website www.comicscreators.org.uk

humour is still very subjective. Rejections are a fact of life for even the most successful cartoonists, but one editor's rejected cartoon may be snapped up by another publication.

One way to lessen the sting is to have several submissions on the go at once. A strong pre-paid envelope will ensure that work comes back in one piece, ready for its next expedition. (Put your name and address on the back of each cartoon in case it gets detached from the main bundle.) If you are sending lots of cartoons back and forth to different publications it is wise to create a filing system. Otherwise you'll inevitably receive the dreaded response 'You've sent this one before ... and it wasn't funny the first time'.

Markets

General gag cartoons

Even in the midst of the modern media storm, the instant appeal of the one-panel cartoon still has its place. Although *Punch* (first launched in 1841), sadly, has folded, magazines like *Private Eye* and the *Spectator* still publish joke or gag cartoons alongside more topical items, and new cartoon magazines continue to appear.

Topical cartoons

Topical cartoons are a good market for the quick-witted artist. Remember that the cartoon must still be topical on the day it is published. This is (relatively) easy if the cartoon is for a newspaper coming out the next day, but a topical cartoon can become very outdated in the time it takes a weekly or fortnightly magazine to publish. Faxing roughs to the editor can save time. If accepted, you may need to produce finished artwork to very tight deadlines.

Try to get your cartoons back after publication – people featured in topical cartoons sometimes ask to buy the original artwork. Be aware also that more and more publications like artwork scanned and emailed. If you're non-technical, either start learning (not as scary as it seems) or find a friendly 'techie' who can help.

Specialist and trade publications

This is an under-exploited market for cartoonists who are able to tailor jokes to particular subjects – but remember you are dealing with an expert audience. A stereotypical cartoon chef may suffice for general cartoons, but you'd better get the terminology and different uniforms right for *Bakery World* or *Catering*.

Try creating your own markets. Think about jobs you've had, past or present, or your particular sports, hobbies and interests. No matter how obscure, there may be a related publication just waiting to be brightened up by your combination of cartoon skills and specialist knowledge.

Regular comic strips and syndication

For regular comic strips or cartoon features, editors need to see that you can produce not only funny material but also that you can maintain a consistent output. Submit a good supply of roughs along with examples of finished cartoons to show that you can do this. The same applies when approaching a syndicate with your strip and feature ideas (see *Syndicates, news and press agencies*, page 133). Cartoons may be in syndication for a long time, and in different countries, so very topical humour and local references are best avoided. If cartoons are syndicated in other languages humour based on verbal puns may not translate very well.

Other

Card and stationery publishers which accept illustrations and verses on page 398 should suggest other markets for cartoons. Cartoons are often used to illustrate books for both adults and children (listings of *Book publishers UK and Ireland* start on page 141 and *Book packagers* start on page 203). Some of the *Art agents and commercial art studios* listed on page 390 represent cartoonists.

Cartoon sites on the internet are some of the most frequently visited and cartoonists selling their wares through this new medium have reported very good responses. Some (e.g. www.cartoonstock.com) even act as cartoon libraries selling work online. Many publications which buy print cartoons also now have their own websites.

Finally ...

The life of a full-time funny person needs serious work as well as humorous invention, but properly researching and tailoring work to specific markets and adopting an organised approach to submissions should greatly reduce your rejection collection.

John Byrne combines his own writing and drawing career with training workshops on cartooning and comedy writing. Visit him at www.webtoonist.com.

See also ...

- *Freelancing for beginners*, page 383
- *Newspapers and magazines which accept cartoons*, page 405
- *Websites for artists*, page 565
- *Digital imaging for writers*, page 571
- *Show me the money!*, page 388

Further reading

Byrne, John, *Drawing Cartoons that Sell*, HarperCollins, 2nd edn, 2001

Byrne, John, *Learn to Draw Cartoons*, HarperCollins, 2nd edn, 1999

Byrne, John, *Learn to Draw Comics*, HarperCollins, 2001

Byrne, John, *Writing Comedy*, A & C Black, 2nd edn, 2002

Byrne, John, *The Secret Cartoonist's Handbook*, Puffin, 2002

Hall, Robin, *The Cartoonist's Workbook*, A & C Black, revised edn, 2000

Whitaker, Steve, *The Encyclopaedia of Cartooning Techniques*, Headline, reprinted 1996 o.p.

Newspapers and magazines which accept cartoons

Listed below are newspapers and magazines which take cartoons – either occasionally, or on a regular basis. Approach in writing in first instance (see listings starting on pages 3, 12 and 21 for addresses) to ascertain the editor's requirements.

Newspapers and colour supplements

(Adelaide) Advertiser
(Brisbane) The Sunday Mail
(Christchurch) The Press
Daily Dispatch
Daily Mirror
Evening Gazette
Express & Echo
The Independent
Independent Newspapers (South Africa) Ltd
Independent Newspapers Gauteng
Independent Newspapers Kwa-Zulu Natal Ltd
Independent on Sunday
(Invercargill) The Southland Times
The Leicester Mercury
Mail on Sunday
(Melbourne) Herald Sun
Morning Star
(New Plymouth) The Daily News
The Star
The Sun
The Sun
Sunday Independent
The Sunday Sun
The Sunday Times Scotland
The Sunday Tribune
The Times
(Wellington) The Evening Post
The Western Mail
Yorkshire Evening Post

Consumer and special interest magazines

Active Life
Aeroplane Monthly
Aquila
Back Street Heroes
Bella
The Big Issue Australia
Bird Watching
Birding World
Boards
Bowls International
Canal & Riverboat
Car
Christian Herald
Church of England Newspaper
Classic Cars
Computer Weekly
Computing
The Countryman
The Cricketer International
Cycling Weekly
Dance Australia
The Dandy
Darts World
Dirt Bike Rider
Dogs Today
Dolly
EA Today Magazine
East Lothian Life
The Erotic Review
Essex Magazine
Football Picture Story Library
Fortean Times
Garden News
Gay Times
Golf Monthly
Golf World
GQ
H&E Naturist
Home and Country
Home Words
Index on Censorship
Ireland of the Welcomes
Ireland's Own
Jewish Telegraph
Kids Alive! (The Young Soldier)
Life & Work: Magazine of the Church of Scotland
Making Music
Modern Woman Nationwide
More!
Motor Caravan Magazine
Mslexia
Musical Opinion
New Internationalist
New Musical Express
New Scientist
New Statesman
New Welsh Review
The Oldie
Opera Now
Organic Gardening
Overland
Park Home & Holiday Caravan
Picture Postcard Monthly
Planet
Poetry Review
Pony Magazine
Pride
Private Eye
Prospect
Red Pepper
Reform
Rugby World
Running Fitness
Scottish Home and Country
Scouting Magazine
Sight and Sound
Ski and Board
Smallholder
The Spectator
The Squash Player
Staple
Suffolk Norfolk Life
The Tablet
that's life!
Today's Fishkeeper
Today's Pilot
Tribune
Trout and Salmon

The Universe
The Vegan
Viz Comic
The Voice
The War Cry
Waterways World
The Weekly News
Weight Watchers Magazine
West Lothian Life
What's on TV
Writers' Forum
Yachting Monthly
Yachting World
Young Writer
Yours

Business and professional magazines

Accountancy
BMA News
Broadcast
Drapers Record
Education Journal
EE Times
Electrical Review
Electrical Times
Hospital Doctor
Hotel and Catering Review
Housebuilder
Irish Medical Times
Nursing Times
PCS View
Pilot
Police Review
Post Magazine & Insurance Week
Printing World
Therapy Weekly
Truck & Driver

Photography and picture research

The freelance photographer

*Becoming a successful freelance photographer is as much about marketing as photographic talent. **Bruce Coleman** and **Ian Thraves** discuss possibilities for the freelance photographer.*

Having an outstanding portfolio is one thing, but to receive regular commissions takes a good business head and sound market knowledge. Although working as a professional photographer can be tough, it is undoubtedly one of the most interesting and rewarding ways of earning a living.

Entering professional photography

A good starting point is to embark on one of the many college courses available, which range from GCSE to degree level, and higher. These form a good foundation, though most teach only the technical aspects of photography and very few cover the basics of running a business. But a good college course will provide students with the opportunity to become familiar with photographic equipment and develop skills without the restrictions and pressures found in the workplace.

In certain fields, such as commercial photography, it is possible to learn the trade as an assistant to an established photographer. A photographer's assistant will undertake many varied tasks, including preparing camera equipment and lighting, building sets, obtaining props and organising locations, as well as general mundane chores. It usually takes only a year or two for an assistant to become a fully competent photographer, having during that time learnt many technical aspects of a particular field of photography and the fundamentals of running a successful business. There is, however, the danger of a long-standing assistant becoming a clone of the photographer worked for, and it is for this reason that some assistants prefer to gain experience with other photographers rather than working for just one for a long period of time. The Association of Photographers can help place an assistant.

However, in other fields of photography, such as photojournalism or wildlife photography, an assistant is not generally required, and photographers in these fields have to learn for themselves as they work.

Identifying your market

From the outset, identify which markets are most suitable for the kind of subjects you photograph. Study each market carefully and only offer images which suit the client's in-house requirements.

Usually photographers who specialise in a particular field do better than those who generalise. By concentrating on one or two subject areas they become expert at what they do. Those who make a name for themselves are invariably specialists, and it is far easier for the images of, for example, an exceptional fashion photographer or an award-winning wildlife photographer to be remembered than the work of someone who covers a broad range of subjects.

In addition, photographers who produce work with individual style (e.g. by experimenting with camera angles or manipulating film to create unusual effects) are far more likely to make an impact. Alternative images which attract attention and can help sell a product are always sought after. This is especially true of advertising photography, but applies also to other markets such as book and magazine publishers, who are always seeking eye-catching images to use on front covers.

Promoting yourself

Effective self-promotion tells the market who you are and what service you offer. A first step should be to create an outstanding portfolio of images, tailored to appeal to the targeted market. Photographers targeting a few different markets should create an individual portfolio for each rather than presenting a single general one, including only a few relevant images. A portfolio containing between 10 and 20 images is enough for a potential client to judge a photographer's abilities.

Images should be presented in a format which the client is used to handling. Transparencies (perhaps duplicated to a larger size for easier viewing and general impact) are usually suitable for the editorial markets, but often more general companies prefer to view high-quality prints. Images can also be presented on CD-Rom and, unlike a traditional portfolio, can be left with potential clients to keep and refer to. Any published material (often referred to as 'tear sheets') should also be added to a portfolio. Tear sheets are often presented mounted and laminated in plastic.

Business cards and letterheads should be designed to reflect style and professionalism. Consider using a good graphic designer to design a logo for use on cards, letterheads and any other promotional literature. Many photographers produce postcard-size business cards and include an image as well as their name and logo.

Other than word of mouth, advertising is probably the best way of making your services known to potential clients. For a local market, a business directory such as *Yellow Pages* is a good start. Specialist directories in which photographers can advertise include *The Creative Handbook* and *Contact Photographers* (see page 410).

Cold calling by telephone is probably the most cost-effective and productive way of making contacts, and these should be followed up by an appointment for a personal visit (if possible) in order to show a portfolio of images. This helps to ensure you will not be forgotten.

Many photographers now use the internet as an alternative medium to promote themselves. A cleverly designed website is a stylish and cost-effective way to expose a photographer's portfolio to a global market, as well as being a convenient way for a potential client to view a photographer's work. A personal website address can be added to business stationery and to other forms of advertising together with the usual address and telephone number information.

Creating a website is usually much cheaper than advertising using conventional published print media. However, its design should be carefully composed and is probably best left to a professional website designer (see *Setting up a website*, page 556). Although many images and details about your business can be placed on a website, one limiting factor is the time it can take to download the images due to the size of the files. Unless this is a relatively quick process the viewer may lose patience and cancel access to the site.

A well-organised exhibition of images is a very effective way of bringing your work to the attention of current and potential new clients. Throw a preview party with refreshments for friends, colleagues and specially invited guests from the industry. A show which is well reviewed by critics who write for newspapers and magazines can generate additional interest. Many photographic organisations have regular exhibitions. An excellent example is the Photographers Gallery in London, where work selected by the gallery board is exhibited free.

As a photographer's career develops, the budget for self-promotion should increase. Many established photographers

Professional organisations

The Association of Photographers
Chief executive Gwen Thomas,
81 Leonard Street, London EC2A 4QS
tel 020-7739 6669 *fax* 020-7739 8707
email general@aophoto.co.uk
website www.aophoto.co.uk
See page 487.

British Institute of Professional Photography
Fox Talbot House, Amwell End, Ware, Herts. SG12 9HN
tel (01920) 464011
email bipp@compuserve.com
website www.bipp.com
See page 487.

Master Photographers Association
Hallmark House, 1 Chancery Lane, Darlington, Co. Durham DL1 5QP
tel (01325) 356555 *fax* (01325) 357813
email generalenquiries@mpauk.com
website www.mpauk.com
See page 487.

The Royal Photographic Society
The Octagon, Milsom Street, Bath BA1 1DN
tel (01225) 462841 *fax* (01225) 448688
email rps@rps.org
website www.rps.org
See page 487.

BAPLA (British Association of Picture Libraries and Agencies)
See page 462.

will go as far as producing full-colour mailers, posters, and even calendars, which all contain examples of their work.

Digital photography

Digital photography and image-enhancement and manipulation using computer technology are now widely used in the photographic industry. Since the cost of digital cameras and other hardware can be considerably cheaper than using large quantities of film, many studio photographers are now using this technology.

There are various levels of quality produced by digital cameras and photographers should consider the requirements of their market prior to investing in expensive hardware which is prone to rapid change and improvement. At the cheaper level (£2000–£5000) the 35mm style digital cameras manufactured by companies such as Nikon and Canon can produce outstanding quality images suitable for many end uses. Cameras like these are now used predominantly for press and PR work, where maximum quality is not paramount and speed and convenience are the priority.

At a higher level, many commercial studio photographers have invested in a 'digital capture back', which is a high-quality chip which can be adapted to fit many of the conventional studio cameras. This system is far more expensive (the chip alone starts at around £10,000), but is capable of producing file sizes which closely compare in quality to a high-resolution scan from large format film. Thus the images are suitable for any end use, such as top-quality advertisements. Photographers thinking of supplying stock libraries with digital images should realise that it is this kind of quality which is normally required, as stock libraries are looking to supply a diverse range of markets, including advertising.

Image-enhancement and manipulation using a computer program such as Adobe Photoshop provides photographers with an on-screen darkroom where the possibilities for creating imaginative images are endless. As well as being useful for retouching purposes and creating photo compositions, it provides the photographer with an opportunity to create more unusual images. It is therefore especially useful for targeting the advertising market, where fantasy images are more important than reality.

Using a stock library

As well as undertaking commissions, photographers have the option of selling their images through a photographic stock library or agency. There are many stock libraries in the UK, some specialising in specific subject areas, such as wildlife photography, and others covering general subjects (see *Picture agencies and libraries*, page 412).

Stock libraries are fiercely competitive, all fighting for a share of the market, and it is therefore best to aim to place images with an established name, although competition amongst photographers will be strong. Each stock library has different specific requirements and established markets, so contact them first before making a submission. Some libraries will ask to see a few hundred images from a photographer in order to judge for consistency of quality and saleability. Stock libraries selling images through catalogues or over the internet will often consider an initial submission of just a few images, knowing that it is possible to accumulate significant fees from a small number of outstanding individual images marketed this way.

Images placed with a library remain the property of the photographer and libraries do not normally sell images outright to clients, but lease them for a specific use for a fee, from which commission is deducted. This means that a single image can accumulate many sales over a period of time. The commission rate is usually about 50% of every sale generated by the library. This may sound high, but it should be borne in mind that the library takes on all overheads, marketing costs and other responsibilities involved in the smooth running of a business, allowing the photographer the freedom to spend more time taking pictures.

Photographers should realise, however, that stock photography is a long-term investment and it can take some time for sales to build up to a significant income. Clearly, photographers who supply the right images for the market, and are prolific, are those who do well, and there are a good number of photographers who make their entire living as full-time stock photographers, never having to undertake commissioned work.

Royalty-free CD companies

Many stock libraries are now marketing royalty-free images on CD-Rom. These companies usually obtain images by purchasing them from photographers for a flat fee. Once a CD has been purchased by a client (usually at very low cost) they, in effect, own the images on the CD and are therefore able to reproduce them as many times as they wish, paying no further fees. Some royalty-free companies, however, do pay to photographers royalties related to CD sales in addition to a flat fee for the images. A typical CD usually contains approximately one hundred high-resolution reproduction-quality images in a variety of subject areas, including most specialist subjects.

Although photographers may be tempted to sell images to these companies in order to gain an instant fee, they should be aware that placing images with a traditional stock library can be far more fruitful financially in the long term, since a good image can accumulate very high fees over a period of time and go on selling for many years to come. Furthermore, the photographer always retains the rights to his or her own images.

Useful information

Bureau of Freelance Photographers
Focus House, 497 Green Lanes, London N13 4BP
tel 020-8882 3315 *fax* 020-8886 5174
website www.thebfp.com
Chief Executive John Tracy
Helps the freelance photographer by providing information on markets and a free advisory service. Publishes *Market Newsletter* (monthly). Membership: £45 p.a.

Directories

Reed Business Information
Windsor Court, East Grinstead House, Wood Street, East Grinstead, West Sussex RH19 1XA
tel (01342) 332034 *fax* (01342) 332037
Publishes *The Creative Handbook*.

Elfande Ltd
Surrey House, 31 Church Street, Leatherhead, Surrey KT22 8EF
tel (01372) 220300 *fax* (01372) 220340
email mail@contact-uk.com
website www.contact-uk.com
Publishes *Contact Photographers*.

Running your own library

Photographers choosing to market their own images or start up their own library have the advantage of retaining a full fee for every picture sale they make. But it is unlikely that an individual photographer could ever match the rates of an established library, or make the same volume of sales per image. However, the internet has opened a new marketing avenue for photographers, who now have the opportunity to sell their images worldwide. Previously, only an established stock library would have been able to do this. Before embarking on establishing a home library, photographers should be aware that the business of marketing images is essentially a desk job which involves a considerable amount of paperwork and time, which could be spent taking pictures.

When setting up a picture library, your first consideration should be whether to build up a library of your own images, or to take on other contributing photographers. Many photographers running their own libraries submit additional images to bigger libraries to increase the odds of making a good income. Often, a photographer's personal library is made up of work rejected by the larger libraries, which are usually only interested in images that will regularly sell and generate a high turnover. However, occasional sales can generate a significant amount of income for the individual. Furthermore, a photographer with a library of specialised subjects stands a good chance of gaining recognition with niche markets, which can be very lucrative if the competition for those particular subjects is low.

If you take on contributing photographers, the responsibility for another's work becomes yours, so it is important to draw up a contract with terms of business for both your contributing photographers and your clients. Loss or damage of images is the most important consideration when sending pictures to clients (most libraries will charge clients a fee of £400–£600 per image for loss or damage of originals). It is often worth checking that a company wishing to receive transparencies does have adequate insurance to cover these fees, which can amount to a considerable figure if a large quantity of images is lost or damaged. On no account should images be sent to companies which refuse to take responsibility for loss or damage, nor to private individuals, unless they are working on a freelance basis for an established company. It should also be clearly stated in your terms that all pictures in the client's possession become the client's responsibility until they are returned and inspected for damage by the library. Many libraries are now taking a safer approach to distributing images by scanning them first and then supplying them as digital files either on CD or direct to clients, usually via ISDN lines. In addition to being a much cheaper way of distributing images, the problem of loss or damage or original material is also eliminated.

Reproduction fees should also be established on a strict basis, bearing in mind that you owe it to your contributing photographers to command fees which are as high as possible when selling the rights to their images. It is also essential that you control how pictures will be used and the amount of exposure they will receive. The fees should be established according to the type of client using the image and how the image itself will be reproduced. Important factors to consider are where the image will appear, to what size it will be reproduced, the size of the print run, and the territorial rights required by the client. Many libraries also apply holding fees in cases where clients hold on to pictures for periods of time longer than a month.

Bruce Coleman is Managing Director of the Bruce Coleman Collection and past President of the British Association of Picture Libraries.
Ian Thraves is a freelance photographer and former picture editor at the Bruce Coleman Collection (www.thravesphoto.co.uk).

Picture agencies and libraries

As well as supplying images to picture editors, picture researchers and others who use pictures, picture agencies and libraries provide a service to the freelance photographer as one way of selling their work. Most of the picture agencies and libraries listed in this section take work from other photographers.

If you want to introduce your work to a library or agency, send tear sheets, colour photocopies, disks or CDs that do not need to be returned. Never send unsolicited transparencies. Picture agencies and libraries are approached by photographers daily so do your homework to find the best agency to work for you, and consider which work they would most be interested in marketing. Remember that libraries are only interested in images that will sell. If you are approached by an agency, ask to see their terms and conditions. Members of BAPLA have signed a code of conduct that promotes fair dealing with photographers and customers.

To find agencies and libraries which cover specific subjects, start by referring to the *Picture agencies and libraries by subject area* on page 445, or see the listing for BAPLA on page 462.

See also ...

- *Card and stationery publishers which accept photographs*, page 452
- *Syndicates, news and press agencies*, page 133
- *The freelance photographer*, page 407
- *The picture research revolution*, page 454
- *National newspapers UK and Ireland*, page 3
- *Magazines by subject area*, page 113

**Member of the British Association of Picture Libraries and Agencies (BAPLA)*

A-Z Botanical Collection Ltd

192 Goswell Road, London EC1V 7DT
tel 020-7253 0991 *fax* 020-7253 0992
email azbotanical@yahoo.com
website www.a-z.picture-library.com
Library Manager James Wakefield

Colour transparencies of plant life worldwide, including named gardens, habitats, gardening, still life, romantic seasonal shots, fungi, pests and diseases, etc (6 x 6cm, 35mm, 5 x 4in).

A.A. & A. Ancient Art & Architecture Collection*

Suite 1, 1st Floor, 410-420 Rayners Lane, Pinner, Middlesex HA5 5DY
tel 020-8429 3131 *fax* 020-8429 4646
email library@aaacollection.co.uk
website www.aaacollection.com

Specialises in the history of civilisations of the Middle East, Mediterranean countries, Europe, Asia, Americas, from ancient times to recent past, their arts, architecture, beliefs and peoples.

Abode Interiors Picture Library*

Albion Court, 1 Pierce Street, Macclesfield, Cheshire SK11 6ER
tel (01625) 500070 *fax* (01625) 500910
email abodepix@appleonline.net
website www.abodepix.co.uk
Contact Judi Goodwin

Colour photo library specialising in English and Scottish house interiors of all styles, types and periods. High quality material only; terms by agreement. Please phone before sending material. Founded 1993.

Academic File News Photos

Eastern Art Publishing Group, PO Box 13666, 27 Wallorton Gardens, London SW14 8WF
tel 020-8392 1122 *fax* 020-8392 1422

email afis@eapgroup.com
website www.eapgroup.com
Director Sajid Rizvi

Daily news coverage in UK and general library of arts, cultures, people and places, with special reference to the Middle East, North Africa and Asia. New photographers welcomed to cover UK and abroad. Sample pictures accepted over email. Founded 1985.

Ace Photo Agency*

Satellite House, 2 Salisbury Road, London SW19 4EZ
tel 020-8944 9944 *fax* 020-8944 9940
email info@acestock.com
website www.acestock.com

General library: people, industry, business, travel, commerce, skies, sport, music and natural history. Worldwide syndication. Sae for enquiries. Very selective editing policy. Terms: 50%. Founded 1980.

Action Plus*

54-58 Tanner Street, London SE1 3PH
tel 020-7403 1558 *fax* 020-7403 1526
email info@actionplus.co.uk
website www.actionplus.co.uk

Specialist sports and action picture library. Comprehensive collection of creative images, including all aspects of 130 professional and amateur sports worldwide. Covers all age groups, all ethnic groups and all levels of ability. 35mm colour stock and online digital archive accessible by ISDN or modem. Terms: 50%. Founded 1986.

Lesley and Roy Adkins Picture Library

Ten Acre Wood, Heath Cross, Whitestone, Exeter EX4 2HW
tel (01392) 811357 *fax* (01392) 811435
email mail@adkinsarchaeology.com
website www.adkinsarchaeology.com

Colour library covering archaeology and heritage; prehistoric, Roman, Greek, Egyptian and medieval sites and monuments; landscape, countryside, architecture, towns, villages and religious monuments. Founded 1989.

Aerofilms*

Aerofilms Ltd, Gate Studios, Station Road, Borehamwood, Herts. WD6 1EJ
tel 020-8207 0666 *fax* 020-8207 5433
email library@aerofilms.com

Comprehensive library – over 2.5 million photos going back to 1919 – of vertical and oblique aerial photographs of UK; large areas with complete cover. Founded 1919.

Air Photo Supply

42 Sunningvale Avenue, Biggin Hill, Kent TN16 3BX
tel (01959) 574872
email norman.rivett@virgin.net

Aircraft and associated subjects, Southeast England, colour and monochrome. No other photographers' material required. Founded 1963.

AKG London*

(The Arts and History Picture Library)
5 Melbray Mews, 158 Hurlingham Road, London SW6 3NS
tel 020-7610 6103 *fax* 020-7610 6125
email enquiries@akg-london.co.uk
website www.akg-london.co.uk

Principal subjects covered: art, archaeology and history. Exclusive UK and US representative for the Archiv für Kunst und Geschichte (AKG) with full access to the 10 million images held by AKG Berlin. Also exclusively represents the Erich Lessing Cultureand Fine Art Archives in the UK. Founded 1994.

Bryan and Cherry Alexander Photography*

Higher Cottage, Manston, Sturminster Newton, Dorset DT10 1EZ
tel (01258) 473006 *fax* (01258) 473333
email alexander@arcticphoto.co.uk
website www.arcticphoto.co.uk

Polar regions with emphasis on indigenous peoples of the North. Landscape and wildlife: Alaska to Siberia and Antarctica. Founded 1973.

Rev. J. Catling Allen

7 St Barnabas, The Beauchamp Community, Newland, Malvern WR13 5AX
tel (01684) 899390

Library of colour transparencies (35mm) and b&w photos of Bible Lands, including archaeological sites and the religions of Christianity, Islam and Judaism. Medieval abbeys and priories, cathedrals and churches in Britain. Also historic, rural and scenic Britain. (Not an agent or buyer.)

Allied Artists

5 Fauconberg Road, London W4 3JZ
tel 020-8995 5500 *fax* 020-8995 8844
email info@alliedartists.ltd.uk

website www.alliedartists.ltd.uk
Contacts Gary Mills (director), Mary Burtenshaw
Agency for illustrators specialising in a wide range of styles for magazines, books, children's books and advertising. Large colour library. Founded 1983.

Allsport UK

3 Greenlea Park, Prince George's Road, London SW19 2JD
tel 020-8685 1010 *fax* 020-8648 5240
email allsportlondon@gettyimages.com
website www.allsport.com
International sport and leisure. Part of Getty Images (UK) Ltd. Founded 1968.

American History Picture Library

3 Barton Buildings, Bath BA1 2JR
tel (01225) 334213 *fax* (01225) 480554
Photographs, engravings, colour transparencies covering the exploration and social, political and military history of North America from 15th to 20th century: conquistadors, civil war, railroads, the Great Depression, advertisements, Prohibition and gangsters, moon landings and space.

AMIS

(Atlas Mountains Information Services)
26 Kirkcaldy Road, Burntisland, Fife KY3 9HQ
tel (01592) 873546
Proprietor Hamish Brown MBE, FRSGS
Picture library on Moroccan sites, topography, mountains, travel. Illustration service. Commissions undertaken. No pictures purchased.

Ancient Egypt Picture Library

6 Branden Drive, Knutsford, Cheshire WA16 8EJ
tel/fax (01565) 633106
email BobEgyptPL@aol.com
Images of Egypt, including most of the ancient sites and views of modern Egypt. All photographs (over 30,000 colour transparencies) taken by an Egyptologist, who can also provide full historical/archaeological information. Founded 1996.

Andalucía Slide Library

Apto 499, Estepona, Málaga 29680, Spain
tel (34) 952-793647 *fax* (34) 952-880138
email info@andaluciaslidelibrary.com
website www.andaluciaslidelibrary.com
Contact Michelle Chaplow
Colour transparencies (35mm and medium format) covering all aspects of Andalucía and Spain, principally its geography and culture. Also images of Portugal, Madeira, Malta. Commissions undertaken. Founded 1991.

Andes Press Agency*

26 Padbury Court, London E2 7EH
tel 020-7613 5417 *fax* 020-7739 3159
email apa@andespressagency.com
Director Carlos Reyes
Social, political and economic aspects of Latin America, Africa, Asia, Middle East, Europe and Britain; specialises in Latin America and contemporary world religions. Founded 1983.

Heather Angel/Natural Visions*

Highways, 6 Vicarage Hill, Farnham, Surrey GU9 8HJ
tel (01252) 716700 *fax* (01252) 727464
email hangel@naturalvisions.co.uk
website www.naturalvisions.co.uk
Colour transparencies (35mm and 2¼in square) with worldwide coverage of natural history and biological subjects including animals, plants, natural habitats (deserts, polar regions, rainforests, wetlands, etc), landscapes, gardens, close-ups and underwater images; also man's impact on the environment – pollution, acid rain, urban wildlife, etc. Large China file including pandas in all seasons. Extensive water file (liquid, solid and vapour). Pictures cannot be supplied *gratis* for personal use.

Animal Photography*

4 Marylebone Mews, New Cavendish Street, London W1G 8PY
tel 020-7935 0503 *fax* 020-7487 3038
email thompson@animal-photography.co.uk
website www.animal-photography.co.uk
Horses, dogs, cats, small pets, East Africa, Galapagos. Other photographers' work not represented. Founded 1955.

Aquarius Library*

PO Box 5, Hastings, East Sussex TN34 1HR
tel (01424) 721196 *fax* (01424) 717704
email aquarius.lib@clara.net
website www.aquariuscollection.com
Contact David Corkill
Showbusiness specialist library with over one million colour and b&w images: film stills, classic portraiture, candids, archive material to present. New material added every week. Archival situation stills for advertising and magazine illustration use. Also TV, vintage pop,

opera, ballet and stage. Worldwide representation and direct sales. Division of SPM London Ltd.

Aquila Wildlife Images

PO Box 1, Studley, Warks. B80 7JG
tel (01527) 852357
email interbirdnet @birder.co.uk

Specialists in ornithological subjects, but covering all aspects of natural history, also pets and landscapes, in both colour and b&w.

Arcaid Architectural Photography and Picture Library*

The Factory, 2 Acre Road, Kingston, Surrey KT2 6EF
tel 020-8546 4352 *fax* 020-8541 5230
email arcaid@arcaid.co.uk
website www.arcaid.co.uk
www.alamy.com/arcaid

'The built environment' – international collection: architecture, interior design, lifestyle interiors, gardens, travel, museums, historic and contemporary. Terms: 50%.

Archivio Veneziano – see Venice Picture Library

Arctic Camera

66 Ashburnham Grove, London SE10 8UJ
tel/fax 020-8692 7651
email Derek.Fordham@btinternet.com
Contact Derek Fordham

Colour transparencies of all aspects of Arctic life and environment. Founded 1978.

Ardea Wildlife & Pets*

35 Brodrick Road, London SW17 7DX
tel 020-8672 2067 *fax* 020-8672 8787
email ardea@ardea.co.uk
website www.ardea.co.uk
Contact Sophie Napier

Specialist worldwide natural history photographic library of animals, birds, plants, fish, insects, reptiles, worldwide scenics and domestic pets.

The Associated Press Ltd

News Photo Department, The Associated Press House, 12 Norwich Street, London EC4A 1BP
tel 020-7427 4260/4266, 020-7427 4269 (library manager) *fax* 020-7427 4269
email london_photolibrary@ap.org
website www.apwideworld.com

News, features, sports, 20th century history, personalities.

Australia Pictures

28 Sheen Common Drive, Richmond, London TW10 5BN
tel/fax 020-7602 1989
Contact John Miles

Comprehensive library covering Australia, Aboriginals and their art, indigenous peoples, underwater, Tibet, Peru, Bolivia, Iran, Irian Jaya, Pakistan, Yemen. Founded 1988.

Aviation Picture Library (Austin J. Brown)*

116 The Avenue, St Stephen's, London W13 8 JX
tel 020-8566 7712 *cellphone* (07860) 670073 *fax* 020-8566 7714
email avpix@aol.com
website www.aviationpictures.com

Worldwide aviation photographic library, including dynamic views of aircraft. Aerial and travel library including Europe, Caribbean, USA, and East and West Africa. Material taken since 1960. Specialising in air-to-air and air-to-ground commissions. Chief photographers for *Flyer* magazine. Founded 1970.

B. & B. Photographs

Prospect House, Clifford Chambers, Stratford upon Avon, Warks. CV37 8HX
tel (01789) 298106 *fax* (01789) 292450
email BandBPhotographs@btinternet.com

35mm/medium format colour library of horticulture (especially pests and diseases) and geography (worldwide), natural history and biological education. Other photographers' work not represented. Founded 1974.

Bandphoto Agency

(division of UPPA Ltd)
29-31 Saffron Hill, London EC1N 8SW
tel 020-7421 6000 *fax* 020-7421 6006

International news and feature picture service for British and overseas publishers.

Barnaby's Picture Library – see Mary Evans Picture Library

Barnardo's Photographic Archive

Tanners Lane, Barkingside, Ilford, Essex IG6 1QG
tel 020-8550 8822 *fax* 020-8550 0429

Extensive collection of b&w and colour images dating from 1874 to the present day covering social history with the emphasis on children and child care. Also 300 films dating from 1905. Founded 1874.

BBC Natural History Unit Picture Library*

BBC Broadcasting House, Whiteladies Road, Bristol BS8 2LR
tel 0117-974 6720 *fax* 0117-923 8166
email info@naturepl.com
website www.naturepl.com

Photographs illustrating all aspects of nature: mammals, birds, insects, reptiles, marine life, plants, landscapes, indigenous peoples, environmental issues and wildlife filming. Recently renamed the Nature Picture Library.

Dr Alan Beaumont

52 Squires Walk, Lowestoft, Suffolk NR32 4LA
tel (01502) 560126
email embeaumont@supernet.com

Worldwide collection of monochrome prints and colour transparencies (35mm and 6 x 7cm) of natural history, countryside, windmills and aircraft. Brochure and subject lists available. No other photographers required.

Bee Photographs – see Heritage & Natural History Photography

Stephen Benson Slide Bureau

45 Sugden Road, London SW11 5EB
tel 020-7223 8635

World: agriculture, archaeology, architecture, commerce, everyday life, culture, environment, geography, science, tourism. Speciality: South America, the Caribbean, Australasia, Nepal, Turkey, Israel and Egypt. Assignments undertaken.

Bird Images

28 Carousel Walk, Sherburn in Elmet, North Yorkshire LS25 6LP
tel/fax (01977) 684666
Principal P. Doherty

Specialist in the birds of Britain and Europe, including video footage from Europe and North America. Expert captioning service available. Founded 1989.

John Birdsall Photography*

75 Raleigh Street, Nottingham NG7 4DL
tel 0115-978 2645 *fax* 0115-978 5546
email photos@johnbirdsall.co.uk
website www.johnbirdsall.co.uk
Contact Clare Marsh

Contemporary social documentary library covering children, youth, old age, health, disability, education, housing, work; also Nottingham and surrounding area; Spain, Cuba, India – commissions and stock pictures. Online catalogue searchable in both English and German. Founded 1980.

The Anthony Blake Photo Library*

20 Blades Court, Deodar Road, London SW15 2NU
tel 020-8877 1123 *fax* 020-8877 9787
email info@abpl.co.uk
website www.abpl.co.uk

Food and wine images from around the world, including raw ingredients, finished dishes, shops, restaurants, markets, agriculture and viticulture. Commissions undertaken. Contributors welcome. Brochure available.

Sarah Boait Photography and Picture Library

tel/fax (01409) 281354
email sarahboait@compuserve.com

Covers the British Isles, especially the West Country and locations from legend and folklore; also world travel, world religions. No contributors' work accepted.

Bodleian Library*

Oxford OX1 3BG

Published slides and filmstrips
tel (01865) 277214/277152
fax (01865) 277187
email slidesales@bodley.ox.ac.uk
websites www.bodley.ox.ac.uk/dept/scwmss/wmss/medieval/browse.htm
www.bodley.ox.ac.uk/dept/scwmss/wmss/medieval/slides/cumulative.htm
www.bodley.ox.ac.uk/dept/scwmss/wmss/Orderforms2002-UK-EU.pdf
www.bodley.ox.ac.uk/dept/scwmss/wmss/Orderforms2002-World.pdf

Imaging service
tel (01865) 277215/277061
fax (01865) 287127
email repro@bodley.ox.ac.uk
website www.bodley.ox.ac.uk/dept/imaging

Published slides and manuscripts: Library of 32,000 35mm colour transparencies in slides or filmstrips for immediate sale (not hire). There is an iconographical index to the images, which are mostly from medieval manuscripts.

Imaging service: Large format transparencies more suitable for reproduction are available to order, as are copies, photographs and microfilm of any other items from the Bodleian's vast collections.

BookArt & Architecture Picture Library
1 Woodcock Lodge, Epping Green, Hertford SG13 8ND
tel (01707) 875253 *fax* (01707) 875286
email sharpd@globalnet.co.uk
Modern and historic buildings, landscapes, works of named architects in Great Britain, Europe, Scandinavia, North America, India, Southeast Asia, Japan, North and East Africa; modern sculpture. Listed under style, place and personality. Founded 1991.

Boxing Picture Library
3 Barton Buildings, Bath BA1 2JR
tel (01225) 334213 *fax* (01225) 480554
Prints, engravings and photos of famous boxers, boxing personalities and famous fights from 18th century to recent years.

The Bridgeman Art Library*
17-19 Garway Road, London W2 4PH
tel 020-7727 4065 *fax* 020-7792 8509
email london@bridgeman.co.uk
website www.bridgeman.co.uk
Source of fine art images for publication. Acts as an agent for thousands of museums, galleries and private collections throughout the world. Every subject, era and style represented from cave paintings to pop art and beyond, including many historical events and personalities. Also offers research service and acts as copyright agent to a growing number of artists. Images may be viewed and ordered online. Printed catalogues available. Founded 1972.

Britain on View*
43 Drury Lane, London WC2B 5RT
tel 020-7836 6608 *fax* 020-7836 6553
email cdubyk-yates@bta.org.uk
website www.britainonview.com
Photo library of the British Tourist Authority. British culture, society, events, landscapes, towns and villages, tourist attractions.

British Library Picture Library*
96 Euston Road, London NW1 2DB
tel 020-7412 7614 *fax* 020-7412 7771
email bl-repro@bl.uk
website www.bl.uk
Illustrative and historical material from manuscripts, printed books, oriental and Indian items, maps, music and stamps. In addition to the stock collection, images from 15 million books can be sourced. Founded 1996.

David Broadbent/Peak District Pictures
12 Thomas Street, Glossop, Derbyshire SK13 8QN
tel/fax (01457) 862997
email info@davidbroadbent.com
website www.davidbroadbent.com
The Peak District fully covered, landscape, natural history, birds a speciality. Commissions undertaken. New material welcome. Terms: 50%. Founded 1989.

David Broadbent/Birds
Highly stylised and pictorial library of British birds, bird reserves and important wildlife landscapes.

Hamish Brown, Scottish Photographic
26 Kirkcaldy Road, Burntisland, Fife KY3 9HQ
tel (01592) 873546
Picture library on Scottish sites, topography, mountains, travel. Book illustrations. Commissions undertaken. No pictures purchased.

Butterflies
27 Lucastes Lane, Haywards Heath, West Sussex RH16 1LE
tel (01444) 454254
Proprietors Dr J. Tampion, Mrs M.D. Tampion
Worldwide: butterflies, silkmoths, hawkmoths, adults, larvae, pupae, their foodplants, poisonous plants, wild, garden, greenhouse and tropical plants, botanical and gardening science, ecology, environment. Articles and line illustrations also available; commissions undertaken. No new photographers required. Founded 1990.

Caledonia Light Images
80 McBain Place, Kinross, Perthshire KY13 8QZ
tel (01577) 864861
email admin@caledonialight.co.uk
website www.caledonialight.co.uk
Proprietor Stuart McAleese
Colour transparencies of Scotland's natural heritage, countryside, archaeology, landscapes and ecosystems. Collections feature mountaineering, Slovenia, Ireland and European travel. Founded 2000.

Camera Press Ltd*
21 Queen Elizabeth Street, London SE1 2PD
tel 020-7378 1300 *fax* 020-7278 5126

B&w prints and colour transparencies including up-to-date coverage of British royalty, portraits of world statesmen, politicians, entertainers, reportage, humour, nature, pop, features. Terms: 50%. Founded 1947.

CartoonStock*
Studio X, 25 Horsell Road, London N5 1XL
tel 020-7700 7080 *fax* 020-7700 7090
email admin@cartoonstock.com
website www.cartoonstock.com
Director Joel Mishon
Library of cartoons and comic illustration. B&w and colour cartoons by over 170 cartoonists whose work appears in national and overseas newspapers and magazines and other publications. Full database may be searched online. Founded 1998.

Cephas Picture Library*
Hurst House, 157 Walton Road, East Molesey, Surrey KT8 0DX
tel 020-8979 8647 or 07000 CEPHAS *fax* 020-8224 8095
email mickrock@cephas.co.uk
website www.cephas.co.uk
Comprehensive library of food and drink photos: wine and vineyards, spirits, beer and cider, food and drink worldwide. Free catalogue available; specialist knowledge.

Chrysalis Images
64 Brewery Road, London N7 9NT
tel 020-7697 3000 *fax* 020-7697 3001
email tforshaw@chrysalisbooks.co.uk
Picture Manager Terry Forshaw
General collection including cookery, crafts, history, military, natural history, space, transport and travel. Founded 1996.

COI Photo Library – see Stockwave

Michael Cole Camerawork*
The Coach House, 27 The Avenue, Beckenham, Kent BR3 2DP
tel/fax 020-8658 6120
website www.tennisphotos.com
Probably the largest and most comprehensive tennis library in the world comprising over half a million colour and b&w images. Includes over 50 years of the Wimbledon Championships. All grand slam and major events covered. Founded 1945.

Bruce Coleman Inc.
117 East 24th Street, New York, NY 10010-2919, USA
tel 212-979-6252 *fax* 212-979-5468
email norman@bciusa.com
website www.bciusa.com
President Norman Owen Tomalin
Specialises in the natural world and travel destinations around it. All subjects required. Traditional colour transparencies and digital stock media.

Bruce Coleman The Natural World
16 Chiltern Business Village, Arundel Road, Uxbridge UB8 2SN
tel (01895) 467990 *fax* (01895) 467955
email library@brucecoleman.co.uk
website www.brucecoleman.co.uk
Creative images of nature, animals, landscapes, space and wildlife. Catalogues available.

Collections*
13 Woodberry Crescent, London N10 1PJ
tel 020-8883 0083 *fax* 020-8883 9215
The British Isles only: places, people, buildings, industry, leisure; specialist collections on customs, castles, bridges, London, plus an extensive collection on Ireland. Founded 1990.

Colorific/Getty Images News Services*
3 Greenlea Park, Prince George's Road, London SW19 2JD
tel 020-7515 3000 *fax* 020-8648 2184
email david.leverton@gettyimages.com
website www.newsmakers.com
Handles the work of international celebrity and features photographers. Most subjects currently on file, upwards of 250,000 images. Represents the following agencies: Contact Press Images (New York/Paris), Visages (Los Angeles), Regards (Paris), Saola (Paris). Also represents *Sports Illustrated*.

Dee Conway Ballet & Dance Picture Library
110 Sussex Way, London N7 6RR
tel 020-7272 7845 *fax* 020-7272 7966
email library@ddance.co.uk
website www.ddance.co.uk
Proprietor Dee Conway
Classical ballet, modern dance, flamenco, tango, rock, jive, mime; dance from India, Africa, Russia, China, Japan, Thailand; informal class pictures of

dance, music and drama. Colour and b&w images. Founded 1995.

Thomas Cook Archives

19-21 Coningsby Road, Peterborough PE3 8SB
tel (01733) 402025 *fax* (01733) 402026
email paul.smith-archives@thomascook.com
Company Archivist Paul Smith

History of travel and tourism in the late 19th and early 20th centuries: posters, photos, brochure covers (1851–1960). Founded 1999.

Corbis*

111 Salusbury Road, London NW6 6RG
tel 020-7644 7400 *fax* 020-7644 7401
email info@corbis.com
website www.corbis.com

Over 2.1 million images available online from a total of 65 million. The images are from professional photographers, museums, cultural institutions and public and private collections worldwide including the Bettmann Archive, Ansel Adams, Lynn Goldsmith, the Turnley Collection and Hulton Deutsch. Covers a wide range of subjects including celebrities and news. Founded 1989.

Sylvia Cordaiy Photo Library

45 Rotherstone, Devizes, Wilts. SN10 2DD
tel (01380) 728327 *fax* (01380) 728328
email sylviacordaiy@compuserve.com
website www.sylvia-cordaiy.com

Worldwide travel and architecture, global environmental topics, wildlife and domestic animals, veterinary, comprehensive UK files, Paul Kaye b&w archive. Terms: 50%. Founded 1990.

Country Collections Photolibrary

Unit 9, Ditton Priors Trading Estate, Bridgnorth, Shropshire WV16 6SS
tel (01746) 712533, 861330
Contact Robert Foster

Specialises in Celtic culture from stone circles to the present day. Also an expanding collection of rivers and streamside vegetation. Colour transparencies. Founded 1985.

Crafts Council Picture Library*

44A Pentonville Road, London N1 9BY
tel 020-7806 2503 *fax* 020-7833 4479
email photostore@craftscouncil.org.uk
website www.craftscouncil.org.uk/photostore

Comprehensive source of visual material for contemporary British crafts. Spanning the last 30 years, subject areas cover: jewellery, ceramics, furniture, glass, woodwork, paperwork, bookbinding, domestic objects, decorative forms, lettering, textiles, fashion accessories, basketry, musical instruments and public art. Images can be accessed through Photostore, the Council's interactive database, open during working hours (no appointment necessary) and through regional terminals. Founded 1973.

Peter Cumberlidge Photo Library

Sunways, Slapton, Kingsbridge, Devon TQ7 2PR
tel (01548) 580461 *fax* (01548) 580588
email info@petercumberlidge.co.uk
Contact Jane Cumberlidge

Nautical, travel and coastal colour transparencies 35mm and 6 x 6cm. Specialities: boats, harbours, marinas, inland waterways. Travel and holiday subjects in Northern Europe, the Mediterranean, and New England, USA. No other photographers' material required. Founded 1982.

Sue Cunningham Photographic*

56 Chatham Road, Kingston-upon-Thames, Surrey KT1 3AA
tel 020-8541 3024 *fax* 020-8541 5388
email pictures@scphotographic.com
website www.scphotographic.com

International coverage on many subjects: Latin America, Africa and Eastern Europe. Also Western Europe, London (including aerial).

Das Photo

Chalet le Pin, Domaine de Bellevue 181, 6940 Septon, Belgium
tel/fax (32) 86-322426
Old School House, Llanfilo, Brecon, Powys LD3 0RH
email dasphotogb@aol.com

Arab countries, Americas, Europe, Caribbean, Southeast Asia, Amazon, world festivals, archaeology, people, biblical, education, schools, modern languages. Founded 1975.

Barry Davies

Dyffryn, Bolahaul Road, Cwmffrwd, Carmarthen, Carmarthenshire SA31 2LW
tel/fax (01267) 233625

Natural history, landscape, Egypt, children, outdoor activities and general subjects. Formats 35mm, 6 x 6cm, 6 x 7cm, 6 x 17cm, 5 x 4in. Other photographers' work not accepted. Founded 1983.

Dennis Davis Photography

9 Great Burrow Rise, Northam, Bideford, Devon EX39 1TB
tel (01237) 475165

Gardens, wild and garden flowers, domestic livestock including rare breeds and poultry, agricultural landscapes, architecture – interiors and exteriors, landscape, coastal, rural life. Commissions welcomed. No other photographers required. Founded 1984.

James Davis Travel Photography

65 Brighton Road, Shoreham, West Sussex BN43 6RE
tel (01273) 452252 *fax* (01273) 440116
email library@eyeubiquitous.com
website www.eyeubiquitous.com
Proprietor Paul Seheult

Stock transparency library specialising in worldwide travel photos.

Peter Dazeley*

The Studios, 5 Heathmans Road, London SW6 4TJ
tel 020-7736 3171 *fax* 020-7371 8876
email dazeleyp@aol.com

Extensive golf library dating from 1970. Colour and b&w coverage of major tournaments, with over 250,000 images of players, courses worldwide, action shots, portraits, trophies, including miscellaneous images: clubs, balls and teaching shots.

George A. Dey

Drumcairn, Aberdeen Road, Laurencekirk, Kincardineshire AB30 1AJ
tel (01561 37) 8845

Scottish Highland landscapes, Highland Games, forestry, seabirds, castles of Northeast Scotland, gardens, spring, autumn, winter scenes, veteran cars, North Holland, New Zealand (North Island). Mostly 35mm, some 6 x 6cm. Founded 1980.

Douglas Dickins Photo Library

2 Wessex Gardens, London NW11 9RT
tel 020-8455 6221

Worldwide collection of colour transparencies (mostly 6 x 6cm, some 35mm) and b&w prints (10 x 8in originals), specialising in Asia, particularly India and Indonesia; also USA, Canada, France, Austria and Switzerland, Japan, China, Burma. Founded 1946.

C.M. Dixon*

The Orchard, Marley Lane, Kingston, Canterbury, Kent CT4 6JH
tel (01227) 830075 *fax* (01227) 831135

Europe, Iceland, Jordan, Sri Lanka, Tunisia, Turkey, former USSR. Main subjects include agriculture, ancient art, archaeology, architecture, clouds, geography, geology, history, horses, industry, meteorology, mosaics, mountains, mythology, occupations, people.

Earth Images Picture Library

PO Box 43, Keynsham, Bristol BS31 2TH
tel/fax 0117-986 1144/(01275) 839643
Director Richard Arthur

Earth from Space (satellite remote sensing); earth science and art-in-science imagery – from cosmic to sub-atomic. Founded 1989.

Ecoscene*

The Oasts, Headley Lane, Passfield, Liphook, Hants GU30 7RX
tel (01428) 751056 *fax* (01428) 751057
email sally@ecoscene.com
website www.ecoscene.com
Contact Sally Morgan

Specialists in environment and wildlife. Subjects include agriculture, conservation, energy, industry, pollution, habitats and habitat loss, sustainability, wildlife; worldwide coverage. Terms: 55% to photographer. Founded 1987.

Edinburgh Photographic Library*

Mercat International, 14 Garscube Terrace, Edinburgh EH12 6BQ
tel 0131-337 7615 *fax* 0131-337 0303
email epl@mercat.co.uk
website www.mercat.co.uk
Proprietor James Young

15,000 colour transparency images of Scotland – castles, scenic, mountains, festivals, pipe bands. Founded 1986.

Education Photos*

April Cottage, Warners Lane, Albury Heath, Guildford, Surrey GU5 9DE
tel/fax (01483) 203846
email johnwalmsley@educationphotos.co.uk
website www.educationphotos.co.uk
Proprietor John Walmsley

Colour transparencies of education, careers, portraits of ordinary people. Commissions undertaken. Founded 1987.

English Heritage Photo Library*

23 Savile Row, London W1S 2ET
tel 020-7973 3338/3339 *fax* 020-7973 3027

Wide range of high quality colour transparencies, ranging from ancient monuments to artefacts, legendary castles to stone circles, elegant interiors to industrial architecture and post-war listed buildings.

Environmental Investigation Agency*

62-63 Upper Street, London N1 0NY
tel 020-7354 7960 *fax* 020-7354 7961
email communications@eia-international.org
website www.eia-international.org
Communications Manager Mary Rice

Specialists in images of the illegal trade in endangered species, ozone-depleting substances and illegal logging; also animals in their natural environment. Founded 1984.

Greg Evans International Photo Library*

ICS House, 32 Crossways, Silwood Road, Sunninghill, Ascot, Berks. SL5 0PL
tel 020-7636 8238 *fax* 020-7637 1439
email greg@gregevans.net
website www.gregevans.net

Comprehensive, general colour library with over 300,000 transparencies. Subjects include: abstract, aircraft, arts, animals, beaches, business, children, computers, couples, families, food/restaurant, women, industry, skies, sports (action and leisure), UK scenics, worldwide travel. Visitors welcome; combined commissions undertaken. No search fee. Photographers' submissions welcome. Searchable website. Free brochure/CD-Rom. Founded 1979.

Mary Evans Picture Library*

59 Tranquil Vale, London SE3 0BS
tel 020-8318 0034 *fax* 020-8852 7211
email lib@mepl.co.uk
website www.mepl.co.uk

Millions of historical illustrations documenting social, political, cultural, technical, geographical and biographical themes from ancient times to the 1970s. Photographs, original prints, and ephemera backed by a large international book and magazine collection. Special collections include the Sigmund Freud Collection, the Women's Library, the Meledin Collection (20th-century Russian history) and individual photographers active from the 1930s to the 1970s. Recent acquisitions include the Weimar Archive and Barnaby's Picture Library, which incorporates the Mustograph Agency. Colour brochure available. Compilers of the *Picture Researcher's Handbook*, published every 3 years by Pira International (www.piranet.com).

Exile Images

1 Mill Row, West Hill Road, Brighton BN1 3SU
tel (01273) 208741 *fax* (01273) 382782
email pics@exileimages.co.uk
website www.exileimages.co.uk
Contact Howard Davies

Colour and b&w photos documenting refugees, asylum seekers, displaced peoples and conflicts worldwide. Also documentary photos of rural and urban lives in developing countries. Photos from 1988. CD-Rom available through website. Founded 2000.

Eyeline Photography

259 London Road, Cheltenham, Glos. GL52 6YG
tel (01242) 513567
email colin.jarman@btinternet.com

Sailing. Founded 1979.

FAMOUS Pictures & Features Agency*

13 Harwood Road, London SW6 4QP
tel 020-7731 9333 *fax* 020-7731 9330
email info@famous.uk.com
website www.famous.uk.com

Colour pictures and features library covering music, film and TV personalities. Terms: 50%. Founded 1990.

Feature-Pix Colour Library – see World Pictures

Financial Times Pictures*

Number One, Southwark Bridge, London SE1 9HL
tel 020-7873 3671 *fax* 020-7873 4606
email photosynd@ft.com

Colour and b&w library serving the *Financial Times*. Specialises in world business, industry and commerce; world politicians and statespeople; cities and countries; plus many other subjects. Also *FT* maps and graphics. All material available in colour and b&w, print and electronic formats. Library updated daily.

Fine Art Photographic Library*
Rawlings House, 2A Milner Street, London SW3 2PU
tel 020-7589 3127 *fax* 020-7584 1944
email info@fineartphotolibrary.com

Holds over 25,000 transparencies of paintings by British and European artists, from Old Masters to contemporary. Free brochure. CD-Rom available. Founded 1980.

FirePix International*
68 Arkles Lane, Anfield, Liverpool L4 2SP
tel/fax 0151-260 0111
email info@firepix.com
website www.firepix.com
Contact Tony Myers ARPS, GIFireE

Holds 23,000 images of fire and fire-fighters at work in the UK, USA, Japan and China. Established by photographer Tony Myers after 28 years in service with the British Fire Service. Many images are stored digitally; CD-Rom available. Founded 1995.

Fogden Wildlife Photographs*
Flat 1, 78 High Street, Perth PH1 5TH
tel/fax (01738) 580811
email susan.fogden@virgin.net
website www.fogdenphotos.com
Library Manager Susan Fogden

Wide coverage of natural history, including camouflage, warning coloration, mimicry, breeding strategies, feeding, animal/plant relationships, environmental studies, especially in rainforests and deserts. Founded 1980.

Christine Foord
155B City Way, Rochester, Kent ME1 2BE
tel/fax (01634) 847348

Colour picture library of over 1000 species of wild flowers. Also British insects, garden flowers, pests and diseases, lichen, mosses and cacti.

Forest Life Picture Library*
Forestry Commission, 231 Corstorphine Road, Edinburgh EH12 7AT
Picture Researcher Neill Campbell
tel 0131-314 6411
email neill.campbell@forestry.gsi.gov.uk
Business Manager Douglas Green
tel 0131-314 6200 *fax* 0131-314 6285
email douglas.green@forestry.gsi.gov.uk

Tree species, forest and woodland views and management, landscapes, wildlife, flora and fauna, conservation, sport and leisure. Founded 1983.

Werner Forman Archive*
36 Camden Square, London NW1 9XA
tel 020-7267 1034 *fax* 020-7267 6026
email wfa@btinternet.com
website www.werner-forman-archive.com

Art, architecture, archaeology, history and peoples of ancient, oriental and primitive cultures. Founded 1975.

Format Photographers*
19 Arlington Way, London EC1R 1UY
tel 020-7833 0292 *fax* 020-7833 0381
email format@formatphotogs.demon.co.uk
website www.formatphotographers.co.uk
Contact Maggie Murray

A library and agency representing the work of 20 women documentary photographers. The images, mainly from the last 20 years, are constantly updated and offer a unique perspective of the world. Subjects covered: social and political life in Britain and abroad, health, education, women's issues, work, the elderly and the very young, disability, gay and lesbian, Black and Asian culture, the environment, housing and homelessness, transport and leisure. Countries from Albania to Zambia. Colour and b&w. Commissions undertaken. Founded 1983.

Fortean Picture Library*
Henblas, Mwrog Street, Ruthin LL15 1LG
tel (01824) 707278 *fax* (01824) 705324
email janet.bord@forteanpix.demon.co.uk
website www.forteanpix.demon.co.uk

Colour and b&w pictures covering strange phenomena: UFOs, Loch Ness Monster, ghosts, Bigfoot, witchcraft, etc; also antiquities (especially in Britain – prehistoric and Roman sites, castles, churches).

Fotoccompli – The Picture Library
35 Birch Croft Road, Sutton Coldfield B75 6BP
tel 0121-378 1064
email djgriffiths@lineone.net
website www.fotoccompli.com

Comprehensive library, ranging from abstracts to zoology, with added specialism of the building and construction industries. Terms: 50%. Minimum retention period: 3 years. Founded 1989.

Fotomas Index*

12 Pickhurst Rise, West Wickham, Kent BR4 0AL
tel 020-8776 2772 *fax* 020-8776 2236

Specialises in supplying pre-20th century (mostly pre-Victorian) illustrative material to publishing and academic worlds, and for TV and advertising. Complete production back-up for interior décor, exhibitions and locations.

Fotosports International

The Barn, Swanbourne, Bucks. MK17 0SL
tel (01296) 720773 *fax* (01296) 728181
email info@fotosports.com
website www.fotosports.com
Contact Roger Parker, Partner

250,000 b&w photos and 250,000 colour transparencies of sports: soccer (domestic, foreign, World Cup 1970s to present), tennis majors, Formula One motor racing, American football (inc. Superbowl) 1985–95; some golf, rugby, cricket. Founded 1968.

Freelance Focus

39 Scotts Garth Close, Tickton, Beverley, East Yorkshire HU17 9RQ
tel/fax (01964) 501729
Contact Gary Hicks

UK/international network of photographers. Stock pictures covering most subjects, worldwide, at competitive rates. Assignments undertaken for all types of clients. Founded 1988.

Frontline Photo Press Agency

18 Wall Street, Norwood, SA 5067
postal address PO Box 162, Kent Town, SA 5071, Australia
tel (08) 8333 2691 *fax* (08) 8364 0604
email info@frontline.net.au
website www.frontline.net.au
Photo Editor Carlo Irlitti

Stock photo agency, picture library and photographic press agency with 400,000 images. Covers sport, people, personalities, travel, scenics, environmental, agricultural, industrial, natural history, concepts, science, medicine, social documentary and press images. Seeking worldwide stock contributors. Assignments undertaken. Prefers high resolution image files on CD-Rom. Write, fax or email for submission guidelines, photo requirements and other details. Terms: 60% to photographer (stock); assignment rates negotiable. Founded 1988.

John Frost Newspapers

22B Rosemary Avenue, Enfield, Middlesex EN2 0SS
tel 020-8366 1392/0946 *fax* 020-8366 1379
website www.johnfrostnewspapers.co.uk

Headline stories from 80,000 British and overseas newspapers and 100,000 press cuttings reporting events since 1850.

Brian Gadsby Picture Library

17 route des Pyrénées, 65700 Labatut-Riviere, Hautes Pyrénées, France
tel (33) 5 62 96 38 44
email GadsbyJB@aol.com

Colour transparencies (6 x 4.5cm, 35mm) and b&w prints. Wide range of subjects but emphasis on travel and the environment: UK, Europe (particularly France), Ecuador and Galapagos Islands, Patagonia, Sri Lanka. Natural history: mainly birds and plant life (wild and garden). Large wildfowl file. Catalogue on request by picture researchers. No other photographers' material required.

Andrew N. Gagg's Photo Flora*

Town House Two, Fordbank Court, Henwick Road, Worcester WR2 5PF
tel (01905) 748515
email a.n.gagg@ntlworld.com
website http://homepage.ntlworld.com/a.n.gagg/photo/photoflora.html
Contact Andrew N. Gagg

Comprehensive collection of British and European wild plants. Travel: Egypt, India, Tibet, China, Nepal, Thailand, Mexico, Vietnam and Cambodia. Founded 1982.

Galaxy Picture Library*

1 Milverton Drive, Ickenham, Uxbridge, Middlesex UB10 8PP
tel (01895) 637463 *fax* (01895) 623277
email robin@galaxypix.com
website www.galaxypix.com
Contact Robin Scagell

Astronomy: specialities include the night sky, amateur astronomy, astronomers and observatories. Founded 1992.

Garden Matters Photographic Library*

Marlham, Henley's Down, Battle, East Sussex TN33 9BN
tel (01424) 830566 *fax* (01424) 830224
email gardens@gmpix.com
website www.gmpix.com
Contact Dr John Feltwell

Plants 10,000 Over 10,000 scientifically

named species and cultivars of garden flowers, wild plants, trees (over 1000 species), grasses, crops, herbs, spices, houseplants, carnivorous plants, climbers (especially Clematis), roses, geraniums and pelargoniums, and pests.

General gardening How-to, gardening techniques, garden design and embellishments, cottage gardens, USA designer-gardens, 200 garden portfolios from 16 states in the USA, 100 portfolios from 12 European countries. Several photographers now represented. Founded 1993.

Colin Garratt – see Railways – Milepost 92½

Genesis Space Photo Library*

Greenbanks, Robins Hill, Raleigh, Bideford, Devon EX39 3PA
tel (01237) 471960 *fax* (01237) 472060
email tim@spaceport.co.uk
website www.spaceport. co.uk
Contact Tim Furniss

Specialises in rockets, spacecraft, spacemen, Earth, Moon, planets, stars, galaxies, the Universe. Founded 1990.

Geo Aerial Photography*

4 Christian Fields, London SW16 3JZ
tel/fax 020-8764 6292, 0115-981 9418
email geo-aerial@geo-group.co.uk
website www.geo-group.co.uk
Director J.F.J. Douglas

Air-to-air and air-to-ground colour library: natural and cultural/man-made landscapes and individual features. Subjects from UK, Scandinavia, Middle East, Asia and Africa. Commissions undertaken. Terms: 50%. Founded 1992.

GeoScience Features*

(incorporates K.S.F. and RIDA photolibraries)
6 Orchard Drive, Wye, Kent TN25 5AU
tel/fax (01233) 812707
email gsf@geoscience.demon.co.uk
website www.geoscience.demon.co.uk
Director Dr Basil Booth

Colour library (35mm to 5 x 4in). Animals, biology, birds, botany, chemistry, earth science, ecology, environment, geology, geography, habitats, landscapes, macro/micro, peoples, plants, travel, sky, weather, wildlife and zoology; Americas, Africa, Australasia, Europe, India, Southeast Asia. Over a third of a million colour images available as film or high resolution digital images. CD-Rom.

Geoslides*

4 Christian Fields, London SW16 3JZ
tel/fax 020-8764 6292 or 0115-981 9418
email geoslides@geo-group.co.uk
website www.geo-group.co.uk
Library Director John Douglas

Broadly based and substantial collections from Africa, Asia, Antarctic, Arctic and sub-Arctic areas, Australia (Blackwood Collection). Worldwide commissions undertaken. Terms: 50% on UK sales. Founded 1968.

Mark Gerson Photography

3 Regal Lane, Regents Park Road, London NW1 7TH
tel 020-7286 5894 *fax* 020-7267 9246
email mark.gerson@virgin.net

Portrait photographs of personalities, mainly literary, in colour and b&w from 1950 to the present. No other photographers' material required.

Getty Images*

101 Bayham Street, London NW1 0AG
tel 0800-376 7977 *fax* 020-7544 3334
email sales@gettyimages.co.uk
website www.gettyimages.co.uk

Still and moving imagery for the advertising, publishing and corporate sector. Online searching and purchase available.

John Glover Photography

The Oast Houses, Headley Lane, Passfield, Hants GU30 7RX
tel (01428) 751925 *mobile* (07973) 307078
fax (01428) 751191
email john@glovphot.demon.co.uk
website www.glovphot.demon.co.uk

Gardens and gardening, from overall views of gardens to plant portraits with Latin names; UK landscapes including ancient sites, Stonehenge, etc. Founded 1979.

Martin and Dorothy Grace

40 Clipstone Avenue, Mapperley, Nottingham NG3 5JZ
tel 0115-920 8248 *fax* 0115-962 6802
email graces@lineone.net

General British natural history, specialising in native trees, shrubs, flowers, ferns, habitats and ecology. Founded 1984.

Tim Graham Picture Library

31 Ferncroft Avenue, London NW3 7PG
tel 020-7435 7693 *fax* 020-7431 4312

Royal Family in this country and on tours; background pictures on royal homes, staff, hobbies, sports, cars, etc; English and foreign country scenes; international Heads of State, VIPs and celebrities. Founded 1978.

Angela Hampton – Family Life Picture Library

Holly Tree House, The Street, Walberton, Arundel, West Sussex BN18 0PH
tel/fax (01243) 555952
Proprietor Angela Hampton

Contemporary lifestyle images including pregnancy, childbirth, babies and children, parenting, behaviour, education, medical, holidays, pets, families, couples, teenagers, women's health, men's health, retirement. Also domestic and farm animals. Over 50,000 colour transparencies. Founded 1991.

Robert Harding Picture Library*

58-59 Great Marlborough Street, London W1F 7JY
tel 020-7478 4000 *fax* 020-7631 1070
email info@robertharding.com
website www.robertharding.com

Picture library with extensive range of subjects, including rights protected and royalty free, in particular travel, lifestyle, business and industry, botany, science and medical. Full e-commerce website with over 70,000 searchable images. Free catalogue.

Harper Horticultural Slide Library

219 Robanna Drive, Seaford, VA 23696, USA
tel 757-898-6453 *fax* 757-890-9378
email pamharper@mindspring.com

160,000 35mm slides of plants, gardens and native habitats.

Jason Hawkes Library*

Unit 46, 124-128 Barlby Road, London W10 6BL
tel 020-8960 7525 *fax* 020-8960 7253
email library@jasonhawkes.com
website www.jasonhawkes.com
Library Manager Chris Lacey

Aerial photography of London and Britain; also Europe, USA and Australia. Online searchable database of over 8000 images. Founded 1998.

Heritage & Natural History Photography

37 Plainwood Close, Summersdale, Chichester, West Sussex PO19 4YB
tel/fax (01243) 533822
Contact Dr John B. Free

Archaeology, history, agriculture: Arabia, China, India, Iran, Ireland, Japan, Kenya, Mediterranean countries, Mexico, Nepal, North America, Oman, Russia, Thailand, UK. Bees and bee keeping, insects and small invertebrates, tropical crops and flowers.

Pat Hodgson Library & Picture Research Agency

Jasmine Cottage, Spring Grove Road, Richmond, Surrey TW10 6EH
tel/fax 020-8940 5986
email pat.hodgpix@virgin.net

Small collection of b&w historical engravings, book illustrations, ephemera, etc; some colour and modern photos. Subjects include history, Victoriana, ancient civilisations, occult, travel. Text written and research undertaken on any subject.

Holt Studios International Ltd*

The Courtyard, 24 High Street, Hungerford, Berks. RG17 0NF
tel (01488) 683523 *fax* (01488) 683511
email library@holt-studios.co.uk
website www.holt-studios.co.uk

110,000 pictures on worldwide agriculture, horticulture, crops and associated pests (and their predators), diseases and deficiencies, farming people and practices, livestock, machinery, landscapes, diverse environments, natural flora and fauna. Extensive gardens and garden plants collection. Founded 1981.

Horizon International

Horizon International Images Ltd, Horizon House, Route de Picaterre, Alderney, Guernsey GY9 3UP
tel (01481) 822587 *fax* (01481) 823880
email mail@hrz
website www.hrzn.com

Specialist stock library. Images include leisure and lifestyle, business and industry, science and medicine, environment and nature, world travel. Founded 1978.

David Hosking FRPS

Pages Green House, Wetheringsett, Stowmarket, Suffolk IP14 5QA
tel (01728) 861113 *fax* (01728) 860222
email pictures@flpa-images.co.uk
website www.flpa-images.co.uk

Natural history subjects, especially birds covering whole world. Also Dr D.P. Wilson's unique marine photo collection.

Houses & Interiors Photographic Features Agency

192 Goswell Road, London EC1V 7DT
tel 020-7253 0991 *fax* 020-7253 0992
website www.a-z.picture-library.com
Contact Val Jones

Stylish house interiors and exteriors, people in their homes and gardens, home dossiers, renovations, architectural details, interior design, gardens and houseplants. Also step-by-step photographic sequences of DIY subjects, fresh and dried flower arrangements and gardening techniques. Food. Colour only. Commissions undertaken. Terms: 50%, negotiable. Founded 1985.

Hulton Archive

Unique House, 21-31 Woodfield Road, London W9 2BA
tel 020-7266 2662 *fax* 020-7266 3154
website www.hultonarchive.com

Over 15 million b&w and colour images. Specialises in social history, royalty, transport, war, fashion, sport, entertainment, people, places and early photography. Collections include *Picture Post*, *Express*, *Evening Standard*, Keystone, Fox and Topical Press. Publisher of CD-Roms for creative image access.

Hutchison Picture Library*

118B Holland Park Avenue, London W11 4UA
tel 020-7229 2743 *fax* 020-7792 0259
email library@hutchisonpic.demon.co.uk
website www.hutchisonpictures.co.uk

General colour library; worldwide subjects: agriculture, the environment, festivals, human relationships, industry, landscape, peoples, religion, towns, travel. Founded 1976.

The Illustrated London News Picture Library*

20 Upper Ground, London SE1 9PF
tel 020-7805 5585 *fax* 020-7805 5905
email iln.pictures@ilng.co.uk
website www.ilng.co.uk

Engravings, photos, illustrations in b&w and colour from 1842 to present day, especially 19th and 20th century social history, wars, portraits, royalty.

The Image Bank – see Getty Images

Image Diggers

618B Finchley Road, London NW11 7RR
tel/fax 020-8455 4564
email ziph@macunlimited.net
Contact Neil Hornick

Stills archive covering performing arts, popular culture, human interest, natural history, architecture, nautical, children and people, strange phenomena, etc. Also audio and video for research purposes, books, and ephemera including magazines, comic books, sheet music, postcards. Founded 1980.

Imagefile*

79 Merrion Square South, Dublin 2, Republic of Ireland
tel (01) 6766850 *fax* (01) 6624476
email info@imagefile.ie
website www.imagefile.ie

Over 150,000 images provided by overseas agents of general material covering 32 countries. Also holds Irish collection of traditional and contemporary icons – from pubs to dolmens, gardens to traditional music – and covers the Irish landscape. Comprehensive searchable website. Images can be sent as digital previews or hi-res scans. Founded 1978.

Imagefinder Pte Ltd

228A South Bridge Road, Singapore 058777
tel (65) 324 3747 *fax* (65) 324 3748
email imagef@mbox4.singnet.com.sg
Director Rashidah Hamid

General photo library with strong focus on Asian-related material. Founded 1998.

Images of Africa Photobank*

11 The Windings, Lichfield, Staffs. WS13 7EX
tel (01543) 262898 *fax* (01543) 417154
email info@imagesofafrica.co.uk
website www.imagesofafrica.co.uk
Library Manager Jacquie Shipton, *Proprietor* David Keith Jones FRPS

135,000 images covering 19 African countries: Botswana, Chad, Egypt, Ethiopia, Kenya, Lesotho, Madagascar, Malawi, Mali, Namibia, Rwanda, South Africa, Swaziland, Tanzania, Uganda, Zaire, Zambia, Zanzibar and Zimbabwe. Specialities: wildlife, people, landscapes, tourism, hotels and lodges, National Parks and Reserves. Terms: 50%. Founded 1983.

ImageState Ltd*

Ramillies House, 1-2 Ramillies Street, London W1F 7LN
Office Manager Julie Chamberlain

Supplier of contemporary rights-protected and royalty-free images, footage and music. Subjects include people, business, UK and world travel, industry and sport. Founded 1983.

Imperial War Museum*

Photograph Archive, Austral Street, London SE11 4SL
tel 020-7416 5333/8 *fax* 020-7416 5355
email photos@iwm.org.uk
website www.iwm.org.uk

National archive of over 6 million photos, dealing with conflict in the 20th century involving the armed forces of Britain and the Commonwealth countries. Open by appointment Mon–Fri. Prints made to order. Founded 1917.

International Press Agency (Pty) Ltd

PO Box 67, Howard Place 7450, South Africa
tel (021) 531 1926 *fax* (021) 531 8789
email inpra@iafrica.com

Press photos for South African market. Founded 1934.

Isle of Wight Photo Library – see S. & O. Mathews

Isle of Wight Pictures

60 York Street, Cowes, Isle of Wight PO31 7BS
tel (01983) 290366 *mobile* (07768) 877914 *fax* (01983) 290366
email patrick@patrickeden.co.uk
website www.patrickeden.co.uk
Proprietor Patrick Eden

Covers all aspects of the Isle of Wight, including landscape, aerial, industry, agriculture, tourism, Cowes Week, nautical aspects. Over 5000 pictures; any picture not on file can be shot to order. All images available as originals or in digital formats. Founded 1985.

Japan Archive

9 Victoria Drive, Horsforth, Leeds LS18 4PN
tel 0113-258 3244 *fax* 0113-216 3441
email stephen.turnbull@virgin.net
website www.stephenturnbull.com
Contact S.R. Turnbull

Japan: modern, daily life, architecture, religion, history, personalities, gardens, natural world; European castles. Founded 1993.

Jazz Index

26 Fosse Way, London W13 0BZ
tel 020-8998 1232 *fax* 020-8998 2880
email christianhim@jazzindex.co.uk
website www. jazzindex.co.uk

Photo library of jazz, blues and contemporary musicians. Also atmospheric photos of club interiors and 'still life' of instruments. Photos sold on behalf of photographers. Terms: 50%. Founded 1979.

Joefilmbase.com

1 Town Mead Business Centre, William Morris Way, London SW6 2SZ
tel/fax 020-7751 0007
email joefilmbase@btconnect.com
website www.joefilmbase.com

General library: fashion, catwalk, people, business, ideas, art photos, business, traders, travel, dance, concerts, cars, boats, lifestyle, nature, worldwide. Transparencies only: 35mm, 6 x 7cm, etc. Founded 1991.

J.S. Library International

101A Brondesbury Park, London NW2 5JL
tel 020-8451 2668 *fax* 020-8459 0223/8517
email js@online24.co.uk

The J.S. Royal collection, Art collection, Hollywood collection, Celebrity service, particularly authors. Travel, fauna and flora and general pictures. New photographers and material required. Assignments worldwide undertaken. Founded 1979.

Just Europe

50 Basingfield Road, Thames Ditton, Surrey KT7 0PD
tel/fax 020-8398 2468
email justeurope@altavista.com

Specialises in Europe – major cities, towns, people and customs. Assignments undertaken; background information available; advice/research service. Founded 1989.

Katz Pictures Ltd*

109 Clifton Street, London EC2A 4LD
tel 020-7749 6000 *fax* 020-7749 6001
email info@katzpictures.com
website www.katzpictures.com

Images of people and world events from 1900s to contemporary.

Kilmartin House Trust

Kilmartin House, Kilmartin, Argyll PA31 8RQ
tel (01546) 510278 *fax* (01546) 510330
email museum@kilmartin.org
website www.kilmartin.org
Contact D.J. Adams McGilp

Ancient monuments, archaeological sites;

artefacts and excavations. Aerial photographs of Mid Argyll. Colour prints and transparencies. Publishers of historical/archaeological works, including fiction. Founded 1994.

Lakeland Life Picture Library

Langsett, Lyndene Drive, Grange-over-Sands, Cumbria LA11 6QP
tel (015395) 33565 (answerphone)

English Lake District: industries, crafts, sports, shows, customs, architecture, people. Also provides colour and b&w, illustrated articles. Not an agency. Catalogue available. Founded 1979.

Frank Lane Picture Agency Ltd*

Pages Green House, Wetheringsett, Stowmarket, Suffolk IP14 5QA
tel (01728) 860789 *fax* (01728) 860222
email pictures@flpa-images.co.uk
website www.flpa-images.co.uk

Natural history, ecology, environment, farming, geography, trees and weather.

Michael Leach

Brookside, Kinnerley, Oswestry SY10 8DB
tel (01691) 682639 *fax* (01691) 682003
email mike.leach@lineone.net
website www.michael-leach.co.uk

General worldwide wildlife and natural history subjects, with particular emphasis on mammals (especially great apes) and urban wildlife. Comprehensive collection of owls from all over the world. No other photographers required.

Lebrecht Music Collection*

58B Carlton Hill, London NW8 0ES
tel 020-7625 5341 and 020-7372 8233
fax 020-7625 5341
email pictures@lebrecht.co.uk
website www.lebrecht.co.uk
Director Elbie Lebrecht

Colour and b&w images of classical music from antiquity to the 21st century: composers, musicians, opera singers, musical scores, concert halls and opera houses, instruments, world music. Founded 1992.

Dave Lewis Nostalgia Collection

20 The Avenue, Starbeck, Harrogate, North Yorkshire HG1 4QD
tel/fax (01423) 888642
email lewisattic@btinternet.com
website www.harrogate.com/davel

A collection of advertising, packaging, points of sale and magazine reference from 1800–1970s. Founded 1995.

Link Picture Library*

33 Greyhound Road, London W6 8NH
tel 020-7381 2261/2433 *fax* 020-7385 6244
email lib@linkpics.demon.co.uk
website www.linkpicturelibrary.com
Proprietor Orde Eliason

Specialist archives on Central and Southern Africa, India, Southeast Asia and Israel. Commissions accepted. Terms: 50%. Founded 1982.

Elizabeth Linley Collection

The Elizabeth Linley Studio, 29 Dewlands, Godstone, Surrey RH9 8BS
tel (01883) 742702, 742451
Contact Audrey I.B. Thomas

Prints, b&w photos and colour transparencies of 18th- and 19th-century artists, portraits, illustrations, theatre, society events, architecture.

London Metropolitan Archives

(formerly Greater London Record Office)
40 Northampton Road, London EC1R 0HB
tel 020-7332 3820 *minicom* 020-7278 8703
fax 020-7833 9136
email ask.lma@corpoflondon.gov.uk

Over 350,000 photographic prints and 1,500,000 negatives of London and the London area from *c.*1860 to 1986. Especially strong on local authority projects, including schools, public housing and open spaces.

Lonely Planet Images*

Australia 90 Maribrynong Street, Footscray, Victoria 3011
tel (03) 8379 8181 *fax* (03) 8379 8182
email lpi@lonelyplanet.com.au
website www.lonelyplanetimages.com
Contact Ellen Burrows
USA Lonely Planet Images/Photo 20-20, 150 Linden Street, Oakland, California 94607
tel 510-547-2020 *fax* 510-547-2496
email lpi@lonelyplanet.com
Contact Jain Lemos
UK/Europe 10A Spring Place, London NW5 3BH
tel 020-7428 4800 *fax* 020-7428 4828
email lpi@lonelyplanet.co.uk
Contact Miranda Duffy

Online library of travel-related imagery. Searchable website.

The Billie Love Historical Collection

Reflections, 3 Winton Street, Ryde, Isle of Wight PO33 2BX
tel (01983) 812572 *fax* (01983) 616515
Proprietor Billie Love

Photos (late 19th century–1930s), engravings, coloured lithographs, covering subjects from earliest times, people, places and events up to the Second World War; also more recent material. Founded 1969.

Ludvigsen Library Ltd

Scoles Gate, Hawkedon, Suffolk IP29 4AU
tel/fax (01284) 789246
email karlcars@btinternet.com
Photographic resources Karl Ludvigsen

Specialist automotive and motor racing photo library. Includes much rare and unpublished material from John Dugdale, Edward Eves, Max le Grand, Peter Keen, Karl Ludvigsen, Rodolfo Mailander, Ove Nielsen, Stanley Rosenthall and others. Founded 1984.

The MacQuitty International Collection*

7 Elm Lodge, River Gardens, Stevenage Road, London SW6 6NZ
tel/fax 020-7385 5606
email miranda.macquitty@btinternet.com

300,000 photos covering aspects of life in 70 countries: archaeology, art, buildings, flora and fauna, gardens, museums, people and occupations, scenery, religions, methods of transport, surgery, acupuncture, funeral customs, fishing, farming, dancing, music, crafts, sports, weddings, carnivals, food, drink, jewellery and oriental subjects. Period: 1920 to present day.

Mander & Mitchenson Theatre Collection*

Jerwood Library of the Performing Arts, King Charles Building, Old Royal Naval College, London SE10 9JF
tel 020-8305 3893 *fax* 020-8305 3993
email rmangan@tcm.ac.uk

Prints, drawings, photos, programmes, etc, theatre, opera, ballet, music hall, and other allied subjects including composers, playwrights, etc. All periods.

Mansell Collection – see Rex Features Ltd

Marine Wildlife Photo Agency

Vine Villa, Mount Road, Llanfairfechan, North Wales LL33 0DW
tel/fax (01248) 681361
email info@marinewildlife.co.uk
website www.marinewildlife.co.uk
Proprietor Paul Kay

35mm and medium format images of UK and Irish (temperate) marine life and associated subjects (coastal services, environmental issues, etc). Subjects range from straight animal/plant portraits through to abstracts; also underwater scenic photos. Founded 1992.

John Massey Stewart Picture Library

20 Hillway, London N6 6QA
tel 020-8341 3544 *fax* 020-8341 5292
email jms@gn.apc.org

Large collection Russia/USSR, including topography, people, culture, Siberia, plus Russian and Soviet history, 3000 pre-revolutionary PCs, etc. Also Britain, Europe (including Bulgaria, Poland, Slovenia and Turkey), Alaska, USA, Israel, Sinai desert, etc; and classical composers (portraits, houses, graves, monuments, etc).

S. & O. Mathews

The Old Rectory, Calbourne, Isle of Wight PO30 4JE
tel (01983) 531247 *fax* (01983) 531253
email oliver@mathews-photography.com

Gardens, plants and landscapes.

Chris Mattison

138 Dalewood Road, Sheffield S8 0EF
tel/fax 0114-236 4433
email chris.mattison@btinternet.com
website www.chris.mattison.btinternet.co.uk

Colour library specialising in reptiles and amphibians; other natural history subjects; habitats and landscapes in Africa, Southeast Asia, South America, USA, Mexico, Mediterranean. Captions or detailed copy supplied if required. No other photographers' material required.

Bill Meadows Picture Library

11 Begonia Close, St Peters, Worcester WR5 3LZ
tel (01905) 350801
Proprietor Bill Meadows

Aspects of Great Britain: general scenic including towns and villages; buildings and monuments; agricultural, industrial and building sites; urban scenes and services; misuse of the environment, vandalism, etc; recreational, 'people at play'; natural history subjects. 20,000 b&w photographs and 50,000 (6 x 6cm and 35mm) colour transparencies. Founded 1968.

Medimage

32 Brooklyn Road, Coventry CV1 4JT
tel/fax (01203) 668562
email chambersking@ntlworld.com

Contact Anthony King
Specialist library of medium format transparencies of subjects in Mediterranean countries and the Czech Republic: agriculture, architecture, crafts, festivals, flora, industry, landscapes, markets, portraits, recreation, seascapes, sport and transport. Commissions undertaken. Other photographers' work not accepted. Founded 1992.

Merseyside Photo Library
Suite 6, Egerton House, Tower Road, Birkenhead, Wirral CH41 1FN
tel 0151-650 6975 *fax* 0151-650 6976
email ron@merseywide.demon.co.uk
Operated by Ron Jones Associates
Library specialising in images of Liverpool and Merseyside but includes other destinations. Founded 1989.

Microscopix
Middle Travelly, Beguildy, Nr Knighton, Powys LD7 1UW
tel (01547) 510242 *fax* (01547) 510317
email semages@microscopix.co.uk
website www.microscopix.co.uk
Scientific photo library specialising in scanning electron micrographs and photomicrographs for technical and aesthetic purposes. Commissioned work, both biological and non-biological, undertaken offering a wide variety of applicable microscopical techniques. Founded 1986.

Military History Picture Library
3 Barton Buildings, Bath BA1 2JR
tel (01225) 334213 *fax* (01225) 480554
Prints, engravings, photos, colour transparencies covering all aspects of warfare and uniforms from ancient times to the present.

Mirrorpix*
One Canada Square, Canary Wharf, London E14 5AP
tel 020-7293 3700 *fax* 020-7293 2712
email desk@mirrorpix.com
website www.mirrorpix.com
Contact Sales desk
Specialises in current affairs, personalities, royalty, sport, cinema. Agents for Trinity Mirror Newspapers.

Monitor Picture Library
Monitor Press Features Ltd, The Forge, Roydon, Harlow, Essex CM19 5HH
tel (01279) 792700 *fax* (01279) 792600
email sales@monitorpicturelibrary.com
website www.monitorpicturelibrary.com
Contact Will Carleton, Stewart White
UK and international personalities 1850–1994. B&w and colour.

Motorcycles Unlimited
48 Lemsford Road, St Albans, Herts. AL1 3PR
tel (01727) 869001 *fax* (01727) 869014
email rolandbrown@motobike.demon.co.uk
Owner Roland Brown
Motorbikes of all kinds, from latest roadsters to classics, racers to tourers. Detailed information available on all machines pictured. Founded 1993.

Motoring Picture Library*
National Motor Museum, Beaulieu, Hants SO42 7ZN
tel (01590) 614656 *fax* (01590) 612655
email motoring.pictures@beaulieu.co.uk
website www.alamy.com www.heritage-images.com
All aspects of motoring, cars, commercial vehicles, motor cycles, personalities, etc. Illustrations of period scenes and motor sport. Also large library of 5 x 4in and smaller colour transparencies of veteran, vintage and modern cars, commercial vehicles and motorcycles. Over 800,000 images in total.

Mountain Dynamics
Heathcourt, Morven Way, Monaltrie, Ballater AB35 5SF
tel (013397) 55081 *fax* (013397) 55526
email gpa@globalnet.co.uk
Proprietor Graham P. Adams
Scottish and European mountains – from ground to summits – in panoramic (6 x 17cm), 5 x 4in and medium format. Commissions undertaken. Terms: 50%. Founded 1990.

Mountain Visions and Faces
25 The Mallards, Langstone, Havant, Hants PO9 1SS
tel 020 0317 8441
email mtvisions@hotmail.com
website www.mountainvisions.co.uk
Contact Graham Elson and Roslyn Elson
Colour transparencies of mountaineering, skiing, and tourism in Europe, Africa, Himalayas, Arctic, Far East, South America and Australia. Does not act as agent for other photographers. Founded 1984.

The Mustograph Agency – see Mary Evans Picture Library

National Maritime Museum Picture Library*

National Maritime Museum, Greenwich, London SE10 9NF
email picturelibrary@nmm.ac.uk
website www.nmm.ac.uk
Contact David Taylor *tel* 020-8312 6631, Chris Rich *tel* 020-8312 6704

Maritime, transport, time and space and historic photographs.

National Museums & Galleries of Northern Ireland, Ulster Folk & Transport Museum

153 Bangor Road, Cultra, Holywood, Co. Down BT18 0EU, Northern Ireland
tel 028-9042 8428 *fax* 028-9042 8728
email t.kenneth.anderson@talk21.com
Head of Dept of Photography T.K. Anderson

Photographs from 1850s to the present day, including the work of W.A. Green, Rose Shaw and R.J. Welsh while he was under contract to Harland and Wolff Ltd. Subjects include Belfast shipbuilding (80,000 photographs, including 70 original negatives of the *Titanic*), road and rail transport, folk life, agriculture and the linen industry. B&w and colour (35mm, medium and large format). Founded 1962.

National Portrait Gallery Picture Library*

St Martin's Place, London WC2H 0HE
tel 020-7312 2474 *fax* 020-7312 2464
email picturelibrary@npg.org.uk
website www.npg.org.uk
Contact Tom Morgan

Portraits of the makers of British history, medieval to the present. The most comprehensive collection in the world: paintings, drawings, sculptures, engravings and photographs. Images supplied with definitive captions and rights clearance.

Natural Image

31 Shaftesbury Road, Poole, Dorset BH15 2LT
tel (01202) 675916 *fax* (01202) 242944
email bob.gibbons@which.net
Contact Dr Bob Gibbons

Colour library covering natural history, habitats, countryside and gardening (UK and worldwide); special emphasis on conservation. Commissions undertaken. Terms: 50%. Founded 1982.

The Nature and Landscape File

24 Southleigh Crescent, Leeds LS11 5TW
tel 0113-2715535 *mobile* (07866) 057823
website www.photosource.co.uk/photosource/Nature&Landscape.htm
Proprietor Dr Mark Lucock

Natural history subjects and landscapes from around the world, especially the UK, southern Europe, North America. Specialises in photomacrographic images. 30,000 large- and small-format colour transparencies. Founded 1997.

Nature Picture Library – see BBC Natural History Unit Picture Library

New Blitz Literary & TV Agency

Via di Panico 67, 00186 Rome, Italy
postal address CP 30047-00193, Rome 47, Italy
tel/fax (06) 686 4859
email blitzgacs@inwind.it
Contact Giovanni A.S. Congiu

News and general library.

Peter Newark Picture Library

3 Barton Buildings, Bath BA1 2JR
tel (01225) 334213 *fax* (01225) 480554

One million pictures: engravings, prints, paintings and photographs on all aspects of world history from ancient times to the present.

NHPA*

(Natural History Photographic Agency)
57 High Street, Ardingly, West Sussex RH17 6TB
tel (01444) 892514 *fax* (01444) 892168
email nhpa@nhpa.co.uk
website www.nhpa.co.uk

Represents more than 120 of the world's leading natural history photographers covering a wide range of wildlife, marine life, domestic animals and pets, plants, landscapes and environmental subjects. Specialisations include the unique high-speed photography of Stephen Dalton, comprehensive coverage on North America and Africa, and the ANT collection of Australasian material (for which NHPA is UK agent). Recent acquisitions include work from new contributors on Madagascar, Antarctica, East African wildlife and both UK and tropical marine life. Pictures are generally supplied to commercial companies only and are sent to freelance writers and artists by agreement with the publisher or commissioning company.

Northern Picture Library – see Stockwave

Operation Raleigh – see Raleigh International Picture Library

Christine Osborne Pictures

53A Crimsworth Road, London SW8 4RJ
tel/fax 020-7720 6951
email copix@clara.co.uk co@worldreligions.co.uk
website www.worldreligions.co.uk
www.middleeastpictures.com

The managerial library for Middle East Pictures founded 1984 and World Religions (2001). Specialist stock on the developing world: Middle East/Arabia, North Africa, Central Asian Republics, Southeast Asia, South Asia and Indian Ocean islands. Travel, culture, crafts, agriculture and food. Major files on world religions – places of worship, rites of passage, sacred sites and pilgrimage. Welcomes enquiries from photographers covering these subjects. Member of the British Guild of Travel Writers and Fellow of the Royal Geographical Society. Specialises in illustrated editorial features. French and Spanish spoken.

Oxford Scientific Films Ltd, Photo Library*

(incorporating the Survival Anglia Photo Library)
Lower Road, Long Hanborough, Oxon OX29 8LL
tel (01993) 881881 *fax* (01993) 882808
email photo.library@osf.uk.com
website www.osf.uk.com

350,000 colour transparencies of wildlife, underwater, natural science, plants, gardens, landscapes, habitats, agriculture, fossils, dinosaur illustrations, domestic animals, tribal people, weather, space and environmental images supplied by over 300 photographers worldwide. UK agents for Animals Animals, New York; Okapia, Frankfurt; Dinodia, India; Garden Image, Canada.

PA Photos*

292 Vauxhall Bridge Road, London SW1V 1AE
tel 020-7963 7032/34/35 *fax* 020-7963 7066
email paphotos.research@pa.press.net
website www.paphotos.com

Over 6 million photos dating from the turn of the 20th century, covering news, sport, royalty and showbiz. Library updated daily. Searches undertaken, or customers are welcome to visit.

PAL (Performing Arts Library)*

1st Floor, Production House, 25 Hackney Road, London E2 7NX
tel 020-7749 4850 *fax* 020-7749 4858
email admin@peformingartslibrary.com
website www.performingartslibrary.com

Continually updated specialist image collection covering classical music, opera, theatre, musicals, instruments, festivals, venues, circus, ballet and contemporary dance. Almost one million images from late 19th century onwards.

Panos Pictures*

1 Chapel Court, Borough High Street, London SE1 1HH
tel 020-7234 0010 *fax* 020-7357 0094
email pics@panos.co.uk
website www.panos.co.uk

Third World and Eastern European documentary photos focusing on social, political and economic issues with a special emphasis on environment and development. Files on agriculture, conflict, education, energy, environment, family life, festivals, food, health, industry, landscape, people, politics, pollution, refugees, religions, rural life, transport, urban life, water, weather. Terms: 50%. Founded 1986.

Papilio Natural History & Travel Library

The Oasts, Headley Lane, Liphook, Hants GU30 7RX
tel (01428) 751056 *fax* (01428) 751057
email library@papiliophotos.com
website www.papiliophotos.com
Contacts Vicki Coombs (library), Robert Pickett

Worldwide coverage of natural history and travel; commissions undertaken. More than 100,000 images held. Colour catalogue available. Founded 1988.

Ann and Bury Peerless*

22 King's Avenue, Minnis Bay, Birchington-on-Sea, Kent CT7 9QL
tel (01843) 841428 *fax* (01843) 848321

Art, craft (including textiles), archaeology, architecture, dance, iconography, miniature paintings, manuscripts, museum artefacts, social, cultural, agricultural, industrial, historical, political, educational, geographical subjects and travel in India, Pakistan, Bangladesh, Afghanistan, Burma, Cambodia, China, Egypt, Hong Kong,

Indonesia (Borobudur, Java), Iran, Israel, Kenya, Libya, Malta, Malaysia, Morocco, Nepal, Russia (Moscow, St Petersburg, Samarkand and Bukhara, Uzbekistan), Sri Lanka, Spain, Sudan, Taiwan, Thailand, Tunisia, Uganda, Vietnam, Zambia and Zimbabwe. Specialist material on historical and world religions: Hinduism, Buddhism, Jainism, Judaism, Christianity, Confucianism, Islam, Sikhism, Taoism, Zoroastrianism (Parsees of India).

Chandra S. Perera Cinetra

437 Pethiyagoda, Kelaniya-11600, Sri Lanka
tel (94) 1-911885 *fax* (94) 1-323910, 674737, 674738
email cinetraww@dialoguesl.net comsvc01@slt.lk
Cinetra Worldwide Createch (Pvt) Ltd
126/3rd Floor, 10B, YMBA Building, Fort, Colombo 1, Sri Lanka
tel/fax (94) 1-323910
Managing Director Chandra S. Perera

B&w and colour library including news, wildlife, religious, social, political, sports, adventure, environmental, forestry, nature and tourism. Photographic and journalistic features on any subject. Founded 1958.

Photo Link

126 Quarry Lane, Northfield, Birmingham B31 2QD
tel 0121-475 8712 *fax* 0121-604 0480
email vines@aviationphotolink.co.uk
website www.aviationphotolink.co.uk
Contact Mike Vines

Colour and b&w aviation library, covering subjects from 1909 to the present day. Specialises in air-to-air photography. Assignments undertaken. Over 10,000 aviation images from around the world are added every year. Can also research, advise and write aviation stories and press releases. Founded 1990.

Photo Resources

The Orchard, Marley Lane, Kingston, Canterbury, Kent CT4 6JH
tel (01227) 830075 *fax* (01227) 831135

Ancient civilisations, art, archaeology, world religions, myth, and museum objects covering the period from 30,000 BC to AD 1900. European birds, butterflies, trees.

Photofusion*

17A Electric Lane, London SW9 8LA
tel 020-7738 5774 *fax* 020-7738 5509
email library@photofusion.org
website www.photofusion.org

Covers all aspects of UK contemporary life with an emphasis on social issues. Catalogue available. Photographers available for commission.

The Photographers' Library*

81A Endell Street, London WC2H 9AJ
tel 020-7836 5591 *fax* 020-7379 4650

Requires transparency material on business, lifestyles, worldwide travel, industry, agriculture, sport, scenic. Colour only. Terms: 50%. Founded 1978.

The Photolibrary Wales*

2 Bro-nant, Church Road, Pentyrch, Cardiff CF15 9QG
tel 029-2089 0311 *fax* 029-2089 2650
email info@photolibrarywales.com
website www.photolibrarywales.com
Director Steve Benbow

Comprehensive collection of contemporary images of Wales. Subjects include landscape, lifestyle, current affairs, sport, industry, people. Over 100 photographers represented. Digital files and transmission available. Colour transparencies and b&w prints. Commission: 50%. Founded 1998.

Pictor International Ltd

Lymehouse Studios, 30-31 Lyme Street, London NW1 0EE
tel 020-7482 0478 *fax* 020-7267 1396
email info@pictor.com
website www.pictor.com

Offices and agents in over 20 countries. All subjects. Terms: 50%.

The Picture Company

100 Pondcroft Road, Knebworth, Herts SG3 6DE
tel (01438) 814418 *mobile* (07850) 971491 *fax* (01438) 814418
email chrisbonass@hotmail.co.uk
website www.flightonfilm.co.uk
Contact Chris Bonass

Colour transparencies (2¼ x 2¼in and 35mm) of people and places worldwide. Taken by award-winning film and TV cameraman and largely unseen and unpublished. Also aviation pictures old and new, including air-to-air photography and a unique archive on 16mm film and broadcast videotape. Used by BBC, C4, etc. Assignments undertaken. Founded 1993.

Picture Research Service

Rich Research, One Bradby, 77 Carlton Hill, London NW8 9XE

tel/fax 020-7624 7755
Contact Diane Rich
Visuals found for all sectors of the media and publishing. Artwork and photography commissioned. Rights and permissions negotiated.

Picturepoint Ltd – see Topham Picturepoint

Picturesmiths Ltd*

Manor Farm Cottage, Main Road, Curbridge, Witney, Oxon OX29 7NT
tel (01993) 771907 *fax* (01993) 706383
email roger@picturesmiths.co.uk
website www.picturesmiths.co.uk
Managing Director Roger M. Smith
Plant photography, from portraits, close-ups and macrophotography to plant associations, colour themes and garden scenes. Also prehistoric archaeology, medieval castles, butterflies, military aircraft, firefighting, Falkland Islands wildlife. Colour transparencies. Founded 1997.

Sylvia Pitcher Photo Library

75 Bristol Road, London E7 8HG
tel/fax 020-8552 8308
email SPphotolibrary@aol.com
Musicians: blues, jazz, old-time country and bluegrass, cajun and zydeco, soul and gospel, pop (1960s and 1970s), plus related ephemera. Views and details of the USA: countryside, 'small-town America', shacks, railroads, rural Americana. Archival: early 20th century – mainly cottonfields, riverboats and various cities in the USA. 1960s–1970s: girls (both white and black) and couples. Founded 1968.

Pixfeatures

5 Latimer Road, Barnet, Herts. EN5 5NU
tel 020-8449 9946 *fax* 020-8441 2725
Contact Peter Wickman
Historical pictures and features covering big news events, royalty, showbiz. Travel (all countries). National newspapers' extensive collection of people in the news to 1970. *Stern* magazine features (before 1985). Documentary and historical photos. Special collections: Dukes of Windsor and Kent, Kennedys, Beatles, Keeler/Levy, trainrobbers, Second World War/Nazis. Terms: 50%.

Popperfoto (Paul Popper Ltd)*

The Old Mill, Overstone Farm, Overstone, Northampton NN6 0AB
tel (01604) 670670 *fax* (01604) 670635
email popperfoto@msn.com
website www.popperfoto.com
www.thegalleryatpopperfoto.com
Over 14 million images, covering 150 years of photographic history. Unrivalled archival material, world-famous sports library and extensive stock photography. Credit line includes Reuters, Bob Thomas Sports Photography, UPI, AFP and EPA, Acme, INP, Planet, Paul Popper, Exclusive News Agency, Victory Archive, Odhams Periodicals Library, *Illustrated*, Harris Picture Agency, and H.G. Ponting which holds the Scott 1910–12 Antarctic expedition material.

Colour from 1940, b&w from 1870 to present. Major subjects covered worldwide include: events, personalities, wars, royalty, sport, politics, transport, crime, history and social conditions. Popperfoto policy is to make material available, same day, to clients throughout the world. Mac-desk accessible. Researchers welcome by appointment. Free catalogue available.

POPPERFOTO Online includes half a million photos with delivery of full resolution images. *The Gallery at POPPERFOTO* features limited edition, hand-printed fine art photographs which can also be ordered online.

Premaphotos Wildlife*

Amberstone, 1 Kirland Road, Bodmin, Cornwall PL30 5JQ
tel (01208) 78258 *fax* (01208) 72302
email pics@premaphotos.co.uk
website www.premaphotos.co.uk
Contact Dr Rod Preston-Mafham
Library of 35mm transparencies; wide range of natural history subjects from around the world, including camouflage, mimicry, warning coloration, parental care, courtship, mating, flowers, fruits, fungi, habitats (particularly rainforests and deserts), and many more. Specialists in invertebrate behaviour and cacti. Captions and copy can be provided. Founded 1978.

Press Association Photos – see PA Photos

Press Features Syndicate

9 Paradise Close, Eastbourne,
East Sussex BN20 8BT
tel (01323) 728760

For full details see page 137.

PSP Image Library

49 Palmerston Avenue, Goring by Sea,
West Sussex BN12 4RN
tel (01903) 503147
email enquiries@peterstiles.com
website www.peterstiles.com

Stock image library specialising in pictures of plants, flowers, watergardening and most horticultural/gardening subjects. Also pictorial views of the Channel Islands and UK, tropical marine aquarium fish and invertebrates. Illustrated garden articles and commissioned horticultural photography.

Public Record Office Image Library*

Public Record Office, Ruskin Avenue, Kew,
Surrey TW9 4DU
tel 020-8392 5225 *fax* 020-8392 5266
email image-library@pro.gov.uk
website www.pro.gov.uk/imagelibrary

Unique collection of millions of historical documents on a wide range of formats from 1066 to 1960s. Special collections include: Victorian and Edwardian advertisements and photographs, Second World War propaganda, military history, maps, decorative and technical designs and medieval illuminations. Founded 1995.

Punch Cartoon Library & Archive*

Until Sept 2002 Suite 5, 3 Hans Crescent,
London SW1X 0LN
tel 020-7225 6710/6793 *fax* 020-7225 6712
email punch.library@harrods.com

Comprehensive collection of cartoons and illustrations, indexed under subject categories: humour, historical events, politics, fashion, sport, personalities, etc.

Railways – Milepost 92½*

Milepost 92½, Newton Harcourt, Leics. LE8 9FH
tel 0116-259 2068 *fax* 0116-259 3001
email contacts@milepost92-half.co.uk
website www.milepost92-half.co.uk

Comprehensive library representing all aspects of modern railway operations and scenic pictures from the UK and abroad. Includes Colin Garratt's collection of world steam trains as well as archive b&w photos. Welcomes contributing photographers and also archives, and markets picture collections on behalf of individuals. Founded 1969.

Raleigh International Picture Library

Raleigh House, 27 Parson's Green Lane,
London SW6 4HZ
tel 020-7371 8585
email press@raleigh.org.uk
website www.raleighinternational.org
Contact Marie Watton

Stock colour images from around the world, especially remote landscapes, people and flora/fauna. Updated from expeditions 11 times a year. Open to researchers by appointment only, Mon–Fri, 9.30am–4.00pm.

Redferns Music Picture Library*

7 Bramley Road, London W10 6SZ
tel 020-7792 9914 *fax* 020-7792 0921
email info@redferns.com
website www.musicpictures.com
Contact Dede Millar

All styles of music, from 1920s jazz to current Top 10, plus instruments, crowds, festivals and atmospherics. Brochure available. Pictures can be researched and sent digitally through website.

Retna Pictures Ltd*

53-56 Great Sutton Street, London EC1V 0DG
tel 020-7608 4800 *fax* 020-7608 4805
email londonlife@retna.com
website www.retna.com

Two libraries: celebrity (early and contemporary music, films and personalities) and lifestyle (people, family life, work, leisure and food). Founded 1984.

Retrograph Nostalgia Archive

164 Kensington Park Road, London W11 2ER
tel 020-7727 9378 *fax* 020-7229 3395
email retropix1@aol.com
website www.retrograph.com

Worldwide advertising, packaging, posters, postcards, decorative and fine art illustrations from 1880–1970. Special collections include Victoriana illustrations and scraps (1860–1901), fashion and beauty (1880–1975), RetroTravel Archive: travel and tourism, RetroGourmet Archive: food and drink (1890–1950). Research service and Image Consultancy services; RetroMontages: Victoriana montage design service. Free colour leaflets. Founded 1984.

Rex Features Ltd

18 Vine Hill, London EC1R 5DZ
tel 020-7278 7294 *fax* 020-7837 4812
email rex@rexfeatures.com
website www.rexfeatures.com
www.timepix.com
Editorial Director Mike Selby, *Library Sales Manager* Glen Marks

International news and features photo agency and picture library serving more than 30 countries, and representing hundreds of photographers. Covers celebrity, news, human interest, pop and showbiz, etc. UK representative of TimePix, the picture archive of Time Inc. which includes the Mansell Collection, the British archive of historical images. Founded 1953.

Ritmeyer Archaeological Design

50 Tewit Well Road, Harrogate, North Yorkshire HG2 8JJ
tel (01423) 530143
email ritmeyer@ntlworld.com
website www.templemountonline.com
Contact Leen and Kathleen Ritmeyer

Colour transparencies of the archaeology of the Holy Land with the emphasis on Jerusalem and the Temple Mount. Architectural reconstruction drawings of ancient sites, such as temples, synagogues, mosques and churches. Special collection of scenes of Jewish temple ritual illustrated on to-scale model of the first century temple in Jerusalem. Drawing commissions undertaken. Founded 1983.

Ann Ronan Picture Library

Old Church Studios, Clifton, Deddington, Banbury, Oxon OX15 0PE
tel (01869) 338883 *fax* (01869) 338887

Woodcuts, engravings, etc social and political history plus history of science and technology, including military and space, literature and music.

Roundhouse Ornithology Collection

Mathry Hill House, Mathry, Pembrokeshire SA62 5HB
tel/fax (01348) 837008
email john@stewartsmith.fsnet.co.uk
Contact John Stewart-Smith

Colour library specialising in birds of UK, Europe, Middle East (especially), North Africa, Far East and South America. Founded 1991.

Royal Geographical Society Picture Library*

1 Kensington Gore, London SW7 2AR
tel 020-7591 3060 *fax* 020-7591 3061
email pictures@rgs.org
website www.rgs.org/picturelibrary
Contact Picture Library Manager

Worldwide coverage of geography, travel, exploration, expeditions and cultural environment from 1870s to the present. Founded 1830.

The Royal Photographic Society*

The Octagon, Milsom Street, Bath BA1 1DN
tel (01225) 462841 *fax* (01225) 469880
email sam@collection.rps.org
Contact Sam Johnson

History of photography from 1827 to the present day. Founded 1853.

The Royal Society for Asian Affairs

2 Belgrave Square, London SW1X 8PJ
tel 020-7235 5122 *fax* 020-7259 6771
email info@rsaa.org.uk
website www.rsaa.org.uk

Library of 19th and 20th century books on Asia, mainly central Asia and archive of original 19th and 20th century b&w photos, glass slides, etc, of Asia. Publishes *Asian Affairs* (3 p.a.).

Royal Society of Chemistry Library and Information Centre

Burlington House, Piccadilly, London W1J 0BA
tel 020-7440 3373 *fax* 020-7287 9798
email library@rsc.org
website www.rsc.org

Covers all aspects of chemistry information. Images collection dating from 1538 includes prints and photographs of famous chemists, *Vanity Fair* cartoons, scenes, lantern slides of similar subjects and colour photomicrographs of crystal structures. Founded 1841.

Royalpics – see Stockwave

RSPCA Photolibrary*

RSPCA Trading Ltd, Wilberforce Way, Southwater, Horsham, West Sussex RH13 7WN
tel 0870-754 0150 *fax* 0870-753 0048
email pictures@rspcaphotolibrary.com
website www.rspcaphotolibrary.com
Manager Andrew Forsyth

A comprehensive collection of natural history pictures representing the work of over 400 photographers, including the Wild Images collection. Includes wild, domestic and farm animals, birds, marine life, veterinary work, animal welfare and environmental issues and a record of the work of the RSPCA. Founded 1993.

Dawn Runnals Photographic Library

5 St Marys Terrace, Kenwyn Road, Truro, Cornwall TR1 3SW
tel (01872) 279353

General library: land and seascapes, flora and fauna, sport, animals, people, buildings, boats, harbours, miscellaneous section; details of other subjects on application. Other photographers' work not accepted. Sae appreciated with enquiries. Founded 1985.

Russia and Eastern Images*

Sonning, Cheapside Lane, Denham, Uxbridge, Middlesex UB9 5AE
tel (01895) 833508 *fax* (01895) 831957
email easteuropix@btinternet.com
Library Manager Mark Wadlow

Architecture, cities, landscapes, people and travel images covering Russia and the former Soviet Union. Excellent background knowledge available and Russian language spoken. Founded 1988.

S & G Press Agency Ltd

63 Gee Street, London EC1V 3RS
tel 020-7336 0632 *fax* 020-7253 8419

Press photos and vast photo library. Send photos, but negatives preferred.

Salamander Picture Library – see Chrysalis Images

Peter Sanders Photography Ltd*

24 Meades Lane, Chesham, Bucks. HP5 1ND
tel (01494) 773674, 771372 *fax* (01494) 773674
email photos@petersanders.com
website www.petersanders.com

Specialises in cultures, lifestyles, architecture, landscapes, festivals and industry. Countries included: the Middle East (including Saudi Arabia), Africa – North, East and West, the Far East (including China). Founded 1987.

Steffi Schubert, Wildlife Conservation Collection Photographic Library

Bramble Cottage, Foxhill, St Cross, South Elmham, Harleston, Norfolk IP20 0NX
tel/fax (01986) 782279

All aspects of British wildlife and fauna. Founded 1990.

Science Photo Library*

327-9 Harrow Road, London W9 3RB
tel 020-7432 1100 *fax* 020-7286 8668
email info@sciencephoto.com
website www.sciencephoto.com

Subjects include the human body, health and medicine, research, genetics, technology and industry, space exploration and astronomy, earth science, satellite imagery, environment, nature and wildlife and the history of science. Over 100,000 images available online. Founded 1979.

Science & Society Picture Library*

Science Museum, Exhibition Road, London SW7 2DD
tel 020-7942 4400 *fax* 020-7942 4401
email piclib@nmsi.ac.uk
website www.nmsi.ac.uk/piclib/

Subjects include: science and technology, medicine, industry, transport, social documentary and the media. Extensive collection; images drawn from the Science Museum in London, the National Railway Museum in York and the National Museum of Photography, Film and Television in Bradford. Free brochure available. Founded 1993.

Scope Features

26 St Cross Street, London EC1N 8UH
tel 020-7405 2997 *fax* 020-7831 4549
email scope.features@btconnect.com

Colour images of personalities, particularly TV personalities. Scope Beauty: colour situations/beauty pictures.

Scotland in Focus Picture Library

Unit 5, Langlee Centre, Marigold Drive, Galashiels, Selkirkshire TD1 2LP
tel (01896) 755124 *fax* (01896) 752370
email library@scotfocus.sol.co.uk
website www.scotfocus.com

Specialist library offering thousands of stock images to illustrate every aspect of Scottish life and work.

Scottish Wildlife Library

Environmental and natural history. All Scottish material required on 35mm and upwards, medium format preferred. Photographers must enclose return postage. Terms: 50%. Founded 1988.

SCR Photo Library

Society for Co-operation in Russian and Soviet Studies, 320 Brixton Road, London SW9 6AB
tel 020-7274 2282 *fax* 020-7274 3230
email ruslibrary@scrss.co.uk

website www.scrss.co.uk
Russian and Soviet life and history. Comprehensive coverage of cultural subjects: art, theatre, folk art, costume, music; agriculture and industry, architecture, armed forces, education, history, places, politics, science, sport. Also material on contemporary life in Russia, the CIS and the Baltic states; posters and theatre props, artistic reference, advice. Research by appointment only. Founded 1924.

Seaco Picture Library*
Sea Containers House, 20 Upper Ground, London SE1 9PF
tel 020-7805 5831/5834 *fax* 020-7805 5807
Stills and video footage of: container shipping; fast ferries and ports; produce and fruit farming; Orient-Express. Hotels and resorts in Botswana, South Africa, Portugal, USA, Brazil, Peru, Italy and Australia. Founded 1995.

Sealand Aerial Photography Ltd
Unit 2, Breadbares Barns, Clay Lane, Chichester, West Sussex PO18 8DJ
tel (01243) 576688 *fax* (01243) 575528
Aerial photo coverage of any subject that can be photographed from the air in the UK. Most stock on 2¼in format colour negative/transparency. Subjects constantly updated from new flying. Founded 1976.

Mick Sharp Photography
Eithinog, Waun, Penisarwaun, Caernarfon, Gwynedd LL55 3PW
tel/fax (01286) 872425
email mick.jean@virgin.net
Archaeology, ancient monuments, buildings, churches, countryside, environment, history, landscape, past cultures and topography. Emphasis on British Isles, but material also from other countries. Access to other specialist collections on related subjects. B&w prints from 5 x 4in negatives, and 35mm and 6 x 4.5cm colour transparencies. Founded 1981.

Shout Picture Library
Mordene House, Merritts Hill, Illogan, Redruth, Cornwall TR16 4DF
tel (01209) 210525
email john@shoutpictures.com
website www.shoutpictures.com
Contact John Callan
Specialises in the emergency services: fire, police and ambulance. Also hospital, medical and trauma. Commissions accepted. Founded 1994.

Brian and Sal Shuel – see Collections

Sites, Sights and Cities
1 Manchester Court, Moreton-in-Marsh, Glos. GL56 0BY
tel/fax (01608) 652829
email paul.dev@tesco.net
Director Paul Devereux
Ancient monuments, mainly in Britain, Egypt, Greece and USA; city features in UK, Europe and USA; general nature shots. Founded 1990.

Skishoot – Offshoot*
Hall Place, Upper Woodcott, Whitchurch, Hants RG28 7PY
tel (01635) 255527 *fax* (01635) 255528
email skishootsnow@aol.com
website www.skishoot.net
Librarians Jo Crossley, Kate Parker
Library specialising in all aspects of skiing and snowboarding. Also France, all year round. Assignments undertaken. Terms: 50%. Founded 1986.

Skyscan Photolibrary*
Oak House, Toddington, Cheltenham, Glos. GL54 5BY
tel (01242) 621357 *fax* (01242) 621343
email info@skyscan.co.uk
website www.skyscan.co.uk
Specialist aerial photolibrary now covering air-to-ground, aviation and aerial sports. Contributing photographers work from planes, helicopters, masts, balloons, gliders and other aerial platforms. Images can be placed in-house on an agency basis or retained by the photographer and requested for use on a brokerage basis; both terms: 50%. Founded 1984.

The Harry Smith Collection Horticultural Photographic Library*
Mayfield Studio, South Hanningfield Road, Wickford, Essex SS11 7PF
tel (01268) 710044 *fax* (01268) 710122
email hsmithhortphoto@aol.com
website www.harrysmithcollection.co.uk
Partners Françoise Davis and Lisa Smith
All aspects of horticulture, including large and small gardens, specialist sections on all subjects including trees, fruit, vegetables, herbs, cacti, orchids, grasses, cultivated and wild flowers from all over the world, pests and diseases, action shots.Founded 1974.

Patrick Smith Associates

c/o Arioma, PO Box 53,
Aberystwyth SY24 5WG
tel (01970) 871296 *fax* (01970) 871733

South London 1950–1977, mid-Wales, aviation; also The Patrick Smith Collection of London photos, now in the Museum of London. Founded 1964.

Snookerimages (Eric Whitehead Photography)

Postal Buildings, Ash Street, Bowness on Windermere, Cumbria LA23 3EB
tel (015394) 48894 *mobile* (07768) 808249
fax (015394) 48294
email eric@snookerimages.co.uk
website www.snookerimages.co.uk
Contact Eric Whitehead

Specialist picture library covering the sport of snooker. Over 20,000 images of all the professional players dating from 1984 to the present day: players away from the table in locations throughout the world as well as action images.

Society for Anglo-Chinese Understanding

Sally & Richard Greenhill Photo Library, 357 Liverpool Road, London N1 1NL
tel 020-7607 8549 *fax* 020-7607 7151
email sr.greenhill@virgin.net

Colour and b&w prints of China, late 1960s–1989. Founded 1965.

Society for Co-operation in Russian and Soviet Studies – see SCR Photo Library

Spectrum Colour Library

41-42 Berners Street, London W1T 3NB
tel 020-7637 1587 *fax* 020-7637 3681
website www.spectrumcolourlibrary.com

Extensive general library of high-quality transparencies, for worldwide marketing, including electronically. Photographer's information pack available. Purchases photos and collections of photos.

Sporting Pictures (UK) Ltd*

7A Lambs Conduit Passage,
London WC1R 4RG
tel 020-7405 4500 *fax* 020-7831 7991
email photos@sportingpictures.demon.co.uk
website www.sporting-pictures.com
Director Crispin J. Thruston, *Librarian* Peter Hermanstein

Specialises in sports, sporting events, sportspersons, amateur sport.

The Still Moving Picture Company*

157 Broughton Road, Edinburgh EH7 4JJ
tel 0131-557 9697 *fax* 0131-557 9699
email info@stillmovingpictures.com
website www.stillmovingpictures.com

Over 100,000 pictures of Scotland and all things Scottish; sport (Allsport agent for Scotland). Founded 1991.

STILL PICTURES The Whole Earth Photo Library*

199 Shooters Hill Road, London SE3 8UL
tel 020-8858 8307 *fax* 020-8858 2049
email info@stillpictures.com
website www.stillpictures.com
Proprietor Mark Edwards

Specialises in people and the environment; the Third World; nature; wildlife and habitats. Includes industry, agriculture, indigenous peoples and cultures, nature and endangered species. Terms: 50%. Founded 1970.

Stockwave

Headquarters Aylesbury office
tel (01296) 747878 *fax* (01296) 748648
email enquiries@stockwave.com
website www.stockwave.com www.royalpics.com

Collections encompassing Britain, Europe and the world. British events (including social calendar), social/political news, government, politicians, industrial, tourism, science and technology, defence, lifestyle, Royal family, film and stage personalities.

John Blake Picture Library

General topography of England, Europe and the rest of the world. Landscapes, architecture, churches, gardens, countryside, towns and villages. Horse trials covered including Badminton and Gatcombe Park.

COI Photo Library

Includes many important and previously unseen images of Britain's government, political events, interior views of the Houses of Parliament and 10 Downing Street, etc, British Royal archives, Festival of Britain, industrial and manufacturing archives, agriculture, education, defence.

Northern Picture Library

Northern England scenery; cities of Northern England and Scotland; architecture and industrial scenes of Northern England past and present.

Royalpics
Dedicated site for Royal pictures from Stockwave, COI Archives and other major photo libraries.

Tony Stone Images
101 Bayham Street, London NW1 0AG
tel 020-7544 3333 *fax* 020-7544 3334
email info@tonystone.com
website www.tonystone.com
Contact Creative Dept
International photo library. Subjects required: travel, people, natural history, commerce, industry, technology, sport, concepts, etc. Terms: variable.

Survival Anglia Photo Library – see **Oxford Scientific Films Ltd**

Sutcliffe Gallery
1 Flowergate, Whitby, North Yorkshire YO21 3BA
tel (01947) 602239 *fax* (01947) 820287
email photographs@sutcliffe-gallery.fsnet.co.uk
website www.sutcliffe-gallery.fsnet.co.uk
Collection of 19th century photography, all by Frank M. Sutcliffe HON FRPS (1853–1941), especially inshore fishing boats and fishing community; also farming interests. Period covered 1872–1910.

Syndication International – see **Mirrorpix**

Charles Tait Photo Library
Kelton, St Ola, Orkney KW15 1TR
tel (01856) 873738 *fax* (01856) 875313
email charles.tait@zetnet.co.uk
website www.charles-tait.co.uk
Colour photo library specialising in the Scottish islands, especially Orkney, Shetland, the Western Isles (including outliers) and Caithness. Archaeology, landscapes, seascapes, wildlife, crafts, industries, events, transport, and sites of interest. Also mainland Scotland and Hadrian's Wall, plus France and Venice. Over 100,000 images in formats ranging from 35mm to 5 x 4in, including 70mm panoramic. Images available to browse online, on CD and by email. Publisher of postcards, calendars, guidebooks. Founded 1978.

The Tank Museum Archive & Reference Library
The Tank Museum, Bovington, Dorset BH20 6JG
tel (01929) 462398 *fax* (01929) 462410
email librarian@tankmuseum.co.uk
website www.tankmuseum.co.uk
International collection, from 1900 to present, of armoured fighting vehicles and military transport, including tanks, armoured cars, personnel carriers, cars, lorries and tractors, First and Second World War Royal Armoured Corps War Diaries. Founded *c*.1946.

Telegraph Colour Library*
101 Bayham Street, London NW1 0AG
tel 020-7859 8900 *fax* 020-7859 8901
Contemporary and archive rights-managed international images covering real people, real issues and real lives from a British perspective. Subjects include industry, business, leisure and sport, animals, medical, nature, space, travel. Fast despatch in any format.

Theatre Museum
National Museum of the Performing Arts, 1E Tavistock Street, London WC2E 7PA
tel 020-7943 4700 *fax* 020-7943 4777
website http://theatremuseum.org
In addition to extensive public displays on live entertainment and education programme, the Museum has an unrivalled collection of programmes, playbills, prints, photos, videos, texts and press cuttings relating to performers and productions from the 17th century onwards. Available by appointment (book 3 weeks in advance), free of charge through the Study Room. Open Wed–Fri 10.30am–4.30pm. Reprographic services available.

Tibet Pictures
28 Sheen Common Drive, Richmond, Surrey TW10 5BN
tel/fax 020-7602 1989
Contact Jonathan Miller
Specialises in the people, architecture, history, religion and politics of Tibet. Also Yemen. Colour and b&w. Founded 1992.

Topham Picturepoint*
PO Box 33, Edenbridge, Kent TN8 5PB
tel (01732) 863939 *fax* (01732) 860215
email admin@topfoto.co.uk
website www.topfoto.co.uk
Eight million contemporary and historical images. Delivery online if requested. New photographers – sample submission of 50 transparencies; 5-year contract, 50% commission.

B.M. Totterdell Photography*

Constable Cottage, Burlings Lane, Knockholt, Kent TN14 7PE
tel/fax (01959) 532001
email btrial@btinternet.com

Specialist volleyball library, covering all aspects of the sport. Founded 1989.

Transworld/Scope – see Scope Features

Travel Ink Photo & Feature Library*

The Old Coach House, 14 High Street, Goring-on-Thames, Nr Reading, Berks. RG8 9AR
tel (01491) 873011 *fax* (01491) 875558
email info@travel-ink.co.uk
website www.travel-ink.co.uk

Travel, tourism and lifestyles covering around 150 countries – including the UK. Specialist sections include Hong Kong (including construction of the Tsing Ma Bridge), North Wales and Greece. Founded 1988.

Travel Photo International

9 Halsall Green, Wirral CH63 9NA
tel/fax 0151-334 2300

Touristic interest including scenery, towns, monuments, historic buildings, archaeological sites, local people. Specialises in travel brochures and books. Terms: 50%.

TRH Pictures*

Bradley's Close, 74-77 White Lion Street, London N1 9PF
tel 020-7520 7647 *fax* 020-7520 7606
email trh@trhpictures.co.uk
website www.trhpictures.co.uk
Director Ted Nevill

Specialises in colour transparencies and b&w photos of the history of civil and military aviation, modern warfare from the American Civil War, transport on land and sea, and the exploration of space. Commission: 50%. Founded 1983.

Tropix Photo Library*

156 Meols Parade, Meols, Wirral CH47 6AN
tel/fax 0151-632 1698
email tropixphoto@talk21.com
website www.tropix.co.uk

All aspects of tropics, sub-tropics and non-tropical developing countries. Plus MerseySlides: photos of Liverpool. Positive, progressive and model-released images. Preliminary enquiry in writing essential, preferably by email. Visit website for full submission guidelines. No unsolicited material. Terms: 50%. Founded 1982.

True North Picture Source

26 New Road, Hebden Bridge, West Yorkshire HX7 8EF
tel (01422) 845532
email john@trunorth.demon.co.uk
Proprietor John Morrison

The life and landscape of the North of England. No other photographers' work required. 30,000 transparencies (35mm and medium format). Commissions undertaken. Founded 1992.

Ulster Folk & Transport Museum – see National Museums & Galleries of Northern Ireland, Ulster Folk & Transport Museum

Universal Pictorial Press & Agency Ltd (UPPA)*

29-31 Saffron Hill, London EC1N 8SW
tel 020-7421 6000 *fax* 020-7421 6006
email postmaster@uppa.demon.co.uk

Photo library containing notable Royal, political, company, academic, legal, diplomatic, church, military, pop, arts, entertainment and sports personalities and well-known views and buildings. Commercial, industrial, corporate and public relations photo assignments undertaken. Founded 1929.

Colin Varndell Natural History Photography

The Happy Return, Whitecross, Netherbury, Bridport, Dorset DT6 5NH
tel (01308) 488341
email colin_varndell@hotmail.com
Proprietor Colin Varndell

UK wildlife and landscape with particular emphasis on birds, mammals, butterflies, wild flowers and habitats. 110,000 colour transparencies. Founded 1980.

Venice Picture Library*

(formerly Archivio Veneziano)
c/o The Bridgeman Art Library, 17-19 Garway Road, London W2 4PH
tel 020-7727 4065 *fax* 020-7792 8509
email info@bridgeman.co.uk
website www.bridgeman.co.uk
Contact Michelle Wood

Specialises in Venice, covering most aspects of the city, islands and lagoon, especially architecture and the environment. Founded 1990.

John Vickers Theatre Collection
27 Shorrolds Road, London SW6 7TR
tel 020-7385 5774

Archives of British theatre and portraits of actors, writers and musicians by John Vickers from 1938–1974.

Vidocq Photo Library
162 Burwell Meadow, Witney, Oxon OX28 5JJ
tel/fax (01993) 778518
email vidocq@which.net

Specialist in photographs for language and educational text books. Detailed coverage of France. Assignments undertaken. Founded 1983.

Visions in Golf
Noblethorpe Hall, Silkstone, Barnsley, South Yorkshire S75 4NG
tel (01226) 791001 *fax* (0870) 831 1941
email mark@visionsingolf.freeserve.co.uk
Proprietor Mark Newcombe

Every aspect of worldwide golf, including an archive dating back to the late 19th century and world-famous golf courses. Over 250,000 colour transparencies and 5000 b&w images. Commission: 50%. Founded 1984.

Christopher Ware Photography
65 Trinity Street, Barry, South Glamorgan CF62 7EX
tel (01446) 732816 *fax* (01446) 413471
Proprietor Christopher Ware

Colour and b&w photos of industry and transport of the southeast Wales area; also civil and military aircraft. Commissions undertaken. Founded 1970.

Simon Warner
Whitestone Farm, Stanbury, Keighley, West Yorkshire BD22 0JW
tel/fax (01535) 644644
email photos@simonwarner.co.uk
website www.simonwarner.co.uk

Landscape photographer with own stock pictures of northern England, North Wales and Northwest Scotland.

Waterways Photo Library*
39 Manor Court Road, London W7 3EJ
tel 020-8840 1659 *fax* 020-8567 0605
email watphot39@aol.com
Contact Derek Pratt

British inland waterways; canals, rivers; bridges, aqueducts, locks and all waterside architectural features; watersports; waterway holidays, boats, fishing; town and countryside scenes. No other photographers' work required. Founded 1976.

The Weimar Archive – see Mary Evans Picture Library

Welfare History Picture Library
Heatherbank Museum of Social Work, Caledonian University, Cowcaddens Road, Glasgow G4 0BA
tel 0141-331 8637 *fax* 0141-331 3005
email a.ramage@gcal.ac.uk
website www.lib.gcal.ac.uk/heatherbank/

Social history and social work, especially child welfare, poorhouses, prisons, hospitals, slum clearance, women's movement, social reformers and their work. Catalogue on request and on website. Founded 1975.

Wellcome Trust Medical Photographic Library*
210 Euston Road, London NW1 2BE
fax 020-7611 8348 fax 020-7611 8577
email photolib@wellcome.ac.uk
website www.medphoto.wellcome.ac.uk
Library Manager Catherine Draycott

Medical and social history; contemporary clinical and general medicine. Over 170,000 images. Founded 1936; renamed 1992.

Richard Welsby Photography
1 Breadalbane Terrace, Edinburgh EH11 2BW
tel/fax 0131-337 9975
email richard.welsby@orkney.com
website www.richardwelsby.com
Contact Richard Welsby

Specialist library of the Orkney Islands: business and industry, scenics, geology, archaeology and historic; wide coverage of flowers, plants and other natural history subjects; aerials. Founded 1984.

Westcountry Pictures
10 Headon Gardens, Countess Wear, Exeter, Devon EX2 6LE
tel (01392) 426640 *fax* (01392) 209080
email petercooper@eclipse.co.uk
website www.westcountrypictures.co.uk
Contact Peter Cooper

All aspects of Devon and Cornwall – culture, places, industry and leisure. Founded 1989.

Western Americana Picture Library
3 Barton Buildings, Bath BA1 2JR
tel (01225) 334213 *fax* (01225) 480554

Prints, engravings, photos and colour

transparencies on the American West, cowboys, gunfighters, Indians, including pictures by Frederic Remington and Charles Russell, etc.

Roy J. Westlake ARPS

West Country Photo Library, 31 Redwood Drive, Plympton, Plymouth PL7 2FS
tel/fax (01752) 336444

Specialises in all aspects of Devon, Cornwall, Dorset, Somerset and Wiltshire. Medium format transparencies of landscapes, seascapes, architecture, etc. Other photographers' work not required. Founded 1960.

Eric Whitehead Photography – see Snookerimages

Wilderness Photographic Library*

Mill Barn, Broad Raine, Sedbergh, Cumbria LA10 5ED
tel (015396) 20196 *fax* (015396) 21293
email wildernessphoto@bt.internet.com
Director John Noble FRGS

Specialist library in mountain and wilderness regions, especially polar. Associated aspects of people, places, natural history, geographical features, exploration and mountaineering, adventure sports, travel.

Wildlife Matters Photographic Library*

Marlham, Henley's Down, Battle, East Sussex TN33 9BN
tel (01424) 830566 *fax* (01424) 830224
email gardens@gmpix.com
website www.gmpix.com
Contact Dr John Feltwell

Ecology, conservation and environment; habitats and pollution; agriculture and horticulture; general natural history, entomology; Mediterranean wildlife; rainforests (Amazon, Central America, Costa Rica and Indonesia); aerial pics of countryside UK, Europe, USA. Founded 1980.

David Williams Picture Library*

50 Burlington Avenue, Glasgow G12 0LH
tel 0141-339 7823 *fax* 0141-337 3031

Specialises in travel photography; wide coverage of Scotland, Iceland and Spain. Also other European countries and Western USA and Canada. Subjects include: cities, towns, villages, 'tourist haunts', buildings, landscapes and natural features; geology and physical geography of Scotland and Iceland. Commissions undertaken. Catalogue available. Founded 1989.

The Neil Williams Classical Collection

22 Avon, Hockley, Tamworth, Staffs. B77 5QA
tel/fax (01827) 286086
email TNWCC@aol.com
website http://members.aol.com/TNWCC/TNWCC.htm
Proprietor Neil Williams BA Hons, DiPMus, Dip EurHum

Specialises in classical music ephemera, including portraits of composers, musicians, conductors, opera singers, ballet stars, impresarios, and music-related literary figures. Old and sometimes rare photographs, postcards, antique prints, cigarette cards, stamps, concert programmes, Victorian newspapers, etc. Also modern photographs of composer references such as museums, statues, memorials, etc.

Other subjects: music in art, musical instruments, manuscripts, concert halls, opera houses and other music venues. Founded 1996.

S. & I. Williams, Power Pix International Picture Library

Castle Lodge, Wenvoe, Cardiff CF5 6AD
tel/fax (029) 2059 5163

Worldwide travel, people and views, girl and 'mood-pix', sub-aqua, aircraft, flora, fauna, agriculture, children. Agents worldwide. Founded 1968.

Windrush Photos*

99 Noah's Ark, Kemsing, Sevenoaks, Kent TN15 6PD
tel (01732) 763486 *fax* (01732) 763285
email windrushphotos@hotmail.com
Owner David Tipling

Worldwide wildlife and landscapes; birds a speciality. Captioning and text services; ornithological consultancy. Photographic and features commissions undertaken. Terms: 50%. Founded 1991.

Tim Woodcock

59 Stoodham, South Petherton, Somerset TA13 5AS
tel (01460) 242788
email tim@timwoodcock.co.uk
website www.timwoodcock.co.uk

British and Eire landscape, seascape,

architecture and heritage; children, parenthood, adults and education; gardens and containers; mountain biking. Location commissions undertaken. Terms: 50%. Founded 1983.

Woodmansterne Publications Ltd

1 The Boulevard,
Blackmoor Lane, Watford,
Herts. WD18 8UW
tel (01923) 200600 *fax* (01923) 200601
email johanna@woodmansterne.co.uk

Britain, Europe, Holy Land; architecture, cathedral and stately home interiors; general art subjects; museum collections; volcanoes, transport, Space; opera and ballet; major state occasions; British heritage, contemporary artists.

World Pictures*

(formerly Feature-Pix Colour Library)
85A Great Portland Street,
London W1W 7LT
tel 020-7437 2121/436 0440 *fax* 020-7439 1307
email worldpictures@btinternet.com
website www.worldpictures.co.uk
Directors David Brenes, Carlo Irek

Over 600,000 medium and large format colour transparencies aimed at travel and travel-related markets. Extensive coverage of cities, countries and specific resort areas, together with material of an emotive nature, i.e. children, couples and families on holiday, all types of winter and summer sporting activities, motoring abroad, etc. Terms: 50%; major contributing photographers 60%.

Murray Wren Picture Library

3 Hallgate, London SE3 9SG
tel 020-8852 7556
email murraywren@aol.com

Outdoor nudes; nudist holiday resorts and activities in Europe and elsewhere; historic and erotic art of the nude through the ages. No new photographers required.

The Allan Wright Photo Library

The Stables, Parton, Castle Douglas,
Kirkcudbrightshire DG7 3NB
tel (016444) 470260 *fax* (016444) 470202
email allan@lyricalscotland.com
website www.lyricalscotland.com

Source of 'Lyrical Scotland' range of images featuring all of Scotland. Founded 1986.

Gordon Wright Scottish Photo Library

25 Mayfield Road, Edinburgh EH9 2NQ
tel 0131-667 1300 *fax* 0131-667 1459
email info@scottish-books-photos.co.uk
website www.scottish-books-photos.co.uk
Managing Director Gordon Wright

Specialist library illustrating Scotland: cities, towns and villages; landscapes and landmarks including the Orkney Islands; Scottish nationalism, personalities and writers. 56,000 b&w photos and 11,000 colour transparencies. Founded 1960.

Yemen Pictures

Flat 2, Auriol Mansions, Edith Road,
London W14 0ST
tel/fax 020-7602 1989
Contact John Miles

Specialist colour library of Yemen, covering all aspects of culture, people, architecture, dance, qat and music. Also Africa, Australia, Middle East and Asia. Founded 1995.

York Archaeological Trust Picture Library

Cromwell House, 13 Ogleforth, York YO1 7FG
tel (01904) 663000 *fax* (01904) 663024
email enquiries@yorkarchaeology.co.uk
website www.yorkarchaeology.co.uk
Picture Librarian H. Dawson

York archaeology covering Romans, Dark Ages, Vikings and Middle Ages; traditional crafts; scenes of York and Yorkshire. Founded 1987.

Yorkshire Now!

4 Keelham Place, Denholme, Bradford,
West Yorks. BD13 4HL
tel/fax (01274) 831652
email melvyn@mynstrel.fsworld.co.uk
Proprietor Melvyn Strelitze

B&w and colour images and videos of towns, cities, industries, etc in Yorkshire. Commissions undertaken. Founded 1998.

Zoological Society of London*

Regent's Park, London NW1 4RY
tel 020-7449 6293 *fax* 020-7586 5743
email library@zsl.org
website www.zsl.org/library
Librarian Ann Sylph

Archive collection of photographs, paintings and prints, from the 16th century onwards, covering almost all vertebrate animals, many now extinct or rare, plus invertebrates. Founded 1826.

Picture agencies and libraries by subject area

This index gives the major subject area(s) only of each entry in the main listing which begins on page 412, and should be used with discrimination.

Aerial photography

Aerofilms
Aviation Picture Library (Austin J. Brown)
Sue Cunningham Photographic
Geo Aerial Photography
Jason Hawkes Library
Sealand Aerial Photography Ltd
Skyscan Photolibrary

Africa

Academic File News Photos
AMIS
Ancient Egypt Picture Library
Andes Press Agency
Animal Photography
Sue Cunningham Photographic
C.M. Dixon
Geoslides
Images of Africa Photobank
Link Picture Library
Tibet Pictures
Yemen Pictures

Agriculture and farming

Stephen Benson Slide Bureau
The Anthony Blake Photo Library
Dennis Davis Photography
Ecoscene
Heritage & Natural History Photography
Holt Studios International Ltd
Frank Lane Picture Agency Ltd
Seaco Picture Library
Sutcliffe Gallery

Aircraft and aviation

Air Photo Supply
Aviation Picture Library (Austin J. Brown)
Dr Alan Beaumont
Photo Link
The Picture Company
Skyscan Photolibrary
Patrick Smith Associates
TRH Pictures

Archaeology, antiquities, ancient monuments and heritage

A.A. & A. Ancient Art & Architecture Collection
Lesley and Roy Adkins Picture Library
AKG London
Rev. J. Catling Allen
Ancient Egypt Picture Library
Stephen Benson Slide Bureau
Sarah Boait Photography and Picture Library
Caledonia Light Images
Country Collections Photolibrary
C.M. Dixon
English Heritage Photo Library
Werner Forman Archive
Fortean Picture Library
John Glover Photography
Heritage & Natural History Photography
Kilmartin House Trust
Photo Resources
Ritmeyer Archaeological Design
Mick Sharp Photography
Sites, Sights and Cities
Travel Photo International
Woodmansterne Publications Ltd
York Archaeological Trust Picture Library

Architecture, houses and interiors

A.A. & A. Ancient Art & Architecture Collection
Abode Interiors Picture Library
Rev. J. Catling Allen
Arcaid Architectural Photography and Picture Library
Stephen Benson Slide Bureau
BookArt & Architecture Picture Library
Sylvia Cordaiy Photo Library
Dennis Davis Photography
English Heritage Photo Library
Werner Forman Archive
Houses & Interiors Photographic Features Agency
Mick Sharp Photography
Venice Picture Library
Woodmansterne Publications Ltd

Art, sculpture and crafts

AKG London
Allied Artists
Bodleian Library
BookArt & Architecture Picture Library
The Bridgeman Art Library
Crafts Council Picture Library
Fine Art Photographic Library
Werner Forman Archive
National Portrait Gallery Picture Library
Ann and Bury Peerless
Photo Resources
Retrograph Nostalgia Archive
Venice Picture Library

Asia

Academic File News Photos
Andes Press Agency
Australia Pictures
Das Photo
Douglas Dickins Photo Library
C.M. Dixon
Andrew N. Gagg's Photo Flora
Geoslides
Imagefinder Pte Ltd
Japan Archive
Link Picture Library
Christine Osborne Pictures
Ann and Bury Peerless
The Royal Society for Asian Affairs
Society for Anglo-Chinese Understanding
Tibet Pictures
Travel Ink Photo & Feature Library
Yemen Pictures

Australia and New Zealand

Australia Pictures
George A. Dey
Frontline Photo Press Agency
Geoslides
Yemen Pictures

Britain (see also Ireland, Scotland, Wales)

Air Photo Supply
Rev. J. Catling Allen
John Birdsall Photography
Sarah Boait Photography and Picture Library
Britain on View
David Broadbent/Peak District Pictures
COI Photo Library
Collections
English Heritage Photo Library
Jason Hawkes Library
Isle of Wight Photo Library
Isle of Wight Pictures
Lakeland Life Picture Library
S. & O. Mathews
Bill Meadows Picture Library
Merseyside Photo Library
Photofusion
Skyscan Photolibrary
True North Picture Source
Simon Warner
Westcountry Pictures
Roy J. Westlake ARPS
Tim Woodcock
Woodmansterne Publications Ltd
York Archaeological Trust Picture Library
Yorkshire Now!

Business, industry and commerce

Ace Photo Agency
Financial Times Pictures
Fotoccompli – The Picture Library
Horizon International
The Photographers' Library
Christopher Ware Photography

Camping and caravanning

Children and people (see also Social issues)

Barnardo's Photographic Archive
Das Photo
Barry Davies
Format Photographers
Angela Hampton – Family Life Picture Library

Cities and towns (see also London)

Lesley and Roy Adkins Picture Library
Financial Times Pictures
Bill Meadows Picture Library
Sites, Sights and Cities
Skyscan Photolibrary

Civilisations, cultures and way of life

A.A. & A. Ancient Art & Architecture Collection
Bryan and Cherry Alexander Photography
Andalucía Slide Library
Australia Pictures
Dee Conway Ballet & Dance Picture Library
Country Collections Photolibrary
Werner Forman Archive
Angela Hampton – Family Life Picture Library
Imagefile
Christine Osborne Pictures
Photo Resources
Royal Geographical Society Picture Library
Peter Sanders Photography Ltd
STILL PICTURES The Whole Earth Photo Library
Tibet Pictures

Countryside and rural life (see also Landscapes)

Andalucía Slide Library
Dr Alan Beaumont
Forest Life Picture Library
National Museums & Galleries of Northern Ireland, Ulster Folk & Transport Museum
Wildlife Matters Photographic Library

Developing countries

BBC Natural History Unit Picture Library
Exile Images
Geoslides
Christine Osborne Pictures
Panos Pictures
STILL PICTURES The Whole Earth Photo Library
Tropix Photo Library

Environment, conservation, ecology and habitats

Heather Angel/Natural Visions
Arctic Camera
BBC Natural History Unit Picture Library
Butterflies
Sylvia Cordaiy Photo Library
Ecoscene
Environmental Investigation Agency
Fogden Wildlife Photographs
Forest Life Picture Library
Brian Gadsby Picture Library
GeoScience Features
Martin and Dorothy Grace
Harper Horticultural Slide Library
Holt Studios International Ltd
Horizon International
Frank Lane Picture Agency Ltd
Chris Mattison
Natural Image
NHPA
Oxford Scientific Films Ltd, Photo Library

Panos Pictures
Premaphotos Wildlife
STILL PICTURES The Whole Earth Photo Library
Tropix Photo Library
Colin Varndell Natural History Photography
Wildlife Matters Photographic Library

Europe and Eastern Europe (excluding UK and Ireland)

Andalucía Slide Library
Andes Press Agency
John Birdsall Photography
Caledonia Light Images
Sue Cunningham Photographic
Das Photo
C.M. Dixon
Just Europe
John Massey Stewart Picture Library
Medimage
Panos Pictures
Russia and Eastern Images
Skishoot – Offshoot
Charles Tait Photo Library
Venice Picture Library
Vidocq Photo Library
The Weimar Archive
David Williams Picture Library

Fashion and lifestyle

Joefilmbase.com

Food and drink

The Anthony Blake Photo Library
Cephas Picture Library
Retrograph Nostalgia Archive

Gardens, gardening and horticulture (see also Plant life)

A-Z Botanical Collection Ltd
Arcaid Architectural Photography and Picture Library
Butterflies
Dennis Davis Photography
Forest Life Picture Library
Garden Matters Photographic Library
John Glover Photography
Harper Horticultural Slide Library
Holt Studios International Ltd
Houses & Interiors Photographic Features Agency
S. & O. Mathews
Natural Image
PSP Image Library
The Harry Smith Collection Horticultural Photographic Library
Tim Woodcock

General and stock libraries

Ace Photo Agency
Stephen Benson Slide Bureau
Chrysalis Images
Bruce Coleman Inc.
Colorific/Getty Images News Services
Corbis
Barry Davies
C.M. Dixon
Greg Evans International Photo Library
Fotoccompli – The Picture Library
Freelance Focus
Frontline Photo Press Agency
GeoScience Features
Geoslides
Getty Images
Robert Harding Picture Library
Horizon International
Hulton Archive
Hutchison Picture Library
Image Diggers
Imagefinder Pte Ltd
ImageState Ltd
Joefilmbase.com
The MacQuitty International Collection
Chandra S. Perera Cinetra
Photofusion
The Photographers' Library
Pictor International Ltd
Popperfoto (Paul Popper Ltd)
Raleigh International Picture Library
Retna Pictures Ltd
Dawn Runnals Photographic Library
S & G Press Agency Ltd
Spectrum Colour Library
Tony Stone Images
Telegraph Colour Library
Topham Picturepoint
Universal Pictorial Press & Agency Ltd (UPPA)
S. & I. Williams, Power Pix International Picture Library
Woodmansterne Publications Ltd

Geography, biogeography and topography

Arctic Camera
B. & B. Photographs
GeoScience Features
Geoslides
John Massey Stewart Picture Library
Royal Geographical Society Picture Library
Mick Sharp Photography

Glamour, moods and nudes

Scope Features
S. & I. Williams, Power Pix International Picture Library
Murray Wren Picture Library

Health and medicine

Education Photos
Angela Hampton – Family Life Picture Library
Science Photo Library
Science & Society Picture Library
Shout Picture Library
Wellcome Trust Medical Photographic Library

High-tech, high-speed, macro/micro, special effects and step-by-step

Earth Images Picture Library
GeoScience Features
Getty Images
Houses & Interiors Photographic Features Agency
Microscopix
The Nature and Landscape File
NHPA
Oxford Scientific Films Ltd, Photo Library

History

AKG London
American History Picture Library
The Associated Press Ltd
Barnaby's Picture Library
Bodleian Library
British Library Picture Library
Chrysalis Images
Mary Evans Picture Library
John Frost Newspapers
Heritage & Natural History Photography
Pat Hodgson Library & Picture Research Agency
Katz Pictures Ltd
Dave Lewis Nostalgia Collection
Elizabeth Linley Collection
London Metropolitan Archives
The Billie Love Historical Collection
National Museums & Galleries of Northern Ireland, Ulster Folk & Transport Museum
Peter Newark Picture Library
Sylvia Pitcher Photo Library
Pixfeatures
Public Record Office Image Library
Retrograph Nostalgia Archive
Ann Ronan Picture Library
The Royal Photographic Society
The Royal Society for Asian Affairs
Royal Society of Chemistry Library and Information Centre
SCR Photo Library
The Tank Museum Archive & Reference Library
Topham Picturepoint
The Weimar Archive

Illustrations, prints, engravings, lithographs and cartoons

Allied Artists
American History Picture Library
Barnaby's Picture Library
Bodleian Library
British Library Picture Library
CartoonStock
Mary Evans Picture Library
Fotomas Index
Pat Hodgson Library & Picture Research Agency
The Illustrated London News Picture Library
Katz Pictures Ltd
Elizabeth Linley Collection
The Billie Love Historical Collection
National Portrait Gallery Picture Library
Peter Newark Picture Library
Public Record Office Image Library
Punch Cartoon Library & Archive
Retrograph Nostalgia Archive
Ann Ronan Picture Library
Royal Society of Chemistry Library and Information Centre
Western Americana Picture Library
Zoological Society of London

Ireland

Collections
Heritage & Natural History Photography
Imagefile
National Museums & Galleries of Northern Ireland, Ulster Folk & Transport Museum
The Weimar Archive

Landscapes and scenics

Lesley and Roy Adkins Picture Library
Andalucía Slide Library
Ardea Wildlife & Pets
BookArt & Architecture Picture Library
Bruce Coleman The Natural World
Barry Davies
George A. Dey
John Glover Photography
Isle of Wight Photo Library
Isle of Wight Pictures
S. & O. Mathews
Bill Meadows Picture Library
Medimage
The Nature and Landscape File
The Photolibrary Wales
PSP Image Library
Railways – Milepost 92½
Raleigh International Picture Library
Charles Tait Photo Library
Simon Warner
Richard Welsby Photography
Roy J. Westlake ARPS
Windrush Photos
The Allan Wright Photo Library

Latin America

Andes Press Agency
Sue Cunningham Photographic
Das Photo

London

Jason Hawkes Library
The Illustrated London News Picture Library
London Metropolitan Archives
Patrick Smith Associates

Middle East

Academic File News Photos
Ancient Egypt Picture Library
Australia Pictures
Stephen Benson Slide Bureau
Das Photo
Barry Davies
Link Picture Library
Christine Osborne Pictures
Ann and Bury Peerless
Yemen Pictures

Military and armed forces

Air Photo Supply
Chrysalis Images
Imperial War Museum
Military History Picture Library
Public Record Office Image Library
The Tank Museum Archive & Reference Library

Mountains

AMIS
Hamish Brown, Scottish Photographic
Mountain Dynamics
Mountain Visions and Faces
Royal Geographical Society Picture Library
Wilderness Photographic Library

Natural history (see also Environment, Plant life)

A-Z Botanical Collection Ltd
Heather Angel/Natural Visions
Animal Photography
Aquila Wildlife Images
Ardea Wildlife & Pets
B. & B. Photographs
BBC Natural History Unit Picture Library
Dr Alan Beaumont
Bird Images
David Broadbent/Peak District Pictures
Butterflies
Bruce Coleman Inc.
Bruce Coleman The Natural World
Sylvia Cordaiy Photo Library
Barry Davies
Ecoscene
Environmental Investigation Agency
Fogden Wildlife Photographs
Christine Foord
Forest Life Picture Library
Brian Gadsby Picture Library
GeoScience Features
Martin and Dorothy Grace
Robert Harding Picture Library
Heritage & Natural History Photography
David Hosking FRPS
Image Diggers
Frank Lane Picture Agency Ltd
Michael Leach
Chris Mattison
Natural Image
The Nature and Landscape File
NHPA
Oxford Scientific Films Ltd, Photo Library
Papilio Natural History & Travel Library
Photo Resources
Premaphotos Wildlife
PSP Image Library
Roundhouse Ornithology Collection
RSPCA Photolibrary
Steffi Schubert, Wildlife Conservation Collection Photographic Library
Scotland in Focus Picture Library
STILL PICTURES The Whole Earth Photo Library
Colin Varndell Natural History Photography
Richard Welsby Photography
Wildlife Matters Photographic Library
Windrush Photos
Zoological Society of London

Nautical and marine

Peter Cumberlidge Photo Library
National Maritime Museum Picture Library
National Museums & Galleries of Northern Ireland, Ulster Folk & Transport Museum
Seaco Picture Library

News, features and photo features

Academic File News Photos
The Associated Press Ltd
Bandphoto Agency
Corbis
Financial Times Pictures
Frontline Photo Press Agency
John Frost Newspapers
International Press Agency (Pty) Ltd
Mirrorpix
New Blitz Literary & TV Agency
PA Photos
Chandra S. Perera Cinetra
Pixfeatures
Press Features Syndicate
S & G Press Agency Ltd
Topham Picturepoint

North America

American History Picture Library
Douglas Dickins Photo Library
Sylvia Pitcher Photo Library
Western Americana Picture Library

Nostalgia, ephemera and advertising

Fotomas Index
Dave Lewis Nostalgia Collection
Retrograph Nostalgia Archive

Performing arts (theatre, dance, music)

Aquarius Library
Camera Press Ltd
Dee Conway Ballet & Dance Picture Library
FAMOUS Pictures & Features Agency
Image Diggers
Jazz Index
Lebrecht Music Collection
Link Picture Library
Mander & Mitchenson Theatre Collection
PA Photos
PAL (Performing Arts Library)
Sylvia Pitcher Photo Library
Redferns Music Picture Library
Retna Pictures Ltd
Theatre Museum
John Vickers Theatre Collection
The Neil Williams Classical Collection

Personalities and portraits (see also Royalty)

Aquarius Library
The Associated Press Ltd
Camera Press Ltd
Corbis
FAMOUS Pictures & Features Agency
Financial Times Pictures
Mark Gerson Photography
Tim Graham Picture Library
Pat Hodgson Library & Picture Research Agency
J.S. Library International
Mander & Mitchenson Theatre Collection
Mirrorpix
Monitor Picture Library
National Portrait Gallery Picture Library
PAL (Performing Arts Library)
Pixfeatures
Popperfoto (Paul Popper Ltd)
Punch Cartoon Library & Archive
Retna Pictures Ltd
The Royal Photographic Society
Royal Society of Chemistry Library and Information Centre
Scope Features
Topham Picturepoint
Universal Pictorial Press & Agency Ltd (UPPA)
John Vickers Theatre Collection

Plant life (see also Gardens)

A-Z Botanical Collection Ltd
Heather Angel/Natural Visions
Ardea Wildlife & Pets
B. & B. Photographs
Butterflies
Christine Foord
Andrew N. Gagg's Photo Flora
Garden Matters Photographic Library
John Glover Photography
Martin and Dorothy Grace
Harper Horticultural Slide Library
Heritage & Natural History Photography
NHPA
Picturesmiths Ltd
Premaphotos Wildlife
The Harry Smith Collection Horticultural Photographic Library
Richard Welsby Photography

Polar and Arctic

Bryan and Cherry Alexander Photography
Arctic Camera
Geoslides
Popperfoto (Paul Popper Ltd)
Royal Geographical Society Picture Library
Wilderness Photographic Library

Religions and religious monuments

Lesley and Roy Adkins Picture Library
Rev. J. Catling Allen
Andes Press Agency
Sarah Boait Photography and Picture Library
Christine Osborne Pictures
Ann and Bury Peerless
Photo Resources
Ritmeyer Archaeological Design
Peter Sanders Photography Ltd

Royalty

Camera Press Ltd
Tim Graham Picture Library
J.S. Library International
Mirrorpix
Monitor Picture Library
Pixfeatures

Russia

C.M. Dixon
John Massey Stewart Picture Library
Russia and Eastern Images
SCR Photo Library

Science, technology and meteorology

Ace Photo Agency
Earth Images Picture Library
GeoScience Features
Horizon International
Frank Lane Picture Agency Ltd
Microscopix
Oxford Scientific Films Ltd, Photo Library
Ann Ronan Picture Library
Royal Society of Chemistry Library and Information Centre
Science Photo Library
Science & Society Picture Library

Scotland

Hamish Brown, Scottish Photographic
George A. Dey
Edinburgh Photographic Library
Kilmartin House Trust
Scotland in Focus Picture Library
The Still Moving Picture Company
Charles Tait Photo Library
Simon Warner
Richard Welsby Photography
David Williams Picture Library
The Allan Wright Photo Library
Gordon Wright §Scottish Photo Library

Social issues and social history

Barnardo's Photographic Archive
John Birdsall Photography
COI Photo Library
Education Photos
Mary Evans Picture Library
Exile Images
FirePix International
Format Photographers
Hulton Archive
The Illustrated London News Picture Library
Imperial War Museum
Elizabeth Linley Collection
London Metropolitan Archives
Photofusion
Ann Ronan Picture Library
RSPCA Photolibrary
Science & Society Picture Library
Shout Picture Library
Stockwave
Welfare History Picture Library
Wellcome Trust Medical Photographic Library

South America

Animal Photography
Australia Pictures
Stephen Benson Slide Bureau
Das Photo
David Hosking FRPS

Space and astronomy

Bruce Coleman The Natural World
Earth Images Picture Library
Galaxy Picture Library
Genesis Space Photo Library
National Maritime Museum Picture Library
Oxford Scientific Films Ltd, Photo Library
Science Photo Library
TRH Pictures

Sport and leisure

Action Plus
Allsport UK
The Associated Press Ltd
Boxing Picture Library
Caledonia Light Images
Michael Cole Camerawork
Sylvia Cordaiy Photo Library
Peter Dazeley
George A. Dey
Eyeline Photography
Fotosports International
Frontline Photo Press Agency
Isle of Wight Pictures
Ludvigsen Library Ltd
Mirrorpix
Mountain Visions and Faces
PA Photos
Popperfoto (Paul Popper Ltd)
Skishoot – Offshoot
Skyscan Photolibrary
Snookerimages (Eric Whitehead Photography)
Sporting Pictures (UK) Ltd

The Still Moving Picture Company
B.M. Totterdell Photography
Universal Pictorial Press & Agency Ltd (UPPA)
Visions in Golf
Waterways Photo Library
Tim Woodcock
World Pictures

Strange phenomena, occult and mystical

Fortean Picture Library
Image Diggers
Sites, Sights and Cities

Transport (cars and motoring, railways)

Das Photo
George A. Dey
Ludvigsen Library Ltd
Motorcycles Unlimited
Motoring Picture Library
National Museums & Galleries of Northern Ireland, Ulster Folk & Transport Museum
Railways – Milepost 92½
Science & Society Picture Library
Seaco Picture Library
TRH Pictures
Christopher Ware Photography

Travel and tourism

Ace Photo Agency
Arcaid Architectural Photography and Picture Library
Aviation Picture Library (Austin J. Brown)
Sarah Boait Photography and Picture Library
Britain on View
Bruce Coleman Inc.
Thomas Cook Archives
Sylvia Cordaiy Photo Library
Peter Cumberlidge Photo Library
James Davis Travel Photography
Douglas Dickins Photo Library
C.M. Dixon
Ecoscene
Greg Evans International Photo Library
Format Photographers
Brian Gadsby Picture Library
Andrew N. Gagg's Photo Flora
Robert Harding Picture Library
Hutchison Picture Library
The Illustrated London News Picture Library
J.S. Library International
Just Europe
Lonely Planet Images
Mountain Visions and Faces
Papilio Natural History & Travel Library
The Photographers' Library
The Picture Company
Raleigh International Picture Library
Royal Geographical Society Picture Library
Seaco Picture Library
Spectrum Colour Library
Charles Tait Photo Library
Telegraph Colour Library
Travel Ink Photo & Feature Library
Travel Photo International
Wilderness Photographic Library
World Pictures

Wales

The Photolibrary Wales
Patrick Smith Associates
Travel Ink Photo & Feature Library
Christopher Ware Photography
Simon Warner

Waterways

Country Collections Photolibrary
Peter Cumberlidge Photo Library
Waterways Photo Library
Roy J. Westlake ARPS

Card and stationery publishers which accept photographs

Before submitting work, photographers are advised to ascertain requirements, including terms and conditions. Only top quality material should be submitted; inferior work is never accepted. Postage for return of material should be enclosed.

**Member of the Greeting Card Association*

Britannia Products Ltd

Dawson Lane, Dudley Hill, Bradford,
West Yorkshire BD4 6HW
tel (01274) 784200 *fax* (01274) 651218
Managing Director Steve McNally

Designs and manufactures greetings cards, giftwrap and calendars. Submit transparencies (5 x 4in). Brands: Fine Art Graphics, Paws for Thought, The Comedy Club, Just Kiddin', Academy, Mother Earth, Animates, Fleurs, Truffles. Division of Hallmark Cards (Holdings) Ltd. Founded 1980.

Card Connection Ltd*

Park House, South Street, Farnham,
Surrey GU9 7QQ
tel (01252) 892300 *fax* (01252) 892363
email ho@cardconnection.co.uk
Managing Director Adrian Atkinson, *Senior Product and Marketing Manager* Alison Mahoney

Cute, humour, traditional, floral, contemporary, photography. Submit colour copies or 5 x 4in transparencies of originals. Humour and sentimental verse. Founded 1992.

Caspari Ltd*

9 Shire Hill, Saffron Walden, Essex CB11 3AP
tel (01799) 513010 *fax* (01799) 513101
Managing Director Keith Entwisle

Traditional fine art/classic images; 5 x 4in transparencies. No verses. Founded 1990.

Chapter and Verse (International) Ltd

Granta House, 96 High Street, Linton,
Cambs. CB1 6JT
tel (01223) 891951 *fax* (01223) 894137
email sales@chapter-and-verse.sagehost.co.uk

Buildings, animals, flowers, scenic, or domestic subjects in series, suitable for greetings cards and postcards. All sizes of transparency. No verses. Founded 1981.

Hallmark Cards Plc*

Bingley Road, West Yorkshire BD9 8SD
Submissions Mr Richmond Denton

All subjects suitable for greetings cards considered.

Images & Editions*

Bourne Road, Essendine, Nr Stamford,
Lincs. PE9 4UW
tel (01780) 757118 *fax* (01780) 754629
Contact Joanne Forrow (director)

Greetings cards, giftwrap, gift products and social stationery: flowers, gardens and landscape, animals, especially cats and dogs. Any format accepted; transparencies preferred. Founded 1984.

Nigel Quiney Publications Ltd

Cloudesley House, Shire Hill, Saffron Walden,
Essex CB11 3FB
tel (01799) 520200 *fax* (01799) 520100
Contact Ms J. Arkinstall, Product & Marketing Director

Everyday and seasonal greetings cards and giftwrap including fine art, photog raphic, humour, fun art, contemporary and cute. Submit colour copies, photographs or transparencies: no original artwork.

J. Salmon Ltd

100 London Road, Sevenoaks, Kent TN13 1BB
tel (01732) 452381 *fax* (01732) 450951

Picture postcards, calendars and local view booklets.

Santoro Graphics Ltd

Rotunda Point, 11 Hartfield Crescent, London SW19 3RL
tel 020-8781 110 *fax* 020-8781 1101
email enquiries@santorographics.com
website www.santorographics.com
Directors L. Santoro, M. Santoro

Publishers of innovative and award-winning designs for greetings cards, giftwrap and gift stationery. Bold contemporary images with an international appeal. Subjects covered: black and white, colour floral, quirky and humorous, whimsical, 'Fifties, 'Seventies, futuristic! All formats accepted in both b&w and colour; transparencies ideally 5 x 4in but will accept 35mm. Founded 1985.

Scandecor Ltd

3 The Ermine Centre, Hurricane Close, Huntingdon, Cambs. PE29 6WY
tel (01480) 456395 *fax* (01480) 456269
Managing Director Derek Shirley

Transparencies all sizes. Founded 1967.

Twin Oaks Publishing **– see Nigel Quiney Publications Ltd**

The picture research revolution

***Julian Jackson** describes how picture researchers have had to change the way they work since entering the 'digital age'.*

Picture researchers find the images you see in books, magazines, on television shows and videos, and now on CD-Roms and the internet. For many years picture research was a relatively static profession. The procedures for contacting picture suppliers didn't change very much. The researcher would phone or fax a supplier with a request then a package of transparencies or prints would arrive in the post. Since entering the 'digital age' this has changed dramatically. Now picture researchers need to learn new skills in addition to the old ones. They need considerable internet search competencies. They also need enough technological knowledge to check that digital files are of sufficient quality for their use, which may be for a much wider variety of media. In an era of rapid technological change they need to keep an eye out for developments such as new file formats or software.

Traditional picture research

There are two sorts of researchers: freelances, and salaried staff, sometimes called 'in-house' researchers. The way they both approach a job is the same. Generally most picture research assignments follow this pattern:

1. Briefing and creation of picture list.
2. The picture researcher contacts picture libraries, press agencies, photographers, museums, galleries or other picture sources, by phone, fax, email or personal visit.
3. Photography is commissioned, if appropriate.
4. Pictures arrive and are 'booked in'.
5. A preliminary selection is made, usually by the picture researcher, designer and editor working in concert.
6. Rejected pictures are returned to the library.
7. A final selection is made.
8. The picture researcher negotiates the fees, creates a list of contributors to be credited, and checks the proofs.
9. The picture researcher returns all the remaining unused pictures, and those used when they return from the printers or other production organisations.
10. The picture researcher keeps records and sends complementary copies or 'tearsheets' (the page that the supplier's picture was used on) to the various suppliers of the pictures.

This is a broad view of how all picture research assignments work, whether for traditional media such as books, or new media like CD-Roms. In some cases there might already be a fee structure in place so the researcher does not have to do fee negotiation.

Skills required

Picture researchers need to be organised, diligent, capable of leaps of the imagination when necessary ("I bet there's a museum devoted to shopping bags somewhere!"), and above all *diplomatic*. They need the ability to wheedle images out of sometimes unresponsive people: professional image libraries pride themselves on swift, efficient service, but picture researchers have to deal with museum staff, private collectors, individual photographers, PR people, and the odd complete nutter who just happens to own the rights to *the picture you must have*. Of all

Courses and training

London School of Publishing
David Game House, 69 Notting Hill Gate, London W11 3JS
tel 020-7221 3399 *fax* 020-7243 1730
email lsp@easynet.co.uk
website www.publishing-school.co.uk
A 10-week evening course suitable for anyone wanting to pursue a career in picture research.

The Publishing Training Centre at Book House
45 East Hill, London SW18 2QZ
tel 020-8874 2718 *fax* 020-8870 8985
email publishing.training@bookhouse.co.uk
One-day picture research course suitable for those already working in publishing, aimed at those who already have some picture research experience.

Useful organisations

The Picture Research Association
See page 487.

BAPLA (British Association of Picture Libraries and Agencies)
See page 462.

The Association of Photographers
See page 487.

DACS (Design and Artists Copyright Society)
See page 642.

the skills necessary, this is the most vital.

A good picture researcher also needs diligence and good organisation. Diligence means keeping tabs on the pictures so they do not get lost. Though theoretically this isn't difficult, with large amounts of material and perhaps over-eager designers who take pictures from the files without telling you, transparencies do get lost. It isn't even necessary to lose the transparency: taking one out of its mount to scan, then losing the mount is often enough to mean hours of searching through delivery notes in order to track down which library it came from.

Though this is not often evident to outsiders, pictures are *valuable*. If a photographer has trekked to the Grand Canyon at dawn, and you lose the original, that picture is gone forever. A £400 replacement fee is not really too much in that particular case but some loss fees are much higher. While the occasional picture may go astray, the more a picture researcher keeps control over the situation, the fewer catastrophes will happen. For example, only give the designers selected images and keep the 'rejects', and note which images they have retained.

If you are a freelance and working from home there could be significant costs if you lose some pictures, so you need to take a careful look at your house contents insurance to see if that eventuality is covered. Once you deliver material to the client, then their insurance should cover it, but this is a point to note.

The digital wave

Digitisation of files and the advent of the internet in general has caused a revolution in picture research. Agonised waits for a package of transparencies to arrive from Inner Mongolia are a thing of the past; now pictures can be sent by ISDN in seconds. Commissioning a photographer is streamlined when you can look at his or her portfolio online. Email is particularly convenient for dealing with suppliers in different time zones.

Like the famous 'butterfly' chaos theory, digitisation has caused a tornado which is roaring through the industry. Deadlines are shorter, leaving less time for considered decisions. Unlike transparencies, digital files can be unusable for a variety of invisible factors: for example, bad scanning, wrong resolution, corruption. These problems usually become evident at the last possible moment. Old-style picture researchers would have rejected a bad transparency or print at an early stage so these problems would have been avoided.

In recent years, picture researchers have had to learn powerful computer search skills and develop understandings of many technological concepts. For some

Useful directories

Picture Researcher's Handbook
by Hilary and Mary Evans, 7th edn, Pira
No picture researcher should be without this invaluable and comprehensive source of picture libraries worldwide. The book clearly lists where picture libraries are, the subjects they cover and addresses, websites, email addresses, telephone and fax numbers.

BAPLA Directory
BAPLA, 18 Vine Hill, London EC1R 5DZ
tel 020-7713 1780 *fax* 020-7713 1211
Lists all the current members of the British Association of Picture Libraries and Agencies (BAPLA).

Picture Research in a Digital Age
by Julian Jackson
website www.julianjackson.co.uk/pic_res_dig.htm
This e-book covers digital photography, scanning, searching the internet, and many other important topics to enable researchers to get the best out of the digital age. It is available online, and can be downloaded immediately.

this has been a difficult process that has lessened the enjoyment of the job. Unfortunately, one of the spin-offs from digitisation has been that employers may mistakenly believe that a researcher can do his or her job from behind a computer. However, it is estimated that only 3–5% of the pictures of major collections are currently digitised. The personal visit to a source to find images, and forge a relationship with the people there – often experts in their subject – is still an essential part of the job.

Old style *v.* digital

There are advantages and disadvantages to both ways of working. Most picture researchers will continue to handle prints and transparencies in the conventional manner alongside downloading, modifying, and transmitting digital files from their computer.

- One distinct advantage of digital files is that they can be instantly downloaded from the web or sent via ISDN, ADSL or other means.
- Working with digital files means that there are no time-consuming and tedious returns to do.
- Analogue media – prints, negatives and transparencies – can be immediately assessed for quality. To assess the quality of a digital file, further investigation is required.
- Intricate keywording systems often fail to find pictures which the library holds. Phoning the library's experienced staff may well be a better use of your time than spending hours wrestling with an online search system.
- Sometimes it is hard to keep track of digital files on a computer system, especially if the file name is just a number, as opposed to a descriptive name, such as 'Picture of Paris.jpg'.
- Negotiating fees remains the same. It is what the picture is *used* for, not whether it is analogue or digital, that is the main criterion.

Picture research now

Picture research has changed. Old-style methods of receiving transparencies in the post and viewing them on a lightbox are still valid, but the speed and convenience of digital files means that online picture research is becoming more and more of a necessity for researchers. Modern researchers need high levels of computer search skills to enable them to find the pictures they want, whether it's by searching the web generally, or accessing the online search systems of picture libraries.

Julian Jackson is a writer, internet expert and consultant to the UK picture research industry. He has close links with many companies and organisations within the photographic industry. His website is www.julianjackson.co.uk.

Societies, prizes and festivals

Societies, associations and clubs

The societies, associations and clubs listed here will be of interest to both writers and artists. They include appreciation societies devoted to specific authors, professional bodies and national institutions. Some also offer prizes and awards (see page 512).

Academi (Welsh Academy)
Main Office 3rd Floor, Mount Stuart House, Mount Stuart Square, Cardiff CF10 5FQ
tel 029-2047 2266 *fax* 029-2049 2930
email post@academi.org
website www.academi.org
North West Wales Office Ty Newydd, Llanystumdwy, Cricieth, Gwynedd LL52 0LW
tel (01766) 522817 *fax* (01766) 523095
email academi.gog@dial.pipex.com
South West Wales Office Dylan Thomas Centre, Somerset Place, Swansea SA1 1RR
tel (01792) 463980 *fax* (01792) 463993
email academi.dylan.thomas@business.ntl.com
North East Wales Office Yr Hen Garchar, 46 Clwyd Street, Ruthin, Denbighshire LL15 1HP
tel (01824) 708218 *fax* (01824) 708202
email academi@denbighshire.gov.uk
Chief Executive Peter Finch
Membership Associate: £15 p.a. (waged), £7.50 (unwaged)

Academi is shorthand for Yr Academi Gymreig, the national society of writers in Wales, which exists to promote literature in Wales and to assist in maintaining its standards by providing a forum for writers. With funds mostly provided from public sources, it has been constitutionally independent since 1978. It runs courses, competitions (including the Cardiff International Poetry Competition), conferences, tours by authors, festivals and represents the interests of Welsh writers and Welsh writing both inside Wales and beyond. Its publications include *Taliesin* (3 p.a.), a literary journal in the Welsh language; *A470* (bi-monthly), a literature information magazine; *The Oxford Companion to the Literature of Wales*, *The Welsh Academy English-Welsh Dictionary*, and a variety of translated works.

In 1998 Academi took on a much enlarged role when it won the Arts Council of Wales's franchise to provide a Welsh National Literature Promotion Agency. It now administers a range of schemes including Writers on Tour, Writers Residencies, Writing Squads for young people, has field workers based in North West, North East and West Wales, and co-ordinates a number of literature development projects. It promotes an annual literary festival and runs a dedicated programme of literary activity. In addition, the Academi is in receipt of a lottery grant to publish the first *Encyclopaedia of Wales*. Founded 1959.

Academic Writers Group – see The Society of Authors, page 504

Acrylic Painters' Association, National (NAPA)
134 Rake Lane, Wallasey, Wirral, Merseyside CH45 1JW
tel/fax 0151-639 2980
Membership The Executive Council, c/o Alan Edwards, 6 Berwyn Boulevard, Bebington, Wirral CH63 5LR
tel 0151-645 8433
email napainfo@yahoo.com
website www.art-arena.com/napa
www.napa-inter.org
www.watercolour-online.com/NAPA
President Alwyn Crawshaw, *Director/Founder* Kenneth J. Hodgson

Promotes interest in, and encourages excellence and innovation in, the work of painters in acrylic. Holds an annual exhibition and regional shows: awards are made. Worldwide membership. Publishes a newsletter known as the *International Napa Newspages*. American Division established 1995. Founded 1985.

Agricultural Journalists, Guild of
Hon. General Secretary Don Gomery, Charmwood, 47 Court Meadow, East Sussex TN6 3LQ
tel (01892) 853187 *fax* (01892) 853551
email don.gomery@farmline.com
website www.gaj.org.uk
President Tony Pexton, *Chairman* Tim Angelbeck

Established to promote a high standard among journalists who specialise in agricultural matters and to assist them to increase their sources of information and technical knowledge.

American Correspondents in London, Association of (AACL)
Secretary Elizabeth Lea, c/o Time Magazine, Brettenham House, Lancaster Place, London WC2E 7TL
tel 020-7322 1084 *fax* 020-7322 1230

American Publishers, Association of Inc.
71 Fifth Avenue, New York, NY 10003, USA
tel 212-255-0200 *fax* 212-255-7007
website www.publishers.org
President and Ceo Patricia S. Schroeder

Founded 1970.

American Society of Composers, Authors and Publishers
One Lincoln Plaza, New York, NY 10023, USA
tel 212-621-6000 *fax* 212-874 8480
President and Chairman Marilyn Bergman

American Society of Indexers (ASI)
10200 West 44th Avenue, Suite 304, Wheat Ridge, CO 80033, USA
tel 303-463-2887 *fax* 303-422-8894
email info@asindexing.org
website www.asindexing.org

Aims to increase awareness of the value of high-quality indexes and indexing; offer members access to educational resources that enable them to strengthen their indexing performance; keep members up to date on indexing technology; defend and safeguard the professional interests of indexers.

Art and Design, National Society for Education in
The Gatehouse, Corsham Court, Corsham, Wilts. SN13 0BZ
tel (01249) 714825 *fax* (01249) 716138
website www.nsead.org
General Secretary Dr John Steers NDD, ATC, AE, PhD

The leading national authority concerned with art, craft and design across all phases of education in the UK. Offers the benefits of membership of a professional association, a learned society and a trade union. Has representatives on National and Regional Committees concerned with Art and Design Education. Publishes *Journal of Art and Design Education* (3 p.a.), (Blackwells). Founded 1888.

Art Club, New English
17 Carlton House Terrace, London SW1Y 5BD
tel 020-7930 6844 *fax* 020-7839 7830
President Ken Howard RA

For all those interested in the art of painting, and the promotion of fine arts. Open Annual Exhibition at the Mall Galleries, The Mall, London SW1, open to all working in painting, drawing, pastels and prints.

Art Historians, Association of (AAH)
70 Cowcross Street, London EC1M 6EJ
tel 020-7490 3211 *fax* 020-7490 3277
email admin@aah.org.uk
website www.aah.org.uk
Administrator Claire Davies
Membership Various options for personal membership; corporate membership available

Formed to promote the study of art history and ensure wider public recognition of the field. Publishes *Art History* journal, *The Art Book* magazine, *Bulletin* newsletter. Annual conference and bookfair in March/April. Founded 1974.

Artists, Federation of British
17 Carlton House Terrace, London SW1Y 5BD
tel 020-7930 6844 *fax* 020-7839 7830
website www.mallgalleries.org.uk

Administers 9 major National Art Societies at The Mall Galleries, The Mall, London SW1.

Artists, The International Guild of
Briargate, 2 The Brambles, Ilkley, West Yorkshire LS29 9DH
Director Leslie Simpson FRSA

Organises 4 seasonal exhibitions per year for 3 national societies: Society of Miniaturists, British Society of Painters in Oils, Pastels & Acrylics and British Watercolour Society. Promotes these 3 societies in countries outside the British Isles.

Artists, Royal Birmingham Society of
4 Brook Street, St Paul's, Birmingham B3 1SA
tel 0121-236 4353 *fax* 0121-236 4555
Membership Friends £18 p.a.

The Society has 2 floors of exhibition space and a craft gallery in the city centre. Members (RBSA) and Associates (ARBSA) are elected annually. Holds 3 Open Exhibitions: 2 all-media exhibitions (Spring and Summer) and Pastel & Drawing (December) – send sae for schedules, available 6 weeks prior to Exhibition. A further Open £1000 First Prize Exhibition is held (June/July) for works in any media. Other substantial money prizes can be won with no preference given to Members and Associates. Also a varying programme of exhibitions throughout the year, including the Autumn Exhibition, open to Members and Associates, and 2 Friends Exhibitions (February and August). Friends of the RBSA are entitled to attend various functions and to submit work for the Annual Exhibitions.

Artists, Royal Society of British
17 Carlton House Terrace, London SW1Y 5BD
tel 020-7930 6844 *fax* 020-7839 7830
President Cav. Romeo di Girolamo, *Keeper* Alfred Daniels

Incorporated by Royal Charter for the purpose of encouraging the study and practice of the arts of painting, sculpture and architectural designs. Annual Open Exhibition at the Mall Galleries, The Mall, London SW1, open to artists working in any 2- or 3-dimensional medium.

Artists Agents, Society of
44 Brookbank Avenue, London W7 3DW
tel/fax 020-8575 6572
email careyb@thesaa.com
website www.thesaa.com
Contact Carey Bennett

Formed to promote professionalism in the illustration industry and to forge closer links between clients and artists through an agreed set of guidelines. The Society believes in an ethical approach through proper terms and conditions, thereby protecting the interests of the artists and clients. Founded 1992.

Artists Association of Ireland
43 Temple Bar, Dublin 2, Republic of Ireland
tel (01) 8740529 *fax* (01) 6771585
email info@artistsireland.com
website www.artistsireland.com
Contact Administrator
Membership £45 p.a.

Information and advice resource for professional visual artists in Ireland. Publishes *Art Bulletin* (6 p.a.), available on subscription. Founded 1981.

Arts Boards – see Regional Arts Offices

Arts Club
40 Dover Street, London W1S 4NP
tel 020-7499 8581 *fax* 020-7409 0913
Club Secretary Tony Derrett

For all those connected with or interested in the arts, literature and science. Founded 1863.

The Arts Council/An Chomhairle Ealaíon
Literature Officer, 70 Merrion Square, Dublin 2, Republic of Ireland
tel (01) 6180200 *fax* (01) 6761302
website www.artscouncil.ie
Literature Officer Sinéad MacAodha, *Visual Arts Officer* Oliver Dowling

The national development agency for the arts in Ireland. Founded 1951.

Arts Council of England
14 Great Peter Street, London SW1P 3NQ
tel 020-7333 0100, *Information Desk* 020-7973 6517
fax 020-7973 6590
email enquiries@artscouncil.org.uk
website www.artscouncil.org.uk
Chairman Gerry Robinson, *Chief Executive* Peter Hewitt, *Executive Director of Arts* Kim Evans, *Director of Literature* Gary McKeone, *Director of Visual Arts* Marjorie Allthorpe-Guyton

To develop, sustain and champion the arts and to increase their accessibility to the public. The Arts Council of England is the national policy body for the arts in England. On 1 April 2002, the Arts Council of England and the 10 Regional Arts Boards (RABs) joined together to form a single development organisation for the arts. It champions the arts – promoting artistic endeavour in its own right and for its importance to social, economic and spiritual wellbeing. It distributes public money from government and from the National Lottery to artists and arts organisations, both directly and through its 9 regional arts offices. It works independently and at arms' length from the government. The arts with which the Council is mainly concerned are dance, drama, literature, music and opera, collaborative arts, the visual arts, including new media, photography, architecture, crafts, and artists' film and video.

Within literature, 15 annual writers' awards are given competitively (see also page 513). Subsidies are provided to literary organisations and magazines, and schemes include support for translation, writers' residencies in prisons, tours by authors and the promotion of literature in libraries and education. The Visual Arts Department is committed to the long-term improvement of visual artists' and makers' economic standing and working conditions in England. It now has responsibility for crafts and funds the Crafts Council.

Arts Council of Northern Ireland

MacNeice House, 77 Malone Road, Belfast BT9 6AQ
tel 028-9038 5200 *fax* 028-90661715
website www.artscouncil-ni.org
Chief Executive Brian Ferran, *Literature Officer* Ciaran Carson, *Visual Arts Officer* Paula Campbell

Promotes and encourages the arts throughout Northern Ireland. Artists in drama, dance, music and jazz, literature, the visual arts, traditional arts and community arts, can apply for support for specific schemes and projects. The value of the grant will be set according to the aims of the application. Applicants must have contributed regularly to the artistic activities of the community, with residency of at least one year in Northern Ireland.

Arts Council of Wales

9 Museum Place, Cardiff CF10 3NX
tel 029-2037 6500 *fax* 029-2022 1447
email information@ccc-acw.org.uk
website www.ccc-acw.org.uk
Chairman Sybil Crouch, *Chief Executive* Peter Tyndall, *Deputy Chief Executive* Frances Medley, *Senior Literature Officer* Tony Bianchi, *Senior Officer: Dance* Anna Holmes, *Senior Visual Arts and Crafts Officer* vacant

National organisation with specific responsibility for the funding and development of the arts in Wales. ACW receives funding from the National Assembly for Wales and also distributes the National Lottery funds in Wales to the arts. From these resources, ACW makes grants to support arts activity and facilities. Some of the funds are allocated in the form of annual revenue grants to full-time arts organisations; also operates schemes which provide financial and other forms of support for individual activities or projects. Undertakes this work in both the English and Welsh languages.

North Wales Regional Office
36 Princes Drive, Colwyn Bay LL29 8LA
tel (01492) 533440 *fax* (01492) 533677

West Wales Regional Office
6 Gardd Llydaw, Jackson Lane, Carmarthen SA31 1QD
tel (01267) 234248 *fax* (01267) 233084

Asian Affairs, The Royal Society for

2 Belgrave Square, London SW1X 8PJ
tel 020-7235 5122 *fax* 020-7259 6771
email info@rsaa.org.uk
website www.rsaa.org.uk
President The Lord Denman CBE, MC TD, *Chairman of Council* Sir Donald Hawley KCMG, MBE, *Secretary* David Easton MA, FRSA, FRGS
Membership £55 p.a. London, £45 more than 60 miles from London and overseas, £10 up to age 25

For the study of all Asia past and present; fortnightly lectures, etc; library. Publishes *Asian Affairs* (3 p.a.), free to members. Founded 1901.

Aslib (The Association for Information Management)

Staple Hall, Stone House Court, London EC3A 7PB
tel 020-7903 0000 *fax* 020-7903 0011
email aslib@aslib.com
website www.aslib.com
Ceo Roger Bowes

Actively promotes best practice in the management of information resources. It represents its members and lobbies on all aspects of the management of and legislation concerning information at local, national and international levels. Aslib provides consultancy and information services, professional development training, conferences, specialist recruitment, internet products, and publishes primary and secondary journals, conference proceedings, Directories and monographs. Founded 1924.

The Jane Austen Society

Acting Secretary Maggie Lane, 1 Brookleaze, Sea Mills, Bristol BS9 2ET
email mlane@bgs.bristol.sch.uk
website www.janeaustensociety.org.uk
Membership £10p.a. UK, £150 life; £12 overseas, £180 life

Founded in 1940 to promote interest in, and enjoyment of, Jane Austen's novels and letters. Twelve branches in UK.

Australia Council

PO Box 788, Strawberry Hills, NSW 2012, Australia
located at 372 Elizabeth Street, Surry Hills, NSW 2010
tel (02) 9215 9000 *fax* (02) 9215 9111
email mail@ozco.gov.au
website www.ozco.gov.au
Chairperson Dr Margaret Seares

Provides a broad range of support for the arts in Australia, embracing music, theatre, literature, visual arts, crafts, Aboriginal arts, community and new media arts. It has 8 major Funds: Literature, Visual Arts/Craft, Music, Theatre, Dance, New Media, Community Cultural Development, Major Organisations, as well as the Aboriginal and Torres Strait Islander Arts Board.

The Literature Fund's chief objective is to support the writing of all forms of creative literature – novels, short stories, poetry, plays and literary non-fiction. It also assists with the publication of literary magazines, has a book publishing subsidies programme, and initiates and supports projects of many kinds designed to promote Australian literature both within Australia and abroad.

Australian Copyright Council

Secretary Stella Collier, PO Box 1986, Strawberry Hills, NSW 2012
tel (02) 9318 1788 *fax* (02) 9698 3536
email info@copyright.org.au
website www.copyright.org.au

An independent non-profit organisation which aims to assist creators and other copyright owners to exercise their rights effectively; raise awareness in the community generally about the importance of copyright; research and identify areas of copyright law which are inadequate or unfair; seek changes to law and practice to enhance the effectiveness and fairness of copyright; foster cooperation amongst bodies representing creators and owners of copyright.

The Council comprises 23 organisations or associations of owners and creators of copyright material, including the Australian Society of Authors, the Australian Writers Guild and the Australian Book Publishers Association. Founded 1968.

Australian Library and Information Association

PO Box E441, Kingston, ACT 2604, Australia
tel (02) 6285 1877 *fax* (02) 6282 2249
email enquiry@alia.org.au
website www.alia.org.au/
Executive Director Jennefer Nicholson

Aims to promote and improve the services of libraries and other information agencies; to improve the standard of library and information personnel and foster their professional interests; to represent the interests of members to governments, other organisations and the community; and to encourage people to contribute to the improvement of library and information services by supporting the association.

Australian Publishers Association (APA)

60/89 Jones Street, Ultimo, NSW 2007, Australia
tel (02) 9281 9788 *fax* (02) 9281 1073
email apa@publishers.asn.au
website www.publishers.asn.au

The Australian Society of Authors

PO Box 1566, Strawberry Hills NSW 2012, Australia
tel (02) 9318 0877 *fax* (02) 9318 0530
email asa@asauthors.org
website www.asauthors.org
located at 98 Pitt Street, Redfern NSW 2016
Executive Director José Borghino

Authors, The Society of – see page 504

Authors' Agents, The Association of

2nd Floor, Drury House, 34-43 Russell Street, London WC2B 5HA
tel 020-7344 1000 *fax* 020-7836 9541
email aaa@pfd.co.uk
website www.agentsassoc.co.uk
President Jonathan Lloyd, *Vice President* Julian Alexander, *Treasurer* Barbara Levy, *Secretary* Simon Trewin

Maintains a code of professional practice to which all members commit themselves; holds regular meetings to discuss matters of common professional interest; provides a vehicle for representing the view of authors' agents in discussion of matters of common interest with other professional bodies. Founded 1974.

Authors' Club (at The Arts Club)

40 Dover Street, London W1S 4NP
tel 020-7499 8581 *fax* 020-7409 0913
Secretary Ann de La Grange
Membership Apply to Secretary

Founded by Sir Walter Besant, the Authors' Club welcomes as members writers, publishers, critics, journalists, academics and anyone involved with literature. Administers the Authors' Club Best First Novel Award and the Sir Banister Fletcher Award. Founded 1891.

Authors' Licensing and Collecting Society Ltd (ALCS) – see page 640

Authors' Representatives Inc., Association of

PO Box 237201, Ansonia Station, New York, NY 10023, USA
tel 212-252-3695
website www.aar-online.org

Founded 1991.

Aviation Artists, The Guild of

(incorporating the Society of Aviation Artists)
The Bondway Business Centre, 71 Bondway, Vauxhall Cross, London SW8 1SQ
tel/fax 020-7735 0634
email admin@gava.org.uk
website www.gava.org.uk
President Michael Turner PGAvA, *Secretary* Ian Burnstock
Membership £40 p.a. Associates, £55 Members (by invitation), £20 non-exhibiting artists and friends

Formed in 1971 to promote aviation art through the organisation of exhibitions and meetings. Holds annual open exhibition in July in London; £1000 for 'Aviation Painting of the Year'. Quarterly members' journal.

AXIS

Visual Arts Information Service, Leeds Metropolitan University, 8 Queen Square, Leeds LS2 8AJ
tel 0113-245 7946 *fax* 0113-245 7950
Axis Information Service 0930-170130 (UK only 50p/min)
email axis@lmu.ac.uk
website www.axisartists.org.uk

Provides information on contemporary artists and makers living/working in Britain to national and international clients. The Axis database features 14,000+ images by over 4000 artists (professionals and recent graduates). The database can be accessed in 4 different ways: on CD-Rom, online, at Axispoint host organisations throughout the UK, and on the Axis Information Service line. Printouts of artist CVs, artwork images, and contact details are available to potential buyers, commissioners, exhibitors and collaborators. Axis receives funding from the Arts Councils of England, Scotland and Wales, and 7 Regional Arts Offices. Founded 1991.

BAFTA (British Academy of Film and Television Arts)

195 Piccadilly, London W1J 9LN
tel 020-7734 0022 *fax* 020-7437 0473
email deborahb@bafta.org
website www.bafta.org
Chief Executive Amanda Berry
Membership £195 p.a., £98 under age 30/overseas, £88 country

The pre-eminent organisation in the UK for film, TV and interactive entertainment, recognising and promoting the achievement and endeavour of industry practitioners. BAFTA Awards are awarded annually by members to their peers in recognition of their skills and expertise. The Academy's premises provide club facilities with a 200-seat cinema and 40-seat preview theatre. Provides a full and varied programme of industry-related events, masterclasses, seminars and panel discussions, which are open to both members and non-members. Founded 1947.

BANA (Bath Area Network for Artists)

16A Broad Street, Bath BA1 5LY
tel (01225) 396425
email donna.baber@virgin.net
website www.artuk.co.uk
Membership Secretary Ione Parkin, 15 Kensington Gardens, Bath BA1 6LH
tel (01225) 482170
email ioneparkin@netscapeonline.co.uk
Membership £10 p.a.

Aims to raise the profile of arts activity in Bath and North East Somerset; to establish and strengthen links between individual artists, artists' groups and arts promoters; and to advocate for increased investment in local arts activities. Membership fee includes registration on database, newsletter, web space and more. Founded 1999.

BAPLA (British Association of Picture Libraries and Agencies)

18 Vine Hill, London EC1R 5DZ
tel 020-7713 1780 *fax* 020-7713 1211
email enquiries@bapla.org.uk
website www.bapla.org.uk
Chief Executive Linda Royles

Represents the interests of the British picture library industry. Works on UK and worldwide levels on issues such as copyright, industry statistics and technology. It offers researchers free telephone referrals from its database, and through its website,from over 400 members. Publishes a *Directory,* the definitive guide to UK picture libraries, and *Light Box* (quarterly) magazine. Founded 1975.

The Beckford Society

Secretary Sidney Blackmore, 15 Healey Street, London NW1 8SR
tel 020-7267 7750 *fax* (01985) 213239
email sidney.blackmore@btinternet.com
Membership £10 p.a. minimum

Aims to promote an interest in the life and works of William Beckford of Fonthill (1760–1844) and his circle. Encourages Beckford studies and scholarship through exhibitions, lectures and publications, including *The Beckford Journal* (annual) and occasional newsletters. Founded 1995.

Thomas Lovell Beddoes Society

11 Laund Nook, Belper, Derbyshire DE56 1GY
tel (01773) 828066
email john@beddoes.demon.co.uk
website www.nortexinfo.net/mcdaniel/ tlb.htm

Aims to promote an interest in the life and works of Thomas Lovell Beddoes (1803–1849). The Society promotes and undertakes Beddoes studies, and disseminates and publishes useful research. Founded 1994.

Beer Writers, British Guild of

Secretary Barry Bremner
tel (01462) 685844 *fax* (01462) 685783
email beer@bremner.tv
website www.beerguild.com
Membership £30 p.a

Aims to improve standards in beer writing and at the same time extend public knowledge of beers and brewing. The Gold and Silver Tankard Awards are given annually to writers and broadcasters judged to have made the most valuable contribution to this end. Publishes a directory of members with details of their publications and their particular areas of interest, which is circulated to the media. Founded 1988.

The Arnold Bennett Society

Secretary Jean Potter, 106 Scotia Road, Burslem, Stoke-on-Trent ST6 4ET
tel (01782) 816311
Membership £7 p.a. individuals, £9 p.a. family (plus £2 if living outside EC)

Aims to promote the study and appreciation of the life, works and times not only of Arnold Bennett (1867–1931) himself, but also of other provincial writers with particular relationship to North Staffordshire.

The E.F. Benson Society

The Old Coach House, High Street, Rye, East Sussex TN31 7JF
tel (01797) 223114
Secretary Allan Downend
Membership £7.50 p.a. single, £8.50 2 people at same address, £12.50 overseas

To promote interest in the author E.F. Benson and the Benson family. Arranges annual literary evening, annual outing to Rye (July), talks on the Bensons and exhibitions. Archive includes the Austin Seckersen Collection, transcriptions of the Benson diaries and letters. Publishes postcards, anthologies of Benson's works, a Benson biography and an annual journal, *The Dodo.* Also sells out-of-print Bensons to members. Founded 1984.

E.F. Benson: The Tilling Society

5 Friars Bank, Guestling, Hastings, East Sussex TN35 4EJ
fax (01424) 813237
Secretaries Cynthia and Tony Reavell
Membership £8 p.a., £10 overseas; full starters membership (inc. all back newsletters) £32, overseas £36

To bring together enthusiasts, wherever they may live, for E.F. Benson and his Mapp & Lucia novels; annual gathering in Rye. Publishes 2 journal-length newsletters a year. Founded 1982.

Bibliographical Society

c/o Wellcome Library, 183 Euston Road, London NW1 2BE
tel 020-7611 7244 *fax* 020-7611 8703
email jm93@dial.pipex.com
President M.M. Foot, *Hon. Secretary* D. Pearson

Acquisition and dissemination of information upon subjects connected with historical bibliography. Founded 1892.

The Blackpool Art Society

The Studio, Wilkinson Avenue, Blackpool FY3 9HB
President Kenneth Weigh
Hon. Secretary Wendy Slattery, 33 Leighton Avenue, Fleetwood, Lancs FY7 8BP

tel (01253) 773769
Summer and autumn exhibition (members' work only). Studio meetings, practicals, lectures, etc, out-of-door sketching, workshops. Founded 1884.

Books Across the Sea
The English-Speaking Union of the Commonwealth, Dartmouth House, 37 Charles Street, London W1J 5ED
tel 020-7529 1550 *fax* 020-7495 6108
email esu@esu.org
website www.esu.org
The English Speaking Union of the United States, 144 East 39th Street, New York, NY 10016, USA
tel 212-818-1200 *fax* 212-867-4177
email info@english-speakingunion.org
World voluntary organisation devoted to the promotion of international understanding and friendship. Exchanges books with its corresponding BAS Committees in New York, Russia and Australia. The books are selected to reflect the life and culture of each country and the best of its recent publishing and writing. New selections are announced by bulletin, *The Ambassador Booklist*.

The Booksellers Association of the United Kingdom & Ireland Ltd
272 Vauxhall Bridge Road, London SW1V 1BA
tel 020-7834 5477 *fax* 020-7834 8812
email mail@booksellers.org.uk
Chief Executive T.E. Godfray
Founded 1895.

Booktrust
(formerly the National Book League, founded 1925)
Book House, 45 East Hill, London SW18 2QZ
tel 020-8516 2977 *fax* 020-8516 2998
email info@booktrust.org.uk
website www.booktrust.org.uk
www.booktrusted.com
Chairman Trevor Glover, *Executive Director* Chris Meade
Membership Booktrust subscription: £25 p.a.
Booktrust is an independent charity bringing books and people together. It exists to open up the world of books and reading to people of all ages and cultures. Its services and activities include the Book Information Service, a unique specialist information service for all queries on books and reading (business callers are charged at £1.50 per minute on 0906-516 1193, weekdays 10am–1pm. Booktrust administers a number of literary prizes, including the Orange, Booker, Commonwealth and Nestlé Prizes and runs a series of reader development projects.

The Children's Literature Team at Booktrust offers advice and information on all aspects of children's reading and books. The booktrusted.com website is dedicated to children's books and resources for professionals working with young readers, including annotated book lists, information about organisations concerned with children's books, publishers, children's book news and much more. Booktrust also produces a range of publications and resource materials for National Children's Book Week. Subscribers receive 4 issues of *Children's Books News* and a copy of *100 Best Books 2002*. Booktrust also coordinates the national Bookstart (books for babies) programme which gives free advice and books to parents/carers attending their baby's health checks.

The George Borrow Society
Hon. Secretary Ms K.J. Cann, 21 Mulberry Close, Cambridge CB4 2AS
website www.clough5.fsnet.co.uk/gb.html
Membership £12.50 p.a.
Promotes knowledge of the life and works of George Borrow (1803–81), traveller and author. Publishes *Bulletin* (bi-annual). Founded 1991.

Botanical Artists, The Society of
Executive Secretary Mrs Pam Henderson, 1 Knapp Cottages, Wyke, Gillingham, Dorset SP8 4NQ
tel (01747) 825718, 020-7222 2723 (during exhibitions)
email pam@soc-botanical-artists.org
website www.soc-botanical-artists.org
Founder President Suzanne Lucas FLS, PRMS, FPSBA, *Hon. Treasurer* Pamela Davis, *Executive Vice President* Margaret Stevens
Membership Through selection. £100 p.a.; £20 lay members
Aims to encourage the art of botanical painting. Annual Open Exhibition held after Easter at the Westminster Gallery, Central Hall Westminster, Storey's Gate, London SW1H 9NH; hand in February/March. Information and entrance forms available from the Executive Secretary from January, on receipt of sae. Founded 1985.

British Academy
10 Carlton House Terrace, London SW1Y 5AH
tel 020-7969 5200 *fax* 020-7969 5300
email secretary@britac.ac.uk
website www.britac.ac.uk
President Viscount Runciman, *Humanities Vice-President* The Revd Prof John Morrill, *Social Sciences Vice-President* tba, *Treasurer* Prof R.J.P. Kain, *Foreign Secretary* Prof C.N.J. Mann, *Publications Secretary* Dr D.J. McKitterick, *Secretary* P.W.H. Brown CBE, *Research Grants Officer* Prof R.J. Bennett

The national Academy for the humanities and social sciences: an independent and self-governing fellowship of scholars, elected for distinction and achievement in one or more branches of the academic disciplines that make up the humanities and social sciences. Its primary purpose is to promote research and scholarship in those areas: through research grants and other awards, the sponsorship of a number of research projects and of research institutes overseas; the award of prizes and medals; and the publication both of sponsored lectures and seminar papers and of fundamental texts and research aids prepared under the direction of Academy committees. It also acts as a forum for the discussion of issues of interest and concern to scholars in the humanities and the social sciences, and it provides advice to the Government and other public bodies. Founded 1901.

British Academy of Composers and Songwriters
British Music House, 25-27 Berners Street, London W1T 3LR
tel 020-7636 2929 *fax* 020-7636 2212
email info@britishacademy.com
website www.britishacademy.com
Contact Fergal Kilroy, Head of Membership

The Academy represents the interests of composers and songwriters across all genres, providing advice on professional and artistic matters. It administers a number of major awards and events, including the prestigious Ivor Novello Awards, and publishes *The Works* magazine (quarterly).

British American Arts Association (BAAA) – see Centre for Creative Communities

The British Council
10 Spring Gardens, London SW1A 2BN
tel 020-7930 8466 *fax* 020-7839 6347
website www.britcoun.org/ www.britishcouncil.org/arts/literature
Chair Baroness Helena Kennedy, *Director-General* David Green, *Director of Literature* Margaret Meyer, *Director, Arts* Sue Harrison

The British Council promotes Britain abroad, by providing access to British ideas, talent and experience in education and training, books and the English language, information, the arts, the sciences and technology. The Council is an authority on teaching English as a second or foreign language and gives advice and information on curriculum, methodology, materials and testing. It also promotes British literature overseas through writers' tours, academic visits, seminars and exhibitions. The Council works in 109 countries where it runs over 220 libraries and resource centres and 138 teaching centres.

The Council's lending and reference libraries throughout the world stock material appropriate to the Council's priorities in individual countries. Where appropriate the libraries act as showcases for the latest British publications. They vary in size from small reference collections and information centres to comprehensive libraries equipped with reference works, CD-Rom, online facilities and a selection of British periodicals. Bibliographies of British books on special subjects are prepared on request.

The Council organises book and virtual exhibitions for overseas, ranging from small specialist displays to larger exhibitions at major international book fairs. The Council publishes *New Writing*, an annual anthology; a series of literary bibliographies, including *Eyes Wide Open: New Fiction from the UK 1999-2001*; and exhibitions on literary topics such as translation. It provides a range of online resources on its literature website, including directories of postgraduate and short courses in literature and creative writing. In 2002 a literary conference website and a contemporary writers website will be launched.

The Visual Arts Department, part of the Council's Arts Division, develops and enlarges overseas knowledge and appreciation of British achievement in the fields of painting, sculpture, printmaking, design, photography, the crafts and architecture, working closely with the Council's overseas offices and with professional colleagues in Britain and abroad.

The Council helps manage book aid projects for developing countries. In 2001/2002 the Council also supported over 3000 events in the visual arts, film and TV, drama, literature, dance and music, ranging from the classical to the contemporary.

Further information about the work of the British Council is available from the Press and Public Relations Department at the headquarters in London or from British Council offices and libraries overseas.

British Film Institute (BFI)
21 Stephen Street, London W1T 1LN
tel 020-7255 1444 *24-hour BFI Events Line* 0870-240 4050 *fax* 020-7436 0439
website www.bfi.org.uk
Chair Joan Bakewell CBE, *Director* Jon Teckman

The BFI offers opportunities for people to experience, learn and discover more about the world of film and moving image culture. It incorporates the BFI National Library, the magazine *Sight and Sound* (monthly), the BFI National Film Theatre, the annual London Film Festival, and the BFI London IMAX, and provides advice and support for regional cinemas and film festivals across the UK. The BFI also undertakes the preservation of, and promotes access to films, TV programmes, computer games, museum collections, stills, posters and designs, and other special collections. Founded 1933.

British Interactive Media Association (BIMA)
Briarlea House, Southend Road, Billericay, Essex CM11 2PR
tel 020-7436 8250 *fax* (01277) 658107
email info@bima.co.uk
website www.bima.co.uk
Office Administrator Janice Cable
Membership Open to any organisation or individual with an interest in multimedia. £650 p.a. commercial, £300 institutional, £160 individual + VAT

BIMA was established to promote a wider understanding of the benefits of interactive multimedia to industry, government and education and to provide a regular forum for the exchange of views amongst members. Publishes regular newsletters. Founded 1984.

Broadcasting Entertainment Cinematograph and Theatre Union (BECTU), Writers Section
111 Wardour Street, London W1V 4AY
tel 020-7437 8506 *fax* 020-7437 8268
email info@bectu.org.uk
website www.bectu.org.uk
General Secretary R. Bolton

To defend the interests of writers in film, TV and radio. By virtue of its industrial strength, the Union is able to help its writer members to secure favourable terms and conditions. In cases of disputes with employers, the Union can intervene in order to ensure an equitable settlement. Its production agreement with PACT lays down minimum terms for writers working in the documentary area. Founded 1946.

Broadcasting Group – see the Society of Authors, page 504

The Brontë Society
Membership Secretary The Brontë Parsonage Museum, Haworth, Keighley, West Yorkshire BD22 8DR
tel (01535) 642323 *fax* (01535) 647131
email bronte@bronte.prestel.co.uk
website www.bronte.org.uk

Acquisition, preservation, illustration of the memoirs and literary remains of the Brontë family; exhibitions of MSS and other subjects. Publishes *Brontë Studies* (3 p.a.) and *The Brontë Gazette* (bi-annual). Its Museum is open throughout the year.

The Browning Society
Secretary Ralph Ensz, 163 Wembley Hill Road, Wembley Park, Middlesex HA9 8EL
tel 020-8904 8401
website www.ucl.ac.uk/~ucleslе
Membership £15 p.a.

Aims to widen the appreciation and understanding of the lives and poetry of Robert Browning and Elizabeth Barrett Browning, and other Victorian writers and poets. Founded 1881; refounded 1969.

The John Buchan Society
Membership Secretary Russell Paterson, Limpsfield, 16 Ranfurly Road, Bridge of Weir, Renfrewshire PA11 3EL

tel (01505) 613116
Membership £10 p.a. full/overseas; other rates on application

Promotes a wider understanding and appreciation of the life and works of John Buchan. Encourages publication of a complete annotated edition of Buchan's works, and supports the John Buchan Centre and Museum at Broughton, Borders. Holds regular meetings and social gatherings; produces a Newsletter and a Journal. Founded 1979.

Byron Society (International)
Byron House, 6 Gertrude Street, London SW10 0JN
tel 020-7352 5112 *fax* 020-7352 1226
Hon. Director Mrs Elma Dangerfield CBE
Membership £20 p.a.

To promote research into the life and works of Lord Byron by seminars, discussions, lectures and readings. Publishes *The Byron Journal* (annual, £5.50 plus postage). Founded 1971.

Randolph Caldecott Society
Secretary Kenn Oultram, Clatterwick House, Little Leigh, Northwich, Cheshire CW8 4RJ
tel (01606) 891303 (office), 781731 (evening)
Membership £7-£10 p.a.

To encourage an interest in the life and works of Randolph Caldecott, the Victorian artist, illustrator and sculptor. Meetings held in Chester and London. Founded 1983.

Canada, Writers Guild of
123 Edward Street, Suite 1225, Toronto, Ontario M5G 1E2, Canada
tel 416-979-7907 *toll free* 1-800-567-9974
fax 416-979-9273
email info@wgc.ca
website www.wgc.ca
Executive Director Maureen Parker
Membership $150 p.a. plus 2% of fees earned in the Guild's jurisdiction

Represents over 1700 professional writers of film, TV, animation, radio, documentary and multimedia. Negotiates and administers collective agreements with independent producers as well as the CBC, TVO and NFB. The Guild also publishes *Canadian Screenwriter* magazine.

Canada, The Writers' Union of
40 Wellington Street East, 3rd Floor, Toronto, Ontario M5E 1C7, Canada
tel 416-703-8982 *fax* 416-504-7656
email info@writersunion.ca
website www.writersunion.ca

Canadian Authors Association
PO Box 419, Campbellford, Ontario K0L 1L0, Canada
tel 705-653-0323 *fax* 705-653-0593
email canauth@redden.on.ca
website www.CanAuthors.org/national.html
President Gillian Foss, *Administrator* Alec McEachern

Canadian Magazine Publishers Association
130 Spadina Avenue, Suite 202, Toronto, Ontario M5V 2L4, Canada
tel 416-504-0274 *fax* 416-504-0437
email cmpainfo@cmpa.ca
website www.cmpa.ca www.magomania.com
President Mark Jamison

Founded 1973.

Canadian Poets, League of
54 Wolseley Street, 3rd Floor, Toronto, Ontario M5T 1A5, Canada
tel 416-504-1657 *fax* 416-504 0096
email league@poets.ca
website www.poets.ca
Executive Director Edita Page

To promote the interests of poets and to advance Canadian poetry in Canada and abroad. Administers 3 annual awards; operates the 'Poetry Spoken Here' webstore; runs National Poetry Month; publishes a newsletter and *Poetry Markets for Canadians, Who's Who in The League of Canadian Poets, Poets in the Classroom* (teaching guide). Promotes and sells members' poetry books. Founded 1966.

Canadian Publishers, Association of
110 Eglinton Avenue West, Suite 401, Toronto, Ontario M4R 1A3, Canada
tel 416-487-6116 *fax* 416-487-8815
email info@canbook.org
website www.publishers.ca
Executive Director Monique Smith

Founded 1976; formerly Independent Publishers Association, 1971.

Canadian Publishers' Council
250 Merton Street, Suite 203, Toronto, Ontario M4S 1B1, Canada
tel 416-322-7011 *fax* 416-322-6999
email pubadmin@pubcouncil.ca
website www.pubcouncil.ca
Executive Director Jacqueline Hushion

Career Development Group
(formerly Association of Assistant Librarians)
c/o The Library Association, 7 Ridgmount Street, London WC1E 7AE

President Anne Partridge BSc, MSc *Hon. Secretary* Joanna Ball BA, MA, ALA

Publishes bibliographical aids, the journal *Impact*, works on librarianship; and runs educational courses. Founded 1895.

Careers Writers' Association

Membership Secretary Anne Goodman, 16 Caewal Road, Llandaff, Cardiff CF5 2BT
tel 029-2054 3444 *fax* 029-2056 6363
email anne.goodman5@ntlworld.com
Membership £20 p.a.

Society for established writers on the inter-related topics of education, training and careers. Holds occasional meetings on subjects of interest to members, and circulates details of members to information providers. Founded 1979.

(Daresbury) Lewis Carroll Society

Secretary Kenn Oultram, Clatterwick House, Little Leigh, Northwich, Cheshire CW8 4RJ
tel (01606) 891303 (office), 781731 (evening)
Membership £5 p.a.

To encourage an interest in the life and works of Lewis Carroll, author of *Alice's Adventures.* Meetings at Carroll's birth village (Daresbury, Cheshire). Elects an annual 'Alice', who is available for public engagements. Founded 1970.

The Lewis Carroll Society

Secretary Alan White, 69 Cromwell Road, Hertford, Herts. SG13 7DP
email alanwhite@tesco.net
website http://aznet.co.uk/lcs
Membership £13 p.a. UK, £15 Europe, £17 elsewhere; special rates for institutions

To promote interest in the life and works of Lewis Carroll (Revd Charles Lutwidge Dodgson) and to encourage research. Activities include regular meetings, exhibitions, and a publishing programme that includes the first annotated, unexpurgated edition of his diaries in 9 volumes, the Society's journal *The Carrollian* (2 p.a.), a newsletter, *Bandersnatch* (quarterly) and the *Lewis Carroll Review* (occasional). Founded 1969.

Cartoonists Club of Great Britain

Secretary Richard Tomes, 29 Ulverley Crescent, Olton, Solihull, West Midlands B92 8BJ
tel 0121-706 7652
email r.tomes@btinternet.com
website www.ccgb.org.uk
Membership Fee on joining: full, provisional, or associate £50; thereafter £35 p.a.

Aims to encourage social contact between members and endeavours to promote the professional standing and prestige of cartoonists.

Centerprise Literature Development Project

Centerprise Trust, 136-138 Kingsland High Street, London E8 2NS
tel 020-7254 9632 ext. 211, 214 *fax* 020-7923 1951
email sharon.centerlit@care4free.net
eva.centerlit@care4free.net
Contact Eva, Sharon

An advice and resource centre for writers of fiction and poetry, servicing Central, East and North London. Runs courses and workshops in creative writing, organises poetry and book readings, discussions and debates on literary and relevant issues, writers' surgeries, and telephone information on resources for writers in London. Publishes *Calabash* newsletter for Writers of Black and Asian origin. Funded by London Arts. See also page 574. Founded 1995.

Centre for Creative Communities (CCC)

118 Commercial Street, London E1 6NF
tel 020-7247 5385 *fax* 020-7247 5256
email info@creativecommunities.org.uk
website www.creativecommunities.org.uk
Director Jennifer Williams

A non-profit-making organisation working in the field of arts, education and community development. Conducts research, organises conferences, produces a quarterly newsletter and is part of an international network of arts and education organisations. Maintains a specialised arts, education and community development library. CCC is not a grant-giving organisation.

The Chesterton Society

Hon. Secretary Robert Hughes KHS, 11 Lawrence Leys, Bloxham, Nr Banbury, Oxon OX15 4NU
tel (01295) 720869
Membership £12.50 p.a.

To promote interest in the life and work of G.K. Chesterton and those associated with him or influenced by his writings. Two lectures a year. Publishes the *Chesterton Quarterly Review* (4 p.a.). Founded 1974.

Children's Book Circle

c/o Lucy Firth, David Higham Associates, 5-8 Lower John Street, London W1F 9HA
tel 020-7434 5915 *fax* 020-7437 1072

email lucyfirth@davidhigham.co.uk
Membership Secretary Jo Williamson
tel 020-8307 4680
Membership £15 p.a. if working inside M25; £12 outside

Provides a discussion forum for anybody involved with children's books. Monthly meetings are addressed by a panel of invited speakers and topics focus on current and controversial issues. Holds the annual Patrick Hardy lecture and administers the EleanorFarjeon Award. Founded 1962.

Children's Books History Society

Secretary Mrs Pat Garrett, 25 Field Way, Hoddesdon, Herts. EN11 0QN
tel/fax (01992) 464885
email cbhs@abcgarrett.demon.co.uk
Membership £10 p.a.; apply for overseas rates

Aims 'to promote an appreciation of children's books, and to study their history, bibliography and literary content'. Holds approx. 6 meetings and produces 3 substantial *Newsletters* and an occasional paper per year. The Harvey Darton Award is givenbiennially for a book that extends knowledge of British children's literature of the past. Founded 1969.

Children's Writers and Illustrators Group – see the Society of Authors, page 504

Christian Literature, United Society for

Albany House, 67 Sydenham Road, Guildford, Surrey GU1 3RY
tel (01483) 888580 *fax* (01483) 888581
email headoffice@feedtheminds.org
website www.feedtheminds.org
Chairman John Clark

To aid Christian literature principally in the world's poorest countries. Founded 1799.

Christian Writers, Association of

Administrator Mrs J.L. Kyriacou, All Saints Vicarage, 43 All Saints Close, Edmonton, London N9 9AT
tel 020-8884 4348
email admin@christianwriters.org.uk
Membership £17 p.a. (£15 DD)

Aims to see the quality of writing in every area of the media, either overtly Christian or shaped by a Christian perspective, reaching the widest range of people across the UK and beyond. To inspire and equip people to use their talents and skills with integrity to devise, write and market excellent material which comes from a Christian world view. Founded 1971.

CILIP: Chartered Institute of Library and Information Professionals

7 Ridgmount Street, London WC1E 7AE
tel 020-7255 0500, *textphone* 020-7255 0505
fax 020-7255 0501
email info@cilip.org.uk
website www.cilip.org.uk
Chief Executive Bob McKee PhD, FRSA, MCLIP
Membership Varies according to income

CILIP was formed on 1 April 2002 following the unification of the Institution of Information Scientists and the Library Association. It is the leading membership body for library and information professionals, with around 23,000 members in the UK and overseas. Its monthly magazine *Update* is distributed free to members. The IIS was originally founded in 1958 and the LA in 1877.

Civil and Public Service Writers, The Society of

Secretary Mrs J.M. Hykin, 17 The Green, Corby Glen, Grantham, Lincs. NG33 4NP
Membership £15 p.a.; Poetry Workshop add £3

Welcomes serving and retired members of the Civil Service, Armed Forces, Post Office and BT, the nursing profession, and other public servants. Members can be aspiring or published writers. Holds annual competitions for short stories, articles and poetry, plus occasional for longer works. Offers postal folios for short stories and articles; holds AGM and occasional meetings; publishes *The Civil Service Author* (quarterly) magazine. Send sae for details. Founded 1935.

The John Clare Society

The Stables, 1A West Street, Helpston, Peterborough PE6 7DU
tel/fax (01733) 252678
email moyse.helpston@talk21.com
website http://vzone.virgin.net/linda.curry/jclaresociety
Membership £9.50 p.a. UK individual; other rates on application

Promotes a wider appreciation of the life and works of the poet John Clare. Founded 1981.

Classical Association

Secretary (Council) Dr M. Schofield, St John's College, Cambridge CB2 1TP

Publicity Officer Ward House, Walkhampton, Devon PL20 6JY
Administrator Clare Roberts, Senate House, Malet Street, London WC1E 7HU
tel 020-7862 8706 *fax* 020-7862 8729
email croberts@sas.ac.uk
website www.sas.ac.uk/icls/classass

To promote and sustain interest in classical studies, to maintain their rightful position in universities and schools, and to give scholars and teachers opportunities for meeting and discussing their problems.

Clé: The Irish Book Publishers' Association

43-44 Temple Bar, Dublin 2, Republic of Ireland
tel (01) 6707 393 *fax* (01) 6707 642
email info@publishingireland.com
website www.publishingireland.com
President Sara Wilbourne, *Executive Director* Orla Martin

The William Cobbett Society

Chairman Molly Townsend, 10 Grenehurst Way, Petersfield, Hants GU31 4AZ
tel (01730) 262060
Membership £8 p.a.

To make the life and work of William Cobbett better known. Founded 1976.

The Wilkie Collins Society

Membership Secretary Paul Lewis, 4 Ernest Gardens, London W4 3QU
email paul@paullewis.co.uk
website www.wilkiecollins.org
Chairman Andrew Gasson
Membership £10 p.a. EU, £18 international

To promote interest in the life and works of Wilkie Collins. Publishes a newsletter, an occasional scholarly journal and reprints of Collins's lesser known works. Founded 1981.

Comedy Writers Association UK (CWAUK)

Membership Secretary Mary Gamon, 12 Erskine Road, Colwyn Bay, Conwy, North Wales LL29 8EV
email info@cwauk.co.uk
website www.cwauk.co.uk
Membership £36 p.a. + one-off £5 registration fee. Open to everyone interested in comedy writing

The largest group of independent comedy writers in the UK with contacts around the world. Holds one-day seminars with invited industry speakers. Advice on writing and career development. Monthly newsletter and monthly market information. Founded 1981.

Comedy Writers, British Society of

President Kenneth Rock, 61 Parry Road, Ashmore Park, Wolverhampton, West Midlands WV11 2PS
tel/fax (01902) 722729
email info@bscw.co.uk
website www.bscw.co.uk
Membership £75 p.a. full, £40 p.a. subscriber

Aims to bring together writers and industry representatives in order to develop new projects and ideas. Holds an annual international comedy conference, networking days and workshops to train new writers to professional standards. A script reading service is available. Founded 1999.

Comhairle nan Leabhraichean/The Gaelic Books Council

22 Mansfield Street, Glasgow G11 5QP
tel 0141-337 6211 *fax* 0141-353 0515
email fios@gaelicbooks.net
website www.gaelicbooks.net
Chair Donalda MacKinnon

Stimulates Scottish Gaelic publishing by awarding publication grants for new books, commissioning authors and providing editorial services and general assistance to writers and readers. Has its own bookshop of all Gaelic and Gaelic-related books in printand runs a book club; catalogue available. Founded 1968.

Comics Creators Guild

(formerly Society for Strip Illustration)
Postal address only 22 St James' Mansions, West End Lane, London NW6 2AA
website www.comicscreators.org.uk

Open to all those concerned with, or interested in, professional comics creation. Holds monthly meetings and publishes a newsletter (monthly), a Directory of Members' Work, Submission Guidelines for the major comics publishers, sample scripts for artists, a 'Guide to Contracts' and 'Getting Started in Comics', a beginners' guide to working in the industry, and *Comics Forum* (quarterly), a magazine of art and criticism.

Commonwealth Institute

Kensington High Street, London W8 6NQ
tel 020-7603 4535 *fax* 020-7602 7374
email info@commonwealth.org.uk
website www.commonwealth.org.uk/
Chief Executive David French

Promotes Commonwealth education and

culture in the UK. The Resource Centre offers services to teachers and school groups, and includes a specialist Literature Collection. Open to the public Mon–Sat, 10am–4pm. Founded 1962.

Commonwealth Secretariat – see page 608

Communicators in Business, The British Association of

42 Borough High Street, London SE1 1XW
tel 020-7378 7139 *fax* 020-7378 7140
email enquiries@bacb.org
website www.bacb.org.uk

Aims to be the market leader for those involved in corporate media management and practice by providing professional, authoritative, dynamic, supportive and innovative services. Founded 1949.

The Joseph Conrad Society (UK)

The Conradian, Dr Allan Simmons, Dept of English, St Mary's College, Twickenham, Middlesex TW1 4SX
Chairman Keith Carabine, *President* Philip Conrad, *Secretary* Hugh Epstein, *Editor* Allan Simmons

Maintains close and friendly links with the Conrad family. Activities include an annual international conference; publication of *The Conradian* and a series of pamphlets; and maintenance of a study centre at the Polish Cultural Centre, 238–246 King Street, London W6 0RF. Administers the Juliet McLauchlan Prize: £100 annual award for the winner of an essay competition. Founded 1973.

Copyright Clearance Center Inc.

222 Rosewood Drive, Danvers, MA 01923, USA
tel 978-750-8400 *fax* 978-750-4470
website www.copyright.com

Copyright Council, The British

Copyright House, 29-33 Berners Street, London W1T 3AB
tel (01986) 788 122 *fax* (01986) 788 847
email copyright@bcc2.demon.co.uk
Vice-Presidents Geoffrey Adams, Maureen Duffy, *Chairman* Prof Gerald Dworkin, *Vice Chairmen* Gwen Thomas, David Lester, Kate Pool, *Secretary* Janet Ibbotson, *Treasurer* Hugh Jones

Aims to defend and foster the true principles of creators' copyright and their acceptance throughout the world, to bring together bodies representing all who are interested in the protection of such copyright, and to keep watch on any legal or other changes which may require an amendment of the law.

The Copyright Licensing Agency Ltd (CLA) – see page 638

Crime Writers' Association

website www.thecwa.co.uk
Membership Associate membership open to publishers, journalists, booksellers specialising in crime literature

For professional writers of crime novels, short stories, plays for stage, TV and radio, or of other serious works on crime. Publishes *Red Herrings* (monthly), available to members only. Founded 1953.

The Critics' Circle

Contact Catherine Cooper, Administrator, c/o 69 Marylebone Lane, London W1U 2PH
tel 020-7224 1410 (office hours)
President Jane Edwardes, *Hon. General Secretary* Charles Hedges
Membership By invitation of the Council

Aims to promote the art of criticism, to uphold its integrity in practice, to foster and safeguard the professional interests of its members, to provide opportunities for social intercourse among them, and to support the advancement of the arts. Such invitations are issued only to persons engaged professionally, regularly and substantially in the writing or broadcasting of criticism of drama, music, films, dance and the visual arts. Founded 1913.

Cyngor Llyfrau Cymru – see Welsh Books Council

Deaf Broadcasting Council

70 Blacketts Wood Drive, Chorleywood, Rickmansworth, Herts. WD3 5QQ
tel (01923) 284538 (text phone only)
email rmyers@waitrose.com
website www.deafbroadcastingcouncil.org.uk
Secretary Ruth Myers

Design and Artists Copyright Society Ltd (DACS) – see page 642

Designers, The Chartered Society of

3 Bermondsey Street, London SE1 3UW
tel 020-7357 8088 *fax* 020-7407 9878
email csd@csd.org.uk
website www.designweb.co.uk/csd
Director Brian Lymbery

Works to promote and regulate standards of competence, professional conduct and integrity, including representation on government and official bodies, design education and awards. The services to members include general information, publications, guidance on copyright and other professional issues, access to professional indemnity insurance, as well as the membership magazine *csd*. Activities in the regions are included in an extensive annual programme of events and training courses.

Designers in Ireland, Institute of
8 Merrion Square, Dublin 2, Republic of Ireland
tel (01) 7167885 *fax* (01) 7168736
Membership E171 p.a. full, E57 associate
Irish design profession's representative body, covering every field of design. Details from the honorary secretary. Founded 1972.

Dickens Fellowship
The Dickens House, 48 Doughty Street, London WC1N 2LX
tel 020-7405 2127 *fax* 020-7831 5175
Joint Hon. Secretaries Dr Tony Williams, Thelma Grove
Membership On application
Based in house occupied by Dickens 1837–9; publishes *The Dickensian* (3 p.a.). Founded 1902.

Directory & Database Publishers Association
Secretary Rosemary Pettit, PO Box 23034, London W6 0RJ
tel 020-8846 9707
Membership £120-£1200 p.a.
Maintains a code of professional practice; aims to raise the standard and professional status of UK directory and database publishing and to protect (and promote) the legal, statutory and common interests of directory publishers; provides for the exchange of technical, commercial and management information between members. Founded 1970.

'Sean Dorman' Manuscript Society
Cherry Trees, Crosemere Road, Cockshutt, Ellesmere, Shropshire SY12 0JP
tel (01939) 270293
Director Mary Driver
Provides mutual help among writers and aspiring writers in the UK. By means of circulating MSS parcels, members receive constructive criticism of their own work and read and comment on the work of others. Each 'Circulator' has up to 9 participants and members' contributions may be in any medium: short stories, chapters of a novel, poetry, magazine articles, etc. Send sae for full details and application form. Founded 1957.

The Arthur Conan Doyle Society
Organisers Christopher and Barbara Roden, PO Box 1360, Ashcroft, B.C., Canada V0K 1A0
tel 250-453-2045 *fax* 250-453-2075
email ashtree@ash-tree.bc.ca
website www.ash-tree.bc.ca/acdsocy.html
Membership £16 p.a. (airmail extra)
Promotes the study of the life and works of Sir Arthur Conan Doyle. Publishes *ACD* journal (bi-annual) and occasional reprints of Conan Doyle material. Occasional conventions. Founded 1989.

Early English Text Society
Christ Church, Oxford OX1 1DP
website www.eets.org.uk
Hon. Director Prof John Burrow *Executive Secretary* R.F.S. Hamer
Membership £15 p.a.
To bring unprinted early English literature within the reach of students in sound texts. Founded 1864.

The Eckhart Society
Summa, 22 Tippings Lane, Woodley, Reading, Berks. RG5 4RX
tel 0118-9690118
email ashleyyoung@aysumma.demon.co.uk
website www.eckhartsociety.org
Secretary Ashley Young
Membership £15 p.a.; £8 OAPs/students
Aims to promote the understanding and appreciation of Eckhart's writings and their importance for Christian thought and practice; to facilitate scholarly research into Eckhart's life and works; and to promote the study of Eckhart's teaching as a contribution to inter religious dialogue. Founded 1987.

Edinburgh Bibliographical Society
c/o National Library of Scotland, George IV Bridge, Edinburgh EH1 1EW
tel 0131-226-4531
Secretary Dr W. McDougall, *Treasurer* P. Freshwater
Membership £10 p.a., £15 institutions; £5 full-time students
Encourages bibliographical activity through organising talks for members, particularly on bibliographical topics relating

to Scotland, and visits to libraries. Also publishes *Transactions* (generally every 3 years, free to members) and other occasional publications. Founded 1890.

Editors and Proofreaders, Society for (SfEP)

(formerly Society of Freelance Editors and Proofreaders)
Office Riverbank House, 1 Putney Bridge Approach, London SW6 3JD
tel 020-7736 3278
email admin@sfep.org.uk
website www.sfep.org.uk

Works to promote high editorial standards and achieve recognition of its members' professional status, through local and national meetings, an annual conference, an email newsletter, a regular magazine and a programme of reasonably priced workshops/training sessions. These sessions help newcomers to acquire basic skills, enable experienced editors to update their skills or broaden their competence, and also cover aspects of professional practice or business for the self-employed. An annual Directory of members' services is available. The Society supports moves towards recognised standards of training and accreditation for editors and proofreaders and has developed its own Accreditation in Proofreading qualification. It has close links with the Publishing Training Centre and the Society of Indexers, is represented on the BSI Technical Committee dealing with copy preparation and proof correction (BS 5261), and works to foster good relations with all relevant bodies and organisations in the UK and worldwide. Founded 1988.

Editors, Society of

Director Bob Satchwell, University Centre, Granta Place, Mill Lane, Cambridge CB2 1RU
tel (01223) 304080 *fax* (01223) 304090
email info@societyofeditors.org
website www.societyofeditors.org
Membership £200 p.a.

Formed from the merger of the Guild of Editors and the Association of British Editors, the Society has more than 450 members in national, regional and local newspapers, magazines, broadcasting, new media, journalism education and media law, campaigning for media freedom. Publishes *Briefing* (monthly). Founded 1999.

Educational Writers Group – see the Society of Authors, page 504

The George Eliot Fellowship

Secretary Mrs K.M. Adams,
71 Stepping Stones Road, Coventry CV5 8JT
tel 024-7659 2231
President Jonathan G. Ouvry
Membership £10 p.a.

Promotes an interest in the life and work of George Eliot (1819–80) and helps to extend her influence; arranges meetings; produces an annual journal, a quarterly newsletter and other publications. Awards the annual George Eliot Fellowship Prize (£250) for an essay on Eliot's life or work, which must be previously unpublished and not exceed 2500 words. Founded 1930.

English Association

University of Leicester, University Road, Leicester LE1 7RH
tel 0116-252 3982 *fax* 0116-252 2301
email engassoc@le.ac.uk
website www.le.ac.uk/engassoc/
Chair Elaine Treharne, *Chief Executive* Helen Lucas

Aims to further knowledge, understanding and enjoyment of English literature and the English language, by working towards a fuller recognition of English as an essential element in education and in the community at large; by encouraging the study of English literature and language by means of conferences, lectures and publications; and by fostering the discussion of methods of teaching English of all kinds.

English Regional Arts Boards – see Regional Arts Offices

English Speaking Board (International) Ltd

26A Princes Street, Southport PR8 1EQ
tel (01704) 501730 *fax* (01704) 539637
email admin@esbuk.org
website www.esbuk.org
President Christabel Burniston MBE, *Chairman* Prof Andrew Trott
Membership £25 p.a. individuals, £50 corporate

Aims to foster all activities concerned with oral communication. Offers assessment qualifications in practical speaking and listening skills for candidates at all levels in schools, vocational and business contexts; also for those with learning difficulties and those for whom English is an acquired language. Also provides training courses in teaching and delivery of oral communication. Offers membership to all those concerned with the development and expression of the English language. Members receive *Speaking English* (2 p.a.); articles are invited on any special aspect of spoken English.

The English-Speaking Union

Dartmouth House, 37 Charles Street, London W1J 5ED
tel 020-7529 1550 *fax* 020-7495 6108
email esu@esu.org
website www.esu.org
Director-General Mrs Valerie Mitchell OBE
Membership Various categories

Aims to promote international understanding and human achievement through the widening use of the English language throughout the world. The ESU is an educational charity which sponsors scholarships and exchanges, educational programmes promoting the effective use of English, and a wide range of international and cultural events. Members contribute to its work across the world. Administers the Marsh Biography Award. See also Books Across the Sea. Founded 1918.

European Broadcasting Union

PO Box 45, Ancienne Route 17A, CH-1218 Grand Saconnex (Geneva), Switzerland
tel (22) 7172111 *fax* (22) 7174000
email ebu@ebu.ch
website www.ebu.ch
Secretary-General Mr Jean Stock

The EBU is the largest professional association of national broadcasters. Working on behalf of its members in the European area, the EBU negotiates broadcasting rights for major sports events; operates the Eurovision and Euroradio networks; organises programme exchanges; stimulates and coordinates co-productions; and provides a full range of other operational, commercial, technical, legal and strategic services. Founded 1950.

European Publishers, Federation of

204 avenue de Tervuren, 1150 Brussels, Belgium
tel (2) 770 11 10 *fax* (2) 771 20 71
email malemann@fep_fee.be
website www.fep_fee.be
President Michael Gill, *Director* Mechthild von Alemann

Represents the interests of European publishers on EU affairs; informs members on the development of EU policies which could affect the publishing industry. Founded 1967.

Fabian Society

11 Dartmouth Street, London SW1H 9BN
tel 020-7227 4900 *fax* 020-7976 7153
email info@fabian-society.org.uk
website www.fabian-society.org.uk
General Secretary Michael Jacobs

Current affairs, political thought, economics, education, environment, foreign affairs, social policy. Also controls NCLC Publishing Society Ltd. Founded 1884.

Fantasy Society, The British

201 Reddish Road, South Reddish, Stockport SK5 7HR
tel 0161-476 5368 (after 6pm)
email faliol@yahoo.com
website www.britishfantasy.org.uk
President Ramsey Campbell, *Secretary* Robert Parkinson
Membership £25 p.a.

For devotees of fantasy, horror and related fields, in literature, art and the cinema. Publications include *British Fantasy Newsletter* (bi-monthly) featuring news and reviews and several annual booklets, including: *Dark Horizons*; *Masters of Fantasy* on individual authors. There is a small-press library and an annual convention and fantasy awards sponsored by the Society. Founded 1971.

Federation Against Copyright Theft Ltd (FACT)

7 Victory Business Centre, Worton Road, Isleworth, Middlesex TW7 6DB
tel 020-8568 6646 *fax* 020-8560 6364
email investigator@fact-uk.org.uk
Contact David Lowe, Director General

FACT aims to protect the interests of its members and others against infringement in the UK of copyright in cinematograph films, TV programmes and all forms of audiovisual recording. Founded 1982.

The Copyright Hotline offers advice and information to anyone who wants to use film, music or software copyrights. It is part of a collective initiative by FACT, Federation Against Software Theft (FAST), Music Publishers Association (MPA), Mechanical Copyright Protection Society (MCPS), Performing Right Society (PRS) and British Music Rights (BMR).

Financial Journalists' Group
Secretary, c/o Association of British Insurers, 51 Gresham Street, London EC2V 7HQ
tel 020-7216 7410
Chairman Chris Wheal
Membership No fee

Aims to give journalists working in the area of, or with an interest in, finance and financial services, a forum to learn more about some of the issues involved, and meet colleagues with similar interests. Founded 1997.

The Fine Art Trade Guild
16-18 Empress Place, London SW6 1TT
tel 020-7381 6616 *fax* 020-7381 2596
email information@fineart.co.uk
website www.fineart.co.uk
Managing Director Rosie Sumner

Promotes the sale of fine art prints and picture framing in the UK and overseas markets; establishes and raises standards amongst members and communicates these to the buying public. The Guild publishes *The Directory* and *Art Business Today*, the trade's longest established magazine and various specialist books. Founded 1910.

First Film Foundation
Director Jonathan Rawlinson, 9 Bourlet Close, London W1W 7BP
tel 020-7580 2111 *fax* 020-7580 2116
email info@firstfilm.demon.co.uk
website www.firstfilm.co.uk

A charity that exists to help new British writers, producers and directors make their first feature film. Provides a range of unique educational and promotional programmes that give film-makers the contacts, knowledge and experience they need to achieve this goal. Founded 1987.

FOCAL International Ltd (Federation of Commercial AudioVisual Libraries International Ltd)
Pentax House, South Hill Avenue, South Harrow, Middlesex HA2 0DU
tel 020-8423 5853 *fax* 020-8933 4826
email info@focalint.org
website www.focalint.org
*Commerical Manager*Anne Johnson

Founded 1985.

The Folklore Society
The Warburg Institute, Woburn Square, London WC1E 0AB
tel 020-7862 8564
email folklore.society@talk21.com
website www.folklore-society.com
Hon. Secretary Dr Juliette Wood

Collection, recording and study of folklore. Founded 1878.

Food Writers, Guild of
Administrator Christina Thomas, 48 Crabtree Lane, London SW6 6LW
tel 020-7610 1180 *fax* 020-7610 0299
email gfw@gfw.co.uk
website www.gfw.co.uk
Membership £70 p.a.

Aims to bring together professional food writers including journalists, broadcasters and authors, to print and issue an annual list of members, to extend the range of members' knowledge and experience by arranging discussions, tastings and visits, and to encourage the development of new writers by every means including competitions and awards. There are 7 awards for 2003 and entry is not restricted to members of the Guild. Founded 1984.

Foreign Press Association in London
Registered Office 11 Carlton House Terrace, London SW1Y 5AJ
tel 020-7930 0445 *fax* 020-7925 0469
email secretariat@foreign-press.org.uk
website www.foreign-press.org.uk
President Tine van Houts, *General Manager* Bob Jenner
Membership Entrance fee: £152; £128 p.a. Full membership open to overseas professional journalists residing in the UK; Associate membership available for British press and freelance journalists

Aims to promote the professional interests of its members. Founded 1888.

Free Painters & Sculptors
Registered office 14 John Street, London WC1N 2EB
Hon. Secretary Owen Legg, 152 Hadlow Road, Tonbridge, Kent TN9 1PB
Membership Secretary Teresa Cooke, 2 Exbury House, 16 Rampayne Street, London SW1V 2QR

Promotes group shows 4 times a year in prestigious galleries in London. Sponsors all that is exciting in contemporary art.

Freelance Editors, Proofreaders and Indexers, Association of
Contact Grainne Farren, 74 George's Avenue, Blackrock, Co. Dublin, Republic of Ireland
Chair Helen Litton
tel (01) 2692214 *fax* (01) 2692214
email helenlitton@clubi.ie
website www.publishingireland.com

Provides information to publishers on freelances through a list of members and their qualifications. Also protects the interests of freelances, and provides social contact for isolated workers.

Freelance Journalists, Association of
President Martin Scholes, 2 Glen Cottages, Brick Hill Lane, Beverley Glen, Ketley, Telford, Shrops. TF2 6SB
email afj@yahoo.com
website http://afj.home-page.org
Membership £30 p.a.
Aims to foster the interests of freelance journalists and news photographers, especially those on a low income, including those working as stringers, local correspondents, writers for specialist fields, etc. Founded 1996.

Freelance Photographers, Bureau of
Focus House, 497 Green Lanes, London N13 4BP
tel 020-8882 3315 *fax* 020-8886 5174
website www.thebfp.com
Chief Executive John Tracy
Membership £45 p.a.
To help the freelance photographer by providing information on markets, and free advisory service. Publishes *Market Newsletter* (monthly). Founded 1965.

French Publishers' Association
(Syndicat National de l'Edition)
115 Blvd St Germain, 75006 Paris, France
tel (1) 44 41 40 50 *fax* (1) 44 41 40 77
website www.sne.fr

The Gaelic Books Council – see Comhairle nan Leabhraichean

Garden Writers Guild
Administrator Angela Clarke, c/o Institute of Horticulture, 14-15 Belgrave Square, London SW1X 8PS
tel/fax 020-7245 6943
email gwg@horticulture.org.uk
website www.gardenwriters.co.uk
Membership £40 p.a.
Aims to raise the standards of gardening communicators. Administers annual awards to encourage excellence in garden writing, trade and consumer press journalism, TV and radio broadcasting, as well as garden photography. Founded 1991.

The Gaskell Society
Far Yew Tree House, Over Tabley, Knutsford, Cheshire WA16 0HN
tel (01565) 634668
email JoanLeach@aol.com
website www.gaskellsociety.users.btopenworld.com
Hon. Secretary Mrs Joan Leach
Membership £12 p.a., £16 corporate and overseas
Promotes and encourages the study and appreciation of the work and life of Elizabeth Cleghorn Gaskell. Holds regular meetings in Knutsford, London, Manchester and Bath, visits and residential conferences; produces an annual Journal and bi-annual Newsletters. Founded 1985.

Gay Authors Workshop
Kathryn Byrd, BM Box 5700, London WC1N 3XX
tel 020-8520 5223
Membership £7 p.a., £3 unwaged
To encourage writers who are lesbian, gay or bisexual. Quarterly newsletter. Founded 1978.

General Practitioners Writers Association
President Dr Robin Hull, West Carnliath, Strathtay, Pitlochry, Perthshire PH9 0PG
tel (01887) 840380
Aims to improve the writing by, for, from or about general medical practice. Publishes *The GP Writer* (2 p.a.); register of members' writing interests is sent to medical editors and publishers. Founded 1985.

German Publishers' and Booksellers' Association
(Börsenverein des Deutschen Buchhandels e.V.)
Postfach 100442, 60004 Frankfurt am Main, Germany
tel (069) 13060 *fax* (069) 1306201
email info@boev.de
website www.boersenverein.de
General Manager Dr Harald Heker

Graphic Fine Art, Society of
15 Willow Way, Hatfield, Herts AL10 9QD
President David Brooke
Membership By election

Graphical, Paper & Media Union
Keys House, 63-67 Bromham Road, Bedford MK40 2AG
tel (01234) 351521 *fax* (01234) 270580
email general@gpmu.org.uk
website www.gpmu.org.uk
General Secretary Tony Dubbins

Graham Greene Birthplace Trust
Secretary Ken Sherwood, Rhenigidale, Ivy House Lane, Berkhamsted, Herts. HP4 2PP
tel (01442) 865158
email secretary@grahamgreenebt.org
website www.grahamgreenebt.org

Membership £7.50 p.a., £18 3 years

To study the works of Graham Greene (1904–91). The Trust promotes the Annual Graham Greene Festival, a Spring lecture, Graham Greene trails. It publishes a quarterly newsletter, occasional papers, videos and CDs, and maintains a small archive. It administers the annual Graham Greene Awards of £350 for projects which, in the Trustees' opinion, would have met with Greene's approval (closing date: 30 November). Founded 1997.

The Greeting Card Association

United House, North Road, London N7 9DP
tel/fax 020-7619 0396
Administrator Sharon Little

Official magazine: *Progressive Greetings Worldwide* (12 p.a.). See page 397.

Guernsey Arts Council

St James Concert and Assembly Hall, St Peter Port, Guernsey, CI
email brijen@onetel.net.uk eales@guernsey.net
Secretary Elizabeth Eales *tel* (01481) 263189

Haiku Society, The British

Secretary David Walker, Lenacre Ford, Woolhope, Hereford HR1 4RF
tel (01432) 860328
email davidwalker@btinternet.com
website www.britishhaikusociety.org
Membership £25 p.a. UK, £28 Europe, £32 rest of world, £20 concession/unwaged

Aims to pioneer the appreciation and writing of haiku, senryu, renku and tanka in the UK and the rest of Europe, and to establish links with haiku societies throughout the world. Publishes the journal *Blithe Spirit*, and a newsletter, *The Brief*, and holds national events. Administers the biennial Sasakawa Prize (worth £2500), James W. Hackett International Award and the Nobuyuki Yuasa International English Haibun Contest. Founded 1990.

Hakluyt Society

c/o The Map Library, The British Library, 96 Euston Road, London NW1 2DB
tel (01428) 641850 *fax* (01428) 641933
email office@hakluyt.com
website www.hakluyt.com
President Sarah Tyacke CB, *Hon. Secretary* Dr Andrew Cook

Publication of original narratives of voyages, travels, naval expeditions, and other geographical records. Founded 1846.

The Thomas Hardy Society Ltd

PO Box 1438, Dorchester, Dorset DT1 1YH
tel/fax (01305) 251501
Membership £18 p.a., £22.50 overseas

Publishes *The Thomas Hardy Journal* (3 p.a.). Biennial conference in Dorchester, 2004. Founded 1967.

Harleian Society

College of Arms, Queen Victoria Street, London EC4V 4BT
tel 020-7236 7728 *fax* 020-7248 6448
Chairman J. Brooke-Little CVO, MA, FSA, *Hon. Secretary* T.H.S. Duke, Chester Herald of Arms

Instituted for transcribing, printing and publishing the heraldic visitations of Counties, Parish Registers and any manuscripts relating to genealogy, family history and heraldry. Founded 1869.

Health Writers, Guild of

Administrator Jatinder Dua, 1 Broadmead Close, Hampton, Middlesex TW12 3RT
tel/fax 020-8941 2977
email admin@healthwriters.com
website www.healthwriters.com
Membership £40 plus VAT p.a.

Brings together professional journalists dedicated to providing accurate, broad-based information about health and related subjects to the public. Publishes a directory of members. Founded 1995.

Heraldic Arts, Society of

46 Reigate Road, Reigate, Surrey RH2 0QN
tel (01737) 242945
website www.heraldic-arts.com
Secretary John Ferguson ARCA, SHA, DFACH, FRSA, FHS
Membership £12 p.a. associate, £17 craft

Aims to serve the interests of heraldic artists, craftsmen, designers and writers, to provide a 'shop window' for their work, to obtain commissions on their behalf and to act as a forum for the exchange of information and ideas. Also offers an information service to the public. Candidates for admission as craft members should be artists or craftsmen whose work comprises a substantial element of heraldry and is of a sufficiently high standard to satisfy the requirements of the society's advisory council. Founded 1987.

The James Hilton Society

Hon. Secretary Dr J.R. Hammond, 49 Beckingthorpe Drive, Bottesford, Nottingham NG13 0DN

Membership £10 p.a.

Aims to promote interest in the life and work of novelist and scriptwriter James Hilton (1900–54). Publishes quarterly newsletter and organises conferences. Founded 2000.

Historical Novel Society

Secretary Richard Lee, Marine Cottage, The Strand, Starcross, Devon EX6 8NY
tel (01626) 891962
email histnovel@aol.com
website www.historicalnovelsociety.com
Membership £18 p.a.

Promotes the historical novel via short story competitions, conferences, a society magazine *Solander* (2 p.a.) and reviews (*Historical Novels Review*, quarterly). Membership is open to all and includes eminent novelists. Founded 1997.

The Sherlock Holmes Society of London

General enquiries Heather Owen, 64 Graham Road, London SW19 3SS
tel/fax 020-8540 7657
email abcc@msn.com
website www.sherlock-holmes.org.uk
Membership R.J. Ellis, 13 Crofton Avenue, Orpington, Kent BR6 8DU
tel/fax (01689) 811314
President A.D. Howlett MA, LLB, *Chairman* Peter L. Horrocks MA
Membership £14 p.a. UK/Europe, £18 Far East, US$30.50 USA

Aims to bring together those who have a common interest as readers and students of the literature of Sherlock Holmes, and to encourage the pursuit of knowledge of the public and private lives of Sherlock Holmes and Dr Watson. Membership includes *The Sherlock Holmes Journal* (2 p.a.). Founded 1951.

Hopkins Society

Secretary Oughtrington Rectory, Lymm, Cheshire WA13 9JB
website www.hopkinsoc.freeserve.co.uk
Membership £7 p.a., £10 outside Europe

To promote and celebrate the work of the poet, Gerard Manley Hopkins, to inform members about the latest publications about Hopkins and to support educational projects concerning his work. Annual lecture held in North Wales in the spring; publishes a newsletter (2 p.a.) Founded 1990.

Horror Writers Association (HWA)

PO Box 50577, Palo Alto, CA 94303, USA
email hwa@horror.org
website www.horror.org
UK Jo Fletcher, 24 Pearl Road, London E17 4QZ
Membership $55 p.a. North America, $65/£45 elsewhere

A worldwide organisation of writers and publishing professionals dedicated to promoting the interests of writers of horror and dark fantasy. There are 3 levels of membership: for new writers, established writers and non-writing horror professionals. Founded 1980s.

Housman Society

80 New Road, Bromsgrove, Worcs. B60 2LA
tel (01527) 874136 *fax* (01527) 837274
email info@housman-society.co.uk
website www.housman-society.co.uk /
Chairman Jim Page
Membership £10 p.a.

Aims to foster interest in and promote knowledge of A.E. Housman and his family. Sponsors a lecture at the Hay Festival and the biennial National Poetry Competition (£1000). Founded 1973.

Hesketh Hubbard Art Society

17 Carlton House Terrace, London SW1Y 5BD
tel 020-7930 6844 *fax* 020-7839 7830
website www.mallgalleries.org.uk
President Simon Whittle

Weekly life drawing classes open to all.

Illustrators, The Association of

81 Leonard Street, London EC2A 4QS
tel 020-7613 4328 *fax* 020-7613 4417
website www.aoisupplement.co.uk
Contact Membership Secretary

To support illustrators, promote illustration and encourage professional standards in the industry. Publishes bimonthly magazine; presents an annual programme of events; annual competition, exhibition and tour of Images – the Best of British Illustration; call for entries late spring. Founded 1973.

Indexers, Society of – see page 593

Indian Publishers, The Federation of

18/1-C Institutional Area, Aruna Asaf Ali Marg (near JNU), New Delhi 110067, India
tel 6964847, 6852263 *fax* 91-11-6864054
email fipl@satyam.net.in
website www.federationofindianpublishers.com

The Irish Book Publishers' Association – see Clé

The Irish Copyright Licensing Agency
19 Parnell Square, Dublin 1, Republic of Ireland
tel (01) 8729202 *fax* (01) 8722035
email icla@esatlink.com
Executive Director Samantha Holman
Licences schools and other users of copyright material to photocopy extracts of such material, and distributes the monies collected to the authors and publishers whose works have been copied. Founded 1992.

Irish Playwrights and Screenwriters Guild
(formerly the Society of Irish Playwrights)
Irish Writers' Centre, 19 Parnell Square, Dublin 1, Republic of Ireland
tel (01) 8721302 *fax* (01) 8726282
email moffatts@intigo.ie
Secretary Sean Moffatt

Irish Translators' Association
Irish Writers' Centre, 19 Parnell Square, Dublin 1, Republic of Ireland
tel (01) 8721302 *fax* (01) 8726282
email translation@eircom.net
website http://translatorsassociation.ie
Hon. Secretary Miriam Lee
Membership E30 p.a. ordinary, E15 student, E80 corporate
Promotes translation in Ireland, the translation of Irish authors abroad and the practical training of translators, and promotes the interests of translators. Catalogues the works of translators in areas of Irish interest; secures the awarding of prizes and bursaries for translators; and maintains a detailed register of translators. Founded 1986.

Irish Writers' Union/Comhar na Scríbhneoirí
Irish Writers' Centre, 19 Parnell Square, Dublin 1, Republic of Ireland
tel (01) 8721302 *fax* (01) 8726282
Chairman Tony Hickey, *Secretary* Helen Brennan
The Union aims to advance the cause of writing as a profession, to achieve better remuneration and more favourable conditions for writers and to provide a means for the expression of the collective opinion of writers on matters affecting their profession. Founded 1986.

The Richard Jefferies Society
Hon. Secretary Phyllis Treitel, Eidsvoll, Bedwells Heath, Boars Hill, Oxford OX1 5JE
tel (01865) 735678
Membership £7 p.a. Worldwide membership
Promotes interest in the life, works and associations of the naturalist and novelist, Richard Jefferies; helps to preserve buildings and memorials, and co-operates in the development of a Museum in his birthplace. Arranges regular meetings in Swindon, and occasionally elsewhere; organises outings and displays; publishes a Journal and Newsletter in spring and an Annual Report in September. Founded 1950.

The Johnson Society
Johnson Birthplace Museum, Breadmarket Street, Lichfield, Staffs. WS13 6LG
tel (01543) 264972
Hon. General Secretary Norma Hooper
To encourage the study of the life and works of Dr Samuel Johnson; to preserve the memorials, associations, books, manuscripts, letters of Dr Johnson and his contemporaries; to work with the local council in the preservation of his birthplace.

Johnson Society of London
Secretary Mrs Zandra O'Donnell MA, 255 Baring Road, London SE12 0BQ
tel 020-8851 0173
President The Viscountess Eccles
To study the life and works of Dr Johnson, and to perpetuate his memory in the city of his adoption. Founded 1928.

Journalists, British Association of
General Secretary Steve Turner, 88 Fleet Street, London EC4Y 1PJ
tel 020-7353 3003 *fax* 020-7353 2310
Membership £12.50 per month national newspaper staff, national broadcasting staff and national news agency staff; £7.50 p.m. other seniors including magazine journalists, PRs, freelances; £5 p.m. under age 24
Aims to protect and promote the industrial and professional interests of journalists. Founded 1992.

Journalists, The Chartered Institute of
General Secretary Christopher Underwood FCIJ, FRSA, 2 Dock Offices, Surrey Quays Road, London SE16 2XU
tel 020-7252 1187 *fax* 020-7232 2302
email memberservices@ioj.co.uk
Membership £170 p.a. maximum, £85 trainees, £115 affiliate
The senior organisation of the profession, founded in 1884 and incorporated by Royal Charter in 1890. The Chartered Institute maintains an employment register and has accumulated funds for the

assistance of members. A Freelance Division links editors and publishers with freelances and a Directory is published of freelance writers, with their specialisations. There are special sections for broadcasters, motoring correspondents, public relations practitioners and overseas members. Occasional contributors to the media may qualify for election as Affiliates.

Journalists Ltd, National Council for the Training of (NCTJ)
Latton Bush Centre, Southern Way, Harlow, Essex CM18 7BL
tel (01279) 430009 *fax* (01279) 438008
email info@nctj.com
website www.nctj.com
Training Director Sally Mellis

A registered charity which aims to advance the education and training of trainee journalists, including press photographers. Full-time courses run at 28 colleges/universities in the UK. Distance learning courses also available in newspaper and magazine journalism and subediting. Founded 1952.

The Sheila Kaye-Smith Society
Secretary Grace Chatfield, 5 Leeds Close, Ore Village, Hastings, East Sussex TN35 5BX
tel (01424) 437413 *fax* (01424) 883268
Membership £6 p.a. single, £9 joint

Aims to stimulate and widen interest in the work of the Sussex writer and novelist, Sheila Kaye-Smith (1887–1956). Produces *The Gleam* (annual) and occasional papers, and organises talks. Founded 1987.

Keats-Shelley Memorial Association
Hon. Secretary David Leigh-Hunt, 1 Satchwell Walk, Leamington Spa, Warks. CV32 4QE
tel (01926) 427400 *fax* (01926) 335133
Chairman Hon. Mrs H. Cullen
Membership £10 p.a. minimum

Owns and supports house in Rome where John Keats died as a museum open to the public, and celebrates the poets Keats, Shelley and Leigh Hunt. Occasional meetings; poetry competitions; annual *Review*, 2 literary awards, and progress reports. Founded 1903.

Kent and Sussex Poetry Society
Hon. Secretary Joyce Mandel Walter, 23 Arundel Road, Tunbridge Wells, Kent TN1 1TB
email walter.scape@which.net
President Laurence Lerner, *Chairman* Clive Eastwood
Membership £10 p.a. full, £5 country members/concessions

Based in Tunbridge Wells, the society was formed in 1946 to create a greater interest in Poetry. Well-known poets address the Society, a Folio of members' work is produced and a full programme of recitals, discussions, competitions and readings is provided. See page 526 for details of Open Poetry Competition.

The Kipling Society
Hon. Secretary Jane Keskar, 6 Clifton Road, London W9 1SS
tel 020-7286 0194
email jane@keskar.fsworld.co.uk
website www.kipling.org.uk
Membership Details on application

Aims to honour and extend the influence of Rudyard Kipling (1865–1936), to assist in the study of his writings, to hold discussion meetings, to publish a quarterly journal, and to maintain a Kipling Library in London and a Kipling Room in The Grange, Rottingdean, near Brighton.

The Lancashire Authors' Association
General Secretary Eric Holt, 5 Quakerfields, Westhoughton, Bolton BL5 2BJ
tel (01942) 791390
Membership £9 p.a.

'For writers and lovers of Lancashire literature and history.' Publishes *The Record* (quarterly). Founded 1909.

The D.H. Lawrence Society
Secretary Ron Faulks, 24 Briarwood Avenue, Nottingham NG3 6JQ
tel 0115-950 3008
Membership £11 p.a. UK, £13 Europe, £16 rest of world (under review)

Aims to bring together people interested in D.H. Lawrence (1885–1930), to encourage study of his work, and to provide information and guides for people visiting Eastwood. Founded 1974.

The T.E. Lawrence Society
PO Box 728, Oxford OX2 6YP
website www.telawrencesociety.org
Membership £18 p.a., £23 overseas

Promotes the memory of T.E. Lawrence and furthers knowledge by research into his life; publishes *Journal* (bi-annual) and *Newsletter* (quarterly). Founded 1985.

Learned and Professional Society Publishers, The Association of
Secretary-General Sally Morris, South House, The Street, Clapham, Worthing, West Sussex BN13 3UU
tel (01903) 871 686 *fax* (01903) 871457
email sec-gen@alpsp.org
website www.alpsp.org
Membership Open to non-for-profit publishers and allied organisations

Represents non-for-profit publishers of scholarly and professional information. Founded 1972.

Librarians, Association of Assistant – see Career Development Group

Limners, The Society of
Founder/President Elizabeth Davys Wood MBE, 2 Glentrammon Close, Green Street Green, Orpington, Kent BR6 6DL
tel (01689) 851158
email dionevenables@clara.net
Membership £30 p.a., £15 Friends (open to non-exhibitors); £45, £20 overseas

Aims to promote an interest in miniature painting (in any medium), calligraphy and heraldry and encourage their development to a high standard. New members are elected after the submission of 4 works of acceptable standard and guidelines are provided fornew artists. Members receive up to 4 newsletters a year and 2 annual exhibitions are arranged. Founded 1986.

Linguists, Institute of
Saxon House, 48 Southwark Street, London SE1 1UN
tel 020-7940 3100 *fax* 020-7940 3101
email info@iol.org.uk
website www.iol.org.uk

Professional association for translators, interpreters and language tutors with 'Find-a-Linguist' website service. International language examinations run by its Educational Trust. One subsidiary NRPSI Ltd manages the National Register of Public Service Interpreters. Another, Language Services Ltd, offers customised assessments and services.

Literacy Trust, National
Swire House, 59 Buckingham Gate, London SW1E 6AJ
tel 020-7828 2435 *fax* 020-7931 9986
email contact@literacytrust.org.uk
website www.literacytrust.org.uk www.rif.org.uk
Director Neil McClelland, *PA* Jacky Taylor

A registered charity that aims to make an independent, strategic contribution to the creation of a society in which all can enjoy the appropriate skills, confidence and pleasures of literacy to support their educational, economic, social and cultural goals. Maintains an extensive website with literacy issues, research news and a database detailing literacy practice nationwide; promotes and facilitates literacy partnerships; organises an annual conference, courses and training events; publishes quarterly magazine *Literacy Today* (£18 p.a.). Organised and implemented the National Year of Reading 1998–9 and is coordinating the National Reading Campaign. Runs Reading is Fundamental, UK which provides books free to children. Founded 1993.

Literary Societies, Alliance of
Secretary Rosemary Culley, 22 Belmont Grove, Havant, Hants PO9 3PU
tel 023-9247 5855 *fax* (0870) 056 0330
email rosemary@sndc.demon.co.uk
website www.sndc.demon.co.uk
Open Book, Greta, Sandford Avenue, Church Stretton, Shropshire SY6 7AB
tel (01694) 722821
Editor Thelma Thompson

Aims to enable close cooperation between societies so that the ideas for expansion to membership and the preservation of our literary heritage can flourish. Produces an annual handbook and newsletters (2 p.a.).

Literature, Royal Society of
Somerset House, Strand, London WC2R 1LA
tel 020-7845 4676 *fax* 020-7845 4679
email info@rslit.org
Chairman of Council Ronald Harwood CBE, FRSL, *Secretary* Maggie Fergusson
Membership £30 p.a.

For the promotion of literature and encouragement of writers by way of lectures, discussions, readings, and by publications. Administers the Royal Society of Literature Award under the W.H. Heinemann Bequest, the V.S. Pritchett Memorial Prize and the Winifred Holtby Memorial Prize. Founded 1820.

Little Theatre Guild of Great Britain
Public Relations Officer Michael Shipley, 121 Darwen Road, Bromley Cross, Bolton BL7 9BG
tel (01204) 304103

Aims to promote closer co-operation

amongst the little theatres constituting its membership; to act as co-ordinating and representative body on behalf of the little theatres; to maintain and advance the highest standards in the art of theatre; and to assist in encouraging the establishment of other little theatres. Yearbook available to non-members £5.

Marine Artists, Royal Society of
17 Carlton House Terrace, London SW1Y 5BD
tel 020-7930 6844 *fax* 020-7839 7830
President Bert Wright

To promote and encourage marine painting. Open Annual Exhibition at the Mall Galleries, London for any artists whose main interest is the sea, or tidal waters, or some object essentially connected therewith.

The Marlowe Society
Secretary Carolyn Barford, 27 Blois Road, Steeple Bumpstead, Suffolk CB9 7BN
tel (01227) 451467
Membership £12 p.a., £7 concessions, £15/$26 overseas

To extend appreciation and widen recognition of Christopher Marlowe (1564–93) as the foremost poet and dramatist preceding Shakespeare, whose development he influenced. Holds meetings and cultural visits, and issues a bi-annual magazine. Founded 1955.

The John Masefield Society
Chairman Peter J.R. Carter, The Frith, Ledbury, Herefordshire HR8 1LW
tel (01531) 633800 *fax* (01531) 631647
email petercarter@btinternet.com
website http://my.genie.co.uk/masefield
Membership £5 p.a., £10 overseas, £8 family/institutions

To stimulate interest in and public awareness and enjoyment of the life and works of the poet John Masefield. Holds an annual lecture and other, less formal, readings and gatherings; publishes an annual journal and frequent newsletters. Founded 1992.

Mechanical-Copyright Protection Society Ltd (MCPS)
Copyright House, 29-33 Berners Street, London W1T 3AB
tel 020-7580 5544, 020-8769 4400
fax 020-7306 4455 020-8769 8792
website www.mcps.co.uk
Chief Executive John Hutchinson

The Media Society
Secretary Peter Dannheisser, 56 Roseneath Road, London SW11 6AQ
tel/fax 020-7223 5631
Membership £35 p.a.

To promote and encourage collective and independent research into the standards, performance, organisation and economics of the media and hold regular discussions, debates, etc. on subjects of topical or special interest and concern to print and broadcast journalists and others working in or with the media. Founded 1973.

Mediawatch-UK
(formerly National Viewers' and Listeners' Association)
Director John C. Beyer, 3 Willow House, Kennington Road, Ashford, Kent TN24 0NR
tel (01233) 633936 *fax* (01233) 633836
email info@mediawatchuk.org
website www.mediawatchuk.org
Chairman John Milton Whatmore
Membership £10 p.a.

Aims to encourage viewers and listeners to react effectively to programme content; to initiate and stimulate public discussion and parliamentary debate concerning the effects of broadcasting, and other mass media, on the individual, the family and society; to secure – then uphold – effective legislation to control obscenity and pornography in the media. Founded 1965.

Medical Journalists Association
Hon. Secretary Sue Lowell, 101 Cambridge Gardens, London W10 6JE
tel 020-8968 1614 *fax* 020-8968 7910
email sue4382@aol.com
Chairman John Illman
Membership £30 p.a.

Aims to improve the quality and practice of health and medical journalism. Administers major awards for health and medical journalism and broadcasting. Publishes The *MJA Directory* and *MJA News* newsletter. Founded 19[illegible].

Medical Writers Group – see the Society of Authors, page 504

Miniature Painters, Sculptors and Gravers, The Royal Society of
Executive Secretary Mrs Pam Henderson, 1 Knapp Cottages, Wyke, Gillingham, Dorset SP8 4NQ
tel (01747) 825718; 020-7222 2723 (during exhibitions)

email hendersons@dial.pipex.com
website www.royal-miniature-society.org.uk
President Suzanne Lucas FLS, PRMS, FPSBA, *Treasurer* Alastair MacDonald, *Hon. Secretary* Pauline Gyles
Membership By selection and standard of work over a period of years (ARMS associate, RMS full member)

Annual Open Exhibition in November at the Westminster Gallery in London. Hand in Sept/Oct; schedules available in July (send sae). Applications and enquiries to the Executive Secretary. Founded 1895.

Miniaturists, British Society of
Director Margaret Simpson, Briargate, 2 The Brambles, Ilkley, West Yorkshire LS29 9DH
Membership By selection

'The world's oldest miniature society.' Holds 2 open exhibitions p.a. Founded 1895.

Miniaturists, The Hilliard Society of
The Executive Officer Pauline Warner, Priory Lodge, 7 Priory Road, Wells, Somerset BA5 1SR
tel/fax (01749) 674472
website www.art-in-miniature.org
President Heather O. Catchpole RMS, pHSF, MASSA, MASF
Membership from £25 p.a.

Founded to increase knowledge and promote the art of miniature painting. Annual Exhibition held in June at Wells; seminars; Young People's Awards (11–19 years); Newsletter. Member of the World Federation of Miniaturists. Founded 1982.

William Morris Society
Kelmscott House, 26 Upper Mall, London W6 9TA
tel 020-8741 3735 *fax* 020-8748 5207
email william.morris@care4free.net
website www.morrissociety.org
Secretary Peter Faulkner

To spread knowledge of the life, work and ideas of William Morris; publishes *Newsletter* (quarterly) and *Journal* (2 p.a.). Library and collections open to the public Thu and Sat, 2–5pm. Founded 1955.

Motoring Artists, The Guild of
Administrator David Purvis, 71 Brook Court, Watling Street, Radlett, Herts. WD7 7JA
tel (01923) 853803
email sharon@scott-fairweather.freeserve.co.uk
website www.newspress.co.uk/guild
Membership £27.50 p.a., £22.50 associate, £18 friend

To promote, publicise and develop motoring fine art; to build a recognised group of artists interested in motoring art, holding events and exchanging ideas and support; to hold motoring art exhibitions. Founded 1986.

Motoring Writers, The Guild of
Contact General Secretary, 30 The Cravens, Smallfield, Surrey RH6 9QS
tel (01342) 843294 *fax* (01342) 844093

To raise the standard of motoring journalism. For writers, broadcasters, photographers on matters of motoring, but who are not connected with the motor industry.

Music Publishers Association Ltd
3rd Floor, Strandgate, 18-20 York Buildings, London WC2N 6JU
tel 020-7839 7779 *fax* 020-7839 7776
email info@mpaonline.org.uk
Chief Executive Sarah Faulder
Membership Details on request

Trade organisation representing over 200 UK music publisher members: promotes and safeguards its members' interests in copyright, trade and related matters. Subcommittees and groups deal with particular interests. Founded 1881.

Musical Association, The Royal
Secretary Dr Jeffrey Dean, 4 Chandos Road, Chorlton-Cum-Hardy, Manchester M21 0ST
tel 0161-861 7542 *fax* 0161-861 7543
email dean@okeghem.demon.co.uk
website http://pages.britishlibrary.net/rma.news/index.htm

Musicians, Incorporated Society of
10 Stratford Place, London W1C 1AA
tel 020-7629 4413 *fax* 020-7408 1538
email membership@ism.org
website www.ism.org
President 2001-02: John Stephens OBE, *Chief Executive* Neil Hoyle
Membership £103 p.a.

Professional body for musicians. Aims to promote the art of music; protect the interests and raise the standards of the musical profession; provide services, support and advice for its members. Publishes *Music Journal* (12 p.a.); Yearbook and 3 Registers of Specialists annually.

National Campaign for the Arts (NCA)
Pegasus House, 37-43 Sackville Street, London W1S 3EH
tel 020-7333 0375 *fax* 020-7333 0660
Director Victoria Todd, *Deputy Director* Anna Leatherdale
Membership £50 p.a., £25 unwaged; special rates for organisations

Independent advocacy and lobbying organisation that exists to promote the interests of the arts world in all its diversity. It is funded through membership subscriptions to ensure its independence. Founded 1985.

National Union of Journalists
Head Office Headland House,
308-312 Gray's Inn Road, London WC1X 8DP
tel 020-7278 7916 *fax* 020-7837 8143
email acorn.house@nuj.org.uk

Trade union for working journalists with 28,000 members and 147 branches throughout the UK and the Republic of Ireland, and in Paris, Brussels, Geneva and the Netherlands. It covers the newspaper press, news agencies and broadcasting, the major part of periodical and book publishing, and a number of public relations departments and consultancies, information services and Prestel-Viewdata services. Administers disputes, unemployment, benevolent and provident benefits. Official publications: *The Journalist* (bi-monthly), *Freelance Directory*, *Freelance Fees Guide* and policy pamphlets.

National Viewers' and Listeners' Association – see Mediawatch-UK

NCTJ – see Journalists Ltd, National Council for the Training of

The Edith Nesbit Society
21 Churchfields, West Malling, Kent ME19 6RJ
email mmccarthy30@hotmail.com
website www.imagix.dial.pipex.com
Membership £6 p.a.; £12 organisations/overseas

Aims to promote an interest in the life and works of Edith Nesbit (1858–1924) by means of talks, a regular newsletter and and other publications, and visits to relevant places. Founded 1996.

New Science Fiction Alliance (NSFA)
Chris Reed, BBR, PO Box 625, Sheffield S1 3GY
website www.bbr-online.com/catalogue
Publicity Officer Chris Reed

The NSFA is committed to supporting the work of new writers and artists by promoting independent and small press publications worldwide. It was founded by a group of independent publishers to give writers the opportunity to explore the small press and find the right market for their material. It offers a mail order service for magazines. Founded 1989.

New Writing North
7-8 Trinity Chare, Quayside,
Newcastle upon Tyne NE1 3DF
tel 0191-232 9991 *fax* 0191-230 1883
email subtext.nwn@virgin.net
website www.newwritingnorth.com
Director Claire Malcolm, *Administrator* John McGagh

The literature development agency for the Northern Arts region. Offers advice and support to writers of poetry, prose and plays. See website. Founded 1996.

Book Publishers Association of New Zealand Inc.
PO Box 36477, Northcote, Auckland 1309, New Zealand
tel (09) 480-2711 *fax* (09) 480-1130
email bpanz@copyright.co.nz
President Kevin Chapman

Copyright Council of New Zealand Inc.
PO Box 36477, Northcote, Auckland 1309, New Zealand
tel (09) 480-2711 *fax* (09) 480-1130
Chairman Terence O'Neill-Joyce, *Secretary* Kathy Sheat

New Zealand Writers Guild
PO Box 47886, Ponsonby, Auckland, New Zealand
tel (09) 360-1408 *fax* (09) 360-1409
email info@nzwritersguild.org.nz
website www.nzwritersguild.org.nz
Membership NZ$150-$400 full, $90 associate

Aims to represent the interests of New Zealand writers (TV, film, radio and theatre); to establish and improve minimum conditions of work and rates of compensation for writers; to provide professional services for members. Founded 1975.

Newspaper Press Fund
Dickens House, 35 Wathen Road, Dorking, Surrey RH4 1JY
tel (01306) 887511 *fax* (01306) 888212
website www.foundation.reuters.com/npf
Secretary David Ilott

For the relief of hardship amongst journalists, their widows and dependants. Financial assistance and retirement housing are provided.

The Newspaper Publishers Association Ltd
34 Southwark Bridge Road, London SE1 9EU
tel 020-7207 2200 *fax* 020-7928 2067

Newspaper Society

Bloomsbury House, 74-77 Great Russell Street, London WC1B 3DA
tel 020-7636 7014 *fax* 020-7631 5119
AdDoc DX35701 Bloomsbury
email ns@newspapersoc.org.uk
website www.newspapersoc.org.uk
Director David Newell

Oil Painters, Royal Institute of

17 Carlton House Terrace, London SW1Y 5BD
tel 020-7930 6844 *fax* 020-7839 7830
President Olwen Tarrant

Promotes and encourages the art of painting in oils. Open Annual Exhibition at the Mall Galleries, London.

Oils, Pastels and Acrylics, British Society of Painters in

Briargate, 2 The Brambles, Ilkley, West Yorkshire LS29 9DH
Director Margaret Simpson
Membership By selection

Promotes interest and encourages high quality in the work of painters in these media. Holds 2 open exhibitions p.a. Founded 1988.

Outdoor Writers' Guild

Secretary Terry Marsh, PO Box 520, Bamber Bridge, Preston, Lancs. PR5 8LF
tel/fax (01772) 696732
email info@owg.org.uk
website www.owg.org.uk
Membership £60 p.a.

Aims to promote and maintain a high professional standard among writers, illustrators and photographers who specialise in outdoor activities; represents members' interests to representative bodies in the outdoor leisure industry; circulates members with news of media opportunities; provides a forum for members to meet colleagues and others in the outdoor leisure industry. Presents annual literary and photographic awards. Founded 1980.

Wilfred Owen Association

192 York Road, Shrewsbury SY1 3QH
tel/fax (01743) 460089
Membership £4 p.a. (£6 overseas), £10 groups/institutions, £2 concessions

To commemorate the life and work of Wilfred Owen, and to encourage and enhance appreciation of his work through visits, public events and a newsletter. Founded 1989.

PACT (Producers Alliance for Cinema and Television)

45 Mortimer Street, London W1W 8HJ
tel 020-7331 6030 *fax* 020-7331 6700
email enquiries@pact.co.uk
website www.pact.co.uk
Chief Executive John McVay, *Membership Officer* David Alan Mills

Pact Scotland
249 West George Street, Glasgow G2 4QE
tel 0141-302 1720 *fax* 0141-302 1721
email margaret@pactscot.co.uk
website www.pactscot.co.uk
Head of Nations & Regions Margaret Scott

The main trade association for feature film and independent TV production companies. Represents the interests of over 1000 production companies throughout the UK: promotes and protects the commercial interests of its members; lobbies government and regulators on their behalf; negotiates terms of trade with broadcasters; provides a range of membership services including advice on business affairs, industrial relations and legal advice; operates a copyright registration service for members' proposals and treatments for films and TV programmes. Its representative office in Glasgow serves the interests of its Scottish members.

Painter-Printmakers, Royal Society of

Bankside Gallery, 48 Hopton Street, London SE1 9JH
tel 020-7928 7521
email info@banksidegallery.com
website www.banksidegallery.com
President Prof David L. Carpanini Hon. RWS, RBA, RWA, NEAC
Membership Open to British and overseas artists. An election of Associates is held annually; for particulars apply to the Secretary

The Society organises workshops and lectures on original printmaking; holds one members' exhibition per year. Friends of the RE open to all those interested in artists' original printmaking. Founded 1880.

Painters, Sculptors and Printmakers, National Society of

Hon. Secretary Gwen Spencer, 122 Copse Hill, London SW20 0NL
tel 020-8946 7878
website www.nationalsociety.co.uk

An annual exhibition at the Westminster Galleries (26 November–1 December 2002). Not an open exhibition but artists are welcome to apply for membership. Newsletter (2 p.a.) for members. Founded 1930.

The Pastel Society

17 Carlton House Terrace, London SW1Y 5BD
tel 020-7930 6844 *fax* 020-7839 7830
President Thomas Coates

Pastel and drawings in pencil or chalk. Annual Exhibition open to all artists working in dry media held at the Mall Galleries, London. Members elected from approved candidates' list. Founded 1899.

The Mervyn Peake Society

Secretary Yvonne McLean, Rupera, Trinity Road, Mistley, Manningtree CO11 2HL
Hon. President Sebastian Peake, *Chairman* Brian Sibley
Membership £12 p.a. UK and Europe, £5 students, £16 all other countries

Devoted to recording the life and works of Mervyn Peake; publishes a journal and newsletter. Founded 1975.

PEN, International

International Secretary Terry Carlbom, 9-10 Charterhouse Buildings, Goswell Road, London EC1M 7AT
tel 020-7253 4308 *fax* 020-7253 5711
email intpen@dircon.co.uk
website www.oneworld.org/internatpen
International President Homero Aridjis
Membership See below for English Centre; for Scottish and Irish Centres apply to them direct

A world association of writers. PEN was founded in 1921 by C.A. Dawson Scott under the presidency of John Galsworthy, to promote friendship and understanding between writers and to defend freedom of expression within and between all nations.

The initials PEN stand for Poets, Playwrights, Editors, Essayists, Novelists – but membership is open to all writers of standing (including translators), whether men or women, without distinction of creed or race, who subscribe to these fundamental principles. PEN takes no part in state or party politics. The International PEN Writers in Prison Committee works on behalf of writers imprisoned for exercising their right to freedom of expression, a right implicit in the PEN Charter to which all members subscribe. The International PEN Translations and Linguistic Rights Committee strives to promote the translations of works by writers in the lesser-known languages and to defend those languages. The Writers for Peace Committee exists to find ways in which writers can work for peaceful coexistence in the world. The Women Writers' Committee works to promote women's writing and publishing in developing countries. The Writers in Exile Network helps exiled writers. International Congresses are held most years. The 67th Congress was held in Moscow in 2000 and the 68th will be held in Ohrid, Macedonia in 2002.

Membership of any one Centre implies membership of all Centres; at present 132 autonomous Centres exist throughout the world. Membership of the English Centre is £30 p.a. for country members, £35 for London and overseas members (add £5 when paying by cheque).

Associate membership is available for writers not yet eligible for full membership and for persons connected with literature. The English Centre has a programme of literary lectures, discussion, dinners and parties. A yearly Writers' Day is open to the public as are some literary lectures.

English PEN Centre

email enquiries@pen.org.uk
President Victoria Glendinning
Executive Director Diana Reich, 152-6 Kentish Town Road, London NW1 9QB
tel 020-7267 9444 *fax* 020-7267 9304
email enquiries@pen.org.uk

Scottish PEN Centre

President Simon Berry, Greenleaf Editorial, 126 West Princess Street, Glasgow G4 9DB
tel/fax 0141-564 1958
email greenenter@aol.com

Irish PEN Centre

President John B. Keane
Secretary Arthur Flynn, 26 Rosslyn, Killarney Road, Bray, Co. Wicklow, Republic of Ireland
tel (353) 1 282 8053

Performing Right Society Ltd (PRS)

Copyright House, 29-33 Berners Street, London W1T 3AB
tel 020-7580 5544 020-8769 4400
fax 020-7306 4455 020-8769 8792
website www.prs.co.uk
Chief Executive John Hutchinson

Periodical Publishers Association
Queens House, 28 Kingsway, London WC2B 6JR
tel 020-7404 4166 *fax* 020-7404 4167
email info1@ppa.co.uk
website www.ppa.co.uk
Chief Executive Ian Locks

The Personal Managers' Association Ltd
Liaison Secretary Angela Adler,
1 Summer Road, East Molesey, Surrey KT8 9LX
tel/fax 020-8398 9796
email aadler@thepma.com

Association of theatrical agents in the theatre, film and entertainment world generally.

Photographers, The Association of
Co-Secretary Gwen Thomas, 81 Leonard Street, London EC2A 4QS
tel 020-7739 6669 *fax* 020-7739 8707
email general@aophoto.co.uk
website www.aophoto.co.uk
Membership £90-£412.50 p.a. depending on turnover

To protect and promote the interests of fashion advertising and editorial photographers. Founded 1968.

Photographers Association, Master
Hallmark House, 1 Chancery Lane, Darlington, Co. Durham DL1 5QP
tel (01325) 356555 *fax* (01325) 357813
email generalenquiries@mpauk.com
website www.mpa@mpauk.com
Membership £110 p.a.

To promote and protect professional photographers. Members qualify for awards of Licentiate, Associate and Fellowship.

Photographic Society, The Royal
The Octagon, Milsom Street, Bath BA1 1DN
tel (01225) 462841 *fax* (01225) 448688
email rps@rps.org
website www.rps.org

Open membership organisation which promotes the art and science of photography and electronic imagery; publishes *The RPS Journal* (monthly) and *Imaging Science Journal* (quarterly). Founded 1853.

Photography, British Institute of Professional
Fox Talbot House, Amwell End, Ware, Herts. SG12 9HN
tel (01920) 464011
email bipp@compuserve.com
website www.bipp.com

To represent all who practise photography as a profession in any field; to improve the quality of photography; establish recognised examination qualifications and a high standard of conduct; to safeguard the interests of the public and the profession. Admission can be obtained either via examinations, or by submission of work and other information to the appropriate examining board. Fellows, Associates and Licentiates are entitled to the designation Incorporated Photographer or Incorporated Photographic Technician. Organises numerous meetings and conferences in various parts of the country throughout the year; publishes *The Photographer* journal (10 p.a.), and an annual Register of Members and *Guide to Buyers of Photography*, plus various pamphlets and leaflets on professional photography. Founded 1901, incorporated 1921.

Picture Libraries and Agencies, British Association of – see BAPLA

The Picture Research Association
(formerly SPREd)
2 Culver Drive, Oxted, Surrey RH8 9HP
tel (01883) 730123 *fax* (01883) 730144
email pra@lippmann.co.uk
website www.picture-research.org.uk
Chair Charlotte Lippmann

Professional organisation of picture researchers and picture editors. Its aims are:

- to promote the recognition of picture research, management, editing, picture buying and supplying as a profession requiring particular skills and knowledge;
- to bring together all those involved in the picture profession and provide a forum for information exchange and interaction;
- to encourage publishers, TV and video production organisations, internet companies, and any other users of images to use the PRA freelance register and engage a member of PRA to obtain them, thus ensuring that professional standards are maintained;
- to advise those specifically wishing to embark on a profession in the research and supply of pictures for all types of visual media information, providing guidelines and standards in so doing.

Player-Playwrights
Secretary Peter Thompson, 9 Hillfield Park, London N10 3QT
tel 020-8883 0371
email p-p@dial.pipex.com
Membership £10 in first year and £6 thereafter (plus £1.50 per attendance)
Meets on Monday evenings upstairs at the Horse and Groom, 128 Great Portland Street, London W1. The society reads, performs and discusses plays and scripts submitted by members, with a view to assisting the writers in improving and marketing their work. Newcomers and new acting members are always welcome. Founded 1948.

Playwrights Trust, New – see Writernet

Poetry Book Society
Book House, 45 East Hill, London SW18 2QZ
tel 020-8870 8403 *fax* 020-8877 1615
email info@poetrybooks.co.uk
website www.poetrybooks.co.uk
Chair Maura Dooley, *Director* Clare Brown
Foremost in getting books of new poetry to readers through quarterly selections, special offers, and 300-strong backlist which it sells at favourable rates to members. Website features over 1000 post-1950s poetry books for sale. Publishes *Bulletin* (quarterly) and runs the annual T.S. Eliot Prize for the best collection of new poetry. Operates as a charitable Book Club with annual membership (£10, £32, £125) open to all. Education resources for secondary schools and Children's Poetry Bookshelf for primary schools and libraries.

The Poetry Society
22 Betterton Street, London WC2H 9BX
tel 020-7420 9880 *fax* 020-7240 4818
email info@poetrysociety.org.uk
website www.poetrysociety.org.uk
Subscriptions Subscriptions and Membership Dept, Freepost 5410, London WC2H 9BR
tel 020-7420 9881 *fax* 020-7240 4818
Chair Richard Price, *Director* Christina Patterson
Membership Open to all; national membership
Aims to help poets and poetry thrive in Britain today. Publishes *Poetry Review* (quarterly) and *Poetry News* (quarterly), has an information and imagination service, runs promotions and educational projects, helps to co-ordinate National Poetry Day and the annual National Poetry Competition (see page 531). Provides a unique critical service, Poetry Prescription, where poetry of up to 100 lines is appraised by a chosen poet. Runs the Poetry Café at its premises in Covent Garden, which is also a venue for regular and one-off events, and is also available for hire for small readings and seminars (contact Jess York, *tel* 020-7420 9887). Founded 1909.

The John Polidori Literary Society
Contact The Secretary, PO Box 6078, Nottingham NG16 4HX
Founder/President Franklin Charles Bishop
Membership By invitation only
Promotes and encourages the appreciation of the life and works of Anglo-Italian John William Polidori MD (1795–1821) – novelist, poet, tragedian, philosopher, diarist, essayist, reviewer, traveller and one of the youngest ever students to obtain a medical degree at the age of 19. He introduced into English literature the icon of the vampire portrayed as an aristocratic, handsome seducer both cynical and amoral with his seminal work *The Vampyre – A Tale* (1819). The Society has a programme of republishing Polidori's literary works, including a recently found cache of previously unknown letters. The Society houses a collection of rare letters and memorabilia connected with Polidori. International membership. Founded 1990.

Portrait Painters, Royal Society of
17 Carlton House Terrace, London SW1Y 5BD
tel 020-7930 6844 *fax* 020-7839 7830
President Paul Brason
Annual Exhibition at the Mall Galleries, London, of members' work and that of selected non-members. Three high-profile artists' awards are made: the Ondaatje Prize for Portraiture (£10,000), the Carroll Foundation Young Portrait Painters Award (£3000), and the Prince of Wales Award for Portrait Drawing (£2000). Also commissions consultancy service. Founded 1891.

The Beatrix Potter Society
The Administrator, 9 Broadfields, Harpenden, Herts AL5 2HJ
tel (01582) 769755
email jenny@beatrixpottersociety.org.uk
website www.beatrixpottersociety.org.uk

Chairman Judy Taylor
Membership £15 p.a. UK, £20 overseas

Promotes the study and appreciation of the life and works of Beatrix Potter as author, artist, diarist, farmer and conservationist. Founded 1980.

The Powys Society

Hon. Secretary Chris Gostick, Old School House, George Green Road, George Green, Wexham, Bucks. SL3 6BJ
tel (01753) 578632
email gostick@altavista.net
website www.powys-society.telinco.co.uk

Aims to promote the greater public recognition and enjoyment of the writings, thought and contribution to the arts of the Powys family, particularly John Cowper (1872–1963), Theodore (1875–1953) and Llewelyn (1884–1939) Powys, and the many other family members and their close friends. Publishes an annual scholarly journal (*The Powys Journal*) and 3 newsletters per year, and holds an annual weekend conference in August, as well as other activities. Founded 1967.

Press Agencies, National Association of

The Administrator, 41 Lansdowne Crescent, Leamington Spa, Warks. CV32 4PR
tel (01926) 424181 *fax* (01926) 424760
Membership £250 p.a.

Trade association representing the interests of the leading national news and photographic agencies. Founded 1983.

The Press Complaints Commission

Director Guy Black, 1 Salisbury Square, London EC4Y 8JB
tel 020-7353 1248
Helpline tel 020-7353 3732
fax 020-7353 8355
email pcc@pcc.org.uk
website www.pcc.org.uk
Acting Chairman Prof Robert Pinker

Independent body founded to oversee self-regulation of the Press. Deals with complaints by the public about the contents and conduct of British newspapers and magazines and advises editors on journalistic ethics. Complaints must be about the failure of newspapers or magazines to follow the letter or spirit of a Code of Practice, drafted by newspaper and magazine editors, adopted by the industry and supervised by the Commission. Founded 1991.

The J.B. Priestley Society

Secretary Rod Slater, 54 Framingham Road, Sale, Greater Manchester M33 3RJ
tel 0161-962 1477 (evening) *fax* 0161-905 3103
email priestleysociety@slatersweb.demon.co.uk
Membership £10 p.a. single, £15 family, £5 concessions

Aims to widen the knowledge, understanding and appreciation of the published works of J.B. Priestley (1894–1984) and to promote the study of his life and career. Holds lectures and discussions and shows films. Publishes a newsletter. Organises walks to areas with Priestley connections, Annual Priestley Night and other social events. Founded 1997.

Printmakers Council

Clerkenwell Workshops, 31 Clerkenwell Close, London EC1R 0AT
tel/fax 020-7250 1927
President Stanley Jones, *Chair* Sheila Sloss
Membership £55 p.a., £27.50 students

Artist-led group which aims 'to promote the use of both traditional and innovative printmaking techniques by:
- holding exhibitions of prints;
- providing information on prints and printmaking to both its membership and the public;
- encouraging co-operation and exchanges between members, other associations and interested individuals.'

Founded 1965.

Private Libraries Association

Ravelston, South View Road, Pinner, Middlesex HA5 3YD
website www.the-old-school.demon.co.uk/pla.htm
President Colin Franklin, *Hon. Editors* David Chambers and Paul W. Nash, *Hon. Secretary* Frank Broomhead
Membership £25 p.a.

International society of book collectors and private libraries. Publications include *The Private Library* (quarterly), annual *Private Press Books*, and other books on book collecting. Founded 1956.

The Publishers Association

29B Montague Street, London WC1B 5BH
tel 020-7691 9191 *fax* 020-7691 9199
email mail@publishers.org.uk
website www.publishers.org.uk
Chief Executive Ronnie Williams OBE, *Director of International and Trade Divisions (BDCI)* Ian Taylor, *Director of Educational, Academic and Professional Publishing* Graham Taylor

Founded 1896.

Publishers Association, International

3 avenue de Miremont, CH-1206 Geneva, Switzerland
tel (022) 346-30-18 *fax* (022) 347-57-17
President Pere Vicens, *Secretary-General* Mr Benoît Müller

Founded 1896.

Publishers Guild, Independent

PO Box 93, Royston, Herts. SG8 5GH
tel (01763) 247014 *fax* (01763) 246293
Membership £85 plus VAT p.a. Open to new and established publishers and book packagers; supplier membership is available to specialists in fields allied to publishing (but not printers and binders)

Provides an information and contact network for independent publishers. The IPG also voices the concerns of member companies with the book trade. Founded 1962.

Publishers Licensing Society Ltd (PLS)

5 Dryden Street, London WC2E 9NB
tel 020-7829 8486 *fax* 020-7829 8488
email pls@pls.org.uk
website www.pls.org.uk
Chairman Robert Kiernan, *Chief Executive* Jens Bammel

PLS has mandates from over 1600 publishers. These non-exclusive licences allow PLS to include those publishers' works as part of the repertoire offered to licensees by CLA. The licences permit photocopying and some digitisation of parts of copyright works. The money collected from these licences is shared between publishers and authors and PLS has responsibility for distributing the publishers' share to the mandating companies. PLS represents the interests of a wide range of publishers from the multinationals to the single-title publisher. Founded 1981.

Publishers Publicity Circle

Secretary/Treasurer Heather White, 65 Airedale Avenue, London W4 2NN
tel 020-8994 1881
email ppc-@lineone.net
website www.publisherspublicitycircle.co.uk

Enables all book publicists to meet and share information regularly. Monthly meetings provide a forum for press journalists, TV and radio researchers and producers to meet publicists collectively. Awards are presented for the best PR campaigns. Monthly newsletter includes recruitment advertising. Founded 1955.

The Radclyffe International Philosophical Association

BM-RIPhA, Old Gloucester Street, London WC1N 3XX
email riphassoc@aol.com
President William Mann FRIPhA, *Secretary General* John Khasseyan FRIPhA
Membership £30 p.a. (Fellows, Members and Associates)

Aims to dignify those achievements which might otherwise escape formal recognition; to promote the interests and talent of its members; to encourage their good fellowship; and to form a medium for the exchange of ideas between members. Published authors and artists usually enter at Fellowship level. Founded 1955.

The Radio Academy

5 Market Place, London W1W 8AE
email info@radioacademy.org
website www.radioacademy.org
Director John Bradford

The professional association for those engaged in the UK radio industry with over 2000 individual members and 30 corporate patrons. Organises conferences, seminars, debates, the annual UK Radio Festival and social events for members; publishes *Off Air* (monthly) newsletter and an annual *Yearbook*. Provides administrative support for the Student Radio Association and the Radio Studies Network and organises a series of regional training events for those interested in getting into radio.

Railway Artists, Guild of

Chief Executive Officer F.P. Hodges HON. GRA, 45 Dickins Road, Warwick CV34 5NS
tel (01926) 499246
email frank.hodges@tinyworld.co.uk
website www.railart.co.uk

Aims to forge a link between artists depicting railway subjects and to give members a corporate identity; also stages railway art exhibitions and members' meetings. Founded 1979.

Regional Arts Offices

website www.arts.org.uk

On 1 April 2002 the English Regional Arts Boards (RABs) joined together with the Arts Council of England to form a single development organisation for the arts in England. At the same time, regional boundaries were redrawn to complement existing Government Office boundaries and the 3 RABs in the south of England formed 2 new regional arts councils covering the same area. The objective is to build a national force for the arts which will deliver more funding and increased profile to artists and arts organisations, benefiting audiences everywhere.

While the new structure is being set up, services continue as usual in the fields of arts development, arts funding and audience building. The role of the new organisation includes providing advice and information, commissioning new creative work and conducting research. It promotes the case for the arts, creates partnerships and works to lever in new money for the arts. It works closely with local government, with regional agencies and with other sectors such as education, regeneration and health.

Funds, which come from Government and the National Lottery, are mainly used to invest in arts organisations and individual artists working in a wide variety of art forms. Investment is also made in strategic and developmental work such as training artists to work in schools, audience development and improving business skills.

Wales and Scotland do not have regional offices but work directly through the Arts Council of Wales and the Scottish Arts Council.

East England Arts
Eden House, 48-49 Bateman Street, Cambridge CB2 1LR
tel (01223) 454400 *fax* (0870) 2421271
email info@eearts.co.uk
Regional Executive Director Andrea Stark

Bedfordshire, Cambridgeshire, Essex, Hertfordshire, Norfolk and Suffolk; unitary authorities of Luton, Peterborough, Southend-on-Sea, Thurrock.

East Midlands Arts
Mountfields House, Epinal Way, Loughborough, Leics LE11 0QE
tel (01509) 218292 *fax* (01509) 262214
email info@em-arts.co.uk
Regional Executive Director Laura Dyer

Derbyshire (including High Peak District), Leicestershire, Lincolnshire, Northamptonshire and Nottinghamshire; unitary authorities of Derby, Leicester, Nottingham, Rutland.

London Arts
2 Pear Tree Court, London EC1R 0DS
tel 020-7608 6100 *fax* 020-7608 4100
email info@lonab.co.uk
text phone 020-7608 4101
Chief Executive Nigel Pittman

The area of the 32 London Boroughs and the City of London.

North West Arts
Manchester House, 22 Bridge Street, Manchester M3 3AB
tel 0161-834 6644 *fax* 0161-834 6969
email info@nwarts.co.uk
Regional Executive Director Michael Eakin

Cheshire, Cumbria, Lancashire; unitary authorities of Blackburn with Darwen, Blackpool, Halton, Warrington; metropolitan districts of Bolton, Bury, Knowsley, Liverpool, Manchester, Oldham, Rochdale, St Helens, Salford, Sefton, Stockport, Tameside, Trafford, Wigan, Wirral.

Northern Arts
Central Square, North Street, Newcastle upon Tyne NE1 3PJ
tel 0191-255 8500 *fax* 0191-230 1020
email info@northernarts.org.uk
Regional Executive Director Andrew Dixon

Durham, Northumberland, metropolitan districts of Newcastle, Gateshead, Sunderland, North Tyneside and South Tyneside; unitary authorities of Darlington, Hartlepool, Middlesbrough, Redcar and Cleveland, Stockton.

South West Arts
Bradninch Place, Gandy Street, Exeter EX4 3LS
tel (01392) 218188 *fax* (01392) 413554
email info@swa.co.uk
Regional Executive Director Nick Capaldi

Cornwall, Devon, Wiltshire (from 1 April 2003), Dorset (including Districts of Bournemouth, Christchurch and Poole from 1 April 2003), Gloucestershire, Somerset; non-metropolitan districts of Bristol, Bath and North-East Somerset, South Gloucestershire, North Somerset, Swindon, Plymouth, Torbay

Southern and South East Arts
Winchester office 13 St Clement Street, Winchester, Hants SO23 9DQ
tel (01962) 855099 *fax* (01962) 861186
email infowin@ssea.co.uk
Tunbridge Wells office Union House, Eridge Road, Tunbridge Wells, Kent TN4 8HF
tel (01892) 507200 *fax* (0870) 2421259
textphone (01892) 525831
email infotw@ssea.co.uk

Regional Executive Director Felicity Harvest

Buckinghamshire, East Sussex, Isle of Wight, Kent, Oxfordshire, Surrey and West Sussex; the non-metropolitan districts of Bracknell Forest, Brighton and Hove, the Medway Towns, Milton Keynes, Portsmouth, Reading, Slough, Southampton, West Berkshire, Windsor, Maidenhead and Wokingham. On 1 April 2003 Wiltshire, Swindon, Bournemouth, Poole and Christchurch will transfer to South West Arts.

West Midlands Arts
82 Granville Street, Birmingham B1 2LH
tel 0121-631 3121 *fax* 0121-643 7239
email info@west-midlands-arts.co.uk
textphone 0121-643 2815
Regional Executive Director Sally Luton

Worcestershire, Shropshire, Staffordshire, Warwickshire; unitary authorities of Herefordshire, Stoke-on-Trent, Telford and Wrekin; metropolitan districts of Birmingham, Coventry, Dudley, Sandwell, Solihull, Walsall, Wolverhampton.

Yorkshire Arts
21 Bond Street, Dewsbury, West Yorkshire WF13 1AX
tel (01924) 455555 *fax* (01924) 466522
email info@yarts.co.uk
textphone (01924) 438585
Regional Executive Director Andy Carver

North Yorkshire; unitary authorities of East Riding, Kingston-upon-Hull, North and North East Lincolnshire, York; metropolitan districts of Barnsley, Bradford, Calderdale, Doncaster, Kirklees, Leeds, Rotherham, Sheffield, Wakefield.

Ridley Art Society
50 Crowborough Road, London SW17 9QQ
tel 020-8682 1212
email ridley@artboy.demon.co.uk
President Ken Howard RA, *Chairman* dickon

Represents a wide variety of attitudes towards the making of art. In recent years has sought to encourage young artists. At least one central London exhibition annually. Founded 1889.

The Romantic Novelists' Association
Chairman Jean Chapman, 3 Arnesby Lane, Peatling Magna, Leicester LE8 5UN
tel/fax 020-7736 4968
website www.rna-uk.org
Hon. Secretary Mary de Laszlo, 57 Coniger Road, London SW6 3TB

To raise the prestige of Romantic Authorship. Open to romantic and historical novelists. See also page 533.

Royal Academy of Arts
Piccadilly, London W1J 0BD
tel 020-7300 8000 *fax* 020-7300 8001
website www.royalacademy.org.uk
President Prof Phillip King, *Keeper* Brendan Neiland RA

Academicians (RA) are elected from the most distinguished artists in the UK. Major loan exhibitions throughout the year with the Annual Summer Exhibition, June to August. Also runs art schools for 60 post-graduate students in painting and sculpture.

The Royal Literary Fund
3 Johnson's Court, off Fleet Street, London EC4A 3EA
tel 020-7353 7150 *fax* 020-7353 1350
email egunnrlf@globalnet.co.uk
President His Honour Sir Stephen Tumim, *General Secretary* Eileen Gunn

Founded in 1790, the Fund is the oldest and largest charity serving literature, set up to help writers and their families who face hardship. It does not offer grants to writers who can earn their living in other ways, nor does it provide financial support for writing projects. But it sustains authors who have for one reason or another fallen on hard times – illness, family misfortune, or sheer loss of writing form. Applicants must have published work of approved literary merit, which may include important contributions to periodicals. The literary claim of every new applicant must be accepted by the General Committee before the question of need can be considered.

The Royal Society
6-9 Carlton House Terrace, London SW1Y 5AG
tel 020-7451 2500 *fax* 020-7930 2170
email press@royalsoc.ac.uk
website www.royalsoc.ac.uk
President Lord May of Oxford AC, Kt, PRS, *Treasurer* Sir Eric Ash CBE, FRS, *Biological Secretary* Prof P.P.G. Bateson FRS, *Physical Secretary* Prof John Enderby CBE, FRS, *Foreign Secretary* Prof Dame Julia Higgins DBE, FRS, FREng, *Executive Secretary* Mr S. Cox CVO

Royal Society for the encouragement of Arts, Manufactures and Commerce (RSA)
8 John Adam Street, London WC2N 6EZ
tel 020-7930 5115 *fax* 020-7839 5805

email editor@rsa.org.uk
website www.rsa.org.uk
Chairman of Council Dr Neil Cross, *Director* Penny Egan, *Commercial Director* Chris Bond, *Programme Director* Dr Geoffrey Botting, *Communication Director* Paul Crake, *Director of Finance* Bernard Kelly, *Editor, RSA Journal* Bruce Willan, *Press Officer* Barbara Ormston

With over 20,000 Fellows, the RSA sustains a forum for people from all walks of life to come together to address issues, shape new ideas and stimulate action. It works through projects, award schemes and its lecture programme, the proceedings of which are recorded in *RSA Journal*. Founded 1754.

The Ruskin Society

Hon. Secretary Dr C.J. Gamble, 49 Hallam Street, London W1W 6JP
Membership £10 p.a.

Aims to encourage a wider understanding of John Ruskin (1819–1900) and his contemporaries. Organises lectures and events which seek to explain to the public the nature of Ruskin's theories and to place these in a modern context. Affiliated to the Ruskin Foundation. Founded 1997.

The Ruskin Society of London

Membership Secretary Mrs A. Hardy, 351 Woodstock Road, Oxford OX2 7NX
tel (01865) 310987/515962 *fax* (01865) 240448
Chairman and General Secretary Miss O.E. Forbes-Madden
Membership £10 p.a.

Promotes literary and biographical interest in John Ruskin and his contemporaries. The Society publishes an annual *Ruskin Gazette* free to members. Members are also affiliated to other literary societies. Founded 1985.

SAA (Society for All Artists)

PO Box 50, Newark, Notts. NG23 5GY
tel (01949) 844050 *fax* (01949) 844051
email inspiration@saa.co.uk
website www.saa.co.uk
Membership £20-£42 p.a. including paintings exhibition insurance and third party public liability, £27.50 overseas

Aims to 'inform, encourage and inspire all who want to paint', from complete beginners to professionals; to promote friendship and companionship amongst fellow artists. Holds meetings and events locally and nationally, organises painting holidays, workshops, local and international exhibitions and competitions, publishes newsletter *Paint* (quarterly) and *SAA Home Shopping* catalogue. Founded 1992.

The Malcolm Saville Society

Secretary Mark O'Hanlon, 10 Bilford Road, Worcester WR3 8QA
email mystery@witchend.demon.co.uk
website www.witchend.demon.co.uk
Membership £7.50 p.a. UK and EU, £12 outside EU

Aims to remember and promote interest in the work of Malcolm Saville (1901–82), children's author. Regular social activities, book search, library, contact directory and magazine (3 p.a.). Founded 1994.

The Dorothy L. Sayers Society

Chairman Christopher J. Dean, Rose Cottage, Malthouse Lane, Hurstpierpoint, West Sussex BN6 9JY
tel (01273) 833444 *fax* (01273) 835988
website www.sayers.org.uk/
Secretaries Lenelle Davis, Jasmine Simeone
Membership £14 p.a. UK, £16.50 Europe, $28 USA

To promote and encourage the study of the works of Dorothy L. Sayers; to collect relics and reminiscences about her and make them available to students and biographers; to hold an annual seminar and other meetings; to publish proceedings, pamphlets and a bi-monthly bulletin. Founded 1976.

Scattered Authors Society

Secretary Anne Cassidy, 150 Wanstead Lane, Ilford, Essex IG1 3SG
email anne.cassidy@cwcom.net

Aims to provide a forum for informal discussion, contact and support for professional writers in children's fiction. Founded 1998.

Science Fiction Association Ltd, The British

Membership Secretary Paul Billinger, 1 Long Row Close, Everdon, Daventry, Northants. NN11 3BE
email bsfa@enterprise.net
President Arthur C. Clarke

For authors, publishers, booksellers and readers of science fiction, fantasy and allied genres. Publishes *Matrix*, an informal magazine of news and information; *Focus*, an amateur writers' magazine; *Vector*, a critical magazine and The Orbiter Service, a network of postal writers workshops. Founded 1958.

Science Writers, Association of British
c/o British Association for the Advancement of Science, 23 Savile Row, London W1X 2NB
tel 020-7439 1205 *fax* 020-7973 3051
email absw@absw.org.uk
website www.absw.org.uk
Chairman Pallab Ghosh, *Administrator* Barbara Drillsma

Association of science writers, editors, and radio, film and TV producers concerned with the presentation and communication of science, technology and medicine. Aims to improve the standard of science writing and to assist its members in their work.

Scottish Academy, Royal
Administrative Offices 17 Waterloo Place, Edinburgh EH1 3BG
tel 0131-558 7097 *fax* 0131-557 6417
email info@royalscottishacademy.org
President Ian McKenzie Smith OBE, PRSA,
Secretary Bill Scott RSA,
Treasurer Isi Metzstein OBE, RSA

Academicians (RSA) and Associates (ARSA) and non-members may exhibit in the Annual Exhibition of Painting, Sculpture and Architecture, held approximately mid April to July; Festival Exhibition August/October. Other artists' societies' annual exhibitions, normally between October and January. Royal Scottish Academy Student Competition held in March. Founded 1826.

Scottish Arts Club
24 Rutland Square, Edinburgh EH1 2BW
tel 0131-229 8157 *fax* 0131-229 8887
Hon. Secretary Mhairi Kerr
tel 0131-229 8157
Membership £330 p.a. full; reductions available

Art, literature, music.

Scottish Arts Council
12 Manor Place, Edinburgh EH3 7DD
tel 0131-226 6051
Chairman James Boyle, *Director* Tessa Jackson, *Head of Literature* Jenny Brown, *Head of Visual Arts* Amanda Catto

Principal channel for government funding of the arts in Scotland, the Scottish Arts Council is funded by the Scottish Executive. It aims to develop and improve the knowledge, understanding and practice of the arts, and to increase their accessibility throughout Scotland. It offers about 1300 grants a year to artists and arts organisations concerned with the visual arts, drama, dance and mime, literature, music, festivals, and traditional, ethnic and community arts. It is also the distributor of National Lottery funds to the arts in Scotland.

Scottish Book Marketing Group
Scottish Book Centre, 137 Dundee Street, Edinburgh EH11 1BG
tel 0131-228 6866 *fax* 0131-228 3220
email allan@scottishbooks.org
Co-ordinator Allan Shanks

Co-operative venture set up by the Scottish Publishers Association and the Booksellers Association (Scottish Branch) which aims to promote Scottish books through member booksellers. Founded 1986.

Scottish Book Trust
The Scottish Book Centre, 137 Dundee Street, Edinburgh EH11 1BG
tel 0131-229 3663 *fax* 0131-228 4293
email info@scottishbooktrust.com
website www.scottishbooktrust.com

With a particular responsibility towards Scottish writing, the Trust exists to promote literature and reading, and aims to reach (and create) a wider reading public than has existed before. It also organises exhibitions, readings and storytellings, administers the Writers in Scotland scheme, operates an extensive children's reference library available to everyone and administers literary prizes, including the Blue Peter Book Awards and the Fidler Award. The Trust also publishes posters, literary guides and Directories and advises other relevant art organisations. Founded 1960.

Scottish Daily Newspaper Society
48 Palmerston Place, Edinburgh EH12 5DE
tel 0131-220 4353 *fax* 0131-220 4344
email info@sdns.org.uk
Director J.B. Raeburn FCIS

Scottish Literary Studies, Association for (ASLS)
c/o Dept of Scottish History, 9 University Gardens, University of Glasgow G12 8QH
tel 0141-330 5309
email d.jones@scothist.arts.gla.ac.uk
website www.asls.org.uk
Hon. President Dorothy McMillan, *Hon. Secretary* Jim Alison, *Publishing Manager* Duncan Jones
Membership £34 p.a. individuals, £10 UK students, £63 corporate

Promotes the study, teaching and writing of Scottish literature and furthers the study of the languages of Scotland. Publishes annually an edited text of Scottish literature, an anthology of new Scottish writing, a series of academic journals and a Newsletter (2 p.a.). Also publishes *Scotnotes* – comprehensive study guides to major Scottish writers – literary texts and commentary cassettes designed to assist the classroom teacher, and a series of occasional papers. Organises 3 conferences a year. Founded 1970.

Scottish Newspaper Publishers Association
48 Palmerston Place, Edinburgh EH12 5DE
tel 0131-220 4353 *fax* 0131-220 4344
email info@snpa.org.uk
website www.snpa.org.uk
Director J.B. Raeburn FCIS

Scottish Publishers Association
Scottish Book Centre, 137 Dundee Street, Edinburgh EH11 1BG
tel 0131-228 6866 *fax* 0131-228 3220
email enquiries@scottishbooks.org
website www.scottishbooks.org
Director Lorraine Fannin, *Administrator* Carol Lothian, *Marketing Manager* Alison Rae, *Scottish Book Marketing Group/Training Manager* Allan Shanks, *Projects Assistant* Caroline Taylor
Founded 1973.

Scottish Screen
249 West George Street, Glasgow G2 4QE
tel 0141-302 1700 *fax* 0141-302 1711
email info@scottishscreen.com
website www.scottishscreen.com
Information Manager Isabella Edgar
Responsible to the Scottish parliament for developing all aspects of screen industry and culture in Scotland through script and company development, short film production, distribution of National Lottery production finance, training, education, exhibition funding, the Film Commission locations support, and the Scottish Screen Archive. Founded 1997.

Screenwriters' Workshop
(formerly London Screenwriters' Workshop)
Suffolk House, 1-8 Whitfield Place, London W1T 5JU
tel 020-7387 5511
email screenoffice@tisali.co.uk
website www.lsw.org.uk
Contact The Secretary
Membership £40 p.a.
Forum for contact, information and tuition, the SW helps new and established writers work successfully in the film and TV industry, and organises a continuous programme of activities, events, courses and seminars, all of which are reduced to members and open to non-members at reasonable rates. The SW is the largest screenwriting group in Europe and supports Euroscript, a Media II-funded organisation developing scripts for film and TV throughout the EU. Founded 1983.

Scribes and Illuminators, Society of (SSI)
Hon. Secretary 6 Queen Square, London WC1N 3AT
email scribe@calligraphyonline.org
website www.calligraphyonline.org
Membership £27 Lay members; £22 Friends
Aims to advance the crafts of writing and illumination. Holds regular exhibitions, provides opportunities for discussion, demonstration and sharing of research. Founded 1921.

SCRIBO
Contact K. & P. Sylvester, Flat 1, 31 Hamilton Road, Bournemouth BH1 4EQ
Membership Joining fee: £5 (send sae); no annual subscription
A postal forum for novelists (published and unpublished), SCRIBO aims to give friendly, informed encouragement and help, to discuss all matters of interest to novelists and to offer criticism via MSS folios: crime/thrillers, fantasy/sci-fi, mainstream, aga-saga/popular women's fiction, 2 literary folios (mostly graduates writing serious fiction). Porn is not accepted. Founded 1971.

The Shaw Society
Secretary Barbara Smoker, 51 Farmfield Road, Downham, Bromley, Kent BR1 4NF
tel 020-8697 3619
email anthnyellis@aol.com
Membership £15/$30 p.a.
Improvement and diffusion of knowledge of the life and works of Bernard Shaw and his circle. Meetings in London; annual festival at Ayot St Lawrence in July; publishes *The Shavian*.

The Society of Authors – see page 504

Society of Young Publishers
Contact The Secretary, c/o The Bookseller, Endeavour House, 189 Shaftesbury Avenue, London WC2H 8TJ

email thesyp@thesyp.org.uk
website www.thesyp.org.uk
Membership Open to anyone employed in publishing or hoping to be soon; Associate membership available to those over the age of 35

Organises monthly speaker meetings at which senior figures talk on topics of key importance to the industry today, and social and other events. Runs a job database which matches candidates with potential employers. London meetings are held at Foyles Art Gallery, usually on the last Wednesday of the month at 6.30pm. Also a branch in Oxford. Founded 1949.

Songwriters & Composers, The Guild of International

Sovereign House, 12 Trewartha Road, Praa Sands, Penzance, Cornwall TR20 9ST
tel (01736) 762826 *fax* (01736) 763328
email songmag@aol.com
website www.songwriters-guild.co.uk
Secretary Carole Ann Jones
Membership £40 p.a. UK, £50 EU/overseas

Gives advice to members on contractual and copyright matters; assists with protection of members rights; assists with analysis of members' works; international collaboration register free to members; outlines requirements to record companies, publishers, artists. Publishes *Songwriting & Composing* (quarterly).

South Africa, Publishers' Association of (PASA)

PO Box 22640, Fish Hoek 7974, South Africa
tel (021) 782-7677 *fax* (021) 782-7679
email pasa@publishsa.co.za
website www.publishsa.co.za/

South African Writers' Circle

Secretary Ann Carter, PO Box 115, Hillcrest 3650, South Africa
tel (031) 7655706
email brianduc@mweb.co.za
website www.sawc.sos.co.za
Membership R85 p.a. local, R130 overseas

Aims to help and encourage all writers, new and experienced, in the art of writing. Publishes a monthly *Newsletter*, and runs competitions with prizes for the winners. Founded 1960.

South & Mid Wales Association of Writers (SAMWAW)

Secretary Julian Rosser, c/o IMC Consulting Group, Denham House, Lambourne Crescent, Cardiff CF14 5ZW
tel 029-2076 1170 *fax* 029-2076 1304
email info@imcconsultinggroup.co.uk
Membership £10 p.a. single, £15 joint

Aims to encourage the art of writing in all its forms, for both beginners and established writers. Offers a range of courses (see page 575). Publishes a newsletter and runs competitions, including the Mathew Prichard Award for Short Story Writing (see page 534). Founded 1965.

Southwest Scriptwriters

Secretary John Colborn *tel* 0117-909 5522
email southwest_scriptwriters@hotmail.com
website www.southwest-scriptwriters.co.uk
Membership £5 p.a.

Workshops members' drama scripts for stage, screen, radio and TV with the aim of improving their chances of professional production, meeting at the Bristol Old Vic. Also hosts regular talks by professional dramatists. Presents short annual seasons of script-in-hand performances of members' work at a major Bristol venue. Bi-monthly newsletter. Founded 1994.

Spanish Publishers' Association, Federation of

(Federación de Gremios de Editores de España)
Cea Bermúdez, 44-2° Dcha. 28003 Madrid, Spain
tel (91) 534 51 95 *fax* (91) 535 26 25
email fgee@fujitsu.es
President Emiliano Martinez, *Secretary* Antonio Avila

Spoken Word Publishing Association (SWPA)

Administrator Zoe Howes, Macmillan Audio Books, 20 New Wharf Road, London N1 9RR
tel 020-7014 6041
website www.swpa.co.uk
Membership £50-£600 p.a. + VAT

The UK trade association for the spoken word industry, SWPA brings together all those involved – publishers, performers, producers, distributors, retailers, manufacturers. It aims to increase the profile of the spoken word in the media, the retail trade and among the general public, and to provide a forum for discussion. Founded 1994.

Sports Writers' Association of Great Britain (SWA)

Secretary Trevor Bond, 244 Perry Street, Billericay, Essex CM12 0QP
tel (01277) 651708 *fax* (01277) 622890

Membership £23.50 p.a.

Represents sports journalists across the country and is Britain's voice in international sporting affairs. Offers advice to members covering major events, acts as a consultant to organisers of major sporting events on media requirements. Member of the BOA Press Advisory Committee. Founded 1948.

SPREd (Society of Picture Researchers and Editors) – see The Picture Research Association

Stationers and Newspaper Makers, Worshipful Company of

Stationers' Hall, London EC4M 7DD
tel 020-7248 2934 *fax* 020-7489 1975
Master Robert J. Russell,
Clerk Brig. Denzil Sharp AFC

One of the Livery Companies of the City of London. Connected with the printing, publishing, bookselling, newspaper and allied trades. Founded 1557.

The Robert Louis Stevenson Club

Secretary Margaret Bean, c/o 37 Lauder Road, Edinburgh EH9 1UE
tel 0131-667 6256 *fax* 0131-662 0353
email mbeanconferences@compuserve.com
Membership £15 p.a., £100 10 years, £180 life

Aims to foster interest in Stevenson's life (1850–94) and works through various events and its newsletter. Founded 1920.

Strip Illustration, Society for – now Comics Creators Guild

Sussex Authors, The Society of

Secretary Michael Legat, Bookends, Lewes Road, Horsted Keynes, Haywards Heath, West Sussex RH17 7DP
tel/fax (01825) 790755
email michael@bookends.claranet.com
Membership £10 p.a. Open to writers living in Sussex who have had at least one book commercially published or who have worked extensively in journalism, radio, TV or the theatre

Aims to encourage social contact between members, and to promote interest in literature and authors. Founded 1969.

Sussex Playwrights' Club

Hon. Secretary, 2 Brunswick Mews, Hove, East Sussex BN3 1HD
website www.newventure.org.uk

See 'features' page on website.

Swedish Publishers' Association

(Svenska Förläggareföreningen)
Drottninggaten 97, 2 tr., 113 60 Stockholm, Sweden
tel 08-736 19 40 *fax* 08-736 19 44
email svf@forlagskansli.se
website www.forlagskansli.se
Director Kristina Ahlinder

Founded 1843.

Television Society, Royal

Holborn Hall, 100 Gray's Inn Road, London WC1X 8AL
tel 020-7430 1000 *fax* 020-7430 0924
email membership@rts.org.uk
website www.rts.org.uk
Chief Executive Simon Albury, *Membership Services Manager* Deborah Halls
Membership £70 p.a.

The Society is a unique, central, independent forum to debate the art, science and politics of TV. Holds awards, conferences, dinners, lectures and workshops. Founded 1927.

The Tennyson Society

Hon. Secretary Kathleen Jefferson, Brayford House, Lucy Tower Street, Lincoln LN1 1XN
tel (01522) 552851 *fax* (01522) 552858
email linnet@lincolnshire.gov.uk
website www.tennysonsociety.org.uk
Membership £8 p.a., £10 family, £15 institutions

Promotes the study and understanding of the life and work of the poet Alfred, Lord Tennyson and supports the Tennyson Research Centre in Lincoln; holds lectures, visits and seminars; publishes the *Tennyson Research Bulletin* (annual), Monographs and Occasional Papers; tapes/recordings available. Founded 1960.

Theatre Exchange, International

Registered office Drama Association of Wales, Cardiff
email aled.daw@virgin.net
Secretariat 20 Abbey Road, Grimsby DN32 0HW
tel (01472) 343424

To encourage, foster and promote exchanges of theatre; student, educational, adult, theatre activities at international level. To organise international seminars, workshops, courses and conferences, and to collect and collate information of all types for national and international dissemination.

Theatre Research, The Society for

c/o The Theatre Museum, 1E Tavistock Street, London WC2E 7PR
email e.cottis@btinternet.com

website www.str.org.uk
Hon. Secretaries Eileen Cottis and Frances Dann

Publishes annual volumes and journal (3 p.a.), *Theatre Notebook*, holds lectures and makes annual research grants (current total sum approx. £4000). Starting in 1998, the Society's 50th anniversary, it awards an annual prize of £400 for the best book published in English on the historical or current practice of the British theatre.

Theatre Writers' Union – incorporated into The Writers' Guild of Great Britain, page 506

Angela Thirkell Society

Chairman Mrs I.J. Cox, 32 Murvagh Close, Cheltenham, Glos. GL53 7QY
tel (01242) 251604
email penny.aldred@tesco.net
website www.angelathirkell.org
Secretary Mrs P. Aldred, 54 Belmont Park, London SE13 5BN
tel 020-8244 9339
Membership £7 p.a.

Aims 'to honour the memory of Angela Thirkell (1890–1960) as a writer, and to make her works available to new generations'. Publishes an *Annual Journal*, and encourages Thirkell studies. Founded 1980.

The Edward Thomas Fellowship

Butler's Cottage, Halswell House, Goathurst, Nr Bridgwater, Somerset TA5 2DH
tel (01278) 662856
Hon. Secretary Richard N. Emeny
Membership £7 p.a.

To perpetuate the memory of Edward Thomas, poet and writer, foster an interest in his life and work, to assist in the preservation of places associated with him and to arrange events which extend fellowship amongst his admirers. Founded 1980.

The Tolkien Society

Secretary Sally Kennett, 210 Prestbury Road, Cheltenham, Glos. GL52 3ER
website www.tolkiensociety.org
Membership Secretary Trevor Reynolds, 65 Wentworth Crescent, Ash Vale, Surrey GU12 5LF
email trevor@caerlas.demon.co.uk

Translation & Interpreting, The Institute of (ITI)

Contact The Secretary, Exchange House, 494 Midsummer Boulevard, Milton Keynes MK9 2EA
tel 020-7713 7600 *fax* 020-7713 7650
email info@iti.org.uk
website www.iti.org.uk

The ITI is a professional association of translators and interpreters which aims to promote the highest standards in translating and interpreting. It has a strong corporate membership and runs professional development courses and conferences, sometimes in conjunction with its language, regional and subject networks. Membership is open to those with a genuine and proven involvement in translation and interpreting of all kinds, but particularly technical and commercial translation. As a full and active member of the International Federation of Translators, it maintains good contacts with translators and interpreters worldwide. ITI's directory of members (online and in CD-Rom) and its bi-monthly bulletin are available from the Secretariat.

The Translators Association

84 Drayton Gardens, London SW10 9SB
tel 020-7373 6642
email info@societyofauthors.org
website www.societyofauthors.org
Membership £75 p.a. (£70 DD), including membership of the Society of Authors

Specialist unit within the membership of the Society of Authors (see page 504), exclusively concerned with the interests and special problems of translators into English whose work is published or performed commercially in Great Britain and English-speaking countries overseas. Members are entitled to general and legal advice on all questions connected with their work, including remuneration and contractual arrangements with publishers, editors, broadcasting organisations. Publishes a *Quick Guide* to literary translation (£2 to non-members). Administers a range of translation prizes. Founded 1958

Travel Writers, The British Guild of

Hon. Secretary Melissa Shales, 91 Amesbury Avenue, London SW2 3AF
tel/fax 020-8674 7406
email m.shales@virgin.net
website www.bgtw.org

Arranges meetings, discussions and visits for its 220 members (who are all professional travel journalists) to promote and encourage the public's interest in travel. Publishes a monthly newsletter (for members only) and an annual *Yearbook,* which contains details of members and lists travel industry PRs and contacts. Annual awards for journalism (members only) and the travel trade.

The Trollope Society

9A North Street, London SW4 0HN
tel 020-7720 6789 *fax* 020-978 1815
email trolsoc@barset.fsnet.co.uk
Chairman John Letts, *Secretary* Phyllis Eden
Membership £24 p.a., £240 life

Has produced the first ever complete edition of the novels of Anthony Trollope (48 vols now available). New 3-year extension will make this into the 'Complete Works' (60 vols by 2004). Founded 1987.

The Turner Society

BCM Box Turner, London WC1N 3XX
Chairman Eric Shanes
Membership £15 p.a.

To foster a wider appreciation of all facets of Turner's work; to encourage exhibitions of his paintings, drawings and engravings. Publishes *Turner Society News* (3 p.a.). Founded 1975.

Typographic Designers, International Society of

Hon. Secretary Helen Cornish, Chapelfield Cottage, Randwick, Stroud, Glos. GL6 6HS
tel (01453) 759311 *fax* (01453) 767466
email helen.randwick@virgin.net
President Colin Banks FSTD, *Chair* Freda Sack FSTD

Advises and acts on matters of professional and educational practice, provides a better understanding of the typographic craft and the rapidly changing technology in the graphic industries by lectures, discussions and through the journal *Typographic.* Students of typography and graphic design are encouraged to gain membership of the Society by entering the annual student assessment project. Founded 1928.

Vampire Research Society

International Secretary Dennis Crawford, PO Box 542, London N6 5FZ
email vampireresearchsociety@gothicpress.freeserve.co.uk
Membership By invitation

The Society's sole purpose is to study and investigate vampirological phenomena, and publishes its research findings in books and academic reports. Holds the largest archive of vampire-related material in the world, to which membership allows access. Publishes a newsletter. Not affiliated to any other vampire interest group and remains aloof from the wider subculture. Founded 1970.

Ver Poets

Organiser/Editor May Badman, Haycroft, 61-63 Chiswell Green Lane, St Albans, Herts. AL2 3AL
tel (01727) 867005
Membership £12.50 p.a. UK, £15/$30 overseas

Encourages the writing and study of poetry as a part of our culture. Help and advice, assessment and comment on work are available on request. Holds meetings (fortnightly) in St Albans; organises workshops and competitions for members, and produces anthologies of members' work. The annual Open Competition (October) is also open to non-members. Founded 1966.

Visiting Arts

11 Portland Place, London W1B 1EJ
tel 020-7389 3019 *fax* 020-7389 3016
email visiting.arts@britishcouncil.org
website www.visitingarts.org.uk
Director Terry Sandell OBE

The national agency for promoting the flow of international arts into the UK and developing related cultural links abroad to help build cultural awareness, positive cultural relations and fostering mutually beneficial arts contacts at national, regional, local and institutional levels. Activities include providing advice, information, training, consultancy, publications, special projects and project development and covers the performing arts, visual, applied and media arts, crafts, design, literature, film, architecture and some museum activity.

Visiting Arts is an independent educational charity jointly funded by the Arts Council of England, the Scottish Arts Council, the Arts Council of Wales and the Arts Council of Northern Ireland, the Foreign and Commonwealth Office and the British Council. Founded 1977.

Visual Communication Association, International (IVCA)

19 Pepper Street, Glengall Bridge, London E14 9RP
tel 020-7512 0571 *fax* 020-7512 0591
email info@ivca.org
website www.ivca.org
Membership Secretary Nick Gardiner

Membership From £175 p.a.

For those who use or supply visual communication. Aims to promote the industry and provide a collective voice; provides a range of services, publications and events to help existing and potential users to make the most of what video, film, multimedia andlive events can offer their business. Founded 1987.

Voice of the Listener & Viewer (VLV)
101 King's Drive, Gravesend, Kent DA12 5BQ
tel (01474) 352835
Chairman Jocelyn Hay, *Administrative Secretary* Linda Forbes

Independent association representing the citizen and consumer interest in broadcasting and the interests of listeners and viewers on all broadcasting issues at UK and European level. Concerned to maintain the principle of public service plus independence, quality and diversity in British broadcasting. Has over 2000 individual members, nearly 30 charities as corporate members and more than 50 colleges in academic membership. Holds frequent public conferences all over UK. Maintains a panel of speakers. Holds the archives of the former Broadcasting Research Unit (1980–90), British Action for Children's Television (BACTV) 1988–94, as well as its own archive. Publishes a quarterly newsletter and briefings on broadcasting developments. Founded 1983.

Wales, Arts Council of – see Arts Council of Wales

The Walmsley Society
Secretary Fred Lane, April Cottage, 1 Brand Road, Hampden Park, Eastbourne, East Sussex BN22 9PX
Membership Secretary Mrs Elizabeth Buckley, 21 The Crescent, Hipperholm, Halifax, West Yorkshire HX3 8NQ

Aims to promote and encourage an appreciation of the literary and artistic heritage left to us by Leo and J. Ulric Walmsley. Founded 1985.

Water Colours, Royal Institute of Painters in
17 Carlton House Terrace, London SW1Y 5BD
tel 020-7930 6844 *fax* 020-7839 7830
website www.mallgalleries.org.uk
President Ronald Maddox Hon. RWS
Membership Elected from approved candidates' list

The Institute promotes the appreciation of watercolour painting in its traditional and contemporary forms, primarily by means of an annual exhibition at the Mall Galleries, London SW1 of members' and non-members' work and also by members' exhibitions at selected venues in Britain and abroad. Founded 1831.

Watercolour Society, British
Director Margaret Simpson, Briargate, 2 The Brambles, Ilkley, West Yorkshire LS29 9DH
tel (01943) 609075

Promotes the best in traditional watercolour painting. Holds 2 open exhibitions a year. Founded 1830.

Watercolour Society, Royal
Bankside Gallery, 48 Hopton Street, London SE1 9JH
tel 020-7928 7521
email info@banksidegallery.com
website www.banksidegallery.com
President Francis Bowyer PPRWS
Membership Open to British and overseas artists. Election of Associates held annually; write to the Secretary for particulars

Arranges lectures on watercolour paintings; organises residential/non-residential courses; holds open exhibition in summer. Exhibitions: spring and autumn. Friends of the RWS open to all those interested in watercolour painting. Founded 1804.

Mary Webb Society
Secretary Sue Higginbotham, 8 The Knowe, Willaston, Neston, Cheshire CH64 1TA
tel 0151-327 5843
email suehigginbotham@yahoo.co.uk
website www.marywebb.2ya.com

For devotees of the literature and works of Mary Webb and of the beautiful Shropshire countryside of her novels. Publishes an annual journal, organises summer schools and other events in various locations related to Webb's life and works. Archives, lectures; tours arranged for individuals and groups. Founded 1972.

The H.G. Wells Society
Hon. General Secretary J.R. Hammond, 49 Beckingthorpe Drive, Bottesford, Nottingham NG13 0DN
website http://hgwellsusa.50megs.com
Membership £16 p.a., £20 corporate

Promotes an active interest in and an appreciation of the life, work and thought of H.G. Wells. Publishes *The*

Wellsian (annual) and *The Newsletter* (bi-annual). Founded 1960.

Welsh Academy – see Academi

Welsh Books Council/Cyngor Llyfrau Cymru
Castell Brychan, Aberystwyth,
Ceredigion SY23 2JB
tel (01970) 624151 *fax* (01970) 625385
email castellbrychan@cllc.org.uk
website www.cllc.org.uk www.gwales.com
Director Gwerfyl Pierce Jones

Founded in 1961 to promote Welsh-language and English-language books of Welsh interest. Editorial, design, marketing, distribution and children's books promotion services provided for publishers.

The West Country Writers' Association
Acting Secretary Bob Cooper, Taylor's Cottage, Little Wittenham, Abingdon, Oxon OX14 4RD
tel (01865) 407827
website www.westcountrywriters.co.uk
President Christopher Fry FRSL DLitt,
Chair Dr David Keep
Membership Open to published authors, £10 p.a.

To foster love of literature in the West Country and to give authors an opportunity of meeting to exchange news and views. Holds Annual Weekend Congress and Regional Meetings. Newsletter (2 p.a.).

West of England Academy, Royal
Queens Road, Clifton, Bristol BS8 1PX
tel 0117-973 5129 *fax* 0117-923 7874
website www.rwa.org.uk
President Derek Balmer, *Academy Secretary* Rachel Fear

To advance the education of the public in the fine arts and in particular to promote the appreciation and practice of the fine arts and to encourage and develop talent in the fine arts. Founded 1844.

The Oscar Wilde Society
100 Peacock Street, Gravesend, Kent DA12 1EQ
tel (01474) 535 978
email vanessa@salome.co.uk
Secretary Vanessa Harris

To promote knowledge, appreciation and study of the life, personality and works of the writer and wit Oscar Wilde (1854–1900). Activities include meetings, lectures, readings and exhibitions, and visits to associated locations. Members receive a journal, *The Wildean* (2 p.a.), and a newsletter, *Intentions* (6 p.a.). Founded 1990.

Wildlife Artists, Society of
17 Carlton House Terrace, London SW1Y 5BD
tel 020-7930 6844 *fax* 020-7839 7830
President Bruce Pearson

To promote and encourage the art of wildlife painting and sculpture. Open Annual Exhibition at the Mall Galleries, The Mall, London SW1, for any artist whose work depicts wildlife subjects (botanical and domestic animals are not admissable).

Charles Williams Society
Secretary Richard Sturch, 35 Broomfield, Stacey Bushes, Milton Keynes MK12 6HA

To promote interest in the life and work of Charles Walter Stansby Williams (1886–1945) and to make his writings more easily available. Founded 1975.

The Henry Williamson Society
General Secretary Sue Cumming,
7 Monmouth Road, Dorchester, Dorset DT1 2DE
tel (01305) 264092
email zseagull@aol.com
website www.hwsoc.org.uk
Membership Secretary Margaret Murphy,
16 Doran Drive, Redhill, Surrey RH1 6AX
tel (01737) 763228
email mm@misterman.freeserve.co.uk
Chairman Margaret White
Membership £12 p.a.

Aims to encourage a wider readership and greater understanding of the literary heritage left by Henry Williamson. Two meetings annually; also weekend activities. Publishes an annual journal. Founded 1980.

Circle of Wine Writers
Secretary John Radford, 121 Brighton Road, Worthing, West Sussex BN11 2ES
tel (07000) 790148 *fax* (01903) 602574
email john@johnradford.com
website www.circleofwinewriters.org
Membership By election, £45 p.a.

An association for those engaged in communicating about wines and spirits. Produces *Circle Update* newsletter (5 p.a.), organises tasting sessions as well as a programme of meetings and talks. Founded 1960.

The P.G. Wodehouse Society (UK)
Details Tony Ring, 34 Longfield,
Great Missenden, Bucks. HP16 0EG
tel (01494) 864848 *fax* (01494) 863048
email tring@sauce34.freeserve.co.uk
website www.eclipse.co.uk/wodehouse

Membership £15 p.a.

Aims to promote enjoyment of P.G. Wodehouse (1881–1975). Publishes *Wooster Sauce* (quarterly) and *By The Way* papers (3 p.a.) which cover diverse subjects of Wodehousean interest. Holds events, entertainments and meetings throughout Britain. Founded 1997.

Women Artists, The Society of

Executive Secretary 1 Knapp Cottages, Wyke, Gillingham, Dorset SP8 4NQ
tel (01747) 825718 *fax* (01747) 826835
email hendersons@dial.pipex.com
website www.society-women-artists.org.uk
President Elizabeth Meek RMS, HS, FRSA
Membership Election by invitation, based on work submitted to the exhibition

Founded in 1855 when women were not considered as serious contributors to art and could not compete for professional honours, the Society continues to promote art by women. Receiving day end January for annual open exhibition held just before Easter at Westminster Gallery, Central Hall Westminster, Storey's Gate, London SW1H 9NH.

Women in Publishing

c/o The Publishers Association,
29B Montague Street, London WC1B 5BH
email wipub@hotmail.com
website www.cyberiacafe.net/wip/
Membership £25 p.a.

Promotes the status of women within publishing; encourages networking and mutual support among women; provides a forum for the discussion of ideas, trends and subjects to women in the trade; offers practical training for career and personal development; supports and publicises women's achievements and successes. Each year WiP presents 2 awards: the Pandora Award is given in recognition of significant personal contributions to women in publishing, and the New Venture Award is presented to a recent venture which reflects the interests and concerns of women or minority groups in the 21st century. Founded 1979.

Women Writers and Journalists, Society of

Secretary Jennie Davidson, 4 Larch Way, Haywards Heath, West Sussex RH16 3TY
tel (01444) 416866
email swwriters@aol.com
Membership £35 p.a. town, £30 country, £25 overseas; £20 joining fee

For women writers: lectures, monthly workshops/speakers; members' postal critique service. *The Woman Writer* (4 p.a.). Founded 1894.

Women Writers Network

Membership Secretary Cathy Smith, 23 Prospect Road, London NW2 2JU
tel 020-7794 5861
Membership £40 p.a.; meetings only: £5 at door

London-based network serving both salaried and independent women writers from all disciplines, and providing a forum for the exchange of information, support and networking opportunities. Holds monthly meetings, workshops and publishes a newsletter and members' online Directory. Send sae for information. Founded 1985.

Virginia Woolf Society of Great Britain

Details Stuart N. Clarke, Fairhaven, Charnleys Lane, Banks, Southport PR9 8HJ
tel/fax (01903) 764655
email snclarke@talk21.com
website http://orlando.jp.org/vwsgb/
Membership £12 p.a., £15 overseas

Acts as a forum for British admirers of Virginia Woolf (1882–1941) to meet, correspond and share their enjoyment of her work. Publishes the *Virginia Woolf Bulletin*. Founded 1998.

Worker Writers and Community Publishers, The Federation of

Burslem School of Art, Queen Street, Stoke-on-Tent ST6 3EJ
tel/fax (01782) 822327
email thefwwcp@tislali.co.uk
website www.thefwwcp.org.uk
Membership £40 p.a. funded groups; £20 unfunded

A network of writers groups and community publishers which promotes working-class writing and publishing. Founded 1976.

Writernet

(formerly New Playwrights Trust)
Cabin V, Clarendon Buildings, 25 Horsell Road, London N5 1XL
tel 020-7609 7474 *fax* 020-7609 7557
email writernet@btinternet.com
website www.writernet.org.uk
Executive Director Jonathan Meth
Membership Rates on application

Research and development organisation

for writers and aspiring writers for all forms of live and recorded performance, and those interested in developing and producing new work. Services include script-reading; information guides; 6-weekly *Newsletter*.

The Writers Advice Centre for Children's Books
The Courtyard Studio, 43 Lesbourne Road, Reigate, Surrey RH2 7JS
tel (01737) 242999
email WritersAdvice@aol.com
Director Cherith Baldry

Editorial and marketing advice to children's writers. Founded 1994.

Writers' Circles Handbook
Contact Jill Dick, Oldacre, Horderns Park Road, Chapel-en-le-Frith, High Peak SK23 9SY
tel (01298) 812305
email jillie@cix.co.uk oldacre@bt.internet.com
website www.btinternet.com/~oldacre

Handbook for writers' circles with information, articles, and a comprehensive list of all known circles and groups meeting in the UK. Some overseas entries too. Regular free updates available after initial purchase. Contact author Jill Dick for details.

Writers' Groups, National Association of
The Arts Centre, Biddick Lane, Washington, Tyne and Wear NE38 8AB
tel 0191-416 9751 *fax* 0191-431 1263
Secretary Brian Lister
Membership £20 p.a. plus £5 registration per group; £10 Associate individuals

Aims 'to advance the education of the general public throughout the UK, including the Channel Islands, by promoting the study and art of writing in all its aspects.' Founded 1995.

Writers Guild of America, East Inc. (WGAE)
Executive Director Mona Mangan, 555 West 57 Street, Suite 1230, New York, NY 10019, USA
tel 212-767-7800
Membership 1.5% of covered earnings

Writers Guild of America, West Inc. (WGA)
Executive Director John McLean, 7000 West 3rd Street, Los Angeles, CA 90048, USA
tel 323-951-4000 *fax* 323-782-4800
website www.wga.org
Membership $2500 initiation, $25 quarterly, 1.5% of income annually

The Writers' Guild of Great Britain – see page 506

Writers in Oxford
Membership Secretary Brian Levison, 6 Princes Street, Oxford OX4 1DD
tel (01865) 791202
email brian@levison.fslife.co.uk
Membership £20 p.a.

To promote valuable discussion and social meetings among all kinds of published writers in and around Oxfordshire. Activities include: topical lunches and dinners, where subjects important to the writer are discussed; showcase evenings; parties. Termly newsletter, *The Oxford Writer*. Founded 1992.

Yachting Journalists' Association
3 Friars Lane, Maldon, Essex CM9 6AG
tel (01621) 855943 *fax* (01621) 852212
email yjauk@cs.com
Secretary Peter Cook
Membership £30 p.a.

Aims to further the interests of yachting, sail and power, and yachting journalism. Members vote annually for the Yachtsman of the Year, headline title of the British Nautical Awards, and the Young Sailor of the Year Award. Founded 1969.

The Yorkshire Dialect Society
Hon. Secretary Michael Park, 51 Stepney Avenue, Scarborough YO12 5BW
Membership £7 p.a. (£10 from 1 Jan 2003)

Aims to encourage interest in: dialect speech, the writing of dialect verse, prose and drama; the publication and circulation of dialect literature; the study of the origins and the history of dialect and kindred subjects. Organises meetings; publishes *Transactions* (annual) and *The Summer Bulletin* free to members; list of other publications on request. Founded 1897.

Francis Brett Young Society
Secretary Mrs J. Hadley, 92 Gower Road, Halesowen, West Midlands B62 9BT
tel 0121-422 8969
website www.fbysociety.co.uk
Membership £7 p.a., £70 p.a. life

To provide opportunities for members to meet, correspond, and to share the enjoyment of the author's works. Journal published 2 p.a. Founded 1979.

The Society of Authors

The Society of Authors is an independent trade union, representing writers' interests in all aspects of the writing profession, particularly publishing, but also broadcasting, television and films, theatre and translation.

Founded over 100 years ago by Walter Besant, the Society now has more than 7000 members. It has a professional staff, responsible to a Management Committee of 12 authors, and a Council (an advisory body meeting twice a year) consisting of 60 eminent writers. There are specialist groups within the Society to serve particular needs: the Academic Writers Group, the Broadcasting Group, the Children's Writers and Illustrators Group, the Educational Writers Group, the Medical Writers Group and the Translators Association (see page 498). There are also groups representing Scotland and the North of England.

> "When we begin working, we are so poor and so busy that we have neither the time nor the means to defend ourselves against the commercial organisations which exploit us. When we become famous, we become famous suddenly, passing at one bound from the state in which we are, as I have said, too poor to fight our own battles, to a state in which our time is so valuable that it is not worth our while wasting any of it on lawsuits and bad debts. We all, eminent and obscure alike, need the Authors' Society. We all owe it a share of our time, our means, our influence"
>
> – *Bernard Shaw*

What the Society does for members

Through its permanent staff (including a solicitor), the Society is able to give its members a comprehensive personal and professional service covering the business aspects of authorship, including:

- providing information about agents, publishers, and others concerned with the book trade, journalism, broadcasting and the performing arts;
- advising on negotiations, including the individual vetting of contracts, clause by clause, and assessing their terms both financial and otherwise;
- taking up complaints on behalf of members on any issue concerned with the business of authorship;
- pursuing legal actions for breach of contract, copyright infringement, and the non-payment of royalties and fees, when the risk and cost preclude individual action by a member and issues of general concern to the profession are at stake;
- holding conferences, seminars, meetings and social occasions;
- producing a comprehensive range of publications, free of charge to members, including the Society's quarterly journal, *The Author*. *Quick Guides* cover many aspects of the profession such as: copyright, publishing contracts, libel, income tax, VAT, authors' agents, permissions, indexing, and the protection of titles. The Society also publishes occasional papers on subjects such as film agreements, packaged books, revised editions, multimedia, and vanity publishing.

Further membership benefits

Members have access to:

- the Retirement Benefit Scheme;
- a group Medical Insurance Scheme with BUPA;
- the Pension Fund (which offers discretionary pensions to a number of members)

- the Contingency Fund (which provides financial relief for authors or their dependents in sudden financial difficulties);
- automatic free membership of the Authors' Licensing and Collecting Society (ALCS);
- books at special rates;
- membership of the Royal Over-Seas League at a discount;
- use of the Society's photocopier at special rates.

The Society frequently secures improved conditions and better returns for members. It is common for members to report that, through the help and facilities offered, they have saved more, and sometimes substantially more, than their annual subscriptions (which are an allowable expense against income tax).

What the Society does for authors

The Society lobbies Members of Parliament, Ministers and Government Departments on all issues of concern to writers. Recent issues have included the operation and funding of Public Lending Right, the threat of VAT on books, copyright legislation and European Community initiatives. Concessions have also been obtained under various Finance Acts.

The Society litigates in matters of importance to authors. For example, the Society backed Andrew Boyle when he won his appeal against the Inland Revenue's attempt to tax the Whitbread Award.

The Society campaigns for better terms for writers. With the Writers' Guild, it has negotiated 'minimum terms agreements' with many leading publishers. The translators' section of the Society has also drawn up a minimum terms agreement for translators which has been adopted by Faber & Faber, and has been used on an individual basis by a number of other publishers.

The Society is recognised by the BBC for the purpose of negotiating rates for writers' contributions to radio drama, as well as for the broadcasting of published material. It was instrumental in setting up the ALCS (see page 640), which collects and distributes fees from reprography and other methods whereby copyright material is exploited without direct payment to the originators.

The Society keeps in close touch with the Arts Councils, the Association of Authors' Agents, the British Council, the Broadcasting Entertainment Cinematograph and Theatre Union, the Institute of Translation and Interpreting, the Department for Culture, Media and Sport, the National Union of Journalists, the Publishers Association and the Writers' Guild of Great Britain.

The Society is a member of the European

Membership

The Society of Authors
84 Drayton Gardens, London SW10 9SB
tel 020-7373 6642
email info@societyofauthors.org
website www.societyofauthors.org
General Secretary Mark Le Fanu

Membership at the discretion of the Committee of Management is open to authors who have had a full-length work published, broadcast or performed commercially in the UK. It is also open to authors who have had a full-length work accepted for publication, but not yet published; and those authors who have had occasional items broadcast or performed, or translations, articles, illustrations or short stories published. The owner or administrator of a deceased author's copyrights can become a member on behalf of the author's estate.

The annual subscription (which is tax deductible under Schedule D) is £75 (£70 by direct debit after the first year), and there are special joint membership terms for husband and wife. Authors under 35, who are not yet earning a significant income from their writing, may apply for membership at a lower subscription of £55. Authors over 65 may apply to pay at the reduced rate after their first year of membership.

Contact the Society for a free membership booklet and copy of *The Author*.

Writers Congress, the British Copyright Council and the National Book Committee.

Awards

The Society of Authors administers:
• Travelling Scholarships which give honorary awards;
• four prizes for novels: the Betty Trask Awards, the Encore Award, the McKitterick Prize and the Sagittarius Prize;
• two prizes for a full-length published work: the Somerset Maugham Awards and the *Sunday Times* Young Writer of the Year Award;
• two poetry awards: the Eric Gregory Awards and the Cholmondeley Awards;
• the Tom-Gallon Award for short story writers;
• the Authors' Foundation and Kathleen Blundell Trust, which give grants to published authors working on their next book;
• the Margaret Rhondda Award for women journalists;
• awards for translations from French, German, Italian, Dutch, Portuguese, Spanish, Swedish and Japanese into English;
• the Francis Head Bequest for assisting authors who, through physical mishap, are temporarily unable to maintain themselves or their families.

The Writers' Guild of Great Britain

The Writers' Guild of Great Britain is the writers' trade union and is affiliated to the TUC.

The Writers' Guild of Great Britain is the writers' trade union, affiliated to the TUC, and represents writers' interests in film, television, radio, theatre and publishing. Formed in 1959 as the Screenwriters' Guild, the union gradually extended into all areas of freelance writing activity and copyright protection. In 1974, when book authors and stage dramatists became eligible for membership, substantial numbers joined. In June 1997 the Theatre Writers' Union membership unified with that of the Writers' Guild to create a larger, more powerful writers' union.

Apart from necessary dealings with Government and policies on legislative matters affecting writers, the Guild is, by constitution, non-political, has no involvement with any political party, and members pay no political levy.

The Guild employs a permanent secretary and staff and is administered by an Executive Council of 26 members. The Guild has a national and regional/branch structure with committees representing Scotland, Wales, London and the South East, the North West, the North East, the Midlands and the South West of England.

The Guild comprises practising professional writers in all media, united in common concern for one another and regulating the conditions under which they work.

The Writers' Guild and agreements

The Guild's basic function is to negotiate minimum terms in those areas in which its members work. Those agreements form the basis of the individual contracts signed by members. Further details are given below. The Guild also gives individual advice to its members on contracts and other matters which the writer encounters in his or her professional life.

Television

The Guild has national agreements with the BBC, the ITV companies, PACT (Producers Alliance for Cinema and Television) and TAC (representing Welsh language television producers). These agreements regulate minimum fees and going rates, copyright licence, credit terms and conditions for television plays, series and serials, dramatisations and adaptations. One of the Guild's most important achievements has been the establishment of pension rights for members. The BBC pays an additional 8% of the going rate on the understanding that the Guild member pays 5% of his or her fee. ITV companies now pay an additional 8% and the writer 5%.

The advent of digital and cable television channels and the creation of the BBC's commercial arm has seen the Guild in constant negotiation. The Guild now has agreements for all of the BBC's digital channels and for its joint venture channels.

In 1997, the Guild negotiated substantial revised terms and conditions for writers who are commissioned by the ITV companies. The new agreement includes a provision for the non-arms length sale of material to digital and cable channels, thus ensuring that writers receive market prices for the use of their material on these new channels.

Film

On 11 March 1985, an important agreement was signed with the two producer organisations: the British Film and Television Producers' Association and the Independent Programme Producers Association (now known as PACT, the Producers' Alliance for Cinema and Television). Since then there has been an industrial agreement which covers both independent television productions and independent film productions. Pension fund contributions have been negotiated for Guild members in the same way as for the BBC and ITV. The Agreement was renegotiated in February 1992 and negotiations on an updated agreement are in progress.

Radio

The Guild has a standard agreement for Radio Drama with the BBC, establishing a fee structure which is annually reviewed. The current agreement includes a Code of Practice which is important for establishing good working conditions for the writer working for the BBC. In December 1985 the BBC agreed to extend the pension scheme already established for television writers to include radio writers. In 1994 a comprehensive revision of the Agreement was undertaken. The Guild negotiated special agreements for the new daily serial on Radio 4, the new World Service soap *West Way*, the BBC Radio Wales soap *Station Road*, and for the online streaming of BBC Radio services.

Books

The Guild fought long, hard and successfully for the loans-based Public Lending Right to reimburse authors for books lent in libraries. This is now law and the Guild is constantly in touch with the Registrar of the scheme, which is administered from offices in Stockton-on-Tees.

The Guild, together with the Society of Authors, has drawn up a draft Minimum Terms Book Agreement which has been widely circulated amongst publishers. A new model contract is in preparation.

Theatre

In 1979 the Guild, together with the Theatre Writers' Union, negotiated the first ever industrial agreement for theatre writers. The Theatres National Committee Agreement covers the Royal Shakespeare Company, the National Theatre Company and the English Stage Company.

In June 1986, a new agreement was signed with the Theatrical Management Association, which covers some 95 provincial theatres. In 1993, this agreement was comprehensively revised and included a provision for a year-on-year increase in fees in line with the Retail Price Index.

After many years of negotiation, an agreement was concluded in 1991 between the Guild and the Independent Theatre Council, which represents some 200 of the smaller and fringe theatres as well as educational, touring companies.

Other activities

The Guild is in constant touch with Government and national institutions wherever and whenever the interests of writers are in question or are being discussed. The Guild holds cross-party Parliamentary lobbies with Equity and the Musicians Union to ensure that the various art forms they represent are properly cared for.

Working with the Federation of Entertainment Unions, the Guild makes its views known to Government bodies on a broader basis. It keeps in touch with the Arts Councils of Great Britain, the Independent Television Commission and other national bodies.

The Guild has close working relationships with Equity and the Musicians' Union and have agreed to work closely together where they share a common interest.

Internationally, the Guild plays a leading role in the International Affiliation of Writers' Guilds, which includes the American Guilds East and West, the Canadian Guilds (French and English), and the Australian and New Zealand Guilds. When it is possible to make common cause, the Guilds act accordingly.

The Guild takes a leading role in the European Writers' Congress, which is becoming increasingly important and successful. The Guild is becoming more involved with matters at European level where the harmonisation of copyright law and the regulation of a converged audiovisual/telecommunications are of immediate interest.

Membership

The Writers' Guild of Great Britain
(incorporating the Theatre Writers' Union)
430 Edgware Road, London W2 1EH
tel 020-7723 8074 *fax* 020-7706 2413
email admin@writersguild.org.uk
website www.writersguild.org.uk
General Secretary Bernie Corbett

Membership of the Guild is open to all persons entitled to claim a single piece of written work of any length for which payment has been received under written contract in terms not less favourable than those existing in current minimum terms agreements negotiated by the Guild. Candidate membership (£55) is open to all those who are taking their first steps into writing but who have not yet received a contract.

The minimum subscription is currently £125 plus 1% of that part of an author's income earned from professional writing sources in the previous calendar year with a cap of £1250.

All Full members are automatically members of the Authors Licensing and Collecting Society (ALCS). The Guild is a corporate member of the ALCS and maintains its links through representation on its board.

Members receive the *Writers' Bulletin*, which carries articles, letters and reports written by members.They are entitled to various other benefits, such as free entry to the British Library reading rooms, and reduced entry to the National Film Theatre.

Membership activities

The Guild in its day-to-day work takes up problems on behalf of individual members, gives advice on contracts, and helps with any problems which affect the lives of its members as professional writers. It now has a legal hotline so that members can quickly and easily seek legal advice.

Regular Craft Meetings are held by all the Guild's specialist committees. This gives Guild members the opportunity of meeting those who control, work within, or affect the sphere of writing within which they work.

In conclusion

The writer is an isolated individual in a world in which individual voices are not always heard. The Guild brings together those writers in order to make common cause in respect of the many vitally important matters which are susceptible to influence only from the position of the collective strength which the Guild enjoys.

Writers' circles

Writers' circles have much to offer writers whether they are beginners or full-time published writers. Members can offer criticism of each others' work, share knowledge and ideas, and arrange for speakers to visit them. ***Jill Dick*** *sets the scene.*

"Once I had joined a writers' circle," says a now well-established author, "I never looked back. As a beginner I was bursting with enthusiasm but had no idea how to channel it onto the right lines – and, more importantly, I lacked practical knowledge." A playwright remembers his early experience of a circle: "I found a small group with several members able and willing to give me real help... until then I'd had no success in selling my work. There really is no substitute for hands-on guidance and talking through your problems with other folk who have the experience to steer you."

Are you a member of a writers' circle? Or are you struggling alone, in need of help with your writing but unsure where and how to find it? Perhaps, like one poet with much published verse to her credit, you are already finding that contact with other writers is a spur to working even harder, to gaining more success, and to enjoying greater fulfillment in your writing. For writing is essentially a lonely business. Only you can decide what you are going to write – novels, short stories, articles, poems, plays, television sit-coms or any other *genre* that stirs your imagination – and if you are going to make a success of it you will spend most of your time at work, in solitude.

Maybe you won't notice the hours and days pass by when all is going well, when you're in full flow, and your fingers can't write or type quickly enough. Even then, perhaps especially then, the need for the stimulation of others who understand what you are doing can be invaluable, as many professional writers agree. "If I can't get out and meet other people every now and then," claims a leading novelist, "my characters and I become the only people in our little world, and that's not good for either of us."

What are writers' circles?

Writers' circles vary in size and are generally open to all levels of writers, from beginners to those who write full-time. Members are like-minded souls and often good friends through love of the craft of writing.

Members of Wrekin Writers (one of many well-run circles) are aged from 18 to 80 and some members' work has been published while others write purely for pleasure. The circle's policy is that a writer is someone who *writes* and its encouragement for members to take prepared work to monthly meetings spurs them into persisting with their current projects. "If it weren't for the circle," says one member, "I'd be a writer but not such a happy one."

Tips and hints from circle members often bring out others' talent. "I knew that whatever I wanted to write needed a strong opening," confessed one determined article writer," but I couldn't begin without a lot of waffle, as if I had to get it out of my system at first. The real story would begin in about paragraph five. Then I listened to a circle discussion about intros – opening words and sentences – and suddenly I realised how to clear my mind and get straight to the point. After some practice at home I mastered it, and this knowledge has stood me in good stead with editors ever since."

Most circles vary their programmes according to members' needs. For example, interviewing techniques may be discussed, or guidelines may be given on how to write query letters to editors. Other topics may include information on competitions to enter, news of writing successes and an exchange of market information (editors move, editorial policies change, titles merge, new ones are launched and others fold – market study never ends). The *Writers' & Artists' Yearbook* and other published guides may be studied and recent editions of books and magazines borrowed or lent.

Popular meetings give members the chance of hearing visiting speakers – a well-known writer's advice may put newcomers on the right tracks – while others offer time for general discussion on such topics as the use of illustrations, syndicating published work, the cost of vanity publishing and self-publishing, writing to deadlines, and the importance (or unimportance) of grammar – the list of likely topics for mutual discussion and enlightenment is endless. Practical sessions led by experts may cover income tax, VAT, copyright problems and keeping accounts. Getting to grips with the business side of being a writer is essential if you're working on your own.

The best circles are comprehensive and versatile in their activities. Their members may invite and visit other circles, providing the opportunity to benefit from sharing working experiences: they may hold brainstorming sessions and specialist 'surgeries' on a one-to-one member-and-expert basis; they may also create circle newsletters and publish members' work. They are imaginative, vigorous and well-organised – small wonder such groups wean successful writers.

The pros and cons

The internet offers contact with other writers through online circles but browsing, like writing, is a solitary occupation. It can be more beneficial to go to a writers' circle and meet other people there. The most valuable outcome of joining a circle can be seeing afresh what you are writing, or want to write, through new eyes.

One lady who'd thought of herself only as a non-fiction writer realised she had a gift for comedy writing through success in a circle's monthly competition. "I felt I ought to enter to support the circle," she said when the results were announced, "but I had no idea how much I would enjoy this type of writing." Another member had never tackled poetry, afraid of putting his emotions into words, but discovered a surge of delight with his first steps into writing poems.

The snags? Of course all writers' circles are not the same, and not all offer unalloyed help to other writers. Because they vary widely it is wise to establish the aims, scope and working structure of any you may consider joining. Do you want to take part in workshops – generally practical working sessions where written work is prepared and criticised among members? Maybe your novel is not moving forward and words from a distinguished visiting novelist will show you the path to follow. Some circles divide their members into small groups according to their writing proclivities or levels of skill: you may find a group dedicated to your particular field more stimulating – and less time-wasting – than joining a larger class with varied interests.

Further information

The Writers' Circles Handbook
Contact Jill Dick, Oldacre, Horderns Park Road, Chapel-en-le-Frith, High Peak SK23 9SY
tel (01298) 812305
email jillie@cix.co.uk
website www.btinternet.com/~oldacre
Contains invaluable information, articles, and a comprehensive list of all known circles and groups meeting in the UK, with some overseas entries. Regular free updates are available after initial purchase.

Starting a circle

If there isn't a circle in your neighbourhood perhaps you could start one. Many writers' circles exist because a group of frustrated writers couldn't find one and decided to start their own. Does initial research indicate enough writers will be attracted to a new circle to make it viable? Where will meetings be held, how frequently and at what charge? Remember to consider the cost of refreshments and expenses incurred in hiring or acquiring a meeting place. Helpful members may offer their own homes as venues but while such offers may be financial lifelines, normal social pleasantries may stifle the circle's wider activities. Printing, publicity, advertising and guest speakers can be costly; how much will writers be prepared to pay for membership and when? Once goals are planned, meetings must be carefully structured and timed. This calls for sound practical sense, patience and – at times – unlimited tact: everything depends on those at the top.

Pitfalls include the burden of dominant individuals spoiling meetings for others, a disregard for commercial marketing and too much talking about writing rather than doing it. Well-established groups may, without intention, deter newcomers who are essential for a breath of fresh air. The most widespread criticism is that written work is always pronounced excellent, members being too polite to say otherwise. It's hard to accept, but only comment by folk who really know what they are talking about is to everyone's ultimate advantage.

A well-run circle can transform a writer's life, enriching working practice and extending writing horizons. I believe no writer is ever bored even though we spend a lot of time alone. With a writers' circle within reach no writer need ever be lonely. Good writing!

Jill Dick has spent many years working for national, regional and local newspapers as a feature writer, columnist, reviewer and departmental editor. She is compiler/editor of *The Writers' Circles Handbook* and her published books include *Freelance Writing for Newspapers* and *Writing for Magazines*, both now in second editions and published by A & C Black.

Prizes and awards

This list provides details of many British prizes, competitions and awards for writers and artists, including grants, bursaries and fellowships, as well as details of major international prizes. See page 541 for a quick reference to its contents.

ABSW/Glaxo Science Writers Awards

Details Barbara Drillsma, Association of British Science Writers, 23 Savile Row, London W1X 2NB
tel 020-7439 1205 *fax* 020-7973 3051

Awards are given to the writers who, in the opinion of the judges, have done most to enhance the quality of science journalism. Entries will be accepted from specialist writers, newspaper reporters and freelances. There are 7 categories, each worth £2500. Organised in conjunction in the Association of British Science Writers. Closing date: 31 January. Founded 1966.

J.R. Ackerley Prize for Autobiography

Information PEN, 152-6 Kentish Town Road, London NW1 9QB
tel 020-7267 9444 *fax* 020-7267 9304

An annual prize given for an outstanding work of literary autobiography written in English and published during the previous year by an author of British nationality or an author who has been a long-term resident in the UK. No submissions please – books are nominated by the judges only. First awarded in 1982.

The Alexander Prize

Literary Director, Royal Historical Society, University College London, Gower Street, London WC1E 6BT
tel 020-7387 7532 *fax* 020-7387 7532
email royalhistsoc@ucl.ac.uk
website www.rhs.ac.uk

An annual award of £250 or a silver medal for a paper based on original historical research. Candidates must either be under the age of 35 or be registered for a higher degree now or within the last 3 years. Closing date: 1 November each year.

Further information

In the UK, details of awards for novels, short stories and works of non-fiction, as they are offered, will be found in such journals as *The Author*.

Booktrust

Book House, 45 East Hill, London SW18 2QZ
tel 020-8516 2977 *fax* 020-8516 2998
email info@booktrust.org.uk
website www.booktrust.org.uk

The website has full details of literary prizes, awards and grants to writers.

The Hans Christian Andersen Medals

Details International Board on Books for Young People, Nonnenweg 12, Postfach, CH-4003 Basel, Switzerland
tel (61) 272 29 17 *fax* (61) 272 27 57
email ibby@eye.ch
website www.ibby.org

The Medals are awarded every 2 years to a living author and an illustrator who by the outstanding value of their work are judged to have made a lasting contribution to literature for children and young people.

Artists' Residencies in Tuscany

Enquiries 31 Addison Avenue, London W11 4QS
email rmka101@ucl.ac.uk
website www.geocities.com/bgomperts/Artists_in_Tuscany.html

Annual bursaries (value up to £2000) provide board, lodging and studio facilities at the Centro Verrocchio in Italy. Also, small grants to support experimental projects on specified themes. Available by competitive application. Open to artists aged 25–45 (UK only). Funded by the Juliet Gomperts Memorial

Trust. Closing date: end of January. Send sae for further details.

The Arts Council/An Chomhairle Ealaíon, Ireland

Details The Arts Council/An Chomhairle Eala'on, 70 Merrion Square, Dublin 2, Republic of Ireland
tel (01) 618 0200 *fax* (01) 676 1302, 661 0349
email info@artscouncil.ie
website www.artscouncil.ie

Owing to an overhaul of all funding to individuals, there are changes in the way literature awards are organised. Information on these changes is available from the Arts Council.

Arts Council of England

Details The Literature Dept, Arts Council of England, 14 Great Peter Street, London SW1P 3NQ
tel 020-7973 6442
email info.literature@artscouncil.org.uk
website www.artscouncil.org.uk

The Literature Dept of the Arts Council of England administers 4 main award schemes which operate nationally. These are the Writers' Awards, the David Cohen British Literature Prize, the Independent Foreign Fiction Prize and the Raymond Williams Community Publishing Prize. See the separate entries for details. For details of all Literature funding schemes, contact the Literature Dept or visit the Arts Council website publications list.

Arts Council of England Children's Award

Details Theatre Writing Dept, Arts Council of England, 14 Great Peter Street, London SW1P 3NQ
tel 020-7973 6431
email info.drama@artscouncil.org.uk

An award of £6000 will be made for a playwright who writes for children up to the age of 12. Plays must have been produced professionally between 1 July 2002 and 30 June 2003 and must be at least 45 minutes long. It may be a first, second or third production of a play written within the last 10 years. Closing date: 4 July 2003.

Arts Council of England Writers' Awards

The Literature Dept, Arts Council of England, 14 Great Peter Street, London SW1P 3NQ
tel 020-7973 6442
email info.literature@artscouncil.org.uk
website www.artscouncil.org.uk

The Arts Council of England offers 15 awards annually of £7000 each for writers who need finance for a period of concentrated work on their next book. These Awards are open to writers who have been previously published in book form. Poetry, fiction, autobiography, biography, drama intended for publication, literature for young people, and other creative works are eligible. At least one award will be reserved specifically for a writer of Literature for Young People and the Clarissa Luard Award will be made to a fiction writer under 35 years of age. The Award winners will be determined by a panel of 3 judges, who are themselves writers.

The Arts Council of Wales Awards to Writers

Literature Department, The Arts Council of Wales, Museum Place, Cardiff CF10 3NX
tel 029-2037 6500 *fax* 029-2022 1447
email information@ccc-acw.org.uk
website www.ccc-acw.org.uk

Book of the Year Award

A £3000 prize is awarded to winners, in Welsh and English, and £1000 to 4 other short-listed authors for works of exceptional merit by Welsh authors (by birth or residence) published during the previous calendar year in the categories of poetry, fiction and creative non-fiction.

Bursaries

Bursaries totalling about £75,000 are awarded annually to authors writing in both Welsh and English. Write for further details of the Council's policies.

Arvon Foundation International Poetry Competition

Details Arvon Foundation Poetry Competition, 2nd Floor, 42A Buckingham Palace Road, London SW1W 0RE
tel 020-7931 7611
email london@arvonfoundation.org

A biennial competition for previously unpublished poems written in English. First prize £5000, plus at least £5000 in other cash prizes. Next competition: spring 2004. Founded in 1980.

The Asham Award

Details The Administrator, Asham Literary Endowment Trust, c/o Lewes House, 32 High Street, Lewes, East Sussex BN7 2LX

tel (01273) 484400 *fax* (01273) 484373
email carole.buchan@lewes.gov.uk

A biennial national short story competition for women writers over the age of 18 and currently resident in the UK who have not previously had a novel or anthology published. Winners receive a cash prize and inclusion in an anthology published by Serpent's Tail. Next competition will be launched in October 2002. Founded 1996.

The Society of Authors and The Royal Society of Medicine Medical Book Awards

Details The Secretary, MWG, The Society of Authors, 84 Drayton Gardens, London SW10 9SB
tel 020-7373 6642
email info@societyofauthors.org
website www.societyofauthors.org

Entries should be submitted by the publisher. Closing date for submissions of medical text books: 31 May. The Medical Writers Group of the Society of Authors administers the prizes sponsored by the Royal Society of Medicine.

Authors' Club Awards

Details Ann de La Grange, Secretary, Authors' Club, 40 Dover Street, London W1S 4NP
tel 020-7499 8581 *fax* 020-7409 0913

Best First Novel Award

An award of £1000 is presented at a dinner held in the Club, to the author of the most promising first novel published in the UK during each year. Entries (one from each publisher's imprint) are accepted during October and November and must be full-length novels – short stories are not eligible. Instituted by Lawrence Meynell in 1954.

Sir Banister Fletcher Award for Authors' Club

The late Sir Banister Fletcher, a former President of both the Authors' Club and the Royal Institute of British Architects instituted an annual prize 'for the book on architecture or the arts most deserving'. The award is made on the recommendation of the Professional Literature Committee of RIBA, to whom nominations for eligible titles (i.e. those written by British authors or those resident in the UK and published under a British imprint) should be submitted by the end of May of the year after publication. The prize of £1000 is awarded by the Authors' Club during September. First awarded in 1954.

The Authors' Foundation

The Society of Authors, 84 Drayton Gardens, London SW10 9SB
tel 020-7373 6642
email info@societyofauthors.org
website www.societyofauthors.org

Grants are available to novelists, poets and writers of non-fiction who are published authors working on their next book. The aim is to provide funding (in addition to a proper advance) for research, travel or other necessary expenditure. Closing dates: 30 April and 31 October. Send sae for an information sheet. Founded in 1984 to mark the centenary of the Society of Authors.

The Aventis Prizes for Science Books

Details Copus, c/o The Royal Society, 6-9 Carlton House Terrace, London SW1Y 5AG
tel 020-7451 2579 *fax* 020-7451 2693
email booksprize@copus.org.uk
website www.aventissciencebookprizes.com

These annual prizes reward books that make science more accessible to readers of all ages and backgrounds. Prizes of up to a total of £30,000 are awarded in 2 categories: General (£10,000) for a book with a general readership; and Junior (£10,000) for a book written for people aged under 14. Up to 5 shortlisted authors in each category receive £1000.

Eligible books should be written in English and their first publication in the UK must have been between 1 January and 31 December 2002. Seven copies of each entry should be supplied with a fully completed entry form. Publishers may submit any number of books for each prize. Entries may cover any aspect of science and technology but educational textbooks published for professional or specialist audiences are not eligible. The Prizes are organised by Copus – The Science Communication Partnership – and are sponsored by Aventis Pharma Ltd. Founded 1988.

BA/Book Data Author of the Year

Details The Booksellers Association of the UK and Ireland Ltd, 272 Vauxhall Bridge Road, London SW1V 1BA

tel 020-7834 5477 fax 020-7834 8812
This annual award of £1000 is judged by members of the Booksellers Association (3200 bookshops) in a postal ballot. Any living, British or Irish published writer is eligible and the award is given to the author judged to have had the most impact in the year. Founded in 1993.

BAFTA (British Academy of Film and Television Arts) Awards
Chief Executive Amanda Berry, 195 Piccadilly, London W1J 9LN
tel 020-7734 0022 *fax* 020-7494 2759
email suev@bafta.org
website www.bafta.org
The pre-eminent organisation in the UK for film, TV and interactive, recognising and promoting the achievement and endeavour of industry practitioners. BAFTA Awards are awarded annually by members to their peers in recognition of their skills and expertise. Founded 1947.

Verity Bargate Award
Details The Literary Officer, Soho Theatre and Writers' Centre, 21 Dean Street, London W1D 3NE
email writers@sohotheatre.com
website www.sohotheatre.com
A biennial award, set up in honour of the company's co-founder, is made to the writer of a new and previously unperformed full-length play. Writers with 3 or more professional productions to their credit are ineligible. The prize (£1500) represents an option to produce the play by Soho Theatre Company. Next award: 2004.

The BBC Four Samuel Johnson Prize for Non-Fiction
Details Booksellers Association, Minster House, 272 Vauxhall Bridge Road, London SW1V 1BA
tel 020-7834 5477 *fax* 020-7834 8812
email sharon.down@booksellers.org.uk
A prize of £30,000 will be awarded to the winning writer of a non-fiction book in the areas of current affairs, history, politics, science, sport, travel, biography, autobiography and the arts. Each shortlisted author will receive £1000. Books must be published in English in the UK between 1 May 2002 and 30 April 2003, and authors must be alive when the books are submitted. Books must not be written by more than 2 authors. Both hardback and paperback originals are eligible. Founded 1998.

The David Berry Prize
Council of the Royal Historical Society, University College London, Gower Street, London WC1E 6BT
tel 020-7387 7532 *fax* 020-7387 7532
email royalhistsoc@ucl.ac.uk
website www.rhs.ac.uk
Candidates may select any subject dealing with Scottish history. Value of prize: £250. Closing date: 31 October each year.

Besterman/McColvin Medals – see The CILIP/Whitaker Reference Awards

BG Wildlife Photographer of the Year
Details BG Wildlife Photographer of the Year, The Natural History Museum, Cromwell Road, London SW7 5BD
tel 020-7942 5015 *fax* 020-7942 5084
email wildphoto@nhm.ac.uk
website www.nhm.ac.uk/wildphoto
An annual award given to the photographer whose individual image is judged to be the most striking and memorable. The overall adult winner receives a bronze trophy and £2000. The Young Wildlife Photographer of the Year receives a bronze trophy of an ibis and £500, plus a day out with a photographer. Open to all ages. Closing date: April 2003. Sponsored by BG Group; 2003 marks 20 years of the Competition.

The Bisto Book of the Year Awards
Details The Administrator, Children's Books Ireland, 17 Lower Camden Street, Dublin 2, Republic of Ireland
tel (01) 872 5854 *fax* (01) 872 5854
email childrensbooksire@eircom.net
Annual awards open to authors and/or illustrators who were born in Ireland, or who were living in Ireland at the time of a book's publication.

The Bisto Book of the Year Award
An award of E3000 is presented to the overall winner (text and/or illustration).

Bisto Merit Awards
A prize fund of E2400 is divided between 3 authors and/or illustrators.

Bisto Eilís Dillon Award
An award of E1000 is presented to an author for a first children's book.

Closing date: 31 January 2003 for work published between 1 January and 31 December 2002. Founded 1990.

The James Tait Black Memorial Prizes

Submissions Department of English Literature, David Hume Tower, George Square, Edinburgh EH8 9JX
tel 0131-650 3619 *fax* 0131-650 6898
website www.ed.ac.uk/englit/jtbinf.htm

Two prizes of £3000 are awarded annually: one for the best biography or work of that nature, the other for the best novel, published during the calendar year. The adjudicator is the Professor of English Literature in the University of Edinburgh. Eligible novels and biographies are those written in English and usually first published in Britain in the year of the award. Both prizes may go to the same author, but neither to the same author a second time. Publishers should submit a copy of any appropriate biography, or work of fiction, as early as possible with a note of the date of publication, marked 'James Tait Black Prize'. Closing date for submissions: 30 September. Founded in memory of a partner in the publishing house of A & C Black, these prizes were instituted in 1918.

The Kathleen Blundell Trust

Kathleen Blundell Trust, The Society of Authors, 84 Drayton Gardens, London SW10 9SB
tel 020-7373 6642
email info@societyofauthors.org
website www.societyofauthors.org

Awards are given to published writers under the age of 40 to assist them with their next book. The author's work must 'contribute to the greater understanding of existing social and economic organisation', but fiction is not excluded. Closing dates: 30 April and 31 October. Send sae for an information sheet.

The Boardman Tasker Prize

Details Maggie Body, Pound House, Llangennith, Swansea SA3 1JQ
email margaretbody@lineone.net
website www.boardmantasker.co.uk

This annual prize of £2000 is given for a work of fiction, non-fiction or poetry, the central theme of which is concerned with the mountain environment. Authors of any nationality are eligible but the work must be published or distributed in the UK. Entries from publishers only. Founded in 1983.

The Booker Prize

Booktrust, Book House, 45 East Hill, London SW18 2QZ
tel 020-8516 2973/2972 *fax* 020-8516 2978
email kate@booktrust.org.uk
Contact Kate Mervyn-Jones, Tarryn McKay

This annual prize for fiction of £26,000, including £1000 to each of 6 shortlisted authors, is awarded to the best novel published each year. It is open to novels written in English by citizens of the British Commonwealth and Republic of Ireland and published for the first time in the UK by a British publisher, although previous publication of a book outside the UK does not disqualify it. Entries only from UK publishers who may each submit not more than 2 novels with scheduled publication dates between 1 October of the previous year and 30 September of the current year, but the judges may also ask for other eligible novels to be submitted to them. In addition, publishers may submit eligible titles by authors who have been shortlisted or won the Booker Prize previously. Sponsored by Booker plc.

BP Portrait Award

Details National Portrait Gallery, St Martin's Place, London WC2H 0HE
tel 020-7306 0055 *fax* 020-7306 0056
website www.npg.org.uk

An annual award to encourage young artists (aged 18–40) to focus upon and develop the theme of portraiture within their work. 1st prize: £25,000 plus at the judges' discretion a commission worth £3000 to be agreed between the NPG and the artist; 2nd prize £5000; 3rd prize: £3000; commendation: up to 5 entrants may be awarded £1000 each. Closing date: March/April. A selection of entrants' work is exhibited at the National Portrait Gallery between June and October. Founded 1978.

Alfred Bradley Bursary Award

Details BBC Radio Drama Department, BBC North, New Broadcasting House, Oxford Road, Manchester M60 1SJ
tel 0161-244 4255

This biennial bursary of £6000 (over 2 years, plus a full commission for a radio play) is awarded to a writer resident or born in the North of England who has had a small amount of work published or produced. The scheme also allows for a group of finalists to receive small bursaries and develop ideas for radio drama commissions. Next closing date: November 2002. Founded in 1992.

The Branford Boase Award

Details The Administrator, 18 Grosvenor Road, Portswood, Southampton SO17 1RT
tel 023-8055 5057 *fax* 023-8055 5057
email locol@csi.com

An annual award of £1000 is made to a first-time writer of a full-length children's novel (age 7+) published in the preceding year; the editor is also recognised. Its aim is to encourage new writers for children and to recognise the role of perceptive editors in developing new talent. The Award was set up in memory of the outstanding children's writer Henrietta Branford and the gifted editor and publisher Wendy Boase who both died in 1999. Closing date: 28 March 2003. Founded 2000.

The Bridport Prize

Details Bridport Arts Centre, South Street, Bridport, Dorset DT6 3NR
tel (01308) 459444 *fax* (01308) 459166
email info@bridport-arts.com
website www.bridportprize.org.uk

Annual prizes are awarded for poetry and short stories – 1st £3000, 2nd £1000, 3rd £500 in both categories. Entries should be in English, original work, typed or clearly written, and never published, read on radio/TV/stage or entered for any other current competition. Closing date: 30 June each year. Winning stories are read by leading London literary agent, without obligation, and an anthology of winning entries is published each autumn. Send sae for entry form.

The British Academy Book Prize

Details External Relations, The British Academy, 10 Carlton House Terrace, London SW1Y 5AH
tel 020-7969 5263 *fax* 020-7969 5414
email jbreckon@britac.ac.uk
website www.britac.ac.uk

Aims to increase the public appreciation of the humanities and social sciences by celebrating outstanding scholarly works that are accessible to the non-specialist. Eligible books must be published in English in the UK; the author may be of any nationality. The award is £2500. Closing date: 20 February 2003. Founded 2001.

British Academy Medals and Prizes

The British Academy, 10 Carlton House Terrace, London SW1Y 5AH
tel 020-7969 5200 *fax* 020-7969 5300
email secretary@britac.ac.uk

A number of medals and prizes are awarded for outstanding work in various fields of the humanities on the recommendation of specialist committees: Burkitt Medal for Biblical Studies; Derek Allen Prize (made annually in turn in musicology, numismatics and Celtic studies); Sir Israel Gollancz Prize (in English studies); Grahame Clark Medal for Prehistoric Archaeology; Kenyon Medal for Classical Studies; Rose Mary Crawshay Prize (for English literature); Serena Medal for Italian Studies; Leverhulme Medal and Prize.

The British Academy Research Awards

Details/application form The British Academy, 10 Carlton House Terrace, London SW1Y 5AH
tel 020-7969 5200 *fax* 020-7969 5300
email secretary@britac.ac.uk
website www.britac.ac.uk

These awards are made quarterly to scholars conducting advanced academic research in the humanities and social sciences, and normally resident in the UK. Applications are accepted for travel and maintenance expenses in connection with an approved programme of research. There are also awards for attendance at scholarly conferences overseas; and for postdoctoral fellowships, research readerships and research professorships.

British Book Awards

Details Merric Davidson, PO Box 60, Cranbrook, Kent TN17 2ZR
tel (01580) 212041 *fax* (01580) 212041
email nibbies@mdla.co.uk

Presented annually, major categories include: Author of the Year, Publisher of the Year, Bookseller of the Year, Children's Book of the Year. Founded 1989.

British Fantasy Awards

Details Robert Parkinson, Secretary, The British Fantasy Society, 201 Reddish Road, South Reddish, Stockport SK5 7HR
email faliol@yahoo.com

website www.britishfantasysociety.org.uk
Members of the British Fantasy Society vote annually for the best novel, short fiction, artist, small press and anthology of the preceding year. A further award, the Committee Award, is decided separately. The awards take the form of a statuette. Closing date for nominations: end August each year. Founded in 1972.

The Caine Prize for African Writing
Details Nick Elam, Administrator, 2 Drayson Mews, London W8 4LY
tel 020-7376 0440 *fax* 020-7938 3728
email caineprize@jftaylor.com
An annual award of $15,000 for a short story published in English (may be a translation into English) by an African writer in the 5 years before the closing date, and not previously submitted. Submissions only by publishers. Closing date: 31 January each year. Founded 1999.

Cardiff International Poetry Competition
Details/entry form Cardiff International Poetry Competition, PO Box 438, Cardiff CF10 5YA
Eight prizes totalling £5000 are awarded annually for unpublished poetry written in English (prizes: 1st £3000; 2nd £700; 3rd £300; plus 5 prizes of £200). Closing date: 1 November 2002.

Carnegie Medal – see The CILIP Carnegie and Kate Greenaway Awards

Children's Book Award
Details Marianne Adey, The Old Malt House, Aldbourne, Marlborough, Wilts. SN8 2DW
tel (01672) 540629 *fax* (01672) 541280
This award is given annually to authors of works of fiction for children published in the UK. Children participate in the judging of the award. 'Pick of the Year' booklist is published in conjunction with the award. Founded in 1980 by the Federation of Children's Book Groups.

The Children's Laureate
Details The Administrator, 18 Grosvenor Road, Portswood, Southampton SO17 1RT
tel 023-8055 5057 *fax* 023-8055 5057
email locol@csi.com
A biennial award of £10,000 to honour a writer or illustrator of children's books for a lifetime's achievement – highlights the importance of children's book creators in making readers of the future. Children's Laureates: Quentin Blake (1999–2001), Anne Fine (2001–3). Founded 1998.

Cholmondeley Awards
Administered by The Society of Authors, 84 Drayton Gardens, London SW10 9SB
These honorary awards are to recognise the achievement and distinction of individual poets. Submissions are not accepted. Total value of awards about £8000. Established by the then Dowager Marchioness of Cholmondeley in 1965.

The CILIP Carnegie and Kate Greenaway Awards
email marketing@cilip.org.uk
website www.ckg.org.uk
Recommendations for the following 2 awards are invited from members of CILIP (the Chartered Institute of Library and Information Professionals), who are asked to submit a preliminary list of not more than 2 titles for each award, accompanied by a 50-word appraisal justifying the recommendation of each book. The awards are selected by the Youth Libraries Group of CILIP.

Carnegie Medal
Awarded annually for an outstanding book for children (fiction or non-fiction) written in English and first published in the UK during the preceding year or co-published elsewhere within a 3-month time lapse.

Kate Greenaway Medal
Awarded annually for an outstanding illustrated book for children first published in the UK during the preceding year or co-published elsewhere within a 3-month time lapse. Books intended for older as well as younger children are included, and reproduction will be taken into account. The Colin Mears Award (£5000) is awarded annually to the winner of the Kate Greenaway Medal.

The CILIP/Whitaker Reference Awards
email marketing@cilip.org.uk
website www.cilip.org.uk

The Besterman/McColvin Medals
Awarded annually for outstanding works of reference published in the UK during the preceding year. There are 2 categories, one for electronic formats and one

for printed works. Recommendations are invited from Members of CILIP (the Chartered Institute of Library and Information Professionals), publishers and others, who are asked to submit a preliminary list of not more than 3 titles. Winners receive a cash prize of £500, a certificate and a prestigious golden medal.

The Walford Award

Awarded annually to an individual who has made a sustained and continued contribution to the science and art of British bibliography over a period of years. The bibliographer's work can encompass effort in the history, classification and description of printed, written, audio-visual and machine-readable materials. Recommendations may be made for the work of a living person or persons, or for an organisation. The award can be made to a British bibliographer or to a person or organisation working in the UK. The winner receives a cash prize of £500.

The Wheatley Medal

Awarded annually for an outstanding index published during the preceding year. Printed indexes to any type of publication may be submitted for consideration, providing that the whole work, including the index, or the index alone has originated in the UK. Recommendations for the award are invited from members of CILIP and the Society of Indexers, publishers and others. The final selection is made by a committee consisting of representatives of the CILIP Cataloguing and Indexing Group and the Society of Indexers.

The Citigroup Private Bank Photography Prize 2003

Information The Photographers' Gallery, 5 Great Newport Street, London WC2H 7HY
tel 020-7831 1772 *fax* 020-7836 9704
website www.photonet.org.uk

An annual prize of £15,000 is awarded to the individual who is judged to have made the most significant contribution to the medium of photography over the previous year. Anyone who has exhibited or published a substantial body of work in the UK in the year prior to the award is eligible. Runners up are awarded £1500 each. Nominations deadline: September 2002. Founded 1996.

Arthur C. Clarke Award

Details Paul Kincaid, 60 Bournemouth Road, Folkestone, Kent CT19 5AZ
email clarke@appomattox.demon.co.uk

An annual award of £2002 plus engraved bookend is given for the best science fiction novel with first UK publication during the previous calendar year. Titles are submitted by publishers. Founded 1985.

The David Cohen British Literature Prize

Details The Literature Dept, Arts Council of England, 14 Great Peter Street, London SW1P 3NQ
tel 020-7973 6442
email info.literature@artscouncil.org.uk
website www.artscouncil.org.uk

This prize of £30,000 is awarded every 2 years to a living writer, novelist, short story writer, poet, essayist or dramatist in recognition of a lifetime's substantial body of achievement. Work must be written primarily in English and the writer must be a British citizen. In addition, the Arts Council will make available an extra £10,000 to enable the winner to encourage reading or writing among younger people. The final choice of winner is determined by a distinguished jury on the basis of its collective reading. The winner of the 2003 prize will be announced in March 2003.

Commonwealth Writers Prize

Details/entry form Booktrust, Book House, 45 East Hill, London SW18 2QZ
tel 020-8516 2973/2972 *fax* 020-8516 2978
email kate@booktrust.org.uk
Contact Kate Mervyn-Jones, Tarryn McKay

This annual award is for the best work of fiction in English by a citizen of the Commonwealth published in the year prior to the award. A prize of £10,000 is awarded for best book entry and a prize of £3000 for best first published book, selected from 8 regional winners who each receive prizes of £1000. Sponsored by the Commonwealth Foundation.

The Duff Cooper Prize

Details Artemis Cooper, 54 St Maur Road, London SW6 4DP
tel 020-7736 3729 *fax* 020-7731 7638

An annual prize for a literary work in the field of biography, history, politics or poetry published in English or French and submitted by a recognised publisher during the previous 12 months. The prize of £3000 comes from a Trust Fund established by thefriends and admirers of Duff Cooper, 1st Viscount Norwich (1890–1954) after his death.

The Rose Mary Crawshay Prizes

The British Academy, 10 Carlton House Terrace, London SW1Y 5AH
tel 020-7969 5200 *fax* 020-7969 5300
email secretary@britac.ac.uk

One or more prizes are awarded each year to women of any nationality who, in the judgement of the Council of the British Academy, have written or published within the 3 calendar years immediately preceding the date of the award an historical or critical work of sufficient value on any subject connected with English literature, preference being given to a work regarding Byron, Shelley or Keats. Founded in 1888.

The John D. Criticos Prize

Coordinator Michael Moschos, The London Hellenic Society, 11 Stormont Road, London N6 4NS
tel 020-7626 0006 *fax* 020-7626 0601

A prize of £10,000 will be awarded to an artist, writer or researcher for an original work on Hellenic culture. Areas of particular interest are archaeology, art, art history, history and literature. No application necessary: send 2 copies of book plus covering letter. Closing date: 31 January. Founded 1996.

CWA Awards

website www.thecwa.co.uk

Awards for crime writing: the Cartier Diamond Dagger; the Creasey Dagger; the Macallan Gold Dagger and Silver Dagger for Fiction; the Macallan Gold Dagger for Non-Fiction; the Macallan Short Story Dagger; the CWA Ellis Peters Historical Dagger; the DebutDagger; the Ian Fleming Steel Dagger. See website for details.

The David St John Thomas Charitable Trust Competitions & Awards

The David St John Thomas Charitable Trust, PO Box 6055, Nairn IV12 4YB
tel (01667) 453351
Contact Lorna Edwardson (Competition & Awards Manager)

Programme of writing competitions and awards totalling £20,000–£30,000. Regular competitions are the annual ghost story and annual love story (each 1600–1800 words with £1000 1st prize) and the open poetry competition (up to 32 lines, total prize money £1200). Publication of winning entries is guaranteed, usually in *Writers' News/Writing Magazine* and/or an annual anthology. The Self-Publishing Awards are open to anyone who has self-published a book during the preceding calendar year, with 4 categories each with £250 prize. The overall winner is declared Self-Publisher of the Year with a total award of £1000. For full details of these and other awards, including an annual writers' groups anthology and letter-writer of the year send a large sae.

The Rhys Davies Trust

Details Prof Meic Stephens, The Secretary, The Rhys Davies Trust, 10 Heol Don, Whitchurch, Cardiff CF14 2AU
tel 029-2062 3359 *fax* 029-2052 9202
email meic@heoldon.fsnet.co.uk

The Trust aims to foster Welsh writing in English and offers financial assistance to English-language literary projects in Wales, directly or in association with other bodies.

The Dundee Book Prize

Details Deborah Kennedy, Dundee City Council, Economic Development, 3 City Square, Dundee DD1 3BA
tel (01382) 434275 *fax* (01382) 434096
email deborah.kennedy@dundeecity.gov.uk
website www.dundeecity.gov.uk

A biennial prize (£6000 and the chance of publication by Polygon) awarded for an unpublished novel. Next award: 2004. Founded 1996.

The T.S. Eliot Prize

Applications Poetry Book Society, Book House, 45 East Hill, London SW18 2QZ
tel 020-8870 8403
email info@poetrybooks.co.uk
website www.poetrybooks.co.uk

An annual prize of £10,000 is awarded to the best collection of new poetry published in the UK or the Republic of Ireland during the year. Submissions are invited from publishers in the summer. Donated by Valerie Eliot. Founded in 1993.

Encore Award
Details Awards Secretary, The Society of Authors, 84 Drayton Gardens, London SW10 9SB
tel 020-7373 6642
email info@societyofauthors.org
website www.societyofauthors.org

This annual award of £10,000 is for the best second novel of the year. The work submitted must be: a novel by one author who has had one (and only one) novel published previously, and in the English language, first published in the UK. Entries should be submitted by the publisher. Closing date: 30 November.

European Jewish Publication Society Grants
Details Dr Colin Shindler, Editorial Director, European Jewish Publication Society, PO Box 19948, London N3 3ZJ
tel 020-8346 1668 *fax* 020-8346 1776
email cs@ejps.org.uk
website www.ejps.org.uk

Awards of up to £3000 are given to publishers to assist in the publication of books of Jewish interest, including fiction, non-fiction and poetry. Translations from other languages are considered eligible. Founded 1995.

European Publishers Award for Photography
Details Dewi Lewis Publishing, 8 Broomfield Road, Heaton Moor, Stockport SK4 4ND
tel 0161-442 9450 *fax* 0161-442 9450
email mail@dewilewispublishing.com
website www.dewilewispublishing.com

Annual competition for the best set of photographs suitable for publication as a book. All photographic material must be completed and unpublished in book form and be original. Projects conceived as anthologies are not acceptable. Copyright must belong to the photographer. Closing date: 31 January. Founded 1994.

Christopher Ewart-Biggs Memorial Prize
Details The Secretary, Memorial Prize, Flat 3, 149 Hamilton Terrace, London NW8 9QS
fax 020-7328 0699

This prize of £5000 is awarded once every 2 years to the writer, of any nationality, whose work is judged to contribute most to:
- peace and understanding in Ireland;
- to closer ties between the peoples of Britain and Ireland;
- or to cooperation between the partners of the European Union.

Eligible works must be published during the 2 years to 31 December 2002. Closing date: 31 December 2002.

The Geoffrey Faber Memorial Prize

An annual prize of £1000 is awarded in alternate years for a volume of verse and for a volume of prose fiction, first published originally in the UK during the 2 years preceding the year in which the award is given which is, in the opinion of the judges, of the greatest literary merit. Eligible writers must be not more than 40 years old at the date of publication of the book and a citizen of the UK and Colonies, of any other Commonwealth state or of the Republic of Ireland. The 3 judges are reviewers of poetry or fiction who are nominated each year by the literary editors of newspapers and magazines which regularly publish such reviews. Faber and Faber invite nominations from reviewers and literary editors. No submissions for the prize are to be made. Established in 1963 by Faber and Faber Ltd, as a memorial to the founder and first Chairman of the firm.

The Alfred Fagon Award
Details c/o Cruickshank Cazenove Ltd, 97 Old South Lambeth Road, London SW8 1XU
tel 020-7735 2933 *fax* 020-7820 1081

An annual award of £2500 for the best new play (which need not have been produced) for the theatre in English. TV and radio plays and film scripts will not be considered. Writers from the Caribbean or with Caribbean antecedents are eligible. Applicants should submit 2 copies of their play plus sae for return of script and a CV which includes details of the writer's Caribbean connection and a brief history of the play. Closing date: 29 August 2003. Founded 1997.

Fallen Leaves Short Story Competition
Details Cork Campus Radio, Level 3, Áras na Mac Léinn, University College Cork, Cork City, Republic of Ireland
tel (021) 4902170 *fax* (021) 4903108
email radio@ucc.ie
Contact Sinéad O'Donnell, Station Manager

Fallen Leaves is a short story radio series devised to provide new and innovative

Irish short story writers with an opportunity to write for radio. Stories should be 1800–2000 words long and unpublished. Fee: £4 for the first story and £2 for each subseqent story. Founded 1996.

The Eleanor Farjeon Award

An annual prize of (minimum) £750 may be given to a librarian, teacher, author, artist, publisher, reviewer, TV producer or any other person working with or for children through books. Sponsored by Scholastic Ltd. Instituted in 1965 by the Children's Book Circle for distinguished services to children's books and named after the much-loved children's writer.

The Fidler Award

Administered by Scottish Book Trust,
The Scottish Book Centre, 137 Dundee Street,
Edinburgh EH11 1BG
tel 0131-229 3663

An annual award for an unpublished novel for children aged 8–12 years, to encourage authors new to writing for this age group. The award is currently without a sponsor and entrants should contact Scottish Book Trust before submitting MSS.

The Fish Short Story Prize

Durrus, Bantry, Co. Cork, Republic of Ireland
tel (353) 27 61246
email info@fishpublishing.com
website www.fishpublishing.com
Contact Clem Cairns

An annual international award which aims to discover, encourage and publish exciting new literary talent. Previously unpublished stories of up to 5000 words are eligible. 1st prize: £1000 (E1500); 2nd prize: one week residence at Anam Cara Writers' and Artists' Retreat, West Cork. The best 15–20 stories are published in an anthology. Entry fee: £10 (E14) for the first, £7 (E9) for subsequent entries. Concession rate: £7 (E9). Closing date: 30 November. Critiques available all year for £30 (E40). Winners announced at the annual West Cork Literary Festival, June/July. Founded 1994.

E.M. Forster Award

The distinguished English author, E.M. Forster, bequeathed the American publication rights and royalties of his posthumous novel *Maurice* to Christopher Isherwood, who transferred them to the American Academy of Arts and Letters (633 West 155th Street, New York, NY 10032, USA), for the establishment of an E.M. Forster Award, currently $15,000, to be given annually to a British or Irish writer for a stay in the USA. Applications for this award are not accepted.

Forward Poetry Prizes

Details Forward Poetry Prize Administrator,
Colman Getty PR, 17-18 Margaret Street,
London W1W 8RP
tel 020-7631 2666 *fax* 020-7631 2699

Three prizes are awarded annually:

- The Forward Prize for best collection of poetry published between 1 October and 30 September (£10,000);
- The Waterstones Prize for best first collection of poetry published between 1 October and 30 September (£5000); and
- The Tolman Cunard Prize for best individual poem, published but not as part of a collection between 1 May 2002 and 30 April 2003 (£1000).

All poems entered are also considered for inclusion in the *Forward Book of Poetry*, an annual anthology. Entries must be submitted by book publishers and editors of newspapers, periodicals and magazines in the UK and Eire. Entries from poets will not be accepted. Established 1992.

Miles Franklin Literary Award

Details Permanent Trustee Company Ltd,
35 Clarence Street, Sydney, NSW 2001, Australia
email linda.ingalelo@permanentgroup.com.au

This annual award of $28,000 is for a novel or play first published in the preceding year, which presents Australian life in any of its phases. More than one entry may be submitted by each author, and collaborations between 2 or more authors are eligible. Biographies, collections of short stories or children's books are not eligible. Closing date: approx. 15 December. Founded in 1957.

The Lionel Gelber Prize

Details Prize Manager, The Lionel Gelber Prize,
c/o Munk Center for International Studies,
1 Devonshire Place, Toronto, Ontario M5S 3K7,
Canada
tel 416-656-3722 *fax* 416-658-5205
email meisner@interlog.com

This international prize of $50,000 is

awarded annually in Canada to the author of the year's most outstanding work of non-fiction in the field of international relations. Submissions must be published in English or in English translation between 1 September and 31 August of the following year. Submissions deadline: 31 May, i.e. 3 months before the end of the period in question. Books must be submitted by the publisher. Established in 1989.

The Gilchrist-Fisher Award

Contact Matthew Sturgis, 33 Warren Street, London W1T 5NQ

Biennial prize (approx. £3500) awarded to a young artist (aged under 30) for landscape painting. Award exhibition for finalists held at Rebecca Hossack Gallery, London W1. Founded 1987.

Gladstone History Book Prize

Submissions Executive Secretary, Royal Historical Society, University College London, Gower Street, London WC1E 6BT
email royalhistsoc@ucl.ac.uk

An annual award (value £1000) for a history book. The book must:
• be on any historical subject which is not primarily related to British history;
• be its author's first solely written history book;
• have been published in English during the calendar year of 2002 by a scholar normally resident in the UK;
• be an original and scholarly work of historical research.
Three non-returnable copies of an eligible book should be submitted before 31 December.

Glenfiddich Food & Drink Awards

Details The Glenfiddich Awards, 4 Bedford Square, London WC1B 3RA
tel 020-7255 1100 *fax* 020-7631 0602

Awards are given annually to recognise excellence in writing, publishing and broadcasting relating to the subjects of food and drink. £1000 is given to each of 12 categories, together with a case of Glenfiddich single malt Scotch whisky and an award. The overall winner receives The Glenfiddich Trophy and an additional £3000. Founded in 1970.

Kate Greenaway Medal – see The CILIP Carnegie and Kate Greenaway Awards

E.C. Gregory Trust Fund

Details Awards Secretary, The Society of Authors, 84 Drayton Gardens, London SW10 9SB
tel 020-7373 6642
email info@societyofauthors.org
website www.societyofauthors.org

A number of substantial awards are made annually for the encouragement of young poets who can show that they are likely to benefit from an opportunity to give more time to writing. An eligible candidate must:
• be a British subject by birth but not a national of Eire or any of the British dominions or colonies and be ordinarily resident in the UK or Northern Ireland;
• be under the age of 30 on 31 March in the year of the Award (i.e. the year following submission).
Send sae for entry form. Closing date: 31 October.

Griffin Poetry Prize

Details The Griffin Trust for Excellence in Poetry, 6610 Edwards Boulevard, Mississauga, Ontario, Canada L5T 2V6
tel 905-565-5993 *fax* 905-564 3645
website www.griffinpoetryprize.com

Two annual prizes of C$40,000 will be awarded for collections of poetry published in English during the preceding year. One prize will go to a living Canadian poet, the other to a living poet from any country. Collections of poetry translated into English from other languages are also eligible and will be assessed for their literary quality in English. Submissions only from publishers. Closing date: 31 December. Founded 2000.

The Guardian Children's Fiction Prize

tel 020-7239 9694
email books@guardian.co.uk

The *Guardian's* annual prize of £1500 is for a work of children's fiction (for children over 8; no picture books) published by a British or Commonwealth writer. The winning book is chosen by the Children's Book Editor together with a team of 3–4 other authors of children's books.

The Guardian First Book Award

Contact Claire Armitstead
tel 020-7239 9694 *fax* 020-7713 4366
email books@guardian.co.uk
Submissions Literary Editor, The Guardian,

119 Farringdon Road, London EC1R 3ER

Open to first-time authors published in English in the UK across all genres of writing, the award will recognise and reward new writing by honouring an author's first book. The winner will receive £10,000 plus an advertising package within the *Guardian* and the *Observer.* In addition, an endowment of £1000 worth of books will be made by the *Guardian* to a UK school of the author's choice. Publishers may submit up to 3 titles per imprint with publication dates between January and December 2000. Closing date: late July.

The Paul Hamlyn Foundation Awards to Artists

Details The Administrator, 18 Queen Anne's Gate, London SW1H 9AA
tel 020-7227 3500 *fax* 020-7222 0601
email information@phf.org.uk

Five awards of £30,000 spread over 3 years will be made to visual artists in 2003 to support the creative process. Strength of talent, promise and need, as well as achievement, are all assessed. Nominations are made by a nationwide panel of 20 artists and others. The scheme is not open to application. Founded 1993.

The Hawthornden Prize

Details The Administrator, 42A Hays Mews, Berkeley Square, London W1J 5QA

This prize is awarded annually to the author of what, in the opinion of the Committee, is the best work of imaginative literature published during the preceding calendar year by a British author. Books do not have to be specially submitted.

Hawthornden Writers' Fellowships

Details The Administrator, Hawthornden Castle International Retreat for Writers, Hawthornden Castle, Lasswade, Midlothian EH18 1EG
tel 0131-440 2180

Applications are invited from novelists, poets, dramatists and other creative writers whose work has already been published. Four-week fellowships are offered to those working on a current project.

The Felicia Hemans Prize for Lyrical Poetry

Submissions The Registrar, The University of Liverpool, PO Box 147, Liverpool L69 3BX
tel 0151-794 2458 *fax* 0151-794 3765
email wilderc@liv.ac.uk

This annual prize of books or money, open to past and present members and students of the University of Liverpool only, is awarded for a lyrical poem, the subject of which may be chosen by the competitor. Only one poem, either published or unpublished, may be submitted. The prize shall not be awarded more than once to the same competitor. Poems, endorsed 'Hemans Prize', must be sent on or before 1 May.

Heywood Hill Literary Prize

Administration Heywood Hill Booksellers, 10 Curzon Street, London W1J 5HH

An award of £12,000 is given annually to a person chosen for their lifetime's contribution to the enjoyment of books. No applications. Established in 1995.

William Hill Sports Book of the Year Award

Details Graham Sharpe, William Hill Organisation, Greenside House, 50 Station Road, London N22 4TP
tel 020-8918 3731

This award is given annually in November for a book with a sporting theme (record books and listings excluded). The title must be in the English language, and published for the first time in the UK during the relevant calendar year. Total value of prize is £15,000, including £12,000 in cash. An award for the best cover design has total value of £1000. Founded in 1989.

The Calvin and Rose G. Hoffman Memorial Prize for Distinguished Publication on Christopher Marlowe

Applications The Headmaster, The King's School, Canterbury, Kent CT1 2ES
tel (01227) 595501 *fax* (01227) 595595

This annual prize of between £5000 and £6000 is awarded to the best unpublished work that examines the life and works of Christopher Marlowe and the relationship between the works of Marlowe and Shakespeare. Closing date: 1 September.

The Winifred Holtby Memorial Prize

Submissions The Royal Society of Literature, Somerset House, Strand, London WC2R 1LA
tel 020-7845 4676 *fax* 020-7845 4679
email info@rslit.org

This prize (value £1000) is awarded for the best regional novel of the year written in the English language. The writer must be of British or Irish nationality, or a citizen of the Commonwealth. Translations, unless made by the author of the work, are not eligible for consideration. If in any year it is considered that no regional novel is of sufficient merit the prize may be awarded to an author, qualified as aforesaid, of a literary work of non-fiction or poetry, concerning a regional subject. Novels published during the current year should be submitted between 1 October and 15 December. Contact the Secretary for details.

L. Ron Hubbard's Writers and Illustrators of the Future Contests
Administrator Andrea Grant-Webb, PO Box 218, East Grinstead, West Sussex RH19 4GH
Aims to encourage new and aspiring writers and illustrators of science fiction, fantasy and horror. In addition to the quarterly prizes there is an annual prize of £2500 for each contest. All 24 winners are invited to the annual L. Ron Hubbard Achievement Awards, which include a series of writers' and illustrators' workshops, and their work is published in an anthology. Write for an entry form.

Writers of the Future Contest
Entrants should submit a short story of up to 10,000 words or a novelette of less than 17,000 words. Prizes of £640 (1st), £480 (2nd) and £320 (3rd) are awarded each quarter. Founded 1984.

Illustrators of the Future Contest
Entrants should submit three black and white illustrations on different themes. Three prizes of £320 are awarded each quarter. Founded 1988.

Hunting Art Prizes
Details Parker Harris Partnership, PO Box 279, Esher, Surrey KT10 8YZ
tel (01372) 462190 *fax* (01372) 460032
email hap@parkerharris.co.uk
website www.parkerharris.co.uk
An annual national art competition open to all artists resident in the UK. Total prize monies: £24,000. Entry fee is £10 (£4 students) per work and artists may submit up to 3 works. Closing date: end November 2002. An exhibition will be held at the Royal College of Art in early 2003. Established 1980.

Images – The Best of British Illustration
Details Association of Illustrators, 81 Leonard Street, London EC2A 4QS
tel 020-7613 4328 *fax* 020-7613 4417
email info@a-o-illustrators.demon.co.uk
website www.aoisupplement.co.uk
Contact Events & Exhibitions Manager
Illustrators are invited to submit work for possible inclusion in the *Images Annual*, a jury-selected showcase of the best of contemporary British illustration. Selected work forms the Images exhibition, which tours the UK. UK illustrators or illustrators working for UK clients are all eligible. Send sae for entry form in the Spring. Founded 1976.

The Richard Imison Memorial Award
Details/entry form The Secretary, The Broadcasting Committee, The Society of Authors, 84 Drayton Gardens, London SW10 9SB
tel 020-7373 6642
email info@societyofauthors.org
website www.societyofauthors.org
This annual prize of £1500 is awarded to any new writer of radio drama first transmitted within the UK during the period 1 January–31 December 2002 by a writer new to radio. Founded in 1993.

Independent Foreign Fiction Prize
Details The Literature Dept, Arts Council of England, 14 Great Peter Street, London SW1P 3NQ
tel 020-7973 6442
email info.literature@artscouncil.org.uk
website www.artscouncil.org.uk
A prize of £10,000, split equally between author and translator, awarded to the best contemporary work of literary fiction in translation published in the UK. This prize, awarded in conjunction with the *Independent*, underlines the Literature Dept'scommitment to raising the profile of literature in translation and the work of literary translators.

Insight Guides Travel Photography Prize
Details APA Publications (UK) Ltd, 58 Borough High Street, London SE1 1XF
tel 020-7403 0284 *fax* 020-7403 0290
website www.insightguides.com
An annual competition open to amateur and professional photographers resident in the UK (theme to be announced in 2002). First prize is a commission to photograph

for an Insight Guide worth £3000; 11 other prizes of equipment and film. Closing date: September 2002. Founded 2000.

International IMPAC Dublin Literary Award

Details The International IMPAC Dublin Literary Award Office, Dublin City Council Library & Archive, Administrative Headquarters, Pearse Street, Dublin 2, Republic of Ireland
tel (01) 664 4800 *fax* (01) 676 1628
email dubaward@iol.ie
website www.impacdublinaward.ie

An annual award of E100,000 is presented to the author of a work of fiction, written and published in the English language or written in a language other than English and published in English translation, which in the opinion of the judges is of high literary merit and constitutes a lasting contribution to world literature. Nominations are accepted from library systems of major cities from all over the world, regardless of national origin of the author or the place of publication. Founded in 1995.

International Playwriting Festival

Details/entry form Festival Administrator, Warehouse Theatre, Dingwall Road, Croydon CR0 2NF
tel 020-8681 1257 *fax* 020-8688 6699
email warehous@dircon.co.uk
website www.warehousetheatre.co.uk

An annual competition for full-length unperformed plays, judged by a panel of theatre professionals. Selected plays are given rehearsed readings during the festival week in November. Entries are welcome from all parts of the world. For further details and entry forms send an sae. Deadline for entries: usually by the end of June. Founded 1985.

Irish Times Literary Prizes

Details Gerard Cavanagh (Administrator), Paul Anderson (Co-ordinator)
tel (3531) 679 2022 *fax* (3531) 670 9383
email gcavanagh@irish-times.ie

These 5 biennial prizes are awarded from nominations submitted by literary editors, critics, writers and academics. The 2003 Irish Literature Prizes are £5000 each for 4 categories and are open only to Irish authors:

- fiction (a novel, novella or a collection of short stories);
- non-fiction (history, biography, autobiography, criticism, politics, sociological interest, travel, current affairs and belles-lettres);
- poetry (a collection of works, a long poem or sequence of poems or revised/updated edition of previously published selection or collection of a poet's work);
- Irish language (works of fiction, non-fiction or poetry written in the Irish language).

A separate International Fiction Prize of £7500 is also awarded (novels, novellas, short stories), open to authors of any nationality for work in the English language. Work must be first published between 31 July 2001 and 1 August 2003, and apart from the Irish language prize, all entries must have been originally published in English.

Jewish Quarterly Literary Prizes

Details The Administrator, Jewish Quarterly, PO Box 2078, London W1A 1JR
tel 020-7629 5004 *fax* 020-7629 5110

Prizes are awarded annually for a work of fiction (£4000) and non-fiction (£4000) which best stimulate an interest in and awareness of themes of Jewish concern among a wider reading public. Founded in 1977.

The Petra Kenney Poetry Competition

Details Morgan Kenney, Danny, Hurstpierpoint, East Sussex BN6 9BB
fax (01273) 831889
email morgan@petrapoetrycompetition.co.uk
website www.petrapoetrycompetition.co.uk

This annual competition is for unpublished poems on any theme and in any style, and is open to everyone. Poems should be no more than 80 lines. Prizes: £1000 (1st), £500 (2nd), £250 (3rd), 3 at £125; also an inscribed Royal Brierley crystal vase to each winner and publication in *Writers' Forum* magazine. Entry fee: £3 per poem. Closing date: 1 December each year. Founded 1995.

Kent and Sussex Poetry Society Open Poetry Competition

Submissions The Organiser, 13 Ruscombe Close, Southborough, Tunbridge Wells, Kent TN4 0SG

This competition is open to all unpublished poems, no longer than 40 lines in length. Prizes: 1st £500, 2nd £200, 3rd £100, 4th 4 at £50. Closing date: 31 January. Entries should include an entry fee of £3 per poem, the author's name and address and a list of poems submitted. Founded in 1985.

The John Kobal Foundation Photographic Portrait Grants
Details The John Kobal Foundation, PO Box 3838, London EC1R 0XN
tel 020-7278 8482 *fax* 020-7278 8482
Portrait photography is defined here as 'photography concerned with portraying people with the emphasis on their identity as individuals' and applications for grants towards portrait photographic projects are accepted throughout the year.

Kraszna-Krausz Awards
Details Andrea Livingstone, Administrator, Kraszna-Krausz Foundation, 122 Fawnbrake Avenue, London SE24 0BZ
tel 020-7738 6701 *fax* 020-7738 6701
email awards@k-k.org.uk
website www.k-k.org.uk
Awards totalling over £10,000 are made each year, alternating annually between the best books on:

- moving image (film, TV and video): culture and history; business, techniques and technology (2003);
- still photography: art, culture and history; craft, technology and scientific (2004).

The prize in each category will be awarded to the best book published in the preceding 2 years. Closing date: 1 July. The Foundation is also open to applications for grants (UK only) concerned with the literature of photography and the moving image. Instituted in 1985.

The Lady Short Story Competition
The Lady, 39-40 Bedford Street, London WC2E 9ER
Open to anyone, details are published in an October issue of *The Lady*. First prize is £1000. Subjects for short stories change each year. Further information in the relevant issue – please do not contact the magazine office directly in connection with the competition.

The Laing Art Competition
Details Parker Harris Partnership, PO Box 279, Esher, Surrey KT10 8YZ
tel (01372) 462190 *fax* (01372) 460032
email laing@parkerharris.co.uk
website www.parkerharris.co.uk
An annual national open art competition of seascape and landscape painting open to all artists resident in the UK. 1st prize: £4000; 2 highly commended prizes: £1000. Winning entries will be exhibited in April at the Mall Galleries, London. Founded 1972.

Langhe Ceretto Prize for Food and Wine Culture, The International
Details Segreteria del Premio, Ceretto, Loc. San Cassiano 34, 12051 Alba, Italy
tel (0) 173 282582 *fax* (0) 173 282383
email ceretto@ceretto.com
website www.ceretto.com
This Prize is awarded for the work judged best at dealing with a topic relating to a historic, scientific, dietological, gastronomic or sociological aspect of food and wine (It.L 15,000,000). Publishers should send 11 copies to the Prize Secretariat. See website for details. Founded 1991.

Leverhulme Research Fellowships and Grants
The Leverhulme Trust, 1 Pemberton Row, London EC4A 3BG
tel 020-7822 6477 *fax* 020-7822 5084
email jcater@leverhulme.org.uk
website www.leverhulme.org.uk
The Leverhulme Trustees offer annually approx. 120 Fellowships and Grants to individuals in aid of original research – not for study of any sort. These awards are not available as replacement for past support from other sources. Applications will be considered in all subject areas. Total Fellowship/Grant monies for 2002 was £20,000 for a Fellowship and £17,800 for a Grant. Completed application forms must be received by mid November 2002 for 2003 awards. Founded 1933.

London Arts
Details Sarah Sanders, Senior Literature Administrator, London Arts, 2 Pear Tree Court, London EC1R 0DS
tel 020-7608 6100 *fax* 020-7608 4100
email sarah.sanders@lonab.co.uk
website www.arts.org.uk/londonarts
London Arts is the Regional Arts Office for the Capital, covering 32 boroughs and the City of London. Grants are available to support a variety of literature projects, focusing on 3 main areas:

- live literature, including storytelling;

• support for small presses and literary magazines in the publishing of new or under-represented creative writing;
• bursaries for writers who have published one book and are working on their second work of fiction or poetry.

There are 2 deadlines each year for applications. Contact Literature Unit for more information and an application form.

The London New Writing Competition
Entry form London Arts, 2 Pear Tree Court, London EC1R 0DS
tel 020-7608 6100 *fax* 020-7340 1092
email sarah.sanders@lonab.co.uk

Open to adults resident in Greater London, this biennial competition offers awards of E300 each (plus publication in an anthology) for the best creative pieces about London. Next closing date: January 2004. Founded in 1992.

London Press Club Awards
Details The Hon. Secretary, London Press Club, St Bride Institute, 14 Bride Lane, Fleet Street, London EC4Y 8EQ
tel 020-7353 7086/7 *fax* 020-7353 7087
email lpressclub@aol.com

From 2001 3 new awards were introduced, sponsored by Consignia plc: Business Journalist of the Year, New Media Journalist of the Year and Broadcasting Journalist of the Year.

Scoop of the Year Award
Chosen by a panel of senior editors, this annual award of a bronze statuette is given for the reporting scoop of the year, appearing in either a newspaper or electronic media. Founded 1990.

Edgar Wallace Award
Chosen by a panel of senior editors, this annual award of a silver inkstand is given for outstanding writing or reporting by a journalist. Founded 1990.

London Writers Competition
Details Arts Office, Room 224A, Wandsworth Town Hall, High Street, London SW18 2PU
tel 020-8871 8711
email arts@wandsworth.gov.uk
website www.wandsworth.gov.uk

Open to writers who live, work or study in the Greater London Area. Awards are made annually in 3 classes (Poetry, Short Story and Play) and prizes total £1000 in each class. Entries must be previously unpublished work. Judging is under the chairmanship of Martyn Goff.

The Sir William Lyons Award
Details General Secretary, 30 The Cravens, Smallfield, Surrey RH6 9QS
tel (01342) 843294 *fax* (01342) 844093
email sharon@scott-fairweather.freeserve.co.uk
website www.newspress.co.uk/guild

This annual award (trophy, £1000 and 2 years' probationary membership of The Guild of Motoring Writers) was set up to encourage young people in automotive journalism, including broadcasting, and to foster interest in motoring and the motor industry through these media. Open to any person of British nationality resident in the UK aged 17–23, it consists of writing 2 essays and an interview with the Award Committee.

The Macallan/Scotland on Sunday Short Story Competition
Details The Administrator, The Macallan/ Scotland on Sunday Short Story Competition, 108 Holyrood Road, Edinburgh EH8 8AS

These annual prizes (1st £6000; 2nd £2000; 4 runners up £500 each; publication of winning entries in *Scotland on Sunday*) are awarded for the best short story of less than 3000 words written by a person born in Scotland, now living in Scotland or by a Scot living abroad. The best 20 stories will be published in a special collection. Instituted 1990.

The McKitterick Prize
Details Awards Secretary, The Society of Authors, 84 Drayton Gardens, London SW10 9SB
tel 020-7373 6642
email info@societyofauthors.org
website www.societyofauthors.org

This annual award of £4000 is open to first published novels and unpublished typoscripts by authors over the age of 40. Closing date: 20 December. Endowed by the late Tom McKitterick. Send sae for entry form.

The Enid McLeod Literary Prize
Details Executive Secretary, Franco-British Society, Room 623, Linen Hall, 162-168 Regent Street, London W1R 5TB
tel 020-7734 0815 *fax* 020-7734 0815

This annual prize of £250 is given for a full-length work of literature which contributes most to Franco-British understanding. It must be first published in the UK between 1 January and 31 December, and written in English by a citizen of the UK, BritishCommonwealth, the Republic of Ireland, Pakistan, Bangladesh or South Africa. Closing date: 31 December.

Bryan MacMahon Short Story Award

Writers' Week, 24 The Square, Listowel, Co. Kerry, Republic of Ireland
tel (353) 6821074 *fax* (353) 6822893
email writersweek@eircom.net
website www.writersweek.ie

An annual award for the best short story (up to 3000 words) on any subject. Prize: E2000. Entry fee: E6.50. Closing date: 1 March. Founded 1971.

The Macmillan Prize for Children's Picture Book Illustration

Applications Marketing Dept, Macmillan Children's Books, 20 New Wharf Road, London N1 9RR

Three prizes are awarded annually for unpublished children's book illustrations by art students in higher education establishments in the UK. Prizes: £1000 (1st), £500 (2nd) and £250 (3rd).

Macmillan Silver Pen Award for Fiction

Details PEN, 152-6 Kentish Town Road, London NW1 9QB
tel 020-7267 9444 *fax* 020-7267 9304

This award of £500 is given annually for an outstanding collection of short stories written in English and published during the previous year by an author of British nationality or an author who has been a long-term resident in the UK. No submissions please – books are nominated by members of the PEN Executive Committee and by the Vice President of PEN. Sponsored by Macmillan since 1986. Founded in 1969.

The Mail on Sunday/John Llewellyn Rhys Prize

Entry form The Mail on Sunday/John Llewellyn Rhys Prize, c/o Booktrust, Book House, 45 East Hill, London SW18 2QZ
tel 020-8516 2973/2972 *fax* 020-8516 2978
email kate@booktrust.org.uk
Contact Kate Mervyn-Jones, Tarryn McKay

This annual prize of £5000 (plus £500 to each shortlisted author) is offered to the author of the most promising literary work of any kind published for the first time during the current year. The author must be a citizen of the UK or the Commonwealth, and not have passed his/her 35th birthday by the date of the publication of the work submitted. Publishers only may submit books. Inaugurated in memory of the writer John Llewellyn Rhys.

Marsh Award for Children's Literature in Translation

Administered by National Centre for Research in Children's Literature, Digby Stuart College, University of Surrey, Roehampton, Roehampton Lane, London SW15 5PU
tel 020-8392 3008
Contact Dr Gillian Lathey

This biennial award of £750 is given to the translator of a book for children (aged 4–16) from a foreign language into English and published in the UK by a British publisher. Electronic books, and encyclopedias and other reference books, are not eligible. Next award: January 2003. Founded in 1996.

Marsh Biography Award

Administered by The English-Speaking Union, Dartmouth House, 37 Charles Street, London W1J 5ED
tel 020-7529 1550 *fax* 020-7495 6108
email tim_rolph@esu.org

This major national biography prize of £4000 plus a trophy is presented every 2 years. Entries must be serious biographies written by British authors and published in the UK. Next award: October 2003. Founded 1985–6.

The Somerset Maugham Awards

Details Awards Secretary, The Society of Authors, 84 Drayton Gardens, London SW10 9SB
tel 020-7373 6642
email info@societyofauthors.org
website www.societyofauthors.org

These annual awards, totalling about £12,000, are for writers under the age of 35. Candidates must be British subjects by birth, and ordinarily resident in the UK or Northern Ireland. Poetry, fiction, non-fiction, belles-lettres or philosophy, but not dramatic works, are eligible. Entries should be submitted by the publisher. Closing date: 20 December.

MCA Management Thinking Awards

Details Sarah Taylor, Management Consultancies Association, 2nd Floor, 49 Whitehall, London SW1A 2BX

tel 020-7321 3990
email sarah.taylor@mca.org.uk
Prizes of £5000 are given to books, articles and essays which contribute stimulating, original and progressive ideas on management issues.

Meyer-Whitworth Award

Details Theatre Writing Section, Drama Department, Arts Council of England, 14 Great Peter Street, London SW1P 3NQ
tel 020-7973 6431
email info.drama@artscouncil.org.uk
Set up to help further the careers of UK contemporary playwrights who are not yet established, this award of up to £8000 is given annually for an English-language play which shows writing of individual quality and the promise of a developing new talent. Candidates will have had no more than 2 of their plays professionally produced. Nominated plays must have been produced professionally in the UK for the first time between 1 August 2002 and 31 July 2003; closing date: 29 August 2003.

Millfield Arts Projects

Atkinson Gallery, Millfield, Butleigh Road, Street, Somerset BA16 0YD
tel (01458) 442291 *fax* (01458) 447276
email lag@millfield.somerset.sch.uk
website www.millfield.somerset.sch.uk
Director of Art Len Green
'The mandate of the Millfield Arts Project programme is to search for, promote and support, primarily but not exclusively, young aspiring artists at local, regional, national and international levels.' In a professional art context MAP offers:
• Sculpture Commission. Artists work on campus for 8 weeks (£7500). Deadline for entries: mid January.
• Summer Show. An open exhibition. Application forms available: March
• Six Gallery exhibitions selected by the Director of Art. Interested artists should send slides and CV to the Director of Art.

Mind Book of the Year

Details Anny Brackx, Information Department, Granta House, 15-19 Broadway, London E15 4BQ
tel 020-8519 2122 *fax* 020-8522 1725
This £1000 award is given to the author of any book (fiction or non-fiction) published in the UK in the current year which outstandingly furthers public understanding of the prevention, causes, treatment or experience of mental health problems. Entries by 31 December. Administered by Mind, the National Association for Mental Health. Inaugurated in memory of Sir Allen Lane in 1981.

The Oscar Moore Screenwriting Prize

Details The Oscar Moore Foundation, 33-39 Bowling Green Lane, London EC1R 0DA
tel 020-7505 8080 *fax* 020-7505 8087
email annmarie.oconnor@media.emap.com
website www.screendaily.com
The Foundation works to build for a Europe-wide culture of screenwriting excellence and to this end makes this annual award (£10,000) to finance the first draft of a promising screenplay. A different genre is chosen for each year.

John Moores Liverpool Exhibition

The Walker, William Brown Street, Liverpool L3 8EL
tel 0151-478 4199 *fax* 0151-478 4190
email stephen.guy@nmgm.org
website www.nmgm.org.uk
Contact Stephen Guy
Biennial painting exhibition open to any artist living or working in the UK. Cash prize of £25,000 plus acquisition (by gift) of prize-winning painting by the Walker. Exhibition 14 Sept–8 Dec 2002. Founded 1957.

Shiva Naipaul Memorial Prize

Details The Spectator, 56 Doughty Street, London WC1N 2LL
This annual prize of £3000 is given to an English language writer of any nationality under the age of 35 for an essay of not more than 4000 words giving the most acute and profound observation of a culture alien to the writer. Founded 1985.

The National Art Library Illustration Awards

Enquiries The National Art Library, Victoria and Albert Museum, South Kensington, London SW7 2RL
tel 020-7942 2414
website www.nal.vam.ac.uk
Contact Dr Leo De Freitas *tel/fax* (01295) 256110
These annual awards are given to practising book and magazine illustrators, for work first published in Great Britain in the 12 months preceding the judging of the awards. Book covers, illustrations of a purely technical nature and photographs

together with works produced as limited editions are excluded. Cover illustrations to magazines are eligible. Sponsored by The Enid Linder Foundation.

National Poetry Competition

Contact Competition Organiser, The Poetry Society, 22 Betterton Street, London WC2H 9BX
tel 020-7420 9880 *fax* 020-7240 4818
email info@poetrysociety.org.uk
website www.poetrysociety.org.uk

One of Britain's major annual open poetry competitions. Poems on any theme, up to 40 lines. Prizes: 1st £5000, 2nd £1000, 3rd £500, plus 10 commendations of £50. All poems will be read by a team of poetry specialists before the final judging process. Forrules and entry form send an sae. Entries also accepted via the website. Closing date: 31 October each year.

The Natural World Book Prize

(in partnership with The Wildlife Trusts)
Details/entry form Booktrust, Book House, 45 East Hill, London SW18 2QZ
tel 020-8516 2973/2972 *fax* 020-8516 2978
email kate@booktrust.org.uk
Contacts Kate Mervyn-Jones, Tarryn McKay

Awards of £5000 to the winner and £1000 to the runner up for an adult book which most imaginatively promotes the conservation of the natural environment and all its animals and plants. Books must have been published between 1 June and the following 31 May. An amalgamation of the BP Conservation Book Prize and the Natural World Book of the Year Award. Sponsored by BP and Subbuteo Books.

The Néstle Smarties Book Prize

Details Booktrust, Book House, 45 East Hill, London SW18 2QZ
tel 020-8516 2973/2972 *fax* 020-8516 2978
email kate@booktrust.org.uk
Contact Kate Mervyn-Jones, Tarryn McKay

A prize (Gold Award) of £2500 is awarded to each of the 3 age category winners (0–5, 6–8 and 9–11 years). Runners-up (Silver Award) receive £1500 each, and third prize (Bronze Award) winners receive £500 each. Eligible books must be published in the UK in the 12 months ending 30 September of the year of presentation and be a work of fiction or poetry for children written in English by a citizen or resident of the UK. Closing date for entries: 31 July of the year of presentation. Sponsored by Nestlé Smarties. Established in 1985.

New Millennial Science Essay Competition

Details The Wellcome Trust, 210 Euston Road, London NW1 2BE
tel 020-7611 7221 *fax* 020-7611 8269
email r.birse@wellcome.ac.uk
website www.wellcome.ac.uk/ScienceEssay

Postgraduate students (in science, engineering or technology) currently writing up their theses are invited to write an entertaining essay on the possible impact of their research on society of no more than 700 words. The aim is to make the research topic interesting and accessible to a wider non-specialist audience. Applicants must be registered at an internationally recognised institution. The competition is open from mid March to mid May each year. A collaboration between the Wellcome Trust and *New Scientist* magazine. Prizes: £1500 and publication in *New Scientist* (1st), £750 (2nd), two 3rd prizes of £375 each. All winners, including the next 10 best essays, receive a one-year subscription to *New Scientist*. Founded 1993.

The New Writer Prose and Poetry Prizes

Details The New Writer Poetry Prizes, PO Box 60, Cranbrook, Kent TN17 2ZR
tel (01580) 212626 *fax* (01580) 212041
email info@thenewwriter.com
website www.thenewwriter.com

Short stories up to 5000 words, novellas, essays and articles; poets may submit either one or a collection of 6–10 previously unpublished poems. Total prize money £2500 as well as publication for the prize-winners in the *New Writer* magazine. Entry fees: £3 per poem; £10 for a collection of 6–10 poems. Send for an entry form or visit the website for information about the short fiction and non-fiction sections. Closing date: 30 November 2002. Founded 1997.

The Nobel Prize in Literature

Awarding authority Swedish Academy, Box 2118, S-10313 Stockholm, Sweden
tel (08) 10-65-24 *fax* (08) 24-42-25
email sekretariat@svenskaakademien.se
website www.svenskaakademien.se

This is one of the awards stipulated in

the will of the late Alfred Nobel, the Swedish scientist who invented dynamite. No direct application for a prize will be taken into consideration. For authors writing in English it was bestowed upon Rudyard Kipling in 1907, W.B. Yeats in 1923, George Bernard Shaw in 1925, Sinclair Lewis in 1930, John Galsworthy in 1932, Eugene O'Neill in 1936, Pearl Buck in 1938, T.S. Eliot in 1948, William Faulkner in 1949, Bertrand Russell in 1950, Sir Winston Churchill in 1953, Ernest Hemingway in 1954, John Steinbeck in 1962, Samuel Beckett in 1969, Patrick White in 1973, Saul Bellow in 1976, William Golding in 1983, Wole Soyinka in 1986, Joseph Brodsky in 1987, Nadine Gordimer in 1991, Derek Walcott in 1992, Toni Morrison in 1993, Seamus Heaney in 1995 and V.S. Naipaul in 2001.

Northern Rock Foundation Writer Award

Details New Writing North, 7-8 Trinity Chare, Quayside, Newcastle Upon Tyne NE1 3DF
tel 0191-232 9991 *fax* 0191-230 1883
email subtext.nwn@virgin.net
website www.newwritingnorth.com

An annual award of £20,000 p.a. for a 3-year period (i.e. £60,000) designed to release a writer from commitments such as teaching to devote time to a major work. Eligible are writers of poetry, prose, children's books and biography with at least 2 books published by a recognised publisher. Writers must reside in Northumberland, Tyne & Wear, County Durham or Teesside. Closing date: see website. Founded 2002.

Northern Writers' Awards

Administered by New Writing North, 7-8 Trinity Chare, Quayside, Newcastle upon Tyne NE1 3DF
tel 0191-232 9991 *fax* 0191-230 1883
email subtext.nwn@virgin.net
website www.newwritingnorth.com
Contact John McGagh

Awards (from £1500 to £8000) are aimed at developing writers at 2 different stages in their careers. A panel of professional writers shortlists and makes minor awards once a year. Applicants must be resident in the Northern Arts region (Northumberland, Tyne & Wear, Durham, Teesside). See website for details. Deadline for all applications: 31 January.

The Observer Hodge Award/Exhibition

Details The Observer Hodge Award, The Observer, 119 Farringdon Road, London EC1R 3ER
tel 020-7886 9305 *fax* 020-7837 1267
email annfarragher@guardian.co.uk
website www.observer.co.uk/hodgeaward
Contact Ann Farragher

Set up in memory of David Hodge who died aged 30, this annual award is given to student and professional photographers under 30. First prize: £4000 plus an expenses-paid assignment for the *Observer*; best student prize: £2000. Next awards to be launched February 2003; deadline: 30 June 2003. Founded 1986.

P.J. O'Connor Awards

P.J. O'Connor Awards, RTE Radio Drama, Donnybrook, Dublin 4, Republic of Ireland
tel (01) 2083111 *fax* (01) 2082045
Producer in Charge Michael Campion

An annual competition for a 30-minute original radio play, open to unproduced writers born in or living in Ireland. Prizes: £2000 (1st), £1500 (2nd), £750 (3rd). Closing date: November 2000.

Orange Prize for Fiction

Orange Prize for Fiction, Booktrust, Book House, 45 East Hill, London SW18 2QZ
tel 020-8516 2973/2972 *fax* 020-8516 2978
email kate@booktrust.org.uk
Contact Kate Mervyn-Jones, Tarryn McKay

This award of £30,000 is for a full-length novel written in English by a woman of any nationality and first published in the UK between 1 April and the following 31 March.

George Orwell Memorial Prize

Details Simage Communications Ltd, Fulton House, Fulton Road, Wembley Park, Middlesex HA9 0TF
tel 020-8584 0444 *fax* 020-8584 0443
email orwell@simage-comms.co.uk
website www.simage-comms.co.uk
Contact Sue Dowsott

Two prizes of £1000 each are awarded in March/April each year – one for the best political book, and one for best political journalism – of the previous year, giving equal merit to content and good style accessible to the general public. Founded in 1993.

Catherine Pakenham Memorial Award

Entry form Charlotte Ibarra, Corporate Affairs Dept, The Sunday Telegraph, 1 Canada Square, Canary Wharf, London E14 5DT *email* charlotte.ibarra@telegraph.co.uk

This award is open to young women journalists aged 18–25 who have at least one piece of published work. Entrants are asked to submit a non-fiction 750–2000-word article by 5 May 2003. The winner will receive £1000 and the chance to write for a *Telegraph* publication. Three runners-up each receive £200. Entry forms are available after 1 January. Founded in 1970 in memory of Catherine Pakenham, who died in a car crash whilst working for the *Telegraph Magazine*.

The Parker Romantic Novel of the Year Award

Details Joan Emery, 2 Broad Oak Lane, Wigginton, York YO32 2SB
tel (01904) 765035
website www.rna-uk.org

This annual award of £10,000 for the best romantic novel of the year is open to both members and non-members of the Romantic Novelists' Association, provided non-members are domiciled in the UK. Novels must be published between the previous 1 December and 30 November of the year of entry. Three copies of the novel are required. Entry forms and details are available from July onwards.

New Writers' Award

Margaret James, 21 Copse Way, Finchampstead, Berks. RG40 4EJ
tel (01189) 733942
email margaret@jamesk.freeserve.co.uk

For writers previously unpublished in the adult novel field and who are probationary members of the Association. MSS can be submitted until the end of September under the New Writers' Scheme. All receive a critique. Any MSS which have passed through the Scheme and which are subsequently accepted for publication become eligible for the Award.

Peterloo Poets Open Poetry Competition

Details Peterloo Poets, The Old Chapel, Sand Lane, Calstock, Cornwall PL18 9QX

This annual competition offers a first prize of £2000 and 14 other prizes totalling £2100. There is also a 15–19 age group section with 5 prizes each of £100. Closing date: 1 March 2003. Founded in 1986.

The Poetry Business Book & Pamphlet Competition

Competition Administrator The Poetry Business, The Studio, Byram Arcade, Westgate, Huddersfield HD1 1ND
tel (01484) 434840 *fax* (01484) 426566
email edit@poetrybusiness.co.uk
website www.poetrybusiness.co.uk
Directors Peter Sansom, Janet Fisher

An annual award is made for a poetry collection. The judges select up to 5 short collections for publication as pamphlets; on further submission of more poems, one of these will be selected for a full-length collection to be published under the Poetry Business's Smith/Doorstop imprint. All winners share a cash prize of £1000. Poets over the age of 18 writing in English from anywhere in the world are eligible. Closing date: 31 October. Founded 1986.

Poetry Life Open Poetry Competition

Details 1 Blue Ball Corner, Water Lane, Winchester, Hants SO23 0ER
email adrian.abishop@virgin.net
website http://freespace.virgin.net/poetry.life/

Competitions are held 3 times a year with a first prize of £500. Any style is acceptable with an 80-line limit on each poem. Poems must be previously unpublished (in book form) and must not have won a prize in another competition. All winning poems are published in *Poetry Life* magazine and on its website. Send sae for further details. Founded 1994.

The Portico Prize

Details Miss Emma Marigliano, Librarian, Portico Library, 57 Mosley Street, Manchester M2 3HY
tel 0161-236 6785 *fax* 0161-236 6803

This biennial prize of £3000 is awarded for a published work of fiction or non-fiction, of general interest and literary merit set wholly or mainly in the North-West of England (Lancashire, Manchester, Liverpool, High Peak of Derbyshire, Cheshire and Cumbria). Next award: 2004. Founded in 1985.

Dennis Potter Play of the Year Award

Details Jeremy Howe, BBC Broadcasting House, Whiteladies Road, Bristol BS8 2LR

Information about this award is obtainable from the above office after October 2000. Founded in 1994.

The Mathew Prichard Award for Short Story Writing

Details The Competition Secretary, The Mathew Prichard Award, 2 Rhododendron Close, Cyncoed, Cardiff CF23 7HS

Total prize money of £2000 is awarded annually in this open competition for original short stories in English of not more than 2500 words. Adjudication is organised in May each year by the South and Mid Wales Association of Writers. Send sae for entry form.

The V.S. Pritchett Memorial Prize

Details The Royal Society of Literature, Somerset House, Strand, London WC2R 1LA
tel 020-7845 4676 *fax* 020-7845 4679
email info@rslit.org
website www.rslit.org

An annual prize of £1000 is awarded for a previously unpublished short story of up to 5000 words. Entry fee: £5 per story. For entry forms contact the Secretary. Founded 1999.

The Real Writers/The Book Pl@ce Short Story Awards

(formerly The Real Writers Short Story Competition)
PO Box 170, Chesterfield, Derbyshire S40 1FE
tel (01246) 238492 *fax* (01246) 238492
email realwrtrs@aol.com
website www.real-writers.com

First prize: £2500 plus 10 regional awards. Send sae for entry form. Optional critiques. Entry fee: £5. Closing date: 30 September. Founded 1994.

Trevor Reese Memorial Prize

Details Events and Publicity Officer, Institute of Commonwealth Studies, 28 Russell Square, London WC1B 5DS
tel 020-7862 8825 *fax* 020-7862 8820
email skearins@sas.ac.uk
website www.sas.ac.uk/commonwealthstudies/

This prize of £1000 is awarded biennially, usually for a scholarly work by a single author in the field of Imperial and Commonwealth history. The next award (for a book published in 2000 or 2001) will be given in 2003.

The Margaret Rhondda Award

Details Awards Secretary, The Society of Authors, 84 Drayton Gardens, London SW10 9SB
tel 020-7373 6642
email info@societyofauthors.org
website www.societyofauthors.org

This award is given every 3 years to a woman writer as a grant-in-aid towards the expenses of a research project in journalism, in recognition of the service which women journalists give to the public through journalism. Send sae for entry form. Closing date for next award: 20 December 2004. First awarded in July 1968 on the tenth anniversary of Lady Rhondda's death.

The Rooney Prize for Irish Literature

Details J.A. Sherwin, Strathin, Templecarrig, Delgany, Co. Wicklow, Republic of Ireland
tel (01) 287 4769 *fax* (01) 287 2595
email jsherwin@iol.ie

An annual prize to encourage young Irish writing talent. E7500 is awarded to an individual, who must be Irish, published and under 40 years of age. The prize is non-competitive and there is no application procedure or entry form. Founded in 1976 by Daniel M. Rooney, Pittsburgh, Pennsylvania.

The Royal Society of Literature Award under the W.H. Heinemann Bequest

Details/Submissions The Secretary, Royal Society of Literature, Somerset House, Strand, London WC2R 1LA
tel 020-7845 4676 *fax* 020-7845 4679
email info@rslit.org

Works of any kind of literature may be submitted by publishers under this award of £5000, which aims to encourage genuine contributions to literature. Books must be written in the English language and have been published in the previous year. Translations are not eligible for consideration, nor are single poems, nor collections of pieces by more than one author, nor may individuals put forward their own work. Entries published during the current year should be submitted between 1 October and 15 December.

RSPCA Young Photographer Awards

Details Publications Department, RSPCA, Wilberforce Way, Southwater, Horsham, West Sussex RH13 9RS
tel (0870) 7540145 *fax* (0870) 7530048
email publications@rspca.org.uk

Annual awards are made for animal photographs taken by young people in 2 age categories: under 12 and 12–18. Prizes: overall winner (£250 cash, £300 camera, and £250 books), age group winners

(£100 cash, £180 camera, £100 books). Four runners-up in each age group receive £150 camera, £50 cash and £50 worth of books. Sponsored by Olympus. Closing date for entries: 16 September 2002. Founded 1994.

Runciman Award

Details The Administrator, The Anglo-Hellenic League, 16-18 Paddington Street, London W1U 5AS
tel 020-7486 9410

An annual prize of not less than £5000 for a work wholly or mainly about some aspect of Greece or the Hellenic scene, which has been published in its first English edition in the UK during the previous year and listed in *Whitaker's Books in Print*. The Award may be given for a work of fiction, drama or non-fiction; concerned academically or non-academically with the history of any period; biography or autobiography, the arts, archaeology; a guidebook or a translation from the Greek of any period. Established 1985.

Sainsbury's Baby Book Award

Booktrust, Book House, 45 East Hill, London SW18 2QZ
tel 020-8516 2973 *fax* 020-8516 2978
email kate@booktrust.org.uk
website www.booktrust.org.uk

An annual award of £2000 for the author and/or illustrator of the best book for babies under one year of age. Closing date: 1 June 2003.

Alastair Salvesen Art Scholarship

The Royal Scottish Academy, The Mound, Edinburgh
Reply to Admin Secretary, 17 Waterloo Place, Edinburgh EH1 3BG
tel 0131-558 7097 *fax* 0131-557 6417

The Scholarship consists of 2 parts:

• A 3–6 months travel scholarship of up to £10,000 depending on the plan submitted; and

• An exhibition in Nov/Dec organised by the Royal Scottish Academy.

Applicants must be painters aged 25–35 who have been trained at one of the 4 Scottish colleges of art; are currently living and working in Scotland; have worked for a minimum of 3 years outside a college or student environment; and have during 2002 had work accepted for an exhibition in the Annual Exhibition organised by certain Scottish institutes or, in a recognised gallery, have held a one-artist exhibition or participated in a group exhibition. Application forms available in December. Founded 1989.

The Scottish Arts Council

Contact Jenny Brown, Literature Director, The Scottish Arts Council, 12 Manor Place, Edinburgh EH3 7DD
tel 0131-226 6051
email jenny.brown@scottisharts.org.uk

A limited number of writers' bursaries – up to £15,000 each – are offered to enable professional writers based in Scotland, including writers for children, to devote more time to writing. Priority is given to writers of fiction and verse and playwrights, but writers of literary non-fiction are also considered. Applications may be discussed with Jenny Brown.

Scottish Book Awards

Gavin Wallace, Literature Officer, The Scottish Arts Council, 12 Manor Place, Edinburgh EH3 7DD
tel 0131-226 6051
email gavin.wallace@scottisharts.org.uk

Up to 7 awards ranging from £2000 to £10,000 are made in the spring to new and established authors of published books in recognition of high standards of writing, for both adults and children. Preference is given to literary fiction and poetry, but literary non-fiction is also considered. Authors should be Scottish, resident in Scotland or have published books of Scottish interest. Entries from publishers only. Guidelines available on request.

The Scottish Book of the Year and Scottish First Book

Details The Saltire Society, 9 Fountain Close, 22 High Street, Edinburgh EH1 1TF
tel 0131-556 1836 *fax* 0131-557 1675
email saltire@saltire.org.uk
website www.saltire-society.demon.co.uk

These 2 annual awards (£5000 and £1500) are open to any author of Scottish descent or living in Scotland, or for a book by anyone which deals with the work or life of a Scot or with a Scottish problem, event or situation. Nominations are made by literary editors of Scottish newspapers and periodicals. Supported by Consignia. Established in 1982 and 1988 respectively.

The André Simon Memorial Fund Book Awards

Details Tessa Hayward, 5 Sion Hill Place, Bath BA1 5SJ
tel (01225) 336305 *fax* (01225) 421862
email tessa@tantraweb.co.uk

Two awards (£2000 each) are given annually, one each for the best new book on food and on drink, plus one Special Commendation of £1000 in either category. Closing date: November each year. Founded in 1978.

Singer & Friedlander/Sunday Times Watercolour Competition

Details Parker Harris Partnership, PO Box 279, Esher, Surrey KT10 8YZ
tel (01372) 462190 *fax* (01372) 460032
email sf@parkerharris.co.uk
website www.parkerharris.co.uk

An annual competition 'to promote the continuance of the British tradition of fine watercolour painting'. Total prize money: £30,000. Open to artists born or resident in the UK. Closing date: mid June 2003. Winning entries will be exhibited in London, Manchester, Leeds and Birmingham. Launched 1987.

WHSmith Book Awards

Details WHSmith PLC, Nations House, 103 Wigmore Street, London W1U 1WH
tel 020-7514 9623 *fax* 020-7514 9635
email elizabeth.walker@group-whsmith.co.uk
website www.whsmith.co.uk
Contact Elizabeth Walker, Book Awards Manager

An award voted for by the public celebrating excellence in published works across a broad spectrum of subjects. There are 9 Award categories in total. The 8 new categories are: Biography/Autobiography, Children's Book of the Year, Fiction, Travel Writing, Business, General Knowledge, New Talent and Home & Leisure. The ninth category incorporates the long-standing WHSmith Literary Award.

WHSmith Thumping Good Read Award

Details Award Administrator, WHSmith, Greenbridge Road, Swindon, Wilts. SN3 3LD
tel (01793) 616161 *fax* (01793) 562590

An annual award of £5000 is presented to the best popular fiction author of the year. The award is judged by a panel of WHS customers. Founded 1992.

The Jill Smythies Award

The Linnean Society of London, Burlington House, Piccadilly, London W1J 0BF
tel 020-7434 4479 *fax* 020-7287 9364
email john@linnean.org
website www.linnean.org

Established in honour of Jill Smythies whose career as a botanical artist was cut short by an accident to her right hand. The rubic states that 'the Award, to be made by Council usually annually consisting of a silver medal and a purse (currently £1000) … is for published illustrations, such as drawings and paintings, in aid of plant identification, with the emphasis on botanical accuracy and the accurate portrayal of diagnostic characteristics. Illustrations of cultivars of garden origin are not eligible.' Closing date for nominations: 30 September. Founded 1988.

Sony Radio Academy Awards

Details Sony Radio Academy Awards Secretariat, Zafer Associates, 47-48 Chagford Street, London NW1 6EB
tel 020-7723 0106 *fax* 020-7724 6163
email secretariat@radioawards.org

'The Sony Radio Academy Awards celebrate excellence in broadcast work. They reward creative achievement through imagination, originality, wit and integrity. The Awards offer an opportunity to enter work in a range of categories which reflect today's local, regional and national radio. The Awards are for everyone regardless of resources – for stations big and small, for a team or for one person with a microphone.' Send for further information. Founded 1982.

The Spoken Word Awards

Contact The Spoken Word Publishing Association, c/o Zoe Howes, Macmillan Publishers Ltd, 20 New Wharf Road, London N1 9RR
tel 020-7014 6041 *fax* 020-7014 6141
email z.howes@macmillan.co.uk
website www.swpa.co.uk

Annual awards are made for excellence in the spoken word industry. There are over 40 judges from all areas of the industry including audiobook reviewers, radio broadcasters, producers, abridgers, etc. Closing date: end May 2003.

The Stern Silver Pen Award for Non-Fiction

Details PEN, 152-6 Kentish Town Road, London NW1 9QB
tel 020-7267 9444 *fax* 020-7267 9304

This award of £1000 is given annually for an outstanding work of non-fiction written in English and published during the previous year by an author of British nationality or an author who has been a long-term resident in the UK. No submissions please – books are nominated by members of the PEN Executive Committee and by the Vice President of PEN. Sponsored by the Stern family since 1996. Founded in 1969.

The Sunday Times Young Writer of the Year Award

Details The Society of Authors, 84 Drayton Gardens, London SW10 9SB
tel 020-7373 6642
email info@societyofauthors.org
website www.societyofauthors.org

Annual award to published fiction and non-fiction writers under the age of 35. The panel consists of *Sunday Times* journalists and critics. Entry by publishers. Closing date: 20 December. Established 1991.

Tabla Poetry Competition

Tabla, Dept of English, University of Bristol, 3-5 Woodland Road, Bristol BS8 1TB
fax 0117-928 8860
email stephen.james@bris.ac.uk
website www.bris.ac.uk/tabla

An annual competition for poems of any length and on any subject. Selected entries are published alongside work by established authors in the annual *Tabla Book of New Verse*. Prizes: £500 (1st), £200 (2nd), £100 (3 runners up). Closing date: 1 March.

TAPS (Television Arts Performance Showcase)

Shepperton Studios, Studios Road, Shepperton, Middlesex TW17 0QD
tel (01932) 592151, 593321 *fax* (01932) 592233
email taps@tvarts.demon.co.uk
website www.tvarts.demon.co.uk

A national scheme promoting new writers for film and TV. Open to any British scriptwriter with less than 2 hours work broadcast on network TV. Will accept either full-length drama (min. 1 hour), comedy (30 mins) or shorts (10 mins). Scripts can be submitted at any time throughout the year. Selected scripts are showcased by professional actors to industry executives culminating in the annual Writer of the Year Awards. TAPS also runs training workshops and is building a National Writers Database.

Reginald Taylor and Lord Fletcher Essay Competition

Submissions Dr Martin Henig, Hon. Editor, British Archaeological Association, Institute of Archaeology, 36 Beaumont Street, Oxford OX1 2PG

A prize of a medal and £300 is awarded biennially for the best unpublished essay of high scholarly standard, not exceeding 7500 words, which shows original research on a subject of archaeological, art-historical or antiquarian interest within the period from the Roman era to AD 1830. The successful competitor will be invited to read the essay before the Association and the essay may be published in the Association's *Journal*. Competitors should notify the Hon. Editor in advance of the intended subject of their work. Next award: autumn 2004. The essay should be submitted not later than 1 June 2004, enclosing an sae. Founded in memory of E. Reginald Taylor FSA and Lord Fletcher FSA.

Theatre Research Book Prize, Society for

Details The Society for Theatre Research, c/o The Theatre Museum, 1E Tavistock Street, London WC2E 7PR
email e.cottis@btinternet.com
website www.str.org.uk

An annual award (£400) is given to the author whose book, in the opinion of the judges, is the best original research into any aspect of the history and technique of the British theatre. Books must have been published in English in the preceding calendaryear. Founded 1997.

The Thomas Cook Travel Book Award

Details Travel Book Award, Thomas Cook Publishing, PO Box 227, Thorpe Wood, Peterborough PE3 6PU
tel (01733) 402009 *fax* (01733) 416688
email joan.lee@thomascook.com

This annual award (£10,000) is given to encourage the art of travel writing and to inspire the wish to travel. Travel narrative books (150pp minimum) written in English and published between 1 January and 31 December of the preceding year are eligible. Established in 1980.

The Times Educational Supplement Book Awards

Details The Administrator, TES Book Awards, The Times Educational Supplement, Admiral House, 66-68 East Smithfield, London E1W 1BX
tel 020-7782 3269 *fax* 020-7782 3200
email friday@tes.co.uk

At the time of going to press, the TES Book Awards were under review.

Tir Na N-og Awards

Details Welsh Books Council, Castell Brychan, Aberystwyth, Ceredigion SY23 2JB
tel (01970) 624151 *fax* (01970) 625385
email menna.lloydwilliams@cllc.org.uk
website www.cllc.org.uk

There are 3 annual awards to children's authors and illustrators: best original Welsh fiction, including short stories and picture books; best original Welsh non-fiction book of the year; best English book with an authentic Welsh background. Total prize value is £3000. Founded 1976.

The Tom-Gallon Trust

Details Awards Secretary, The Society of Authors, 84 Drayton Gardens, London SW10 9SB
tel 020-7373 6642
email info@societyofauthors.org
website www.societyofauthors.org

A biennial award of £1000 is made to fiction writers of limited means who have had at least one short story accepted for publication. Send sae for entry form. Next closing date: 20 September 2002.

The Translators Association Awards

Details Dorothy Sym, The Translators Association, 84 Drayton Gardens, London SW10 9SB
tel 020-7373 6642
email info@societyofauthors.org
website www.societyofauthors.org

The Translators Association of the Society of Authors administers a number of prizes for published translations into English. They include prizes for translations of Dutch and Flemish, French, German, Greek, Italian, Japanese, Portuguese, Spanish and Swedish works. Entries should be submitted by the publisher.

The Betty Trask Awards

Details Awards Secretary, The Society of Authors, 84 Drayton Gardens, London SW10 9SB
tel 020-7373 6642
email info@societyofauthors.org
website www.societyofauthors.org

These awards are for the benefit of young authors under the age of 35 and are given on the strength of a first novel (published or unpublished) of a romantic or traditional nature. It is expected that prizes totalling at least £25,000 will be presented each year. The winners are required to use the money for a period or periods of foreign travel. Send sae for entry form. Closing date: 31 January. Made possible through a generous bequest from Miss Betty Trask.

The Travelling Scholarships

Administered by The Society of Authors, 84 Drayton Gardens, London SW10 9SB

These are honorary awards established in 1944 by an anonymous benefactor. Submissions are not accepted.

The Trewithen Poetry Prize

Details The Competition Secretary, Chy-an-Dour, Trewithen Moor, Stithians, Truro, Cornwall TR3 7DU
website www.trewithenpoetry.co.uk

An annual prize to promote poetry with a rural theme. Poems can reflect contemporary rural living, environmental concerns, or any other aspect of nature or rural life in any country. Total prize money: £800. In addition, prize-winners will have their poems published in the *Trewithen Chapbook*, a biennial limited edition publication. Entry fee: £3.50. Send sae for entry form or see website. Closing date: 31 October each year.

'Charles Veillon' European Essay Prize

Details The Secretary, Charles Veillon Foundation, CH 1017 Lausanne, Switzerland
tel (021) 706 9029

A prize of 30,000 Swiss francs is awarded annually to a European writer or essayist for essays offering a critical look at modern society's way of life and ideology. Founded in 1975.

Ver Poets Open Competition

Organiser May Badman, Ver Poets, 61-63 Chiswell Green Lane, St Albans, Herts. AL2 3AL
tel (01727) 867005

A competition open to all for poems of up to 30 lines of any genre or subject matter, which must be unpublished work in English. Prizes: £500 (1st), £300 (2nd), £100 (2 x 3rd). Entry fee: £3 per poem with 2 copies of each poem (each year a gift to charity is made); send sae for entry form. Closing date 30 April each year.

The Walford Award – see The CILIP/Whitaker Reference Awards

David Watt Prize

Details/entry form The Administrator, The David Watt Prize, Rio Tinto plc, 6 St James's Square, London SW1Y 4LD
email davidwattprize@riotinto.com

An annual award (£7500) initiated to commemorate the life and work of David Watt. Open to writers currently engaged in writing for English language newspapers and journals on international and national affairs. The winners are judged as having made 'outstanding contributions towards the greater understanding of national, international or global issues'. Entries must have been published during the year preceding the award. Final entry date: 31 March.

Wellcome Trust Prize

Details The Wellcome Trust, 210 Euston Road, London NW1 2BE
tel 020-7611 7221 *fax* 020-7611 8269
email r.birse@wellcome.ac.uk
website www.wellcome.ac.uk

A bi-annual prize of £25,000 (paid quarterly over one year) gives the opportunity for a professional life scientist to take a break from their normal routine to write a popular book about their work which will educate, captivate and inspire the non-specialist lay reader. The winning work will be published by either HarperCollins or Weidenfeld & Nicolson. Applicants must be resident in the UK and have not previously published a popular science book. Founded 1997.

The Wheatley Medal – see The CILIP/Whitaker Reference Awards

Whitaker Gold and Platinum Book Awards

tel (01252) 742555 *fax* (01252) 742556
email gold&platinumawards@whitaker.co.uk

The awards are a recognition of sales purchases of a book by the general public. Eligible books are those priced at £4.99 or above that reach 500,000 unit sales (Gold) or 1,000,000 unit sales (Platinum) as measured by Whitaker BookTrack within a 5-year period. All qualifying titles receive an award, funded for the author by their publisher. Founded 2001.

Whitbread Book Awards

Details Denise Bayat, The Booksellers Association, Minster House, 272 Vauxhall Bridge Road, London SW1V 1BA
tel 020-7834 5477 *fax* 020-7834 8812
email denise.bayat@booksellers.co.uk
website www.whitbread-bookawards.co.uk

The awards celebrate and promote the most enjoyable contemporary British writing. Judged in 2 stages and offering a total of £50,000 prize money, the awards are open to 5 categories: Novel, First Novel, Biography, Poetry and Children's. The Novel, First Novel, Biography and Poetry Awards are judged by a panel of 3 judges and the winner in each category receives an award of £5000. Three adult judges and 2 young judges select a shortlist of 4 books for the Children's Book Award. The final judges then select the Whitbread Children's Book of the Year, worth £5000, and then choose the Whitbread Book of the Year from the winners of all categories. The winner receives a cheque for £25,000. Writers must have lived in Great Britain or Ireland for 3 or more years. Submissions must be received from publishers. Closing date: early July.

The Whitfield Prize

Submissions Executive Secretary, Royal Historical Society, University College London, Gower Street, London WC1E 6BT
tel 020-7387 7532 *fax* 020-7387 7532
email royalhistsoc@ucl.ac.uk
website www.rhs.ac.uk

The Prize (value £1000) is announced in July each year for the best work on a subject within a field of British history. It must be its author's first solely written history book, an original and scholarly work of historical research and have been published in the UK in the preceding calendar year. Three non-returnable copies of an eligible book should be submitted before 31 December to the Executive Secretary.

John Whiting Award

Details Writing Theatre Dept, Arts Council of England, 14 Great Peter Street, London SW1P 3NQ
tel 020-7973 6431
email info.drama@artscouncil.org.uk

This prize of £6000 is given annually. Plays must have been written during 2002 and 2003 and writers should have received during 2002 and 2003 either Arts Council theatre writing support or had a commission or premier production by a theatre company in receipt of annual subsidy from either the Arts Council or a Regional Arts Office. Closing date: 9 January 2004. Founded 1965.

The Raymond Williams Community Publishing Prizes

Details The Literature Dept, Arts Council of England, 14 Great Peter Street, London SW1P 3NQ
tel 020-7973 6442
email info.literature@artscouncil.org.uk
website www.artscouncil.org.uk

These annual prizes are awarded to non-profit making publishers for works of outstanding imaginative and creative quality which reflect the voices and experiences of the people of particular communities. 1st prize: £2000 to publisher, £1000 to writer/group. Runner-up: £1500 to publisher, £500 to writer/group. Founded in 1990.

David T.K. Wong Fellowship

Details David T.K. Wong Fellowship, School of English & American Studies, University of East Anglia, Norwich NR4 7TJ
tel (01603) 592810 *fax* (01603) 507728
email v.striker@vea.ac.uk
website www.uea.ac.uk/eas/fellowships/wong/wongfell.htm

Founded by David Wong, retired senior civil servant, journalist and businessman, the annual Fellowship (worth £25,000) at the University of East Anglia will give writers of exceptional talent the chance to produce a work of fiction in English which deals seriously with some aspect of life in the Far East. Residential: October–June. Write for centres and full details. Closing date: 31 October each year. Founded 1997.

The David T.K. Wong Prize for Short Fiction

tel 020-7253 4308 *fax* 020-7253 5711
email intpen@dircon.co.uk
website www.oneworld.org/internatpen

A biennial prize to promote literary excellence in the form of a short story (max. 6000 words) written in English. Unpublished stories are welcome from writers worldwide but entries must incorporate one or more of International PEN's ideals as set out in its charter. Entries should come from the applicant's local PEN Centre. Closing date *circa* 30 September 2002 but check with local centre (see website for centres, charter and full details). Founded 2000.

Write A Story for Children Competition

Entry forms The Academy of Children's Writers, PO Box 95, Huntingdon, Cambs. PE28 5RL
tel (01487) 832752
email per_ardua@lycos.co.uk

Three prizes are awarded annually (1st £1000, 2nd £200, 3rd £100) for a short story for children, maximum 1000 words, by an unpublished writer of children's fiction. Send sae for details. Founded in 1984.

Writers' Forum Short Story Competition

Details Writers' International Ltd, PO Box 3229, Bournemouth BH1 1ZS
tel (01202) 589828 *fax* (01202) 587758
email writintl@globalnet.co.uk
website www.worldwidewriters.com

Writers' Forum (10 p.a.) is an anthology of short stories from the winners of its competitions. Prizes range from £150 to £250 in each issue with an annual trophy and a cheque for £1000 for the best story of the year. Entry fee: £10 to non-subscribers of *Writers' Forum*; £6 to subscribers.

Yorkshire Post Book of the Year

Submissions Margaret Brown, Yorkshire Post Literary Awards, Yorkshire Post Newspapers Ltd, PO Box 168, Wellington Street, Leeds LS1 1RF
tel (01423) 772217 *fax* (01423) 772217

A prize of £1200 annually for the Best Book, either fiction or non-fiction. Submissions are accepted only from publishers, and authors should be British or resident in the UK. Next closing date: 31 December.

Young Writers' Season

Details Young Writers' Season, Royal Court Young Writers' Programme, Sloane Square, London SW1W 8AS
tel 020-7565 5034 *fax* 020-7565 5001

Anyone aged 25 or under can submit a

play on any subject. A selection of plays is professionally presented by the Royal Court Theatre with the writers fully involved in rehearsal and production. Pre-Festival Development Workshops are run by professional theatre practitioners and designed to help everyone attending to write a play.

Prizes and awards by subject area

This list provides a quick reference to the main listings of prizes, competitions and awards which starts on page 512.

Biography

J.R. Ackerley Prize for Autobiography
The James Tait Black Memorial Prizes
The Duff Cooper Prize
Marsh Award for Children's Literature in Translation
Northern Rock Foundation Writer Award
The Royal Society of Literature Award under the W.H. Heinemann Bequest
Runciman Award
The Scottish Writer of the Year Award
Whitbread Book Awards

Children

The Hans Christian Andersen Medals
Arts Council of England Children's Award
BG Wildlife Photographer of the Year
The Bisto Book of the Year Awards
Children's Book Award
The Children's Laureate
The CILIP Carnegie and Kate Greenaway Awards
The Eleanor Farjeon Award
The Fidler Award
The Guardian Children's Fiction Prize
The Macmillan Prize for Children's Picture Book Illustration
The Kurt Maschler Award
The Néstle Smarties Book Prize
Northern Rock Foundation Writer Award
Sainsbury's Baby Book Award
The Signal Poetry for Children Award
The Times Educational Supplement Book Awards
Tir Na N-og Awards
Write A Story for Children Competition

Drama – theatre, TV and radio

Arts Council of England Children's Award
BAFTA (British Academy of Film and Television Arts) Awards
Verity Bargate Award
The Samuel Beckett Award
The David Cohen British Literature Prize
Miles Franklin Literary Award
The Richard Imison Memorial Award
LAB/LBC London Radio Playwrights' Festival
Meyer-Whitworth Award
P.J. O'Connor Awards
Dennis Potter Play of the Year Award
Sony Radio Academy Awards
TAPS (Television Arts Performance Showcase)
John Whiting Award
Young Writers' Season

Essays

The David Cohen British Literature Prize
Shiva Naipaul Memorial Prize
New Millennial Science Essay Competition
Reginald Taylor and Lord Fletcher Essay Competition
T.E. Utley Memorial Fund Award
'Charles Veillon' European Essay Prize

Fiction

Authors' Club Awards
The James Tait Black Memorial Prizes
The Booker Prize
The Raymond Chandler Society's 'Marlowe' Award for Best International Crime Novel
Arthur C. Clarke Award
The David Cohen British Literature Prize
Commonwealth Writers Prize
CWA Awards
The Dundee Book Prize
Encore Award
Christopher Ewart-Biggs Memorial Prize
The Geoffrey Faber Memorial Prize
Miles Franklin Literary Award
The Guardian First Book Award
The Hawthornden Prize
The Winifred Holtby Memorial Prize
International IMPAC Dublin Literary Award
Irish Times Literary Prizes

Japan Festival Awards
Jewish Quarterly Literary Prizes
The Lichfield Prize
London Arts
The McKitterick Prize
The Enid McLeod Literary Prize
Macmillan Silver Pen Award for Fiction
The Mail on Sunday/John Llewellyn Rhys Prize
The Somerset Maugham Awards
Mind Book of the Year
Orange Prize for Fiction
The Parker Romantic Novel of the Year Award
The Portico Prize
Runciman Award
The Scottish Arts Council
The Scottish Writer of the Year Award
WHSmith Book Awards
The Sunday Times Young Writer of the Year Award
The Betty Trask Awards
Whitbread Book Awards
David T.K. Wong Fellowship
Yorkshire Post Book of the Year

Fine art – see Visual art

Grants, bursaries and fellowships

The Arts Council/An Chomhairle Ealaíon, Ireland
Arts Council of England
The Arts Council of Wales Awards to Writers
The Authors' Foundation
The Kathleen Blundell Trust
Alfred Bradley Bursary Award
The British Academy Research Awards
The Rhys Davies Trust
European Jewish Publication Society Grants
E.M. Forster Award
E.C. Gregory Trust Fund
Hawthornden Writers' Fellowships
Leverhulme Research Fellowships and Grants
London Arts
Northern Writers' Awards
The Margaret Rhondda Award
The Scottish Arts Council
The Travelling Scholarships
Wellcome Trust Prize
David T.K. Wong Fellowship

Illustration

The Hans Christian Andersen Medals
The Bisto Book of the Year Awards
British Fantasy Awards
The Eleanor Farjeon Award
L. Ron Hubbard's Writers and Illustrators of the Future Contests
Images – The Best of British Illustration
The Macmillan Prize for Children's Picture Book Illustration
The Kurt Maschler Award
The National Art Library Illustration Awards
Sainsbury's Baby Book Award
The Jill Smythies Award
Tir Na N-og Awards

Journalism

ABSW/Glaxo Science Writers Awards
London Press Club Awards
George Orwell Memorial Prize
Catherine Pakenham Memorial Award
The Margaret Rhondda Award
The Scottish Writer of the Year Award
Edgar Wallace Award

Non-fiction

The Alexander Prize
The Society of Authors and The Royal Society of Medicine Medical Book Awards
Authors' Club Awards
The Aventis Prizes for Science Books
The BBC Four Samuel Johnson Prize for Non-Fiction
The David Berry Prize
The British Academy Book Prize
British Academy Medals and Prizes
The CILIP/Whitaker Reference Awards
The Duff Cooper Prize
The Rose Mary Crawshay Prizes
The John D. Criticos Prize
CWA Awards
Christopher Ewart-Biggs Memorial Prize
Gladstone History Book Prize
Glenfiddich Food & Drink Awards
The Calvin and Rose G. Hoffman Memorial Prize for Distinguished Publication on Christopher Marlowe
Irish Times Literary Prizes
Japan Festival Awards
Jewish Quarterly Literary Prizes
Kraszna-Krausz Awards
Langhe Ceretto Prize for Food and Wine Culture, The International
The Enid McLeod Literary Prize
The Mail on Sunday/John Llewellyn Rhys Prize
The Somerset Maugham Awards
MCA Management Thinking Awards
Mind Book of the Year
The Natural World Book Prize
Northern Rock Foundation Writer Award
The Portico Prize
Trevor Reese Memorial Prize
The Royal Society of Literature Award under the W.H. Heinemann Bequest
Runciman Award
The Scottish Arts Council
The André Simon Memorial Fund Book Awards
WHSmith Book Awards
The Stern Silver Pen Award for Non-Fiction
The Sunday Times Young Writer of the Year Award
Theatre Research Book Prize, Society for
The Thomas Cook Travel Book Award
The Times Educational Supplement Book Awards
David Watt Prize
The Whitfield Prize
Yorkshire Post Book of the Year

Photography – see Visual art

Poetry

The Arts Council/An Chomhairle Ealaíon, Ireland
Arts Council of England
The Arts Council of Wales Awards to Writers
Arvon Foundation International Poetry Competition
The Bridport Prize
Cardiff International Poetry Competition
Cholmondeley Awards
The David Cohen British Literature Prize
The David St John Thomas Charitable Trust Competitions & Awards
The T.S. Eliot Prize
The Geoffrey Faber Memorial Prize
Forward Poetry Prizes
The Felicia Hemans Prize for Lyrical Poetry
Irish Times Literary Prizes
The Petra Kenney Poetry Competition
Kent and Sussex Poetry Society Open Poetry Competition
London Arts
London Writers Competition
The Somerset Maugham Awards
National Poetry Competition
The Néstle Smarties Book Prize
The New Writer Prose and Poetry Prizes
Northern Rock Foundation Writer Award
Peterloo Poets Open Poetry Competition
The Poetry Business Book & Pamphlet Competition
Poetry Life Open Poetry Competition
The Royal Society of Literature Award under the W.H. Heinemann Bequest
Runciman Award
The Scottish Arts Council
The Scottish Writer of the Year Award
The Signal Poetry for Children Award
Stand Magazine Awards
Tabla Poetry Competition
The Trewithen Poetry Prize
Ver Poets Open Competition
Whitbread Book Awards

Short stories

The Bridport Prize
The David Cohen British Literature Prize
CWA Awards
The David St John Thomas Charitable Trust Competitions & Awards
The Fish Short Story Prize
The Martin Healy Short Story Award
L. Ron Hubbard's Writers and Illustrators of the Future Contests
The Lady Short Story Competition
London Writers Competition
The Macallan/Scotland on Sunday Short Story Competition
Bryan MacMahon Short Story Award
Macmillan Silver Pen Award for Fiction
The Mathew Prichard Award for Short Story Writing
The Real Writers/The Book Pl@ce Short Story Awards
The Scottish Writer of the Year Award
Stand Magazine Awards
The Tom-Gallon Trust
Write A Story for Children Competition
Writers' Forum Short Story Competition

Translation

Marsh Award for Children's Literature in Translation
The Translators Association Awards

Specialist

BA/Book Data Author of the Year
The Boardman Tasker Prize
British Academy Medals and Prizes
British Book Awards
British Fantasy Awards
The CILIP/Whitaker Reference Awards
The David St John Thomas Charitable Trust Competitions & Awards
The Lionel Gelber Prize
Heywood Hill Literary Prize
William Hill Sports Book of the Year Award
The London New Writing Competition
The Enid McLeod Literary Prize
The Somerset Maugham Awards
The Nobel Prize in Literature
The Portico Prize
The Rooney Prize for Irish Literature
Runciman Award
The Scottish Arts Council
The Scottish Book of the Year and Scottish First Book
The Seebohm Trophy – Age Concern Book of the Year
Sony Radio Academy Awards
The Spoken Word Awards
The Times Educational Supplement Book Awards
Whitaker Gold and Platinum Book Awards

Visual art

Artists' Residencies in Tuscany
BG Wildlife Photographer of the Year
BG Young Wildlife Photographer of the Year
BP Portrait Award
The Citigroup Private Bank Photography Prize 2003
The John D. Criticos Prize
The Gilchrist-Fisher Award
The Paul Hamlyn Foundation Awards to Artists
Hunting Art Prizes
Images – The Best of British Illustration
The John Kobal Foundation Photographic Portrait Grants
The Laing Art Competition
Millfield Arts Projects
John Moores Liverpool Exhibition
The Observer Hodge Award/Exhibition
RSPCA Young Photographer Awards
Alastair Salvesen Art Scholarship
Singer & Friedlander/Sunday Times Watercolour Competition

Literature festivals

There are hundreds of arts festivals held in the UK each year – too many to mention in this Yearbook and many of which are not applicable specifically to writers. We give here a selection of literature festivals and general arts festivals which include literature events. Space constraints and the nature of an annual publication together determine that only brief details are given; contact festival organisers for a full programme of events. The British Council will supply a list of forthcoming literature festivals on receipt of a large sae.

The Academi Ty Newydd Festival

3rd Floor, Mount Stuart House,
Mount Stuart Square, Cardiff CF10 5FQ
tel (02920) 472266 *fax* (02920) 492930
email post@academi.org
website www.academi.org
Contact Peter Finch, Chief Executive
Takes place April 2003 (biennual)

Events are centred on the writing centre at Llanystumdwy in Gwynedd and feature a mix of Welsh and English events including Poetry Stomps and guest readers. The Academi, the Welsh National Literature Promotion Agency and Ty Newydd work together to create this festival.

Aldeburgh Poetry Festival

Aldeburgh Poetry Trust, Goldings, Goldings Lane, Leiston, Suffolk IP16 4EB
tel (01379) 668345
email njaffa@aldeburghpoetryfestival.org
Festival Director Naomi Jaffa
Takes place First weekend in Nov

Contemporary poetry festival. Includes readings, workshops, a public masterclass, a lecture and a children's event. Twenty international and national poets as well as fringe events and a writer-in-residence. Aldeburgh Festival Prize for the year's best first collection.

Aspects Festival

North Down Heritage Centre, The Castle, Bangor, Co. Down BT20 4BT
tel (028) 91 271200 *fax* (028) 91 271370
Festival Director Kenneth Irvine
Contact Paula Clamp (Arts Officer)
Takes place 25–29 Sept 2002

An annual celebration of contemporary Irish writing with novelists, poets, playwrights and non-fiction writers. Includes readings, discussions, workshops and a children's day.

Ballymena Arts Festival

Ballymena Borough Council, Ardeevin,
80 Galgorm Road, Ballymena,
Co. Antrim BT42 1AB
tel (01266) 660300 *fax* (01266) 660400
Takes place Oct

Bath Literature Festival

Bath Festivals Trust, 5-6 Broad Street,
Bath BA1 5LJ
tel (01225) 462231 *fax* (01225) 445551
email nicola.bennett@bathfestivals.org.uk
website www.bathlitfest.org.uk
Director Nicola Bennett
Takes place 1–9 March 2003

An annual 9-day festival with leading guest writers. Includes readings, debates, discussions and workshops, and children's activities. Education & Community Programme includes author visits to schools and a children's writing competition. Each year has achosen theme.

Belfast Festival at Queen's

Festival House, 25 College Gardens,
Belfast BT9 6BS
tel 028-9066 7687 *fax* 028-9066 3733
email festival@gub.ac.uk
website www.belfastfestival.com
Director Stella Hall
Takes place 25 Oct–10 Nov 2002

The largest annual arts event in Ireland. Includes literature events. Programme available mid-September.

Book Now!

Education, Arts & Leisure Department,
London Borough of Richmond upon Thames,
Regal House, London Road,
Twickenham TW1 3QB
tel 020-8381 6138 *fax* 020-8891 7904
website www.richmond.gov.uk
Head of Arts Daryl Frazer
Takes place Throughout Nov

An annual literature festival covering a broad range of subjects. Leading British and overseas guest writers and poets hold discussions, talks, debates and workshops and give readings. There are also exhibitions, storytelling sessions and a schools programme.

Brighton Festival

12A Pavilion Buildings, Castle Square,
Brighton BN1 1EE
tel (01273) 700747 *fax* (01273) 707505
email info@brighton-festival.org.uk
website www.brighton-festival.org.uk
Takes place May

An annual general arts festival with a large literature programme. Leading guest writers cover a broad range of subjects in a diverse programme of events. Programme published end of February.

Cambridge Conference of Contemporary Poetry

c/o Dr Rod Mengham, Jesus College,
Cambridge CB5 8BL
tel (01223) 339493
email r.mengham@jesus.cam.ac.uk
Kevin Nolan, 2 Bells Close, West Road,
Saffron Walden, Essex CB11 3DU
email k.nolan@virgin.net
website www.cccp-online.org
Takes place April

An annual weekend of poetry readings, discussion and performance of international poetry in the modernist tradition.

Canterbury Festival

Festival Office, Christ Church Gate,
The Precincts, Canterbury, Kent CT1 2EE
tel (01227) 452853 *fax* (01227) 781830
email info@canterburyfestival.co.uk
Takes place 12–26 Oct 2002

An annual general arts festival with a literature programme. Programme published in July.

Chaucer Festival

Chaucer Heritage Trust, Chaucer Centre,
22 St Peter's Street, Canterbury, Kent CT1 2BQ
tel 020-7229 0635 *fax* (01227) 761416
Director Martin Starkie,
Manager and Events Organiser Zoran Tesic
tel (01227) 470379
Takes place Spring, Summer and Autumn

An annual festival which includes commemoration services, theatre productions, exhibitions, readings, recitals, Chaucer site visits, medieval fairs, costumed cavalcades, educational programmes for schools. Takes place in London, Canterbury and the County of Kent in the Spring (Easter Chaucer Pilgrimage), Summer (June–July), and Autumn (Oct).

Cheltenham Festival of Literature

Town Hall, Imperial Square, Cheltenham,
Glos. GL50 1QA
tel (01242) 227979 (box office), 237377 (brochure), 263494 (festival office)
fax (01242) 256457
email sarahsm@cheltenham.gov.uk
website www.cheltenhamfestivals.co.uk
Festival Director Sarah Smyth
Takes place 11–20 Oct 2002

This annual festival is the largest of its kind in Europe. Events include talks and lectures, poetry readings, novelists in conversation, exhibitions, discussions, workshops and a large bookshop. *Book It!* is a festival for children within the main festival with an extensive programme of events and a multimedia room. Brochures are available in August.

Chester Literature Festival

8 Abbey Square, Chester CH1 2HU
tel (01244) 319985 *fax* (01244) 341200
Festival Administrator Freda Hadwen
Takes place 5–20 Oct 2002

An annual festival with events featuring international and national writers, events by local literary groups, events for children, a Literary Lunch, workshops and competitions.

Chichester Festivities

Canon Gate House, South Street, Chichester,
West Sussex PO19 1PU
tel (01243) 785718 *fax* (01243) 528356
email info@chifest.org.uk
website www.chifest.org.uk
Takes place June/July

City of London Festival

Bishopsgate Hall, 230 Bishopsgate,
London EC2M 4HW
tel 020-7377 0540 *fax* 020-7377 1972
email admin@colf.org

website www.colf.org
Takes place 23 June–10 July 2003 (provisional)

An annual multi-arts festival with a programme of literary events. Programme published in April.

City Voice

Central Library, Calverley Street, Leeds LS1 3AB
tel 0113-247 8421
website www.leeds.gov.uk/wordarena
Contact Festival Organiser
Takes place May/June

An annual 2-week celebration of the voices of the city – provides a platform for Leeds writers alongside established names.

The Cúirt International Festival of Literature

Galway Arts Centre, 47 Dominick Street, Galway, Republic of Ireland
tel (091) 565886 *fax* (091) 568642
email gac@indigo.ie
website www.galwayartscentre.ie
Director Helen Carey, *Coordinator and Progammer* Maura Kennedy
Takes place April

An annual week-long festival to celebrate writing, bringing together national and international writers to promote literary discussion. Events include readings, performances, workshops, seminars, lectures, poetry slams and talks. The festival is renowned for its convivial atmosphere ('cúirt' means a 'bardic court or gathering').

Durham Literature Festival 2002

c/o Durham City Arts Ltd, Byland Lodge, Hawthorn Terrace, Durham DH1 4TD
tel 0191-301 8830 *fax* 0191-301 8821
Festival Coordinator Alison Lister
Takes place June–July

Edinburgh International Book Festival

Scottish Book Centre, 137 Dundee Street, Fountainbridge, Edinburgh EH11 1BG
tel 0131-228 5444 *fax* 0131-228 4333
email admin@edbookfest.co.uk
website www.edbookfest.co.uk
Director Catherine Lockerbie
Takes place 10–30 Aug 2003

Now established as Europe's largest book event for the public. In addition to a unique independent bookselling operation, over 400 writers contribute to the programme of events. Programme details available in June.

Edinburgh International Festival

The Hub, Edinburgh's Festival Centre, Castlehill, Royal Mile, Edinburgh EH1 2NE
tel 0131-473 2000 *fax* 0131-473 2002
email eif@eif.co.uk
website www.eif.co.uk
Takes place 10–30 Aug 2003

An annual international arts festival including world class theatre, dance, opera and music. Programme published late March.

Everybody's Reading

Leicester City Council, 12th Floor, Block A, New Walk Centre, Welford Place, Leicester LE1 6ZG
Contact Sarah Butler
Takes place June

Exeter Festival

Festival Office, Civic Centre, Exeter EX1 1JJ
tel (01392) 265200 *fax* (01392) 265265
website www.exeter.gov.uk
Festival Manager Lesley Waters
Takes place July

An annual general arts festival which includes a programme of literary activities. Programme of events available in April.

Federation of Worker Writers and Community Publishers Festival of Writing

Burslem School of Art, Queen Street, Stoke-on-Trent ST6 3EJ
tel/fax (01782) 822327
email thefwwcp@tislali.co.uk
website www.thefwwcp.org.uk
Takes place April

Female Eye National Festival of Women's Writing

Female Eye, Watersmead, Norwood Green Hill, Halifax, West Yorkshire HX3 8QX
tel/fax (01274) 670181
Takes place June

Festival at the Edge

c/o 3 Highpoint, Little Wenlock, Telford, Shrops. TF6 5BT
tel (01952) 504882
email info@festivalattheedge.org
website www.festivalattheedge.org
Contact Jackie Douglas
Takes place Third full weekend of July

Guildford Book Festival

c/o Arts Office, University of Surrey, Guildford GU2 7XH
tel (01483) 879167
email book-festival-director@surrey.ac.uk

website www.guildford.org.uk
Festival Director Glenis Pycraft
Takes place 20 Oct–3 Nov 2002

A varied programme with over 60 events held at different venues in Guildford, including readings, discussions, literary lunches and teas, performance poetry, workshops, competitions. High profile authors and a writer in residence. Many children's events. Held annually, its aim is to involve, instruct and entertain all who care about literature and to encourage in children a love of reading. Founded 1990.

Harrogate International Festival

1 Victoria Avenue, Harrogate,
North Yorkshire HG1 1EQ
tel (01423) 562303 *fax* (01423) 521264
email info@harrogate-festival.org.uk
website www.harrogate-festival.org.uk
Takes place July/Aug

An annual international multi-arts festival. Programme available in May.

Hastings International Poetry Festival

c/o The Snoring Cat, 16 Marianne Park,
Dudley Road, Hastings, East Sussex TN35 5PU
tel/fax (01424) 428855
Organiser and Editor of First Time Josephine Austin
Takes place 2–3 Nov 2002

Started in 1968, this national festival is now held in the Sussex Hall, White Rock Theatre. Includes the prize-giving of the *Hastings National Poetry Competition*. Poems are invited for consideration for the bi-annual *First Time* poetry magazine. Please include sae.

Ilkley Literature Festival

The Manor House, Ilkley LS29 9DT
tel (01943) 601210 *fax* (01943) 817079
email admin@ilkleyliteraturefestival.org.uk
website www.ilkleyliteraturefestival.org.uk
Festival Director Dominic Gregory
Takes place Oct

The north of England's oldest and largest literature festival organises a full programme of writing and reading events.

International Playwriting Festival

Warehouse Theatre, Dingwall Road,
Croydon CR0 2NF
tel 020-8681 1257 *fax* 020-8688 6699
email warehous@dircon.co.uk
website www.warehousetheatre.co.uk
Festival Administrator Carolyn Braby
Takes place Nov

An annual competition for full-length unperformed plays (see page 526). The weekend festival includes readings of selected plays and work from the leading Italian festival, the Premio Candoni Arta Terme.

King's Lynn Festival

5 Thoresby College, Queen Street, King's Lynn,
Norfolk PE30 1HX
tel (01553) 767557 *fax* (01553) 767688
website www.kl-festival.freeserve.co.uk
Administrator Joanne Rutterford
Takes place 24 July–2 Aug 2003

An annual general arts festival with literature events featuring leading guest writers.

King's Lynn Festivals

19 Tuesday Market Place, King's Lynn,
Norfolk PE30 1JW
tel (01553) 691661 *fax* (01553) 691779
Chairman Tony Ellis
Takes place Sept/March

Poetry Festival (27–29 Sept 2002). An annual festival which brings 8 published poets to King's Lynn for the weekend for readings and discussions. The King's Lynn Poetry Prize (value £1000) is awarded at the festival.

Fiction Festival (14–16 March 2003). An annual festival which brings 8 published novelists to King's Lynn for the weekend for readings and discussions.

Ledbury Poetry Festival

Town Council Offices, Church Street,
Ledbury HR8 1DH
tel (01531) 634156
email prog@poetry-festival.com
website www.poetry-festival.com
Festival Manager Charles Bennett
Takes place 4–13 July 2003

An annual festival featuring top poets from around the world, together with a poet-in-residence programme, competitions (send sae for entry form), workshops and exhibitions. Full programme available in May.

Lincolnshire Literature Festival

Education and Cultural Services Directorate,
Lincolnshire County Council, County Offices,
Lincoln LN1 1YL
tel (01522) 552831 *fax* (01522) 552811
email david.lambert@lincolnshire.gov.uk
County Arts Development Officer David Lambert
County Literature Development Officer Paul Sutherland, PO Box 3, District Council Offices,

Kesteven Street, Sleaford, Lincs. NG34 7EF
tel (01529) 414155
email paul_sutherland@n-kesteven.gov.uk
Takes place Throughout the year

A monthly series of varied literary events. Occasional festivals, tours, publications in Lincolnshire; work with East Midlands Arts.

Lit Up!

The Plough Arts Centre, 9-11 Fore Street, Torrington, Devon EX38 8HQ
tel (01805) 622552 *fax* (01805) 622113
Contact Richard Wolfenden-Brown
Takes place Throughout the year

An occasional literature programme including workshops, readings, performances and exhibitions, as part of a larger programme of arts work, including community and educational workshops, projects and residencies.

Litfest

Sun Street Studios, 23-29 Sun Street, Lancaster LA1 1EW
tel (01524) 62166
email andy.dorby@litfest.org
website www.litfest.org
Contact Andrew Darby
Takes place mid Oct

Annual festival featuring readings, performances and workshops by contemporary writers for adults; includes performance of several new commissioned works each year. Litfest also acts as a year-round literature development agency in Lancashire.

Manchester Poetry Festival

114 Fog Lane, Disbury, Manchester M20 6SP
tel 0161-438 0550 *fax* 0161-438 0660
email mpf@rgmevents.co.uk
website www.mpf.co.uk
Festival Director Richard Michael
Takes place 2–10 Nov 2002

An annual festival catering for all tastes, including readings, children's events, slams, workshops and many live events.

Norfolk and Norwich Festival

42-58 St George's Street, Norwich NR3 1AB
tel (01603) 614921 *fax* (01603) 632303
email info@nnfest.demon.co.uk
website www.eab.org.uk/festivals
Artistic Director/Chief Executive Peter Bolton
Takes place May

North East Lincolnshire Annual Literature Festival

Arts Development Unit, North East Lincolnshire Council, Knoll Street, Cleethorpes DN35 8LN
tel (01472) 323007
Contact Arts Development Unit
Takes place Feb/March

Reflecting the heritage and culture of the area, this annual festival aims to make literature accessible to all ages and abilities through a varied and unusual programme. Write or telephone for details.

Off the Shelf Literature Festival

c/o Central Library, Surrey Street, Sheffield S1 1XZ
tel 0114-273 4716 *fax* 0114-273 5009
email off-the-shelf@pop3.poptel.org.uk
website www.offtheshelf.org.uk
Contacts Maria de Souza, Su Walker
Takes place 19 Oct–2 Nov 2002

The festival comprises a wide range of events for adults and children, including author visits, writing workshops, storytelling, competitions, theatre performances and exhibitions. Programme available in September.

Poetry International

Literature Department, Royal Festival Hall, London SE1 8XX
tel 020-7921 0906 *fax* 020-7928 2049
email literature&talks@rfh.org.uk
website www.rfh.org.uk
Takes place 26 Oct–2 Nov 2002 (biennial)

The biggest poetry festival in the British Isles, bringing together a wide range of poets from around the world. Includes readings, workshops, discussions and events for children. The Literature Section also runs a year-round programme of readings, talks and debates.

Royal Court Young Writers' Festival

The Royal Court Young Writers' Programme, Sloane Square, London SW1W 8AS
tel 020-7565 5050
Contact The Administrator
Takes place Biennially

A national festival which anyone up to the age of 25 can enter. Promising plays which arise from the workshops are then developed and performed at the Royal Court's Theatre Upstairs (see page 540).

Royal National Eisteddfod of Wales

40 Parc Ty Glas, Llanishen, Cardiff CF14 5WU
tel 029-2076 3777
email info@eisteddfod.org.uk
website www.eisteddfod.org.uk
Marketing Officer Betsan Williams
Takes place 2–9 Aug 2003

Wales' largest cultural festival, based on 800 years of tradition. Activities include competitions in all aspects of the arts, fringe performances and majestic ceremonies. In addition to activities held in the main pavilion, it houses over 300 trade stands along with a literary pavilion, a music studio, a movement and dance theatre, a rock pavilion and a purpose-built theatre. The event is set in a different location each year, and is set to visit Meifod (Powys) in August 2003.

Rye Festival

PO Box 33, Rye, East Sussex TN31 7YB
tel (01797) 224982 *fax* (01797) 224226
Literary Events Manager Mrs Hilary Brooke
Takes place First 2 weeks of Sept (15 days); Winter Series held last weekend Jan and first weekend Feb (4 days)

An annual festival of 15 literary events featuring novelists, biographers, and political and scientific writers, with book signings and discussions. Runs concurrently with the Rye festival of music and visual arts.

Salisbury Festival

75 New Street, Salisbury, Wilts. SP1 2PH
tel (01722) 332241 *fax* (01722) 410552
Director Trevor Davies
Takes place May/June

An annual general multi-arts festival with a literature programme of events. Programme published in April.

Stratford-upon-Avon Poetry Festival

Shakespeare Centre, Henley Street, Stratford-upon-Avon CV37 6QW
tel (01789) 204016 *fax* (01789) 296083
email info@shakespeare.org.uk
website www.shakespeare.org.uk
Director Roger Pringle
Takes place Usually Sunday evenings throughout July and Aug

An annual festival which aims to present poetry of many different ages and to provide opportunities for readings by contemporary poets. Sponsored by the Shakespeare Birthplace Trust. Founded 1954.

The Sunday Times Hay Festival

Festival Office, Hay-on-Wye HR3 5BX
tel (01497) 821217 *fax* (01497) 821066
email admin@hayfestival.co.uk
website www.hayfestival.co.uk
Takes place May/June

This annual festival aims to celebrate the best in writing and performance from around the world, to commission new work, and to promote and encourage young writers of excellence and potential. Over 200 events in 10 days with leading guest writers. Programme published April.

Swindon Festival of Literature

Lower Shaw Farm, Shaw, Swindon, Wilts. SN5 5PJ
tel/fax (01793) 771080
email swindonlitfest@lsfarm.globalnet.co.uk
website www.swindonfestivalofliterature.co.uk
Festival Director Matt Holland
Takes place Starts at dawn on 1 May for 10–14 days

An annual celebration of literature – prose, poetry, drama and storytelling – by readings, discussions, performances, talks, etc, indoors and out.

Dylan Thomas – The Celebration 2002

The Dylan Thomas Centre, Somerset Place, Swansea SA1 1RR
tel (01792) 463980 *fax* (01792) 463993
email dylan.thomas@cableol.co.uk
website www.dylanthomas.org
Events Manager David Woolley
Takes place 27 Oct–9 Nov 2002

An annual festival celebrating the life and work of Swansea's most famous son. Performances, lectures, debates, poetry, music and film.

Warwick & Leamington Festival

Warwick Arts Society, Pageant House, 2 Jury Street, Warwick CV34 4EW
tel (01926) 410747 *fax* (01926) 409050
email admin@warwickarts.org.uk
website www.warwickarts.org.uk
Festival Director Richard Phillips
Takes place First half of July

A music festival which includes some literature and poetry events: readings, performances and workshops.

Ways With Words Literature Festival

Droridge Farm, Dartington, Totnes, Devon TQ9 6JQ
tel (01803) 867311 *fax* (01803) 863688
email admin@wayswithwords.co.uk
website www.wayswithwords.co.uk
Contact Kay Dunbar
Takes place 10 days in middle of July each year

200 speakers give readings, talks, interviews, discussions, seminars, workshops with leading guest writers. Also organises Words by the Water: a Cumbrian literature festival (March) and Sole Bay Literature Festival, Southwold (Nov), as

well as writing courses and writing and painting holidays in Italy.

Wells Festival of Literature

Tower House, St Andrew Street, Wells, Somerset BA5 2UN
tel (01749) 673385
website www.somersite.co.uk/wellsfest.htm
Takes place Late Oct

This annual festival features leading guest writers and poets; includes writing workshops and competitions. The main venue is the historic Bishop's Palace, Wells.

Young Readers UK

Literature Office, Central Library, Chamberlain Square, Birmingham B3 3HQ
tel 0121-303 3368 *fax* 0121-303 2981
email anne-everall@birmingham.gov.uk
website www.youngreadersuk.org
Director Annie Everall
Takes place May/June

An annual festival targeted at young people aged 0–19 and adults who care for or work with them. It aims to motivate them to enjoy reading and through this to encourage literacy; to provide imaginative access to books, writers and storytellers; to encourage families to share reading for pleasure; to provide a national focus for the celebration of books and reading for children and young people and help raise the media profile of children's books and writing. Approximately 170 events.

Writers and artists online

E-publishing

E-publishers offer a variety of services to authors and have no set standards of quality or provision. ***Jane Dorner*** *looks at the electronic minefield facing authors.*

All major UK publishers have websites on which they promote their books. Some are publishing electronic versions downloadable directly from the web. Some, like Random House, are sharing the revenue from e-titles 50–50 with their authors. This is still basically traditional publishing, and all the brand name expectations apply.

There's another, new, set of e-publishers which do not have an established track record – there has been no time for the investment in a brand (high standards, quality provision, peer review, integrity). Some are genuine publishers operating in the new environment and some come perilously close to vanity publishers eager to make money out of the unwary. Others offer useful services to self-publishers. And some call themselves publishers, but are effectively book showrooms. The boundaries can sometimes be so vague that it is difficult to be dogmatic about what value they provide.

For example, one e-publisher offers a core free service, but that is only if you throw a completely finished, edited file into a standard template; anything individual or quality-vetted costs £200 and upwards. Another charges £40 to act as an e-agent, showcasing a synopsis and first chapter and targeting agents and publishers with an email alerter. A third requires £99 to turn your book into an electronic format, plus minimal marketing, and charges a flat rate of nearly £5 a book of which £2 goes to the author. Some take anything they are offered (within the bounds of censorship) and others have strict filtering systems. Not many provide editing, design or quality control.

Until new reputations form, writers will have to look closely at the new e-publisher's websites, read carefully through submission statements, look for an online contract or terms and conditions and judge for themselves. Enter into an email dialogue and get as much information as you can before you submit anything.

The most obvious appeal is to writers who have unpublished works, out-of-print works whose rights have reverted to them, or previously published materials that could have a renewed life in a new format.

E-formats

The choice of formats is diverse, including:

- book-a-likes – book-sized electronic devices with screens of varying sizes designed for reading continuous texts – the texts displayed on them are e-books;
- personal organisers like the Palm Pilot, Handspring, Jornada or Psion, also able to carry e-books;
- any platform using Adobe Portable Document Format (PDF), which is a universal standard for preserving the original appearance (fonts, formatting, colours and graphics) of any source document, regardless of the application and platform used to create it;
- notebook PCs using Microsoft Reader format – electronic reading software designed for easy screen reading;
- coded web pages (in HTML or XML, the coding used by software browsers);
- plain vanilla text (ASCII);
- Tablet PC – a textbook and notebook rolled into one.

All content can be downloaded into the reading devices from a website and can be paid for at that time. These formats are relatively cheap for a publisher to produce – but only assuming they do nothing to add to the editorial value. None of the electronic formats are secure from plagiarists, though some make a better attempt at security than others. At present, PDF files are the most secure (though hackable), with options ranging from preventing text selection (so users cannot cut and paste), disabling reading on screen (so only one print copy can be made), or, conversely, disabling printing, to password-protection. All these possibilities can form part of your email discussion.

The question here is whether yours is the sort of book that people will want to read from screens – small or large.

Print On Demand

E-publishers are also offering Print On Demand services for good quality paper copies in runs of 1 to 250. This has a double appeal to authors:

- for self-publishing; and
- for bringing an out-of-print book back into circulation.

The self-publishing route is attractive. There's a set-up cost and a per title cost, but they're generally lower than the self-publishing options that have been available up to now. This option may well be of interest to authors who don't mind doing their own promotion. Print On Demand offers a potentially viable digital production model to the publishing industry as a whole. If the technology settles and origination costs come down a little lower than they are now, we could see certain types of book being ordered on the internet for collection an hour later at the local bookshop where it is bound and printed. Authors in some genres may be able to bypass publishers.

Out-of-print publishing is more complex. It is unlikely that the author will have a digital copy of a former work. Corrections, design and late changes to the latest version of either the author's or the editor's file is not the final version. This means a published copy must be scanned in and converted. To do this with acceptable accuracy requires a sophisticated scanner and two copies of the book with cut spines, merged and assembled in book order. There are two problems. With older books, the author may only have one precious copy and may not be willing to cut it up. With newer books, the chances are the rights have reverted, but the typographical right still belongs to the publisher for 25 years after publication. It's arguable that scanning violates that right.

Marketing

The listing below offers just some of the new e-publishers which are offering services to authors who would like to sell or resell their works in one of the formats described. Some market in the same way as traditional publishers. Many new e-publishers double as online booksellers, so they are not publishers in the sense we have been used to – although they also promote their best-selling authors more aggressively than the ones no one has heard of. The difference is that they can offer showcase capacity to any author, well known or not. Most guarantee visitors against pornography and real rubbish, but it's fairly rudimentary quality control. Showcasing is generally just that – a space on the bookshelf. And in this environment bookshelving is infinitely expandable. Most are sited in the US, but that doesn't matter since this is global exposure anyway.

Websites

Note, this is a fast-moving area and more online publishers will spring up and some of these will disappear. In all cases, authors should check all details of the contracts.

Allandale Online Publishing

www.allandale.co.uk/
Academic books in politics and international relations.

Artemis Press

www.artemispress.com/
Women's fiction, 40% royalty; contract and submission details online; exclusive rights requested.

Atlantic Bridge
www.atlanticbridge.net/
Seeks science fiction, horror, romance and mystery writers; non-exclusive contract and submission details online; 30% royalty.

Authors Direct
www.wordwizard.com/adindex.htm
A self-publishing showcase linking to UK authors' websites; connects to word wizard club.

Author's Studio
www.theauthorsstudio.org/
Community of small presses owned and operated by commercial authors.

Avid Press
www.avidpress.com/
Seeking high-quality fiction novels to be published in ebook and/or print format; romance, mystery, gothic genre bias.

Back-in-Print (UK)
www.backinprint.co.uk/
Out-of-print titles brought back into print in small print runs; sensible rights advice.

Black Sheep Books
http://blacksheepbooks.co.uk/
Crime/thriller and children's publishing.

Book4Publishing
www.book4publishing.com/
Shropshire-based e-agent which showcases synopsis and first chapter and then auto-targets publishers and agents; £39.95 fee.

BookLocker
www.booklocker.com/
E-book publisher offering 70% royalties to authors only requesting non-exclusive rights. Authors are free to list and sell their books elsewhere.

Book-on-Disk
www.book-on-disc.com/
Creates e-books in downloadable or disk format; pays royalties and appears to have been vetted by the American Guild of Writers; authors retain copyright. Not a vanity press.

Books on Line
www.books-on-line.com/
Public domain titles as well as opportunities to offer your own work.

Boson Books
www.cmonline.com/boson/
Electronic book imprint of C&M Online Media Inc.; eclectic list.

Centre House Press
www.centrehousepress.co.uk/
Publishes excerpts of literary works of all types, where the respective authors intend later full production in book form.

Crowsnest Books
www.computercrowsnest.com/
Science fiction, fantasy, horror, adventure, war, crime and thriller novels; some non-fiction.

Diskus Publishing
www.diskuspublishing.com/
Indiana-based romantic fiction niche publisher. Books for several e-reader formats can be downloaded for about £6.30 a book. Said to publish about 5% of submissions.

Domhan Books
www.domhanbooks.com/
Multicategory genre listing for publications in a variety of formats.

Eastgate
www.eastgate.com/
New hypertext technologies; publication of serious hypertext, fiction and non-fiction: serious, interactive writing.

eBook Palace
www.ebookpalace.com/
Visitor-submitted directory of e-books; authors can list their own.

eBookAd
www.ebookad.com/
A clearing house for all kinds of e-book information; appears to be pitched at publishers.

eBooks.com
www.ebooks.com/
Internet Digital Bookstore. Invites authors to let publisher or agent know about it; authors should check rights deals with their publishers.

EBooks on the Net
www.ebooksonthe.net/
Non-mainstream genres.

eBookWeb
www.ebookweb.org/
Central source for news and information on all aspects of electronic publishing.

Electronic Literature Organisation
www.eliterature.org/
Promotes new media writing.

Electronic Publishers Coalition
www.epccentral.org/
Educates the reading public – consumers, retailers and distributors – on the changing face of electronic books.

ENovel
http://ssl.enovel.com/
Free service offering 50% royalty on books, stories, novellas and subscriptions stories – beware the click copyright though as it's not necessary.

FictionWise
www.fictionwise.com/
Independent eBook publisher and distributor. Work must be previously published fiction works from established authors. Does not accept unsolicited material or work from new writers.

Fiction Works
www.fictionworks.com/
E-books and audio book opportunities; submissions in certain genres only.

1stBooks Library
www.1stbooks.com/
E-book distributor; offers books in PDF format; a 40% deal to established authors; motley collection.

Great Unpublished
www.greatunpublished.com/
Integrated community of writers, readers and professional editors, self-publishing venue and bookstore. Also provides a POD service. Operates a 2-tiered system: basic kit and special imprint program.

Infopost
www.infopost.com/
Digital everything marketplace and portal; opportunities for authors to sell directly.

iUniverse
www.iuniverse.com/
A service for redeploying out-of-print books; check the author contract carefully.

Microsoft Reader
www.microsoft.com/reader/authors
The page about the Reader (e-books designed to be read on pocket PCs) aimed at authors; keep your eye on this one.

My Publish
www.mypublish.com/
Sales resource for digital content.

Neighborhood Press
www.neighborhoodpress.com/
All types of fiction, from political mysteries to western historical romances.

nctLibrary
www.netlibrary.com/
Free and purchasable titles using the Knowledge Station software; expanding into hand-held computers; check the licensing agreements before signing up titles.

Netspace Publishing
www.netspace-publishing.co.uk/
Publishes electronic versions of texts not placed anywhere else. All books sold for £2.99; author gets £1.

New Concepts Publishing
www.newconceptspublishing.com/
Specialises in romance writers seeking publication; inexpensive for buyers; not obvious what the advantages to sellers are.

No Spine
www.nospine.com/
A UK self-publishing facilitator that takes 20% of whatever an author charges to cover e-commerce and web overheads. Quotes *Writers & Artists' Yearbook* profusely. Track record unknown.

Online Originals
www.onlineoriginals.com/
One of the higher-profile venues for new writers wanting to get published; UK based.

Open eBook initiative
www.openebook.org/
Format specifications, sponsored by the National Institute of Standards and Technology.

Overdrive Systems
www.overdrive.com/news/index.htm
How to publish with Microsoft Reader and other *soi-disant* e-publishing solutions.

Palm Digital Media
www.peanutpress.com/
E-books for hand-held computers; has published Palm versions of books by well-known authors.

Paperbackwriters
www.paperbackwriters.co.uk/
Showcase focusing exclusively on aspiring novelists in any genre looking for a publisher.

Pigeonhole Press
www.pigeonholepress.com/
For niche markets.

PublishingOnline
www.publishingonline.com/
An electronic publisher; no clear specialism; has a sample contract online.

Pulpless
www.pulpless.com/
Non-paper book publisher which claims to publish only established professional authors; check sample contract before proceeding.

Questia
www.questia.com/
Dallas-based company which is looking for authors' out-of-print non-fiction (mostly textbooks); be sure you own the rights to scan before negotiations begin.

ReadMyWriting
www.readmywriting.com/
Stated aim is to bring together authors, literary agents and publishers to enable the efficient publication of their work through the internet.

Reedmee
www.reedmee.com/
Sheffield-based company specialising in non-fiction e-books.

Replica Books
www.replicabooks.com/
Would you like to see an out-of-print book back on the shelf? See what their terms are.

Roaming Reader
www.roamingreader.com/
The classics delivered to your mobile phone; no e-roaming originals yet.

SellYourBooks
www.sellyourbooks.co.uk/
Perth-based web publisher charging £57 handling fee for MS formatting and showcasing books.

Small Press Center
www.smallpress.org/
New-York-based non-profit institution for independent publishers; useful articles and information for small publishers.

Treeless Press
www.treelesspress.com/
Non-exclusive publishing deal with Rocket eBooks.

UK Children's Books
www.ukchildrensbooks.co.uk/
Listings of authors, illustrators and publishers.

Unlimited Publishing
www.unlimitedpublishing.com/
A Print On Demand system for new and out-of-print titles; will cost authors a minimum of $800 as long as they use Word or similar.

Virtual Bookworm
www.virtualbookworm.com/
Print On Demand and e-book supplier.

Virtual Volumes
www.virtualvolumes.com/
UK-based publisher offering a serious service for the 'manuscript in a drawer'.

Write Online
www.write-on-line.co.uk/
E-texts and traditional print works for the academic market. Aim to secure hard-copy contracts.

Writers Co-operative
www.books-4u-online.com/
www.rabbitbooks.com/
Mixed collection of UK self-publishing writers' work and its authors publishing venue.

WritersServices.com
www.writersservices.com/
Offers editorial services and advice from well-known writers; pitched largely at unpublished authors.

Xlibris
www.xlibris.com/
Self-publishing centre; says it exists solely to serve and empower authors – at a price.

Zoetrope Stories
www.all-story.com
Authors submit and critique each others' stories; seemingly no remuneration.

Setting up a website

Computer users who have email almost certainly have web space available to them. ***Jane Dorner*** *explains the points for writers and artists to consider when setting up a personal website and how to best make it work for them.*

This article assumes that readers are familiar with websites and have used the internet for research. To set up your own website the main investment you need to make is in time, perhaps more than you initially think. The process may have its frustrating moments, but it is ultimately creative.

Personal websites

A website can be a useful self-publicity medium for writers. It can be especially useful if you self-publish, but equally worthwhile for showing the world a portfolio of your accomplishments. Many writers are polymaths and the web shows up such diversity to advantage.

A personal website can be set up to demonstrate your writing or illustration style(s) and areas of interest with examples of work so that commissioning editors can see if they are choosing the right writer or artist for the job. You can include an outline of your skills and achievements, and list your publications – or you could even offer a personal syndication service for stories, articles, photographs or illustrations (if first or resale rights are yours).

You need to let people know that your website exists – there is no point having a wonderful site if no one visits it – for which old-fashioned marketing techniques are necessary. Posting your site on the web and registering hopefully with a few (or even a hundred) search engines is no substitute for careful targeting, although it is helpful once initial contact has been made. Refer potential clients to your website, and make sure it attracts them sufficiently to explore it.

Skills required

In order to create the website yourself, you will need to have:

- a capacity for logical thinking;
- secure language expertise;
- some technical understanding;
- good visual sense;
- patience; and
- familiarity with applicable law.

If you don't have (or can't acquire) these skills then it is worth thinking about asking someone else to build the site for you. Expect to pay for at least one day of a professional designer's time (between £250 and £450) to create a modest suite of individually tailored pages with some attention to what you want and need. Bear in mind that the less you pay, the more likely it is that your material is simply being poured into a standard template.

Planning a website

Whether you get involved with the technological side or not, you will still have to plan and write the copy yourself. Writing for the web is a new art form that uses writerly skills: it is genuinely creative; requires writers, not programmers; and needs editors with an understanding of traditional editorial values.

Writing the text for a website is like any other writing project. The more effort that goes into the planning stage, the better the result. You need to identify who you are targeting and be clear about the purpose of the website. For instance, is it your calling card; a PR brochure; a sales outlet; an information resource; a literary club or part of a network; a designer's showcase; or a medium of self-expression? The website needs to be planned and created accordingly. For example, if you just want a simple calling card, then a single screen – called a splash page – might suffice. It would have your name, perhaps a photograph of you, a few lines about your specialist skills and interests, possibly some work you have had published, and your contact details. You can then be found by anyone who uses the internet; your personal front cover is on the world bookshelf.

Writing for screen reading

If you write for radio, you will have an advantage over other writers. Writing for the web is a bit like writing for broadcasting: the style has to compensate for the loss of the visual impact of words. It's a common mistake to cut and paste from documents created for print because the text will not read as well on a website.

The average adult spends eight hours a week reading as opposed to 27 hours watching television. And that's reading from paper – reading from a screen has so far proved less efficient than paper.

When writing the introductory text for a website, aim for the reluctant reader with a less than three-minute attention span and use easy words and short sentences. As readers delve deeper into a site, their acceptance of more discursive reading matter increases. Once they are committed to the subject material, you can write in your normal style and assume they will print out the text and read from paper. Take writing for radio or television as the paradigm and then make it even simpler. Here are a few pointers:

- **Use the tadpole or pyramid structure**. Hit your reader with the main points at the top of the page (people are reluctant to scroll). Use interior pages to unfold details.
- **Be concise**. The overall length of a radio or television piece is about a third of a print article; a web page should be even shorter. Cut every word that doesn't contribute. A good web page length is under 300 words – it is better to divide anything longer than that into sub-topics.
- **Write short paragraphs**. Paragraph breaks refresh the eye: between two and five sentences is enough.
- **Write simple sentences**. Ideas are easier to digest in a simple subject-verb-object progression. Make subclauses into separate sentences. Use one idea per sentence and make them under the 17-word print average.
- **Use the present or present perfect tense**. The web is here and now. Keep passives away.
- **Be consistent**. Use the same font, type size, alignment and background colour throughout your site. Or use different colour bands to denote different 'areas' (novels, poetry, teaching and so on). Remember that capital letters onscreen look like SHOUTING.
- **Consider navigation**. If a visitor makes Choice A here, what are the ramifications for Choice B there? Web writing is not static, but writing dynamically is something that most writers have not learned. It is, perhaps, something we will all have to discover as we progress into the web publishing age.
- **Links**. Don't link every prompt phrase that leads somewhere else. If you want readers to stay with you to absorb your point, put the link outside the main text area. Don't link just because you can.
- **Define the main areas of your site**. Consider synonyms for your top level labels (the four to six main areas of your site). How often have you got lost in a website simply because the way in which your mind works isn't the same as the mindset of the person who created it? Try to second guess what visitors to your site will want to see when they come to each page then find a single word that most unambiguously describes it.

Websites for design

Art and the Zen of Web Sites
www.tlc-systems.com/webtips.shtml
Why the web is not a place to show off artistic skills.

Creating Graphics for the Web
www.widearea.co.uk/designer/
Information on GIFs, JPEGs, anti-aliasing and other design matters.

Killer Sites
www.killersites.com/
Website of *Creating Killer Web Sites* by David Siegal. Both book and site are full of information for designers.

Web-safe colours
www.visibone.com/colorlab/

Web-safe fonts
www.microsoft.com/truetype/fontpack/default.htm

Useful websites

Amazon Bookshop Associates Scheme
www.amazon.co.uk/associates/
For linking to sales of your own (or recommended) books.

Alert Box
www.useit.com/alertbox/
Web usability and readability analysis. Opinionated but pertinent.

The CGI Resource Index
www.cgi-resources.com/
Scripts that you can buy (some are free), e.g. automatic forms and page counters.

Coffee Cup
www.coffeecup.com/
Web creation software.

1st Site Free
www.1stsitefree.com/
Create a website in 7 easy steps. A good starting point; links to useful tools.

FTP Explorer
www.ftpx.com/
File transfer software for PCs.

The HTML Writers Guild
www.hwg.org/
Free membership and access to resources.

Netfinder
www.ozemail.com.au/~pli/netfinder/
File transfer software for Macs.

Pedalo
www.pedalo.co.uk/
Website promotion services to writers.

Site Aid
www.siteaid.com/
Freeware HTML editor. Looks similar to Microsoft's FrontPage.

UK2.Net
http://uk2.net/
Inexpensive domain registration and web forwarding.

Validator
http://validator.w3.org/
Free online validation of HTML code.

Web Style Guide
www.uncle-netword.com/webstyle/
Opinionated view of how to write for the web.

Yale Style Manual
http://info.med.yale.edu/caim/manual/
Excellent guide to aspects of web writing.

Web Services for Writers
www.nothingnet.co.uk/webservices/forwriters/
Get a suite of 5 pages for £49.

Designing for screens

The first thing to remember about designing for screens is that you cannot control how the screen page will look as there are so many variables, such as screen resolution and type of web browser. You should therefore test your design on several platforms. Design depends on purpose, but here are a few good practice points:

Colour. Have a white or pale cream background and black or very dark type (studies show that sharp contrasts aid readability). Use 'web-safe' colours (see box). There are 216 of them based on RGB, which simply stands for Red, Green, Blue – nature's three primary colours. Monitors and television sets transmit RGB – after all colour is light – so the only colours available are the ones that standard monitors can transmit.

Fonts. How typefaces appear onscreen depends on which ones are on that particular system, not what you specify on yours. The ones you can rely on to look good on screens – and are universally available – are known as 'web-safe' fonts (see box).

Line length. Put the text in invisible tables so that the line length is limited to about 10 words in standard browsers – this is an optimum reading line length. If you do not set a limit, the chances are that at high screen resolutions readers might get a line length of 25 words on the default reading typeface. This leads to what is known as 'regression pauses' while the reader struggles to make sense of the text.

Page size. A reasonable rule of thumb is to make each page a maximum of 35K. People don't like watching a blank screen and research suggests that 10 seconds is as long as most people will wait for the screen to be filled. Standard dialup connections download at around 4–5K a second, so that means the first 20K or so need to be interesting enough to grab the viewer's attention. A short text page with three or four thumbnail-sized graphics will generally load fast.

Graphics. Every graphic must speak: make sure its iconography is clear and unambiguous. Remember that when you insert a picture it is good form to give an explanatory note in the ALT (Alternative) command. This pops up as a little yellow box hovering over the image area and presents an opportunity to preview in words what the picture illustrates.

Artist's portfolio. A gallery of small thumbnail illustrations is useful for showcasing an artist's range of work, with a click-link to larger pictures. Take care not to offer high-quality graphics that could be plagiarised: most internet graphics are in JPEG format, which is 72 dpi and not suitable for print reproduction. It's advisable to watermark all artwork.

Animation. Bullet points or graphic elements help pick out key words but animations should be avoided. Studies show that the message is lost when television images fail to reinforce spoken words. The same is true of the web.

Frames. Using frames can be an elegant solution to navigation problems, but for the user it's not ideal. Because the page name on the URL never varies, the visitor never knows where they are. They cannot bookmark a particular page, or find it again on a second visit and that can be very frustrating.

Going online

Once you have the planning, writing and graphics of your website organised, you need a little basic technical understanding to get it online. Your service provider will have a starter kit of instructions – although whether they make sense is another matter. You may well have to turn to other sources for instruction.

The internet is chock-a-block with instructional material. Try 1st Site Free (see page 558), which outlines and expands on seven easy steps – plan, design, code, upload, test, promote and maintain.

An alternative is to use software that 'talks you through' setting up a small site with what are called 'wizards'. Wizards come in software programs such as FrontPage (part of Microsoft Office Premium) and its free look-a-like Site Aid. Both resemble word processors and keep the coding hidden from view. Hard core web designers will sneer at these programs, because programmers like to control the way the code works themselves. What they do not realise is that writers want to concentrate on the words, not the coding, and as long as it functions, the refinements of the underlying structure are of less importance. For artists who are more concerned with design, the best package is Dreamweaver (which is expensive and not easy to learn).

Once the pages are ready, the next step is to transmit them to the service provider's machines. The mechanics of this are frequently opaque even when you are offered a handy button that says 'Publish'. The chances are that your service provider will not have the extensions that make the 'Publish' button work and you will have to acquire a (free) File Transfer Protocol (ftp) program. If you are technophobe, this may seem frightening at first. However, it is really very simple and once you have successfully transferred (or uploaded) the pages from your computer to the web space on the remote server, you will wonder what the problem was. For this transfer process you will need to know the host name, your user ID and your password, information available from your provider.

HTML

If you want to learn HTML (HyperText Markup Language) – the code that tags elements such as text, links and graphics so that browser software will know how to display a document – then you need only a plain text program, like Notepad, and an HTML primer (there are plenty online as well as in printed form). Find some website pages which you like and look at their source code to see how they have been constructed (click the subsidiary button of the mouse, usually the right button, and select View Source). If the originators have used JavaScript or Cascading Style Sheets, this may well be more code than you want to know about so look at simple pages first.

Going a step further

You may wish to have a web address or URL that is short or memorable so that it is easier for people to find your website. You can choose this domain name yourself, and is now relatively cheap (see box on page 558).

It is probably best to leave e-commerce (having a secure site that can handle credit card sales) till later. In the meantime, however, a simple way to boost your income is to become an Amazon Associate. If your book titles are linked to Amazon, you'll make 15% on a direct sale made from your site.

Websites for writers

***The Internet: A Writer's Guide** by Jane Dorner (www.internetwriter.co.uk) is published by A & C Black and has the full listing of over 1000 resources for writers from which the sites below have been selected.*

New to the internet

Acronym Expander
www.ucc.ie/info/net/acronyms/index.html
Web abbreviations and acronyms.

BBC Web Wise
www.bbc.co.uk/education/webwise/
How to get started on the internet.

FAQ
www.faqs.org/
Frequently Asked Questions on just about anything to do with the internet.

Google
www.google.com/
The current favourite amongst search engines.

How Stuff Works
www.howstuffworks.com/
Fairly technical explanations about how the internet works, and much more.

Fact finding online

Ananova (UK Press Association)
www.ananova.net/
Latest stories from the UK's top news and information websites; useful free daily round-up of news, sport and information by email.

Ask Oxford
www.askoxford.com/
Various bits from the language dictionaries; changing word news and word-based interest.

Bartlett's Familiar Quotations
www.bartleby.com/

Bibliomania
www.bibliomania.com/
Excellent full text with a good word or phrase retrieval; includes the wonderful *Brewer's Dictionary of Phrase & Fable* (which no author can do without).

Bookworks
www.bookworks.org.uk/
Text-related projects including internet and new media projects.

British Library
http://portico.bl.uk/
Free search for material held in the major Reference and Document Supply collections of the British Library.

CIA World Factbook
www.cia.gov/cia/publications/factbook/
Statistical data about countries and other useful data.

Crossref
www.crossref.org/
A collaborative reference linking service for researchers.

Encyclopaedia Britannica
www.britannica.com/
Full text and searching, together with a huge resource of information, grammar and reference links. Some free; premium subscription.

Fonts
www.cuycoskywarn.org/utils/fonts/fonts.htm
Downloadable fonts for you to use for your own e-books.

Free Pint
www.freepint.com/
Free bi-monthly email newsletter with tips and articles on finding reliable sites and searching more effectively. Written by information professionals.

Response Source
http://sourcewire.com/frames/pr
UK journalists can request business information in a single step from over 300 organisations.

Roget's Thesaurus
http://humanities.uchicago.edu/forms_unrest/ROGET.html
1911 version (out of copyright, and inevitably out of currency too).

WISDOM: Knowledge & Literature Search
http://thinkers.net/
Links to writing and literature sites under the headings Creativity, Literature, Authors, Thoughts, Publishing, Words, Languages.

Interactivity

Alt-X
www.altx.com/
Online publishing network – 'where the digerati meet the literati'.

Electronic Poetry Center
http://wings.buffalo.edu/epc/

E-Zone
http://ezone.org
Literary site that includes an e-zine 'entryzone'; some permanent hypertext works.

Hyperizons: the Search for Hypertext Fiction
www.duke.edu/~mshumate/hyperfic.html

Plexus
www.plexus.org/
Interface to a flux of ideas contained in the writings and visual works of several artists and writers.

Writing communities

Bloomsbury Magazine
www.bloomsburymagazine.com/writersarea/
Writers' area; advice and resources for authors.

E-Writers
http://e-writers.net
Community, competitions and advice – weekly online publishing newsletter.

Fiction Writer's Connection
www.fictionwriters.com
Provides help with novel writing and information on finding agents and editors and getting published; has a mailing list of 3000+.

For writers
www.forwriters.com
Self-help; links and professional markets.

HackWriters
www.hackwriters.com/
UK-based free internet magazine devoted to good writing on any subject. No fees; forum of exchange.

Literati Club
www.emeraldinsight.com/literaticlub
Site for journal authors.

Littoral
www.littoral.org.uk
Arts trust which aims to develop new arts projects.

Live Literature Network
www.liveliterature.net/
Database of writers offering live events in the UK.

Mystic Ink
www.mystic-ink.com/
Community areas for e-writers.

National Association for Literature Development
www.literaturedevelopment.com/development/

Online Writing Community
http://trace.ntu.ac.uk
Centre of experimental writing in the UK; also has courses.

StudioNotes
www.studionotes.com/
Service in entertainment industry to provide aspiring writers the opportunity to develop and market their material; costly.

Word Circuits
www.wordcircuits.com/
A community as well as a gallery of new fiction and poetry.

Writernet
www.writernet.org.uk/
British community, mostly for writers working in theatre, TV, radio, film, live art and performance poetry; a professional network.

Writers Net
www.writers.net
US-based forum for writers, editors, agents and publishers. Participants exchange ideas about the writing life and the business of writing.

Writelink
www.writelink.co.uk/
Resource site linking to paying markets, competitions, reference sites, software and so on.

Writers on the Net
www.writers.com
Busy community offering online (paid for) classes.

New media writing prizes

Electronic Literature Awards
www.eliterature.org/
One for fiction and one for poetry.

Eppie Awards for E-books
http://members.aol.com/seriouslywhacked/eppie_awards.htm
21 fiction and non-fiction categories.

Gutenberg-e
www.theaha.org/prizes/gutenberg/
A prize competition for the best history dissertations in fields where the traditional monograph has now become endangered.

Independent e-Book Awards
www.e-book-awards.com/indie-intro.shtml
For self- or independently published e-books and digital stories.

International eBook Award Foundation
www.iebaf.org
For fiction and non-fiction (not necessarily experimental) at the Frankfurt and Bologna Book Fairs.

Media Arts Plaza Awards
http://plaza.bunka.go.jp/english/

Java Museum Online Awards
www.javamuseum.org/
For innovative new media installations.

The trAce/Alt-X International Hypertext Competition
http://trace.ntu.ac.uk/comp.cfm

Miscellany

Dying Words
www.corsinet.com/braincandy/dying.html
For the historical novelist.

Eponym
www.eponym.org/
Aimed at new parents and handy for finding a name for a character; names from just about everywhere in the world at different times in history.

Famous Birthdays
www.famousbirthdays.com/
Month-by-month and day-by-day listing of birth dates, historical and in the media.

Famous Firsts
www.corsinet.com/trivia/1-triv.html
People-who-did-something-first arranged in ascending date order.

Literary Calendar: An Almanac of Literary Information
http://litcal.yasuda-u.ac.jp/lc
Significant literary events.

Lives
http://amillionlives.com/
Links to biographies, autobiographies, memoirs, diaries, letters, narratives and oral histories.

Perpetual Virtual Calendars
www.vpcalendar.net/
A historical or science fiction novelist's dream: verify any date or day of the week in the 20th and 21st centuries.

Research-it
www.itools.com/research-it
Little battery of dictionaries and acronym converters.

Rhyming dictionary
www.link.cs.cmu.edu/dougb/rhyme-doc.html

Time Zone Converter
www.timezoneconverter.com/
What time it is or will be anywhere in the world.

Who is or Was
www.biography.com/
Good for checking people's dates; incorporates the *Cambridge Dictionary of American Biography*.

World Wide Words
www.quinion.com/words/
Verbal cornucopia for anyone interested in words; circulates a newsletter.

Texts online

Electronic Text Center
http://etext.lib.virginia.edu/english.html
Collection of online English language texts; links to other texts online by subject or by author.

The English Server
http://eserver.org/
Large collection of interesting resources.

Etext Archives
www.etext.org
Archives of religious, political, legal and fanzine text.

Oxford Text Archive
www.ota.ahds.ac.uk/
Distributes more than 2500 resources in over 25 different languages for study purposes only.

Project Gutenberg
www.gutenberg.net/
The official sites (many mirrors all over the world); vast library of e-texts, mostly public domain; all in plain text format.

Shakespeare Resources
www.shakespeare.com/
Links to many other sites.

E-publishing – see page 551

Writing tools

Screenwriting

Creativity Unleashed
www.cul.co.uk/
Software to stimulate creative thinking.

Dramatica
www.dramatica.com/
Screenplay software; not free – compare it with ScreenForge below.

Final Draft
www.finaldraft.com/
Apparently the bees knees of scripting software – expensive (about £150), high functionality and cross-platform compatibility.

ScreenForge
www.apotheosispictures.com/
Almostfree Hollywood scriptwriting format bolt-on for Word.

Scrnplay.dot
www.erols.com/lehket/Dale/scrnplay.html
Free template for Word 6/7 for screenplay writers; both this and ScreenForge are worth looking at.

Storyware

Alice
www.cs.virginia.edu/~alice/
Software program for storyboard modelling; quite technical but interesting.

Brutus Story Generator
www.rpi.edu/dept/ppcs/BRUTUS/brutus.html#Sample

Creativity Unleashed
www.cul.co.uk/
Software to stimulate creative thinking, originally intended for business.

StoryBoard Quick
www.powerproduction.com/
Storyboard software for films, animation, games and other uses.

Storycraft Writer's Software
www.writerspage.com/
Fiction-writing program that claims to turn ideas into complete novels, screenplays, plays or short stories.

Web Store for Writers and Creative Pros
www.masterfreelancer.com/
Plots Unlimited, Writer's Software Companion and other software aids.

Word-processing aids

Tricks and Trinkets
www.tricksandtrinkets.com/pk/
To make word processing easier, e.g. autotext for often-used phrases.

WordTips
www.VitalNews.com/wordtips/
How to get the best out of Microsoft Word; useful tips, many a real boon for writers.

Setting up a website – see page 556

Jane Dorner is the author of 19 books and represents authors' interests on the Boards of ALCS and CLA. She is author of ***The Internet: A Writer's Guide*** (A & C Black) (www.internetwriter.co.uk) which has the full listing of over 1000 resources for writers. The following genre areas have substantial listings: academic writing; business writing; children's writing; crime writing and mystery; fantasy; fiction; health writers; historical research; horror; interactive fiction and experimental forms; journalism; literature festivals; literature resources; mystery; poetry; prizes; residencies; romance; science fiction, fantasy and horror; specialist subjects; screen, TV and playwriting; translation; travel writing; STM writers; technical writing; women's and gender issues; writing courses and many other themes.

Websites for artists

Studio space is expensive and is seldom close to those who buy or market artists' work. Total immersion in creating makes it difficult to spend time out of the studio in the name of business and still meet deadlines. The internet can provide many resources for artists and ***Alison Baverstock*** *introduces some useful websites.*

In theory, the web should be an ideal way for artists to obtain support but in practice there are relatively few good information sites for visual artists. Ironically, most of the organisations that are involved in visual arts have not developed sites that are particularly useful to artists. They tend to have websites that are used more for marketing their own organisations than providing free information online. However, several of the regional arts offices sites are useful, as are some of the government sites, and some organisation sites provide links to places for further 'digging'. The following list of web addresses will be useful as a starting point.

General sites

AN: The Artists Information Company

www.anweb.co.uk
A very broad site, covering all aspects of being an artist from current events to developing and maintaining good business practice. Initial section headings are:
• Forum – an interactive space for artists to seek and exchange advice on practice, career, project and business issues
• Practice – practical information and examples on showing, selling, commissions, residencies, production and collaboration
• Career – information on developing a career as an artist: first steps, looking at yourself, skills, developing a career, portfolio careers
• Business – valuable know-how and tips on becoming and being self employed, accounts, tax, contracts, promotion and insurance
• Contacts – over 1000 links to visual arts organisations in the UK and internationally which offer email and web links
• Artists – artists tell the real story of practice: their approaches, achievements and setbacks
• Research – introducing research on visual arts and artists' practice.
There are also two sister sites:
www.workingwithartists.co.uk and
www.artistscareers.co.uk.
AN publishes *AN Magazine*, which specifically caters for the needs of visual and applied artists.

Art Train

www.arttrain.org.uk
A searchable database of courses and training providers in Scotland.

Artifact

www.artifact.ie
An online register representing work by over 1000 contemporary professional artists based in the Republic of Ireland and Northern Ireland.

The Arts Council

www.artscouncil.org.uk
Offers useful information on public policy towards the arts and current funding (such as which areas of the arts each organisation handles). The 'news and information' section offers useful statistics on the arts in England as well as links to other sites.

The Arts Council of Northern Ireland

www.artscouncil-ni.org
Information on arts policy, funding schemes and contacts in Northern Ireland and the Republic.

The Arts Council of Wales

www.ccc-acw.org.uk
Information on arts policy, funding schemes and contacts in Wales.

AXIS for Information on Visual Artists

www.axisartists.org.uk
The largest interactive database of contemporary British art on the internet.

Birkbeck College, University of London

www.bbk.ac.uk/lib/artlibgu/html
Offers details of art libraries in London.

Center for Safety in the Arts
http://artswire.org:70/1/csa
Based in the USA but includes excellent information on health and safety in the visual arts.

The Crafts Council
www.craftscouncil.org.uk
Offers services for both makers and members of the public interested in craft practice and purchase.

Cultural Enterprise – Menter Diwylliannol
www.cultural-enterprise.com
Information on business support for creative industries in Wales.

Culture, Media and Sport, Dept of
www.culture.gov.uk
Holds the latest research reports on the creative industries.

Cywaith Cymru – Artworks Wales
www.cywaithcymru.org
Listings of public art and residency projects in Wales.

Design and Artists Copyright Society
www.dacs.co.uk .
Information on copyright and intellectual property.

The Gallery Channel UK
www.thegallerychannel.co.uk
An excellent and almost comprehensive exhibition listings website.

Inland Revenue
www.inlandrevenue.gov.uk
Useful information on tax, national insurance and self-assessment – particularly helpful if you are new to being self employed.

Institute of International Visual Arts (inIVA)
www.iniva.org
A contemporary visual arts organisation with a special interest in new technologies, commissioning site-specific artworks and international collaborations.

Intellectual Property
www.intellectual-property.gov.uk
The Government's information site on copyright and other intellectual property rights.

International Association of Residential Arts Centres
www.resartis.org
An online directory of residency centres worldwide.

International Cultural Desk
www.icd.org.uk
Offers international opportunities for Scottish artists.

Metier
www.metier.org.uk
The national training organisation for the arts and entertainment industries, representing 500,000 people involved in the arts (including visual arts and all aspects of arts management).

National Disability Arts Forum
www.ndaf.org
Offers disability arts news and information on opportunities and contacts.

National Statistics: the official UK statistics site
www.statistics.gov.uk
Publishes a range of general and specific statistics on the arts.

Public Art South West
www.publicartonline.org.uk
Offers information on contacts, opportunities and practical advice on public art.

Regional Arts Offices
www.arts.org.uk
Offers access to the Arts Council of England's 9 reorganised regional offices in England for useful information on funding schemes, opportunities and who to contact to find out more.

The Scottish Arts Council
www.sac.org.uk
Information on arts policy, funding schemes and contacts in Scotland.

Trans Artists
www.transartists.nl
Netherlands-based site providing information on international artists-in-residence and exchange programmes, finances, cultural institutes (with links to their websites).

xrefer The web's reference engine
http://w1.xrefer.com
Free access online to over 50 reference titles including *The Bloomsbury Guide to Art*, *The Oxford Dictionary of Art* and the *Grove Concise Dictionary of Music*.

Your Creative Future
www.yourcreativefuture.org
A career-planning site for those involved in the arts.

After 10 years in publishing **Alison Baverstock** set up her own marketing consultancy, specialising in running campaigns for the book trade and training publishers to market more effectively. She is a well-established speaker on the book business and has written widely on how to market books. Her most recent title is *Marketing Your Book: An Author's Guide* (A & C Black, 2001).

Resources for writers

The writer's toolkit

Sooner or later, whatever the nature of their work, all writers must do some research. When they confront the sheer volume of information currently available in printed and manuscript form, as well as on the internet, this can seem a daunting task. ***Ann Hoffmann*** *looks at the skills involved and recommends a number of standard sources.*

Throughout the centuries writers have relied for their research on their own curiosity and observation skills. They have also fed voraciously on the knowledge and output of others. The earliest storytellers gathered their material through a combination of oral enquiry and attentive listening, each one in turn 'embroidering' in varying degrees what they had learnt. These tales later came to be written down and laboriously copied again and again in manuscript form, with little or no regard for accuracy or spelling. A new dimension was added in the wake of Caxton: the newspaper and the printed book, so that by the mid-18th century Samuel Johnson would speak of a writer turning over 'half a library' to make one book. Clearly the great Doctor had in mind a private collection of a few hundred books – nothing like the vast libraries and databases available to us today.

We live in an age of 'information overload'. Books galore, websites, and internet 'newsgroups' are on offer on every subject under the sun. The skill no longer lies in *finding* the information, but in *finding it quickly* and, most importantly, *sorting out the authoritative from the inaccurate*. At the same time, because so few of us today maintain proper diaries, and most choose to telephone rather than write a personal letter, there is already a serious dearth of information at the disposal of biographers, social historians and writers of historical fiction, from the mid-20th century onwards. Thus the traditional skills of looking and listening have come back into their own. Today's researchers cannot safely rely only on books and manuscripts, or even on the web, but must look closely at video and film and – the novelist and the dramatist especially – listen to tape recordings and to the spoken word. They must also master the art of the interview.

Photocopying and microfilming techniques have relieved us of the laborious chore of copying by hand – with all the risks of error that that involved. Information technology (IT) enables us to obtain instantly, in the comfort of our own study, the most up-to-the-minute factual information on record, from anywhere in the world. Another bonus is that we can keep abreast of current research – new discoveries and theories which so often shed a different, if controversial, light on historical events and people, and will be reflected in our creative work.

That said, writers should not regard the internet as a substitute for the library or archive centre, or other resources, but think of it rather as a springboard or first port of call. They should also be wary of using any material that does not come from an authoritative source.

Using the internet as a research tool

The internet is a global network of computers. Its most useful component for research is the World Wide Web (usually referred to as the 'web' or 'WWW'). This is the world's fastest-growing information research source. It is open 24 hours a day, 365 days a year.

To access the web, you must go online. The basic requirements for this are a personal computer, a telephone line and a modem. You then sign up with an Internet Service Provider (ISP), who supplies the necessary software to connect your computer with their own, through which you are able to access the worldwide network. If you are not yet online, you can gain access through your local library, university or college, or at one of the growing number of cybercafés.

The choice of ISP is wide open, and it is best to take the recommendation of a fellow writer. Some providers offer a 'free' service, in which case you incur telephone charges for every minute you spend online. Others quote a range of subscription rates, from the flat rate 'anytime' to 'off-peak', and/or a fixed number of hours online per month, with no additional charge for telephone calls. The speed of connection and the time it takes for data to reach you are important factors, as is the facility of a 24-hour technical support service at a local call rate. Basically you get what you pay for, i.e. the fee-paying ISPs are usually the least complicated to use and may offer additional services. There is no difficulty about changing your ISP, should you wish to do so later.

The amount of information online is huge. It is accessed with the aid of 'web browser' software, such as Microsoft Internet Explorer or Netscape Navigator, provided free of charge by the ISP. When a web page address, known as a URL (Uniform Resource Locator) and starting usually with http://www, is typed in, the required page appears on screen. Each page displayed contains useful 'hyperlinks' (cross-references) to other web pages.

If you do not know the URL, or you are conducting a search by subject, you can enlist the help of one or more of the 'search engines' on the web: when you type in a keyword or topic, all relevant sites found are displayed. As each search engine is different, a knowledge of how they operate is essential if you wish to speed up your research.

The secret of successful, economic researching on the web is to *be specific.* Refining searches down to the *precise* information required not only saves time and money, but also avoids the chore of having to wade through a mass of superfluous, irrelevant material. It is very important to keep a record of the path to your information, by using the 'Bookmark' or 'Favourite' facilities on the browser program. The maintenance of a personal website address book is also recommended.

There are two other internet resources of immense value to the writer: the 'Usenet' discussion or newsgroups, and email. The Deja News website points the way to over 20,000 newsgroups on numerous subjects. Messages 'posted' will be read by all members of the group, and much information not available elsewhere may be forthcoming. Some groups produce a useful 'Frequently Asked Questions' (FAQ) information list. Email scarcely needs any recommendation here. It is fast, it is cheap, and it is indispensable.

Useful manuals catering specifically for the writer are: *Books and Publishing on the Internet* by Roger Ferneyhough (Internet Handbooks, Plymouth, 2000); *The Internet: A Writer's Guide* by Jane Dorner (A & C Black, London, 2nd edn, 2001); *A Writer's Guide to the Internet* by Trevor Lockwood and Karen Scott (Allison & Busby, London, 2000); *The Internet Writer's Handbook 2001–2002* by Karen Scott (Allison & Busby, London, 2001); and *The Internet for Writers* by Nick Daws (Internet Handbooks, Plymouth, 1999).

Using libraries and archive centres

Although, thanks to IT, much preparatory catalogue searching can be done online, the bulk of a writer's research is carried out in a reference library or archive centre. Nearly every country in the world has its national library and its national archives collection. Their catalogues – nowadays online – are among the most valuable of all research tools.

In the United Kingdom we have the British Library and the Public Record Office; there are also six copyright libraries (The British Library, London; The Bodleian Library, Oxford; Cambridge University

Library, Cambridge; The National Library of Wales, Aberystwyth; The National Library of Scotland, Edinburgh; Trinity College Library, Dublin), each of which has received one free copy of every book published here since the early 18th century. Among other major collections are the British Library Newspaper Library and the British Library National Sound Archive. We also have an excellent public library lending system which, if unable to meet a user's needs from its local stock, will obtain books on loan from other libraries or through the British Library Document Supply Service.

The advantage of using the local library, especially if it has a reference section, is that you have access to the stacks and can browse at will, whereas at the British Library and copyright libraries a limited number of books are on the open shelves: the rest have to be ordered, which means either entering author, title or keyword on the computer terminal or filling in a docket and waiting for the book to be delivered to the counter or your desk.

To search official or genealogical records you may need to visit the Public Record Office (PRO) at Kew, the Family Records Centre in London, or a local country record office or archives centre. The whereabouts of private papers can be ascertained by consulting the indexes at the National Register of Archives in London. A useful inexpensive publication, regularly updated, is the PRO/Royal Commission on Historic Manuscripts' *Record Repositories in Great Britain*.

Admission to the British Library and most of the sources mentioned above is free, with the exception of the Bodleian and Cambridge University Library, which currently make a modest charge, but you will need a reader's ticket (ask for details in advance). If you are a graduate you will be able to use any university library. Professional bodies with specialist collections will usually grant bona fide researchers access on application. There are also a small number of private subscription libraries in London and the major cities.

There are no formalities at the Family Records Centre or county record offices, but you must book in advance to secure a seat, especially if you wish to use a computer or microfilm reader. Laptops are permitted in most libraries and archive centres, but you will almost certainly be restricted to note-taking in pencil and, if handling fragile documents, you may be issued with gloves.

Major UK sources

The British Library

96 Euston Road, London NW1 2DB
tel 020-7412 7676 (general enquiries)
fax 020-7412 7609
email readerservices-enquiries@bl.uk
reader-admissions@bl.uk
website www.bl.uk

The British Library Public Catalogue (BLPC)

website http://blpc.bl.uk

The British Library National Sound Archive

96 Euston Road, London NW1 2DB
tel 020-7412 7440 *fax* 020-7412 7441
email nsa@bl.uk
website www.bl.uk/collections/sound-archive

The British Library Newspaper Library

Colindale Avenue, London NW9 5HE
tel 020-7412 7353
fax 020-7412 7379
email newspaper@bl.uk
website www.bl.uk/collections/newspaper

Family Records Centre

1 Myddleton Street, London EC1R 1UW
tel 020-8392 5300 (general enquiries)
fax 020-8392 5307
email enquiry@pro.gov.uk
website www.familyrecords.gov.uk

National Register of Archives, Royal Commission on Historical Manuscripts

Quality House, Quality Court, Chancery Lane, London WC2A 1HP
tel 020-7242 1198 *fax* 020-7831 3550
email nra@hmc.gov.uk
website www.hmc.gov.uk

Public Record Office

Ruskin Avenue, Kew, Richmond, Surrey TW9 4DU
tel 020-8876 3444 *fax* 020-8878 8905
email enquiry@pro.gov.uk
website www.pro.gov.uk

Selected titles for the bookshelf

Brewer's Dictionary of Phrase & Fable
Britain: An Official Handbook
The Cassell Dictionary of Slang (Jonathan Green)
Chambers Biographical Dictionary
The Chronology of Words & Phrases (L. & R. Flavell)
The Companion to British History (C. Arnold-Baker)
Fowler's Modern English Usage
The Hutchinson Chronology of World History
Mind the Gaffe: The Penguin Guide to Modern Errors in English (R.L. Trask)
The New Shell Book of Firsts (ed. P. Robertson)
The Oxford Companion to English Literature (ed. M. Drabble)
Pears Cyclopedia
Roget's Thesaurus (ed. B. Kirkpatrick)
The Statesman's Year Book
The Times Atlas of the World (compact edition)
Whitaker's Almanack
Who's Who
The Writers' & Artists' Yearbook
The Writer's Handbook

On CD-Rom

Encyclopedia Britannica
The Writers Shelf (16 reference titles marketed by Oxford University Press on one disk)
Who Was Who 1897–1996

If you are very rich you may subscribe to *The Oxford English Dictionary* online; otherwise make do with the *New Shorter OED* or the *Concise OED* and consult the main version at the library.

The golden rule of research is *accuracy*. When transcribing or taking notes, you should check carefully all dates, figures and unusual names, and *keep a meticulous record of all sources*. Take full advantage of photocopying and filming facilities: the rule of thumb is that if copying by hand is likely to take more than 10 minutes, it is worth the expense. (A photocopy is an accurate copy!)

The Aslib Directory of Information Sources in the United Kingdom, published biennially, should be available for consultation in every reference library. *Walford's Guide to Reference Material* (3 vols), regularly updated, is a standard work.

Indexes and bibliographies

A well-constructed index should lead the researcher directly to the subject matter required. A good bibliography suggests avenues of further search.

As well as indexes to individual books, the various indexes to newspapers and periodicals are of tremendous value. Outstanding among these are *The Times Index* (from 1906, with an unofficial earlier version from 1790) and *The British Humanities Index*, formerly known as the *Subject Index to Periodicals*, from 1915. There are of course subject indexes in many fields, too numerous to list here.

The British National Bibliography, known as the *BNB*, published since 1950, is available online and on CD-Rom. The best international source is *The World Bibliographical Series* launched in 1977 by Clio Press of Oxford.

The writer's bookshelf

Much reference material is now published in electronic as well as in printed form. Shelf space (and possibly also money!) may be saved by buying, say, your main encyclopedia, thesaurus and dictionary on CD-Rom; but it is advisable to keep a concise edition (hardback or paperback) at your elbow for quick reference. Some standard reference titles are marketed, three or more together, as a compendium, at a very reasonable price; and from time to time the book clubs come up with excellent offers. Buying books online may also carry worthwhile discounts. Your minimum needs are:

- an up-to-date English dictionary;
- a thesaurus;
- a guide to English usage;

• an up-to-date atlas (also a historical atlas if you write about the past);
• an encyclopedia (or two) – the best you can afford!
• a dictionary of quotations;
• a dictionary of dates;
• a concise world history and/or chronology;
• a biographical dictionary; and
• a current *Yearbook*.

Add to these according to your field of writing and your pocket: for the modern novelist perhaps a dictionary of slang; the historical novelist something on costume, the history of food, the cost of living in centuries past; and so on.

The easiest way to acquire a title that is out of print is to contact your local secondhand bookdealer or one of the major booksellers, such as Waterstone's, who operate a book-search service. Or you can use an independent searcher. Now that most bookfinders use the internet, obtaining out-of-print books is much faster – and cheaper – than it used to be.

Ann Hoffmann is a professional writer researcher of many years' standing and the author of five non-fiction books. Her *Research for Writers* (A & C Black, 6th edn 1999) includes chapters on research methods, basic sources, research for modern and historical fiction writers, biographers, local and family historians, as well as an up-to-date listing by subject of major sources.

Digital imaging for writers

The way in which images are presented can sway an editor's decision to use an article. ***David Askham*** *explains how to transfer images to a computer and suggests ways to arrange them for best effect.*

An editor, who regularly commissioned me to produce profiles of small gardens, telephoned me as soon as he received one of my proposals. He said, "When I first read your letter, I was convinced that it would not be suitable for our British readers. Then I turned the page and said 'WOW!' Please go ahead with the feature."

So what tipped the scales?

Admittedly the subject was a rather unusual one, in fact a so-called 'shade garden'. Furthermore, it was located far away in Australia! Because of this, I suspected that the proposal would fail if I sent words alone. I could have sent accompanying small colour prints to illustrate the potential of the article, but they would have lacked impact and risked becoming separated from my proposal. So I tried an experiment. I scanned a selection of photographs and compiled a simple but bold and colourful composite A4 sheet which formed part of my brief proposal. It worked and I have used variants of this idea with success ever since.

But the advantages of digital photography outlined above do not end there because once pictures are filed on a writer's personal computer they are available for a variety of useful purposes. They can serve as inspiration, providing quick recall of a scene or a person's facial features or attire. It is like revisiting a location or experiencing an unexpected reunion with an old friend. Digital images are quick visual references; they can jog a writer's memory and inspire. Let us look at the subject in a little more detail.

Technical aspects

Most writers will be familiar with cameras which use conventional film, either black and white or colour. These films produce negatives from which prints are produced; or transparencies which can be projected (for lecture purposes) or used by publishers to provide illustrations in print. In contrast, a new generation of cameras has arrived which do not use film, but instead record and store images digitally on special reusable memory. These varying forms of photographic images must then be transferred to a personal computer so that they may be cropped, modified and integrated into the desired documents, such as a proposal. If the source is a digital camera it is relatively straightforward to transfer images using the computer software which came with the camera. Using the connecting cables supplied, images are 'down-loaded' into the computer or into special camera memory adapters which are inserted into a conventional floppy disk drive. The whole chain is digital which makes it so easy.

However, you do not necessarily need a digital camera to transfer images to your computer. You can work with prints which you already have – or could produce at will in the future. Or you can digitise your existing colour (or black and white) slides or negatives. For the latter operation your pictures need to be scanned and recorded on a CD, a process which has become increasingly available at most processing laboratories. Alternatively, with the right equipment, you can do the whole process yourself.

Possibly the easier and cheaper method is to buy a flatbed scanner which will produce digital files from your original colour or black and white prints. Flatbed scanners have tumbled in price over the past few years and are now often bundled with new computers. Alternatively, they can be bought for well under £100 although, like most consumer goods, it does not pay to buy the cheapest available. Take advice from a knowledgeable friend or trusted dealer.

If you wish to work from negatives or colour slides, you will need to buy a film scanner. These are more expensive (from £150 up to £1000 or more), but they give superior results particularly if you want to produce photo-realistic prints from a colour printer, say for promotional or exhibition purposes.

Initially, you can achieve commendable results by using your existing camera and having selected images scanned onto a CD by a processing laboratory. Then you can extract copies of the desired pictures from the CD and place them in your chosen document file. When you feel more confident and can justify the expense, you can then shop around for a suitable scanner to use at home.

Before moving on, I think a word is needed on the relative merits of using conventional film or digital cameras. The latter have developed rapidly over recent years. However, except for the top-priced models (£2000–£5000), results of consumer digital cameras are only just beginning to compare favourably with film and fall well short if big enlargements are needed in print. Like-for-like, they are also more expensive. Within a year or so, however, I expect the gap will close.

Using visual references

In addition to my example of the use of photographs in a book or article proposal, digital pictures are also a valuable aid to many forms of research and writing. For example, the value of tape-recorded research or interview notes is significantly enhanced if you add thumbnail pictures to enrich and augment the narrative information. Words and pictures which are integrated in this way have to be more reliable than unaided human memory when writing begins, particularly if there is a significant time interval between research and writing. But it is in the production of proposals, those all important selling documents, where digital imaging comes into its own.

However, I do not advocate using any old pictures. They have to be directly relevant to the subject being proposed and they must be of good quality. Therefore, it is worthwhile budgeting for your photography and providing high quality pictures using conventional cameras and films at the outset. You will then have confidence in being able to deliver high quality images to the editor.

Computing and software

Unless you are a computer buff, eyes can easily glaze when faced with yet more software to master. Unfortunately, some knowledge is essential but I will keep it simple.

Most modern computers can handle graphics which includes digital photographs and drawings. Indeed most modern word processing software, such as WordPerfect, can integrate pictures directly into documents. Provided you know the filename of the required picture, or can find it by exploring the file listing hierarchy, you merely have to point to INSERT ... GRAPHICS ... FROM FILE and select the appropriate file. (The commands may be slightly different in other word processing programs.) The photograph then appears and you can adjust both its size and position within the document.

Ideally you will have made any cropping or other adjustments using the picture management software which may have been delivered with your digital camera or scanner. If the pictures supplied by your film processor were delivered on a CD, you may find a simple program included on the disk. Alternatively, you may choose to buy a picture processing program, such as Paint Shop Pro or Photoshop, which possess enormous capabilities for enhancing and transforming digital images, way beyond what you require initially. Photoshop is expensive, although a limited edition of the program is bundled with some scanners and is perfectly adequate for first-time users. Consider buying one or two magazines which specialise in digital photography to study reviews and tables of available digital hardware and software. A study of analytical reports can be very helpful in short-listing potential solutions.

One last word on specialist software. Be prepared to invest plenty of time if you wish to explore digital image processing capabilities beyond basic cropping of your photographs. It can be very rewarding, but it takes time to learn and is beyond the scope of this article.

Adding visual elements

A simple example was given earlier of how you can add photographs to a text document. Sometimes it is better to devote an A4 page exclusively to the visual side of your proposals. Although this can be done using a word processor, a publishing program such as Microsoft Home Publishing is more adept and flexible for designing layout and adding captions. However, you will soon find that you are straying into the realms of graphic design which appears to be much easier than it really is.

Working out the relative sizes of your pictures on the page and their positions can be extremely time consuming. It requires patience and discipline. My advice is to keep things as simple as possible before tackling more ambitious layouts. Avoid trying to include too many pictures on a page; six should be a maximum. Try to vary their individual sizes so that there is variety. Your aim should be to present just sufficient visual information to whet an editor's appetite with the whole effect being easy on the eye. There is no doubt that in a highly competitive world digital imaging can endow a writer with a competitive edge. Take heart and inspiration from my experience and see if your success rate improves.

David Askham is author of *Photo Libraries and Agencies* (BFP Books) and has been illustrating his written work for over 35 years. His photographs have been published worldwide in books, brochures, magazines and newspapers, many through international agencies.

Creative writing courses

Full details of courses are available on application to the institution. Anyone wishing to participate should first satisfy themselves as to content and quality. For day and evening courses consult your local Adult Education Centre.

Alston Hall Residential College for Adult Education

Alston Lane, Longridge, Preston PR3 3BP
tel (01772) 784661 *fax* (01772) 785835
email alston.hall@ed.lancscc.gov.uk
website www.alstonhall.u-net.com

Annual Writers' Conference

Chinook, Southdown Road, Winchester, SO21 2BY
tel (01962) 712307
email Writerconf@aol.com
website www.gmp.co.uk/writers/conference
Conference Director Barbara Large MBE, FRSA
Venue King Alfred's College, Winchester – 27–29 June 2003

Mini courses and workshops, lectures, seminars, one-to-one appointments with agents and commissioning editors, Bookfair, 15 writing competitions; followed by week-long workshops 30 June–4 July.

The Arvon Foundation

Lumb Bank, Heptonstall, Hebden Bridge, West Yorkshire HX7 6DF
tel/fax (01422) 843714
email l-bank@arvonfoundation.org
website www.arvonfoundation.org
Contact Ann Anderton
Moniack Mhor, Teavarran, Kiltarlity, Beauly, Inverness-shire IV4 7HT
tel (01463) 741675 *fax* (01463) 741733
email m-mhor@arvonfoundation.org
Contact Chris Aldridge
The Arvon Foundation, Totleigh Barton, Sheepwash, Beaworthy, Devon EX21 5NS
tel (01409) 231338 *fax* (01409) 231144
email t-barton@arvonfoundation.org
Contact Julia Wheadon

Belstead House Education & Conference Centre (Residential Courses)

Belstead, Ipswich, Suffolk IP8 3NA
tel (01473) 686321 *fax* (01473) 686664
email belsteadhouse@talk21.com

Burton Manor College

Burton, Neston, Cheshire CH64 5SJ
tel 0151-336 5172 *fax* 0151-336 6586
email enquiry@burtonmanor.com
website www.burtonmanor.com
Principal Keith Chandler

Centerprise Literature Development Project

136 Kingsland High Street, London E8 2NS
tel 020-7254 9632 ext. 211, 214 *fax* 020-7923 1951
email eva.centerlit@care4free.net
sharon.centerlit@care4free.net

See also page 468.

Creative in Calvados

1 Ormelie Terrace, Joppa, Edinburgh EH15 2EX
tel 0131-669 4025
email steveharvey@creativeincalvados.co.uk
website www.creativeincalvados.co.uk
Contact Stephen Harvey

Midweek and long weekend courses in poetry, songwriting/music, scriptwriting, drama and prose. Takes place in Normandy.

Dingle Writing Courses Ltd

Ballyneanig, Ballyferriter, Tralee, Co Kerry, Republic of Ireland
tel 66 9154990 *fax* 66 9154992
email info@dinglewriting.com
website www.dinglewriting.com
Directors Abigail Joffe, Nicholas McLachlan

The Earnley Concourse

Earnley Trust Ltd, Earnley, Chichester, West Sussex PO20 7JL
tel (01243) 670392 *fax* (01243) 670832
email info@earnley.co.uk
website www.earnley.co.uk

Far West

23 Chapel Street, Penzance, Cornwall TR18 4AP
tel (01736) 363146 *fax* (01736) 331131
email farwest@waitrose.com
website www.writing-courses-cornwall.com
Contact Angela Stoner

The Indian King Arts Centre
Fore Street, Camelford, Cornwall PL32 9PG
tel (01840) 212111
email info@indianking.co.uk
website www.indianking.co.uk

Summer Academy, Keynes College
The University, Canterbury, Kent CT2 7NP
tel (01227) 470404/823473 *fax* (01227) 784338
email summeracademy@ukc.ac.uk
website www.ukc.ac.uk/sa/index.html
Contact Andrea McDonnell

Knuston Hall
Irchester, Wellingborough, Northants. NN29 7EU
tel (01933) 312104 *fax* (01933) 357596
email enquiries@knustonhall.org.uk
website www.knustonhall.org.uk
Contact Daphne Brittin

Lancaster University
Dept of Continuing Education, Lonsdale College, Lancaster University LA1 4YN
tel (01524) 592624 *fax* (01524) 592448
email Conted@lancaster.ac.uk
website www.lancs.ac.uk/users/conted/index.htm

Missenden Abbey
Great Missenden, Bucks HP16 0BN
tel (01494) 862904 *fax* (01494) 890087
email conedchil@buckscc.gov.uk
website www.aredu.org.uk/missendenabbey

The Old Rectory Adult Education College
Fittleworth, Pulborough, West Sussex RH20 1HU
tel/fax (01798) 865306
email oldrectory@mistral.co.uk
website www.oldrectory.mistral.co.uk

Open Studies – Part-time Courses for Adults: Office of Lifelong Learning
University of Edinburgh, 11 Buccleuch Place, Edinburgh EH8 9LW
tel 0131-650 4400 *fax* 0131-667 6097
email oll@ed.ac.uk
website www.lifelong.ed.ac.uk

South and Mid Wales Association of Writers
c/o IMC Consulting Group, Denham House, Lambourne Crescent, Cardiff CF14 5ZW
tel 029-2076 1170 *fax* 029-2076 1304
Contact Julian Rosser

Southern Writers' Conference
Stable House, Home Farm, Coldharbour Lane, Dorking, Surrey RH4 3JG
Contact Lucia White

Ty Newydd
Ty Newydd, National Creative Writing Centre of Wales, Llanystumdwy, Cricieth, Gwynedd LL52 0LW
tel (01766) 522811 *fax* (01766) 523095
email tynewydd@dial.pipex.com
website www.tynewydd.org

University of Nottingham Study Tours
School of Continuing Education, University of Nottingham, Jubilee Campus, Wollaton Road, Nottingham NG8 1BB
tel 0115-951 6526 *fax* 0115-951 6556
email re-studytours@nottingham.ac.uk
Administrator Sylvia Stephens

Urchfont Manor College
Urchfont, Devizes, Wilts. SN10 4RG
tel (01380) 840495 *fax* (01380) 840005
email urchfont@wccyouth.org.uk

Wedgwood Memorial College
Station Road, Barlaston, Stoke-on-Trent ST12 9DG
tel (01782) 372105/373427 *fax* (01782) 372393

Writers' Summer School, Swanwick
Contact The Secretary, PO Box 5532, Heanor DE75 7YF
website www.wss.org.uk

Editorial, literary and production services

The following specialists offer a wide variety of services to writers (both new and established), to publishers, journalists and others. Services include advice on manuscripts, editing and book production, indexing, translation, research and writing. For an index of the services offered here, see page 590.

'A Feature Factory' Editorial Services

4 St Andrews Court,
Norwich NR7 0EW
tel (01603) 435229 *mobile* (07890) 182492
fax (01603) 435229
email editorial@fdsltd.com
Editors Dr Dennis Chaplin, Sara de Villeurbanne

Contract magazine/book publishing, editorial consultancy and troubleshooting, DTP (Quark/Photoshop), proofreading, sub-editing, legal copy checks, typesetting, advertisement design, copywriting, features, broadcast backgrounders, news releases, autobiography ghostwriting, novel/script editing, brochures, leaflets, research projects, tourist guides, editorial/journalism training. Researchers often needed (send CV and samples).

Aaron Editorial

19 Albemarle Road, Gorleston-on-Sea,
Norfolk NR31 7AR
tel/fax (01493) 444556
email aared@onetel.net.uk
Contact Eldo Barkhuizen

Copy-editing, onscreen editing, writing, Americanising/Anglicising. All subjects (especially philosophy and biblical studies) covered. Established 1997.

Abbey Writing Services

Twitchen Cottage, Holcombe Rogus, Wellington,
Somerset TA21 0PT
tel/fax (01823) 672762
email john.mcilwain@virgin.net
Director John McIlwain

Comprehensive non-fiction writing, project management and editorial service. Educational consultants. Lexicography. Founded 1989.

Academic File

(in association with The Centre for Near East Afro-Asia Research – NEAR)
27 Wallorton Gardens, PO Box 13666,
London SW14 8WF
tel 020-8392 1122 *fax* 020-8392 1422
email afis@eapgroup.com
website www.eapgroup.com
Director Sajid Rizvi

Research, advisory and consultancy services related to politics, economics and societies of the Near and Middle East, Asia and North Africa and related issues in Europe. Risk analysis, editorial assessment, editing, contract publishing, design and production. Founded 1985.

Advice and Criticism Service

1 Beechwood Court, Syderstone, Norfolk PE31 8TR
tel (01485) 578594 *fax* (01485) 578138
email hilary@hilaryjohnson.demon.co.uk
website www.hilaryjohnson.demon.co.uk
Contact Hilary Johnson

Authors' consultant: detailed and constructive assessment of typescripts/practical advice regarding publication. Former organiser of Romantic Novelists' Association's New Writers' Scheme, adjudicator of literary awards and publishers' reader. Specialities: crime/thrillers/popular women's fiction. Advice also available on science fiction/fantasy, children's books, TV/radio/film scripts, poetry and non-fiction.

AFI Research – Richard M. Bennett Associates

The Ground Floor, 27 The Avenue,
Newton Abbot TQ12 2BZ
tel/fax (01626) 335040
email afi@supanet.com
Senior Associate Richard Bennett

OSINT, strategic forecasting conflict, intelligence, security and defence information. Commentary, articles and briefings for the news media worldwide.

Amolibros

5 Saxon Close, Watchet, Somerset TA23 0BN
tel/fax (01984) 633713
email amolibros@aol.com
website www.amolibros.co.uk
Managing Consultant Jane Tatam

A self-publishing consultancy/packager. Also offers copy-editing, proofreading, typesetting, advice on marketing and sales. Established 1992.

Anchor Editorial Services

Anchor House, 5 High Street, Dulverton, Somerset TA22 9HB
tel/fax (01398) 324350
Editorial Director Leigh-Anne Perryman, *Photographic Director* Martyn Collins

A complete editorial, research and photographic service for company brochures and magazines; guidebooks, publicity leaflets and tourism projects; press releases and newsletters. Established 1998.

Angel Books

6 Lancaster Road, Harrogate, North Yorkshire HG2 0EZ
tel (01423) 566804
Contact Angela Sibson BA, AFBPsS

Professional author (20 titles) and tutor in creative writing offers comprehensive, sympathetic assessment of fiction MSS. Revision suggested with a view to getting into print. Special interests: psychological suspense, crime, thrillers, women's, teenage. Established 1994.

Arioma Editorial Services

PO Box 53, Aberystwyth, Ceredigion SY24 5WG
tel (01970) 871296 *fax* (01970) 871733
Proprietor Moira W. Smith

Research, co-writing, ghostwriting, DTP, complete book production service. Specialities: military, naval, aviation history and autobiography.

Arkst Publishing

1 Lindsey House, Lloyds's Place, London SE3 0QF
tel 020-8297 9997 *fax* 020-8318 4359
email jim@arkst.demon.co.uk
Director James H. Willis MA, FRCP (Edin.)

Independent appraisal of MSS – fiction and non-fiction. Founded 1995.

Authors' Advisory Service

24 Lyndale Avenue, Childs Hill, London NW2 2QA
tel 020-7794 3285

All typescripts professionally evaluated in depth by long-established publishers' reader specialising in constructive advice to new writers and with wide experience of current literary requirements. Founded 1972.

Authors' Aid

11 Orchard Street, Fearnhead, Warrington, Cheshire WA2 0PL
tel (01925) 838431
email chris.sawyer@btinternet.com
website www.authorsaid.co.uk
Partners Chris Sawyer and Deborah Ramage

Appraisal and editorial services. Offers honest, constructive feedback and detailed guidance on style, presentation, characterisation, plot, construction, marketability, etc. A personalised service by a publishing professional with the clear aim of maximising the writer's chances of publication. Other services: rewriting, proofreading, ghostwriting, word processing, commissioned work. Write, phone or email before sending work. Established 1991.

Authors Appraisal Service

12 Hadleigh Gardens, Boyatt Wood, Eastleigh, Hants SO50 4NP
Literary consultant J. Evans

Professional writer offers critical appraisal of MSS – fiction only. Specialises in romantic and historical fiction. Competitive rates. Preliminary letter essential and sae for reply. Founded 1988.

AuthorsOnLine Ltd

15 Maidenhead Street, Hertford SG14 1DW
tel (01992) 586788 *fax* (01992) 586787
email theeditor@authorsonline.co.uk
website www.authorsonline.co.uk
Contact Richard Fitt (editor)

Publishes MSS (including short stories and poetry) on the AuthorsOnLine website. Offers full publishing facilities on a print-on-demand basis for authors of 'special interest' books. Authors retain control of editorial content and copyright, leaving them free to pursue hard copy contracts. Works closely with publishers and literary agents. New and established authors welcome. Fee for book-length MS: eformat £95 plus £10 p.a.; POD £495 including eformat. Founded 1997.

Authors' Research Services
32 Oak Village, London NW5 4QN
tel 020-7284 4316
email rmwindserv@aol.com
Contact Richard Wright
Offers comprehensive research service to writers, academics and business people worldwide, including fact checking, bibliographical references and document supply. Specialises in English history, social sciences, business. Founded 1966.

Anne Barclay Enterprises
The Old Farmhouse, Hexworthy, Yelverton, Devon PL20 6SD
tel/fax (01364) 631 405
email anne@theswiftgroup.co.uk
website www.theswiftgroup.co.uk
Typing MSS and audio transcription through to full editorial services – appraisal, editing, research, feature writing, co-writing and ghostwriting. Special interests: food, travel, crime, memoirs. Founded 1996.

Richard A. Beck
49 Curzon Avenue, Stanmore, Middlesex HA7 2AL
tel 020-8933 9787 *fax* 020-8904 5182
email rbeck@bushinternet.com
Editing, proofreading, indexing, research, writing and rewriting. Reduced rates for new authors, senior citizens, the unemployed, etc. Founded 1991.

Beswick Writing Services
19 Haig Road, Stretford M32 0DS
tel 0161-865 1259
Contact Francis Beswick
Editing, research, information books. Special interests: religious, philosophical and educational. Expertise in correspondence courses and Open Learning materials. Founded 1988.

Black Ace Book Production
PO Box 6557, Forfar DD8 2YS
tel (01307) 465096 *fax* (01307) 465494
website www.blackacebooks.com
Directors Hunter Steele, Boo Wood
Book production and text processing, including text capture (or scanning), editing, proofing to camera-ready/film, printing and binding, jacket artwork and design. Delivery of finished books; can sometimes help with distribution. Founded 1990.

Blair Services
Blair Cottage, Aultgrishan, Melvaig, Gairloch, Wester Ross IV21 2DZ
tel/fax (01445) 771228
email BlairServices@aultgrisham.freeserve.co.uk
Director Ian Mertling-Blake MA, DPhil
Editing and revision: fiction and non-fiction (such as prospectus for schools and other educational purposes). Also specialist academic revision for books/ articles on archaeology and associated subjects. Founded 1992.

Book Data Ltd
Globe House, 1 Chertsey Road, Twickenham TW1 1LR
tel 020-8843 8600 *fax* 020-8843 8744
email biblio@bookdata.co.uk
website www.bookdata.co.uk www.ehaus.co.uk
Book Data is the leading supplier of high-quality, content-rich book information and other published media to the book industry. Information taken from publishers is used to create a unique title record which includes bibliographic details, text summaries, tables of contents, extensive subject-related information, market-rights details, jacket images, author interviews, etc. This information is made available through record supply, CD-Rom and online (BookFind-Online) to booksellers, librarians and publishers internationally.

e-haus is Book Data's web services department; it creates and maintains internet sites for the book industry.

The Book Guild Ltd
Temple House, 25 High Street, Lewes, East Sussex BN7 2LU
tel (01273) 472534 *fax* (01273) 476472
email info@bookguild.co.uk
website www.bookguild.co.uk
Directors G.M. Nissen CBE (chairman), Carol Biss (managing), Anthony Nissen, Jane Nissen, David Ross, Paul White (financial), Janet Wrench (production)
Offers a range of publishing options:
• Comprehensive package for authors incorporating editorial, design, production, marketing, publicity and distribution.
• Editorial and production only for authors requiring private editions.
• A complete service for companies and organisations requiring books for internal

or promotional purposes – from brief to finished book. Founded 1982.

Book Production Consultants plc
25-27 High Street, Chesterton, Cambridge CB4 1ND
tel (01223) 352790 *fax* (01223) 460718
email tl@bpccam.co.uk
website www.bpccam.co.uk
Directors A.P. Littlechild, C.S. Walsh
Complete publishing service: writing, editing, designing, illustrating, translating, indexing, photography; production management of printing and binding; specialised sales and distribution; advertising sales. For books, journals, manuals, reports, magazines, catalogues, electronic media. Founded 1973.

Book-in-Hand Ltd
20 Shepherds Hill, London N6 5AH
tel/fax 020-8341 7650
Contact Ann Kritzinger
Production of cost-effective short-run books for small and self-publishers, from typescript (or disk) to bound copies (hardbacks or paperbacks, sewn or unsewn). Enquiries with sae, or by fax.

Brackley Proofreading Services
PO Box 5920, Brackley, Northants. NN13 6YB
tel/fax (01280) 703355
email brackleyproof@LineOne.net
Proofreading. Founded 2000.

Brooke Projects
21 Barnfield, Urmston, Manchester M41 9EW
tel 0161-746 8140 *fax* 0161-746 8132
email urmston@brooke.u-net.com
Research, editing and contract writing. Specialises in business, management, tourism, history, biography and social science.

Mrs D. Buckmaster
51 Chatsworth Road, Torquay, Devon TQ1 3BJ
tel/fax (01803) 294663
General editing of non-fiction, with particular attention to clarity of expression and meaning, grammar, punctuation and flow. Experience editing architecture, photography, financial, religious, natural health and human potential MSS. Founded 1966.

John Button – Editorial Services
Tower House, 6 Burnham Court, Martello Bay, Clacton on Sea, Essex CO15 1RE
tel (01255) 470404
Copy-editing and proofreading, specialising in government committee of enquiry reports, legal, financial, taxation, business education and corporate identity publications; Legal Reference Library series. Founded 1991.

Causeway Resources
8 The Causeway, Teddington, Middlesex TW11 0HE
tel/fax 020-8977 8797
Director Keith Skinner
Genealogical, biographical and historical research, specialising in police history and true crime research. Founded 1989.

Vanessa Charles
38 Ham Common, Richmond, Surrey TW10 7JG
tel/fax 020-8940 9225
email 101361,1176@compuserve.com
Design and book production services. Founded 1975.

Chase Publishing Services
Mead, Fortescue, Sidmouth, Devon EX10 9QG
tel/fax (01395) 514709
email r.addicott@btinternet.com
Proprietor Ray Addicott
Coordinates a network of specialists in academic bookwork taking raw MSS through to finished books. Services include copy-editing and proofreading, design, typesetting, indexing and a full production service. Founded 1989.

Barbara Cheney
16 Watson Road, Westcott, Nr Dorking, Surrey RH4 3QW
tel (01306) 889164
email barscheney@aol.com
Copy-editing, proofreading, layout and design. Books (up to 704pp), directories, magazines, newsletters, annual reports, prospectuses, catalogues, leaflets. Clients include publishers, institutes and government departments. Freelance since 1987.

Karyn Claridge Book Production
244 Bromham Road, Biddenham, Bedford MK40 4AA
tel (01234) 347909
email kclaridge@eddisonsadd.co.uk
Complete book production management service offered from MS to bound copies; graphic services available; sourcing service for interactive book projects. Founded 1989.

Johnathon Clifford

27 Mill Road, Fareham, Hants PO16 0TH
tel/fax (01329) 822218
website http://ourworld.compuserve.com/homepages/johnathonclifford

Offers a free, unbiased advice service for anyone looking for a publisher or who has experienced difficulties with a publishing house. Has extensive knowledge of vanity publishing and acted as adviser to the Advertising Standards Authority regarding the wording of the 'Advice Note Vanity Publishing July 1997'. See website for his report on the government White Paper against rogue traders and its effectiveness where authors are concerned. Established 1994.

Combrógos

Dr Meic Stephens, 10 Heol Don, Whitchurch, Cardiff CF14 2AU
tel 029-2062 3359 *fax* 029-2052 9202
email meic@heoldon.fsnet.co.uk

Specialises in books (including fiction and poetry) about Wales or by Welsh authors, providing a full editorial service and undertaking arts and media research. Founded 1990.

Cornerstones

PO Box 22534, London W8 4GP
tel 020-7727 2478 *fax* 020-7727 6983
email helen@cornerstones.co.uk
kidscorner@cornerstones.co.uk
website www.cornerstones.co.uk
Proprietor Helen Corner

Specialist team of readers (authors, editors and literary reviewers) provides literary guidance and constructive assessment of MSS for published or unpublished authors. Strong contacts with agents and publishers. Established 1998.

Kids' Corner (children's division)
All age ranges of children's fiction, from picture books to teenage.

Ingrid Cranfield

16 Myddelton Gardens, London N21 2PA
tel/fax 020-8360 2433
email ingrid_cranfield@hotmail.com

Advisory and editorial services for authors, publishers and media, including critical assessment, rewriting, proofreading, copy-editing, indexing, research, interviews, transcripts. Special interests: geography, travel, exploration, adventure (own archives), language, education, youth training, art and architecture (including Japanese). Translations from German and French. Not an employer or agency. Founded 1972.

David A. Cross

University College, The Castle, Durham DH1 3RW
tel 0191-374 4585

Research and information service; editing texts, specialising in art history, biography and genealogy; creative writing tutorials; lectures on artists and writers of the Lake District (especially George Romney and John Ruskin).

D & N Publishing

5 The Green, Baydon, Marlborough, Wilts. SN8 2JW
tel/fax (01672) 540556
email dandnpub@aol.com
Partners David and Namrita Price-Goodfellow

Complete project management including some or all of the following: commissioning, editing, picture research, illustration and design, page layout, proofreading, indexing, printing and repro. All stages managed in-house and produced on Apple Macs running the latest software. Founded 1991.

David Wineman, Solicitors

Craven House, 121 Kingsway, London WC2B 6NX
tel 020-7400 7800 *fax* 020-7400 7890
email law@davidwineman.co.uk
website www.davidwineman.co.uk
Contact Irving David, Mark Waring

A broadly based media law firm. Offers legal advice to authors, illustrators, photographers, composers, songwriters and their agents on all forms of publishing agreement, including negotiation and review of commercial terms, where required, with book andmusic publishers, film, TV and theatrical production companies, packagers and merchandisers. Founded 1981.

Meg Davies

31 Egerton Road, Ashton, Preston, Lancs. PR2 1AJ
tel (01772) 725120 *mobile* (07789) 433254
fax (01772) 723853
email megindex@aol.com
website www.megindex.com

Indexing at general and post-graduate level in the arts and humanities. Also proofreading and copy-editing. Registered with Society of Indexers since 1971.

Rosemary Dooley
Crag House, Witherslack, Grange-over-Sands, Cumbria LA11 6RW
tel (015395) 52286 *fax* (015395) 52013
email musicbks @rdooley.demon.co.uk
website www.booksonmusic.co.uk
Proprietor Rosemary Dooley
Collaborative publishers' exhibitions: music books. Founded 1985.

Editorial Solutions
537 Antrim Road, Belfast BT15 3BU
tel 028-9077 2300 *fax* 028-9078 1356
email inbox@editorialsolutions.com
website www.editorialsolutions.com
Partners Sheelagh Hughes, Michael Johnston
Offers a comprehensive editorial and publications service, including news and feature writing, copywriting, editing and copy-editing, proofreading, publication design, page layout and complete publication management, and online publications. Qualified journalists. Specialisms: business, public sector, education, religious communications, multimedia.

Editorial/Visual Research
21 Leamington Road Villas, London W11 1HS
tel 020-7727 4920 *mobile* (07973) 820020
Contact Angela Murphy
Comprehensive research service including historical, literary, film and picture research for writers, publishers, film and TV companies. Services also include copy-writing, editing, and travel and feature writing. Founded 1973.

Lewis Esson Publishing
45 Brewster Gardens, London W10 6AQ
tel 020-7854 0668 *fax* 020-8968 1623
email lewisesson@supanet.com
Project management of illustrated books in areas of food, art and interior design; editing and writing of food books; copywriting, especially in the area of food packaging and FMCGs. Founded 1989.

Finers Stephens Innocent
179 Great Portland Street, London W1N 6LS
tel 020-7323 4000 *fax* 020-7344 5600
email nsolomon@fsilaw.co.uk
website www.fsilaw.co.uk
Contact Nicola Solomon, Partner
Services include: drafting and negotiating agency and publishing agreements; advice on copyright and moral rights, libel reading, defamation advice and insurance; breaches or termination of contract; errors in printing and failure or refusal to publish or delay in publishing; debt collection for payment of royalties, commission or fees, including suing or insolvency proceedings where necessary; injunctions; preparation of wills, administering artistic and literary estates; permissions, rights, copyright infringement and negligent misstatement; electronic rights and international sales. Solicitors to the Society of Authors, the Writers' Guild, the British Association of Picture Libraries and Agencies and the Association of Illustrators.

First Edition Translations Ltd
6 Wellington Court, Wellington Street, Cambridge CB1 1HZ
tel (01223) 356733 *fax* (01223) 321488/316232
email info@firstedit.co.uk
website www.firstedit.co.uk
Directors Sheila Waller, Jeremy Waller
Translation, interpreting, voice-over recording, editing, proofreading, Americanisation, DTP; books, manuals, reports, journals and promotional material. Founded 1981.

FJN Associates
Little Theobald, Sandy Cross, Heathfield, East Sussex TN21 8BT
tel (01435) 866653 *fax* (01435) 868998
email fred@nixonf.freeserve.co.uk
Partners Frederick J. Nixon, Brenda Mellen Nixon
Comprehensive DTP and editorial service including magazine and newsletter design and production; advice to authors, editing and preparation of manuscripts for submission to publishers/ editors; proofreading. Founded 1990.

Christine Foley Secretarial Services
Glyndedwydd, Login, Whitland, Carmarthenshire SA34 0TN
tel/fax (01994) 448414
Partners Christine Foley, Michael Foley
Word processing service: preparation of MSS from handwritten/typed notes and audio-transcription. Complete secretarial support. Founded 1991.

***the* Freelance Editorial Service**
45 Bridge Street, Musselburgh, Midlothian EH21 6AA
tel 0131-663 1238
Contact Bill Houston BSc, DipLib, MPhil
Editing, proofreading, indexing, abstract-

ing, translations, bibliographies; particularly scientific and medical. Founded 1975.

Freelance Market News

Sevendale House, 7 Dale Street,
Manchester M1 1JB
tel 0161-228 2362 *fax* 0161-228 3533
email fmn@writersbureau.com
website www.writersbureau.com
Contact Angela Cox, Editor

A monthly market newsletter. A good rate of pay made for news of editorial requirements. Information on UK and overseas publications with editorial content, submission requirements and contact details. Founded 1968.

Freelance Services

41A Newal Road, Ballymoney,
Co. Antrim BT53 6HB
tel 028-2766 2953 *fax* 028-2766 5019
website www.joanshannon.co.uk
Contact Joan Shannon

Writing, editorial and desktop design service. Commercial, industrial, scenic, fine art and natural light photography. Postcard publisher. Founded 1991.

Shelagh Furness

Hallgarth Farmhouse, The Hallgarth, Durham,
Co. Durham DH1 3BJ
tel 0191-384 3840

Research, editorial and information services. Experienced book and journal editor; online and library research; specialises in current affairs, geopolitics, environment and information systems. Founded 1992.

Geo Group & Associates

4 Christian Fields, London SW16 3JZ
tel 020-8764 6292 *fax* 0115-981 9418
email publishing@geo-group.co.uk
website www.geo-group.co.uk

Publishing services. From copy-editing and proofreading to complete package. Research and publishing consultancy. Low cost, quality, short-run printing. Publishing imprint: Nyala Publishing. Two photo libraries (including aerial); photography commissioned. Special rates to author-publishers. Established 1968.

C.N. Gilmore

27 Salisbury Street, Bedford MK41 7RE
tel (01234) 346142
email Intel_Thug@compuserve.com

Sub-editing, slush-pile reading, reviewing. Will also collaborate. Undertakes work in all scholarly and academic fields as well as fiction and practical writing. Specialises in editing translated works. Founded 1987.

Graham-Cameron Publishing

The Studio, 23 Holt Road, Sheringham,
Norfolk NR26 8NB
tel (01263) 821333 *fax* (01263) 821334
Partners Helen Graham-Cameron, Mike Graham-Cameron

Complete editorial, including writing, editing, illustration and production services. Absolutely no unsolicited MSS. Founded 1984.

Bernard Hawton

6 Merdon Court, Merdon Avenue,
Chandler's Ford, Hants SO53 1FP
tel 023-8026 7400
email bernardhawton@hotmail.com

Proofreading, copy-editing.

Antony Hemans

Maranatha, 1 Nettles Terrace, Guildford,
Surrey GU1 4PA
tel (01483) 574511

Biographical and historical research, specialising in industrial archaeology – railways, canals and shipping, air, military and naval operations – genealogy and family history. Founded 1981.

Rosemary Horstmann

122 Mayfield Court, 27 West Savile Terrace,
Edinburgh EH9 3DR
tel 0131-667 1377

Broadcasting scripts evaluated; general consultancy on editorial and marketing matters.

E.J. Hunter

6 Dorset Road, London N22 7SL
tel 020-8889 0370

Editing, copy-editing, appraisal of MSS. Special interests: novels, short stories, drama, children's stories; primary education, complementary medicine, New Age.

Hurst Village Publishing

Henry and Elizabeth Farrar, High Chimneys,
Davis Street, Hurst, Reading RG10 0TH
tel 0118-9345211 *fax* 0118-9342073
email henry@heritagesites.eu.com

Offers design, photography, typesetting using the latest desktop publishing programs, photographic equipment and high resolution colour and laser printers. Founded 1989.

Indexers, Society of – see page 593

Indexing Specialists (UK) Ltd

202 Church Road, Hove, East Sussex BN3 2DJ
tel (01273) 738299 *fax* (01273) 323309
email richardr@indexing.co.uk
website www.indexing.co.uk
Director Richard Raper BSc, DTA

Indexes for all types: books, journals and reference publications on professional, scientific and general subjects; copy-editing, proofreading services; consultancy on indexing and electronic indexing. Founded 1965.

The Information Bureau

(formerly Daily Telegraph Information Bureau)
51 The Business Centre, 103 Lavender Hill, London SW11 5QL
tel 020-7924 4414 *fax* 020-7924 4456
email infobureau@dial.pipex.com
website www.infobureau.co.uk
Contact Jane Hall

Offers an on-demand research service on a variety of subjects including current affairs, business, marketing, history, the arts, media and politics. Resources include range of cuttings amassed by the bureau since 1948.

Library Research Agency

Burberry, Devon Road, Salcombe, Devon TQ8 8HJ
tel (01548) 842769 *fax* (01548) 842933
Directors D.J. Langford MA, B. Langford

Research and information service for writers, journalists, artists, businessmen from libraries, archives, museums, record offices and newspapers in UK, USA and Europe. Sources may be in English, French, German, Russian, Serbo-Croat, Bulgarian, and translations made if required. Founded 1974.

The Literary Consultancy (TLC)

Diorama Arts Centre, 34 Osnaburgh Street, London NW1 3ND
tel/fax 020-7813 4330
email swifttlc@dircon.co.uk
website www.literaryconsultancy.co.uk
Director Rebecca Swift, *Administrator* Rebecca de Saintonge

Offers a detailed assessment of fiction, non-fiction and autobiography from a team of professional editors and writers. Fees based on length. Quick turnaround. Personal links with agents and publishers. Approved by the Arts Council of England. Established 1996.

Dr Kenneth Lysons

Lathom, Scotchbarn Lane, Whiston, Nr Prescot, Merseyside L35 7JB
tel 0151-426 5513 *fax* 0151-430 6934
email lysons@literaryservices.co.uk
Contact Dr Kenneth Lysons MA, MEd, DPA, DMA, FCIS, FInstPS, FBIM

Company and institutional histories, support material for organisational management and supervisory training, house journals, research and reports service. Full secretarial support. Founded 1986.

Duncan McAra

28 Beresford Gardens, Edinburgh EH5 3ES
tel/fax 0131-552 1558
email duncanmcara@hotmail.com

Consultancy on all aspects of general trade publishing; editing; proof correction. Main subjects include art, architecture, archaeology, biography, military, Scottish and travel. See also page 358. Founded 1988.

McText

Denmill, Tough, By Alford, Aberdeenshire AB33 8EP
tel/fax (019755) 62582
email d@mctext.com
website www.mctext.com
Partners K. and Duncan McArdle

Proofreading, copy-editing, website proofing. Specialist interests: archaeology, equestrian, oil-related commerce. Founded 1986.

Manuscript Appraisals

Lanetrees, Simpson Cross, Haverfordwest, Pembs. SA62 6AE
tel/fax (01437) 710534
email manuscript_app@hotmail.com
Proprietor Norman Price *Consultants* Ray Price, Mary Hunt

Independent appraisal of authors' MSS (fiction and non-fiction, but no poetry) with full editorial guidance and advice. In-house editing, copy-editing, rewriting and proofreading if required. Overseas enquiries welcome. Interested in the work of new writers. Founded 1984.

Marlinoak

22 Eve's Croft, Birmingham B32 3QL
tel/fax 0121-475 6139
Proprietor Hazel J. Billing JP, BA, DipEd

Preparation of scripts, plays, books, MSS service, proofreading; also audio-transcription, word processing. Founded 1984.

Susan Moore Editorial Services
65 Albion Road, London N16 9PP
tel/fax 020-7923 2480
email NCLWebb@compuserve.com
Troubleshooting service for publishers, packagers and agents: co-authorship with specialists, translation fine tuning. Founded 1994.

Murder Files
81 Churchfields Drive, Bovey Tracey TQ13 9QU
tel (01626) 833487 *fax* (01626) 835797
email enquiry@murderfiles.com
website www.murderfiles.com
Director Paul Williams
Crime writer and researcher specialising in UK murders. Holds information on thousands of well-known and less well-known murders dating from 1400 to the present day. Copies of press cuttings available from 1920 to date. Details of executions, particularly at the Tyburn and Newgate. Information on British Hangmen. Specialist in British police murders since 1700. Service available to general enquirers, writers, TV, radio, video, etc. Founded 1994.

Elizabeth Murray
3 Gower Mews Mansions, Gower Mews, London WC1E 6HR
tel/fax 020-7636 3761
email MurraySearch@aol.com
Literary, biographical, historical, crime, military, cinema, genealogy research for authors, journalists, radio and TV from UK, European and USA sources. Founded 1975.

My Word!
138 Railway Terrace, Rugby, Warks. CV21 3HN
tel (01788) 571294 *fax* (01788) 550957
email enquiries@myword.co.uk
website www.myword.co.uk
Partners Roddie Grant, Janet Grant
Specialises in typesetting and website solutions. Produces materials for printing and websites, e.g. magazines, newsletters, books, brochures, leaflets, conference and sales literature. Founded 1994.

Paul Nash
Munday House, Aberdalgie, Perth PH2 0QB
tel/fax (01738) 621584
email paulnash@zetnet.co.uk
Indexer specialising in sciences, engineering, technology, environmental science. Registered with the Society of Indexers. Winner of Library Association Wheatley Medal (1992) for outstanding index. Founded 1979.

Peter Nickol
50 St Leonards Road, Exeter EX2 4LS
tel/fax (01392) 255512
email pnickol@ninoakes.freeserve.co.uk
Editing and page layout; typesetting and music engraving; copyright licensing; project management including mixed media coordination, CD recording and production. Specialises in music and music education. Established 1987.

Nidaba Publishing Services
68 Bramblebury Road, London SE18 7TG
tel 020-8317 3767
email ali.glen@virgin.net
Contact Ali Glenny PhD Eng. Lit.
Copy-editing, proofreading and onscreen text correction (Word, Quark). Established 1997.

Paul H. Niekirk
40 Rectory Avenue, High Wycombe, Bucks. HP13 6HW
tel (01494) 527200
Text editing for works of reference and professional and management publications, particularly texts on law; freelance writing. Founded 1976.

Northern Writers Advisory Services
77 Marford Crescent, Sale, Cheshire M33 4DN
tel 0161-969 1573
email grovesjill@aol.com
Proprietor Jill Groves
Offers copy-editing and typesetting to small publishers, societies and authors. Local history only. Founded 1986.

Oriental Languages Bureau
Lakshmi Building, Sir P. Mehta Road, Fort, Bombay 400001, India
tel 2661258/2665640 *fax* 2664598
email icsolb@vsnl.net
Proprietor Rajan K. Shah
Undertakes translations, phototypesetting-DTP, artwork and printing in all Indian languages and a few foreign languages.

Ormrod Research Services
Weeping Birch, Burwash, East Sussex TN19 7HG
tel/fax (01435) 882541
Comprehensive research service: literary, historical, academic, biographical, commercial. Critical reading with report

(novels, theses, non-fiction), editing, indexing, proofreading, ghostwriting. Founded 1982.

Oxford Designers & Illustrators

(formerly Oxford Illustrators and Oxprint Design)
Aristotle House, Aristotle Lane, Oxford OX2 6TR
tel (01865) 512331 *fax* (01865) 512408
email name@odi-illustration.co.uk
website www.oxford-illustrators.co.uk
Directors Peter Lawrence, Richard Corfield, Andrew King

Over 30 years' experience in the design, typesetting and illustration of educational and general books. In-house artists for all subjects including scientific and technical, medical, natural history, cartoons, maps and diagrams. Full project management and repro service. Not an agency.

Pages Editorial & Publishing Services

Ballencrieff Cottage, Ballencrieff Toll, Bathgate, West Lothian EH48 4LD
tel (01506) 632728 *fax* (01506) 635444
email suse@pages.clara.net
Director Susan Coon

Editorial and production service of magazines/newspapers for companies or for commercial distribution. Founded 1995.

Pagewise

2 Butlers Close, Amersham, Bucks. HP6 5PY
tel/fax (01494) 729760
email info@pagewise.co.uk
Director Monica Bratt

Specialist service for self publishers: design, typesetting, editing and indexing, proofreading and production services. Founded 1999.

Geoffrey D. Palmer

47 Burton Fields Road, Stamford Bridge, York YO41 1JJ
tel (01759) 372874
email gdp@lineone.net
website www.geoffreydpalmer.co.uk

Editorial and production services, including STM and general copy-editing, on-screen editing, artwork editing, proofreading and indexing. Pre-press project management. Founded 1987.

Roger Palmer Ltd

Antonia House, 262 Holloway Road, London N7 6NE
tel 020-7609 4828 *fax* 020-7609 4878
email contracts@rogerpalmerltd.co.uk
Contact Peter Palmer

Drafts, advises on and negotiates all media contracts for publishers, packagers, agents, authors and others; operates complete outsourced contracts department functions for publishers; undertakes contractual audits and devises contracts and permissions systems; provides advice on copyright and related issues; provides training and seminars. Special terms for members of the Society of Authors and the Writers' Guild of Great Britain. Founded 1993.

Phoenix 2

Lantern House, Lodge Drove, Woodfalls, Salisbury, Wilts SP5 2NH
tel (01725) 512200 *fax* (01725) 511819
email walker@phoenix2.prestel.co.uk
Partners Bryan Walker, Amanda Walker

Writing, editing, sub-editing, typesetting and design of magazines, newsletters, journals, brochures and promotional literature. Specialist areas are business, tourism, social affairs and education. Founded 1994.

Christopher Pick

41 Chestnut Road, London SE27 9EZ
tel 020-8761 2585 *fax* 020-8761 6388
email cpick@netcomuk.co.uk

Publications consultancy, project management, writing and editing for companies and public-sector and voluntary-sector agencies: e.g. annual reports, brochures and booklets, information materials, websites, strategy documents, research reports, books, organisational histories. Extensive expertise and experience in presenting information clearly and concisely for non-specialist readers.

Picture Research Agency

Jasmine Cottage, Spring Grove Road, Richmond, Surrey TW10 6EH
tel/fax 020-8940 5986
email pat.hodgpix@virgin.net
Contact Pat Hodgson

Illustrations found for books, films and TV. Written research also undertaken particularly on historical subjects, including photographic and film. Small picture library.

Picture Research Service – see Rich Research

Reginald Piggott

Decoy Lodge, Decoy Road, Potter Heigham, Norfolk NR29 5LX
tel (01692) 670384

Cartographer to the University Presses

and academic publishers in Britain and overseas. Maps and diagrams for academic and educational books. Founded 1962.

Plum Communications

Fountain Head, Morchard Bishop, Crediton, Devon EX17 6NW
tel/fax (01363) 877463
email stephanie.plum@virgin.net
Contact Stephanie Walshe

Proofreading and copy editing (hard copy and onscreen), copywriting, ghost writing, rewriting, indexing, page layout, research, project management. Backlog reading, appraisal of fiction and non-fiction MSS with report (write, phone or email first), website authoring. Complete marketing service and production of all promotional material, training manuals, strategy documents, research reports and company histories. Founded 1990.

Keith Povey Editorial Services

Stoneleigh House, South Brentor, Tavistock, Devon PL19 0NW
tel (01822) 810190 *fax* (01822) 810191
email Povedservs@aol.com

Copy-editing, indexing, proofreading, publisher/author liaison. Partnership with T & A Typesetting Services (*tel* 01706 861662) – specialist book typesetting to final output of any kind, graphic design.

David Price

4 Harbidges Lane, Long Buckby, Northampton NN6 7QL
tel/fax (01327) 844119
email dprice@macunlimited.net
website www.cancanplus.net

Copy-editing, proofreading, research, writing, rewriting. Special interests: fine art (particularly modern art), operetta and musicals, modern European history (including the former Soviet Union), alternative health. Founded 1995.

Victoria Ramsay

Abbots Rest, Chilbolton, Stockbridge, Hants SO20 6BE
tel (01264) 860251 *fax* (01264) 860026
email victoredit@supanet.com

Freelance editing, copy-editing and proofreading; non-fiction research and writing of promotional literature and pamphlets. Any non-scientific subject undertaken. Special interests: education, cookery, travel, Africa and Caribbean and works in translation. Established 1981.

Reading and Righting (Robert Lambolle Services)

618B Finchley Road, London NW11 7RR
tel/fax 020-8455 4564
email ziph@macunlimited.net

MSS/script advisory and evaluation service: fiction, non-fiction, stage plays and screenplays; editorial services; one-to-one tutorials, creative writing courses and lectures. Send sae for leaflet. Founded 1987.

Repertoire

21 Hindsleys Place, London SE23 2NF
tel 020-8244 5816
email theentertainer@yahoo.co.uk
Contact John Parker

Editing, proofreading and advice for all writers. Plus anything written to order: fillers, humour, editorials, reports, brochures, trade press, arts, reviews, photo features, interviews, assignments. Fast turnaround; competitive rates. Established 1991.

S. Ribeiro, Literary Services

42 West Heath Court, North End Road, London NW11 7RG
tel 020-8458 9082
email sribeiroeditor@aol.com
Contact S. Ribeiro

MSS reading and appraisal with detailed analysis and guidance in submission to agents and publishers. Sensitive editing to publication standard. Also rewriting, Americanisation, idiom for translations. Copywriting: synopses, reviews and book jackets. Creative writing tutor. Special experience: fiction and general non-fiction, memoirs, poetry. Published and new writers, including overseas, welcome. Guidance for self-publishing. Send sae or telephone for leaflet. Established 1986.

Rich Research

One Bradby, 77 Carlton Hill, London NW8 9XE
tel/fax 020-7624 7755
Contact Diane Rich

Picture research service. Visuals found for all sectors of the media and publishing. Artwork and photography commissioned. Rights and permissions negotiated. Founded 1978.

Anton Rippon Press Services

Breedon House, 3 The Parker Centre, Derby DE21 4SZ

tel (01332) 384235 *cellphone* (07702) 693864
fax (01332) 364063/521548
email anton@breedonpublishing.co.uk
General feature and sports writing for newspapers and magazines. Ghostwriting (preliminary letter essential). Radio and film documentary treatments and scripts. Complete book production service. Part of the Breedon Publishing Group.

Sandhurst Editorial Consultants

36 Albion Road, Sandhurst, Berks. GU47 9BP
tel (01252) 877645 *fax* (01252) 890508
email mail@sand-con.demon.co.uk
website www.sand-con.demon.co.uk
Partners Lionel Browne, Janet Browne
Specialists in technical, professional and reference work. Project management, editorial development, writing, rewriting, copy-editing, proofreading, and general editorial consultancy. Founded 1991.

Sandton Literary Agency

PO Box 785799, Sandton 2146, South Africa
tel (011) 442-8624
Directors J. Victoria Canning, M. Sutherland
Evaluating, editing and/or indexing book MSS. Preparing reports, company histories, house journals, etc. Critical but constructive advice to writers. Lecture agents. Please write or phone first. Founded 1982.

SciText

18 Barton Close, Landrake, Saltash, Cornwall PL12 5BA
tel/fax (01752) 851451
email bg@scitext.fsnet.co.uk
Contact Dr Brian Gee
Proofreading and editing in science, chemical and electrical engineering and the history of science and technology; IBM compatible PC. Founded 1988.

SfEP (Society for Editors and Proofreaders) – see page 473

Gill Shepherd

87 Elm Park Mansions, Park Walk, London SW10 0AP
tel 020-7352 1770
email rgbshepherd@msn.com
Research, fact checking, rewriting for authors. Specialises in history, politics, biography and genealogy. Established 1985.

Small Print

The Old School House, 74 High Street, Swavesey, Cambridge CB4 5QU
tel (01954) 231713 *fax* (01954) 205061
email info@smallprint.co.uk
website www.smallprint.co.uk
Proprietor Naomi Laredo
Editorial, design, page layout, project management, and audio production services, specialising in ELT and foreign language courses for secondary schools and home study; also phrase books, travel guides, general humanities. Translation from/to and editing in many European and Asian languages. Photography and picture research. Founded 1986.

Special Edition Pre-press Services

Partners Romilly Hambling, 17 Almorah Road, London N1 3ER
tel/fax 020-7226 5339
email mail@special-edition.co.uk
website www.special-edition.co.uk
and Corinne Orde, 2 Caledonian Wharf, London E14 3EW
tel/fax 020-7987 9600
Integrated editing and page make-up for publishers of general and STM titles. Design and project management undertaken. See website for downloadable brochure. Established 1993.

Mrs Gene M. Spencer

63 Castle Street, Melbourne, Derbyshire DE73 1DY
tel (01332) 862133
Editing, copy-editing and proofreading; feature writing; theatrical profiles; book reviews; freelance writing. Founded 1970.

SPREd (Society of Picture Researchers and Editors) – now The Picture Research Association – see p 487

StorytrackS

PO Box 3155, Glastonbury, Somerset BA16 0WB
tel (01395) 279659
email storytracks@aol.com
website www.storytracks.net
Directors Marina Oliver, Margaret James, Chris Dukes
A team of widely published authors offer honest appraisals of MSS: constructive comment on content and structure and help to improve writing style. Guidance is based on extensive experience and sound market awareness. Also offers ghostwriting services, advice on self-publishing and editorial assistance. Founded 2001.

Strand Editorial Services

16 Mitchley View, South Croydon, Surrey CR2 9HQ
tel 020-8657 1247 *fax* 020-8651 3525
Joint Principals Derek and Irene Bradley

Provide a comprehensive service to publishers, editorial departments, and public relations and advertising agencies. Proofreading and copy-editing a speciality. Founded 1974.

Success Writing Bureau

Thirsol House, Earby, Barnoldswick, Lancs BB18 6NE
tel/fax (01282) 842495
Contact John O'Toole

MSS appraisal with agency links where applicable. Home study courses in journalism/article writing, short story, radio, TV and novel writing. Speedy turnaround. John O'Toole tutorials since 1965; bureau founded 1980.

Hans Tasiemka Archives

80 Temple Fortune Lane, London NW11 7TU
tel 020-8455 2485 *fax* 020-8455 0231
Proprietor Mrs Edda Tasiemka

Comprehensive newspaper cuttings library from 1850s to the present day on all subjects for writers, publishers, picture researchers, film and TV companies. Founded 1950.

Lyn M. Taylor

(Eve-Line Editorial/Proofs)
Mill of Auldallan, Balintore, By Kirriemuir, Angus DD8 5JS
tel (01575) 560 380 *fax* (01575) 560 780
email LynTaylor@compuserve.com

General comprehensive editorial service for publishers: copy-editing (hard copy or onscreen) and proofreading in all subjects. Specialises in scientific and medical books, journals and reports. Formatting, coding.

Tecmedia Ltd

Bruce House, 258 Bromham Road, Biddenham, Beds. MK40 4AA
tel (01234) 325223 *fax* (01234) 353524
email jojobaxter@cs.com
Managing Director J.D. Baxter

Specialists in the design, development and production of information packages, newsletters and promotional material. Founded 1972.

Teral Research Services

111 The Avenue, Bournemouth, Dorset BH9 2UX
tel (01202) 519220
45 Forest View Road, Bournemouth BH9 3BH
tel (01202) 516834 *fax* (01202) 516834
Contact Alan C. Wood, Terry C. Treadwell

Research and consultancy on military aviation, army, navy, defence, space, weapons (new and antique), police, intelligence, medals, uniforms and armour. Founded 1980.

Thoughtbubble Ltd

58-60 Fitzroy Street, London W1T 5BU
tel 020-7387 8890 *fax* 020-7383 2220
email enquiries@thoughtbubble.net
website www.thoughtbubble.net
Contact James Maltby

Website design and development, database integration, Flash animation, audio/video editing and production, e-commerce, intranet design and development, software development, print design, CD-Rom design and production. Also presentation, training and website hosting. Founded 1997.

Felicity Trotman

Downside, Chicklade, Salisbury, Wilts. SP3 5SU
tel/fax (01747) 820503
email f.trotman@btinternet.com

For publishers only: editing, copy-editing, proofreading, writing, rewriting. Specialises in children's books, fiction and non-fiction, all ages. Established 1982.

John Vickers

27 Shorrolds Road, London SW6 7TR
tel 020-7385 5774

Archives of British Theatre photographs by John Vickers, from 1938-1974.

Gordon R. Wainwright

22 Hawes Court, Sunderland SR6 8NU
tel/fax 0191-548 9342
email gordon@gordonwainwright.co.uk
website www.gordonwainwright.co.uk

Criticism, advice and revision for non-fiction authors; internet information detective; grant applications writer; non-fiction authors' publishing consultant. Established 1961.

Caroline White

78 Howard Road, London E17 4SQ
tel 020-8521 5791
email cwhite@bmjgroup.com

Research and writing of features for newspapers, magazines and radio, specialising in health and medicine; also travel. Corporate literature and reports. Press and public relations. Written and spoken Italian, Spanish and French. Founded 1985.

Derek Wilde

59 Victoria Road, Woodbridge, Suffolk IP12 1EL
tel/fax (01394) 384557
email jill001@aol.com

Copy-editing, proofreading, indexing, research. Particular expertise in directories and reference books. Special interests: higher education, performing arts, travel and transport. Languages: French and Latin plus some knowledge of German and Italian. Established 1991.

David L. Williams

7 Buckbury Heights, Newport, Isle of Wight PO30 2LX
tel (01983) 528729 *fax* (01983) 822116
email davidw@genpix.fsnet.co.uk

Complete research and information service (pictures and text) specialising in transport – particularly maritime and aviation – history and genealogy. Member of the Picture Research Association. Established 1982.

David Winpenny

33 St Marygate, Ripon, North Yorkshire HG4 1LX
tel (01765) 608320 *fax* (01765) 607641
email david@dwpr.freeserve.co.uk
website www.dwpr.org.uk

Writer and editor, including research and writing of features, news stories, brochures, speeches, advertising copy. Special interest in country walks, architectural history, the arts, music, landscape, heritage, business and the North. Founded 1991.

Rita Winter Editorial Services

'Kilrubie', Eddleston, Peeblesshire EH45 8QP
tel/fax (01721) 730353
email rita@ednet.co.uk

On-screen editing, copy-editing and proofreading (English and Dutch). Academic and general material, books, dictionaries, company literature. Special interests: art, art history, exhibition catalogues.

Witan Publishing Services

Cherry Tree House, 8 Nelson Crescent, Cotes Heath, via Stafford ST21 6ST
tel (01782) 791673
Director Jeff Kent

Editing, proofreading, typesetting, publishing advice, design and artwork, printing, marketing, publicity, repping, distribution advice. Established 1980.

WORDSmith

2 The Island, Thames Ditton, Surrey KT7 0SH
tel/fax 020-8339 0945
email ws@good-writing-matters.com
website www.good-writing-matters.com
Partners Michael Russell and Elaine Russell

Copy-editing on paper and onscreen: all areas including film scripts. Specialises in new writer fiction, rewriting and abridging. Also short-run publishing for new writing, as Riverside Press. Founded 1984.

Wordwise

37 Elmthorpe Road, Wolvercote, Oxford OX2 8PA
tel (01865) 510098 *fax* (01865) 310556
email wordwise@mendes.demon.co.uk
Director Valerie Mendes

Specialises in creative writing projects for children and young adults. Founded 1990.

WordWise

66 Russell Road, Lee-on-the-Solent, Hants PO13 9HP
tel 023-9235 9960 *fax* 023-9255 4842
email martyn@wordwise.co.uk
website www.wordwise.co.uk
Contact Martyn Yeo

The following services are offered to publishers only: copy-editing, indexing, HTML and SGML mark-up, data entry, database publishing, typesetting, project management. Member of SfEP. Established 1984.

Richard M. Wright

32 Oak Village, London NW5 4QN
tel 020-7284 4316
email rmwindserv@aol.com

Indexing, copy-editing, specialising in politics, history, business, social sciences. Founded 1977.

Write on...

62 Kiln Lane, Oxford OX3 8EY
tel/fax (01865) 744336
email Writeon1989@aol.com
Director Yvonne Newman

Non-fiction book planning workshops and one-to-one consultations. Send sae for details. Founded 1989.

The Writers' Exchange

14 Old School Mews, Bacup,
Lancs. OL13 0QN
tel (01706) 877480, 217083
email writers'exchange@j-m-wright.freeserve.co.uk
website www.world-wide-words.co.uk
Secretary Mike Wright

Copywriting, ghostwriting, DTP, internet publishing and editorial services, including appraisal service for amateur writers preparing to submit material to literary agents/publishers. Offers 'constructive, objective evaluation service, particularly for those who cannot get past the standard rejection slip barrier, or who have had work rejected by publishers and need an impartial view of why it did not sell'. Novels, short stories, film, TV, radio and stage plays. Send sae for details. Founded 1977.

The Written Word

43 Green Lane, Beaumont, Lancaster LA1 2ES
tel/fax (01524) 35215
email steve@ashton01.freeserve.co.uk
Contact Steve Ashton

Script evaluation service (£45 articles, £120 for 3 chapters and synopsis of book). Editorial services by arrangement. Founded 1999.

Hans Zell, Publishing Consultant

Glais Bheinn, Lochcarron, Ross-shire IV54 8YB
tel (01520) 722951 *fax* (01520) 722953
email hzell@dial.pipex.com
website www.hanszell.co.uk/

Consultancies, project evaluations, market assessments, feasibility studies, research and surveys, funding proposals, freelance editorial work, commissioning, journals management, internet training. Specialises in services to publishers and the book community in Third World countries and provides specific expertise in these areas. Also mailing list services. Founded 1987.

Editorial, literary and production services by specialisation

Addresses for editorial, literary and production services start on page 576.

Complete editorial, literary and book production services

'A Feature Factory' Editorial Services
Academic File
Anchor Editorial Services
The Book Guild Ltd
Book Production Consultants plc
Chase Publishing Services
Karyn Claridge Book Production
D & N Publishing
Editorial Solutions
Geo Group & Associates
Graham-Cameron Publishing
Oxford Designers & Illustrators
Pages Editorial & Publishing Services
Pagewise
Keith Povey Editorial Services
Anton Rippon Press Services

Advisory and consultancy services, critical assessments, reports

Academic File
Advice and Criticism Service
Amolibros
Angel Books
Arkst Publishing
Authors' Advisory Service
Authors' Aid
Authors Appraisal Service
Johnathon Clifford
Cornerstones
Ingrid Cranfield
FJN Associates
Geo Group & Associates
C.N. Gilmore
Rosemary Horstmann
E.J. Hunter
Indexing Specialists (UK) Ltd
The Literary Consultancy (TLC)
Duncan McAra
Manuscript Appraisals
Ormrod Research Services
Christopher Pick
Reading and Righting (Robert Lambolle Services)
S. Ribeiro, Literary Services
Sandhurst Editorial Consultants
Sandton Literary Agency
Storytracks
Success Writing Bureau
Teral Research Services
Felicity Trotman

Gordon R. Wainwright
Witan Publishing Services
Wordwise
Write on...
The Writers' Exchange
Hans Zell, Publishing Consultant

Editing, copy-editing, proofreading

Aaron Editorial
Abbey Writing Services
Amolibros
Arkst Publishing
Authors' Aid
Richard A. Beck
Beswick Writing Services
Black Ace Book Production
Blair Services
The Book Guild Ltd
Brooke Projects
Mrs D. Buckmaster
John Button – Editorial Services
Barbara Cheney
Combrógos
Ingrid Cranfield
David A. Cross
Meg Davies
Editorial Solutions
Editorial/Visual Research
Lewis Esson Publishing
First Edition Translations Ltd
FJN Associates
the Freelance Editorial Service
Freelance Services
C.N. Gilmore
Bernard Hawton
E.J. Hunter
Indexing Specialists (UK) Ltd
Duncan McAra
McText
Manuscript Appraisals
Marlinoak
My Word!
Peter Nickol
Nidaba Publishing Services
Paul H. Niekirk
Northern Writers Advisory Services
Ormrod Research Services
Geoffrey D. Palmer
Phoenix 2
Christopher Pick
Plum Communications
Keith Povey Editorial Services
David Price
Victoria Ramsay
Reading and Righting (Robert Lambolle Services)
S. Ribeiro, Literary Services
Sandhurst Editorial Consultants
Sandton Literary Agency
SciText
Small Print
Mrs Gene M. Spencer
Strand Editorial Services
Lyn M. Taylor
Felicity Trotman
Derek Wilde
David Winpenny
Rita Winter Editorial Services
Witan Publishing Services
WordWise
Richard M. Wright
The Writers' Exchange
Hans Zell, Publishing Consultant

Design, typing, word processing, DTP, book production

'A Feature Factory' Editorial Services
Arioma Editorial Services
Authors' Aid
Black Ace Book Production
The Book Guild Ltd
Book-in-Hand Ltd
Vanessa Charles
Barbara Cheney
Editorial Solutions
First Edition Translations Ltd
FJN Associates
Christine Foley Secretarial Services
Freelance Services
Shelagh Furness
Hurst Village Publishing
Marlinoak
My Word!
Peter Nickol
Nidaba Publishing Services
Northern Writers Advisory Services
Oriental Languages Bureau
Phoenix 2
Small Print
Special Edition Pre-press Services
Tecmedia Ltd
Witan Publishing Services
The Writers' Exchange

Research and/or writing, rewriting, picture research

'A Feature Factory' Editorial Services
Aaron Editorial
Abbey Writing Services
Academic File
AFI Research – Richard M. Bennett Associates
Arioma Editorial Services
Authors' Research Services
Richard A. Beck
Beswick Writing Services
Blair Services
Brooke Projects
Causeway Resources
Combrógos
Ingrid Cranfield
David A. Cross
Editorial Solutions
Editorial/Visual Research
Lewis Esson Publishing
Freelance Services
Shelagh Furness
Geo Group & Associates
Antony Hemans
The Information Bureau
Library Research Agency
Dr Kenneth Lysons
Manuscript Appraisals
Susan Moore Editorial Services
Murder Files
Elizabeth Murray
Paul H. Niekirk
Ormrod Research Services
Phoenix 2
Christopher Pick
Picture Research Agency
David Price
Victoria Ramsay
Repertoire
S. Ribeiro, Literary Services
Rich Research
Anton Rippon Press Services
Sandhurst Editorial Consultants
Sandton Literary Agency
Gill Shepherd
Small Print
Mrs Gene M. Spencer
Teral Research Services
Felicity Trotman
Gordon R. Wainwright
Caroline White
David L. Williams
David Winpenny
Wordwise
The Writers' Exchange
Hans Zell, Publishing Consultant

Indexing

Richard A. Beck
Ingrid Cranfield
Meg Davies
the Freelance Editorial Service
Indexers, Society of
Indexing Specialists (UK) Ltd
Paul Nash
Ormrod Research Services
Geoffrey D. Palmer
Keith Povey Editorial Services
Sandton Literary Agency
David L. Williams
WordWise
Richard M. Wright

Translations

Ingrid Cranfield
First Edition Translations Ltd
the Freelance Editorial Service
Oriental Languages Bureau
Small Print

Specialist services

Archives

Book Data Ltd
The Information Bureau
Murder Files
Hans Tasiemka Archives
John Vickers

Cartography

Reginald Piggott

Cassettes, visual aids

Small Print

Contracts and copyright services

Peter Nickol
Geoffrey D. Palmer

Ghostwriting

Authors Aid
Anne Barclay Enterprises
Plum Communications
Anton Rippon Press Services
StorytrackS
The Writers' Exchange

Interpreting

First Edition Translations Ltd

Legal services

David Wineman, Solicitors
Finers Stephens Innocent

Media and publicity services

Book Data Ltd
Rosemary Dooley
Freelance Market News
Plum Communications

Multimedia/websites/internet/database services

AuthorsOnLine Ltd
Editorial Solutions
McText
My Word!
Peter Nickol
Thoughtbubble Ltd
WordWise
Hans Zell, Publishing Consultant

Indexing

A good index is a joy to the user of a non-fiction book; a bad index will downgrade an otherwise good book. The function of indexes, together with the skills needed to compile them, are examined here.

An index is a detailed key to the contents of a document, in contrast to a contents list, which gives only the titles of the parts into which the document is divided (e.g. chapters). Precisely, an index is 'A systematic arrangement of entries designed to enable users to locate information in a document'. The document may be a book, a series of books, an issue of a periodical, a run of several volumes of a periodical, an audiotape, a map, a film, a picture, a computer disk, an object, or any other information source in print or non-print form.

The objective of an index is to guide enquirers to information on given subjects in a document by providing the terms of their choice (single words, phrases, abbreviations, acronyms, dates, names, and so on) in an appropriately organised list which refers them to specific locations using page, column, section, frame, figure, table, paragraph, line or other appropriate numbers.

An index differs from a catalogue, which is a record of the documents held in a particular collection, such as a library; though a catalogue may require an index, for example to guide searchers from subject words to class numbers.

A document may have separate indexes for different classes of heading, so that personal names are distinguished from subjects, for example, or a single index in which all classes of heading are interfiled.

The Society of Indexers

The Society of Indexers is a non-profit organisation founded in 1957 and is the only autonomous professional body for indexers in the UK. It is affiliated with the American Society of Indexers, the Australian Society of Indexers, the China Society of Indexers, the Indexing and Abstracting Society of Canada, and the Association of Southern African Indexers and Bibliographers, and has close ties with the Chartered Institute of Library and Information Professionals (CILIP) and the Society for Editors and Proofreaders (SfEP).

The main objectives of the Society are to promote all types of indexing standards and techniques and the role of indexers in the organisation of knowledge; to provide, promote and recognise facilities for both the initial and the further training of indexers; to establish criteria for assessing indexing standards; and to conduct research and publish guidance, ideas and information about indexing. It seeks to establish good relationships between indexers, librarians, publishers and authors, both to advance good indexing and to improve the role and wellbeing of indexers.

Services to indexers

The Society publishes a learned journal *The Indexer* (2 p.a.), a newsletter and *Occasional Papers in Indexing*. Meetings are held regularly on a wide range of subjects while local and special interest groups provide the chance for members to meet to discuss common interests. A two-day conference is held every year. All levels of training are supported by regular workshops held at venues throughout the country.

Professional competence is recognised in two stages by the Society. Accredited

Indexers who have completed the open-learning course qualification (see below) have shown theoretical competence in indexing while Registered Indexers have proved their experience and competence in practical indexing through an assessment procedure and admission to the Register of Indexers. The services of Registered Indexers are actively promoted by the Society while all trained and experienced members have the opportunity of an annual entry in *Indexers Available*, a directory published by the Society and distributed without charge to over 1000 publishers to help them find an indexer.

The Society sets annually recommended minimum rates for indexing (£15–£20 per hour; £1.20–£2 per page in 2002) and provides advice on the business side of indexing to its members.

Further information

Society of Indexers, Globe Centre,
Penistone Road, Sheffield S6 3AE
tel 0114-281 3060 *fax* 0114-281 3061
email admin@socind.demon.co.uk
website www.socind.demon.co.uk
Administrator Wendy Burrow
Registrar Elizabeth Wallis *tel* 020-8940 4771
Membership £50 p.a. UK/Europe, £65 overseas; £100 corporate, £125 overseas

Contact the Administrator for further information. Enquiries from publishers and authors seeking to commission an indexer should be made to the Registrar.

Services to publishers and authors

Anyone who commissions indexes needs to be certain of engaging a professional indexer working to the highest standards and able to meet deadlines.

Indexers Available, now searchable on the Society's website, lists only members of the Society and gives basic contact details, subject specialisms and indexing experience. Those accepted for listing need to fall into the following categories:

- Registered Indexers who have had their competence in practical indexing recognised by the Society;
- Accredited Indexers who have passed the Society's tests of technical competence; and
- others who have successfully completed other recognised training courses.

Advice on the selection of indexers is available from the Registrar, who may also be able to suggest names of professionals able to undertake related tasks such as thesaurus construction, terminology control or database indexing. The Registrar will also advise on relations with indexers.

The Society co-operates with CILIP in the award of the Wheatley Medal for an outstanding index.

Training in indexing

The Society's course (in printed and electronic format) is based on the principle of open learning with Units, tutorial support and formal tests all available separately so that individuals can learn in their own way and at their own pace. The Units cover four core subjects and contain practical exercises and self-administered tests. Members of the Society receive a substantial discount on the cost although anyone can purchase the Units. Only members of the Society can apply for the formal tests or for tutorial support.

Further reading

British Standards Institution, *British Standard recommendations for examining documents, determining their subjects and selecting indexing terms*, BSI, 1984 (BS6529:1984)

Information and documentation – guidelines for the content, organization and presentation of indexes (ISO 999:1996)

Correcting proofs

The following notes and table are extracted from BS 5261 Part 2: 1976 (1995) and are reproduced by permission of the British Standards Institution.

4 Marks for copy preparation and proof correction

4.1 The marks to be used for marking up copy for composition and for the correction of printers' proofs shall be as shown in Table 1 (see pages 597–606).

4.2 The marks in Table 1 are classified in three groups as follows:
(a) Group A: general.
(b) Group B: deletion, insertion and substitution.
(c) Group C: positioning and spacing.

4.3 Each item in Table 1 is given a simple alpha-numeric serial number denoting the classification group to which it belongs and its position within the group.

4.4 The marks have been drawn keeping the shapes as simple as possible and using sizes which relate to normal practice. The shapes of the marks should be followed exactly by all who make use of them.

4.5 For each marking-up or proof correction instruction a distinct mark is to be made:
(a) in the text: to indicate the exact place to which the instruction refers;
(b) in the margin: to signify or amplify the meaning of the instruction.
It should be noted that some instructions have a combined textual and marginal mark.

4.6 Where a number of instructions occur in one line, the marginal marks are to be divided between the left and right margins where possible, the order being from left to right in both margins.

4.7 Specification details, comments and instructions may be written on the copy or proof to complement the textual and marginal marks. Such written matter is to be clearly distinguishable from the copy and from any corrections made to the proof. Normally this is done by encircling the matter and/or by the appropriate use of colour (see below).

4.8 Proof corrections shall be made in coloured ink thus:
(a) printer's literal errors marked by the printer for correction: green;
(b) printer's literal errors marked by the customer and his agents for correction: red;
(c) alterations and instructions made by the customer and his agents: black or dark blue.

Further information

British Standards Institution (BSI)
Technical Information Group,
389 Chiswick High Road, London W4 4AL
tel 020-8996 7111 *fax* 020-8996 7048
Customer Services tel 020-8996 9001
fax 020-8996 7001
email info@bsi.org.uk
website www.bsi.org.uk/

BSI is the independent national body responsible for preparing British Standards. It presents the UK view on standards in Europe and at the international level. It is incorporated by Royal Charter.

For a complete standard, contact Customer Services.

5 Proofing procedure

5.1 The printer should supply the customer with proofs. The number of proofs required will depend upon the nature of the job and should be agreed between customer and printer.

5.2 One of the proofs to be supplied shall be the printer's marked proof on which he has marked literal errors and queries for the customer's attention. The printer should date and indicate the status of this proof, e.g. first galley proof, revised galley proof, page proof, etc.

5.3 The printer's marked proof shall be returned to the printer by the customer or his agent with all additional corrections marked on it, integrating those made by author, editor, designer, publisher, etc. It thus becomes a master reference for the next stage of the job.

5.4 The customer should keep a copy of the printer's marked proof, as returned to the printer, for his own reference.

5.5 Where the printer has drawn attention to any particular point on the printer's marked proof by means of a query (see Table 1, mark A4), it is essential that the appropriate authority should settle the query by writing a clear instruction on the proof or, if the matter is already correct, strike through the query.

5.6 The following additional information should be entered on the printer's marked proof before returning it:

(a) *Either* that a revised set of proofs is required (indicate whether these are to be supplied in galley/slip, page, imposed page or book form); *or* that the job is approved for press (indicate whether approval is subject to final corrections being made).

(b) The signature and status of the person who is returning the printer's marked proof.

(c) The date on which the printer's marked proof is returned to the printer; this clearly identifies the position of the proof in the production sequence.

'able 1. Classified list of marks

OTE. The letters M and P in the notes column indicate marks for arking-up copy and for correcting proofs respectively.

roup A General

umber	Instruction	Textual mark	Marginal mark	Notes
1	Correction is concluded	None	/	P Make after each correction
2	Leave unchanged	- - - - - - under characters to remain	✓	M P
3	Remove extraneous marks	Encircle marks to be removed	X	P e.g. film or paper edges visible between lines on bromide or diazo proofs
3.1	Push down risen spacing material	Encircle blemish	⊥	P
4	Refer to appropriate authority anything of doubtful accuracy	Encircle word(s) affected	?	P

roup B Deletion, insertion and substitution

	Insert in text the matter indicated in the margin	⋏	New matter followed by ⋏	M P Indentical to B2
	Insert additional matter identified by a letter in a diamond	⋏	⋏ Followed by for example Ⓐ	M P The relevant section of the copy should be supplied with the corresponding letter marked on it in a diamond e.g. Ⓐ
	Delete	/ through character(s) or ├──┤ through words to be deleted	ꝺ	M P
	Delete and close up	/ through character or ├──┤ through characters e.g. charaácter charaeacter	ꝺ	M P

Table 1 *(continued)*

Number	Instruction	Textual mark	Marginal mark	Notes
B5	Substitute character or substitute part of one or more word(s)	/ through character or ├──┤ through word(s)	New character or new word(s)	M P
B6	Wrong fount. Replace by character(s) of correct fount	Encircle character(s) to be changed	⊗	P
B6.1	Change damaged character(s)	Encircle character(s) to be changed	X	P This mark is identical to A3
B7	Set in or change to italic	——— under character(s) to be set or changed	⊔⊔	M P Where space does not per[mit] textual marks encircle the affected area instead
B8	Set in or change to capital letters	≡ under character(s) to be set or changed	≡	
B9	Set in or change to small capital letters	= under character(s) to be set or changed	=	
B9.1	Set in or change to capital letters for initial letters and small capital letters for the rest of the words	≡ under initial letters and = under rest of the word(s)	≡	
B10	Set in or change to bold type	∿∿∿ under character(s) to be set or changed	∿	
B11	Set in or change to bold italic type	∿∿∿ (with line above) under character(s) to be set or changed	⊔⊔ ∿	
B12	Change capital letters to lower case letters	Encircle character(s) to be changed	≢	P For use when B5 is inappropriate

'able 1 *(continued)*

umber	Instruction	Textual mark	Marginal mark	Notes
12.1	Change small capital letters to lower case letters	Encircle character(s) to be changed	≠	P For use when B5 is inappropriate
13	Change italic to upright type	Encircle character(s) to be changed	⊔	P
14	Invert type	Encircle character to be inverted	↻	P
15	Substitute or insert character in 'superior' position	/ through character or ⅄ where required	⅂ under character e.g. 2	P
16	Substitute or insert character in 'inferior' position	/ through character or ⅄ where required	L over character e.g. 2	P
7	Substitute ligature e.g. ffi for separate letters	⊢⊣ through characters affected	⌒ ‿ e.g. ffi	P
7.1	Substitute separate letters for ligature	⊢⊣	Write out separate letters	P
8	Substitute or insert full stop or decimal point	/ through character or ⅄ where required	⊙	M P
8.1	Substitute or insert colon	/ through character or ⅄ where required	(:)	M P
8.2	Substitute or insert semi-colon	/ through character or ⅄ where required	;	M P

Table 1 *(continued)*

Number	Instruction	Textual mark	Marginal mark	Notes
B18.3	Substitute or insert comma	/ through character or ⋏ where required	,	M P
B18.4	Substitute or insert apostrophe	/ through character or ⋏ where required	’	M P
B18.5	Substitute or insert single quotation marks	/ through character or ⋏ where required	‘ and/or ’	M P
B18.6	Substitute or insert double quotation marks	/ through character or ⋏ where required	“ and/or ”	M P
B19	Substitute or insert ellipsis	/ through character or ⋏ where required	•••	M P
B20	Substitute or insert leader dots	/ through character or ⋏ where required	(•••)	M P Give the measure of the leader when necessa
B21	Substitute or insert hyphen	/ through character or ⋏ where required	|–|	M P
B22	Substitute or insert rule	/ through character or ⋏ where required	|—|	M P Give the size of the rule the marginal mark e.g. |1 em| |4 mm|

Table 1 *(continued)*

Number	Instruction	Textual mark	Marginal mark	Notes
B23	Substitute or insert oblique	/ through character or where required	/	M P
Group C	**Positioning and spacing**			
C1	Start new paragraph			M P
C2	Run on (no new paragraph)			M P
C3	Transpose characters or words	between characters or words, numbered when necessary		M P
C4	Transpose a number of characters or words	3 2 1	123	M P To be used when the sequence cannot be clearly indicated by the use of C3. The vertical strokes are made through the characters or words to be transposed and numbered in the correct sequence
C5	Transpose lines			M P
C6	Transpose a number of lines		3 2 1	P To be used when the sequence cannot be clearly indicated by C5. Rules extend from the margin into the text with each line to be transposed numbered in the correct sequence
C7	Centre	[enclosing matter to be centred]	[ ]	M P
C8	Indent			P Give the amount of the indent in the marginal mark

Table 1 *(continued)*

Number	Instruction	Textual mark	Marginal mark	Notes
C9	Cancel indent			P
C10	Set line justified to specified measure	and/or		P Give the exact dimensions when necessary
C11	Set column justified to specified measure			M P Give the exact dimensions when necessary
C12	Move matter specified distance to the right	enclosing matter to be moved to the right		P Give the exact dimensions when necessary
C13	Move matter specified distance to the left	enclosing matter to be moved to the left		P Give the exact dimensions when necessary
C14	Take over character(s), word(s) or line to next line, column or page			P The textual mark surrounds the matter to be taken over and extends into the margin
C15	Take back character(s), word(s), or line to previous line, column or page			P The textual mark surround the matter to be taken back and extends into the margin
C16	Raise matter	over matter to be raised under matter to be raised		P Give the exact dimensions when necessary. (Use C28 for insertion of space betw lines or paragraphs in text)
C17	Lower matter	over matter to be lowered under matter to be lowered		P Give the exact dimensions when necessary. (Use C29 for reduction of space between lines or paragraph in text)
C18	Move matter to position indicated	Enclose matter to be moved and indicate new position		P Give the exact dimensions when necessary

Table 1 *(continued)*

Number	Instruction	Textual mark	Marginal mark	Notes
C19	Correct vertical alignment			P
C20	Correct horizontal alignment	Single line above and below misaligned matter e.g. misaligned		P The marginal mark is placed level with the head and foot of the relevant line
C21	Close up. Delete space between characters or words	linking characters		M P
C22	Insert space between characters	between characters affected		M P Give the size of the space to be inserted when necessary
C23	Insert space between words	between words affected		M P Give the size of the space to be inserted when necessary
C24	Reduce space between characters	between characters affected		M P Give the amount by which the space is to be reduced when necessary
C25	Reduce space between words	between words affected		M P Give amount by which the space is to be reduced when necessary
C26	Make space appear equal between characters or words	between characters or words affected		M P
C27	Close up to normal interline spacing	(each side of column linking lines)		M P The textual marks extend into the margin

Marked galley proof of text

At the sign of the red pale

The Life and Work of William Caxton by H W Larken

[An Extract]

Few people, even in the field of printing, have any clear conception of what William Caxton did or, indeed, of what he was. Much of this lack of knowledge is due to the absence of information that can be counted as factual and the consequent tendency to vague generalsation.

Though it is well known that Caxton was born in the county of Kent, there is no information as to the precise place. In his prologue to the History of Troy, William Caxton wrote for in France I was never and was born and learned my English in Kent in the Weald where I doubt not is spoken as broad and rudeEnglish as in any place of England.[1] During the fifteenth century there were a great number of Flemish cloth weavers in Kent; most of them had come to England at the instigation of Edward III with the object of teaching their craft to the English. So successful was this venture thaf the English cloth trade flourished and the agents who sold the cloth (the mercers) became very wealthy people. There have bl There have been many speculations concerning the origin of the Caxton family and much research has been carried out. It is assumed often that Caxton's family must have been connected with the wool trade in order to have secured his apprenticeship to an influential merchant.

W. Blyth Crotch (Prologues and Epilogues of William Caxton) suggests that the origin of the name Caxton (of which there are several variations in spelling) may be traced to Cambridgeshire but notes that many writers have suggested that Caxton was connected with a family at Hadlow or alternatively a family in Canterbury.

Of the Canterbury connection a William Caxton became freeman of the City in 1431 and William Pratt, a mercer who was the printer's friend, was born there. H. R. Plomer suggests that Pratt and Caxton might possibly have been schoolboys together, perhaps at the school St. Alphege. In this parish there lived a John Caxton who used as his mark three cakes over a barrel (or tun) and who is mentioned in an inscription on a monument in the church of St. Alphege.

In 1941, Alan Keen (an authority on manuscripts) secured some documents concerning Caxton; these are now in the BRITISH MUSEUM. Discovered in the library of Earl Winterton at Shillinglee Park by Richard Holworthy, the documents cover the period 1420 to 1467. One of Winterton's ancestors purchased the manor of West Wratting from a family named Caxton, the property being situated in the Weald of Kent.

There is also record of a property mentioning Philip Caxton and his wife Dennis who had two sons, Philip (born in 1413) and William

Particularly interesting in these documents is one recording that Philip Caxton junior sold the manor of Little Wratting to John Christemasse of London in 1436 the deed having been witnessed by two aldermen, one of whom was Robert Large, the printer's employer. Further, in 1439 the other son, William Caxton, con Wratting to John Christemasse, and an indenture of 1457 concerning this property mentions one William Caxton veyed his rights in the manor Buntes Hall at Little alias Causton. It is an interesting coincidence to note that the lord of the manor of Little Wratting was the father of Margaret, Duchess of Burgundy.

In 1420, a Thomas Caxton of Tenterden witnessed the will of a fellow townsman; he owned property in Kent and appears to have been a person of some importance.

[1] See 'William Caxton'.

Ⓐ attached to Christchurch Monastery in the parish of

Revised galley proof of text incorporating corrections

At the Sign of the Red Pale

The Life and Work of William Caxton, *by H W Larken*

An Extract

Few people, even in the field of printing, have any clear conception of what William Caxton did or, indeed, of what he was. Much of this lack of knowledge is due to the absence of information that can be counted as factual and the consequent tendency to vague generalisation.

Though it is well known that Caxton was born in the county of Kent, there is no information as to the precise place. In his prologue to the *History of Troy*, William Caxton wrote '. . . for in France I was never and was born and learned my English in Kent in the Weald where I doubt not is spoken as broad and rude English as in any place of England.'

During the fifteenth century there were a great number of Flemish cloth weavers in Kent; most of them had come to England at the instigation of Edward III with the object of teaching their craft to the English. So successful was this venture that the English cloth trade flourished and the agents who sold the cloth (the mercers) became very wealthy people.

There have been many speculations concerning the origin of the Caxton family and much research has been carried out. It is often assumed that Caxton's family must have been connected with the wool trade in order to have secured his apprenticeship to an influential merchant.

W. Blyth Crotch (*Prologues and Epilogues of William Caxton*) suggests that the origin of the name Caxton (of which there are several variations in spelling) may be traced to Cambridgeshire but notes that many writers have suggested that Caxton was connected with a family at Hadlow or alternatively a family in Canterbury.

Of the Canterbury connection: a William Caxton became freeman of the City in 1431 and William Pratt, a mercer who was the printer's friend, was born there. H. R. Plomer[1] suggests that Pratt and Caxton might possibly have been schoolboys together, perhaps at the school attached to Christchurch Monastery in the parish of St. Alphege. In this parish there lived a John Caxton who used as his mark three cakes over a barrel (or tun) and who is mentioned in an inscription on a monument in the church of St. Alphege.

In 1941, Alan Keen (an authority on manuscripts) secured some documents concerning Caxton; these are now in the British Museum. Discovered in the library of Earl Winterton at Shillinglee Park by Richard Holworthy, the documents cover the period 1420 to 1467. One of Winterton's ancestors purchased the manor of West Wratting from a family named Caxton, the property being situated in the Weald of Kent. There is also record of a property mentioning Philip Caxton and his wife Dennis who had two sons, Philip (born in 1413) and William.

Particularly interesting in these documents is one recording that Philip Caxton junior sold the manor of Little Wratting to John Christemasse of London in 1436—the deed having been witnessed by two aldermen, one of whom was Robert Large, the printer's employer. Further, in 1439, the other son, William Caxton, conveyed his rights in the manor Bluntes Hall at Little Wratting to John Christemasse, and an indenture of 1457 concerning this property mentions one William Caxton alias Causton. It is an interesting coincidence to note that the lord of the manor of Little Wratting was the father of Margaret, Duchess of Burgundy.

In 1420, a Thomas Caxton of Tenterden witnessed the will of a fellow townsman; he owned property in Kent and appears to have been a person of some importance.

[1] See 'William Caxton'.

Table 1 *(continued)*

Number	Instruction	Textual mark	Marginal mark	Notes
C28	Insert space between lines or paragraphs		or	M P The marginal mark extends between the lines of text. Give the size of the space t be inserted when necessary
C29	Reduce space between lines or paragraphs		or	M P The marginal mark extend between the lines of text. Give the amount by which the space is to be reduced when necessary

Government offices and public services

Enquiries to any of the following bodies should be sent to the Public Relations Officer, accompanied by a sae. The names and addresses of many other public bodies can be found in Whitaker's Almanack.

Advertising Standards Authority
2 Torrington Place,
London WC1E 7HW
tel 020-7580 5555 *fax* 020-7631 3051
email enquiries@asa.org.uk
website www.asa.org.uk

Agriculture, Fisheries and Food, Ministry of – see DEFRA: Department for Environment, Food and Rural Affairs

American Embassy
24 Grosvenor Square, London W1A 1AE
tel 020-7499 9000
website www.usembassy.org.uk

Apsley House, The Wellington Museum
Hyde Park Corner, London W1J 7NT
tel 020-7499 5676 *fax* 020-7493 6576
website www.apsleyhouse.org.uk
Open Tues–Sun, 11am–5pm.

Architecture and the Built Environment, Commission for
The Tower Building, 11 York Road,
London SE1 7NX
tel 020-7960 2400 *fax* 020-7960 2444
email enquiries@cabe.org.uk
website www.cabe.org.uk

Arts Council of England – see page 459

Arts Council of Northern Ireland
MacNeice House, 77 Malone Road,
Belfast BT9 6AQ
tel 028-9038 5200 *fax* 028-9066 1715
website www.artscouncil-ni.org

Arts Council of Wales
9 Museum Place, Cardiff CF10 3NX
tel 029-2037 6500 *fax* 029-2022 1447
email information@ccc-acw.org.uk
website www.ccc-acw.org.uk
North Wales Regional Office
36 Prince's Drive,
Colwyn Bay LL29 8LA
tel (01492) 533440 *fax* (01492) 533677
West Wales Regional Office
6 Gardd Llydaw, Jackson's Lane,
Carmarthen SA31 1QD
tel (01267) 234248 *fax* (01267) 233084

Australian High Commission
Australia House, Strand, London WC2B 4LA
tel 020-7379 4334 *fax* 020-7240 5333
website www.australia.org.uk

Austrian Embassy
18 Belgrave Mews West, London SW1X 8HU
tel 020-7235 3731 *fax* 020-7344 0292
email embassy@austria.org.uk
website www.austria.org.uk
Austrian Cultural Forum, 28 Rutland Gate,
London SW7 1PQ
tel 020-7584 8653 *fax* 020-7225 0470
email culture@austria.org.uk

The Bank of England
Threadneedle Street, London EC2R 8AH
tel 020-7601 4444 *fax* 020-7601 4771
website www.bankofengland.co.uk

Belgian Embassy
103 Eaton Square, London SW1W 9AB
tel 020-7470 3700 *fax* 020-7259 6213
email info@belgium-embassy.co.uk
website www.belgium-embassy.co.uk

Benefits Agency, Pensions and Overseas Benefits Directorate (POD) – see Social Security, Department of

Bodleian Library
Oxford OX1 3BG
tel (01865) 277000 *fax* (01865) 277182
email enquiries@bodley.ox.ac.uk
website www.bodley.ox.ac.uk

Bosnia-Herzegovina, Embassy of
320 Regent Street, London W1R 5AB
tel 020-7255 3758 *fax* 020-7255 3760

British Broadcasting Corporation
Broadcasting House, London W1A 1AA
tel 020-7580 4468
website www.bbc.co.uk

The British Council – see page 465

British Film Commission
10 Little Portland Street, London W1W 7JG
tel 020-7861 7860 *fax* 020-7861 7864
email info@bfc.co.uk
website www.bfc.co.uk

British Film Institute – see page 466

The British Library
96 Euston Road, London NW1 2DB
tel 020-7412 7332 *fax* 020-7412 7340
website www.bl.uk

British Library Document Supply Centre
Boston Spa, Wetherby, West Yorkshire LS23 7BQ
tel (01937) 546060 *fax* (01937) 546333
email dsc-customer-services@bl.uk
website www.bl.uk

British Library Newspaper Library
Colindale Avenue, London NW9 5HE
tel 020-7412 7353 *fax* 020-7412 7379
email newspaper@bl.uk
website www.bl.uk/collections/newspaper/

British Museum
Great Russell Street, London WC1B 3DG
tel 020-7323 8000
email information@thebritishmuseum.ac.uk
website www.thebritishmuseum.ac.uk

British Railways Board – see Strategic Rail Authority

British Standards Institution
Technical Information Group,
389 Chiswick High Road, London W4 4AL
tel 020-8996 7111 *fax* 020-8996 7048
email info@bsi.org.uk
website www.bsi.org.uk/

British Tourist Authority
Thames Tower, Black's Road, London W6 9EL
tel 020-8846 9000 *fax* 020-8563 0302
website www.visitbritain.com
www.britishtouristauthority.org

Broadcasting Standards Commission
7 The Sanctuary, London SW1P 3JS
tel 020-7808 1000 *fax* 020-7233 0397
website www.bsc.org.uk

Bulgaria, Embassy of the Republic of
186-188 Queen's Gate, London SW7 5HL
tel 020-7584 9400/9433, 020-7581 3144 (5 lines)
fax 020-7584 4948
email bgembasy@globalnet.co.uk

The Cabinet Office
70 Whitehall, London SW1A 2AS
tel 020-7276 1234
website www.cabinet-office.gov.uk

Cadw: Welsh Historic Monuments
Crown Building, Cathays Park, Cardiff CF10 3NQ
tel 029-2050 0200 *fax* 029-2082 6375
email cadw@wales.gsi.gov.uk
website www.cadw.wales.gov.uk

Canadian High Commission
Cultural Affairs Section, Canada House,
Trafalgar Square, London SW1Y 5BJ
tel 020-7258 6412 *fax* 020-7258 6434
Contact Literature Officer

Central Office of Information – see COI Communications

Centre for Information on Language Teaching and Research (CILT)
20 Bedfordbury, London WC2N 4LB
tel 020-7379 5101 *fax* 020-7379 5082
email library@cilt.org.uk
website www.cilt.org.uk

Charity Commission
Head Office Harmsworth House,
13-15 Bouverie Street, London EC4Y 8DP
tel (0870) 3330123 *fax* 020-7674 2300
email feedback@charity-commission.gsi.gov.uk
website www.charity-commission.gsi.gov.uk
2nd Floor, 20 King's Parade, Queen's Dock,
Liverpool L3 4DQ
tel (0870) 3330123 *fax* 0151-703 1555
Woodfield House, Tangier, Taunton TA1 4BL
tel (0870) 3330123 *fax* (01823) 345003

The Coal Authority
200 Lichfield Lane, Mansfield, Notts. NG18 4RG
tel (01623) 427162 *fax* (01623) 622072
email thecoalauthority@coal.gov.uk
website www.coal.gov.uk

COI Communications
Hercules House, Hercules Road, London SE1 7DU
tel 020-7928 2345

College of Arms (or Heralds' College)
Queen Victoria Street, London EC4V 4BT
tel 020-7248 2762 *fax* 020-7248 6448
email enquiries@college-of-arms.gov.uk
website www.college-of-arms.gov.uk

Committee on Standards in Public Life
35 Great Smith Street, London SW1P 3BQ
tel 020-7276 2595 *fax* 020-7276 2585
email nigel.wicks@gtnet.gov.uk
website www.public-standards.gov.uk

Commonwealth Institute – see page 470

Commonwealth Secretariat
Marlborough House, Pall Mall, London SW1Y 5HX
tel 020-7839 3411 *fax* 020-7839 9081
email info@commonwealth.int
website www.thecommonwealth.org

Competition Commission
(formerly Monopolies and Mergers Commission)
New Court, 48 Carey Street, London WC2A 2JT
tel 020-7271 0243 *fax* 020-7271 0367
email info@competition-commission.org.uk
website www.competition-commission.org.uk

Consignia Headquarters
5th Floor, 148 Old Street, London EC1V 9HQ
tel 020-7490 2888

Contributions Agency, International Services (InS) – see Inland Revenue, Board of

Copyright Directorate – see under Patent Office

Copyright Tribunal
Room 1/8, Harmsworth House,
13-15 Bouverie Street, London EC4Y 8DP
tel 020-7596 6510 *textphone* (08459) 222250
fax 020-7596 6526
email copyright.tribunal@patent.gov.uk
website www.patent.gov.uk/copy/tribunal/index.htm

Countryside Agency
John Dower House, Crescent Place, Cheltenham, Glos. GL50 3RA
tel (01242) 521381 *fax* (01242) 584270
website www.countryside.gov.uk

Court of the Lord Lyon
HM New Register House, Edinburgh EH1 3YT
tel 0131-556 7255 *fax* 0131-557 2148

Crafts Council
Resource Centre, 44A Pentonville Road, London N1 9BY
tel 020-7806 2501 *fax* 020-7833 4479
email reference@craftscouncil.org.uk
website www.craftscouncil.org.uk

Croatia, Embassy of the Republic of
21 Conway Street, London W1T 6BN
tel 020-7387 1790 *fax* 020-7387 3289

Culture, Media and Sport, Department for
2-4 Cockspur Street, London SW1Y 5DH
tel 020-7211 6200

Cyprus High Commission
93 Park Street, London W1K 7ET
tel 020-7499 8272 *fax* 020-7491 0691
email cyphclondon@dial.pipex.com
presscounsellor@chclondon.com (press office)
website www.pio.gov.cy

Czech Republic, Embassy of the
26 Kensington Palace Gardens, London W8 4QY
tel 020-7243 1115 *fax* 020-7727 9654
email london@embassy.mzv.cz
website www.czechembassy.org.uk

Royal Danish Embassy
55 Sloane Street, London SW1X 9SR
tel 020-7333 0200 *fax* 020-7333 0270
email lonamb@um.dk
website www.denmark.org.uk

Data Protection Commissioner, Office of the – see Information Commissioner's Office

Defence, Ministry of
Metropole Building, Northumberland Avenue, London WC2N 5BP
tel 020-7218 9000
website www.mod.uk/

DEFRA: Department for Environment, Food and Rural Affairs
3-8 Whitehall Place, London SW1A 2HH
tel 020-7270 8000, *Helpline* (0845) 9335577
fax 020-7270 8419
website www.defra.gov.uk

Design Council
34 Bow Street, London WC2E 7DL
tel 020-7420 5200 *fax* 020-7420 5300
website www.designcouncil.org.uk

DFID: Department for International Development
1 Palace Street, London SW1E 5HE
tel 020-7023 0000
email enquiry@dfid.gov.uk
website www.dfid.gov.uk
Abercrombie House, Eaglesham Road, East Kilbride, Glasgow G75 8EA
tel (01355) 844000
Public Enquiry Point tel (0845) 300 4100 (local rate) *tel* (01355) 843132 (for enquiries from overseas)

DTI: Department of Trade and Industry
1 Victoria Street, London SW1H 0ET
tel 020-7215 5000 (general enquiries)
minicom/textphone 020-7215 6740
fax 020-7222 0612
website www.dti.gov.uk

Economic and Social Research Council
Polaris House, North Star Avenue, Swindon, Wilts. SN2 1UJ
tel (01793) 413000 *fax* (01793) 413130
email exrel@esrc.ac.uk
website www.esrc.ac.uk

Education and Skills, Department for
Sanctuary Buildings, Great Smith Street, London SW1P 3BT
tel (0870) 0012345 (switchboard)
0800-000 2288 (public enquiries)

Electricity & Gas Regulation Northern Ireland, Office of (OFREG)
Brookmount Buildings, 42 Fountain Street, Belfast BT1 5EE
tel 028-9031 1575 *fax* 028-9031 1740
email ofreg@nics.gov.uk
website http://ofreg.nics.gov.uk/

Engineering and Physical Sciences Research Council
Polaris House, North Star Avenue, Swindon, Wilts. SN2 1ET
tel (01793) 444000
email infoline@epsrc.ac.uk
website www.epsrc.ac.uk
Press Officer Jane Reck *tel* (01793) 444312
email jane.reck@epsrc.ac.uk

English Heritage
23 Savile Row, London W1S 2ET
tel 020-7973 3000 *fax* 020-7973 3001
website www.english-heritage.org.uk

English Tourism Council
Thames Tower, Black's Road, London W6 9EL
tel 020-8563 3000 *fax* 020-8563 0302
website www.englishtourism.org.uk

The Environment Agency
Head Office Rio House, Waterside Drive, Aztec West, Almondsbury, Bristol BS32 4UD
tel (01454) 624400 *fax* (01454) 624409
website www.environment-agency.gov.uk

Equal Opportunities Commission
Arndale House, Arndale Centre, Manchester M4 3EQ
tel (0845) 601 5901 *fax* 0161-838 8303
email info@eoc.org.uk
website www.eoc.org.uk

The European Commission
8 Storey's Gate, London SW1P 3AT
tel 020-7973 1992 *fax* 020-7973 1900
email eu-uk-press@cec.eu.int
website www.cec.org.uk

European Parliament
UK Office 2 Queen Anne's Gate, London SW1H 9AA
tel 020-7227 4300 *fax* 020-7227 4302
library fax 020-7227 4301
website www.europarl.org.uk

Fair Trading, Office of
Fleetbank House, 2-6 Salisbury Square, London EC4Y 8SX
tel 020-7211 8000 *fax* 020-7211 8800
email enquiries@oft.gov.uk
website www.oft.gov.uk

Film Classification, British Board of
3 Soho Square, London W1D 3HD
tel 020-7440 1570 *fax* 020-7287 0141
email webmaster@bbfc.co.uk
website www.bbfc.co.uk
Director Robin Duval

Finland, Embassy of
38 Chesham Place, London SW1X 8HW
tel 020-7838 6200 *fax* 020-7235 3680 (general) 020-7259 5602 (press and information office)
website www.finemb.org.uk

Foreign and Commonwealth Office
King Charles Street, London SW1A 2AH
tel 020-7270 3000
website www.fco.gov.uk

Forestry Commission
231 Corstorphine Road, Edinburgh EH12 7AT
tel 0131-334 0303 *fax* 0131-334 4473
email info@forestry.gov.uk
website www.forestry.gov.uk

French Embassy
58 Knightsbridge, London SW1X 7JT
tel 020-7073 1000
website www.ambafrance-uk.org
Cultural Department 23 Cromwell Road, London SW7 2EL
tel 020-7073 1300

Gas and Electricity Markets, Office of (OFGEM)
Head Office 9 Millbank, London SW1P 3GE
tel 020-7901 7000
website www.ofgem.gov.uk
OFGEM Scotland Regents Court, 70 West Regent Street, Glasgow G2 2QZ
tel 0141-331 2678

German Embassy
23 Belgrave Square, London SW1X 8PZ
tel 020-7824 1300 *fax* 020-7824 1435
email mail@german-embassy.org.uk
website www.german-embassy.org.uk

Greece, Embassy of
Press and Information Office, 1A Holland Park, London W11 3TP
tel 020-7727 3071 *fax* 020-7727 8960
email pressoffice@greekembassy.org.uk

Hayward Gallery
Belvedere Road, London SE1 8XZ
tel 020-7928 3144 *fax* 020-7401 2664
website www.haywardgallery.org.uk

Health, Department of
Richmond House, 79 Whitehall, London SW1A 2NS
tel 020-7210 3000
website www.doh.gov.uk

Health and Safety Executive
Rose Court, 2 Southwark Bridge, London SE1 9HS
tel (08701) 545500 *fax* (02920) 859260

email hseinformationservices@natbrit.com
website www.hse.gov.uk

Historic Scotland
Longmore House, Salisbury Place,
Edinburgh EH9 1SH
tel 0131-668 8600 *fax* 0131-668 8699
website www.historic-scotland.gov.uk

Historical Manuscripts Commission
Quality House, Quality Court, Chancery Lane,
London WC2A 1HP
tel 020-7242 1198 *fax* 020-7831 3550
email nra@hmc.gov.uk
website www.hmc.gov.uk

HMSO Books – see The Stationery Office

Home Office
Queen Anne's Gate, London SW1H 9AT
tel 020-7273 3757
Director, Communication B. Butler

Housing Corporation
149 Tottenham Court Road,
London W1T 7BN
tel 020-7393 2000 *fax* 020-7393 2111
email enquiries@housingcorp.qsx.gov.uk
website www.housingcorp.gov.uk

Hungary, Embassy of the Republic of
35 Eaton Place, London SW1X 8BY
tel 020-7235 5218 *fax* 020-7823 1348
email office@huemblon.org.uk
website www.huemblon.org.uk

Independent Television Commission
33 Foley Street, London W1W 7TL
tel 020-7255 3000 *fax* 020-7306 7800
email publicaffairs@itc.org.uk
website www.itc.org.uk

High Commission of India, Press & Information Wing
India House, Aldwych, London WC2B 4NA
tel 020-7836 8484 ext 147, 286, 327
fax 020-7836 2632
email 106167.1470@compuserve.com

Information Commissioner's Office
(formerly Office of the Data Protection
Commissioner)
Wycliffe House, Water Lane, Wilmslow,
Cheshire SK9 5AF
tel (01625) 545745(enquiries) (01625) 545700
(switchboard) *fax* (01625) 524510
email data@dataprotection.gov.uk
website www.dataprotection.gov.uk

The Inland Revenue
Visitors Centre, Ground Floor, SW Wing,
Bush House, Strand, London WC2B 4RD
tel 020-7438 6420/5
website www.inlandrevenue.gov.uk
Inland Revenue, National Insurance
Contributions Office, International Services,
Benton Park View, Longbenton,
Newcastle Upon Tyne NE98 1ZZ
tel 0191-225 4811 *fax* 0191-225 0067
email internationalservices.ir.sbg@ir.gsi.gov.uk

Contact Inland Revenue, International Services (InS) for queries about working abroad and paying NI contributions.

International Services – see Inland Revenue, Board of

Ireland, Embassy of
17 Grosvenor Place, London SW1X 7HR
tel 020-7235 2171 *fax* 020-7245 6961
Passport and Visa Office Montpelier House,
106 Brompton Road, London SW3 1JJ
tel 020-7225 7700 *fax* 020-7225 7777

Israel, Embassy of
2 Palace Green, London W8 4QB
tel 020-7957 9500 *fax* 020-7957 9555
email info-assist@london.mfa.gov.il
website www.israel-embassy.org.uk

Italian Embassy
14 Three Kings Yard, Davies Street,
London W1K 4EH
tel 020-7312 2200 *fax* 020-7312 2230
email emblondon@embitaly.org.uk
website www.embitaly.org.uk

Japan, Embassy of
101-104 Piccadilly, London W1J 7JT
tel 020-7465 6500 *fax* 020-7491 9347 (information)
020-7491 9348 (other departments)
email jicc@jicc.demon.co.uk
website www.embjapan.org.uk

HM Land Registry
Lincoln's Inn Fields, London WC2A 3PH
tel 020-7917 8894 *fax* 020-7917 5934
email michele.bennett@landreg.gsi.gov.uk
website www.landreg.gov.uk

Law Commission
Conquest House, 37-38 John Street,
Theobalds Road, London WC1N 2BQ
tel 020-7453 1220 *fax* 020-7453 1297
email secretary@lawcommission.gsi.gov.uk
website www.lawcom.gov.uk

Covers England and Wales.

The Legal Deposit Office
The British Library, Boston Spa, Wetherby,
West Yorkshire LS23 7BY
tel (01937) 546267/546268 *fax* (01937) 546176

Legal Services Commission
(formerly Legal Aid Board)
85 Gray's Inn Road, London WC1X 8TX
tel 020-7759 0000

Legal Services Ombudsman, Office of the
3rd Floor, Sunlight House, Quay Street, Manchester M3 3JZ
tel 0161-839 7262, *Lo call* 0845-6010794 (charged at local rate) *fax* 0161-832 5446
email lso@olso.gsi.gov.uk
website www.olso.org

London Museum – see Museum of London

London Records Office, Corporation of
Guildhall, London EC2P 2EJ
tel 020-7332 1251 *fax* 020-7710 8682
email CLRO@corpoflondon.gov.uk
website www.cityoflondon.gov.uk/archives/clro

Luxembourg, Embassy of
27 Wilton Crescent, London SW1X 8SD
tel 020-7235 6961 *fax* 020-7235 9734

Malta High Commission
Malta House, 36-38 Piccadilly, London W1J 0LE
tel 020-7292 4800 *fax* 020-7734 1831

Medical Research Council
20 Park Crescent, London W1B 1AL
tel 020-7636 5422 *fax* 020-7436 6179
email firstname.surname@headoffice.mrc.ac.uk
website www.mrc.ac.uk

Millennium Commission
Portland House, Stag Place, London SW1E 5EZ
tel 020-7880 2001 *Information line* 020-7880 2030
fax 020-7880 2000
email info@millennium.gov.uk
website www.millennium.gov.uk

Monopolies and Mergers Commission – now Competition Commission

Museum of London
London Wall, London EC2Y 5HN
tel 020-7600 3699 *fax* 020-7600 1058
email info@museumoflondon.org
website www.museumoflondon.org

National Audit Office
157-197 Buckingham Palace Road, London SW1W 9SP
tel 020-7798 7000 *fax* 020-7798 7070
email enquiries@nao.gsi.gov.uk
Audit House, 23-24 Park Place, Cardiff CF1 3BA
tel 029-2037 8661 *fax* 029-2067 8501

National Consumer Council
20 Grosvenor Gardens, London SW1W 0DH
tel 020-7730 3469 *fax* 020-7730 0191
email info@ncc.org.uk
website www.ncc.org.uk

National Gallery
Trafalgar Square, London WC2N 5DN
tel 020-7747 2885 *fax* 020-7747 2423
email information@ng-london.org.uk
website www.nationalgallery.org.uk

National Lottery Commission
101 Wigmore Street, London W1U 1QU
tel 020-7016 3400 *fax* 020-7016 3464
email publicaffairs@natlotcomm.gov.uk
website www.natlotcomm.gov.uk

National Maritime Museum
Greenwich, London SE10 9NF
tel 020-8858 4422 *fax* 020-8312 6632
email research@nmm.ac.uk
website www.nmm.ac.uk www.port.nmm.ac.uk (gateway site for maritime information)
www.rog.nmm.ac.uk (for astronomy information)

The National Monuments Record
English Heritage, National Monuments Record Centre, Kemble Drive, Swindon, Wilts. SN2 2GZ
tel (01793) 414600 *fax* (01793) 414606
email nmrinfo@english-heritage.org.uk
website www.english-heritage.org.uk

Natural Environment Research Council
Polaris House, North Star Avenue, Swindon, Wilts. SN2 1EU
tel (01793) 411500 *fax* (01793) 411501
email requests@nerc.ac.uk
website www.nerc.ac.uk

The Natural History Museum
Cromwell Road, London SW7 5BD
tel 020-7942 5000

Royal Netherlands Embassy
38 Hyde Park Gate, London SW7 5DP
tel 020-7590 3200 *fax* 020-7581 0053 (Press and cultural affairs)
email cultural@netherlands-embassy.org.uk
website www.netherlands-embassy.org.uk

New Zealand High Commission
New Zealand House, Haymarket, London SW1Y 4TQ
tel 020-7930 8422 *fax* 020-7839 4580
website www.nzembassy.com/britain

Northern Ireland Assembly
Parliament Buildings, Belfast BT4 3XX
tel 028-9052 1333

Northern Ireland Office
11 Millbank, London SW1P 4PN
tel 020-7210 3000
Castle Buildings, Belfast BT4 3ST
tel 028-9052 0700
website www.nio.gov.uk

Northern Ireland Tourist Board
59 North Street, Belfast, Northern Ireland BT1 1NB
tel 028-9023 1221 *fax* 028-9024 0960
email info@nitb.com
website www.discovernorthernireland.com

Royal Norwegian Embassy
25 Belgrave Square, London SW1X 8QD
tel 020-7591 5500 *fax* 020-7245 6993
email emb.london@mfa.no
website www.norway.org.uk/

Royal Observatory of Greenwich – see National Maritime Museum

Oftel – see Telecommunications, Office of

OFWAT – see Water Services, Office of

Ordnance Survey
Romsey Road, Maybush, Southampton SO16 4GU
tel 023-8079 2000, *Press Officer tel* 023-8079 2635, *Customer Help Line* (08456) 050505
fax 023-8079 2615
email enquiries@ordsvy.gov.uk
website www.ordnancesurvey.co.uk

Particle Physics and Astronomy Research Council (PPARC)
Polaris House, North Star Avenue, Swindon, Wilts. SN2 1SZ
tel (01793) 442000 *fax* (01793) 442002
email pr.pus@pparc.ac.uk
website www.pparc.ac.uk

Patent Office
General enquiries (designs, patents, trade marks), Concept House, Cardiff Road, Newport, South Wales NP10 8QQ
tel (0645) 500505 *text phone* (0645) 222250
email enquiries@patent.gov.uk
website www.patent.gov.uk
Copyright enquiries Copyright Directorate, The Patent Office, Room 1/10, Harmsworth House, 13-15 Bouverie Street, London EC4Y 8DP
tel 020-7596 6566 {textphone} (0645) 222250
fax 020-7596 6526
email copyright@patent.gov.uk
website www.patent.gov.uk www.intellectual-property.gov.uk

Pensions Ombudsman, The
11 Belgrave Road, London SW1V 1RB
tel 020-7834 9144 *fax* 020-7821 0065
email enquiries@pensions-ombudsman.org.uk
website www.pensions-ombudsman.org.uk
Ombudsman David Laverick

Pensions and Overseas Benefits Directorate (POD) – see Social Security, Department of

PLR Office – see page 626

Poland, Embassy of the Republic of
47 Portland Place, London W1B 1JH
tel (0870) 774 2700 *fax* 020-7323 4018
email polishembassy@polishembassy.org.uk
website www.home.btclick.com/polishembassy/index.htm
Polish Cultural Institute 34 Portland Place, London W1B 1HQ
tel (0870) 7742 900 *fax* 020-7637 2190
email pci@polishculture.org.uk
website www.polishculture.org.uk

Police Complaints Authority
10 Great George Street, London SW1P 3AE
tel 020-7273 6450 *fax* 020-7273 6401
website www.pca.gov.uk

Portuguese Embassy
11 Belgrave Square, London SW1X 8PP
tel 020-7235 5331 *fax* 020-7245 1287
020-7235 0739
email Portembassy-London@dialin.net

Post Office Headquarters – see Consignia Headquarters

Privy Council Office
2 Carlton Gardens, London SW1Y 5AA
tel 020-7210 1033 *fax* 020-7210 1071
email jackie.lindsay@cabinet-office.x.gsi.gov.uk
website www.privy-council.org.uk

Public Guardianship Office
Archway Tower, 2 Junction Road, London N19 5SZ
tel 020-7664 7000 *fax* 020-7664 7705
website www.guardianship.gov.uk

Public Record Office
Ruskin Avenue, Kew, Richmond, Surrey TW9 4DU
tel 020-8876 3444 *fax* 020-8878 8905
website www.pro.gov.uk

Public Trust Office – see Public Guardianship Office

Qualifications and Curriculum Authority (QCA)
83 Piccadilly, London W1J 8QA
tel 020-7509 5555 *fax* 020-7509 6666
email info@qca.org.uk
website www.qca.org.uk
Chairman Sir William Stubbs, *Chief Officer* Beverley Evans

Racial Equality, Commission for
Elliot House, 10-12 Allington Street, London SW1E 5EH
tel 020-7828 7022 *fax* 020-7630 7605

The Radio Authority
Holbrook House, 14 Great Queen Street, London WC2B 5DG
tel 020-7430 2724 *fax* 020-7405 7062
email info@radioauthority.org.uk
website www.radioauthority.org.uk

Regional Arts Offices – see page 490

Romania, Embassy of
4 Palace Green, London W8 4QD
tel 020-7937 9666 *fax* 020-7937 8069
email romania@roemb.demon.uk.co

Royal Commission on the Ancient and Historical Monuments of Scotland
(with National Monuments Record of Scotland)
John Sinclair House, 16 Bernard Terrace, Edinburgh EH8 9NX
tel 0131-662 1456 *fax* 0131-662 1477/1499
email postmaster@rcahms.gov.uk
website www.rcahms.gov.uk

Royal Commission on the Ancient and Historical Monuments of Wales
(with National Monuments Record of Wales)
Crown Building, Plas Crug, Aberystwyth, Ceredigion SY23 1NJ
tel (01970) 621200 *fax* (01970) 627701
email nmr.wales@rcahmw.org.uk
website www.rcahmw.org.uk

Royal Commission on the Historical Monuments of England – merged with English Heritage

Royal fine art commission for Scotland
Bakehouse Close, 146 Canongate, Edinburgh EH8 8DD
tel 0131-556 6699 *fax* 0131-556 6633
email plan@RoyfinartcomforSco.gov.uk
website www.RoyfinartcomforSco.gov.uk

Royal Mint
Llantrisant, Pontyclun CF72 8YT
tel (01443) 222111
email linda.doster@royalmint.gov.uk
website www.royalmint.com

Royal National Theatre Board
South Bank, London SE1 9PX
tel 020-7452 3333 *fax* 020-7452 3344
website www.nationaltheatre.org.uk

Russian Federation, Embassy of the
13 Kensington Palace Gardens, London W8 4QX
tel 020-7229 2666 *fax* 020-7727 8625

Science Museum
Exhibition Road, London SW7 2DD
tel (0870) 870 4868
email sciencemuseum@nmsi.ac.uk
website www.sciencemuseum.org.uk

The Scotland Office
Dover House, Whitehall, London SW1A 2AU
tel 020-7270 3000
website www.scottishsecretary.gov.uk

Scotland, The National Archives of
HM General Register House, Edinburgh EH1 3YY
tel 0131-535 1314 *fax* 0131-535 1360
email enquiries@nas.gov.uk
website www.nas.gov.uk

Scotland, National Galleries of
National Gallery of Scotland
The Mound, Edinburgh EH2 2EL
Scottish National Portrait Gallery
1 Queen Street, Edinburgh EH2 1JD
Scottish National Gallery of Modern Art
Belford Road, Edinburgh EH4 3DR
The Dean Gallery Belford Road, Edinburgh EH4 3DS
tel 0131-624 6200, 0131-624 6332 (press office)
fax 0131-343 3250 (press office)
email pressinfo@nationalgalleries.org
website www.nationalgalleries.org

Scotland, National Library of
George IV Bridge, Edinburgh EH1 1EW
tel 0131-226 4531 *fax* 0131-622 4803
email enquiries@nls.uk
website www.nls.uk

Scottish Arts Council
12 Manor Place, Edinburgh EH3 7DD
tel 0131-226 6051 *Help Desk tel* 0131-240 2443
fax 0131-225 9833
email help.desk@scottisharts.org.uk
website www.scottisharts.org.uk

The Scottish Executive
St Andrew's House, Regent Road, Edinburgh EH1 1DG
tel 0131-556 8400
website www.scotland.gov.uk

Scottish Law Commission
140 Causewayside, Edinburgh EH9 1PR
tel 0131-668 2131 *fax* 0131-662 4900
email info@scotlawcom.gov.uk
website www.scotlawcom.gov.uk

Scottish Legal Aid Board
44 Drumsheugh Gardens, Edinburgh EH3 7SW
tel 0131-226 7061 *fax* 0131-220 4878
website www.slab.org.uk

Scottish Natural Heritage
12 Hope Terrace, Edinburgh EH9 2AS
tel 0131-447 4781 *fax* 0131-446 2279 (press office)
website www.snh.org.uk

The Scottish Office – see The Scotland Office

The Scottish Parliament
Edinburgh EH99 1SP
tel 0131-348 5000 (public information service)
fax 0131-348 5601
email sp.info@scottish.parliament.uk
website www.scottish parliament.uk

Serpentine Gallery
Kensington Gardens, London W2 3XA
tel 020-7402 6075,
Public information 020-7298 1501
fax 020-7402 4103

Singapore High Commission
9 Wilton Crescent, London SW1X 8SP
tel 020-7235 8315 *fax* 020-7245 6583
email info@singaporehc.org.uk
website www.mfa.gov.sg

Slovak Republic, Embassy of the
25 Kensington Palace Gardens, London W8 4QY
tel 020-7243 0803 *fax* 020-7313 6481
email mail@slovakembassy.co.uk
website www.slovakembassy.co.uk

Slovenia, Embassy of
10 Little College Street, London SW1P 3SH
tel 020-7222 5400 *fax* 020-7222 5277
email vlo@mzz-dkp.gov.si
website www.embassy-slovenia.org.uk

Social Security, Department of
Richmond House, 79 Whitehall,
London SW1A 2NS
tel 020-7238 0800
POD at DSS, Benefits Agency,
Tyneview Park, Whitley Road,
Newcastle Upon Tyne NE98 1BA
tel 0191-218 7777 *fax* 0191-218 7293
email pod-customer-care-ba@ms04.dss.qsi.gov.uk
Contact Benefits Agency, Pensions and Overseas Benefits Directorate (POD) for queries about benefits being paid abroad.

South Africa, Republic of
South African High Commission, South Africa House, Trafalgar Square, London WC2N 5DP
tel 020-7451 7299 *fax* 020-7451 7283/7284
email general@southafricahouse.com
website www.southafricahouse.com

Spanish Embassy
39 Chesham Place, London SW1X 8SB
tel 020-7235 5555 *fax* 020-7259 5392

Sport England
16 Upper Woburn Place, London WC1H 0QP
tel 020-7273 1500 *fax* 020-7383 5740
email info@sportengland.org
website www.sportengland.org

Sri Lanka, High Commission of the Democratic Socialist Republic of
13 Hyde Park Gardens, London W2 2LU
tel 020-7262 1841 *fax* 020-7262 7970

Standards in Education, Office for (OFSTED)
Alexandra House, 33 Kingsway, London WC2B 6SE
tel 020-7421 6800 *fax* 020-7421 6707

The Stationery Office
PO Box 291, Norwich NR3 1GN
tel (0870) 600 5522
website www.clickkso.com

Strategic Rail Authority
55 Victoria Street, London SW1H 0EU
tel 020-7654 6000 *fax* 020-7654 6010
website www.sra.gov.uk

Sweden, Embassy of
11 Montagu Place, London W1H 2AL
tel 020-7917 6400 *fax* 020-7917 6477
email embassy@swednet.org.uk
website www.swedish-embassy.org.uk

Swiss Embassy Cultural Section
16-18 Montagu Place,
London W1H 2BQ
tel 020-7616 6000 *fax* 020-7616 6097
email swissembassy@lon.rep.admin.ch
website www.swissembassy.org.uk

Tate
Tate Britain
Millbank, London SW1P 4RG
tel 020-7887 8008, 020-7887 8000 (admin)
email information@tate.org.uk
website www.tate.org.uk
Tate Modern, Bankside,
London SE1 9TG
tel 020-7887 8008
Tate Liverpool, Albert Dock,
Liverpool L3 4BB
tel 0151-702 7400
Tate St Ives, Porthmeor Beach, St Ives,
Cornwall TR26 1TG
tel (01736) 796226

Telecommunications, Office of
50 Ludgate Hill, London EC4M 7JJ
tel 020-7634 8700 *fax* 020-7634 8943
email infocent@oftel.gov.uk
website www.oftel.gov.uk

Theatre Museum – **see page 440**

Transport for London
Windsor House, 42-50 Victoria Street,
London SW1H 0TL
tel 020-7941 4500
website www.transportforlondon.gov.uk

HM Treasury
Parliament Street, London SW1P 3AG
tel 020-7270 5000, *Press Office tel* 020-7270 5238
fax 020-7270 5244
website www.hm-treasury.gov.uk

Trinity House, Corporation of
Tower Hill, London EC3N 4DH
tel 020-7481 6900 *fax* 020-7480 7662
email howard.cooper@thls.org
website www.trinityhouse.co.uk

Turkish Embassy
43 Belgrave Square, London SW1X 8PA
tel 020-7393 0202 *fax* 020-7393 0066
email info@turkishembassy.co.uk

Victoria and Albert Museum
South Kensington, London SW7 2RL
tel 020-7942 2000
website www.vam.ac.uk

Visiting Arts
11 Portland Place, London W1B 1EJ
tel 020-7389 3019 *fax* 020-7389 3016
email visiting.arts@britishcouncil.org
website www.visitingarts.org.uk
Director T. Sandell OBE

VisitScotland
23 Ravelston Terrace, Edinburgh EH4 3TP
tel 0131-332 2433 *fax* 0131-343 1513
email info@visitscotland.com
website www.visitscotland.com

Vocational Qualifications, National Council for (NCVQ) – see Qualifications and Curriculum Authority

The Wales Office
Gwydyr House, Whitehall, London SW1A 2ER
tel 020-7270 0549 *fax* 020-7270 0568
website www.walesoffice.gov.uk

Wales, National Assembly for
Public Information and Education Services, Cardiff Bay, Cardiff CF99 1NA
tel 029-2089 8200
email Assembly.Info@wales.gsi.gov.uk
website www.wales.gov.uk

Wales, The National Library of
Aberystwyth, Ceredigion SY23 3BU
email holi@llgc.org.uk
website www.llgc.org.uk

Wales Tourist Board
Brunel House, 2 Fitzalan Road, Cardiff CF24 0UY
tel 029-2047 5214 *fax* 029-2048 2436
email info@tourism.wales.gov.uk
website www.visitwales.com

Water Services, Office of (OFWAT)
Centre City Tower, 7 Hill Street, Birmingham B5 4UA
tel 0121-625 1300 *fax* 0121-625 1400
email enquiries@ofwat.gsi.gov.uk
website www.ofwat.gov.uk

Women's National Commission
Cabinet Office, 1st Floor, 35 Great Smith Street, London SW1P 3BQ
tel 020-7276 2555 *fax* 020-7276 2563
website www.thewnc.org.uk

Yugoslavia, Embassy of the Federal Republic of
5-7 Lexham Gardens, London W8 5JJ
tel 020-7370 6105 *fax* 020-7370 3838
email londre@jugisek.demon.co.uk
website www.yugoslavembassy.org.uk

Publishing practice

Publishing agreements

Publisher's agreements are not a standard form. Before signing one, the author must check it carefully, taking nothing for granted. ***Michael Legat*** *navigates the reader through this complex document.*

Any author, presented with so complex a document as a publisher's agreement, should read it carefully before signing, making sure that every clause is understood, and not taking anything for granted. Bear in mind that there is no such thing as a standard form. A given publisher's 'standard' contract may not only differ substantially from those of other publishers, but will often vary from author to author and from book to book. Don't be fooled into believing that it is a standard form because it appears to have been printed – most agreements are individually produced on a word processor to give exactly that effect.

A fair and reasonable agreement

You should be able to rely on your agent, if you have one, to check the agreement for you, or – if you are a member – you can get it vetted by the Society of Authors or the Writers' Guild of Great Britain. But if you are on your own, you must either go to one of the solicitors who specialise in publishing business (probably expensive) or Do It Yourself. In the latter case it will help to compare the contract you have been offered, clause by clause, with a typical Minimum Terms Agreement such as those printed in my own books, *An Author's Guide to Publishing* and *Understanding Publishers' Contracts*.

Minimum Terms Agreement

The Minimum Terms Agreement (MTA), developed jointly by the Society of Authors and the Writers' Guild, is signed by a publisher on the one hand and the Society and the Guild on the other. It is not an agreement between a publisher and an individual author. It commits the publisher to offering his or her authors terms which are at least as good as those in the MTA. The intention is that only members of the Society and the Guild should be eligible for this special treatment, but in practice publishers who sign the agreement tend to offer its terms to all their authors. There is no standard MTA, and most signatory publishers have insisted on certain variations in the agreement; nevertheless, the more important basic principles have always been accepted. It must be pointed out that the MTA does not usually apply to:

- books in which illustrations take up 40% or more of the space;
- specialist works on the visual arts in which illustrations fill 25% or more of the space;
- books involving three or more participants in royalties; or
- technical books, manuals and reference books.

Since its origins in 1980, comparatively few publishers have signed a Minimum Terms Agreement, although the signatories include several major publishing houses. Some publishers have refused, claiming to treat their authors quite well enough already, while others say that each author and each book is so different that standard terms cannot be laid down. Nonetheless, the MTA has been a resounding success. Almost all non-signatory publishers have adopted some or all of its provisions, and even in the case of the excluded books mentioned above, the terms have tended to improve. All authors can now argue, from a position of some strength, that their own agreements should meet the MTA's standards.

The provisions of the MTA

The MTA is a royalty agreement (usually the most satisfactory form for an author), and it lays down the minimum acceptable royalties on sales, and the levels at which the rate should rise. These royalties are expressed as percentages of the book's retail price but can easily be adjusted to apply to royalties based on price received, a system to which a number of publishers are changing, increasing the percentages so that the author's earnings are not adversely affected. The MTA also covers the size of the advance (calculated in accordance with the expected initial print quantity and retail price), and recommended splits between publisher and author of moneys from the sale of subsidiary rights (including US and translation rights).

However, the MTA is not by any means concerned solely with money, but with fairness to the author in all clauses of a publishing agreement, special attention being paid to provisions designed to make the author/publisher relationship more of a partnership than it has often been in the past. While recognising the publisher's right to take final decisions on such matters as print quantity, publication date, retail price, jacket or cover design, wording of the blurb, promotion and publicity, and remaindering, the MTA insists that the author has a right to consultation (which should not be an empty formality but should mean that serious consideration is given to his or her views), in all such cases. Also the author's approval must be sought for the sale of any subsidiary rights.

Some essential clauses

Any publisher's agreement you sign should contain, in addition to acceptable financial terms, clauses covering:

- **Rights licensed.** A clear definition of which rights you are licensing to the publisher. The publisher will normally require volume rights but the agreement must specify whether such rights will apply in all languages (or perhaps only in English) and throughout the world (or only in an agreed list of territories). The duration of the publisher's licence should be spelt out; commonly this is for the period of copyright (currently the author's lifetime plus 70 years), although some publishers now accept a shorter term. A list of those subsidiary rights of which control is granted to the publisher must be included (make sure that the splits of moneys earned from these rights are in accordance with, or approximate reasonably to, those in the MTA, especially in the currently growing area of merchandising).
- **Publication date.** Commitment by the publisher to publication of the book by a specific date (usually within a year or 18 months from the delivery of the typescript). Avoid signing an agreement which is vague on this point, saying, for instance, only that the book will be published 'within a reasonable period'.
- **Copyright.** Confirmation that in all copies of the book the publisher will print a copyright notice in the author's name and a statement that the author has asserted his or her 'Right of Paternity' (the right to be identified as the author in future exploitation of the material in any form), and that a similar commitment will be required from any subsidiary licensee.
- **Fees and permissions.** Clarification, if the book is to include a professionally prepared index or material the copyright of which does not belong to the author, of whether the author or the publisher will be responsible for the fees (or if costs are to be shared, in what proportions) and the clearance of permissions.
- **Acceptable accounting procedures.** Most publishers divide the year into two six-month periods, accounting to the author, and paying any sums due, three months after the end of each period. Look askance at any less frequent accounting or longer delay after the royalty period. The publisher should also agree to pay the author the due share of any subsidiary moneys promptly on

receipt, provided that the advance on the book has been earned.

• **Termination.** A clear definition of the various conditions under which the agreement shall be terminated, with reversion of rights to the author.

Clauses to question

You can question anything in a publisher's agreement before you sign it. Provided that you do so politely and are not just being difficult, the publisher should be prepared to answer every query, to explain, and where possible to meet your objections. Most publishing contracts are not designed to exploit the author unfairly, but you should watch out for:

• **Rights assigned elsewhere.** It is unwise to accept a clause which allows the publisher to assign the rights in your book to another firm or person without your approval.

• **Non-publication.** The contract for a commissioned book often includes wording which alludes to the publisher's acceptance of the work, implying that there is no obligation to publish it if he or she deems it unacceptable. It may be understandable that the publisher wants an escape route in case the author turns in an inferior work, but he or she should be obliged to justify the rejection, and to give the author an opportunity to revise the work to bring it up to standard. If, having accepted the book, the publisher then wishes to cancel the contract prior to publication, the author can usually expect to receive financial compensation, which should be non-returnable even if the book is subsequently placed with another publisher. However, this point is not normally covered in a publishing agreement.

• **Sole publisher.** Some agreements prohibit the author from writing similar material for any other publisher. This may clearly affect the author's earning ability.

• **Editing consultation.** Don't agree to the publisher's right to edit your work without any requirement for him or her to obtain your approval of any changes made.

• **Royalty rate.** While it is normal practice for an agreement to allow the publisher to pay a lower royalty on books which are sold at high trade discounts, such sales are more frequently made nowadays than in the past, and you should therefore make sure the royalty rate on high discount sales is not unfairly low.

• **Future books.** The Society of Authors and the Writers' Guild are both generally opposed to clauses giving the publisher the right to publish the author's next work, feeling that this privilege should be earned by the publisher's handling of the earlier book. If you accept an option clause, at least make sure that it leaves all terms for a future book to be agreed.

Electronic and other multimedia rights

The importance of electronic, digital and other multimedia rights, which already require a carefully worded clause in a contract, is likely to increase in years to come, when the only form of publication for a book may be on the internet or whatever may replace it as technology develops. In the meantime publishers, on the one hand, and literary agents and authors' organisations on the other, are in dispute about these rights, including other rights as yet unknown.

The two main issues are concerned with control of the rights and with royalties. Should these rights remain in the direct control of the author (possibly negotiating through an agent) or, as publishers maintain, be regarded as a part of volume rights, and therefore licensed to the publisher? If the publisher controls the rights, should the author receive a royalty of 15% or thereabouts on the publisher's receipts from sales of these rights, or at least 50% of the income, as the Society of Authors and the Association of Authors' Agents insist is fair? Until some agreement has been reached on these and other matters, it is advisable for authors to seek advice on suitable wording of the relevant clause from a literary agent or the Society of Authors or any other established body representing writers.

Joint and multiple authorship

In the case of joint authorship (a work so written that the individual contributions of the authors cannot be readily separated), the first written agreement should be between the authors themselves, setting out the proportions in which any moneys earned by the book will be split, specifying how the authors' responsibilities are to be shared, and especially laying down the procedure to be adopted should the authors ever find themselves in dispute. The terms of any publishing agreement which they sign (each author having an identical copy) should reflect their joint understanding. The total earnings should not be less than would be paid were the book by a single author, and the authors should have normal rights of consultation.

In the case of multiple authorship (when the work of each contributor can be clearly separated), each author is likely to have an individual contract, and may not be aware of what terms are offered to the others involved. Because of the possibility of disagreement between the authors, the publisher will probably offer little in the way of consultation. All the individual author can do is to ensure that the agreement appears to be fair in relation to the amount of work contributed, and that the author's responsibilities indicated by the contract refer only to his or her work.

Outright sale

As a general rule no author should agree to surrender his or her copyright to the publisher, although this may be unavoidable in the case of a book with many contributors, such as an encyclopedia. Even then, give up your copyright with great reluctance and only after an adequate explanation from the publisher of why you should (and probably a substantial financial inducement, including, if possible, provision for the payment of a further fee each time the book is reprinted). The agreement itself will probably be no more than a brief and unequivocal letter.

Subsidies and vanity publishing

Few commercial publishers will be interested in publishing your book on a subsidy basis (i.e. with a contribution from you towards costs), unless perhaps it is of a serious, highly specialised nature, such as an academic monograph, when a publisher who is well established within that particular field will certainly behave with probity and offer a fair contract. Vanity publishers, on the other hand, will accept your book with enthusiasm, ask for 'a small contribution to production costs' (which turns out to be a very substantial sum, not a penny of which you are likely to see again), and will fail to achieve any sales for your book apart from the copies which you yourself buy. If you want to put your own money into the publication of your book, try self-publishing (see page 251) – you will be far better off than going to a vanity house. How do you tell which are the vanity publishers? That's easy – they're the ones who put advertisements in the papers saying things like, 'Authors Wanted!'. Regular publishers don't need to do that.

Michael Legat became a full-time writer after a long and successful publishing career. He is the author of a number of highly regarded books on publishing and writing.

Further reading

Clark, Charles (ed.), *Publishing Agreements: A Book of Precedents*, Butterworths, 6th edn, 2002

Flint, Michael F., *A User's Guide to Copyright*, Butterworths, 5th edn, 2000

Legat, Michael, *An Author's Guide to Publishing*, Robert Hale, 3rd edn revised, 1998

Legat, Michael, *Understanding Publishers' Contracts*, Robert Hale, 2nd edn revised, 2002

Unwin, Sir Stanley, *The Truth About Publishing*, Unwin Hyman, 8th edn, 1976, o.p.

Frequently asked questions about ISBNs

The Standard Book Numbering Agency receives a large number of enquiries about the ISBN system. The most frequently asked questions are answered here.

What is an ISBN?

An ISBN (International Standard Book Number) is a 10-digit product number used by publishers, booksellers and libraries for ordering, listing and stock control purposes. It enables them to identify a specific edition of a specific title in a specific format from a particular publisher.

The 10 digits are always divided into four parts, separated by spaces or hyphens. The four parts can be of varying length and are as follows:

- Group Identifier – Identifies a national, geographic or language grouping of publishers. It tells you which of these groupings the publisher belongs to (not the language of the book).
- Publisher Prefix – Identifies a specific publisher or imprint.
- Title Number – Identifies a specific edition of a specific title in a specific format.
- Check Digit – This is always and only the final digit which mathematically validates the rest of the number. It is calculated using a Modulus 11 system with weights 10–12.

Do all books need to have an ISBN?

There is no legal requirement for an ISBN and it conveys no form of legal or copyright protection. It is a product number.

What can be gained from using an ISBN?

If you wish to sell your publication through major bookselling chains, or internet booksellers, they will require you to have an ISBN to assist their internal processing and ordering systems.

The ISBN also provides access to Bibliographic Databases such as Whitaker BookBank, which are organised using ISBNs as references. These databases are used by the book trade and libraries to provide information for customers. The ISBN therefore provides access to additional marketing tools which could help sales of your product.

Where can we get an ISBN?

ISBN prefixes are assigned to publishers in the country in which the publisher is based by the national agency for that country. In the UK and Republic of Ireland this agency is the Standard Book Numbering Agency Ltd which is a wholly owned subsidiary of J. Whitaker & Sons Ltd. The Agency introduces new publishers to the system, assigns prefixes to new and existing publishers and deals with any queries or problems in using the system. The Standard Book Numbering Agency Ltd was the first ISBN Agency in the world. Publishers based elsewhere will not be able to get numbers from the UK Agency but should contact them for details of the relevant Agency.

Who is eligible for ISBNs?

Any publisher which is publishing a qualifying product for general sale or distribution to the market is eligible (see 'Which products do not qualify for ISBNs?').

What is a publisher?

It is sometimes difficult to decide who the publisher is and who their agent may be, but the publisher is generally the person or body which takes the financial risk in making a product available. For example, if a product went on sale and sold no copies at all, the publisher is usually the person or body which loses money. If you get paid anyway, you are likely to be a designer, printer, author or consultant of some kind.

How long does it take to get an ISBN?
In the UK the Standard service time is 10 working days. There is also a Fast Track service, which is a three-working day processing period.

How much does it cost to get an ISBN?
In the UK there is a registration fee which is payable by all new publishers. The fees are £57.50 plus VAT for the Standard service and £91 plus VAT for the Fast Track service. A publisher prefix unique to you will be provided and allows for 10 ISBNs. Larger allocations are available where appropriate.

What if we only want one ISBN?
ISBNs are only available in blocks. The smallest block is 10 numbers. It is not possible to obtain a single ISBN.

Which products do not qualify for ISBNs?
Calendars; diaries; greetings cards, videos for entertainment; documentaries on video/CD-Rom; computer games; computer application programs; items which are available to a restricted group of people, e.g. a history of a golf club which is only for sale to members, or an educational course book only available to those registered as students on the course.

Contact details

ISBN Agency
Woolmead House West, Bear Lane, Farnham, Surrey GU9 7LG
tel (01252) 742590 *fax* (01252) 742526
email isbn@whitaker.co.uk
website www.whitaker.co.uk/isbn.htm

Can I turn my ISBN into a barcode?
Where a product carries a barcode and an ISBN, the barcode is derived from the ISBN and includes the Bookland Prefix (978). The barcode also contains a check digit which is derived by a different calculation method from that used for ISBNs. Further information about barcoding for books is available on the Book Industry Communication website (www.bic.org.uk).

What is an ISSN?
An International Standard Serial Number is the numbering system for journals, magazines, periodicals, newspapers and newsletters. It is administered by the British Library (*tel* (01937) 546959).

Public Lending Right

Under the PLR system, payment is made from public funds to authors (writers, translators, illustrators and some editors/compilers) whose books are lent out from public libraries. Payment is made once a year, in February, and the amount authors receive is proportionate to the number of times (established from a sample) that their books were borrowed during the previous year (July to June).

The legislation

PLR was created, and its principles established, by the Public Lending Right Act 1979 (HMSO, 30p). The Act required the rules for the administration of PLR to be laid down by a scheme. That was done in the Public Lending Right Scheme 1982 (HMSO, £2.95), which includes details of transfer (assignment), transmission after death, renunciation, trusteeship, bankruptcy, etc. Amending orders made in 1983, 1984, 1988, 1989 and 1990 were consolidated in December 1990 (SI 2360, £3.90). Some further amendments affecting author eligibility came into effect in December 1991 (SI 2618, £1), July 1997 (SI 1576, £1.10), December 1999 (SI 420, £1) and July 2000 (SI 933, £1.50).

How the system works

From the applications he receives, the Registrar of PLR compiles a register of authors and books which is held on computer. A representative sample of book issues is recorded, consisting of all loans from selected public libraries. This is then multiplied in proportion to total library lending to produce, for each book, an estimate of its total annual loans throughout the country. Each year the computer compares the register with the estimated loans to discover how many loans are credited to each registered book for the calculation of PLR payments. The computer does this using code numbers – in most cases the ISBN printed in the book.

Parliament allocates a sum each year (£7,000,000 for 2002–3) for PLR. This Fund pays the administrative costs of PLR and reimburses local authorities for recording loans in the sample libraries. The remaining money is then divided by the total registered loan figure in order to work out how much can be paid for each estimated loan of a registered book.

Limits on payments

Bottom limit. If all the registered interests in an author's books score so few loans that they would earn less than £5 in a year, no payment is due.

Top limit. If the books of one registered author score so high that the author's PLR earnings for the year would exceed £6000, then only £6000 is paid. No author can earn more than £6000 in PLR in any one year.

Money that is not paid out because of these limits belongs to the Fund and increases the amounts paid that year to other authors.

The sample

The basic sample represents only public libraries (no academic, school, private or commercial libraries are included) and only loans made over the counter (not consultations of books on library premises). It follows that only those books which are loaned from public libraries can earn PLR and make an application worthwhile.

The sample consists of the entire loans

Summary of the 19th year's results

Registration: authors. When registration closed for the 19th year (30 June 2001) the number of shares in books registered was 334,936 for 34,220 authors. This included some 400 European authors registering for the first time this year.

Eligible loans. Of the 430 million estimated loans from UK libraries, 193 million belong to books on the PLR register. The loans credited to registered books – 45% of all library borrowings – qualify for payment. The remaining 55% of loans relate to books that are ineligible for various reasons, to books written by dead or foreign authors, and to books that have simply not been applied for.

Money and payments. PLR's administrative costs are deducted from the fund allocated to the Registrar annually by Parliament. Operating the Scheme this year cost £726,228, representing some 13.9% of the PLR fund. The Rate per Loan for 2001–2 increased to 2.67 pence and was calculated to distribute all the £4,503,593 available. The total of PLR distribution and costs is therefore the full £5,201,000 which the Government provided in 2001–2.

The numbers of authors in various payment categories are as follows:

*169	payments at	5000–6000
272	payments between	2500–4999.99
584	payments between	1000–2499.99
750	payments between	500–999.99
3,400	payments between	100–499.99
12,406	payments between	5–99.99
17,581	TOTAL	

There were also 16,639 registered authors whose books earned them nil payment. As a result of the £6000 maximum payment rule around £500,000 became available for redistribution to other authors.

* includes 130 authors where the maximum threshold applied.

records for a year from libraries in 30 public library authorities spread through England, Scotland, Wales and Northern Ireland. Sample loans represent 10% of the national total. Several computerised sampling points in an authority contribute loans data ('multi-site' sampling). This change has been introduced gradually, and began in July 1991. The aim has been to increase the sample without any significant increase in costs. In order to counteract sampling error, libraries in the sample change every two to three years. Loans are totalled every 12 months for the period 1 July to 30 June.

An author's entitlement to PLR depends, under the 1979 Act, on the loans accrued by his or her books in the sample. This figure is multiplied to produce first regional and then finally national estimated loans.

ISBNs

PLR depends on the use of code numbers to identify books lent and to correlate loans with entries on the register so that payment can be made. The system uses the International Standard Book Number (ISBN), which is required for all new registrations. Different editions (e.g. 1st, 2nd, hardcover, paperback, large print) of the same book have different ISBNs.

Authorship

In the PLR system the author of a book is the writer, illustrator, translator, compiler, editor or reviser. Authors must be named on the book's title page, or be able to prove authorship by some other means (e.g. receipt of royalties). The ownership of copyright has no bearing on PLR eligibility.

Co-authorship/illustrators. In the PLR system the authors of a book are those writers, translators, editors, compilers and illustrators as defined above. Authors must apply for registration before their books can earn PLR. There is no restriction on the number of authors who can register shares in any one book as long as they satisfy the eligibility criteria.

Writers and/or illustrators. At least one must be eligible and they must jointly agree what share of PLR each will take. This agreement is necessary even if one or two are ineligible or do not wish to register for PLR. Share sizes should be based on contribution. The eligible authors will receive the share(s) specified in the application. PLR can be any whole percentage. Detailed advice is available from the PLR office.

Translators. Translators may apply, with-

Most borrowed authors in UK public libraries

Based on PLR sample loans July 2000–June 2001. Includes all writers, both registered and unregistered, but not illustrators where the book has a separate writer. Writing names are used; pseudonyms have not been combined.

Most borrowed authors

1. Catherine Cookson
2. Danielle Steel
3. Josephine Cox
4. Dick Francis
5. Jack Higgins
6. Agatha Christie
7. Ruth Rendell
8. Patricia Cornwell
9. Audrey Howard
10. Emma Blair
11. Maeve Binchy
12. John Grisham
13. Mary Higgins Clark
14. Bernard Cornwell
15. Mary Jane Staples
16. Harry Bowling
17. Barbara Taylor Bradford
18. Jessica Stirling
19. Lyn Andrews
20. Virginia Andrews

Most borrowed children's authors

1. R.L. Stine
2. Jacqueline Wilson
3. Janet & Allan Ahlberg
4. Lucy Daniels
5. Roald Dahl
6. Mick Inkpen
7. Enid Blyton
8. Eric Hill
9. Dick King-Smith
10. Nick Butterworth
11. John Cunliffe
12. Joan Jonker
13. Roderick Hunt
14. Shirley Hughes
15. Martin Waddell
16. Terry Deary
17. Ann M. Martin
18. Rod Campbell
19. David McKee
20. Colin & Jacqui Hawkins

out reference to other authors, for a 30% fixed share (to be divided equally between joint translators).

Editors and compilers. An editor or compiler may apply, either with others or without reference to them, to register a 20% share. Unless in receipt of royalties an editor must have written at least 10% of the book's content or more than 10 pages of text in addition to normal editorial work. The share of joint editors/compilers is 20% in total to be divided equally. An application from an editor or compiler to register a greater percentage share must be accompanied by supporting documentary evidence of actual contribution.

Dead or missing co-authors. Where it is impossible to agree shares with a co-author because that person is dead or untraceable, then the surviving co-author or co-authors may submit an application without the dead or missing co-author but must name the co-author and provide supporting evidence as to why that co-author has not agreed shares. The living co-author(s) will then be able to register a share in the book which will be 20% for the illustrator (or illustrators) and the residual percentage for the writer (or writers). If this percentage is to be divided between more than one writer or illustrator, then this will be in equal shares unless some other apportionment is requested and agreed by the Registrar.

The PLR Office keeps a file of missing authors (mostly illustrators) to help locate co-authors. Help is also available from publishers, the writers' organisations, and the Association of Illustrators.

Life and death. Authors can only be registered for PLR during their lifetime. However, for authors so registered, books can later be registered if first published within one year before their death or 10 years afterwards. New versions of titles registered by the author can be registered posthumously.

Residential qualifications. With effect from 1 July 2000, PLR is open to authors living in the European Economic Area (i.e. EU member states plus Norway, Liechtenstein and Iceland). A resident in these countries (for PLR purposes) has his or her only or principal home there. The United Kingdom does not include the Channel Islands or the Isle of Man.

Eligible books

In the PLR system each separate edition of a book is registered and treated as a separate book. A book is eligible for PLR registration provided that:

- it has an eligible author (or co-author);
- it is printed and bound (paperbacks counting as bound);
- copies of it have been put on sale (i.e. it is not a free handout and it has already been published);
- it is not a newspaper, magazine, journal or periodical;
- the authorship is personal (i.e. not a company or association) and the book is not crown copyright;
- it is not wholly or mainly a musical score;
- it has an ISBN.

Notification and payment

Every registered author receives from the Registrar an annual statement of estimated loans for each book and the PLR due.

Sampling arrangements

To help minimise the unfairnesses that arise inevitably from a sampling system, the Scheme specifies the eight regions within which authorities and sampling points have to be designated and includes libraries of varying size. Part of the sample drops out by rotation each year to allow fresh libraries to be included. The following library authorities have been designated for the year beginning 1 July 2002 (all are multi-site authorities):

- London – Kingston upon Thames, Bexley, Brent, Southwark;
- Metropolitan Boroughs – Bradford, Leeds, Sheffield, The Wirral, Stockport;
- Counties: Northern – Stockton on Tees, Lancashire, Durham;
- Counties: South West – Warwickshire, Devon, Somerset, Southampton;
- Counties: South East – Hertfordshire, Milton Keynes/Bucks, Essex, Bedfordshire/Luton, Northamptonshire;
- Scotland– West Lothian, Dundee, South Lanarkshire;
- Northern Ireland – North-Eastern Education & Library Board (NEELB), Belfast;
- Wales – Flintshire, Cardiff, Carmarthenshire.

Participating local authorities are reimbursed on an actual cost basis for additional expenditure incurred in providing loans data to the PLR Office. The extra PLR work mostly consists of modifications to computer programs to accumulate loans data in the local authority computer and to transmit the data to the PLR Office at Stockton-on-Tees.

Reciprocal arrangements

In 1981–2 reciprocal arrangements with West Germany were sought by British writers to help ensure that they did not lose the German PLR payments they had enjoyed since 1974 under international copyright law. The German Scheme, although loan based, is very different in most other respects and operates under German copyright law. Reciprocity was brought into effect in January 1985. Authors can apply for German PLR through the Authors' Licensing and Collecting Society. (Further information on PLR schemes internationally and recent developments within the EC towards wider recognition of PLR is available from the PLR Office or on the international website.)

Further information

Public Lending Right

PLR Office, Richard House, Sorbonne Close, Stockton-on-Tees TS17 6DA
tel (01642) 604699 *fax* (01642) 615641
websites www.plr.uk.com
www.plrinternational.com
Contact The Registrar

Application forms, information, publications and a copy of its *Annual Report* are all obtainable from the PLR Office. See website for further information on eligibility for PLR, loans statistics and forthcoming developments.

PLR Advisory Committee

Advises the Secretary of State for Culture, Media and Sport and the Registrar on the operation of the PLR scheme.

Copyright and libel

Copyright questions

Copyright is a vital part of any writer's assets, and should never be assigned or sold without due consideration and the advice of a competent authority, such as the Society of Authors, the Writers' Guild of Great Britain, or the National Union of Journalists. ***Michael Legat*** *answers some of the most commonly asked questions about copyright.*

Is there a period of time after which the copyright expires?
Copyright in the European Union lasts for the lifetime of the author and for a further 70 years from the end of the year of death, or, if the work is first published posthumously, for 70 years from the end of the year of publication. In most other countries of the world copyright exists similarly for the lifetime and for either 50 years or 70 years after death or posthumous publication.

If I want to include an extract from a book, poem or article, do I have to seek copyright? How much may be used without permission? What happens if I apply for copyright permission but do not get a reply?
It is essential to seek permission to quote from another author's work, unless that author has been dead for 70 years or more, or 70 years or more has passed from the date of publication of a work published posthumously. Only if you are quoting for purposes of criticism or review are you allowed to do so without obtaining permission, and even then the Copyright, Designs and Patents Act of 1988 restricts you to 400 words of prose in a single extract from a copyright work, or a series of extracts of up to 300 words each, totalling no more than 800 words, or up to 40 lines of poetry, which must not be more than 25% of the poem. However, a quotation of no more than, say, half a dozen words may usually be used without permission since it will probably not extend beyond a brief and familiar reference, as, for example, Rider Haggard's well-known phrase, 'she who must be obeyed'. If in doubt, always check. If you do not get a reply when you ask for permission to quote, insert a notice in your work saying that you have tried without success to contact the copyright owner, and would be pleased to hear from him or her so that the matter could be cleared up – and keep a copy of all the relevant correspondence, in order to back up your claim of having tried to get in touch.

If a newspaper pays for an article and I then want to sell the story to a magazine, am I free under the copyright law to do so?
Yes, provided that you have not granted copyright or exclusive use to the newspaper. When selling your work to newspapers or magazines make it clear, in writing, that you are selling only First or Second Serial Rights, not your copyright.

If I agree to have an article published for no payment do I retain any rights over how it appears?
Whether or not you are paid for the work has no bearing on the legal situation. However, the Moral Rights which apply to books, plays, television and radio scripts, do not cover you against a failure to acknowledge you as the author of an article, nor against the mutilation of your text, when it is published in a newspaper or magazine.

I want to publish a photograph that was taken in 1950. I am not sure how to

contact the photographer or even if he is still alive. Am I allowed to go ahead and publish it?
The Copyright, Designs and Patents Act of 1988 works retrospectively, so a photograph taken in 1950 is bound to be in copyright until at least 2020, and the copyright will be owned by the photographer, even though, when it was taken, the copyright would have belonged to the person who commissioned it, according to the laws then in place. You should therefore make every effort to contact the photographer, keeping copies of any relevant correspondence, and in case of failure take the same course of action as described above in relation to a textual extract the copyright owner of which you have been unable to trace.

I recently read an article on the same subject as one I have written. It contained many identical facts. Did this writer breach my copyright? What if I send ideas for an article to a magazine editor and those ideas are used despite the fact that I was not commissioned? May I sue the magazine?
Facts are normally in the public domain and may be used by anyone. However, if your article contains a fact which you have discovered and no one else has published, there could be an infringement of copyright if the author who uses it fails to attribute it to you. There is no copyright in ideas, so you cannot sue a writer or a journal for using ideas that you have put forward; in any case you would find it very difficult to prove that the idea belonged to you and to no one else. There is also no copyright in titles.

Does being paid a kill fee affect my copyright in a given piece?
No, provided that you have not sold the magazine or newspaper your copyright.

Do I need to copyright a piece of writing physically – whether an essay or a novel – or is it copyrighted automatically? Does it have to carry the © symbol?
Anything that you write is your copyright, assuming that it is not copied from the work of someone else, as soon as you have written it on paper or recorded it on the disk of a computer or on tape, or broadcast it. It is not essential for the work to carry the © symbol, although its inclusion may act as a warning and help to stop another writer from plagiarising it.

Am I legally required to inform an interviewee that our conversation is being recorded?
The interviewee owns the copyright of any words that he or she speaks as soon as they are recorded on your tape. Unless you have received permission to use those words in direct quotation, you could be liable to an action for infringement of copyright. You should therefore certainly inform the interviewee that the conversation is being recorded and seek permission to quote what is said directly.

More and more newspapers and magazines have versions both in print and on the internet. How can I ensure that my work is not published on the internet without my permission?
Make sure that any clause granting electronic rights to anyone in any agreement that you sign in respect of your work specifies not only the proportion of any fees received which you will get, but that your agreement must be sought before the rights are sold. Copyright extends to electronic rights, and therefore to publication on the internet, in just the same way as to other uses of the material.

I commissioned a designer to design a business card for me, and I paid her well. Does the design belong to me or to her?
Copyright would belong to the designer, and not to the person who commissioned it (as is also true in the case of a photograph, copyright in which belongs to the photographer). However, copyright in the business card might be transferred to you if a court considered you to have gained beneficially from the card.

Michael Legat became a full-time writer after a long and successful publishing career. He is the author of a number of highly regarded books on publishing and writing.

British copyright law

In this article, ***Amanda Michaels*** *describes the main types of work which may qualify for copyright protection, or related protection as a design, together with some of the main problems which may be faced by readers of this Yearbook in terms of protecting their own works or avoiding infringement of existing works in the UK. This is a technical area of the law, and one which is constantly developing; in an article of this length, it is not possible to deal fully with all the complexities of the law. It must also be emphasised that copyright is national in scope, and whilst works of UK authors will be protected in many other countries of the world, foreign laws may deal differently with questions of subsistence, ownership and infringement.*

Copyright is a creation of statute, now shaped and influenced significantly by EU harmonisation measures. On 1 August 1989, the Copyright, Designs & Patents Act 1988 ('the Act') replaced the Copyright Act 1956, which in turn replaced the Copyright Act 1911. All three Acts are still relevant to copyright today. Whilst the Act to a large degree restated the existing law, it was also innovative, in particular in the creation of a new 'design right' offering protection (generally speaking in lieu of copyright) for many industrial or commercial designs, and in the wider protection of moral rights.

A number of EU Directives affecting copyright law have taken effect since 1989. In particular, on 1 January 1996 significant changes were made to the duration of copyright protection, so that copyright in respect of most works (see below) was extended from 'life of the author' plus 50 years to life plus 70 years. Further changes came into force on 1 January 1998, when a new 'database right' was created. Others are in the pipeline.

Continuing relevance of old law

In this article, I discuss the law as it currently stands, but where a work was created prior to 1 August 1989 it will always be necessary to consider the law in force at the time of creation (or possibly first publication) in order to assess the existence or scope of any rights. Particular difficulties may arise with foreign works, which may qualify for protection in the UK as a matter of international obligation. Each Act has contained transitional provisions and these, as well as the substantive provisions of any relevant earlier Act will need to be considered where, for instance, use is sought to be made of an earlier work and it is necessary to decide whether permission is needed and if so, who may grant it. Equally, publishing or licence agreements designed for use under older Acts and prior to the development of modern technologies may be unsuitable for current use.

Copyright protection of works

Copyright protects the particular form in which the author's idea has been expressed, not the idea itself. Generally speaking, plots or artistic ideas are not protected by copyright, but what is protected is the particular manner in which the idea is presented. See now *Designers Guild Limited* v. *Russell Williams (Textiles) Limited* [2001] FSR 113 in which a fairly simple fabric design was found to be original and to have been copied. Of course, if someone has written an outline, script or screenplay for a television show, film, etc and that idea is confidential, then dual protection may arise in the confidential idea embodied in the documents and in the literary (and sometimes artistic) works in which the idea has taken material form. But, if the idea is used, but not the form, then a remedy could at best lie in only breach of confidence, not in copyright infringement. Copyright prevents the copying of the *material form* in which the idea has been presented, or of a substantial part of it, measured in terms of quality, not quantity.

S.1 of the Act sets out a number of different categories of works which can be the subject of copyright protection. These are:

- original literary, dramatic, musical or artistic works,
- sound recordings, films, broadcasts or cable programmes, and
- typographical arrangements of published editions.

These works are further defined in ss.3–8 (see box for examples).

Definitions under the Act

Literary work is defined as: 'any work, other than a dramatic or musical work, which is written, spoken or sung, and accordingly includes: (a) a table or compilation other than a database, (b) a computer program, (c) preparatory design material for a computer program and (d) a database.'

A musical work means: 'a work consisting of music, exclusive of any words or action intended to be sung, spoken or performed with the music.'

An artistic work means: '(a) a graphic work, photograph, sculpture or collage, irrespective of artistic quality, (b) a work of architecture being a building or model for a building, or (c) a work of artistic craftsmanship.'

These categories of work are not mutually exclusive, e.g. a film may be protected both as a film and as a dramatic work. See *Norowzian v. Arks* [2000] FSR 363.

However, none of these works are protected before being reduced into tangible form. S.3(2) specifically provides that no copyright shall subsist in a literary, musical or artistic work until it has been recorded in writing or otherwise.

On the other hand, all that is required to achieve copyright protection is to record the original work in any appropriate medium. Once that has been done, copyright will subsist in the work (assuming that the qualifying features set out below are present) without any formality of registration or otherwise. There is, for instance, no need for it to be published in any way for the protection to attach to it. Please note, however, that the law of the United States does differ on this – see page 644. However, there can be a real benefit in keeping a proper record of the creation of a work. Drafts or preliminary sketches should be kept and dated, so as to be able to show the development of a work. It may also be beneficial (especially where works are to be submitted to potential publishers or purchasers) to take a complete copy of the documents and send them to oneself or lodge them with a responsible third party, sealed and dated, so as to be able to provide cogent evidence of what your work was at that date. Such evidence may help prove one's independent title either as claimant or defendant in a copyright infringement (or indeed breach of confidence) action.

Originality

In order to gain copyright protection, literary, dramatic, artistic and musical works must be original. Sound recordings or films which are copies of pre-existing sound recordings or films, broadcasts which infringe rights in another broadcast or cable programmes which consist of immediate retransmissions of broadcasts are not protected by copyright.

Just as the law protects the form, rather than the idea, originality relates to the 'expression of the thought', rather than to the thought itself. A work need not be original in the sense of showing innovative artistic, literary or cultural merit, but only to have been the product of skill and labour on the part of the author. This can be seen for instance in the definition of certain artistic works, and in the fact that copyright protects works such as compilations (like football pools coupons or directories) and tables (including mathematical tables).

There may be considerable difficulty, at times, in deciding whether a work is of sufficient originality, or has original features, where there is a series of similar designs or amendments of existing works. See *L.A. Gear Inc.* [1992] FSR 121 and *Biotrading* [1998] FSR 109. A new edition or an adaptation of an existing work may obtain a new copyright depending upon the scope of the changes to the work; this will not affect the earlier copyright protection. See *Cala Homes* [1995] FSR 818. What is clear, though, is that merely making a 'slavish copy' of a drawing will not create an original work: see *Interlego AG* [1989] AC 217. On the other hand, if the work gives particular expression to a commonplace idea or an old tale, copyright may subsist in it (see *Christoffer* v. *Poseidon Film Distributors Limited* (6/10/99) in which it was held that a script for an animated film of a story from Homer's *Odyssey* was an original literary work). Copyright protection will be limited to the original features of the work, or those features created or chosen by the author's input of skill and labour. See *Biotrading* above.

'Works' comprising the titles of books or periodicals, or advertising slogans, which may have required a good deal of original thought, generally are not accorded copyright protection, because they are too short to be deemed literary works.

Qualification

The Act is limited in its effects to the UK (and to colonies to which it may be extended by Order). It is aimed primarily at protecting the works of British citizens, or works which were first published here. However, in line with the requirements of various international conventions, copyright protection in the UK is also accorded to the works of nationals of many foreign states, as well as to works first published in those states, on a reciprocal basis.

As for works of nationals of other member states of the European Union, there is a principle of equal treatment, so that protection must be offered to such works here: see *Phil Collins* [1993] 2 CMLR 773.

The importance of these rules mainly arises when one is trying to find out whether a foreign work is protected by copyright here, for instance, if one wishes to make a film based upon a foreign novel.

Ownership

The general rule is that the copyright in a work will first be owned by its author, the author being the creator of the work, or in the case of a film or sound recording the person who makes the arrangements necessary for it to be made. The 'principal director' of a film is deemed to be its author or one of its authors.

One important exception to the general rule is that the copyright in a work made by an employee in the course of his or her employment will belong to their employer, subject to any agreement to the contrary. However, this rule does not apply to freelance designers, journalists, etc, and not even to nominally self-employed company directors. This obviously may lead to problems if the question of copyright ownership is not dealt with when an agreement is made to create, purchase or use a work (see box, page 633).

Where a work is produced by several people who collaborate in such a way that each one's contribution is not distinct from that of the other(s), then they will be the joint authors of the work. Where two people collaborate to write a song, one producing the lyrics and the other the music, there will be two separate copyright works, the copyright of which will be owned by each of the authors separately. But where two people write a play, each rewriting what the other produces, there will be a joint work.

The importance of knowing whether the work is joint or not arises:

- in working out the duration of the copyright, and
- from the fact that joint works can only be exploited with the agreement of all the joint authors, so that all of them have

to join in any licence, although each of them can sue for infringement without joining the other(s) as a claimant in the proceedings.

Duration of copyright

As a result of the amendments brought into effect on 1 January 1996, copyright in literary, dramatic, musical or artistic works expires at the end of the period of 70 years from the end of the calendar year in which the author dies (s.12(1)). Where there are joint authors, then the 70 years runs from the death of the last of them to die. If the author is unknown, there will be 70 years protection from the date the work was first made or (where applicable) first made available to the public. Previously, the protection was for 'life plus 50'.

The extended 70-year term also applies to films, and runs from the end of the calendar year in which the death occurs of the last to die of the principal director, the author of the screenplay, the dialogue or the composer of any music created for the film (s.13B). This obviously may be a nightmare to establish, and there are certain presumptions in s.66A which may help someone wishing to use material from an old film.

However, sound recordings are still protected by copyright only for 50 years from the year of making or release (s.13A); similarly, broadcasts, cable programmes and computer-generated works still get only 50 years protection.

The new longer term applies without difficulty to works created after 1 January 1996 and to works in copyright on 31 December 1995. The owner of that extended copyright will be the person who owned it on 31 December 1995, unless that person had only a limited term of ownership, in which case the extra 20 years will be added on to the reversionary term.

Where copyright had expired here, but the author died between 50 and 70 years ago, the position is more complicated. EC Directive 93/98 provided that if a work was protected by copyright anywhere in the European Union on 1 July 1995, copyright revives for it in any other state until the end of the same 70-year period. Differences in national laws may make it necessary to look at the position in the states offering a longer term of protection, namely Germany, France and Spain.

Ownership of the revived term of copyright will belong to the person who was the owner of the copyright when the initial term expired, save that if that person died (or a company, etc, ceased to exist) before 1 January 1996, then the revived term will vest in the author's personal representatives, and in the case of a film, in the principal director's personal representatives.

Any licence affecting a copyright work which subsisted on 31 December 1995 and was then for the full term of the copyright, continues to have effect during any extended term of copyright, subject to any agreement to the contrary (paragraph 21 of the Regulations).

The increased term offered to works of other EU nationals as a result of the Term Directive is not offered automatically to the nationals of other states, but will only apply where an equally long term is offered in their state of origin.

Where acts are carried out in relation to such revived copyright works, pursuant to things done whilst they were in the public domain, protection from infringement is available. A licence as of right may also be available, on giving notice to the copyright owner and paying a royalty.

Dealing with copyright works

Ownership of the copyright in a work confers upon the owner the exclusive right to deal with the work in a number of ways, and essentially stops all unauthorised exploitation of the work. Ownership of the copyright is capable of being separated from ownership of the material form in which the work is embodied, depending upon the terms of any agreement or the circumstances. Buying a copy of a book does not transfer the ownership of the copyright in the underlying work, but purchasing an original manuscript or a unique piece of sculpture might do so.

Copyright works can be exploited by their owners in two ways:

- Assignment: rights in a work may be sold, with the owner retaining no interest in it (except, possibly, for payment by way of royalties or some reversionary rights in certain agreed circumstances) – see box; or
- Licensing: the owner may grant a licence to another to exploit the right, whilst retaining overall ownership (see box, page 634).

Agreements dealing with copyright should make it clear whether an assignment or a licence is being granted. There may be significant advantages in granting a licence rather than an assignment, for where an assignee sells the rights to a third party, or perhaps the rights of an insolvent assignee are sold, it may prove impossible to require a purchaser to pay royalties or abide by other contractual obligations on the part of the original assignee (*Barker* v. *Stickney* [1919] 1 KB 121). If the agreement is unclear, the Court is likely to find that the grantee took the minimum rights necessary for his intended use of the work (*Ray* v. *Classic FM plc* [1998] FSR 622). The question of moral rights (see below) will also have to be considered by parties negotiating an assignment or licence.

Both assignments and licences can, and frequently do, split up the various rights contained within the copyright. So, for instance, a licence might be granted to one person to publish a novel in book form, another person might be granted the film, television and video rights, and yet another the right to translate the novel into other languages.

Assignments and licences may also confer rights according to territory, dividing the USA from the EU or different EU countries one from the other. Any such agreement would have to take into account divergences between different national copyright laws. Furthermore, when seeking to divide rights between different territories of the EU there is a danger of infringing the competition rules of the EU. Professional advice should be taken as breach of these rules would render the parties liable to a fine, as well as making the agreement void in whole or in part.

Licences can, of course, be of varying lengths. There is no need for a licence to be granted for the whole term of copyright. Well-drafted licences will provide for termination on breach, including the failure of the licensee to exploit the work, and on the insolvency of the licensee and will specify whether the rights may be assigned or sub-licensed.

Copyright may be assigned by will. A bequest of an original document, etc embodying an unpublished copyright work will carry the copyright.

Assignments

In an assignment, rights in the work are sold, with the owner retaining no interest in it (except, possibly, for payment by way of royalties).

An assignment must be in writing, signed by or on behalf of the assignor, but no other formality is required. One can make an assignment of future copyright (under s.91). Where the author of a projected work agrees in writing that he will assign the rights in a future work to another, the copyright vests in the assignee immediately upon the creation of the work, without further formalities.

These rules do not affect the common law as to beneficial interests in copyright. One possibility may be that a court will, in the right circumstances, find or infer an agreement to assign the copyright in a work, e.g. where a sole trader had title to the copyright used in his business later incorporated his business and allowed the company to exploit the software as if it were its own, an agreement to assign was inferred (see *Lakeview Computers plc* 26/11/99). Alternatively, if the court finds that a work was commissioned to be made, and that there was a common intention that the purchaser should own the copyright, the court may order the author to assign the copyright to him. 'Commission' in this context means only to order a particular piece of work to be done: see *Apple Corps Ltd* v. *Cooper* [1993] FSR 286 (on the 1956 Act).

Licensing

A licence is granted to another to exploit the right whilst retaining overall ownership.

Licences do not need to take any form in particular, and may indeed be granted orally. However, an exclusive licence (i.e. one which excludes even the copyright owner himself from exploiting the work) must be in writing, if the licensee is to enjoy rights in respect of infringements concurrent with those of the copyright owner.

Infringement

The main type of infringement is what is commonly thought of as plagiarism, that is, copying the work. In fact, copyright confers on the owner the exclusive right to do a number of specified acts, so that anyone doing those acts without his permission will infringe. It is important to note that it is not necessary to copy a work exactly or use all of it; it is sufficient if a substantial part is used. That question is to be judged on a qualitative not a quantitative basis, bearing in mind that it is the skill and labour of the author which is to be protected (see *Ravenscroft* v. *Herbert* [1980] RPC 193 and *Designers Guild*).

The form of infringement common to all forms of copyright works is that of copying. This means reproducing the work in any material form. It is important to note that primary infringement, such as copying, can be done innocently of any intention to infringe.

Infringement may occur where an existing work provides the inspiration for a later one, if copying results, e.g. by including edited extracts from a history book in a novel (*Ravenscroft*), using a photograph as the inspiration for a painting (*Baumann* v. *Fussell* [1978] RPC 485), or words from a verse of a song for another (*Ludlow Music* v. *Williams* [2001] FSR 271). Infringement will not necessarily be prevented merely by the application of significant new skill and labour by the infringer, nor by a change of medium.

In the case of a two-dimensional artistic work, reproduction can mean making a copy in three dimensions, and vice versa. However, s.51 of the Act provides that in the case of a 'design document or model' (for definition, see page 636) for something which is not *itself* an artistic work, it is no infringement to make an article to that design. This means that whilst it would be an infringement of copyright to make an article from a design drawing for, say, a sculpture, it will not be an infringement of copyright to make a handbag from a copy of the design drawing for it, or from a handbag which one has purchased. Instead, such designs are generally protected by design right or as registered designs (for both see below).

Copying a film, broadcast or cable programme can include making a copy of the whole or a substantial part of any image from it (see s.17(4)). This means that copying one frame of the film will be an infringement. It is not an infringement of copyright in a film (though there would probably be an infringement of the copyright in underlying works) to reshoot the film (*Norowzian*).

Copying is generally proved by showing substantial similarities between the original and the alleged copy, plus an opportunity to copy. Surprisingly often, minor errors in the original are reproduced by an infringer.

Copying need not be direct, so that, for instance, where the copyright is in a fabric design, copying the material without ever having seen the original drawing will still be an infringement, as will 'reverse engineering' of industrial designs e.g. to make unlicensed spare parts (*British Leyland* [1984] FSR 591; also *Mars* v. *Teknowledge* [2000] FSR 138).

Issuing copies of a work to the public when they have not previously been put into circulation in the UK is also an infringement of all types of work.

Other acts which may amount to an infringement depend upon the nature of the work. It will be an infringement of the copyright in a literary, dramatic or musical work to perform it in public, whether by live performance or by playing recordings. Similarly, it is an infringement of the copyright in a sound recording, film, broadcast or cable programme to play or show it in public. Many copyright works will also be infringed by the rental or lending of copies of the work.

One rather different form of infringement is to make an adaptation of a literary, dramatic or musical work. An adaptation includes, in the case of a literary work, a translation, in the case of a non-dramatic work, making a dramatic work of it, and vice versa. A transcription or arrangement of a musical work is an adaptation of it.

There are also a number of 'secondary' infringements – see box.

Exceptions to infringement

The Act provides a large number of exceptions to the rules on infringement. They are far too numerous to be dealt with here in full, but they include:

- fair dealing with literary, dramatic, musical or artistic works for the purpose of research or private study;
- fair dealing for the purpose of criticism or review or reporting current events, as to which there have been a number of important decisions recently (*Pro Sieben Media* [1999] FSR 610; *Hyde Park* v. *Yelland* [2001] Ch. 143; *NLA* v. *Marks & Spencer Plc* [2001] Ch. 257);
- incidental inclusion of a work in an artistic work, sound recording, film, broadcast or cable programme;
- educational exceptions (see ss.32–36);
- exceptions for libraries (see ss.37–44) and public administration (see ss.45–50);
- backing-up, or converting a computer program or accessing a licensed database (see s.50A–D);
- dealing with a work where the author cannot be identified and the work seems likely to be out of copyright;
- public recitation, if accompanied by a sufficient acknowledgement;
- various e-commerce, transient use, etc exceptions based upon Directive 2001/29/EC (which should be brought into effect in the UK soon).

The effect of the Human Rights Act on copyright in relation to the right to free speech seems likely to be limited, as sufficient protection is to be found in the fair dealing provisions: *Ashdown* v. *Telegraph Group Limited* [2001] 2 WLR 967.

There is no defence of parody.

'Secondary' infringements

Secondary infringements consist not of making infringing copies, but of dealing with them in some way. It is an infringement to import an infringing copy into the UK, and to possess in the course of business, or to sell, hire, offer for sale or hire, or distribute in the course of trade an infringing copy. However, none of these acts will be an infringement unless the alleged infringer knew or had reason to believe that the articles were infringing copies. What is sufficient knowledge will depend upon the facts of each case (see *LA Gear Inc.* [1992] FSR 121 and *ZYX Records* v. *King* [1997] 2 All ER 132, *Pensher Security* [2000] RPC 249). Merely putting someone on notice of a dispute as to ownership of copyright may not suffice to give him or her reason to believe in infringement for this purpose: *Hutchison* [1995] FSR 365.

Other secondary infringements consist of permitting a place to be used for a public performance in which copyright is infringed and supplying apparatus to be used for infringing public performance, again, in each case, with safeguards for innocent acts.

Remedies for infringements

The copyright owner will usually want to prevent the repetition or continuation of the infringement and compensation.

In almost all cases an injunction will be sought to stop the infringement. The Courts have useful powers to grant an injunction at an early stage, indeed, even before any infringement takes place, if a real threat of damage can be shown. Such an interim injunction can be applied for on three days notice (or without notice in appropriate cases), but will not be granted unless the claimant has a reasonably good case and can show that he would suffer 'unquantifiable' damage if the defendant's activities continued pending trial. Delay in bringing an interim application may be fatal to its success. An injunction may not be granted where the claimant clearly only wants financial compensation (*Ludlow Music*).

Financial compensation may be sought

in one of two forms. Firstly, damages. These will usually be calculated upon evidence of the loss caused to the claimant, sometimes based upon loss of business, at others upon the basis of what would have been a proper licence fee for the defendant's acts. Additional damages may be awarded in rare cases for flagrant infringements.

Damages will not be awarded for infringement where the infringer did not know, and had no reason to believe, that copyright subsisted in the work. This exception is of limited use to a defendant, though, in the usual situation where the work was of such a nature that he should have known that copyright would subsist in it.

The alternative to damages is an account of profits, that is, the net profits made by the infringer by virtue of his illicit exploitation of the copyright. Where an account of profits is sought, no award of flagrant damages can be made. See *Redrow Homes Ltd* [1998] FSR 345.

A copyright owner may also apply for delivery up of infringing copies.

Finally, there are various criminal offences relating to the making, importation, possession, sale, hire, distribution, etc of infringing copies.

Design right

Many industrial designs are excluded from copyright protection, by s.51. Alternatively, the term of copyright protection is limited to 25 years from first industrial exploitation, by s.52. However, they may instead be protected by the 'design right' created by ss.213–64. Like copyright, design right does not depend upon registration, but upon the creation of a suitable design by a qualified person.

Design right is granted to original designs consisting of the shape or configuration (internal or external) of the whole or part of an article, not being merely 'surface decoration'. A design is not original if it was commonplace in the design field in question at the time of its creation. In *Farmers Build* [1999] RPC 461, 'commonplace' was defined as meaning a design of a type which would excite no 'peculiar attention' amongst those in the trade, or one which amounts to a run-of-the-mill combination of well-known features. Designs are not protected if they consist of a method or principle of construction, or are dictated by the shape, etc of an article to which the new article is to be connected or of which it is to form part, the so-called 'must-fit' and 'must-match' exclusions. In *Ocular Sciences* [1997] RPC 289, these exclusions had a devastating effect upon numerous design rights claimed for contact lens designs.

Design right subsists in designs made by or for qualifying persons (see, broadly, 'Qualification' on page 631) or first marketed in the UK or EU or any other country to which the provision may be extended by Order.

Design right lasts only 15 years from the end of the year in which it was first recorded or an article made to the design, or (if shorter) 10 years from the end of the year in which articles made according to the design were first sold or hired out. During the last five years of the term of protection, a licence to use the design can be obtained 'as of right' but against payment of a proper licence fee. Hence, design right may give only five years 'absolute' protection, as opposed to the 'life plus 70' of copyright.

The designer will be the owner of the right, unless it was commissioned, in which case the commissioner will be the first owner. An employee's designs made in the course of employment will belong to the employer.

The right given to the owner of a design right is the exclusive right to reproduce the design for commercial purposes. The rules as to assignments, licensing and infringement, both primary and secondary, are substantially similar to those described above in relation to copyright, as are the remedies available.

There have recently been significant changes to the law on registered designs, which coexist with the right given by the unregistered design right discussed above. The Registered Design Act 1949 has been amended (and expanded) in line with EU legislation, and now permits the registration of designs consisting of the appearance of the whole or any part of a product resulting from features of the product itself, such as shape, materials, etc or from the ornamentation of the product. It covers industrial or handicraft items, their packaging or get-up, etc. Designs must be novel and not solely dictated by function. The range of designs which may be registered is wider than under the old law, and designs need *not* necessarily have 'eye appeal'. Such designs provide a monopoly right renewable for up to 25 years. For further explanation see the useful guidance on the Patent Office website. A Community registered design is also in the offing.

Moral rights

The Act also provides for the protection of certain so-called 'moral rights'.

The right of 'paternity' is for the author of a copyright literary, dramatic, musical or artistic work, or the director of a copyright film, to be identified as the author/director, largely whenever the work is commercially exploited (s.77).

However, the right does not arise unless it has been 'asserted' by appropriate words in writing, or in the case of an artistic work by ensuring that the artist's name appears on the frame, etc (see end). There are exceptions to the right, in particular where first ownership of the copyright vested in the author's or director's employer.

The right of 'integrity' protects one's work from 'derogatory treatment', meaning an addition to, deletion from, alteration or adaptation of a work which amounts to distortion or mutilation of the work or is otherwise prejudicial to the honour or reputation of the author/director.

Again, infringement of the right takes place when the maltreated work is published commercially or performed or exhibited in public. There are various exceptions set out in s.81 of the Act, in particular where the publication is in a newspaper, etc, and the work was made for inclusion in it or made available with the author's consent.

Where the copyright in the work vested first in the author's or director's employer, he or she has no right to 'integrity' unless identified at the time of the relevant act or on published copies of the work.

These rights subsist for as long as the copyright in the work subsists.

A third moral right conferred by the Act is not to have a literary, dramatic, musical or artistic work falsely attributed to one as author, or to have a film falsely attributed to one as director, again where the work in question is published, etc. This right subsists until 20 years after a person's death.

None of these rights can be assigned during the person's lifetime, but all of them either pass on the person's death as directed by his or her will or fall into his residuary estate.

A fourth but rather different moral right is conferred by s.85. It gives a person who has commissioned the taking of photographs for private purposes a right to prevent copies of the work being issued to the public, etc.

The remedies for breach of these moral rights again include damages and an injunction, although s.103(2) specifically foresees the granting of an injunction qualified by a right to the defendant to do the acts complained of, if subject to a suitable disclaimer.

Moral rights are exercisable in relation to works in which the copyright has revived subject to any waiver or assertion of the right made before 1 January 1996 (see details as to who may exercise rights in paragraph 22 of the Regulations).

NOTICE

AMANDA LOUISE MICHAELS, hereby asserts and gives notice of her right under s.77 of the Copyright, Designs & Patents Act 1988 to be identified as the author of the foregoing article.

AMANDA MICHAELS

Amanda L. Michaels is a barrister in private practice in London, and specialises in copyright, designs, trade marks, and similar intellectual property and 'media' work. She is author of *A Practical Guide to Trade Mark Law* (Sweet & Maxwell, 3rd edn 2001).

Further reading

Garnett, Rayner James and Davies, *Copinger and Skone James on Copyright*, Sweet & Maxwell, 14th edn, 1999 and Supplement 2002

Laddie, Prescott and Vitoria, *The Modern Law of Copyright*, Butterworths, 3rd edn, 2000

Flint, *A User's Guide to Copyright*, Butterworths, 5th edn, 2000

Bainbridge, David, *Intellectual Property*, Pearson Education, 5th edn, 2002

Copyright Acts

Copyright, Designs and Patents Act 1998

The Duration of Copyright and Rights in Performances Regulations 1995 (SI 1995 No 3297)

see also Numerous Orders in Council

The Copyright Licensing Agency Ltd

The Copyright Licensing Agency (CLA) collects and distributes money on behalf of artists, writers and publishers for the photocopying of their work. CLA operates on a non-profit basis, and issues licences to schools, further and higher education, business and government bodies so that such organisations can access the copyright material in books, journals, law reports, magazines and periodicals.

Why was CLA established?

CLA was established in 1982 by its members, the Authors' Licensing and Collecting Society (ALCS) and the Publishers Licensing Society (PLS) to promote and enforce the intellectual property rights of British rightsholders both at home and abroad. CLA also has close ties with the Design and Artists Copyright Society (DACS), which represents artists and illustrators.

ALCS has two corporate members – the Society of Authors and the Writers' Guild of Great Britain. It also has a large number of individual authors as members and affiliations with the National Union of Journalists and the Chartered Institute of Journalists. PLS members are the Publishers Association, the Periodical Publishers Association and the Association of Learned and Professional Society Publishers.

How CLA helps artists and writers

CLA allows licensed users access to over 16 million titles worldwide. In return CLA ensures artists and writers, along with publishers, are fairly recompensed by the licence fees, which CLA collects and forwards to its members for onward distribution to artists, writers and publishers.

The collective management of licensing schemes means that CLA can provide users with the simplest and most cost-effective means of obtaining authorisation for photocopying, while copy limits ensure fair recompense is maintained for rightsholders.

CLA is currently developing licences which will enable the electrocopying and digitisation of existing print material. The licence will enable users to scan, store and electronically send extracts from copyright works.

Licence to copy

CLA's licensees fall into three main categories:
- education (schools, further and higher education);
- government (central, local, public bodies); and
- business (business, industry, professionals).

CLA develops licences to meet the specific needs of each sector and groupings within each sector. Depending on the requirement, there are both blanket and transactional licences available. Every licence allows the photocopying of most books, journals, magazines and periodicals published in the UK.

An international dimension

Many countries have established equivalents to CLA and the number of such agencies is set to grow. Nearly all these agencies, including CLA, are members of the International Federation of Reproduction Rights Organisations (IFRRO).

Through reciprocal arrangements with these organisations, any CLA licence also allows copying from an expanding list of publications in other countries. Currently these countries are: Australia, Canada (including Quebec), Denmark, Finland, France, Germany, Greece, Iceland, Ireland, The Netherlands, New Zealand, Norway, South Africa, Spain, Sweden, Switzerland and the USA.

CLA receives monies from these organisations for the copying of UK material abroad and forwards it to rightsholders.

Distribution

The fees collected from licensees are forwarded to artists, authors and publishers, via ALCS, DACS and PLS respectively, and are based on statistical surveys and records of copying activity. Since CLA had its first distribution in 1986–7, £129 million has been distributed. For the year ending 31 March 2001, £23 million was returned to rightsholders.

Respecting copyright

CLA also believes it is important to raise awareness of the copyright in published material and the need to protect the creativity of artists, authors and publishers. To this end, CLA organises a range of activities such as copyright workshops in schools, seminars for businesses and institutions and an extensive exhibition programme. A comprehensive website is regularly updated and a bi-annual newsletter, *Clarion*, is posted to all licensees and to those individuals and groups concerned with copyright.

Protecting creativity

CLA believes in working together with all sectors to take into account their differing needs, meaning legal action is rare. However, organisations – especially in the business sector – need to be made aware that copyright is a legally enforceable right enshrined in statute law, not a voluntary option. CLA's recently restructured compliance division aims to continue the education programme. However, as a last resort it has the power to take legal proceedings on behalf of rightsholders.

Further information

The Copyright Licensing Agency Ltd
90 Tottenham Court Road, London W1T 4LP
tel 020-7631 5555 *fax* 020-7631 5500
email cla@cla.co.uk
website www.cla.co.uk
CBC House, 24 Canning Street,
Edinburgh EH3 8E9
tel 0131-272 2711 *fax* 0131-272 2811

The Authors' Licensing and Collecting Society Ltd (ALCS)

The Authors' Licensing and Collecting Society Ltd is the UK rights management society that acts to ensure writers are fairly compensated whenever their works are copied, broadcast or recorded.

ALCS has upwards of 18,000 members and collects and distributes fees of around £10 million each year. Its aims are:
- to ensure hard-to-collect revenues due to authors are efficiently collected and speedily distributed;
- to protect and promote authors' rights;
- to campaign for new licensing schemes;
- to identify and develop new sources of income for writers;
- to foster an awareness of intellectual property issues among the writing community.

Formed in 1997, ALCS is internationally recognised as a leading authority on copyright matters and authors' collective interests. It maintains a close watching brief on all matters affecting copyright, both in the UK and abroad, and makes regular representations to the UK government and the EU.

The ALCS Mandate

Members grant to ALCS the right to administer on their behalf those rights that they aren't able to exercise as an individual; that are best handled on a collective basis; and where the law stipulates that they must be administered collectively.

ALCS maximises the amount of fees due to writers, and ensures they receive their money quickly and cost effectively. It has a highly specialised knowledge of audiovisual and text-based repertoires, a sophisticated membership database, efficient distribution and accounting systems, an extensive network of international contacts, and reciprocal agreements with foreign collection societies.

Collecting and distributing fees

ALCS collects fees owing to writers from a variety of sources:

Photocopying is its largest source of income. It is administered by the Copyright Licensing Agency (CLA) which issues licences to users who photocopy from books, periodicals and journals. The licence fee paid by each organisation is based on the number of people who benefit from photocopying, and on the numbers of copies they make per year. Overseas payments also flow through CLA.

Digitisation. Since 1999, the CLA has offered licences to educational establishments for storing and using digital versions of authors' printed works which have been scanned into a computer. Digitisation fees are split 50:50 between authors and publishers.

Foreign Public Lending Right. The Public Lending Right (PLR) system pays authors whose books are borrowed from public libraries. Through a reciprocal agreement between ALCS and VG Wort (the German collecting society), ALCS members receive payment whenever their books are borrowed from German libraries. It is hoped that this will also include the Netherlands in the near future. (Note: ALCS does not administer the UK Public Lending Right.)

Cable retransmission is the simultaneous showing of one country's television signals in another country, via a cable network. Cable companies pay a central collecting organisation a percentage of their subscription fees, which must be collectively administered. ALCS receives the writers' share of these fees for British terrestrial programmes which contain literary and dramatic material.

Educational recording. ALCS, together with the main broadcasters and other rights holders, set up the Educational Recording Agency (ERA) in 1989 to offer licences to educational establishments that wish to record programmes to show to their students. ERA collects fees from the licensees and pays ALCS the amount due to its members for the use of their literary works.

BBC Prime. ALCS licenses BBC Worldwide Ltd for every transmission which includes literary and dramatic material. This licence covers the direct reception and cable retransmission of BBC Prime – the BBC's entertainment satellite channel – throughout Europe and Africa.

Blank tape and machine levy. A number of European countries levy a charge on sales of blank tapes which compensates rights owners for the private copying of their works. The fees due to UK writers are collected by sister societies and sent to ALCS.

Miscellaneous literary rights. Fees are collected from a number of miscellaneous sources, which include readings of excerpts of literary works broadcast on television and radio, or read aloud at literary festivals.

How ALCS is financed

ALCS is a non-profit-making, non-union organisation and is financed by:

1. **Membership fees**. Members who live in the UK and other EU countries pay an annual subscription of £7.50. UK residents have to pay VAT on this sum. Members who are not resident in the EU pay a subscription of £10.
2. **Commission fees**. ALCS charges 11% commission on all fees distributed to members. Associate members (who don't pay an annual subscription fee) are charged 14% commission. On certain sources of income, the Society deducts a further 0.5% for the ALCS legal fund.

How ALCS is run

ALCS policy is controlled by a non-executive Management Council. There are 12 council members. Four are elected by ALCS members, four are nominated by the Society of Authors and four by the Writers' Guild of Great Britain.

The core activity of ALCS is the collection and distribution of money owed to members on its database. It also tracks down non-member authors for whom fees have been collected but who are unaware they are owed money.

Membership

The Authors' Licensing and Collecting Society Ltd (ALCS)

Marlborough Court, 14-18 Holborn, London EC1N 2LE
tel 020-7395 0600 *fax* 020-7395 0660
email alcs@alcs.co.uk
website www.alcs.co.uk
Chief Executive Officer Dafydd Wyn Phillips

Membership is open to the following groups of writers and successors to their estates: novelists; non-fiction authors; poets; playwrights; business, academic and technical authors; scriptwriters; journal contributors; freelance journalists; and translators. There are 3 membership categories: ordinary members (writers); successor members (heirs); and associate members (writers and their successors who do not elect to join as ordinary members; or individuals who do not qualify for full membership).

Members of the Society of Authors and the Writers' Guild of Great Britain are entitled to become ordinary members of ALCS at no annual charge. A special associate members arrangement exists for freelance journalists who are members of the National Union of Journalists, the Chartered Institute of Journalists, the British Association of Journalists, and for members of the British Comedy Writers' Association.

The Design and Artists Copyright Society Ltd (DACS)

The Design and Artists Copyright Society Ltd (DACS) is the copyright and collecting society for visual artists in the UK. It is an independent, non-profit-making society open to all artists and photographers.

About DACS

Founded in 1983, DACS works to create a fair working environment for visual creators by administering and protecting copyright on behalf of its members, and by lobbying for all artists at both national and international levels on rights-related issues. It is the only organisation working for artists and photographers in the UK that deals solely with copyright and artists' rights. DACS is part of a national framework of UK artists' and photographers' professional associations and trade unions, which ensures a consistent approach to all copyright and rights-related issues in the UK. Any individual or business based in the UK that wishes to reproduce an artistic work by a member must apply to DACS for permission to do so.

Copyright

Copyright is a right granted to creators under law. Copyright in all artistic works is established from the moment of creation – the only qualification required is that the work must be original. DACS' activities complement those of other UK collecting societies, such as the Performing Rights Society (PRS) and the Authors' Licensing and Copyright Society (ALCS).

DACS administers copyright in the UK on behalf of its members. This principally involves providing users of visual works (such as a publisher) with licences for inclusion of works of art in various products, such as books and posters. Permission to reproduce a work is normally granted in return for a fee. DACS charges fees calculated according to published tariffs or via negotiation for merchandising and advertising uses. Each licence granted to a publisher, film producer, or any other user is legally binding.

Often professional and commercial artists create their works as a result of a commission, and they may directly administer and control their primary rights in these works. However, individual creators are often unable to control their secondary rights, and a system of Collective Administration has been established, so that these rights are administered on behalf of many creators by one collecting society. In the UK, DACS is the collecting society for visual artists' secondary rights. The Payback campaign seeks to unite artists with monies collected in this manner. It is not necessary to be a member of DACS to benefit from Payback since DACS represents the entire visual artists' repertoire in the UK.

Additional benefits

All members of DACS are entitled to assistance and advice regarding copyright matters. Joining an organisation set up to protect and administer artists' copyright helps strengthen one's position as an independent artist, and promotes the rights of artists as a group.

Worldwide protection

DACS represents 40,000 artists through reciprocal representation agreements with visual arts collecting societies throughout Europe and internationallly.

Membership

The Design and Artists Copyright Society Ltd (DACS)

Parchment House, 13 Northburgh Street, London EC1V 0JP
tel 020-7336 8811 *fax* 020-7336 8822
email info@dacs.org.uk
website www.dacs.org.uk

Membership is open to any visual artist of any discipline who is resident in the UK or the Republic of Ireland. Currently DACS represents artists from a wide variety of disciplines: fine art, photography, sculpture, illustration, textiles, glass and ceramics, to name but a few. Contact DACS for a membership application pack.

In the UK, DACS represents the copyright interests of artists from all over the world and in turn societies abroad represent DACS' members there. Artists and photographers therefore benefit from a global network of societies that provides administration and copyright protection.

Artists' rights

DACS is currently working towards the successful implementation of *droit de suite*, or the Artist's Resale Right. This right ensures that artists receive a percentage of the revenue each time a work is sold after the first sale, a right enjoyed by artists across Europe.

As new issues and technologies affecting copyright and artists' rights arise, such as the internet, DACS and its sister societies develop systems to protect their members' interests while encouraging creativity. As part of an international network, DACS can keep abreast of the global issues affecting artists and ensure that artists are represented at all levels, and on every major area of concern.

Structure

DACS is governed by a Council of Management, which consists of elected members of the Society. The Council is responsible for making all major policy and financial decisions at DACS. The day-to-day running of the Society is carried out by the Chief Executive in conjunction with a specialised staff experienced in copyright matters.

As a non-profit-making society, DACS is financed primarily by commission deducted from the fees and royalties that it collects. Other income is derived from membership fees.

US copyright law

Gavin McFarlane, barrister, introduces US copyright law and points out the differences, and similarities, of British copyright law.

International copyright

International copyright conventions

There is no general principle of international copyright which provides a uniform code for the protection of right owners throughout the world. There are, however, two major international copyright conventions which lay down certain minimum standards for member states, in particular requiring member states to accord to right owners of other member states the same protection which is granted to their own nationals. One is the higher standard Berne Convention of 1886, the most recent revision of which was signed in Paris in 1971. The other is the Universal Copyright Convention signed in 1952 with lower minimum standards, and sponsored by Unesco. This also was most recently revised in Paris in 1971, jointly with the Berne Convention. To this latter Convention the United States has belonged since 1955. On 16 November 1988, the Government of the United States deposited its instrument of accession to the Paris Revision of the Berne Convention. The Convention entered into force as regards the United States on 1 March 1989. Together with certain new statutory provisions made in consequence of accession to Berne, this advances substantially the process of overhaul and modernisation of US copyright law which was begun in the 1970s.

Effect on British copyright owners

The copyright statute of the United States having been brought into line with the requirements of the Berne compliance with the formalities required by American law has been largely removed. The Berne Convention Implementation Act of 1988 makes statutory amendments to the way foreign works are now treated in US law. These are now inserted in the US codified law as Title 17 – The Copyright Act. 'Foreign works' are works having a country of origin other than the United States. The formalities which were for so long a considerable handicap for foreign copyright owners in the American system have now become optional, though not removed altogether. The new system provides incentives to encourage foreign right owners to continue to comply with formalities on a voluntary basis, in particular notice, renewal and registration.

US copyright law – summary

Introduction of new law

After many years of debate, the new Copyright Statute of the United States was passed on 19 October 1976. The greater part of its relevant provisions came into force on 1 January 1978. It has extended the range of copyright protection, and further eased the requirements whereby British authors can obtain copyright protection in America. New Public Law 100–568 of 31 October 1988 has made further amendments to the Copyright Statute which were necessary to enable ratification of the Berne Convention to take place. The Universal Copyright Convention is now for all practical purposes moribund. The problems which derived from the old system of common law copyright no longer exist.

The rights of a copyright owner

(1) To reproduce the copyrighted work in copies or phonorecords.
(2) To prepare derivative works based upon the copyrighted work.
(3) To distribute copies or phonorecords of the copyrighted work to the public by sale or other transfer of ownership, or by rental, lease or lending.
(4) In the case of literary, musical, dramatic and choreographic works, pantomimes, and motion pictures and other audiovisual works, but not sound recordings, to perform the copyrighted work publicly. However, in 1995 Congress granted a limited performance right to sound recordings in digital format in an interactive medium.
(5) In the case of literary, musical, dramatic, and choreographic works, pantomimes, and pictorial, graphic, or sculptural works, including the individual images of a motion picture or other audiovisual work, to display the copyrighted work publicly.
(6) By the Record Rental Amendment Act 1984, s.109 of the Copyright Statute is amended. Now, unless authorised by the owners of copyright in the sound recording and the musical works thereon, the owner of a phonorecord may not, for direct or indirect commercial advantage, rent, lease or lend the phonorecord. A compulsory licence under s.115(c) includes the right of a maker of a phonorecord of non-dramatic musical work to distribute or authorise the distribution of the phonorecord by rental, lease, or lending, and an additional royalty is payable in respect of that. This modifies the 'first sale doctrine', which otherwise permits someone buying a copyright work to hire or sell a lawfully purchased copy to third parties without compensating the copyright owners, and without his or her consent.
(7) A further exception to the 'first sale doctrine' and s.109 of the Copyright Act is made by the Computer Software Rental Amendments Act. A similar restriction has been placed on the unauthorised rental, lease or lending of software, subject to certain limited exceptions. Both the phonorecord and software exceptions to the first sale doctrine terminated, and were extended by Congress on 1 October 1997.
(8) The Semiconductor Chip Protection Act 1984 adds to the Copyright Statute a new chapter on the protection of semiconductor chip products.
(9) The Visual Artists Rights Act 1990 has added moral rights to the various economic rights listed above. These moral rights are the right of integrity, and the right of attribution or paternity. A new category of 'work of visual art' is defined broadly as paintings, drawings, prints and sculptures, with an upper limit of 200 copies. Works generally exploited in mass market copies such as books, newspapers, motion pictures and electronic information services are specifically excluded from these moral rights provisions. Where they apply, they do so only in respect of works created on or after 1 June 1991, and to certain works previously created where title has not already been transferred by the author.

Manufacturing requirements

With effect from 1 July 1986, these ceased to have effect. Prior to 1 July 1986, the importation into or public distribution in the United States of a work consisting preponderantly of non-dramatic literary material that was in the English language and protected under American law was prohibited unless the portions consisting of such material had been manufactured in the United States or Canada. This provision did not apply where, on the date when importation was sought or public distribution in the United States was made, the author of any substantial part of such material was not a national of the United States or, if a national, had been domiciled outside the United States for a continuous period of at least one year immediately preceding that date.

Since 1 July 1986, there is no manufacturing requirement in respect of works of British authors. With American ratification of the Berne Convention, the formalities previously required in relation to copyright notice, deposit and registration have been greatly modified.

Works protected in American law

Works of authorship include:

- Literary works. Note: Computer programs are classified as literary works for the purposes of United States copyright. In *Whelan Associates Inc.* v. *Jaslow Dental Laboratory Inc.* (1987) FSR1, it was held that the copyright of a computer program could be infringed even in the absence of copying of the literal code if the structure was part of the expression of the idea behind a program rather than the idea itself.
- Musical works, including any accompanying words.
- Dramatic works, including any accompanying music.
- Pantomimes and choreographic works.
- Pictorial, graphic and sculptural works.
- Motion pictures and other audiovisual works. Note: copyright in certain motion pictures has been extended by the North American Free Trade Agreement Information Act 1993.
- Sound recordings, but copyright in sound recordings is not to include a right of public performance.
- Architectural works: the design of a building as embodied in any tangible medium of expression, including a building, architectural plans or drawings. The Architectural Works Copyright Protections Act applies this protection to works created on or after 1 December 1990.

Formalities

Notice of copyright. Whenever a work protected by the American Copyright Statute is published in the United States or elsewhere by authority of the copyright owner, a notice of copyright should be placed on all publicly distributed copies. This should consist of:

- either the symbol © or the word 'Copyright' or the abbreviation 'Copr.' plus
- the year of first publication of the work, plus
- the name of the copyright owner.

Since the Berne Amendments, both US and works of foreign origin which were first published in the US after 1 March 1989 without having notice of copyright placed on them will no longer be unprotected. In general, authors are advised to place copyright notices on their works, as this is a considerable deterrent to plagiarism. Damages may well be lower in a case where no notice of copyright was placed on the work.

Deposit. The owner of copyright or the exclusive right of publication in a work published with notice of copyright in the United States must within three months of such publication deposit in the Copyright Office for the use or disposition of the Library of Congress two complete copies of the best edition of the work (or two records, if the work is a sound recording). Failure to comply with the deposit requirements does not result in the loss of copyright, but a court could assess fines and issue an injunction.

Registration. Registration for copyright in the United States is optional. However, any owner of copyright in a work first published outside the United States may register a work by making application to the Copyright Office with the appropriate fee, and by depositing one complete copy of the work. This requirement of deposit may be satisfied by using copies deposited for the Library of Congress. Whilst registration is still a requirement for works of US origin and from non-Berne countries as a precondition to filing an infringement action, it is no longer necessary for foreign works from Berne countries. But as a matter of practice there are procedural advantages in any litigation where there has been registration. The United States has interpreted the Berne Convention as allowing formalities which are not in themselves conditions for obtaining copyright protection, but which lead to improved protection. The law allows statutory damages and attorneys' fees only if the work was registered prior to the infringement.

Restoration of copyright

Works by non-US authors which lost copyright protection in the United States because of failure to comply with any of these formalities may have had protection automatically restored in certain circumstances. Works claiming restoration must still be in copyright in their country of origin. If a work succeeds in having copyright restored, it will last for the remainder of the period to which it would originally have been entitled in the United States.

Duration of copyright

Copyright in a work created on or after 1 January 1978 endures for a term of the life of the author, and a period of 50 years after the author's death. The further amendments made by Public Law 100–568 of 31 October 1988 have enabled the government to ratify the higher standard Berne Convention. Copyright in a work created before 1 January 1978, but not published or copyrighted before then, subsists from 1 January 1978, and lasts for the life of the author and a post-mortem period of 50 years.

Any copyright, the first term of which under the previous law was still subsisting on 1 January 1978, shall endure for 28 years from the date when it was originally secured, and the copyright proprietor or his or her representative may apply for a further term of 47 years within one year prior to the expiry of the original term. Until 1992, application for renewal and extension was required. Failure to do so produced disastrous results with some material of great merit passing into the public domain in error. By Public Law 102–307 enacted on 26 June 1992, there is no longer necessity to make a renewal registration in order to obtain the longer period of protection. Now renewal copyright vests automatically in the person entitled to renewal at the end of the 28th year of the original term of copyright.

The duration of any copyright, the renewal term of which was subsisting at any time between 31 December 1976 and 31 December 1977, or for which renewal registration was made between those dates, is extended to endure for a term of 75 years from the date copyright was originally secured.

All terms of copyright provided for by the sections referred to above run to the end of the calendar year in which they would otherwise expire.

Public performance

Under the previous American law the provisions relating to performance in public were less generous to right owners than those existing in United Kingdom copyright law. In particular, performance of a musical work was formerly only an infringement if it was 'for profit'. Moreover, the considerable American coin-operated record-playing machine industry (juke boxes) had obtained an exemption from being regarded as instruments of profit, and accordingly their owners did not have to pay royalties for the use of copyright musical works.

Now by the new law one of the exclusive rights of the copyright owner is, in the case of literary, musical, dramatic and choreographic works, pantomimes, and motion pictures and other audiovisual works, to perform the work publicly, without any requirement of such performance being 'for profit'. By Section 114 however, the exclusive rights of the owner of copyright in a sound recording are specifically stated not to include any right of public performance, although this provision was modified in 1995.

The position of coin-operated record players (juke boxes) is governed by the new Section 116A, inserted by Public Law 100–568 of 31 October 1988. It covers the position of negotiated licences. Limitations are placed on the exclusive right if licences are not negotiated.

Mechanical right

Where sound recordings of a non-dramatic musical work have been distributed to the public in the United States with the authority of the copyright owner, any other person may, by following the provisions of the law, obtain a compulsory licence to make and distribute sound recordings of the work. This right is known in the United Kingdom as 'the mechanical right'. Notice must be served on the copyright owner, who is entitled to a royalty in respect of each of his or her works recorded of either two and three fourths cents or one half of one cent per minute of playing time or fraction thereof, whichever amount is the larger. These rates are adjusted periodically by the Copyright Arbitration Royalty Panels (CARP). Failure to serve or file the required notice forecloses the possibility of a compulsory licence and, in the absence of a negotiated licence, renders the making and distribution of such records actionable as acts of infringement.

Transfer of copyright

Under the previous American law copyright was regarded as indivisible, which meant that on the transfer of copyright, where it was intended that only film rights or some other such limited right be transferred, the entire copyright nevertheless had to be passed. This led to a cumbersome procedure whereby the author would assign the whole copyright to his or her publisher, who would return to the author by means of an exclusive licence those rights which it was not meant to transfer.

Now it is provided by Section 201(d) of the Copyright Statute that (1) the ownership of a copyright may be transferred in whole or in part by any means of conveyance or by operation of law, and may be bequeathed by will or pass as personal property by the applicable laws of intestate succession, and (2) any of the exclusive rights comprised in a copyright (including any subdivision of any of the rights set out in 'The rights of a copyright owner' above) may be transferred as provided in (1) above and owned separately. The owner of any particular exclusive right is entitled, to the extent of that right, to all the protection and remedies accorded to the copyright owner by that Statute. This removes the difficulties which existed under the previous law, and brings the position much closer to that existing in the copyright law of the United Kingdom. All transfers and assignments of copyright must be recorded in the US Copyright Office to have full legal effect.

Copyright Arbitration Royalty Panels

In 1993, the Copyright Royalty Tribunal which had been established by the Copyright Act was eliminated by Congress. In its place a new administrative mechanism was established in the Copyright Office with the purpose of making adjustments of reasonable copyright royalty rates in respect of the exercise of certain rights, mainly affecting the musical interests. The newly formed Copyright Arbitration Royalty Panels are constituted on an ad hoc basis and perform in the United States a function similar to the Copyright Tribunal in the United Kingdom.

The new American law spells out the economic objectives which the CARP is to apply in calculating the relevant rates. These are:

- to maximise the availability of creative works to the public;
- to afford the copyright owner a fair return for his or her creative work and the copyright user a fair income under existing economic conditions;
- to reflect the relative roles of the copyright owner and the copyright user in the product made available to the public with respect to relative creative contribution, technological contribution, capital investment, cost, risk, and contribution to the opening of new markets for creative expression and media for their communication;
- to minimise any disruptive impact on the structure of the industries involved and on generally prevailing industry practices.

Every final determination of the CARP shall be published in the Federal Register. It shall state in detail the criteria that the CARP determined to be applicable to the particular proceeding, the various facts that it found relevant to its determination in that proceeding, and the specific reasons for its determination. Any final decision of the CARP in a proceeding may be appealed to the United States Court of Appeals by an aggrieved party, within 30 days after its publication in the Federal Register.

Fair use

One of the most controversial factors which held up the revision of the American copyright law for at least a decade was the extent to which a balance should be struck between the desire of copyright owners to benefit from their works by extending copyright protection as far as possible, and the pressure from users of copyright to obtain access to copyright material as cheaply as possible – if not completely freely.

The new law provides by Section 107 that the fair use of a copyright work, including such use by reproduction of excerpts, for purposes such as criticism, comment, news reporting, teaching (including multiple copies for classroom use), scholarship or research is not an infringement of copyright. In determining whether the use made of a work in any particular case is a fair use, the factors to be considered include:

- the purpose and character of the use, including whether such use is of a commercial nature or is for non-profit educational purposes;
- the nature of the copyrighted work;
- the amount and substantiality of the portion used in relation to the copyrighted work as a whole; and
- the effect of the use upon the potential market for or value of the copyrighted work.

It is not an infringement of copyright for a library or archive, or any of its employees acting within the scope of their employment, to reproduce or distribute no more than one copy of a work, if:

- the reproduction or distribution is made without any purpose of direct or indirect commercial advantage;
- the collections of the library or archive are either open to the public or available not only to researchers affiliated with the library or archive or with the institution of which it is a part, but also to other persons doing research in a specialised field; and
- the reproduction or distribution of the work includes a notice of copyright.

It is not generally an infringement of copyright if a performance or display of a work is given by instructors or pupils in the course of face-to-face teaching activities of a non-profit educational institution, in a classroom or similar place devoted to instruction.

Nor is it an infringement of copyright to give a performance of a non-dramatic literary or musical work or a dramatico-musical work of a religious nature in the course of services at a place of worship or other religious assembly.

It is also not an infringement of copyright to give a performance of a non-dramatic literary or musical work other than in a transmission to the public, without any purpose of direct or indirect commercial advantage and without payment of any fee for the performance to any of the performing artists, promoters or organisers if either:

Criminal proceedings in respect of copyright

- Anyone who infringes a copyright wilfully and for purposes of commercial advantage and private financial gain shall be fined not more than $10,000 or imprisoned for not more than 3 years, or both. However, if the infringement relates to copyright in a sound recording or a film, the infringer is liable to a fine of not more than $250,000 or imprisonment for not more than 5 years or both on a first offence, which can be increased to a fine of up to $250,000 or imprisonment for not more than 10 years or both for a subsequent offence.
- Following a conviction for criminal infringement a court may in addition to these penalties order the forfeiture and destruction of all infringing copies and records, together with implements and equipment used in their manufacture.
- It is also an offence knowingly and with fraudulent intent to place on any article a notice of copyright or words of the same purport, or to import or distribute such copies. A fine is provided for this offence of not more than $2500. The fraudulent removal of a copyright notice also attracts the same maximum fine, as does the false representation of a material particular on an application for copyright representation.

• there is no direct or indirect admission charge; or
• the proceeds, after deducting the reasonable costs of producing the performance, are used exclusively for educational, religious or charitable purposes and not for private financial gain.

In this case the copyright owner has the right to serve notice of objection to the performance in a prescribed form.

Note the important decision of the Supreme Court in *Sony Corporation of America* v. *Universal City Studios* (No. 81–1687, 52 USLW 4090). This decided that the sale of video recorders to the public for the purpose of recording a copyrighted programme from a broadcast signal for private use for time-switching purposes alone (not for archiving or 'librarying') does not amount to contributory infringement of the rights in films which are copied as a result of television broadcasts of them. In 2001 the World Trade Organisation upheld a complaint by the EU that Section 110(5)(B) of the US Copyright Act infringes WTO agreements. The US must now abolish its present exemption from public performance royalties for bars, shops and restaurants.

Remedies for copyright owners

Infringement of copyright

Copyright is infringed by anyone who violates any of the exclusive rights referred to in 'The rights of a copyright owner' (page 645), or who imports copies or records into the United States in violation of the law. The owner of copyright is entitled to institute an action for infringement so long as that infringement is committed while he or she is the owner of the right infringed. Previously, no action for infringement of copyright could be instituted until registration of the copyright claim had been made, but this requirement has been modified now that the United States has ratified the Berne Convention. Under the new provision, US authors must register, or attempt to register, but non-US Berne authors are exempt from this requirement.

Injunctions

Any court having civil jurisdiction under the copyright law may grant interim and final injunctions on such terms as it may deem reasonable to prevent or restrain infringement of copyright. Such injunction may be served anywhere in the United States on the person named. An injunction is operative throughout the whole of the United States, and can be enforced by proceedings in contempt or otherwise by any American court which has jurisdiction over the infringer.

Impounding and disposition

At any time while a copyright action under American law is pending, the court may order the impounding on such terms as it considers reasonable of all copies or records claimed to have been made or used in violation of the copyright owner's exclusive rights; it may also order the impounding of all VCRs, tape recorders, plates, moulds, matrices, masters, tapes, film negatives or other articles by means of which infringing copies or records may be reproduced. A court may order as part of a final judgement or decree the destruction or other disposition of all copies or records found to have been made or used in violation of the copyright owner's exclusive rights. It also has the power to order the destruction of all articles by means of which infringing copies or records were reproduced.

Damages and profits

An infringer of copyright is generally liable either for the copyright owner's actual damage and any additional profits made by the infringer, or for statutory damages.

• The copyright owner is entitled to recover the actual damages suffered by him or her as a result of the infringement, and in addition any profits of the infringer which are attributed to the infringement and are not taken into account in computing the actual damages. In establishing the infringer's profits, the copyright owner is only required to present proof of the infringer's gross revenue, and it is for the infringer to prove his or her deductible expenses and the elements of profit attributable to factors other than the copyright work.

• Except where the copyright owner has persuaded the court that the infringement was committed wilfully, the copyright owner may elect, at any time before final judgement is given, to recover, instead of actual damages and profits, an award of statutory damages for all infringements involved in the action in respect of any one work, which may be between $750 and $30,000 according to what the court considers justified.

• However, where the copyright owner satisfies the court that the infringement was committed wilfully, the court has the discretion to increase the award of statutory damages to not more than $150,000. Where the infringer succeeds in proving that he or she was not aware and had no reason to believe that his or her acts constituted an infringement of copyright, the court has the discretion to reduce the award of statutory damages to not less than $200.

Costs: time limits

In any civil proceedings under American copyright law, the court has the discretion to allow the recovery of full costs by or against any party except the Government of the United States. It may also award a reasonable sum in respect of an attorney's fee. No civil or criminal proceedings in respect of copyright law shall be permitted unless begun within three years after the claim or cause of action arose.

Counterfeiting

By the Piracy and Counterfeiting Amendment Act 1982, pirates and counterfeiters of sound recordings and of motion pictures now face maximum penalties of up to five years imprisonment or fines of up to $250,000.

Colouring films

The United States Copyright Office has decided that adding colour to a black and white film may qualify for copyright protection whenever it amounts to more than a trivial change.

Satellite home viewers

The position of satellite home viewers is controlled by the Satellite Home Viewer Act of 1988. (Title II of Public Law 100–667 of 16 November 1988.) The Copyright Remedy Clarification Act has created s.511 of the Copyright Act, in order to rectify a situation which had developed in case law. By this, the component States of the Union, their agencies and employees are placed in the same position as private individuals and entities in relation to their liability for copyright infringement.

Digital Millennium Copyright Act

The US Congress in 1998 passed new legislation to make clear that the copyright law applies to all works transmitted, or simply made available to, users over the internet.

This measure is unique in that for the first time it gives its copyright owner the right to control access to the digital work, which is so crucial to security on the internet. To allow the United States to ratify two new WIPO (World Intellectual Property Organisation) treaties – the WIPO Copyright Treaty and the WIPO Performance and Phonograms Treaty, negotiated in 1996 – the Digital Millennium Copyright Act (DMCA) makes two changes in US law. First, it outlaws, with substantial criminal and civil penalties, any tampering with copyright management information – the invisible digital coding embedded on sound recordings, software, motion pictures, and databases that identify the owner of the work and stipulate the price and conditions of use. This encoding will help promote e-commerce and curtail internet piracy.

Second, the DMCA prohibits anyone

from disabling anti-copying circuitry in a machine or signal. It also bans the manufacture, sale, and importation of electronic devices that would permit the disabling of that circuitry. Here, too, the DMCA specifies stiff civil and criminal penalties for acts of circumvention and for the manufacture or sale of the devices.

With the DMCA passed, the United States quickly joined the two new WIPO treaties in the hope that its action would serve as an example to other countries.

General observations

The copyright law of the United States was improved as a result of the statute passed by Congress on 19 October 1976. (Title 17, United States Code.) Apart from lifting the general standards of protection for copyright owners to a higher level than that which previously existed, it has on the whole shifted the balance of copyright protection in favour of the copyright owner and away from the copyright user in many of the areas where controversy existed. But most important for British and other non-American authors and publishers, it has gone a long way towards bringing American copyright law up to the same standards of international protection for non-national copyright proprietors which have long been offered by the United Kingdom and the other major countries, both in Europe and elsewhere in the English-speaking world. The ratification by the United States of the Berne Convention with effect from 1 March 1989 was an action which at that time put American copyright law on par with the protection offered by other major countries.

Gavin McFarlane LLM, PhD is a barrister at Temple Chambers, Cardiff. He specialises in international trade law, and is particularly interested in the involvement of the World Trade Organisation in intellectual property matters. He is a visiting professor at London Guildhall University.

Further information

US Copyright Office
website www.loc.gov/copyright
Forms for registration, etc can be obtained online.

Libel

Any writer should be aware of the law of libel. ***Antony Whitaker*** *gives an outline of the main principles, concentrating on points which are most frequently misunderstood. But this article is no more than that, and specific legal advice should be taken when practical problems arise.*

The law discussed is the law of England and Wales. Scotland has its own, albeit somewhat similar, rules. A summary of the main differences between the two systems appears in the box (below). The Defamation Act 1996, designed mainly to streamline and simplify libel litigation, became fully effective in February 2000.

Libel: liability to pay damages

English law draws a distinction between defamation published in permanent form and that which is not. The former is libel, the latter slander. 'Permanent form' includes writing, printing, drawings and photographs and radio and television broadcasts. It follows that it is the law of libel rather than slander which most concerns writers and artists professionally, and the slightly differing rules applicable to slander will not be mentioned in this article.

Publication of a libel can result in a civil action for damages, an injunction to prevent repetition and/or in certain cases a criminal prosecution against those responsible, who include the author (or artist or photographer), the publishers and the editor, if any, of the publication in which the libel appeared. 'Innocent disseminators', such as printers, distributors, broadcasters, internet service providers and retailers, who can show they took reasonable care and had no reason to believe what they were handling contained a libel, are protected under the 1996 Act. Prosecutions are rare. Certain special rules apply to them and these will be explained below after a discussion of the question of civil liability, which in practice arises much more frequently.

Libel claims do not qualify for legal aid, although the closely analagous remedy of malicious falsehood does. Most libel cases are usually heard by a judge and jury, and it is the jury which decides the amount of any award, which is tax-free. It is not necessary for the plaintiff to prove that he or she has actually suffered any loss, because the law presumes damage. While the main purpose of a libel claim is to compensate

English and Scottish law

Much of the terminology of the Scots law of defamation differs from that of English law, and in certain minor respects the law itself is different. North of the border, libel and slander are virtually indistinguishable, both as to the nature of the wrongs and their consequences; and Scots law does not recognise the offence of criminal libel. Where individual English litigants enjoy absolute privilege for what they say in court, their Scottish counterparts have only qualified privilege. 'Exemplary', or 'punitive', damages are not awarded by the Scottish courts. Until recently, libel cases in Scotland were for the most part heard by judges sitting alone, but there is now a marked trend towards trial by jury, which has been accompanied by a significant increase in the levels of damages awarded.

the plaintiff for the injury to his or her reputation, a jury may give additional sums either as 'aggravated' damages, if it appears a defendant has behaved malevolently or spitefully, or as 'exemplary', or 'punitive', damages where a defendant hopes the economic advantages of publication will outweigh any sum awarded. Damages can also be 'nominal' if the libel complained of is trivial. It is generally very difficult to forecast the amounts juries are likely to award, though awards against newspapers disclose a tendency towards considerable generosity. The Court of Appeal has power to reduce excessive awards of damages.

In an action for damages for libel, it is for the plaintiff to establish that the matter he or she complains of: has been published by the defendant; refers to the plaintiff; is defamatory. If this is done, the plaintiff establishes a *prima facie* case. However, the defendant will escape liability if he or she can show he has a good defence. There are five defences to a libel action. They are: Justification; Fair Comment; Privilege; Offer of Amends: ss. 2–4 of the Defamation Act, 1996; Apology, etc, under the Libel Acts, 1843 and 1845. A libel claim can also become barred under the Limitation Acts, as explained below. These matters must now be examined in detail.

The plaintiff's case

The meaning of 'published'

'Published' in the legal sense means communicated to a person other than the plaintiff. Thus the legal sense is wider than the lay sense but includes it. It follows that the content of a book is published in the legal sense when the manuscript is first sent to the publishing firm just as much as it is when the book is later placed on sale to the public. Subject to the 'innocent dissemination' defence referred to above, both types of publication are sufficient for the purpose of establishing liability for libel, but the law differentiates between them, since the scope of publication can properly be taken into account by the jury in considering the actual amount of damages to award. Material placed on the internet is unquestionably 'published' there, and the extent of publication can be judged by the number of visits made to the relevant website. It should be noted that Internet Service Providers can compel website operators to identify the authors of defamatory material anonymously posted to their discussion boards.

Establishing identity

The plaintiff must also establish that the matter complained of refers to him or her. It is of course by no means necessary to mention a person's name before it is clear that he or she is referred to. Nicknames by which he or she is known or corruptions of his name are just two ways in which his or her identity can be indicated. There are more subtle methods. The sole question is whether the plaintiff is indicated to those who read the matter complained of. In some cases he or she will not be unless it is read in the light of facts known to the reader from other sources, but this is sufficient for the plaintiff's purpose. The test is purely objective and does not depend at all on whether the writer intended to refer to the plaintiff.

It is because it is impossible to establish reference to any individual that generalisations, broadly speaking, are not successfully actionable. To say boldly 'All lawyers are crooks' does not give any single lawyer a cause of action, because the statement does not point a finger at any individual. However, if anyone is named in conjunction with a generalisation, then it may lose its general character and become particular from the context. Again, if one says 'One of the X Committee has been convicted of murder' and the X Committee consists of, say, four persons, it cannot be said that the statement is not actionable because no individual is indicated and it could be referring to any of the committee. This is precisely why it is actionable at the suit of each of them as suspicion has been cast on all.

Determining what is defamatory

It is for the plaintiff to show that the matter complained of is defamatory. What is defamatory is decided by the jury except in the extreme cases where the judge rules that the words cannot bear a defamatory meaning. Various tests have been laid down for determining this. It is sufficient that any one test is satisfied. The basic tests are:

- Does the matter complained of tend to lower the plaintiff in the estimation of society?
- Does it tend to bring him or her into hatred, ridicule, contempt, dislike or disesteem with society?
- Does it tend to make him shunned or avoided or cut off from society? The mere fact that what is published is inaccurate is not enough to involve liability; it is the adverse impact on the plaintiff's reputation that matters. For example, merely to overstate a person's income is not defamatory; but it will be if the context implies he has not fully declared it to the tax authorities.

'Society' means right-thinking members of society generally. It is by reference to such people that the above tests must be applied. A libel action against a newspaper which had stated that the police had taken a statement from the plaintiff failed, notwithstanding that the plaintiff gave evidence that his apparent assistance to the police (which he denied) had brought him into grave disrepute with the underworld. It was not by their wrongheaded standards that the matter fell to be judged.

Further, it is not necessary to imply that the plaintiff is at fault in some way in order to defame him. To say of a woman that she has been raped or of someone that he is insane imputes to them no degree of blame, but nonetheless both statements are defamatory. Lawyers disagree over whether the claim that an individual is 'ugly' is, or could be, defamatory.

Sometimes a defamatory meaning is conveyed by words which on the face of them have no such meaning. 'But Brutus is an honourable man' is an example. If a jury finds that words are meant ironically they will consider this ironical sense when determining whether the words are defamatory. In deciding, therefore, whether or not the words are defamatory, the jury seeks to discover what, without straining the words or putting a perverse construction on them, they will be understood to mean. In some cases this may differ substantially from their literal meaning.

Matter may also be defamatory by innuendo. Strictly so called, an innuendo is a meaning that words acquire by virtue of facts known to the reader but not stated in the passage complained of. Words, quite innocent on the face of them, may acquire a defamatory meaning when read in the light of these facts. For example, where a newspaper published a photograph of a man and a woman, with the caption that they had just announced their engagement, it was held to be defamatory of the man's wife since those who knew that she had cohabited with him were led to the belief that she had done so only as his mistress. The newspaper was unaware that the man was already married, but some of its readers were not. In general, however, imputations of unchastity against members of either sex would today be regarded as far less defamatory than they were in 1929 when this case was decided.

Defences to a libel action

Quite apart from the provisions concerning statutory apologies mentioned below, a swift and well publicised apology will always go some way towards assuaging injured feelings and help reduce an award of damages.

Justification

English law does not protect the reputation that a person either does not or should not possess. Stating the truth therefore does not incur liability, and the plea of justification – namely, that what is complained of is true in substance and in fact – is a complete answer to an action for damages. However, this defence is by no means to be undertaken lightly. For instance, to prove one instance of using bad language will be insufficient to justify the allegation that a person is 'foul-mouthed'. It would be necessary to prove several instances, and the defendant is obliged in most cases to particularise in his pleadings giving details, dates and places. However, the requirement that the truth of every allegation must be proved is not absolute, and is qualified by the 'multiple charge – no worse off' defence. This applies where two or more distinct charges are levelled against a plaintiff, and some of what is said turns out to be inaccurate. If his or her reputation in the light of what is shown to be true is made no worse by the unprovable defamatory allegations – for example, mistaken accusations that a convicted pickpocket and car thief is also a shoplifter – the publisher will be safe. This is the extent of the law's recognition that some individuals are so disreputable as to be beyond redemption by awards of damages regardless of what is said about them. Subject to this, however, it is for the defendant to prove that what he or she has published is true, not for the plaintiff to disprove it, though if he can do so, so much the better for him.

One point requires special mention. It is insufficient for the defendant to prove that he or she has accurately repeated what a third person has written or said or that such statements have gone uncontradicted when made on occasions in the past. If X writes 'Y told me that Z is a liar', it is no defence to an action against X merely to prove that Y did say that. X has given currency to a defamatory statement concerning Z and has so made it his own. His only defence is to prove that Z is a liar by establishing a number of instances of Z's untruthfulness. Nor does it help a defence of justification to prove that the defendant genuinely believed what he or she published to be true. This may, however, form part of a qualified privilege defence (see below), and might well be a complete answer in an action, other than a libel action, based on a false but non-defamatory statement. For such statements do not incur liability in the absence of fraud or malice which, in this context, means a dishonest or otherwise improper motive. Bona fide belief, however, may be relevant to the assessment of damages, even in a libel action.

Special care should be taken in relation to references to a person's convictions, however accurately described. Since the Rehabilitation of Offenders Act, 1974, a person's less serious convictions may become 'spent' and thereafter it may involve liability to refer to them. Reference to the Act and orders thereunder must be made in order to determine the position in any particular case.

Fair comment

It is a defence to prove that what is complained of is fair comment made in good faith and without malice on a matter of public interest. 'Fair' in this context means 'honest'. 'Fair comment' means therefore the expression of the writer's genuinely held opinion. It does not necessarily mean opinion with which the jury agree. Comment may therefore be quite extreme and still be 'fair' in the legal sense. However, if it is utterly perverse the jury may be led to think that no one could have genuinely held such views. In such a case the defence would fail, for the comment could not be honest. 'Malice' here includes the popular sense of personal spite, but covers any dishonest or improper motive.

The defence only applies when what is complained of is comment as distinct from a statement of fact. The line between comment and fact is notoriously difficult to draw in some cases. Comment means a statement of opinion. The facts on which comment is made must be stated together with the comment or be sufficiently indicated with it. This is merely another way of saying that it must be clear that the defamatory statement is one of opinion and not of fact, for which the only defence would be the onerous one of justification. The exact extent to which the facts commented on must be stated or referred to is a difficult question, but some help may be derived in answering it by considering the purpose of the rule, which is to enable the reader to exercise his own judgement and to agree or disagree with the comment. It is quite plain that it is not necessary to state every single detail of the facts. In one case it was sufficient merely to mention the name of one of the Press lords in an article about a newspaper though not one owned by him. He was so well known that to mention his name indicated the substratum of fact commented upon, namely his control of his group of newspapers. No universal rule can be laid down, except that, in general, the fuller the facts set out or referred to with the comment, the better. All these facts must be proved to be true subject, however, to the flexibility of the 'proportionate truth' rule. This means that the defence remains available even if, for example, only three out of five factual claims can be proved true, provided that these three are by themselves sufficient to sustain, and are proportionate to, the fairness of the comment. The impact of the two unproven claims would probably fall to be assessed in accordance with the 'multiple charge – no worse off' rule in justification, set out above.

The defence only applies where the matters commented on are of public interest, i.e. of legitimate concern to the public or a substantial section of it. Thus the conduct of national and local government, international affairs, the administration of justice, etc, are all matters of public interest, whereas other people's private affairs may very well not be, although they undoubtedly interest the public, or provoke curiosity.

In addition, matters of which criticism has been expressly or impliedly invited, such as publicly performed plays and published books, are a legitimate subject of comment. Criticism need not be confined merely to their artistic merit but equally may deal with the attitudes to life and the opinions therein expressed.

It is sometimes said that a man's moral character is never a proper subject of comment for the purpose of this defence. This is certainly true where it is a private individual who is concerned, and some authorities say it is the same in the case of a public figure even though his or her character may be relevant to his or her public life. Again, it may in some cases be exceeding the bounds of fair comment to impute a dishonourable motive to a person, as is frequently done by way of inference from facts. In general, the imputation is a dangerous and potentially expensive practice.

Privilege

Privilege in the law of libel is either 'absolute' or 'qualified', and denotes the two levels of protection from liability afforded, in the public interest, to defamatory statements made on certain occasions. Absolute privilege – where the individual defamed has no remedy whatever – has applied to Parliamentary papers published by the direction of either House, or full republications thereof, since early in the 19th century. Following the implementation of section 14 of the 1996 Defamation Act, this privilege also applies to fair, accurate and contemporaneous reports of public judicial proceedings in the United Kingdom, the European Courts of Justice and Human Rights, and any international criminal tribunal established by the Security Council.

Qualified privilege confers protection provided publication is made only for the reason that the privilege is given and not for some wrongful or indirect motive. In October 1999 the House of Lords extended the defence to protect publications where a defamatory mistake on a matter of public concern has been made by a writer who can show he did his best to uncover the truth. He must show he acted responsibly both in checking his sources and, where appropriate, seeking the potential plaintiff's comments. The precise limits of this defence are not clear, and will only become so as other cases are decided in the future.

The defence also applies, under section 15 of the Act, to fair and accurate reports of public proceedings before a legislature, a court, a government inquiry and an international organisation or conference anywhere in the world, and of certain documents, or extracts from such documents, issued by those bodies. While there is no requirement to correct or publish explanations concerning these reports, such an obligation does arise under section 15 in respect of a separate category of reports of notices issued by various bodies within the European Community and of proceedings of certain bodies or organisations within the United Kingdom. Apart from the Act, such privilege also attaches to extracts from Parliamentary papers and fair and accurate reports of Parliamentary proceedings.

This list of privileged occasions is by no means exhaustive, and the second category may now be expanded by an order of the Lord Chancellor. The privilege defence is extended to the media generally, rather than being restricted, as it was hitherto, simply to newspapers.

Offers of Amends under the 1996 Act

Sections 2, 3 and 4 of the 1996 Act offer a flexible method of nipping in the bud potential libel actions by those who have been unintentionally defamed. The range of libel meanings for which this defence caters is much wider than that previously available. It envisages the payment of damages as well as costs, together with the offer of a correction and apology, and the damages figure will be fixed by a judge if the parties cannot agree. He or she will do this bearing in mind the generosity of the correction and apology, and the extent of its publication. While recourse to this defence excludes reliance on the defences of justification, privilege and fair comment, it offers a considerable incentive to settle complaints and will save substantially on costs.

Apology under 1843 and 1845 Acts

This defence is rarely utilised, since if any condition of it is not fulfilled, the plaintiff must succeed and the only question is the actual amount of damages. It only applies to actions in respect of libels in newspapers and periodicals. The defendant pleads that the libel was inserted without actual malice and without gross negligence and that before the action commenced or as soon afterwards as possible he inserted a full apology in the same newspaper, etc, or had offered to publish it in a newspaper, etc, of the plaintiff's choice, where the original newspaper is published at intervals greater than a week. Further a sum must be paid into court with this defence to compensate the plaintiff.

'Fast-track disposal' procedure

In its recognition of the generally cumbersome nature of libel litigation, the 1996 Act provides a simplified mechanism for dealing with less serious complaints. Sections 8, 9 and 10 enable a judge alone to dismiss unrealistic claims at the outset; and he will also be able to dispose 'summarily' of relatively minor, but well-founded, claims, on the basis of an award of up to £10,000, a declaration that the publication was libellous, an order for an apology and an order forbidding repetition.

Limitation and death

The 1996 Act has reduced from three years to one the period within which a libel action must generally be started if it is not to become 'statute-barred' through lapse of time. But successive and subsequent publications, such as the issue of later editions of the same book, or the sale of surplus copies of an old newspaper, or the failure to remove libellous material from the internet, can give rise to fresh claims.

Civil claims for libel cannot be brought on behalf of the dead. If an individual living plaintiff or defendant in a libel case dies before the jury gives their verdict, the action 'abates', i.e. comes to an end, so far as their involvement is concerned, and no rights arising out of it survive either for or against their personal representatives.

Insurance

For an author, the importance of at least an awareness of this branch of law lies first, in the fact that most book contracts contain a clause enabling the publisher to look to him should any libel claims result; and second, in the increasingly large awards of damages. It is therefore advisable to check what libel insurance a publisher carries, and whether it also covers the author who, if he or she is to have the benefit of it, should always alert the publisher to any potential risk. One company which offers libel insurance for authors is Royal Sun Alliance, Professional and Financial Risks, 4th Floor, Leadenhall Court, Leadenhall Street, London EC3V 1PP (*tel* 020-7283 9000). Premiums start at £1000, and can be substantially higher if the book is tendentious or likely to be controversial. The company generally insists on the author obtaining, and paying for, a legal opinion first. Indemnity limits vary between £50,000 and £1 million, and the author is required to bear at least the first £5000 of any loss. It is worth remembering that 'losses' include legal costs as well as damages, which they can often exceed. Libel insurance can also be obtained through a Lloyds broker.

Criminal liability in libel

Whereas the object of a civil action is to obtain compensation for the wrong done or to prevent repetition, the object of criminal proceedings is to punish the wrongdoer by fine or imprisonment or both. There are four main types of writing which may provoke a prosecution: defamatory libel; obscene publications; sedition and incitement to racial hatred; blasphemous libel.

Defamatory libel

The publication of defamatory matter is in certain circumstances a crime as well as a civil wrong. But whereas the principal object of civil proceedings will normally be to obtain compensation, the principal object of a criminal prosecution will be to secure punishment of the accused, for example by way of a fine. Prosecutions are not frequent, but there have been signs of late of a revival of interest. There are important differences between the rules applicable to criminal libel and its civil counterpart. For example, a criminal libel may be 'published' even though only communicated to the person defamed and may be found to have occurred even where the person defamed is dead, or where only a group of persons but no particular individual has been maligned. During election campaigns, it is an 'illegal practice' to publish false statements about the personal character or conduct of a candidate irrespective of whether they are also defamatory.

Obscene publications

It is an offence to publish obscene matter. By the Obscene Publications Act, 1959, matter is obscene if its effect is such as to tend to deprave and corrupt persons who are likely, having regard to all relevant circumstances, to read, see or hear it. 'To deprave and corrupt' is to be distinguished from 'to shock and disgust'. It is a defence to a prosecution to prove that publication of the matter in question is justified as being for the public good, on the ground that it is in the interests of science, literature, art or learning, or of other objects of general concern. Expert evidence may be given as to its literary, artistic, scientific or other merits. Playwrights, directors and producers should note that the Theatres Act, 1968, though designed to afford similar protection to stage productions, does not necessarily prevent prosecutions for indecency under other statutes.

Sedition/incitement to racial hatred

Writings which tend to destroy the peace of the realm may be prosecuted as being seditious or as amounting to incitement to racial hatred. Seditious writings include those which advocate reform by unconstitutional or violent means or incite contempt or hatred for the monarch or Parliament. These institutions may be criticised stringently, but not in a manner which is likely to lead to insurrection or civil commotion or indeed any physical force. Prosecutions are a rarity, but it should be remembered that writers of matter contemptuous of the House of Commons, though not prosecuted for seditious libel are, from time to time, punished by that House for breach of its privileges, although, if a full apology is made, it is often an end of the matter. The Public Order Act 1986 makes it an offence, irrespective of the author's or publisher's intention, to publish, or put on plays containing, threatening, abusive or insulting matter if hatred is likely to be stirred up against any racial group in Great Britain.

Blasphemous libel

Blasphemous libel consists in the vilification of the Christian religion or its ceremonies. Other religions are not protected. The offence lies essentially in the impact of what is said concerning, for instance, God, Christ, the Bible, the Book of Common Prayer, etc; it is irrelevant that the publisher does not intend to shock or arouse resentment. While temperate and sober writings on religious topics however anti-Christian in sentiment will not involve liability, if the discussion is 'so scurrilous and offensive as to pass the limit of decent controversy and to outrage any Christian feeling', it will.

Antony Whitaker OBE, a barrister, is Legal Consultant to City solicitors Theodore Goddard & Co.

Finance for writers and artists

FAQs for writers

***Peter Vaines**, a chartered accountant and barrister, addresses some questions frequently asked by writers.*

What can a working writer claim against tax?

A working writer is carrying on a business and can therefore claim all the expenses which are incurred wholly and exclusively for the purposes of that business. A list showing most of the usual expenses is contained on page 666 of this *Yearbook* but there will be other expenses which can be allowed in special circumstances.

Strictly, only expenses which are incurred for the sole purpose of the business can be claimed; there must be no 'duality of purpose' so an item of expenditure cannot be divided into private and business parts. However, the Inland Revenue is usually quite flexible and is prepared to allow all reasonable expenses (including apportioned sums) where the amounts can be commercially justified.

Allowances can also be claimed for the cost of business assets such as a motor car, personal computers, fax, copying machines and all other equipment (including books) which may be used by the writer. An allowance of 25% of the cost can be claimed on the reducing balance each year and for most assets (except cars) an allowance of 40% can be claimed in the first year of purchase. Some expenditure on information technology now benefits from a special 100% allowance. Further details of the deductions available in respect of capital expenditure may be found on page 667.

Can I request interest on fees owed to me beyond 30 days of my invoice?

Yes. A writer is like any other person carrying on a business and is entitled to charge interest at a rate of 8% over bank base rate on any debt outstanding for more than 30 days – although the period of credit can be varied by agreement between the parties. It is not compulsory to claim the interest; it is up to you to decide whether to enforce the right.

What can I do about bad debts?

A writer is in exactly the same position as anybody else carrying on a business over the payment of his or her invoices. It is generally not commercially sensible to insist on payment in advance but where the work involved is substantial (which will normally be the case with a book), it is usual to receive one third of the fee on signature, one third of the fee on delivery of the manuscript and the remaining one third on publication. On other assignments, perhaps not as substantial as a book, it could be worthwhile seeking 50% of the fee on signature and the other 50% on delivery. This would provide a degree of protection in case of cancellation of the assignment because of changes of policy or personnel at the publisher.

What financial disputes can I take to the Small Claims Court?

If somebody owes you money you can take them to the Small Claims Court, which deals with financial disputes up to £5000. The procedure is much less formal than normal court proceedings and involves little expense. It is not necessary to have a solicitor. You fill in a number of forms, turn up on the day and explain the background to why you are owed the money. Full details of the procedure can be found on:

www.courtservice.gov.uk.

If I receive an advance, can I divide it between two tax years?

Yes. There used to be a system known as 'spreading' but in 2001 a new system called 'averaging' was introduced. This enables writers (and others engaged in the creation of literary, dramatic works or designs) to average the profits of two or more consecutive years if the profits for one year are less than 75% of the profits for the highest year. This relief will apply even if the work takes less than 12 months to create. Both the spreading relief and the averaging relief allow the writer to avoid the higher rates of tax which might arise if the income in respect of a number of years' work were all to be concentrated in a single year.

How do I make sure I am taxed as a self-employed person so that tax and National Insurance Contributions are not deducted at source?

To be taxed as a self-employed person under Schedule D you have to make sure that the contract for the writing cannot be regarded as a contract of employment. This is unlikely to be the case with a professional author. The subject is highly complex but the most important feature is that the publisher must not be in a position to direct or control the author's work. Where any doubt exists, the author might find the publisher deducting tax and National Insurance Contributions as a precaution and that would clearly be highly disadvantageous. The author would be well advised to discuss the position with the publisher before the contract is signed to agree that he or she should be treated as self employed and that no tax or National Insurance Contributions will be deducted from any payments. If such agreement cannot be reached, professional advice should immediately be sought so that the detailed technical position can be explained to the publisher.

Is it a good idea to operate through a limited company?

It can be a good idea for a self-employed writer to operate through a company but generally only where the income is quite large. The costs of operating a company would certainly outweigh any benefit if the writer is paying tax only at the basic rate. Where the writer is paying tax at the higher rate of 40%, being able to retain some of the income in a company at a tax rate of only 19% is obviously attractive. However, this will be entirely ineffective if the writer's contract with the publisher would otherwise be an employment. The whole subject of operating through a company is complex and professional advice is essential.

When does it become necessary to register for VAT?

Where the writer's self-employed income (from all sources, not only writing) exceeds £55,000 in the previous 12 months or is expected to do so in the next 30 days, he or she must register for VAT and add VAT to all his/her fees. The publisher will pay the VAT to the writer, who must pay the VAT over to the Customs and Excise each quarter. Any VAT the writer has paid on business expenses and on the purchase of business assets can be deducted. It will be possible for some authors to take advantage of a new simplified system for VAT payments which applies to small businesses. This involves a flat rate payment of VAT without any need to keep records of VAT on expenses.

If I make a loss from my writing can I get any tax back?

Where a writer makes a loss, the Inland Revenue may suggest that the writing is only a hobby and not a professional activity thereby denying any relief or tax deduction for the loss. However, providing the writing is carried out on a sensible commercial basis with an expectation of profits, any resulting loss can be offset against any other income the writer may have for the same or the previous year.

Peter Vaines FCA, ATII, barrister, is a partner in the international law firm of Haarmann Hemmelrath and writes and speaks widely on tax matters. He is Managing Editor of *Personal Tax Planning Review*, on the Editorial Board of *Taxation*, and tax columnist of *Accountancy* and *New Law Journal*.

Income tax

Despite attempts by successive Governments to simplify our taxation system, the subject has become increasingly complicated. ***Peter Vaines****, a chartered accountant and barrister, gives a broad outline of taxation from the point of view of writers and other creative professionals. The proposals in the April 2002 Budget are broadly reflected in this article.*

How income is taxed

Generally

Authors are usually treated for tax purposes as carrying on a profession and are taxed in a similar fashion to other professionals, i.e. as self-employed persons assessable under Schedule D. This article is directed to self-employed persons only, because if a writer is employed he or she will be subject to the rules of Schedule E where different considerations apply – substantially to his or her disadvantage.

Attempts are often made by employed persons to shake off the status of 'employee' and to attain 'freelance' status so as to qualify for the advantages of Schedule D, such attempts meeting with varying degrees of success. The problems involved in making this transition are considerable and space does not permit a detailed explanation to be made here – individual advice is necessary if difficulties are to be avoided.

Particular attention has been paid by the Inland Revenue to journalists and to those engaged in the entertainment industry with a view to reclassifying them as employees so that PAYE is deducted from their earnings. This blanket treatment has been extended to other areas and, although it is obviously open to challenge by individual taxpayers, it is always difficult to persuade the Inland Revenue to change its views.

There is no reason why employed people cannot carry on a freelance business in their spare time. Indeed, aspiring authors, painters, musicians, etc, often derive so little income from their craft that the financial security of an employment, perhaps in a different sphere of activity, is necessary. The existence of the employment is irrelevant to the taxation of the freelance earnings although it is most important not to confuse the income or expenditure of the employment with the income or expenditure of the self-employed activity. The Inland Revenue is aware of the advantages which can be derived by an individual having 'freelance' income from an organisation of which he or she is also an employee, and where such circumstances are contrived, it can be extremely difficult to convince an Inspector of Taxes that a genuine freelance activity is being carried on. Where the individual operates through a company or partnership providing services personally to a particular client, and would be regarded as an employee if the services were supplied directly by the individual, additional problems arise from the notorious IR35 legislation and professional advice is essential.

For those starting in business or commencing work on a freelance basis the Inland Revenue produces a very useful booklet, *Starting in Business (IR28)*, which is available from any tax office.

Income

For income to be taxable it need not be substantial, nor even the author's only source of income; earnings from casual writing are also taxable but this can be an advantage, because occasional writers do not often make a profit from their writing. The expenses incurred in connection with writing may well exceed any income receivable and the resultant loss may then be used to reclaim tax paid on other income. There may be deducted from the income certain allowable expenses and capital allowances which are set out in more detail below. The possibility of a loss being used as a basis for a tax repayment is fully appreciated by the Inland Revenue, which sometimes attempts to treat casual writing as a hobby so that any losses incurred cannot be used to reclaim tax; of course by the same token any income receivable would not be chargeable to tax. This treatment may sound attractive but it should be resisted vigorously because the Inland Revenue does not hesitate to change its mind when profits begin to arise. In the case of exceptional or non-recurring writing, such as the autobiography of a sports personality or the memoirs of a politician, it could be better to be treated as pursuing a hobby and not as a professional author. Sales of copyright cannot be charged to income tax unless the recipient is a professional author. However, the proceeds of sale of copyright may be charged to capital gains tax, even by an individual who is not a professional author.

Royalties

Where the recipient is a professional author, a series of cases has laid down a clear principle that sales of copyright are taxable as income and not as capital receipts. Similarly, lump sums on account of, or in advance of royalties are also taxable as income in the year of receipt, subject to a claim for spreading relief (see below).

Copyright royalties are generally paid without deduction of income tax. However, if royalties are paid to a person who normally lives abroad, tax will be deducted by the payer or his agent at the time the payment is made unless arrangements are made with the Inland Revenue for payments to be made gross under the terms of a Double Taxation Agreement with the other country.

Arts Council category A awards

- Direct or indirect musical, design or choreographic commissions and direct or indirect commission of sculpture and paintings for public sites.
- The Royalty Supplement Guarantee Scheme.
- The contract writers' scheme.
- Jazz bursaries.
- Translators' grants.
- Photographic awards and bursaries.
- Film and video awards and bursaries.
- Performance Art Awards.
- Art Publishing Grants.
- Grants to assist with a specific project or projects (such as the writing of a book) or to meet specific professional expenses such as a contribution towards copying expenses made to a composer or to an artist's studio expenses.

Arts Council grants

Persons in receipt of grants from the Arts Council or similar bodies will be concerned whether or not such grants are liable to income tax. The Inland Revenue has issued a Statement of Practice after detailed discussions with the Arts Council regarding the tax treatment of such awards. Grants and other receipts of a similar nature have now been divided into two categories (see boxes) – those which are to be treated by the Inland Revenue as chargeable to tax and those which are not. Category A awards are considered to be taxable; awards made under category B are not chargeable to tax.

This Statement of Practice has no legal force and is used merely to ease the administration of the tax system. It is open to anyone in receipt of a grant or award to disregard the agreed statement and challenge the Inland Revenue view on the merits of their particular case. However, it must be recognised that the Inland Revenue does not issue such statements lightly and any challenge to their view would almost certainly involve a lengthy and expensive action through the Courts.

The tax position of persons in receipt of

Arts Council category B awards

- Bursaries to trainee directors.
- Bursaries for associate directors.
- Bursaries to people attending full-time courses in arts administration (the practical training course).
- In-service bursaries to theatre designers and bursaries to trainees on the theatre designers' scheme.
- In-service bursaries for administrators.
- Bursaries for actors and actresses.
- Bursaries for technicians and stage managers.
- Bursaries made to students attending the City University Arts Administration courses.
- Awards, known as the Buying Time Awards, made not to assist with a specific project or professional expenses but to maintain the recipient to enable him or her to take time off to develop his personal talents. These at present include the awards and bursaries known as the Theatre Writing Bursaries, awards and bursaries to composers, awards and bursaries to painters, sculptures and print makers, literature awards and bursaries.

literary prizes will generally follow a decision by the Special Commissioners in connection with the Whitbread Literary Award. In that case it was decided that the prize was not part of the author's professional income and accordingly not chargeable to tax. The precise details are not available because decisions of the Special Commissioners were not, at that time, reported unless an appeal was made to the High Court; the Inland Revenue chose not to appeal against this decision. Details of the many literary awards which are given each year start on page 512, and this decision is of considerable significance to the winners of each of these prizes. It would be unwise to assume that all such awards will be free of tax as the precise facts which were present in the case of the Whitbread award may not be repeated in another case; however it is clear that an author winning a prize has some very powerful arguments in his or her favour, should the Inland Revenue seek to charge tax on the award.

Allowable expenses

To qualify as an allowable business expense, expenditure has to be laid out wholly and exclusively for business purposes. Strictly there must be no 'duality of purpose', which means that expenditure cannot be apportioned to reflect the private and business usage, e.g. food, clothing, telephone, travelling expenses, etc. However, the Inland Revenue does not usually interpret this principle strictly and is prepared to allow all reasonable expenses (including apportioned sums) where the amounts can be commercially justified.

It should be noted carefully that the expenditure does not have to be 'necessary', it merely has to be incurred 'wholly and exclusively' for business purposes. Naturally, however, expenditure of an outrageous and wholly unnecessary character might well give rise to a presumption that it was not really for business purposes. As with all things, some expenses are unquestionably allowable and some expenses are equally unquestionably not allowable – it is the grey area in between which gives rise to all the difficulties and the outcome invariably depends on negotiation with the Inland Revenue.

Great care should be taken when claiming a deduction for items where there is a 'duality of purpose' and negotiations should be conducted with more than usual care and courtesy – if provoked the Inspector of Taxes may well choose to allow nothing. An appeal is always possible although unlikely to succeed as a string of cases in the Courts has clearly demonstrated. An example is the case of *Caillebotte* v. *Quinn* where the taxpayer (who normally had lunch at home) sought to claim the excess cost of meals incurred because he was working a long way from his home. The taxpayer's arguments failed because he did not eat only in order to work, one of the reasons for his eating was in order to sustain his life; a duality of purpose therefore existed and no tax relief was due.

Other cases have shown that expenditure on clothing can also be disallowed if it is the kind of clothing which is in everyday use, because clothing is worn not only to assist

Allowable expenses

(a) Cost of all materials used up in the course of preparation of the work.
(b) Cost of typewriting and secretarial assistance, etc; if this or other help is obtained from one's spouse then it is entirely proper for a deduction to be claimed for the amounts paid for the work. The amounts claimed must actually be paid to the spouse and should be at the market rate although some uplift can be made for unsocial hours, etc. Payments to a wife (or husband) are of course taxable in her (or his) hands and should therefore be most carefully considered. The wife's earnings may also be liable for National Insurance contributions and it is important to take care because otherwise you may find that these contributions may outweigh the tax savings. The impact of the National Minimum Wage should also be considered.
(c) All expenditure on normal business items such as postage, stationery, telephone, email, fax and answering machines, agent's fees, accountancy charges, photography, subscriptions, periodicals, magazines, etc, may be claimed. The cost of daily papers should not be overlooked if these form part of research material. Visits to theatres, cinemas, etc, for research purposes may also be permissible (but not the cost relating to guests). Unfortunately, expenditure on all types of business entertaining is specifically denied tax relief.
(d) If work is conducted at home, a deduction for 'use of home' is usually allowed providing the amount claimed is reasonable. If the claim is based on an appropriate proportion of the total costs of rent, light and heat, cleaning and maintenance, insurance, etc (but not the Council Tax), care should be taken to ensure that no single room is used 'exclusively' for business purposes, because this may result in the Capital Gains Tax exemption on the house as the only or main residence being partially forfeited. However, it would be a strange household where one room was in fact used exclusively for business purposes and for no other purpose whatsoever (e.g. storing personal bank statements and other private papers); the usual formula is to claim a deduction on the basis that most or all of the rooms in the house are used at one time or another for business purposes, thereby avoiding any suggestion that any part was used exclusively for business purposes.
(e) The appropriate business proportion of motor running expenses may also be claimed although what is the appropriate proportion will naturally depend on the particular circumstances of each case; it should be mentioned that the well-known scale benefits, whereby one is taxed according to the size and cost of the car, do not apply to self-employed persons.
(f) It has been long established that the cost of travelling from home to work (whether employed or self-employed) is not an allowable expense. However, if home is one's place of work then no expenditure under this heading is likely to be incurred and difficulties are unlikely to arise.
(g) Travelling and hotel expenses incurred for business purposes will normally be allowed but if any part could be construed as disguised holiday or pleasure expenditure, considerable thought would need to be given to the commercial reasons for the journey in order to justify the claim. The principle of 'duality of purpose' will always be a difficult hurdle in this connection – although not insurmountable.
(h) If a separate business bank account is maintained, any overdraft interest thereon will be an allowable expense. This is the only circumstance in which overdraft interest is allowed for tax purposes and care should be taken to avoid overdrafts in all other circumstances.
(i) Where capital allowances (see page 667) are claimed for a personal computer, fax, modem, television, video, CD or tape player, etc, used for business purposes the costs of maintenance and repair of the equipment may also be claimed.

the pursuit of one's profession but also to accord with public decency. This duality of purpose may be sufficient to deny relief – even where the particular type of clothing is of a kind not otherwise worn by the taxpayer. In the case of *Mallalieu* v. *Drummond* a lady barrister failed to obtain a tax deduction for items of sombre clothing purchased specifically for wearing in Court. The House of Lords decided that a duality of purpose existed because clothing represented part of her needs as a human being.

Despite the above, Inspectors of Taxes are not usually inflexible and the expenses listed in the box (above) are among those generally allowed. Clearly many other allowable items may be claimed in addition to those listed. Wherever there is any reasonable business motive for some expenditure it should be claimed as a deduction although it is necessary to preserve all records relating to the expense. It is sensible to avoid an excess of imagination as this would naturally cause the Inspector of Taxes to doubt the genuineness of other expenses claimed.

The question is often raised whether the whole amount of an expense may be deducted or whether the VAT content must be excluded. Where VAT is reclaimed from the Customs and Excise (on the quarterly returns made by a registered person), the VAT element of the expense cannot be treated as an allowable deduction. Where the VAT is not reclaimed, the whole expense (inclusive of VAT) is allowable for income tax purposes.

Capital allowances

Allowances

Where expenditure of a capital nature is incurred, it cannot be deducted from income as an expense – a separate and sometimes more valuable capital allowance being available instead. Capital allowances are given for many different types of expenditure, but authors and similar professional people are likely to claim only for 'plant and machinery'; this is a very wide expression which may include motor cars, personal computers, fax and photocopying machines, modems, televisions, CD, video and cassette players used for business purposes, books – and even a horse! Plant and machinery generally qualify for a 40% allowance in the year of purchase and 25% of the reducing balance in subsequent years. Expenditure on information technology for the purposes of the business now benefits from a special 100% allowance in the year of purchase. Where the useful life of an asset is expected to be short, it is possible to claim special treatment as a 'short life asset' enabling the allowances to be accelerated.

The reason these allowances can be more valuable than allowable expenses is that they may be wholly or partly disclaimed in any year that full benefit cannot be obtained – ordinary business expenses cannot be similarly disclaimed. Where, for example, the income of an author does not exceed his personal allowances, he would not be liable to tax and a claim for capital allowances would be wasted. If the capital allowances were to be disclaimed their benefit would be carried forward for use in subsequent years. Careful planning with claims for capital allowances is therefore essential if maximum benefit is to be obtained.

As an alternative to capital allowances, claims can be made on the 'renewals' basis whereby all renewals are treated as allowable deductions in the year; no allowance is obtained for the initial purchase, but the cost of replacement (excluding any improvement element) is allowed in full. This basis is no longer widely used, as it is considerably less advantageous than claiming capital allowances as described above.

Leasing is a popular method of acquiring fixed assets, and where cash is not available to enable an outright purchase to be made, assets may be leased over a period of time. Whilst leasing may have financial benefits in certain circumstances, in normal cases there is likely to be no tax advantage in leasing an asset where the alternative of outright purchase is available. Indeed, leasing can be a positive disadvantage in the case of motor cars with a new retail price of more than £12,000. If such a car is leased, only a proportion of the leasing charges will be tax deductible.

Books

The question of whether the cost of books is eligible for tax relief has long been a source of difficulty. The annual cost of replacing books used for the purposes of one's professional activities (e.g. the cost of a new *Writers' & Artists' Yearbook* each year) has always been an allowable expense; the difficulty arose because the initial cost of reference books, etc (e.g. when commencing one's profession) was treated as capital expenditure but no allowances were due as the books were not considered to be 'plant'. However, the matter was clarified by the case of *Munby* v. *Furlong* in which the Court of Appeal decided that the initial cost of law books purchased by a barrister was expenditure on 'plant' and eligible for capital allowances. This is clearly a most important decision, particularly relevant to any person who uses expensive books in the course of exercising his or her profession.

Pension contributions

Personal pensions

Where a self-employed person pays annual premiums under an approved personal pension policy, tax relief may now be obtained each year for the following amounts:

Age at 6/4/2002	Maximum %
35 and under	17.5% (max) £17,010
36 – 45	20% (max) £19,440
46 – 50	25% (max) £24,300
51 – 55	30% (max) £29,160
56 – 60	35% (max) £34,020
61 – 74	40% (max) £38,880

These figures do not apply to existing retirement annuity policies; these remain subject to the old limits which are unchanged.

These arrangements can be extremely advantageous in providing for a pension as premiums are usually paid when the income is high (and the tax relief is also high) and the pension (taxed as earned income when received) usually arises when the income is low and little tax is payable. There is also the opportunity to take part of the pension entitlement as a tax-free lump sum. The reduction in the rates of income tax to a maximum of 40% makes this decision a little more difficult because the tax advantages could go into reverse. When the pension is paid it could, if rates rise again, be taxed at a higher rate than the rate of tax relief at the moment. One would be deferring income in order to pay more tax on it later. However, this involves a large element of guesswork, and many people will be content simply with the long-term pension benefits.

From 6 April 2001 the Stakeholder pension rules came into force allowing payment of up to £3600 to be paid into a Stakeholder pension without the need for any earnings.

Class 4 NI contributions

Allied to pensions is the payment of Class 4 National Insurance contributions, although no pension or other benefit is obtained by the contributions; the Class 4 contributions are designed solely to extract additional amounts from self-employed persons and are payable in addition to the normal Class 2 (self-employed) contributions. The rates are changed each year and for 2002/03 self-employed persons will be obliged to contribute 7% of their profits between the range £4615–£30,420 per annum, a maximum liability of £1806 for 2002/03. This amount is collected in conjunction with the Schedule D income tax liability.

From 6 April 2003 the rate of NIC will go up to 8% and there will be a further 1% charge on the whole of the earnings to correspond with the increase in employees' contributions.

Spreading relief

Relief for copyright payments

For many years special provisions have enabled authors and similar persons engaged on a literary, dramatic, musical or artistic work for a period of more than 12 months, to spread certain amounts received over two or three years depending on the time spent in preparing the work. If the author was engaged on the work for a period exceeding 12 months, the receipt may be spread backwards over two years; if the author was engaged on the work for more than 24 months, the receipt may be spread backwards over three years. (Analogous provisions applied to sums received for the sale of a painting, sculpture or other work of art.) The relief applied to:

- lump sums received on the assignment of copyright, in whole or in part;
- sums received on the grant of any interest in the copyright by licence;
- non-returnable advances on account of royalties;
- any receipts of or on account of royalties or any periodical sums received within two years of first publication.

A claim for spreading relief had to be made within eight years from 5 April following the date of first publication.

Where copyright was assigned (or a licence in it was granted) more than 10 years after the first publication of the work, then the amounts received could qualify for a different spreading relief. The assignment (or licence) must have been for a period of more than two years and the receipt was spread forward over the number of years for which the assignment (or licence) was granted – but with a maximum of six years. The relief was terminated by death, but there were provisions enabling the deceased author's personal representatives to re-spread the amounts if it was to the beneficiaries' advantage.

The above rules were arbitrary and cumbersome, only providing a limited measure of relief in special circumstances. The provisions could sometimes be helpful to repair matters when consideration of the tax position had been neglected.

This system was replaced on 6 April 2001 by a new system of averaging which is simpler. Under these new rules, professional authors and artists engaged in the creation of literary, dramatic works or designs will be able to make a claim to average the profits of two or more consecutive years if the profits for one year are less than 75% of the profits for the highest year. This new relief will apply even if the work took less than 12 months to create and will be available to people who create works in partnership with others.

The purpose of the relief (and of the previous spreading relief) is to enable the creative artist to utilise his allowances fully and to avoid the higher rates of tax which might apply if all the income were to arise in a single year.

Collection of tax

Self-assessment

In 1997, the system of sending in a tax return showing all your income and the Inland Revenue raising an assessment to collect the tax was abolished. So was the idea that you pay tax on your profits for the preceding year. Now, when you send in your tax return you have to work out your own tax liability and send a cheque; this is called 'self-assessment'. If you get it wrong, or if you are late with your tax return or the payment of tax, interest and penalties will be charged.

Under this new system, the Inland Revenue will rarely issue assessments; they are no longer necessary because the idea is that you assess yourself. A new colour-coded tax return is issued, designed to help individuals meet their new tax obligations. This is a daunting task but the term 'self-assessment' is not intended to imply that individuals have to do it themselves; they can (and often will) engage professional help. The term is only intended to convey that it is the taxpayer, and not the Inland Revenue, who is responsible for getting the tax liability right and for it to be paid on time.

The deadline for sending in the tax return is 31 January following the end of the tax year; so for the tax year 2002/03, the tax return has to be submitted to the Inland Revenue by 31 January 2004. If for some reason you are unwilling or unable to calculate the tax payable, you can ask the Inland Revenue to do it for you, in which case it is necessary to send in your tax return by 30 September 2003.

Income tax on self-employed earnings remains payable in two instalments but the payment dates have been moved to 31 January and 31 July each year. Because the accurate figures may not necessarily be known, these payments in January and July will therefore be only payments on account based on the previous year's liability. The final balancing figure will be paid the following 31 January together with the first instalment of the liability for the following year.

When the Inland Revenue receives the self-assessment tax return, it is checked to see if there is anything obviously wrong; if there is, a letter will be sent to you immediately. Otherwise, the Inland Revenue has 12 months from the filing date of 31 January in which to make further enquiries; if it doesn't, it will have no further opportunity to do so and your tax liabilities are final – unless there is something seriously wrong such as the omission of income or capital gains. In that event, the Inland Revenue will raise an assessment later to collect any extra tax together with appropriate penalties. It is essential for the operation of the new system that all records relevant to your tax returns are retained for at least 12 months in case they are needed by the Inland Revenue. For the self-employed, the record-keeping requirement is much more onerous because the records need to be kept for nearly six years. One important change in the rules is that if you claim a tax deduction for an expense, it will be necessary to have a receipt or other document proving that the expenditure has been made. Because the existence of the underlying records is so important to the operation of self-assessment, the Inland Revenue treats them very seriously and there is a penalty of £3000 for any failure to keep adequate records.

Interest

Interest is chargeable on overdue tax at a variable rate, which at the time of writing is 6.5% per annum. It does not rank for any tax relief, which can make the Inland Revenue an expensive source of credit.

However, the Inland Revenue can also be obliged to pay interest (known as repayment supplement) tax-free where repayments are delayed. The rules relating to repayment supplement are less beneficial and even more complicated than the rules for interest payable but they do exist and can be very welcome if a large repayment has been delayed for a long time. Unfortunately, the rate of repayment supplement is only 2.5%, much lower than the rate of interest on unpaid tax.

Value added tax

The activities of writers, painters, composers, etc, are all 'taxable supplies' within the scope of VAT and chargeable at the standard rate. (Zero rating which applies to publishers, booksellers, etc on the supply of books does not extend to the work performed by writers.) Accordingly, authors are obliged to register for VAT if their income for the past 12 months exceeds £55,000 or if their income for the coming month will exceed that figure.

Delay in registering can be a most serious matter because if registration is not effected at the proper time, the Customs and Excise can (and invariably do) claim VAT from all the income received since the date on which registration should have been made. As no VAT would have been included in the amounts received during this period the amount claimed by the Customs and Excise must inevitably come straight from the pocket of the author.

The author may be entitled to seek reimbursement of the VAT from those whom he or she ought to have charged VAT but this is obviously a matter of some difficulty and may indeed damage his commercial relationships. Apart from these disadvantages there is also a penalty for late registration. The rules are extremely harsh and are imposed automatically even in cases of innocent error. It is therefore extremely important to monitor the income very carefully because if in any period of 12 months the income exceeds the £55,000 limit, the Customs and Excise must be notified within 30 days of the end of the period. Failure to do so will give rise to an automatic penalty. It should be emphasised that this is a penalty for failing to submit a form and has nothing to do with any real or potential loss of tax. Furthermore, whether the failure was innocent or deliberate will not matter. Only the existence of a 'reasonable excuse' will be a defence to the penalty. However, a reasonable excuse does not include ignorance, error, a lack of funds or reliance on any third party.

However, it is possible to regard VAT registration as a privilege and not a penalty, because only VAT registered persons can reclaim VAT paid on their expenses such as stationery, telephone, professional fees, etc, and even typewriters and other plant and machinery (excluding cars). However, many find that the administrative inconvenience – the cost of maintaining the necessary records and completing the necessary forms – more than outweighs the benefits to be gained from registration and prefer to stay outside the scope of VAT for as long as possible.

Overseas matters

The general observation may be made that self-employed persons resident and domiciled in the United Kingdom are not well treated with regard to their overseas work, being taxable on their worldwide income. It is important to emphasise that if fees are earned abroad, no tax saving can be achieved merely by keeping the money outside the country. Although exchange control regulations no longer exist to require repatriation of foreign earnings, such income remains taxable in the UK and must be disclosed to the Inland Revenue; the same applies to interest or other income arising on any investment of these earnings overseas. Accordingly, whenever foreign earnings are likely to become substantial, prompt and effective action is required to limit the impact of UK and foreign taxation. In the case of non-resident authors it is important that arrangements concerning writing for publication in the UK, e.g. in newspapers, are undertaken with great care. A case concerning the wife of one of the great train robbers who provided detailed information for a series of articles in a Sunday newspaper is most instructive. Although she was acknowledged to be resident in Canada for all the relevant years, the income from the articles was treated as arising in this country and fully chargeable to UK tax.

The United Kingdom has double taxation agreements with many other countries and these agreements are designed to ensure that income arising in a foreign country is taxed either in that country or in the UK. Where a withholding tax is deducted from payments received from another country (or where tax is paid in full in the absence of a double taxation agreement), the amount of foreign tax paid can usually be set off against the related UK tax liability. Many successful authors can be found living in Eire because of the complete exemption from tax which attaches to works of cultural or artistic merit by persons who are resident there. However, such a step should only be contemplated having careful regard to all the other domestic and commercial considerations and specialist advice is essential if the exemption is to be obtained and kept; a careless breach of the conditions could cause the exemption to be withdrawn with catastrophic consequences.

Further information concerning the precise conditions to be satisfied for exemption for tax in Eire can be obtained from the Revenue Commissioners, Blocks 3–10, Dublin Castle, Dublin 2, or from their website (www.revenue.ie).

Companies

When an author becomes successful the prospect of paying tax at the higher rate may drive him or her to take hasty action such as the formation of companies, etc, which may not always be to his advantage. Indeed some authors seeing the exodus into tax exile of their more successful colleagues even form companies in low tax areas in the naive expectation of saving large amounts of tax. The Inland Revenue is fully aware of the opportunities and have extensive powers to charge tax and combat avoidance. Accordingly, such action is just as likely to increase tax liabilities and generate other costs and should never be contemplated without expert advice; some very expensive mistakes are often made in this area which are not always able to be remedied.

To conduct one's business through the medium of a company can be a most effective method of mitigating tax liabilities, and providing it is done at the right time and under the right circumstances very substantial advantages can be derived. However, if done without due care and attention the intended advantages will simply evaporate. At the very least it is essential to ensure that the company's business is genuine and conducted properly with regard to the realities of the situation. If the author continues his or her activities unchanged, simply paying all the receipts from his work into a company's bank account, he cannot expect to persuade the Inland Revenue that it is the company and not himself who is entitled to, and should be assessed to tax on, that income.

It must be strongly emphasised that many pitfalls exist which can easily eliminate all the tax benefits expected to arise by the formation of the company. For example, company directors are employees of the company and will be liable to pay much higher National Insurance contributions; the company must also pay the employer's proportion of the contribution and a total liability of over 20% of gross salary may arise. This compares most unfavourably with the position of a self-employed person. Moreover, on the commencement of the company's business the individual's profession will cease and the possibility of revisions being made by the Inland Revenue to earlier tax liabilities means that the timing of a change has to be considered very carefully.

The tax return

No mention has been made above of personal reliefs and allowances; this is because these allowances and the rates of tax are subject to constant change and are always set out in detail in the explanatory notes which accompany the Tax Return. The annual Tax Return is an important document and should be completed promptly with extreme care, particularly since the introduction of self-assessment. If filling in the Return is a source of difficulty or anxiety, comfort may be found in the Consumer Association's publication *Money Which? – Tax Saving Guide*; this is published in March of each year and includes much which is likely to be of interest and assistance.

Peter Vaines FCA, ATII, barrister, is a partner in the international law firm of Haarmann Hemmelrath and writes and speaks widely on tax matters. He is Managing Editor of *Personal Tax Planning Review*, on the Editorial Board of *Taxation*, and tax columnist of *Accountancy* and *New Law Journal*.

Social security contributions

*In general, every individual who works in Great Britain either as an employee or as a self-employed person is liable to pay social security contributions. The law governing this subject is complicated and **Peter Arrowsmith** FCA gives here a summary of the position. This article should be regarded as a general guide only.*

All contributions are payable in respect of years ending on 5 April. See box for the classes of contributions.

Employed or self-employed?

The question as to whether a person is employed under a contract *of* service and is thereby an employee liable to Class 1 contributions, or performs services (either solely or in partnership) under a contract *for* service and is thereby self-employed liable to Class 2 and Class 4 contributions, often has to be decided in practice. One of the best guides can be found in the case of *Market Investigations Ltd* v. *Minister of Social Security* (1969 2 WLR 1) when Cooke J. remarked:

'... the fundamental test to be applied is this: "Is the person who has engaged himself to perform these services performing them as a person in business on his own account?" If the answer to that question is "yes", then the contract is a contract for services. If the answer is "no", then the contract is a contract of service. No exhaustive list has been compiled and perhaps no exhaustive list can be compiled of the considerations which are relevant in determining that question, nor can strict rules be laid down as to the relative weight which the various considerations should carry in particular cases. The most that can be said is that control will no doubt always have to be considered, although it can no longer be regarded as the sole determining factor; and that factors which may be of importance are such matters as:

- whether the man performing the services provides his own equipment,
- whether he hires his own helpers,
- what degree of financial risk he takes,
- what degree of responsibility for investment and management he has, and
- whether and how far he has an opportunity of profiting from sound management in the performance of his task.'

The above case has often been considered subsequently – notably in November 1993 by the Court of Appeal in the case of *Hall* v. *Lorimer*. In this case a vision mixer with around 20 clients and undertaking around 120–150 separate engagements per annum was held to be self-employed. This follows the, perhaps surprising, contention of the Inland Revenue that the taxpayer was an employee.

Further guidance

There have been three cases dealing with musicians, in relatively recent times, which provide further guidance on the question as to whether an individual is employed or self-employed.

- ***Midland Sinfonia Concert Society Ltd* v. *Secretary of State for Social Services* (1981 ICR 454).** A musician, employed to play in an orchestra by separate invitation at irregular intervals and remunerated solely in respect of each occasion upon which he does play, is employed under a contract for services. He is therefore self-employed, not an employed earner, for the purposes of the Social Security Contributions and Benefits Act 1992, and the orchestra which engages him is not

Classes of contributions

Class 1 These are payable by employees (primary contributions) and their employers (secondary contributions) and are based on earnings.
Class 1A Payable only by employers in respect of all taxable benefits in kind (cars and fuel only prior to 6 April 2000).
Class 1B Payable only by employers in respect of PAYE Settlement Agreements entered into by them.
Class 2 These are weekly flat rate contributions, payable by the self-employed.
Class 3 These are weekly flat rate. contributions, payable on a voluntary basis in order to provide, or make up entitlement to, certain social security benefits.
Class 4 These are payable by the self-employed in respect of their trading or professional income and are based on earnings.

liable to pay National Insurance contributions in respect of his earnings.

• ***Addison* v. *London Philharmonic Orchestra Ltd* (1981 ICR 261).** This was an appeal to determine whether certain individuals were employees for the purposes of section 11(1) of the Employment Protection (Consolidation) Act 1978.

The Employment Appeal Tribunal upheld the decision of an industrial tribunal that an associate player and three additional or extra players of the London Philharmonic Orchestra were not employees under a contract of service, but were essentially freelance musicians carrying on their own business. The facts found by the industrial tribunal showed that, when playing for the orchestra, each appellant remained essentially a freelance musician, pursuing his or her own profession as an instrumentalist, with an individual reputation, and carrying on his or her own business, and they contributed their own skills and interpretative powers to the orchestra's performances as independent contractors.

• ***Winfield* v. *London Philharmonic Orchestra Ltd* (1979 ICR 726).** This case dealt with the question as to whether an individual was an employee within the meaning of section 30 of the Trade Union and Labour Relations Act 1974. The following remarks by the appeal tribunal are of interest in relation to the status of musicians:

"... making music is an art, and the co-operation required for a performance of Berlioz's *Requiem* is dissimilar to that required between the manufacturer of concrete and the truck driver who takes the concrete where it is needed ... It took the view, as we think it was entitled on the material before it to do, that the company was simply machinery through which the members of the orchestra managed and controlled the orchestra's operation ... In deciding whether you are in the presence of a contract of service or not, you look at the whole of the picture. This picture looks to us, as it looked to the industrial tribunal, like a co-operative of distinguished musicians running themselves with self and mutual discipline, and in no sense like a boss and his musician employees."

Other recent cases have concerned a professional dancer and holiday camp entertainers (all of whom were regarded as employees). In two recent cases income from part-time lecturing was held to be from an employment.

Accordingly, if a person is regarded as an employee under the above rules, he or she will be liable to pay contributions even if his employment is casual, part time or temporary. Furthermore, if a person is an employee and also carries on a trade or profession either solely or in partnership, there will be a liability to more than one class of contributions (subject to certain maxima – see below).

Exceptions

There are certain exceptions to the above rules, those most relevant to artists and writers being:

• The employment of a wife by her husband, or vice versa, is disregarded for social security purposes unless it is for the purposes of a trade or profession (e.g. the employment of his wife by an author would not be disregarded and would result in a liability for contributions if her salary reached the minimum levels).

• The employment of certain relatives in a private dwelling house in which both employee and employer reside is disregarded for social security purposes provided the employment is not for the purposes of a trade or business carried on at those premises by the employer. This would cover the employment of a relative (as defined) as a housekeeper in a private residence.

• In general, lecturers, teachers and instructors engaged by an educational establishment to teach on at least four days in three consecutive months are regarded as employees, although this rule does not apply to fees received by persons giving public lectures.

Freelance film workers

There is a list of grades in the film industry in respect of which PAYE need not be deducted and who are regarded as self-employed for tax purposes.

Further information can be obtained from the Summer 2000 edition of the Inland Revenue guidance notes on the application of PAYE to casual and freelance staff in the film industry. In view of the Inland Revenue announcement that the same status will apply for PAYE and NIC purposes, no liability for employee's and employer's contributions should arise in the case of any of the grades mentioned above.

However, in the film and TV industry this general rule was not always followed in practice. In December 1992, after a long review, the DSS agreed that individuals working behind the camera and who have jobs on the Inland Revenue Schedule D list are self-employed for social security purposes.

There are special rules for, *inter alia*, personnel appearing before the camera, short engagements, payments to limited companies and payments to overseas personalities.

Artistes, performers/non-performers

The status of artistes and performers for tax purposes will depend on the individual circumstances but for social security new regulations which took effect on 17 July 1998 require most actors, musicians or similar performers to be treated as employees for social security purposes, whether or not this status applies under general and/or tax law. It also applies whether or not the individual is supplied through an agency.

Personal service companies

From 6 April 2000, those who have control of their own 'one-man service companies' are subject to special rules. If the work that the owner of the company does for the company's customers would – but for the one-man company – fall to be considered as an employment of that individual (i.e. rather than self-employment), a deemed salary may arise. If it does, then some or all of the income of the company will be treated as salary liable to PAYE and National Insurance contributions. This will be the case whether or not such salary is actually paid by the company. The same situation may arise where the worker owns as little as 5% of the company's share capital.

The calculations required by the Inland Revenue are complicated and have to be done very quickly at the end of each tax year (even if the company's year-end is different). It is essential that affected businesses seek detailed professional advice about these new rules which may, in certain circumstances, also apply to partnerships.

Class 1 contributions

As mentioned above, these are related to earnings, the amount payable depending upon whether the employer has applied for his employees to be 'contracted-out' of the State earnings-related pension scheme; such application can be made where the employer's own pension scheme provides a requisite level of benefits for his or her employees and their dependants or, in the case of a money purchase scheme (COMPS) certain minimum safeguards are covered. Employers with employees contributing to 'stakeholder pension plans' continue to pay the full not contracted-out rate. Such employees have their contracting out arrangements handled separately by government authorities.

Contributions are payable by employees and employers on earnings that exceed the earnings threshold limited in the case of employees' contributions only, to the upper earnings limit. Contributions are normally collected via the PAYE tax deduction machinery, and there are penalties for late submission of returns and for errors therein. From 19 April 1993, interest will be charged automatically on unpaid PAYE and social security contributions.

Employees liable to pay

Contributions are payable by any employee who is aged 16 years and over (even though he or she may still be at school) and who is paid an amount equal to, or exceeding, the earnings threshold (see below). Nationality is irrelevant for contribution purposes and, subject to special rules covering employees not normally resident in Great Britain, Northern Ireland or the Isle of Man, or resident in EEA countries or those with which there are reciprocal agreements, contributions must be paid whether the employee concerned is a British subject or not provided he is gainfully employed in Great Britain.

Employees exempt from liability to pay

Persons over pensionable age (65 for men; 60 – until 2010 – for women) are exempt from liability to pay primary contributions, even if they have not retired. However, the fact that an employee may be exempt from liability does not relieve an employer from liability to pay secondary contributions in respect of that employee.

Employees' (primary) contributions

From 6 April 2002, the rate of employees' contributions on earnings from the earnings threshold to the upper earnings limit is 10% (8.4% for contracted-out employments). Certain married women who made appropriate elections before 12 May 1977 may be entitled to pay a reduced rate of 3.85%. However, they will have no entitlement to benefits in respect of these contributions.

From April 2003, all these rates will increase by 1% and, for the first time, earnings above the upper earnings limit will attract a liability at the rate of 1%.

Employers' (secondary) contributions

All employers are liable to pay contributions on the gross earnings of employees. As mentioned above, an employer's liability is not reduced as a result of employees being exempted from contributions, or being liable to pay only the reduced rate (3.85%) of contributions.

For earnings paid on or after 6 April 2002 employers are liable at a rate of 11.8% on earnings paid above the earnings threshold (without any upper earnings limit), 8.3% where the employment is contracted out (salary related) or 10.8% (money purchase). In addition, special rebates apply in respect of earnings falling between the lower earnings limit and the earnings threshold. This provides, effectively, a negative rate of contribution in that small band of earnings. It should be noted that the contracted-out rates of 8.3% and 10.8% apply only up to the upper earnings limit. Thereafter, the not

Rates of Class 1 contributions and earnings limits from 6 April 2002

Earnings per week	Rates payable on earnings in each band			
	Not contracted-out		Contracted-out	
	Employee	Employer	Employee	Employer
£	%	%	%	%
Below 75.00	—	—	—	—
75.00 – 88.99	—	—	— (*)	— (*)
89.00 – 585.00	10	11.8	8.4	8.3 or 10.8
Over £585.00	—	11.8	—	11.8

* Special rebates deductible in respect of this band of earnings.

contracted-out rate of 11.8% is applicable. From April 2003, all these rates will increase by 1%.

The employer is responsible for the payment of both employees' and employer's contributions, but is entitled to deduct the employees' contributions from the earnings on which they are calculated. Effectively, therefore, the employee suffers a deduction in respect of his or her social security contributions in arriving at his weekly or monthly wage or salary. Special rules apply to company directors and persons employed through agencies.

Items included in, or excluded from, earnings

Contributions are calculated on the basis of a person's gross earnings from his or her employment. This will normally be the figure shown on the tax deduction working sheet, except where the employee pays superannuation contributions and, from 6 April 1987, charitable gifts under payroll giving – these must be added back for the purposes of calculating Class 1 liability.

Earnings include salary, wages, overtime pay, commissions, bonuses, holiday pay, payments made while the employee is sick or absent from work, payments to cover travel between home and office, and payments under the statutory sick pay and statutory maternity pay schemes.

However, certain payments, some of which may be regarded as taxable income for income tax purposes, are ignored for Class 1 purposes. These include:

- certain gratuities paid other than by the employer,
- redundancy payments and some payments in lieu of notice,
- certain payments in kind,
- reimbursement of specific expenses incurred in the carrying out of the employment,
- benefits given on an individual basis for personal reasons (e.g. wedding and birthday presents),
- compensation for loss of office.

IR Booklet CWG 2 (2002 edition) gives a list of items to include in or exclude from earnings for Class 1 contribution purposes. Some such items may, however, be liable to Class 1A contributions.

Maximum contributions

There is a limit to the total liability for social security contributions payable by a person who is employed in more than one employment, or is also self-employed or a partner.

Where only not contracted-out Class 1 contributions, or not contracted-out Class 1 and Class 2 contributions, are payable, the maximum contribution is limited to 53 primary Class 1 contributions at the maximum weekly not contracted-out standard rate. For 2002/03 the maximum will thus be £2628.80.

However, where contracted-out Class 1 contributions are payable, the maximum primary Class 1 contributions payable for 2002/03 where all employments are contracted out are £2207.98.

Where Class 4 contributions are payable in addition to Class 1 and/or Class 2 contributions, the Class 4 contributions are restricted so that they shall not exceed the excess of £1912.35 (i.e. 53 Class 2 contributions plus maximum Class 4 contributions) over the aggregate of the Class 1 and Class 2 contributions.

Miscellaneous rules

There are detailed rules covering a person with two or more employments; where a person receives a bonus or commission in addition to a regular wage or salary; and where a person is in receipt of holiday pay. From 6 April 1991 employers' social security contributions arise under Class 1A in respect of the private use of a company car, and of fuel provided for private use therein. From 6 April 2000, this charge was extended to cover most benefits in kind. The rate is now 11.8%. From 6 April 1999, Class 1B contributions are payable by employers using PAYE Settlement Agreements in respect of small and/or irregular expense payments and benefits, etc. This rate is also currently 11.8%. Both these rates will increase to 12.8% from April 2003.

Class 2 contributions

Class 2 contributions are payable at the weekly rate of £2.00 as from 6 April 2000 and remains at that rate for 2002/03. Exemptions from Class 2 liability are:
- A man over 65 or a woman over 60.
- A person who has not attained the age of 16.
- A married woman or, in certain cases, a widow who elected prior to 12 May 1977 not to pay Class 2 contributions.
- Persons with small earnings (see below).
- Persons not ordinarily self-employed (see below).

Small earnings

Application for a certificate of exception from Class 2 contributions may be made by any person who can show that his or her net self-employed earnings per his profit and loss account (as opposed to taxable profits):
- for the year of application are expected to be less than a specified limit (£4025 in the 2002/03 tax year); or
- for the year preceding the application were less than the limit specified for that year (£3955 for 2001/02) and there has been no material change of circumstances.

Certificates of exception must be renewed in accordance with the instructions stated thereon. At the Inland Revenue's discretion the certificate may commence up to 13 weeks before the date on which the application is made. Despite a certificate of exception being in force, a person who is self-employed is still entitled to pay Class 2 contributions if they wish, in order to maintain entitlement to social security benefits.

Persons not ordinarily self-employed

Part-time self-employed activities (including as a writer or artist) are disregarded for contribution purposes if the person concerned is not ordinarily employed in such activities and has a full-time job as an employee. There is no definition of 'ordinarily employed' for this purpose but a person who has a regular job and whose earnings from spare-time occupation are not expected to be more than £800 per annum may fall within this category. Persons qualifying for this relief do not require certificates of exception but may be well advised to apply for one nonetheless.

Method of payment

From April 1993, Class 2 contributions may be paid by monthly direct debit in arrears or, alternatively, by cheque, bank giro, etc following receipt of a quarterly (in arrears) bill.

Overpaid contributions

If, following the payment of Class 2 contributions, it is found that the earnings are below the exception limit (e.g. the relevant accounts are prepared late), the Class 2 contributions that have been overpaid can be reclaimed, provided a claim is made between 6 April and 31 December immediately following the end of the tax year.

Class 3 contributions

Class 3 contributions are payable voluntarily, at the weekly rate of £6.85 per week from 6 April 2002, by persons aged 16 or over with a view to enabling them to qualify for a limited range of benefits if their contribution record is not otherwise sufficient. In general, Class 3 contributions can be paid by employees, the self-employed and the non employed.

Broadly speaking, no more than 52 Class 3 contributions are payable for any one tax year, and contributions are not payable after the end of the tax year in which the individual concerned reaches the age of 64 (59 for women).

Class 3 contributions may be paid in the same manner as Class 2 (see above) or by annual cheque in arrears.

Class 4 contributions

In addition to Class 2 contributions, self-employed persons are liable to pay Class 4 contributions. These are calculated at the rate of 7% on the amount of profits or gains chargeable to income tax under Schedule D Case I or II which exceed £4615 per annum but which do not exceed £30,420 per annum for 2002/03. Thus the maximum Class 4 contribution is 7% of £25,805 – i.e. £1806.35 for 2002/03. The rate will increase to 8% from April 2003 and there will then also be a 1% charge on profits over the upper limit.

The income tax profit on which Class 4 contributions are calculated is after deducting capital allowances and losses, but before deducting personal tax allowances or retirement annuity or personal pension or stakeholder pension plan premiums.

Class 4 contributions produce no additional benefits, but were introduced to ensure that self-employed persons as a whole pay a fair share of the cost of pensions and other social security benefits yet without those who make only small profits having to pay excessively high flat rate contributions.

Payment of contributions

In general, contributions are now self-assessed and paid to the Inland Revenue together with the income tax under Schedule D Case I or II, and accordingly the contributions are due and payable at the same time as the income tax liability on the relevant profits. Under self-assessment, interim payments of Class 4 contributions are payable at the same time as interim payments of tax.

Class 4 exemptions

The following persons are exempt from Class 4 contributions:

- Men over 65 and women over 60 at the commencement of the year of assessment (i.e. on 6 April).
- An individual not resident in the United Kingdom for income tax purposes in the year of assessment.
- Persons whose earnings are not 'immediately derived' from carrying on a trade, profession or vocation (e.g. sleeping partners and, possibly, limited partners).
- A child under 16 on 6 April of the year of assessment.
- Persons not ordinarily self-employed (see above as for Class 2 contributions).

Further information

Further information can be obtained from the many booklets published by the Inland Revenue, available from local National Insurance Contributions Office sites.

National Insurance Contributions Office, International Services
Newcastle upon Tyne NE98 1ZZ
tel (08459) 154811 (local call rates apply)
Address for enquiries for individuals resident abroad.

Married persons and partnerships

Under independent taxation of husband and wife from 1990/91 onwards, each spouse is responsible for his or her Class 4 liability.

In partnerships, each partner's liability is calculated separately. If a partner also carries on another trade or profession, the profits of all such businesses are aggregated for the purposes of calculating his or her Class 4 liability.

When an assessment has become final and conclusive for the purposes of income tax, it is also final and conclusive for the purposes of calculating Class 4 liability.

Transfer to Inland Revenue

The administrative functions of the former Contributions Agency transferred to the Inland Revenue from 1 April 1999. Responsibility for NIC policy matters was also transferred from DSS Ministers to the Inland Revenue and Treasury Ministers on the same date.

Peter Arrowsmith FCA is a sole practitioner specialising in National Insurance matters. He is chairman of the Employer Issues Committee of the Institute of Chartered Accountants in England and Wales and Consulting Editor to *Tolley's National Insurance Contributions 2002/03*.

Social security benefits

*There are many leaflets produced by the Department of Social Security. However, due to the nature of the subject social security benefits can be quite difficult to understand. In this article, **K.D. Bartlett** FCA has summarised some of the more usual benefits that are available under the Social Security Acts.*

This article deliberately does not cover every aspect of the legislation but the references given should enable the relevant information to be easily traced. These references are to the leaflets issued by the Department of Social Security.

It is usual for only one periodical benefit to be payable at any one time. If the contribution conditions are satisfied for more than one benefit it is the larger benefit that is payable. Benefit rates shown below were those payable from the week commencing 6 April 2002.

Self-employed persons (Class 2 and Class 4 contributors) are covered for all benefits except earnings-related supplements, unemployment benefit, widow's and invalidity pensions, widowed mother's allowance and industrial injury benefits. Most authors are self employed.

Family benefits

Child benefit (Leaflet CH 1) is payable for all children who are either under 16 or under 19 and receiving full-time education at a recognised educational establishment. The rate is £15.75 for the first or eldest child and £10.55 a week for each subsequent child. It is payable to the person who is responsible for the child but excludes foster parents or people exempt from UK tax. Furthermore, one-parent families receive £17.55 per week for the eldest child.

Those with little money may apply for a maternity loan or grant from the social fund. Those claiming Working Families Tax Credit or Disabled Persons Tax Credit can apply for a Sure Start Maternity Grant of £300 for each baby expected, born, adopted or subject to a parental order. Any savings over £500 are taken into account. This grant will only be paid on the provision of a relevant certificate from a doctor, midwife or health visitor.

A guardian's allowance (Leaflet NI 14) is paid at the rate of £9.65 a week. For each subsequent child the rate of benefit is £11.35 a week to people who have taken orphans into their own family. Usually both of the child's parents must be dead and at least one of them must have satisfied a residence condition.

The allowance can only be paid to the person who is entitled to child benefit for the child (or to that person's spouse). It is not necessary to be the legal guardian. The claim should be made within three months of the date of entitlement.

Disability living allowance

Disability living allowance has replaced attendance allowance for disabled people before they reach the age of 65. It has also replaced mobility allowance.

Those who are disabled after reaching 65 may be able to claim attendance allowance. The attendance allowance board decide whether, and for how long, a person is eligible for this allowance. Attendance allowance is not taxable. The care component is divided into three rates whereas the mobility allowance has two rates. The rate of benefit from 6 April 2002 is as follows:

	Per week
Care component	
Higher rate (day and night, or terminally ill)	£56.25
Middle rate (day or night)	£37.65
Lower rate (if need some help during day, or over 16 and need help preparing a meal)	£14.90
Mobility component	
Higher rate (unable or virtually unable to walk)	£39.30
Lower rate (can walk but needs help when outside)	£14.90

Benefits for the ill

Incapacity benefit (Leaflet DS 700) replaced sickness benefit and invalidity benefit. The contribution conditions haven't changed but a new medical test has been brought in which includes a comprehensive questionnaire. The rates from 8 April 2002 are:

Long-term incapacity benefit	£70.95
Short-term incapacity benefit	£53.50
Increase of long-term incapacity benefit for age:	
Higher rate	£14.90
Lower rate	£7.45

Invalid care allowance (Leaflet NI 212) is a taxable benefit paid to people of working age who cannot take a job because they have to stay at home to look after a severely disabled person. The basic allowance is £41.75 per week. An extra £9.65 is paid for the first dependent child and £11.35 for each subsequent child.

Disabled person's tax credit is a benefit for people under pensionable age who cannot work because of physical or mental ill health and do not have sufficient National Insurance contributions to qualify for sickness or invalidity benefit. The basic allowance is £62.10 a week. There are increases of £30.70 a week for adult dependants and £11.65 for each child.

Pensions and widow's benefits

The state pension (Leaflets NP 23, NP 35, NP 31) is divided into two parts – the basic pension, presently £75.50 per week for a single person or £120.70 per week for a married couple.

Women paying standard rate contributions into the scheme are eligible for the same amount of pension as men but five years earlier, from age 60. The Pensions Act 1995 incorporated the provision for an equal state pension age of 65 for men and women to be phased in over a 10-year period beginning 6 April 2010. If a woman stays at home to bring up her children or to look after a person receiving attendance allowance she can have her basic pension rights protected without paying contributions.

The widow's pension and widowed mother's allowance also consists of a basic pension and an additional earnings-related pension. The full amount of the additional pension applies only if the husband has contributed to the new scheme for at least 20 years.

Widow's benefits

From 11 April 1988 there are three main widow's benefits:

Widow's payment, which has replaced the widow's allowance, is currently a lump sum payment of £2000 payable to widows who were bereaved on or after 11 April 1988. It is payable immediately on the death of the husband. Entitlement to this benefit is based on the late husband's contribution record but no payment will be made if the widow is living with another man as husband and wife at the date of death. The late husband must have actually paid contributions on earnings of at least 25 times the weekly or lower earnings limit for a given tax year in any tax year ending before his death (or ending before he reached pensionable age if he was over 65 when he died). The equivalent number of Class 2 or voluntary Class 3 contributions will be sufficient.

When claiming, the widow should complete the form on the back of the death certificate and send it to the local social security office. On receipt of this information the DSS will send the claimant a more detailed form (BD8) which, once completed, has to go back to the social security office. It is important to claim the benefit within 12 months of the husband's death.

Widowed mother's allowance (Leaflet NP 45). Those widowed before 9 April 2001 left with children to look after, are entitled to a widowed mother's allowance provided that her late husband had paid sufficient National Insurance contributions. These contributions are:

- 25 Class 1, 2 or 3 contributions before age 65 and before 6 April 1975; or
- contributions in any one tax year after 6 April 1975 on earnings of at least 25 times the weekly lower earnings limit for that year.

It is important that the widow is looking after either her own child or her husband's child and that the child is under 16 or, if between the age of 16 and 19, is continuing in full-time education.

The allowance stops immediately if the widow remarries and will be suspended if she lives with a man as his wife. From April 2002 the basic allowance is £75.50 with £11.35 increase for each child. Where a husband's contributions only satisfied the first test above, the basic allowance may be payable at a reduced rate. This reduction does not alter the rate of an increase for a child.

Widow's pension (Leaflet NP 45). A widow who is widowed before 9 April 2001 and who is over the age of 45 when her husband dies may be eligible for a widow's pension unless she is eligible for the widowed mother's allowance. In this situation the widow's pension becomes payable when the widowed mother's allowance ends, provided she is still under the age of 65. However, where a woman had been receiving the widowed mother's allowance, she becomes entitled to a widow's pension if she is between the ages of 45 and 65 when the allowance ends, no matter what her age may have been when her husband died. Before 11 April 1988 a widow aged 40 or over could qualify for a widow's pension.

Qualification conditions

- The contributions conditions must be satisfied and these conditions are the same as those for the widowed mother's allowance above.
- The widow must not be receiving the widowed mother's allowance.
- When her husband died she was aged between 45 and 65 or she was entitled to widowed mother's allowance and is aged between 45 and 65 when her widowed mother's allowance finished.

Cessation of widow's pension

- Entitlement finishes if the widowed mother's allowance stops because she has remarried.
- Widow's pension must not be claimed when the payment of the widowed mother's allowance has been suspended because the widow is in pension or is living with a man as his wife.

From 11 April 1988 both the basic and additional pension are paid at a reduced rate if the widow was aged under 55:

- when her husband died, if she did not subsequently become entitled to widowed mother's allowance; or
- when her widowed mother's allowance ceased to be paid. The relevant rates from April 2002 are as follows:

Age related	£	%
Basic	75.50	100
Age 54 (49)	70.22	93
53 (48)	64.93	86
52 (47)	59.65	79
51 (46)	54.36	72
50 (45)	49.08	65
49 (44)	43.79	58
48 (43)	38.51	51
47 (42)	33.22	44
46 (41)	27.94	37
45 (40)	22.65	30

(The ages given in parentheses apply to women for whom widow's pension was payable before 11 April 1988.)

Bereavement payment and benefits

From 9 April 2001 bereavement benefits are payable to both widows and widowers but the benefits are only paid to those without children. Benefits are based on the National Insurance contributions of the deceased. No benefit is payable if the couple were divorced at the date of death or if either of the survivors remarries or cohabits.

Widows and widowers bereaved on or after 9 April 2001 are entitled to a tax-free bereavement payment of £2000.

The death grant to cover funeral expenses was abolished from 6 April 1987. It has been replaced by a funeral payment from the social fund where the claimant is in receipt of income support, income-based Jobseekers' Allowance, Disabled Persons' Tax Credit, Working Families' Tax Credit or housing benefit. The full cost of a reasonable funeral is paid, reduced by any savings of over £500 held by the claimant or his or her family (£1000 for couples over 60).

Working Families' Tax Credit (WFTC)

WFTC replaced Family Credit on 5 October 1999. It entitles families who have at least one partner who works 16 hours or more a week who have at least one child in full-time education up to and including A level or equivalent to claim. Both self-employed and employed people are covered.

WFTC is now administered and paid by the Inland Revenue. An application form can be obtained by phoning the helpline on (0845) 609 5000. WFTC is paid for a fixed period of 26 weeks but the claimant can keep re-applying every 26 weeks. It usually runs for the 26-week period even if the circumstances change. There is an exception to this when the last remaining child leaves full-time education when the family's WFTC is terminated from the pay week following the change. The weekly rates of WFTC effective from 6 April 2002 are:

- £60.00 basic (adult) tax credit (one payable per family);
- £11.65 30-hour tax credit (payable if the claimant or partner is working 30 hours or more a week – one payable per family).

Childcare tax credit

One credit is paid in respect of each child – the amount depends on their age when the WFTC is awarded:

£26.45	From birth to September following 16th birthday
£27.20	From September following 16th birthday to age 18
£135.00	Maximum childcare tax credit (one child only)
£200.00	Maximum childcare tax credit (2 or more children)
£94.50	Applicable amount (i.e. threshold)
55%	Taper
70%	Childcare taper

For each family there is a maximum level of WFTC. If the family's net income exceeds £94.50 per week, 55 pence of every excess £1 is deducted from the maximum WFTC. Net income is earnings (gross pay less tax, National Insurance contributions and half of any occupational or personal pension contributions) and most other forms of income.

Childcare tax credit will be worth up to 70% of eligible childcare costs. The maximum limit for eligible childcare costs will be £135 per week for one child and £200 per week for two or more children. This means that for a family with one child currently paying eligible childcare costs of £135, £94.50 per week childcare will be included in their WFTC award. Eligible childcare means childcare provided by registered childminders, nurseries and out-of-hours clubs on school premises, run by the school or local authority; and childcare schemes run on crown property.

Capital of between £3000 and £8000 will affect the level of income to be taken into account. A weekly income of £1 is assumed for each £250, or part of £250, of capital above £3000.

Disabled Persons' Tax Credit (DPTC)

This is a new tax credit to help people with an illness or disability who are in work. It replaces Disability Working Allowance (DWA), and is administered by the Inland Revenue. It is similar to Working Families' Tax Credit (WFTC), and is paid through the wage packet. It is intended for people with an illness or disability, who work at least 16 hours a week; are resident in the United Kingdom, and entitled to work here; have savings of £16,000 or less; have one of a number of qualifying benefits.

Further information

Further information can be obtained from the local office of the Department of Social Security or from Accountants Digest No. 439 published by the Institute of Chartered Accountants in England and Wales. Readers resident abroad who have queries should write to the Department's Overseas Branch, Newcastle upon Tyne NE98 1BA.

DPTC consists of basic tax credit (£62.10, or £92.80 for a couple) and 30-hour credit (£11.65). Payment is calculated by adding the credits together. If net income of the family is above £94.50 per week, this is reduced by 55 pence for each £1 above £94.50. For single people the threshold is £73.50. A DPTC award will normally last for 26 weeks.

How to apply

Applications are made to the Inland Revenue, which assess and calculate how much DPTC a claimant will receive. For employees payment will be made in the pay packet, and for the self-employed payment will be made directly.

Those who are directly receiving DWA will continue for the full 26-week period. Depending on individual circumstances, a person can then apply for DPTC. An application form for DPTC is automatically sent before an existing DWA award runs out. You cannot receive both DWA and DPTC.

Grants from local authorities

People eligible to claim housing benefit are those who are on a low income, or are in receipt of income support, or share the house with certain other persons who are receiving income support. The maximum benefit entitlement for a liable person claiming will be 100% of the liability.

Effect of the budget on 17 April 2002

The Chancellor announced details of the new child and working tax credits that will replace the existing children's tax credit and working families' tax credit in April 2003.

The child tax credit will be available to couples with children under 16 with joint incomes of up to £58,000 a year gross. Household earnings up to £66,000 will receive some help during the child's first year. Those on low earnings with children will receive the working tax credit as well as the child tax credit. Lone parents and two earner families who pay for childcare may receive an enhanced payment.

The Chancellor intends to bring in a new pension credit in October 2003 to make it easier for the elderly to claim. It is intended to reward those who save for retirement. However, those with moderate savings will be disqualified. Pensioners with income over £58 a week, or a couple with £78 from savings or a private pension will be ineligible.

K.D. Bartlett FCA qualified as a Chartered Accountant in 1969 and became a partner in a predecessor firm of Horwath Clark Whitehill in 1972.

Index